AMERICAN SUBURBS
RATING GUIDE AND FACT BOOK

Ranks 1,770 suburbs
in 50 metropolitan areas

Text by Alan Willis

Statistical data compiled by
Bennett Jacobstein

Toucan Valley Publications

Copyright © 1993 by Toucan Valley Publications, Inc.

Library of Congress Cataloging-in-Publication Data

Willis, Alan, 1948-
    American suburbs rating guide and fact book/ text by Alan Willis ;
statistical data compiled by Bennett Jacobstein. -- 1st ed.
    846 p.   cm.
    Includes index.
    ISBN 0-9634017-5-0
    1. Suburbs--Ratings--United States--Statistics.   I. Jacobstein,
Bennett, 1957-   .   II. Title.
HA214.W55   1993
307.74'0973--dc20   93-4750
                                                                       CIP

Toucan Valley Publications, Inc.
142 N. Milpitas Blvd., Suite 260
Milpitas, CA 95035
(408) 956-9492

Manufactured in the United States of America
First Edition

Minneapolis

Rochester
Buffalo Albany Boston
2 1
3 1. Providence

2. Hartford

3. New York

Milwaukee Detroit
Chicago

Cleveland Pittsburgh
Columbus Philadelphia
4 4. Baltimore
Indian- Dayton 5 5. Washington
apolis Cincinnati

Kansas City
St. Louis Louisville

Richmond
Norfolk

Greensboro
Nashville Charlotte
Memphis

Birmingham Atlanta

New Orleans Jacksonville
Orlando
Tampa
6 6. West Palm Beach
Miami

Contents

Suburbs in American Life

Americans have always had a love affair with the open countryside. When our forebears came to this country, open frontier was there to greet them whether in seventeenth century New England and Virginia or the nineteenth century midwestern prairies and far western mountains. Our culture and character were shaped for nearly four hundred years by the country homestead, with its surrounding acres of crops and livestock. It has only been since the United States Census of 1920 that more Americans have lived in urban rather than rural areas.

As our country's economy became more industrial and more people left the farms for jobs in city factories, the desire to find a home in the wide open spaces continued to live on in the new city dwellers. This desire to leave the dense, cramped quarters of city tenements and row houses became the driving force behind suburban development.

Our first suburbs were originally small outlying towns and villages. What transformed them into suburbs was the development of more rapid and efficient urban public transportation systems. Streetcars and commuter railroad lines extended themselves from the large city into the surrounding small towns, making it attractive for real estate developers to invest in and build residential tracts on open farm land. Improvements in sanitation and the extension of gas and lighting utilities services out from the metropolis also contributed to the development of open land into residential neighborhoods.

The middle class was then as now the target group for the real estate developers' sales pitch. They appealed to urban professionals who longed to raise families in a place with strong community values and who wanted the slower-paced life style of a small town, while still being only a short traveling distance from their city jobs. By the 1880's the new street and interurban railroads made this dream possible for America's professionals, and suburban America was born.

The advent of the automobile and construction of highways and superhighways further encouraged suburban development. By the late 1960's, whole new suburbs were springing up, utilities and all, from open land close to superhighways. These new real estate developer creations sported fanciful names, with streets named after children or relatives, baseball players, movie stars, even children's story book characters. The superhighway, twenty to thirty miles commute from the work place, became the suburb's umbilical cord to the life-sustaining city.

Suburbs have continued to fan further and further out in an ever-larger circumference from the metropolitan core. As suburbs "fill up" and stop expanding in population, they lose favor to newer ones adjacent to large tracts of open land. Older suburbs, locked in by housing and commercial development, often lose their luster and risk decline. The children of parents who moved in the 1940's to a nearby suburb will themselves move to the newer outer suburbs featuring modern homes and shopping centers. Small towns even further out, known as exurbs, are also experiencing rapid growth from this migratory pattern. Near suburbs, as a result, can find their populations aging, and the viability of businesses dependent upon younger consumers threatened.

A recent and accelerating trend in the development of suburbs is the relocation of large corporations away from the metropolitan core. Tax incentives offered by suburban governments, cheaper office space, and lower cost of living are some factors which have encouraged the likes of Exxon to move its corporate headquarters from New York City to the Dallas suburb of Irving, Texas, and Sears from Chicago to Hoffman Estates, Illinois. Rockwell International (Seal Beach, California) and IBM (Armonk, New York) are two other examples of Fortune 500 corporations whose corporate headquarters are found in suburbs. This trend, in turn, pushes suburban growth even further outward from the core, as wage earners take up residence in the exurbs to commute to suburban jobs.

The dynamic of outward expansion can only be expected to continue into the next century, as succeeding generations of Americans chase the perimeter of suburban development, trying to combine the advantages of the countryside with such urban amenities as well-financed schools, state-of-the-art healthcare, a wide variety of shopping, and reasonable distances to jobs. The 1990 Census tells us that more Americans now live in the suburbs than in either the city or country. Just as in 1920 the United States became an urban nation, it has now become a suburban nation, with a suburban culture. Suburbs are where we, as Americans, increasingly now live and work, for better or worse.

This book is intended to be an aid to those who need to relocate to another part of the country, to urban studies professionals, and to others needing data on suburbs throughout the nation and their quality of life. The suburbs of the fifty largest metropolitan areas in the country have been chosen to be analyzed and ranked from best to worst, overall and in seven individual evaluation categories. These categories are **economics, affordable housing, crime, open spaces, education, commute,** and **community stability.**

Under **economics**, median household income and the percentage of families above the poverty level are analyzed because adequate family income is a key indicator of the ability of a suburb's residents to afford a comfortable lifestyle. Under **affordable housing**, median home value and median rent are chosen. Both of these statistics reveal the ability of residents to find and upkeep reasonably-priced shelter. **Crime** is an indicator of how safe a place is to live, and also reveals difference in types of crime between suburbs. Both violent and property crime rates are analyzed. With **open spaces**, population density and the average number of rooms per house are used. Room to breathe is a major factor in the livability of a suburb. Almost everyone recognizes the desirability of good public schools. This is addressed in the **education** category. Reporting the percentage of high school-aged youth currently enrolled in or graduated from high school and the percentage of adults age 25 or over who have a college degree shows how important schools are to a particular suburb, and how much its people value education. The larger the number of college graduates in a community, the more likely its citizens will demand college-bound curricula from its public high schools. The **commute** time to and from work is important as a lifestyle factor. The longer the commute time, the more stress on the people living in a community, and the less likely the people there will be very happy. Easy commutes are prized. In addition to the average length of a commute, the percentage of workers commuting on public transportation is included. The more people use public transportation, the more relief there is from traffic gridlock, and the cleaner the air is. Finally, **community stability** is important because it gives a sense of how friendly and community-minded a suburb's people are likely to be. The longer people live in a suburb, the more financial and emotional investment they have in that community. Advantages traditionally associated with the small town, such as friendliness, looking out for your neighbor, community spirit, and strong community values are characteristic of places where people have lived a number of years. The number of years residents have lived in the same house and in the same county are used as community stability measurements.

How to Use the Data

INCLUSION

The fifty largest metropolitan areas based on 1990 U.S. Census Bureau population figures are included. Metropolitan areas are those defined by the Office of Management and Budget as either Metropolitan Statistical Areas (MSA's) or Consolidated Metropolitan Statistical Areas (CMSA's) as of June 30, 1989. Each MSA consists of one or more counties (and in a few cases, independent cities). In some cases MSA's located near each other are combined into a single CMSA. MSA's and CMSA's may include counties in more than one state. For the New England states, New England County Metropolitan Areas (NECMA's) are used instead of MSA's or CMSA's.

For each of the fifty metropolitan areas all suburbs with a 1990 population of 10,000 or greater located in the metropolitan area are included. A suburb is defined as any "place" in the metropolitan area except those included in the name of the metropolitan area. A "place" is defined by the U.S. Bureau of the Census as "census designated places and incorporated places." Census designated places are "densely settled concentrations of population that are identified by name, but are not legally incorporated places." Incorporated places are "those reported to the Census Bureau as legally in existence on January 1, 1990, under the laws of their respective States as cities, boroughs, towns, and villages, with the following exceptions: the towns in the New England States, New York, and Wisconsin, and the boroughs in New York."

RANKING AND SCORING

For each suburb, 22 separate ranks and scores are given: a composite rank and score, a rank and score for each of the seven categories (described in the next section), and a rank and score for each of the 14 individual statistics (two statistics for each of the seven categories). All ranks are based on scores with the highest score getting the highest rank (one = the highest rank). Scores for the 14 individual statistics are based on the percentile of the range of possible values. The suburb with the most favorable value for a given statistic gets a score of 100, and the suburb with the least favorable value for that statistic gets a score of 0. If the most favorable value for a particular statistic is 80%, and the least favorable value is 60%, then a suburb with a value of 65% would get a score of 25 (65 is 25% of the range between 60% and 80%). Scores for the seven categories are the average (mean) of the scores for the two statistics that make up each category. The composite score is the average of the seven category scores. In some cases, statistics for the **crime** category were not available (see next section), and in those cases the average score of the other six categories was used to determine the composite score. The reason scores were used instead of simply ranking by the value of the statistic, is to avoid penalizing a suburb if it had a value lower than many other suburbs, but only slightly lower.

3

ARRANGEMENT OF DATA

The fifty metropolitan areas are arranged alphabetically. For each metropolitan area there are four sections.

Part I: Metropolitan Area Description

This section lists the state(s) and county(ies) included in the metropolitan area, the total population, the population of all suburbs, the population of each city included in the metropolitan area name (but **not** included in the book), and a general description of the metropolitan area suburbs.

Part II: Metropolitan Area Map

The map for each metropolitan area includes all counties in the metropolitan area, each city included in the metropolitan area name, and an identifying number for the approximate location of each suburb in the metropolitan area. The Metropolitan Area Suburb Alphabetical Index (see Part III) includes the map number corresponding to each suburb.

Part III: Metropolitan Area Suburb Alphabetical Index

This part contains a table with the following elements:

SUBURB	PAGE	MAP NO.	STATE	COUNTY	POPU-LATION	RANK
ADDISON	131	1	Illinois	Du Page	32,058	97 / 138

Sample

Suburb is the name of the suburb.

Page is the page that contains the detailed information for the suburb (see part IV).

Map No. is the location number on the Metropolitan Area Map (see part II) that corresponds to the suburb.

State is the state in which the suburb is located.

County is the county in which the suburb is located. If the suburb is located in more than one county, then the county containing the largest percentage of the population of the suburb is listed.

Population is the 1990 population according to the U.S. Bureau of the Census.

Rank is the composite rank for the suburb (one = highest) followed by the total number of suburbs in the metropolitan area.

Part IV: Metropolitan Area Suburb Rankings

The Suburb Rankings section lists each suburb in composite rank order. For each suburb the following elements are given:

Composite: Rank 4 / 138 *Score* 69.04 **HINSDALE (IL)**

CATEGORY	RANK	SCORE	STATISTIC	VALUE	RANK	SCORE
Economics	8	71.70	Median Household Income	$68,518	7	49.6
			% of Families Above Poverty Level	98.3%	40	93.8
Affordable Housing	130	47.75	Median Home Value	$284,300	136	46.4
			Median Rent	$650	110	49.1
Crime	5	97.50	Violent Crimes per 10,000 Population	4	3	99.7
			Property Crimes per 10,000 Population	171	5	95.3
Open Spaces	17	72.85	Population Density (Persons/Sq. Mile)	3456	58	73.8
			Average Rooms per Housing Unit	6.7	12	71.9
Education	5	85.60	% High School Enrollment/Completion	99.0%	7	95.6
			% College Graduates	60.8%	4	75.6
Commute	8	47.80	Average Work Commute in Minutes	27	58	31.8
			% Commuting on Public Transportation	17.5%	8	63.8
Community Stability	78	60.05	% Living in Same House as in 1979	42.1%	51	58.5
			% Living in Same County as in 1985	74.3%	106	61.6

Sample

Composite Rank is the overall rank for the suburb (one = highest) followed by the total number of suburbs in the metropolitan area.

Composite Score is the overall score for the suburb (the average of the category scores).

{Suburb Name} is listed above each table. The state abbreviation follows the suburb name when the metropolitan area crosses state lines.

Category is the category for the corresponding two statistics (see page 5 for information on the seven categories).

Rank (column 2) is the rank for the corresponding category.

Score (column 3) is the score for the corresponding category.

Statistic is the statistics used for each category. Unless otherwise indicated, all data is from the *1990 Summary Tape File 3A* by the U.S. Bureau of the Census. Also, unless otherwise indicated, the highest value equals the most favorable score.

Economics:
> **Median Household Income** is the 1989 value.
> **% of Families Above the Poverty level** is based on definitions used by the U.S. Bureau of the Census.

5

Affordable Housing:

Median Home Value (lowest value equals most favorable score) is the value of owner-occupied or for-sale housing units as reported by owner. The U.S. Bureau of the Census reports all values over $500,000 as $500,001.

Median Rent (lowest value equals most favorable score) is the monthly rent. All values over $1,000 are reported as $1,001.

Crime:

Crime data is from the *1991 Uniform Crime Reports* by the U.S. Federal Bureau of Investigation. Data is not available for many suburbs. Value, Rank, and Score are replaced with "N/A" when the data is not available. Additionally, if at least 50% of a metropolitan area does **not** have crime statistics available, then the Crime Ranks and Scores for the entire metropolitan area are not calculated and are listed as "N/A". Forcible rape figures for Illinois are not available. The national average for forcible rape as a percentage of all uniform crimes is 1%. This figure has been used to adjust the Illinois data in order to allow it to be compared with other states.

Violent Crimes per 10,000 Population (lowest value equals most favorable score) includes murder, forcible rape, robbery, and aggravated assault.

Property Crimes per 10,000 Population (lowest value equals most favorable score) includes burglary, larceny-theft, and motor vehicle theft.

Open Spaces:

Population Density (lowest value equals most favorable score) is the number of persons divided by the land area in square miles (water area is excluded).

Average Rooms per Housing Unit includes living rooms, dining rooms, kitchens, bedrooms, finished recreation rooms, enclosed porches suitable for year-round use, and lodger's rooms. The U.S. Bureau of the Census reports all housing units with more than 9 rooms as 9 rooms.

Education:

% High School Enrollment/Completion includes all persons ages 16-19 who are either currently enrolled in high school or have already graduated.

% College Graduates includes all persons age 25 or over who have a four-year college degree.

Commute:

Average work commute in minutes (lowest value equals most favorable score) includes all persons who work outside their home and is for the commute from home to work.

% Commuting on Public Transportation includes those commuting by bus, trolley, streetcar, subway, elevated railroad, or ferryboat.

Community Stability:

> **% Living in Same House as in 1979** includes all households that lived in the same housing unit in 1990 as they did in 1979.
>
> **% Living in Same County as in 1985** includes all persons age 5 or older who lived in the same county in 1990 as they did in 1985.

Value is the actual data for the statistics listed above.

Rank (column 6) is the rank for the corresponding statistic.

Score (column 7) is the score for the corresponding statistic.

GETTING THE MOST FROM THIS BOOK

Although a high composite ranking speaks well of a suburb, some will find certain categories of statistics important to their particular situation while other categories are not at all important to them. For example, those who need affordable housing and are also especially concerned about education will look for suburbs with favorable rankings in these two categories. Additionally, those interested in renting rather than purchasing a home will consider suburbs that rank favorably in rent values, rather than in the affordable housing category as a whole.

In addition to rankings, this book is a valuable source of nearly 25,000 statistical facts about the American suburbs.

NOTES

Statistics for the Miami-Fort Lauderdale metropolitan area are pre-Hurricane Andrew (August, 1992). Some of the suburbs were severely damaged by the hurricane.

Statistics for suburbs that have a significant college or university population may be impacted by that fact, and may not be completely representative of the permanent population of the suburb.

Factors which are relevant to a metropolitan area as a whole rather than to individual suburbs (e.g. major cultural events, weather) are purposely not included, since they do not significantly differentiate one suburb from another.

Metropolitan Area Description
ALBANY-SCHENECTADY-TROY

STATE: New York
COUNTIES: Albany, Greene, Montgomery, Rensselaer, Saratoga, Schenectady

TOTAL POPULATION: 874,304

POPULATION IN SUBURBS: 653,387   (74.7%)

POPULATION IN Albany: 101,082   (11.6%)
POPULATION IN Schenectady: 65,566   (7.5%)
POPULATION IN Troy: 54,269   (6.2%)

The ALBANY-SCHENECTADY-TROY metropolitan area is located in the eastern part of New York state north of the city of New York and along the Hudson River. The suburbs range geographically from Saratoga Springs in the north (33 miles from Albany), to Amsterdam in the west (36 miles from Albany). The area is growing in population and had an increase of 4.6% between 1980 and 1990. The greatest growth occurred north along Interstate 87 in Saratoga County. Additionally, Saratoga County was the second fastest growing county in the state. Summer time high temperatures average in the 80's and winter time lows average in the teens. The area is known primarily as the seat of New York state government. General Electric, founded by Thomas Edison, has many important divisions located in the suburbs.

Loudonville is the overall highest rated suburb and also has the highest scores in economics, open spaces, and education. **Amsterdam** is the suburb with the most affordable housing. The top rated commute belongs to **Watervliet**. The number one rating in community stability goes to **Rotterdam**. Crime rankings were not available for the area.

The highest ranked suburb overall which also has an affordable housing score of at least 50.00 is **Rotterdam**.

The highest ranked suburb in the education category which also has an affordable housing score of at least 50.00 is also **Rotterdam**.

The county whose suburbs have the highest average overall score is **Schenectady County** (53.92)

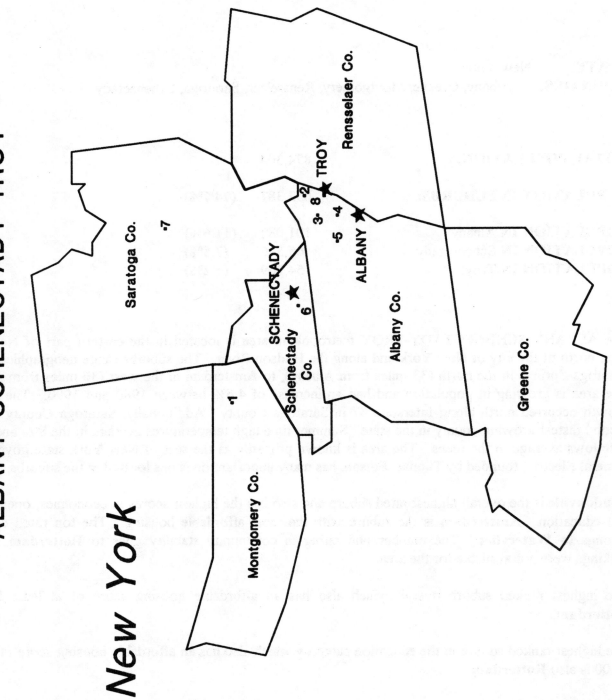

Metropolitan Area Map
ALBANY-SCHENECTADY-TROY

New York

Saratoga Co.
•7

Montgomery Co.

Schenectady
Co.
SCHENECTADY
•6
★

Albany Co.

Greene Co.

•3 •8
•5
•4
ALBANY
★

•2
TROY
★

Rensselaer Co.

Metropolitan Area Suburb Alphabetical Index
ALBANY-SCHENECTADY-TROY

SUBURB	PAGE	MAP NO.	STATE	COUNTY	POPU-LATION	RANK
AMSTERDAM	13	1	New York	Montgomery	20,714	6 / 8
COHOES	14	2	New York	Albany	16,825	8 / 8
LATHAM	12	3	New York	Albany	10,131	3 / 8
LOUDONVILLE	12	4	New York	Albany	10,822	1 / 8
ROESSLEVILLE	13	5	New York	Albany	10,753	4 / 8
ROTTERDAM	12	6	New York	Schenectady	21,228	2 / 8
SARATOGA SPRINGS	14	7	New York	Saratoga	25,001	7 / 8
WATERVLIET	13	8	New York	Albany	11,061	5 / 8

Metropolitan Area Suburb Rankings
ALBANY-SCHENECTADY-TROY

Composite: *Rank* 1 / 8 *Score* 72.94   **LOUDONVILLE**

CATEGORY	RANK	SCORE	STATISTIC	VALUE	RANK	SCORE
Economics	1	98.25	Median Household Income	$52,591	1	100.0
			% of Families Above Poverty Level	97.9%	3	96.5
Affordable Housing	8	0.00	Median Home Value	$141,300	8	0.0
			Median Rent	$618	8	0.0
Crime	N/A	N/A	Violent Crimes per 10,000 Population	N/A	N/A	N/A
			Property Crimes per 10,000 Population	N/A	N/A	N/A
Open Spaces	1	91.45	Population Density (Persons/Sq. Mile)	2177	3	82.9
			Average Rooms per Housing Unit	6.9	1	100.0
Education	1	100.00	% High School Enrollment/Completion	98.7%	1	100.0
			% College Graduates	38.8%	1	100.0
Commute	3	53.40	Average Work Commute in Minutes	15	1	100.0
			% Commuting on Public Transportation	2.3%	5	6.8
Community Stability	2	94.55	% Living in Same House as in 1979	60.7%	2	97.8
			% Living in Same County as in 1985	89.2%	2	91.3

Composite: *Rank* 2 / 8 *Score* 53.92   **ROTTERDAM**

CATEGORY	RANK	SCORE	STATISTIC	VALUE	RANK	SCORE
Economics	3	66.55	Median Household Income	$32,928	3	35.4
			% of Families Above Poverty Level	98.0%	2	97.7
Affordable Housing	4	60.35	Median Home Value	$89,200	3	73.4
			Median Rent	$485	5	47.3
Crime	N/A	N/A	Violent Crimes per 10,000 Population	4	N/A	N/A
			Property Crimes per 10,000 Population	339	N/A	N/A
Open Spaces	4	51.20	Population Density (Persons/Sq. Mile)	3061	4	71.2
			Average Rooms per Housing Unit	5.8	3	31.2
Education	4	43.35	% High School Enrollment/Completion	96.1%	2	79.0
			% College Graduates	12.3%	5	7.7
Commute	7	2.05	Average Work Commute in Minutes	20	7	0.0
			% Commuting on Public Transportation	2.1%	7	4.1
Community Stability	1	100.00	% Living in Same House as in 1979	61.3%	1	100.0
			% Living in Same County as in 1985	90.9%	1	100.0

Composite: *Rank* 3 / 8 *Score* 52.58   **LATHAM**

CATEGORY	RANK	SCORE	STATISTIC	VALUE	RANK	SCORE
Economics	2	79.95	Median Household Income	$40,395	2	59.9
			% of Families Above Poverty Level	98.2%	1	100.0
Affordable Housing	7	31.85	Median Home Value	$115,000	7	37.0
			Median Rent	$543	6	26.7
Crime	N/A	N/A	Violent Crimes per 10,000 Population	N/A	N/A	N/A
			Property Crimes per 10,000 Population	N/A	N/A	N/A
Open Spaces	2	60.60	Population Density (Persons/Sq. Mile)	2115	2	83.7
			Average Rooms per Housing Unit	5.9	2	37.5
Education	3	64.65	% High School Enrollment/Completion	93.6%	4	58.9
			% College Graduates	30.3%	3	70.4
Commute	5	23.40	Average Work Commute in Minutes	18	4	40.0
			% Commuting on Public Transportation	2.3%	5	6.8
Community Stability	5	55.05	% Living in Same House as in 1979	44.2%	5	38.3
			% Living in Same County as in 1985	85.4%	5	71.8

Metropolitan Area Suburb Rankings
ALBANY-SCHENECTADY-TROY

Composite: Rank 4 / 8 *Score* 49.44   **ROESSLEVILLE**

CATEGORY	RANK	SCORE	STATISTIC	VALUE	RANK	SCORE
Economics	4	52.30	Median Household Income	$30,284	5	26.7
			% of Families Above Poverty Level	96.3%	4	77.9
Affordable Housing	6	43.05	Median Home Value	$93,000	5	68.0
			Median Rent	$567	7	18.1
Crime	N/A	N/A	Violent Crimes per 10,000 Population	N/A	N/A	N/A
			Property Crimes per 10,000 Population	N/A	N/A	N/A
Open Spaces	6	31.25	Population Density (Persons/Sq. Mile)	3718	6	62.5
			Average Rooms per Housing Unit	5.3	7	0.0
Education	5	32.35	% High School Enrollment/Completion	92.6%	6	50.8
			% College Graduates	14.1%	4	13.9
Commute	2	73.90	Average Work Commute in Minutes	17	2	60.0
			% Commuting on Public Transportation	8.3%	2	87.8
Community Stability	3	63.80	% Living in Same House as in 1979	48.2%	3	52.7
			% Living in Same County as in 1985	86.0%	3	74.9

Composite: Rank 5 / 8 *Score* 40.81   **WATERVLIET**

CATEGORY	RANK	SCORE	STATISTIC	VALUE	RANK	SCORE
Economics	6	13.05	Median Household Income	$25,852	6	12.1
			% of Families Above Poverty Level	90.8%	6	14.0
Affordable Housing	3	77.10	Median Home Value	$81,400	2	84.4
			Median Rent	$422	3	69.8
Crime	N/A	N/A	Violent Crimes per 10,000 Population	N/A	N/A	N/A
			Property Crimes per 10,000 Population	N/A	N/A	N/A
Open Spaces	8	0.00	Population Density (Persons/Sq. Mile)	8443	8	0.0
			Average Rooms per Housing Unit	5.3	7	0.0
Education	6	31.35	% High School Enrollment/Completion	93.9%	3	61.3
			% College Graduates	10.5%	7	1.4
Commute	1	80.00	Average Work Commute in Minutes	17	2	60.0
			% Commuting on Public Transportation	9.2%	1	100.0
Community Stability	6	43.35	% Living in Same House as in 1979	42.0%	6	30.3
			% Living in Same County as in 1985	82.4%	7	56.4

Composite: Rank 6 / 8 *Score* 38.27   **AMSTERDAM**

CATEGORY	RANK	SCORE	STATISTIC	VALUE	RANK	SCORE
Economics	8	0.00	Median Household Income	$22,166	8	0.0
			% of Families Above Poverty Level	89.6%	8	0.0
Affordable Housing	1	100.00	Median Home Value	$70,300	1	100.0
			Median Rent	$337	1	100.0
Crime	N/A	N/A	Violent Crimes per 10,000 Population	5	N/A	N/A
			Property Crimes per 10,000 Population	210	N/A	N/A
Open Spaces	5	42.20	Population Density (Persons/Sq. Mile)	3474	5	65.7
			Average Rooms per Housing Unit	5.6	4	18.7
Education	7	7.90	% High School Enrollment/Completion	87.3%	7	8.1
			% College Graduates	12.3%	5	7.7
Commute	6	16.75	Average Work Commute in Minutes	19	5	20.0
			% Commuting on Public Transportation	2.8%	4	13.5
Community Stability	4	62.75	% Living in Same House as in 1979	48.2%	3	52.7
			% Living in Same County as in 1985	85.6%	4	72.8

Metropolitan Area Suburb Rankings
ALBANY-SCHENECTADY-TROY

Composite: Rank 7 / 8 Score 34.40   **SARATOGA SPRINGS**

CATEGORY	RANK	SCORE	STATISTIC	VALUE	RANK	SCORE
Economics	5	40.00	Median Household Income	$30,938	4	28.8
			% of Families Above Poverty Level	94.0%	5	51.2
Affordable Housing	5	48.55	Median Home Value	$108,500	6	46.2
			Median Rent	$475	4	50.9
Crime	N/A	N/A	Violent Crimes per 10,000 Population	122	N/A	N/A
			Property Crimes per 10,000 Population	637	N/A	N/A
Open Spaces	3	53.15	Population Density (Persons/Sq. Mile)	880	1	100.0
			Average Rooms per Housing Unit	5.4	5	6.3
Education	2	64.70	% High School Enrollment/Completion	93.4%	5	57.3
			% College Graduates	30.8%	2	72.1
Commute	8	0.00	Average Work Commute in Minutes	20	7	0.0
			% Commuting on Public Transportation	1.8%	8	0.0
Community Stability	8	0.00	% Living in Same House as in 1979	33.6%	8	0.0
			% Living in Same County as in 1985	71.4%	8	0.0

Composite: Rank 8 / 8 Score 30.29   **COHOES**

CATEGORY	RANK	SCORE	STATISTIC	VALUE	RANK	SCORE
Economics	7	4.70	Median Household Income	$24,319	7	7.1
			% of Families Above Poverty Level	89.8%	7	2.3
Affordable Housing	2	78.55	Median Home Value	$89,900	4	72.4
			Median Rent	$380	2	84.7
Crime	N/A	N/A	Violent Crimes per 10,000 Population	96	N/A	N/A
			Property Crimes per 10,000 Population	243	N/A	N/A
Open Spaces	7	29.25	Population Density (Persons/Sq. Mile)	4496	7	52.2
			Average Rooms per Housing Unit	5.4	5	6.3
Education	8	0.00	% High School Enrollment/Completion	86.3%	8	0.0
			% College Graduates	10.1%	8	0.0
Commute	4	30.25	Average Work Commute in Minutes	19	5	20.0
			% Commuting on Public Transportation	4.8%	3	40.5
Community Stability	7	39.00	% Living in Same House as in 1979	39.3%	7	20.6
			% Living in Same County as in 1985	82.6%	6	57.4

14

Metropolitan Area Description
ATLANTA

STATE: Georgia

COUNTIES: Barrow, Butts, Cherokee, Clayton, Cobb, Coweta, De Kalb, Douglas, Fayette, Forsyth, Fulton, Gwinnett, Henry, Newton, Paulding, Rockdale, Spalding, Walton

TOTAL POPULATION: 2,833,511

POPULATION IN SUBURBS: 2,439,494 (86.1%)

POPULATION IN Atlanta: 394,017 (13.9%)

The ATLANTA metropolitan area is located in the northwestern part of Georgia. The suburbs range geographically from Alpharetta in the north (53 miles from Atlanta), to Douglasville in the west (24 miles from Atlanta), to Griffin in the south (38 miles from Atlanta), and to Covington in the east (32 miles from Atlanta). The area is growing rapidly in population and had an increase of 32.5% between 1980 and 1990. All of the increase occurred in the suburbs, as the population of the city of Atlanta decreased by 7.3%. Summer time high temperatures average in the 80's and winter time lows average in the 40's. The area is looked upon by business as a good place for relocation. In 1991, *Fortune* magazine rated the metropolitan area number one for business. Public transportation in the area is provided by a 32-mile rapid rail transit system (MARTA) and extensive connector bus routes.

Dunwoody is the overall highest rated suburb and also has the highest score in economics. **Griffin** is the suburb with the most affordable housing. The number one rating in education belongs to **Druid Hills**. The top rated commute goes to **College Park**. The suburb with the most open spaces is **Peachtree City**. Finally, **Covington** receives the number one rating in community stability. Crime rankings were not available for the area.

The highest ranked suburb overall which also has an affordable housing score of at least 50.00 is **Mableton**.

The highest ranked suburb in the education category which also has an affordable housing score of at least 50.00 is **Redan**.

The county whose suburbs have the highest average overall score is **Newton County** (52.59).

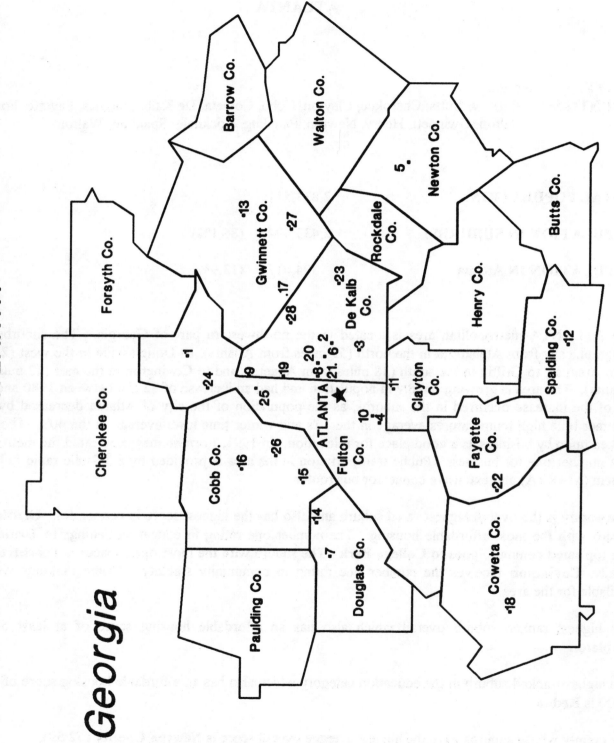

Metropolitan Area Map
ATLANTA

Georgia

Cherokee Co.

Forsyth Co.

Barrow Co.

Walton Co.

Newton Co.

5.

Gwinnett Co.
•13
•27
•17
•28

Rockdale
Co.

Butts Co.

Cobb Co.
•1
•24
•9
•19
•25
•26
•16

De Kalb
Co.
•23

Henry Co.

Spalding Co.
•12

Paulding Co.

Douglas Co.
•7
•15
•14

ATLANTA
Fulton
Co.
•20
•8 •2
•21 •6
•10
•4

Clayton
Co.
•11

Fayette
Co.

Coweta Co.
•18
•22

Metropolitan Area Suburb Alphabetical Index
ATLANTA

SUBURB	PAGE	MAP NO.	STATE	COUNTY	POPU-LATION	RANK
ALPHARETTA	24	1	Georgia	Fulton	13,002	19 / 28
BELVEDERE PARK	25	2	Georgia	De Kalb	18,089	24 / 28
CANDLER-MCAFEE	21	3	Georgia	De Kalb	29,491	10 / 28
COLLEGE PARK	26	4	Georgia	Fulton	20,457	27 / 28
COVINGTON	20	5	Georgia	Newton	10,026	8 / 28
DECATUR	23	6	Georgia	De Kalb	17,336	17 / 28
DOUGLASVILLE	24	7	Georgia	Douglas	11,635	21 / 28
DRUID HILLS	19	8	Georgia	De Kalb	12,174	5 / 28
DUNWOODY	18	9	Georgia	De Kalb	26,302	1 / 28
EAST POINT	21	10	Georgia	Fulton	34,402	12 / 28
FOREST PARK	23	11	Georgia	Clayton	16,925	16 / 28
GRIFFIN	23	12	Georgia	Spalding	21,347	18 / 28
LAWRENCEVILLE	25	13	Georgia	Gwinnett	16,848	22 / 28
LITHIA SPRINGS	24	14	Georgia	Douglas	11,403	20 / 28
MABLETON	19	15	Georgia	Cobb	25,725	6 / 28
MARIETTA	27	16	Georgia	Cobb	44,129	28 / 28
MOUNTAIN PARK	18	17	Georgia	Gwinnett	11,025	3 / 28
NEWNAN	22	18	Georgia	Coweta	12,497	15 / 28
NORTH ATLANTA	26	19	Georgia	De Kalb	27,812	25 / 28
NORTH DECATUR	19	20	Georgia	De Kalb	13,936	4 / 28
NORTH DRUID HILLS	22	21	Georgia	De Kalb	14,170	13 / 28
PEACHTREE CITY	21	22	Georgia	Fayette	19,027	11 / 28
REDAN	26	23	Georgia	De Kalb	24,376	26 / 28
ROSWELL	20	24	Georgia	Fulton	47,923	9 / 28
SANDY SPRINGS	22	25	Georgia	Fulton	67,842	14 / 28
SMYRNA	25	26	Georgia	Cobb	30,981	23 / 28
SNELLVILLE	20	27	Georgia	Gwinnett	12,084	7 / 28
TUCKER	18	28	Georgia	De Kalb	25,781	2 / 28

Metropolitan Area Suburb Rankings
ATLANTA

Composite: Rank 1 / 28 *Score* 67.36   **DUNWOODY**

CATEGORY	RANK	SCORE	STATISTIC	VALUE	RANK	SCORE
Economics	1	100.00	Median Household Income	$68,269	1	100.0
			% of Families Above Poverty Level	99.2%	1	100.0
Affordable Housing	27	16.20	Median Home Value	$174,500	27	32.4
			Median Rent	$728	28	0.0
Crime	N/A	N/A	Violent Crimes per 10,000 Population	N/A	N/A	N/A
			Property Crimes per 10,000 Population	N/A	N/A	N/A
Open Spaces	2	78.90	Population Density (Persons/Sq. Mile)	2177	18	57.8
			Average Rooms per Housing Unit	7.4	1	100.0
Education	3	85.15	% High School Enrollment/Completion	94.7%	6	85.8
			% College Graduates	54.9%	2	84.5
Commute	12	46.25	Average Work Commute in Minutes	21	6	76.9
			% Commuting on Public Transportation	2.9%	12	15.6
Community Stability	7	77.65	% Living in Same House as in 1979	42.6%	5	83.9
			% Living in Same County as in 1985	73.5%	9	71.4

Composite: Rank 2 / 28 *Score* 62.20   **TUCKER**

CATEGORY	RANK	SCORE	STATISTIC	VALUE	RANK	SCORE
Economics	5	74.45	Median Household Income	$46,714	6	54.5
			% of Families Above Poverty Level	98.1%	4	94.4
Affordable Housing	21	47.00	Median Home Value	$110,700	21	68.1
			Median Rent	$630	23	25.9
Crime	N/A	N/A	Violent Crimes per 10,000 Population	N/A	N/A	N/A
			Property Crimes per 10,000 Population	N/A	N/A	N/A
Open Spaces	7	65.55	Population Density (Persons/Sq. Mile)	2145	16	58.7
			Average Rooms per Housing Unit	6.6	4	72.4
Education	8	64.20	% High School Enrollment/Completion	92.2%	8	75.0
			% College Graduates	37.4%	9	53.4
Commute	16	38.00	Average Work Commute in Minutes	23	10	61.5
			% Commuting on Public Transportation	2.7%	13	14.5
Community Stability	3	84.00	% Living in Same House as in 1979	44.8%	3	89.4
			% Living in Same County as in 1985	76.6%	7	78.6

Composite: Rank 3 / 28 *Score* 58.16   **MOUNTAIN PARK**

CATEGORY	RANK	SCORE	STATISTIC	VALUE	RANK	SCORE
Economics	3	79.65	Median Household Income	$49,711	4	60.8
			% of Families Above Poverty Level	98.9%	2	98.5
Affordable Housing	22	46.00	Median Home Value	$99,100	19	74.6
			Median Rent	$662	26	17.4
Crime	N/A	N/A	Violent Crimes per 10,000 Population	N/A	N/A	N/A
			Property Crimes per 10,000 Population	N/A	N/A	N/A
Open Spaces	6	70.80	Population Density (Persons/Sq. Mile)	1900	13	65.7
			Average Rooms per Housing Unit	6.7	3	75.9
Education	9	58.45	% High School Enrollment/Completion	92.1%	9	74.6
			% College Graduates	31.2%	14	42.3
Commute	26	15.60	Average Work Commute in Minutes	28	23	23.1
			% Commuting on Public Transportation	1.5%	16	8.1
Community Stability	6	78.45	% Living in Same House as in 1979	45.4%	2	91.0
			% Living in Same County as in 1985	71.1%	13	65.9

Composite: *Rank* 4 / 28 *Score* 56.91 — NORTH DECATUR

CATEGORY	RANK	SCORE	STATISTIC	VALUE	RANK	SCORE
Economics	10	61.70	Median Household Income	$36,333	11	32.6
			% of Families Above Poverty Level	97.4%	7	90.8
Affordable Housing	19	49.35	Median Home Value	$103,700	20	72.1
			Median Rent	$627	22	26.6
Crime	N/A	N/A	Violent Crimes per 10,000 Population	N/A	N/A	N/A
			Property Crimes per 10,000 Population	N/A	N/A	N/A
Open Spaces	18	35.95	Population Density (Persons/Sq. Mile)	2776	22	40.9
			Average Rooms per Housing Unit	5.4	13	31.0
Education	4	81.75	% High School Enrollment/Completion	96.1%	3	91.8
			% College Graduates	47.7%	5	71.7
Commute	13	44.45	Average Work Commute in Minutes	23	10	61.5
			% Commuting on Public Transportation	5.1%	9	27.4
Community Stability	12	68.25	% Living in Same House as in 1979	37.1%	9	70.1
			% Living in Same County as in 1985	71.3%	12	66.4

Composite: *Rank* 5 / 28 *Score* 56.18 — DRUID HILLS

CATEGORY	RANK	SCORE	STATISTIC	VALUE	RANK	SCORE
Economics	12	57.75	Median Household Income	$37,186	10	34.4
			% of Families Above Poverty Level	95.5%	14	81.1
Affordable Housing	25	42.95	Median Home Value	$162,800	26	38.9
			Median Rent	$550	15	47.0
Crime	N/A	N/A	Violent Crimes per 10,000 Population	N/A	N/A	N/A
			Property Crimes per 10,000 Population	N/A	N/A	N/A
Open Spaces	20	34.15	Population Density (Persons/Sq. Mile)	2904	24	37.3
			Average Rooms per Housing Unit	5.4	13	31.0
Education	1	100.00	% High School Enrollment/Completion	98.0%	1	100.0
			% College Graduates	63.6%	1	100.0
Commute	3	67.75	Average Work Commute in Minutes	18	1	100.0
			% Commuting on Public Transportation	6.6%	8	35.5
Community Stability	19	34.45	% Living in Same House as in 1979	31.0%	16	54.8
			% Living in Same County as in 1985	48.6%	26	14.1

Composite: *Rank* 6 / 28 *Score* 54.98 — MABLETON

CATEGORY	RANK	SCORE	STATISTIC	VALUE	RANK	SCORE
Economics	13	55.70	Median Household Income	$35,027	13	29.8
			% of Families Above Poverty Level	95.6%	13	81.6
Affordable Housing	9	76.00	Median Home Value	$75,500	10	87.9
			Median Rent	$485	9	64.1
Crime	N/A	N/A	Violent Crimes per 10,000 Population	N/A	N/A	N/A
			Property Crimes per 10,000 Population	N/A	N/A	N/A
Open Spaces	8	64.85	Population Density (Persons/Sq. Mile)	1220	7	84.9
			Average Rooms per Housing Unit	5.8	9	44.8
Education	18	37.15	% High School Enrollment/Completion	88.9%	13	60.8
			% College Graduates	15.0%	22	13.5
Commute	23	20.35	Average Work Commute in Minutes	26	19	38.5
			% Commuting on Public Transportation	0.4%	23	2.2
Community Stability	9	75.85	% Living in Same House as in 1979	39.7%	7	76.6
			% Living in Same County as in 1985	75.1%	8	75.1

Composite: *Rank* 7 / 28 *Score* 54.27   **SNELLVILLE**

CATEGORY	RANK	SCORE	STATISTIC	VALUE	RANK	SCORE
Economics	6	72.80	Median Household Income	$46,875	5	54.8
			% of Families Above Poverty Level	97.4%	7	90.8
Affordable Housing	17	52.90	Median Home Value	$96,300	17	76.2
			Median Rent	$616	21	29.6
Crime	N/A	N/A	Violent Crimes per 10,000 Population	2	N/A	N/A
			Property Crimes per 10,000 Population	358	N/A	N/A
Open Spaces	3	77.15	Population Density (Persons/Sq. Mile)	1324	8	81.9
			Average Rooms per Housing Unit	6.6	4	72.4
Education	12	52.00	% High School Enrollment/Completion	93.0%	7	78.4
			% College Graduates	21.8%	16	25.6
Commute	28	3.85	Average Work Commute in Minutes	30	27	7.7
			% Commuting on Public Transportation	0.0%	27	0.0
Community Stability	13	66.90	% Living in Same House as in 1979	35.1%	12	65.1
			% Living in Same County as in 1985	72.3%	11	68.7

Composite: *Rank* 8 / 28 *Score* 52.59   **COVINGTON**

CATEGORY	RANK	SCORE	STATISTIC	VALUE	RANK	SCORE
Economics	26	4.30	Median Household Income	$21,344	26	0.9
			% of Families Above Poverty Level	81.1%	26	7.7
Affordable Housing	2	95.75	Median Home Value	$58,100	4	97.6
			Median Rent	$372	2	93.9
Crime	N/A	N/A	Violent Crimes per 10,000 Population	N/A	N/A	N/A
			Property Crimes per 10,000 Population	N/A	N/A	N/A
Open Spaces	11	58.20	Population Density (Persons/Sq. Mile)	836	4	95.7
			Average Rooms per Housing Unit	5.1	20	20.7
Education	24	17.55	% High School Enrollment/Completion	82.4%	20	32.8
			% College Graduates	8.7%	27	2.3
Commute	9	48.05	Average Work Commute in Minutes	19	3	92.3
			% Commuting on Public Transportation	0.7%	20	3.8
Community Stability	1	91.70	% Living in Same House as in 1979	42.4%	6	83.4
			% Living in Same County as in 1985	85.9%	1	100.0

Composite: *Rank* 9 / 28 *Score* 52.50   **ROSWELL**

CATEGORY	RANK	SCORE	STATISTIC	VALUE	RANK	SCORE
Economics	4	79.50	Median Household Income	$52,205	3	66.1
			% of Families Above Poverty Level	97.8%	5	92.9
Affordable Housing	24	44.00	Median Home Value	$142,100	25	50.5
			Median Rent	$586	18	37.5
Crime	N/A	N/A	Violent Crimes per 10,000 Population	16	N/A	N/A
			Property Crimes per 10,000 Population	474	N/A	N/A
Open Spaces	5	73.40	Population Density (Persons/Sq. Mile)	1471	10	77.8
			Average Rooms per Housing Unit	6.5	6	69.0
Education	5	77.55	% High School Enrollment/Completion	95.0%	5	87.1
			% College Graduates	45.6%	6	68.0
Commute	25	16.95	Average Work Commute in Minutes	28	23	23.1
			% Commuting on Public Transportation	2.0%	15	10.8
Community Stability	24	23.60	% Living in Same House as in 1979	17.9%	23	21.9
			% Living in Same County as in 1985	53.5%	23	25.3

Composite: *Rank* 10 / 28 *Score* 51.86   **CANDLER-MCAFEE**

CATEGORY	RANK	SCORE	STATISTIC	VALUE	RANK	SCORE
Economics	20	32.45	Median Household Income	$30,378	18	20.0
			% of Families Above Poverty Level	88.4%	21	44.9
Affordable Housing	8	76.40	Median Home Value	$61,300	6	95.8
			Median Rent	$512	10	57.0
Crime	N/A	N/A	Violent Crimes per 10,000 Population	N/A	N/A	N/A
			Property Crimes per 10,000 Population	N/A	N/A	N/A
Open Spaces	26	22.40	Population Density (Persons/Sq. Mile)	4225	28	0.0
			Average Rooms per Housing Unit	5.8	9	44.8
Education	16	39.35	% High School Enrollment/Completion	91.1%	10	70.3
			% College Graduates	12.1%	25	8.4
Commute	8	48.85	Average Work Commute in Minutes	29	26	15.4
			% Commuting on Public Transportation	15.3%	3	82.3
Community Stability	1	91.70	% Living in Same House as in 1979	49.0%	1	100.0
			% Living in Same County as in 1985	78.7%	5	83.4

Composite: *Rank* 11 / 28 *Score* 51.17   **PEACHTREE CITY**

CATEGORY	RANK	SCORE	STATISTIC	VALUE	RANK	SCORE
Economics	2	83.10	Median Household Income	$53,514	2	68.8
			% of Families Above Poverty Level	98.7%	3	97.4
Affordable Housing	26	36.85	Median Home Value	$118,200	22	63.9
			Median Rent	$691	27	9.8
Crime	N/A	N/A	Violent Crimes per 10,000 Population	3	N/A	N/A
			Property Crimes per 10,000 Population	144	N/A	N/A
Open Spaces	1	87.80	Population Density (Persons/Sq. Mile)	816	3	96.3
			Average Rooms per Housing Unit	6.8	2	79.3
Education	6	75.65	% High School Enrollment/Completion	97.3%	2	97.0
			% College Graduates	37.9%	8	54.3
Commute	24	19.50	Average Work Commute in Minutes	26	19	38.5
			% Commuting on Public Transportation	0.1%	26	0.5
Community Stability	28	4.15	% Living in Same House as in 1979	12.5%	26	8.3
			% Living in Same County as in 1985	42.5%	28	0.0

Composite: *Rank* 12 / 28 *Score* 50.56   **EAST POINT**

CATEGORY	RANK	SCORE	STATISTIC	VALUE	RANK	SCORE
Economics	23	21.25	Median Household Income	$26,787	23	12.4
			% of Families Above Poverty Level	85.5%	23	30.1
Affordable Housing	5	82.55	Median Home Value	$63,400	7	94.7
			Median Rent	$461	5	70.4
Crime	N/A	N/A	Violent Crimes per 10,000 Population	156	N/A	N/A
			Property Crimes per 10,000 Population	836	N/A	N/A
Open Spaces	21	32.95	Population Density (Persons/Sq. Mile)	2500	19	48.7
			Average Rooms per Housing Unit	5.0	23	17.2
Education	21	27.10	% High School Enrollment/Completion	83.0%	19	35.3
			% College Graduates	18.0%	18	18.9
Commute	4	67.70	Average Work Commute in Minutes	25	15	46.2
			% Commuting on Public Transportation	16.6%	2	89.2
Community Stability	11	71.80	% Living in Same House as in 1979	32.7%	14	59.0
			% Living in Same County as in 1985	79.2%	4	84.6

Metropolitan Area Suburb Rankings
ATLANTA

Composite: Rank 13 / 28 *Score* 50.46   **NORTH DRUID HILLS**

CATEGORY	RANK	SCORE	STATISTIC	VALUE	RANK	SCORE
Economics	11	60.85	Median Household Income	$35,534	12	30.9
			% of Families Above Poverty Level	97.4%	7	90.8
Affordable Housing	20	48.90	Median Home Value	$123,700	24	60.9
			Median Rent	$588	19	36.9
Crime	N/A	N/A	Violent Crimes per 10,000 Population	N/A	N/A	N/A
			Property Crimes per 10,000 Population	N/A	N/A	N/A
Open Spaces	23	28.05	Population Density (Persons/Sq. Mile)	2847	23	38.9
			Average Rooms per Housing Unit	5.0	23	17.2
Education	7	72.10	% High School Enrollment/Completion	90.2%	11	66.4
			% College Graduates	51.1%	4	77.8
Commute	6	60.60	Average Work Commute in Minutes	20	5	84.6
			% Commuting on Public Transportation	6.8%	7	36.6
Community Stability	20	32.25	% Living in Same House as in 1979	25.5%	17	41.0
			% Living in Same County as in 1985	52.7%	24	23.5

Composite: Rank 14 / 28 *Score* 49.98   **SANDY SPRINGS**

CATEGORY	RANK	SCORE	STATISTIC	VALUE	RANK	SCORE
Economics	7	71.05	Median Household Income	$45,226	7	51.3
			% of Families Above Poverty Level	97.4%	7	90.8
Affordable Housing	28	15.05	Median Home Value	$232,200	28	0.0
			Median Rent	$614	20	30.1
Crime	N/A	N/A	Violent Crimes per 10,000 Population	N/A	N/A	N/A
			Property Crimes per 10,000 Population	N/A	N/A	N/A
Open Spaces	14	56.55	Population Density (Persons/Sq. Mile)	1806	12	68.3
			Average Rooms per Housing Unit	5.8	9	44.8
Education	2	86.10	% High School Enrollment/Completion	95.9%	4	90.9
			% College Graduates	53.1%	3	81.3
Commute	15	40.70	Average Work Commute in Minutes	23	10	61.5
			% Commuting on Public Transportation	3.7%	11	19.9
Community Stability	22	30.40	% Living in Same House as in 1979	20.3%	20	27.9
			% Living in Same County as in 1985	56.8%	21	32.9

Composite: Rank 15 / 28 *Score* 49.03   **NEWNAN**

CATEGORY	RANK	SCORE	STATISTIC	VALUE	RANK	SCORE
Economics	27	2.40	Median Household Income	$20,993	27	0.2
			% of Families Above Poverty Level	80.5%	27	4.6
Affordable Housing	3	93.45	Median Home Value	$55,700	2	99.0
			Median Rent	$395	3	87.9
Crime	N/A	N/A	Violent Crimes per 10,000 Population	92	N/A	N/A
			Property Crimes per 10,000 Population	885	N/A	N/A
Open Spaces	13	57.40	Population Density (Persons/Sq. Mile)	1012	6	90.7
			Average Rooms per Housing Unit	5.2	18	24.1
Education	27	8.25	% High School Enrollment/Completion	74.8%	27	0.0
			% College Graduates	16.7%	21	16.5
Commute	7	50.00	Average Work Commute in Minutes	18	1	100.0
			% Commuting on Public Transportation	0.0%	27	0.0
Community Stability	4	82.70	% Living in Same House as in 1979	37.7%	8	71.6
			% Living in Same County as in 1985	83.2%	3	93.8

Composite: **Rank** 16 / 28 **Score** 48.31   **FOREST PARK**

CATEGORY	RANK	SCORE	STATISTIC	VALUE	RANK	SCORE
Economics	21	30.85	Median Household Income	$25,982	24	10.7
			% of Families Above Poverty Level	89.6%	19	51.0
Affordable Housing	4	83.10	Median Home Value	$53,900	1	100.0
			Median Rent	$477	6	66.2
Crime	N/A	N/A	Violent Crimes per 10,000 Population	N/A	N/A	N/A
			Property Crimes per 10,000 Population	N/A	N/A	N/A
Open Spaces	17	43.90	Population Density (Persons/Sq. Mile)	1969	14	63.7
			Average Rooms per Housing Unit	5.2	18	24.1
Education	25	14.20	% High School Enrollment/Completion	81.4%	25	28.4
			% College Graduates	7.4%	28	0.0
Commute	14	40.80	Average Work Commute in Minutes	22	7	69.2
			% Commuting on Public Transportation	2.3%	14	12.4
Community Stability	8	77.00	% Living in Same House as in 1979	43.0%	4	84.9
			% Living in Same County as in 1985	72.5%	10	69.1

Composite: **Rank** 17 / 28 **Score** 48.30   **DECATUR**

CATEGORY	RANK	SCORE	STATISTIC	VALUE	RANK	SCORE
Economics	24	20.50	Median Household Income	$26,803	22	12.4
			% of Families Above Poverty Level	85.2%	24	28.6
Affordable Housing	7	76.55	Median Home Value	$95,300	16	76.8
			Median Rent	$439	4	76.3
Crime	N/A	N/A	Violent Crimes per 10,000 Population	N/A	N/A	N/A
			Property Crimes per 10,000 Population	N/A	N/A	N/A
Open Spaces	27	14.60	Population Density (Persons/Sq. Mile)	4169	27	1.6
			Average Rooms per Housing Unit	5.3	16	27.6
Education	15	44.30	% High School Enrollment/Completion	81.7%	24	29.7
			% College Graduates	40.5%	7	58.9
Commute	2	69.20	Average Work Commute in Minutes	23	10	61.5
			% Commuting on Public Transportation	14.3%	4	76.9
Community Stability	14	64.65	% Living in Same House as in 1979	34.9%	13	64.6
			% Living in Same County as in 1985	70.6%	14	64.7

Composite: **Rank** 18 / 28 **Score** 47.62   **GRIFFIN**

CATEGORY	RANK	SCORE	STATISTIC	VALUE	RANK	SCORE
Economics	25	4.85	Median Household Income	$20,915	28	0.0
			% of Families Above Poverty Level	81.5%	25	9.7
Affordable Housing	1	98.75	Median Home Value	$58,300	5	97.5
			Median Rent	$349	1	100.0
Crime	N/A	N/A	Violent Crimes per 10,000 Population	151	N/A	N/A
			Property Crimes per 10,000 Population	988	N/A	N/A
Open Spaces	16	46.70	Population Density (Persons/Sq. Mile)	1652	11	72.7
			Average Rooms per Housing Unit	5.1	20	20.7
Education	28	6.25	% High School Enrollment/Completion	74.8%	27	0.0
			% College Graduates	14.4%	23	12.5
Commute	10	47.25	Average Work Commute in Minutes	19	3	92.3
			% Commuting on Public Transportation	0.4%	23	2.2
Community Stability	5	81.90	% Living in Same House as in 1979	37.0%	10	69.8
			% Living in Same County as in 1985	83.3%	2	94.0

Metropolitan Area Suburb Rankings
ATLANTA

Composite: *Rank* 19 / 28 *Score* 45.99   **ALPHARETTA**

CATEGORY	RANK	SCORE	STATISTIC	VALUE	RANK	SCORE
Economics	8	70.90	Median Household Income	$44,335	8	49.5
			% of Families Above Poverty Level	97.7%	6	92.3
Affordable Housing	23	44.55	Median Home Value	$119,500	23	63.2
			Median Rent	$630	23	25.9
Crime	N/A	N/A	Violent Crimes per 10,000 Population	12	N/A	N/A
			Property Crimes per 10,000 Population	341	N/A	N/A
Open Spaces	4	74.15	Population Density (Persons/Sq. Mile)	684	1	100.0
			Average Rooms per Housing Unit	5.9	7	48.3
Education	11	53.85	% High School Enrollment/Completion	87.6%	14	55.2
			% College Graduates	36.9%	10	52.5
Commute	21	22.50	Average Work Commute in Minutes	26	19	38.5
			% Commuting on Public Transportation	1.2%	17	6.5
Community Stability	27	10.00	% Living in Same House as in 1979	12.1%	27	7.3
			% Living in Same County as in 1985	48.0%	27	12.7

Composite: *Rank* 20 / 28 *Score* 45.58   **LITHIA SPRINGS**

CATEGORY	RANK	SCORE	STATISTIC	VALUE	RANK	SCORE
Economics	15	52.50	Median Household Income	$32,954	16	25.4
			% of Families Above Poverty Level	95.2%	15	79.6
Affordable Housing	12	69.35	Median Home Value	$71,100	8	90.4
			Median Rent	$545	14	48.3
Crime	N/A	N/A	Violent Crimes per 10,000 Population	N/A	N/A	N/A
			Property Crimes per 10,000 Population	N/A	N/A	N/A
Open Spaces	10	59.55	Population Density (Persons/Sq. Mile)	739	2	98.4
			Average Rooms per Housing Unit	5.1	20	20.7
Education	23	19.40	% High School Enrollment/Completion	82.2%	21	31.9
			% College Graduates	11.3%	26	6.9
Commute	22	20.85	Average Work Commute in Minutes	26	19	38.5
			% Commuting on Public Transportation	0.6%	21	3.2
Community Stability	15	51.85	% Living in Same House as in 1979	31.5%	15	56.0
			% Living in Same County as in 1985	63.2%	17	47.7

Composite: *Rank* 21 / 28 *Score* 44.23   **DOUGLASVILLE**

CATEGORY	RANK	SCORE	STATISTIC	VALUE	RANK	SCORE
Economics	19	33.10	Median Household Income	$30,275	19	19.8
			% of Families Above Poverty Level	88.7%	20	46.4
Affordable Housing	10	74.80	Median Home Value	$80,300	12	85.2
			Median Rent	$484	8	64.4
Crime	N/A	N/A	Violent Crimes per 10,000 Population	N/A	N/A	N/A
			Property Crimes per 10,000 Population	N/A	N/A	N/A
Open Spaces	9	59.75	Population Density (Persons/Sq. Mile)	970	5	91.9
			Average Rooms per Housing Unit	5.3	16	27.6
Education	22	24.40	% High School Enrollment/Completion	82.2%	21	31.9
			% College Graduates	16.9%	20	16.9
Commute	19	24.45	Average Work Commute in Minutes	25	15	46.2
			% Commuting on Public Transportation	0.5%	22	2.7
Community Stability	16	48.85	% Living in Same House as in 1979	25.5%	17	41.0
			% Living in Same County as in 1985	67.1%	15	56.7

Composite: **Rank** 22 / 28 *Score* 43.47   **LAWRENCEVILLE**

CATEGORY	RANK	SCORE	STATISTIC	VALUE	RANK	SCORE
Economics	16	49.40	Median Household Income	$34,826	14	29.4
			% of Families Above Poverty Level	93.2%	16	69.4
Affordable Housing	13	67.75	Median Home Value	$88,500	15	80.6
			Median Rent	$520	11	54.9
Crime	N/A	N/A	Violent Crimes per 10,000 Population	48	N/A	N/A
			Property Crimes per 10,000 Population	592	N/A	N/A
Open Spaces	12	57.65	Population Density (Persons/Sq. Mile)	1365	9	80.8
			Average Rooms per Housing Unit	5.5	12	34.5
Education	20	27.45	% High School Enrollment/Completion	81.8%	23	30.2
			% College Graduates	21.3%	17	24.7
Commute	20	23.65	Average Work Commute in Minutes	25	15	46.2
			% Commuting on Public Transportation	0.2%	25	1.1
Community Stability	18	34.95	% Living in Same House as in 1979	19.6%	21	26.1
			% Living in Same County as in 1985	61.5%	18	43.8

Composite: **Rank** 23 / 28 *Score* 42.95   **SMYRNA**

CATEGORY	RANK	SCORE	STATISTIC	VALUE	RANK	SCORE
Economics	14	55.25	Median Household Income	$33,863	15	27.3
			% of Families Above Poverty Level	95.9%	12	83.2
Affordable Housing	15	64.90	Median Home Value	$78,800	11	86.0
			Median Rent	$562	17	43.8
Crime	N/A	N/A	Violent Crimes per 10,000 Population	57	N/A	N/A
			Property Crimes per 10,000 Population	836	N/A	N/A
Open Spaces	24	26.35	Population Density (Persons/Sq. Mile)	2724	21	42.4
			Average Rooms per Housing Unit	4.8	25	10.3
Education	13	46.60	% High School Enrollment/Completion	85.4%	15	45.7
			% College Graduates	34.1%	12	47.5
Commute	18	33.70	Average Work Commute in Minutes	23	10	61.5
			% Commuting on Public Transportation	1.1%	19	5.9
Community Stability	21	30.90	% Living in Same House as in 1979	19.6%	21	26.1
			% Living in Same County as in 1985	58.0%	19	35.7

Composite: **Rank** 24 / 28 *Score* 42.53   **BELVEDERE PARK**

CATEGORY	RANK	SCORE	STATISTIC	VALUE	RANK	SCORE
Economics	22	25.95	Median Household Income	$27,853	20	14.7
			% of Families Above Poverty Level	86.9%	22	37.2
Affordable Housing	11	74.50	Median Home Value	$57,300	3	98.1
			Median Rent	$535	12	50.9
Crime	N/A	N/A	Violent Crimes per 10,000 Population	N/A	N/A	N/A
			Property Crimes per 10,000 Population	N/A	N/A	N/A
Open Spaces	25	23.90	Population Density (Persons/Sq. Mile)	3630	25	16.8
			Average Rooms per Housing Unit	5.4	13	31.0
Education	26	11.80	% High School Enrollment/Completion	78.2%	26	14.7
			% College Graduates	12.4%	24	8.9
Commute	11	46.75	Average Work Commute in Minutes	28	23	23.1
			% Commuting on Public Transportation	13.1%	5	70.4
Community Stability	10	72.30	% Living in Same House as in 1979	35.4%	11	65.8
			% Living in Same County as in 1985	76.7%	6	78.8

Metropolitan Area Suburb Rankings
ATLANTA

Composite: **Rank** 25 / 28 **Score** 41.80   **NORTH ATLANTA**

CATEGORY	RANK	SCORE	STATISTIC	VALUE	RANK	SCORE
Economics	17	41.25	Median Household Income	$31,014	17	21.3
			% of Families Above Poverty Level	91.6%	17	61.2
Affordable Housing	16	60.85	Median Home Value	$98,400	18	75.0
			Median Rent	$551	16	46.7
Crime	N/A	N/A	Violent Crimes per 10,000 Population	N/A	N/A	N/A
			Property Crimes per 10,000 Population	N/A	N/A	N/A
Open Spaces	28	13.40	Population Density (Persons/Sq. Mile)	3640	26	16.5
			Average Rooms per Housing Unit	4.8	25	10.3
Education	14	46.45	% High School Enrollment/Completion	84.5%	17	41.8
			% College Graduates	36.1%	11	51.1
Commute	5	67.15	Average Work Commute in Minutes	22	7	69.2
			% Commuting on Public Transportation	12.1%	6	65.1
Community Stability	25	21.70	% Living in Same House as in 1979	20.7%	19	28.9
			% Living in Same County as in 1985	48.8%	25	14.5

Composite: **Rank** 26 / 28 **Score** 41.78   **REDAN**

CATEGORY	RANK	SCORE	STATISTIC	VALUE	RANK	SCORE
Economics	9	67.45	Median Household Income	$41,802	9	44.1
			% of Families Above Poverty Level	97.4%	7	90.8
Affordable Housing	18	51.30	Median Home Value	$82,300	13	84.1
			Median Rent	$658	25	18.5
Crime	N/A	N/A	Violent Crimes per 10,000 Population	N/A	N/A	N/A
			Property Crimes per 10,000 Population	N/A	N/A	N/A
Open Spaces	15	47.90	Population Density (Persons/Sq. Mile)	2542	20	47.5
			Average Rooms per Housing Unit	5.9	7	48.3
Education	10	56.60	% High School Enrollment/Completion	90.2%	11	66.4
			% College Graduates	33.7%	13	46.8
Commute	27	10.50	Average Work Commute in Minutes	31	28	0.0
			% Commuting on Public Transportation	3.9%	10	21.0
Community Stability	26	16.95	% Living in Same House as in 1979	9.2%	28	0.0
			% Living in Same County as in 1985	57.2%	20	33.9

Composite: **Rank** 27 / 28 **Score** 41.49   **COLLEGE PARK**

CATEGORY	RANK	SCORE	STATISTIC	VALUE	RANK	SCORE
Economics	28	1.35	Median Household Income	$22,194	25	2.7
			% of Families Above Poverty Level	79.6%	28	0.0
Affordable Housing	6	77.50	Median Home Value	$73,500	9	89.0
			Median Rent	$478	7	66.0
Crime	N/A	N/A	Violent Crimes per 10,000 Population	189	N/A	N/A
			Property Crimes per 10,000 Population	1,603	N/A	N/A
Open Spaces	22	30.20	Population Density (Persons/Sq. Mile)	2087	15	60.4
			Average Rooms per Housing Unit	4.5	28	0.0
Education	19	29.75	% High School Enrollment/Completion	84.6%	16	42.2
			% College Graduates	17.1%	19	17.3
Commute	1	73.10	Average Work Commute in Minutes	25	15	46.2
			% Commuting on Public Transportation	18.6%	1	100.0
Community Stability	17	37.05	% Living in Same House as in 1979	17.6%	25	21.1
			% Living in Same County as in 1985	65.5%	16	53.0

Metropolitan Area Suburb Rankings
ATLANTA

Composite: *Rank* 28 / 28 *Score* 39.46   **MARIETTA**

CATEGORY	RANK	SCORE	STATISTIC	VALUE	RANK	SCORE
Economics	18	34.85	Median Household Income	$27,371	21	13.6
			% of Families Above Poverty Level	90.6%	18	56.1
Affordable Housing	14	66.15	Median Home Value	$85,300	14	82.4
			Median Rent	$539	13	49.9
Crime	N/A	N/A	Violent Crimes per 10,000 Population	168	N/A	N/A
			Property Crimes per 10,000 Population	1,174	N/A	N/A
Open Spaces	19	34.20	Population Density (Persons/Sq. Mile)	2166	17	58.1
			Average Rooms per Housing Unit	4.8	25	10.3
Education	17	38.10	% High School Enrollment/Completion	83.9%	18	39.2
			% College Graduates	28.2%	15	37.0
Commute	17	37.85	Average Work Commute in Minutes	22	7	69.2
			% Commuting on Public Transportation	1.2%	17	6.5
Community Stability	23	25.60	% Living in Same House as in 1979	17.9%	23	21.9
			% Living in Same County as in 1985	55.2%	22	29.3

Metropolitan Area Description
BALTIMORE

STATE: Maryland

COUNTIES: Anne Arundel, Baltimore, Carroll, Harford, Howard, Queen Anne's

INDE-PENDENT CITIES: Baltimore

TOTAL POPULATION: 2,382,172

POPULATION IN SUBURBS: 1,646,158 (69.1%)

POPULATION IN Baltimore: 736,014 (30.9%)

The BALTIMORE metropolitan area is located in the northeastern part of Maryland along the Chesapeake Bay. The suburbs range geographically from Westminster in the northwest (32 miles from Baltimore), to Parole in the south (30 miles from Baltimore), and to Aberdeen in the east (31 miles from Baltimore). The area is growing in population and had an increase of 8.3% between 1980 and 1990. Summer time high temperatures average in the 80's and winter time lows average in the 20's. The suburb of Columbia has attracted many companies including General Electric, Bendix, and the Applied Physics Laboratory of Johns Hopkins University. AAI Corporation, one of Maryland's largest employers, is located in Cockeysville. Westinghouse has major divisions in the area employing over 17,000 persons. Public transportation in the area is provided by the Baltimore Metro Subway System and by many bus routes.

Lutherville-Timonium is the overall highest rated suburb and also has the highest score in community stability. **Severna Park** receives the highest score in economics. **Essex** is the suburb with the most affordable housing. The number one rating in education belongs to **Mays Chapel**. The top rated commute goes to **Lansdowne-Baltimore Highlands**. Finally, **Bel Air North** is the number one rated suburb in open spaces. Crime rankings were not available for the area.

The highest ranked suburb overall which also has an affordable housing score of at least 50.00 is **Lutherville-Timonium**.

The highest ranked suburb in the education category which also has an affordable housing score of at least 50.00 is **Towson**.

The county whose suburbs have the highest average overall score is **Baltimore County** (56.65).

Metropolitan Area Map
BALTIMORE

Harford Co.

Queen Anne's Co.

•1

•6

•5

•21

•14.

•35

•27

17

•8 31

40

13

BALTIMORE

32

•44

•10

•26 25.

•24

36

•37 46. 9•

•3

•15

•16

•28

Howard Co. 11•

•38

Carroll Co.

•45

•29

Baltimore Co.

39

•20 22

•4

•33 •2

•19

•43 •34

•42

•23 7

18

•41 •30

•12

Anne Arundel Co.

Maryland

Metropolitan Area Suburb Alphabetical Index
BALTIMORE

SUBURB	PAGE	MAP NO.	STATE	COUNTY	POPU-LATION	RANK
ABERDEEN	42	1	Maryland	Harford	13,087	33 / 46
ANNAPOLIS	45	2	Maryland	Anne Arundel	33,187	40 / 46
ARBUTUS	36	3	Maryland	Baltimore	19,750	13 / 46
ARNOLD	38	4	Maryland	Anne Arundel	20,261	19 / 46
BEL AIR NORTH	37	5	Maryland	Harford	14,880	16 / 46
BEL AIR SOUTH	40	6	Maryland	Harford	26,421	26 / 46
BROOKLYN PARK	38	7	Maryland	Anne Arundel	10,987	21 / 46
CARNEY	44	8	Maryland	Baltimore	25,578	37 / 46
CATONSVILLE	33	9	Maryland	Baltimore	35,233	5 / 46
COCKEYSVILLE	43	10	Maryland	Baltimore	18,668	35 / 46
COLUMBIA	40	11	Maryland	Howard	75,883	27 / 46
CROFTON	42	12	Maryland	Anne Arundel	12,781	31 / 46
DUNDALK	37	13	Maryland	Baltimore	65,800	17 / 46
EDGEWOOD	44	14	Maryland	Harford	23,903	39 / 46
ELKRIDGE	45	15	Maryland	Howard	12,953	42 / 46
ELLICOTT CITY	38	16	Maryland	Howard	41,396	20 / 46
ESSEX	46	17	Maryland	Baltimore	40,872	44 / 46
FERNDALE	41	18	Maryland	Anne Arundel	16,355	29 / 46
GLEN BURNIE	43	19	Maryland	Anne Arundel	37,305	34 / 46
GREEN HAVEN	46	20	Maryland	Anne Arundel	14,416	45 / 46
JOPPATOWNE	36	21	Maryland	Harford	11,084	14 / 46
LAKE SHORE	35	22	Maryland	Anne Arundel	13,269	10 / 46
LANSDOWNE-BALTIMORE HIGHLANDS	42	23	Maryland	Baltimore	15,509	32 / 46
LOCHEARN	34	24	Maryland	Baltimore	25,240	8 / 46
LUTHERVILLE-TIMONIUM	32	25	Maryland	Baltimore	16,442	1 / 46
MAYS CHAPEL	32	26	Maryland	Baltimore	10,132	2 / 46
MIDDLE RIVER	45	27	Maryland	Baltimore	24,616	41 / 46
MILFORD MILL	41	28	Maryland	Baltimore	22,547	30 / 46
NORTH LAUREL	44	29	Maryland	Howard	15,008	38 / 46
ODENTON	36	30	Maryland	Anne Arundel	12,833	15 / 46
OVERLEA	35	31	Maryland	Baltimore	12,137	11 / 46
PARKVILLE	39	32	Maryland	Baltimore	31,617	24 / 46
PAROLE	40	33	Maryland	Anne Arundel	10,054	25 / 46
PASADENA	34	34	Maryland	Anne Arundel	10,012	9 / 46
PERRY HALL	39	35	Maryland	Baltimore	22,723	22 / 46
PIKESVILLE	33	36	Maryland	Baltimore	24,815	6 / 46
RANDALLSTOWN	34	37	Maryland	Baltimore	26,277	7 / 46
REISTERSTOWN	39	38	Maryland	Baltimore	19,314	23 / 46
RIVIERA BEACH	41	39	Maryland	Anne Arundel	11,376	28 / 46
ROSEDALE	35	40	Maryland	Baltimore	18,703	12 / 46
SEVERN	43	41	Maryland	Anne Arundel	24,499	36 / 46
SEVERNA PARK	33	42	Maryland	Anne Arundel	25,879	4 / 46
SOUTH GATE	47	43	Maryland	Anne Arundel	27,564	46 / 46
TOWSON	32	44	Maryland	Baltimore	49,445	3 / 46
WESTMINSTER	46	45	Maryland	Carroll	13,068	43 / 46
WOODLAWN	37	46	Maryland	Baltimore	32,907	18 / 46

Metropolitan Area Suburb Rankings
BALTIMORE

Composite: Rank 1 / 46 *Score* 72.84   LUTHERVILLE-TIMONIUM

CATEGORY	RANK	SCORE	STATISTIC	VALUE	RANK	SCORE
Economics	12	76.70	Median Household Income	$51,265	11	65.0
			% of Families Above Poverty Level	98.1%	18	88.4
Affordable Housing	31	52.75	Median Home Value	$149,500	38	34.5
			Median Rent	$544	19	71.0
Crime	N/A	N/A	Violent Crimes per 10,000 Population	N/A	N/A	N/A
			Property Crimes per 10,000 Population	N/A	N/A	N/A
Open Spaces	10	76.05	Population Density (Persons/Sq. Mile)	2212	17	80.1
			Average Rooms per Housing Unit	6.8	6	72.0
Education	5	78.80	% High School Enrollment/Completion	97.6%	5	91.1
			% College Graduates	40.4%	10	66.5
Commute	13	56.85	Average Work Commute in Minutes	21	3	91.7
			% Commuting on Public Transportation	2.6%	21	22.0
Community Stability	1	95.90	% Living in Same House as in 1979	57.7%	2	99.5
			% Living in Same County as in 1985	84.6%	2	92.3

Composite: Rank 2 / 46 *Score* 64.15   MAYS CHAPEL

CATEGORY	RANK	SCORE	STATISTIC	VALUE	RANK	SCORE
Economics	2	95.55	Median Household Income	$60,848	2	91.1
			% of Families Above Poverty Level	99.4%	1	100.0
Affordable Housing	43	19.65	Median Home Value	$166,100	43	21.1
			Median Rent	$782	43	18.2
Crime	N/A	N/A	Violent Crimes per 10,000 Population	N/A	N/A	N/A
			Property Crimes per 10,000 Population	N/A	N/A	N/A
Open Spaces	9	78.35	Population Density (Persons/Sq. Mile)	2700	23	72.7
			Average Rooms per Housing Unit	7.1	2	84.0
Education	1	93.30	% High School Enrollment/Completion	100.0%	1	100.0
			% College Graduates	51.2%	2	86.6
Commute	14	55.35	Average Work Commute in Minutes	21	3	91.7
			% Commuting on Public Transportation	2.3%	22	19.0
Community Stability	32	42.70	% Living in Same House as in 1979	22.3%	39	14.2
			% Living in Same County as in 1985	76.7%	20	71.2

Composite: Rank 3 / 46 *Score* 62.82   TOWSON

CATEGORY	RANK	SCORE	STATISTIC	VALUE	RANK	SCORE
Economics	20	65.80	Median Household Income	$41,635	23	38.7
			% of Families Above Poverty Level	98.6%	9	92.9
Affordable Housing	30	53.35	Median Home Value	$133,800	32	47.1
			Median Rent	$595	28	59.6
Crime	N/A	N/A	Violent Crimes per 10,000 Population	N/A	N/A	N/A
			Property Crimes per 10,000 Population	N/A	N/A	N/A
Open Spaces	30	48.05	Population Density (Persons/Sq. Mile)	3521	32	60.1
			Average Rooms per Housing Unit	5.9	28	36.0
Education	3	86.35	% High School Enrollment/Completion	99.0%	2	96.3
			% College Graduates	45.7%	5	76.4
Commute	4	65.35	Average Work Commute in Minutes	21	3	91.7
			% Commuting on Public Transportation	4.3%	13	39.0
Community Stability	24	58.00	% Living in Same House as in 1979	42.5%	11	62.9
			% Living in Same County as in 1985	69.9%	34	53.1

Metropolitan Area Suburb Rankings
BALTIMORE

Composite: *Rank* 4 / 46 *Score* 62.04   **SEVERNA PARK**

CATEGORY	RANK	SCORE	STATISTIC	VALUE	RANK	SCORE
Economics	1	97.30	Median Household Income	$64,088	1	100.0
			% of Families Above Poverty Level	98.8%	4	94.6
Affordable Housing	46	10.10	Median Home Value	$177,500	44	12.0
			Median Rent	$827	45	8.2
Crime	N/A	N/A	Violent Crimes per 10,000 Population	N/A	N/A	N/A
			Property Crimes per 10,000 Population	N/A	N/A	N/A
Open Spaces	2	91.65	Population Density (Persons/Sq. Mile)	2003	15	83.3
			Average Rooms per Housing Unit	7.5	1	100.0
Education	6	77.30	% High School Enrollment/Completion	94.5%	15	79.7
			% College Graduates	44.9%	6	74.9
Commute	40	24.65	Average Work Commute in Minutes	28	36	33.3
			% Commuting on Public Transportation	2.0%	26	16.0
Community Stability	10	71.25	% Living in Same House as in 1979	41.2%	15	59.8
			% Living in Same County as in 1985	81.0%	10	82.7

Composite: *Rank* 5 / 46 *Score* 61.98   **CATONSVILLE**

CATEGORY	RANK	SCORE	STATISTIC	VALUE	RANK	SCORE
Economics	24	59.50	Median Household Income	$39,340	28	32.4
			% of Families Above Poverty Level	97.9%	19	86.6
Affordable Housing	22	69.20	Median Home Value	$110,200	24	66.1
			Median Rent	$538	15	72.3
Crime	N/A	N/A	Violent Crimes per 10,000 Population	N/A	N/A	N/A
			Property Crimes per 10,000 Population	N/A	N/A	N/A
Open Spaces	20	59.75	Population Density (Persons/Sq. Mile)	2515	20	75.5
			Average Rooms per Housing Unit	6.1	20	44.0
Education	16	67.10	% High School Enrollment/Completion	96.6%	7	87.5
			% College Graduates	29.7%	18	46.7
Commute	11	58.15	Average Work Commute in Minutes	22	7	83.3
			% Commuting on Public Transportation	3.7%	14	33.0
Community Stability	23	58.20	% Living in Same House as in 1979	40.8%	17	58.8
			% Living in Same County as in 1985	71.6%	29	57.6

Composite: *Rank* 6 / 46 *Score* 61.81   **PIKESVILLE**

CATEGORY	RANK	SCORE	STATISTIC	VALUE	RANK	SCORE
Economics	19	67.00	Median Household Income	$48,425	14	57.2
			% of Families Above Poverty Level	96.8%	27	76.8
Affordable Housing	36	44.00	Median Home Value	$151,900	41	32.6
			Median Rent	$614	33	55.4
Crime	N/A	N/A	Violent Crimes per 10,000 Population	N/A	N/A	N/A
			Property Crimes per 10,000 Population	N/A	N/A	N/A
Open Spaces	17	63.10	Population Density (Persons/Sq. Mile)	2072	16	82.2
			Average Rooms per Housing Unit	6.1	20	44.0
Education	8	74.65	% High School Enrollment/Completion	92.5%	23	72.3
			% College Graduates	46.0%	4	77.0
Commute	8	61.65	Average Work Commute in Minutes	22	7	83.3
			% Commuting on Public Transportation	4.4%	11	40.0
Community Stability	21	60.45	% Living in Same House as in 1979	42.2%	13	62.2
			% Living in Same County as in 1985	72.0%	28	58.7

Metropolitan Area Suburb Rankings
BALTIMORE

Composite: *Rank* 7 / 46 *Score* 61.80   **RANDALLSTOWN**

CATEGORY	RANK	SCORE	STATISTIC	VALUE	RANK	SCORE
Economics	18	67.95	Median Household Income	$46,190	17	51.1
			% of Families Above Poverty Level	97.7%	21	84.8
Affordable Housing	21	70.00	Median Home Value	$103,200	22	71.7
			Median Rent	$556	21	68.3
Crime	N/A	N/A	Violent Crimes per 10,000 Population	N/A	N/A	N/A
			Property Crimes per 10,000 Population	N/A	N/A	N/A
Open Spaces	14	69.45	Population Density (Persons/Sq. Mile)	2556	22	74.9
			Average Rooms per Housing Unit	6.6	11	64.0
Education	19	61.35	% High School Enrollment/Completion	91.9%	26	70.1
			% College Graduates	32.9%	14	52.6
Commute	22	39.65	Average Work Commute in Minutes	28	36	33.3
			% Commuting on Public Transportation	5.0%	6	46.0
Community Stability	20	62.40	% Living in Same House as in 1979	41.3%	14	60.0
			% Living in Same County as in 1985	74.3%	23	64.8

Composite: *Rank* 8 / 46 *Score* 61.19   **LOCHEARN**

CATEGORY	RANK	SCORE	STATISTIC	VALUE	RANK	SCORE
Economics	33	48.25	Median Household Income	$39,619	26	33.1
			% of Families Above Poverty Level	95.3%	35	63.4
Affordable Housing	11	79.15	Median Home Value	$85,400	8	86.0
			Median Rent	$538	15	72.3
Crime	N/A	N/A	Violent Crimes per 10,000 Population	N/A	N/A	N/A
			Property Crimes per 10,000 Population	N/A	N/A	N/A
Open Spaces	34	44.35	Population Density (Persons/Sq. Mile)	4531	42	44.7
			Average Rooms per Housing Unit	6.1	20	44.0
Education	21	56.50	% High School Enrollment/Completion	93.7%	20	76.8
			% College Graduates	24.1%	22	36.2
Commute	2	70.85	Average Work Commute in Minutes	27	29	41.7
			% Commuting on Public Transportation	10.4%	1	100.0
Community Stability	14	68.05	% Living in Same House as in 1979	47.3%	8	74.5
			% Living in Same County as in 1985	73.1%	26	61.6

Composite: *Rank* 9 / 46 *Score* 60.32   **PASADENA**

CATEGORY	RANK	SCORE	STATISTIC	VALUE	RANK	SCORE
Economics	10	79.25	Median Household Income	$51,816	9	66.5
			% of Families Above Poverty Level	98.5%	10	92.0
Affordable Housing	34	49.00	Median Home Value	$141,600	35	40.8
			Median Rent	$606	31	57.2
Crime	N/A	N/A	Violent Crimes per 10,000 Population	N/A	N/A	N/A
			Property Crimes per 10,000 Population	N/A	N/A	N/A
Open Spaces	5	82.60	Population Density (Persons/Sq. Mile)	1351	7	93.2
			Average Rooms per Housing Unit	6.8	6	72.0
Education	28	48.95	% High School Enrollment/Completion	90.0%	30	63.1
			% College Graduates	23.3%	24	34.8
Commute	33	29.50	Average Work Commute in Minutes	26	26	50.0
			% Commuting on Public Transportation	1.3%	33	9.0
Community Stability	8	72.60	% Living in Same House as in 1979	41.0%	16	59.3
			% Living in Same County as in 1985	82.2%	6	85.9

Metropolitan Area Suburb Rankings
BALTIMORE

Composite: Rank 10 / 46 *Score* 60.12   **LAKE SHORE**

CATEGORY	RANK	SCORE	STATISTIC	VALUE	RANK	SCORE
Economics	7	81.50	Median Household Income	$51,516	10	65.7
			% of Families Above Poverty Level	99.1%	3	97.3
Affordable Housing	39	35.35	Median Home Value	$140,000	34	42.1
			Median Rent	$735	41	28.6
Crime	N/A	N/A	Violent Crimes per 10,000 Population	N/A	N/A	N/A
			Property Crimes per 10,000 Population	N/A	N/A	N/A
Open Spaces	4	83.00	Population Density (Persons/Sq. Mile)	1302	5	94.0
			Average Rooms per Housing Unit	6.8	6	72.0
Education	25	52.45	% High School Enrollment/Completion	94.0%	18	77.9
			% College Graduates	19.1%	29	27.0
Commute	43	13.00	Average Work Commute in Minutes	29	43	25.0
			% Commuting on Public Transportation	0.5%	45	1.0
Community Stability	2	95.40	% Living in Same House as in 1979	54.1%	4	90.8
			% Living in Same County as in 1985	87.5%	1	100.0

Composite: Rank 11 / 46 *Score* 59.99   **OVERLEA**

CATEGORY	RANK	SCORE	STATISTIC	VALUE	RANK	SCORE
Economics	26	55.30	Median Household Income	$36,283	33	24.0
			% of Families Above Poverty Level	97.9%	19	86.6
Affordable Housing	12	78.85	Median Home Value	$87,500	10	84.3
			Median Rent	$533	14	73.4
Crime	N/A	N/A	Violent Crimes per 10,000 Population	N/A	N/A	N/A
			Property Crimes per 10,000 Population	N/A	N/A	N/A
Open Spaces	31	46.90	Population Density (Persons/Sq. Mile)	3935	37	53.8
			Average Rooms per Housing Unit	6.0	26	40.0
Education	27	49.35	% High School Enrollment/Completion	94.3%	17	79.0
			% College Graduates	15.2%	36	19.7
Commute	21	44.85	Average Work Commute in Minutes	24	15	66.7
			% Commuting on Public Transportation	2.7%	20	23.0
Community Stability	6	84.70	% Living in Same House as in 1979	50.3%	6	81.7
			% Living in Same County as in 1985	82.9%	5	87.7

Composite: Rank 12 / 46 *Score* 59.53   **ROSEDALE**

CATEGORY	RANK	SCORE	STATISTIC	VALUE	RANK	SCORE
Economics	28	54.20	Median Household Income	$39,398	27	32.5
			% of Families Above Poverty Level	96.7%	29	75.9
Affordable Housing	16	75.05	Median Home Value	$94,300	15	78.9
			Median Rent	$543	18	71.2
Crime	N/A	N/A	Violent Crimes per 10,000 Population	N/A	N/A	N/A
			Property Crimes per 10,000 Population	N/A	N/A	N/A
Open Spaces	22	58.05	Population Density (Persons/Sq. Mile)	2739	24	72.1
			Average Rooms per Housing Unit	6.1	20	44.0
Education	36	36.65	% High School Enrollment/Completion	89.0%	33	59.4
			% College Graduates	12.1%	39	13.9
Commute	19	47.85	Average Work Commute in Minutes	24	15	66.7
			% Commuting on Public Transportation	3.3%	17	29.0
Community Stability	5	85.40	% Living in Same House as in 1979	54.1%	4	90.8
			% Living in Same County as in 1985	80.0%	11	80.0

Metropolitan Area Suburb Rankings
BALTIMORE

***Composite:** **Rank** 13 / 46 **Score** 59.42*   **ARBUTUS**

CATEGORY	RANK	SCORE	STATISTIC	VALUE	RANK	SCORE
Economics	31	48.50	Median Household Income	$35,227	37	21.1
			% of Families Above Poverty Level	96.7%	29	75.9
Affordable Housing	8	83.70	Median Home Value	$91,800	12	80.9
			Median Rent	$474	9	86.5
Crime	N/A	N/A	Violent Crimes per 10,000 Population	N/A	N/A	N/A
			Property Crimes per 10,000 Population	N/A	N/A	N/A
Open Spaces	25	51.75	Population Density (Persons/Sq. Mile)	3041	26	67.5
			Average Rooms per Housing Unit	5.9	28	36.0
Education	32	41.15	% High School Enrollment/Completion	89.7%	32	62.0
			% College Graduates	15.5%	35	20.3
Commute	3	67.35	Average Work Commute in Minutes	21	3	91.7
			% Commuting on Public Transportation	4.7%	8	43.0
Community Stability	18	64.10	% Living in Same House as in 1979	46.9%	9	73.5
			% Living in Same County as in 1985	70.5%	31	54.7

***Composite:** **Rank** 14 / 46 **Score** 58.24*   **JOPPATOWNE**

CATEGORY	RANK	SCORE	STATISTIC	VALUE	RANK	SCORE
Economics	22	62.15	Median Household Income	$42,941	22	42.2
			% of Families Above Poverty Level	97.4%	23	82.1
Affordable Housing	19	71.85	Median Home Value	$101,900	20	72.7
			Median Rent	$544	19	71.0
Crime	N/A	N/A	Violent Crimes per 10,000 Population	N/A	N/A	N/A
			Property Crimes per 10,000 Population	N/A	N/A	N/A
Open Spaces	13	70.50	Population Density (Persons/Sq. Mile)	1627	9	89.0
			Average Rooms per Housing Unit	6.3	16	52.0
Education	26	50.00	% High School Enrollment/Completion	94.0%	18	77.9
			% College Graduates	16.5%	33	22.1
Commute	37	25.35	Average Work Commute in Minutes	27	29	41.7
			% Commuting on Public Transportation	1.3%	33	9.0
Community Stability	11	69.60	% Living in Same House as in 1979	42.3%	12	62.4
			% Living in Same County as in 1985	78.8%	14	76.8

***Composite:** **Rank** 15 / 46 **Score** 58.17*   **ODENTON**

CATEGORY	RANK	SCORE	STATISTIC	VALUE	RANK	SCORE
Economics	15	71.60	Median Household Income	$47,200	15	53.9
			% of Families Above Poverty Level	98.2%	15	89.3
Affordable Housing	28	53.65	Median Home Value	$121,300	28	57.2
			Median Rent	$638	35	50.1
Crime	N/A	N/A	Violent Crimes per 10,000 Population	N/A	N/A	N/A
			Property Crimes per 10,000 Population	N/A	N/A	N/A
Open Spaces	3	83.60	Population Density (Persons/Sq. Mile)	958	2	99.2
			Average Rooms per Housing Unit	6.7	9	68.0
Education	29	44.55	% High School Enrollment/Completion	90.6%	28	65.3
			% College Graduates	17.4%	30	23.8
Commute	31	30.35	Average Work Commute in Minutes	27	29	41.7
			% Commuting on Public Transportation	2.3%	22	19.0
Community Stability	17	65.25	% Living in Same House as in 1979	40.8%	17	58.8
			% Living in Same County as in 1985	76.9%	18	71.7

Metropolitan Area Suburb Rankings
BALTIMORE

Composite: Rank 16 / 46 *Score* 56.92   **BEL AIR NORTH**

CATEGORY	RANK	SCORE	STATISTIC	VALUE	RANK	SCORE
Economics	8	80.15	Median Household Income	$52,488	8	68.3
			% of Families Above Poverty Level	98.5%	10	92.0
Affordable Housing	27	56.85	Median Home Value	$132,900	31	47.8
			Median Rent	$567	24	65.9
Crime	N/A	N/A	Violent Crimes per 10,000 Population	N/A	N/A	N/A
			Property Crimes per 10,000 Population	N/A	N/A	N/A
Open Spaces	1	92.00	Population Density (Persons/Sq. Mile)	906	1	100.0
			Average Rooms per Housing Unit	7.1	2	84.0
Education	10	71.95	% High School Enrollment/Completion	98.3%	3	93.7
			% College Graduates	31.6%	16	50.2
Commute	46	7.15	Average Work Commute in Minutes	31	44	8.3
			% Commuting on Public Transportation	1.0%	40	6.0
Community Stability	36	33.40	% Living in Same House as in 1979	29.5%	29	31.6
			% Living in Same County as in 1985	63.2%	39	35.2

Composite: Rank 17 / 46 *Score* 56.41   **DUNDALK**

CATEGORY	RANK	SCORE	STATISTIC	VALUE	RANK	SCORE
Economics	39	35.30	Median Household Income	$31,120	42	9.9
			% of Families Above Poverty Level	95.0%	38	60.7
Affordable Housing	2	96.00	Median Home Value	$68,000	1	100.0
			Median Rent	$449	4	92.0
Crime	N/A	N/A	Violent Crimes per 10,000 Population	N/A	N/A	N/A
			Property Crimes per 10,000 Population	N/A	N/A	N/A
Open Spaces	43	29.30	Population Density (Persons/Sq. Mile)	4935	44	38.6
			Average Rooms per Housing Unit	5.5	38	20.0
Education	41	21.70	% High School Enrollment/Completion	84.3%	40	42.1
			% College Graduates	5.3%	44	1.3
Commute	6	64.15	Average Work Commute in Minutes	22	7	83.3
			% Commuting on Public Transportation	4.9%	7	45.0
Community Stability	4	92.00	% Living in Same House as in 1979	55.9%	3	95.2
			% Living in Same County as in 1985	83.3%	3	88.8

Composite: Rank 18 / 46 *Score* 56.38   **WOODLAWN**

CATEGORY	RANK	SCORE	STATISTIC	VALUE	RANK	SCORE
Economics	25	59.00	Median Household Income	$40,941	24	36.8
			% of Families Above Poverty Level	97.3%	25	81.2
Affordable Housing	17	72.60	Median Home Value	$94,800	16	78.5
			Median Rent	$563	23	66.7
Crime	N/A	N/A	Violent Crimes per 10,000 Population	N/A	N/A	N/A
			Property Crimes per 10,000 Population	N/A	N/A	N/A
Open Spaces	24	52.75	Population Density (Persons/Sq. Mile)	3429	31	61.5
			Average Rooms per Housing Unit	6.1	20	44.0
Education	23	54.30	% High School Enrollment/Completion	90.7%	27	65.7
			% College Graduates	27.7%	20	42.9
Commute	15	53.35	Average Work Commute in Minutes	24	15	66.7
			% Commuting on Public Transportation	4.4%	11	40.0
Community Stability	29	46.25	% Living in Same House as in 1979	35.0%	25	44.8
			% Living in Same County as in 1985	67.9%	36	47.7

Metropolitan Area Suburb Rankings
BALTIMORE

Composite: Rank 19 / 46 *Score* 55.50   **ARNOLD**

CATEGORY	RANK	SCORE	STATISTIC	VALUE	RANK	SCORE
Economics	6	84.75	Median Household Income	$56,196	6	78.4
			% of Families Above Poverty Level	98.4%	13	91.1
Affordable Housing	42	24.05	Median Home Value	$147,800	37	35.9
			Median Rent	$809	44	12.2
Crime	N/A	N/A	Violent Crimes per 10,000 Population	N/A	N/A	N/A
			Property Crimes per 10,000 Population	N/A	N/A	N/A
Open Spaces	5	82.60	Population Density (Persons/Sq. Mile)	1876	13	85.2
			Average Rooms per Housing Unit	7.0	4	80.0
Education	13	69.80	% High School Enrollment/Completion	92.6%	22	72.7
			% College Graduates	40.6%	9	66.9
Commute	42	19.15	Average Work Commute in Minutes	28	36	33.3
			% Commuting on Public Transportation	0.9%	42	5.0
Community Stability	27	52.65	% Living in Same House as in 1979	29.7%	28	32.0
			% Living in Same County as in 1985	77.5%	16	73.3

Composite: Rank 20 / 46 *Score* 55.20   **ELLICOTT CITY**

CATEGORY	RANK	SCORE	STATISTIC	VALUE	RANK	SCORE
Economics	4	86.70	Median Household Income	$58,261	3	84.1
			% of Families Above Poverty Level	98.2%	15	89.3
Affordable Housing	41	31.30	Median Home Value	$189,500	45	2.3
			Median Rent	$592	27	60.3
Crime	N/A	N/A	Violent Crimes per 10,000 Population	N/A	N/A	N/A
			Property Crimes per 10,000 Population	N/A	N/A	N/A
Open Spaces	7	81.05	Population Density (Persons/Sq. Mile)	1290	4	94.1
			Average Rooms per Housing Unit	6.7	9	68.0
Education	4	79.80	% High School Enrollment/Completion	95.1%	11	81.9
			% College Graduates	46.4%	3	77.7
Commute	41	24.35	Average Work Commute in Minutes	27	29	41.7
			% Commuting on Public Transportation	1.1%	39	7.0
Community Stability	39	28.00	% Living in Same House as in 1979	27.5%	34	26.7
			% Living in Same County as in 1985	61.0%	41	29.3

Composite: Rank 21 / 46 *Score* 54.82   **BROOKLYN PARK**

CATEGORY	RANK	SCORE	STATISTIC	VALUE	RANK	SCORE
Economics	40	32.20	Median Household Income	$31,756	40	11.7
			% of Families Above Poverty Level	94.1%	39	52.7
Affordable Housing	5	91.05	Median Home Value	$80,900	5	89.6
			Median Rent	$447	3	92.5
Crime	N/A	N/A	Violent Crimes per 10,000 Population	N/A	N/A	N/A
			Property Crimes per 10,000 Population	N/A	N/A	N/A
Open Spaces	34	44.35	Population Density (Persons/Sq. Mile)	3746	34	56.7
			Average Rooms per Housing Unit	5.8	30	32.0
Education	46	8.75	% High School Enrollment/Completion	77.4%	45	16.6
			% College Graduates	5.1%	45	0.9
Commute	11	58.15	Average Work Commute in Minutes	22	7	83.3
			% Commuting on Public Transportation	3.7%	14	33.0
Community Stability	3	94.40	% Living in Same House as in 1979	57.9%	1	100.0
			% Living in Same County as in 1985	83.3%	3	88.8

Composite: Rank 22 / 46 *Score* 54.58   **PERRY HALL**

CATEGORY	RANK	SCORE	STATISTIC	VALUE	RANK	SCORE
Economics	14	73.65	Median Household Income	$47,116	16	53.6
			% of Families Above Poverty Level	98.7%	7	93.7
Affordable Housing	26	57.45	Median Home Value	$114,500	26	62.6
			Median Rent	$628	34	52.3
Crime	N/A	N/A	Violent Crimes per 10,000 Population	N/A	N/A	N/A
			Property Crimes per 10,000 Population	N/A	N/A	N/A
Open Spaces	21	58.15	Population Density (Persons/Sq. Mile)	3249	29	64.3
			Average Rooms per Housing Unit	6.3	16	52.0
Education	17	65.40	% High School Enrollment/Completion	96.5%	8	87.1
			% College Graduates	28.1%	19	43.7
Commute	34	29.15	Average Work Commute in Minutes	28	36	33.3
			% Commuting on Public Transportation	2.9%	19	25.0
Community Stability	31	43.65	% Living in Same House as in 1979	27.2%	35	26.0
			% Living in Same County as in 1985	73.0%	27	61.3

Composite: Rank 23 / 46 *Score* 54.53   **REISTERSTOWN**

CATEGORY	RANK	SCORE	STATISTIC	VALUE	RANK	SCORE
Economics	30	48.75	Median Household Income	$37,023	31	26.1
			% of Families Above Poverty Level	96.2%	32	71.4
Affordable Housing	13	76.45	Median Home Value	$102,100	21	72.6
			Median Rent	$502	10	80.3
Crime	N/A	N/A	Violent Crimes per 10,000 Population	N/A	N/A	N/A
			Property Crimes per 10,000 Population	N/A	N/A	N/A
Open Spaces	38	41.60	Population Density (Persons/Sq. Mile)	3844	36	55.2
			Average Rooms per Housing Unit	5.7	31	28.0
Education	22	56.05	% High School Enrollment/Completion	93.6%	21	76.4
			% College Graduates	23.8%	23	35.7
Commute	17	49.85	Average Work Commute in Minutes	27	29	41.7
			% Commuting on Public Transportation	6.2%	3	58.0
Community Stability	25	54.50	% Living in Same House as in 1979	32.3%	27	38.3
			% Living in Same County as in 1985	76.5%	21	70.7

Composite: Rank 24 / 46 *Score* 54.51   **PARKVILLE**

CATEGORY	RANK	SCORE	STATISTIC	VALUE	RANK	SCORE
Economics	36	44.90	Median Household Income	$33,242	39	15.7
			% of Families Above Poverty Level	96.5%	31	74.1
Affordable Housing	10	82.70	Median Home Value	$86,200	9	85.4
			Median Rent	$503	11	80.0
Crime	N/A	N/A	Violent Crimes per 10,000 Population	N/A	N/A	N/A
			Property Crimes per 10,000 Population	N/A	N/A	N/A
Open Spaces	46	14.00	Population Density (Persons/Sq. Mile)	7467	46	0.0
			Average Rooms per Housing Unit	5.7	31	28.0
Education	24	53.20	% High School Enrollment/Completion	95.4%	10	83.0
			% College Graduates	17.2%	31	23.4
Commute	9	58.50	Average Work Commute in Minutes	23	13	75.0
			% Commuting on Public Transportation	4.6%	9	42.0
Community Stability	7	73.75	% Living in Same House as in 1979	47.6%	7	75.2
			% Living in Same County as in 1985	77.1%	17	72.3

Composite: **Rank** 25 / 46 **Score** 52.68   **PAROLE**

CATEGORY	RANK	SCORE	STATISTIC	VALUE	RANK	SCORE
Economics	5	85.20	Median Household Income	$57,156	4	81.1
			% of Families Above Poverty Level	98.2%	15	89.3
Affordable Housing	45	12.75	Median Home Value	$192,400	46	0.0
			Median Rent	$749	42	25.5
Crime	N/A	N/A	Violent Crimes per 10,000 Population	N/A	N/A	N/A
			Property Crimes per 10,000 Population	N/A	N/A	N/A
Open Spaces	8	79.45	Population Density (Persons/Sq. Mile)	975	3	98.9
			Average Rooms per Housing Unit	6.5	12	60.0
Education	9	74.05	% High School Enrollment/Completion	94.5%	15	79.7
			% College Graduates	41.4%	8	68.4
Commute	39	25.15	Average Work Commute in Minutes	28	36	33.3
			% Commuting on Public Transportation	2.1%	24	17.0
Community Stability	34	39.50	% Living in Same House as in 1979	26.5%	36	24.3
			% Living in Same County as in 1985	70.5%	31	54.7

Composite: **Rank** 26 / 46 **Score** 52.38   **BEL AIR SOUTH**

CATEGORY	RANK	SCORE	STATISTIC	VALUE	RANK	SCORE
Economics	11	76.95	Median Household Income	$49,202	12	59.3
			% of Families Above Poverty Level	98.8%	4	94.6
Affordable Housing	23	66.50	Median Home Value	$119,400	27	58.7
			Median Rent	$529	12	74.3
Crime	N/A	N/A	Violent Crimes per 10,000 Population	N/A	N/A	N/A
			Property Crimes per 10,000 Population	N/A	N/A	N/A
Open Spaces	12	74.20	Population Density (Persons/Sq. Mile)	1670	12	88.4
			Average Rooms per Housing Unit	6.5	12	60.0
Education	15	67.90	% High School Enrollment/Completion	94.9%	12	81.2
			% College Graduates	34.0%	13	54.6
Commute	44	8.65	Average Work Commute in Minutes	31	44	8.3
			% Commuting on Public Transportation	1.3%	33	9.0
Community Stability	43	20.05	% Living in Same House as in 1979	22.2%	40	14.0
			% Living in Same County as in 1985	59.8%	42	26.1

Composite: **Rank** 27 / 46 **Score** 52.37   **COLUMBIA**

CATEGORY	RANK	SCORE	STATISTIC	VALUE	RANK	SCORE
Economics	9	80.10	Median Household Income	$55,419	7	76.3
			% of Families Above Poverty Level	97.6%	22	83.9
Affordable Housing	40	32.00	Median Home Value	$150,900	40	33.4
			Median Rent	$726	38	30.6
Crime	N/A	N/A	Violent Crimes per 10,000 Population	N/A	N/A	N/A
			Property Crimes per 10,000 Population	N/A	N/A	N/A
Open Spaces	19	60.00	Population Density (Persons/Sq. Mile)	3270	30	64.0
			Average Rooms per Housing Unit	6.4	14	56.0
Education	2	91.70	% High School Enrollment/Completion	95.5%	9	83.4
			% College Graduates	58.4%	1	100.0
Commute	29	32.15	Average Work Commute in Minutes	28	36	33.3
			% Commuting on Public Transportation	3.5%	16	31.0
Community Stability	44	18.25	% Living in Same House as in 1979	20.7%	41	10.4
			% Living in Same County as in 1985	59.8%	42	26.1

Metropolitan Area Suburb Rankings
BALTIMORE

Composite: Rank 28 / 46 *Score* 52.28   **RIVIERA BEACH**

CATEGORY	RANK	SCORE	STATISTIC	VALUE	RANK	SCORE
Economics	16	68.50	Median Household Income	$43,340	21	43.3
			% of Families Above Poverty Level	98.7%	7	93.7
Affordable Housing	25	59.50	Median Home Value	$97,800	18	76.0
			Median Rent	$670	36	43.0
Crime	N/A	N/A	Violent Crimes per 10,000 Population	N/A	N/A	N/A
			Property Crimes per 10,000 Population	N/A	N/A	N/A
Open Spaces	27	48.75	Population Density (Persons/Sq. Mile)	4744	43	41.5
			Average Rooms per Housing Unit	6.4	14	56.0
Education	30	42.70	% High School Enrollment/Completion	90.3%	29	64.2
			% College Graduates	16.0%	34	21.2
Commute	37	25.35	Average Work Commute in Minutes	27	29	41.7
			% Commuting on Public Transportation	1.3%	33	9.0
Community Stability	12	68.90	% Living in Same House as in 1979	39.2%	21	54.9
			% Living in Same County as in 1985	81.1%	9	82.9

Composite: Rank 29 / 46 *Score* 52.12   **FERNDALE**

CATEGORY	RANK	SCORE	STATISTIC	VALUE	RANK	SCORE
Economics	27	54.65	Median Household Income	$37,443	30	27.2
			% of Families Above Poverty Level	97.4%	23	82.1
Affordable Housing	15	76.00	Median Home Value	$95,800	17	77.7
			Median Rent	$529	12	74.3
Crime	N/A	N/A	Violent Crimes per 10,000 Population	N/A	N/A	N/A
			Property Crimes per 10,000 Population	N/A	N/A	N/A
Open Spaces	39	38.05	Population Density (Persons/Sq. Mile)	4048	38	52.1
			Average Rooms per Housing Unit	5.6	35	24.0
Education	38	28.00	% High School Enrollment/Completion	85.8%	37	47.6
			% College Graduates	9.1%	41	8.4
Commute	20	47.65	Average Work Commute in Minutes	22	7	83.3
			% Commuting on Public Transportation	1.6%	30	12.0
Community Stability	13	68.40	% Living in Same House as in 1979	40.5%	20	58.1
			% Living in Same County as in 1985	79.5%	12	78.7

Composite: Rank 30 / 46 *Score* 51.39   **MILFORD MILL**

CATEGORY	RANK	SCORE	STATISTIC	VALUE	RANK	SCORE
Economics	37	43.10	Median Household Income	$36,170	34	23.7
			% of Families Above Poverty Level	95.2%	36	62.5
Affordable Housing	18	72.50	Median Home Value	$88,400	11	83.6
			Median Rent	$587	26	61.4
Crime	N/A	N/A	Violent Crimes per 10,000 Population	N/A	N/A	N/A
			Property Crimes per 10,000 Population	N/A	N/A	N/A
Open Spaces	37	42.25	Population Density (Persons/Sq. Mile)	3232	28	64.5
			Average Rooms per Housing Unit	5.5	38	20.0
Education	20	57.90	% High School Enrollment/Completion	94.9%	12	81.2
			% College Graduates	23.2%	25	34.6
Commute	4	65.35	Average Work Commute in Minutes	27	29	41.7
			% Commuting on Public Transportation	9.3%	2	89.0
Community Stability	41	27.25	% Living in Same House as in 1979	29.2%	30	30.8
			% Living in Same County as in 1985	58.9%	44	23.7

Metropolitan Area Suburb Rankings
BALTIMORE

Composite: **Rank** 31 / 46 *Score* 50.03   **CROFTON**

CATEGORY	RANK	SCORE	STATISTIC	VALUE	RANK	SCORE
Economics	3	88.95	Median Household Income	$56,651	5	79.7
			% of Families Above Poverty Level	99.2%	2	98.2
Affordable Housing	44	16.25	Median Home Value	$152,000	42	32.5
			Median Rent	$864	46	0.0
Crime	N/A	N/A	Violent Crimes per 10,000 Population	N/A	N/A	N/A
			Property Crimes per 10,000 Population	N/A	N/A	N/A
Open Spaces	11	75.50	Population Density (Persons/Sq. Mile)	2544	21	75.0
			Average Rooms per Housing Unit	6.9	5	76.0
Education	11	71.85	% High School Enrollment/Completion	92.1%	24	70.8
			% College Graduates	43.8%	7	72.9
Commute	45	8.50	Average Work Commute in Minutes	32	46	0.0
			% Commuting on Public Transportation	2.1%	24	17.0
Community Stability	35	39.15	% Living in Same House as in 1979	29.1%	32	30.6
			% Living in Same County as in 1985	67.9%	36	47.7

Composite: **Rank** 32 / 46 *Score* 49.97   **LANSDOWNE-BALTIMORE HIGHLANDS**

CATEGORY	RANK	SCORE	STATISTIC	VALUE	RANK	SCORE
Economics	42	22.25	Median Household Income	$30,705	44	8.8
			% of Families Above Poverty Level	92.2%	42	35.7
Affordable Housing	4	92.90	Median Home Value	$74,600	3	94.7
			Median Rent	$453	5	91.1
Crime	N/A	N/A	Violent Crimes per 10,000 Population	N/A	N/A	N/A
			Property Crimes per 10,000 Population	N/A	N/A	N/A
Open Spaces	42	32.05	Population Density (Persons/Sq. Mile)	3784	35	56.1
			Average Rooms per Housing Unit	5.2	43	8.0
Education	45	14.60	% High School Enrollment/Completion	80.8%	42	29.2
			% College Graduates	4.6%	46	0.0
Commute	1	71.00	Average Work Commute in Minutes	20	1	100.0
			% Commuting on Public Transportation	4.6%	9	42.0
Community Stability	15	67.00	% Living in Same House as in 1979	45.8%	10	70.8
			% Living in Same County as in 1985	73.7%	24	63.2

Composite: **Rank** 33 / 46 *Score* 49.62   **ABERDEEN**

CATEGORY	RANK	SCORE	STATISTIC	VALUE	RANK	SCORE
Economics	45	17.35	Median Household Income	$30,043	45	7.0
			% of Families Above Poverty Level	91.3%	43	27.7
Affordable Housing	6	90.45	Median Home Value	$84,300	6	86.9
			Median Rent	$440	2	94.0
Crime	N/A	N/A	Violent Crimes per 10,000 Population	75	N/A	N/A
			Property Crimes per 10,000 Population	729	N/A	N/A
Open Spaces	36	44.05	Population Density (Persons/Sq. Mile)	2476	19	76.1
			Average Rooms per Housing Unit	5.3	41	12.0
Education	37	32.75	% High School Enrollment/Completion	86.6%	36	50.6
			% College Graduates	12.6%	38	14.9
Commute	16	50.00	Average Work Commute in Minutes	20	1	100.0
			% Commuting on Public Transportation	0.4%	46	0.0
Community Stability	19	63.10	% Living in Same House as in 1979	36.1%	22	47.5
			% Living in Same County as in 1985	79.5%	12	78.7

Metropolitan Area Suburb Rankings
BALTIMORE

Composite: **Rank** 34 / 46 *Score* 48.98   **GLEN BURNIE**

CATEGORY	RANK	SCORE	STATISTIC	VALUE	RANK	SCORE
Economics	34	45.60	Median Household Income	$36,032	35	23.3
			% of Families Above Poverty Level	95.8%	33	67.9
Affordable Housing	14	76.15	Median Home Value	$92,900	13	80.0
			Median Rent	$538	15	72.3
Crime	N/A	N/A	Violent Crimes per 10,000 Population	N/A	N/A	N/A
			Property Crimes per 10,000 Population	N/A	N/A	N/A
Open Spaces	32	45.80	Population Density (Persons/Sq. Mile)	3034	25	67.6
			Average Rooms per Housing Unit	5.6	35	24.0
Education	44	15.45	% High School Enrollment/Completion	78.4%	44	20.3
			% College Graduates	10.3%	40	10.6
Commute	23	39.35	Average Work Commute in Minutes	24	15	66.7
			% Commuting on Public Transportation	1.6%	30	12.0
Community Stability	9	71.55	% Living in Same House as in 1979	40.6%	19	58.3
			% Living in Same County as in 1985	81.8%	8	84.8

Composite: **Rank** 35 / 46 *Score* 48.74   **COCKEYSVILLE**

CATEGORY	RANK	SCORE	STATISTIC	VALUE	RANK	SCORE
Economics	35	45.20	Median Household Income	$36,386	32	24.3
			% of Families Above Poverty Level	95.6%	34	66.1
Affordable Housing	33	49.95	Median Home Value	$149,500	38	34.5
			Median Rent	$569	25	65.4
Crime	N/A	N/A	Violent Crimes per 10,000 Population	N/A	N/A	N/A
			Property Crimes per 10,000 Population	N/A	N/A	N/A
Open Spaces	29	48.25	Population Density (Persons/Sq. Mile)	1662	11	88.5
			Average Rooms per Housing Unit	5.2	43	8.0
Education	7	75.90	% High School Enrollment/Completion	96.8%	6	88.2
			% College Graduates	38.8%	11	63.6
Commute	18	48.65	Average Work Commute in Minutes	22	7	83.3
			% Commuting on Public Transportation	1.8%	29	14.0
Community Stability	42	24.50	% Living in Same House as in 1979	18.7%	44	5.5
			% Living in Same County as in 1985	66.3%	38	43.5

Composite: **Rank** 36 / 46 *Score* 48.69   **SEVERN**

CATEGORY	RANK	SCORE	STATISTIC	VALUE	RANK	SCORE
Economics	32	48.30	Median Household Income	$44,870	18	47.5
			% of Families Above Poverty Level	93.7%	40	49.1
Affordable Housing	29	53.30	Median Home Value	$130,100	30	50.1
			Median Rent	$609	32	56.5
Crime	N/A	N/A	Violent Crimes per 10,000 Population	N/A	N/A	N/A
			Property Crimes per 10,000 Population	N/A	N/A	N/A
Open Spaces	15	68.60	Population Density (Persons/Sq. Mile)	1877	14	85.2
			Average Rooms per Housing Unit	6.3	16	52.0
Education	30	42.70	% High School Enrollment/Completion	88.6%	34	57.9
			% College Graduates	19.4%	28	27.5
Commute	24	37.35	Average Work Commute in Minutes	24	15	66.7
			% Commuting on Public Transportation	1.2%	37	8.0
Community Stability	33	41.90	% Living in Same House as in 1979	28.8%	33	29.9
			% Living in Same County as in 1985	70.2%	33	53.9

Metropolitan Area Suburb Rankings
BALTIMORE

Composite: *Rank* 37 / 46 *Score* 48.24 — **CARNEY**

CATEGORY	RANK	SCORE	STATISTIC	VALUE	RANK	SCORE
Economics	21	63.50	Median Household Income	$40,310	25	35.0
			% of Families Above Poverty Level	98.5%	10	92.0
Affordable Housing	20	70.65	Median Home Value	$100,200	19	74.1
			Median Rent	$561	22	67.2
Crime	N/A	N/A	Violent Crimes per 10,000 Population	N/A	N/A	N/A
			Property Crimes per 10,000 Population	N/A	N/A	N/A
Open Spaces	26	49.05	Population Density (Persons/Sq. Mile)	3658	33	58.1
			Average Rooms per Housing Unit	6.0	26	40.0
Education	42	20.35	% High School Enrollment/Completion	72.9%	46	0.0
			% College Graduates	26.5%	21	40.7
Commute	28	35.15	Average Work Commute in Minutes	25	22	58.3
			% Commuting on Public Transportation	1.6%	30	12.0
Community Stability	28	50.75	% Living in Same House as in 1979	32.4%	26	38.6
			% Living in Same County as in 1985	73.6%	25	62.9

Composite: *Rank* 38 / 46 *Score* 47.00 — **NORTH LAUREL**

CATEGORY	RANK	SCORE	STATISTIC	VALUE	RANK	SCORE
Economics	13	76.30	Median Household Income	$48,712	13	58.0
			% of Families Above Poverty Level	98.8%	4	94.6
Affordable Housing	38	37.90	Median Home Value	$145,000	36	38.1
			Median Rent	$694	37	37.7
Crime	N/A	N/A	Violent Crimes per 10,000 Population	N/A	N/A	N/A
			Property Crimes per 10,000 Population	N/A	N/A	N/A
Open Spaces	16	67.75	Population Density (Persons/Sq. Mile)	1466	8	91.5
			Average Rooms per Housing Unit	6.1	20	44.0
Education	14	68.15	% High School Enrollment/Completion	94.7%	14	80.4
			% College Graduates	34.7%	12	55.9
Commute	32	30.15	Average Work Commute in Minutes	28	36	33.3
			% Commuting on Public Transportation	3.1%	18	27.0
Community Stability	45	1.75	% Living in Same House as in 1979	17.5%	45	2.7
			% Living in Same County as in 1985	50.3%	45	0.8

Composite: *Rank* 39 / 46 *Score* 45.91 — **EDGEWOOD**

CATEGORY	RANK	SCORE	STATISTIC	VALUE	RANK	SCORE
Economics	41	30.40	Median Household Income	$34,699	38	19.7
			% of Families Above Poverty Level	92.8%	41	41.1
Affordable Housing	7	88.45	Median Home Value	$84,900	7	86.4
			Median Rent	$456	6	90.5
Crime	N/A	N/A	Violent Crimes per 10,000 Population	N/A	N/A	N/A
			Property Crimes per 10,000 Population	N/A	N/A	N/A
Open Spaces	18	60.80	Population Density (Persons/Sq. Mile)	1328	6	93.6
			Average Rooms per Housing Unit	5.7	31	28.0
Education	33	39.35	% High School Enrollment/Completion	89.9%	31	62.7
			% College Graduates	13.2%	37	16.0
Commute	35	29.00	Average Work Commute in Minutes	26	26	50.0
			% Commuting on Public Transportation	1.2%	37	8.0
Community Stability	40	27.45	% Living in Same House as in 1979	25.9%	37	22.9
			% Living in Same County as in 1985	62.0%	40	32.0

Composite: **Rank** 40 / 46 *Score* 45.56   ANNAPOLIS

CATEGORY	RANK	SCORE	STATISTIC	VALUE	RANK	SCORE
Economics	43	19.45	Median Household Income	$35,516	36	21.9
			% of Families Above Poverty Level	90.1%	45	17.0
Affordable Housing	32	51.15	Median Home Value	$137,400	33	44.2
			Median Rent	$602	29	58.1
Crime	N/A	N/A	Violent Crimes per 10,000 Population	121	N/A	N/A
			Property Crimes per 10,000 Population	707	N/A	N/A
Open Spaces	44	24.95	Population Density (Persons/Sq. Mile)	5246	45	33.9
			Average Rooms per Housing Unit	5.4	40	16.0
Education	18	61.45	% High School Enrollment/Completion	92.0%	25	70.5
			% College Graduates	32.8%	15	52.4
Commute	7	63.50	Average Work Commute in Minutes	23	13	75.0
			% Commuting on Public Transportation	5.6%	4	52.0
Community Stability	26	52.85	% Living in Same House as in 1979	29.2%	30	30.8
			% Living in Same County as in 1985	78.1%	15	74.9

Composite: **Rank** 41 / 46 *Score* 45.11   MIDDLE RIVER

CATEGORY	RANK	SCORE	STATISTIC	VALUE	RANK	SCORE
Economics	44	17.85	Median Household Income	$30,747	43	8.9
			% of Families Above Poverty Level	91.2%	44	26.8
Affordable Housing	3	93.55	Median Home Value	$72,200	2	96.6
			Median Rent	$456	6	90.5
Crime	N/A	N/A	Violent Crimes per 10,000 Population	N/A	N/A	N/A
			Property Crimes per 10,000 Population	N/A	N/A	N/A
Open Spaces	41	36.70	Population Density (Persons/Sq. Mile)	3173	27	65.4
			Average Rooms per Housing Unit	5.2	43	8.0
Education	43	19.50	% High School Enrollment/Completion	82.7%	41	36.2
			% College Graduates	6.1%	42	2.8
Commute	25	37.15	Average Work Commute in Minutes	25	22	58.3
			% Commuting on Public Transportation	2.0%	26	16.0
Community Stability	16	65.90	% Living in Same House as in 1979	35.8%	24	46.7
			% Living in Same County as in 1985	81.9%	7	85.1

Composite: **Rank** 42 / 46 *Score* 44.66   ELKRIDGE

CATEGORY	RANK	SCORE	STATISTIC	VALUE	RANK	SCORE
Economics	23	62.05	Median Household Income	$44,781	19	47.3
			% of Families Above Poverty Level	96.8%	27	76.8
Affordable Housing	37	42.35	Median Home Value	$122,800	29	55.9
			Median Rent	$734	40	28.8
Crime	N/A	N/A	Violent Crimes per 10,000 Population	N/A	N/A	N/A
			Property Crimes per 10,000 Population	N/A	N/A	N/A
Open Spaces	23	56.40	Population Density (Persons/Sq. Mile)	1643	10	88.8
			Average Rooms per Housing Unit	5.6	35	24.0
Education	12	70.50	% High School Enrollment/Completion	98.1%	4	93.0
			% College Graduates	30.4%	17	48.0
Commute	26	36.65	Average Work Commute in Minutes	25	22	58.3
			% Commuting on Public Transportation	1.9%	28	15.0
Community Stability	46	0.00	% Living in Same House as in 1979	16.4%	46	0.0
			% Living in Same County as in 1985	50.0%	46	0.0

Metropolitan Area Suburb Rankings
BALTIMORE

Composite: **Rank** 43 / 46 **Score** 44.53 **WESTMINSTER**

CATEGORY	RANK	SCORE	STATISTIC	VALUE	RANK	SCORE
Economics	38	36.00	Median Household Income	$31,298	41	10.4
			% of Families Above Poverty Level	95.1%	37	61.6
Affordable Housing	9	83.05	Median Home Value	$93,600	14	79.4
			Median Rent	$473	8	86.7
Crime	N/A	N/A	Violent Crimes per 10,000 Population	35	N/A	N/A
			Property Crimes per 10,000 Population	724	N/A	N/A
Open Spaces	33	44.85	Population Density (Persons/Sq. Mile)	2366	18	77.7
			Average Rooms per Housing Unit	5.3	41	12.0
Education	35	38.80	% High School Enrollment/Completion	85.2%	39	45.4
			% College Graduates	21.9%	26	32.2
Commute	27	35.35	Average Work Commute in Minutes	24	15	66.7
			% Commuting on Public Transportation	0.8%	43	4.0
Community Stability	38	29.15	% Living in Same House as in 1979	20.2%	43	9.2
			% Living in Same County as in 1985	68.4%	35	49.1

Composite: **Rank** 44 / 46 **Score** 44.22 **ESSEX**

CATEGORY	RANK	SCORE	STATISTIC	VALUE	RANK	SCORE
Economics	46	0.00	Median Household Income	$27,486	46	0.0
			% of Families Above Poverty Level	88.2%	46	0.0
Affordable Housing	1	96.45	Median Home Value	$76,800	4	92.9
			Median Rent	$413	1	100.0
Crime	N/A	N/A	Violent Crimes per 10,000 Population	N/A	N/A	N/A
			Property Crimes per 10,000 Population	N/A	N/A	N/A
Open Spaces	45	24.15	Population Density (Persons/Sq. Mile)	4301	39	48.3
			Average Rooms per Housing Unit	5.0	46	0.0
Education	39	26.95	% High School Enrollment/Completion	87.1%	35	52.4
			% College Graduates	5.4%	43	1.5
Commute	10	58.35	Average Work Commute in Minutes	24	15	66.7
			% Commuting on Public Transportation	5.4%	5	50.0
Community Stability	22	59.45	% Living in Same House as in 1979	36.0%	23	47.2
			% Living in Same County as in 1985	76.9%	18	71.7

Composite: **Rank** 45 / 46 **Score** 43.48 **GREEN HAVEN**

CATEGORY	RANK	SCORE	STATISTIC	VALUE	RANK	SCORE
Economics	17	68.20	Median Household Income	$44,053	20	45.3
			% of Families Above Poverty Level	98.4%	13	91.1
Affordable Housing	35	48.75	Median Home Value	$108,100	23	67.8
			Median Rent	$730	39	29.7
Crime	N/A	N/A	Violent Crimes per 10,000 Population	N/A	N/A	N/A
			Property Crimes per 10,000 Population	N/A	N/A	N/A
Open Spaces	28	48.50	Population Density (Persons/Sq. Mile)	4515	41	45.0
			Average Rooms per Housing Unit	6.3	16	52.0
Education	40	24.80	% High School Enrollment/Completion	80.0%	43	26.2
			% College Graduates	17.2%	31	23.4
Commute	36	26.50	Average Work Commute in Minutes	26	26	50.0
			% Commuting on Public Transportation	0.7%	44	3.0
Community Stability	30	44.15	% Living in Same House as in 1979	24.7%	38	20.0
			% Living in Same County as in 1985	75.6%	22	68.3

Metropolitan Area Suburb Rankings
BALTIMORE

Composite: **Rank** 46 / 46   *Score* 42.82   **SOUTH GATE**

CATEGORY	RANK	SCORE	STATISTIC	VALUE	RANK	SCORE
Economics	29	54.00	Median Household Income	$38,594	29	30.3
			% of Families Above Poverty Level	96.9%	26	77.7
Affordable Housing	24	60.95	Median Home Value	$112,800	25	64.0
			Median Rent	$603	30	57.9
Crime	N/A	N/A	Violent Crimes per 10,000 Population	N/A	N/A	N/A
			Property Crimes per 10,000 Population	N/A	N/A	N/A
Open Spaces	40	37.65	Population Density (Persons/Sq. Mile)	4363	40	47.3
			Average Rooms per Housing Unit	5.7	31	28.0
Education	34	38.95	% High School Enrollment/Completion	85.6%	38	46.9
			% College Graduates	21.3%	27	31.0
Commute	29	32.15	Average Work Commute in Minutes	25	22	58.3
			% Commuting on Public Transportation	1.0%	40	6.0
Community Stability	37	33.20	% Living in Same House as in 1979	20.7%	41	10.4
			% Living in Same County as in 1985	71.0%	30	56.0

Metropolitan Area Description
BIRMINGHAM

STATE: Alabama
COUNTIES: Blount, Jefferson, St. Clair, Shelby, Walker

TOTAL POPULATION: 907,810

POPULATION IN SUBURBS: 641,842   (70.7%)

POPULATION IN Birmingham: 265,968   (29.3%)

The BIRMINGHAM metropolitan area is located in the central part of Alabama. The suburbs range geographically from Jasper in the northwest (46 miles from Birmingham), to Alabaster in the south (22 miles from Birmingham), and to Pinson-Clay-Chalkville in the east (20 miles from Birmingham). The area is growing in population and had an increase of 2.7% between 1980 and 1990. Summer time high temperatures average in the 90's and winter time lows average in the 40's. The area, traditionally known for its steel manufacturing, has recently been attracting new business in the health care and medical research fields. The suburb of Bessemer recently built the Greenwood Exchange business park and announced Baxter Health Care as its first tenant in 1990. Public transportation in the area is provided by Metro Area Express (MAX) buses.

Mountain Brook is the overall highest rated suburb and also has the highest scores in economics, education, and open spaces. **Bessemer** is the suburb with the most affordable housing. **Vestavia Hills** is rated the safest suburb with the lowest crime rate. The top rated commute belongs to **Fairfield**. Finally, the number one rating in community stability goes to **Hueytown**.

The highest ranked suburb overall which also has an affordable housing score of at least 50.00 is **Forestdale**.

The highest ranked suburb in the education category which also has an affordable housing score of at least 50.00 is **Homewood**.

The county whose suburbs have the highest average overall score is **Walker County** (53.46).

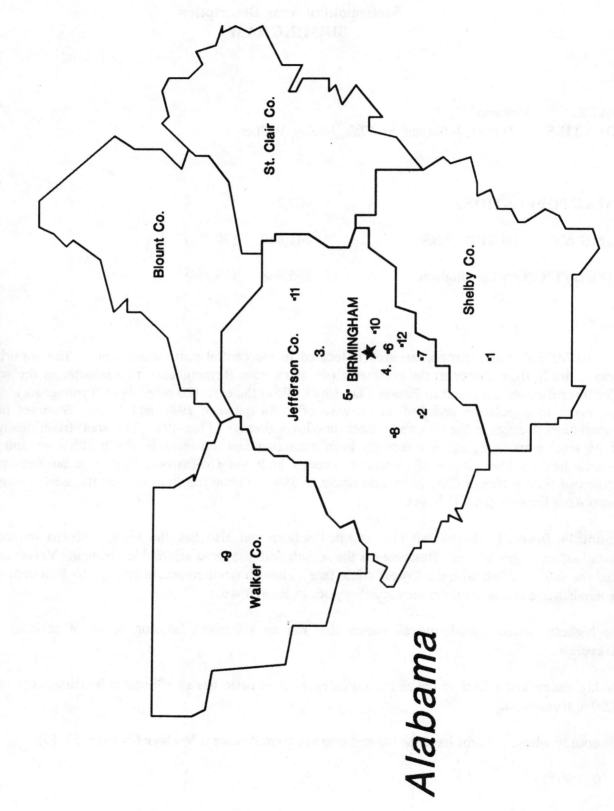

Metropolitan Area Map
BIRMINGHAM

St. Clair Co.

Blount Co.

Jefferson Co.

Walker Co.

Shelby Co.

BIRMINGHAM

*11

*10

*12

3.

*6

4.

*7

5*

*2

*8

*9

*1

Alabama

Metropolitan Area Suburb Alphabetical Index
BIRMINGHAM

SUBURB	PAGE	MAP NO.	STATE	COUNTY	POPU-LATION	RANK
ALABASTER	54	1	Alabama	Shelby	14,732	8 / 12
BESSEMER	55	2	Alabama	Jefferson	33,497	10 / 12
CENTER POINT	55	3	Alabama	Jefferson	22,658	12 / 12
FAIRFIELD	55	4	Alabama	Jefferson	12,200	11 / 12
FORESTDALE	52	5	Alabama	Jefferson	10,395	3 / 12
HOMEWOOD	54	6	Alabama	Jefferson	22,922	7 / 12
HOOVER	53	7	Alabama	Jefferson	39,788	6 / 12
HUEYTOWN	53	8	Alabama	Jefferson	15,280	5 / 12
JASPER	53	9	Alabama	Walker	13,553	4 / 12
MOUNTAIN BROOK	52	10	Alabama	Jefferson	19,810	1 / 12
PINSON-CLAY-CHALKVILLE	54	11	Alabama	Jefferson	10,987	9 / 12
VESTAVIA HILLS	52	12	Alabama	Jefferson	19,749	2 / 12

Metropolitan Area Suburb Rankings
BIRMINGHAM

Composite: Rank 1 / 12 *Score* 72.26   **MOUNTAIN BROOK**

CATEGORY	RANK	SCORE	STATISTIC	VALUE	RANK	SCORE
Economics	1	100.00	Median Household Income	$65,372	1	100.0
			% of Families Above Poverty Level	98.6%	1	100.0
Affordable Housing	12	5.65	Median Home Value	$191,400	12	0.0
			Median Rent	$474	10	11.3
Crime	3	95.75	Violent Crimes per 10,000 Population	4	1	100.0
			Property Crimes per 10,000 Population	196	3	91.5
Open Spaces	1	81.70	Population Density (Persons/Sq. Mile)	1706	7	63.4
			Average Rooms per Housing Unit	7.3	1	100.0
Education	1	100.00	% High School Enrollment/Completion	98.3%	1	100.0
			% College Graduates	67.4%	1	100.0
Commute	4	50.00	Average Work Commute in Minutes	16	1	100.0
			% Commuting on Public Transportation	0.0%	9	0.0
Community Stability	5	72.75	% Living in Same House as in 1979	44.6%	6	65.8
			% Living in Same County as in 1985	87.5%	7	79.7

Composite: Rank 2 / 12 *Score* 59.41   **VESTAVIA HILLS**

CATEGORY	RANK	SCORE	STATISTIC	VALUE	RANK	SCORE
Economics	2	83.35	Median Household Income	$49,858	2	68.4
			% of Families Above Poverty Level	98.2%	2	98.3
Affordable Housing	11	19.40	Median Home Value	$132,700	11	38.8
			Median Rent	$500	12	0.0
Crime	1	96.20	Violent Crimes per 10,000 Population	9	2	97.8
			Property Crimes per 10,000 Population	154	2	94.6
Open Spaces	5	58.00	Population Density (Persons/Sq. Mile)	2237	9	46.0
			Average Rooms per Housing Unit	6.7	2	70.0
Education	2	75.30	% High School Enrollment/Completion	94.1%	2	74.2
			% College Graduates	53.2%	2	76.4
Commute	6	41.65	Average Work Commute in Minutes	18	3	83.3
			% Commuting on Public Transportation	0.0%	9	0.0
Community Stability	9	41.95	% Living in Same House as in 1979	35.1%	8	35.2
			% Living in Same County as in 1985	77.7%	10	48.7

Composite: Rank 3 / 12 *Score* 56.90   **FORESTDALE**

CATEGORY	RANK	SCORE	STATISTIC	VALUE	RANK	SCORE
Economics	6	64.75	Median Household Income	$34,855	6	37.8
			% of Families Above Poverty Level	96.7%	6	91.7
Affordable Housing	6	64.30	Median Home Value	$69,100	7	80.8
			Median Rent	$390	4	47.8
Crime	N/A	N/A	Violent Crimes per 10,000 Population	N/A	N/A	N/A
			Property Crimes per 10,000 Population	N/A	N/A	N/A
Open Spaces	3	63.40	Population Density (Persons/Sq. Mile)	1297	5	76.8
			Average Rooms per Housing Unit	6.3	3	50.0
Education	5	37.60	% High School Enrollment/Completion	91.2%	5	56.4
			% College Graduates	18.5%	6	18.8
Commute	10	16.65	Average Work Commute in Minutes	24	8	33.3
			% Commuting on Public Transportation	0.0%	9	0.0
Community Stability	2	94.70	% Living in Same House as in 1979	53.2%	2	93.5
			% Living in Same County as in 1985	92.6%	3	95.9

Metropolitan Area Suburb Rankings
BIRMINGHAM

Composite: **Rank** 4 / 12 **Score** 53.46   **JASPER**

CATEGORY	RANK	SCORE	STATISTIC	VALUE	RANK	SCORE
Economics	10	32.90	Median Household Income	$22,476	10	12.5
			% of Families Above Poverty Level	87.9%	10	53.3
Affordable Housing	3	85.80	Median Home Value	$56,700	4	89.0
			Median Rent	$310	2	82.6
Crime	7	50.75	Violent Crimes per 10,000 Population	134	7	43.0
			Property Crimes per 10,000 Population	645	6	58.5
Open Spaces	6	55.00	Population Density (Persons/Sq. Mile)	592	1	100.0
			Average Rooms per Housing Unit	5.5	10	10.0
Education	6	32.60	% High School Enrollment/Completion	90.0%	6	49.1
			% College Graduates	16.9%	8	16.1
Commute	5	46.75	Average Work Commute in Minutes	19	4	75.0
			% Commuting on Public Transportation	0.5%	5	18.5
Community Stability	6	70.45	% Living in Same House as in 1979	44.9%	5	66.8
			% Living in Same County as in 1985	85.7%	8	74.1

Composite: **Rank** 5 / 12 **Score** 53.07   **HUEYTOWN**

CATEGORY	RANK	SCORE	STATISTIC	VALUE	RANK	SCORE
Economics	9	53.40	Median Household Income	$29,080	9	26.0
			% of Families Above Poverty Level	94.2%	8	80.8
Affordable Housing	5	65.60	Median Home Value	$54,000	3	90.8
			Median Rent	$407	7	40.4
Crime	5	75.70	Violent Crimes per 10,000 Population	59	6	75.9
			Property Crimes per 10,000 Population	414	5	75.5
Open Spaces	9	40.70	Population Density (Persons/Sq. Mile)	1767	8	61.4
			Average Rooms per Housing Unit	5.7	8	20.0
Education	10	18.25	% High School Enrollment/Completion	87.3%	10	32.5
			% College Graduates	9.6%	11	4.0
Commute	9	18.50	Average Work Commute in Minutes	24	8	33.3
			% Commuting on Public Transportation	0.1%	7	3.7
Community Stability	1	99.35	% Living in Same House as in 1979	55.2%	1	100.0
			% Living in Same County as in 1985	93.5%	2	98.7

Composite: **Rank** 6 / 12 **Score** 50.57   **HOOVER**

CATEGORY	RANK	SCORE	STATISTIC	VALUE	RANK	SCORE
Economics	3	77.20	Median Household Income	$44,747	3	57.9
			% of Families Above Poverty Level	97.8%	3	96.5
Affordable Housing	10	28.90	Median Home Value	$111,800	10	52.6
			Median Rent	$488	11	5.2
Crime	4	85.75	Violent Crimes per 10,000 Population	16	3	94.7
			Property Crimes per 10,000 Population	396	4	76.8
Open Spaces	7	52.35	Population Density (Persons/Sq. Mile)	1668	6	64.7
			Average Rooms per Housing Unit	6.1	4	40.0
Education	3	65.80	% High School Enrollment/Completion	93.0%	4	67.5
			% College Graduates	45.8%	3	64.1
Commute	7	33.35	Average Work Commute in Minutes	20	5	66.7
			% Commuting on Public Transportation	0.0%	9	0.0
Community Stability	11	10.65	% Living in Same House as in 1979	25.1%	11	2.9
			% Living in Same County as in 1985	68.1%	11	18.4

Composite: **Rank** 7 / 12 *Score* 50.35   **HOMEWOOD**

CATEGORY	RANK	SCORE	STATISTIC	VALUE	RANK	SCORE
Economics	7	60.50	Median Household Income	$30,516	8	28.9
			% of Families Above Poverty Level	96.8%	5	92.1
Affordable Housing	9	51.70	Median Home Value	$88,900	9	67.7
			Median Rent	$418	8	35.7
Crime	6	70.00	Violent Crimes per 10,000 Population	43	5	82.9
			Property Crimes per 10,000 Population	665	7	57.1
Open Spaces	11	8.65	Population Density (Persons/Sq. Mile)	3110	11	17.3
			Average Rooms per Housing Unit	5.3	11	0.0
Education	4	65.10	% High School Enrollment/Completion	93.8%	3	72.4
			% College Graduates	42.0%	4	57.8
Commute	3	62.95	Average Work Commute in Minutes	16	1	100.0
			% Commuting on Public Transportation	0.7%	3	25.9
Community Stability	10	33.55	% Living in Same House as in 1979	28.9%	10	15.2
			% Living in Same County as in 1985	78.7%	9	51.9

Composite: **Rank** 8 / 12 *Score* 46.80   **ALABASTER**

CATEGORY	RANK	SCORE	STATISTIC	VALUE	RANK	SCORE
Economics	5	67.30	Median Household Income	$39,261	4	46.8
			% of Families Above Poverty Level	95.8%	7	87.8
Affordable Housing	8	54.65	Median Home Value	$77,300	8	75.4
			Median Rent	$422	9	33.9
Crime	2	96.05	Violent Crimes per 10,000 Population	22	4	92.1
			Property Crimes per 10,000 Population	80	1	100.0
Open Spaces	2	64.40	Population Density (Persons/Sq. Mile)	782	2	93.8
			Average Rooms per Housing Unit	6.0	5	35.0
Education	7	30.85	% High School Enrollment/Completion	87.4%	9	33.1
			% College Graduates	24.4%	5	28.6
Commute	11	14.35	Average Work Commute in Minutes	25	10	25.0
			% Commuting on Public Transportation	0.1%	7	3.7
Community Stability	12	0.00	% Living in Same House as in 1979	24.2%	12	0.0
			% Living in Same County as in 1985	62.3%	12	0.0

Composite: **Rank** 9 / 12 *Score* 45.43   **PINSON-CLAY-CHALKVILLE**

CATEGORY	RANK	SCORE	STATISTIC	VALUE	RANK	SCORE
Economics	4	68.50	Median Household Income	$37,469	5	43.1
			% of Families Above Poverty Level	97.2%	4	93.9
Affordable Housing	7	63.60	Median Home Value	$66,800	6	82.4
			Median Rent	$397	6	44.8
Crime	N/A	N/A	Violent Crimes per 10,000 Population	N/A	N/A	N/A
			Property Crimes per 10,000 Population	N/A	N/A	N/A
Open Spaces	4	58.80	Population Density (Persons/Sq. Mile)	969	4	87.6
			Average Rooms per Housing Unit	5.9	6	30.0
Education	9	24.40	% High School Enrollment/Completion	87.9%	8	36.2
			% College Graduates	14.8%	9	12.6
Commute	12	3.70	Average Work Commute in Minutes	28	12	0.0
			% Commuting on Public Transportation	0.2%	6	7.4
Community Stability	8	53.55	% Living in Same House as in 1979	31.3%	9	22.9
			% Living in Same County as in 1985	88.9%	6	84.2

Metropolitan Area Suburb Rankings
BIRMINGHAM

Composite: *Rank* 10 / 12 *Score* 44.26   **BESSEMER**

CATEGORY	RANK	SCORE	STATISTIC	VALUE	RANK	SCORE
Economics	12	0.00	Median Household Income	$16,331	12	0.0
			% of Families Above Poverty Level	75.7%	12	0.0
Affordable Housing	1	100.00	Median Home Value	$40,100	1	100.0
			Median Rent	$270	1	100.0
Crime	8	8.60	Violent Crimes per 10,000 Population	232	9	0.0
			Property Crimes per 10,000 Population	1,208	8	17.2
Open Spaces	8	45.50	Population Density (Persons/Sq. Mile)	866	3	91.0
			Average Rooms per Housing Unit	5.3	11	0.0
Education	12	0.00	% High School Enrollment/Completion	82.0%	12	0.0
			% College Graduates	7.2%	12	0.0
Commute	2	63.45	Average Work Commute in Minutes	23	6	41.7
			% Commuting on Public Transportation	2.3%	2	85.2
Community Stability	3	92.25	% Living in Same House as in 1979	50.4%	3	84.5
			% Living in Same County as in 1985	93.9%	1	100.0

Composite: *Rank* 11 / 12 *Score* 42.51   **FAIRFIELD**

CATEGORY	RANK	SCORE	STATISTIC	VALUE	RANK	SCORE
Economics	11	18.60	Median Household Income	$21,085	11	9.7
			% of Families Above Poverty Level	82.0%	11	27.5
Affordable Housing	2	87.20	Median Home Value	$49,900	2	93.5
			Median Rent	$314	3	80.9
Crime	9	1.55	Violent Crimes per 10,000 Population	225	8	3.1
			Property Crimes per 10,000 Population	1,443	9	0.0
Open Spaces	12	7.50	Population Density (Persons/Sq. Mile)	3636	12	0.0
			Average Rooms per Housing Unit	5.6	9	15.0
Education	8	29.05	% High School Enrollment/Completion	88.8%	7	41.7
			% College Graduates	17.1%	7	16.4
Commute	1	70.85	Average Work Commute in Minutes	23	6	41.7
			% Commuting on Public Transportation	2.7%	1	100.0
Community Stability	4	82.85	% Living in Same House as in 1979	47.9%	4	76.5
			% Living in Same County as in 1985	90.5%	4	89.2

Composite: *Rank* 12 / 12 *Score* 42.44   **CENTER POINT**

CATEGORY	RANK	SCORE	STATISTIC	VALUE	RANK	SCORE
Economics	8	56.85	Median Household Income	$32,469	7	32.9
			% of Families Above Poverty Level	94.2%	8	80.8
Affordable Housing	4	65.70	Median Home Value	$63,000	5	84.9
			Median Rent	$393	5	46.5
Crime	N/A	N/A	Violent Crimes per 10,000 Population	N/A	N/A	N/A
			Property Crimes per 10,000 Population	N/A	N/A	N/A
Open Spaces	10	28.40	Population Density (Persons/Sq. Mile)	2668	10	31.8
			Average Rooms per Housing Unit	5.8	7	25.0
Education	11	12.40	% High School Enrollment/Completion	84.0%	11	12.3
			% College Graduates	14.7%	10	12.5
Commute	8	23.60	Average Work Commute in Minutes	25	10	25.0
			% Commuting on Public Transportation	0.6%	4	22.2
Community Stability	7	67.70	% Living in Same House as in 1979	39.7%	7	50.0
			% Living in Same County as in 1985	89.3%	5	85.4

BOSTON-LAWRENCE-SALEM-LOWELL-BROCKTON

STATE: Massachusetts
COUNTIES: Essex, Middlesex, Norfolk, Plymouth, Suffolk

TOTAL POPULATION: 3,783,817

POPULATION IN SUBURBS: 2,905,009   (76.8%)

POPULATION IN Boston: 574,283   (15.2%)
POPULATION IN Lawrence: 70,207   (1.9%)
POPULATION IN Salem: 38,091   (1.0%)
POPULATION IN Lowell: 103,439   (2.7%)
POPULATION IN Brockton: 92,788   (2.5%)

The BOSTON-LAWRENCE-SALEM-LOWELL-BROCKTON metropolitan area is located in the eastern part of Massachusetts along the Atlantic Ocean. The suburbs range geographically from Amesbury in the north (38 miles from Boston), to Marlborough in the west (30 miles from Boston), and to Abington in the south (19 miles from Boston). The area is growing in population and had an increase of 3.3% between 1980 and 1990. Summer time high temperatures average in the 80's and winter time lows average in the 20's. Many high tech companies are located in the area including Digital Equipment in Maynard and Raytheon in Lexington. Well known colleges found in the suburbs include Harvard University in Cambridge, Wellesley College in Wellesley, and Brandeis University in Waltham. Public transportation in the area is provided by the Massachusetts Bay Transportation Authority using subways, trolleys and buses.

Lynnfield is the overall highest rated suburb and also has the highest score in open spaces. **Wellesley** receives the highest scores in both economics and education. **Lynn** is the suburb with the most affordable housing. **Reading** is rated the safest suburb with the lowest crime rate. The top rated commute belongs to **Cambridge**. Finally, the number one rating in community stability goes to **Wilmington**.

The highest ranked suburb overall which also has an affordable housing score of at least 50.00 is **Lynnfield.**

The highest ranked suburb in the education category which also has an affordable housing score of at least 50.00 is **Cambridge.**

The county whose suburbs have the highest average overall score is **Norfolk County** (63.10).

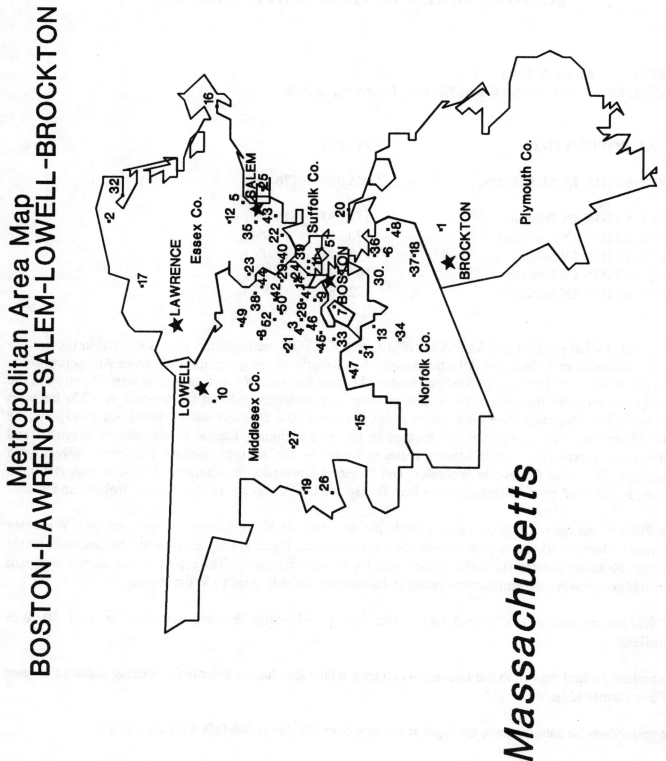

Metropolitan Area Map
BOSTON-LAWRENCE-SALEM-LOWELL-BROCKTON

Massachusetts

Metropolitan Area Suburb Alphabetical Index
BOSTON-LAWRENCE-SALEM-LOWELL-BROCKTON

SUBURB	PAGE	MAP NO.	STATE	COUNTY	POPU-LATION	RANK
ABINGTON	69	1	Massachusetts	Plymouth	13,817	25 / 52
AMESBURY	73	2	Massachusetts	Essex	12,109	39 / 52
ARLINGTON	67	3	Massachusetts	Middlesex	44,630	21 / 52
BELMONT	65	4	Massachusetts	Middlesex	24,720	13 / 52
BEVERLY	68	5	Massachusetts	Essex	38,195	24 / 52
BRAINTREE	65	6	Massachusetts	Norfolk	33,836	15 / 52
BROOKLINE	75	7	Massachusetts	Norfolk	54,718	44 / 52
BURLINGTON	64	8	Massachusetts	Middlesex	23,302	12 / 52
CAMBRIDGE	77	9	Massachusetts	Middlesex	95,802	49 / 52
CHELMSFORD	64	10	Massachusetts	Middlesex	32,388	10 / 52
CHELSEA	78	11	Massachusetts	Suffolk	28,710	52 / 52
DANVERS	67	12	Massachusetts	Essex	24,174	20 / 52
DEDHAM	67	13	Massachusetts	Norfolk	23,782	19 / 52
EVERETT	74	14	Massachusetts	Middlesex	35,701	41 / 52
FRAMINGHAM	74	15	Massachusetts	Middlesex	64,994	42 / 52
GLOUCESTER	71	16	Massachusetts	Essex	28,716	33 / 52
HAVERHILL	75	17	Massachusetts	Essex	51,418	43 / 52
HOLBROOK	68	18	Massachusetts	Norfolk	11,041	22 / 52
HUDSON	66	19	Massachusetts	Middlesex	14,267	16 / 52
HULL	77	20	Massachusetts	Plymouth	10,466	50 / 52
LEXINGTON	62	21	Massachusetts	Middlesex	28,974	5 / 52
LYNN	77	22	Massachusetts	Essex	81,245	51 / 52
LYNNFIELD	61	23	Massachusetts	Essex	11,274	1 / 52
MALDEN	76	24	Massachusetts	Middlesex	53,884	46 / 52
MARBLEHEAD	64	25	Massachusetts	Essex	19,971	11 / 52
MARLBOROUGH	75	26	Massachusetts	Middlesex	31,813	45 / 52
MAYNARD	72	27	Massachusetts	Middlesex	10,325	35 / 52
MEDFORD	69	28	Massachusetts	Middlesex	57,407	26 / 52
MELROSE	63	29	Massachusetts	Middlesex	28,150	8 / 52
MILTON	61	30	Massachusetts	Norfolk	25,725	3 / 52
NEEDHAM	62	31	Massachusetts	Norfolk	27,557	6 / 52
NEWBURYPORT	74	32	Massachusetts	Essex	16,317	40 / 52
NEWTON	66	33	Massachusetts	Middlesex	82,585	17 / 52
NORWOOD	70	34	Massachusetts	Norfolk	28,700	28 / 52
PEABODY	69	35	Massachusetts	Essex	47,039	27 / 52
QUINCY	73	36	Massachusetts	Norfolk	84,985	37 / 52
RANDOLPH	72	37	Massachusetts	Norfolk	30,093	34 / 52
READING	61	38	Massachusetts	Middlesex	22,539	2 / 52
REVERE	76	39	Massachusetts	Suffolk	42,786	47 / 52
SAUGUS	70	40	Massachusetts	Essex	25,549	30 / 52
SOMERVILLE	76	41	Massachusetts	Middlesex	76,210	48 / 52
STONEHAM	68	42	Massachusetts	Middlesex	22,203	23 / 52
SWAMPSCOTT	66	43	Massachusetts	Essex	13,650	18 / 52
WAKEFIELD	65	44	Massachusetts	Middlesex	24,825	14 / 52
WALTHAM	72	45	Massachusetts	Middlesex	57,878	36 / 52
WATERTOWN	73	46	Massachusetts	Middlesex	33,284	38 / 52
WELLESLEY	63	47	Massachusetts	Norfolk	26,615	9 / 52
WEYMOUTH	71	48	Massachusetts	Norfolk	54,063	32 / 52
WILMINGTON	63	49	Massachusetts	Middlesex	17,654	7 / 52
WINCHESTER	62	50	Massachusetts	Middlesex	20,267	4 / 52
WINTHROP	71	51	Massachusetts	Suffolk	18,127	31 / 52

SUBURB	PAGE	MAP NO.	STATE	COUNTY	POPU-LATION	RANK
WOBURN	70	52	Massachusetts	Middlesex	35,943	29 / 52

Metropolitan Area Suburb Rankings
BOSTON-LAWRENCE-SALEM-LOWELL-BROCKTON

Composite: Rank 1 / 52 *Score* 76.23   **LYNNFIELD**

CATEGORY	RANK	SCORE	STATISTIC	VALUE	RANK	SCORE
Economics	6	78.45	Median Household Income	$58,561	6	61.9
			% of Families Above Poverty Level	97.9%	10	95.0
Affordable Housing	34	70.00	Median Home Value	$258,100	46	50.1
			Median Rent	$580	5	89.9
Crime	4	93.95	Violent Crimes per 10,000 Population	8	4	96.3
			Property Crimes per 10,000 Population	169	6	91.6
Open Spaces	1	99.75	Population Density (Persons/Sq. Mile)	1111	3	99.5
			Average Rooms per Housing Unit	7.0	1	100.0
Education	13	65.70	% High School Enrollment/Completion	95.4%	20	79.7
			% College Graduates	40.9%	14	51.7
Commute	44	37.85	Average Work Commute in Minutes	24	30	68.8
			% Commuting on Public Transportation	3.0%	41	6.9
Community Stability	3	87.90	% Living in Same House as in 1979	58.9%	2	96.1
			% Living in Same County as in 1985	86.0%	21	79.7

Composite: Rank 2 / 52 *Score* 73.66   **READING**

CATEGORY	RANK	SCORE	STATISTIC	VALUE	RANK	SCORE
Economics	7	75.60	Median Household Income	$52,783	12	51.2
			% of Families Above Poverty Level	99.0%	1	100.0
Affordable Housing	39	65.50	Median Home Value	$206,500	39	71.5
			Median Rent	$706	34	59.5
Crime	1	98.45	Violent Crimes per 10,000 Population	7	3	96.9
			Property Crimes per 10,000 Population	117	1	100.0
Open Spaces	9	84.90	Population Density (Persons/Sq. Mile)	2271	16	92.9
			Average Rooms per Housing Unit	6.4	8	76.9
Education	17	60.85	% High School Enrollment/Completion	94.9%	23	77.3
			% College Graduates	36.7%	16	44.4
Commute	34	43.80	Average Work Commute in Minutes	23	13	75.0
			% Commuting on Public Transportation	4.9%	35	12.6
Community Stability	4	86.50	% Living in Same House as in 1979	52.7%	9	75.8
			% Living in Same County as in 1985	91.6%	2	97.2

Composite: Rank 3 / 52 *Score* 73.11   **MILTON**

CATEGORY	RANK	SCORE	STATISTIC	VALUE	RANK	SCORE
Economics	10	73.90	Median Household Income	$53,130	11	51.9
			% of Families Above Poverty Level	98.1%	7	95.9
Affordable Housing	41	55.60	Median Home Value	$221,200	41	65.4
			Median Rent	$763	42	45.8
Crime	9	90.60	Violent Crimes per 10,000 Population	25	16	85.9
			Property Crimes per 10,000 Population	146	3	95.3
Open Spaces	3	93.45	Population Density (Persons/Sq. Mile)	1973	13	94.6
			Average Rooms per Housing Unit	6.8	3	92.3
Education	9	75.40	% High School Enrollment/Completion	98.6%	3	95.2
			% College Graduates	43.1%	11	55.6
Commute	23	49.65	Average Work Commute in Minutes	24	30	68.8
			% Commuting on Public Transportation	10.9%	16	30.5
Community Stability	15	73.20	% Living in Same House as in 1979	54.6%	4	82.0
			% Living in Same County as in 1985	81.1%	37	64.4

Metropolitan Area Suburb Rankings
BOSTON-LAWRENCE-SALEM-LOWELL-BROCKTON

Composite: *Rank* 4 / 52 *Score* 72.66   **WINCHESTER**

CATEGORY	RANK	SCORE	STATISTIC	VALUE	RANK	SCORE
Economics	3	86.50	Median Household Income	$65,994	3	75.7
			% of Families Above Poverty Level	98.4%	4	97.3
Affordable Housing	48	29.55	Median Home Value	$292,700	49	35.7
			Median Rent	$856	47	23.4
Crime	3	96.30	Violent Crimes per 10,000 Population	8	4	96.3
			Property Crimes per 10,000 Population	140	2	96.3
Open Spaces	6	87.60	Population Density (Persons/Sq. Mile)	3356	31	86.7
			Average Rooms per Housing Unit	6.7	4	88.5
Education	5	83.90	% High School Enrollment/Completion	97.9%	5	91.8
			% College Graduates	54.8%	5	76.0
Commute	21	50.20	Average Work Commute in Minutes	23	13	75.0
			% Commuting on Public Transportation	9.2%	22	25.4
Community Stability	14	74.55	% Living in Same House as in 1979	49.6%	14	65.7
			% Living in Same County as in 1985	87.2%	15	83.4

Composite: *Rank* 5 / 52 *Score* 71.84   **LEXINGTON**

CATEGORY	RANK	SCORE	STATISTIC	VALUE	RANK	SCORE
Economics	2	87.55	Median Household Income	$67,389	2	78.3
			% of Families Above Poverty Level	98.3%	5	96.8
Affordable Housing	51	20.10	Median Home Value	$281,900	47	40.2
			Median Rent	$953	52	0.0
Crime	2	97.40	Violent Crimes per 10,000 Population	2	1	100.0
			Property Crimes per 10,000 Population	149	4	94.8
Open Spaces	4	92.15	Population Density (Persons/Sq. Mile)	1767	9	95.8
			Average Rooms per Housing Unit	6.7	4	88.5
Education	7	82.75	% High School Enrollment/Completion	96.0%	18	82.6
			% College Graduates	58.7%	3	82.9
Commute	33	43.95	Average Work Commute in Minutes	23	13	75.0
			% Commuting on Public Transportation	5.0%	34	12.9
Community Stability	10	78.95	% Living in Same House as in 1979	54.0%	7	80.1
			% Living in Same County as in 1985	85.4%	23	77.8

Composite: *Rank* 6 / 52 *Score* 70.48   **NEEDHAM**

CATEGORY	RANK	SCORE	STATISTIC	VALUE	RANK	SCORE
Economics	4	80.75	Median Household Income	$60,357	4	65.2
			% of Families Above Poverty Level	98.2%	6	96.3
Affordable Housing	47	32.75	Median Home Value	$255,800	44	51.0
			Median Rent	$893	51	14.5
Crime	5	92.65	Violent Crimes per 10,000 Population	11	9	94.5
			Property Crimes per 10,000 Population	174	7	90.8
Open Spaces	7	87.10	Population Density (Persons/Sq. Mile)	2185	15	93.4
			Average Rooms per Housing Unit	6.5	6	80.8
Education	4	85.60	% High School Enrollment/Completion	99.0%	2	97.1
			% College Graduates	53.7%	8	74.1
Commute	24	49.50	Average Work Commute in Minutes	24	30	68.8
			% Commuting on Public Transportation	10.8%	17	30.2
Community Stability	27	65.00	% Living in Same House as in 1979	51.6%	11	72.2
			% Living in Same County as in 1985	79.0%	40	57.8

Metropolitan Area Suburb Rankings
BOSTON-LAWRENCE-SALEM-LOWELL-BROCKTON

Composite: Rank 7 / 52 *Score* 70.47   **WILMINGTON**

CATEGORY	RANK	SCORE	STATISTIC	VALUE	RANK	SCORE
Economics	10	73.90	Median Household Income	$52,189	13	50.1
			% of Families Above Poverty Level	98.5%	3	97.7
Affordable Housing	21	77.65	Median Home Value	$174,900	22	84.7
			Median Rent	$660	22	70.6
Crime	18	72.65	Violent Crimes per 10,000 Population	42	24	75.5
			Property Crimes per 10,000 Population	304	17	69.8
Open Spaces	5	90.40	Population Density (Persons/Sq. Mile)	1027	1	100.0
			Average Rooms per Housing Unit	6.5	6	80.8
Education	46	37.60	% High School Enrollment/Completion	91.1%	45	58.9
			% College Graduates	20.6%	42	16.3
Commute	38	41.10	Average Work Commute in Minutes	23	13	75.0
			% Commuting on Public Transportation	3.1%	40	7.2
Community Stability	1	100.00	% Living in Same House as in 1979	60.1%	1	100.0
			% Living in Same County as in 1985	92.5%	1	100.0

Composite: Rank 8 / 52 *Score* 70.27   **MELROSE**

CATEGORY	RANK	SCORE	STATISTIC	VALUE	RANK	SCORE
Economics	16	63.20	Median Household Income	$44,109	18	35.1
			% of Families Above Poverty Level	97.1%	17	91.3
Affordable Housing	22	77.25	Median Home Value	$195,400	37	76.2
			Median Rent	$628	16	78.3
Crime	10	90.35	Violent Crimes per 10,000 Population	9	7	95.7
			Property Crimes per 10,000 Population	210	11	85.0
Open Spaces	38	62.70	Population Density (Persons/Sq. Mile)	5993	40	71.6
			Average Rooms per Housing Unit	5.8	20	53.8
Education	18	59.60	% High School Enrollment/Completion	96.3%	15	84.1
			% College Graduates	31.4%	20	35.1
Commute	13	58.05	Average Work Commute in Minutes	24	30	68.8
			% Commuting on Public Transportation	16.5%	13	47.3
Community Stability	5	80.75	% Living in Same House as in 1979	50.8%	12	69.6
			% Living in Same County as in 1985	89.9%	5	91.9

Composite: Rank 9 / 52 *Score* 68.57   **WELLESLEY**

CATEGORY	RANK	SCORE	STATISTIC	VALUE	RANK	SCORE
Economics	1	99.30	Median Household Income	$79,111	1	100.0
			% of Families Above Poverty Level	98.7%	2	98.6
Affordable Housing	52	20.15	Median Home Value	$344,800	51	14.0
			Median Rent	$844	46	26.3
Crime	N/A	N/A	Violent Crimes per 10,000 Population	N/A	N/A	N/A
			Property Crimes per 10,000 Population	N/A	N/A	N/A
Open Spaces	2	95.45	Population Density (Persons/Sq. Mile)	2614	24	90.9
			Average Rooms per Housing Unit	7.0	1	100.0
Education	1	100.00	% High School Enrollment/Completion	99.6%	1	100.0
			% College Graduates	68.5%	1	100.0
Commute	17	52.45	Average Work Commute in Minutes	23	13	75.0
			% Commuting on Public Transportation	10.7%	18	29.9
Community Stability	41	44.05	% Living in Same House as in 1979	48.8%	16	63.1
			% Living in Same County as in 1985	68.5%	50	25.0

Metropolitan Area Suburb Rankings
BOSTON-LAWRENCE-SALEM-LOWELL-BROCKTON

Composite: *Rank* 10 / 52 *Score* 68.56 **CHELMSFORD**

CATEGORY	RANK	SCORE	STATISTIC	VALUE	RANK	SCORE
Economics	9	74.40	Median Household Income	$53,956	8	53.4
			% of Families Above Poverty Level	98.0%	8	95.4
Affordable Housing	32	71.95	Median Home Value	$177,900	27	83.4
			Median Rent	$702	32	60.5
Crime	16	77.50	Violent Crimes per 10,000 Population	29	17	83.4
			Property Crimes per 10,000 Population	293	15	71.6
Open Spaces	8	85.40	Population Density (Persons/Sq. Mile)	1429	5	97.7
			Average Rooms per Housing Unit	6.3	9	73.1
Education	16	61.00	% High School Enrollment/Completion	94.6%	25	75.8
			% College Graduates	37.7%	15	46.2
Commute	41	38.40	Average Work Commute in Minutes	23	13	75.0
			% Commuting on Public Transportation	1.3%	49	1.8
Community Stability	16	71.25	% Living in Same House as in 1979	47.2%	22	57.8
			% Living in Same County as in 1985	87.6%	13	84.7

Composite: *Rank* 11 / 52 *Score* 66.83 **MARBLEHEAD**

CATEGORY	RANK	SCORE	STATISTIC	VALUE	RANK	SCORE
Economics	12	73.80	Median Household Income	$53,333	10	52.2
			% of Families Above Poverty Level	98.0%	8	95.4
Affordable Housing	43	49.00	Median Home Value	$254,700	43	51.5
			Median Rent	$760	41	46.5
Crime	8	91.00	Violent Crimes per 10,000 Population	15	11	92.0
			Property Crimes per 10,000 Population	179	8	90.0
Open Spaces	15	74.95	Population Density (Persons/Sq. Mile)	4408	34	80.7
			Average Rooms per Housing Unit	6.2	12	69.2
Education	6	82.95	% High School Enrollment/Completion	97.9%	5	91.8
			% College Graduates	53.7%	8	74.1
Commute	51	28.65	Average Work Commute in Minutes	29	51	37.5
			% Commuting on Public Transportation	7.3%	29	19.8
Community Stability	22	67.45	% Living in Same House as in 1979	46.2%	25	54.6
			% Living in Same County as in 1985	86.2%	20	80.3

Composite: *Rank* 12 / 52 *Score* 66.27 **BURLINGTON**

CATEGORY	RANK	SCORE	STATISTIC	VALUE	RANK	SCORE
Economics	8	74.45	Median Household Income	$55,952	7	57.1
			% of Families Above Poverty Level	97.2%	14	91.8
Affordable Housing	44	48.90	Median Home Value	$191,100	35	78.0
			Median Rent	$871	49	19.8
Crime	N/A	N/A	Violent Crimes per 10,000 Population	N/A	N/A	N/A
			Property Crimes per 10,000 Population	N/A	N/A	N/A
Open Spaces	10	81.90	Population Density (Persons/Sq. Mile)	1973	13	94.6
			Average Rooms per Housing Unit	6.2	12	69.2
Education	14	65.00	% High School Enrollment/Completion	97.7%	9	90.8
			% College Graduates	33.7%	19	39.2
Commute	28	47.65	Average Work Commute in Minutes	21	4	87.5
			% Commuting on Public Transportation	3.3%	39	7.8
Community Stability	7	79.70	% Living in Same House as in 1979	52.0%	10	73.5
			% Living in Same County as in 1985	88.0%	12	85.9

Composite: *Rank* 13 / 52 *Score* 65.94   **BELMONT**

CATEGORY	RANK	SCORE	STATISTIC	VALUE	RANK	SCORE
Economics	13	73.75	Median Household Income	$53,488	9	52.5
			% of Families Above Poverty Level	97.9%	10	95.0
Affordable Housing	50	26.25	Median Home Value	$304,400	50	30.8
			Median Rent	$863	48	21.7
Crime	6	92.10	Violent Crimes per 10,000 Population	8	4	96.3
			Property Crimes per 10,000 Population	192	10	87.9
Open Spaces	17	74.30	Population Density (Persons/Sq. Mile)	5310	39	75.5
			Average Rooms per Housing Unit	6.3	9	73.1
Education	10	73.95	% High School Enrollment/Completion	93.8%	31	72.0
			% College Graduates	54.7%	6	75.9
Commute	14	57.10	Average Work Commute in Minutes	23	13	75.0
			% Commuting on Public Transportation	13.8%	14	39.2
Community Stability	28	64.15	% Living in Same House as in 1979	48.3%	17	61.4
			% Living in Same County as in 1985	81.9%	36	66.9

Composite: *Rank* 14 / 52 *Score* 65.85   **WAKEFIELD**

CATEGORY	RANK	SCORE	STATISTIC	VALUE	RANK	SCORE
Economics	19	63.10	Median Household Income	$43,960	19	34.9
			% of Families Above Poverty Level	97.1%	17	91.3
Affordable Housing	30	73.15	Median Home Value	$189,000	33	78.8
			Median Rent	$673	26	67.5
Crime	N/A	N/A	Violent Crimes per 10,000 Population	N/A	N/A	N/A
			Property Crimes per 10,000 Population	N/A	N/A	N/A
Open Spaces	21	72.30	Population Density (Persons/Sq. Mile)	3324	30	86.9
			Average Rooms per Housing Unit	5.9	17	57.7
Education	23	54.90	% High School Enrollment/Completion	96.3%	15	84.1
			% College Graduates	26.0%	29	25.7
Commute	19	50.95	Average Work Commute in Minutes	22	7	81.2
			% Commuting on Public Transportation	7.6%	26	20.7
Community Stability	6	80.70	% Living in Same House as in 1979	50.5%	13	68.6
			% Living in Same County as in 1985	90.2%	4	92.8

Composite: *Rank* 15 / 52 *Score* 65.71   **BRAINTREE**

CATEGORY	RANK	SCORE	STATISTIC	VALUE	RANK	SCORE
Economics	20	62.90	Median Household Income	$44,734	17	36.3
			% of Families Above Poverty Level	96.7%	23	89.5
Affordable Housing	17	80.70	Median Home Value	$167,600	18	87.7
			Median Rent	$647	19	73.7
Crime	24	61.50	Violent Crimes per 10,000 Population	37	21	78.5
			Property Crimes per 10,000 Population	461	30	44.5
Open Spaces	12	76.75	Population Density (Persons/Sq. Mile)	2436	20	92.0
			Average Rooms per Housing Unit	6.0	16	61.5
Education	37	44.65	% High School Enrollment/Completion	93.0%	36	68.1
			% College Graduates	23.4%	33	21.2
Commute	30	45.35	Average Work Commute in Minutes	24	30	68.8
			% Commuting on Public Transportation	8.0%	24	21.9
Community Stability	2	88.15	% Living in Same House as in 1979	55.9%	3	86.3
			% Living in Same County as in 1985	89.3%	7	90.0

Metropolitan Area Suburb Rankings
BOSTON-LAWRENCE-SALEM-LOWELL-BROCKTON

Composite: *Rank* 16 / 52 *Score* 65.58   **HUDSON**

CATEGORY	RANK	SCORE	STATISTIC	VALUE	RANK	SCORE
Economics	16	63.20	Median Household Income	$43,600	21	34.2
			% of Families Above Poverty Level	97.3%	13	92.2
Affordable Housing	11	85.85	Median Home Value	$162,700	14	89.8
			Median Rent	$613	13	81.9
Crime	7	91.55	Violent Crimes per 10,000 Population	19	13	89.6
			Property Crimes per 10,000 Population	157	5	93.5
Open Spaces	27	68.90	Population Density (Persons/Sq. Mile)	2496	22	91.6
			Average Rooms per Housing Unit	5.6	26	46.2
Education	35	46.40	% High School Enrollment/Completion	94.6%	25	75.8
			% College Graduates	21.0%	39	17.0
Commute	47	37.50	Average Work Commute in Minutes	23	13	75.0
			% Commuting on Public Transportation	0.7%	51	0.0
Community Stability	25	65.65	% Living in Same House as in 1979	42.5%	34	42.5
			% Living in Same County as in 1985	88.9%	9	88.8

Composite: *Rank* 17 / 52 *Score* 65.05   **NEWTON**

CATEGORY	RANK	SCORE	STATISTIC	VALUE	RANK	SCORE
Economics	5	79.10	Median Household Income	$59,719	5	64.1
			% of Families Above Poverty Level	97.7%	12	94.1
Affordable Housing	49	26.60	Median Home Value	$290,400	48	36.6
			Median Rent	$884	50	16.6
Crime	15	78.15	Violent Crimes per 10,000 Population	23	14	87.1
			Property Crimes per 10,000 Population	308	18	69.2
Open Spaces	14	76.45	Population Density (Persons/Sq. Mile)	4572	37	79.8
			Average Rooms per Housing Unit	6.3	9	73.1
Education	3	87.45	% High School Enrollment/Completion	98.5%	4	94.7
			% College Graduates	57.2%	4	80.2
Commute	16	56.05	Average Work Commute in Minutes	23	13	75.0
			% Commuting on Public Transportation	13.1%	15	37.1
Community Stability	36	51.55	% Living in Same House as in 1979	47.1%	23	57.5
			% Living in Same County as in 1985	75.1%	46	45.6

Composite: *Rank* 18 / 52 *Score* 64.94   **SWAMPSCOTT**

CATEGORY	RANK	SCORE	STATISTIC	VALUE	RANK	SCORE
Economics	14	69.10	Median Household Income	$50,191	14	46.4
			% of Families Above Poverty Level	97.2%	14	91.8
Affordable Housing	45	46.65	Median Home Value	$224,800	42	63.9
			Median Rent	$831	45	29.4
Crime	11	85.70	Violent Crimes per 10,000 Population	6	2	97.5
			Property Crimes per 10,000 Population	279	14	73.9
Open Spaces	16	74.75	Population Density (Persons/Sq. Mile)	4476	35	80.3
			Average Rooms per Housing Unit	6.2	12	69.2
Education	12	66.30	% High School Enrollment/Completion	94.6%	25	75.8
			% College Graduates	43.8%	10	56.8
Commute	37	41.70	Average Work Commute in Minutes	26	46	56.2
			% Commuting on Public Transportation	9.8%	20	27.2
Community Stability	18	70.35	% Living in Same House as in 1979	47.7%	19	59.5
			% Living in Same County as in 1985	86.5%	19	81.2

Metropolitan Area Suburb Rankings
BOSTON-LAWRENCE-SALEM-LOWELL-BROCKTON

Composite: **Rank** 19 / 52 *Score* 64.92   **DEDHAM**

CATEGORY	RANK	SCORE	STATISTIC	VALUE	RANK	SCORE
Economics	15	63.35	Median Household Income	$45,687	15	38.1
			% of Families Above Poverty Level	96.5%	25	88.6
Affordable Housing	25	74.95	Median Home Value	$175,200	23	84.6
			Median Rent	$682	29	65.3
Crime	N/A	N/A	Violent Crimes per 10,000 Population	N/A	N/A	N/A
			Property Crimes per 10,000 Population	N/A	N/A	N/A
Open Spaces	11	81.05	Population Density (Persons/Sq. Mile)	2275	17	92.9
			Average Rooms per Housing Unit	6.2	12	69.2
Education	36	46.30	% High School Enrollment/Completion	92.4%	42	65.2
			% College Graduates	27.0%	24	27.4
Commute	26	48.30	Average Work Commute in Minutes	23	13	75.0
			% Commuting on Public Transportation	7.9%	25	21.6
Community Stability	12	75.55	% Living in Same House as in 1979	54.6%	4	82.0
			% Living in Same County as in 1985	82.6%	33	69.1

Composite: **Rank** 20 / 52 *Score* 63.84   **DANVERS**

CATEGORY	RANK	SCORE	STATISTIC	VALUE	RANK	SCORE
Economics	18	63.15	Median Household Income	$43,759	20	34.5
			% of Families Above Poverty Level	97.2%	14	91.8
Affordable Housing	26	74.15	Median Home Value	$188,300	32	79.1
			Median Rent	$666	24	69.2
Crime	30	52.55	Violent Crimes per 10,000 Population	34	18	80.4
			Property Crimes per 10,000 Population	584	34	24.7
Open Spaces	13	76.60	Population Density (Persons/Sq. Mile)	1820	10	95.5
			Average Rooms per Housing Unit	5.9	17	57.7
Education	19	57.80	% High School Enrollment/Completion	97.3%	11	88.9
			% College Graduates	26.6%	26	26.7
Commute	31	45.10	Average Work Commute in Minutes	21	4	87.5
			% Commuting on Public Transportation	1.6%	47	2.7
Community Stability	11	77.50	% Living in Same House as in 1979	49.4%	15	65.0
			% Living in Same County as in 1985	89.3%	7	90.0

Composite: **Rank** 21 / 52 *Score* 63.34   **ARLINGTON**

CATEGORY	RANK	SCORE	STATISTIC	VALUE	RANK	SCORE
Economics	24	61.60	Median Household Income	$43,309	24	33.7
			% of Families Above Poverty Level	96.7%	23	89.5
Affordable Housing	40	58.95	Median Home Value	$210,500	40	69.9
			Median Rent	$754	40	48.0
Crime	12	84.40	Violent Crimes per 10,000 Population	35	19	79.8
			Property Crimes per 10,000 Population	185	9	89.0
Open Spaces	41	49.50	Population Density (Persons/Sq. Mile)	8610	46	56.7
			Average Rooms per Housing Unit	5.5	29	42.3
Education	11	66.35	% High School Enrollment/Completion	95.3%	22	79.2
			% College Graduates	41.9%	12	53.5
Commute	15	56.25	Average Work Commute in Minutes	25	39	62.5
			% Commuting on Public Transportation	17.4%	11	50.0
Community Stability	24	66.30	% Living in Same House as in 1979	47.3%	21	58.2
			% Living in Same County as in 1985	84.3%	28	74.4

Composite: Rank 22 / 52 Score 62.84   **HOLBROOK**

CATEGORY	RANK	SCORE	STATISTIC	VALUE	RANK	SCORE
Economics	40	52.55	Median Household Income	$37,775	39	23.4
			% of Families Above Poverty Level	95.0%	39	81.7
Affordable Housing	2	95.10	Median Home Value	$138,500	2	99.8
			Median Rent	$578	4	90.4
Crime	N/A	N/A	Violent Crimes per 10,000 Population	N/A	N/A	N/A
			Property Crimes per 10,000 Population	N/A	N/A	N/A
Open Spaces	22	71.75	Population Density (Persons/Sq. Mile)	1501	6	97.3
			Average Rooms per Housing Unit	5.6	26	46.2
Education	41	40.10	% High School Enrollment/Completion	93.7%	32	71.5
			% College Graduates	16.3%	47	8.7
Commute	42	38.45	Average Work Commute in Minutes	26	46	56.2
			% Commuting on Public Transportation	7.6%	26	20.7
Community Stability	9	79.10	% Living in Same House as in 1979	54.1%	6	80.4
			% Living in Same County as in 1985	85.4%	23	77.8

Composite: Rank 23 / 52 Score 62.78   **STONEHAM**

CATEGORY	RANK	SCORE	STATISTIC	VALUE	RANK	SCORE
Economics	26	60.70	Median Household Income	$43,343	23	33.7
			% of Families Above Poverty Level	96.3%	27	87.7
Affordable Housing	37	66.55	Median Home Value	$192,500	36	77.4
			Median Rent	$722	37	55.7
Crime	17	75.65	Violent Crimes per 10,000 Population	11	9	94.5
			Property Crimes per 10,000 Population	385	25	56.8
Open Spaces	35	63.75	Population Density (Persons/Sq. Mile)	3618	33	85.2
			Average Rooms per Housing Unit	5.5	29	42.3
Education	20	57.25	% High School Enrollment/Completion	97.9%	5	91.8
			% College Graduates	24.3%	30	22.7
Commute	29	46.75	Average Work Commute in Minutes	22	7	81.2
			% Commuting on Public Transportation	4.8%	36	12.3
Community Stability	20	68.80	% Living in Same House as in 1979	45.1%	27	51.0
			% Living in Same County as in 1985	88.2%	11	86.6

Composite: Rank 24 / 52 Score 62.48   **BEVERLY**

CATEGORY	RANK	SCORE	STATISTIC	VALUE	RANK	SCORE
Economics	39	53.60	Median Household Income	$39,603	35	26.8
			% of Families Above Poverty Level	94.7%	40	80.4
Affordable Housing	18	79.60	Median Home Value	$177,000	25	83.8
			Median Rent	$640	18	75.4
Crime	13	80.65	Violent Crimes per 10,000 Population	17	12	90.8
			Property Crimes per 10,000 Population	300	16	70.5
Open Spaces	32	65.10	Population Density (Persons/Sq. Mile)	2474	21	91.7
			Average Rooms per Housing Unit	5.4	33	38.5
Education	21	55.65	% High School Enrollment/Completion	95.9%	19	82.1
			% College Graduates	28.0%	23	29.2
Commute	32	44.55	Average Work Commute in Minutes	23	13	75.0
			% Commuting on Public Transportation	5.4%	33	14.1
Community Stability	33	58.20	% Living in Same House as in 1979	41.5%	35	39.2
			% Living in Same County as in 1985	85.2%	27	77.2

Metropolitan Area Suburb Rankings
BOSTON-LAWRENCE-SALEM-LOWELL-BROCKTON

Composite: *Rank* 25 / 52 *Score* 62.05   **ABINGTON**

CATEGORY	RANK	SCORE	STATISTIC	VALUE	RANK	SCORE
Economics	29	59.45	Median Household Income	$42,730	29	32.6
			% of Families Above Poverty Level	96.0%	32	86.3
Affordable Housing	6	88.25	Median Home Value	$154,000	7	93.4
			Median Rent	$608	11	83.1
Crime	N/A	N/A	Violent Crimes per 10,000 Population	N/A	N/A	N/A
			Property Crimes per 10,000 Population	N/A	N/A	N/A
Open Spaces	19	73.95	Population Density (Persons/Sq. Mile)	1389	4	97.9
			Average Rooms per Housing Unit	5.7	23	50.0
Education	31	49.55	% High School Enrollment/Completion	96.7%	13	86.0
			% College Graduates	18.8%	46	13.1
Commute	48	35.90	Average Work Commute in Minutes	25	39	62.5
			% Commuting on Public Transportation	3.8%	38	9.3
Community Stability	26	65.20	% Living in Same House as in 1979	45.7%	26	52.9
			% Living in Same County as in 1985	85.3%	26	77.5

Composite: *Rank* 26 / 52 *Score* 61.67   **MEDFORD**

CATEGORY	RANK	SCORE	STATISTIC	VALUE	RANK	SCORE
Economics	38	53.80	Median Household Income	$38,859	36	25.4
			% of Families Above Poverty Level	95.1%	38	82.2
Affordable Housing	23	75.40	Median Home Value	$182,700	30	81.4
			Median Rent	$665	23	69.4
Crime	22	62.25	Violent Crimes per 10,000 Population	72	29	57.1
			Property Crimes per 10,000 Population	319	19	67.4
Open Spaces	39	55.90	Population Density (Persons/Sq. Mile)	7055	41	65.6
			Average Rooms per Housing Unit	5.6	26	46.2
Education	25	53.60	% High School Enrollment/Completion	96.6%	14	85.5
			% College Graduates	23.7%	31	21.7
Commute	9	63.10	Average Work Commute in Minutes	23	13	75.0
			% Commuting on Public Transportation	17.8%	10	51.2
Community Stability	21	67.65	% Living in Same House as in 1979	47.1%	23	57.5
			% Living in Same County as in 1985	85.4%	23	77.8

Composite: *Rank* 27 / 52 *Score* 61.50   **PEABODY**

CATEGORY	RANK	SCORE	STATISTIC	VALUE	RANK	SCORE
Economics	34	57.20	Median Household Income	$39,800	34	27.2
			% of Families Above Poverty Level	96.2%	28	87.2
Affordable Housing	12	84.15	Median Home Value	$176,600	24	84.0
			Median Rent	$603	10	84.3
Crime	26	60.75	Violent Crimes per 10,000 Population	24	15	86.5
			Property Crimes per 10,000 Population	520	32	35.0
Open Spaces	24	69.75	Population Density (Persons/Sq. Mile)	2869	27	89.5
			Average Rooms per Housing Unit	5.7	23	50.0
Education	40	41.50	% High School Enrollment/Completion	92.6%	41	66.2
			% College Graduates	20.9%	41	16.8
Commute	36	42.10	Average Work Commute in Minutes	22	7	81.2
			% Commuting on Public Transportation	1.7%	46	3.0
Community Stability	13	75.05	% Living in Same House as in 1979	47.7%	19	59.5
			% Living in Same County as in 1985	89.5%	6	90.6

Metropolitan Area Suburb Rankings
BOSTON-LAWRENCE-SALEM-LOWELL-BROCKTON

Composite: *Rank* 28 / 52 *Score* 61.26   **NORWOOD**

CATEGORY	RANK	SCORE	STATISTIC	VALUE	RANK	SCORE
Economics	23	61.80	Median Household Income	$42,805	28	32.7
			% of Families Above Poverty Level	97.0%	19	90.9
Affordable Housing	36	67.90	Median Home Value	$177,800	26	83.5
			Median Rent	$736	39	52.3
Crime	14	80.30	Violent Crimes per 10,000 Population	36	20	79.1
			Property Crimes per 10,000 Population	232	12	81.5
Open Spaces	33	64.35	Population Density (Persons/Sq. Mile)	2737	25	90.2
			Average Rooms per Housing Unit	5.4	33	38.5
Education	33	47.75	% High School Enrollment/Completion	93.0%	36	68.1
			% College Graduates	27.0%	24	27.4
Commute	26	48.30	Average Work Commute in Minutes	24	30	68.8
			% Commuting on Public Transportation	10.0%	19	27.8
Community Stability	32	58.40	% Living in Same House as in 1979	44.5%	31	49.0
			% Living in Same County as in 1985	82.2%	34	67.8

Composite: *Rank* 29 / 52 *Score* 61.11   **WOBURN**

CATEGORY	RANK	SCORE	STATISTIC	VALUE	RANK	SCORE
Economics	32	58.25	Median Household Income	$42,679	30	32.5
			% of Families Above Poverty Level	95.5%	36	84.0
Affordable Housing	31	72.35	Median Home Value	$171,500	21	86.1
			Median Rent	$710	36	58.6
Crime	N/A	N/A	Violent Crimes per 10,000 Population	N/A	N/A	N/A
			Property Crimes per 10,000 Population	N/A	N/A	N/A
Open Spaces	30	66.00	Population Density (Persons/Sq. Mile)	2834	26	89.7
			Average Rooms per Housing Unit	5.5	29	42.3
Education	32	48.30	% High School Enrollment/Completion	94.4%	29	74.9
			% College Graduates	23.7%	31	21.7
Commute	18	51.85	Average Work Commute in Minutes	20	2	93.8
			% Commuting on Public Transportation	4.0%	37	9.9
Community Stability	19	69.90	% Living in Same House as in 1979	45.1%	27	51.0
			% Living in Same County as in 1985	88.9%	9	88.8

Composite: *Rank* 30 / 52 *Score* 60.39   **SAUGUS**

CATEGORY	RANK	SCORE	STATISTIC	VALUE	RANK	SCORE
Economics	25	60.75	Median Household Income	$41,919	31	31.1
			% of Families Above Poverty Level	96.9%	20	90.4
Affordable Housing	9	86.80	Median Home Value	$166,700	17	88.1
			Median Rent	$598	8	85.5
Crime	35	35.30	Violent Crimes per 10,000 Population	50	25	70.6
			Property Crimes per 10,000 Population	737	37	0.0
Open Spaces	20	73.20	Population Density (Persons/Sq. Mile)	2325	19	92.6
			Average Rooms per Housing Unit	5.8	20	53.8
Education	44	38.35	% High School Enrollment/Completion	93.0%	36	68.1
			% College Graduates	16.2%	48	8.6
Commute	25	49.15	Average Work Commute in Minutes	22	7	81.2
			% Commuting on Public Transportation	6.4%	31	17.1
Community Stability	8	79.20	% Living in Same House as in 1979	52.9%	8	76.5
			% Living in Same County as in 1985	86.7%	18	81.9

Metropolitan Area Suburb Rankings
BOSTON-LAWRENCE-SALEM-LOWELL-BROCKTON

Composite: **Rank** 31 / 52   *Score* 60.14   **WINTHROP**

CATEGORY	RANK	SCORE	STATISTIC	VALUE	RANK	SCORE
Economics	36	55.50	Median Household Income	$37,240	41	22.4
			% of Families Above Poverty Level	96.5%	25	88.6
Affordable Housing	28	73.70	Median Home Value	$181,700	29	81.9
			Median Rent	$681	28	65.5
Crime	N/A	N/A	Violent Crimes per 10,000 Population	N/A	N/A	N/A
			Property Crimes per 10,000 Population	N/A	N/A	N/A
Open Spaces	44	46.15	Population Density (Persons/Sq. Mile)	9116	47	53.8
			Average Rooms per Housing Unit	5.4	33	38.5
Education	24	54.75	% High School Enrollment/Completion	97.8%	8	91.3
			% College Graduates	21.7%	36	18.2
Commute	5	69.10	Average Work Commute in Minutes	25	39	62.5
			% Commuting on Public Transportation	26.0%	5	75.7
Community Stability	29	61.65	% Living in Same House as in 1979	41.5%	35	39.2
			% Living in Same County as in 1985	87.4%	14	84.1

Composite: **Rank** 32 / 52   *Score* 59.87   **WEYMOUTH**

CATEGORY	RANK	SCORE	STATISTIC	VALUE	RANK	SCORE
Economics	27	60.45	Median Household Income	$41,586	32	30.5
			% of Families Above Poverty Level	96.9%	20	90.4
Affordable Housing	19	77.95	Median Home Value	$156,600	10	92.3
			Median Rent	$689	30	63.6
Crime	20	71.10	Violent Crimes per 10,000 Population	37	21	78.5
			Property Crimes per 10,000 Population	342	22	63.7
Open Spaces	36	63.10	Population Density (Persons/Sq. Mile)	3178	29	87.7
			Average Rooms per Housing Unit	5.4	33	38.5
Education	33	47.75	% High School Enrollment/Completion	94.9%	23	77.3
			% College Graduates	21.7%	36	18.2
Commute	43	38.30	Average Work Commute in Minutes	26	46	56.2
			% Commuting on Public Transportation	7.5%	28	20.4
Community Stability	30	60.45	% Living in Same House as in 1979	44.8%	30	50.0
			% Living in Same County as in 1985	83.2%	32	70.9

Composite: **Rank** 33 / 52   *Score* 59.51   **GLOUCESTER**

CATEGORY	RANK	SCORE	STATISTIC	VALUE	RANK	SCORE
Economics	46	43.75	Median Household Income	$32,690	47	14.0
			% of Families Above Poverty Level	93.2%	45	73.5
Affordable Housing	8	87.70	Median Home Value	$178,100	28	83.4
			Median Rent	$571	2	92.0
Crime	25	60.70	Violent Crimes per 10,000 Population	89	32	46.6
			Property Crimes per 10,000 Population	273	13	74.8
Open Spaces	26	69.00	Population Density (Persons/Sq. Mile)	1106	2	99.5
			Average Rooms per Housing Unit	5.4	33	38.5
Education	48	34.30	% High School Enrollment/Completion	89.8%	47	52.7
			% College Graduates	20.4%	43	15.9
Commute	21	50.20	Average Work Commute in Minutes	20	2	93.8
			% Commuting on Public Transportation	2.9%	42	6.6
Community Stability	17	70.90	% Living in Same House as in 1979	43.9%	32	47.1
			% Living in Same County as in 1985	90.8%	3	94.7

Metropolitan Area Suburb Rankings
BOSTON-LAWRENCE-SALEM-LOWELL-BROCKTON

Composite: *Rank* 34 / 52 *Score* 57.70   **RANDOLPH**

CATEGORY	RANK	SCORE	STATISTIC	VALUE	RANK	SCORE
Economics	28	60.35	Median Household Income	$43,244	26	33.5
			% of Families Above Poverty Level	96.2%	28	87.2
Affordable Housing	29	73.50	Median Home Value	$155,000	9	93.0
			Median Rent	$729	38	54.0
Crime	N/A	N/A	Violent Crimes per 10,000 Population	N/A	N/A	N/A
			Property Crimes per 10,000 Population	N/A	N/A	N/A
Open Spaces	25	69.40	Population Density (Persons/Sq. Mile)	2987	28	88.8
			Average Rooms per Housing Unit	5.7	23	50.0
Education	26	52.45	% High School Enrollment/Completion	96.8%	12	86.5
			% College Graduates	21.8%	35	18.4
Commute	49	32.65	Average Work Commute in Minutes	27	50	50.0
			% Commuting on Public Transportation	5.8%	32	15.3
Community Stability	34	57.85	% Living in Same House as in 1979	47.9%	18	60.1
			% Living in Same County as in 1985	78.3%	42	55.6

Composite: *Rank* 35 / 52 *Score* 57.57   **MAYNARD**

CATEGORY	RANK	SCORE	STATISTIC	VALUE	RANK	SCORE
Economics	31	58.80	Median Household Income	$43,253	25	33.6
			% of Families Above Poverty Level	95.5%	36	84.0
Affordable Housing	14	82.40	Median Home Value	$168,900	19	87.2
			Median Rent	$631	17	77.6
Crime	N/A	N/A	Violent Crimes per 10,000 Population	N/A	N/A	N/A
			Property Crimes per 10,000 Population	N/A	N/A	N/A
Open Spaces	18	74.20	Population Density (Persons/Sq. Mile)	1971	12	94.6
			Average Rooms per Housing Unit	5.8	20	53.8
Education	49	33.65	% High School Enrollment/Completion	86.6%	50	37.2
			% College Graduates	28.5%	22	30.1
Commute	40	38.70	Average Work Commute in Minutes	23	13	75.0
			% Commuting on Public Transportation	1.5%	48	2.4
Community Stability	35	57.65	% Living in Same House as in 1979	40.4%	38	35.6
			% Living in Same County as in 1985	86.0%	21	79.7

Composite: *Rank* 36 / 52 *Score* 56.56   **WALTHAM**

CATEGORY	RANK	SCORE	STATISTIC	VALUE	RANK	SCORE
Economics	37	55.10	Median Household Income	$38,514	38	24.8
			% of Families Above Poverty Level	95.8%	33	85.4
Affordable Housing	35	68.85	Median Home Value	$190,000	34	78.4
			Median Rent	$707	35	59.3
Crime	18	72.65	Violent Crimes per 10,000 Population	10	8	95.1
			Property Crimes per 10,000 Population	426	27	50.2
Open Spaces	40	51.45	Population Density (Persons/Sq. Mile)	4558	36	79.8
			Average Rooms per Housing Unit	5.0	43	23.1
Education	27	51.20	% High School Enrollment/Completion	94.6%	25	75.8
			% College Graduates	26.5%	28	26.6
Commute	11	58.70	Average Work Commute in Minutes	19	1	100.0
			% Commuting on Public Transportation	6.5%	30	17.4
Community Stability	47	38.00	% Living in Same House as in 1979	38.5%	41	29.4
			% Living in Same County as in 1985	75.4%	45	46.6

Composite: *Rank* 37 / 52 *Score* 56.31   QUINCY

CATEGORY	RANK	SCORE	STATISTIC	VALUE	RANK	SCORE
Economics	42	50.15	Median Household Income	$35,858	44	19.9
			% of Families Above Poverty Level	94.7%	40	80.4
Affordable Housing	16	81.20	Median Home Value	$159,500	12	91.1
			Median Rent	$657	21	71.3
Crime	21	66.45	Violent Crimes per 10,000 Population	41	23	76.1
			Property Crimes per 10,000 Population	385	25	56.8
Open Spaces	43	46.20	Population Density (Persons/Sq. Mile)	5063	38	77.0
			Average Rooms per Housing Unit	4.8	50	15.4
Education	30	50.25	% High School Enrollment/Completion	95.4%	20	79.7
			% College Graduates	23.2%	34	20.8
Commute	12	58.65	Average Work Commute in Minutes	25	39	62.5
			% Commuting on Public Transportation	19.0%	8	54.8
Community Stability	44	41.30	% Living in Same House as in 1979	38.7%	40	30.1
			% Living in Same County as in 1985	77.3%	44	52.5

Composite: *Rank* 38 / 52 *Score* 55.30   WATERTOWN

CATEGORY	RANK	SCORE	STATISTIC	VALUE	RANK	SCORE
Economics	22	62.00	Median Household Income	$43,490	22	34.0
			% of Families Above Poverty Level	96.8%	22	90.0
Affordable Housing	42	54.70	Median Home Value	$196,600	38	75.7
			Median Rent	$813	44	33.7
Crime	28	57.45	Violent Crimes per 10,000 Population	52	26	69.3
			Property Crimes per 10,000 Population	454	29	45.6
Open Spaces	42	47.10	Population Density (Persons/Sq. Mile)	8098	45	59.6
			Average Rooms per Housing Unit	5.3	39	34.6
Education	15	61.10	% High School Enrollment/Completion	93.3%	34	69.6
			% College Graduates	41.4%	13	52.6
Commute	10	62.35	Average Work Commute in Minutes	23	13	75.0
			% Commuting on Public Transportation	17.3%	12	49.7
Community Stability	42	42.40	% Living in Same House as in 1979	39.1%	39	31.4
			% Living in Same County as in 1985	77.6%	43	53.4

Composite: *Rank* 39 / 52 *Score* 55.20   AMESBURY

CATEGORY	RANK	SCORE	STATISTIC	VALUE	RANK	SCORE
Economics	43	50.00	Median Household Income	$36,937	43	21.9
			% of Families Above Poverty Level	94.2%	44	78.1
Affordable Housing	5	91.10	Median Home Value	$145,500	5	96.9
			Median Rent	$599	9	85.3
Crime	N/A	N/A	Violent Crimes per 10,000 Population	N/A	N/A	N/A
			Property Crimes per 10,000 Population	N/A	N/A	N/A
Open Spaces	34	63.70	Population Density (Persons/Sq. Mile)	2280	18	92.8
			Average Rooms per Housing Unit	5.3	39	34.6
Education	38	43.90	% High School Enrollment/Completion	93.5%	33	70.5
			% College Graduates	21.2%	38	17.3
Commute	46	37.65	Average Work Commute in Minutes	23	13	75.0
			% Commuting on Public Transportation	0.8%	50	0.3
Community Stability	39	44.85	% Living in Same House as in 1979	31.7%	50	7.2
			% Living in Same County as in 1985	86.9%	17	82.5

Metropolitan Area Suburb Rankings
BOSTON-LAWRENCE-SALEM-LOWELL-BROCKTON

Composite: *Rank* 40 / 52 *Score* 55.12 **NEWBURYPORT**

CATEGORY	RANK	SCORE	STATISTIC	VALUE	RANK	SCORE
Economics	35	55.90	Median Household Income	$38,618	37	25.0
			% of Families Above Poverty Level	96.1%	30	86.8
Affordable Housing	13	83.80	Median Home Value	$171,200	20	86.2
			Median Rent	$615	14	81.4
Crime	N/A	N/A	Violent Crimes per 10,000 Population	N/A	N/A	N/A
			Property Crimes per 10,000 Population	N/A	N/A	N/A
Open Spaces	28	68.50	Population Density (Persons/Sq. Mile)	1950	11	94.7
			Average Rooms per Housing Unit	5.5	29	42.3
Education	22	55.05	% High School Enrollment/Completion	93.0%	36	68.1
			% College Graduates	35.3%	18	42.0
Commute	50	30.65	Average Work Commute in Minutes	26	46	56.2
			% Commuting on Public Transportation	2.4%	45	5.1
Community Stability	48	36.80	% Living in Same House as in 1979	33.4%	48	12.7
			% Living in Same County as in 1985	80.0%	39	60.9

Composite: *Rank* 41 / 52 *Score* 54.82 **EVERETT**

CATEGORY	RANK	SCORE	STATISTIC	VALUE	RANK	SCORE
Economics	49	38.80	Median Household Income	$30,786	49	10.5
			% of Families Above Poverty Level	91.8%	49	67.1
Affordable Housing	7	87.80	Median Home Value	$154,500	8	93.2
			Median Rent	$611	12	82.4
Crime	N/A	N/A	Violent Crimes per 10,000 Population	N/A	N/A	N/A
			Property Crimes per 10,000 Population	N/A	N/A	N/A
Open Spaces	48	34.35	Population Density (Persons/Sq. Mile)	10553	48	45.6
			Average Rooms per Housing Unit	5.0	43	23.1
Education	47	36.45	% High School Enrollment/Completion	94.0%	30	72.9
			% College Graduates	11.3%	52	0.0
Commute	7	64.30	Average Work Commute in Minutes	23	13	75.0
			% Commuting on Public Transportation	18.6%	9	53.6
Community Stability	23	67.20	% Living in Same House as in 1979	45.1%	27	51.0
			% Living in Same County as in 1985	87.2%	15	83.4

Composite: *Rank* 42 / 52 *Score* 53.61 **FRAMINGHAM**

CATEGORY	RANK	SCORE	STATISTIC	VALUE	RANK	SCORE
Economics	30	59.20	Median Household Income	$42,965	27	33.0
			% of Families Above Poverty Level	95.8%	33	85.4
Affordable Housing	33	71.50	Median Home Value	$184,300	31	80.8
			Median Rent	$695	31	62.2
Crime	31	51.60	Violent Crimes per 10,000 Population	93	33	44.2
			Property Crimes per 10,000 Population	371	24	59.0
Open Spaces	37	62.85	Population Density (Persons/Sq. Mile)	2587	23	91.1
			Average Rooms per Housing Unit	5.3	39	34.6
Education	28	50.95	% High School Enrollment/Completion	90.9%	46	58.0
			% College Graduates	36.4%	17	43.9
Commute	45	37.70	Average Work Commute in Minutes	24	30	68.8
			% Commuting on Public Transportation	2.9%	42	6.6
Community Stability	43	41.50	% Living in Same House as in 1979	37.7%	43	26.8
			% Living in Same County as in 1985	78.5%	41	56.2

Metropolitan Area Suburb Rankings
BOSTON-LAWRENCE-SALEM-LOWELL-BROCKTON

Composite: **Rank** 43 / 52 *Score* 53.41   **HAVERHILL**

CATEGORY	RANK	SCORE	STATISTIC	VALUE	RANK	SCORE
Economics	45	46.35	Median Household Income	$36,945	42	21.9
			% of Families Above Poverty Level	92.6%	47	70.8
Affordable Housing	3	93.65	Median Home Value	$140,800	4	98.9
			Median Rent	$586	6	88.4
Crime	34	36.95	Violent Crimes per 10,000 Population	68	28	59.5
			Property Crimes per 10,000 Population	648	35	14.4
Open Spaces	31	65.85	Population Density (Persons/Sq. Mile)	1543	8	97.1
			Average Rooms per Housing Unit	5.3	39	34.6
Education	39	43.05	% High School Enrollment/Completion	93.2%	35	69.1
			% College Graduates	21.0%	39	17.0
Commute	35	43.60	Average Work Commute in Minutes	22	7	81.2
			% Commuting on Public Transportation	2.7%	44	6.0
Community Stability	40	44.40	% Living in Same House as in 1979	34.3%	46	15.7
			% Living in Same County as in 1985	83.9%	29	73.1

Composite: **Rank** 44 / 52 *Score* 53.33   **BROOKLINE**

CATEGORY	RANK	SCORE	STATISTIC	VALUE	RANK	SCORE
Economics	21	62.35	Median Household Income	$45,598	16	37.9
			% of Families Above Poverty Level	96.1%	30	86.8
Affordable Housing	46	34.00	Median Home Value	$378,500	52	0.0
			Median Rent	$671	25	68.0
Crime	27	59.05	Violent Crimes per 10,000 Population	54	27	68.1
			Property Crimes per 10,000 Population	427	28	50.0
Open Spaces	47	39.50	Population Density (Persons/Sq. Mile)	8059	44	59.8
			Average Rooms per Housing Unit	4.9	45	19.2
Education	2	90.95	% High School Enrollment/Completion	97.6%	10	90.3
			% College Graduates	63.7%	2	91.6
Commute	2	83.20	Average Work Commute in Minutes	24	30	68.8
			% Commuting on Public Transportation	33.3%	2	97.6
Community Stability	51	4.25	% Living in Same House as in 1979	32.1%	49	8.5
			% Living in Same County as in 1985	60.5%	52	0.0

Composite: **Rank** 45 / 52 *Score* 53.12   **MARLBOROUGH**

CATEGORY	RANK	SCORE	STATISTIC	VALUE	RANK	SCORE
Economics	33	57.45	Median Household Income	$41,315	33	30.0
			% of Families Above Poverty Level	95.7%	35	84.9
Affordable Housing	27	73.95	Median Home Value	$166,600	16	88.1
			Median Rent	$705	33	59.8
Crime	N/A	N/A	Violent Crimes per 10,000 Population	N/A	N/A	N/A
			Property Crimes per 10,000 Population	N/A	N/A	N/A
Open Spaces	29	67.85	Population Density (Persons/Sq. Mile)	1509	7	97.2
			Average Rooms per Housing Unit	5.4	33	38.5
Education	42	39.45	% High School Enrollment/Completion	89.7%	48	52.2
			% College Graduates	26.6%	26	26.7
Commute	39	40.60	Average Work Commute in Minutes	22	7	81.2
			% Commuting on Public Transportation	0.7%	51	0.0
Community Stability	46	39.40	% Living in Same House as in 1979	34.3%	46	15.7
			% Living in Same County as in 1985	80.7%	38	63.1

Composite: **Rank** 46 / 52 **Score** 52.69   **MALDEN**

CATEGORY	RANK	SCORE	STATISTIC	VALUE	RANK	SCORE
Economics	44	48.25	Median Household Income	$34,344	45	17.0
			% of Families Above Poverty Level	94.5%	42	79.5
Affordable Housing	15	81.35	Median Home Value	$162,300	13	89.9
			Median Rent	$651	20	72.8
Crime	29	52.75	Violent Crimes per 10,000 Population	93	33	44.2
			Property Crimes per 10,000 Population	357	23	61.3
Open Spaces	49	32.30	Population Density (Persons/Sq. Mile)	10587	49	45.4
			Average Rooms per Housing Unit	4.9	45	19.2
Education	45	37.65	% High School Enrollment/Completion	91.3%	44	59.9
			% College Graduates	20.1%	44	15.4
Commute	6	68.55	Average Work Commute in Minutes	25	39	62.5
			% Commuting on Public Transportation	25.6%	6	74.6
Community Stability	38	48.00	% Living in Same House as in 1979	38.3%	42	28.8
			% Living in Same County as in 1985	82.0%	35	67.2

Composite: **Rank** 47 / 52 **Score** 51.11   **REVERE**

CATEGORY	RANK	SCORE	STATISTIC	VALUE	RANK	SCORE
Economics	50	37.75	Median Household Income	$30,659	50	10.2
			% of Families Above Poverty Level	91.4%	50	65.3
Affordable Housing	10	85.95	Median Home Value	$158,100	11	91.7
			Median Rent	$620	15	80.2
Crime	33	45.35	Violent Crimes per 10,000 Population	75	31	55.2
			Property Crimes per 10,000 Population	517	31	35.5
Open Spaces	45	41.90	Population Density (Persons/Sq. Mile)	7230	42	64.6
			Average Rooms per Housing Unit	4.9	45	19.2
Education	50	24.75	% High School Enrollment/Completion	88.8%	49	47.8
			% College Graduates	12.3%	50	1.7
Commute	8	63.45	Average Work Commute in Minutes	25	39	62.5
			% Commuting on Public Transportation	22.2%	7	64.4
Community Stability	31	58.60	% Living in Same House as in 1979	43.0%	33	44.1
			% Living in Same County as in 1985	83.9%	29	73.1

Composite: **Rank** 48 / 52 **Score** 49.58   **SOMERVILLE**

CATEGORY	RANK	SCORE	STATISTIC	VALUE	RANK	SCORE
Economics	48	41.70	Median Household Income	$32,455	48	13.5
			% of Families Above Poverty Level	92.4%	48	69.9
Affordable Housing	20	77.80	Median Home Value	$164,400	15	89.1
			Median Rent	$677	27	66.5
Crime	23	61.65	Violent Crimes per 10,000 Population	73	30	56.4
			Property Crimes per 10,000 Population	322	20	66.9
Open Spaces	52	9.60	Population Density (Persons/Sq. Mile)	18537	52	0.0
			Average Rooms per Housing Unit	4.9	45	19.2
Education	28	50.95	% High School Enrollment/Completion	92.9%	40	67.6
			% College Graduates	30.9%	21	34.3
Commute	3	81.40	Average Work Commute in Minutes	24	30	68.8
			% Commuting on Public Transportation	32.1%	3	94.0
Community Stability	49	23.95	% Living in Same House as in 1979	34.6%	45	16.7
			% Living in Same County as in 1985	70.5%	49	31.2

Metropolitan Area Suburb Rankings
BOSTON-LAWRENCE-SALEM-LOWELL-BROCKTON

Composite: Rank 49 / 52 *Score* 48.29   **CAMBRIDGE**

CATEGORY	RANK	SCORE	STATISTIC	VALUE	RANK	SCORE
Economics	47	43.25	Median Household Income	$33,140	46	14.8
			% of Families Above Poverty Level	92.8%	46	71.7
Affordable Housing	24	75.30	Median Home Value	$256,800	45	50.6
			Median Rent	$538	1	100.0
Crime	36	32.85	Violent Crimes per 10,000 Population	105	35	36.8
			Property Crimes per 10,000 Population	558	33	28.9
Open Spaces	51	10.40	Population Density (Persons/Sq. Mile)	14888	51	20.8
			Average Rooms per Housing Unit	4.4	52	0.0
Education	8	79.55	% High School Enrollment/Completion	96.3%	15	84.1
			% College Graduates	54.2%	7	75.0
Commute	1	93.75	Average Work Commute in Minutes	21	4	87.5
			% Commuting on Public Transportation	34.1%	1	100.0
Community Stability	52	2.95	% Living in Same House as in 1979	29.5%	52	0.0
			% Living in Same County as in 1985	62.4%	51	5.9

Composite: Rank 50 / 52 *Score* 46.79   **HULL**

CATEGORY	RANK	SCORE	STATISTIC	VALUE	RANK	SCORE
Economics	41	51.35	Median Household Income	$37,683	40	23.2
			% of Families Above Poverty Level	94.5%	42	79.5
Affordable Housing	38	65.65	Median Home Value	$153,300	6	93.7
			Median Rent	$797	43	37.6
Crime	32	46.05	Violent Crimes per 10,000 Population	120	36	27.6
			Property Crimes per 10,000 Population	337	21	64.5
Open Spaces	22	71.75	Population Density (Persons/Sq. Mile)	3520	32	85.8
			Average Rooms per Housing Unit	5.9	17	57.7
Education	43	39.25	% High School Enrollment/Completion	92.1%	43	63.8
			% College Graduates	19.7%	45	14.7
Commute	52	12.45	Average Work Commute in Minutes	35	52	0.0
			% Commuting on Public Transportation	9.0%	23	24.9
Community Stability	45	41.00	% Living in Same House as in 1979	41.1%	37	37.9
			% Living in Same County as in 1985	74.6%	47	44.1

Composite: Rank 51 / 52 *Score* 38.59   **LYNN**

CATEGORY	RANK	SCORE	STATISTIC	VALUE	RANK	SCORE
Economics	51	23.70	Median Household Income	$28,553	51	6.3
			% of Families Above Poverty Level	86.1%	51	41.1
Affordable Housing	1	95.65	Median Home Value	$138,100	1	100.0
			Median Rent	$574	3	91.3
Crime	37	0.65	Violent Crimes per 10,000 Population	165	37	0.0
			Property Crimes per 10,000 Population	729	36	1.3
Open Spaces	46	41.10	Population Density (Persons/Sq. Mile)	7513	43	63.0
			Average Rooms per Housing Unit	4.9	45	19.2
Education	51	9.35	% High School Enrollment/Completion	81.7%	51	13.5
			% College Graduates	14.3%	49	5.2
Commute	20	50.65	Average Work Commute in Minutes	23	13	75.0
			% Commuting on Public Transportation	9.5%	21	26.3
Community Stability	37	49.00	% Living in Same House as in 1979	37.4%	44	25.8
			% Living in Same County as in 1985	83.6%	31	72.2

Composite: **Rank** 52 / 52 **Score** 33.73   **CHELSEA**

CATEGORY	RANK	SCORE	STATISTIC	VALUE	RANK	SCORE
Economics	52	0.00	Median Household Income	$25,144	52	0.0
			% of Families Above Poverty Level	77.1%	52	0.0
Affordable Housing	4	93.15	Median Home Value	$138,500	2	99.8
			Median Rent	$594	7	86.5
Crime	N/A	N/A	Violent Crimes per 10,000 Population	N/A	N/A	N/A
			Property Crimes per 10,000 Population	N/A	N/A	N/A
Open Spaces	50	17.40	Population Density (Persons/Sq. Mile)	13112	50	31.0
			Average Rooms per Housing Unit	4.5	51	3.8
Education	52	0.60	% High School Enrollment/Completion	78.9%	52	0.0
			% College Graduates	12.0%	51	1.2
Commute	4	69.70	Average Work Commute in Minutes	25	39	62.5
			% Commuting on Public Transportation	26.4%	4	76.9
Community Stability	50	21.55	% Living in Same House as in 1979	29.6%	51	0.3
			% Living in Same County as in 1985	74.2%	48	42.8

Metropolitan Area Description
BUFFALO-NIAGARA FALLS

STATE: New York
COUNTIES: Erie, Niagara

TOTAL POPULATION:	1,189,288	
POPULATION IN SUBURBS:	799,325	(67.2%)
POPULATION IN Buffalo:	328,123	(27.6%)
POPULATION IN Niagara Falls:	61,840	(5.2%)

The BUFFALO-NIAGRA FALLS metropolitan area is located in the northwestern part of New York along Lake Erie and the Canadian border. The suburbs range geographically from Lockport in the north (40 miles from Buffalo), to Hamburg in the south (21 miles from Buffalo), and to Lancaster in the east (8 miles from Buffalo). The area is shrinking in population and had a decrease of 4.3% between 1980 and 1990. Summer time high temperatures average in the 70's and winter time lows average in the teens. Major employers in the suburban area include Peter J. Schmitt Company located in Cheektowaga. Many Canadian companies have opened in the area due to the Free Trade Agreement between the United States and Canada. Operating and labor costs are less expensive in the Buffalo area than in Ontario Province, making the area attractive to Canadian business.

Tonawanda is the overall highest rated suburb. **Hamburg** receives the highest scores in both economics and education. **Lackawanna** is the suburb with the most affordable housing and also has the top rated commute. **Lancaster** is rated the safest suburb with the lowest crime rate. Finally, the number one rating in both open spaces and community stability goes to **West Seneca**.

The highest ranked suburb overall which also has an affordable housing score of at least 50.00 is **North Tonawanda**.

The highest ranked suburb in the education category which also has an affordable housing score of at least 50.00 is also **North Tonawanda**.

The county whose suburbs have the highest average overall score is **Erie County** (57.57).

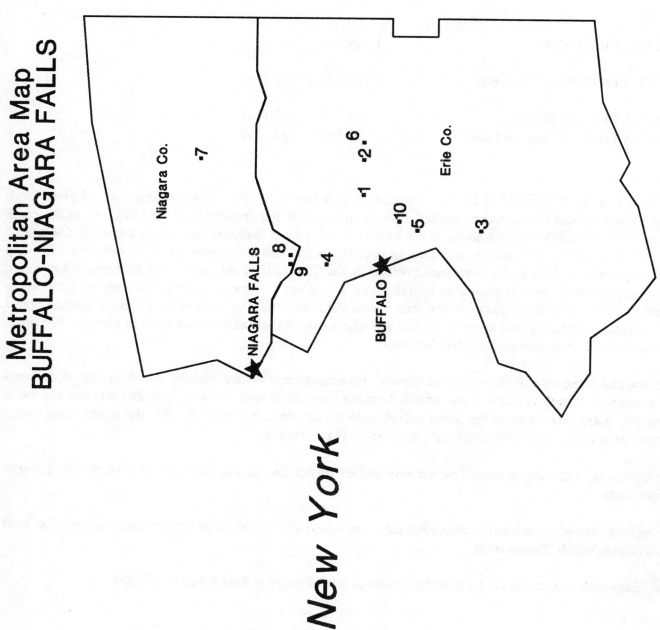

Metropolitan Area Map
BUFFALO-NIAGARA FALLS

New York

Niagara Co.

Erie Co.

NIAGARA FALLS

BUFFALO

•7

•8
•9
•4

•6
•2
•1
•10
•5
•3

Metropolitan Area Suburb Alphabetical Index
BUFFALO-NIAGARA FALLS

SUBURB	PAGE	MAP NO.	STATE	COUNTY	POPU-LATION	RANK
CHEEKTOWAGA	84	1	New York	Erie	84,387	7 / 10
DEPEW	83	2	New York	Erie	17,673	6 / 10
HAMBURG	83	3	New York	Erie	10,442	4 / 10
KENMORE	82	4	New York	Erie	17,180	3 / 10
LACKAWANNA	84	5	New York	Erie	20,585	9 / 10
LANCASTER	83	6	New York	Erie	11,940	5 / 10
LOCKPORT	85	7	New York	Niagara	24,426	10 / 10
NORTH TONAWANDA	84	8	New York	Niagara	34,989	8 / 10
TONAWANDA	82	9	New York	Erie	65,284	1 / 10
WEST SENECA	82	10	New York	Erie	47,866	2 / 10

Metropolitan Area Suburb Rankings
BUFFALO-NIAGARA FALLS

Composite: **Rank** 1 / 10 *Score* 65.67   **TONAWANDA**

CATEGORY	RANK	SCORE	STATISTIC	VALUE	RANK	SCORE
Economics	3	74.55	Median Household Income	$31,185	3	61.2
			% of Families Above Poverty Level	96.3%	3	87.9
Affordable Housing	8	23.25	Median Home Value	$74,000	8	32.1
			Median Rent	$422	6	14.4
Crime	4	79.45	Violent Crimes per 10,000 Population	28	4	85.0
			Property Crimes per 10,000 Population	277	4	73.9
Open Spaces	3	73.45	Population Density (Persons/Sq. Mile)	3757	7	84.4
			Average Rooms per Housing Unit	5.7	4	62.5
Education	3	52.80	% High School Enrollment/Completion	92.0%	7	55.6
			% College Graduates	22.2%	3	50.0
Commute	3	65.10	Average Work Commute in Minutes	18	2	75.0
			% Commuting on Public Transportation	3.8%	3	55.2
Community Stability	3	91.10	% Living in Same House as in 1979	55.6%	1	100.0
			% Living in Same County as in 1985	94.2%	6	82.2

Composite: **Rank** 2 / 10 *Score* 61.64   **WEST SENECA**

CATEGORY	RANK	SCORE	STATISTIC	VALUE	RANK	SCORE
Economics	2	90.55	Median Household Income	$34,399	2	81.1
			% of Families Above Poverty Level	97.6%	1	100.0
Affordable Housing	9	7.95	Median Home Value	$78,900	9	15.9
			Median Rent	$436	10	0.0
Crime	5	76.05	Violent Crimes per 10,000 Population	26	3	86.6
			Property Crimes per 10,000 Population	306	5	65.5
Open Spaces	1	93.75	Population Density (Persons/Sq. Mile)	2238	1	100.0
			Average Rooms per Housing Unit	5.9	2	87.5
Education	6	41.80	% High School Enrollment/Completion	92.9%	6	60.6
			% College Graduates	15.4%	5	23.0
Commute	8	23.70	Average Work Commute in Minutes	20	8	25.0
			% Commuting on Public Transportation	1.9%	5	22.4
Community Stability	1	97.65	% Living in Same House as in 1979	55.2%	2	97.8
			% Living in Same County as in 1985	96.0%	2	97.5

Composite: **Rank** 3 / 10 *Score* 61.52   **KENMORE**

CATEGORY	RANK	SCORE	STATISTIC	VALUE	RANK	SCORE
Economics	4	72.00	Median Household Income	$30,674	4	58.0
			% of Families Above Poverty Level	96.1%	5	86.0
Affordable Housing	5	44.25	Median Home Value	$71,300	7	41.1
			Median Rent	$390	5	47.4
Crime	3	80.85	Violent Crimes per 10,000 Population	36	5	78.7
			Property Crimes per 10,000 Population	245	2	83.0
Open Spaces	10	37.50	Population Density (Persons/Sq. Mile)	11958	10	0.0
			Average Rooms per Housing Unit	5.8	3	75.0
Education	2	70.00	% High School Enrollment/Completion	95.2%	3	73.3
			% College Graduates	26.4%	2	66.7
Commute	2	70.70	Average Work Commute in Minutes	19	3	50.0
			% Commuting on Public Transportation	5.9%	2	91.4
Community Stability	8	55.35	% Living in Same House as in 1979	45.2%	9	43.8
			% Living in Same County as in 1985	92.4%	8	66.9

Metropolitan Area Suburb Rankings
BUFFALO-NIAGARA FALLS

Composite: **Rank** 4 / 10 ***Score*** 60.88   **HAMBURG**

CATEGORY	RANK	SCORE	STATISTIC	VALUE	RANK	SCORE
Economics	1	97.20	Median Household Income	$37,448	1	100.0
			% of Families Above Poverty Level	97.0%	2	94.4
Affordable Housing	10	5.15	Median Home Value	$83,700	10	0.0
			Median Rent	$426	8	10.3
Crime	7	54.40	Violent Crimes per 10,000 Population	45	8	71.7
			Property Crimes per 10,000 Population	405	8	37.1
Open Spaces	2	90.15	Population Density (Persons/Sq. Mile)	4154	8	80.3
			Average Rooms per Housing Unit	6.0	1	100.0
Education	1	100.00	% High School Enrollment/Completion	100.0%	1	100.0
			% College Graduates	34.8%	1	100.0
Commute	9	15.50	Average Work Commute in Minutes	21	10	0.0
			% Commuting on Public Transportation	2.4%	4	31.0
Community Stability	7	63.75	% Living in Same House as in 1979	47.2%	7	54.6
			% Living in Same County as in 1985	93.1%	7	72.9

Composite: **Rank** 5 / 10 ***Score*** 54.90   **LANCASTER**

CATEGORY	RANK	SCORE	STATISTIC	VALUE	RANK	SCORE
Economics	7	66.40	Median Household Income	$29,618	6	51.5
			% of Families Above Poverty Level	95.6%	7	81.3
Affordable Housing	4	48.75	Median Home Value	$68,900	5	49.0
			Median Rent	$389	4	48.5
Crime	1	96.45	Violent Crimes per 10,000 Population	18	2	92.9
			Property Crimes per 10,000 Population	186	1	100.0
Open Spaces	5	63.70	Population Density (Persons/Sq. Mile)	4434	9	77.4
			Average Rooms per Housing Unit	5.6	5	50.0
Education	10	12.70	% High School Enrollment/Completion	82.0%	10	0.0
			% College Graduates	16.0%	4	25.4
Commute	10	13.35	Average Work Commute in Minutes	20	8	25.0
			% Commuting on Public Transportation	0.7%	9	1.7
Community Stability	6	82.95	% Living in Same House as in 1979	49.3%	6	65.9
			% Living in Same County as in 1985	96.3%	1	100.0

Composite: **Rank** 6 / 10 ***Score*** 54.48   **DEPEW**

CATEGORY	RANK	SCORE	STATISTIC	VALUE	RANK	SCORE
Economics	5	70.95	Median Household Income	$30,637	5	57.8
			% of Families Above Poverty Level	95.9%	6	84.1
Affordable Housing	6	28.90	Median Home Value	$70,600	6	43.4
			Median Rent	$422	6	14.4
Crime	6	58.00	Violent Crimes per 10,000 Population	38	6	77.2
			Property Crimes per 10,000 Population	399	7	38.8
Open Spaces	4	68.55	Population Density (Persons/Sq. Mile)	3488	6	87.1
			Average Rooms per Housing Unit	5.6	5	50.0
Education	7	35.55	% High School Enrollment/Completion	93.6%	5	64.4
			% College Graduates	11.3%	8	6.7
Commute	6	27.60	Average Work Commute in Minutes	19	3	50.0
			% Commuting on Public Transportation	0.9%	7	5.2
Community Stability	2	91.80	% Living in Same House as in 1979	54.6%	3	94.6
			% Living in Same County as in 1985	95.0%	5	89.0

Metropolitan Area Suburb Rankings
BUFFALO-NIAGARA FALLS

Composite: **Rank** 7 / 10 *Score* 53.34   **CHEEKTOWAGA**

CATEGORY	RANK	SCORE	STATISTIC	VALUE	RANK	SCORE
Economics	6	67.50	Median Household Income	$29,068	8	48.1
			% of Families Above Poverty Level	96.2%	4	86.9
Affordable Housing	7	26.70	Median Home Value	$68,800	4	49.3
			Median Rent	$432	9	4.1
Crime	8	50.05	Violent Crimes per 10,000 Population	42	7	74.0
			Property Crimes per 10,000 Population	443	9	26.1
Open Spaces	6	63.20	Population Density (Persons/Sq. Mile)	3315	3	88.9
			Average Rooms per Housing Unit	5.5	7	37.5
Education	5	42.25	% High School Enrollment/Completion	96.2%	2	78.9
			% College Graduates	11.0%	9	5.6
Commute	5	36.20	Average Work Commute in Minutes	19	3	50.0
			% Commuting on Public Transportation	1.9%	5	22.4
Community Stability	4	87.50	% Living in Same House as in 1979	52.7%	4	84.3
			% Living in Same County as in 1985	95.2%	4	90.7

Composite: **Rank** 8 / 10 *Score* 52.15   **NORTH TONAWANDA**

CATEGORY	RANK	SCORE	STATISTIC	VALUE	RANK	SCORE
Economics	8	64.40	Median Household Income	$29,576	7	51.2
			% of Families Above Poverty Level	95.2%	8	77.6
Affordable Housing	3	51.40	Median Home Value	$67,600	3	53.3
			Median Rent	$388	3	49.5
Crime	2	88.65	Violent Crimes per 10,000 Population	9	1	100.0
			Property Crimes per 10,000 Population	265	3	77.3
Open Spaces	7	62.45	Population Density (Persons/Sq. Mile)	3464	5	87.4
			Average Rooms per Housing Unit	5.5	7	37.5
Education	4	47.20	% High School Enrollment/Completion	95.0%	4	72.2
			% College Graduates	15.2%	6	22.2
Commute	7	25.00	Average Work Commute in Minutes	19	3	50.0
			% Commuting on Public Transportation	0.6%	10	0.0
Community Stability	9	25.95	% Living in Same House as in 1979	46.7%	8	51.9
			% Living in Same County as in 1985	84.5%	10	0.0

Composite: **Rank** 9 / 10 *Score* 48.15   **LACKAWANNA**

CATEGORY	RANK	SCORE	STATISTIC	VALUE	RANK	SCORE
Economics	10	0.00	Median Household Income	$21,310	10	0.0
			% of Families Above Poverty Level	86.9%	10	0.0
Affordable Housing	1	94.05	Median Home Value	$57,100	2	88.1
			Median Rent	$339	1	100.0
Crime	9	20.85	Violent Crimes per 10,000 Population	136	10	0.0
			Property Crimes per 10,000 Population	389	6	41.7
Open Spaces	9	44.20	Population Density (Persons/Sq. Mile)	3363	4	88.4
			Average Rooms per Housing Unit	5.2	10	0.0
Education	9	17.20	% High School Enrollment/Completion	88.2%	8	34.4
			% College Graduates	9.6%	10	0.0
Commute	1	75.00	Average Work Commute in Minutes	19	3	50.0
			% Commuting on Public Transportation	6.4%	1	100.0
Community Stability	5	85.75	% Living in Same House as in 1979	51.1%	5	75.7
			% Living in Same County as in 1985	95.8%	3	95.8

Metropolitan Area Suburb Rankings
BUFFALO-NIAGARA FALLS

Composite: **Rank** 10 / 10 **Score** 38.64   **LOCKPORT**

CATEGORY	RANK	SCORE	STATISTIC	VALUE	RANK	SCORE
Economics	9	16.10	Median Household Income	$25,000	9	22.9
			% of Families Above Poverty Level	87.9%	9	9.3
Affordable Housing	2	87.65	Median Home Value	$53,500	1	100.0
			Median Rent	$363	2	75.3
Crime	10	13.00	Violent Crimes per 10,000 Population	103	9	26.0
			Property Crimes per 10,000 Population	534	10	0.0
Open Spaces	8	59.30	Population Density (Persons/Sq. Mile)	2862	2	93.6
			Average Rooms per Housing Unit	5.4	9	25.0
Education	8	21.10	% High School Enrollment/Completion	86.3%	9	23.9
			% College Graduates	14.2%	7	18.3
Commute	4	51.70	Average Work Commute in Minutes	17	1	100.0
			% Commuting on Public Transportation	0.8%	8	3.4
Community Stability	10	21.60	% Living in Same House as in 1979	37.1%	10	0.0
			% Living in Same County as in 1985	89.6%	9	43.2

Metropolitan Area Description
CHARLOTTE-GASTONIA-ROCK HILL

STATE: North Carolina
COUNTIES: Cabarrus, Gaston, Lincoln, Mecklenburg, Rowan, Union

STATE: South Carolina
COUNTIES: York

TOTAL POPULATION:	1,162,093	
POPULATION IN SUBURBS:	669,784	(57.6%)
POPULATION IN Charlotte (NC):	395,934	(34.1%)
POPULATION IN Gastonia (NC):	54,732	(4.7%)
POPULATION IN Rock Hill (SC):	41,643	(3.6%)

The CHARLOTTE-GASTONIA-ROCK HILL metropolitan area is located in the southcentral part of North Carolina and the northcentral part of South Carolina. The suburbs range geographically from Salisbury (NC) in the northeast (42 miles from Charlotte), to Monroe (NC) in the south (26 miles from Charlotte). The area is growing rapidly in population and had an increase of 19.6% between 1980 and 1990. Summer time high temperatures average in the 80's and winter time lows average in the 30's. Major employers in the area include PCA National and Harris-Teeter, both located in the suburb of Matthews (NC). Grocery giant Food Lion is located in Salisbury (NC).

Mint Hill (NC) is the overall highest rated suburb and also has the highest scores in education and open spaces. **Matthews** (NC) receives the highest score in economics and is also rated the safest suburb with the lowest crime rate. **Kannapolis** (NC) is the suburb with the most affordable housing and also ranks number one in community stability. Finally, the top rated commute belongs to **Salisbury** (NC).

The highest ranked suburb overall which also has an affordable housing score of at least 50.00 is **Salisbury** (NC).

The highest ranked suburb in the education category which also has an affordable housing score of at least 50.00 is also **Salisbury** (NC).

The county whose suburbs have the highest average overall score is **Rowan County** (NC) (59.08).

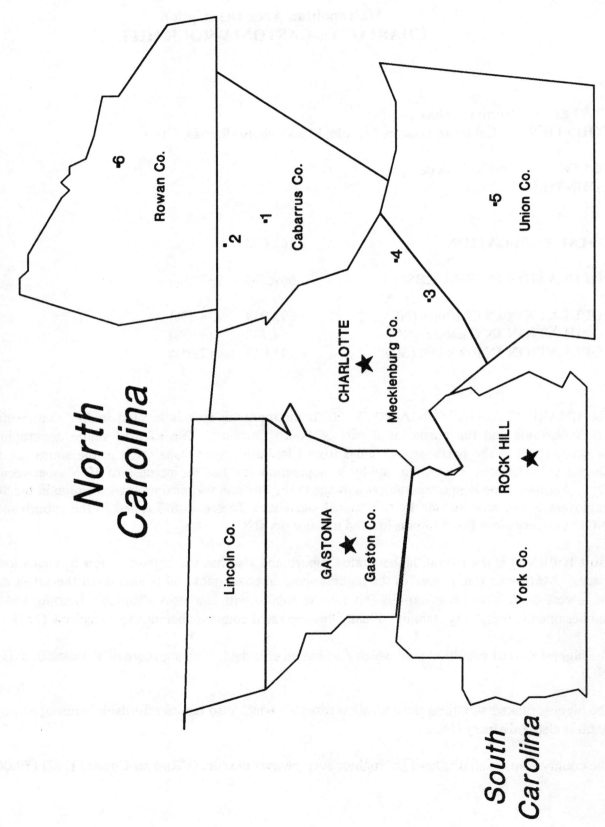

Metropolitan Area Map
CHARLOTTE-GASTONIA-ROCK HILL

North Carolina

South Carolina

Rowan Co.

Cabarrus Co.

Union Co.

Mecklenburg Co.

CHARLOTTE

Lincoln Co.

GASTONIA
Gaston Co.

ROCK HILL

York Co.

•1
•2
•3
•4
•5
•6

Metropolitan Area Suburb Alphabetical Index
CHARLOTTE-GASTONIA-ROCK HILL

SUBURB	PAGE	MAP NO.	STATE	COUNTY	POPU-LATION	RANK
CONCORD	91	1	North Carolina	Cabarrus	27,347	5 / 6
KANNAPOLIS	91	2	North Carolina	Cabarrus	29,696	4 / 6
MATTHEWS	90	3	North Carolina	Mecklenburg	13,651	3 / 6
MINT HILL	90	4	North Carolina	Mecklenburg	11,567	1 / 6
MONROE	91	5	North Carolina	Union	16,127	6 / 6
SALISBURY	90	6	North Carolina	Rowan	23,087	2 / 6

Metropolitan Area Suburb Rankings
CHARLOTTE-GASTONIA-ROCK HILL

Composite: **Rank** 1 / 6 **Score** 64.72   **MINT HILL** (NC)

CATEGORY	RANK	SCORE	STATISTIC	VALUE	RANK	SCORE
Economics	2	94.75	Median Household Income	$47,976	2	89.5
			% of Families Above Poverty Level	99.4%	1	100.0
Affordable Housing	5	11.65	Median Home Value	$97,700	5	23.3
			Median Rent	$609	6	0.0
Crime	N/A	N/A	Violent Crimes per 10,000 Population	N/A	N/A	N/A
			Property Crimes per 10,000 Population	N/A	N/A	N/A
Open Spaces	1	100.00	Population Density (Persons/Sq. Mile)	640	1	100.0
			Average Rooms per Housing Unit	6.7	1	100.0
Education	1	69.95	% High School Enrollment/Completion	93.5%	1	100.0
			% College Graduates	19.8%	3	39.9
Commute	5	23.10	Average Work Commute in Minutes	28	6	0.0
			% Commuting on Public Transportation	0.6%	2	46.2
Community Stability	2	88.85	% Living in Same House as in 1979	41.4%	3	77.7
			% Living in Same County as in 1985	83.4%	1	100.0

Composite: **Rank** 2 / 6 **Score** 59.08   **SALISBURY** (NC)

CATEGORY	RANK	SCORE	STATISTIC	VALUE	RANK	SCORE
Economics	5	11.00	Median Household Income	$24,081	4	6.0
			% of Families Above Poverty Level	89.4%	5	16.0
Affordable Housing	2	91.15	Median Home Value	$54,500	2	87.5
			Median Rent	$353	2	94.8
Crime	4	36.55	Violent Crimes per 10,000 Population	92	4	63.1
			Property Crimes per 10,000 Population	1,065	4	10.0
Open Spaces	5	30.30	Population Density (Persons/Sq. Mile)	1411	5	38.4
			Average Rooms per Housing Unit	5.3	3	22.2
Education	3	65.90	% High School Enrollment/Completion	92.2%	2	88.9
			% College Graduates	20.7%	2	42.9
Commute	1	100.00	Average Work Commute in Minutes	15	1	100.0
			% Commuting on Public Transportation	1.3%	1	100.0
Community Stability	4	78.65	% Living in Same House as in 1979	41.4%	3	77.7
			% Living in Same County as in 1985	79.2%	5	79.6

Composite: **Rank** 3 / 6 **Score** 51.14   **MATTHEWS** (NC)

CATEGORY	RANK	SCORE	STATISTIC	VALUE	RANK	SCORE
Economics	1	97.50	Median Household Income	$50,980	1	100.0
			% of Families Above Poverty Level	98.8%	2	95.0
Affordable Housing	6	5.00	Median Home Value	$113,400	6	0.0
			Median Rent	$582	5	10.0
Crime	1	100.00	Violent Crimes per 10,000 Population	26	1	100.0
			Property Crimes per 10,000 Population	343	1	100.0
Open Spaces	2	70.00	Population Density (Persons/Sq. Mile)	1113	2	62.2
			Average Rooms per Housing Unit	6.3	2	77.8
Education	2	66.25	% High School Enrollment/Completion	85.6%	3	32.5
			% College Graduates	38.0%	1	100.0
Commute	6	19.25	Average Work Commute in Minutes	27	5	7.7
			% Commuting on Public Transportation	0.4%	3	30.8
Community Stability	6	0.00	% Living in Same House as in 1979	19.8%	6	0.0
			% Living in Same County as in 1985	62.8%	6	0.0

Metropolitan Area Suburb Rankings
CHARLOTTE-GASTONIA-ROCK HILL

Composite: *Rank* 4 / 6 *Score* 50.94   **KANNAPOLIS** (NC)

CATEGORY	RANK	SCORE	STATISTIC	VALUE	RANK	SCORE
Economics	4	13.05	Median Household Income	$22,369	6	0.0
			% of Families Above Poverty Level	90.6%	4	26.1
Affordable Housing	1	100.00	Median Home Value	$46,100	1	100.0
			Median Rent	$339	1	100.0
Crime	2	95.95	Violent Crimes per 10,000 Population	34	2	95.5
			Property Crimes per 10,000 Population	372	2	96.4
Open Spaces	6	0.00	Population Density (Persons/Sq. Mile)	1892	6	0.0
			Average Rooms per Housing Unit	4.9	6	0.0
Education	6	3.40	% High School Enrollment/Completion	82.6%	4	6.8
			% College Graduates	7.7%	6	0.0
Commute	2	50.00	Average Work Commute in Minutes	19	3	69.2
			% Commuting on Public Transportation	0.4%	3	30.8
Community Stability	1	94.15	% Living in Same House as in 1979	47.6%	1	100.0
			% Living in Same County as in 1985	81.0%	3	88.3

Composite: *Rank* 5 / 6 *Score* 48.70   **CONCORD** (NC)

CATEGORY	RANK	SCORE	STATISTIC	VALUE	RANK	SCORE
Economics	3	21.35	Median Household Income	$25,473	3	10.8
			% of Families Above Poverty Level	91.3%	3	31.9
Affordable Housing	3	80.50	Median Home Value	$59,900	3	79.5
			Median Rent	$389	3	81.5
Crime	3	78.15	Violent Crimes per 10,000 Population	53	3	84.9
			Property Crimes per 10,000 Population	572	3	71.4
Open Spaces	4	33.85	Population Density (Persons/Sq. Mile)	1254	4	51.0
			Average Rooms per Housing Unit	5.2	4	16.7
Education	5	11.70	% High School Enrollment/Completion	81.8%	6	0.0
			% College Graduates	14.8%	4	23.4
Commute	4	30.75	Average Work Commute in Minutes	20	4	61.5
			% Commuting on Public Transportation	0.0%	6	0.0
Community Stability	3	84.60	% Living in Same House as in 1979	41.6%	2	78.4
			% Living in Same County as in 1985	81.5%	2	90.8

Composite: *Rank* 6 / 6 *Score* 33.64   **MONROE** (NC)

CATEGORY	RANK	SCORE	STATISTIC	VALUE	RANK	SCORE
Economics	6	1.35	Median Household Income	$23,153	5	2.7
			% of Families Above Poverty Level	87.5%	6	0.0
Affordable Housing	4	73.10	Median Home Value	$62,600	4	75.5
			Median Rent	$418	4	70.7
Crime	5	0.00	Violent Crimes per 10,000 Population	205	5	0.0
			Property Crimes per 10,000 Population	1,145	5	0.0
Open Spaces	3	37.45	Population Density (Persons/Sq. Mile)	1163	3	58.2
			Average Rooms per Housing Unit	5.2	4	16.7
Education	4	11.85	% High School Enrollment/Completion	81.9%	5	0.9
			% College Graduates	14.6%	5	22.8
Commute	3	46.15	Average Work Commute in Minutes	18	2	76.9
			% Commuting on Public Transportation	0.2%	5	15.4
Community Stability	5	65.60	% Living in Same House as in 1979	33.2%	5	48.2
			% Living in Same County as in 1985	79.9%	4	83.0

Metropolitan Area Description
CHICAGO-GARY-LAKE COUNTY

STATE: Illinois
COUNTIES: Cook, Du Page, Grundy, Kane, Kendall, Lake, McHenry, Will

STATE: Indiana
COUNTIES: Lake, Porter

STATE: Wisconsin
COUNTIES: Kenosha

TOTAL POPULATION: 8,065,633

POPULATION IN SUBURBS: 5,165,261 (64.0%)

POPULATION IN Chicago (IL): 2,783,726 (34.5%)
POPULATION IN Gary (IN): 116,646 (1.4%)

The CHICAGO-GARY-LAKE COUNTY metropolitan area is located in the northeastern part of Illinois, the southwestern part of Wisconsin, and the northwestern part of Indiana along Lake Michigan. The suburbs range geographically from Kenosha (WI) in the north (60 miles from Chicago), to Woodstock (IL) in the west (60 miles from Chicago), to Joliet (IL) in the south (37 miles from Chicago), and to Valparaiso (IN) in the east (54 miles from Chicago). The area is growing in population and had an increase of 1.6% between 1980 and 1990. Summer time high temperatures average in the 80's and winter time lows average in the teens. Many high tech companies have located along interstate 88 in DuPage and Kane Counties. The area has been nicknamed "Silicon Prairie." Public transportation in the area is provided by the Chicago Transit Authority utilizing a network of buses, subways, and elevated trains.

Winnetka (IL) is the overall highest rated suburb and also has the highest scores in economics and education. **East Chicago** (IN) is the suburb with the most affordable housing. **Lake Forest** (IL) is rated the safest suburb with the lowest crime rate. The top rated commute belongs to **Evanston** (IL). **Goodings Grove** (IL) receives the highest score in open spaces. Finally, the number one rating in community stability goes to **Norridge** (IL).

The highest ranked suburb overall which also has an affordable housing score of at least 50.00 is **South Holland** (IL).

The highest ranked suburb in the education category which also has an affordable housing score of at least 50.00 is **River Forest** (IL).

The county whose suburbs have the highest overall score is **Kenosha County** (WI) (58.59).

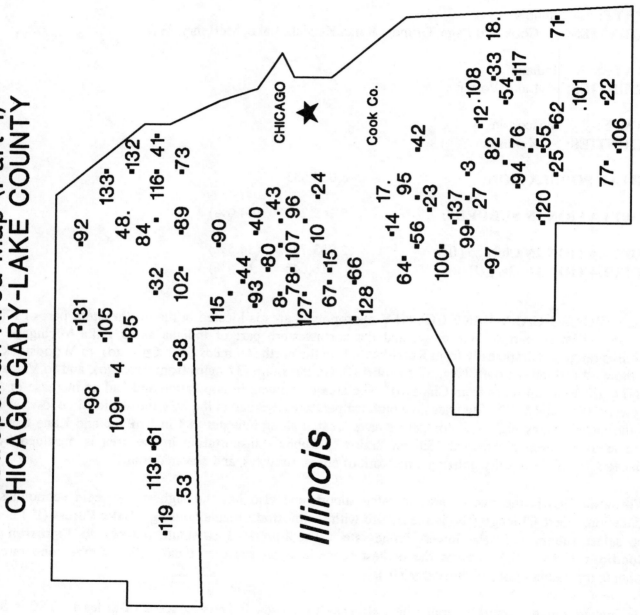

Metropolitan Area Map (Part 1)
CHICAGO-GARY-LAKE COUNTY

CHICAGO

Cook Co.

Illinois

Metropolitan Area Map (Part 2)
CHICAGO-GARY-LAKE COUNTY

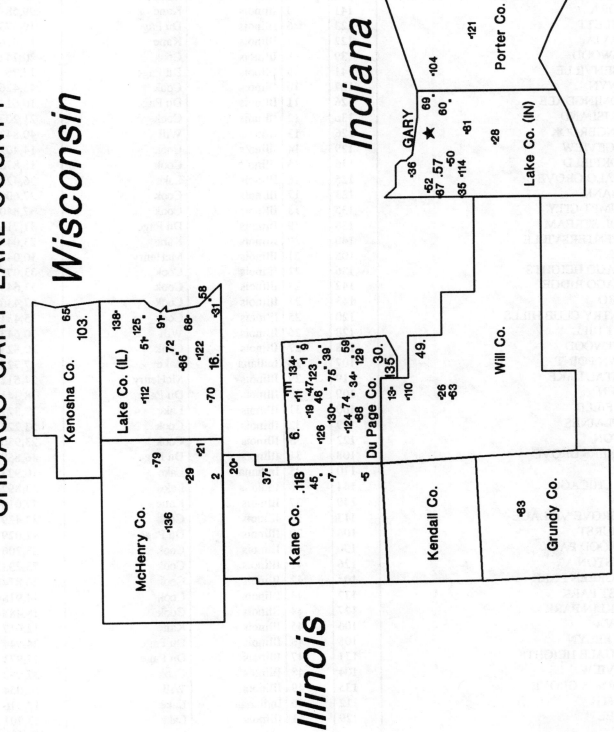

Wisconsin

Illinois

Indiana

Kenosha Co. 65 103.

McHenry Co. ·136

Lake Co. (IL) 138· 125· 9+ 5+ 72 ·86 ·68 ·122 16. ·112 ·70 58 ·31

·79 ·29 ·21 2 ·20

Kane Co. ·118 37· 45· ·7 ·5

111 134· 1 9 ·19 ·47 123 59 46· 75· 39 129 ·130 34· ·124 74· 88 ·126 6.

Du Page Co. 30. 13· ·135 ·110 49.

Kendall Co.

Grundy Co. ·83

GARY ★ ·36 ·52 57 69. ·50 67 ·35 ·114 60· ·81 ·28

Porter Co. ·104 ·121

Lake Co. (IN)

Will Co. ·26 ·63

Metropolitan Area Suburb Alphabetical Index
CHICAGO-GARY-LAKE COUNTY

SUBURB	PAGE	MAP NO.	STATE	COUNTY	POPU-LATION	RANK
ADDISON	131	1	Illinois	Du Page	32,058	97 / 138
ALGONQUIN	124	2	Illinois	McHenry	11,663	76 / 138
ALSIP	132	3	Illinois	Cook	18,227	101 / 138
ARLINGTON HEIGHTS	111	4	Illinois	Cook	75,460	39 / 138
AURORA	141	5	Illinois	Kane	99,581	128 / 138
BARTLETT	123	6	Illinois	Du Page	19,373	74 / 138
BATAVIA	122	7	Illinois	Kane	17,076	72 / 138
BELLWOOD	139	8	Illinois	Cook	20,241	122 / 138
BENSENVILLE	141	9	Illinois	Du Page	17,767	129 / 138
BERWYN	127	10	Illinois	Cook	45,426	86 / 138
BLOOMINGDALE	126	11	Illinois	Du Page	16,614	84 / 138
BLUE ISLAND	136	12	Illinois	Cook	21,203	112 / 138
BOLINGBROOK	126	13	Illinois	Will	40,843	82 / 138
BRIDGEVIEW	129	14	Illinois	Cook	14,402	92 / 138
BROOKFIELD	116	15	Illinois	Cook	18,876	53 / 138
BUFFALO GROVE	125	16	Illinois	Lake	36,427	81 / 138
BURBANK	123	17	Illinois	Cook	27,600	73 / 138
CALUMET CITY	135	18	Illinois	Cook	37,840	111 / 138
CAROL STREAM	138	19	Illinois	Du Page	31,716	119 / 138
CARPENTERSVILLE	140	20	Illinois	Kane	23,049	126 / 138
CARY	108	21	Illinois	McHenry	10,043	29 / 138
CHICAGO HEIGHTS	136	22	Illinois	Cook	33,072	114 / 138
CHICAGO RIDGE	142	23	Illinois	Cook	13,643	131 / 138
CICERO	143	24	Illinois	Cook	67,436	135 / 138
COUNTRY CLUB HILLS	120	25	Illinois	Cook	15,431	66 / 138
CREST HILL	128	26	Illinois	Will	10,643	90 / 138
CRESTWOOD	128	27	Illinois	Cook	10,823	88 / 138
CROWN POINT	107	28	Indiana	Lake	17,728	27 / 138
CRYSTAL LAKE	119	29	Illinois	McHenry	24,512	63 / 138
DARIEN	109	30	Illinois	Du Page	18,341	33 / 138
DEERFIELD	100	31	Illinois	Lake	17,327	6 / 138
DES PLAINES	109	32	Illinois	Cook	53,223	31 / 138
DOLTON	122	33	Illinois	Cook	23,930	71 / 138
DOWNERS GROVE	108	34	Illinois	Du Page	46,858	29 / 138
DYER	110	35	Indiana	Lake	10,923	35 / 138
EAST CHICAGO	144	36	Indiana	Lake	33,892	137 / 138
ELGIN	140	37	Illinois	Kane	77,010	125 / 138
ELK GROVE VILLAGE	113	38	Illinois	Cook	33,429	45 / 138
ELMHURST	106	39	Illinois	Du Page	42,029	22 / 138
ELMWOOD PARK	130	40	Illinois	Cook	23,206	96 / 138
EVANSTON	126	41	Illinois	Cook	73,233	83 / 138
EVERGREEN PARK	104	42	Illinois	Cook	20,874	17 / 138
FOREST PARK	137	43	Illinois	Cook	14,918	116 / 138
FRANKLIN PARK	127	44	Illinois	Cook	18,485	85 / 138
GENEVA	106	45	Illinois	Kane	12,617	23 / 138
GLEN ELLYN	105	46	Illinois	Du Page	24,944	21 / 138
GLENDALE HEIGHTS	131	47	Illinois	Du Page	27,973	99 / 138
GLENVIEW	104	48	Illinois	Cook	37,093	16 / 138
GOODINGS GROVE	135	49	Illinois	Will	14,054	110 / 138
GRIFFITH	112	50	Indiana	Lake	17,916	42 / 138
GURNEE	129	51	Illinois	Lake	13,701	90 / 138

Metropolitan Area Suburb Alphabetical Index
CHICAGO-GARY-LAKE COUNTY

SUBURB	PAGE	MAP NO.	STATE	COUNTY	POPU-LATION	RANK
HAMMOND	139	52	Indiana	Lake	84,236	121 / 138
HANOVER PARK	137	53	Illinois	Cook	32,895	117 / 138
HARVEY	144	54	Illinois	Cook	29,771	138 / 138
HAZEL CREST	120	55	Illinois	Cook	13,334	64 / 138
HICKORY HILLS	114	56	Illinois	Cook	13,021	48 / 138
HIGHLAND	107	57	Indiana	Lake	23,696	26 / 138
HIGHLAND PARK	102	58	Illinois	Lake	30,575	11 / 138
HINSDALE	100	59	Illinois	Du Page	16,029	4 / 138
HOBART	108	60	Indiana	Lake	21,822	28 / 138
HOFFMAN ESTATES	125	61	Illinois	Cook	46,561	79 / 138
HOMEWOOD	101	62	Illinois	Cook	19,278	9 / 138
JOLIET	137	63	Illinois	Will	76,836	115 / 138
JUSTICE	141	64	Illinois	Cook	11,137	127 / 138
KENOSHA	131	65	Wisconsin	Kenosha	80,352	98 / 138
LA GRANGE	105	66	Illinois	Cook	15,362	19 / 138
LA GRANGE PARK	104	67	Illinois	Cook	12,861	18 / 138
LAKE FOREST	101	68	Illinois	Lake	17,836	8 / 138
LAKE STATION	138	69	Indiana	Lake	13,899	118 / 138
LAKE ZURICH	119	70	Illinois	Lake	14,947	61 / 138
LANSING	113	71	Illinois	Cook	28,086	44 / 138
LIBERTYVILLE	116	72	Illinois	Lake	19,174	52 / 138
LINCOLNWOOD	107	73	Illinois	Cook	11,365	25 / 138
LISLE	121	74	Illinois	Du Page	19,512	68 / 138
LOMBARD	128	75	Illinois	Du Page	39,408	89 / 138
MARKHAM	117	76	Illinois	Cook	13,136	57 / 138
MATTESON	118	77	Illinois	Cook	11,378	60 / 138
MAYWOOD	142	78	Illinois	Cook	27,139	132 / 138
MCHENRY	134	79	Illinois	McHenry	16,177	108 / 138
MELROSE PARK	143	80	Illinois	Cook	20,859	133 / 138
MERRILLVILLE	110	81	Indiana	Lake	27,257	36 / 138
MIDLOTHIAN	125	82	Illinois	Cook	14,372	80 / 138
MORRIS	118	83	Illinois	Grundy	10,270	59 / 138
MORTON GROVE	103	84	Illinois	Cook	22,408	15 / 138
MOUNT PROSPECT	118	85	Illinois	Cook	53,170	58 / 138
MUNDELEIN	134	86	Illinois	Lake	21,215	107 / 138
MUNSTER	102	87	Indiana	Lake	19,949	10 / 138
NAPERVILLE	112	88	Illinois	Du Page	85,351	41 / 138
NILES	114	89	Illinois	Cook	28,284	46 / 138
NORRIDGE	124	90	Illinois	Cook	14,459	78 / 138
NORTH CHICAGO	144	91	Illinois	Lake	34,978	136 / 138
NORTHBROOK	102	92	Illinois	Cook	32,308	12 / 138
NORTHLAKE	117	93	Illinois	Cook	12,505	56 / 138
OAK FOREST	111	94	Illinois	Cook	26,203	38 / 138
OAK LAWN	112	95	Illinois	Cook	56,182	40 / 138
OAK PARK	123	96	Illinois	Cook	53,648	74 / 138
ORLAND PARK	111	97	Illinois	Cook	35,720	36 / 138
PALATINE	121	98	Illinois	Cook	39,253	67 / 138
PALOS HEIGHTS	103	99	Illinois	Cook	11,478	14 / 138
PALOS HILLS	113	100	Illinois	Cook	17,803	42 / 138
PARK FOREST	117	101	Illinois	Cook	24,656	55 / 138
PARK RIDGE	103	102	Illinois	Cook	36,175	13 / 138

Metropolitan Area Suburb Alphabetical Index
CHICAGO-GARY-LAKE COUNTY

SUBURB	PAGE	MAP NO.	STATE	COUNTY	POPU-LATION	RANK
PLEASANT PRAIRIE	106	103	Wisconsin	Kenosha	11,961	24 / 138
PORTAGE	124	104	Indiana	Porter	29,060	77 / 138
PROSPECT HEIGHTS	138	105	Illinois	Cook	15,239	120 / 138
RICHTON PARK	119	106	Illinois	Cook	10,523	62 / 138
RIVER FOREST	101	107	Illinois	Cook	11,669	7 / 138
RIVERDALE	140	108	Illinois	Cook	13,671	124 / 138
ROLLING MEADOWS	130	109	Illinois	Cook	22,591	94 / 138
ROMEOVILLE	133	110	Illinois	Will	14,074	104 / 138
ROSELLE	120	111	Illinois	Du Page	20,819	65 / 138
ROUND LAKE BEACH	142	112	Illinois	Lake	16,434	130 / 138
SCHAUMBURG	133	113	Illinois	Cook	68,586	105 / 138
SCHERERVILLE	133	114	Indiana	Lake	19,926	103 / 138
SCHILLER PARK	134	115	Illinois	Cook	11,189	106 / 138
SKOKIE	109	116	Illinois	Cook	59,432	32 / 138
SOUTH HOLLAND	100	117	Illinois	Cook	22,105	5 / 138
ST. CHARLES	115	118	Illinois	Kane	22,501	50 / 138
STREAMWOOD	135	119	Illinois	Cook	30,987	109 / 138
TINLEY PARK	114	120	Illinois	Cook	37,121	47 / 138
VALPARAISO	115	121	Indiana	Porter	24,414	49 / 138
VERNON HILLS	136	122	Illinois	Lake	15,319	113 / 138
VILLA PARK	121	123	Illinois	Du Page	22,253	69 / 138
WARRENVILLE	116	124	Illinois	Du Page	11,333	54 / 138
WAUKEGAN	139	125	Illinois	Lake	69,392	123 / 138
WEST CHICAGO	132	126	Illinois	Du Page	14,796	102 / 138
WESTCHESTER	105	127	Illinois	Cook	17,301	20 / 138
WESTERN SPRINGS	99	128	Illinois	Cook	11,984	2 / 138
WESTMONT	132	129	Illinois	Du Page	21,228	100 / 138
WHEATON	110	130	Illinois	Du Page	51,464	34 / 138
WHEELING	129	131	Illinois	Cook	29,911	93 / 138
WILMETTE	99	132	Illinois	Cook	26,690	3 / 138
WINNETKA	99	133	Illinois	Cook	12,174	1 / 138
WOOD DALE	115	134	Illinois	Du Page	12,425	51 / 138
WOODRIDGE	130	135	Illinois	Du Page	26,256	95 / 138
WOODSTOCK	122	136	Illinois	McHenry	14,353	70 / 138
WORTH	127	137	Illinois	Cook	11,208	87 / 138
ZION	143	138	Illinois	Lake	19,775	134 / 138

Metropolitan Area Suburb Rankings
CHICAGO-GARY-LAKE COUNTY

Composite: **Rank** 1 / 138 *Score* 74.63   **WINNETKA (IL)**

CATEGORY	RANK	SCORE	STATISTIC	VALUE	RANK	SCORE
Economics	1	98.75	Median Household Income	$118,456	1	100.0
			% of Families Above Poverty Level	99.2%	7	97.5
Affordable Housing	137	22.80	Median Home Value	$480,500	137	4.2
			Median Rent	$705	120	41.4
Crime	20	93.75	Violent Crimes per 10,000 Population	8	14	98.6
			Property Crimes per 10,000 Population	258	22	88.9
Open Spaces	3	86.50	Population Density (Persons/Sq. Mile)	3185	53	76.1
			Average Rooms per Housing Unit	7.5	2	96.9
Education	1	100.00	% High School Enrollment/Completion	100.0%	1	100.0
			% College Graduates	79.2%	1	100.0
Commute	6	52.25	Average Work Commute in Minutes	33	134	4.5
			% Commuting on Public Transportation	27.2%	1	100.0
Community Stability	61	68.35	% Living in Same House as in 1979	42.4%	49	59.1
			% Living in Same County as in 1985	84.1%	72	77.6

Composite: **Rank** 2 / 138 *Score* 71.11   **WESTERN SPRINGS (IL)**

CATEGORY	RANK	SCORE	STATISTIC	VALUE	RANK	SCORE
Economics	5	74.25	Median Household Income	$67,454	8	48.5
			% of Families Above Poverty Level	99.8%	1	100.0
Affordable Housing	133	41.60	Median Home Value	$193,100	128	66.0
			Median Rent	$878	135	17.2
Crime	9	95.85	Violent Crimes per 10,000 Population	6	10	99.1
			Property Crimes per 10,000 Population	207	12	92.6
Open Spaces	22	71.30	Population Density (Persons/Sq. Mile)	4559	96	64.5
			Average Rooms per Housing Unit	6.9	6	78.1
Education	8	80.90	% High School Enrollment/Completion	98.3%	11	92.6
			% College Graduates	56.0%	8	69.2
Commute	10	45.35	Average Work Commute in Minutes	28	82	27.3
			% Commuting on Public Transportation	17.4%	9	63.4
Community Stability	11	88.50	% Living in Same House as in 1979	57.3%	8	87.7
			% Living in Same County as in 1985	91.3%	42	89.3

Composite: **Rank** 3 / 138 *Score* 69.99   **WILMETTE (IL)**

CATEGORY	RANK	SCORE	STATISTIC	VALUE	RANK	SCORE
Economics	6	74.15	Median Household Income	$71,274	6	52.4
			% of Families Above Poverty Level	98.8%	17	95.9
Affordable Housing	134	36.65	Median Home Value	$278,300	135	47.7
			Median Rent	$818	133	25.6
Crime	17	93.95	Violent Crimes per 10,000 Population	7	12	98.9
			Property Crimes per 10,000 Population	256	20	89.0
Open Spaces	27	69.65	Population Density (Persons/Sq. Mile)	4939	111	61.2
			Average Rooms per Housing Unit	6.9	6	78.1
Education	3	87.75	% High School Enrollment/Completion	99.1%	6	96.1
			% College Graduates	63.7%	3	79.4
Commute	7	50.35	Average Work Commute in Minutes	29	101	22.7
			% Commuting on Public Transportation	21.3%	5	78.0
Community Stability	34	77.40	% Living in Same House as in 1979	48.3%	24	70.4
			% Living in Same County as in 1985	88.3%	55	84.4

Metropolitan Area Suburb Rankings
CHICAGO-GARY-LAKE COUNTY

Composite: **Rank** 4 / 138 *Score* 69.04   **HINSDALE** (IL)

CATEGORY	RANK	SCORE	STATISTIC	VALUE	RANK	SCORE
Economics	8	71.70	Median Household Income	$68,518	7	49.6
			% of Families Above Poverty Level	98.3%	40	93.8
Affordable Housing	130	47.75	Median Home Value	$284,300	136	46.4
			Median Rent	$650	110	49.1
Crime	5	97.50	Violent Crimes per 10,000 Population	4	3	99.7
			Property Crimes per 10,000 Population	171	5	95.3
Open Spaces	17	72.85	Population Density (Persons/Sq. Mile)	3456	58	73.8
			Average Rooms per Housing Unit	6.7	12	71.9
Education	5	85.60	% High School Enrollment/Completion	99.0%	7	95.6
			% College Graduates	60.8%	4	75.6
Commute	8	47.80	Average Work Commute in Minutes	27	58	31.8
			% Commuting on Public Transportation	17.5%	8	63.8
Community Stability	78	60.05	% Living in Same House as in 1979	42.1%	51	58.5
			% Living in Same County as in 1985	74.3%	106	61.6

Composite: **Rank** 5 / 138 *Score* 68.80   **SOUTH HOLLAND** (IL)

CATEGORY	RANK	SCORE	STATISTIC	VALUE	RANK	SCORE
Economics	48	60.15	Median Household Income	$45,211	53	26.1
			% of Families Above Poverty Level	98.4%	35	94.2
Affordable Housing	29	81.50	Median Home Value	$90,000	44	88.2
			Median Rent	$466	21	74.8
Crime	65	86.95	Violent Crimes per 10,000 Population	18	56	95.7
			Property Crimes per 10,000 Population	403	71	78.2
Open Spaces	19	71.50	Population Density (Persons/Sq. Mile)	3033	46	77.4
			Average Rooms per Housing Unit	6.5	16	65.6
Education	57	54.15	% High School Enrollment/Completion	96.7%	23	85.6
			% College Graduates	21.0%	72	22.7
Commute	45	33.60	Average Work Commute in Minutes	27	58	31.8
			% Commuting on Public Transportation	9.9%	41	35.4
Community Stability	6	93.75	% Living in Same House as in 1979	59.6%	5	92.1
			% Living in Same County as in 1985	95.1%	15	95.4

Composite: **Rank** 6 / 138 *Score* 68.74   **DEERFIELD** (IL)

CATEGORY	RANK	SCORE	STATISTIC	VALUE	RANK	SCORE
Economics	4	74.50	Median Household Income	$71,966	4	53.1
			% of Families Above Poverty Level	98.8%	17	95.9
Affordable Housing	129	48.35	Median Home Value	$231,400	130	57.8
			Median Rent	$723	125	38.9
Crime	7	96.70	Violent Crimes per 10,000 Population	3	1	100.0
			Property Crimes per 10,000 Population	197	9	93.4
Open Spaces	5	80.35	Population Density (Persons/Sq. Mile)	3168	52	76.3
			Average Rooms per Housing Unit	7.1	4	84.4
Education	6	81.55	% High School Enrollment/Completion	97.5%	19	89.1
			% College Graduates	59.6%	5	74.0
Commute	28	36.20	Average Work Commute in Minutes	28	82	27.3
			% Commuting on Public Transportation	12.5%	24	45.1
Community Stability	72	63.50	% Living in Same House as in 1979	44.6%	42	63.3
			% Living in Same County as in 1985	75.6%	99	63.7

Metropolitan Area Suburb Rankings
CHICAGO-GARY-LAKE COUNTY

Composite: *Rank* 7 / 138 *Score* 68.17   **RIVER FOREST** (IL)

CATEGORY	RANK	SCORE	STATISTIC	VALUE	RANK	SCORE
Economics	9	70.70	Median Household Income	$62,469	9	43.5
			% of Families Above Poverty Level	99.3%	3	97.9
Affordable Housing	126	52.15	Median Home Value	$256,600	132	52.4
			Median Rent	$630	99	51.9
Crime	97	78.65	Violent Crimes per 10,000 Population	30	92	92.3
			Property Crimes per 10,000 Population	582	100	65.0
Open Spaces	37	64.65	Population Density (Persons/Sq. Mile)	4648	100	63.7
			Average Rooms per Housing Unit	6.5	16	65.6
Education	4	85.80	% High School Enrollment/Completion	99.5%	3	97.8
			% College Graduates	59.5%	6	73.8
Commute	5	53.55	Average Work Commute in Minutes	24	30	45.5
			% Commuting on Public Transportation	16.9%	11	61.6
Community Stability	51	71.70	% Living in Same House as in 1979	43.3%	47	60.8
			% Living in Same County as in 1985	87.2%	60	82.6

Composite: *Rank* 8 / 138 *Score* 67.92   **LAKE FOREST** (IL)

CATEGORY	RANK	SCORE	STATISTIC	VALUE	RANK	SCORE
Economics	2	85.40	Median Household Income	$94,824	2	76.1
			% of Families Above Poverty Level	98.5%	29	94.7
Affordable Housing	138	16.70	Median Home Value	$500,001	138	0.0
			Median Rent	$762	130	33.4
Crime	1	99.70	Violent Crimes per 10,000 Population	5	7	99.4
			Property Crimes per 10,000 Population	107	1	100.0
Open Spaces	2	93.85	Population Density (Persons/Sq. Mile)	1089	3	93.9
			Average Rooms per Housing Unit	7.4	3	93.8
Education	2	89.30	% High School Enrollment/Completion	99.2%	5	96.5
			% College Graduates	65.7%	2	82.1
Commute	16	40.25	Average Work Commute in Minutes	29	101	22.7
			% Commuting on Public Transportation	15.9%	13	57.8
Community Stability	101	50.25	% Living in Same House as in 1979	37.8%	72	50.3
			% Living in Same County as in 1985	67.3%	125	50.2

Composite: *Rank* 9 / 138 *Score* 67.70   **HOMEWOOD** (IL)

CATEGORY	RANK	SCORE	STATISTIC	VALUE	RANK	SCORE
Economics	33	62.50	Median Household Income	$47,064	44	27.9
			% of Families Above Poverty Level	99.1%	8	97.1
Affordable Housing	68	73.10	Median Home Value	$98,800	58	86.3
			Median Rent	$573	75	59.9
Crime	85	83.00	Violent Crimes per 10,000 Population	18	56	95.7
			Property Crimes per 10,000 Population	510	91	70.3
Open Spaces	41	64.10	Population Density (Persons/Sq. Mile)	3682	70	71.9
			Average Rooms per Housing Unit	6.2	32	56.3
Education	15	71.10	% High School Enrollment/Completion	99.3%	4	96.9
			% College Graduates	38.0%	26	45.3
Commute	12	42.60	Average Work Commute in Minutes	31	121	13.6
			% Commuting on Public Transportation	19.6%	7	71.6
Community Stability	33	77.50	% Living in Same House as in 1979	46.5%	32	67.0
			% Living in Same County as in 1985	90.5%	44	88.0

Metropolitan Area Suburb Rankings
CHICAGO-GARY-LAKE COUNTY

Composite: *Rank* 10 / 138 *Score* 67.56   **MUNSTER** (IN)

CATEGORY	RANK	SCORE	STATISTIC	VALUE	RANK	SCORE
Economics	26	63.65	Median Household Income	$48,483	40	29.4
			% of Families Above Poverty Level	99.3%	3	97.9
Affordable Housing	64	74.00	Median Home Value	$100,400	61	86.0
			Median Rent	$558	66	62.0
Crime	34	91.50	Violent Crimes per 10,000 Population	12	31	97.4
			Property Crimes per 10,000 Population	302	39	85.6
Open Spaces	26	70.05	Population Density (Persons/Sq. Mile)	2645	38	80.7
			Average Rooms per Housing Unit	6.3	25	59.4
Education	27	63.35	% High School Enrollment/Completion	97.2%	20	87.8
			% College Graduates	33.2%	39	38.9
Commute	85	28.10	Average Work Commute in Minutes	25	35	40.9
			% Commuting on Public Transportation	4.5%	87	15.3
Community Stability	17	82.30	% Living in Same House as in 1979	55.8%	9	84.8
			% Living in Same County as in 1985	85.5%	67	79.8

Composite: *Rank* 11 / 138 *Score* 66.22   **HIGHLAND PARK** (IL)

CATEGORY	RANK	SCORE	STATISTIC	VALUE	RANK	SCORE
Economics	7	73.60	Median Household Income	$71,905	5	53.0
			% of Families Above Poverty Level	98.4%	35	94.2
Affordable Housing	131	47.50	Median Home Value	$257,000	133	52.3
			Median Rent	$696	118	42.7
Crime	17	93.95	Violent Crimes per 10,000 Population	9	19	98.3
			Property Crimes per 10,000 Population	248	17	89.6
Open Spaces	7	78.30	Population Density (Persons/Sq. Mile)	2538	33	81.6
			Average Rooms per Housing Unit	6.8	8	75.0
Education	17	70.60	% High School Enrollment/Completion	93.6%	68	72.1
			% College Graduates	55.9%	9	69.1
Commute	32	35.10	Average Work Commute in Minutes	28	82	27.3
			% Commuting on Public Transportation	11.9%	26	42.9
Community Stability	68	64.50	% Living in Same House as in 1979	46.2%	36	66.4
			% Living in Same County as in 1985	74.9%	103	62.6

Composite: *Rank* 12 / 138 *Score* 66.17   **NORTHBROOK** (IL)

CATEGORY	RANK	SCORE	STATISTIC	VALUE	RANK	SCORE
Economics	3	75.40	Median Household Income	$73,362	3	54.5
			% of Families Above Poverty Level	98.9%	15	96.3
Affordable Housing	136	30.45	Median Home Value	$272,400	134	49.0
			Median Rent	$916	137	11.9
Crime	23	93.05	Violent Crimes per 10,000 Population	8	14	98.6
			Property Crimes per 10,000 Population	277	27	87.5
Open Spaces	8	78.20	Population Density (Persons/Sq. Mile)	2561	34	81.4
			Average Rooms per Housing Unit	6.8	8	75.0
Education	9	80.30	% High School Enrollment/Completion	98.3%	11	92.6
			% College Graduates	55.1%	10	68.0
Commute	81	28.50	Average Work Commute in Minutes	29	101	22.7
			% Commuting on Public Transportation	9.6%	43	34.3
Community Stability	35	77.30	% Living in Same House as in 1979	45.9%	39	65.8
			% Living in Same County as in 1985	91.0%	43	88.8

Composite: **Rank** 13 / 138 *Score* 65.99   **PARK RIDGE** (IL)

CATEGORY	RANK	SCORE	STATISTIC	VALUE	RANK	SCORE
Economics	17	65.40	Median Household Income	$52,817	20	33.7
			% of Families Above Poverty Level	99.1%	8	97.1
Affordable Housing	118	59.10	Median Home Value	$185,100	126	67.7
			Median Rent	$640	103	50.5
Crime	27	92.30	Violent Crimes per 10,000 Population	11	22	97.7
			Property Crimes per 10,000 Population	284	31	86.9
Open Spaces	62	57.35	Population Density (Persons/Sq. Mile)	5272	117	58.4
			Average Rooms per Housing Unit	6.2	32	56.3
Education	33	61.10	% High School Enrollment/Completion	94.9%	50	77.7
			% College Graduates	37.4%	29	44.5
Commute	23	37.40	Average Work Commute in Minutes	26	48	36.4
			% Commuting on Public Transportation	10.7%	31	38.4
Community Stability	9	89.25	% Living in Same House as in 1979	54.7%	10	82.7
			% Living in Same County as in 1985	95.3%	12	95.8

Composite: **Rank** 14 / 138 *Score* 65.71   **PALOS HEIGHTS** (IL)

CATEGORY	RANK	SCORE	STATISTIC	VALUE	RANK	SCORE
Economics	16	66.15	Median Household Income	$58,707	13	39.7
			% of Families Above Poverty Level	98.0%	48	92.6
Affordable Housing	124	54.80	Median Home Value	$160,500	116	73.0
			Median Rent	$739	127	36.6
Crime	3	98.85	Violent Crimes per 10,000 Population	4	3	99.7
			Property Crimes per 10,000 Population	134	3	98.0
Open Spaces	14	75.05	Population Density (Persons/Sq. Mile)	3301	54	75.1
			Average Rooms per Housing Unit	6.8	8	75.0
Education	34	60.95	% High School Enrollment/Completion	96.1%	34	83.0
			% College Graduates	33.2%	39	38.9
Commute	118	19.95	Average Work Commute in Minutes	29	101	22.7
			% Commuting on Public Transportation	5.0%	78	17.2
Community Stability	13	84.20	% Living in Same House as in 1979	49.0%	22	71.8
			% Living in Same County as in 1985	95.8%	7	96.6

Composite: **Rank** 15 / 138 *Score* 65.22   **MORTON GROVE** (IL)

CATEGORY	RANK	SCORE	STATISTIC	VALUE	RANK	SCORE
Economics	50	60.05	Median Household Income	$47,808	43	28.7
			% of Families Above Poverty Level	97.7%	66	91.4
Affordable Housing	100	64.00	Median Home Value	$150,200	111	75.3
			Median Rent	$624	95	52.7
Crime	52	89.05	Violent Crimes per 10,000 Population	11	22	97.7
			Property Crimes per 10,000 Population	373	64	80.4
Open Spaces	60	57.90	Population Density (Persons/Sq. Mile)	4399	94	65.8
			Average Rooms per Housing Unit	6.0	40	50.0
Education	39	59.20	% High School Enrollment/Completion	96.4%	28	84.3
			% College Graduates	29.6%	51	34.1
Commute	53	32.40	Average Work Commute in Minutes	26	48	36.4
			% Commuting on Public Transportation	8.0%	55	28.4
Community Stability	5	93.95	% Living in Same House as in 1979	59.7%	4	92.3
			% Living in Same County as in 1985	95.2%	13	95.6

Metropolitan Area Suburb Rankings
CHICAGO-GARY-LAKE COUNTY

Composite: *Rank* 16 / 138 *Score* 65.16   **GLENVIEW (IL)**

CATEGORY	RANK	SCORE	STATISTIC	VALUE	RANK	SCORE
Economics	13	68.55	Median Household Income	$59,020	12	40.0
			% of Families Above Poverty Level	99.1%	8	97.1
Affordable Housing	132	44.35	Median Home Value	$233,400	131	57.4
			Median Rent	$777	132	31.3
Crime	13	94.65	Violent Crimes per 10,000 Population	7	12	98.9
			Property Crimes per 10,000 Population	237	14	90.4
Open Spaces	23	71.20	Population Density (Persons/Sq. Mile)	3104	49	76.8
			Average Rooms per Housing Unit	6.5	16	65.6
Education	16	70.70	% High School Enrollment/Completion	96.6%	24	85.2
			% College Graduates	46.2%	19	56.2
Commute	43	33.80	Average Work Commute in Minutes	27	58	31.8
			% Commuting on Public Transportation	10.0%	40	35.8
Community Stability	48	72.85	% Living in Same House as in 1979	43.1%	48	60.5
			% Living in Same County as in 1985	88.8%	52	85.2

Composite: *Rank* 17 / 138 *Score* 65.06   **EVERGREEN PARK (IL)**

CATEGORY	RANK	SCORE	STATISTIC	VALUE	RANK	SCORE
Economics	73	56.10	Median Household Income	$38,834	82	19.6
			% of Families Above Poverty Level	98.0%	48	92.6
Affordable Housing	32	81.00	Median Home Value	$87,800	41	88.7
			Median Rent	$477	23	73.3
Crime	97	78.65	Violent Crimes per 10,000 Population	25	78	93.7
			Property Crimes per 10,000 Population	600	104	63.6
Open Spaces	112	45.50	Population Density (Persons/Sq. Mile)	6577	128	47.3
			Average Rooms per Housing Unit	5.8	56	43.7
Education	42	58.90	% High School Enrollment/Completion	98.6%	10	93.9
			% College Graduates	21.9%	69	23.9
Commute	25	36.90	Average Work Commute in Minutes	29	101	22.7
			% Commuting on Public Transportation	14.1%	17	51.1
Community Stability	3	98.40	% Living in Same House as in 1979	63.3%	2	99.2
			% Living in Same County as in 1985	96.4%	4	97.6

Composite: *Rank* 18 / 138 *Score* 64.86   **LA GRANGE PARK (IL)**

CATEGORY	RANK	SCORE	STATISTIC	VALUE	RANK	SCORE
Economics	55	59.05	Median Household Income	$43,466	61	24.3
			% of Families Above Poverty Level	98.3%	40	93.8
Affordable Housing	74	70.75	Median Home Value	$140,400	103	77.4
			Median Rent	$543	59	64.1
Crime	6	97.25	Violent Crimes per 10,000 Population	4	3	99.7
			Property Crimes per 10,000 Population	178	6	94.8
Open Spaces	104	47.65	Population Density (Persons/Sq. Mile)	5711	122	54.7
			Average Rooms per Housing Unit	5.7	63	40.6
Education	46	58.25	% High School Enrollment/Completion	94.8%	51	77.3
			% College Graduates	33.4%	38	39.2
Commute	19	39.45	Average Work Commute in Minutes	26	48	36.4
			% Commuting on Public Transportation	11.8%	28	42.5
Community Stability	21	81.65	% Living in Same House as in 1979	50.0%	16	73.7
			% Living in Same County as in 1985	91.5%	40	89.6

Composite: *Rank* 19 / 138 *Score* 64.55   **LA GRANGE (IL)**

CATEGORY	RANK	SCORE	STATISTIC	VALUE	RANK	SCORE
Economics	46	60.55	Median Household Income	$52,467	21	33.4
			% of Families Above Poverty Level	96.8%	87	87.7
Affordable Housing	95	65.55	Median Home Value	$165,900	121	71.9
			Median Rent	$578	77	59.2
Crime	43	90.45	Violent Crimes per 10,000 Population	24	74	94.0
			Property Crimes per 10,000 Population	285	33	86.9
Open Spaces	71	55.15	Population Density (Persons/Sq. Mile)	6153	126	50.9
			Average Rooms per Housing Unit	6.3	25	59.4
Education	37	60.00	% High School Enrollment/Completion	91.5%	86	62.9
			% College Graduates	46.9%	18	57.1
Commute	9	46.70	Average Work Commute in Minutes	27	58	31.8
			% Commuting on Public Transportation	16.9%	11	61.6
Community Stability	47	73.45	% Living in Same House as in 1979	43.9%	45	62.0
			% Living in Same County as in 1985	88.6%	53	84.9

Composite: *Rank* 20 / 138 *Score* 64.31   **WESTCHESTER (IL)**

CATEGORY	RANK	SCORE	STATISTIC	VALUE	RANK	SCORE
Economics	47	60.50	Median Household Income	$44,635	56	25.5
			% of Families Above Poverty Level	98.7%	19	95.5
Affordable Housing	114	60.45	Median Home Value	$125,600	86	80.6
			Median Rent	$713	122	40.3
Crime	26	92.45	Violent Crimes per 10,000 Population	14	40	96.9
			Property Crimes per 10,000 Population	270	23	88.0
Open Spaces	85	51.65	Population Density (Persons/Sq. Mile)	5506	121	56.4
			Average Rooms per Housing Unit	5.9	48	46.9
Education	29	62.35	% High School Enrollment/Completion	99.0%	7	95.6
			% College Graduates	25.8%	63	29.1
Commute	53	32.40	Average Work Commute in Minutes	25	35	40.9
			% Commuting on Public Transportation	6.8%	63	23.9
Community Stability	7	90.40	% Living in Same House as in 1979	57.9%	7	88.9
			% Living in Same County as in 1985	92.9%	30	91.9

Composite: *Rank* 21 / 138 *Score* 64.26   **GLEN ELLYN (IL)**

CATEGORY	RANK	SCORE	STATISTIC	VALUE	RANK	SCORE
Economics	19	64.95	Median Household Income	$51,916	24	32.8
			% of Families Above Poverty Level	99.1%	8	97.1
Affordable Housing	96	65.05	Median Home Value	$163,200	119	72.5
			Median Rent	$589	80	57.6
Crime	33	91.55	Violent Crimes per 10,000 Population	12	31	97.4
			Property Crimes per 10,000 Population	301	37	85.7
Open Spaces	53	60.90	Population Density (Persons/Sq. Mile)	4055	83	68.7
			Average Rooms per Housing Unit	6.1	37	53.1
Education	13	72.50	% High School Enrollment/Completion	95.9%	39	82.1
			% College Graduates	51.3%	12	62.9
Commute	26	36.60	Average Work Commute in Minutes	28	82	27.3
			% Commuting on Public Transportation	12.7%	22	45.9
Community Stability	84	58.25	% Living in Same House as in 1979	36.3%	77	47.4
			% Living in Same County as in 1985	78.9%	85	69.1

Metropolitan Area Suburb Rankings
CHICAGO-GARY-LAKE COUNTY

Composite: *Rank* 22 / 138   *Score* 64.22   **ELMHURST (IL)**

CATEGORY	RANK	SCORE	STATISTIC	VALUE	RANK	SCORE
Economics	24	63.80	Median Household Income	$49,611	32	30.5
			% of Families Above Poverty Level	99.1%	8	97.1
Affordable Housing	88	67.05	Median Home Value	$134,300	95	78.7
			Median Rent	$605	85	55.4
Crime	41	90.65	Violent Crimes per 10,000 Population	10	20	98.0
			Property Crimes per 10,000 Population	333	49	83.3
Open Spaces	57	59.00	Population Density (Persons/Sq. Mile)	4142	86	68.0
			Average Rooms per Housing Unit	6.0	40	50.0
Education	35	60.75	% High School Enrollment/Completion	95.1%	49	78.6
			% College Graduates	36.2%	31	42.9
Commute	27	36.50	Average Work Commute in Minutes	25	35	40.9
			% Commuting on Public Transportation	9.0%	47	32.1
Community Stability	50	71.80	% Living in Same House as in 1979	49.2%	21	72.2
			% Living in Same County as in 1985	80.3%	80	71.4

Composite: *Rank* 23 / 138   *Score* 62.94   **GENEVA (IL)**

CATEGORY	RANK	SCORE	STATISTIC	VALUE	RANK	SCORE
Economics	29	63.10	Median Household Income	$49,755	30	30.7
			% of Families Above Poverty Level	98.7%	19	95.5
Affordable Housing	103	62.90	Median Home Value	$148,900	109	75.5
			Median Rent	$641	105	50.3
Crime	31	91.60	Violent Crimes per 10,000 Population	11	22	97.7
			Property Crimes per 10,000 Population	303	40	85.5
Open Spaces	11	76.20	Population Density (Persons/Sq. Mile)	1922	19	86.8
			Average Rooms per Housing Unit	6.5	16	65.6
Education	19	69.30	% High School Enrollment/Completion	97.6%	17	89.5
			% College Graduates	40.9%	22	49.1
Commute	55	32.25	Average Work Commute in Minutes	24	30	45.5
			% Commuting on Public Transportation	5.5%	72	19.0
Community Stability	112	45.20	% Living in Same House as in 1979	33.1%	86	41.3
			% Living in Same County as in 1985	66.6%	127	49.1

Composite: *Rank* 24 / 138   *Score* 62.81   **PLEASANT PRAIRIE (WI)**

CATEGORY	RANK	SCORE	STATISTIC	VALUE	RANK	SCORE
Economics	79	54.90	Median Household Income	$40,145	78	20.9
			% of Families Above Poverty Level	97.1%	79	88.9
Affordable Housing	31	81.10	Median Home Value	$85,300	38	89.2
			Median Rent	$479	25	73.0
Crime	50	89.15	Violent Crimes per 10,000 Population	14	40	96.9
			Property Crimes per 10,000 Population	359	54	81.4
Open Spaces	15	73.45	Population Density (Persons/Sq. Mile)	371	1	100.0
			Average Rooms per Housing Unit	5.9	48	46.9
Education	66	48.45	% High School Enrollment/Completion	95.7%	40	81.2
			% College Graduates	15.7%	94	15.7
Commute	102	25.00	Average Work Commute in Minutes	23	16	50.0
			% Commuting on Public Transportation	0.4%	138	0.0
Community Stability	62	67.60	% Living in Same House as in 1979	43.5%	46	61.2
			% Living in Same County as in 1985	81.9%	74	74.0

Metropolitan Area Suburb Rankings
CHICAGO-GARY-LAKE COUNTY

Composite: **Rank** 25 / 138 *Score* 62.44   **LINCOLNWOOD (IL)**

CATEGORY	RANK	SCORE	STATISTIC	VALUE	RANK	SCORE
Economics	15	66.50	Median Household Income	$57,309	15	38.3
			% of Families Above Poverty Level	98.5%	29	94.7
Affordable Housing	135	32.25	Median Home Value	$200,100	129	64.5
			Median Rent	$1,001	138	0.0
Crime	100	77.95	Violent Crimes per 10,000 Population	25	78	93.7
			Property Crimes per 10,000 Population	620	109	62.2
Open Spaces	24	70.90	Population Density (Persons/Sq. Mile)	4278	91	66.8
			Average Rooms per Housing Unit	6.8	8	75.0
Education	25	63.80	% High School Enrollment/Completion	94.8%	51	77.3
			% College Graduates	41.8%	20	50.3
Commute	58	31.25	Average Work Commute in Minutes	25	35	40.9
			% Commuting on Public Transportation	6.2%	69	21.6
Community Stability	4	94.45	% Living in Same House as in 1979	59.4%	6	91.7
			% Living in Same County as in 1985	96.2%	5	97.2

Composite: **Rank** 26 / 138 *Score* 62.42   **HIGHLAND (IN)**

CATEGORY	RANK	SCORE	STATISTIC	VALUE	RANK	SCORE
Economics	74	55.35	Median Household Income	$39,437	80	20.2
			% of Families Above Poverty Level	97.5%	70	90.5
Affordable Housing	33	80.80	Median Home Value	$71,800	24	92.1
			Median Rent	$504	38	69.5
Crime	84	83.15	Violent Crimes per 10,000 Population	27	86	93.1
			Property Crimes per 10,000 Population	470	87	73.2
Open Spaces	76	54.00	Population Density (Persons/Sq. Mile)	3482	59	73.6
			Average Rooms per Housing Unit	5.5	80	34.4
Education	70	47.70	% High School Enrollment/Completion	94.4%	60	75.5
			% College Graduates	18.9%	81	19.9
Commute	57	31.70	Average Work Commute in Minutes	23	16	50.0
			% Commuting on Public Transportation	4.0%	97	13.4
Community Stability	12	84.25	% Living in Same House as in 1979	53.8%	12	81.0
			% Living in Same County as in 1985	90.2%	47	87.5

Composite: **Rank** 27 / 138 *Score* 62.38   **CROWN POINT (IN)**

CATEGORY	RANK	SCORE	STATISTIC	VALUE	RANK	SCORE
Economics	76	55.05	Median Household Income	$37,539	86	18.3
			% of Families Above Poverty Level	97.8%	63	91.8
Affordable Housing	27	81.95	Median Home Value	$79,200	35	90.5
			Median Rent	$476	22	73.4
Crime	12	95.25	Violent Crimes per 10,000 Population	12	31	97.4
			Property Crimes per 10,000 Population	201	10	93.1
Open Spaces	42	63.90	Population Density (Persons/Sq. Mile)	2247	27	84.1
			Average Rooms per Housing Unit	5.8	56	43.7
Education	81	43.40	% High School Enrollment/Completion	91.8%	82	64.2
			% College Graduates	20.9%	73	22.6
Commute	93	26.30	Average Work Commute in Minutes	23	16	50.0
			% Commuting on Public Transportation	1.1%	135	2.6
Community Stability	54	70.80	% Living in Same House as in 1979	41.3%	59	57.0
			% Living in Same County as in 1985	88.4%	54	84.6

Metropolitan Area Suburb Rankings
CHICAGO-GARY-LAKE COUNTY

Composite: **Rank** 28 / 138 *Score* 62.19   **HOBART** (IN)

CATEGORY	RANK	SCORE	STATISTIC	VALUE	RANK	SCORE
Economics	101	50.10	Median Household Income	$34,602	108	15.4
			% of Families Above Poverty Level	96.1%	99	84.8
Affordable Housing	8	87.05	Median Home Value	$52,400	6	96.3
			Median Rent	$445	14	77.8
Crime	57	88.35	Violent Crimes per 10,000 Population	19	64	95.4
			Property Crimes per 10,000 Population	361	56	81.3
Open Spaces	44	62.80	Population Density (Persons/Sq. Mile)	1413	7	91.2
			Average Rooms per Housing Unit	5.5	80	34.4
Education	85	40.80	% High School Enrollment/Completion	93.4%	71	71.2
			% College Graduates	11.7%	108	10.4
Commute	96	26.10	Average Work Commute in Minutes	24	30	45.5
			% Commuting on Public Transportation	2.2%	124	6.7
Community Stability	25	80.15	% Living in Same House as in 1979	51.3%	15	76.2
			% Living in Same County as in 1985	88.1%	57	84.1

Composite: **Rank** 29 / 138 *Score* 62.09   **CARY** (IL)

CATEGORY	RANK	SCORE	STATISTIC	VALUE	RANK	SCORE
Economics	20	64.80	Median Household Income	$50,804	28	31.7
			% of Families Above Poverty Level	99.3%	3	97.9
Affordable Housing	85	67.60	Median Home Value	$123,100	82	81.1
			Median Rent	$614	88	54.1
Crime	2	99.50	Violent Crimes per 10,000 Population	3	1	100.0
			Property Crimes per 10,000 Population	120	2	99.0
Open Spaces	13	75.20	Population Density (Persons/Sq. Mile)	2166	23	84.8
			Average Rooms per Housing Unit	6.5	16	65.6
Education	17	70.60	% High School Enrollment/Completion	100.0%	1	100.0
			% College Graduates	34.9%	34	41.2
Commute	120	19.65	Average Work Commute in Minutes	32	126	9.1
			% Commuting on Public Transportation	8.5%	50	30.2
Community Stability	127	37.30	% Living in Same House as in 1979	27.0%	117	29.6
			% Living in Same County as in 1985	64.1%	131	45.0

Composite: **Rank** 29 / 138 *Score* 62.09   **DOWNERS GROVE** (IL)

CATEGORY	RANK	SCORE	STATISTIC	VALUE	RANK	SCORE
Economics	35	61.90	Median Household Income	$48,226	41	29.1
			% of Families Above Poverty Level	98.5%	29	94.7
Affordable Housing	83	68.70	Median Home Value	$143,900	105	76.6
			Median Rent	$566	73	60.8
Crime	73	85.70	Violent Crimes per 10,000 Population	16	44	96.3
			Property Crimes per 10,000 Population	444	81	75.1
Open Spaces	46	62.00	Population Density (Persons/Sq. Mile)	3433	57	74.0
			Average Rooms per Housing Unit	6.0	40	50.0
Education	30	61.95	% High School Enrollment/Completion	94.5%	59	76.0
			% College Graduates	40.0%	24	47.9
Commute	40	34.35	Average Work Commute in Minutes	27	58	31.8
			% Commuting on Public Transportation	10.3%	37	36.9
Community Stability	77	60.00	% Living in Same House as in 1979	38.0%	71	50.7
			% Living in Same County as in 1985	79.0%	84	69.3

Composite: *Rank* 31 / 138 *Score* 61.95   **DES PLAINES** (IL)

CATEGORY	RANK	SCORE	STATISTIC	VALUE	RANK	SCORE
Economics	57	58.85	Median Household Income	$42,176	68	23.0
			% of Families Above Poverty Level	98.5%	29	94.7
Affordable Housing	79	69.40	Median Home Value	$130,300	91	79.5
			Median Rent	$577	76	59.3
Crime	59	88.15	Violent Crimes per 10,000 Population	18	56	95.7
			Property Crimes per 10,000 Population	370	61	80.6
Open Spaces	67	55.95	Population Density (Persons/Sq. Mile)	3749	75	71.3
			Average Rooms per Housing Unit	5.7	63	40.6
Education	71	47.35	% High School Enrollment/Completion	93.4%	71	71.2
			% College Graduates	21.6%	70	23.5
Commute	47	33.30	Average Work Commute in Minutes	25	35	40.9
			% Commuting on Public Transportation	7.3%	57	25.7
Community Stability	22	80.65	% Living in Same House as in 1979	48.3%	24	70.4
			% Living in Same County as in 1985	92.3%	35	90.9

Composite: *Rank* 32 / 138 *Score* 61.84   **SKOKIE** (IL)

CATEGORY	RANK	SCORE	STATISTIC	VALUE	RANK	SCORE
Economics	72	56.40	Median Household Income	$42,276	67	23.1
			% of Families Above Poverty Level	97.3%	73	89.7
Affordable Housing	107	62.70	Median Home Value	$148,800	108	75.6
			Median Rent	$645	107	49.8
Crime	56	88.55	Violent Crimes per 10,000 Population	15	43	96.6
			Property Crimes per 10,000 Population	371	62	80.5
Open Spaces	109	46.75	Population Density (Persons/Sq. Mile)	5915	123	52.9
			Average Rooms per Housing Unit	5.7	63	40.6
Education	31	61.75	% High School Enrollment/Completion	95.4%	46	79.9
			% College Graduates	36.7%	30	43.6
Commute	29	36.25	Average Work Commute in Minutes	27	58	31.8
			% Commuting on Public Transportation	11.3%	29	40.7
Community Stability	24	80.45	% Living in Same House as in 1979	50.0%	16	73.7
			% Living in Same County as in 1985	90.0%	48	87.2

Composite: *Rank* 33 / 138 *Score* 61.71   **DARIEN** (IL)

CATEGORY	RANK	SCORE	STATISTIC	VALUE	RANK	SCORE
Economics	31	63.00	Median Household Income	$52,875	19	33.8
			% of Families Above Poverty Level	97.9%	57	92.2
Affordable Housing	104	62.80	Median Home Value	$158,800	114	73.4
			Median Rent	$628	98	52.2
Crime	4	97.65	Violent Crimes per 10,000 Population	8	14	98.6
			Property Crimes per 10,000 Population	152	4	96.7
Open Spaces	39	64.45	Population Density (Persons/Sq. Mile)	3959	79	69.5
			Average Rooms per Housing Unit	6.3	25	59.4
Education	23	67.25	% High School Enrollment/Completion	98.2%	13	92.1
			% College Graduates	35.8%	33	42.4
Commute	111	21.95	Average Work Commute in Minutes	30	113	18.2
			% Commuting on Public Transportation	7.3%	57	25.7
Community Stability	91	54.90	% Living in Same House as in 1979	37.4%	74	49.5
			% Living in Same County as in 1985	73.5%	109	60.3

Metropolitan Area Suburb Rankings
CHICAGO-GARY-LAKE COUNTY

Composite: **Rank** 34 / 138 **Score** 61.69   **WHEATON (IL)**

CATEGORY	RANK	SCORE	STATISTIC	VALUE	RANK	SCORE
Economics	28	63.25	Median Household Income	$52,208	22	33.1
			% of Families Above Poverty Level	98.2%	45	93.4
Affordable Housing	108	62.65	Median Home Value	$148,600	107	75.6
			Median Rent	$646	108	49.7
Crime	25	92.85	Violent Crimes per 10,000 Population	10	20	98.0
			Property Crimes per 10,000 Population	274	26	87.7
Open Spaces	49	61.55	Population Density (Persons/Sq. Mile)	4648	100	63.7
			Average Rooms per Housing Unit	6.3	25	59.4
Education	14	72.35	% High School Enrollment/Completion	96.4%	28	84.3
			% College Graduates	49.4%	15	60.4
Commute	40	34.35	Average Work Commute in Minutes	27	58	31.8
			% Commuting on Public Transportation	10.3%	37	36.9
Community Stability	116	44.85	% Living in Same House as in 1979	28.6%	108	32.6
			% Living in Same County as in 1985	71.5%	113	57.1

Composite: **Rank** 35 / 138 **Score** 61.30   **DYER (IN)**

CATEGORY	RANK	SCORE	STATISTIC	VALUE	RANK	SCORE
Economics	48	60.15	Median Household Income	$44,358	58	25.2
			% of Families Above Poverty Level	98.6%	23	95.1
Affordable Housing	17	83.90	Median Home Value	$87,200	40	88.8
			Median Rent	$436	12	79.0
Crime	14	94.55	Violent Crimes per 10,000 Population	6	10	99.1
			Property Crimes per 10,000 Population	242	15	90.0
Open Spaces	21	71.45	Population Density (Persons/Sq. Mile)	1955	20	86.6
			Average Rooms per Housing Unit	6.2	32	56.3
Education	102	33.30	% High School Enrollment/Completion	88.9%	102	51.5
			% College Graduates	15.3%	96	15.1
Commute	117	20.00	Average Work Commute in Minutes	28	82	27.3
			% Commuting on Public Transportation	3.8%	101	12.7
Community Stability	66	65.75	% Living in Same House as in 1979	45.6%	40	65.3
			% Living in Same County as in 1985	77.1%	97	66.2

Composite: **Rank** 36 / 138 **Score** 61.14   **MERRILLVILLE (IN)**

CATEGORY	RANK	SCORE	STATISTIC	VALUE	RANK	SCORE
Economics	89	52.95	Median Household Income	$36,221	101	17.0
			% of Families Above Poverty Level	97.1%	79	88.9
Affordable Housing	35	80.05	Median Home Value	$62,000	11	94.2
			Median Rent	$530	52	65.9
Crime	92	80.10	Violent Crimes per 10,000 Population	59	111	84.0
			Property Crimes per 10,000 Population	430	80	76.2
Open Spaces	33	66.60	Population Density (Persons/Sq. Mile)	879	2	95.7
			Average Rooms per Housing Unit	5.6	74	37.5
Education	77	44.35	% High School Enrollment/Completion	94.0%	63	73.8
			% College Graduates	15.1%	97	14.9
Commute	100	25.35	Average Work Commute in Minutes	24	30	45.5
			% Commuting on Public Transportation	1.8%	130	5.2
Community Stability	32	78.60	% Living in Same House as in 1979	49.0%	22	71.8
			% Living in Same County as in 1985	88.9%	51	85.4

Composite: **Rank** 36 / 138 **Score** 61.14 **ORLAND PARK** (IL)

CATEGORY	RANK	SCORE	STATISTIC	VALUE	RANK	SCORE
Economics	25	63.70	Median Household Income	$51,748	25	32.7
			% of Families Above Poverty Level	98.5%	29	94.7
Affordable Housing	99	64.10	Median Home Value	$152,000	112	74.9
			Median Rent	$620	91	53.3
Crime	39	90.75	Violent Crimes per 10,000 Population	11	22	97.7
			Property Crimes per 10,000 Population	326	45	83.8
Open Spaces	19	71.50	Population Density (Persons/Sq. Mile)	2674	39	80.5
			Average Rooms per Housing Unit	6.4	22	62.5
Education	32	61.30	% High School Enrollment/Completion	97.6%	17	89.5
			% College Graduates	28.8%	54	33.1
Commute	130	17.25	Average Work Commute in Minutes	32	126	9.1
			% Commuting on Public Transportation	7.2%	60	25.4
Community Stability	82	59.35	% Living in Same House as in 1979	28.1%	113	31.7
			% Living in Same County as in 1985	89.9%	49	87.0

Composite: **Rank** 38 / 138 **Score** 60.57 **OAK FOREST** (IL)

CATEGORY	RANK	SCORE	STATISTIC	VALUE	RANK	SCORE
Economics	63	58.20	Median Household Income	$43,387	62	24.2
			% of Families Above Poverty Level	97.9%	57	92.2
Affordable Housing	61	74.60	Median Home Value	$103,700	64	85.3
			Median Rent	$544	60	63.9
Crime	47	89.60	Violent Crimes per 10,000 Population	18	56	95.7
			Property Crimes per 10,000 Population	331	46	83.5
Open Spaces	74	54.45	Population Density (Persons/Sq. Mile)	4851	109	62.0
			Average Rooms per Housing Unit	5.9	48	46.9
Education	88	39.80	% High School Enrollment/Completion	91.1%	90	61.1
			% College Graduates	17.8%	86	18.5
Commute	64	30.55	Average Work Commute in Minutes	30	113	18.2
			% Commuting on Public Transportation	11.9%	26	42.9
Community Stability	36	76.80	% Living in Same House as in 1979	42.1%	51	58.5
			% Living in Same County as in 1985	94.9%	17	95.1

Composite: **Rank** 39 / 138 **Score** 60.51 **ARLINGTON HEIGHTS** (IL)

CATEGORY	RANK	SCORE	STATISTIC	VALUE	RANK	SCORE
Economics	26	63.65	Median Household Income	$51,331	27	32.2
			% of Families Above Poverty Level	98.6%	23	95.1
Affordable Housing	123	55.90	Median Home Value	$168,900	123	71.2
			Median Rent	$711	121	40.6
Crime	44	90.20	Violent Crimes per 10,000 Population	14	40	96.9
			Property Crimes per 10,000 Population	331	46	83.5
Open Spaces	70	55.25	Population Density (Persons/Sq. Mile)	4665	102	63.6
			Average Rooms per Housing Unit	5.9	48	46.9
Education	24	65.55	% High School Enrollment/Completion	96.3%	31	83.8
			% College Graduates	39.5%	25	47.3
Commute	79	29.15	Average Work Commute in Minutes	28	82	27.3
			% Commuting on Public Transportation	8.7%	49	31.0
Community Stability	70	63.90	% Living in Same House as in 1979	35.7%	79	46.3
			% Living in Same County as in 1985	86.5%	62	81.5

Metropolitan Area Suburb Rankings
CHICAGO-GARY-LAKE COUNTY

Composite: *Rank* 40 / 138 *Score* 60.43   **OAK LAWN (IL)**

CATEGORY	RANK	SCORE	STATISTIC	VALUE	RANK	SCORE
Economics	75	55.20	Median Household Income	$38,665	85	19.5
			% of Families Above Poverty Level	97.6%	68	90.9
Affordable Housing	58	74.95	Median Home Value	$106,900	67	84.6
			Median Rent	$534	56	65.3
Crime	38	91.35	Violent Crimes per 10,000 Population	19	64	95.4
			Property Crimes per 10,000 Population	279	28	87.3
Open Spaces	124	40.40	Population Density (Persons/Sq. Mile)	6690	130	46.4
			Average Rooms per Housing Unit	5.5	80	34.4
Education	79	44.05	% High School Enrollment/Completion	93.1%	75	69.9
			% College Graduates	17.6%	87	18.2
Commute	82	28.40	Average Work Commute in Minutes	28	82	27.3
			% Commuting on Public Transportation	8.3%	52	29.5
Community Stability	10	88.65	% Living in Same House as in 1979	53.6%	13	80.6
			% Living in Same County as in 1985	95.9%	6	96.7

Composite: *Rank* 41 / 138 *Score* 60.41   **NAPERVILLE (IL)**

CATEGORY	RANK	SCORE	STATISTIC	VALUE	RANK	SCORE
Economics	10	69.55	Median Household Income	$60,979	11	42.0
			% of Families Above Poverty Level	99.1%	8	97.1
Affordable Housing	122	56.05	Median Home Value	$176,200	124	69.7
			Median Rent	$698	119	42.4
Crime	29	92.10	Violent Crimes per 10,000 Population	11	22	97.7
			Property Crimes per 10,000 Population	290	35	86.5
Open Spaces	16	72.95	Population Density (Persons/Sq. Mile)	3055	47	77.2
			Average Rooms per Housing Unit	6.6	14	68.7
Education	10	79.20	% High School Enrollment/Completion	98.0%	14	91.3
			% College Graduates	54.4%	11	67.1
Commute	92	27.20	Average Work Commute in Minutes	30	113	18.2
			% Commuting on Public Transportation	10.1%	39	36.2
Community Stability	133	25.85	% Living in Same House as in 1979	18.5%	135	13.2
			% Living in Same County as in 1985	60.1%	133	38.5

Composite: *Rank* 42 / 138 *Score* 60.24   **GRIFFITH (IN)**

CATEGORY	RANK	SCORE	STATISTIC	VALUE	RANK	SCORE
Economics	92	52.50	Median Household Income	$36,562	99	17.3
			% of Families Above Poverty Level	96.8%	87	87.7
Affordable Housing	18	83.40	Median Home Value	$64,300	18	93.7
			Median Rent	$478	24	73.1
Crime	87	81.75	Violent Crimes per 10,000 Population	39	101	89.7
			Property Crimes per 10,000 Population	462	86	73.8
Open Spaces	58	58.50	Population Density (Persons/Sq. Mile)	2055	21	85.7
			Average Rooms per Housing Unit	5.4	90	31.3
Education	89	38.75	% High School Enrollment/Completion	92.0%	80	65.1
			% College Graduates	13.2%	103	12.4
Commute	52	32.45	Average Work Commute in Minutes	23	16	50.0
			% Commuting on Public Transportation	4.4%	90	14.9
Community Stability	44	74.35	% Living in Same House as in 1979	45.6%	40	65.3
			% Living in Same County as in 1985	87.7%	59	83.4

Metropolitan Area Suburb Rankings
CHICAGO-GARY-LAKE COUNTY

Composite: **Rank** 42 / 138 *Score* 60.24   **PALOS HILLS** (IL)

CATEGORY	RANK	SCORE	STATISTIC	VALUE	RANK	SCORE
Economics	57	58.85	Median Household Income	$41,416	72	22.2
			% of Families Above Poverty Level	98.7%	19	95.5
Affordable Housing	71	72.05	Median Home Value	$125,300	85	80.6
			Median Rent	$547	63	63.5
Crime	8	96.40	Violent Crimes per 10,000 Population	8	14	98.6
			Property Crimes per 10,000 Population	185	7	94.2
Open Spaces	81	52.20	Population Density (Persons/Sq. Mile)	4273	90	66.9
			Average Rooms per Housing Unit	5.6	74	37.5
Education	59	51.90	% High School Enrollment/Completion	95.5%	42	80.3
			% College Graduates	21.6%	70	23.5
Commute	119	19.75	Average Work Commute in Minutes	29	101	22.7
			% Commuting on Public Transportation	4.9%	79	16.8
Community Stability	55	70.50	% Living in Same House as in 1979	37.7%	73	50.1
			% Living in Same County as in 1985	92.3%	35	90.9

Composite: **Rank** 44 / 138 *Score* 60.05   **LANSING** (IL)

CATEGORY	RANK	SCORE	STATISTIC	VALUE	RANK	SCORE
Economics	77	55.00	Median Household Income	$36,641	97	17.4
			% of Families Above Poverty Level	98.0%	48	92.6
Affordable Housing	37	79.90	Median Home Value	$77,000	34	91.0
			Median Rent	$509	42	68.8
Crime	94	79.60	Violent Crimes per 10,000 Population	20	67	95.1
			Property Crimes per 10,000 Population	594	102	64.1
Open Spaces	93	50.60	Population Density (Persons/Sq. Mile)	4287	92	66.8
			Average Rooms per Housing Unit	5.5	80	34.4
Education	74	45.25	% High School Enrollment/Completion	94.3%	61	75.1
			% College Graduates	15.5%	95	15.4
Commute	73	30.15	Average Work Commute in Minutes	26	48	36.4
			% Commuting on Public Transportation	6.8%	63	23.9
Community Stability	27	79.85	% Living in Same House as in 1979	46.5%	32	67.0
			% Living in Same County as in 1985	93.4%	26	92.7

Composite: **Rank** 45 / 138 *Score* 60.01   **ELK GROVE VILLAGE** (IL)

CATEGORY	RANK	SCORE	STATISTIC	VALUE	RANK	SCORE
Economics	39	61.20	Median Household Income	$48,863	37	29.8
			% of Families Above Poverty Level	98.0%	48	92.6
Affordable Housing	102	63.70	Median Home Value	$137,800	99	77.9
			Median Rent	$647	109	49.5
Crime	70	86.55	Violent Crimes per 10,000 Population	19	64	95.4
			Property Crimes per 10,000 Population	409	75	77.7
Open Spaces	48	61.85	Population Density (Persons/Sq. Mile)	3110	50	76.8
			Average Rooms per Housing Unit	5.9	48	46.9
Education	50	56.50	% High School Enrollment/Completion	96.1%	34	83.0
			% College Graduates	26.5%	61	30.0
Commute	85	28.10	Average Work Commute in Minutes	25	35	40.9
			% Commuting on Public Transportation	4.5%	87	15.3
Community Stability	74	62.15	% Living in Same House as in 1979	34.8%	82	44.5
			% Living in Same County as in 1985	85.5%	67	79.8

Composite: *Rank* 46 / 138 *Score* 59.97   NILES (IL)

CATEGORY	RANK	SCORE	STATISTIC	VALUE	RANK	SCORE
Economics	77	55.00	Median Household Income	$38,718	84	19.5
			% of Families Above Poverty Level	97.5%	70	90.5
Affordable Housing	86	67.40	Median Home Value	$139,600	102	77.5
			Median Rent	$591	81	57.3
Crime	60	87.90	Violent Crimes per 10,000 Population	11	22	97.7
			Property Crimes per 10,000 Population	404	73	78.1
Open Spaces	114	45.05	Population Density (Persons/Sq. Mile)	4847	108	62.0
			Average Rooms per Housing Unit	5.3	98	28.1
Education	63	50.95	% High School Enrollment/Completion	95.5%	42	80.3
			% College Graduates	20.2%	76	21.6
Commute	58	31.25	Average Work Commute in Minutes	26	48	36.4
			% Commuting on Public Transportation	7.4%	56	26.1
Community Stability	18	82.25	% Living in Same House as in 1979	49.4%	20	72.6
			% Living in Same County as in 1985	92.9%	30	91.9

Composite: *Rank* 47 / 138 *Score* 59.70   TINLEY PARK (IL)

CATEGORY	RANK	SCORE	STATISTIC	VALUE	RANK	SCORE
Economics	54	59.55	Median Household Income	$43,198	63	24.0
			% of Families Above Poverty Level	98.6%	23	95.1
Affordable Housing	70	72.15	Median Home Value	$116,000	76	82.6
			Median Rent	$560	69	61.7
Crime	45	90.25	Violent Crimes per 10,000 Population	17	51	96.0
			Property Crimes per 10,000 Population	317	43	84.5
Open Spaces	55	60.00	Population Density (Persons/Sq. Mile)	3545	63	73.1
			Average Rooms per Housing Unit	5.9	48	46.9
Education	69	47.95	% High School Enrollment/Completion	94.7%	55	76.9
			% College Graduates	18.2%	85	19.0
Commute	99	25.45	Average Work Commute in Minutes	31	121	13.6
			% Commuting on Public Transportation	10.4%	36	37.3
Community Stability	73	62.55	% Living in Same House as in 1979	30.2%	97	35.7
			% Living in Same County as in 1985	91.4%	41	89.4

Composite: *Rank* 48 / 138 *Score* 59.67   HICKORY HILLS (IL)

CATEGORY	RANK	SCORE	STATISTIC	VALUE	RANK	SCORE
Economics	83	54.35	Median Household Income	$41,872	70	22.7
			% of Families Above Poverty Level	96.4%	94	86.0
Affordable Housing	54	76.10	Median Home Value	$113,600	72	83.1
			Median Rent	$507	40	69.1
Crime	28	92.15	Violent Crimes per 10,000 Population	13	35	97.1
			Property Crimes per 10,000 Population	280	29	87.2
Open Spaces	90	50.80	Population Density (Persons/Sq. Mile)	4596	99	64.1
			Average Rooms per Housing Unit	5.6	74	37.5
Education	83	43.10	% High School Enrollment/Completion	93.5%	69	71.6
			% College Graduates	14.9%	99	14.6
Commute	108	22.25	Average Work Commute in Minutes	27	58	31.8
			% Commuting on Public Transportation	3.8%	101	12.7
Community Stability	31	78.95	% Living in Same House as in 1979	44.6%	42	63.3
			% Living in Same County as in 1985	94.6%	20	94.6

Metropolitan Area Suburb Rankings
CHICAGO-GARY-LAKE COUNTY

Composite: *Rank* 49 / 138 *Score* 59.37   VALPARAISO (IN)

CATEGORY	RANK	SCORE	STATISTIC	VALUE	RANK	SCORE
Economics	115	46.05	Median Household Income	$31,602	117	12.3
			% of Families Above Poverty Level	94.9%	109	79.8
Affordable Housing	13	85.85	Median Home Value	$72,200	26	92.0
			Median Rent	$431	9	79.7
Crime	67	86.85	Violent Crimes per 10,000 Population	26	83	93.4
			Property Crimes per 10,000 Population	374	65	80.3
Open Spaces	69	55.40	Population Density (Persons/Sq. Mile)	2406	29	82.7
			Average Rooms per Housing Unit	5.3	98	28.1
Education	44	58.55	% High School Enrollment/Completion	96.6%	24	85.2
			% College Graduates	27.9%	58	31.9
Commute	30	36.15	Average Work Commute in Minutes	19	2	68.2
			% Commuting on Public Transportation	1.5%	133	4.1
Community Stability	108	46.75	% Living in Same House as in 1979	31.5%	92	38.2
			% Living in Same County as in 1985	70.4%	116	55.3

Composite: *Rank* 50 / 138 *Score* 59.36   ST. CHARLES (IL)

CATEGORY	RANK	SCORE	STATISTIC	VALUE	RANK	SCORE
Economics	44	60.65	Median Household Income	$46,655	46	27.5
			% of Families Above Poverty Level	98.3%	40	93.8
Affordable Housing	89	66.80	Median Home Value	$137,100	98	78.1
			Median Rent	$604	84	55.5
Crime	65	86.95	Violent Crimes per 10,000 Population	18	56	95.7
			Property Crimes per 10,000 Population	403	71	78.2
Open Spaces	30	68.85	Population Density (Persons/Sq. Mile)	2186	24	84.6
			Average Rooms per Housing Unit	6.1	37	53.1
Education	48	57.65	% High School Enrollment/Completion	93.7%	64	72.5
			% College Graduates	36.1%	32	42.8
Commute	60	31.15	Average Work Commute in Minutes	23	16	50.0
			% Commuting on Public Transportation	3.7%	103	12.3
Community Stability	119	43.45	% Living in Same House as in 1979	28.2%	112	31.9
			% Living in Same County as in 1985	70.2%	117	55.0

Composite: *Rank* 51 / 138 *Score* 59.30   WOOD DALE (IL)

CATEGORY	RANK	SCORE	STATISTIC	VALUE	RANK	SCORE
Economics	65	58.05	Median Household Income	$43,048	64	23.9
			% of Families Above Poverty Level	97.9%	57	92.2
Affordable Housing	91	66.55	Median Home Value	$120,000	81	81.8
			Median Rent	$634	101	51.3
Crime	30	91.90	Violent Crimes per 10,000 Population	13	35	97.1
			Property Crimes per 10,000 Population	288	34	86.7
Open Spaces	52	61.05	Population Density (Persons/Sq. Mile)	2918	44	78.4
			Average Rooms per Housing Unit	5.8	56	43.7
Education	58	53.40	% High School Enrollment/Completion	97.0%	22	86.9
			% College Graduates	18.9%	81	19.9
Commute	77	29.40	Average Work Commute in Minutes	25	35	40.9
			% Commuting on Public Transportation	5.2%	76	17.9
Community Stability	93	54.75	% Living in Same House as in 1979	39.0%	67	52.6
			% Living in Same County as in 1985	71.4%	114	56.9

Metropolitan Area Suburb Rankings
CHICAGO-GARY-LAKE COUNTY

Composite: Rank 52 / 138 *Score* 59.27   **LIBERTYVILLE** (IL)

CATEGORY	RANK	SCORE	STATISTIC	VALUE	RANK	SCORE
Economics	12	68.85	Median Household Income	$61,632	10	42.6
			% of Families Above Poverty Level	98.6%	23	95.1
Affordable Housing	117	59.70	Median Home Value	$188,000	127	67.1
			Median Rent	$627	96	52.3
Crime	N/A	N/A	Violent Crimes per 10,000 Population	N/A	N/A	N/A
			Property Crimes per 10,000 Population	N/A	N/A	N/A
Open Spaces	9	77.60	Population Density (Persons/Sq. Mile)	2341	28	83.3
			Average Rooms per Housing Unit	6.7	12	71.9
Education	21	68.20	% High School Enrollment/Completion	94.7%	55	76.9
			% College Graduates	48.7%	16	59.5
Commute	84	28.30	Average Work Commute in Minutes	25	35	40.9
			% Commuting on Public Transportation	4.6%	85	15.7
Community Stability	97	53.00	% Living in Same House as in 1979	33.8%	85	42.6
			% Living in Same County as in 1985	75.4%	100	63.4

Composite: Rank 53 / 138 *Score* 59.26   **BROOKFIELD** (IL)

CATEGORY	RANK	SCORE	STATISTIC	VALUE	RANK	SCORE
Economics	86	53.45	Median Household Income	$37,232	90	18.0
			% of Families Above Poverty Level	97.1%	79	88.9
Affordable Housing	66	73.35	Median Home Value	$104,200	65	85.2
			Median Rent	$561	70	61.5
Crime	24	92.80	Violent Crimes per 10,000 Population	11	22	97.7
			Property Crimes per 10,000 Population	271	24	87.9
Open Spaces	118	42.70	Population Density (Persons/Sq. Mile)	6140	125	51.0
			Average Rooms per Housing Unit	5.5	80	34.4
Education	103	32.50	% High School Enrollment/Completion	87.3%	110	44.5
			% College Graduates	19.3%	79	20.5
Commute	18	39.50	Average Work Commute in Minutes	25	35	40.9
			% Commuting on Public Transportation	10.6%	33	38.1
Community Stability	23	80.55	% Living in Same House as in 1979	48.3%	24	70.4
			% Living in Same County as in 1985	92.2%	37	90.7

Composite: Rank 54 / 138 *Score* 59.23   **WARRENVILLE** (IL)

CATEGORY	RANK	SCORE	STATISTIC	VALUE	RANK	SCORE
Economics	23	63.95	Median Household Income	$49,091	34	30.0
			% of Families Above Poverty Level	99.3%	3	97.9
Affordable Housing	115	59.90	Median Home Value	$116,100	77	82.6
			Median Rent	$735	126	37.2
Crime	15	94.45	Violent Crimes per 10,000 Population	4	3	99.7
			Property Crimes per 10,000 Population	253	19	89.2
Open Spaces	28	69.10	Population Density (Persons/Sq. Mile)	2127	22	85.1
			Average Rooms per Housing Unit	6.1	37	53.1
Education	45	58.30	% High School Enrollment/Completion	94.7%	55	76.9
			% College Graduates	33.8%	36	39.7
Commute	95	26.20	Average Work Commute in Minutes	26	48	36.4
			% Commuting on Public Transportation	4.7%	83	16.0
Community Stability	120	42.70	% Living in Same House as in 1979	23.3%	129	22.5
			% Living in Same County as in 1985	75.1%	101	62.9

Metropolitan Area Suburb Rankings
CHICAGO-GARY-LAKE COUNTY

Composite: *Rank* 55 / 138 *Score* 58.96 **PARK FOREST** (IL)

CATEGORY	RANK	SCORE	STATISTIC	VALUE	RANK	SCORE
Economics	88	53.15	Median Household Income	$36,995	92	17.8
			% of Families Above Poverty Level	97.0%	83	88.5
Affordable Housing	16	84.00	Median Home Value	$58,400	9	95.0
			Median Rent	$479	25	73.0
Crime	64	87.00	Violent Crimes per 10,000 Population	29	89	92.6
			Property Crimes per 10,000 Population	359	54	81.4
Open Spaces	81	52.20	Population Density (Persons/Sq. Mile)	5001	112	60.7
			Average Rooms per Housing Unit	5.8	56	43.7
Education	85	40.80	% High School Enrollment/Completion	89.4%	101	53.7
			% College Graduates	24.9%	65	27.9
Commute	83	28.45	Average Work Commute in Minutes	31	121	13.6
			% Commuting on Public Transportation	12.0%	25	43.3
Community Stability	64	67.10	% Living in Same House as in 1979	40.2%	64	54.9
			% Living in Same County as in 1985	85.2%	70	79.3

Composite: *Rank* 56 / 138 *Score* 58.90 **NORTHLAKE** (IL)

CATEGORY	RANK	SCORE	STATISTIC	VALUE	RANK	SCORE
Economics	94	52.40	Median Household Income	$35,129	106	15.9
			% of Families Above Poverty Level	97.1%	79	88.9
Affordable Housing	24	82.65	Median Home Value	$91,200	47	88.0
			Median Rent	$448	15	77.3
Crime	48	89.45	Violent Crimes per 10,000 Population	13	35	97.1
			Property Crimes per 10,000 Population	354	53	81.8
Open Spaces	102	48.15	Population Density (Persons/Sq. Mile)	4118	85	68.2
			Average Rooms per Housing Unit	5.3	98	28.1
Education	106	30.80	% High School Enrollment/Completion	89.8%	97	55.5
			% College Graduates	8.5%	129	6.1
Commute	75	29.85	Average Work Commute in Minutes	22	8	54.5
			% Commuting on Public Transportation	1.8%	130	5.2
Community Stability	30	79.00	% Living in Same House as in 1979	46.3%	35	66.6
			% Living in Same County as in 1985	92.6%	33	91.4

Composite: *Rank* 57 / 138 *Score* 58.79 **MARKHAM** (IL)

CATEGORY	RANK	SCORE	STATISTIC	VALUE	RANK	SCORE
Economics	132	30.90	Median Household Income	$31,233	121	12.0
			% of Families Above Poverty Level	87.6%	134	49.8
Affordable Housing	59	74.70	Median Home Value	$51,800	5	96.4
			Median Rent	$622	93	53.0
Crime	102	76.85	Violent Crimes per 10,000 Population	84	123	76.9
			Property Crimes per 10,000 Population	421	78	76.8
Open Spaces	35	65.90	Population Density (Persons/Sq. Mile)	2518	32	81.8
			Average Rooms per Housing Unit	6.0	40	50.0
Education	98	34.25	% High School Enrollment/Completion	91.3%	88	62.0
			% College Graduates	8.8%	128	6.5
Commute	67	30.40	Average Work Commute in Minutes	29	101	22.7
			% Commuting on Public Transportation	10.6%	33	38.1
Community Stability	2	98.55	% Living in Same House as in 1979	62.2%	3	97.1
			% Living in Same County as in 1985	97.9%	1	100.0

Metropolitan Area Suburb Rankings
CHICAGO-GARY-LAKE COUNTY

Composite: **Rank** 58 / 138 *Score* 58.68   **MOUNT PROSPECT** (IL)

CATEGORY	RANK	SCORE	STATISTIC	VALUE	RANK	SCORE
Economics	51	59.80	Median Household Income	$46,508	47	27.4
			% of Families Above Poverty Level	97.9%	57	92.2
Affordable Housing	98	64.15	Median Home Value	$154,500	113	74.3
			Median Rent	$615	89	54.0
Crime	55	88.50	Violent Crimes per 10,000 Population	17	51	96.0
			Property Crimes per 10,000 Population	365	58	81.0
Open Spaces	96	49.95	Population Density (Persons/Sq. Mile)	5165	114	59.3
			Average Rooms per Housing Unit	5.7	63	40.6
Education	64	49.60	% High School Enrollment/Completion	91.6%	84	63.3
			% College Graduates	30.9%	45	35.9
Commute	71	30.35	Average Work Commute in Minutes	26	48	36.4
			% Commuting on Public Transportation	6.9%	62	24.3
Community Stability	60	68.40	% Living in Same House as in 1979	41.3%	59	57.0
			% Living in Same County as in 1985	85.5%	67	79.8

Composite: **Rank** 59 / 138 *Score* 58.66   **MORRIS** (IL)

CATEGORY	RANK	SCORE	STATISTIC	VALUE	RANK	SCORE
Economics	118	44.70	Median Household Income	$31,699	116	12.4
			% of Families Above Poverty Level	94.2%	115	77.0
Affordable Housing	7	88.45	Median Home Value	$71,000	23	92.3
			Median Rent	$396	3	84.6
Crime	78	85.10	Violent Crimes per 10,000 Population	17	51	96.0
			Property Crimes per 10,000 Population	457	82	74.2
Open Spaces	66	56.15	Population Density (Persons/Sq. Mile)	1862	18	87.3
			Average Rooms per Housing Unit	5.2	106	25.0
Education	80	43.65	% High School Enrollment/Completion	93.4%	71	71.2
			% College Graduates	16.0%	91	16.1
Commute	35	34.85	Average Work Commute in Minutes	19	2	68.2
			% Commuting on Public Transportation	0.8%	136	1.5
Community Stability	86	57.70	% Living in Same House as in 1979	36.0%	78	46.8
			% Living in Same County as in 1985	78.6%	88	68.6

Composite: **Rank** 60 / 138 *Score* 58.65   **MATTESON** (IL)

CATEGORY	RANK	SCORE	STATISTIC	VALUE	RANK	SCORE
Economics	61	58.55	Median Household Income	$48,085	42	29.0
			% of Families Above Poverty Level	96.9%	84	88.1
Affordable Housing	52	76.40	Median Home Value	$86,800	39	88.9
			Median Rent	$544	60	63.9
Crime	128	50.60	Violent Crimes per 10,000 Population	44	106	88.3
			Property Crimes per 10,000 Population	1,288	131	12.9
Open Spaces	12	75.35	Population Density (Persons/Sq. Mile)	1762	15	88.2
			Average Rooms per Housing Unit	6.4	22	62.5
Education	56	54.35	% High School Enrollment/Completion	95.3%	47	79.5
			% College Graduates	25.9%	62	29.2
Commute	76	29.55	Average Work Commute in Minutes	32	126	9.1
			% Commuting on Public Transportation	13.8%	19	50.0
Community Stability	66	65.75	% Living in Same House as in 1979	33.1%	86	41.3
			% Living in Same County as in 1985	91.9%	38	90.2

Metropolitan Area Suburb Rankings
CHICAGO-GARY-LAKE COUNTY

Composite: *Rank* 61 / 138 *Score* 58.60 **LAKE ZURICH** (IL)

CATEGORY	RANK	SCORE	STATISTIC	VALUE	RANK	SCORE
Economics	11	68.90	Median Household Income	$58,422	14	39.4
			% of Families Above Poverty Level	99.4%	2	98.4
Affordable Housing	106	62.75	Median Home Value	$159,900	115	73.2
			Median Rent	$627	96	52.3
Crime	36	91.45	Violent Crimes per 10,000 Population	13	35	97.1
			Property Crimes per 10,000 Population	299	36	85.8
Open Spaces	4	82.60	Population Density (Persons/Sq. Mile)	2638	37	80.8
			Average Rooms per Housing Unit	7.1	4	84.4
Education	22	67.90	% High School Enrollment/Completion	97.1%	21	87.3
			% College Graduates	40.4%	23	48.5
Commute	136	11.10	Average Work Commute in Minutes	32	126	9.1
			% Commuting on Public Transportation	3.9%	99	13.1
Community Stability	134	25.50	% Living in Same House as in 1979	23.6%	126	23.0
			% Living in Same County as in 1985	53.6%	137	28.0

Composite: *Rank* 62 / 138 *Score* 58.55 **RICHTON PARK** (IL)

CATEGORY	RANK	SCORE	STATISTIC	VALUE	RANK	SCORE
Economics	82	54.40	Median Household Income	$38,721	83	19.5
			% of Families Above Poverty Level	97.2%	77	89.3
Affordable Housing	43	78.50	Median Home Value	$74,500	33	91.5
			Median Rent	$533	55	65.5
Crime	80	84.70	Violent Crimes per 10,000 Population	40	103	89.4
			Property Crimes per 10,000 Population	378	66	80.0
Open Spaces	87	51.45	Population Density (Persons/Sq. Mile)	3711	72	71.6
			Average Rooms per Housing Unit	5.4	90	31.3
Education	72	47.00	% High School Enrollment/Completion	93.0%	77	69.4
			% College Graduates	22.4%	68	24.6
Commute	31	35.70	Average Work Commute in Minutes	32	126	9.1
			% Commuting on Public Transportation	17.1%	10	62.3
Community Stability	85	58.10	% Living in Same House as in 1979	29.9%	100	35.1
			% Living in Same County as in 1985	86.3%	64	81.1

Composite: *Rank* 63 / 138 *Score* 58.36 **CRYSTAL LAKE** (IL)

CATEGORY	RANK	SCORE	STATISTIC	VALUE	RANK	SCORE
Economics	44	60.65	Median Household Income	$46,197	48	27.1
			% of Families Above Poverty Level	98.4%	35	94.2
Affordable Housing	93	66.15	Median Home Value	$119,700	80	81.8
			Median Rent	$640	103	50.5
Crime	58	88.20	Violent Crimes per 10,000 Population	11	22	97.7
			Property Crimes per 10,000 Population	396	69	78.7
Open Spaces	18	72.35	Population Density (Persons/Sq. Mile)	1735	14	88.4
			Average Rooms per Housing Unit	6.2	32	56.3
Education	47	58.05	% High School Enrollment/Completion	96.2%	32	83.4
			% College Graduates	28.5%	56	32.7
Commute	104	22.80	Average Work Commute in Minutes	28	82	27.3
			% Commuting on Public Transportation	5.3%	74	18.3
Community Stability	124	40.30	% Living in Same House as in 1979	26.1%	119	27.8
			% Living in Same County as in 1985	68.9%	121	52.8

Metropolitan Area Suburb Rankings
CHICAGO-GARY-LAKE COUNTY

Composite: *Rank* 64 / 138 *Score* 58.16   **HAZEL CREST (IL)**

CATEGORY	RANK	SCORE	STATISTIC	VALUE	RANK	SCORE
Economics	109	48.65	Median Household Income	$40,369	77	21.2
			% of Families Above Poverty Level	94.0%	117	76.1
Affordable Housing	56	75.40	Median Home Value	$67,600	20	93.0
			Median Rent	$588	79	57.8
Crime	106	75.00	Violent Crimes per 10,000 Population	76	120	79.1
			Property Crimes per 10,000 Population	502	90	70.9
Open Spaces	59	58.25	Population Density (Persons/Sq. Mile)	3953	78	69.6
			Average Rooms per Housing Unit	5.9	48	46.9
Education	65	49.25	% High School Enrollment/Completion	94.8%	51	77.3
			% College Graduates	19.9%	77	21.2
Commute	70	30.30	Average Work Commute in Minutes	32	126	9.1
			% Commuting on Public Transportation	14.2%	16	51.5
Community Stability	57	70.30	% Living in Same House as in 1979	37.1%	76	48.9
			% Living in Same County as in 1985	92.8%	32	91.7

Composite: *Rank* 65 / 138 *Score* 58.12   **ROSELLE (IL)**

CATEGORY	RANK	SCORE	STATISTIC	VALUE	RANK	SCORE
Economics	34	62.15	Median Household Income	$50,802	29	31.7
			% of Families Above Poverty Level	98.0%	48	92.6
Affordable Housing	110	62.15	Median Home Value	$125,000	84	80.7
			Median Rent	$689	116	43.6
Crime	11	95.45	Violent Crimes per 10,000 Population	12	31	97.4
			Property Crimes per 10,000 Population	195	8	93.5
Open Spaces	54	60.50	Population Density (Persons/Sq. Mile)	4525	95	64.7
			Average Rooms per Housing Unit	6.2	32	56.3
Education	40	59.15	% High School Enrollment/Completion	96.5%	26	84.7
			% College Graduates	29.2%	52	33.6
Commute	107	22.35	Average Work Commute in Minutes	29	101	22.7
			% Commuting on Public Transportation	6.3%	67	22.0
Community Stability	114	45.10	% Living in Same House as in 1979	28.7%	106	32.8
			% Living in Same County as in 1985	71.7%	111	57.4

Composite: *Rank* 66 / 138 *Score* 58.06   **COUNTRY CLUB HILLS (IL)**

CATEGORY	RANK	SCORE	STATISTIC	VALUE	RANK	SCORE
Economics	69	56.65	Median Household Income	$45,284	52	26.1
			% of Families Above Poverty Level	96.7%	90	87.2
Affordable Housing	84	68.60	Median Home Value	$72,700	27	91.9
			Median Rent	$677	114	45.3
Crime	62	87.35	Violent Crimes per 10,000 Population	31	94	92.0
			Property Crimes per 10,000 Population	341	50	82.7
Open Spaces	31	68.55	Population Density (Persons/Sq. Mile)	3364	56	74.6
			Average Rooms per Housing Unit	6.4	22	62.5
Education	87	40.70	% High School Enrollment/Completion	90.6%	92	59.0
			% College Graduates	20.8%	75	22.4
Commute	113	20.35	Average Work Commute in Minutes	34	136	0.0
			% Commuting on Public Transportation	11.3%	29	40.7
Community Stability	69	64.20	% Living in Same House as in 1979	30.9%	94	37.0
			% Living in Same County as in 1985	92.6%	33	91.4

Composite: *Rank* 67 / 138 *Score* 57.85   PALATINE (IL)

CATEGORY	RANK	SCORE	STATISTIC	VALUE	RANK	SCORE
Economics	38	61.50	Median Household Income	$48,668	39	29.6
			% of Families Above Poverty Level	98.2%	45	93.4
Affordable Housing	112	61.25	Median Home Value	$149,300	110	75.5
			Median Rent	$665	111	47.0
Crime	54	88.65	Violent Crimes per 10,000 Population	16	44	96.3
			Property Crimes per 10,000 Population	365	58	81.0
Open Spaces	65	56.50	Population Density (Persons/Sq. Mile)	3984	80	69.3
			Average Rooms per Housing Unit	5.8	56	43.7
Education	55	54.50	% High School Enrollment/Completion	91.8%	82	64.2
			% College Graduates	37.6%	28	44.8
Commute	89	27.85	Average Work Commute in Minutes	27	58	31.8
			% Commuting on Public Transportation	6.8%	63	23.9
Community Stability	92	54.70	% Living in Same House as in 1979	30.3%	96	35.9
			% Living in Same County as in 1985	81.6%	75	73.5

Composite: *Rank* 68 / 138 *Score* 57.84   LISLE (IL)

CATEGORY	RANK	SCORE	STATISTIC	VALUE	RANK	SCORE
Economics	39	61.20	Median Household Income	$49,712	31	30.6
			% of Families Above Poverty Level	97.8%	63	91.8
Affordable Housing	111	61.40	Median Home Value	$163,100	118	72.5
			Median Rent	$641	105	50.3
Crime	50	89.15	Violent Crimes per 10,000 Population	16	44	96.3
			Property Crimes per 10,000 Population	351	52	82.0
Open Spaces	72	54.75	Population Density (Persons/Sq. Mile)	3302	55	75.1
			Average Rooms per Housing Unit	5.5	80	34.4
Education	11	77.55	% High School Enrollment/Completion	98.7%	9	94.3
			% College Graduates	49.7%	14	60.8
Commute	49	33.05	Average Work Commute in Minutes	27	58	31.8
			% Commuting on Public Transportation	9.6%	43	34.3
Community Stability	132	27.80	% Living in Same House as in 1979	14.7%	136	6.0
			% Living in Same County as in 1985	66.9%	126	49.6

Composite: *Rank* 69 / 138 *Score* 57.83   VILLA PARK (IL)

CATEGORY	RANK	SCORE	STATISTIC	VALUE	RANK	SCORE
Economics	62	58.40	Median Household Income	$41,316	74	22.1
			% of Families Above Poverty Level	98.5%	29	94.7
Affordable Housing	65	73.70	Median Home Value	$108,100	70	84.3
			Median Rent	$550	64	63.1
Crime	91	80.60	Violent Crimes per 10,000 Population	23	73	94.3
			Property Crimes per 10,000 Population	556	96	66.9
Open Spaces	87	51.45	Population Density (Persons/Sq. Mile)	4816	107	62.3
			Average Rooms per Housing Unit	5.7	63	40.6
Education	91	38.60	% High School Enrollment/Completion	89.6%	99	54.6
			% College Graduates	20.9%	73	22.6
Commute	67	30.40	Average Work Commute in Minutes	24	30	45.5
			% Commuting on Public Transportation	4.5%	87	15.3
Community Stability	52	71.65	% Living in Same House as in 1979	48.1%	28	70.1
			% Living in Same County as in 1985	81.4%	77	73.2

Composite: **Rank** 70 / 138 *Score* 57.76   **WOODSTOCK** (IL)

CATEGORY	RANK	SCORE	STATISTIC	VALUE	RANK	SCORE
Economics	116	45.60	Median Household Income	$31,458	118	12.2
			% of Families Above Poverty Level	94.7%	111	79.0
Affordable Housing	40	78.90	Median Home Value	$92,800	49	87.6
			Median Rent	$499	35	70.2
Crime	39	90.75	Violent Crimes per 10,000 Population	16	44	96.3
			Property Crimes per 10,000 Population	308	42	85.2
Open Spaces	56	59.55	Population Density (Persons/Sq. Mile)	1429	8	91.0
			Average Rooms per Housing Unit	5.3	98	28.1
Education	78	44.15	% High School Enrollment/Completion	93.5%	69	71.6
			% College Graduates	16.5%	89	16.7
Commute	37	34.60	Average Work Commute in Minutes	21	6	59.1
			% Commuting on Public Transportation	3.1%	112	10.1
Community Stability	100	50.75	% Living in Same House as in 1979	28.5%	109	32.4
			% Living in Same County as in 1985	78.9%	85	69.1

Composite: **Rank** 71 / 138 *Score* 57.66   **DOLTON** (IL)

CATEGORY	RANK	SCORE	STATISTIC	VALUE	RANK	SCORE
Economics	97	50.75	Median Household Income	$36,724	95	17.5
			% of Families Above Poverty Level	95.9%	105	84.0
Affordable Housing	35	80.05	Median Home Value	$64,600	19	93.7
			Median Rent	$526	49	66.4
Crime	118	68.90	Violent Crimes per 10,000 Population	53	109	85.7
			Property Crimes per 10,000 Population	756	122	52.1
Open Spaces	98	49.45	Population Density (Persons/Sq. Mile)	5287	118	58.3
			Average Rooms per Housing Unit	5.7	63	40.6
Education	73	45.30	% High School Enrollment/Completion	95.2%	48	79.0
			% College Graduates	12.6%	105	11.6
Commute	91	27.30	Average Work Commute in Minutes	32	126	9.1
			% Commuting on Public Transportation	12.6%	23	45.5
Community Stability	20	81.85	% Living in Same House as in 1979	46.8%	31	67.6
			% Living in Same County as in 1985	95.5%	11	96.1

Composite: **Rank** 72 / 138 *Score* 57.64   **BATAVIA** (IL)

CATEGORY	RANK	SCORE	STATISTIC	VALUE	RANK	SCORE
Economics	41	61.10	Median Household Income	$45,005	55	25.9
			% of Families Above Poverty Level	98.9%	15	96.3
Affordable Housing	76	70.00	Median Home Value	$137,800	99	77.9
			Median Rent	$557	65	62.1
Crime	41	90.65	Violent Crimes per 10,000 Population	17	51	96.0
			Property Crimes per 10,000 Population	306	41	85.3
Open Spaces	38	64.55	Population Density (Persons/Sq. Mile)	2470	30	82.2
			Average Rooms per Housing Unit	5.9	48	46.9
Education	84	42.05	% High School Enrollment/Completion	87.6%	109	45.9
			% College Graduates	32.7%	42	38.2
Commute	51	32.85	Average Work Commute in Minutes	22	8	54.5
			% Commuting on Public Transportation	3.4%	106	11.2
Community Stability	121	42.30	% Living in Same House as in 1979	27.7%	114	30.9
			% Living in Same County as in 1985	69.4%	119	53.7

Metropolitan Area Suburb Rankings
CHICAGO-GARY-LAKE COUNTY

Composite: **Rank** 73 / 138 *Score* 57.42   **BURBANK** (IL)

CATEGORY	RANK	SCORE	STATISTIC	VALUE	RANK	SCORE
Economics	84	54.15	Median Household Income	$37,449	87	18.2
			% of Families Above Poverty Level	97.4%	72	90.1
Affordable Housing	41	78.60	Median Home Value	$88,900	43	88.4
			Median Rent	$509	42	68.8
Crime	103	76.30	Violent Crimes per 10,000 Population	59	111	84.0
			Property Crimes per 10,000 Population	533	94	68.6
Open Spaces	123	40.45	Population Density (Persons/Sq. Mile)	6671	129	46.5
			Average Rooms per Housing Unit	5.5	80	34.4
Education	93	37.35	% High School Enrollment/Completion	93.1%	75	69.9
			% College Graduates	7.5%	132	4.8
Commute	101	25.05	Average Work Commute in Minutes	27	58	31.8
			% Commuting on Public Transportation	5.3%	74	18.3
Community Stability	8	90.05	% Living in Same House as in 1979	54.1%	11	81.6
			% Living in Same County as in 1985	97.0%	3	98.5

Composite: **Rank** 74 / 138 *Score* 57.24   **BARTLETT** (IL)

CATEGORY	RANK	SCORE	STATISTIC	VALUE	RANK	SCORE
Economics	29	63.10	Median Household Income	$51,524	26	32.4
			% of Families Above Poverty Level	98.3%	40	93.8
Affordable Housing	87	67.30	Median Home Value	$130,700	92	79.5
			Median Rent	$607	87	55.1
Crime	53	88.75	Violent Crimes per 10,000 Population	16	44	96.3
			Property Crimes per 10,000 Population	362	57	81.2
Open Spaces	6	78.50	Population Density (Persons/Sq. Mile)	1382	5	91.4
			Average Rooms per Housing Unit	6.5	16	65.6
Education	61	51.60	% High School Enrollment/Completion	93.3%	74	70.7
			% College Graduates	28.4%	57	32.5
Commute	133	12.30	Average Work Commute in Minutes	34	136	0.0
			% Commuting on Public Transportation	7.0%	61	24.6
Community Stability	125	39.15	% Living in Same House as in 1979	24.8%	122	25.3
			% Living in Same County as in 1985	69.0%	120	53.0

Composite: **Rank** 74 / 138 *Score* 57.24   **OAK PARK** (IL)

CATEGORY	RANK	SCORE	STATISTIC	VALUE	RANK	SCORE
Economics	81	54.70	Median Household Income	$40,453	76	21.3
			% of Families Above Poverty Level	96.9%	84	88.1
Affordable Housing	72	71.40	Median Home Value	$139,500	101	77.6
			Median Rent	$535	57	65.2
Crime	120	66.95	Violent Crimes per 10,000 Population	75	118	79.4
			Property Crimes per 10,000 Population	724	121	54.5
Open Spaces	135	17.25	Population Density (Persons/Sq. Mile)	11402	135	6.4
			Average Rooms per Housing Unit	5.3	98	28.1
Education	12	73.10	% High School Enrollment/Completion	96.2%	32	83.4
			% College Graduates	51.2%	13	62.8
Commute	2	57.50	Average Work Commute in Minutes	28	82	27.3
			% Commuting on Public Transportation	23.9%	3	87.7
Community Stability	79	59.75	% Living in Same House as in 1979	32.0%	91	39.2
			% Living in Same County as in 1985	85.8%	66	80.3

Metropolitan Area Suburb Rankings
CHICAGO-GARY-LAKE COUNTY

Composite: **Rank** 76 / 138   *Score* 57.11   **ALGONQUIN (IL)**

CATEGORY	RANK	SCORE	STATISTIC	VALUE	RANK	SCORE
Economics	21	64.40	Median Household Income	$53,665	18	34.6
			% of Families Above Poverty Level	98.4%	35	94.2
Affordable Housing	69	72.45	Median Home Value	$134,600	96	78.6
			Median Rent	$527	50	66.3
Crime	20	93.75	Violent Crimes per 10,000 Population	11	22	97.7
			Property Crimes per 10,000 Population	245	16	89.8
Open Spaces	10	76.45	Population Density (Persons/Sq. Mile)	2235	26	84.2
			Average Rooms per Housing Unit	6.6	14	68.7
Education	52	55.50	% High School Enrollment/Completion	93.7%	64	72.5
			% College Graduates	32.9%	41	38.5
Commute	134	12.20	Average Work Commute in Minutes	31	121	13.6
			% Commuting on Public Transportation	3.3%	108	10.8
Community Stability	135	25.00	% Living in Same House as in 1979	21.7%	131	19.4
			% Living in Same County as in 1985	55.2%	136	30.6

Composite: **Rank** 77 / 138   *Score* 56.88   **PORTAGE (IN)**

CATEGORY	RANK	SCORE	STATISTIC	VALUE	RANK	SCORE
Economics	121	42.35	Median Household Income	$33,118	114	13.9
			% of Families Above Poverty Level	92.7%	122	70.8
Affordable Housing	9	86.90	Median Home Value	$62,300	12	94.2
			Median Rent	$432	10	79.6
Crime	82	84.00	Violent Crimes per 10,000 Population	24	74	94.0
			Property Crimes per 10,000 Population	460	84	74.0
Open Spaces	51	61.30	Population Density (Persons/Sq. Mile)	1395	6	91.3
			Average Rooms per Housing Unit	5.4	90	31.3
Education	97	35.25	% High School Enrollment/Completion	91.6%	84	63.3
			% College Graduates	9.3%	125	7.2
Commute	87	28.15	Average Work Commute in Minutes	23	16	50.0
			% Commuting on Public Transportation	2.1%	127	6.3
Community Stability	76	60.20	% Living in Same House as in 1979	39.5%	65	53.6
			% Living in Same County as in 1985	77.5%	94	66.8

Composite: **Rank** 78 / 138   *Score* 56.74   **NORRIDGE (IL)**

CATEGORY	RANK	SCORE	STATISTIC	VALUE	RANK	SCORE
Economics	87	53.10	Median Household Income	$35,766	102	16.5
			% of Families Above Poverty Level	97.3%	73	89.7
Affordable Housing	76	70.00	Median Home Value	$134,600	96	78.6
			Median Rent	$562	71	61.4
Crime	101	77.85	Violent Crimes per 10,000 Population	26	83	93.4
			Property Crimes per 10,000 Population	618	108	62.3
Open Spaces	129	33.40	Population Density (Persons/Sq. Mile)	7975	131	35.5
			Average Rooms per Housing Unit	5.4	90	31.3
Education	109	29.50	% High School Enrollment/Completion	88.3%	105	48.9
			% College Graduates	11.5%	112	10.1
Commute	44	33.85	Average Work Commute in Minutes	26	48	36.4
			% Commuting on Public Transportation	8.8%	48	31.3
Community Stability	1	99.45	% Living in Same House as in 1979	63.7%	1	100.0
			% Living in Same County as in 1985	97.2%	2	98.9

Metropolitan Area Suburb Rankings
CHICAGO-GARY-LAKE COUNTY

Composite: **Rank** 79 / 138 *Score* 56.64   **HOFFMAN ESTATES** (IL)

CATEGORY	RANK	SCORE	STATISTIC	VALUE	RANK	SCORE
Economics	32	62.95	Median Household Income	$49,475	33	30.4
			% of Families Above Poverty Level	98.7%	19	95.5
Affordable Housing	113	61.00	Median Home Value	$133,100	94	78.9
			Median Rent	$693	117	43.1
Crime	35	91.40	Violent Crimes per 10,000 Population	18	56	95.7
			Property Crimes per 10,000 Population	282	30	87.1
Open Spaces	34	66.00	Population Density (Persons/Sq. Mile)	2493	31	82.0
			Average Rooms per Housing Unit	6.0	40	50.0
Education	68	48.05	% High School Enrollment/Completion	90.1%	95	56.8
			% College Graduates	33.5%	37	39.3
Commute	121	19.60	Average Work Commute in Minutes	28	82	27.3
			% Commuting on Public Transportation	3.6%	104	11.9
Community Stability	106	47.50	% Living in Same House as in 1979	25.6%	120	26.9
			% Living in Same County as in 1985	78.3%	89	68.1

Composite: **Rank** 80 / 138 *Score* 56.59   **MIDLOTHIAN** (IL)

CATEGORY	RANK	SCORE	STATISTIC	VALUE	RANK	SCORE
Economics	92	52.50	Median Household Income	$37,042	91	17.8
			% of Families Above Poverty Level	96.7%	90	87.2
Affordable Housing	26	82.30	Median Home Value	$74,400	32	91.6
			Median Rent	$479	25	73.0
Crime	108	74.65	Violent Crimes per 10,000 Population	42	104	88.9
			Property Crimes per 10,000 Population	644	111	60.4
Open Spaces	113	45.45	Population Density (Persons/Sq. Mile)	5129	113	59.6
			Average Rooms per Housing Unit	5.4	90	31.3
Education	113	28.00	% High School Enrollment/Completion	87.7%	108	46.3
			% College Graduates	11.2%	113	9.7
Commute	48	33.25	Average Work Commute in Minutes	27	58	31.8
			% Commuting on Public Transportation	9.7%	42	34.7
Community Stability	26	79.95	% Living in Same House as in 1979	44.6%	42	63.3
			% Living in Same County as in 1985	95.8%	7	96.6

Composite: **Rank** 81 / 138 *Score* 56.48   **BUFFALO GROVE** (IL)

CATEGORY	RANK	SCORE	STATISTIC	VALUE	RANK	SCORE
Economics	14	66.85	Median Household Income	$56,011	17	37.0
			% of Families Above Poverty Level	99.0%	14	96.7
Affordable Housing	125	53.40	Median Home Value	$164,100	120	72.3
			Median Rent	$754	129	34.5
Crime	9	95.85	Violent Crimes per 10,000 Population	5	7	99.4
			Property Crimes per 10,000 Population	212	13	92.3
Open Spaces	47	61.90	Population Density (Persons/Sq. Mile)	4560	97	64.4
			Average Rooms per Housing Unit	6.3	25	59.4
Education	20	69.05	% High School Enrollment/Completion	95.5%	42	80.3
			% College Graduates	47.4%	17	57.8
Commute	129	17.30	Average Work Commute in Minutes	30	113	18.2
			% Commuting on Public Transportation	4.8%	81	16.4
Community Stability	131	31.00	% Living in Same House as in 1979	20.9%	133	17.9
			% Living in Same County as in 1985	63.5%	132	44.1

Composite: **Rank** 82 / 138 **Score** 56.45   **BOLINGBROOK** (IL)

CATEGORY	RANK	SCORE	STATISTIC	VALUE	RANK	SCORE
Economics	56	58.95	Median Household Income	$46,166	49	27.0
			% of Families Above Poverty Level	97.6%	68	90.9
Affordable Housing	60	74.65	Median Home Value	$94,400	53	87.3
			Median Rent	$558	66	62.0
Crime	22	93.40	Violent Crimes per 10,000 Population	24	74	94.0
			Property Crimes per 10,000 Population	204	11	92.8
Open Spaces	35	65.90	Population Density (Persons/Sq. Mile)	3627	65	72.4
			Average Rooms per Housing Unit	6.3	25	59.4
Education	75	45.05	% High School Enrollment/Completion	91.9%	81	64.6
			% College Graduates	23.1%	67	25.5
Commute	131	16.55	Average Work Commute in Minutes	30	113	18.2
			% Commuting on Public Transportation	4.4%	90	14.9
Community Stability	122	40.65	% Living in Same House as in 1979	28.7%	106	32.8
			% Living in Same County as in 1985	66.2%	129	48.5

Composite: **Rank** 83 / 138 **Score** 56.28   **EVANSTON** (IL)

CATEGORY	RANK	SCORE	STATISTIC	VALUE	RANK	SCORE
Economics	99	50.45	Median Household Income	$41,115	75	21.9
			% of Families Above Poverty Level	94.7%	111	79.0
Affordable Housing	116	59.75	Median Home Value	$181,600	125	68.5
			Median Rent	$636	102	51.0
Crime	122	65.75	Violent Crimes per 10,000 Population	69	114	81.1
			Property Crimes per 10,000 Population	779	123	50.4
Open Spaces	134	24.00	Population Density (Persons/Sq. Mile)	9448	133	23.0
			Average Rooms per Housing Unit	5.2	106	25.0
Education	7	81.10	% High School Enrollment/Completion	97.8%	15	90.4
			% College Graduates	58.0%	7	71.8
Commute	1	63.45	Average Work Commute in Minutes	27	58	31.8
			% Commuting on Public Transportation	25.9%	2	95.1
Community Stability	103	49.45	% Living in Same House as in 1979	31.1%	93	37.4
			% Living in Same County as in 1985	74.2%	108	61.5

Composite: **Rank** 84 / 138 **Score** 56.20   **BLOOMINGDALE** (IL)

CATEGORY	RANK	SCORE	STATISTIC	VALUE	RANK	SCORE
Economics	22	64.00	Median Household Income	$51,975	23	32.9
			% of Families Above Poverty Level	98.6%	23	95.1
Affordable Housing	120	57.95	Median Home Value	$147,400	106	75.9
			Median Rent	$715	124	40.0
Crime	109	74.50	Violent Crimes per 10,000 Population	27	86	93.1
			Property Crimes per 10,000 Population	705	117	55.9
Open Spaces	25	70.25	Population Density (Persons/Sq. Mile)	2600	36	81.1
			Average Rooms per Housing Unit	6.3	25	59.4
Education	43	58.65	% High School Enrollment/Completion	96.1%	34	83.0
			% College Graduates	29.7%	50	34.3
Commute	110	22.05	Average Work Commute in Minutes	28	82	27.3
			% Commuting on Public Transportation	4.9%	79	16.8
Community Stability	110	46.00	% Living in Same House as in 1979	26.8%	118	29.2
			% Living in Same County as in 1985	75.0%	102	62.8

Composite: *Rank* 85 / 138 *Score* 55.94   FRANKLIN PARK (IL)

CATEGORY	RANK	SCORE	STATISTIC	VALUE	RANK	SCORE
Economics	104	49.55	Median Household Income	$34,379	110	15.1
			% of Families Above Poverty Level	95.9%	105	84.0
Affordable Housing	21	82.70	Median Home Value	$98,300	57	86.4
			Median Rent	$436	12	79.0
Crime	95	78.75	Violent Crimes per 10,000 Population	39	101	89.7
			Property Crimes per 10,000 Population	543	95	67.8
Open Spaces	116	43.70	Population Density (Persons/Sq. Mile)	4053	82	68.7
			Average Rooms per Housing Unit	5.0	123	18.7
Education	125	20.10	% High School Enrollment/Completion	84.3%	125	31.4
			% College Graduates	10.5%	118	8.8
Commute	42	33.95	Average Work Commute in Minutes	22	8	54.5
			% Commuting on Public Transportation	4.0%	97	13.4
Community Stability	15	82.85	% Living in Same House as in 1979	52.2%	14	77.9
			% Living in Same County as in 1985	90.4%	45	87.8

Composite: *Rank* 86 / 138 *Score* 55.91   BERWYN (IL)

CATEGORY	RANK	SCORE	STATISTIC	VALUE	RANK	SCORE
Economics	108	48.60	Median Household Income	$31,326	119	12.0
			% of Families Above Poverty Level	96.2%	96	85.2
Affordable Housing	21	82.70	Median Home Value	$90,300	45	88.1
			Median Rent	$448	15	77.3
Crime	77	85.30	Violent Crimes per 10,000 Population	26	83	93.4
			Property Crimes per 10,000 Population	416	77	77.2
Open Spaces	136	14.60	Population Density (Persons/Sq. Mile)	11662	137	4.2
			Average Rooms per Housing Unit	5.2	106	25.0
Education	92	38.15	% High School Enrollment/Completion	91.2%	89	61.6
			% College Graduates	15.0%	98	14.7
Commute	14	42.20	Average Work Commute in Minutes	27	58	31.8
			% Commuting on Public Transportation	14.5%	15	52.6
Community Stability	27	79.85	% Living in Same House as in 1979	46.5%	32	67.0
			% Living in Same County as in 1985	93.4%	26	92.7

Composite: *Rank* 87 / 138 *Score* 55.86   WORTH (IL)

CATEGORY	RANK	SCORE	STATISTIC	VALUE	RANK	SCORE
Economics	111	47.90	Median Household Income	$35,658	103	16.4
			% of Families Above Poverty Level	94.8%	110	79.4
Affordable Housing	46	78.05	Median Home Value	$95,700	55	87.0
			Median Rent	$507	40	69.1
Crime	15	94.45	Violent Crimes per 10,000 Population	5	7	99.4
			Property Crimes per 10,000 Population	249	18	89.5
Open Spaces	119	42.55	Population Density (Persons/Sq. Mile)	4704	103	63.2
			Average Rooms per Housing Unit	5.1	113	21.9
Education	119	24.90	% High School Enrollment/Completion	85.9%	113	38.4
			% College Graduates	12.5%	106	11.4
Commute	94	26.35	Average Work Commute in Minutes	27	58	31.8
			% Commuting on Public Transportation	6.0%	71	20.9
Community Stability	37	76.85	% Living in Same House as in 1979	41.5%	58	57.4
			% Living in Same County as in 1985	95.6%	9	96.3

Metropolitan Area Suburb Rankings
CHICAGO-GARY-LAKE COUNTY

Composite: ***Rank*** 88 / 138 *Score* 55.85   **CRESTWOOD** (IL)

CATEGORY	RANK	SCORE	STATISTIC	VALUE	RANK	SCORE
Economics	112	47.00	Median Household Income	$35,414	105	16.2
			% of Families Above Poverty Level	94.4%	114	77.8
Affordable Housing	50	76.75	Median Home Value	$93,000	50	87.6
			Median Rent	$530	52	65.9
Crime	19	93.80	Violent Crimes per 10,000 Population	8	14	98.6
			Property Crimes per 10,000 Population	256	20	89.0
Open Spaces	106	47.05	Population Density (Persons/Sq. Mile)	3652	67	72.2
			Average Rooms per Housing Unit	5.1	113	21.9
Education	115	26.30	% High School Enrollment/Completion	87.0%	111	43.2
			% College Graduates	11.0%	114	9.4
Commute	66	30.45	Average Work Commute in Minutes	28	82	27.3
			% Commuting on Public Transportation	9.4%	46	33.6
Community Stability	59	69.60	% Living in Same House as in 1979	34.6%	83	44.1
			% Living in Same County as in 1985	94.9%	17	95.1

Composite: ***Rank*** 89 / 138 *Score* 55.66   **LOMBARD** (IL)

CATEGORY	RANK	SCORE	STATISTIC	VALUE	RANK	SCORE
Economics	53	59.65	Median Household Income	$44,210	60	25.1
			% of Families Above Poverty Level	98.4%	35	94.2
Affordable Housing	97	64.45	Median Home Value	$117,600	78	82.3
			Median Rent	$668	112	46.6
Crime	104	75.90	Violent Crimes per 10,000 Population	22	70	94.6
			Property Crimes per 10,000 Population	687	114	57.2
Open Spaces	90	50.80	Population Density (Persons/Sq. Mile)	4234	88	67.2
			Average Rooms per Housing Unit	5.5	80	34.4
Education	59	51.90	% High School Enrollment/Completion	92.8%	78	68.6
			% College Graduates	30.4%	48	35.2
Commute	90	27.45	Average Work Commute in Minutes	27	58	31.8
			% Commuting on Public Transportation	6.6%	66	23.1
Community Stability	81	59.45	% Living in Same House as in 1979	38.9%	68	52.4
			% Living in Same County as in 1985	77.3%	95	66.5

Composite: ***Rank*** 90 / 138 *Score* 55.62   **CREST HILL** (IL)

CATEGORY	RANK	SCORE	STATISTIC	VALUE	RANK	SCORE
Economics	98	50.40	Median Household Income	$30,794	125	11.5
			% of Families Above Poverty Level	97.2%	77	89.3
Affordable Housing	15	84.45	Median Home Value	$63,800	15	93.8
			Median Rent	$464	20	75.1
Crime	107	74.75	Violent Crimes per 10,000 Population	52	108	86.0
			Property Crimes per 10,000 Population	602	105	63.5
Open Spaces	96	49.95	Population Density (Persons/Sq. Mile)	1487	9	90.5
			Average Rooms per Housing Unit	4.7	135	9.4
Education	82	43.25	% High School Enrollment/Completion	94.8%	51	77.3
			% College Graduates	10.8%	116	9.2
Commute	61	30.80	Average Work Commute in Minutes	22	8	54.5
			% Commuting on Public Transportation	2.3%	122	7.1
Community Stability	88	55.75	% Living in Same House as in 1979	37.2%	75	49.1
			% Living in Same County as in 1985	74.8%	104	62.4

Composite: *Rank* 90 / 138 *Score* 55.62   GURNEE (IL)

CATEGORY	RANK	SCORE	STATISTIC	VALUE	RANK	SCORE
Economics	43	60.70	Median Household Income	$49,069	35	30.0
			% of Families Above Poverty Level	97.7%	66	91.4
Affordable Housing	94	65.65	Median Home Value	$129,100	89	79.8
			Median Rent	$633	100	51.5
Crime	111	72.90	Violent Crimes per 10,000 Population	35	98	90.9
			Property Crimes per 10,000 Population	718	119	54.9
Open Spaces	32	68.15	Population Density (Persons/Sq. Mile)	1237	4	92.6
			Average Rooms per Housing Unit	5.8	56	43.7
Education	26	63.75	% High School Enrollment/Completion	96.0%	37	82.5
			% College Graduates	37.8%	27	45.0
Commute	103	24.00	Average Work Commute in Minutes	25	35	40.9
			% Commuting on Public Transportation	2.3%	122	7.1
Community Stability	129	34.20	% Living in Same House as in 1979	20.6%	134	17.3
			% Living in Same County as in 1985	67.8%	124	51.1

Composite: *Rank* 92 / 138 *Score* 55.61   BRIDGEVIEW (IL)

CATEGORY	RANK	SCORE	STATISTIC	VALUE	RANK	SCORE
Economics	105	49.40	Median Household Income	$33,652	112	14.4
			% of Families Above Poverty Level	96.0%	102	84.4
Affordable Housing	38	79.20	Median Home Value	$93,000	50	87.6
			Median Rent	$495	34	70.8
Crime	99	78.20	Violent Crimes per 10,000 Population	33	96	91.4
			Property Crimes per 10,000 Population	581	99	65.0
Open Spaces	103	47.75	Population Density (Persons/Sq. Mile)	3484	60	73.6
			Average Rooms per Housing Unit	5.1	113	21.9
Education	111	29.35	% High School Enrollment/Completion	89.6%	99	54.6
			% College Graduates	7.0%	134	4.1
Commute	80	28.65	Average Work Commute in Minutes	25	35	40.9
			% Commuting on Public Transportation	4.8%	81	16.4
Community Stability	38	76.70	% Living in Same House as in 1979	41.8%	54	58.0
			% Living in Same County as in 1985	95.1%	15	95.4

Composite: *Rank* 93 / 138 *Score* 55.49   WHEELING (IL)

CATEGORY	RANK	SCORE	STATISTIC	VALUE	RANK	SCORE
Economics	71	56.65	Median Household Income	$39,848	79	20.7
			% of Families Above Poverty Level	98.0%	48	92.6
Affordable Housing	101	64.05	Median Home Value	$113,800	73	83.1
			Median Rent	$679	115	45.0
Crime	46	89.95	Violent Crimes per 10,000 Population	18	56	95.7
			Property Crimes per 10,000 Population	321	44	84.2
Open Spaces	101	48.40	Population Density (Persons/Sq. Mile)	3696	71	71.8
			Average Rooms per Housing Unit	5.2	106	25.0
Education	38	59.50	% High School Enrollment/Completion	96.4%	28	84.3
			% College Graduates	30.0%	49	34.7
Commute	105	22.85	Average Work Commute in Minutes	26	48	36.4
			% Commuting on Public Transportation	2.9%	116	9.3
Community Stability	107	47.05	% Living in Same House as in 1979	23.4%	128	22.6
			% Living in Same County as in 1985	80.4%	79	71.5

Metropolitan Area Suburb Rankings
CHICAGO-GARY-LAKE COUNTY

Composite: **Rank** 94 / 138 *Score* 55.00   **ROLLING MEADOWS** (IL)

CATEGORY	RANK	SCORE	STATISTIC	VALUE	RANK	SCORE
Economics	42	60.85	Median Household Income	$45,764	51	26.6
			% of Families Above Poverty Level	98.6%	23	95.1
Affordable Housing	105	62.85	Median Home Value	$127,300	88	80.2
			Median Rent	$676	113	45.5
Crime	76	85.75	Violent Crimes per 10,000 Population	21	68	94.9
			Property Crimes per 10,000 Population	424	79	76.6
Open Spaces	93	50.60	Population Density (Persons/Sq. Mile)	4287	92	66.8
			Average Rooms per Housing Unit	5.5	80	34.4
Education	101	33.65	% High School Enrollment/Completion	85.3%	118	35.8
			% College Graduates	27.6%	59	31.5
Commute	50	33.00	Average Work Commute in Minutes	23	16	50.0
			% Commuting on Public Transportation	4.7%	83	16.0
Community Stability	83	58.30	% Living in Same House as in 1979	34.2%	84	43.4
			% Living in Same County as in 1985	81.4%	77	73.2

Composite: **Rank** 95 / 138 *Score* 54.84   **WOODRIDGE** (IL)

CATEGORY	RANK	SCORE	STATISTIC	VALUE	RANK	SCORE
Economics	59	58.80	Median Household Income	$44,570	57	25.4
			% of Families Above Poverty Level	97.9%	57	92.2
Affordable Housing	75	70.25	Median Home Value	$119,600	79	81.8
			Median Rent	$581	78	58.7
Crime	69	86.75	Violent Crimes per 10,000 Population	25	78	93.7
			Property Crimes per 10,000 Population	381	67	79.8
Open Spaces	64	57.00	Population Density (Persons/Sq. Mile)	3502	61	73.4
			Average Rooms per Housing Unit	5.7	63	40.6
Education	49	57.35	% High School Enrollment/Completion	94.7%	55	76.9
			% College Graduates	32.4%	43	37.8
Commute	116	20.10	Average Work Commute in Minutes	30	113	18.2
			% Commuting on Public Transportation	6.3%	67	22.0
Community Stability	130	33.60	% Living in Same House as in 1979	21.2%	132	18.4
			% Living in Same County as in 1985	66.4%	128	48.8

Composite: **Rank** 96 / 138 *Score* 54.78   **ELMWOOD PARK** (IL)

CATEGORY	RANK	SCORE	STATISTIC	VALUE	RANK	SCORE
Economics	103	49.80	Median Household Income	$34,410	109	15.2
			% of Families Above Poverty Level	96.0%	102	84.4
Affordable Housing	56	75.40	Median Home Value	$115,500	74	82.7
			Median Rent	$514	45	68.1
Crime	73	85.70	Violent Crimes per 10,000 Population	27	86	93.1
			Property Crimes per 10,000 Population	401	70	78.3
Open Spaces	138	10.95	Population Density (Persons/Sq. Mile)	12152	138	0.0
			Average Rooms per Housing Unit	5.1	113	21.9
Education	76	44.90	% High School Enrollment/Completion	93.7%	64	72.5
			% College Graduates	16.9%	88	17.3
Commute	36	34.75	Average Work Commute in Minutes	27	58	31.8
			% Commuting on Public Transportation	10.5%	35	37.7
Community Stability	19	81.95	% Living in Same House as in 1979	47.5%	29	68.9
			% Living in Same County as in 1985	94.8%	19	95.0

Metropolitan Area Suburb Rankings
CHICAGO-GARY-LAKE COUNTY

Composite: Rank 97 / 138 Score 54.62 ADDISON (IL)

CATEGORY	RANK	SCORE	STATISTIC	VALUE	RANK	SCORE
Economics	85	53.90	Median Household Income	$41,375	73	22.2
			% of Families Above Poverty Level	96.3%	95	85.6
Affordable Housing	67	73.20	Median Home Value	$124,700	83	80.7
			Median Rent	$531	54	65.7
Crime	73	85.70	Violent Crimes per 10,000 Population	24	74	94.0
			Property Crimes per 10,000 Population	414	76	77.4
Open Spaces	87	51.45	Population Density (Persons/Sq. Mile)	3717	73	71.6
			Average Rooms per Housing Unit	5.4	90	31.3
Education	104	32.35	% High School Enrollment/Completion	88.2%	106	48.5
			% College Graduates	16.1%	90	16.2
Commute	78	29.30	Average Work Commute in Minutes	23	16	50.0
			% Commuting on Public Transportation	2.7%	119	8.6
Community Stability	87	56.45	% Living in Same House as in 1979	35.4%	81	45.7
			% Living in Same County as in 1985	77.7%	92	67.2

Composite: Rank 98 / 138 Score 54.36 KENOSHA (WI)

CATEGORY	RANK	SCORE	STATISTIC	VALUE	RANK	SCORE
Economics	128	34.30	Median Household Income	$27,770	132	8.5
			% of Families Above Poverty Level	90.1%	128	60.1
Affordable Housing	4	89.60	Median Home Value	$58,000	8	95.1
			Median Rent	$400	5	84.1
Crime	90	80.75	Violent Crimes per 10,000 Population	29	89	92.6
			Property Crimes per 10,000 Population	529	93	68.9
Open Spaces	108	46.70	Population Density (Persons/Sq. Mile)	3730	74	71.5
			Average Rooms per Housing Unit	5.1	113	21.9
Education	107	30.60	% High School Enrollment/Completion	88.6%	104	50.2
			% College Graduates	12.2%	107	11.0
Commute	34	34.95	Average Work Commute in Minutes	20	5	63.6
			% Commuting on Public Transportation	2.1%	127	6.3
Community Stability	71	63.60	% Living in Same House as in 1979	38.4%	69	51.4
			% Living in Same County as in 1985	83.0%	73	75.8

Composite: Rank 99 / 138 Score 54.21 GLENDALE HEIGHTS (IL)

CATEGORY	RANK	SCORE	STATISTIC	VALUE	RANK	SCORE
Economics	64	58.15	Median Household Income	$42,822	65	23.7
			% of Families Above Poverty Level	98.0%	48	92.6
Affordable Housing	81	68.90	Median Home Value	$105,200	66	84.9
			Median Rent	$623	94	52.9
Crime	31	91.60	Violent Crimes per 10,000 Population	16	44	96.3
			Property Crimes per 10,000 Population	284	31	86.9
Open Spaces	111	45.65	Population Density (Persons/Sq. Mile)	5443	120	56.9
			Average Rooms per Housing Unit	5.5	80	34.4
Education	54	54.55	% High School Enrollment/Completion	96.0%	37	82.5
			% College Graduates	23.9%	66	26.6
Commute	114	20.20	Average Work Commute in Minutes	28	82	27.3
			% Commuting on Public Transportation	3.9%	99	13.1
Community Stability	123	40.45	% Living in Same House as in 1979	24.9%	121	25.5
			% Living in Same County as in 1985	70.5%	115	55.4

131

Metropolitan Area Suburb Rankings
CHICAGO-GARY-LAKE COUNTY

Composite: *Rank* 100 / 138 *Score* 54.04   WESTMONT (IL)

CATEGORY	RANK	SCORE	STATISTIC	VALUE	RANK	SCORE
Economics	96	51.25	Median Household Income	$37,315	89	18.1
			% of Families Above Poverty Level	96.0%	102	84.4
Affordable Housing	78	69.90	Median Home Value	$129,200	90	79.8
			Median Rent	$572	74	60.0
Crime	49	89.25	Violent Crimes per 10,000 Population	17	51	96.0
			Property Crimes per 10,000 Population	344	51	82.5
Open Spaces	122	40.55	Population Density (Persons/Sq. Mile)	4803	105	62.4
			Average Rooms per Housing Unit	5.0	123	18.7
Education	41	59.00	% High School Enrollment/Completion	96.5%	26	84.7
			% College Graduates	29.0%	53	33.3
Commute	61	30.80	Average Work Commute in Minutes	28	82	27.3
			% Commuting on Public Transportation	9.6%	43	34.3
Community Stability	126	37.50	% Living in Same House as in 1979	24.0%	125	23.8
			% Living in Same County as in 1985	67.9%	123	51.2

Composite: *Rank* 101 / 138 *Score* 53.85   ALSIP (IL)

CATEGORY	RANK	SCORE	STATISTIC	VALUE	RANK	SCORE
Economics	107	49.30	Median Household Income	$36,764	94	17.5
			% of Families Above Poverty Level	95.2%	107	81.1
Affordable Housing	49	77.60	Median Home Value	$94,500	54	87.2
			Median Rent	$515	46	68.0
Crime	121	66.55	Violent Crimes per 10,000 Population	51	107	86.3
			Property Crimes per 10,000 Population	829	127	46.8
Open Spaces	95	50.25	Population Density (Persons/Sq. Mile)	2889	43	78.6
			Average Rooms per Housing Unit	5.1	113	21.9
Education	94	36.25	% High School Enrollment/Completion	91.0%	91	60.7
			% College Graduates	12.8%	104	11.8
Commute	98	25.70	Average Work Commute in Minutes	29	101	22.7
			% Commuting on Public Transportation	8.1%	53	28.7
Community Stability	53	71.30	% Living in Same House as in 1979	35.7%	79	46.3
			% Living in Same County as in 1985	95.6%	9	96.3

Composite: *Rank* 102 / 138 *Score* 53.59   WEST CHICAGO (IL)

CATEGORY	RANK	SCORE	STATISTIC	VALUE	RANK	SCORE
Economics	106	49.45	Median Household Income	$37,406	88	18.2
			% of Families Above Poverty Level	95.1%	108	80.7
Affordable Housing	62	74.55	Median Home Value	$94,100	52	87.3
			Median Rent	$559	68	61.8
Crime	79	84.85	Violent Crimes per 10,000 Population	18	56	95.7
			Property Crimes per 10,000 Population	459	83	74.0
Open Spaces	61	57.45	Population Density (Persons/Sq. Mile)	1565	12	89.9
			Average Rooms per Housing Unit	5.2	106	25.0
Education	117	25.75	% High School Enrollment/Completion	85.9%	113	38.4
			% College Graduates	13.8%	102	13.1
Commute	46	33.65	Average Work Commute in Minutes	21	6	59.1
			% Commuting on Public Transportation	2.6%	121	8.2
Community Stability	103	49.45	% Living in Same House as in 1979	29.6%	103	34.5
			% Living in Same County as in 1985	76.0%	98	64.4

Metropolitan Area Suburb Rankings
CHICAGO-GARY-LAKE COUNTY

Composite: **Rank** 103 / 138 **Score** 53.49 **SCHERERVILLE (IN)**

CATEGORY	RANK	SCORE	STATISTIC	VALUE	RANK	SCORE
Economics	70	56.60	Median Household Income	$42,658	66	23.5
			% of Families Above Poverty Level	97.3%	73	89.7
Affordable Housing	45	78.30	Median Home Value	$102,300	63	85.6
			Median Rent	$493	32	71.0
Crime	N/A	N/A	Violent Crimes per 10,000 Population	N/A	N/A	N/A
			Property Crimes per 10,000 Population	N/A	N/A	N/A
Open Spaces	43	63.80	Population Density (Persons/Sq. Mile)	1535	11	90.1
			Average Rooms per Housing Unit	5.6	74	37.5
Education	53	54.80	% High School Enrollment/Completion	95.7%	40	81.2
			% College Graduates	25.3%	64	28.4
Commute	122	19.25	Average Work Commute in Minutes	27	58	31.8
			% Commuting on Public Transportation	2.2%	124	6.7
Community Stability	105	48.20	% Living in Same House as in 1979	24.8%	122	25.3
			% Living in Same County as in 1985	80.1%	81	71.1

Composite: **Rank** 104 / 138 **Score** 53.39 **ROMEOVILLE (IL)**

CATEGORY	RANK	SCORE	STATISTIC	VALUE	RANK	SCORE
Economics	80	54.85	Median Household Income	$42,114	69	22.9
			% of Families Above Poverty Level	96.6%	92	86.8
Affordable Housing	109	62.50	Median Home Value	$73,800	30	91.7
			Median Rent	$763	131	33.3
Crime	81	84.25	Violent Crimes per 10,000 Population	22	70	94.6
			Property Crimes per 10,000 Population	461	85	73.9
Open Spaces	29	69.05	Population Density (Persons/Sq. Mile)	1773	16	88.1
			Average Rooms per Housing Unit	6.0	40	50.0
Education	130	18.15	% High School Enrollment/Completion	84.6%	124	32.8
			% College Graduates	6.5%	136	3.5
Commute	128	17.75	Average Work Commute in Minutes	27	58	31.8
			% Commuting on Public Transportation	1.4%	134	3.7
Community Stability	65	67.15	% Living in Same House as in 1979	49.5%	18	72.7
			% Living in Same County as in 1985	74.3%	106	61.6

Composite: **Rank** 105 / 138 **Score** 53.36 **SCHAUMBURG (IL)**

CATEGORY	RANK	SCORE	STATISTIC	VALUE	RANK	SCORE
Economics	52	59.85	Median Household Income	$47,029	45	27.9
			% of Families Above Poverty Level	97.8%	63	91.8
Affordable Housing	121	57.85	Median Home Value	$132,500	93	79.1
			Median Rent	$739	127	36.6
Crime	88	81.70	Violent Crimes per 10,000 Population	25	78	93.7
			Property Crimes per 10,000 Population	518	92	69.7
Open Spaces	84	51.75	Population Density (Persons/Sq. Mile)	3647	66	72.2
			Average Rooms per Housing Unit	5.4	90	31.3
Education	51	56.35	% High School Enrollment/Completion	93.7%	64	72.5
			% College Graduates	34.2%	35	40.2
Commute	112	21.10	Average Work Commute in Minutes	28	82	27.3
			% Commuting on Public Transportation	4.4%	90	14.9
Community Stability	115	44.90	% Living in Same House as in 1979	23.5%	127	22.8
			% Living in Same County as in 1985	77.6%	93	67.0

Composite: *Rank* 106 / 138 *Score* 52.78 **SCHILLER PARK** (IL)

CATEGORY	RANK	SCORE	STATISTIC	VALUE	RANK	SCORE
Economics	102	49.95	Median Household Income	$34,379	110	15.1
			% of Families Above Poverty Level	96.1%	99	84.8
Affordable Housing	53	76.20	Median Home Value	$109,900	71	83.9
			Median Rent	$511	44	68.5
Crime	95	78.75	Violent Crimes per 10,000 Population	36	99	90.6
			Property Crimes per 10,000 Population	556	96	66.9
Open Spaces	127	37.50	Population Density (Persons/Sq. Mile)	4047	81	68.8
			Average Rooms per Housing Unit	4.6	137	6.2
Education	122	21.70	% High School Enrollment/Completion	85.3%	118	35.8
			% College Graduates	9.6%	124	7.6
Commute	22	37.85	Average Work Commute in Minutes	23	16	50.0
			% Commuting on Public Transportation	7.3%	57	25.7
Community Stability	63	67.50	% Living in Same House as in 1979	38.4%	69	51.4
			% Living in Same County as in 1985	87.8%	58	83.6

Composite: *Rank* 107 / 138 *Score* 52.38 **MUNDELEIN** (IL)

CATEGORY	RANK	SCORE	STATISTIC	VALUE	RANK	SCORE
Economics	68	57.45	Median Household Income	$45,947	50	26.8
			% of Families Above Poverty Level	96.9%	84	88.1
Affordable Housing	81	68.90	Median Home Value	$115,900	75	82.6
			Median Rent	$606	86	55.2
Crime	83	83.65	Violent Crimes per 10,000 Population	22	70	94.6
			Property Crimes per 10,000 Population	477	89	72.7
Open Spaces	50	61.45	Population Density (Persons/Sq. Mile)	2818	41	79.2
			Average Rooms per Housing Unit	5.8	56	43.7
Education	108	30.65	% High School Enrollment/Completion	83.0%	129	25.8
			% College Graduates	30.6%	46	35.5
Commute	114	20.20	Average Work Commute in Minutes	27	58	31.8
			% Commuting on Public Transportation	2.7%	119	8.6
Community Stability	118	44.35	% Living in Same House as in 1979	29.8%	101	34.9
			% Living in Same County as in 1985	69.5%	118	53.8

Composite: *Rank* 108 / 138 *Score* 52.37 **MCHENRY** (IL)

CATEGORY	RANK	SCORE	STATISTIC	VALUE	RANK	SCORE
Economics	95	51.40	Median Household Income	$36,838	93	17.6
			% of Families Above Poverty Level	96.2%	96	85.2
Affordable Housing	51	76.70	Median Home Value	$100,100	60	86.0
			Median Rent	$519	47	67.4
Crime	N/A	N/A	Violent Crimes per 10,000 Population	N/A	N/A	N/A
			Property Crimes per 10,000 Population	N/A	N/A	N/A
Open Spaces	40	64.30	Population Density (Persons/Sq. Mile)	1789	17	88.0
			Average Rooms per Housing Unit	5.7	63	40.6
Education	67	48.20	% High School Enrollment/Completion	95.5%	42	80.3
			% College Graduates	16.0%	91	16.1
Commute	122	19.25	Average Work Commute in Minutes	27	58	31.8
			% Commuting on Public Transportation	2.2%	124	6.7
Community Stability	96	54.35	% Living in Same House as in 1979	32.9%	88	40.9
			% Living in Same County as in 1985	78.1%	90	67.8

Metropolitan Area Suburb Rankings
CHICAGO-GARY-LAKE COUNTY

Composite: **Rank** 109 / 138 *Score* 52.26   **STREAMWOOD** (IL)

CATEGORY	RANK	SCORE	STATISTIC	VALUE	RANK	SCORE
Economics	36	61.70	Median Household Income	$48,758	38	29.6
			% of Families Above Poverty Level	98.3%	40	93.8
Affordable Housing	127	50.00	Median Home Value	$107,000	68	84.6
			Median Rent	$891	136	15.4
Crime	37	91.40	Violent Crimes per 10,000 Population	13	35	97.1
			Property Crimes per 10,000 Population	301	37	85.7
Open Spaces	63	57.15	Population Density (Persons/Sq. Mile)	4571	98	64.3
			Average Rooms per Housing Unit	6.0	40	50.0
Education	89	38.75	% High School Enrollment/Completion	90.0%	96	56.3
			% College Graduates	19.9%	77	21.2
Commute	135	11.65	Average Work Commute in Minutes	31	121	13.6
			% Commuting on Public Transportation	3.0%	114	9.7
Community Stability	90	55.15	% Living in Same House as in 1979	30.9%	94	37.0
			% Living in Same County as in 1985	81.5%	76	73.3

Composite: **Rank** 110 / 138 *Score* 52.18   **GOODINGS GROVE** (IL)

CATEGORY	RANK	SCORE	STATISTIC	VALUE	RANK	SCORE
Economics	18	65.35	Median Household Income	$57,098	16	38.1
			% of Families Above Poverty Level	98.0%	48	92.6
Affordable Housing	128	48.85	Median Home Value	$161,200	117	72.9
			Median Rent	$824	134	24.8
Crime	N/A	N/A	Violent Crimes per 10,000 Population	N/A	N/A	N/A
			Property Crimes per 10,000 Population	N/A	N/A	N/A
Open Spaces	1	95.25	Population Density (Persons/Sq. Mile)	1492	10	90.5
			Average Rooms per Housing Unit	7.6	1	100.0
Education	35	60.75	% High School Enrollment/Completion	97.8%	15	90.4
			% College Graduates	27.3%	60	31.1
Commute	138	7.10	Average Work Commute in Minutes	34	136	0.0
			% Commuting on Public Transportation	4.2%	95	14.2
Community Stability	128	35.80	% Living in Same House as in 1979	28.9%	104	33.2
			% Living in Same County as in 1985	60.0%	134	38.4

Composite: **Rank** 111 / 138 *Score* 52.15   **CALUMET CITY** (IL)

CATEGORY	RANK	SCORE	STATISTIC	VALUE	RANK	SCORE
Economics	125	39.75	Median Household Income	$30,138	128	10.8
			% of Families Above Poverty Level	92.2%	123	68.7
Affordable Housing	14	84.90	Median Home Value	$63,500	14	93.9
			Median Rent	$458	19	75.9
Crime	124	63.35	Violent Crimes per 10,000 Population	74	116	79.7
			Property Crimes per 10,000 Population	826	126	47.0
Open Spaces	128	37.30	Population Density (Persons/Sq. Mile)	5206	115	59.0
			Average Rooms per Housing Unit	4.9	131	15.6
Education	99	33.80	% High School Enrollment/Completion	90.6%	92	59.0
			% College Graduates	10.4%	119	8.6
Commute	64	30.55	Average Work Commute in Minutes	29	101	22.7
			% Commuting on Public Transportation	10.7%	31	38.4
Community Stability	41	75.40	% Living in Same House as in 1979	41.8%	54	58.0
			% Living in Same County as in 1985	93.5%	25	92.8

Metropolitan Area Suburb Rankings
CHICAGO-GARY-LAKE COUNTY

Composite: **Rank** 112 / 138 *Score* 52.07   **BLUE ISLAND** (IL)

CATEGORY	RANK	SCORE	STATISTIC	VALUE	RANK	SCORE
Economics	123	40.75	Median Household Income	$29,234	129	9.9
			% of Families Above Poverty Level	92.9%	121	71.6
Affordable Housing	12	86.60	Median Home Value	$64,100	17	93.8
			Median Rent	$433	11	79.4
Crime	115	69.20	Violent Crimes per 10,000 Population	71	115	80.6
			Property Crimes per 10,000 Population	679	113	57.8
Open Spaces	125	38.65	Population Density (Persons/Sq. Mile)	5254	116	58.6
			Average Rooms per Housing Unit	5.0	123	18.7
Education	134	16.30	% High School Enrollment/Completion	82.6%	130	24.0
			% College Graduates	10.4%	119	8.6
Commute	20	38.85	Average Work Commute in Minutes	28	82	27.3
			% Commuting on Public Transportation	13.9%	18	50.4
Community Stability	45	74.15	% Living in Same House as in 1979	40.7%	63	55.9
			% Living in Same County as in 1985	93.2%	28	92.4

Composite: **Rank** 113 / 138 *Score* 52.03   **VERNON HILLS** (IL)

CATEGORY	RANK	SCORE	STATISTIC	VALUE	RANK	SCORE
Economics	37	61.60	Median Household Income	$48,873	36	29.8
			% of Families Above Poverty Level	98.2%	45	93.4
Affordable Housing	119	58.75	Median Home Value	$141,200	104	77.2
			Median Rent	$713	122	40.3
Crime	93	80.15	Violent Crimes per 10,000 Population	16	44	96.3
			Property Crimes per 10,000 Population	595	103	64.0
Open Spaces	45	62.40	Population Density (Persons/Sq. Mile)	2228	25	84.2
			Average Rooms per Housing Unit	5.7	63	40.6
Education	28	62.45	% High School Enrollment/Completion	94.3%	61	75.1
			% College Graduates	41.4%	21	49.8
Commute	122	19.25	Average Work Commute in Minutes	28	82	27.3
			% Commuting on Public Transportation	3.4%	106	11.2
Community Stability	137	19.60	% Living in Same House as in 1979	12.7%	137	2.1
			% Living in Same County as in 1985	59.2%	135	37.1

Composite: **Rank** 114 / 138 *Score* 51.71   **CHICAGO HEIGHTS** (IL)

CATEGORY	RANK	SCORE	STATISTIC	VALUE	RANK	SCORE
Economics	136	19.35	Median Household Income	$27,551	133	8.2
			% of Families Above Poverty Level	82.9%	136	30.5
Affordable Housing	5	89.05	Median Home Value	$61,600	10	94.3
			Median Rent	$402	6	83.8
Crime	127	53.20	Violent Crimes per 10,000 Population	179	129	49.7
			Property Crimes per 10,000 Population	694	116	56.7
Open Spaces	83	51.70	Population Density (Persons/Sq. Mile)	3662	68	72.1
			Average Rooms per Housing Unit	5.4	90	31.3
Education	116	25.85	% High School Enrollment/Completion	86.6%	112	41.5
			% College Graduates	11.6%	110	10.2
Commute	17	39.95	Average Work Commute in Minutes	23	16	50.0
			% Commuting on Public Transportation	8.4%	51	29.9
Community Stability	15	82.85	% Living in Same House as in 1979	49.5%	18	72.7
			% Living in Same County as in 1985	93.6%	24	93.0

Metropolitan Area Suburb Rankings
CHICAGO-GARY-LAKE COUNTY

Composite: *Rank* 115 / 138 *Score* 51.60   **JOLIET** (IL)

CATEGORY	RANK	SCORE	STATISTIC	VALUE	RANK	SCORE
Economics	126	36.50	Median Household Income	$30,967	123	11.7
			% of Families Above Poverty Level	90.4%	126	61.3
Affordable Housing	6	88.70	Median Home Value	$63,900	16	93.8
			Median Rent	$403	7	83.6
Crime	125	56.50	Violent Crimes per 10,000 Population	119	127	66.9
			Property Crimes per 10,000 Population	838	128	46.1
Open Spaces	79	52.35	Population Density (Persons/Sq. Mile)	2762	40	79.7
			Average Rooms per Housing Unit	5.2	106	25.0
Education	118	25.00	% High School Enrollment/Completion	85.3%	118	35.8
			% College Graduates	14.6%	100	14.2
Commute	56	32.10	Average Work Commute in Minutes	22	8	54.5
			% Commuting on Public Transportation	3.0%	114	9.7
Community Stability	58	70.05	% Living in Same House as in 1979	42.1%	51	58.5
			% Living in Same County as in 1985	86.6%	61	81.6

Composite: *Rank* 116 / 138 *Score* 51.41   **FOREST PARK** (IL)

CATEGORY	RANK	SCORE	STATISTIC	VALUE	RANK	SCORE
Economics	110	48.05	Median Household Income	$30,572	127	11.3
			% of Families Above Poverty Level	96.1%	99	84.8
Affordable Housing	42	78.55	Median Home Value	$92,400	48	87.7
			Median Rent	$505	39	69.4
Crime	123	64.15	Violent Crimes per 10,000 Population	74	116	79.7
			Property Crimes per 10,000 Population	804	124	48.6
Open Spaces	133	25.40	Population Density (Persons/Sq. Mile)	6173	127	50.8
			Average Rooms per Housing Unit	4.4	138	0.0
Education	95	35.75	% High School Enrollment/Completion	85.4%	117	36.2
			% College Graduates	30.5%	47	35.3
Commute	4	53.60	Average Work Commute in Minutes	27	58	31.8
			% Commuting on Public Transportation	20.6%	6	75.4
Community Stability	94	54.35	% Living in Same House as in 1979	27.4%	115	30.3
			% Living in Same County as in 1985	84.6%	71	78.4

Composite: *Rank* 117 / 138 *Score* 51.36   **HANOVER PARK** (IL)

CATEGORY	RANK	SCORE	STATISTIC	VALUE	RANK	SCORE
Economics	60	58.65	Median Household Income	$44,237	59	25.1
			% of Families Above Poverty Level	97.9%	57	92.2
Affordable Housing	72	71.40	Median Home Value	$101,600	62	85.7
			Median Rent	$593	82	57.1
Crime	71	86.10	Violent Crimes per 10,000 Population	32	95	91.7
			Property Crimes per 10,000 Population	371	62	80.5
Open Spaces	77	53.50	Population Density (Persons/Sq. Mile)	5434	119	57.0
			Average Rooms per Housing Unit	6.0	40	50.0
Education	112	28.40	% High School Enrollment/Completion	85.5%	115	36.7
			% College Graduates	19.0%	80	20.1
Commute	132	16.20	Average Work Commute in Minutes	30	113	18.2
			% Commuting on Public Transportation	4.2%	95	14.2
Community Stability	113	45.25	% Living in Same House as in 1979	28.3%	111	32.1
			% Living in Same County as in 1985	72.3%	110	58.4

Composite: *Rank* 118 / 138 *Score* 51.33   **LAKE STATION (IN)**

CATEGORY	RANK	SCORE	STATISTIC	VALUE	RANK	SCORE
Economics	127	35.10	Median Household Income	$28,642	131	9.3
			% of Families Above Poverty Level	90.3%	127	60.9
Affordable Housing	3	92.10	Median Home Value	$35,200	1	100.0
			Median Rent	$399	4	84.2
Crime	N/A	N/A	Violent Crimes per 10,000 Population	N/A	N/A	N/A
			Property Crimes per 10,000 Population	N/A	N/A	N/A
Open Spaces	68	55.45	Population Density (Persons/Sq. Mile)	1665	13	89.0
			Average Rooms per Housing Unit	5.1	113	21.9
Education	120	23.80	% High School Enrollment/Completion	88.0%	107	47.6
			% College Graduates	3.9%	138	0.0
Commute	88	28.00	Average Work Commute in Minutes	22	8	54.5
			% Commuting on Public Transportation	0.8%	136	1.5
Community Stability	46	73.55	% Living in Same House as in 1979	46.2%	36	66.4
			% Living in Same County as in 1985	86.0%	65	80.7

Composite: *Rank* 119 / 138 *Score* 51.24   **CAROL STREAM (IL)**

CATEGORY	RANK	SCORE	STATISTIC	VALUE	RANK	SCORE
Economics	66	57.85	Median Household Income	$45,141	54	26.0
			% of Families Above Poverty Level	97.3%	73	89.7
Affordable Housing	89	66.80	Median Home Value	$126,900	87	80.3
			Median Rent	$620	91	53.3
Crime	63	87.20	Violent Crimes per 10,000 Population	21	68	94.9
			Property Crimes per 10,000 Population	385	68	79.5
Open Spaces	73	54.60	Population Density (Persons/Sq. Mile)	4074	84	68.6
			Average Rooms per Housing Unit	5.7	63	40.6
Education	62	51.50	% High School Enrollment/Completion	92.1%	79	65.5
			% College Graduates	32.1%	44	37.5
Commute	127	17.85	Average Work Commute in Minutes	30	113	18.2
			% Commuting on Public Transportation	5.1%	77	17.5
Community Stability	136	22.85	% Living in Same House as in 1979	11.6%	138	0.0
			% Living in Same County as in 1985	64.5%	130	45.7

Composite: *Rank* 120 / 138 *Score* 51.00   **PROSPECT HEIGHTS (IL)**

CATEGORY	RANK	SCORE	STATISTIC	VALUE	RANK	SCORE
Economics	67	57.50	Median Household Income	$41,573	71	22.4
			% of Families Above Poverty Level	98.0%	48	92.6
Affordable Housing	91	66.55	Median Home Value	$166,700	122	71.7
			Median Rent	$562	71	61.4
Crime	68	86.70	Violent Crimes per 10,000 Population	29	89	92.6
			Property Crimes per 10,000 Population	367	60	80.8
Open Spaces	100	48.85	Population Density (Persons/Sq. Mile)	3582	64	72.7
			Average Rooms per Housing Unit	5.2	106	25.0
Education	114	26.70	% High School Enrollment/Completion	81.8%	132	20.5
			% College Graduates	28.7%	55	32.9
Commute	97	25.85	Average Work Commute in Minutes	25	35	40.9
			% Commuting on Public Transportation	3.3%	108	10.8
Community Stability	116	44.85	% Living in Same House as in 1979	21.8%	130	19.6
			% Living in Same County as in 1985	79.5%	83	70.1

Composite: **Rank** 121 / 138 *Score* 50.26   **HAMMOND (IN)**

CATEGORY	RANK	SCORE	STATISTIC	VALUE	RANK	SCORE
Economics	134	29.95	Median Household Income	$26,883	135	7.6
			% of Families Above Poverty Level	88.2%	132	52.3
Affordable Housing	2	92.65	Median Home Value	$44,600	3	98.0
			Median Rent	$377	2	87.3
Crime	126	55.40	Violent Crimes per 10,000 Population	135	128	62.3
			Property Crimes per 10,000 Population	805	125	48.5
Open Spaces	107	46.95	Population Density (Persons/Sq. Mile)	3671	69	72.0
			Average Rooms per Housing Unit	5.1	113	21.9
Education	133	16.60	% High School Enrollment/Completion	83.1%	128	26.2
			% College Graduates	9.2%	126	7.0
Commute	32	35.10	Average Work Commute in Minutes	22	8	54.5
			% Commuting on Public Transportation	4.6%	85	15.7
Community Stability	42	75.20	% Living in Same House as in 1979	47.5%	29	68.9
			% Living in Same County as in 1985	86.5%	62	81.5

Composite: **Rank** 122 / 138 *Score* 50.23   **BELLWOOD (IL)**

CATEGORY	RANK	SCORE	STATISTIC	VALUE	RANK	SCORE
Economics	90	52.70	Median Household Income	$39,396	81	20.2
			% of Families Above Poverty Level	96.2%	96	85.2
Affordable Housing	39	78.95	Median Home Value	$73,600	29	91.7
			Median Rent	$528	51	66.2
Crime	N/A	N/A	Violent Crimes per 10,000 Population	N/A	N/A	N/A
			Property Crimes per 10,000 Population	N/A	N/A	N/A
Open Spaces	131	29.65	Population Density (Persons/Sq. Mile)	8480	132	31.2
			Average Rooms per Housing Unit	5.3	98	28.1
Education	99	33.80	% High School Enrollment/Completion	90.2%	94	57.2
			% College Graduates	11.7%	108	10.4
Commute	72	30.25	Average Work Commute in Minutes	27	58	31.8
			% Commuting on Public Transportation	8.1%	53	28.7
Community Stability	40	76.05	% Living in Same House as in 1979	41.6%	57	57.6
			% Living in Same County as in 1985	94.5%	21	94.5

Composite: **Rank** 123 / 138 *Score* 49.94   **WAUKEGAN (IL)**

CATEGORY	RANK	SCORE	STATISTIC	VALUE	RANK	SCORE
Economics	119	43.05	Median Household Income	$31,315	120	12.0
			% of Families Above Poverty Level	93.5%	119	74.1
Affordable Housing	28	81.80	Median Home Value	$72,000	25	92.1
			Median Rent	$490	31	71.5
Crime	113	70.15	Violent Crimes per 10,000 Population	75	118	79.4
			Property Crimes per 10,000 Population	637	110	60.9
Open Spaces	104	47.65	Population Density (Persons/Sq. Mile)	3131	51	76.6
			Average Rooms per Housing Unit	5.0	123	18.7
Education	123	21.60	% High School Enrollment/Completion	83.9%	127	29.7
			% College Graduates	14.1%	101	13.5
Commute	74	30.05	Average Work Commute in Minutes	23	16	50.0
			% Commuting on Public Transportation	3.1%	112	10.1
Community Stability	89	55.25	% Living in Same House as in 1979	32.6%	89	40.3
			% Living in Same County as in 1985	79.6%	82	70.2

Composite: **Rank** 124 / 138 *Score* 49.79   **RIVERDALE** (IL)

CATEGORY	RANK	SCORE	STATISTIC	VALUE	RANK	SCORE
Economics	133	30.60	Median Household Income	$29,092	130	9.8
			% of Families Above Poverty Level	88.0%	133	51.4
Affordable Housing	19	83.35	Median Home Value	$55,400	7	95.7
			Median Rent	$493	32	71.0
Crime	114	69.40	Violent Crimes per 10,000 Population	88	125	75.7
			Property Crimes per 10,000 Population	608	106	63.1
Open Spaces	117	43.30	Population Density (Persons/Sq. Mile)	3782	76	71.0
			Average Rooms per Housing Unit	4.9	131	15.6
Education	138	4.65	% High School Enrollment/Completion	77.1%	138	0.0
			% College Graduates	10.9%	115	9.3
Commute	13	42.35	Average Work Commute in Minutes	33	134	4.5
			% Commuting on Public Transportation	21.9%	4	80.2
Community Stability	43	74.85	% Living in Same House as in 1979	40.9%	62	56.2
			% Living in Same County as in 1985	93.9%	22	93.5

Composite: **Rank** 125 / 138 *Score* 49.57   **ELGIN** (IL)

CATEGORY	RANK	SCORE	STATISTIC	VALUE	RANK	SCORE
Economics	113	46.40	Median Household Income	$35,554	104	16.3
			% of Families Above Poverty Level	94.1%	116	76.5
Affordable Housing	44	78.40	Median Home Value	$96,300	56	86.9
			Median Rent	$501	37	69.9
Crime	105	75.30	Violent Crimes per 10,000 Population	58	110	84.3
			Property Crimes per 10,000 Population	564	98	66.3
Open Spaces	92	50.75	Population Density (Persons/Sq. Mile)	3510	62	73.4
			Average Rooms per Housing Unit	5.3	98	28.1
Education	127	19.40	% High School Enrollment/Completion	81.6%	133	19.7
			% College Graduates	18.3%	84	19.1
Commute	67	30.40	Average Work Commute in Minutes	23	16	50.0
			% Commuting on Public Transportation	3.3%	108	10.8
Community Stability	109	46.35	% Living in Same House as in 1979	30.0%	99	35.3
			% Living in Same County as in 1985	71.7%	111	57.4

Composite: **Rank** 126 / 138 *Score* 49.44   **CARPENTERSVILLE** (IL)

CATEGORY	RANK	SCORE	STATISTIC	VALUE	RANK	SCORE
Economics	124	40.70	Median Household Income	$36,410	100	17.2
			% of Families Above Poverty Level	91.1%	125	64.2
Affordable Housing	48	77.70	Median Home Value	$79,400	36	90.5
			Median Rent	$537	58	64.9
Crime	89	81.05	Violent Crimes per 10,000 Population	42	104	88.9
			Property Crimes per 10,000 Population	470	87	73.2
Open Spaces	80	52.25	Population Density (Persons/Sq. Mile)	4263	89	67.0
			Average Rooms per Housing Unit	5.6	74	37.5
Education	132	16.70	% High School Enrollment/Completion	84.0%	126	30.1
			% College Graduates	6.4%	137	3.3
Commute	125	18.15	Average Work Commute in Minutes	27	58	31.8
			% Commuting on Public Transportation	1.6%	132	4.5
Community Stability	80	59.50	% Living in Same House as in 1979	41.1%	61	56.6
			% Living in Same County as in 1985	74.8%	104	62.4

Metropolitan Area Suburb Rankings
CHICAGO-GARY-LAKE COUNTY

Composite: **Rank** 127 / 138 *Score* 49.36   **JUSTICE** (IL)

CATEGORY	RANK	SCORE	STATISTIC	VALUE	RANK	SCORE
Economics	100	50.35	Median Household Income	$33,562	113	14.3
			% of Families Above Poverty Level	96.5%	93	86.4
Affordable Housing	55	75.95	Median Home Value	$91,100	46	88.0
			Median Rent	$544	60	63.9
Crime	61	87.85	Violent Crimes per 10,000 Population	30	92	92.3
			Property Crimes per 10,000 Population	332	48	83.4
Open Spaces	115	44.40	Population Density (Persons/Sq. Mile)	3888	77	70.1
			Average Rooms per Housing Unit	5.0	123	18.7
Education	135	14.50	% High School Enrollment/Completion	81.4%	135	18.8
			% College Graduates	11.6%	110	10.2
Commute	125	18.15	Average Work Commute in Minutes	28	82	27.3
			% Commuting on Public Transportation	2.8%	118	9.0
Community Stability	95	54.30	% Living in Same House as in 1979	24.2%	124	24.2
			% Living in Same County as in 1985	88.3%	55	84.4

Composite: **Rank** 128 / 138 *Score* 48.87   **AURORA** (IL)

CATEGORY	RANK	SCORE	STATISTIC	VALUE	RANK	SCORE
Economics	122	41.65	Median Household Income	$35,039	107	15.8
			% of Families Above Poverty Level	91.9%	124	67.5
Affordable Housing	34	80.15	Median Home Value	$81,400	37	90.1
			Median Rent	$499	35	70.2
Crime	119	68.75	Violent Crimes per 10,000 Population	90	126	75.1
			Property Crimes per 10,000 Population	617	107	62.4
Open Spaces	78	53.00	Population Density (Persons/Sq. Mile)	2973	45	77.9
			Average Rooms per Housing Unit	5.3	98	28.1
Education	131	16.75	% High School Enrollment/Completion	80.3%	136	14.0
			% College Graduates	18.6%	83	19.5
Commute	61	30.80	Average Work Commute in Minutes	23	16	50.0
			% Commuting on Public Transportation	3.5%	105	11.6
Community Stability	99	51.00	% Living in Same House as in 1979	30.1%	98	35.5
			% Living in Same County as in 1985	77.3%	95	66.5

Composite: **Rank** 129 / 138 *Score* 48.69   **BENSENVILLE** (IL)

CATEGORY	RANK	SCORE	STATISTIC	VALUE	RANK	SCORE
Economics	91	52.55	Median Household Income	$36,649	96	17.4
			% of Families Above Poverty Level	96.8%	87	87.7
Affordable Housing	80	69.20	Median Home Value	$107,000	68	84.6
			Median Rent	$616	90	53.8
Crime	112	72.60	Violent Crimes per 10,000 Population	37	100	90.3
			Property Crimes per 10,000 Population	719	120	54.9
Open Spaces	110	46.35	Population Density (Persons/Sq. Mile)	3067	48	77.1
			Average Rooms per Housing Unit	4.9	131	15.6
Education	126	19.70	% High School Enrollment/Completion	82.5%	131	23.6
			% College Graduates	15.8%	93	15.8
Commute	38	34.50	Average Work Commute in Minutes	23	16	50.0
			% Commuting on Public Transportation	5.5%	72	19.0
Community Stability	111	45.90	% Living in Same House as in 1979	32.4%	90	39.9
			% Living in Same County as in 1985	68.3%	122	51.9

Composite: *Rank* 130 / 138 *Score* 48.21 **ROUND LAKE BEACH** (IL)

CATEGORY	RANK	SCORE	STATISTIC	VALUE	RANK	SCORE
Economics	114	46.35	Median Household Income	$36,616	98	17.4
			% of Families Above Poverty Level	93.8%	118	75.3
Affordable Housing	63	74.25	Median Home Value	$73,900	31	91.7
			Median Rent	$595	83	56.8
Crime	72	85.85	Violent Crimes per 10,000 Population	25	78	93.7
			Property Crimes per 10,000 Population	405	74	78.0
Open Spaces	75	54.15	Population Density (Persons/Sq. Mile)	4171	87	67.7
			Average Rooms per Housing Unit	5.7	63	40.6
Education	128	19.45	% High School Enrollment/Completion	84.7%	123	33.2
			% College Graduates	8.2%	130	5.7
Commute	137	7.55	Average Work Commute in Minutes	32	126	9.1
			% Commuting on Public Transportation	2.0%	129	6.0
Community Stability	102	49.85	% Living in Same House as in 1979	28.5%	109	32.4
			% Living in Same County as in 1985	77.8%	91	67.3

Composite: *Rank* 131 / 138 *Score* 48.16 **CHICAGO RIDGE** (IL)

CATEGORY	RANK	SCORE	STATISTIC	VALUE	RANK	SCORE
Economics	120	42.75	Median Household Income	$32,790	115	13.5
			% of Families Above Poverty Level	93.0%	120	72.0
Affordable Housing	47	77.90	Median Home Value	$88,800	42	88.5
			Median Rent	$520	48	67.3
Crime	110	73.20	Violent Crimes per 10,000 Population	33	96	91.4
			Property Crimes per 10,000 Population	717	118	55.0
Open Spaces	130	30.25	Population Density (Persons/Sq. Mile)	6135	124	51.1
			Average Rooms per Housing Unit	4.7	135	9.4
Education	110	29.45	% High School Enrollment/Completion	88.7%	103	50.7
			% College Graduates	10.1%	123	8.2
Commute	109	22.15	Average Work Commute in Minutes	29	101	22.7
			% Commuting on Public Transportation	6.2%	69	21.6
Community Stability	75	61.45	% Living in Same House as in 1979	28.8%	105	33.0
			% Living in Same County as in 1985	91.7%	39	89.9

Composite: *Rank* 132 / 138 *Score* 48.03 **MAYWOOD** (IL)

CATEGORY	RANK	SCORE	STATISTIC	VALUE	RANK	SCORE
Economics	130	32.70	Median Household Income	$30,780	126	11.5
			% of Families Above Poverty Level	88.6%	131	53.9
Affordable Housing	21	82.70	Median Home Value	$67,800	21	93.0
			Median Rent	$483	28	72.4
Crime	130	34.20	Violent Crimes per 10,000 Population	253	131	28.6
			Property Crimes per 10,000 Population	923	129	39.8
Open Spaces	132	27.70	Population Density (Persons/Sq. Mile)	10043	134	17.9
			Average Rooms per Housing Unit	5.6	74	37.5
Education	105	31.95	% High School Enrollment/Completion	89.8%	97	55.5
			% College Graduates	10.2%	121	8.4
Commute	11	43.95	Average Work Commute in Minutes	25	35	40.9
			% Commuting on Public Transportation	13.0%	20	47.0
Community Stability	14	83.00	% Living in Same House as in 1979	48.3%	24	70.4
			% Living in Same County as in 1985	95.2%	13	95.6

Metropolitan Area Suburb Rankings
CHICAGO-GARY-LAKE COUNTY

Composite: *Rank* 133 / 138 *Score* 47.80 **MELROSE PARK** (IL)

CATEGORY	RANK	SCORE	STATISTIC	VALUE	RANK	SCORE
Economics	117	45.25	Median Household Income	$30,814	124	11.5
			% of Families Above Poverty Level	94.7%	111	79.0
Affordable Housing	30	81.40	Median Home Value	$99,400	59	86.2
			Median Rent	$453	17	76.6
Crime	129	49.85	Violent Crimes per 10,000 Population	79	122	78.3
			Property Crimes per 10,000 Population	1,173	130	21.4
Open Spaces	126	38.40	Population Density (Persons/Sq. Mile)	4938	110	61.2
			Average Rooms per Housing Unit	4.9	131	15.6
Education	136	12.90	% High School Enrollment/Completion	81.5%	134	19.2
			% College Graduates	8.9%	127	6.6
Commute	39	34.55	Average Work Commute in Minutes	22	8	54.5
			% Commuting on Public Transportation	4.3%	94	14.6
Community Stability	49	72.25	% Living in Same House as in 1979	41.7%	56	57.8
			% Living in Same County as in 1985	89.7%	50	86.7

Composite: *Rank* 134 / 138 *Score* 47.71 **ZION** (IL)

CATEGORY	RANK	SCORE	STATISTIC	VALUE	RANK	SCORE
Economics	129	34.15	Median Household Income	$31,159	122	11.9
			% of Families Above Poverty Level	89.2%	129	56.4
Affordable Housing	25	82.45	Median Home Value	$67,800	21	93.0
			Median Rent	$487	30	71.9
Crime	116	69.10	Violent Crimes per 10,000 Population	76	120	79.1
			Property Crimes per 10,000 Population	661	112	59.1
Open Spaces	86	51.50	Population Density (Persons/Sq. Mile)	2594	35	81.1
			Average Rooms per Housing Unit	5.1	113	21.9
Education	121	21.95	% High School Enrollment/Completion	85.1%	121	34.9
			% College Graduates	10.7%	117	9.0
Commute	105	22.85	Average Work Commute in Minutes	26	48	36.4
			% Commuting on Public Transportation	2.9%	116	9.3
Community Stability	98	52.00	% Living in Same House as in 1979	29.8%	101	34.9
			% Living in Same County as in 1985	78.9%	85	69.1

Composite: *Rank* 135 / 138 *Score* 46.99 **CICERO** (IL)

CATEGORY	RANK	SCORE	STATISTIC	VALUE	RANK	SCORE
Economics	131	31.30	Median Household Income	$27,170	134	7.9
			% of Families Above Poverty Level	88.8%	130	54.7
Affordable Housing	9	86.90	Median Home Value	$73,500	28	91.8
			Median Rent	$415	8	82.0
Crime	86	82.10	Violent Crimes per 10,000 Population	86	124	76.3
			Property Crimes per 10,000 Population	271	24	87.9
Open Spaces	137	12.00	Population Density (Persons/Sq. Mile)	11531	136	5.3
			Average Rooms per Housing Unit	5.0	123	18.7
Education	137	9.10	% High School Enrollment/Completion	80.3%	136	14.0
			% College Graduates	7.1%	133	4.2
Commute	24	37.15	Average Work Commute in Minutes	28	82	27.3
			% Commuting on Public Transportation	13.0%	20	47.0
Community Stability	56	70.40	% Living in Same House as in 1979	39.3%	66	53.2
			% Living in Same County as in 1985	90.3%	46	87.6

Composite: *Rank* 136 / 138 *Score* 46.66   **NORTH CHICAGO** (IL)

CATEGORY	RANK	SCORE	STATISTIC	VALUE	RANK	SCORE
Economics	135	28.00	Median Household Income	$25,500	136	6.2
			% of Families Above Poverty Level	87.6%	134	49.8
Affordable Housing	20	83.05	Median Home Value	$63,400	13	93.9
			Median Rent	$485	29	72.2
Crime	116	69.10	Violent Crimes per 10,000 Population	68	113	81.4
			Property Crimes per 10,000 Population	693	115	56.8
Open Spaces	121	40.95	Population Density (Persons/Sq. Mile)	4711	104	63.2
			Average Rooms per Housing Unit	5.0	123	18.7
Education	96	35.40	% High School Enrollment/Completion	91.4%	87	62.4
			% College Graduates	10.2%	121	8.4
Commute	3	55.20	Average Work Commute in Minutes	12	1	100.0
			% Commuting on Public Transportation	3.2%	111	10.4
Community Stability	138	14.90	% Living in Same House as in 1979	27.1%	116	29.8
			% Living in Same County as in 1985	36.4%	138	0.0

Composite: *Rank* 137 / 138 *Score* 45.77   **EAST CHICAGO** (IN)

CATEGORY	RANK	SCORE	STATISTIC	VALUE	RANK	SCORE
Economics	138	0.00	Median Household Income	$19,391	138	0.0
			% of Families Above Poverty Level	75.5%	138	0.0
Affordable Housing	1	99.30	Median Home Value	$41,800	2	98.6
			Median Rent	$286	1	100.0
Crime	131	32.20	Violent Crimes per 10,000 Population	353	132	0.0
			Property Crimes per 10,000 Population	590	101	64.4
Open Spaces	99	48.90	Population Density (Persons/Sq. Mile)	2830	42	79.1
			Average Rooms per Housing Unit	5.0	123	18.7
Education	129	19.25	% High School Enrollment/Completion	85.1%	121	34.9
			% College Graduates	6.6%	135	3.6
Commute	15	41.55	Average Work Commute in Minutes	19	2	68.2
			% Commuting on Public Transportation	4.4%	90	14.9
Community Stability	29	79.20	% Living in Same House as in 1979	46.2%	36	66.4
			% Living in Same County as in 1985	93.0%	29	92.0

Composite: *Rank* 138 / 138 *Score* 40.70   **HARVEY** (IL)

CATEGORY	RANK	SCORE	STATISTIC	VALUE	RANK	SCORE
Economics	137	4.80	Median Household Income	$23,201	137	3.8
			% of Families Above Poverty Level	76.9%	137	5.8
Affordable Housing	11	86.70	Median Home Value	$50,300	4	96.8
			Median Rent	$453	17	76.6
Crime	132	15.70	Violent Crimes per 10,000 Population	243	130	31.4
			Property Crimes per 10,000 Population	1,463	132	0.0
Open Spaces	120	42.15	Population Density (Persons/Sq. Mile)	4805	106	62.4
			Average Rooms per Housing Unit	5.1	113	21.9
Education	124	21.05	% High School Enrollment/Completion	85.5%	115	36.7
			% College Graduates	8.0%	131	5.4
Commute	21	38.40	Average Work Commute in Minutes	29	101	22.7
			% Commuting on Public Transportation	14.9%	14	54.1
Community Stability	39	76.10	% Living in Same House as in 1979	42.2%	50	58.7
			% Living in Same County as in 1985	93.9%	22	93.5

Metropolitan Area Description
CINCINNATI-HAMILTON

STATE: Kentucky
COUNTIES: Boone, Campbell, Kenton

STATE: Indiana
COUNTIES: Dearborn

STATE: Ohio
COUNTIES: Butler, Clermont, Hamilton, Warren

TOTAL POPULATION: 1,744,124

POPULATION IN SUBURBS: 1,318,716 (75.6%)

POPULATION IN Cincinnati (OH): 364,040 (20.9%)
POPULATION IN Hamilton (OH): 61,368 (3.5%)

The CINCINNATI-HAMILTON metropolitan area is located in the southwestern part of Ohio, the southeastern part of Indiana, and the northcentral part of Kentucky. The suburbs range geographically from Middletown (OH) in the north (35 miles from Cincinnati), to Bridgetown North (OH) in the west (11 miles from Cincinnati), to Independence (KY) in the south (19 miles from Cincinnati), and to Blue Ash (OH) in the east (9 miles from Cincinnati). The area is growing in population and had an increase of 5.1% between 1980 and 1990. Summer time high temperatures average in the 80's and winter time lows average in the 20's. The area is dominated by manufacturing giants including General Electric and Proctor and Gamble. Armco Steel, the state's sixth largest commercial employer, is located in the suburb of Middletown (OH). Public transportation in the area is provided by Queen City Metro buses.

Fort Thomas (KY) is the overall highest rated suburb and is also the safest suburb with the lowest crime rate. **Blue Ash** (OH) receives the highest scores in economics and open spaces. **Covington** (KY) is the suburb with the most affordable housing. The number one rating in education goes to **Oxford** (OH). The top rated commute belongs to **Newport** (KY). Finally, the suburb with the highest rating in community stability is **Bridgetown North** (OH).

The highest ranked suburb overall which also has an affordable housing score of at least 50.00 is **Bridgetown North** (OH).

The highest ranked suburb in the education category which also has an affordable housing score of at least 50.00 is also **Bridgetown North** (OH).

The county whose suburbs have the highest average overall score is **Hamilton County** (OH) (56.40).

Metropolitan Area Map
CINCINNATI–HAMILTON

Ohio

Indiana

Kentucky

Butler Co.

HAMILTON

Warren Co.

Clermont Co.

Campbell Co.

Hamilton Co.

CINCINNATI

Kenton Co.

Boone Co.

Dearborn Co.

-10

-14

-19

-5

-12

-13

-1

-21

-8 -22

-20

-17

-23 -16 -6

-2

-18

-15

-9

-3

-11

-7

-4

Metropolitan Area Suburb Alphabetical Index
CINCINNATI-HAMILTON

SUBURB	PAGE	MAP NO.	STATE	COUNTY	POPU-LATION	RANK
BLUE ASH	149	1	Ohio	Hamilton	11,860	4 / 23
BRIDGETOWN NORTH	148	2	Ohio	Hamilton	11,748	3 / 23
COVINGTON	155	3	Kentucky	Kenton	43,264	22 / 23
ERLANGER	150	4	Kentucky	Kenton	15,979	7 / 23
FAIRFIELD	153	5	Ohio	Butler	39,729	18 / 23
FINNEYTOWN	148	6	Ohio	Hamilton	13,096	2 / 23
FLORENCE	153	7	Kentucky	Boone	18,624	16 / 23
FOREST PARK	151	8	Ohio	Hamilton	18,609	11 / 23
FORT THOMAS	148	9	Kentucky	Campbell	16,032	1 / 23
FRANKLIN	152	10	Ohio	Warren	11,026	13 / 23
INDEPENDENCE	149	11	Kentucky	Kenton	10,444	5 / 23
LEBANON	152	12	Ohio	Warren	10,453	15 / 23
MASON	150	13	Ohio	Warren	11,452	8 / 23
MIDDLETOWN	153	14	Ohio	Butler	46,022	17 / 23
NEWPORT	155	15	Kentucky	Campbell	18,871	23 / 23
NORTH COLLEGE HILL	152	16	Ohio	Hamilton	11,002	14 / 23
NORTHBROOK	154	17	Ohio	Hamilton	11,471	20 / 23
NORWOOD	154	18	Ohio	Hamilton	23,674	19 / 23
OXFORD	154	19	Ohio	Butler	18,937	21 / 23
READING	149	20	Ohio	Hamilton	12,038	6 / 23
SHARONVILLE	151	21	Ohio	Hamilton	13,153	10 / 23
SPRINGDALE	151	22	Ohio	Hamilton	10,621	12 / 23
WHITE OAK	150	23	Ohio	Hamilton	12,430	9 / 23

Metropolitan Area Suburb Rankings
CINCINNATI-HAMILTON

Composite: Rank 1 / 23 *Score* 70.12   **FORT THOMAS (KY)**

CATEGORY	RANK	SCORE	STATISTIC	VALUE	RANK	SCORE
Economics	7	79.80	Median Household Income	$36,977	8	67.1
			% of Families Above Poverty Level	97.1%	5	92.5
Affordable Housing	16	45.30	Median Home Value	$80,000	18	34.0
			Median Rent	$426	13	56.6
Crime	1	99.75	Violent Crimes per 10,000 Population	9	2	99.5
			Property Crimes per 10,000 Population	126	1	100.0
Open Spaces	8	68.50	Population Density (Persons/Sq. Mile)	2839	12	68.6
			Average Rooms per Housing Unit	5.9	5	68.4
Education	4	66.15	% High School Enrollment/Completion	94.9%	7	82.7
			% College Graduates	30.1%	4	49.6
Commute	5	54.00	Average Work Commute in Minutes	20	11	45.5
			% Commuting on Public Transportation	5.1%	3	62.5
Community Stability	7	77.35	% Living in Same House as in 1979	44.0%	6	71.9
			% Living in Same County as in 1985	84.6%	8	82.8

Composite: Rank 2 / 23 *Score* 66.42   **FINNEYTOWN (OH)**

CATEGORY	RANK	SCORE	STATISTIC	VALUE	RANK	SCORE
Economics	3	85.30	Median Household Income	$40,114	2	78.1
			% of Families Above Poverty Level	97.1%	5	92.5
Affordable Housing	18	36.90	Median Home Value	$74,000	17	43.3
			Median Rent	$499	18	30.5
Crime	N/A	N/A	Violent Crimes per 10,000 Population	N/A	N/A	N/A
			Property Crimes per 10,000 Population	N/A	N/A	N/A
Open Spaces	3	81.15	Population Density (Persons/Sq. Mile)	3282	16	62.3
			Average Rooms per Housing Unit	6.5	1	100.0
Education	2	72.95	% High School Enrollment/Completion	96.6%	3	90.2
			% College Graduates	33.0%	3	55.7
Commute	17	27.40	Average Work Commute in Minutes	22	17	27.3
			% Commuting on Public Transportation	2.3%	10	27.5
Community Stability	2	94.85	% Living in Same House as in 1979	54.1%	1	100.0
			% Living in Same County as in 1985	88.8%	6	89.7

Composite: Rank 3 / 23 *Score* 65.72   **BRIDGETOWN NORTH (OH)**

CATEGORY	RANK	SCORE	STATISTIC	VALUE	RANK	SCORE
Economics	5	81.15	Median Household Income	$35,620	10	62.3
			% of Families Above Poverty Level	98.8%	1	100.0
Affordable Housing	12	55.05	Median Home Value	$68,800	12	51.3
			Median Rent	$420	12	58.8
Crime	N/A	N/A	Violent Crimes per 10,000 Population	N/A	N/A	N/A
			Property Crimes per 10,000 Population	N/A	N/A	N/A
Open Spaces	12	63.85	Population Density (Persons/Sq. Mile)	3493	17	59.3
			Average Rooms per Housing Unit	5.9	5	68.4
Education	7	58.40	% High School Enrollment/Completion	98.8%	1	100.0
			% College Graduates	14.5%	14	16.8
Commute	10	36.60	Average Work Commute in Minutes	23	18	18.2
			% Commuting on Public Transportation	4.5%	5	55.0
Community Stability	1	99.30	% Living in Same House as in 1979	53.6%	2	98.6
			% Living in Same County as in 1985	95.1%	1	100.0

Metropolitan Area Suburb Rankings
CINCINNATI-HAMILTON

Composite: Rank 4 / 23 *Score* 61.84   **BLUE ASH (OH)**

CATEGORY	RANK	SCORE	STATISTIC	VALUE	RANK	SCORE
Economics	1	96.70	Median Household Income	$46,339	1	100.0
			% of Families Above Poverty Level	97.3%	3	93.4
Affordable Housing	23	0.00	Median Home Value	$101,900	23	0.0
			Median Rent	$584	23	0.0
Crime	5	75.10	Violent Crimes per 10,000 Population	13	3	97.6
			Property Crimes per 10,000 Population	468	7	52.6
Open Spaces	1	88.25	Population Density (Persons/Sq. Mile)	1550	6	87.0
			Average Rooms per Housing Unit	6.3	2	89.5
Education	3	72.10	% High School Enrollment/Completion	92.9%	9	73.8
			% College Graduates	40.0%	2	70.4
Commute	8	39.90	Average Work Commute in Minutes	18	2	63.6
			% Commuting on Public Transportation	1.4%	14	16.2
Community Stability	14	60.85	% Living in Same House as in 1979	34.6%	15	45.8
			% Living in Same County as in 1985	80.4%	14	75.9

Composite: Rank 5 / 23 *Score* 61.04   **INDEPENDENCE (KY)**

CATEGORY	RANK	SCORE	STATISTIC	VALUE	RANK	SCORE
Economics	10	72.70	Median Household Income	$35,951	9	63.5
			% of Families Above Poverty Level	94.7%	14	81.9
Affordable Housing	13	54.85	Median Home Value	$64,200	9	58.4
			Median Rent	$441	14	51.3
Crime	2	94.40	Violent Crimes per 10,000 Population	8	1	100.0
			Property Crimes per 10,000 Population	207	2	88.8
Open Spaces	4	78.95	Population Density (Persons/Sq. Mile)	637	1	100.0
			Average Rooms per Housing Unit	5.7	7	57.9
Education	12	46.05	% High School Enrollment/Completion	93.9%	8	78.2
			% College Graduates	13.1%	16	13.9
Commute	22	15.60	Average Work Commute in Minutes	25	22	0.0
			% Commuting on Public Transportation	2.6%	9	31.2
Community Stability	12	64.75	% Living in Same House as in 1979	35.8%	13	49.2
			% Living in Same County as in 1985	83.1%	10	80.3

Composite: Rank 6 / 23 *Score* 58.95   **READING (OH)**

CATEGORY	RANK	SCORE	STATISTIC	VALUE	RANK	SCORE
Economics	13	64.95	Median Household Income	$29,647	15	41.4
			% of Families Above Poverty Level	96.2%	10	88.5
Affordable Housing	6	67.25	Median Home Value	$66,700	11	54.6
			Median Rent	$361	4	79.9
Crime	3	85.45	Violent Crimes per 10,000 Population	15	4	96.6
			Property Crimes per 10,000 Population	311	3	74.3
Open Spaces	18	38.30	Population Density (Persons/Sq. Mile)	4121	18	50.3
			Average Rooms per Housing Unit	5.1	19	26.3
Education	16	34.30	% High School Enrollment/Completion	87.9%	17	51.6
			% College Graduates	14.6%	13	17.0
Commute	9	39.30	Average Work Commute in Minutes	18	2	63.6
			% Commuting on Public Transportation	1.3%	15	15.0
Community Stability	5	83.10	% Living in Same House as in 1979	45.0%	5	74.7
			% Living in Same County as in 1985	89.9%	4	91.5

Metropolitan Area Suburb Rankings
CINCINNATI-HAMILTON

Composite: **Rank** 7 / 23 *Score* 58.26   **ERLANGER (KY)**

CATEGORY	RANK	SCORE	STATISTIC	VALUE	RANK	SCORE
Economics	12	70.60	Median Household Income	$33,502	11	54.9
			% of Families Above Poverty Level	95.7%	11	86.3
Affordable Housing	7	63.45	Median Home Value	$64,000	8	58.8
			Median Rent	$394	7	68.1
Crime	8	65.30	Violent Crimes per 10,000 Population	80	14	64.9
			Property Crimes per 10,000 Population	373	5	65.7
Open Spaces	11	64.50	Population Density (Persons/Sq. Mile)	1925	8	81.6
			Average Rooms per Housing Unit	5.5	12	47.4
Education	13	42.40	% High School Enrollment/Completion	90.8%	14	64.4
			% College Graduates	16.2%	11	20.4
Commute	6	40.85	Average Work Commute in Minutes	20	11	45.5
			% Commuting on Public Transportation	3.0%	8	36.2
Community Stability	15	60.70	% Living in Same House as in 1979	36.9%	10	52.2
			% Living in Same County as in 1985	76.3%	18	69.2

Composite: **Rank** 8 / 23 *Score* 58.06   **MASON (OH)**

CATEGORY	RANK	SCORE	STATISTIC	VALUE	RANK	SCORE
Economics	2	87.30	Median Household Income	$39,738	3	76.8
			% of Families Above Poverty Level	98.3%	2	97.8
Affordable Housing	17	38.55	Median Home Value	$82,000	19	30.9
			Median Rent	$455	15	46.2
Crime	4	78.25	Violent Crimes per 10,000 Population	29	9	89.8
			Property Crimes per 10,000 Population	366	4	66.7
Open Spaces	2	84.70	Population Density (Persons/Sq. Mile)	938	2	95.7
			Average Rooms per Housing Unit	6.0	3	73.7
Education	11	47.40	% High School Enrollment/Completion	91.1%	13	65.8
			% College Graduates	20.3%	9	29.0
Commute	21	18.80	Average Work Commute in Minutes	21	15	36.4
			% Commuting on Public Transportation	0.2%	21	1.2
Community Stability	19	51.45	% Living in Same House as in 1979	33.0%	16	41.4
			% Living in Same County as in 1985	71.6%	20	61.5

Composite: **Rank** 9 / 23 *Score* 57.93   **WHITE OAK (OH)**

CATEGORY	RANK	SCORE	STATISTIC	VALUE	RANK	SCORE
Economics	11	72.25	Median Household Income	$33,305	12	54.2
			% of Families Above Poverty Level	96.6%	9	90.3
Affordable Housing	9	58.10	Median Home Value	$70,900	15	48.1
			Median Rent	$394	7	68.1
Crime	N/A	N/A	Violent Crimes per 10,000 Population	N/A	N/A	N/A
			Property Crimes per 10,000 Population	N/A	N/A	N/A
Open Spaces	14	61.85	Population Density (Persons/Sq. Mile)	3035	14	65.8
			Average Rooms per Housing Unit	5.7	7	57.9
Education	10	54.35	% High School Enrollment/Completion	95.0%	6	83.1
			% College Graduates	18.7%	10	25.6
Commute	20	20.35	Average Work Commute in Minutes	23	18	18.2
			% Commuting on Public Transportation	1.9%	13	22.5
Community Stability	6	80.70	% Living in Same House as in 1979	42.7%	7	68.3
			% Living in Same County as in 1985	90.9%	3	93.1

Metropolitan Area Suburb Rankings
CINCINNATI-HAMILTON

Composite: *Rank* 10 / 23 *Score* 55.89   **SHARONVILLE** (OH)

CATEGORY	RANK	SCORE	STATISTIC	VALUE	RANK	SCORE
Economics	8	79.15	Median Household Income	$37,128	6	67.6
			% of Families Above Poverty Level	96.7%	7	90.7
Affordable Housing	20	33.95	Median Home Value	$84,200	20	27.4
			Median Rent	$471	17	40.5
Crime	11	60.50	Violent Crimes per 10,000 Population	23	5	92.7
			Property Crimes per 10,000 Population	643	13	28.3
Open Spaces	7	68.65	Population Density (Persons/Sq. Mile)	1342	4	89.9
			Average Rooms per Housing Unit	5.5	12	47.4
Education	5	62.35	% High School Enrollment/Completion	96.5%	4	89.8
			% College Graduates	23.1%	8	34.9
Commute	12	34.90	Average Work Commute in Minutes	18	2	63.6
			% Commuting on Public Transportation	0.6%	19	6.2
Community Stability	18	51.70	% Living in Same House as in 1979	31.9%	19	38.3
			% Living in Same County as in 1985	73.8%	19	65.1

Composite: *Rank* 11 / 23 *Score* 53.86   **FOREST PARK** (OH)

CATEGORY	RANK	SCORE	STATISTIC	VALUE	RANK	SCORE
Economics	9	76.45	Median Household Income	$37,050	7	67.4
			% of Families Above Poverty Level	95.5%	12	85.5
Affordable Housing	19	34.40	Median Home Value	$65,400	10	56.6
			Median Rent	$550	21	12.2
Crime	14	43.40	Violent Crimes per 10,000 Population	35	10	86.8
			Property Crimes per 10,000 Population	847	16	0.0
Open Spaces	5	70.45	Population Density (Persons/Sq. Mile)	2937	13	67.2
			Average Rooms per Housing Unit	6.0	3	73.7
Education	9	54.30	% High School Enrollment/Completion	92.4%	11	71.6
			% College Graduates	24.1%	6	37.0
Commute	14	32.20	Average Work Commute in Minutes	23	18	18.2
			% Commuting on Public Transportation	3.8%	6	46.2
Community Stability	11	65.85	% Living in Same House as in 1979	36.7%	11	51.7
			% Living in Same County as in 1985	82.9%	11	80.0

Composite: *Rank* 12 / 23 *Score* 53.48   **SPRINGDALE** (OH)

CATEGORY	RANK	SCORE	STATISTIC	VALUE	RANK	SCORE
Economics	6	80.95	Median Household Income	$38,128	5	71.2
			% of Families Above Poverty Level	96.7%	7	90.7
Affordable Housing	21	27.35	Median Home Value	$72,900	16	45.0
			Median Rent	$557	22	9.7
Crime	N/A	N/A	Violent Crimes per 10,000 Population	N/A	N/A	N/A
			Property Crimes per 10,000 Population	N/A	N/A	N/A
Open Spaces	9	68.10	Population Density (Persons/Sq. Mile)	2156	9	78.3
			Average Rooms per Housing Unit	5.7	7	57.9
Education	6	59.35	% High School Enrollment/Completion	95.1%	5	83.6
			% College Graduates	23.2%	7	35.1
Commute	16	29.60	Average Work Commute in Minutes	20	11	45.5
			% Commuting on Public Transportation	1.2%	16	13.7
Community Stability	17	55.50	% Living in Same House as in 1979	32.6%	17	40.3
			% Living in Same County as in 1985	77.2%	17	70.7

Metropolitan Area Suburb Rankings
CINCINNATI-HAMILTON

Composite: Rank 13 / 23 *Score* 51.84   **FRANKLIN (OH)**

CATEGORY	RANK	SCORE	STATISTIC	VALUE	RANK	SCORE
Economics	20	33.10	Median Household Income	$25,569	19	27.0
			% of Families Above Poverty Level	85.0%	21	39.2
Affordable Housing	4	75.85	Median Home Value	$55,600	6	71.8
			Median Rent	$361	4	79.9
Crime	10	61.85	Violent Crimes per 10,000 Population	26	7	91.2
			Property Crimes per 10,000 Population	613	12	32.5
Open Spaces	10	65.95	Population Density (Persons/Sq. Mile)	1354	5	89.8
			Average Rooms per Housing Unit	5.4	14	42.1
Education	18	26.65	% High School Enrollment/Completion	88.3%	16	53.3
			% College Graduates	6.5%	23	0.0
Commute	13	32.40	Average Work Commute in Minutes	18	2	63.6
			% Commuting on Public Transportation	0.2%	21	1.2
Community Stability	10	67.05	% Living in Same House as in 1979	39.6%	8	59.7
			% Living in Same County as in 1985	79.5%	16	74.4

Composite: Rank 14 / 23 *Score* 51.41   **NORTH COLLEGE HILL (OH)**

CATEGORY	RANK	SCORE	STATISTIC	VALUE	RANK	SCORE
Economics	14	61.20	Median Household Income	$28,631	16	37.8
			% of Families Above Poverty Level	95.3%	13	84.6
Affordable Housing	8	60.25	Median Home Value	$53,800	5	74.6
			Median Rent	$456	16	45.9
Crime	N/A	N/A	Violent Crimes per 10,000 Population	N/A	N/A	N/A
			Property Crimes per 10,000 Population	N/A	N/A	N/A
Open Spaces	20	30.25	Population Density (Persons/Sq. Mile)	5988	21	23.7
			Average Rooms per Housing Unit	5.3	16	36.8
Education	15	41.15	% High School Enrollment/Completion	92.5%	10	72.0
			% College Graduates	11.4%	18	10.3
Commute	15	29.70	Average Work Commute in Minutes	23	18	18.2
			% Commuting on Public Transportation	3.4%	7	41.2
Community Stability	4	85.90	% Living in Same House as in 1979	45.6%	4	76.4
			% Living in Same County as in 1985	92.3%	2	95.4

Composite: Rank 15 / 23 *Score* 51.28   **LEBANON (OH)**

CATEGORY	RANK	SCORE	STATISTIC	VALUE	RANK	SCORE
Economics	17	53.20	Median Household Income	$27,095	17	32.4
			% of Families Above Poverty Level	92.9%	15	74.0
Affordable Housing	11	56.30	Median Home Value	$69,500	14	50.2
			Median Rent	$410	10	62.4
Crime	6	71.15	Violent Crimes per 10,000 Population	43	13	82.9
			Property Crimes per 10,000 Population	419	6	59.4
Open Spaces	13	62.30	Population Density (Persons/Sq. Mile)	1127	3	93.0
			Average Rooms per Housing Unit	5.2	18	31.6
Education	14	41.45	% High School Enrollment/Completion	90.4%	15	62.7
			% College Graduates	16.1%	12	20.2
Commute	18	27.25	Average Work Commute in Minutes	19	8	54.5
			% Commuting on Public Transportation	0.1%	23	0.0
Community Stability	20	47.30	% Living in Same House as in 1979	25.3%	22	20.0
			% Living in Same County as in 1985	79.6%	15	74.6

Metropolitan Area Suburb Rankings
CINCINNATI-HAMILTON

Composite: Rank 16 / 23 *Score* 50.76   **FLORENCE (KY)**

CATEGORY	RANK	SCORE	STATISTIC	VALUE	RANK	SCORE
Economics	16	58.55	Median Household Income	$31,270	14	47.1
			% of Families Above Poverty Level	92.0%	17	70.0
Affordable Housing	10	56.35	Median Home Value	$69,200	13	50.7
			Median Rent	$411	11	62.0
Crime	9	62.95	Violent Crimes per 10,000 Population	26	7	91.2
			Property Crimes per 10,000 Population	597	11	34.7
Open Spaces	15	59.55	Population Density (Persons/Sq. Mile)	2247	10	77.0
			Average Rooms per Housing Unit	5.4	14	42.1
Education	17	33.00	% High School Enrollment/Completion	87.5%	18	49.8
			% College Graduates	14.2%	15	16.2
Commute	7	40.35	Average Work Commute in Minutes	19	8	54.5
			% Commuting on Public Transportation	2.2%	11	26.2
Community Stability	21	44.55	% Living in Same House as in 1979	31.1%	20	36.1
			% Living in Same County as in 1985	66.4%	22	53.0

Composite: Rank 17 / 23 *Score* 50.51   **MIDDLETOWN (OH)**

CATEGORY	RANK	SCORE	STATISTIC	VALUE	RANK	SCORE
Economics	18	37.55	Median Household Income	$25,714	18	27.5
			% of Families Above Poverty Level	86.9%	20	47.6
Affordable Housing	5	72.35	Median Home Value	$56,700	7	70.1
			Median Rent	$376	6	74.6
Crime	13	60.10	Violent Crimes per 10,000 Population	40	11	84.4
			Property Crimes per 10,000 Population	589	10	35.8
Open Spaces	16	56.70	Population Density (Persons/Sq. Mile)	2279	11	76.6
			Average Rooms per Housing Unit	5.3	16	36.8
Education	19	23.50	% High School Enrollment/Completion	83.9%	20	33.8
			% College Graduates	12.8%	17	13.2
Commute	11	36.20	Average Work Commute in Minutes	18	2	63.6
			% Commuting on Public Transportation	0.8%	18	8.8
Community Stability	9	67.20	% Living in Same House as in 1979	37.1%	9	52.8
			% Living in Same County as in 1985	83.9%	9	81.6

Composite: Rank 18 / 23 *Score* 50.35   **FAIRFIELD (OH)**

CATEGORY	RANK	SCORE	STATISTIC	VALUE	RANK	SCORE
Economics	4	83.00	Median Household Income	$38,531	4	72.6
			% of Families Above Poverty Level	97.3%	3	93.4
Affordable Housing	22	25.25	Median Home Value	$86,700	22	23.6
			Median Rent	$509	19	26.9
Crime	12	60.15	Violent Crimes per 10,000 Population	40	11	84.4
			Property Crimes per 10,000 Population	588	9	35.9
Open Spaces	6	69.90	Population Density (Persons/Sq. Mile)	1906	7	81.9
			Average Rooms per Housing Unit	5.7	7	57.9
Education	8	56.20	% High School Enrollment/Completion	92.4%	11	71.6
			% College Graduates	25.9%	5	40.8
Commute	19	20.70	Average Work Commute in Minutes	21	15	36.4
			% Commuting on Public Transportation	0.5%	20	5.0
Community Stability	22	37.25	% Living in Same House as in 1979	25.7%	21	21.1
			% Living in Same County as in 1985	66.7%	21	53.4

Metropolitan Area Suburb Rankings
CINCINNATI-HAMILTON

Composite: Rank 19 / 23 *Score* 49.57   NORWOOD (OH)

CATEGORY	RANK	SCORE	STATISTIC	VALUE	RANK	SCORE
Economics	18	37.55	Median Household Income	$22,191	20	15.2
			% of Families Above Poverty Level	89.7%	19	59.9
Affordable Housing	3	86.70	Median Home Value	$51,500	3	78.1
			Median Rent	$318	2	95.3
Crime	7	70.25	Violent Crimes per 10,000 Population	25	6	91.7
			Property Crimes per 10,000 Population	495	8	48.8
Open Spaces	22	10.55	Population Density (Persons/Sq. Mile)	7646	23	0.0
			Average Rooms per Housing Unit	5.0	20	21.1
Education	22	12.20	% High School Enrollment/Completion	80.9%	22	20.4
			% College Graduates	8.4%	21	4.0
Commute	3	59.90	Average Work Commute in Minutes	18	2	63.6
			% Commuting on Public Transportation	4.6%	4	56.2
Community Stability	8	69.85	% Living in Same House as in 1979	35.9%	12	49.4
			% Living in Same County as in 1985	89.2%	5	90.3

Composite: Rank 20 / 23 *Score* 45.38   NORTHBROOK (OH)

CATEGORY	RANK	SCORE	STATISTIC	VALUE	RANK	SCORE
Economics	15	59.85	Median Household Income	$31,393	13	47.5
			% of Families Above Poverty Level	92.5%	16	72.2
Affordable Housing	14	49.80	Median Home Value	$51,500	3	78.1
			Median Rent	$524	20	21.5
Crime	N/A	N/A	Violent Crimes per 10,000 Population	N/A	N/A	N/A
			Property Crimes per 10,000 Population	N/A	N/A	N/A
Open Spaces	17	41.30	Population Density (Persons/Sq. Mile)	5918	20	24.7
			Average Rooms per Housing Unit	5.7	7	57.9
Education	20	21.25	% High School Enrollment/Completion	84.2%	19	35.1
			% College Graduates	10.0%	19	7.4
Commute	23	12.50	Average Work Commute in Minutes	25	22	0.0
			% Commuting on Public Transportation	2.1%	12	25.0
Community Stability	3	87.55	% Living in Same House as in 1979	49.1%	3	86.1
			% Living in Same County as in 1985	88.4%	7	89.0

Composite: Rank 21 / 23 *Score* 43.73   OXFORD (OH)

CATEGORY	RANK	SCORE	STATISTIC	VALUE	RANK	SCORE
Economics	21	31.05	Median Household Income	$17,872	23	0.0
			% of Families Above Poverty Level	90.2%	18	62.1
Affordable Housing	15	46.70	Median Home Value	$85,100	21	26.0
			Median Rent	$396	9	67.4
Crime	N/A	N/A	Violent Crimes per 10,000 Population	N/A	N/A	N/A
			Property Crimes per 10,000 Population	N/A	N/A	N/A
Open Spaces	21	29.00	Population Density (Persons/Sq. Mile)	4319	19	47.5
			Average Rooms per Housing Unit	4.8	21	10.5
Education	1	100.00	% High School Enrollment/Completion	98.8%	1	100.0
			% College Graduates	54.1%	1	100.0
Commute	4	55.60	Average Work Commute in Minutes	14	1	100.0
			% Commuting on Public Transportation	1.0%	17	11.2
Community Stability	23	0.00	% Living in Same House as in 1979	18.1%	23	0.0
			% Living in Same County as in 1985	34.1%	23	0.0

Metropolitan Area Suburb Rankings
CINCINNATI-HAMILTON

Composite: **Rank** 22 / 23 *Score* 40.90   **COVINGTON (KY)**

CATEGORY	RANK	SCORE	STATISTIC	VALUE	RANK	SCORE
Economics	22	19.15	Median Household Income	$21,003	21	11.0
			% of Families Above Poverty Level	82.3%	22	27.3
Affordable Housing	1	97.05	Median Home Value	$41,200	2	94.1
			Median Rent	$305	1	100.0
Crime	16	1.75	Violent Crimes per 10,000 Population	213	16	0.0
			Property Crimes per 10,000 Population	822	15	3.5
Open Spaces	19	33.85	Population Density (Persons/Sq. Mile)	3270	15	62.4
			Average Rooms per Housing Unit	4.7	22	5.3
Education	23	3.45	% High School Enrollment/Completion	76.3%	23	0.0
			% College Graduates	9.8%	20	6.9
Commute	2	68.40	Average Work Commute in Minutes	20	11	45.5
			% Commuting on Public Transportation	7.4%	2	91.3
Community Stability	13	62.65	% Living in Same House as in 1979	35.3%	14	47.8
			% Living in Same County as in 1985	81.4%	13	77.5

Composite: **Rank** 23 / 23 *Score* 40.09   **NEWPORT (KY)**

CATEGORY	RANK	SCORE	STATISTIC	VALUE	RANK	SCORE
Economics	23	1.40	Median Household Income	$18,683	22	2.8
			% of Families Above Poverty Level	76.1%	23	0.0
Affordable Housing	2	95.50	Median Home Value	$37,400	1	100.0
			Median Rent	$330	3	91.0
Crime	15	29.15	Violent Crimes per 10,000 Population	125	15	42.9
			Property Crimes per 10,000 Population	736	14	15.4
Open Spaces	23	5.30	Population Density (Persons/Sq. Mile)	6900	22	10.6
			Average Rooms per Housing Unit	4.6	23	0.0
Education	21	12.50	% High School Enrollment/Completion	81.2%	21	21.8
			% College Graduates	8.0%	22	3.2
Commute	1	77.25	Average Work Commute in Minutes	19	8	54.5
			% Commuting on Public Transportation	8.1%	1	100.0
Community Stability	16	59.50	% Living in Same House as in 1979	32.6%	17	40.3
			% Living in Same County as in 1985	82.1%	12	78.7

Metropolitan Area Description
CLEVELAND-AKRON-LORAIN

STATE: Ohio
COUNTIES: Cuyahoga, Geauga, Lake, Lorain, Medina, Portage, Summit

TOTAL POPULATION:	2,759,823	
POPULATION IN SUBURBS:	1,959,943	(71.0%)
POPULATION IN Cleveland:	505,616	(18.3%)
POPULATION IN Akron:	223,019	(8.1%)
POPULATION IN Lorain:	71,245	(2.6%)

The CLEVELAND-AKRON-LORAIN metropolitan area is located in the northeastern part of Ohio along Lake Erie. The suburbs range geographically from Vermilion in the west (37 miles from Cleveland), to Portage Lakes in the south (44 miles from Cleveland), and to Painesville in the east (33 miles from Cleveland). The area is shrinking in population and had a decrease of 2.6% between 1980 and 1990. Summer time high temperatures average in the 80's and winter time lows average in the teens. Major employers in the area tend to be heavy manufacturers. They include industrial equipment giant Figgie International in Willoughby and chemical manufacturer Lubrizol in Wickliffe. Public transportation in the area is provided by the Greater Cleveland Regional Transit Authority using buses and a rapid transit train service.

Seven Hills is the overall highest rated suburb and also has the highest score in community stability. **Beachwood** receives the highest score in economics. **Barberton** is the suburb with the most affordable housing. The number one score in education goes to **University Heights. Bay Village** is the safest suburb with the lowest crime rate. The top score in open spaces goes to **Solon**. Finally, the top rated commute belongs to **Kent**.

The highest ranked suburb overall which also has an affordable housing score of at least 50.00 is **Seven Hills.**

The highest ranked suburb in the education category which also has an affordable housing score of at least 50.00 is **University Heights**.

The county whose suburbs have the highest average overall score is **Cuyahoga County** (59.20).

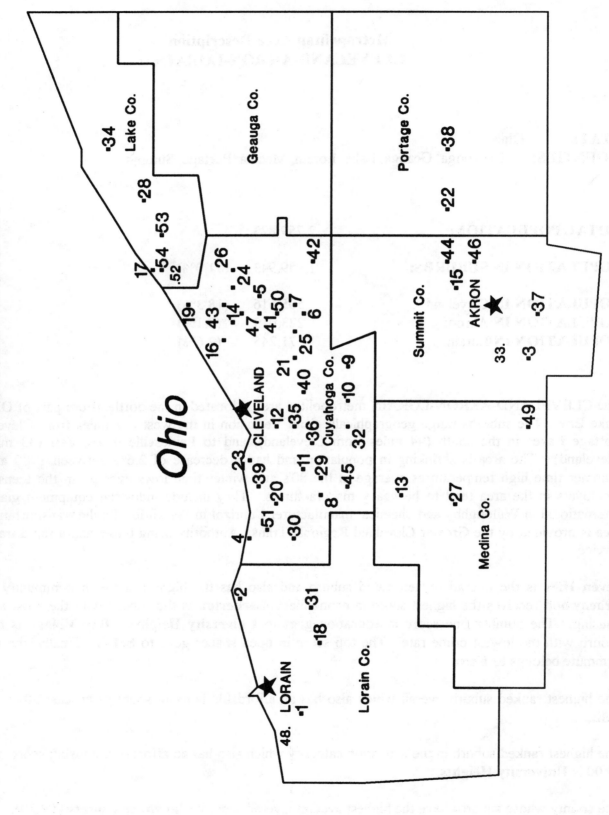

Metropolitan Area Map
CLEVELAND–AKRON–LORAIN

Ohio

Metropolitan Area Suburb Alphabetical Index
CLEVELAND-AKRON-LORAIN

SUBURB	PAGE	MAP NO.	STATE	COUNTY	POPU-LATION	RANK
AMHERST	163	1	Ohio	Lorain	10,332	7 / 54
AVON LAKE	172	2	Ohio	Lorain	15,066	35 / 54
BARBERTON	176	3	Ohio	Summit	27,623	46 / 54
BAY VILLAGE	161	4	Ohio	Cuyahoga	17,000	2 / 54
BEACHWOOD	171	5	Ohio	Cuyahoga	10,677	33 / 54
BEDFORD	172	6	Ohio	Cuyahoga	14,822	36 / 54
BEDFORD HEIGHTS	177	7	Ohio	Cuyahoga	12,131	50 / 54
BEREA	165	8	Ohio	Cuyahoga	19,051	15 / 54
BRECKSVILLE	162	9	Ohio	Cuyahoga	11,818	4 / 54
BROADVIEW HEIGHTS	168	10	Ohio	Cuyahoga	12,219	24 / 54
BROOK PARK	166	11	Ohio	Cuyahoga	22,865	17 / 54
BROOKLYN	173	12	Ohio	Cuyahoga	11,706	39 / 54
BRUNSWICK	175	13	Ohio	Medina	28,230	44 / 54
CLEVELAND HEIGHTS	166	14	Ohio	Cuyahoga	54,052	16 / 54
CUYAHOGA FALLS	171	15	Ohio	Summit	48,950	31 / 54
EAST CLEVELAND	178	16	Ohio	Cuyahoga	33,096	54 / 54
EASTLAKE	170	17	Ohio	Lake	21,161	29 / 54
ELYRIA	176	18	Ohio	Lorain	56,746	48 / 54
EUCLID	175	19	Ohio	Cuyahoga	54,875	45 / 54
FAIRVIEW PARK	164	20	Ohio	Cuyahoga	18,028	11 / 54
GARFIELD HEIGHTS	168	21	Ohio	Cuyahoga	31,739	23 / 54
KENT	177	22	Ohio	Portage	28,835	49 / 54
LAKEWOOD	174	23	Ohio	Cuyahoga	59,718	42 / 54
LYNDHURST	161	24	Ohio	Cuyahoga	15,982	3 / 54
MAPLE HEIGHTS	169	25	Ohio	Cuyahoga	27,089	27 / 54
MAYFIELD HEIGHTS	173	26	Ohio	Cuyahoga	19,847	37 / 54
MEDINA	178	27	Ohio	Medina	19,231	52 / 54
MENTOR	170	28	Ohio	Lake	47,358	28 / 54
MIDDLEBURG HEIGHTS	170	29	Ohio	Cuyahoga	14,702	30 / 54
NORTH OLMSTED	165	30	Ohio	Cuyahoga	34,204	14 / 54
NORTH RIDGEVILLE	174	31	Ohio	Lorain	21,564	41 / 54
NORTH ROYALTON	169	32	Ohio	Cuyahoga	23,197	26 / 54
NORTON	167	33	Ohio	Summit	11,477	19 / 54
PAINESVILLE	178	34	Ohio	Lake	15,699	53 / 54
PARMA	168	35	Ohio	Cuyahoga	87,876	22 / 54
PARMA HEIGHTS	176	36	Ohio	Cuyahoga	21,448	47 / 54
PORTAGE LAKES	171	37	Ohio	Summit	13,373	32 / 54
RAVENNA	175	38	Ohio	Portage	12,069	43 / 54
ROCKY RIVER	167	39	Ohio	Cuyahoga	20,410	20 / 54
SEVEN HILLS	161	40	Ohio	Cuyahoga	12,339	1 / 54
SHAKER HEIGHTS	166	41	Ohio	Cuyahoga	30,831	18 / 54
SOLON	164	42	Ohio	Cuyahoga	18,548	12 / 54
SOUTH EUCLID	163	43	Ohio	Cuyahoga	23,866	8 / 54
STOW	169	44	Ohio	Summit	27,702	25 / 54
STRONGSVILLE	165	45	Ohio	Cuyahoga	35,308	12 / 54
TALLMADGE	163	46	Ohio	Summit	14,870	9 / 54
UNIVERSITY HEIGHTS	162	47	Ohio	Cuyahoga	14,790	6 / 54
VERMILION	172	48	Ohio	Lorain	11,127	34 / 54
WADSWORTH	167	49	Ohio	Medina	15,718	20 / 54
WARRENSVILLE HEIGHTS	177	50	Ohio	Cuyahoga	15,745	51 / 54
WESTLAKE	164	51	Ohio	Cuyahoga	27,018	10 / 54

Metropolitan Area Suburb Alphabetical Index
CLEVELAND-AKRON-LORAIN

SUBURB	PAGE	MAP NO.	STATE	COUNTY	POPU-LATION	RANK
WICKLIFFE	162	52	Ohio	Lake	14,558	5 / 54
WILLOUGHBY	174	53	Ohio	Lake	20,510	40 / 54
WILLOWICK	173	54	Ohio	Lake	15,269	38 / 54

Metropolitan Area Suburb Rankings
CLEVELAND-AKRON-LORAIN

Composite: **Rank** 1 / 54 **Score** 70.12   **SEVEN HILLS**

CATEGORY	RANK	SCORE	STATISTIC	VALUE	RANK	SCORE
Economics	9	84.05	Median Household Income	$42,240	10	68.1
			% of Families Above Poverty Level	98.9%	1	100.0
Affordable Housing	43	58.75	Median Home Value	$104,800	44	48.8
			Median Rent	$498	39	68.7
Crime	3	99.75	Violent Crimes per 10,000 Population	3	3	99.5
			Property Crimes per 10,000 Population	100	1	100.0
Open Spaces	3	86.10	Population Density (Persons/Sq. Mile)	2480	23	81.3
			Average Rooms per Housing Unit	6.9	3	90.9
Education	26	46.90	% High School Enrollment/Completion	95.8%	16	75.8
			% College Graduates	16.8%	32	18.0
Commute	48	16.40	Average Work Commute in Minutes	24	45	22.2
			% Commuting on Public Transportation	2.6%	31	10.6
Community Stability	1	98.90	% Living in Same House as in 1979	70.7%	1	100.0
			% Living in Same County as in 1985	94.2%	5	97.8

Composite: **Rank** 2 / 54 **Score** 68.95   **BAY VILLAGE**

CATEGORY	RANK	SCORE	STATISTIC	VALUE	RANK	SCORE
Economics	4	95.15	Median Household Income	$51,578	4	92.7
			% of Families Above Poverty Level	98.3%	6	97.6
Affordable Housing	49	42.25	Median Home Value	$108,900	46	45.5
			Median Rent	$648	52	39.0
Crime	1	99.80	Violent Crimes per 10,000 Population	2	1	100.0
			Property Crimes per 10,000 Population	102	2	99.6
Open Spaces	8	80.25	Population Density (Persons/Sq. Mile)	3672	38	69.6
			Average Rooms per Housing Unit	6.9	3	90.9
Education	5	75.45	% High School Enrollment/Completion	95.2%	21	71.9
			% College Graduates	49.7%	2	79.0
Commute	44	23.25	Average Work Commute in Minutes	24	45	22.2
			% Commuting on Public Transportation	5.8%	11	24.3
Community Stability	21	66.50	% Living in Same House as in 1979	49.8%	16	53.1
			% Living in Same County as in 1985	85.9%	30	79.9

Composite: **Rank** 3 / 54 **Score** 68.54   **LYNDHURST**

CATEGORY	RANK	SCORE	STATISTIC	VALUE	RANK	SCORE
Economics	14	79.95	Median Household Income	$40,491	15	63.5
			% of Families Above Poverty Level	98.0%	11	96.4
Affordable Housing	46	52.05	Median Home Value	$87,600	37	62.7
			Median Rent	$636	51	41.4
Crime	5	94.05	Violent Crimes per 10,000 Population	3	3	99.5
			Property Crimes per 10,000 Population	161	5	88.6
Open Spaces	20	69.05	Population Density (Persons/Sq. Mile)	3640	36	69.9
			Average Rooms per Housing Unit	6.4	10	68.2
Education	11	65.05	% High School Enrollment/Completion	96.7%	9	81.7
			% College Graduates	33.2%	11	48.4
Commute	29	33.10	Average Work Commute in Minutes	21	17	55.6
			% Commuting on Public Transportation	2.6%	31	10.6
Community Stability	4	86.55	% Living in Same House as in 1979	61.2%	5	78.7
			% Living in Same County as in 1985	92.6%	9	94.4

Metropolitan Area Suburb Rankings
CLEVELAND-AKRON-LORAIN

Composite: **Rank 4 / 54** *Score* 67.44 **BRECKSVILLE**

CATEGORY	RANK	SCORE	STATISTIC	VALUE	RANK	SCORE
Economics	3	97.55	Median Household Income	$53,396	3	97.5
			% of Families Above Poverty Level	98.3%	6	97.6
Affordable Housing	53	21.75	Median Home Value	$144,900	53	16.4
			Median Rent	$708	53	27.1
Crime	2	99.70	Violent Crimes per 10,000 Population	2	1	100.0
			Property Crimes per 10,000 Population	103	3	99.4
Open Spaces	2	97.60	Population Density (Persons/Sq. Mile)	603	2	99.7
			Average Rooms per Housing Unit	7.0	2	95.5
Education	8	74.50	% High School Enrollment/Completion	97.2%	7	85.0
			% College Graduates	41.6%	6	64.0
Commute	41	23.90	Average Work Commute in Minutes	23	39	33.3
			% Commuting on Public Transportation	3.5%	24	14.5
Community Stability	33	57.05	% Living in Same House as in 1979	43.2%	29	38.3
			% Living in Same County as in 1985	84.0%	38	75.8

Composite: **Rank 5 / 54** *Score* 67.41 **WICKLIFFE**

CATEGORY	RANK	SCORE	STATISTIC	VALUE	RANK	SCORE
Economics	28	68.60	Median Household Income	$32,964	33	43.7
			% of Families Above Poverty Level	97.3%	26	93.5
Affordable Housing	20	78.90	Median Home Value	$70,000	20	77.0
			Median Rent	$437	17	80.8
Crime	9	85.55	Violent Crimes per 10,000 Population	19	23	91.3
			Property Crimes per 10,000 Population	208	9	79.8
Open Spaces	28	57.90	Population Density (Persons/Sq. Mile)	3129	32	74.9
			Average Rooms per Housing Unit	5.8	27	40.9
Education	29	44.55	% High School Enrollment/Completion	96.5%	12	80.4
			% College Graduates	11.8%	44	8.7
Commute	4	46.80	Average Work Commute in Minutes	18	2	88.9
			% Commuting on Public Transportation	1.2%	37	4.7
Community Stability	2	89.60	% Living in Same House as in 1979	66.9%	2	91.5
			% Living in Same County as in 1985	89.5%	21	87.7

Composite: **Rank 6 / 54** *Score* 67.09 **UNIVERSITY HEIGHTS**

CATEGORY	RANK	SCORE	STATISTIC	VALUE	RANK	SCORE
Economics	8	84.95	Median Household Income	$43,376	9	71.1
			% of Families Above Poverty Level	98.6%	3	98.8
Affordable Housing	42	59.05	Median Home Value	$89,100	38	61.5
			Median Rent	$559	46	56.6
Crime	13	83.00	Violent Crimes per 10,000 Population	30	31	85.6
			Property Crimes per 10,000 Population	205	8	80.4
Open Spaces	34	54.00	Population Density (Persons/Sq. Mile)	8093	52	26.2
			Average Rooms per Housing Unit	6.7	5	81.8
Education	1	83.40	% High School Enrollment/Completion	98.4%	4	92.8
			% College Graduates	47.0%	3	74.0
Commute	5	46.55	Average Work Commute in Minutes	20	9	66.7
			% Commuting on Public Transportation	6.3%	10	26.4
Community Stability	30	58.70	% Living in Same House as in 1979	49.7%	17	52.9
			% Living in Same County as in 1985	78.8%	47	64.5

Metropolitan Area Suburb Rankings
CLEVELAND-AKRON-LORAIN

Composite: *Rank* 7 / 54 *Score* 65.81   **AMHERST**

CATEGORY	RANK	SCORE	STATISTIC	VALUE	RANK	SCORE
Economics	23	72.85	Median Household Income	$37,695	20	56.2
			% of Families Above Poverty Level	96.3%	35	89.5
Affordable Housing	14	80.70	Median Home Value	$81,500	32	67.7
			Median Rent	$372	4	93.7
Crime	33	62.05	Violent Crimes per 10,000 Population	20	25	90.8
			Property Crimes per 10,000 Population	457	35	33.3
Open Spaces	14	72.85	Population Density (Persons/Sq. Mile)	1469	11	91.2
			Average Rooms per Housing Unit	6.1	19	54.5
Education	19	53.65	% High School Enrollment/Completion	98.0%	6	90.2
			% College Graduates	16.3%	34	17.1
Commute	6	44.65	Average Work Commute in Minutes	18	2	88.9
			% Commuting on Public Transportation	0.2%	53	0.4
Community Stability	13	73.95	% Living in Same House as in 1979	51.6%	13	57.2
			% Living in Same County as in 1985	90.9%	17	90.7

Composite: *Rank* 8 / 54 *Score* 65.26   **SOUTH EUCLID**

CATEGORY	RANK	SCORE	STATISTIC	VALUE	RANK	SCORE
Economics	22	73.80	Median Household Income	$36,119	25	52.0
			% of Families Above Poverty Level	97.8%	16	95.6
Affordable Housing	33	70.25	Median Home Value	$70,800	22	76.3
			Median Rent	$521	41	64.2
Crime	12	83.20	Violent Crimes per 10,000 Population	10	14	95.9
			Property Crimes per 10,000 Population	258	13	70.5
Open Spaces	26	59.65	Population Density (Persons/Sq. Mile)	5094	46	55.7
			Average Rooms per Housing Unit	6.3	13	63.6
Education	12	63.55	% High School Enrollment/Completion	97.2%	7	85.0
			% College Graduates	29.8%	15	42.1
Commute	33	29.00	Average Work Commute in Minutes	22	27	44.4
			% Commuting on Public Transportation	3.3%	26	13.6
Community Stability	11	77.40	% Living in Same House as in 1979	54.1%	11	62.8
			% Living in Same County as in 1985	91.5%	15	92.0

Composite: *Rank* 9 / 54 *Score* 64.36   **TALLMADGE**

CATEGORY	RANK	SCORE	STATISTIC	VALUE	RANK	SCORE
Economics	26	71.70	Median Household Income	$36,979	23	54.3
			% of Families Above Poverty Level	96.2%	36	89.1
Affordable Housing	32	72.05	Median Home Value	$84,400	35	65.3
			Median Rent	$447	23	78.8
Crime	31	65.45	Violent Crimes per 10,000 Population	19	23	91.3
			Property Crimes per 10,000 Population	423	32	39.6
Open Spaces	11	74.60	Population Density (Persons/Sq. Mile)	1110	8	94.7
			Average Rooms per Housing Unit	6.1	19	54.5
Education	21	53.30	% High School Enrollment/Completion	96.7%	9	81.7
			% College Graduates	20.5%	28	24.9
Commute	13	40.40	Average Work Commute in Minutes	19	4	77.8
			% Commuting on Public Transportation	0.8%	42	3.0
Community Stability	14	73.05	% Living in Same House as in 1979	50.7%	14	55.2
			% Living in Same County as in 1985	91.0%	16	90.9

Metropolitan Area Suburb Rankings
CLEVELAND-AKRON-LORAIN

Composite: *Rank* 10 / 54 *Score* 63.31　　**WESTLAKE**

CATEGORY	RANK	SCORE	STATISTIC	VALUE	RANK	SCORE
Economics	7	90.15	Median Household Income	$47,629	7	82.3
			% of Families Above Poverty Level	98.4%	5	98.0
Affordable Housing	50	35.80	Median Home Value	$130,800	50	27.8
			Median Rent	$624	50	43.8
Crime	6	91.20	Violent Crimes per 10,000 Population	6	7	97.9
			Property Crimes per 10,000 Population	183	7	84.5
Open Spaces	12	74.05	Population Density (Persons/Sq. Mile)	1699	14	89.0
			Average Rooms per Housing Unit	6.2	15	59.1
Education	4	76.45	% High School Enrollment/Completion	98.9%	2	96.1
			% College Graduates	37.7%	9	56.8
Commute	35	28.35	Average Work Commute in Minutes	22	27	44.4
			% Commuting on Public Transportation	3.0%	28	12.3
Community Stability	47	47.15	% Living in Same House as in 1979	33.6%	51	16.8
			% Living in Same County as in 1985	84.8%	36	77.5

Composite: *Rank* 11 / 54 *Score* 63.29　　**FAIRVIEW PARK**

CATEGORY	RANK	SCORE	STATISTIC	VALUE	RANK	SCORE
Economics	23	72.85	Median Household Income	$35,549	27	50.5
			% of Families Above Poverty Level	97.7%	19	95.2
Affordable Housing	35	68.60	Median Home Value	$89,800	40	61.0
			Median Rent	$460	29	76.2
Crime	16	81.25	Violent Crimes per 10,000 Population	8	10	96.9
			Property Crimes per 10,000 Population	284	17	65.6
Open Spaces	32	54.35	Population Density (Persons/Sq. Mile)	3857	39	67.8
			Average Rooms per Housing Unit	5.8	27	40.9
Education	17	54.45	% High School Enrollment/Completion	94.9%	23	69.9
			% College Graduates	28.1%	17	39.0
Commute	20	37.30	Average Work Commute in Minutes	22	27	44.4
			% Commuting on Public Transportation	7.2%	7	30.2
Community Stability	12	74.25	% Living in Same House as in 1979	50.3%	15	54.3
			% Living in Same County as in 1985	92.5%	10	94.2

Composite: *Rank* 12 / 54 *Score* 63.22　　**SOLON**

CATEGORY	RANK	SCORE	STATISTIC	VALUE	RANK	SCORE
Economics	2	97.75	Median Household Income	$54,005	2	99.1
			% of Families Above Poverty Level	98.0%	11	96.4
Affordable Housing	52	32.70	Median Home Value	$141,800	52	18.9
			Median Rent	$610	49	46.5
Crime	N/A	N/A	Violent Crimes per 10,000 Population	N/A	N/A	N/A
			Property Crimes per 10,000 Population	N/A	N/A	N/A
Open Spaces	1	98.35	Population Density (Persons/Sq. Mile)	909	3	96.7
			Average Rooms per Housing Unit	7.1	1	100.0
Education	6	75.40	% High School Enrollment/Completion	98.5%	3	93.5
			% College Graduates	38.0%	8	57.3
Commute	43	23.50	Average Work Commute in Minutes	22	27	44.4
			% Commuting on Public Transportation	0.7%	44	2.6
Community Stability	38	51.60	% Living in Same House as in 1979	41.7%	34	35.0
			% Living in Same County as in 1985	80.5%	44	68.2

Metropolitan Area Suburb Rankings
CLEVELAND-AKRON-LORAIN

Composite: *Rank* 12 / 54 *Score* 63.22   **STRONGSVILLE**

CATEGORY	RANK	SCORE	STATISTIC	VALUE	RANK	SCORE
Economics	5	93.90	Median Household Income	$50,916	6	91.0
			% of Families Above Poverty Level	98.1%	10	96.8
Affordable Housing	44	57.90	Median Home Value	$117,000	48	39.0
			Median Rent	$457	28	76.8
Crime	10	84.75	Violent Crimes per 10,000 Population	5	6	98.5
			Property Crimes per 10,000 Population	255	12	71.0
Open Spaces	5	84.45	Population Density (Persons/Sq. Mile)	1433	10	91.6
			Average Rooms per Housing Unit	6.6	6	77.3
Education	13	61.95	% High School Enrollment/Completion	96.6%	11	81.0
			% College Graduates	30.2%	14	42.9
Commute	52	11.50	Average Work Commute in Minutes	25	49	11.1
			% Commuting on Public Transportation	2.9%	29	11.9
Community Stability	44	48.10	% Living in Same House as in 1979	36.2%	44	22.6
			% Living in Same County as in 1985	83.0%	42	73.6

Composite: *Rank* 14 / 54 *Score* 62.51   **NORTH OLMSTED**

CATEGORY	RANK	SCORE	STATISTIC	VALUE	RANK	SCORE
Economics	18	77.85	Median Household Income	$39,657	17	61.3
			% of Families Above Poverty Level	97.5%	24	94.4
Affordable Housing	40	62.50	Median Home Value	$94,100	41	57.5
			Median Rent	$504	40	67.5
Crime	25	70.00	Violent Crimes per 10,000 Population	15	20	93.3
			Property Crimes per 10,000 Population	385	27	46.7
Open Spaces	19	70.05	Population Density (Persons/Sq. Mile)	2972	30	76.5
			Average Rooms per Housing Unit	6.3	13	63.6
Education	15	56.15	% High School Enrollment/Completion	96.3%	13	79.1
			% College Graduates	25.0%	20	33.2
Commute	30	32.00	Average Work Commute in Minutes	22	27	44.4
			% Commuting on Public Transportation	4.7%	15	19.6
Community Stability	19	69.05	% Living in Same House as in 1979	47.8%	20	48.7
			% Living in Same County as in 1985	90.3%	18	89.4

Composite: *Rank* 15 / 54 *Score* 62.27   **BEREA**

CATEGORY	RANK	SCORE	STATISTIC	VALUE	RANK	SCORE
Economics	25	71.75	Median Household Income	$34,695	28	48.3
			% of Families Above Poverty Level	97.7%	19	95.2
Affordable Housing	22	78.40	Median Home Value	$74,100	28	73.6
			Median Rent	$425	14	83.2
Crime	18	80.40	Violent Crimes per 10,000 Population	10	14	95.9
			Property Crimes per 10,000 Population	288	18	64.9
Open Spaces	35	53.90	Population Density (Persons/Sq. Mile)	3492	35	71.4
			Average Rooms per Housing Unit	5.7	32	36.4
Education	14	57.65	% High School Enrollment/Completion	96.1%	15	77.8
			% College Graduates	27.3%	19	37.5
Commute	22	35.25	Average Work Commute in Minutes	21	17	55.6
			% Commuting on Public Transportation	3.6%	23	14.9
Community Stability	31	58.55	% Living in Same House as in 1979	44.5%	24	41.3
			% Living in Same County as in 1985	84.0%	38	75.8

Metropolitan Area Suburb Rankings
CLEVELAND-AKRON-LORAIN

Composite: Rank 16 / 54 *Score* 62.22   **CLEVELAND HEIGHTS**

CATEGORY	RANK	SCORE	STATISTIC	VALUE	RANK	SCORE
Economics	33	67.25	Median Household Income	$36,043	26	51.8
			% of Families Above Poverty Level	94.6%	42	82.7
Affordable Housing	30	73.30	Median Home Value	$71,100	24	76.1
			Median Rent	$489	36	70.5
Crime	11	84.15	Violent Crimes per 10,000 Population	3	3	99.5
			Property Crimes per 10,000 Population	267	14	68.8
Open Spaces	38	49.75	Population Density (Persons/Sq. Mile)	6651	51	40.4
			Average Rooms per Housing Unit	6.2	15	59.1
Education	10	69.15	% High School Enrollment/Completion	94.6%	25	68.0
			% College Graduates	45.0%	4	70.3
Commute	17	37.75	Average Work Commute in Minutes	22	27	44.4
			% Commuting on Public Transportation	7.4%	6	31.1
Community Stability	35	54.20	% Living in Same House as in 1979	39.9%	38	30.9
			% Living in Same County as in 1985	84.8%	36	77.5

Composite: Rank 17 / 54 *Score* 62.06   **BROOK PARK**

CATEGORY	RANK	SCORE	STATISTIC	VALUE	RANK	SCORE
Economics	21	74.85	Median Household Income	$36,612	24	53.3
			% of Families Above Poverty Level	98.0%	11	96.4
Affordable Housing	26	75.25	Median Home Value	$70,900	23	76.2
			Median Rent	$470	32	74.3
Crime	26	68.15	Violent Crimes per 10,000 Population	18	22	91.8
			Property Crimes per 10,000 Population	397	29	44.5
Open Spaces	27	58.90	Population Density (Persons/Sq. Mile)	2925	29	76.9
			Average Rooms per Housing Unit	5.8	27	40.9
Education	43	30.25	% High School Enrollment/Completion	93.4%	34	60.1
			% College Graduates	7.3%	53	0.4
Commute	12	41.00	Average Work Commute in Minutes	20	9	66.7
			% Commuting on Public Transportation	3.7%	20	15.3
Community Stability	5	86.05	% Living in Same House as in 1979	59.4%	6	74.7
			% Living in Same County as in 1985	94.0%	6	97.4

Composite: Rank 18 / 54 *Score* 61.90   **SHAKER HEIGHTS**

CATEGORY	RANK	SCORE	STATISTIC	VALUE	RANK	SCORE
Economics	6	93.35	Median Household Income	$51,128	5	91.5
			% of Families Above Poverty Level	97.7%	19	95.2
Affordable Housing	51	35.75	Median Home Value	$139,000	51	21.2
			Median Rent	$591	48	50.3
Crime	N/A	N/A	Violent Crimes per 10,000 Population	N/A	N/A	N/A
			Property Crimes per 10,000 Population	N/A	N/A	N/A
Open Spaces	22	65.05	Population Density (Persons/Sq. Mile)	4912	45	57.4
			Average Rooms per Housing Unit	6.5	8	72.7
Education	2	82.70	% High School Enrollment/Completion	94.2%	27	65.4
			% College Graduates	61.0%	1	100.0
Commute	9	42.20	Average Work Commute in Minutes	22	27	44.4
			% Commuting on Public Transportation	9.5%	4	40.0
Community Stability	37	52.35	% Living in Same House as in 1979	39.9%	38	30.9
			% Living in Same County as in 1985	83.1%	41	73.8

Metropolitan Area Suburb Rankings
CLEVELAND-AKRON-LORAIN

Composite: **Rank** 19 / 54 **Score** 60.82   **NORTON**

CATEGORY	RANK	SCORE	STATISTIC	VALUE	RANK	SCORE
Economics	31	67.55	Median Household Income	$34,135	29	46.8
			% of Families Above Poverty Level	96.0%	37	88.3
Affordable Housing	19	79.25	Median Home Value	$68,100	18	78.5
			Median Rent	$441	20	80.0
Crime	24	72.50	Violent Crimes per 10,000 Population	20	25	90.8
			Property Crimes per 10,000 Population	345	24	54.2
Open Spaces	9	79.55	Population Density (Persons/Sq. Mile)	573	1	100.0
			Average Rooms per Housing Unit	6.2	15	59.1
Education	48	19.90	% High School Enrollment/Completion	88.3%	50	26.8
			% College Graduates	14.1%	37	13.0
Commute	36	28.25	Average Work Commute in Minutes	21	17	55.6
			% Commuting on Public Transportation	0.3%	51	0.9
Community Stability	10	78.75	% Living in Same House as in 1979	57.8%	8	71.1
			% Living in Same County as in 1985	88.9%	24	86.4

Composite: **Rank** 20 / 54 **Score** 60.22   **ROCKY RIVER**

CATEGORY	RANK	SCORE	STATISTIC	VALUE	RANK	SCORE
Economics	13	80.40	Median Household Income	$40,385	16	63.2
			% of Families Above Poverty Level	98.3%	6	97.6
Affordable Housing	47	49.40	Median Home Value	$122,100	49	34.8
			Median Rent	$522	43	64.0
Crime	N/A	N/A	Violent Crimes per 10,000 Population	N/A	N/A	N/A
			Property Crimes per 10,000 Population	N/A	N/A	N/A
Open Spaces	31	54.50	Population Density (Persons/Sq. Mile)	4294	41	63.5
			Average Rooms per Housing Unit	5.9	25	45.5
Education	3	76.50	% High School Enrollment/Completion	98.1%	5	90.8
			% College Graduates	40.6%	7	62.2
Commute	16	38.15	Average Work Commute in Minutes	22	27	44.4
			% Commuting on Public Transportation	7.6%	5	31.9
Community Stability	26	62.35	% Living in Same House as in 1979	43.0%	31	37.9
			% Living in Same County as in 1985	89.1%	23	86.8

Composite: **Rank** 20 / 54 **Score** 60.22   **WADSWORTH**

CATEGORY	RANK	SCORE	STATISTIC	VALUE	RANK	SCORE
Economics	40	61.25	Median Household Income	$32,141	35	41.5
			% of Families Above Poverty Level	94.2%	44	81.0
Affordable Housing	9	84.35	Median Home Value	$67,500	15	79.0
			Median Rent	$392	8	89.7
Crime	14	82.10	Violent Crimes per 10,000 Population	11	17	95.4
			Property Crimes per 10,000 Population	267	14	68.8
Open Spaces	23	64.10	Population Density (Persons/Sq. Mile)	1871	17	87.3
			Average Rooms per Housing Unit	5.8	27	40.9
Education	25	48.75	% High School Enrollment/Completion	94.7%	24	68.6
			% College Graduates	22.7%	22	28.9
Commute	27	33.80	Average Work Commute in Minutes	20	9	66.7
			% Commuting on Public Transportation	0.3%	51	0.9
Community Stability	46	47.20	% Living in Same House as in 1979	40.4%	37	32.1
			% Living in Same County as in 1985	77.8%	48	62.3

Metropolitan Area Suburb Rankings
CLEVELAND-AKRON-LORAIN

Composite: **Rank** 22 / 54 **Score** 60.20   **PARMA**

CATEGORY	RANK	SCORE	STATISTIC	VALUE	RANK	SCORE
Economics	29	68.20	Median Household Income	$33,281	32	44.5
			% of Families Above Poverty Level	96.9%	29	91.9
Affordable Housing	27	75.00	Median Home Value	$73,400	27	74.2
			Median Rent	$462	30	75.8
Crime	17	80.50	Violent Crimes per 10,000 Population	24	28	88.7
			Property Crimes per 10,000 Population	248	11	72.3
Open Spaces	37	51.70	Population Density (Persons/Sq. Mile)	4397	43	62.5
			Average Rooms per Housing Unit	5.8	27	40.9
Education	35	38.30	% High School Enrollment/Completion	93.6%	31	61.4
			% College Graduates	15.3%	36	15.2
Commute	38	27.70	Average Work Commute in Minutes	23	39	33.3
			% Commuting on Public Transportation	5.3%	13	22.1
Community Stability	9	80.00	% Living in Same House as in 1979	54.6%	10	63.9
			% Living in Same County as in 1985	93.4%	8	96.1

Composite: **Rank** 23 / 54 *Score* 59.89   **GARFIELD HEIGHTS**

CATEGORY	RANK	SCORE	STATISTIC	VALUE	RANK	SCORE
Economics	41	60.35	Median Household Income	$28,694	44	32.4
			% of Families Above Poverty Level	96.0%	37	88.3
Affordable Housing	7	86.60	Median Home Value	$57,900	7	86.7
			Median Rent	$408	12	86.5
Crime	28	67.00	Violent Crimes per 10,000 Population	43	35	79.0
			Property Crimes per 10,000 Population	341	23	55.0
Open Spaces	40	47.20	Population Density (Persons/Sq. Mile)	4390	42	62.6
			Average Rooms per Housing Unit	5.6	37	31.8
Education	45	27.45	% High School Enrollment/Completion	92.2%	41	52.3
			% College Graduates	8.5%	49	2.6
Commute	10	41.40	Average Work Commute in Minutes	21	17	55.6
			% Commuting on Public Transportation	6.5%	8	27.2
Community Stability	3	89.25	% Living in Same House as in 1979	61.3%	4	78.9
			% Living in Same County as in 1985	95.0%	2	99.6

Composite: **Rank** 24 / 54 *Score* 59.76   **BROADVIEW HEIGHTS**

CATEGORY	RANK	SCORE	STATISTIC	VALUE	RANK	SCORE
Economics	19	77.60	Median Household Income	$38,856	19	59.2
			% of Families Above Poverty Level	97.9%	14	96.0
Affordable Housing	48	48.65	Median Home Value	$112,500	47	42.6
			Median Rent	$569	47	54.7
Crime	4	94.10	Violent Crimes per 10,000 Population	6	7	97.9
			Property Crimes per 10,000 Population	152	4	90.3
Open Spaces	13	73.20	Population Density (Persons/Sq. Mile)	935	5	96.4
			Average Rooms per Housing Unit	6.0	22	50.0
Education	15	56.15	% High School Enrollment/Completion	95.6%	19	74.5
			% College Graduates	27.5%	18	37.8
Commute	49	15.10	Average Work Commute in Minutes	25	49	11.1
			% Commuting on Public Transportation	4.6%	17	19.1
Community Stability	36	53.50	% Living in Same House as in 1979	38.4%	42	27.6
			% Living in Same County as in 1985	85.7%	31	79.4

Metropolitan Area Suburb Rankings
CLEVELAND-AKRON-LORAIN

Composite: *Rank* 25 / 54 *Score* 59.22 **STOW**

CATEGORY	RANK	SCORE	STATISTIC	VALUE	RANK	SCORE
Economics	15	78.25	Median Household Income	$39,638	18	61.3
			% of Families Above Poverty Level	97.7%	19	95.2
Affordable Housing	38	65.10	Median Home Value	$83,600	34	66.0
			Median Rent	$521	41	64.2
Crime	19	78.60	Violent Crimes per 10,000 Population	14	19	93.8
			Property Crimes per 10,000 Population	296	19	63.4
Open Spaces	17	72.15	Population Density (Persons/Sq. Mile)	1616	13	89.8
			Average Rooms per Housing Unit	6.1	19	54.5
Education	18	53.95	% High School Enrollment/Completion	94.1%	28	64.7
			% College Graduates	30.4%	13	43.2
Commute	41	23.90	Average Work Commute in Minutes	22	27	44.4
			% Commuting on Public Transportation	0.9%	40	3.4
Community Stability	52	42.60	% Living in Same House as in 1979	34.0%	50	17.7
			% Living in Same County as in 1985	80.2%	45	67.5

Composite: *Rank* 26 / 54 *Score* 59.15 **NORTH ROYALTON**

CATEGORY	RANK	SCORE	STATISTIC	VALUE	RANK	SCORE
Economics	12	81.15	Median Household Income	$40,952	13	64.7
			% of Families Above Poverty Level	98.3%	6	97.6
Affordable Housing	45	57.80	Median Home Value	$107,400	45	46.7
			Median Rent	$497	37	68.9
Crime	7	90.80	Violent Crimes per 10,000 Population	8	10	96.9
			Property Crimes per 10,000 Population	182	6	84.7
Open Spaces	16	72.45	Population Density (Persons/Sq. Mile)	1090	7	94.9
			Average Rooms per Housing Unit	6.0	22	50.0
Education	20	53.60	% High School Enrollment/Completion	96.2%	14	78.4
			% College Graduates	22.6%	23	28.8
Commute	53	7.00	Average Work Commute in Minutes	26	51	0.0
			% Commuting on Public Transportation	3.4%	25	14.0
Community Stability	40	51.25	% Living in Same House as in 1979	35.6%	47	21.3
			% Living in Same County as in 1985	86.5%	27	81.2

Composite: *Rank* 27 / 54 *Score* 59.14 **MAPLE HEIGHTS**

CATEGORY	RANK	SCORE	STATISTIC	VALUE	RANK	SCORE
Economics	38	63.70	Median Household Income	$29,568	40	34.7
			% of Families Above Poverty Level	97.1%	28	92.7
Affordable Housing	6	87.10	Median Home Value	$57,500	6	87.1
			Median Rent	$405	11	87.1
Crime	27	67.40	Violent Crimes per 10,000 Population	26	29	87.7
			Property Crimes per 10,000 Population	383	26	47.1
Open Spaces	44	43.10	Population Density (Persons/Sq. Mile)	5219	49	54.4
			Average Rooms per Housing Unit	5.6	37	31.8
Education	42	30.70	% High School Enrollment/Completion	93.3%	35	59.5
			% College Graduates	8.1%	50	1.9
Commute	18	37.60	Average Work Commute in Minutes	21	17	55.6
			% Commuting on Public Transportation	4.7%	15	19.6
Community Stability	6	84.35	% Living in Same House as in 1979	57.9%	7	71.3
			% Living in Same County as in 1985	94.0%	6	97.4

169

Metropolitan Area Suburb Rankings
CLEVELAND-AKRON-LORAIN

Composite: *Rank* 28 / 54 *Score* 59.10   **MENTOR**

CATEGORY	RANK	SCORE	STATISTIC	VALUE	RANK	SCORE
Economics	11	81.45	Median Household Income	$42,095	11	67.7
			% of Families Above Poverty Level	97.7%	19	95.2
Affordable Housing	41	59.00	Median Home Value	$89,500	39	61.2
			Median Rent	$558	45	56.8
Crime	20	78.55	Violent Crimes per 10,000 Population	11	17	95.4
			Property Crimes per 10,000 Population	305	20	61.7
Open Spaces	7	80.50	Population Density (Persons/Sq. Mile)	1769	15	88.3
			Average Rooms per Housing Unit	6.5	8	72.7
Education	30	41.90	% High School Enrollment/Completion	92.7%	40	55.6
			% College Graduates	22.3%	24	28.2
Commute	45	22.85	Average Work Commute in Minutes	22	27	44.4
			% Commuting on Public Transportation	0.4%	48	1.3
Community Stability	41	49.45	% Living in Same House as in 1979	39.2%	40	29.4
			% Living in Same County as in 1985	81.1%	43	69.5

Composite: *Rank* 29 / 54 *Score* 58.81   **EASTLAKE**

CATEGORY	RANK	SCORE	STATISTIC	VALUE	RANK	SCORE
Economics	30	67.85	Median Household Income	$33,607	30	45.4
			% of Families Above Poverty Level	96.5%	34	90.3
Affordable Housing	18	79.35	Median Home Value	$66,800	13	79.5
			Median Rent	$445	22	79.2
Crime	21	76.80	Violent Crimes per 10,000 Population	17	21	92.3
			Property Crimes per 10,000 Population	307	21	61.3
Open Spaces	30	54.80	Population Density (Persons/Sq. Mile)	3309	33	73.2
			Average Rooms per Housing Unit	5.7	32	36.4
Education	39	33.95	% High School Enrollment/Completion	93.9%	29	63.4
			% College Graduates	9.5%	48	4.5
Commute	32	29.50	Average Work Commute in Minutes	21	17	55.6
			% Commuting on Public Transportation	0.9%	40	3.4
Community Stability	18	69.40	% Living in Same House as in 1979	52.1%	12	58.3
			% Living in Same County as in 1985	86.2%	28	80.5

Composite: *Rank* 30 / 54 *Score* 58.44   **MIDDLEBURG HEIGHTS**

CATEGORY	RANK	SCORE	STATISTIC	VALUE	RANK	SCORE
Economics	20	76.95	Median Household Income	$37,298	22	55.1
			% of Families Above Poverty Level	98.6%	3	98.8
Affordable Housing	39	62.85	Median Home Value	$99,400	43	53.2
			Median Rent	$479	35	72.5
Crime	30	65.75	Violent Crimes per 10,000 Population	6	7	97.9
			Property Crimes per 10,000 Population	455	34	33.6
Open Spaces	21	66.60	Population Density (Persons/Sq. Mile)	1823	16	87.7
			Average Rooms per Housing Unit	5.9	25	45.5
Education	31	41.45	% High School Enrollment/Completion	92.8%	38	56.2
			% College Graduates	21.5%	25	26.7
Commute	40	24.30	Average Work Commute in Minutes	23	39	33.3
			% Commuting on Public Transportation	3.7%	20	15.3
Community Stability	16	71.20	% Living in Same House as in 1979	48.5%	19	50.2
			% Living in Same County as in 1985	91.6%	14	92.2

Metropolitan Area Suburb Rankings
CLEVELAND-AKRON-LORAIN

Composite: *Rank* 31 / 54 *Score* 58.18 **CUYAHOGA FALLS**

CATEGORY	RANK	SCORE	STATISTIC	VALUE	RANK	SCORE
Economics	42	60.25	Median Household Income	$30,895	38	38.2
			% of Families Above Poverty Level	94.5%	43	82.3
Affordable Housing	10	83.65	Median Home Value	$60,700	8	84.5
			Median Rent	$427	15	82.8
Crime	29	66.85	Violent Crimes per 10,000 Population	27	30	87.2
			Property Crimes per 10,000 Population	386	28	46.5
Open Spaces	29	57.05	Population Density (Persons/Sq. Mile)	1917	19	86.8
			Average Rooms per Housing Unit	5.5	39	27.3
Education	27	44.70	% High School Enrollment/Completion	93.8%	30	62.7
			% College Graduates	21.5%	25	26.7
Commute	23	34.65	Average Work Commute in Minutes	20	9	66.7
			% Commuting on Public Transportation	0.7%	44	2.6
Community Stability	29	60.10	% Living in Same House as in 1979	43.0%	31	37.9
			% Living in Same County as in 1985	87.0%	26	82.3

Composite: *Rank* 32 / 54 *Score* 58.10 **PORTAGE LAKES**

CATEGORY	RANK	SCORE	STATISTIC	VALUE	RANK	SCORE
Economics	37	64.25	Median Household Income	$31,778	36	40.6
			% of Families Above Poverty Level	95.9%	39	87.9
Affordable Housing	17	79.90	Median Home Value	$67,200	14	79.2
			Median Rent	$438	18	80.6
Crime	N/A	N/A	Violent Crimes per 10,000 Population	N/A	N/A	N/A
			Property Crimes per 10,000 Population	N/A	N/A	N/A
Open Spaces	24	63.15	Population Density (Persons/Sq. Mile)	1599	12	89.9
			Average Rooms per Housing Unit	5.7	32	36.4
Education	34	38.40	% High School Enrollment/Completion	93.3%	35	59.5
			% College Graduates	16.4%	33	17.3
Commute	23	34.65	Average Work Commute in Minutes	20	9	66.7
			% Commuting on Public Transportation	0.7%	44	2.6
Community Stability	20	68.25	% Living in Same House as in 1979	47.2%	22	47.3
			% Living in Same County as in 1985	90.2%	20	89.2

Composite: *Rank* 33 / 54 *Score* 57.98 **BEACHWOOD**

CATEGORY	RANK	SCORE	STATISTIC	VALUE	RANK	SCORE
Economics	1	99.80	Median Household Income	$54,340	1	100.0
			% of Families Above Poverty Level	98.8%	2	99.6
Affordable Housing	54	0.00	Median Home Value	$165,200	54	0.0
			Median Rent	$845	54	0.0
Crime	N/A	N/A	Violent Crimes per 10,000 Population	N/A	N/A	N/A
			Property Crimes per 10,000 Population	N/A	N/A	N/A
Open Spaces	10	75.45	Population Density (Persons/Sq. Mile)	2332	21	82.7
			Average Rooms per Housing Unit	6.4	10	68.2
Education	9	72.00	% High School Enrollment/Completion	95.7%	17	75.2
			% College Graduates	44.2%	5	68.8
Commute	25	34.20	Average Work Commute in Minutes	21	17	55.6
			% Commuting on Public Transportation	3.1%	27	12.8
Community Stability	22	66.40	% Living in Same House as in 1979	44.1%	28	40.4
			% Living in Same County as in 1985	91.7%	12	92.4

Metropolitan Area Suburb Rankings
CLEVELAND-AKRON-LORAIN

Composite: *Rank* 34 / 54 *Score* 57.95   VERMILION

CATEGORY	RANK	SCORE	STATISTIC	VALUE	RANK	SCORE
Economics	32	67.30	Median Household Income	$37,500	21	55.6
			% of Families Above Poverty Level	93.7%	46	79.0
Affordable Housing	16	80.15	Median Home Value	$63,900	10	81.9
			Median Rent	$449	24	78.4
Crime	34	61.55	Violent Crimes per 10,000 Population	35	34	83.1
			Property Crimes per 10,000 Population	421	30	40.0
Open Spaces	15	72.70	Population Density (Persons/Sq. Mile)	1040	6	95.4
			Average Rooms per Housing Unit	6.0	22	50.0
Education	27	44.70	% High School Enrollment/Completion	95.1%	22	71.2
			% College Graduates	16.9%	31	18.2
Commute	37	27.80	Average Work Commute in Minutes	21	17	55.6
			% Commuting on Public Transportation	0.1%	54	0.0
Community Stability	39	51.45	% Living in Same House as in 1979	44.2%	26	40.6
			% Living in Same County as in 1985	77.8%	48	62.3

Composite: *Rank* 35 / 54 *Score* 57.40   AVON LAKE

CATEGORY	RANK	SCORE	STATISTIC	VALUE	RANK	SCORE
Economics	10	83.75	Median Household Income	$43,660	8	71.9
			% of Families Above Poverty Level	97.8%	16	95.6
Affordable Housing	36	66.50	Median Home Value	$97,200	42	55.0
			Median Rent	$451	25	78.0
Crime	N/A	N/A	Violent Crimes per 10,000 Population	N/A	N/A	N/A
			Property Crimes per 10,000 Population	N/A	N/A	N/A
Open Spaces	4	84.80	Population Density (Persons/Sq. Mile)	1354	9	92.3
			Average Rooms per Housing Unit	6.6	6	77.3
Education	22	51.95	% High School Enrollment/Completion	93.2%	37	58.8
			% College Graduates	31.4%	12	45.1
Commute	50	14.50	Average Work Commute in Minutes	24	45	22.2
			% Commuting on Public Transportation	1.7%	36	6.8
Community Stability	50	42.90	% Living in Same House as in 1979	40.8%	36	33.0
			% Living in Same County as in 1985	73.4%	53	52.8

Composite: *Rank* 36 / 54 *Score* 57.26   BEDFORD

CATEGORY	RANK	SCORE	STATISTIC	VALUE	RANK	SCORE
Economics	35	65.05	Median Household Income	$30,082	39	36.1
			% of Families Above Poverty Level	97.4%	25	94.0
Affordable Housing	23	77.85	Median Home Value	$64,200	11	81.6
			Median Rent	$471	33	74.1
Crime	22	73.30	Violent Crimes per 10,000 Population	21	27	90.3
			Property Crimes per 10,000 Population	334	22	56.3
Open Spaces	43	43.70	Population Density (Persons/Sq. Mile)	2783	27	78.3
			Average Rooms per Housing Unit	5.1	47	9.1
Education	32	40.35	% High School Enrollment/Completion	95.3%	20	72.5
			% College Graduates	11.5%	45	8.2
Commute	18	37.60	Average Work Commute in Minutes	20	9	66.7
			% Commuting on Public Transportation	2.1%	34	8.5
Community Stability	25	63.00	% Living in Same House as in 1979	46.9%	23	46.6
			% Living in Same County as in 1985	85.7%	31	79.4

Composite: **Rank** 37 / 54 *Score* 54.89   **MAYFIELD HEIGHTS**

CATEGORY	RANK	SCORE	STATISTIC	VALUE	RANK	SCORE
Economics	39	62.75	Median Household Income	$28,688	45	32.4
			% of Families Above Poverty Level	97.2%	27	93.1
Affordable Housing	37	66.35	Median Home Value	$77,000	29	71.3
			Median Rent	$535	44	61.4
Crime	15	82.05	Violent Crimes per 10,000 Population	9	12	96.4
			Property Crimes per 10,000 Population	273	16	67.7
Open Spaces	52	32.00	Population Density (Persons/Sq. Mile)	4705	44	59.5
			Average Rooms per Housing Unit	5.0	51	4.5
Education	24	50.75	% High School Enrollment/Completion	95.7%	17	75.2
			% College Graduates	21.3%	27	26.3
Commute	31	29.85	Average Work Commute in Minutes	22	27	44.4
			% Commuting on Public Transportation	3.7%	20	15.3
Community Stability	27	60.45	% Living in Same House as in 1979	44.2%	26	40.6
			% Living in Same County as in 1985	86.1%	29	80.3

Composite: **Rank** 38 / 54 *Score* 54.82   **WILLOWICK**

CATEGORY	RANK	SCORE	STATISTIC	VALUE	RANK	SCORE
Economics	27	70.20	Median Household Income	$33,403	31	44.8
			% of Families Above Poverty Level	97.8%	16	95.6
Affordable Housing	29	73.80	Median Home Value	$67,800	16	78.7
			Median Rent	$497	37	68.9
Crime	N/A	N/A	Violent Crimes per 10,000 Population	N/A	N/A	N/A
			Property Crimes per 10,000 Population	N/A	N/A	N/A
Open Spaces	47	41.25	Population Density (Persons/Sq. Mile)	6068	50	46.1
			Average Rooms per Housing Unit	5.7	32	36.4
Education	44	28.40	% High School Enrollment/Completion	92.0%	42	51.0
			% College Graduates	10.2%	47	5.8
Commute	28	33.35	Average Work Commute in Minutes	21	17	55.6
			% Commuting on Public Transportation	2.7%	30	11.1
Community Stability	8	81.90	% Living in Same House as in 1979	64.2%	3	85.4
			% Living in Same County as in 1985	85.2%	34	78.4

Composite: **Rank** 39 / 54 *Score* 54.65   **BROOKLYN**

CATEGORY	RANK	SCORE	STATISTIC	VALUE	RANK	SCORE
Economics	44	59.30	Median Household Income	$26,818	49	27.5
			% of Families Above Poverty Level	96.7%	31	91.1
Affordable Housing	8	84.40	Median Home Value	$70,300	21	76.7
			Median Rent	$380	6	92.1
Crime	N/A	N/A	Violent Crimes per 10,000 Population	N/A	N/A	N/A
			Property Crimes per 10,000 Population	N/A	N/A	N/A
Open Spaces	46	41.65	Population Density (Persons/Sq. Mile)	2734	26	78.8
			Average Rooms per Housing Unit	5.0	51	4.5
Education	51	16.75	% High School Enrollment/Completion	89.1%	48	32.0
			% College Graduates	7.9%	51	1.5
Commute	8	42.30	Average Work Commute in Minutes	20	9	66.7
			% Commuting on Public Transportation	4.3%	18	17.9
Community Stability	7	83.50	% Living in Same House as in 1979	56.0%	9	67.0
			% Living in Same County as in 1985	95.2%	1	100.0

Metropolitan Area Suburb Rankings
CLEVELAND-AKRON-LORAIN

Composite: **Rank** 40 / 54 *Score* 54.03 **WILLOUGHBY**

CATEGORY	RANK	SCORE	STATISTIC	VALUE	RANK	SCORE
Economics	34	65.70	Median Household Income	$31,693	37	40.3
			% of Families Above Poverty Level	96.7%	31	91.1
Affordable Housing	28	74.85	Median Home Value	$72,700	25	74.8
			Median Rent	$467	31	74.9
Crime	23	73.35	Violent Crimes per 10,000 Population	10	14	95.9
			Property Crimes per 10,000 Population	363	25	50.8
Open Spaces	33	54.25	Population Density (Persons/Sq. Mile)	2017	20	85.8
			Average Rooms per Housing Unit	5.4	41	22.7
Education	41	32.95	% High School Enrollment/Completion	90.8%	45	43.1
			% College Graduates	19.4%	29	22.8
Commute	25	34.20	Average Work Commute in Minutes	20	9	66.7
			% Commuting on Public Transportation	0.5%	47	1.7
Community Stability	50	42.90	% Living in Same House as in 1979	35.3%	48	20.6
			% Living in Same County as in 1985	79.1%	46	65.2

Composite: **Rank** 41 / 54 *Score* 54.01 **NORTH RIDGEVILLE**

CATEGORY	RANK	SCORE	STATISTIC	VALUE	RANK	SCORE
Economics	16	78.10	Median Household Income	$41,095	12	65.1
			% of Families Above Poverty Level	96.7%	31	91.1
Affordable Housing	21	78.75	Median Home Value	$78,600	31	70.0
			Median Rent	$403	10	87.5
Crime	N/A	N/A	Violent Crimes per 10,000 Population	N/A	N/A	N/A
			Property Crimes per 10,000 Population	N/A	N/A	N/A
Open Spaces	6	82.40	Population Density (Persons/Sq. Mile)	921	4	96.6
			Average Rooms per Housing Unit	6.4	10	68.2
Education	47	25.15	% High School Enrollment/Completion	89.9%	47	37.3
			% College Graduates	14.1%	37	13.0
Commute	51	13.25	Average Work Commute in Minutes	24	45	22.2
			% Commuting on Public Transportation	1.1%	39	4.3
Community Stability	48	46.40	% Living in Same House as in 1979	41.9%	33	35.4
			% Living in Same County as in 1985	75.5%	50	57.4

Composite: **Rank** 42 / 54 *Score* 53.76 **LAKEWOOD**

CATEGORY	RANK	SCORE	STATISTIC	VALUE	RANK	SCORE
Economics	46	56.25	Median Household Income	$28,791	43	32.7
			% of Families Above Poverty Level	93.9%	45	79.8
Affordable Housing	15	80.55	Median Home Value	$72,700	25	74.8
			Median Rent	$409	13	86.3
Crime	8	85.75	Violent Crimes per 10,000 Population	9	12	96.4
			Property Crimes per 10,000 Population	233	10	75.1
Open Spaces	53	6.80	Population Density (Persons/Sq. Mile)	10767	54	0.0
			Average Rooms per Housing Unit	5.2	46	13.6
Education	23	51.00	% High School Enrollment/Completion	93.6%	31	61.4
			% College Graduates	29.0%	16	40.6
Commute	2	50.35	Average Work Commute in Minutes	21	17	55.6
			% Commuting on Public Transportation	10.7%	2	45.1
Community Stability	49	45.65	% Living in Same House as in 1979	32.0%	52	13.2
			% Living in Same County as in 1985	85.1%	35	78.1

Metropolitan Area Suburb Rankings
CLEVELAND-AKRON-LORAIN

Composite: **Rank** 43 / 54   *Score* 51.68   **RAVENNA**

CATEGORY	RANK	SCORE	STATISTIC	VALUE	RANK	SCORE
Economics	50	41.75	Median Household Income	$22,999	51	17.4
			% of Families Above Poverty Level	90.5%	48	66.1
Affordable Housing	3	92.40	Median Home Value	$54,600	4	89.4
			Median Rent	$363	3	95.4
Crime	N/A	N/A	Violent Crimes per 10,000 Population	N/A	N/A	N/A
			Property Crimes per 10,000 Population	N/A	N/A	N/A
Open Spaces	39	49.55	Population Density (Persons/Sq. Mile)	2520	24	80.9
			Average Rooms per Housing Unit	5.3	42	18.2
Education	36	35.80	% High School Enrollment/Completion	93.5%	33	60.8
			% College Graduates	12.9%	40	10.8
Commute	11	41.25	Average Work Commute in Minutes	19	4	77.8
			% Commuting on Public Transportation	1.2%	37	4.7
Community Stability	42	49.35	% Living in Same House as in 1979	34.8%	49	19.5
			% Living in Same County as in 1985	85.6%	33	79.2

Composite: **Rank** 44 / 54   *Score* 51.59   **BRUNSWICK**

CATEGORY	RANK	SCORE	STATISTIC	VALUE	RANK	SCORE
Economics	16	78.10	Median Household Income	$40,950	14	64.7
			% of Families Above Poverty Level	96.8%	30	91.5
Affordable Housing	34	69.90	Median Home Value	$83,200	33	66.3
			Median Rent	$474	34	73.5
Crime	N/A	N/A	Violent Crimes per 10,000 Population	N/A	N/A	N/A
			Property Crimes per 10,000 Population	N/A	N/A	N/A
Open Spaces	18	70.30	Population Density (Persons/Sq. Mile)	2457	22	81.5
			Average Rooms per Housing Unit	6.2	15	59.1
Education	33	39.20	% High School Enrollment/Completion	94.5%	26	67.3
			% College Graduates	13.1%	39	11.1
Commute	54	4.45	Average Work Commute in Minutes	26	51	0.0
			% Commuting on Public Transportation	2.2%	33	8.9
Community Stability	45	47.60	% Living in Same House as in 1979	43.2%	29	38.3
			% Living in Same County as in 1985	75.3%	51	56.9

Composite: **Rank** 45 / 54   *Score* 50.36   **EUCLID**

CATEGORY	RANK	SCORE	STATISTIC	VALUE	RANK	SCORE
Economics	47	55.40	Median Household Income	$26,904	48	27.7
			% of Families Above Poverty Level	94.7%	41	83.1
Affordable Housing	12	81.45	Median Home Value	$64,400	12	81.5
			Median Rent	$434	16	81.4
Crime	36	49.65	Violent Crimes per 10,000 Population	34	33	83.6
			Property Crimes per 10,000 Population	551	38	15.7
Open Spaces	51	32.25	Population Density (Persons/Sq. Mile)	5122	48	55.4
			Average Rooms per Housing Unit	5.1	47	9.1
Education	38	34.30	% High School Enrollment/Completion	91.8%	43	49.7
			% College Graduates	17.3%	30	18.9
Commute	21	35.60	Average Work Commute in Minutes	22	27	44.4
			% Commuting on Public Transportation	6.4%	9	26.8
Community Stability	24	63.85	% Living in Same House as in 1979	44.5%	24	41.3
			% Living in Same County as in 1985	88.9%	24	86.4

Metropolitan Area Suburb Rankings
CLEVELAND-AKRON-LORAIN

Composite: **Rank** 46 / 54 **Score** 49.67   **BARBERTON**

CATEGORY	RANK	SCORE	STATISTIC	VALUE	RANK	SCORE
Economics	52	29.20	Median Household Income	$21,688	52	14.0
			% of Families Above Poverty Level	85.1%	52	44.4
Affordable Housing	1	99.35	Median Home Value	$43,100	2	98.7
			Median Rent	$340	1	100.0
Crime	37	47.45	Violent Crimes per 10,000 Population	67	38	66.7
			Property Crimes per 10,000 Population	484	37	28.2
Open Spaces	42	44.05	Population Density (Persons/Sq. Mile)	3640	36	69.9
			Average Rooms per Housing Unit	5.3	42	18.2
Education	52	12.85	% High School Enrollment/Completion	87.9%	51	24.2
			% College Graduates	7.9%	51	1.5
Commute	7	42.95	Average Work Commute in Minutes	19	4	77.8
			% Commuting on Public Transportation	2.0%	35	8.1
Community Stability	15	71.85	% Living in Same House as in 1979	49.0%	18	51.3
			% Living in Same County as in 1985	91.7%	12	92.4

Composite: **Rank** 47 / 54 **Score** 49.31   **PARMA HEIGHTS**

CATEGORY	RANK	SCORE	STATISTIC	VALUE	RANK	SCORE
Economics	36	65.00	Median Household Income	$29,289	41	34.0
			% of Families Above Poverty Level	97.9%	14	96.0
Affordable Housing	25	75.60	Median Home Value	$77,900	30	70.6
			Median Rent	$438	18	80.6
Crime	N/A	N/A	Violent Crimes per 10,000 Population	N/A	N/A	N/A
			Property Crimes per 10,000 Population	N/A	N/A	N/A
Open Spaces	50	36.85	Population Density (Persons/Sq. Mile)	5109	47	55.5
			Average Rooms per Housing Unit	5.3	42	18.2
Education	49	19.45	% High School Enrollment/Completion	87.7%	52	22.9
			% College Graduates	15.7%	35	16.0
Commute	34	28.55	Average Work Commute in Minutes	23	39	33.3
			% Commuting on Public Transportation	5.7%	12	23.8
Community Stability	17	70.40	% Living in Same House as in 1979	47.6%	21	48.2
			% Living in Same County as in 1985	91.8%	11	92.6

Composite: **Rank** 48 / 54 **Score** 49.14   **ELYRIA**

CATEGORY	RANK	SCORE	STATISTIC	VALUE	RANK	SCORE
Economics	49	42.55	Median Household Income	$26,923	47	27.8
			% of Families Above Poverty Level	88.3%	50	57.3
Affordable Housing	4	90.75	Median Home Value	$56,100	5	88.2
			Median Rent	$374	5	93.3
Crime	39	42.40	Violent Crimes per 10,000 Population	55	36	72.8
			Property Crimes per 10,000 Population	571	39	12.0
Open Spaces	36	52.10	Population Density (Persons/Sq. Mile)	2923	28	76.9
			Average Rooms per Housing Unit	5.5	39	27.3
Education	50	18.95	% High School Enrollment/Completion	88.9%	49	30.7
			% College Graduates	11.0%	46	7.2
Commute	15	39.55	Average Work Commute in Minutes	19	4	77.8
			% Commuting on Public Transportation	0.4%	48	1.3
Community Stability	32	57.65	% Living in Same House as in 1979	38.7%	41	28.3
			% Living in Same County as in 1985	89.2%	22	87.0

Composite: **Rank** 49 / 54 **Score** 49.13   KENT

CATEGORY	RANK	SCORE	STATISTIC	VALUE	RANK	SCORE
Economics	53	24.25	Median Household Income	$21,463	53	13.4
			% of Families Above Poverty Level	82.8%	53	35.1
Affordable Housing	11	83.30	Median Home Value	$67,900	17	78.7
			Median Rent	$401	9	87.9
Crime	32	62.30	Violent Crimes per 10,000 Population	32	32	84.6
			Property Crimes per 10,000 Population	421	30	40.0
Open Spaces	48	41.15	Population Density (Persons/Sq. Mile)	3310	34	73.2
			Average Rooms per Housing Unit	5.1	47	9.1
Education	7	74.60	% High School Enrollment/Completion	99.5%	1	100.0
			% College Graduates	33.6%	10	49.2
Commute	1	58.30	Average Work Commute in Minutes	17	1	100.0
			% Commuting on Public Transportation	4.0%	19	16.6
Community Stability	54	0.00	% Living in Same House as in 1979	26.1%	54	0.0
			% Living in Same County as in 1985	49.0%	54	0.0

Composite: **Rank** 50 / 54 **Score** 48.92   BEDFORD HEIGHTS

CATEGORY	RANK	SCORE	STATISTIC	VALUE	RANK	SCORE
Economics	43	59.80	Median Household Income	$28,873	42	32.9
			% of Families Above Poverty Level	95.6%	40	86.7
Affordable Housing	24	77.55	Median Home Value	$68,600	19	78.1
			Median Rent	$456	27	77.0
Crime	35	52.70	Violent Crimes per 10,000 Population	56	37	72.3
			Property Crimes per 10,000 Population	458	36	33.1
Open Spaces	45	41.95	Population Density (Persons/Sq. Mile)	2673	25	79.4
			Average Rooms per Housing Unit	5.0	51	4.5
Education	46	27.20	% High School Enrollment/Completion	90.9%	44	43.8
			% College Graduates	12.8%	41	10.6
Commute	39	26.65	Average Work Commute in Minutes	23	39	33.3
			% Commuting on Public Transportation	4.8%	14	20.0
Community Stability	34	56.60	% Living in Same House as in 1979	36.7%	43	23.8
			% Living in Same County as in 1985	90.3%	18	89.4

Composite: **Rank** 51 / 54 **Score** 47.48   WARRENSVILLE HEIGHTS

CATEGORY	RANK	SCORE	STATISTIC	VALUE	RANK	SCORE
Economics	48	46.60	Median Household Income	$27,893	46	30.3
			% of Families Above Poverty Level	89.7%	49	62.9
Affordable Housing	13	80.80	Median Home Value	$61,500	9	83.8
			Median Rent	$452	26	77.8
Crime	38	46.45	Violent Crimes per 10,000 Population	85	39	57.4
			Property Crimes per 10,000 Population	445	33	35.5
Open Spaces	49	38.05	Population Density (Persons/Sq. Mile)	3934	40	67.0
			Average Rooms per Housing Unit	5.1	47	9.1
Education	40	33.00	% High School Enrollment/Completion	92.8%	38	56.2
			% College Graduates	12.4%	43	9.8
Commute	46	21.30	Average Work Commute in Minutes	26	51	0.0
			% Commuting on Public Transportation	10.1%	3	42.6
Community Stability	23	66.15	% Living in Same House as in 1979	40.9%	35	33.2
			% Living in Same County as in 1985	94.8%	3	99.1

Metropolitan Area Suburb Rankings
CLEVELAND-AKRON-LORAIN

Composite: Rank 52 / 54 ***Score*** 45.88   **MEDINA**

CATEGORY	RANK	SCORE	STATISTIC	VALUE	RANK	SCORE
Economics	45	58.55	Median Household Income	$32,952	34	43.7
			% of Families Above Poverty Level	92.3%	47	73.4
Affordable Housing	31	72.15	Median Home Value	$85,700	36	64.3
			Median Rent	$441	20	80.0
Crime	N/A	N/A	Violent Crimes per 10,000 Population	N/A	N/A	N/A
			Property Crimes per 10,000 Population	N/A	N/A	N/A
Open Spaces	25	61.75	Population Density (Persons/Sq. Mile)	1887	18	87.1
			Average Rooms per Housing Unit	5.7	32	36.4
Education	36	35.80	% High School Enrollment/Completion	90.5%	46	41.2
			% College Graduates	23.5%	21	30.4
Commute	47	17.30	Average Work Commute in Minutes	23	39	33.3
			% Commuting on Public Transportation	0.4%	48	1.3
Community Stability	53	29.70	% Living in Same House as in 1979	27.4%	53	2.9
			% Living in Same County as in 1985	75.1%	52	56.5

Composite: Rank 53 / 54 ***Score*** 44.63   **PAINESVILLE**

CATEGORY	RANK	SCORE	STATISTIC	VALUE	RANK	SCORE
Economics	51	36.15	Median Household Income	$25,007	50	22.7
			% of Families Above Poverty Level	86.4%	51	49.6
Affordable Housing	5	90.15	Median Home Value	$54,100	3	89.8
			Median Rent	$388	7	90.5
Crime	N/A	N/A	Violent Crimes per 10,000 Population	N/A	N/A	N/A
			Property Crimes per 10,000 Population	N/A	N/A	N/A
Open Spaces	41	47.00	Population Density (Persons/Sq. Mile)	3038	31	75.8
			Average Rooms per Housing Unit	5.3	42	18.2
Education	54	5.10	% High School Enrollment/Completion	84.2%	54	0.0
			% College Graduates	12.6%	42	10.2
Commute	13	40.40	Average Work Commute in Minutes	19	4	77.8
			% Commuting on Public Transportation	0.8%	42	3.0
Community Stability	43	49.00	% Living in Same House as in 1979	36.0%	45	22.2
			% Living in Same County as in 1985	84.0%	38	75.8

Composite: Rank 54 / 54 ***Score*** 31.46   **EAST CLEVELAND**

CATEGORY	RANK	SCORE	STATISTIC	VALUE	RANK	SCORE
Economics	54	0.00	Median Household Income	$16,378	54	0.0
			% of Families Above Poverty Level	74.1%	54	0.0
Affordable Housing	2	97.80	Median Home Value	$41,500	1	100.0
			Median Rent	$362	2	95.6
Crime	40	0.00	Violent Crimes per 10,000 Population	197	40	0.0
			Property Crimes per 10,000 Population	635	40	0.0
Open Spaces	54	0.50	Population Density (Persons/Sq. Mile)	10664	53	1.0
			Average Rooms per Housing Unit	4.9	54	0.0
Education	53	11.45	% High School Enrollment/Completion	87.7%	52	22.9
			% College Graduates	7.1%	54	0.0
Commute	3	50.00	Average Work Commute in Minutes	26	51	0.0
			% Commuting on Public Transportation	23.6%	1	100.0
Community Stability	27	60.45	% Living in Same House as in 1979	35.9%	46	22.0
			% Living in Same County as in 1985	94.7%	4	98.9

Metropolitan Area Description
COLUMBUS

STATE: Ohio

COUNTIES: Delaware, Fairfield, Franklin, Licking, Madison, Pickaway, Union

TOTAL POPULATION: 1,377,419

POPULATION IN SUBURBS: 744,509 (54.1%)

POPULATION IN Columbus: 632,910 (45.9%)

The COLUMBUS metropolitan area is located in the central part of Ohio. The suburbs range geographically from Delaware in the north (25 miles from Columbus), to Hilliard in the west (14 miles from Columbus), to Circleville in the south (32 miles from Columbus), and to Newark in the east (37 miles from Columbus). The area is growing in population and had an increase of 10.7% between 1980 and 1990. Summer time high temperatures average in the 80's and winter time lows average in the teens. Honda of America has a major plant in the suburban area. Hamburger giant Wendy's International has its headquarters in the suburb of Dublin. The area has a large supply of well-educated, highly-trained people, and is developing many new high tech industries. In 1992, *Fortune* magazine rated the metropolitan area number six for its pro-business attitude. Public transportation in the area is provided on buses by the Central Ohio Transit Authority

Upper Arlington is the overall highest rated suburb and also has the highest score in education. **Dublin** receives the highest scores in economics and open spaces. **Newark** is the suburb with the most affordable housing. **Gahanna** is rated the safest suburb with the lowest crime rate. The top rated commute belongs to **Bexley**. Finally, the number one rating in community stability goes to **Blacklick Estates**.

The highest ranked suburb overall which also has an affordable housing score of at least 50.00 is **Worthington**.

The highest ranked suburb in the education category which also has an affordable housing score of at least 50.00 is **Bexley**.

The county whose suburbs have the highest average overall score is **Franklin County** (59.83).

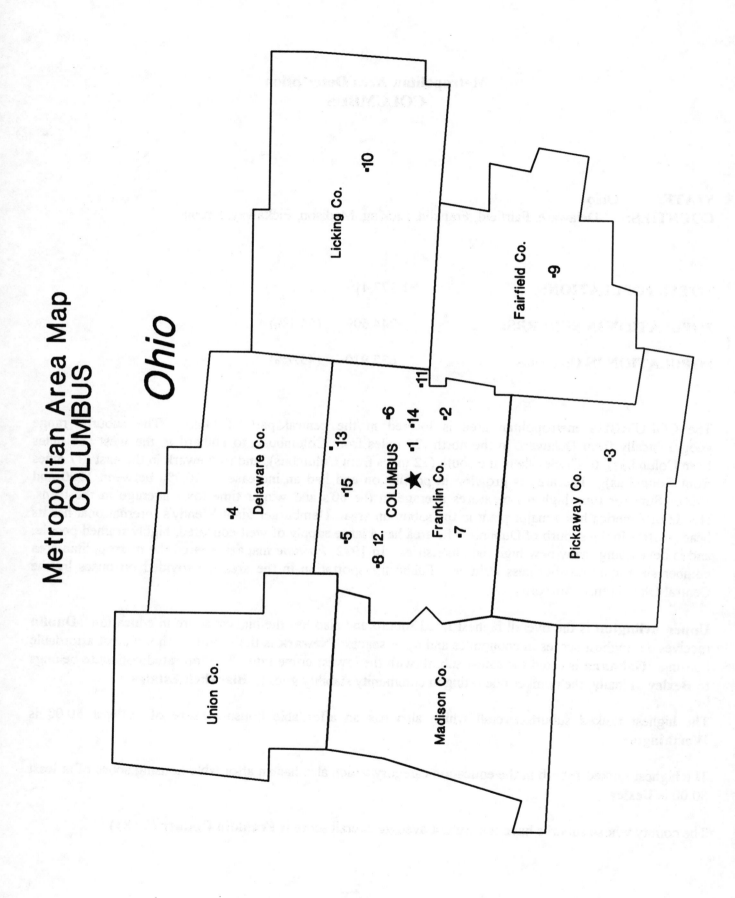

Metropolitan Area Map
COLUMBUS

Ohio

Union Co.

Delaware Co.

•4

•5

•8 12.

•15

•13

Licking Co.

•10

•6
•1 •14

COLUMBUS

★

Franklin Co.

•7

•11

Fairfield Co.

•9

Madison Co.

Pickaway Co.

•3

Metropolitan Area Suburb Alphabetical Index
COLUMBUS

SUBURB	PAGE	MAP NO.	STATE	COUNTY	POPU-LATION	RANK
BEXLEY	182	1	Ohio	Franklin	13,088	3 / 15
BLACKLICK ESTATES	185	2	Ohio	Franklin	10,080	11 / 15
CIRCLEVILLE	185	3	Ohio	Pickaway	11,666	12 / 15
DELAWARE	184	4	Ohio	Delaware	20,030	9 / 15
DUBLIN	184	5	Ohio	Franklin	16,366	8 / 15
GAHANNA	183	6	Ohio	Franklin	27,791	5 / 15
GROVE CITY	183	7	Ohio	Franklin	19,661	6 / 15
HILLIARD	184	8	Ohio	Franklin	11,796	7 / 15
LANCASTER	186	9	Ohio	Fairfield	34,507	14 / 15
NEWARK	186	10	Ohio	Licking	44,389	13 / 15
REYNOLDSBURG	185	11	Ohio	Franklin	25,748	10 / 15
UPPER ARLINGTON	182	12	Ohio	Franklin	34,128	1 / 15
WESTERVILLE	183	13	Ohio	Franklin	30,269	4 / 15
WHITEHALL	186	14	Ohio	Franklin	20,572	15 / 15
WORTHINGTON	182	15	Ohio	Franklin	14,869	2 / 15

Metropolitan Area Suburb Rankings
COLUMBUS

Composite: **Rank** 1 / 15 **Score** 75.03   **UPPER ARLINGTON**

CATEGORY	RANK	SCORE	STATISTIC	VALUE	RANK	SCORE
Economics	2	80.60	Median Household Income	$53,140	2	62.0
			% of Families Above Poverty Level	99.3%	2	99.2
Affordable Housing	14	33.65	Median Home Value	$140,600	14	30.2
			Median Rent	$578	14	37.1
Crime	2	99.00	Violent Crimes per 10,000 Population	12	1	100.0
			Property Crimes per 10,000 Population	304	2	98.0
Open Spaces	6	55.65	Population Density (Persons/Sq. Mile)	3545	12	40.5
			Average Rooms per Housing Unit	6.7	3	70.8
Education	1	100.00	% High School Enrollment/Completion	97.3%	1	100.0
			% College Graduates	59.2%	1	100.0
Commute	3	58.00	Average Work Commute in Minutes	18	2	83.3
			% Commuting on Public Transportation	1.7%	5	32.7
Community Stability	2	98.30	% Living in Same House as in 1979	45.8%	1	100.0
			% Living in Same County as in 1985	88.3%	2	96.6

Composite: **Rank** 2 / 15 **Score** 73.10   **WORTHINGTON**

CATEGORY	RANK	SCORE	STATISTIC	VALUE	RANK	SCORE
Economics	3	74.90	Median Household Income	$49,851	3	55.3
			% of Families Above Poverty Level	98.7%	3	94.5
Affordable Housing	11	57.60	Median Home Value	$118,700	13	46.8
			Median Rent	$465	8	68.4
Crime	3	92.70	Violent Crimes per 10,000 Population	15	4	98.6
			Property Crimes per 10,000 Population	364	3	86.8
Open Spaces	2	70.05	Population Density (Persons/Sq. Mile)	2647	8	60.9
			Average Rooms per Housing Unit	6.9	2	79.2
Education	4	83.25	% High School Enrollment/Completion	94.3%	5	75.0
			% College Graduates	54.8%	4	91.5
Commute	5	44.25	Average Work Commute in Minutes	20	6	50.0
			% Commuting on Public Transportation	2.0%	3	38.5
Community Stability	3	88.95	% Living in Same House as in 1979	42.7%	4	90.9
			% Living in Same County as in 1985	85.2%	4	87.0

Composite: **Rank** 3 / 15 **Score** 71.04   **BEXLEY**

CATEGORY	RANK	SCORE	STATISTIC	VALUE	RANK	SCORE
Economics	5	67.25	Median Household Income	$48,125	5	51.8
			% of Families Above Poverty Level	97.2%	6	82.7
Affordable Housing	13	54.95	Median Home Value	$117,600	12	47.6
			Median Rent	$487	10	62.3
Crime	8	79.85	Violent Crimes per 10,000 Population	30	8	91.5
			Property Crimes per 10,000 Population	464	10	68.2
Open Spaces	13	35.40	Population Density (Persons/Sq. Mile)	5327	15	0.0
			Average Rooms per Housing Unit	6.7	3	70.8
Education	2	98.75	% High School Enrollment/Completion	97.2%	2	99.2
			% College Graduates	58.3%	3	98.3
Commute	1	79.80	Average Work Commute in Minutes	17	1	100.0
			% Commuting on Public Transportation	3.1%	2	59.6
Community Stability	6	81.25	% Living in Same House as in 1979	43.7%	3	93.9
			% Living in Same County as in 1985	79.3%	11	68.6

Composite: **Rank** 4 / 15 *Score* 63.50   **WESTERVILLE**

CATEGORY	RANK	SCORE	STATISTIC	VALUE	RANK	SCORE
Economics	4	71.30	Median Household Income	$48,212	4	52.0
			% of Families Above Poverty Level	98.2%	4	90.6
Affordable Housing	12	56.15	Median Home Value	$107,900	11	55.0
			Median Rent	$505	11	57.3
Crime	4	92.10	Violent Crimes per 10,000 Population	12	1	100.0
			Property Crimes per 10,000 Population	378	4	84.2
Open Spaces	5	61.30	Population Density (Persons/Sq. Mile)	2864	11	55.9
			Average Rooms per Housing Unit	6.6	5	66.7
Education	5	74.40	% High School Enrollment/Completion	95.6%	4	85.8
			% College Graduates	40.1%	5	63.0
Commute	9	31.75	Average Work Commute in Minutes	20	6	50.0
			% Commuting on Public Transportation	0.7%	8	13.5
Community Stability	12	57.50	% Living in Same House as in 1979	30.0%	12	53.8
			% Living in Same County as in 1985	76.9%	12	61.2

Composite: **Rank** 5 / 15 *Score* 62.56   **GAHANNA**

CATEGORY	RANK	SCORE	STATISTIC	VALUE	RANK	SCORE
Economics	6	57.95	Median Household Income	$42,015	6	39.5
			% of Families Above Poverty Level	96.4%	8	76.4
Affordable Housing	8	68.50	Median Home Value	$86,500	10	71.3
			Median Rent	$475	9	65.7
Crime	1	100.00	Violent Crimes per 10,000 Population	12	1	100.0
			Property Crimes per 10,000 Population	293	1	100.0
Open Spaces	3	65.70	Population Density (Persons/Sq. Mile)	2110	5	73.1
			Average Rooms per Housing Unit	6.4	6	58.3
Education	6	54.95	% High School Enrollment/Completion	93.6%	6	69.2
			% College Graduates	28.6%	6	40.7
Commute	12	23.40	Average Work Commute in Minutes	21	11	33.3
			% Commuting on Public Transportation	0.7%	8	13.5
Community Stability	10	67.45	% Living in Same House as in 1979	31.3%	11	57.6
			% Living in Same County as in 1985	82.1%	9	77.3

Composite: **Rank** 6 / 15 *Score* 57.74   **GROVE CITY**

CATEGORY	RANK	SCORE	STATISTIC	VALUE	RANK	SCORE
Economics	10	47.05	Median Household Income	$34,350	10	24.0
			% of Families Above Poverty Level	95.6%	10	70.1
Affordable Housing	7	76.20	Median Home Value	$74,900	8	80.1
			Median Rent	$451	7	72.3
Crime	6	88.40	Violent Crimes per 10,000 Population	21	6	95.8
			Property Crimes per 10,000 Population	395	6	81.0
Open Spaces	7	53.00	Population Density (Persons/Sq. Mile)	1946	4	76.8
			Average Rooms per Housing Unit	5.7	10	29.2
Education	11	21.30	% High School Enrollment/Completion	88.7%	12	28.3
			% College Graduates	15.0%	10	14.3
Commute	6	41.35	Average Work Commute in Minutes	20	6	50.0
			% Commuting on Public Transportation	1.7%	5	32.7
Community Stability	8	76.90	% Living in Same House as in 1979	35.0%	8	68.4
			% Living in Same County as in 1985	84.7%	5	85.4

Metropolitan Area Suburb Rankings
COLUMBUS

Composite: **Rank** 7 / 15 *Score* 55.86   **HILLIARD**

CATEGORY	RANK	SCORE	STATISTIC	VALUE	RANK	SCORE
Economics	9	51.10	Median Household Income	$36,415	8	28.2
			% of Families Above Poverty Level	96.1%	9	74.0
Affordable Housing	10	66.10	Median Home Value	$72,600	7	81.8
			Median Rent	$530	13	50.4
Crime	10	68.55	Violent Crimes per 10,000 Population	82	10	67.0
			Property Crimes per 10,000 Population	454	9	70.1
Open Spaces	4	61.60	Population Density (Persons/Sq. Mile)	1368	2	89.9
			Average Rooms per Housing Unit	5.8	8	33.3
Education	7	47.95	% High School Enrollment/Completion	93.6%	6	69.2
			% College Graduates	21.4%	8	26.7
Commute	10	29.80	Average Work Commute in Minutes	20	6	50.0
			% Commuting on Public Transportation	0.5%	11	9.6
Community Stability	11	65.95	% Living in Same House as in 1979	32.9%	10	62.3
			% Living in Same County as in 1985	79.6%	10	69.6

Composite: **Rank** 8 / 15 *Score* 55.00   **DUBLIN**

CATEGORY	RANK	SCORE	STATISTIC	VALUE	RANK	SCORE
Economics	1	100.00	Median Household Income	$71,996	1	100.0
			% of Families Above Poverty Level	99.4%	1	100.0
Affordable Housing	15	0.00	Median Home Value	$180,300	15	0.0
			Median Rent	$712	15	0.0
Crime	5	88.70	Violent Crimes per 10,000 Population	21	6	95.8
			Property Crimes per 10,000 Population	392	5	81.6
Open Spaces	1	100.00	Population Density (Persons/Sq. Mile)	924	1	100.0
			Average Rooms per Housing Unit	7.4	1	100.0
Education	3	96.30	% High School Enrollment/Completion	96.6%	3	94.2
			% College Graduates	58.4%	2	98.4
Commute	15	0.00	Average Work Commute in Minutes	23	14	0.0
			% Commuting on Public Transportation	0.0%	15	0.0
Community Stability	15	0.00	% Living in Same House as in 1979	11.6%	15	0.0
			% Living in Same County as in 1985	57.2%	15	0.0

Composite: **Rank** 9 / 15 *Score* 52.49   **DELAWARE**

CATEGORY	RANK	SCORE	STATISTIC	VALUE	RANK	SCORE
Economics	11	29.85	Median Household Income	$28,975	11	13.2
			% of Families Above Poverty Level	92.6%	11	46.5
Affordable Housing	6	82.85	Median Home Value	$67,600	6	85.6
			Median Rent	$423	5	80.1
Crime	7	84.50	Violent Crimes per 10,000 Population	15	4	98.6
			Property Crimes per 10,000 Population	452	8	70.4
Open Spaces	8	47.05	Population Density (Persons/Sq. Mile)	1919	3	77.4
			Average Rooms per Housing Unit	5.4	11	16.7
Education	9	38.05	% High School Enrollment/Completion	91.5%	8	51.7
			% College Graduates	20.2%	9	24.4
Commute	8	37.20	Average Work Commute in Minutes	19	4	66.7
			% Commuting on Public Transportation	0.4%	13	7.7
Community Stability	14	47.90	% Living in Same House as in 1979	29.7%	14	52.9
			% Living in Same County as in 1985	71.0%	14	42.9

Metropolitan Area Suburb Rankings
COLUMBUS

Composite: **Rank** 10 / 15   *Score* 51.69   **REYNOLDSBURG**

CATEGORY	RANK	SCORE	STATISTIC	VALUE	RANK	SCORE
Economics	7	57.35	Median Household Income	$37,169	7	29.7
			% of Families Above Poverty Level	97.5%	5	85.0
Affordable Housing	9	67.20	Median Home Value	$77,100	9	78.4
			Median Rent	$510	12	56.0
Crime	9	77.20	Violent Crimes per 10,000 Population	49	9	82.5
			Property Crimes per 10,000 Population	444	7	71.9
Open Spaces	9	45.95	Population Density (Persons/Sq. Mile)	2748	9	58.6
			Average Rooms per Housing Unit	5.8	8	33.3
Education	8	41.95	% High School Enrollment/Completion	91.4%	9	50.8
			% College Graduates	24.7%	7	33.1
Commute	14	17.30	Average Work Commute in Minutes	23	14	0.0
			% Commuting on Public Transportation	1.8%	4	34.6
Community Stability	13	54.85	% Living in Same House as in 1979	30.0%	12	53.8
			% Living in Same County as in 1985	75.2%	13	55.9

Composite: **Rank** 11 / 15   *Score* 51.30   **BLACKLICK ESTATES**

CATEGORY	RANK	SCORE	STATISTIC	VALUE	RANK	SCORE
Economics	8	52.70	Median Household Income	$36,015	9	27.4
			% of Families Above Poverty Level	96.6%	7	78.0
Affordable Housing	5	83.90	Median Home Value	$58,600	5	92.5
			Median Rent	$440	6	75.3
Crime	N/A	N/A	Violent Crimes per 10,000 Population	N/A	N/A	N/A
			Property Crimes per 10,000 Population	N/A	N/A	N/A
Open Spaces	14	34.05	Population Density (Persons/Sq. Mile)	4164	14	26.4
			Average Rooms per Housing Unit	6.0	7	41.7
Education	13	14.15	% High School Enrollment/Completion	88.7%	12	28.3
			% College Graduates	7.6%	15	0.0
Commute	11	23.75	Average Work Commute in Minutes	22	13	16.7
			% Commuting on Public Transportation	1.6%	7	30.8
Community Stability	1	99.25	% Living in Same House as in 1979	45.3%	2	98.5
			% Living in Same County as in 1985	89.4%	1	100.0

Composite: **Rank** 12 / 15   *Score* 48.77   **CIRCLEVILLE**

CATEGORY	RANK	SCORE	STATISTIC	VALUE	RANK	SCORE
Economics	13	12.45	Median Household Income	$24,630	13	4.4
			% of Families Above Poverty Level	89.3%	13	20.5
Affordable Housing	3	95.45	Median Home Value	$55,100	3	95.1
			Median Rent	$366	3	95.8
Crime	N/A	N/A	Violent Crimes per 10,000 Population	N/A	N/A	N/A
			Property Crimes per 10,000 Population	N/A	N/A	N/A
Open Spaces	12	36.45	Population Density (Persons/Sq. Mile)	2853	10	56.2
			Average Rooms per Housing Unit	5.4	11	16.7
Education	10	24.55	% High School Enrollment/Completion	90.1%	10	40.0
			% College Graduates	12.3%	11	9.1
Commute	7	39.10	Average Work Commute in Minutes	19	4	66.7
			% Commuting on Public Transportation	0.6%	10	11.5
Community Stability	4	84.65	% Living in Same House as in 1979	40.4%	5	84.2
			% Living in Same County as in 1985	84.6%	7	85.1

Metropolitan Area Suburb Rankings
COLUMBUS

Composite: Rank 13 / 15 *Score* 47.76   **NEWARK**

CATEGORY	RANK	SCORE	STATISTIC	VALUE	RANK	SCORE
Economics	15	0.65	Median Household Income	$23,062	14	1.3
			% of Families Above Poverty Level	86.7%	15	0.0
Affordable Housing	1	100.00	Median Home Value	$48,700	1	100.0
			Median Rent	$351	1	100.0
Crime	N/A	N/A	Violent Crimes per 10,000 Population	N/A	N/A	N/A
			Property Crimes per 10,000 Population	N/A	N/A	N/A
Open Spaces	11	40.90	Population Density (Persons/Sq. Mile)	2462	7	65.1
			Average Rooms per Housing Unit	5.4	11	16.7
Education	12	18.20	% High School Enrollment/Completion	88.8%	11	29.2
			% College Graduates	11.3%	13	7.2
Commute	4	46.45	Average Work Commute in Minutes	18	2	83.3
			% Commuting on Public Transportation	0.5%	11	9.6
Community Stability	7	80.35	% Living in Same House as in 1979	36.0%	7	71.3
			% Living in Same County as in 1985	86.0%	3	89.4

Composite: Rank 14 / 15 *Score* 42.23   **LANCASTER**

CATEGORY	RANK	SCORE	STATISTIC	VALUE	RANK	SCORE
Economics	14	9.05	Median Household Income	$22,430	15	0.0
			% of Families Above Poverty Level	89.0%	14	18.1
Affordable Housing	2	97.45	Median Home Value	$51,400	2	97.9
			Median Rent	$362	2	97.0
Crime	N/A	N/A	Violent Crimes per 10,000 Population	N/A	N/A	N/A
			Property Crimes per 10,000 Population	N/A	N/A	N/A
Open Spaces	10	41.70	Population Density (Persons/Sq. Mile)	2204	6	70.9
			Average Rooms per Housing Unit	5.3	14	12.5
Education	15	3.90	% High School Enrollment/Completion	85.3%	15	0.0
			% College Graduates	11.6%	12	7.8
Commute	13	17.60	Average Work Commute in Minutes	21	11	33.3
			% Commuting on Public Transportation	0.1%	14	1.9
Community Stability	5	83.65	% Living in Same House as in 1979	39.6%	6	81.9
			% Living in Same County as in 1985	84.7%	5	85.4

Composite: Rank 15 / 15 *Score* 41.30   **WHITEHALL**

CATEGORY	RANK	SCORE	STATISTIC	VALUE	RANK	SCORE
Economics	12	26.00	Median Household Income	$25,943	12	7.1
			% of Families Above Poverty Level	92.4%	12	44.9
Affordable Housing	4	90.25	Median Home Value	$57,300	4	93.5
			Median Rent	$398	4	87.0
Crime	11	0.00	Violent Crimes per 10,000 Population	224	11	0.0
			Property Crimes per 10,000 Population	831	11	0.0
Open Spaces	15	15.10	Population Density (Persons/Sq. Mile)	3998	13	30.2
			Average Rooms per Housing Unit	5.0	15	0.0
Education	14	6.00	% High School Enrollment/Completion	86.0%	14	5.8
			% College Graduates	10.8%	14	6.2
Commute	2	75.00	Average Work Commute in Minutes	20	6	50.0
			% Commuting on Public Transportation	5.2%	1	100.0
Community Stability	9	76.75	% Living in Same House as in 1979	35.0%	8	68.4
			% Living in Same County as in 1985	84.6%	7	85.1

Metropolitan Area Description
DALLAS-FORT WORTH

STATE: Texas
COUNTIES: Collin, Dallas, Denton, Ellis, Johnson, Kaufman, Parker, Rockwall, Tarrant

TOTAL POPULATION:	3,885,415	
POPULATION IN SUBURBS:	2,430,919	(62.6%)
POPULATION IN Dallas:	1,006,877	(25.9%)
POPULATION IN Fort Worth:	447,619	(11.5%)

The DALLAS-FORT WORTH metropolitan area is located in the northeastern part of Texas. The suburbs range geographically from Denton in the north (32 miles from Dallas), to Weatherford in the west (60 miles from Dallas), to Ennis in the south (36 miles from Dallas), and to Terrell in the east (32 miles from Dallas). The area is growing rapidly in population and had an increase of 32.6% between 1980 and 1990. Summer time high temperatures average in the 90's and winter time lows average in the 30's. The suburb of Richardson is the site of a large concentration of telecommunications companies, known as "Telecom Corridor." The international headquarters of Exxon is located in the suburb of Irving. In 1992, *Fortune* magazine rated the metropolitan area number four for its pro-business attitude. Public transportation in the area is provided on buses by the Dallas Area Rapid Transit System.

Colleyville is the overall highest rated suburb. In addition, **Colleyville** receives the highest scores in economics and open spaces, and is rated the safest suburb with the lowest crime rate. **Terrell** is the suburb with the most affordable housing. **University Park** has the highest score in education as well as the top rated commute. Finally, the number one rating in community stability goes to **Forest Hill**.

The highest ranked suburb overall which also has an affordable housing score of at least 50.00 is **Richardson**.

The highest ranked suburb in the education category which also has an affordable housing score of at least 50.00 is also **Richardson**.

The county whose suburbs have the highest average overall score is **Dallas County** (57.79).

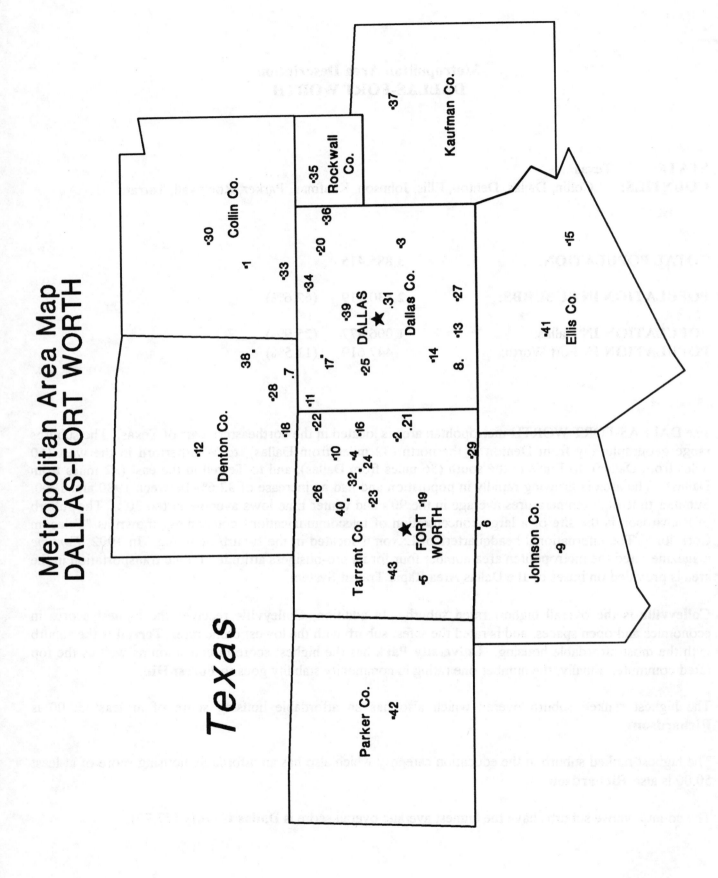

Metropolitan Area Suburb Alphabetical Index
DALLAS-FORT WORTH

SUBURB	PAGE	MAP NO.	STATE	COUNTY	POPU-LATION	RANK
ALLEN	194	1	Texas	Collin	18,309	15 / 43
ARLINGTON	203	2	Texas	Tarrant	261,721	41 / 43
BALCH SPRINGS	203	3	Texas	Dallas	17,406	42 / 43
BEDFORD	197	4	Texas	Tarrant	43,762	23 / 43
BENBROOK	191	5	Texas	Tarrant	19,564	5 / 43
BURLESON	196	6	Texas	Johnson	16,113	19 / 43
CARROLLTON	195	7	Texas	Denton	82,169	18 / 43
CEDAR HILL	193	8	Texas	Dallas	19,976	12 / 43
CLEBURNE	194	9	Texas	Johnson	22,205	13 / 43
COLLEYVILLE	190	10	Texas	Tarrant	12,724	1 / 43
COPPELL	192	11	Texas	Dallas	16,881	9 / 43
DENTON	202	12	Texas	Denton	66,270	38 / 43
DESOTO	192	13	Texas	Dallas	30,544	7 / 43
DUNCANVILLE	191	14	Texas	Dallas	35,748	6 / 43
ENNIS	197	15	Texas	Ellis	13,883	22 / 43
EULESS	198	16	Texas	Tarrant	38,149	26 / 43
FARMERS BRANCH	190	17	Texas	Dallas	24,250	3 / 43
FLOWER MOUND	199	18	Texas	Denton	15,527	28 / 43
FOREST HILL	200	19	Texas	Tarrant	11,482	32 / 43
GARLAND	193	20	Texas	Dallas	180,650	11 / 43
GRAND PRAIRIE	202	21	Texas	Tarrant	99,616	39 / 43
GRAPEVINE	196	22	Texas	Tarrant	29,202	20 / 43
HALTOM CITY	200	23	Texas	Tarrant	32,856	31 / 43
HURST	198	24	Texas	Tarrant	33,574	27 / 43
IRVING	200	25	Texas	Dallas	155,037	33 / 43
KELLER	193	26	Texas	Tarrant	13,683	10 / 43
LANCASTER	195	27	Texas	Dallas	22,117	17 / 43
LEWISVILLE	203	28	Texas	Denton	46,521	40 / 43
MANSFIELD	199	29	Texas	Tarrant	15,607	29 / 43
MCKINNEY	204	30	Texas	Collin	21,283	43 / 43
MESQUITE	196	31	Texas	Dallas	101,484	21 / 43
NORTH RICHLAND HILLS	197	32	Texas	Tarrant	45,895	24 / 43
PLANO	192	33	Texas	Collin	128,713	8 / 43
RICHARDSON	190	34	Texas	Dallas	74,840	2 / 43
ROCKWALL	198	35	Texas	Rockwall	10,486	25 / 43
ROWLETT	195	36	Texas	Dallas	23,260	16 / 43
TERRELL	201	37	Texas	Kaufman	12,490	34 / 43
THE COLONY	201	38	Texas	Denton	22,113	35 / 43
UNIVERSITY PARK	191	39	Texas	Dallas	22,259	4 / 43
WATAUGA	202	40	Texas	Tarrant	20,009	37 / 43
WAXAHACHIE	201	41	Texas	Ellis	18,168	36 / 43
WEATHERFORD	194	42	Texas	Parker	14,804	14 / 43
WHITE SETTLEMENT	199	43	Texas	Tarrant	15,472	30 / 43

Metropolitan Area Suburb Rankings
DALLAS-FORT WORTH

Composite: **Rank** 1 / 43   *Score* 68.53   **COLLEYVILLE**

CATEGORY	RANK	SCORE	STATISTIC	VALUE	RANK	SCORE
Economics	1	100.00	Median Household Income	$77,530	1	100.0
			% of Families Above Poverty Level	99.4%	1	100.0
Affordable Housing	42	35.00	Median Home Value	$189,300	42	43.4
			Median Rent	$647	38	26.6
Crime	1	98.75	Violent Crimes per 10,000 Population	9	2	98.5
			Property Crimes per 10,000 Population	235	2	99.0
Open Spaces	1	94.90	Population Density (Persons/Sq. Mile)	971	15	89.8
			Average Rooms per Housing Unit	7.5	1	100.0
Education	3	74.05	% High School Enrollment/Completion	94.8%	5	89.0
			% College Graduates	45.5%	5	59.1
Commute	28	32.15	Average Work Commute in Minutes	24	19	50.0
			% Commuting on Public Transportation	0.3%	22	14.3
Community Stability	25	44.85	% Living in Same House as in 1979	28.1%	18	52.4
			% Living in Same County as in 1985	64.2%	32	37.3

Composite: **Rank** 2 / 43   *Score* 66.88   **RICHARDSON**

CATEGORY	RANK	SCORE	STATISTIC	VALUE	RANK	SCORE
Economics	9	68.90	Median Household Income	$50,240	7	51.2
			% of Families Above Poverty Level	96.9%	15	86.6
Affordable Housing	35	57.95	Median Home Value	$109,900	36	75.0
			Median Rent	$597	35	40.9
Crime	25	66.55	Violent Crimes per 10,000 Population	40	24	82.5
			Property Crimes per 10,000 Population	610	24	50.6
Open Spaces	18	58.20	Population Density (Persons/Sq. Mile)	2649	33	59.7
			Average Rooms per Housing Unit	6.2	5	56.7
Education	2	76.60	% High School Enrollment/Completion	96.4%	2	93.5
			% College Graduates	45.9%	4	59.7
Commute	3	76.15	Average Work Commute in Minutes	23	17	57.1
			% Commuting on Public Transportation	2.0%	2	95.2
Community Stability	14	63.80	% Living in Same House as in 1979	34.5%	10	65.9
			% Living in Same County as in 1985	74.2%	19	61.7

Composite: **Rank** 3 / 43   *Score* 62.52   **FARMERS BRANCH**

CATEGORY	RANK	SCORE	STATISTIC	VALUE	RANK	SCORE
Economics	21	55.00	Median Household Income	$38,037	22	29.3
			% of Families Above Poverty Level	95.8%	22	80.7
Affordable Housing	30	66.85	Median Home Value	$85,800	30	84.6
			Median Rent	$568	30	49.1
Crime	35	47.40	Violent Crimes per 10,000 Population	38	22	83.5
			Property Crimes per 10,000 Population	915	42	11.3
Open Spaces	21	57.15	Population Density (Persons/Sq. Mile)	2021	26	71.0
			Average Rooms per Housing Unit	5.8	11	43.3
Education	21	51.40	% High School Enrollment/Completion	89.5%	17	74.1
			% College Graduates	25.1%	23	28.7
Commute	2	78.55	Average Work Commute in Minutes	21	5	71.4
			% Commuting on Public Transportation	1.8%	3	85.7
Community Stability	3	81.30	% Living in Same House as in 1979	44.3%	2	86.5
			% Living in Same County as in 1985	80.1%	8	76.1

Metropolitan Area Suburb Rankings
DALLAS-FORT WORTH

Composite: **Rank** 4 / 43 **Score** 62.03   **UNIVERSITY PARK**

CATEGORY	RANK	SCORE	STATISTIC	VALUE	RANK	SCORE
Economics	6	71.90	Median Household Income	$53,614	6	57.2
			% of Families Above Poverty Level	96.9%	15	86.6
Affordable Housing	43	5.45	Median Home Value	$298,300	43	0.0
			Median Rent	$702	42	10.9
Crime	9	80.10	Violent Crimes per 10,000 Population	22	8	91.8
			Property Crimes per 10,000 Population	472	11	68.4
Open Spaces	41	28.35	Population Density (Persons/Sq. Mile)	5975	43	0.0
			Average Rooms per Housing Unit	6.2	5	56.7
Education	1	100.00	% High School Enrollment/Completion	98.7%	1	100.0
			% College Graduates	72.9%	1	100.0
Commute	1	88.10	Average Work Commute in Minutes	17	1	100.0
			% Commuting on Public Transportation	1.6%	4	76.2
Community Stability	17	60.30	% Living in Same House as in 1979	34.9%	9	66.7
			% Living in Same County as in 1985	71.0%	25	53.9

Composite: **Rank** 5 / 43 **Score** 61.68   **BENBROOK**

CATEGORY	RANK	SCORE	STATISTIC	VALUE	RANK	SCORE
Economics	12	65.25	Median Household Income	$45,303	13	42.3
			% of Families Above Poverty Level	97.2%	14	88.2
Affordable Housing	23	79.20	Median Home Value	$84,800	28	85.0
			Median Rent	$483	18	73.4
Crime	4	90.25	Violent Crimes per 10,000 Population	16	4	94.8
			Property Crimes per 10,000 Population	338	5	85.7
Open Spaces	24	51.55	Population Density (Persons/Sq. Mile)	1722	23	76.4
			Average Rooms per Housing Unit	5.3	25	26.7
Education	16	54.55	% High School Enrollment/Completion	86.4%	32	65.4
			% College Graduates	35.2%	10	43.7
Commute	24	35.70	Average Work Commute in Minutes	21	5	71.4
			% Commuting on Public Transportation	0.0%	38	0.0
Community Stability	21	55.25	% Living in Same House as in 1979	29.5%	16	55.4
			% Living in Same County as in 1985	71.5%	23	55.1

Composite: **Rank** 6 / 43 **Score** 61.05   **DUNCANVILLE**

CATEGORY	RANK	SCORE	STATISTIC	VALUE	RANK	SCORE
Economics	17	62.00	Median Household Income	$41,028	19	34.7
			% of Families Above Poverty Level	97.4%	12	89.3
Affordable Housing	27	72.60	Median Home Value	$85,100	29	84.9
			Median Rent	$529	27	60.3
Crime	22	68.15	Violent Crimes per 10,000 Population	38	22	83.5
			Property Crimes per 10,000 Population	593	22	52.8
Open Spaces	28	46.85	Population Density (Persons/Sq. Mile)	3168	39	50.4
			Average Rooms per Housing Unit	5.8	11	43.3
Education	12	59.20	% High School Enrollment/Completion	93.0%	8	83.9
			% College Graduates	29.0%	17	34.5
Commute	10	46.45	Average Work Commute in Minutes	24	19	50.0
			% Commuting on Public Transportation	0.9%	12	42.9
Community Stability	8	72.10	% Living in Same House as in 1979	32.1%	13	60.8
			% Living in Same County as in 1985	83.1%	7	83.4

Metropolitan Area Suburb Rankings
DALLAS-FORT WORTH

Composite: ***Rank*** 7 / 43 ***Score*** 60.27   **DESOTO**

CATEGORY	RANK	SCORE	STATISTIC	VALUE	RANK	SCORE
Economics	11	65.80	Median Household Income	$45,550	12	42.8
			% of Families Above Poverty Level	97.3%	13	88.8
Affordable Housing	25	75.15	Median Home Value	$95,000	32	80.9
			Median Rent	$497	25	69.4
Crime	20	68.90	Violent Crimes per 10,000 Population	26	13	89.7
			Property Crimes per 10,000 Population	630	25	48.1
Open Spaces	11	64.25	Population Density (Persons/Sq. Mile)	1418	21	81.8
			Average Rooms per Housing Unit	5.9	9	46.7
Education	17	54.45	% High School Enrollment/Completion	89.4%	18	73.8
			% College Graduates	29.4%	16	35.1
Commute	19	36.90	Average Work Commute in Minutes	26	31	35.7
			% Commuting on Public Transportation	0.8%	13	38.1
Community Stability	20	56.45	% Living in Same House as in 1979	22.2%	24	40.0
			% Living in Same County as in 1985	78.8%	12	72.9

Composite: ***Rank*** 8 / 43 ***Score*** 60.26   **PLANO**

CATEGORY	RANK	SCORE	STATISTIC	VALUE	RANK	SCORE
Economics	5	74.55	Median Household Income	$53,905	4	57.7
			% of Families Above Poverty Level	97.8%	7	91.4
Affordable Housing	34	58.75	Median Home Value	$113,600	39	73.5
			Median Rent	$586	33	44.0
Crime	18	72.80	Violent Crimes per 10,000 Population	32	18	86.6
			Property Crimes per 10,000 Population	545	20	59.0
Open Spaces	10	66.20	Population Density (Persons/Sq. Mile)	1942	25	72.4
			Average Rooms per Housing Unit	6.3	4	60.0
Education	4	72.45	% High School Enrollment/Completion	93.1%	7	84.2
			% College Graduates	46.6%	3	60.7
Commute	7	53.55	Average Work Commute in Minutes	24	19	50.0
			% Commuting on Public Transportation	1.2%	7	57.1
Community Stability	36	23.55	% Living in Same House as in 1979	17.0%	32	29.1
			% Living in Same County as in 1985	56.3%	39	18.0

Composite: ***Rank*** 9 / 43 ***Score*** 59.48   **COPPELL**

CATEGORY	RANK	SCORE	STATISTIC	VALUE	RANK	SCORE
Economics	2	79.50	Median Household Income	$58,815	2	66.5
			% of Families Above Poverty Level	98.0%	6	92.5
Affordable Housing	37	54.65	Median Home Value	$113,300	38	73.6
			Median Rent	$615	36	35.7
Crime	2	94.65	Violent Crimes per 10,000 Population	6	1	100.0
			Property Crimes per 10,000 Population	310	4	89.3
Open Spaces	8	68.30	Population Density (Persons/Sq. Mile)	1153	17	86.6
			Average Rooms per Housing Unit	6.0	8	50.0
Education	6	66.85	% High School Enrollment/Completion	88.9%	23	72.4
			% College Graduates	47.0%	2	61.3
Commute	16	41.65	Average Work Commute in Minutes	24	19	50.0
			% Commuting on Public Transportation	0.7%	15	33.3
Community Stability	42	10.75	% Living in Same House as in 1979	3.2%	43	0.0
			% Living in Same County as in 1985	57.7%	35	21.5

Composite: **Rank** 10 / 43 *Score* 59.42   **KELLER**

CATEGORY	RANK	SCORE	STATISTIC	VALUE	RANK	SCORE
Economics	4	76.70	Median Household Income	$55,050	3	59.8
			% of Families Above Poverty Level	98.2%	4	93.6
Affordable Housing	33	59.30	Median Home Value	$115,200	40	72.9
			Median Rent	$580	31	45.7
Crime	5	88.90	Violent Crimes per 10,000 Population	49	29	77.8
			Property Crimes per 10,000 Population	227	1	100.0
Open Spaces	3	78.60	Population Density (Persons/Sq. Mile)	747	8	93.9
			Average Rooms per Housing Unit	6.4	3	63.3
Education	13	58.20	% High School Enrollment/Completion	91.8%	11	80.6
			% College Graduates	29.9%	15	35.8
Commute	41	13.10	Average Work Commute in Minutes	28	38	21.4
			% Commuting on Public Transportation	0.1%	33	4.8
Community Stability	28	41.15	% Living in Same House as in 1979	19.5%	29	34.3
			% Living in Same County as in 1985	68.6%	28	48.0

Composite: **Rank** 11 / 43 *Score* 58.95   **GARLAND**

CATEGORY	RANK	SCORE	STATISTIC	VALUE	RANK	SCORE
Economics	26	50.10	Median Household Income	$37,274	24	28.0
			% of Families Above Poverty Level	94.2%	26	72.2
Affordable Housing	20	80.05	Median Home Value	$72,600	17	89.8
			Median Rent	$494	24	70.3
Crime	26	64.70	Violent Crimes per 10,000 Population	48	27	78.4
			Property Crimes per 10,000 Population	607	23	51.0
Open Spaces	34	40.35	Population Density (Persons/Sq. Mile)	3150	37	50.7
			Average Rooms per Housing Unit	5.4	22	30.0
Education	25	47.40	% High School Enrollment/Completion	87.1%	31	67.3
			% College Graduates	24.3%	24	27.5
Commute	5	67.85	Average Work Commute in Minutes	26	31	35.7
			% Commuting on Public Transportation	2.1%	1	100.0
Community Stability	15	62.20	% Living in Same House as in 1979	27.3%	19	50.7
			% Living in Same County as in 1985	79.1%	11	73.7

Composite: **Rank** 12 / 43 *Score* 57.81   **CEDAR HILL**

CATEGORY	RANK	SCORE	STATISTIC	VALUE	RANK	SCORE
Economics	18	60.00	Median Household Income	$41,457	17	35.5
			% of Families Above Poverty Level	96.5%	18	84.5
Affordable Housing	31	64.55	Median Home Value	$84,500	27	85.1
			Median Rent	$586	33	44.0
Crime	10	79.40	Violent Crimes per 10,000 Population	25	10	90.2
			Property Crimes per 10,000 Population	471	10	68.6
Open Spaces	5	69.95	Population Density (Persons/Sq. Mile)	594	5	96.6
			Average Rooms per Housing Unit	5.8	11	43.3
Education	19	53.00	% High School Enrollment/Completion	89.0%	21	72.7
			% College Graduates	28.2%	18	33.3
Commute	26	34.50	Average Work Commute in Minutes	28	38	21.4
			% Commuting on Public Transportation	1.0%	11	47.6
Community Stability	27	43.30	% Living in Same House as in 1979	14.2%	37	23.2
			% Living in Same County as in 1985	74.9%	18	63.4

Metropolitan Area Suburb Rankings
DALLAS-FORT WORTH

Composite: *Rank* 13 / 43 *Score* 57.10   **CLEBURNE**

CATEGORY	RANK	SCORE	STATISTIC	VALUE	RANK	SCORE
Economics	38	28.00	Median Household Income	$26,037	36	7.9
			% of Families Above Poverty Level	89.7%	37	48.1
Affordable Housing	5	97.85	Median Home Value	$52,100	5	98.0
			Median Rent	$398	4	97.7
Crime	28	64.10	Violent Crimes per 10,000 Population	25	10	90.2
			Property Crimes per 10,000 Population	708	29	38.0
Open Spaces	22	55.05	Population Density (Persons/Sq. Mile)	1142	16	86.8
			Average Rooms per Housing Unit	5.2	26	23.3
Education	38	36.15	% High School Enrollment/Completion	85.0%	36	61.4
			% College Graduates	13.2%	37	10.9
Commute	13	42.85	Average Work Commute in Minutes	21	5	71.4
			% Commuting on Public Transportation	0.3%	22	14.3
Community Stability	6	75.70	% Living in Same House as in 1979	39.3%	5	76.0
			% Living in Same County as in 1985	79.8%	9	75.4

Composite: *Rank* 14 / 43 *Score* 57.06   **WEATHERFORD**

CATEGORY	RANK	SCORE	STATISTIC	VALUE	RANK	SCORE
Economics	40	24.05	Median Household Income	$25,208	39	6.4
			% of Families Above Poverty Level	88.5%	40	41.7
Affordable Housing	3	98.60	Median Home Value	$53,500	7	97.5
			Median Rent	$391	2	99.7
Crime	19	71.85	Violent Crimes per 10,000 Population	51	32	76.8
			Property Crimes per 10,000 Population	484	14	66.9
Open Spaces	23	53.85	Population Density (Persons/Sq. Mile)	908	11	91.0
			Average Rooms per Housing Unit	5.0	34	16.7
Education	27	45.70	% High School Enrollment/Completion	90.4%	14	76.6
			% College Graduates	15.8%	34	14.8
Commute	12	44.05	Average Work Commute in Minutes	22	12	64.3
			% Commuting on Public Transportation	0.5%	17	23.8
Community Stability	16	61.35	% Living in Same House as in 1979	35.4%	8	67.8
			% Living in Same County as in 1985	71.4%	24	54.9

Composite: *Rank* 15 / 43 *Score* 56.65   **ALLEN**

CATEGORY	RANK	SCORE	STATISTIC	VALUE	RANK	SCORE
Economics	10	68.35	Median Household Income	$47,869	10	46.9
			% of Families Above Poverty Level	97.5%	10	89.8
Affordable Housing	36	56.50	Median Home Value	$84,100	26	85.3
			Median Rent	$643	37	27.7
Crime	8	80.25	Violent Crimes per 10,000 Population	20	6	92.8
			Property Crimes per 10,000 Population	478	12	67.7
Open Spaces	7	68.35	Population Density (Persons/Sq. Mile)	964	14	90.0
			Average Rooms per Housing Unit	5.9	9	46.7
Education	7	64.75	% High School Enrollment/Completion	95.4%	4	90.7
			% College Graduates	31.9%	13	38.8
Commute	19	36.90	Average Work Commute in Minutes	26	31	35.7
			% Commuting on Public Transportation	0.8%	13	38.1
Community Stability	39	21.45	% Living in Same House as in 1979	13.5%	38	21.7
			% Living in Same County as in 1985	57.6%	36	21.2

Composite: *Rank* 16 / 43 *Score* 56.61   **ROWLETT**

CATEGORY	RANK	SCORE	STATISTIC	VALUE	RANK	SCORE
Economics	7	70.75	Median Household Income	$48,121	9	47.4
			% of Families Above Poverty Level	98.3%	3	94.1
Affordable Housing	40	50.05	Median Home Value	$88,600	31	83.5
			Median Rent	$682	39	16.6
Crime	7	86.10	Violent Crimes per 10,000 Population	25	10	90.2
			Property Crimes per 10,000 Population	367	7	82.0
Open Spaces	4	70.80	Population Density (Persons/Sq. Mile)	1246	18	84.9
			Average Rooms per Housing Unit	6.2	5	56.7
Education	24	50.55	% High School Enrollment/Completion	87.7%	27	69.0
			% College Graduates	27.4%	19	32.1
Commute	34	28.55	Average Work Commute in Minutes	31	42	0.0
			% Commuting on Public Transportation	1.2%	7	57.1
Community Stability	30	39.50	% Living in Same House as in 1979	12.8%	40	20.2
			% Living in Same County as in 1985	73.0%	22	58.8

Composite: *Rank* 17 / 43 *Score* 56.57   **LANCASTER**

CATEGORY	RANK	SCORE	STATISTIC	VALUE	RANK	SCORE
Economics	32	39.30	Median Household Income	$31,489	33	17.6
			% of Families Above Poverty Level	92.1%	32	61.0
Affordable Housing	16	81.10	Median Home Value	$68,200	12	91.6
			Median Rent	$493	23	70.6
Crime	16	74.30	Violent Crimes per 10,000 Population	27	14	89.2
			Property Crimes per 10,000 Population	542	18	59.4
Open Spaces	17	58.45	Population Density (Persons/Sq. Mile)	759	9	93.6
			Average Rooms per Housing Unit	5.2	26	23.3
Education	28	42.50	% High School Enrollment/Completion	87.6%	28	68.7
			% College Graduates	16.8%	32	16.3
Commute	32	29.75	Average Work Commute in Minutes	26	31	35.7
			% Commuting on Public Transportation	0.5%	17	23.8
Community Stability	9	70.60	% Living in Same House as in 1979	28.9%	17	54.1
			% Living in Same County as in 1985	84.6%	3	87.1

Composite: *Rank* 18 / 43 *Score* 56.18   **CARROLLTON**

CATEGORY	RANK	SCORE	STATISTIC	VALUE	RANK	SCORE
Economics	13	64.65	Median Household Income	$45,787	11	43.2
			% of Families Above Poverty Level	96.8%	17	86.1
Affordable Housing	29	67.90	Median Home Value	$99,300	35	79.2
			Median Rent	$542	28	56.6
Crime	24	67.20	Violent Crimes per 10,000 Population	29	17	88.1
			Property Crimes per 10,000 Population	644	27	46.3
Open Spaces	25	50.75	Population Density (Persons/Sq. Mile)	2364	29	64.8
			Average Rooms per Housing Unit	5.6	16	36.7
Education	11	60.25	% High School Enrollment/Completion	89.3%	19	73.5
			% College Graduates	37.4%	6	47.0
Commute	6	60.70	Average Work Commute in Minutes	24	19	50.0
			% Commuting on Public Transportation	1.5%	5	71.4
Community Stability	38	21.80	% Living in Same House as in 1979	14.4%	36	23.6
			% Living in Same County as in 1985	57.1%	37	20.0

Metropolitan Area Suburb Rankings
DALLAS-FORT WORTH

Composite: **Rank** 19 / 43 **Score** 54.94   **BURLESON**

CATEGORY	RANK	SCORE	STATISTIC	VALUE	RANK	SCORE
Economics	29	46.60	Median Household Income	$33,628	30	21.5
			% of Families Above Poverty Level	94.1%	27	71.7
Affordable Housing	20	80.05	Median Home Value	$59,200	9	95.2
			Median Rent	$513	26	64.9
Crime	13	77.90	Violent Crimes per 10,000 Population	20	6	92.8
			Property Crimes per 10,000 Population	514	16	63.0
Open Spaces	13	60.05	Population Density (Persons/Sq. Mile)	955	13	90.1
			Average Rooms per Housing Unit	5.4	22	30.0
Education	33	40.40	% High School Enrollment/Completion	89.0%	21	72.7
			% College Graduates	11.3%	38	8.1
Commute	38	21.45	Average Work Commute in Minutes	25	28	42.9
			% Commuting on Public Transportation	0.0%	38	0.0
Community Stability	18	58.15	% Living in Same House as in 1979	30.2%	15	56.8
			% Living in Same County as in 1985	73.3%	21	59.5

Composite: **Rank** 20 / 43 **Score** 54.92   **GRAPEVINE**

CATEGORY	RANK	SCORE	STATISTIC	VALUE	RANK	SCORE
Economics	8	69.30	Median Household Income	$48,901	8	48.8
			% of Families Above Poverty Level	97.5%	10	89.8
Affordable Housing	26	73.90	Median Home Value	$110,600	37	74.7
			Median Rent	$484	19	73.1
Crime	15	75.45	Violent Crimes per 10,000 Population	33	19	86.1
			Property Crimes per 10,000 Population	500	15	64.8
Open Spaces	12	63.60	Population Density (Persons/Sq. Mile)	934	12	90.5
			Average Rooms per Housing Unit	5.6	16	36.7
Education	10	61.50	% High School Enrollment/Completion	91.4%	13	79.4
			% College Graduates	35.1%	11	43.6
Commute	28	32.15	Average Work Commute in Minutes	24	19	50.0
			% Commuting on Public Transportation	0.3%	22	14.3
Community Stability	43	8.55	% Living in Same House as in 1979	11.3%	42	17.1
			% Living in Same County as in 1985	48.9%	43	0.0

Composite: **Rank** 21 / 43 **Score** 54.66   **MESQUITE**

CATEGORY	RANK	SCORE	STATISTIC	VALUE	RANK	SCORE
Economics	28	47.55	Median Household Income	$35,934	26	25.6
			% of Families Above Poverty Level	93.7%	29	69.5
Affordable Housing	15	84.50	Median Home Value	$68,200	12	91.6
			Median Rent	$469	15	77.4
Crime	30	53.10	Violent Crimes per 10,000 Population	58	33	73.2
			Property Crimes per 10,000 Population	747	33	33.0
Open Spaces	31	44.00	Population Density (Persons/Sq. Mile)	2369	30	64.7
			Average Rooms per Housing Unit	5.2	26	23.3
Education	31	41.35	% High School Enrollment/Completion	86.0%	33	64.2
			% College Graduates	18.3%	31	18.5
Commute	11	46.40	Average Work Commute in Minutes	26	31	35.7
			% Commuting on Public Transportation	1.2%	7	57.1
Community Stability	12	65.70	% Living in Same House as in 1979	25.2%	21	46.3
			% Living in Same County as in 1985	83.8%	5	85.1

Metropolitan Area Suburb Rankings
DALLAS-FORT WORTH

Composite: *Rank* 22 / 43 *Score* 54.35   **ENNIS**

CATEGORY	RANK	SCORE	STATISTIC	VALUE	RANK	SCORE
Economics	42	14.30	Median Household Income	$25,679	37	7.2
			% of Families Above Poverty Level	84.7%	42	21.4
Affordable Housing	6	93.60	Median Home Value	$52,600	6	97.8
			Median Rent	$427	8	89.4
Crime	23	68.10	Violent Crimes per 10,000 Population	45	26	79.9
			Property Crimes per 10,000 Population	566	21	56.3
Open Spaces	20	57.85	Population Density (Persons/Sq. Mile)	829	10	92.4
			Average Rooms per Housing Unit	5.2	26	23.3
Education	41	25.45	% High School Enrollment/Completion	78.6%	41	43.4
			% College Graduates	10.9%	40	7.5
Commute	24	35.70	Average Work Commute in Minutes	21	5	71.4
			% Commuting on Public Transportation	0.0%	38	0.0
Community Stability	2	85.45	% Living in Same House as in 1979	43.0%	3	83.8
			% Living in Same County as in 1985	84.6%	3	87.1

Composite: *Rank* 23 / 43 *Score* 54.29   **BEDFORD**

CATEGORY	RANK	SCORE	STATISTIC	VALUE	RANK	SCORE
Economics	15	64.05	Median Household Income	$42,453	16	37.2
			% of Families Above Poverty Level	97.7%	8	90.9
Affordable Housing	17	80.90	Median Home Value	$95,700	33	80.7
			Median Rent	$456	14	81.1
Crime	12	79.00	Violent Crimes per 10,000 Population	24	9	90.7
			Property Crimes per 10,000 Population	481	13	67.3
Open Spaces	43	26.05	Population Density (Persons/Sq. Mile)	4371	41	28.8
			Average Rooms per Housing Unit	5.2	26	23.3
Education	8	63.90	% High School Enrollment/Completion	93.5%	6	85.4
			% College Graduates	34.3%	12	42.4
Commute	28	32.15	Average Work Commute in Minutes	22	12	64.3
			% Commuting on Public Transportation	0.0%	38	0.0
Community Stability	32	33.95	% Living in Same House as in 1979	15.4%	34	25.7
			% Living in Same County as in 1985	66.2%	31	42.2

Composite: *Rank* 24 / 43 *Score* 54.06   **NORTH RICHLAND HILLS**

CATEGORY	RANK	SCORE	STATISTIC	VALUE	RANK	SCORE
Economics	20	56.40	Median Household Income	$38,354	20	29.9
			% of Families Above Poverty Level	96.2%	19	82.9
Affordable Housing	18	80.45	Median Home Value	$82,200	24	86.0
			Median Rent	$478	17	74.9
Crime	27	64.50	Violent Crimes per 10,000 Population	40	24	82.5
			Property Crimes per 10,000 Population	642	26	46.5
Open Spaces	29	46.05	Population Density (Persons/Sq. Mile)	2518	32	62.1
			Average Rooms per Housing Unit	5.4	22	30.0
Education	26	46.25	% High School Enrollment/Completion	87.5%	29	68.5
			% College Graduates	22.0%	26	24.0
Commute	35	27.40	Average Work Commute in Minutes	24	19	50.0
			% Commuting on Public Transportation	0.1%	33	4.8
Community Stability	19	57.40	% Living in Same House as in 1979	24.0%	23	43.8
			% Living in Same County as in 1985	78.0%	13	71.0

Metropolitan Area Suburb Rankings
DALLAS-FORT WORTH

Composite: **Rank** 25 / 43 **Score** 53.47   **ROCKWALL**

CATEGORY	RANK	SCORE	STATISTIC	VALUE	RANK	SCORE
Economics	19	57.00	Median Household Income	$44,130	14	40.2
			% of Families Above Poverty Level	94.5%	24	73.8
Affordable Housing	32	63.55	Median Home Value	$120,400	41	70.8
			Median Rent	$543	29	56.3
Crime	11	79.25	Violent Crimes per 10,000 Population	27	14	89.2
			Property Crimes per 10,000 Population	465	9	69.3
Open Spaces	6	68.85	Population Density (Persons/Sq. Mile)	715	7	94.4
			Average Rooms per Housing Unit	5.8	11	43.3
Education	14	57.45	% High School Enrollment/Completion	87.5%	29	68.5
			% College Graduates	37.0%	7	46.4
Commute	37	25.00	Average Work Commute in Minutes	28	38	21.4
			% Commuting on Public Transportation	0.6%	16	28.6
Community Stability	37	23.20	% Living in Same House as in 1979	18.4%	30	32.0
			% Living in Same County as in 1985	54.8%	41	14.4

Composite: **Rank** 26 / 43 **Score** 53.37   **EULESS**

CATEGORY	RANK	SCORE	STATISTIC	VALUE	RANK	SCORE
Economics	23	52.80	Median Household Income	$34,950	28	23.8
			% of Families Above Poverty Level	96.0%	21	81.8
Affordable Housing	14	84.95	Median Home Value	$76,100	18	88.5
			Median Rent	$455	13	81.4
Crime	17	74.05	Violent Crimes per 10,000 Population	35	20	85.1
			Property Crimes per 10,000 Population	514	16	63.0
Open Spaces	36	37.30	Population Density (Persons/Sq. Mile)	2378	31	64.6
			Average Rooms per Housing Unit	4.8	39	10.0
Education	15	55.55	% High School Enrollment/Completion	92.1%	10	81.4
			% College Graduates	25.8%	21	29.7
Commute	19	36.90	Average Work Commute in Minutes	22	12	64.3
			% Commuting on Public Transportation	0.2%	27	9.5
Community Stability	33	32.05	% Living in Same House as in 1979	16.5%	33	28.0
			% Living in Same County as in 1985	63.7%	33	36.1

Composite: **Rank** 27 / 43 **Score** 53.36   **HURST**

CATEGORY	RANK	SCORE	STATISTIC	VALUE	RANK	SCORE
Economics	24	51.60	Median Household Income	$37,473	23	28.3
			% of Families Above Poverty Level	94.7%	23	74.9
Affordable Housing	13	85.00	Median Home Value	$83,000	25	85.7
			Median Rent	$445	12	84.3
Crime	36	47.10	Violent Crimes per 10,000 Population	76	36	63.9
			Property Crimes per 10,000 Population	768	34	30.3
Open Spaces	35	39.75	Population Density (Persons/Sq. Mile)	3402	40	46.2
			Average Rooms per Housing Unit	5.5	19	33.3
Education	23	50.60	% High School Enrollment/Completion	90.4%	14	76.6
			% College Graduates	22.4%	25	24.6
Commute	27	34.55	Average Work Commute in Minutes	22	12	64.3
			% Commuting on Public Transportation	0.1%	33	4.8
Community Stability	13	64.90	% Living in Same House as in 1979	33.2%	12	63.2
			% Living in Same County as in 1985	76.2%	17	66.6

Composite: **Rank** 28 / 43 **Score** 52.78   **FLOWER MOUND**

CATEGORY	RANK	SCORE	STATISTIC	VALUE	RANK	SCORE
Economics	3	78.45	Median Household Income	$53,693	5	57.4
			% of Families Above Poverty Level	99.3%	2	99.5
Affordable Housing	41	39.75	Median Home Value	$98,500	34	79.5
			Median Rent	$740	43	0.0
Crime	14	76.85	Violent Crimes per 10,000 Population	67	34	68.6
			Property Crimes per 10,000 Population	343	6	85.1
Open Spaces	2	82.65	Population Density (Persons/Sq. Mile)	485	3	98.6
			Average Rooms per Housing Unit	6.5	2	66.7
Education	5	67.80	% High School Enrollment/Completion	95.6%	3	91.3
			% College Graduates	35.6%	9	44.3
Commute	43	10.70	Average Work Commute in Minutes	30	41	7.1
			% Commuting on Public Transportation	0.3%	22	14.3
Community Stability	41	13.25	% Living in Same House as in 1979	11.5%	41	17.5
			% Living in Same County as in 1985	52.6%	42	9.0

Composite: **Rank** 29 / 43 **Score** 52.67   **MANSFIELD**

CATEGORY	RANK	SCORE	STATISTIC	VALUE	RANK	SCORE
Economics	25	50.30	Median Household Income	$38,108	21	29.5
			% of Families Above Poverty Level	94.0%	28	71.1
Affordable Housing	23	79.20	Median Home Value	$79,100	21	87.3
			Median Rent	$491	22	71.1
Crime	20	68.90	Violent Crimes per 10,000 Population	48	27	78.4
			Property Crimes per 10,000 Population	542	18	59.4
Open Spaces	9	68.35	Population Density (Persons/Sq. Mile)	405	1	100.0
			Average Rooms per Housing Unit	5.6	16	36.7
Education	37	36.40	% High School Enrollment/Completion	81.6%	39	51.8
			% College Graduates	20.0%	28	21.0
Commute	38	21.45	Average Work Commute in Minutes	25	28	42.9
			% Commuting on Public Transportation	0.0%	38	0.0
Community Stability	26	44.10	% Living in Same House as in 1979	20.3%	25	36.0
			% Living in Same County as in 1985	70.3%	27	52.2

Composite: **Rank** 30 / 43 **Score** 52.02   **WHITE SETTLEMENT**

CATEGORY	RANK	SCORE	STATISTIC	VALUE	RANK	SCORE
Economics	36	28.30	Median Household Income	$25,149	40	6.3
			% of Families Above Poverty Level	90.1%	35	50.3
Affordable Housing	4	98.15	Median Home Value	$47,100	1	100.0
			Median Rent	$403	5	96.3
Crime	29	58.15	Violent Crimes per 10,000 Population	28	16	88.7
			Property Crimes per 10,000 Population	789	35	27.6
Open Spaces	40	28.55	Population Density (Persons/Sq. Mile)	3167	38	50.4
			Average Rooms per Housing Unit	4.7	40	6.7
Education	40	32.05	% High School Enrollment/Completion	85.5%	35	62.8
			% College Graduates	6.8%	42	1.3
Commute	8	52.35	Average Work Commute in Minutes	19	2	85.7
			% Commuting on Public Transportation	0.4%	21	19.0
Community Stability	11	66.60	% Living in Same House as in 1979	33.7%	11	64.2
			% Living in Same County as in 1985	77.2%	14	69.0

Metropolitan Area Suburb Rankings
DALLAS-FORT WORTH

Composite: Rank 31 / 43 *Score* 51.81   **HALTOM CITY**

CATEGORY	RANK	SCORE	STATISTIC	VALUE	RANK	SCORE
Economics	34	30.10	Median Household Income	$25,392	38	6.7
			% of Families Above Poverty Level	90.7%	33	53.5
Affordable Housing	2	99.00	Median Home Value	$52,000	4	98.0
			Median Rent	$390	1	100.0
Crime	34	48.20	Violent Crimes per 10,000 Population	50	31	77.3
			Property Crimes per 10,000 Population	855	38	19.1
Open Spaces	38	33.10	Population Density (Persons/Sq. Mile)	2661	34	59.5
			Average Rooms per Housing Unit	4.7	40	6.7
Education	39	32.35	% High School Enrollment/Completion	84.1%	38	58.9
			% College Graduates	9.8%	41	5.8
Commute	13	42.85	Average Work Commute in Minutes	21	5	71.4
			% Commuting on Public Transportation	0.3%	22	14.3
Community Stability	4	77.10	% Living in Same House as in 1979	36.5%	7	70.1
			% Living in Same County as in 1985	83.4%	6	84.1

Composite: Rank 32 / 43 *Score* 51.26   **FOREST HILL**

CATEGORY	RANK	SCORE	STATISTIC	VALUE	RANK	SCORE
Economics	33	35.70	Median Household Income	$32,520	31	19.5
			% of Families Above Poverty Level	90.4%	34	51.9
Affordable Housing	28	71.50	Median Home Value	$53,900	8	97.3
			Median Rent	$580	31	45.7
Crime	41	26.95	Violent Crimes per 10,000 Population	124	40	39.2
			Property Crimes per 10,000 Population	889	41	14.7
Open Spaces	30	45.95	Population Density (Persons/Sq. Mile)	2710	35	58.6
			Average Rooms per Housing Unit	5.5	19	33.3
Education	30	41.85	% High School Enrollment/Completion	90.1%	16	75.8
			% College Graduates	11.2%	39	7.9
Commute	19	36.90	Average Work Commute in Minutes	24	19	50.0
			% Commuting on Public Transportation	0.5%	17	23.8
Community Stability	1	100.00	% Living in Same House as in 1979	50.7%	1	100.0
			% Living in Same County as in 1985	89.9%	1	100.0

Composite: Rank 33 / 43 *Score* 50.71   **IRVING**

CATEGORY	RANK	SCORE	STATISTIC	VALUE	RANK	SCORE
Economics	31	40.05	Median Household Income	$31,767	32	18.1
			% of Families Above Poverty Level	92.3%	30	62.0
Affordable Housing	19	80.10	Median Home Value	$79,000	20	87.3
			Median Rent	$485	20	72.9
Crime	31	51.65	Violent Crimes per 10,000 Population	49	29	77.8
			Property Crimes per 10,000 Population	805	36	25.5
Open Spaces	39	33.05	Population Density (Persons/Sq. Mile)	2293	28	66.1
			Average Rooms per Housing Unit	4.5	43	0.0
Education	36	38.55	% High School Enrollment/Completion	79.8%	40	46.8
			% College Graduates	26.2%	20	30.3
Commute	4	71.40	Average Work Commute in Minutes	21	5	71.4
			% Commuting on Public Transportation	1.5%	5	71.4
Community Stability	29	40.15	% Living in Same House as in 1979	19.8%	26	34.9
			% Living in Same County as in 1985	67.5%	29	45.4

Metropolitan Area Suburb Rankings
DALLAS-FORT WORTH

Composite: **Rank** 34 / 43 *Score* 50.01   **TERRELL**

CATEGORY	RANK	SCORE	STATISTIC	VALUE	RANK	SCORE
Economics	43	0.00	Median Household Income	$21,633	43	0.0
			% of Families Above Poverty Level	80.7%	43	0.0
Affordable Housing	1	99.75	Median Home Value	$47,500	2	99.8
			Median Rent	$391	2	99.7
Crime	39	33.20	Violent Crimes per 10,000 Population	136	41	33.0
			Property Crimes per 10,000 Population	744	32	33.4
Open Spaces	16	58.95	Population Density (Persons/Sq. Mile)	708	6	94.6
			Average Rooms per Housing Unit	5.2	26	23.3
Education	32	41.15	% High School Enrollment/Completion	88.0%	26	69.9
			% College Graduates	14.2%	36	12.4
Commute	18	40.45	Average Work Commute in Minutes	21	5	71.4
			% Commuting on Public Transportation	0.2%	27	9.5
Community Stability	5	76.60	% Living in Same House as in 1979	40.3%	4	78.1
			% Living in Same County as in 1985	79.7%	10	75.1

Composite: **Rank** 35 / 43 *Score* 49.96   **THE COLONY**

CATEGORY	RANK	SCORE	STATISTIC	VALUE	RANK	SCORE
Economics	14	64.35	Median Household Income	$42,743	15	37.8
			% of Families Above Poverty Level	97.7%	8	90.9
Affordable Housing	38	53.00	Median Home Value	$69,900	16	90.9
			Median Rent	$687	40	15.1
Crime	6	86.25	Violent Crimes per 10,000 Population	18	5	93.8
			Property Crimes per 10,000 Population	392	8	78.7
Open Spaces	19	58.25	Population Density (Persons/Sq. Mile)	1897	24	73.2
			Average Rooms per Housing Unit	5.8	11	43.3
Education	20	51.65	% High School Enrollment/Completion	91.6%	12	80.0
			% College Graduates	21.5%	27	23.3
Commute	42	11.90	Average Work Commute in Minutes	31	42	0.0
			% Commuting on Public Transportation	0.5%	17	23.8
Community Stability	35	24.30	% Living in Same House as in 1979	13.0%	39	20.6
			% Living in Same County as in 1985	60.4%	34	28.0

Composite: **Rank** 36 / 43 *Score* 49.46   **WAXAHACHIE**

CATEGORY	RANK	SCORE	STATISTIC	VALUE	RANK	SCORE
Economics	41	15.20	Median Household Income	$24,244	41	4.7
			% of Families Above Poverty Level	85.5%	41	25.7
Affordable Housing	7	92.75	Median Home Value	$61,100	10	94.4
			Median Rent	$421	6	91.1
Crime	42	21.90	Violent Crimes per 10,000 Population	115	39	43.8
			Property Crimes per 10,000 Population	1,003	43	0.0
Open Spaces	13	60.05	Population Density (Persons/Sq. Mile)	583	4	96.8
			Average Rooms per Housing Unit	5.2	26	23.3
Education	35	39.70	% High School Enrollment/Completion	85.9%	34	63.9
			% College Graduates	16.3%	33	15.5
Commute	9	47.60	Average Work Commute in Minutes	19	2	85.7
			% Commuting on Public Transportation	0.2%	27	9.5
Community Stability	10	69.05	% Living in Same House as in 1979	36.6%	6	70.3
			% Living in Same County as in 1985	76.7%	16	67.8

Metropolitan Area Suburb Rankings
DALLAS-FORT WORTH

Composite: *Rank* 37 / 43 *Score* 49.39 **WATAUGA**

CATEGORY	RANK	SCORE	STATISTIC	VALUE	RANK	SCORE
Economics	16	63.90	Median Household Income	$41,096	18	34.8
			% of Families Above Poverty Level	98.1%	5	93.0
Affordable Housing	39	52.60	Median Home Value	$64,900	11	92.9
			Median Rent	$697	41	12.3
Crime	3	94.50	Violent Crimes per 10,000 Population	12	3	96.9
			Property Crimes per 10,000 Population	288	3	92.1
Open Spaces	42	26.30	Population Density (Persons/Sq. Mile)	4900	42	19.3
			Average Rooms per Housing Unit	5.5	19	33.3
Education	29	42.30	% High School Enrollment/Completion	88.3%	24	70.7
			% College Graduates	15.2%	35	13.9
Commute	40	14.30	Average Work Commute in Minutes	27	36	28.6
			% Commuting on Public Transportation	0.0%	38	0.0
Community Stability	23	51.85	% Living in Same House as in 1979	19.8%	26	34.9
			% Living in Same County as in 1985	77.1%	15	68.8

Composite: *Rank* 38 / 43 *Score* 49.03 **DENTON**

CATEGORY	RANK	SCORE	STATISTIC	VALUE	RANK	SCORE
Economics	39	26.50	Median Household Income	$23,156	42	2.7
			% of Families Above Poverty Level	90.1%	35	50.3
Affordable Housing	8	89.45	Median Home Value	$76,400	19	88.3
			Median Rent	$423	7	90.6
Crime	32	51.45	Violent Crimes per 10,000 Population	75	35	64.4
			Property Crimes per 10,000 Population	704	28	38.5
Open Spaces	31	44.00	Population Density (Persons/Sq. Mile)	1259	19	84.7
			Average Rooms per Housing Unit	4.6	42	3.3
Education	9	63.60	% High School Enrollment/Completion	92.2%	9	81.7
			% College Graduates	36.4%	8	45.5
Commute	15	41.70	Average Work Commute in Minutes	20	4	78.6
			% Commuting on Public Transportation	0.1%	33	4.8
Community Stability	34	26.50	% Living in Same House as in 1979	19.6%	28	34.5
			% Living in Same County as in 1985	56.5%	38	18.5

Composite: *Rank* 39 / 43 *Score* 48.66 **GRAND PRAIRIE**

CATEGORY	RANK	SCORE	STATISTIC	VALUE	RANK	SCORE
Economics	30	42.50	Median Household Income	$34,507	29	23.0
			% of Families Above Poverty Level	92.3%	30	62.0
Affordable Housing	10	88.70	Median Home Value	$68,600	14	91.4
			Median Rent	$439	10	86.0
Crime	38	38.15	Violent Crimes per 10,000 Population	97	38	53.1
			Property Crimes per 10,000 Population	823	37	23.2
Open Spaces	27	48.95	Population Density (Persons/Sq. Mile)	1454	22	81.2
			Average Rooms per Housing Unit	5.0	34	16.7
Education	34	40.05	% High School Enrollment/Completion	84.5%	37	60.0
			% College Graduates	19.4%	29	20.1
Commute	32	29.75	Average Work Commute in Minutes	24	19	50.0
			% Commuting on Public Transportation	0.2%	27	9.5
Community Stability	22	52.50	% Living in Same House as in 1979	24.5%	22	44.8
			% Living in Same County as in 1985	73.6%	20	60.2

Metropolitan Area Suburb Rankings
DALLAS-FORT WORTH

Composite: **Rank** 40 / 43 **Score** 47.50 **LEWISVILLE**

CATEGORY	RANK	SCORE	STATISTIC	VALUE	RANK	SCORE
Economics	22	54.05	Median Household Income	$36,006	25	25.7
			% of Families Above Poverty Level	96.1%	20	82.4
Affordable Housing	22	79.45	Median Home Value	$81,500	22	86.3
			Median Rent	$486	21	72.6
Crime	33	51.25	Violent Crimes per 10,000 Population	36	21	84.5
			Property Crimes per 10,000 Population	863	39	18.0
Open Spaces	26	50.40	Population Density (Persons/Sq. Mile)	1289	20	84.1
			Average Rooms per Housing Unit	5.0	34	16.7
Education	22	51.25	% High School Enrollment/Completion	89.2%	20	73.2
			% College Graduates	25.5%	22	29.3
Commute	36	26.20	Average Work Commute in Minutes	25	28	42.9
			% Commuting on Public Transportation	0.2%	27	9.5
Community Stability	40	19.90	% Living in Same House as in 1979	14.7%	35	24.2
			% Living in Same County as in 1985	55.3%	40	15.6

Composite: **Rank** 41 / 43 **Score** 47.39 **ARLINGTON**

CATEGORY	RANK	SCORE	STATISTIC	VALUE	RANK	SCORE
Economics	27	48.35	Median Household Income	$35,048	27	24.0
			% of Families Above Poverty Level	94.3%	25	72.7
Affordable Housing	12	85.35	Median Home Value	$81,900	23	86.1
			Median Rent	$444	11	84.6
Crime	37	39.85	Violent Crimes per 10,000 Population	79	37	62.4
			Property Crimes per 10,000 Population	869	40	17.3
Open Spaces	37	36.70	Population Density (Persons/Sq. Mile)	2815	36	56.7
			Average Rooms per Housing Unit	5.0	34	16.7
Education	18	53.20	% High School Enrollment/Completion	88.2%	25	70.4
			% College Graduates	30.0%	14	36.0
Commute	31	30.95	Average Work Commute in Minutes	23	17	57.1
			% Commuting on Public Transportation	0.1%	33	4.8
Community Stability	31	37.30	% Living in Same House as in 1979	17.7%	31	30.5
			% Living in Same County as in 1985	67.0%	30	44.1

Composite: **Rank** 42 / 43 **Score** 43.69 **BALCH SPRINGS**

CATEGORY	RANK	SCORE	STATISTIC	VALUE	RANK	SCORE
Economics	35	28.80	Median Household Income	$28,734	34	12.7
			% of Families Above Poverty Level	89.1%	39	44.9
Affordable Housing	11	87.80	Median Home Value	$48,100	3	99.6
			Median Rent	$474	16	76.0
Crime	43	17.00	Violent Crimes per 10,000 Population	200	43	0.0
			Property Crimes per 10,000 Population	739	31	34.0
Open Spaces	33	40.90	Population Density (Persons/Sq. Mile)	2161	27	68.5
			Average Rooms per Housing Unit	4.9	38	13.3
Education	42	15.75	% High School Enrollment/Completion	74.4%	42	31.5
			% College Graduates	5.9%	43	0.0
Commute	17	40.50	Average Work Commute in Minutes	27	36	28.6
			% Commuting on Public Transportation	1.1%	10	52.4
Community Stability	7	75.05	% Living in Same House as in 1979	30.8%	14	58.1
			% Living in Same County as in 1985	86.6%	2	92.0

Metropolitan Area Suburb Rankings
DALLAS-FORT WORTH

Composite: *Rank* 43 / 43 *Score* 43.25 **MCKINNEY**

CATEGORY	RANK	SCORE	STATISTIC	VALUE	RANK	SCORE
Economics	37	28.25	Median Household Income	$27,236	35	10.0
			% of Families Above Poverty Level	89.4%	38	46.5
Affordable Housing	9	89.25	Median Home Value	$68,600	14	91.4
			Median Rent	$435	9	87.1
Crime	40	28.35	Violent Crimes per 10,000 Population	163	42	19.1
			Property Crimes per 10,000 Population	711	30	37.6
Open Spaces	15	59.35	Population Density (Persons/Sq. Mile)	479	2	98.7
			Average Rooms per Housing Unit	5.1	33	20.0
Education	43	9.80	% High School Enrollment/Completion	63.2%	43	0.0
			% College Graduates	19.0%	30	19.6
Commute	19	36.90	Average Work Commute in Minutes	22	12	64.3
			% Commuting on Public Transportation	0.2%	27	9.5
Community Stability	24	50.85	% Living in Same House as in 1979	26.6%	20	49.3
			% Living in Same County as in 1985	70.4%	26	52.4

Metropolitan Area Description
DAYTON-SPRINGFIELD

STATE: Ohio
COUNTIES: Clark, Greene, Miami, Montgomery

TOTAL POPULATION:	951,270	
POPULATION IN SUBURBS:	698,739	(73.5%)
POPULATION IN Dayton:	182,044	(19.1%)
POPULATION IN Springfield:	70,487	(7.4%)

The DAYTON-SPRINGFIELD metropolitan area is located in the southwestern part of Ohio. The suburbs range geographically from Piqua in the north (43 miles from Dayton), to Centerville in the south (8 miles from Dayton), and to Xenia in the east (16 miles from Dayton). The area is growing slowly in population and had an increase of 1.0% between 1980 and 1990. Summer time high temperatures average in the 80's and winter time lows average in the 20's. General Motors maintains eight plants in Montgomery County, making the county the largest nucleus of General Motors employees in American outside of Detroit. Paper products producer Mead Corporation has major operations in the suburb of Miamisburg.

Beavercreek is the overall highest rated suburb. In addition, **Beavercreek** receives the highest scores in economics and open spaces, and is rated the safest suburb with the lowest crime rate. **Overlook-Page Manor** is the suburb with the most affordable housing and also has the number one score in community stability. The highest score in education goes to **Centerville**. Finally, the top rated commute belongs to **Shiloh**.

The highest ranked suburb overall which also has an affordable housing score of at least 50.00 is **Overlook-Page Manor**.

The highest ranked suburb in the education category which also has an affordable housing score of at least 50.00 is **Shiloh**.

The county whose suburbs have the highest average overall score is **Montgomery County** (54.07).

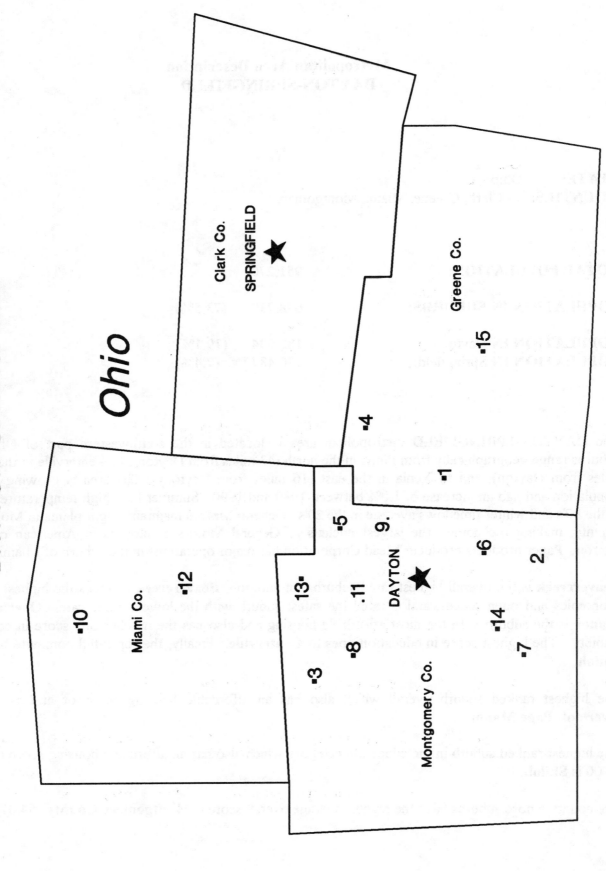

Metropolitan Area Map
DAYTON-SPRINGFIELD

Ohio

Clark Co.
SPRINGFIELD

Greene Co.

Miami Co.

Montgomery Co.
DAYTON

Metropolitan Area Suburb Alphabetical Index
DAYTON-SPRINGFIELD

SUBURB	PAGE	MAP NO.	STATE	COUNTY	POPU-LATION	RANK
BEAVERCREEK	208	1	Ohio	Greene	33,626	1 / 15
CENTERVILLE	208	2	Ohio	Montgomery	21,082	3 / 15
ENGLEWOOD	209	3	Ohio	Montgomery	11,432	6 / 15
FAIRBORN	212	4	Ohio	Greene	31,300	14 / 15
HUBER HEIGHTS	211	5	Ohio	Montgomery	38,696	10 / 15
KETTERING	209	6	Ohio	Montgomery	60,569	5 / 15
MIAMISBURG	211	7	Ohio	Montgomery	17,834	12 / 15
NORTHVIEW	208	8	Ohio	Montgomery	10,337	2 / 15
OVERLOOK-PAGE MANOR	209	9	Ohio	Montgomery	13,242	4 / 15
PIQUA	212	10	Ohio	Miami	20,612	13 / 15
SHILOH	210	11	Ohio	Montgomery	11,607	8 / 15
TROY	210	12	Ohio	Miami	19,478	9 / 15
VANDALIA	210	13	Ohio	Montgomery	13,882	7 / 15
WEST CARROLLTON CITY	211	14	Ohio	Montgomery	14,403	11 / 15
XENIA	212	15	Ohio	Greene	24,664	15 / 15

Metropolitan Area Suburb Rankings
DAYTON-SPRINGFIELD

Composite: **Rank** 1 / 15 **Score** 65.98   **BEAVERCREEK**

CATEGORY	RANK	SCORE	STATISTIC	VALUE	RANK	SCORE
Economics	1	98.15	Median Household Income	$49,143	1	100.0
			% of Families Above Poverty Level	97.4%	3	96.3
Affordable Housing	14	10.95	Median Home Value	$96,900	14	21.9
			Median Rent	$577	15	0.0
Crime	1	100.00	Violent Crimes per 10,000 Population	7	1	100.0
			Property Crimes per 10,000 Population	282	1	100.0
Open Spaces	1	99.50	Population Density (Persons/Sq. Mile)	1306	2	99.0
			Average Rooms per Housing Unit	6.8	1	100.0
Education	2	86.65	% High School Enrollment/Completion	95.9%	3	83.2
			% College Graduates	37.2%	2	90.1
Commute	10	34.90	Average Work Commute in Minutes	18	3	66.7
			% Commuting on Public Transportation	0.3%	12	3.1
Community Stability	13	31.70	% Living in Same House as in 1979	44.3%	2	50.7
			% Living in Same County as in 1985	68.8%	14	12.7

Composite: **Rank** 2 / 15 **Score** 63.58   **NORTHVIEW**

CATEGORY	RANK	SCORE	STATISTIC	VALUE	RANK	SCORE
Economics	2	96.70	Median Household Income	$47,540	2	93.4
			% of Families Above Poverty Level	97.8%	1	100.0
Affordable Housing	13	34.65	Median Home Value	$90,700	13	31.3
			Median Rent	$452	10	38.0
Crime	N/A	N/A	Violent Crimes per 10,000 Population	N/A	N/A	N/A
			Property Crimes per 10,000 Population	N/A	N/A	N/A
Open Spaces	2	76.80	Population Density (Persons/Sq. Mile)	2796	11	53.6
			Average Rooms per Housing Unit	6.8	1	100.0
Education	3	79.35	% High School Enrollment/Completion	96.9%	2	89.7
			% College Graduates	30.6%	3	69.0
Commute	14	21.90	Average Work Commute in Minutes	22	14	0.0
			% Commuting on Public Transportation	1.6%	6	43.8
Community Stability	2	72.10	% Living in Same House as in 1979	43.8%	3	48.9
			% Living in Same County as in 1985	88.3%	2	95.3

Composite: **Rank** 3 / 15 **Score** 60.29   **CENTERVILLE**

CATEGORY	RANK	SCORE	STATISTIC	VALUE	RANK	SCORE
Economics	3	88.55	Median Household Income	$45,424	3	84.6
			% of Families Above Poverty Level	97.0%	5	92.5
Affordable Housing	15	7.30	Median Home Value	$111,300	15	0.0
			Median Rent	$529	13	14.6
Crime	2	94.50	Violent Crimes per 10,000 Population	7	1	100.0
			Property Crimes per 10,000 Population	331	2	89.0
Open Spaces	3	69.60	Population Density (Persons/Sq. Mile)	2356	8	67.0
			Average Rooms per Housing Unit	6.3	3	72.2
Education	1	100.00	% High School Enrollment/Completion	98.5%	1	100.0
			% College Graduates	40.3%	1	100.0
Commute	9	35.40	Average Work Commute in Minutes	20	10	33.3
			% Commuting on Public Transportation	1.4%	7	37.5
Community Stability	14	26.70	% Living in Same House as in 1979	30.5%	15	0.0
			% Living in Same County as in 1985	78.4%	12	53.4

Metropolitan Area Suburb Rankings
DAYTON-SPRINGFIELD

Composite: **Rank** 4 / 15 *Score* 59.46   **OVERLOOK-PAGE MANOR**

CATEGORY	RANK	SCORE	STATISTIC	VALUE	RANK	SCORE
Economics	9	55.25	Median Household Income	$30,472	10	22.6
			% of Families Above Poverty Level	96.5%	9	87.9
Affordable Housing	1	91.25	Median Home Value	$57,000	3	82.5
			Median Rent	$248	1	100.0
Crime	N/A	N/A	Violent Crimes per 10,000 Population	N/A	N/A	N/A
			Property Crimes per 10,000 Population	N/A	N/A	N/A
Open Spaces	15	16.65	Population Density (Persons/Sq. Mile)	4557	15	0.0
			Average Rooms per Housing Unit	5.6	9	33.3
Education	11	33.70	% High School Enrollment/Completion	92.9%	10	63.9
			% College Graduates	10.1%	14	3.5
Commute	2	59.90	Average Work Commute in Minutes	18	3	66.7
			% Commuting on Public Transportation	1.9%	2	53.1
Community Stability	1	100.00	% Living in Same House as in 1979	57.7%	1	100.0
			% Living in Same County as in 1985	89.4%	1	100.0

Composite: **Rank** 5 / 15 *Score* 57.41   **KETTERING**

CATEGORY	RANK	SCORE	STATISTIC	VALUE	RANK	SCORE
Economics	6	66.85	Median Household Income	$34,506	7	39.3
			% of Families Above Poverty Level	97.2%	4	94.4
Affordable Housing	10	45.20	Median Home Value	$76,600	11	52.7
			Median Rent	$453	11	37.7
Crime	4	70.10	Violent Crimes per 10,000 Population	14	4	75.9
			Property Crimes per 10,000 Population	441	8	64.3
Open Spaces	11	39.40	Population Density (Persons/Sq. Mile)	3247	14	39.9
			Average Rooms per Housing Unit	5.7	6	38.9
Education	4	63.55	% High School Enrollment/Completion	93.0%	9	64.5
			% College Graduates	28.6%	4	62.6
Commute	2	59.90	Average Work Commute in Minutes	18	3	66.7
			% Commuting on Public Transportation	1.9%	2	53.1
Community Stability	5	56.90	% Living in Same House as in 1979	40.6%	5	37.1
			% Living in Same County as in 1985	83.9%	10	76.7

Composite: **Rank** 6 / 15 *Score* 54.05   **ENGLEWOOD**

CATEGORY	RANK	SCORE	STATISTIC	VALUE	RANK	SCORE
Economics	4	74.55	Median Household Income	$37,087	5	50.0
			% of Families Above Poverty Level	97.7%	2	99.1
Affordable Housing	11	43.75	Median Home Value	$80,100	12	47.4
			Median Rent	$445	9	40.1
Crime	3	72.80	Violent Crimes per 10,000 Population	13	3	79.3
			Property Crimes per 10,000 Population	432	6	66.3
Open Spaces	6	60.80	Population Density (Persons/Sq. Mile)	2206	5	71.6
			Average Rooms per Housing Unit	5.9	4	50.0
Education	8	49.80	% High School Enrollment/Completion	93.5%	5	67.7
			% College Graduates	19.0%	7	31.9
Commute	13	26.55	Average Work Commute in Minutes	22	14	0.0
			% Commuting on Public Transportation	1.9%	2	53.1
Community Stability	9	50.10	% Living in Same House as in 1979	36.2%	9	21.0
			% Living in Same County as in 1985	84.5%	7	79.2

Metropolitan Area Suburb Rankings
DAYTON-SPRINGFIELD

Composite: Rank 7 / 15 *Score* 53.71 **VANDALIA**

CATEGORY	RANK	SCORE	STATISTIC	VALUE	RANK	SCORE
Economics	7	64.75	Median Household Income	$34,835	6	40.7
			% of Families Above Poverty Level	96.6%	8	88.8
Affordable Housing	8	53.90	Median Home Value	$75,000	10	55.2
			Median Rent	$404	6	52.6
Crime	5	68.75	Violent Crimes per 10,000 Population	19	5	58.6
			Property Crimes per 10,000 Population	376	3	78.9
Open Spaces	5	63.90	Population Density (Persons/Sq. Mile)	1274	1	100.0
			Average Rooms per Housing Unit	5.5	10	27.8
Education	12	31.50	% High School Enrollment/Completion	89.2%	14	40.0
			% College Graduates	16.2%	11	23.0
Commute	6	43.75	Average Work Commute in Minutes	19	8	50.0
			% Commuting on Public Transportation	1.4%	7	37.5
Community Stability	10	49.40	% Living in Same House as in 1979	34.9%	11	16.2
			% Living in Same County as in 1985	85.3%	6	82.6

Composite: Rank 8 / 15 *Score* 53.03 **SHILOH**

CATEGORY	RANK	SCORE	STATISTIC	VALUE	RANK	SCORE
Economics	11	41.00	Median Household Income	$27,011	13	8.2
			% of Families Above Poverty Level	95.0%	10	73.8
Affordable Housing	5	61.15	Median Home Value	$67,000	8	67.3
			Median Rent	$396	5	55.0
Crime	N/A	N/A	Violent Crimes per 10,000 Population	N/A	N/A	N/A
			Property Crimes per 10,000 Population	N/A	N/A	N/A
Open Spaces	13	29.15	Population Density (Persons/Sq. Mile)	3007	13	47.2
			Average Rooms per Housing Unit	5.2	13	11.1
Education	5	59.25	% High School Enrollment/Completion	92.9%	10	63.9
			% College Graduates	26.1%	5	54.6
Commute	1	66.65	Average Work Commute in Minutes	20	10	33.3
			% Commuting on Public Transportation	3.4%	1	100.0
Community Stability	4	61.00	% Living in Same House as in 1979	38.8%	7	30.5
			% Living in Same County as in 1985	87.4%	4	91.5

Composite: Rank 9 / 15 *Score* 50.37 **TROY**

CATEGORY	RANK	SCORE	STATISTIC	VALUE	RANK	SCORE
Economics	12	32.60	Median Household Income	$29,032	11	16.6
			% of Families Above Poverty Level	92.3%	12	48.6
Affordable Housing	4	68.50	Median Home Value	$59,200	4	79.2
			Median Rent	$387	3	57.8
Crime	8	50.75	Violent Crimes per 10,000 Population	26	8	34.5
			Property Crimes per 10,000 Population	429	5	67.0
Open Spaces	8	48.75	Population Density (Persons/Sq. Mile)	2268	6	69.7
			Average Rooms per Housing Unit	5.5	10	27.8
Education	7	50.00	% High School Enrollment/Completion	94.6%	4	74.8
			% College Graduates	16.9%	9	25.2
Commute	5	47.90	Average Work Commute in Minutes	17	2	83.3
			% Commuting on Public Transportation	0.6%	11	12.5
Community Stability	7	54.10	% Living in Same House as in 1979	38.5%	8	29.4
			% Living in Same County as in 1985	84.4%	8	78.8

Metropolitan Area Suburb Rankings
DAYTON-SPRINGFIELD

Composite: Rank 10 / 15 *Score* 49.98   **HUBER HEIGHTS**

CATEGORY	RANK	SCORE	STATISTIC	VALUE	RANK	SCORE
Economics	5	72.05	Median Household Income	$37,912	4	53.4
			% of Families Above Poverty Level	96.8%	7	90.7
Affordable Housing	12	38.25	Median Home Value	$65,200	6	70.1
			Median Rent	$556	14	6.4
Crime	7	60.50	Violent Crimes per 10,000 Population	20	7	55.2
			Property Crimes per 10,000 Population	434	7	65.8
Open Spaces	4	66.05	Population Density (Persons/Sq. Mile)	1862	3	82.1
			Average Rooms per Housing Unit	5.9	4	50.0
Education	9	48.70	% High School Enrollment/Completion	93.5%	5	67.7
			% College Graduates	18.3%	8	29.7
Commute	12	31.80	Average Work Commute in Minutes	21	13	16.7
			% Commuting on Public Transportation	1.7%	5	46.9
Community Stability	12	32.50	% Living in Same House as in 1979	35.4%	10	18.0
			% Living in Same County as in 1985	76.9%	13	47.0

Composite: Rank 11 / 15 *Score* 46.05   **WEST CARROLLTON CITY**

CATEGORY	RANK	SCORE	STATISTIC	VALUE	RANK	SCORE
Economics	8	61.15	Median Household Income	$32,207	9	29.8
			% of Families Above Poverty Level	97.0%	5	92.5
Affordable Housing	9	50.50	Median Home Value	$66,800	7	67.6
			Median Rent	$467	12	33.4
Crime	N/A	N/A	Violent Crimes per 10,000 Population	N/A	N/A	N/A
			Property Crimes per 10,000 Population	N/A	N/A	N/A
Open Spaces	10	40.20	Population Density (Persons/Sq. Mile)	2283	7	69.3
			Average Rooms per Housing Unit	5.2	13	11.1
Education	10	44.90	% High School Enrollment/Completion	93.1%	7	65.2
			% College Graduates	16.7%	10	24.6
Commute	7	42.75	Average Work Commute in Minutes	18	3	66.7
			% Commuting on Public Transportation	0.8%	10	18.8
Community Stability	11	36.80	% Living in Same House as in 1979	30.8%	14	1.1
			% Living in Same County as in 1985	82.9%	11	72.5

Composite: Rank 12 / 15 *Score* 43.12   **MIAMISBURG**

CATEGORY	RANK	SCORE	STATISTIC	VALUE	RANK	SCORE
Economics	10	47.15	Median Household Income	$32,436	8	30.7
			% of Families Above Poverty Level	93.9%	11	63.6
Affordable Housing	7	56.00	Median Home Value	$72,000	9	59.7
			Median Rent	$405	7	52.3
Crime	10	15.40	Violent Crimes per 10,000 Population	35	9	3.4
			Property Crimes per 10,000 Population	605	10	27.4
Open Spaces	7	60.20	Population Density (Persons/Sq. Mile)	1882	4	81.5
			Average Rooms per Housing Unit	5.7	6	38.9
Education	13	31.35	% High School Enrollment/Completion	89.8%	12	43.9
			% College Graduates	14.9%	12	18.8
Commute	8	40.60	Average Work Commute in Minutes	19	8	50.0
			% Commuting on Public Transportation	1.2%	9	31.2
Community Stability	8	51.15	% Living in Same House as in 1979	34.7%	12	15.4
			% Living in Same County as in 1985	86.3%	5	86.9

Metropolitan Area Suburb Rankings
DAYTON-SPRINGFIELD

Composite: Rank 13 / 15 *Score* 38.59   **PIQUA**

CATEGORY	RANK	SCORE	STATISTIC	VALUE	RANK	SCORE
Economics	14	4.65	Median Household Income	$25,026	15	0.0
			% of Families Above Poverty Level	88.1%	14	9.3
Affordable Housing	2	80.85	Median Home Value	$45,500	1	100.0
			Median Rent	$374	2	61.7
Crime	9	16.40	Violent Crimes per 10,000 Population	35	9	3.4
			Property Crimes per 10,000 Population	596	9	29.4
Open Spaces	9	46.45	Population Density (Persons/Sq. Mile)	2783	10	54.0
			Average Rooms per Housing Unit	5.7	6	38.9
Education	15	0.00	% High School Enrollment/Completion	83.0%	15	0.0
			% College Graduates	9.0%	15	0.0
Commute	4	51.55	Average Work Commute in Minutes	16	1	100.0
			% Commuting on Public Transportation	0.3%	12	3.1
Community Stability	3	70.25	% Living in Same House as in 1979	42.9%	4	45.6
			% Living in Same County as in 1985	88.2%	3	94.9

Composite: Rank 14 / 15 *Score* 36.24   **FAIRBORN**

CATEGORY	RANK	SCORE	STATISTIC	VALUE	RANK	SCORE
Economics	13	14.60	Median Household Income	$27,558	12	10.5
			% of Families Above Poverty Level	89.1%	13	18.7
Affordable Housing	6	59.95	Median Home Value	$61,600	5	75.5
			Median Rent	$431	8	44.4
Crime	6	65.05	Violent Crimes per 10,000 Population	19	5	58.6
			Property Crimes per 10,000 Population	409	4	71.5
Open Spaces	14	26.75	Population Density (Persons/Sq. Mile)	2800	12	53.5
			Average Rooms per Housing Unit	5.0	15	0.0
Education	6	51.75	% High School Enrollment/Completion	93.1%	7	65.2
			% College Graduates	21.0%	6	38.3
Commute	11	33.35	Average Work Commute in Minutes	18	3	66.7
			% Commuting on Public Transportation	0.2%	15	0.0
Community Stability	15	2.20	% Living in Same House as in 1979	31.7%	13	4.4
			% Living in Same County as in 1985	65.8%	15	0.0

Composite: Rank 15 / 15 *Score* 30.11   **XENIA**

CATEGORY	RANK	SCORE	STATISTIC	VALUE	RANK	SCORE
Economics	15	1.00	Median Household Income	$25,508	14	2.0
			% of Families Above Poverty Level	87.1%	15	0.0
Affordable Housing	3	72.50	Median Home Value	$52,900	2	88.8
			Median Rent	$392	4	56.2
Crime	11	0.00	Violent Crimes per 10,000 Population	36	11	0.0
			Property Crimes per 10,000 Population	727	11	0.0
Open Spaces	12	38.55	Population Density (Persons/Sq. Mile)	2753	9	54.9
			Average Rooms per Housing Unit	5.4	12	22.2
Education	14	25.60	% High School Enrollment/Completion	89.7%	13	43.2
			% College Graduates	11.5%	13	8.0
Commute	15	18.20	Average Work Commute in Minutes	20	10	33.3
			% Commuting on Public Transportation	0.3%	12	3.1
Community Stability	6	54.95	% Living in Same House as in 1979	39.3%	6	32.4
			% Living in Same County as in 1985	84.1%	9	77.5

Metropolitan Area Description
DENVER-BOULDER

STATE: Colorado
COUNTIES: Adams, Arapahoe, Boulder, Denver, Douglas, Jefferson

TOTAL POPULATION:	1,848,319	
POPULATION IN SUBURBS:	1,297,397	(70.2%)
POPULATION IN Denver:	467,610	(25.3%)
POPULATION IN Boulder:	83,312	(4.5%)

The DENVER-BOULDER metropolitan area is located in the central part of Colorado. The suburbs range geographically from Longmont in the north (37 miles from Denver), to Golden in the west (14 miles from Denver), to Highlands Ranch in the south (16 miles from Denver), and to Aurora in the east (10 miles from Denver). The area is growing in population and had an increase of 14.2% between 1980 and 1990. Summer time high temperatures average in the 80's and winter time lows average in the teens. The suburb of Golden is the home of brewer Adolph Coors Company. Suburban growth, especially the Adams County suburbs of Thornton, Northglenn, and Westminster, will get a large boost from the completion of Denver International Airport in 1993. Public transportation in the area is provided on buses by the Regional Transportation District.

Louisville is the overall highest rated suburb. **Castlewood** receives the highest scores in economics and education. **Commerce City** is the suburb with the most affordable housing and also has the number one score in community stability. **Lafayette** is rated the safest suburb with the lowest crime rate. The top rated commute belongs to **Englewood**. Finally, the number one rating in open spaces goes to **Highlands Ranch**.

The highest ranked suburb overall which also has an affordable housing score of at least 50.00 is **Applewood**.

The highest ranked suburb in the education category which also has an affordable housing score of at least 50.00 is **Littleton**.

The county whose suburbs have the highest average overall score is **Boulder County** (63.88).

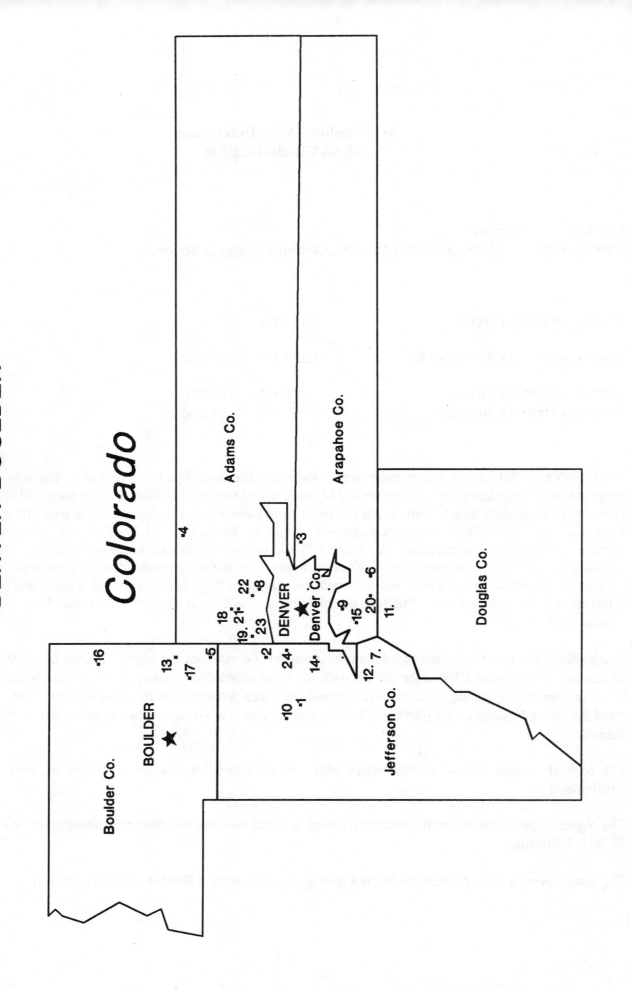

Metropolitan Area Map
DENVER-BOULDER

Colorado

Adams Co.

Arapahoe Co.

Douglas Co.

Jefferson Co.

Boulder Co.

DENVER

Denver Co.

BOULDER

-4

-3

-6

-8
22

18
19. 21.
23

-9
-15
20-
11.

-5
-2
24-
14-

12. 7.

-16

13.
-17

-10
-1

Metropolitan Area Suburb Alphabetical Index
DENVER-BOULDER

SUBURB	PAGE	MAP NO.	STATE	COUNTY	POPU-LATION	RANK
APPLEWOOD	216	1	Colorado	Jefferson	11,069	2 / 24
ARVADA	218	2	Colorado	Jefferson	89,235	9 / 24
AURORA	222	3	Colorado	Arapahoe	222,103	21 / 24
BRIGHTON	221	4	Colorado	Adams	14,203	16 / 24
BROOMFIELD	216	5	Colorado	Boulder	24,638	3 / 24
CASTLEWOOD	217	6	Colorado	Arapahoe	24,392	4 / 24
COLUMBINE	218	7	Colorado	Jefferson	23,969	7 / 24
COMMERCE CITY	223	8	Colorado	Adams	16,466	24 / 24
ENGLEWOOD	220	9	Colorado	Arapahoe	29,387	14 / 24
GOLDEN	219	10	Colorado	Jefferson	13,116	11 / 24
HIGHLANDS RANCH	223	11	Colorado	Douglas	10,181	23 / 24
KEN CARYL	223	12	Colorado	Jefferson	24,391	22 / 24
LAFAYETTE	221	13	Colorado	Boulder	14,548	18 / 24
LAKEWOOD	218	14	Colorado	Jefferson	126,481	8 / 24
LITTLETON	217	15	Colorado	Arapahoe	33,685	6 / 24
LONGMONT	220	16	Colorado	Boulder	51,555	15 / 24
LOUISVILLE	216	17	Colorado	Boulder	12,361	1 / 24
NORTHGLENN	219	18	Colorado	Adams	27,195	12 / 24
SHERRELWOOD	222	19	Colorado	Adams	16,636	19 / 24
SOUTHGLENN	217	20	Colorado	Arapahoe	43,087	5 / 24
THORNTON	222	21	Colorado	Adams	55,031	20 / 24
WELBY	221	22	Colorado	Adams	10,218	17 / 24
WESTMINSTER	220	23	Colorado	Adams	74,625	13 / 24
WHEAT RIDGE	219	24	Colorado	Jefferson	29,419	10 / 24

Metropolitan Area Suburb Rankings
DENVER-BOULDER

Composite: *Rank* 1 / 24 *Score* 70.60   **LOUISVILLE**

CATEGORY	RANK	SCORE	STATISTIC	VALUE	RANK	SCORE
Economics	6	72.70	Median Household Income	$43,379	6	56.0
			% of Families Above Poverty Level	97.2%	7	89.4
Affordable Housing	19	48.45	Median Home Value	$97,300	18	42.8
			Median Rent	$561	19	54.1
Crime	2	93.45	Violent Crimes per 10,000 Population	32	6	86.9
			Property Crimes per 10,000 Population	347	1	100.0
Open Spaces	8	63.35	Population Density (Persons/Sq. Mile)	1611	5	86.7
			Average Rooms per Housing Unit	6.0	10	40.0
Education	5	79.85	% High School Enrollment/Completion	95.3%	4	88.0
			% College Graduates	42.9%	4	71.7
Commute	4	77.00	Average Work Commute in Minutes	21	3	85.7
			% Commuting on Public Transportation	3.4%	7	68.3
Community Stability	21	59.40	% Living in Same House as in 1979	17.0%	21	40.8
			% Living in Same County as in 1985	69.0%	14	78.0

Composite: *Rank* 2 / 24 *Score* 70.21   **APPLEWOOD**

CATEGORY	RANK	SCORE	STATISTIC	VALUE	RANK	SCORE
Economics	7	69.30	Median Household Income	$39,133	7	45.6
			% of Families Above Poverty Level	97.9%	5	93.0
Affordable Housing	18	55.80	Median Home Value	$99,400	20	39.8
			Median Rent	$502	17	71.8
Crime	N/A	N/A	Violent Crimes per 10,000 Population	N/A	N/A	N/A
			Property Crimes per 10,000 Population	N/A	N/A	N/A
Open Spaces	3	72.15	Population Density (Persons/Sq. Mile)	1514	4	88.3
			Average Rooms per Housing Unit	6.4	6	56.0
Education	9	60.30	% High School Enrollment/Completion	91.3%	11	72.0
			% College Graduates	30.2%	9	48.6
Commute	9	68.45	Average Work Commute in Minutes	21	3	85.7
			% Commuting on Public Transportation	2.7%	13	51.2
Community Stability	2	95.25	% Living in Same House as in 1979	40.1%	3	96.2
			% Living in Same County as in 1985	78.8%	2	94.3

Composite: *Rank* 3 / 24 *Score* 68.55   **BROOMFIELD**

CATEGORY	RANK	SCORE	STATISTIC	VALUE	RANK	SCORE
Economics	8	63.95	Median Household Income	$39,067	8	45.5
			% of Families Above Poverty Level	95.8%	9	82.4
Affordable Housing	11	71.75	Median Home Value	$87,700	12	56.4
			Median Rent	$451	9	87.1
Crime	3	92.60	Violent Crimes per 10,000 Population	25	4	91.5
			Property Crimes per 10,000 Population	396	2	93.7
Open Spaces	5	71.65	Population Density (Persons/Sq. Mile)	1104	3	95.3
			Average Rooms per Housing Unit	6.2	8	48.0
Education	8	62.45	% High School Enrollment/Completion	93.4%	6	80.4
			% College Graduates	27.9%	12	44.5
Commute	16	50.70	Average Work Commute in Minutes	24	18	42.9
			% Commuting on Public Transportation	3.0%	11	58.5
Community Stability	16	66.75	% Living in Same House as in 1979	24.8%	16	59.5
			% Living in Same County as in 1985	66.6%	18	74.0

Metropolitan Area Suburb Rankings
DENVER-BOULDER

Composite: **Rank** 4 / 24 **Score** 67.95   **CASTLEWOOD**

CATEGORY	RANK	SCORE	STATISTIC	VALUE	RANK	SCORE
Economics	1	99.25	Median Household Income	$61,410	1	100.0
			% of Families Above Poverty Level	99.0%	3	98.5
Affordable Housing	24	0.00	Median Home Value	$127,400	24	0.0
			Median Rent	$741	24	0.0
Crime	N/A	N/A	Violent Crimes per 10,000 Population	N/A	N/A	N/A
			Property Crimes per 10,000 Population	N/A	N/A	N/A
Open Spaces	4	72.05	Population Density (Persons/Sq. Mile)	3891	18	48.1
			Average Rooms per Housing Unit	7.4	2	96.0
Education	1	100.00	% High School Enrollment/Completion	98.3%	1	100.0
			% College Graduates	58.5%	1	100.0
Commute	8	71.95	Average Work Commute in Minutes	20	1	100.0
			% Commuting on Public Transportation	2.4%	18	43.9
Community Stability	18	64.45	% Living in Same House as in 1979	24.7%	17	59.2
			% Living in Same County as in 1985	64.0%	20	69.7

Composite: **Rank** 5 / 24 **Score** 67.64   **SOUTHGLENN**

CATEGORY	RANK	SCORE	STATISTIC	VALUE	RANK	SCORE
Economics	4	85.55	Median Household Income	$51,612	4	76.1
			% of Families Above Poverty Level	98.3%	4	95.0
Affordable Housing	20	28.80	Median Home Value	$105,000	21	31.8
			Median Rent	$655	21	25.8
Crime	N/A	N/A	Violent Crimes per 10,000 Population	N/A	N/A	N/A
			Property Crimes per 10,000 Population	N/A	N/A	N/A
Open Spaces	7	64.00	Population Density (Persons/Sq. Mile)	4370	22	40.0
			Average Rooms per Housing Unit	7.2	3	88.0
Education	2	83.60	% High School Enrollment/Completion	95.5%	3	88.8
			% College Graduates	46.6%	3	78.4
Commute	12	64.95	Average Work Commute in Minutes	22	10	71.4
			% Commuting on Public Transportation	3.0%	11	58.5
Community Stability	11	78.95	% Living in Same House as in 1979	33.3%	11	79.9
			% Living in Same County as in 1985	69.0%	14	78.0

Composite: **Rank** 6 / 24 **Score** 67.32   **LITTLETON**

CATEGORY	RANK	SCORE	STATISTIC	VALUE	RANK	SCORE
Economics	12	55.50	Median Household Income	$34,006	15	33.1
			% of Families Above Poverty Level	94.9%	11	77.9
Affordable Housing	15	68.25	Median Home Value	$97,300	18	42.8
			Median Rent	$429	7	93.7
Crime	4	88.90	Violent Crimes per 10,000 Population	23	2	92.8
			Property Crimes per 10,000 Population	463	4	85.0
Open Spaces	12	49.90	Population Density (Persons/Sq. Mile)	2730	13	67.8
			Average Rooms per Housing Unit	5.8	12	32.0
Education	6	68.10	% High School Enrollment/Completion	92.7%	8	77.6
			% College Graduates	35.7%	7	58.6
Commute	9	68.45	Average Work Commute in Minutes	21	3	85.7
			% Commuting on Public Transportation	2.7%	13	51.2
Community Stability	14	72.15	% Living in Same House as in 1979	28.5%	13	68.3
			% Living in Same County as in 1985	67.8%	17	76.0

Metropolitan Area Suburb Rankings
DENVER-BOULDER

Composite: **Rank** 7 / 24 **Score** 65.58   **COLUMBINE**

CATEGORY	RANK	SCORE	STATISTIC	VALUE	RANK	SCORE
Economics	3	88.85	Median Household Income	$52,697	3	78.7
			% of Families Above Poverty Level	99.1%	2	99.0
Affordable Housing	22	19.95	Median Home Value	$106,700	22	29.4
			Median Rent	$706	22	10.5
Crime	N/A	N/A	Violent Crimes per 10,000 Population	N/A	N/A	N/A
			Property Crimes per 10,000 Population	N/A	N/A	N/A
Open Spaces	2	75.40	Population Density (Persons/Sq. Mile)	3733	17	50.8
			Average Rooms per Housing Unit	7.5	1	100.0
Education	4	79.90	% High School Enrollment/Completion	96.5%	2	92.8
			% College Graduates	40.3%	5	67.0
Commute	20	38.70	Average Work Commute in Minutes	25	22	28.6
			% Commuting on Public Transportation	2.6%	15	48.8
Community Stability	5	90.70	% Living in Same House as in 1979	39.4%	4	94.5
			% Living in Same County as in 1985	74.3%	9	86.9

Composite: **Rank** 8 / 24 **Score** 64.03   **LAKEWOOD**

CATEGORY	RANK	SCORE	STATISTIC	VALUE	RANK	SCORE
Economics	13	55.35	Median Household Income	$34,054	14	33.3
			% of Families Above Poverty Level	94.8%	12	77.4
Affordable Housing	16	67.15	Median Home Value	$91,200	15	51.4
			Median Rent	$465	12	82.9
Crime	9	71.30	Violent Crimes per 10,000 Population	48	10	76.5
			Property Crimes per 10,000 Population	610	9	66.1
Open Spaces	20	44.75	Population Density (Persons/Sq. Mile)	3100	15	61.5
			Average Rooms per Housing Unit	5.7	14	28.0
Education	10	57.15	% High School Enrollment/Completion	90.0%	14	66.8
			% College Graduates	29.6%	10	47.5
Commute	5	74.70	Average Work Commute in Minutes	22	10	71.4
			% Commuting on Public Transportation	3.8%	5	78.0
Community Stability	12	77.80	% Living in Same House as in 1979	30.9%	12	74.1
			% Living in Same County as in 1985	71.1%	13	81.5

Composite: **Rank** 9 / 24 **Score** 63.97   **ARVADA**

CATEGORY	RANK	SCORE	STATISTIC	VALUE	RANK	SCORE
Economics	9	62.15	Median Household Income	$39,014	9	45.4
			% of Families Above Poverty Level	95.1%	10	78.9
Affordable Housing	13	69.80	Median Home Value	$89,400	14	54.0
			Median Rent	$456	11	85.6
Crime	N/A	N/A	Violent Crimes per 10,000 Population	N/A	N/A	N/A
			Property Crimes per 10,000 Population	N/A	N/A	N/A
Open Spaces	10	50.95	Population Density (Persons/Sq. Mile)	4025	21	45.9
			Average Rooms per Housing Unit	6.4	6	56.0
Education	13	54.20	% High School Enrollment/Completion	90.6%	12	69.2
			% College Graduates	25.0%	14	39.2
Commute	13	59.05	Average Work Commute in Minutes	23	14	57.1
			% Commuting on Public Transportation	3.1%	9	61.0
Community Stability	7	87.70	% Living in Same House as in 1979	35.4%	8	84.9
			% Living in Same County as in 1985	76.5%	4	90.5

Metropolitan Area Suburb Rankings
DENVER-BOULDER

Composite: **Rank** 10 / 24 **Score** 63.96   **WHEAT RIDGE**

CATEGORY	RANK	SCORE	STATISTIC	VALUE	RANK	SCORE
Economics	18	46.35	Median Household Income	$28,338	21	19.3
			% of Families Above Poverty Level	94.0%	14	73.4
Affordable Housing	9	75.10	Median Home Value	$88,500	13	55.3
			Median Rent	$425	6	94.9
Crime	12	59.85	Violent Crimes per 10,000 Population	66	12	64.7
			Property Crimes per 10,000 Population	696	11	55.0
Open Spaces	22	34.95	Population Density (Persons/Sq. Mile)	3314	16	57.9
			Average Rooms per Housing Unit	5.3	20	12.0
Education	12	54.80	% High School Enrollment/Completion	92.9%	7	78.4
			% College Graduates	20.6%	16	31.2
Commute	2	89.20	Average Work Commute in Minutes	21	3	85.7
			% Commuting on Public Transportation	4.4%	2	92.7
Community Stability	8	87.50	% Living in Same House as in 1979	36.1%	7	86.6
			% Living in Same County as in 1985	75.2%	8	88.4

Composite: **Rank** 11 / 24 **Score** 62.49   **GOLDEN**

CATEGORY	RANK	SCORE	STATISTIC	VALUE	RANK	SCORE
Economics	20	42.75	Median Household Income	$29,099	20	21.2
			% of Families Above Poverty Level	92.2%	20	64.3
Affordable Housing	10	72.60	Median Home Value	$93,900	17	47.6
			Median Rent	$416	2	97.6
Crime	5	88.55	Violent Crimes per 10,000 Population	24	3	92.2
			Property Crimes per 10,000 Population	464	5	84.9
Open Spaces	18	46.20	Population Density (Persons/Sq. Mile)	1748	7	84.4
			Average Rooms per Housing Unit	5.2	22	8.0
Education	16	49.20	% High School Enrollment/Completion	84.3%	22	44.0
			% College Graduates	33.4%	8	54.4
Commute	6	73.35	Average Work Commute in Minutes	21	3	85.7
			% Commuting on Public Transportation	3.1%	9	61.0
Community Stability	17	64.80	% Living in Same House as in 1979	25.3%	14	60.7
			% Living in Same County as in 1985	63.5%	21	68.9

Composite: **Rank** 12 / 24 **Score** 62.29   **NORTHGLENN**

CATEGORY	RANK	SCORE	STATISTIC	VALUE	RANK	SCORE
Economics	10	59.90	Median Household Income	$34,726	11	34.9
			% of Families Above Poverty Level	96.3%	8	84.9
Affordable Housing	5	86.55	Median Home Value	$71,100	4	80.0
			Median Rent	$431	8	93.1
Crime	10	70.80	Violent Crimes per 10,000 Population	44	9	79.1
			Property Crimes per 10,000 Population	638	10	62.5
Open Spaces	19	46.00	Population Density (Persons/Sq. Mile)	3897	19	48.0
			Average Rooms per Housing Unit	6.1	9	44.0
Education	20	37.05	% High School Enrollment/Completion	87.1%	17	55.2
			% College Graduates	13.8%	20	18.9
Commute	19	44.60	Average Work Commute in Minutes	24	18	42.9
			% Commuting on Public Transportation	2.5%	17	46.3
Community Stability	4	91.15	% Living in Same House as in 1979	38.4%	5	92.1
			% Living in Same County as in 1985	76.3%	5	90.2

Metropolitan Area Suburb Rankings
DENVER-BOULDER

Composite: Rank 13 / 24 *Score* 60.11 **WESTMINSTER**

CATEGORY	RANK	SCORE	STATISTIC	VALUE	RANK	SCORE
Economics	11	57.55	Median Household Income	$36,716	10	39.7
			% of Families Above Poverty Level	94.4%	13	75.4
Affordable Housing	14	69.35	Median Home Value	$85,600	10	59.4
			Median Rent	$477	15	79.3
Crime	7	77.20	Violent Crimes per 10,000 Population	31	5	87.6
			Property Crimes per 10,000 Population	604	7	66.8
Open Spaces	13	49.40	Population Density (Persons/Sq. Mile)	2785	14	66.8
			Average Rooms per Housing Unit	5.8	12	32.0
Education	14	50.10	% High School Enrollment/Completion	89.1%	15	63.2
			% College Graduates	23.8%	15	37.0
Commute	14	56.80	Average Work Commute in Minutes	24	18	42.9
			% Commuting on Public Transportation	3.5%	6	70.7
Community Stability	20	60.35	% Living in Same House as in 1979	20.5%	19	49.2
			% Living in Same County as in 1985	65.1%	19	71.5

Composite: Rank 14 / 24 *Score* 59.89 **ENGLEWOOD**

CATEGORY	RANK	SCORE	STATISTIC	VALUE	RANK	SCORE
Economics	22	38.50	Median Household Income	$25,422	23	12.2
			% of Families Above Poverty Level	92.3%	19	64.8
Affordable Housing	4	86.60	Median Home Value	$72,500	6	78.0
			Median Rent	$424	5	95.2
Crime	N/A	N/A	Violent Crimes per 10,000 Population	N/A	N/A	N/A
			Property Crimes per 10,000 Population	N/A	N/A	N/A
Open Spaces	24	18.90	Population Density (Persons/Sq. Mile)	4500	23	37.8
			Average Rooms per Housing Unit	5.0	23	0.0
Education	21	36.35	% High School Enrollment/Completion	84.4%	20	44.4
			% College Graduates	19.0%	18	28.3
Commute	1	100.00	Average Work Commute in Minutes	20	1	100.0
			% Commuting on Public Transportation	4.7%	1	100.0
Community Stability	10	79.00	% Living in Same House as in 1979	33.7%	10	80.8
			% Living in Same County as in 1985	68.5%	16	77.2

Composite: Rank 15 / 24 *Score* 58.54 **LONGMONT**

CATEGORY	RANK	SCORE	STATISTIC	VALUE	RANK	SCORE
Economics	15	51.45	Median Household Income	$32,534	17	29.5
			% of Families Above Poverty Level	94.0%	14	73.4
Affordable Housing	12	71.00	Median Home Value	$85,600	10	59.4
			Median Rent	$466	13	82.6
Crime	6	78.35	Violent Crimes per 10,000 Population	41	8	81.0
			Property Crimes per 10,000 Population	535	6	75.7
Open Spaces	21	37.80	Population Density (Persons/Sq. Mile)	3921	20	47.6
			Average Rooms per Housing Unit	5.7	14	28.0
Education	17	41.50	% High School Enrollment/Completion	86.3%	19	52.0
			% College Graduates	20.5%	17	31.0
Commute	15	56.25	Average Work Commute in Minutes	21	3	85.7
			% Commuting on Public Transportation	1.7%	22	26.8
Community Stability	13	73.45	% Living in Same House as in 1979	25.2%	15	60.4
			% Living in Same County as in 1985	74.1%	10	86.5

Metropolitan Area Suburb Rankings
DENVER-BOULDER

Composite: Rank 16 / 24 *Score* 57.91   **BRIGHTON**

CATEGORY	RANK	SCORE	STATISTIC	VALUE	RANK	SCORE
Economics	23	31.00	Median Household Income	$27,126	22	16.3
			% of Families Above Poverty Level	88.5%	23	45.7
Affordable Housing	3	87.55	Median Home Value	$71,600	5	79.3
			Median Rent	$422	3	95.8
Crime	11	60.50	Violent Crimes per 10,000 Population	56	11	71.2
			Property Crimes per 10,000 Population	736	13	49.8
Open Spaces	9	60.95	Population Density (Persons/Sq. Mile)	950	2	97.9
			Average Rooms per Housing Unit	5.6	17	24.0
Education	14	50.10	% High School Enrollment/Completion	94.0%	5	82.8
			% College Graduates	13.0%	21	17.4
Commute	23	28.55	Average Work Commute in Minutes	23	14	57.1
			% Commuting on Public Transportation	0.6%	24	0.0
Community Stability	9	86.70	% Living in Same House as in 1979	35.4%	8	84.9
			% Living in Same County as in 1985	75.3%	7	88.5

Composite: Rank 17 / 24 *Score* 57.85   **WELBY**

CATEGORY	RANK	SCORE	STATISTIC	VALUE	RANK	SCORE
Economics	21	42.40	Median Household Income	$30,282	19	24.0
			% of Families Above Poverty Level	91.5%	21	60.8
Affordable Housing	6	82.05	Median Home Value	$65,800	2	87.5
			Median Rent	$486	16	76.6
Crime	N/A	N/A	Violent Crimes per 10,000 Population	N/A	N/A	N/A
			Property Crimes per 10,000 Population	N/A	N/A	N/A
Open Spaces	16	48.45	Population Density (Persons/Sq. Mile)	2660	11	68.9
			Average Rooms per Housing Unit	5.7	14	28.0
Education	22	33.20	% High School Enrollment/Completion	88.4%	16	60.4
			% College Graduates	6.7%	23	6.0
Commute	17	50.35	Average Work Commute in Minutes	22	10	71.4
			% Commuting on Public Transportation	1.8%	21	29.3
Community Stability	6	90.65	% Living in Same House as in 1979	36.4%	6	87.3
			% Living in Same County as in 1985	78.6%	3	94.0

Composite: Rank 18 / 24 *Score* 57.82   **LAFAYETTE**

CATEGORY	RANK	SCORE	STATISTIC	VALUE	RANK	SCORE
Economics	19	46.20	Median Household Income	$34,182	12	33.6
			% of Families Above Poverty Level	91.1%	22	58.8
Affordable Housing	17	65.50	Median Home Value	$81,300	9	65.5
			Median Rent	$523	18	65.5
Crime	1	94.45	Violent Crimes per 10,000 Population	12	1	100.0
			Property Crimes per 10,000 Population	433	3	88.9
Open Spaces	14	49.15	Population Density (Persons/Sq. Mile)	2109	9	78.3
			Average Rooms per Housing Unit	5.5	19	20.0
Education	18	38.00	% High School Enrollment/Completion	81.1%	23	31.2
			% College Graduates	28.1%	11	44.8
Commute	18	49.30	Average Work Commute in Minutes	23	14	57.1
			% Commuting on Public Transportation	2.3%	20	41.5
Community Stability	19	62.15	% Living in Same House as in 1979	16.2%	22	38.8
			% Living in Same County as in 1985	73.5%	11	85.5

Metropolitan Area Suburb Rankings
DENVER-BOULDER

Composite: *Rank* 19 / 24   *Score* 57.73   **SHERRELWOOD**

CATEGORY	RANK	SCORE	STATISTIC	VALUE	RANK	SCORE
Economics	17	46.85	Median Household Income	$31,049	18	25.9
			% of Families Above Poverty Level	92.9%	18	67.8
Affordable Housing	2	90.30	Median Home Value	$67,500	3	85.1
			Median Rent	$423	4	95.5
Crime	N/A	N/A	Violent Crimes per 10,000 Population	N/A	N/A	N/A
			Property Crimes per 10,000 Population	N/A	N/A	N/A
Open Spaces	23	20.00	Population Density (Persons/Sq. Mile)	6736	24	0.0
			Average Rooms per Housing Unit	6.0	10	40.0
Education	23	27.20	% High School Enrollment/Completion	84.4%	20	44.4
			% College Graduates	8.9%	22	10.0
Commute	11	67.40	Average Work Commute in Minutes	22	10	71.4
			% Commuting on Public Transportation	3.2%	8	63.4
Community Stability	3	94.60	% Living in Same House as in 1979	41.7%	1	100.0
			% Living in Same County as in 1985	75.7%	6	89.2

Composite: *Rank* 20 / 24   *Score* 56.14   **THORNTON**

CATEGORY	RANK	SCORE	STATISTIC	VALUE	RANK	SCORE
Economics	16	51.15	Median Household Income	$34,146	13	33.5
			% of Families Above Poverty Level	93.1%	17	68.8
Affordable Housing	7	77.80	Median Home Value	$75,400	7	73.9
			Median Rent	$469	14	81.7
Crime	8	74.85	Violent Crimes per 10,000 Population	38	7	83.0
			Property Crimes per 10,000 Population	605	8	66.7
Open Spaces	17	46.45	Population Density (Persons/Sq. Mile)	2663	12	68.9
			Average Rooms per Housing Unit	5.6	17	24.0
Education	19	37.10	% High School Enrollment/Completion	87.0%	18	54.8
			% College Graduates	14.1%	19	19.4
Commute	21	36.25	Average Work Commute in Minutes	25	22	28.6
			% Commuting on Public Transportation	2.4%	18	43.9
Community Stability	15	69.35	% Living in Same House as in 1979	22.6%	18	54.2
			% Living in Same County as in 1985	72.9%	12	84.5

Composite: *Rank* 21 / 24   *Score* 55.66   **AURORA**

CATEGORY	RANK	SCORE	STATISTIC	VALUE	RANK	SCORE
Economics	14	52.05	Median Household Income	$33,214	16	31.2
			% of Families Above Poverty Level	93.9%	16	72.9
Affordable Housing	8	76.75	Median Home Value	$79,800	8	67.6
			Median Rent	$455	10	85.9
Crime	13	27.30	Violent Crimes per 10,000 Population	165	14	0.0
			Property Crimes per 10,000 Population	699	12	54.6
Open Spaces	15	48.80	Population Density (Persons/Sq. Mile)	1676	6	85.6
			Average Rooms per Housing Unit	5.3	20	12.0
Education	11	57.00	% High School Enrollment/Completion	91.4%	10	72.4
			% College Graduates	26.3%	13	41.6
Commute	7	72.45	Average Work Commute in Minutes	23	14	57.1
			% Commuting on Public Transportation	4.2%	3	87.8
Community Stability	22	55.30	% Living in Same House as in 1979	19.6%	20	47.0
			% Living in Same County as in 1985	60.3%	23	63.6

Metropolitan Area Suburb Rankings
DENVER-BOULDER

Composite: **Rank** 22 / 24 **Score** 52.63 **KEN CARYL**

CATEGORY	RANK	SCORE	STATISTIC	VALUE	RANK	SCORE
Economics	5	78.80	Median Household Income	$46,896	5	64.6
			% of Families Above Poverty Level	97.9%	5	93.0
Affordable Housing	21	26.90	Median Home Value	$92,900	16	49.0
			Median Rent	$725	23	4.8
Crime	N/A	N/A	Violent Crimes per 10,000 Population	N/A	N/A	N/A
			Property Crimes per 10,000 Population	N/A	N/A	N/A
Open Spaces	6	69.45	Population Density (Persons/Sq. Mile)	2543	10	70.9
			Average Rooms per Housing Unit	6.7	5	68.0
Education	7	67.35	% High School Enrollment/Completion	91.9%	9	74.4
			% College Graduates	36.6%	6	60.3
Commute	24	24.40	Average Work Commute in Minutes	27	24	0.0
			% Commuting on Public Transportation	2.6%	15	48.8
Community Stability	23	48.90	% Living in Same House as in 1979	12.6%	23	30.2
			% Living in Same County as in 1985	62.7%	22	67.6

Composite: **Rank** 23 / 24 **Score** 51.10 **HIGHLANDS RANCH**

CATEGORY	RANK	SCORE	STATISTIC	VALUE	RANK	SCORE
Economics	2	97.10	Median Household Income	$59,039	2	94.2
			% of Families Above Poverty Level	99.3%	1	100.0
Affordable Housing	23	19.25	Median Home Value	$123,100	23	6.1
			Median Rent	$633	20	32.4
Crime	N/A	N/A	Violent Crimes per 10,000 Population	N/A	N/A	N/A
			Property Crimes per 10,000 Population	N/A	N/A	N/A
Open Spaces	1	77.20	Population Density (Persons/Sq. Mile)	2102	8	78.4
			Average Rooms per Housing Unit	6.9	4	76.0
Education	3	83.05	% High School Enrollment/Completion	90.5%	13	68.8
			% College Graduates	57.0%	2	97.3
Commute	22	30.00	Average Work Commute in Minutes	24	18	42.9
			% Commuting on Public Transportation	1.3%	23	17.1
Community Stability	24	0.00	% Living in Same House as in 1979	0.0%	24	0.0
			% Living in Same County as in 1985	22.1%	24	0.0

Composite: **Rank** 24 / 24 **Score** 50.20 **COMMERCE CITY**

CATEGORY	RANK	SCORE	STATISTIC	VALUE	RANK	SCORE
Economics	24	0.00	Median Household Income	$20,427	24	0.0
			% of Families Above Poverty Level	79.4%	24	0.0
Affordable Housing	1	100.00	Median Home Value	$57,000	1	100.0
			Median Rent	$408	1	100.0
Crime	14	19.60	Violent Crimes per 10,000 Population	105	13	39.2
			Property Crimes per 10,000 Population	1,122	14	0.0
Open Spaces	11	50.00	Population Density (Persons/Sq. Mile)	824	1	100.0
			Average Rooms per Housing Unit	5.0	23	0.0
Education	24	0.00	% High School Enrollment/Completion	73.3%	24	0.0
			% College Graduates	3.4%	24	0.0
Commute	3	83.10	Average Work Commute in Minutes	21	3	85.7
			% Commuting on Public Transportation	3.9%	4	80.5
Community Stability	1	98.70	% Living in Same House as in 1979	40.6%	2	97.4
			% Living in Same County as in 1985	82.2%	1	100.0

Metropolitan Area Description
DETROIT-ANN ARBOR

STATE: Michigan
COUNTIES: Lapeer, Livingston, Macomb, Monroe, Oakland, St. Clair, Washtenaw, Wayne

TOTAL POPULATION: 4,665,236

POPULATION IN SUBURBS: 3,527,670 (75.6%)

POPULATION IN Detroit: 1,027,974 (22.0%)
POPULATION IN Ann Arbor: 109,592 (2.3%)

The DETROIT-ANN ARBOR metropolitan area is located in the southeastern part of Michigan along Lake Erie and the Canadian border. The suburbs range geographically from Port Huron in the northeast (57 miles from Detroit), to Ypsilanti in the west (35 miles from Detroit), and to Monroe in the south (37 miles from Detroit). The area is shrinking in population and had a decrease of 1.8% between 1980 and 1990. Summer time high temperatures average in the 80's and winter time lows average in the 20's. Ford Motor Company is the most famous suburban employer, dominating the suburb of Dearborn. Automotive factories are also found in the suburbs of Monroe, Highland Park, Livonia, Plymouth Township, Allen Park, and Ypsilanti. Public transportation in the area is provided on buses by the Detroit Department of Transportation.

Grosse Pointe Farms is the overall highest rated suburb. **Bloomfield Township** receives the highest scores in economics and open spaces. **Highland Park** is the suburb with the most affordable housing. The number one score in education belongs to **Birmingham**. **Grosse Pointe Woods** is the safest suburb with the lowest crime rate. The top rated commute belongs to **Ypsilanti**. Finally, the number one rating in community stability goes to **Allen Park**.

The highest ranked suburb overall which also has an affordable housing score of at least 50.00 is **Plymouth Township**.

The highest ranked suburb in the education category which also has an affordable housing score of at least 50.00 is also **Plymouth Township**.

The county whose suburbs have the highest average overall score is **Wayne County** (57.10).

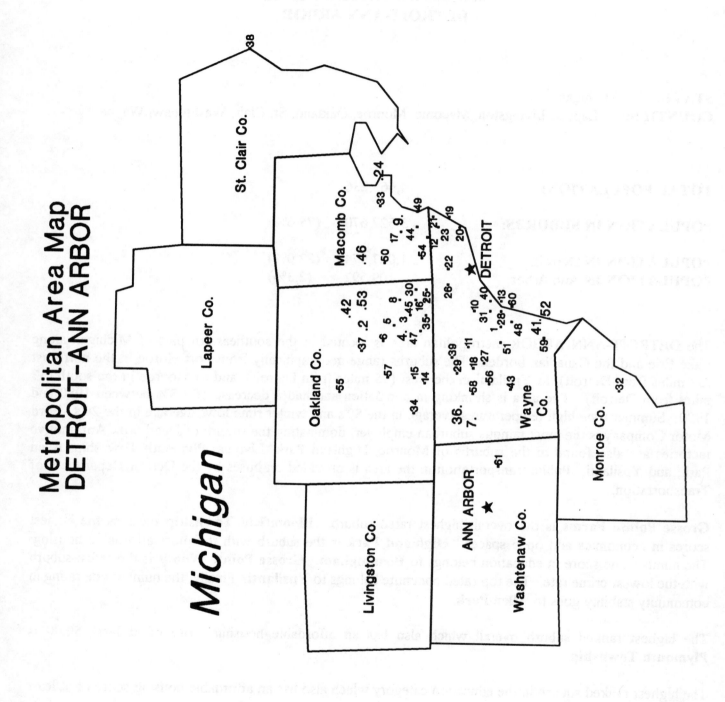

Metropolitan Area Map
DETROIT-ANN ARBOR

Michigan

St. Clair Co.

Lapeer Co.

Macomb Co.

Oakland Co.

Livingston Co.

Washtenaw Co.

Wayne Co.

Monroe Co.

DETROIT

ANN ARBOR

Metropolitan Area Suburb Alphabetical Index
DETROIT-ANN ARBOR

SUBURB	PAGE	MAP NO.	STATE	COUNTY	POPU-LATION	RANK
ALLEN PARK	230	1	Michigan	Wayne	31,092	6 / 61
AUBURN HILLS	242	2	Michigan	Oakland	17,076	40 / 61
BERKLEY	232	3	Michigan	Oakland	16,960	10 / 61
BEVERLY HILLS	229	4	Michigan	Oakland	10,610	2 / 61
BIRMINGHAM	232	5	Michigan	Oakland	19,997	12 / 61
BLOOMFIELD TOWNSHIP	229	6	Michigan	Oakland	42,137	3 / 61
CANTON	236	7	Michigan	Wayne	57,047	22 / 61
CLAWSON	233	8	Michigan	Oakland	13,874	15 / 61
CLINTON	241	9	Michigan	Macomb	85,866	38 / 61
DEARBORN	235	10	Michigan	Wayne	89,286	19 / 61
DEARBORN HEIGHTS	234	11	Michigan	Wayne	60,838	17 / 61
EAST DETROIT	244	12	Michigan	Macomb	35,283	46 / 61
ECORSE	246	13	Michigan	Wayne	12,180	52 / 61
FARMINGTON	235	14	Michigan	Oakland	10,132	21 / 61
FARMINGTON HILLS	239	15	Michigan	Oakland	74,652	31 / 61
FERNDALE	244	16	Michigan	Oakland	25,084	48 / 61
FRASER	238	17	Michigan	Macomb	13,899	29 / 61
GARDEN CITY	233	18	Michigan	Wayne	31,846	13 / 61
GROSSE POINTE FARMS	229	19	Michigan	Wayne	10,092	1 / 61
GROSSE POINTE PARK	232	20	Michigan	Wayne	12,857	11 / 61
GROSSE POINTE WOODS	230	21	Michigan	Wayne	17,715	5 / 61
HAMTRAMCK	249	22	Michigan	Wayne	18,372	61 / 61
HARPER WOODS	241	23	Michigan	Wayne	14,903	39 / 61
HARRISON	247	24	Michigan	Macomb	24,685	56 / 61
HAZEL PARK	247	25	Michigan	Oakland	20,051	55 / 61
HIGHLAND PARK	248	26	Michigan	Wayne	20,121	60 / 61
INKSTER	247	27	Michigan	Wayne	30,772	57 / 61
LINCOLN PARK	240	28	Michigan	Wayne	41,832	34 / 61
LIVONIA	231	29	Michigan	Wayne	100,850	8 / 61
MADISON HEIGHTS	240	30	Michigan	Oakland	32,196	35 / 61
MELVINDALE	245	31	Michigan	Wayne	11,216	51 / 61
MONROE	234	32	Michigan	Monroe	22,902	16 / 61
MOUNT CLEMENS	246	33	Michigan	Macomb	18,405	54 / 61
NOVI	243	34	Michigan	Oakland	32,998	45 / 61
OAK PARK	245	35	Michigan	Oakland	30,462	49 / 61
PLYMOUTH TOWNSHIP	230	36	Michigan	Wayne	23,646	4 / 61
PONTIAC	248	37	Michigan	Oakland	71,166	59 / 61
PORT HURON	242	38	Michigan	St. Clair	33,694	41 / 61
REDFORD	234	39	Michigan	Wayne	54,387	18 / 61
RIVER ROUGE	245	40	Michigan	Wayne	11,314	50 / 61
RIVERVIEW	231	41	Michigan	Wayne	13,894	9 / 61
ROCHESTER HILLS	246	42	Michigan	Oakland	61,766	53 / 61
ROMULUS	241	43	Michigan	Wayne	22,897	37 / 61
ROSEVILLE	244	44	Michigan	Macomb	51,412	47 / 61
ROYAL OAK	238	45	Michigan	Oakland	65,410	28 / 61
SHELBY	235	46	Michigan	Macomb	48,655	20 / 61
SOUTHFIELD	242	47	Michigan	Oakland	75,728	42 / 61
SOUTHGATE	238	48	Michigan	Wayne	30,771	30 / 61
ST. CLAIR SHORES	236	49	Michigan	Macomb	68,107	24 / 61
STERLING HEIGHTS	236	50	Michigan	Macomb	117,810	23 / 61
TAYLOR	243	51	Michigan	Wayne	70,811	44 / 61

Metropolitan Area Suburb Alphabetical Index
DETROIT-ANN ARBOR

SUBURB	PAGE	MAP NO.	STATE	COUNTY	POPU-LATION	RANK
TRENTON	231	52	Michigan	Wayne	20,586	7 / 61
TROY	233	53	Michigan	Oakland	72,884	14 / 61
WARREN	239	54	Michigan	Macomb	144,864	32 / 61
WATERFORD	240	55	Michigan	Oakland	66,692	36 / 61
WAYNE	239	56	Michigan	Wayne	19,899	33 / 61
WEST BLOOMFIELD TOWNSHIP	237	57	Michigan	Oakland	54,843	26 / 61
WESTLAND	243	58	Michigan	Wayne	84,724	43 / 61
WOODHAVEN	237	59	Michigan	Wayne	11,631	25 / 61
WYANDOTTE	237	60	Michigan	Wayne	30,938	27 / 61
YPSILANTI	248	61	Michigan	Washtenaw	24,846	58 / 61

Metropolitan Area Suburb Rankings
DETROIT-ANN ARBOR

Composite: **Rank** 1 / 61 **Score** 70.64   **GROSSE POINTE FARMS**

CATEGORY	RANK	SCORE	STATISTIC	VALUE	RANK	SCORE
Economics	3	87.55	Median Household Income	$66,844	3	76.4
			% of Families Above Poverty Level	98.9%	4	98.7
Affordable Housing	58	25.70	Median Home Value	$171,400	60	21.5
			Median Rent	$721	57	29.9
Crime	14	88.90	Violent Crimes per 10,000 Population	14	5	98.2
			Property Crimes per 10,000 Population	416	17	79.6
Open Spaces	4	80.80	Population Density (Persons/Sq. Mile)	3741	28	61.6
			Average Rooms per Housing Unit	7.3	1	100.0
Education	3	93.85	% High School Enrollment/Completion	96.1%	10	87.7
			% College Graduates	62.1%	1	100.0
Commute	24	33.15	Average Work Commute in Minutes	22	28	54.5
			% Commuting on Public Transportation	2.7%	7	11.8
Community Stability	4	84.55	% Living in Same House as in 1979	55.9%	4	84.0
			% Living in Same County as in 1985	89.2%	20	85.1

Composite: **Rank** 2 / 61 **Score** 68.21   **BEVERLY HILLS**

CATEGORY	RANK	SCORE	STATISTIC	VALUE	RANK	SCORE
Economics	4	84.65	Median Household Income	$61,941	4	69.8
			% of Families Above Poverty Level	99.2%	2	99.5
Affordable Housing	59	24.75	Median Home Value	$153,100	56	30.9
			Median Rent	$791	60	18.6
Crime	2	97.05	Violent Crimes per 10,000 Population	7	3	99.6
			Property Crimes per 10,000 Population	261	5	94.5
Open Spaces	3	82.55	Population Density (Persons/Sq. Mile)	2651	16	75.1
			Average Rooms per Housing Unit	7.0	4	90.0
Education	2	95.90	% High School Enrollment/Completion	99.1%	2	99.6
			% College Graduates	57.5%	4	92.2
Commute	41	27.95	Average Work Commute in Minutes	22	28	54.5
			% Commuting on Public Transportation	0.4%	46	1.4
Community Stability	33	64.60	% Living in Same House as in 1979	45.7%	23	59.3
			% Living in Same County as in 1985	82.9%	43	69.9

Composite: **Rank** 3 / 61 **Score** 67.74   **BLOOMFIELD TOWNSHIP**

CATEGORY	RANK	SCORE	STATISTIC	VALUE	RANK	SCORE
Economics	1	100.00	Median Household Income	$84,494	1	100.0
			% of Families Above Poverty Level	99.4%	1	100.0
Affordable Housing	60	16.40	Median Home Value	$213,000	61	0.0
			Median Rent	$703	56	32.8
Crime	9	91.40	Violent Crimes per 10,000 Population	15	8	98.0
			Property Crimes per 10,000 Population	362	10	84.8
Open Spaces	1	93.50	Population Density (Persons/Sq. Mile)	1689	7	87.0
			Average Rooms per Housing Unit	7.3	1	100.0
Education	4	90.65	% High School Enrollment/Completion	96.0%	11	87.3
			% College Graduates	58.6%	3	94.0
Commute	55	18.65	Average Work Commute in Minutes	24	51	36.4
			% Commuting on Public Transportation	0.3%	50	0.9
Community Stability	34	63.60	% Living in Same House as in 1979	44.0%	28	55.2
			% Living in Same County as in 1985	83.8%	39	72.0

Metropolitan Area Suburb Rankings
DETROIT-ANN ARBOR

Composite: **Rank** 4 / 61 *Score* 66.46   **PLYMOUTH TOWNSHIP**

CATEGORY	RANK	SCORE	STATISTIC	VALUE	RANK	SCORE
Economics	7	79.20	Median Household Income	$53,806	10	58.9
			% of Families Above Poverty Level	99.2%	2	99.5
Affordable Housing	48	53.75	Median Home Value	$126,300	50	44.8
			Median Rent	$517	39	62.7
Crime	7	94.65	Violent Crimes per 10,000 Population	8	4	99.4
			Property Crimes per 10,000 Population	309	8	89.9
Open Spaces	5	78.10	Population Density (Persons/Sq. Mile)	1486	5	89.5
			Average Rooms per Housing Unit	6.3	7	66.7
Education	11	72.70	% High School Enrollment/Completion	96.7%	7	90.1
			% College Graduates	35.8%	11	55.3
Commute	42	27.70	Average Work Commute in Minutes	22	28	54.5
			% Commuting on Public Transportation	0.3%	50	0.9
Community Stability	41	59.15	% Living in Same House as in 1979	38.9%	41	42.9
			% Living in Same County as in 1985	85.2%	37	75.4

Composite: **Rank** 5 / 61 *Score* 66.10   **GROSSE POINTE WOODS**

CATEGORY	RANK	SCORE	STATISTIC	VALUE	RANK	SCORE
Economics	6	79.90	Median Household Income	$55,657	6	61.4
			% of Families Above Poverty Level	98.8%	6	98.4
Affordable Housing	56	31.00	Median Home Value	$133,900	53	40.8
			Median Rent	$775	59	21.2
Crime	1	99.90	Violent Crimes per 10,000 Population	6	2	99.8
			Property Crimes per 10,000 Population	204	1	100.0
Open Spaces	16	62.00	Population Density (Persons/Sq. Mile)	5432	45	40.7
			Average Rooms per Housing Unit	6.8	5	83.3
Education	5	85.10	% High School Enrollment/Completion	99.2%	1	100.0
			% College Graduates	44.6%	7	70.2
Commute	52	22.05	Average Work Commute in Minutes	24	51	36.4
			% Commuting on Public Transportation	1.8%	9	7.7
Community Stability	8	82.75	% Living in Same House as in 1979	55.8%	6	83.8
			% Living in Same County as in 1985	87.8%	25	81.7

Composite: **Rank** 6 / 61 *Score* 65.54   **ALLEN PARK**

CATEGORY	RANK	SCORE	STATISTIC	VALUE	RANK	SCORE
Economics	19	68.05	Median Household Income	$39,925	21	40.3
			% of Families Above Poverty Level	97.8%	16	95.8
Affordable Housing	27	71.15	Median Home Value	$66,600	30	75.6
			Median Rent	$492	29	66.7
Crime	20	86.20	Violent Crimes per 10,000 Population	27	21	95.5
			Property Crimes per 10,000 Population	444	19	76.9
Open Spaces	32	46.50	Population Density (Persons/Sq. Mile)	4437	37	53.0
			Average Rooms per Housing Unit	5.5	20	40.0
Education	24	53.25	% High School Enrollment/Completion	95.2%	15	84.1
			% College Graduates	16.5%	28	22.4
Commute	21	33.60	Average Work Commute in Minutes	21	14	63.6
			% Commuting on Public Transportation	0.9%	23	3.6
Community Stability	1	100.00	% Living in Same House as in 1979	62.5%	1	100.0
			% Living in Same County as in 1985	95.4%	1	100.0

Metropolitan Area Suburb Rankings
DETROIT-ANN ARBOR

Composite: Rank 7 / 61 *Score* 65.52   **TRENTON**

CATEGORY	RANK	SCORE	STATISTIC	VALUE	RANK	SCORE
Economics	20	67.55	Median Household Income	$41,129	18	41.9
			% of Families Above Poverty Level	96.8%	25	93.2
Affordable Housing	25	71.95	Median Home Value	$80,800	39	68.2
			Median Rent	$436	14	75.7
Crime	3	96.80	Violent Crimes per 10,000 Population	20	12	97.0
			Property Crimes per 10,000 Population	239	2	96.6
Open Spaces	22	56.50	Population Density (Persons/Sq. Mile)	2820	17	73.0
			Average Rooms per Housing Unit	5.5	20	40.0
Education	28	49.65	% High School Enrollment/Completion	92.6%	31	73.8
			% College Graduates	18.3%	25	25.5
Commute	24	33.15	Average Work Commute in Minutes	21	14	63.6
			% Commuting on Public Transportation	0.7%	31	2.7
Community Stability	7	83.05	% Living in Same House as in 1979	50.1%	15	70.0
			% Living in Same County as in 1985	93.8%	5	96.1

Composite: Rank 8 / 61 *Score* 64.24   **LIVONIA**

CATEGORY	RANK	SCORE	STATISTIC	VALUE	RANK	SCORE
Economics	12	74.55	Median Household Income	$48,645	12	52.0
			% of Families Above Poverty Level	98.3%	8	97.1
Affordable Housing	46	54.85	Median Home Value	$94,300	45	61.3
			Median Rent	$606	49	48.4
Crime	17	88.40	Violent Crimes per 10,000 Population	28	22	95.3
			Property Crimes per 10,000 Population	397	12	81.5
Open Spaces	13	66.50	Population Density (Persons/Sq. Mile)	2823	18	73.0
			Average Rooms per Housing Unit	6.1	10	60.0
Education	18	57.95	% High School Enrollment/Completion	94.4%	21	81.0
			% College Graduates	23.8%	18	34.9
Commute	36	28.60	Average Work Commute in Minutes	22	28	54.5
			% Commuting on Public Transportation	0.7%	31	2.7
Community Stability	14	78.85	% Living in Same House as in 1979	50.3%	13	70.5
			% Living in Same County as in 1985	90.1%	18	87.2

Composite: Rank 9 / 61 *Score* 63.84   **RIVERVIEW**

CATEGORY	RANK	SCORE	STATISTIC	VALUE	RANK	SCORE
Economics	33	63.35	Median Household Income	$39,735	22	40.1
			% of Families Above Poverty Level	94.3%	39	86.6
Affordable Housing	33	69.35	Median Home Value	$83,300	40	67.0
			Median Rent	$461	19	71.7
Crime	6	95.00	Violent Crimes per 10,000 Population	5	1	100.0
			Property Crimes per 10,000 Population	308	7	90.0
Open Spaces	24	54.45	Population Density (Persons/Sq. Mile)	3152	22	68.9
			Average Rooms per Housing Unit	5.5	20	40.0
Education	22	53.65	% High School Enrollment/Completion	94.8%	18	82.5
			% College Graduates	17.9%	26	24.8
Commute	21	33.60	Average Work Commute in Minutes	21	14	63.6
			% Commuting on Public Transportation	0.9%	23	3.6
Community Stability	16	77.50	% Living in Same House as in 1979	45.8%	22	59.6
			% Living in Same County as in 1985	93.5%	8	95.4

Composite: **Rank** 10 / 61 **Score** 61.76   **BERKLEY**

CATEGORY	RANK	SCORE	STATISTIC	VALUE	RANK	SCORE
Economics	25	65.65	Median Household Income	$36,693	31	36.0
			% of Families Above Poverty Level	97.6%	18	95.3
Affordable Housing	26	71.80	Median Home Value	$64,700	27	76.6
			Median Rent	$490	28	67.0
Crime	5	95.55	Violent Crimes per 10,000 Population	24	14	96.1
			Property Crimes per 10,000 Population	256	4	95.0
Open Spaces	44	37.30	Population Density (Persons/Sq. Mile)	6460	55	27.9
			Average Rooms per Housing Unit	5.7	15	46.7
Education	30	48.20	% High School Enrollment/Completion	90.9%	36	67.1
			% College Graduates	20.5%	22	29.3
Commute	14	38.15	Average Work Commute in Minutes	20	6	72.7
			% Commuting on Public Transportation	0.9%	23	3.6
Community Stability	19	75.70	% Living in Same House as in 1979	50.2%	14	70.2
			% Living in Same County as in 1985	87.6%	26	81.2

Composite: **Rank** 11 / 61 **Score** 61.69   **GROSSE POINTE PARK**

CATEGORY	RANK	SCORE	STATISTIC	VALUE	RANK	SCORE
Economics	10	78.05	Median Household Income	$54,586	9	60.0
			% of Families Above Poverty Level	97.9%	14	96.1
Affordable Housing	52	41.15	Median Home Value	$169,500	59	22.5
			Median Rent	$535	43	59.8
Crime	13	89.15	Violent Crimes per 10,000 Population	19	11	97.2
			Property Crimes per 10,000 Population	401	13	81.1
Open Spaces	14	63.70	Population Density (Persons/Sq. Mile)	5966	52	34.1
			Average Rooms per Housing Unit	7.1	3	93.3
Education	7	78.50	% High School Enrollment/Completion	93.3%	27	76.6
			% College Graduates	50.6%	5	80.4
Commute	31	30.20	Average Work Commute in Minutes	23	43	45.5
			% Commuting on Public Transportation	3.4%	5	14.9
Community Stability	48	51.05	% Living in Same House as in 1979	36.8%	45	37.8
			% Living in Same County as in 1985	80.6%	48	64.3

Composite: **Rank** 12 / 61 **Score** 61.40   **BIRMINGHAM**

CATEGORY	RANK	SCORE	STATISTIC	VALUE	RANK	SCORE
Economics	5	80.80	Median Household Income	$57,573	5	64.0
			% of Families Above Poverty Level	98.5%	7	97.6
Affordable Housing	57	26.00	Median Home Value	$153,900	57	30.5
			Median Rent	$773	58	21.5
Crime	19	87.40	Violent Crimes per 10,000 Population	14	5	98.2
			Property Crimes per 10,000 Population	448	21	76.6
Open Spaces	23	56.40	Population Density (Persons/Sq. Mile)	4183	32	56.1
			Average Rooms per Housing Unit	6.0	11	56.7
Education	1	96.45	% High School Enrollment/Completion	98.2%	3	96.0
			% College Graduates	60.3%	2	96.9
Commute	28	32.50	Average Work Commute in Minutes	21	14	63.6
			% Commuting on Public Transportation	0.4%	46	1.4
Community Stability	49	50.25	% Living in Same House as in 1979	37.0%	44	38.3
			% Living in Same County as in 1985	79.7%	52	62.2

Composite: *Rank* 13 / 61 *Score* 61.16   **GARDEN CITY**

CATEGORY	RANK	SCORE	STATISTIC	VALUE	RANK	SCORE
Economics	22	66.20	Median Household Income	$38,717	26	38.7
			% of Families Above Poverty Level	97.0%	23	93.7
Affordable Housing	21	74.85	Median Home Value	$59,200	22	79.4
			Median Rent	$470	24	70.3
Crime	18	87.75	Violent Crimes per 10,000 Population	25	17	95.9
			Property Crimes per 10,000 Population	416	17	79.6
Open Spaces	41	38.65	Population Density (Persons/Sq. Mile)	5434	46	40.6
			Average Rooms per Housing Unit	5.4	28	36.7
Education	37	40.75	% High School Enrollment/Completion	92.9%	30	75.0
			% College Graduates	7.1%	52	6.5
Commute	42	27.70	Average Work Commute in Minutes	22	28	54.5
			% Commuting on Public Transportation	0.3%	50	0.9
Community Stability	2	92.25	% Living in Same House as in 1979	58.0%	2	89.1
			% Living in Same County as in 1985	93.5%	8	95.4

Composite: *Rank* 14 / 61 *Score* 61.06   **TROY**

CATEGORY	RANK	SCORE	STATISTIC	VALUE	RANK	SCORE
Economics	9	78.70	Median Household Income	$55,407	7	61.1
			% of Families Above Poverty Level	98.0%	12	96.3
Affordable Housing	51	44.80	Median Home Value	$128,800	52	43.5
			Median Rent	$620	51	46.1
Crime	24	84.55	Violent Crimes per 10,000 Population	25	17	95.9
			Property Crimes per 10,000 Population	483	23	73.2
Open Spaces	7	73.85	Population Density (Persons/Sq. Mile)	2173	13	81.0
			Average Rooms per Housing Unit	6.3	7	66.7
Education	8	76.75	% High School Enrollment/Completion	97.0%	4	91.3
			% College Graduates	39.9%	9	62.2
Commute	50	23.00	Average Work Commute in Minutes	23	43	45.5
			% Commuting on Public Transportation	0.2%	55	0.5
Community Stability	53	45.75	% Living in Same House as in 1979	35.0%	49	33.4
			% Living in Same County as in 1985	78.0%	53	58.1

Composite: *Rank* 15 / 61 *Score* 60.84   **CLAWSON**

CATEGORY	RANK	SCORE	STATISTIC	VALUE	RANK	SCORE
Economics	23	66.05	Median Household Income	$36,532	33	35.8
			% of Families Above Poverty Level	98.0%	12	96.3
Affordable Housing	34	69.05	Median Home Value	$71,600	35	73.0
			Median Rent	$502	33	65.1
Crime	8	92.90	Violent Crimes per 10,000 Population	30	23	94.9
			Property Crimes per 10,000 Population	299	6	90.9
Open Spaces	55	29.95	Population Density (Persons/Sq. Mile)	6304	54	29.9
			Average Rooms per Housing Unit	5.2	43	30.0
Education	21	55.90	% High School Enrollment/Completion	96.8%	6	90.5
			% College Graduates	15.8%	30	21.3
Commute	7	41.80	Average Work Commute in Minutes	19	4	81.8
			% Commuting on Public Transportation	0.5%	41	1.8
Community Stability	26	70.25	% Living in Same House as in 1979	45.7%	23	59.3
			% Living in Same County as in 1985	87.6%	26	81.2

Metropolitan Area Suburb Rankings
DETROIT-ANN ARBOR

Composite: **Rank** 16 / 61 *Score* 60.04   **MONROE**

CATEGORY	RANK	SCORE	STATISTIC	VALUE	RANK	SCORE
Economics	52	46.85	Median Household Income	$29,088	48	25.8
			% of Families Above Poverty Level	87.2%	53	67.9
Affordable Housing	18	78.10	Median Home Value	$64,700	27	76.6
			Median Rent	$412	9	79.6
Crime	28	79.30	Violent Crimes per 10,000 Population	64	39	88.0
			Property Crimes per 10,000 Population	510	26	70.6
Open Spaces	18	58.20	Population Density (Persons/Sq. Mile)	2547	15	76.4
			Average Rooms per Housing Unit	5.5	20	40.0
Education	39	40.00	% High School Enrollment/Completion	89.5%	40	61.5
			% College Graduates	14.2%	34	18.5
Commute	4	50.90	Average Work Commute in Minutes	17	1	100.0
			% Commuting on Public Transportation	0.5%	41	1.8
Community Stability	30	66.90	% Living in Same House as in 1979	43.0%	31	52.8
			% Living in Same County as in 1985	87.5%	28	81.0

Composite: **Rank** 17 / 61 *Score* 59.56   **DEARBORN HEIGHTS**

CATEGORY	RANK	SCORE	STATISTIC	VALUE	RANK	SCORE
Economics	32	63.60	Median Household Income	$36,771	30	36.1
			% of Families Above Poverty Level	96.0%	32	91.1
Affordable Housing	35	68.70	Median Home Value	$63,600	26	77.1
			Median Rent	$532	40	60.3
Crime	31	77.45	Violent Crimes per 10,000 Population	55	33	89.8
			Property Crimes per 10,000 Population	567	33	65.1
Open Spaces	38	41.80	Population Density (Persons/Sq. Mile)	5193	43	43.6
			Average Rooms per Housing Unit	5.5	20	40.0
Education	32	46.95	% High School Enrollment/Completion	93.2%	28	76.2
			% College Graduates	13.7%	35	17.7
Commute	36	28.60	Average Work Commute in Minutes	22	28	54.5
			% Commuting on Public Transportation	0.7%	31	2.7
Community Stability	3	89.85	% Living in Same House as in 1979	56.8%	3	86.2
			% Living in Same County as in 1985	92.7%	12	93.5

Composite: **Rank** 18 / 61 *Score* 59.34   **REDFORD**

CATEGORY	RANK	SCORE	STATISTIC	VALUE	RANK	SCORE
Economics	28	65.25	Median Household Income	$37,162	27	36.6
			% of Families Above Poverty Level	97.1%	21	93.9
Affordable Housing	37	67.35	Median Home Value	$57,000	20	80.5
			Median Rent	$570	47	54.2
Crime	34	75.45	Violent Crimes per 10,000 Population	57	34	89.4
			Property Crimes per 10,000 Population	605	37	61.5
Open Spaces	34	45.65	Population Density (Persons/Sq. Mile)	4841	41	48.0
			Average Rooms per Housing Unit	5.6	18	43.3
Education	31	47.00	% High School Enrollment/Completion	93.7%	24	78.2
			% College Graduates	12.6%	39	15.8
Commute	27	32.95	Average Work Commute in Minutes	21	14	63.6
			% Commuting on Public Transportation	0.6%	38	2.3
Community Stability	9	81.75	% Living in Same House as in 1979	53.1%	9	77.2
			% Living in Same County as in 1985	89.7%	19	86.3

Metropolitan Area Suburb Rankings
DETROIT-ANN ARBOR

Composite: *Rank* 19 / 61 *Score* 59.02   **DEARBORN**

CATEGORY	RANK	SCORE	STATISTIC	VALUE	RANK	SCORE
Economics	42	56.80	Median Household Income	$34,909	38	33.6
			% of Families Above Poverty Level	91.8%	45	80.0
Affordable Housing	23	72.75	Median Home Value	$68,800	32	74.4
			Median Rent	$465	21	71.1
Crime	44	66.65	Violent Crimes per 10,000 Population	59	37	89.0
			Property Crimes per 10,000 Population	784	46	44.3
Open Spaces	27	51.25	Population Density (Persons/Sq. Mile)	3664	27	62.5
			Average Rooms per Housing Unit	5.5	20	40.0
Education	27	50.00	% High School Enrollment/Completion	91.3%	33	68.7
			% College Graduates	21.7%	21	31.3
Commute	10	39.75	Average Work Commute in Minutes	20	6	72.7
			% Commuting on Public Transportation	1.6%	14	6.8
Community Stability	18	75.95	% Living in Same House as in 1979	49.4%	16	68.3
			% Living in Same County as in 1985	88.6%	22	83.6

Composite: *Rank* 20 / 61 *Score* 58.90   **SHELBY**

CATEGORY	RANK	SCORE	STATISTIC	VALUE	RANK	SCORE
Economics	13	73.55	Median Household Income	$47,930	13	51.0
			% of Families Above Poverty Level	97.9%	14	96.1
Affordable Housing	47	54.80	Median Home Value	$107,200	48	54.6
			Median Rent	$565	45	55.0
Crime	10	90.90	Violent Crimes per 10,000 Population	25	17	95.9
			Property Crimes per 10,000 Population	351	9	85.9
Open Spaces	8	73.65	Population Density (Persons/Sq. Mile)	1401	4	90.6
			Average Rooms per Housing Unit	6.0	11	56.7
Education	20	56.75	% High School Enrollment/Completion	95.5%	12	85.3
			% College Graduates	19.9%	23	28.2
Commute	59	13.90	Average Work Commute in Minutes	25	57	27.3
			% Commuting on Public Transportation	0.2%	55	0.5
Community Stability	51	48.75	% Living in Same House as in 1979	34.1%	51	31.2
			% Living in Same County as in 1985	81.4%	45	66.3

Composite: *Rank* 21 / 61 *Score* 58.72   **FARMINGTON**

CATEGORY	RANK	SCORE	STATISTIC	VALUE	RANK	SCORE
Economics	18	69.20	Median Household Income	$41,040	19	41.8
			% of Families Above Poverty Level	98.1%	11	96.6
Affordable Housing	50	51.35	Median Home Value	$106,800	47	54.8
			Median Rent	$609	50	47.9
Crime	11	89.55	Violent Crimes per 10,000 Population	15	8	98.0
			Property Crimes per 10,000 Population	401	13	81.1
Open Spaces	30	48.80	Population Density (Persons/Sq. Mile)	3798	29	60.9
			Average Rooms per Housing Unit	5.4	28	36.7
Education	12	71.30	% High School Enrollment/Completion	96.9%	5	90.9
			% College Graduates	33.7%	15	51.7
Commute	34	29.05	Average Work Commute in Minutes	22	28	54.5
			% Commuting on Public Transportation	0.9%	23	3.6
Community Stability	46	51.80	% Living in Same House as in 1979	41.4%	37	48.9
			% Living in Same County as in 1985	76.6%	54	54.7

Metropolitan Area Suburb Rankings
DETROIT-ANN ARBOR

Composite: **Rank** 22 / 61 **Score** 58.68   **CANTON**

CATEGORY	RANK	SCORE	STATISTIC	VALUE	RANK	SCORE
Economics	17	70.15	Median Household Income	$47,009	16	49.8
			% of Families Above Poverty Level	95.8%	33	90.5
Affordable Housing	45	56.95	Median Home Value	$108,600	49	53.9
			Median Rent	$534	42	60.0
Crime	16	88.55	Violent Crimes per 10,000 Population	24	14	96.1
			Property Crimes per 10,000 Population	402	15	81.0
Open Spaces	9	70.80	Population Density (Persons/Sq. Mile)	1585	6	88.3
			Average Rooms per Housing Unit	5.9	13	53.3
Education	17	61.05	% High School Enrollment/Completion	95.0%	16	83.3
			% College Graduates	26.1%	17	38.8
Commute	50	23.00	Average Work Commute in Minutes	23	43	45.5
			% Commuting on Public Transportation	0.2%	55	0.5
Community Stability	55	40.25	% Living in Same House as in 1979	28.2%	55	16.9
			% Living in Same County as in 1985	80.3%	51	63.6

Composite: **Rank** 23 / 61 **Score** 58.62   **STERLING HEIGHTS**

CATEGORY	RANK	SCORE	STATISTIC	VALUE	RANK	SCORE
Economics	16	71.65	Median Household Income	$46,470	17	49.1
			% of Families Above Poverty Level	97.2%	20	94.2
Affordable Housing	44	60.15	Median Home Value	$96,400	46	60.2
			Median Rent	$533	41	60.1
Crime	21	85.10	Violent Crimes per 10,000 Population	33	24	94.3
			Property Crimes per 10,000 Population	455	22	75.9
Open Spaces	21	57.40	Population Density (Persons/Sq. Mile)	3215	23	68.1
			Average Rooms per Housing Unit	5.7	15	46.7
Education	19	57.20	% High School Enrollment/Completion	96.3%	8	88.5
			% College Graduates	18.5%	24	25.9
Commute	54	19.10	Average Work Commute in Minutes	24	51	36.4
			% Commuting on Public Transportation	0.5%	41	1.8
Community Stability	40	59.75	% Living in Same House as in 1979	41.6%	35	49.4
			% Living in Same County as in 1985	83.0%	41	70.1

Composite: **Rank** 24 / 61 **Score** 58.34   **ST. CLAIR SHORES**

CATEGORY	RANK	SCORE	STATISTIC	VALUE	RANK	SCORE
Economics	26	65.50	Median Household Income	$36,929	28	36.3
			% of Families Above Poverty Level	97.4%	19	94.7
Affordable Housing	32	69.50	Median Home Value	$69,200	34	74.2
			Median Rent	$504	36	64.8
Crime	25	84.10	Violent Crimes per 10,000 Population	25	17	95.9
			Property Crimes per 10,000 Population	492	24	72.3
Open Spaces	48	35.75	Population Density (Persons/Sq. Mile)	5906	51	34.8
			Average Rooms per Housing Unit	5.4	28	36.7
Education	33	46.75	% High School Enrollment/Completion	93.1%	29	75.8
			% College Graduates	13.7%	35	17.7
Commute	46	25.25	Average Work Commute in Minutes	23	43	45.5
			% Commuting on Public Transportation	1.2%	18	5.0
Community Stability	10	81.50	% Living in Same House as in 1979	55.9%	4	84.0
			% Living in Same County as in 1985	86.7%	31	79.0

Metropolitan Area Suburb Rankings
DETROIT-ANN ARBOR

Composite: Rank 25 / 61 *Score* 58.26 **WOODHAVEN**

CATEGORY	RANK	SCORE	STATISTIC	VALUE	RANK	SCORE
Economics	15	72.10	Median Household Income	$47,513	15	50.5
			% of Families Above Poverty Level	97.0%	23	93.7
Affordable Housing	40	65.80	Median Home Value	$89,800	43	63.6
			Median Rent	$484	27	68.0
Crime	41	69.10	Violent Crimes per 10,000 Population	34	25	94.1
			Property Crimes per 10,000 Population	786	47	44.1
Open Spaces	15	62.80	Population Density (Persons/Sq. Mile)	1798	9	85.6
			Average Rooms per Housing Unit	5.5	20	40.0
Education	25	51.50	% High School Enrollment/Completion	94.7%	20	82.1
			% College Graduates	15.6%	32	20.9
Commute	47	24.35	Average Work Commute in Minutes	23	43	45.5
			% Commuting on Public Transportation	0.8%	28	3.2
Community Stability	35	62.15	% Living in Same House as in 1979	35.6%	47	34.9
			% Living in Same County as in 1985	91.0%	16	89.4

Composite: Rank 26 / 61 *Score* 58.18 **WEST BLOOMFIELD TOWNSHIP**

CATEGORY	RANK	SCORE	STATISTIC	VALUE	RANK	SCORE
Economics	2	88.75	Median Household Income	$68,661	2	78.8
			% of Families Above Poverty Level	98.9%	4	98.7
Affordable Housing	61	12.75	Median Home Value	$163,700	58	25.5
			Median Rent	$907	61	0.0
Crime	4	96.25	Violent Crimes per 10,000 Population	18	10	97.4
			Property Crimes per 10,000 Population	255	3	95.1
Open Spaces	2	83.20	Population Density (Persons/Sq. Mile)	2007	11	83.1
			Average Rooms per Housing Unit	6.8	5	83.3
Education	6	79.40	% High School Enrollment/Completion	95.0%	16	83.3
			% College Graduates	47.7%	6	75.5
Commute	61	0.45	Average Work Commute in Minutes	28	61	0.0
			% Commuting on Public Transportation	0.3%	50	0.9
Community Stability	52	46.45	% Living in Same House as in 1979	33.0%	52	28.6
			% Living in Same County as in 1985	80.6%	48	64.3

Composite: Rank 27 / 61 *Score* 58.10 **WYANDOTTE**

CATEGORY	RANK	SCORE	STATISTIC	VALUE	RANK	SCORE
Economics	47	52.65	Median Household Income	$28,312	50	24.8
			% of Families Above Poverty Level	92.0%	43	80.5
Affordable Housing	11	82.15	Median Home Value	$49,000	16	84.7
			Median Rent	$412	9	79.6
Crime	15	88.60	Violent Crimes per 10,000 Population	23	13	96.3
			Property Crimes per 10,000 Population	403	16	80.9
Open Spaces	52	34.50	Population Density (Persons/Sq. Mile)	5829	50	35.7
			Average Rooms per Housing Unit	5.3	34	33.3
Education	48	29.85	% High School Enrollment/Completion	87.1%	47	52.0
			% College Graduates	7.8%	50	7.7
Commute	17	35.65	Average Work Commute in Minutes	21	14	63.6
			% Commuting on Public Transportation	1.8%	9	7.7
Community Stability	6	83.30	% Living in Same House as in 1979	50.6%	12	71.2
			% Living in Same County as in 1985	93.5%	8	95.4

Metropolitan Area Suburb Rankings
DETROIT-ANN ARBOR

Composite: **Rank** 28 / 61 *Score* 58.08   **ROYAL OAK**

CATEGORY	RANK	SCORE	STATISTIC	VALUE	RANK	SCORE
Economics	29	65.05	Median Household Income	$36,835	29	36.2
			% of Families Above Poverty Level	97.1%	21	93.9
Affordable Housing	36	68.60	Median Home Value	$74,900	36	71.3
			Median Rent	$497	32	65.9
Crime	26	81.50	Violent Crimes per 10,000 Population	37	27	93.5
			Property Crimes per 10,000 Population	521	28	69.5
Open Spaces	46	36.35	Population Density (Persons/Sq. Mile)	5532	47	39.4
			Average Rooms per Housing Unit	5.3	34	33.3
Education	16	61.65	% High School Enrollment/Completion	94.3%	22	80.6
			% College Graduates	28.4%	16	42.7
Commute	23	33.40	Average Work Commute in Minutes	21	14	63.6
			% Commuting on Public Transportation	0.8%	28	3.2
Community Stability	39	60.00	% Living in Same House as in 1979	42.1%	34	50.6
			% Living in Same County as in 1985	82.7%	44	69.4

Composite: **Rank** 29 / 61 *Score* 57.99   **FRASER**

CATEGORY	RANK	SCORE	STATISTIC	VALUE	RANK	SCORE
Economics	34	63.10	Median Household Income	$36,644	32	35.9
			% of Families Above Poverty Level	95.7%	34	90.3
Affordable Housing	28	70.80	Median Home Value	$77,200	38	70.1
			Median Rent	$462	20	71.5
Crime	29	78.70	Violent Crimes per 10,000 Population	49	32	91.1
			Property Crimes per 10,000 Population	555	30	66.3
Open Spaces	29	50.05	Population Density (Persons/Sq. Mile)	3318	25	66.8
			Average Rooms per Housing Unit	5.3	34	33.3
Education	36	42.05	% High School Enrollment/Completion	91.2%	34	68.3
			% College Graduates	12.6%	39	15.8
Commute	39	28.40	Average Work Commute in Minutes	22	28	54.5
			% Commuting on Public Transportation	0.6%	38	2.3
Community Stability	23	72.80	% Living in Same House as in 1979	46.6%	19	61.5
			% Living in Same County as in 1985	88.8%	21	84.1

Composite: **Rank** 30 / 61 *Score* 56.71   **SOUTHGATE**

CATEGORY	RANK	SCORE	STATISTIC	VALUE	RANK	SCORE
Economics	31	64.35	Median Household Income	$36,526	34	35.8
			% of Families Above Poverty Level	96.7%	26	92.9
Affordable Housing	24	72.40	Median Home Value	$58,500	21	79.8
			Median Rent	$503	35	65.0
Crime	30	77.55	Violent Crimes per 10,000 Population	42	29	92.5
			Property Crimes per 10,000 Population	593	35	62.6
Open Spaces	43	37.80	Population Density (Persons/Sq. Mile)	4488	38	52.3
			Average Rooms per Housing Unit	5.0	52	23.3
Education	43	35.80	% High School Enrollment/Completion	89.4%	41	61.1
			% College Graduates	9.5%	46	10.5
Commute	33	29.30	Average Work Commute in Minutes	22	28	54.5
			% Commuting on Public Transportation	1.0%	20	4.1
Community Stability	11	79.75	% Living in Same House as in 1979	47.4%	17	63.4
			% Living in Same County as in 1985	93.8%	5	96.1

Metropolitan Area Suburb Rankings
DETROIT-ANN ARBOR

Composite: Rank 31 / 61 Score 56.58 — FARMINGTON HILLS

CATEGORY	RANK	SCORE	STATISTIC	VALUE	RANK	SCORE
Economics	11	76.80	Median Household Income	$51,986	11	56.5
			% of Families Above Poverty Level	98.3%	8	97.1
Affordable Housing	55	37.25	Median Home Value	$145,500	55	34.8
			Median Rent	$660	53	39.7
Crime	12	89.35	Violent Crimes per 10,000 Population	24	14	96.1
			Property Crimes per 10,000 Population	385	11	82.6
Open Spaces	11	66.70	Population Density (Persons/Sq. Mile)	2242	14	80.1
			Average Rooms per Housing Unit	5.9	13	53.3
Education	9	74.15	% High School Enrollment/Completion	94.8%	18	82.5
			% College Graduates	42.0%	8	65.8
Commute	49	23.45	Average Work Commute in Minutes	23	43	45.5
			% Commuting on Public Transportation	0.4%	46	1.4
Community Stability	58	28.35	% Living in Same House as in 1979	27.9%	57	16.2
			% Living in Same County as in 1985	70.7%	58	40.5

Composite: Rank 32 / 61 *Score* 56.34 — WARREN

CATEGORY	RANK	SCORE	STATISTIC	VALUE	RANK	SCORE
Economics	37	61.60	Median Household Income	$35,980	36	35.0
			% of Families Above Poverty Level	94.9%	37	88.2
Affordable Housing	29	70.50	Median Home Value	$69,000	33	74.3
			Median Rent	$492	29	66.7
Crime	35	75.10	Violent Crimes per 10,000 Population	82	44	84.3
			Property Crimes per 10,000 Population	559	32	65.9
Open Spaces	33	46.15	Population Density (Persons/Sq. Mile)	4225	34	55.6
			Average Rooms per Housing Unit	5.4	28	36.7
Education	44	35.70	% High School Enrollment/Completion	89.0%	43	59.5
			% College Graduates	10.3%	44	11.9
Commute	24	33.15	Average Work Commute in Minutes	21	14	63.6
			% Commuting on Public Transportation	0.7%	31	2.7
Community Stability	24	72.20	% Living in Same House as in 1979	51.2%	10	72.6
			% Living in Same County as in 1985	83.7%	40	71.8

Composite: Rank 33 / 61 *Score* 54.91 — WAYNE

CATEGORY	RANK	SCORE	STATISTIC	VALUE	RANK	SCORE
Economics	45	54.35	Median Household Income	$31,250	46	28.7
			% of Families Above Poverty Level	91.8%	45	80.0
Affordable Housing	9	83.45	Median Home Value	$47,600	13	85.4
			Median Rent	$400	7	81.5
Crime	37	73.35	Violent Crimes per 10,000 Population	100	47	80.7
			Property Crimes per 10,000 Population	558	31	66.0
Open Spaces	31	46.85	Population Density (Persons/Sq. Mile)	3306	24	67.0
			Average Rooms per Housing Unit	5.1	47	26.7
Education	50	27.40	% High School Enrollment/Completion	85.0%	50	43.7
			% College Graduates	9.8%	45	11.1
Commute	40	28.15	Average Work Commute in Minutes	22	28	54.5
			% Commuting on Public Transportation	0.5%	41	1.8
Community Stability	25	70.80	% Living in Same House as in 1979	42.2%	33	50.8
			% Living in Same County as in 1985	91.6%	15	90.8

Metropolitan Area Suburb Rankings
DETROIT-ANN ARBOR

Composite: *Rank* 34 / 61 *Score* 54.85   **LINCOLN PARK**

CATEGORY	RANK	SCORE	STATISTIC	VALUE	RANK	SCORE
Economics	43	56.60	Median Household Income	$30,638	47	27.9
			% of Families Above Poverty Level	93.8%	41	85.3
Affordable Housing	13	81.80	Median Home Value	$44,100	11	87.2
			Median Rent	$432	13	76.4
Crime	36	74.50	Violent Crimes per 10,000 Population	47	30	91.5
			Property Crimes per 10,000 Population	646	39	57.5
Open Spaces	58	23.05	Population Density (Persons/Sq. Mile)	7153	60	19.4
			Average Rooms per Housing Unit	5.1	47	26.7
Education	53	24.65	% High School Enrollment/Completion	84.9%	51	43.3
			% College Graduates	6.8%	55	6.0
Commute	12	38.85	Average Work Commute in Minutes	20	6	72.7
			% Commuting on Public Transportation	1.2%	18	5.0
Community Stability	5	84.50	% Living in Same House as in 1979	51.2%	10	72.6
			% Living in Same County as in 1985	93.9%	4	96.4

Composite: *Rank* 35 / 61 *Score* 54.56   **MADISON HEIGHTS**

CATEGORY	RANK	SCORE	STATISTIC	VALUE	RANK	SCORE
Economics	44	56.40	Median Household Income	$31,757	44	29.4
			% of Families Above Poverty Level	93.1%	42	83.4
Affordable Housing	22	73.85	Median Home Value	$59,600	23	79.2
			Median Rent	$481	26	68.5
Crime	21	85.10	Violent Crimes per 10,000 Population	37	27	93.5
			Property Crimes per 10,000 Population	447	20	76.7
Open Spaces	47	36.15	Population Density (Persons/Sq. Mile)	4492	39	52.3
			Average Rooms per Housing Unit	4.9	54	20.0
Education	45	33.55	% High School Enrollment/Completion	87.6%	46	54.0
			% College Graduates	11.0%	42	13.1
Commute	15	37.70	Average Work Commute in Minutes	20	6	72.7
			% Commuting on Public Transportation	0.7%	31	2.7
Community Stability	41	59.15	% Living in Same House as in 1979	42.8%	32	52.3
			% Living in Same County as in 1985	81.3%	46	66.0

Composite: *Rank* 36 / 61 *Score* 54.15   **WATERFORD**

CATEGORY	RANK	SCORE	STATISTIC	VALUE	RANK	SCORE
Economics	24	65.75	Median Household Income	$39,463	23	39.7
			% of Families Above Poverty Level	96.3%	29	91.8
Affordable Housing	38	66.80	Median Home Value	$76,000	37	70.7
			Median Rent	$516	38	62.9
Crime	38	73.00	Violent Crimes per 10,000 Population	57	34	89.4
			Property Crimes per 10,000 Population	656	41	56.6
Open Spaces	17	60.80	Population Density (Persons/Sq. Mile)	2128	12	81.6
			Average Rooms per Housing Unit	5.5	20	40.0
Education	46	32.70	% High School Enrollment/Completion	84.9%	51	43.3
			% College Graduates	16.3%	29	22.1
Commute	57	18.20	Average Work Commute in Minutes	24	51	36.4
			% Commuting on Public Transportation	0.1%	59	0.0
Community Stability	36	61.80	% Living in Same House as in 1979	38.0%	42	40.7
			% Living in Same County as in 1985	88.3%	23	82.9

Metropolitan Area Suburb Rankings
DETROIT-ANN ARBOR

Composite: **Rank** 37 / 61 *Score* 53.94   **ROMULUS**

CATEGORY	RANK	SCORE	STATISTIC	VALUE	RANK	SCORE
Economics	50	49.80	Median Household Income	$31,723	45	29.3
			% of Families Above Poverty Level	88.1%	51	70.3
Affordable Housing	14	81.50	Median Home Value	$48,900	15	84.7
			Median Rent	$420	12	78.3
Crime	51	58.05	Violent Crimes per 10,000 Population	108	48	79.1
			Property Crimes per 10,000 Population	860	51	37.0
Open Spaces	12	66.65	Population Density (Persons/Sq. Mile)	638	1	100.0
			Average Rooms per Housing Unit	5.3	34	33.3
Education	52	25.60	% High School Enrollment/Completion	85.8%	48	46.8
			% College Graduates	5.9%	58	4.4
Commute	44	27.25	Average Work Commute in Minutes	22	28	54.5
			% Commuting on Public Transportation	0.1%	59	0.0
Community Stability	28	68.70	% Living in Same House as in 1979	41.3%	38	48.7
			% Living in Same County as in 1985	90.7%	17	88.7

Composite: **Rank** 38 / 61 *Score* 53.77   **CLINTON**

CATEGORY	RANK	SCORE	STATISTIC	VALUE	RANK	SCORE
Economics	30	64.55	Median Household Income	$39,215	24	39.4
			% of Families Above Poverty Level	95.5%	35	89.7
Affordable Housing	39	65.95	Median Home Value	$86,700	42	65.2
			Median Rent	$492	29	66.7
Crime	27	80.75	Violent Crimes per 10,000 Population	48	31	91.3
			Property Crimes per 10,000 Population	514	27	70.2
Open Spaces	26	51.75	Population Density (Persons/Sq. Mile)	3045	21	70.2
			Average Rooms per Housing Unit	5.3	34	33.3
Education	35	42.65	% High School Enrollment/Completion	90.7%	37	66.3
			% College Graduates	14.5%	33	19.0
Commute	53	19.35	Average Work Commute in Minutes	24	51	36.4
			% Commuting on Public Transportation	0.6%	38	2.3
Community Stability	47	51.40	% Living in Same House as in 1979	32.5%	53	27.4
			% Living in Same County as in 1985	85.2%	37	75.4

Composite: **Rank** 39 / 61 *Score* 53.71   **HARPER WOODS**

CATEGORY	RANK	SCORE	STATISTIC	VALUE	RANK	SCORE
Economics	36	61.90	Median Household Income	$33,098	41	31.2
			% of Families Above Poverty Level	96.6%	27	92.6
Affordable Housing	42	64.55	Median Home Value	$66,000	29	75.9
			Median Rent	$576	48	53.2
Crime	54	49.20	Violent Crimes per 10,000 Population	36	26	93.7
			Property Crimes per 10,000 Population	1,196	55	4.7
Open Spaces	50	34.95	Population Density (Persons/Sq. Mile)	5764	49	36.6
			Average Rooms per Housing Unit	5.3	34	33.3
Education	26	50.50	% High School Enrollment/Completion	93.5%	25	77.4
			% College Graduates	17.2%	27	23.6
Commute	17	35.65	Average Work Commute in Minutes	21	14	63.6
			% Commuting on Public Transportation	1.8%	9	7.7
Community Stability	13	79.25	% Living in Same House as in 1979	54.2%	8	79.9
			% Living in Same County as in 1985	86.5%	33	78.6

Composite: *Rank* 40 / 61 *Score* 53.26   AUBURN HILLS

CATEGORY	RANK	SCORE	STATISTIC	VALUE	RANK	SCORE
Economics	39	59.50	Median Household Income	$34,825	39	33.5
			% of Families Above Poverty Level	93.9%	40	85.5
Affordable Housing	41	65.15	Median Home Value	$68,100	31	74.8
			Median Rent	$562	44	55.5
Crime	32	76.25	Violent Crimes per 10,000 Population	77	43	85.4
			Property Crimes per 10,000 Population	546	29	67.1
Open Spaces	20	57.60	Population Density (Persons/Sq. Mile)	1028	2	95.2
			Average Rooms per Housing Unit	4.9	54	20.0
Education	23	53.35	% High School Enrollment/Completion	92.2%	32	72.2
			% College Graduates	23.6%	19	34.5
Commute	29	32.25	Average Work Commute in Minutes	21	14	63.6
			% Commuting on Public Transportation	0.3%	50	0.9
Community Stability	57	28.70	% Living in Same House as in 1979	24.6%	58	8.2
			% Living in Same County as in 1985	74.3%	56	49.2

Composite: *Rank* 41 / 61 *Score* 52.89   PORT HURON

CATEGORY	RANK	SCORE	STATISTIC	VALUE	RANK	SCORE
Economics	56	32.30	Median Household Income	$21,522	56	15.7
			% of Families Above Poverty Level	80.0%	56	48.9
Affordable Housing	5	86.30	Median Home Value	$40,600	10	89.0
			Median Rent	$387	6	83.6
Crime	39	71.10	Violent Crimes per 10,000 Population	92	45	82.3
			Property Crimes per 10,000 Population	621	38	59.9
Open Spaces	35	44.55	Population Density (Persons/Sq. Mile)	4209	33	55.8
			Average Rooms per Housing Unit	5.3	34	33.3
Education	49	27.45	% High School Enrollment/Completion	84.7%	53	42.5
			% College Graduates	10.6%	43	12.4
Commute	3	52.05	Average Work Commute in Minutes	17	1	100.0
			% Commuting on Public Transportation	1.0%	20	4.1
Community Stability	44	56.45	% Living in Same House as in 1979	34.6%	50	32.4
			% Living in Same County as in 1985	87.3%	29	80.5

Composite: *Rank* 42 / 61 *Score* 52.84   SOUTHFIELD

CATEGORY	RANK	SCORE	STATISTIC	VALUE	RANK	SCORE
Economics	21	66.80	Median Household Income	$40,579	20	41.2
			% of Families Above Poverty Level	96.5%	28	92.4
Affordable Housing	49	52.10	Median Home Value	$84,300	41	66.4
			Median Rent	$672	54	37.8
Crime	40	70.45	Violent Crimes per 10,000 Population	75	42	85.8
			Property Crimes per 10,000 Population	671	42	55.1
Open Spaces	24	54.45	Population Density (Persons/Sq. Mile)	2887	19	72.2
			Average Rooms per Housing Unit	5.4	28	36.7
Education	14	66.00	% High School Enrollment/Completion	93.8%	23	78.6
			% College Graduates	34.7%	12	53.4
Commute	35	28.85	Average Work Commute in Minutes	22	28	54.5
			% Commuting on Public Transportation	0.8%	28	3.2
Community Stability	56	31.25	% Living in Same House as in 1979	31.2%	54	24.2
			% Living in Same County as in 1985	69.8%	59	38.3

Metropolitan Area Suburb Rankings
DETROIT-ANN ARBOR

Composite: **Rank** 43 / 61 *Score* 52.79   **WESTLAND**

CATEGORY	RANK	SCORE	STATISTIC	VALUE	RANK	SCORE
Economics	38	60.25	Median Household Income	$34,995	37	33.7
			% of Families Above Poverty Level	94.4%	38	86.8
Affordable Housing	29	70.50	Median Home Value	$62,800	24	77.5
			Median Rent	$512	37	63.5
Crime	33	75.50	Violent Crimes per 10,000 Population	58	36	89.2
			Property Crimes per 10,000 Population	602	36	61.8
Open Spaces	39	39.95	Population Density (Persons/Sq. Mile)	4141	31	56.6
			Average Rooms per Housing Unit	5.0	52	23.3
Education	42	38.25	% High School Enrollment/Completion	89.8%	39	62.7
			% College Graduates	11.4%	41	13.8
Commute	48	23.65	Average Work Commute in Minutes	23	43	45.5
			% Commuting on Public Transportation	0.5%	41	1.8
Community Stability	37	61.45	% Living in Same House as in 1979	37.7%	43	40.0
			% Living in Same County as in 1985	88.3%	23	82.9

Composite: **Rank** 44 / 61 *Score* 52.75   **TAYLOR**

CATEGORY	RANK	SCORE	STATISTIC	VALUE	RANK	SCORE
Economics	48	51.60	Median Household Income	$32,659	42	30.6
			% of Families Above Poverty Level	89.0%	50	72.6
Affordable Housing	17	78.70	Median Home Value	$48,100	14	85.1
			Median Rent	$457	17	72.3
Crime	45	66.40	Violent Crimes per 10,000 Population	63	38	88.2
			Property Crimes per 10,000 Population	781	45	44.6
Open Spaces	28	50.40	Population Density (Persons/Sq. Mile)	2999	20	70.8
			Average Rooms per Housing Unit	5.2	43	30.0
Education	55	19.65	% High School Enrollment/Completion	82.4%	55	33.3
			% College Graduates	6.8%	55	6.0
Commute	36	28.60	Average Work Commute in Minutes	22	28	54.5
			% Commuting on Public Transportation	0.7%	31	2.7
Community Stability	21	73.90	% Living in Same House as in 1979	44.4%	26	56.2
			% Living in Same County as in 1985	91.9%	13	91.6

Composite: **Rank** 45 / 61 *Score* 52.62   **NOVI**

CATEGORY	RANK	SCORE	STATISTIC	VALUE	RANK	SCORE
Economics	14	73.15	Median Household Income	$47,518	14	50.5
			% of Families Above Poverty Level	97.8%	16	95.8
Affordable Housing	54	40.45	Median Home Value	$127,000	51	44.4
			Median Rent	$680	55	36.5
Crime	23	84.60	Violent Crimes per 10,000 Population	14	5	98.2
			Property Crimes per 10,000 Population	506	25	71.0
Open Spaces	10	70.60	Population Density (Persons/Sq. Mile)	1084	3	94.5
			Average Rooms per Housing Unit	5.7	15	46.7
Education	15	64.70	% High School Enrollment/Completion	93.5%	25	77.4
			% College Graduates	33.9%	14	52.0
Commute	56	18.45	Average Work Commute in Minutes	24	51	36.4
			% Commuting on Public Transportation	0.2%	55	0.5
Community Stability	60	16.40	% Living in Same House as in 1979	23.5%	60	5.6
			% Living in Same County as in 1985	65.2%	60	27.2

Metropolitan Area Suburb Rankings
DETROIT-ANN ARBOR

Composite: *Rank* 46 / 61 *Score* 52.60 **EAST DETROIT**

CATEGORY	RANK	SCORE	STATISTIC	VALUE	RANK	SCORE
Economics	35	62.15	Median Household Income	$34,069	40	32.5
			% of Families Above Poverty Level	96.3%	29	91.8
Affordable Housing	19	76.25	Median Home Value	$54,600	18	81.8
			Median Rent	$467	22	70.7
Crime	N/A	N/A	Violent Crimes per 10,000 Population	N/A	N/A	N/A
			Property Crimes per 10,000 Population	N/A	N/A	N/A
Open Spaces	56	29.55	Population Density (Persons/Sq. Mile)	6909	58	22.4
			Average Rooms per Housing Unit	5.4	28	36.7
Education	41	38.50	% High School Enrollment/Completion	91.0%	35	67.5
			% College Graduates	8.9%	47	9.5
Commute	32	29.95	Average Work Commute in Minutes	22	28	54.5
			% Commuting on Public Transportation	1.3%	17	5.4
Community Stability	12	79.20	% Living in Same House as in 1979	55.0%	7	81.8
			% Living in Same County as in 1985	85.7%	36	76.6

Composite: *Rank* 47 / 61 *Score* 51.75 **ROSEVILLE**

CATEGORY	RANK	SCORE	STATISTIC	VALUE	RANK	SCORE
Economics	40	59.45	Median Household Income	$32,337	43	30.2
			% of Families Above Poverty Level	95.1%	36	88.7
Affordable Housing	20	75.45	Median Home Value	$55,000	19	81.6
			Median Rent	$476	25	69.3
Crime	53	56.80	Violent Crimes per 10,000 Population	64	39	88.0
			Property Crimes per 10,000 Population	979	53	25.6
Open Spaces	51	34.90	Population Density (Persons/Sq. Mile)	5236	44	43.1
			Average Rooms per Housing Unit	5.1	47	26.7
Education	47	32.40	% High School Enrollment/Completion	88.8%	45	58.7
			% College Graduates	6.9%	54	6.1
Commute	20	33.85	Average Work Commute in Minutes	21	14	63.6
			% Commuting on Public Transportation	1.0%	20	4.1
Community Stability	27	69.40	% Living in Same House as in 1979	46.0%	21	60.0
			% Living in Same County as in 1985	86.6%	32	78.8

Composite: *Rank* 48 / 61 *Score* 51.51 **FERNDALE**

CATEGORY	RANK	SCORE	STATISTIC	VALUE	RANK	SCORE
Economics	46	52.60	Median Household Income	$28,964	49	25.7
			% of Families Above Poverty Level	91.6%	47	79.5
Affordable Housing	15	80.50	Median Home Value	$38,000	9	90.3
			Median Rent	$467	22	70.7
Crime	42	67.90	Violent Crimes per 10,000 Population	99	46	80.9
			Property Crimes per 10,000 Population	674	43	54.9
Open Spaces	54	30.55	Population Density (Persons/Sq. Mile)	6473	56	27.8
			Average Rooms per Housing Unit	5.3	34	33.3
Education	40	38.60	% High School Enrollment/Completion	89.3%	42	60.7
			% College Graduates	13.0%	37	16.5
Commute	19	35.40	Average Work Commute in Minutes	21	14	63.6
			% Commuting on Public Transportation	1.7%	12	7.2
Community Stability	45	55.05	% Living in Same House as in 1979	39.8%	39	45.0
			% Living in Same County as in 1985	80.9%	47	65.1

Metropolitan Area Suburb Rankings
DETROIT-ANN ARBOR

Composite: **Rank** 49 / 61 *Score* 51.46   **OAK PARK**

CATEGORY	RANK	SCORE	STATISTIC	VALUE	RANK	SCORE
Economics	41	57.35	Median Household Income	$36,090	35	35.2
			% of Families Above Poverty Level	91.6%	47	79.5
Affordable Housing	31	70.10	Median Home Value	$47,400	12	85.5
			Median Rent	$567	46	54.7
Crime	46	65.90	Violent Crimes per 10,000 Population	130	51	74.6
			Property Crimes per 10,000 Population	650	40	57.2
Open Spaces	42	38.00	Population Density (Persons/Sq. Mile)	6079	53	32.7
			Average Rooms per Housing Unit	5.6	18	43.3
Education	29	48.80	% High School Enrollment/Completion	90.5%	38	65.5
			% College Graduates	22.2%	20	32.1
Commute	30	30.65	Average Work Commute in Minutes	22	28	54.5
			% Commuting on Public Transportation	1.6%	14	6.8
Community Stability	50	49.40	% Living in Same House as in 1979	41.6%	35	49.4
			% Living in Same County as in 1985	74.4%	55	49.4

Composite: **Rank** 50 / 61 *Score* 50.57   **RIVER ROUGE**

CATEGORY	RANK	SCORE	STATISTIC	VALUE	RANK	SCORE
Economics	60	17.65	Median Household Income	$17,500	59	10.3
			% of Families Above Poverty Level	70.9%	60	25.0
Affordable Housing	3	96.10	Median Home Value	$22,000	3	98.6
			Median Rent	$325	3	93.6
Crime	48	59.95	Violent Crimes per 10,000 Population	123	49	76.0
			Property Crimes per 10,000 Population	788	48	43.9
Open Spaces	36	44.35	Population Density (Persons/Sq. Mile)	4239	35	55.4
			Average Rooms per Housing Unit	5.3	34	33.3
Education	56	17.50	% High School Enrollment/Completion	81.6%	56	30.2
			% College Graduates	6.1%	57	4.8
Commute	8	40.85	Average Work Commute in Minutes	21	14	63.6
			% Commuting on Public Transportation	4.1%	4	18.1
Community Stability	15	77.60	% Living in Same House as in 1979	44.3%	27	55.9
			% Living in Same County as in 1985	95.1%	2	99.3

Composite: **Rank** 51 / 61 *Score* 50.23   **MELVINDALE**

CATEGORY	RANK	SCORE	STATISTIC	VALUE	RANK	SCORE
Economics	51	48.30	Median Household Income	$26,179	52	21.9
			% of Families Above Poverty Level	89.8%	49	74.7
Affordable Housing	6	84.65	Median Home Value	$37,800	8	90.4
			Median Rent	$416	11	78.9
Crime	49	59.10	Violent Crimes per 10,000 Population	64	39	88.0
			Property Crimes per 10,000 Population	931	52	30.2
Open Spaces	49	35.55	Population Density (Persons/Sq. Mile)	4049	30	57.8
			Average Rooms per Housing Unit	4.7	60	13.3
Education	58	10.55	% High School Enrollment/Completion	78.4%	58	17.5
			% College Graduates	5.4%	59	3.6
Commute	9	39.95	Average Work Commute in Minutes	20	6	72.7
			% Commuting on Public Transportation	1.7%	12	7.2
Community Stability	22	73.50	% Living in Same House as in 1979	43.2%	30	53.3
			% Living in Same County as in 1985	92.8%	11	93.7

Metropolitan Area Suburb Rankings
DETROIT-ANN ARBOR

Composite: *Rank* 52 / 61 *Score* 50.11   **ECORSE**

CATEGORY	RANK	SCORE	STATISTIC	VALUE	RANK	SCORE
Economics	58	23.25	Median Household Income	$18,956	58	12.3
			% of Families Above Poverty Level	74.4%	59	34.2
Affordable Housing	4	92.55	Median Home Value	$25,500	4	96.8
			Median Rent	$358	4	88.3
Crime	43	67.15	Violent Crimes per 10,000 Population	148	53	70.9
			Property Crimes per 10,000 Population	585	34	63.4
Open Spaces	40	39.35	Population Density (Persons/Sq. Mile)	4513	40	52.0
			Average Rooms per Housing Unit	5.1	47	26.7
Education	57	14.50	% High School Enrollment/Completion	81.3%	57	29.0
			% College Graduates	3.3%	61	0.0
Commute	13	38.60	Average Work Commute in Minutes	21	14	63.6
			% Commuting on Public Transportation	3.1%	6	13.6
Community Stability	20	75.35	% Living in Same House as in 1979	43.9%	29	55.0
			% Living in Same County as in 1985	93.6%	7	95.7

Composite: *Rank* 53 / 61 *Score* 50.00   **ROCHESTER HILLS**

CATEGORY	RANK	SCORE	STATISTIC	VALUE	RANK	SCORE
Economics	8	78.80	Median Household Income	$54,996	8	60.5
			% of Families Above Poverty Level	98.3%	8	97.1
Affordable Housing	53	40.90	Median Home Value	$136,700	54	39.4
			Median Rent	$643	52	42.4
Crime	N/A	N/A	Violent Crimes per 10,000 Population	N/A	N/A	N/A
			Property Crimes per 10,000 Population	N/A	N/A	N/A
Open Spaces	6	73.95	Population Density (Persons/Sq. Mile)	1880	10	84.6
			Average Rooms per Housing Unit	6.2	9	63.3
Education	10	73.05	% High School Enrollment/Completion	95.3%	14	84.5
			% College Graduates	39.5%	10	61.6
Commute	60	9.10	Average Work Commute in Minutes	26	59	18.2
			% Commuting on Public Transportation	0.1%	59	0.0
Community Stability	59	24.20	% Living in Same House as in 1979	24.4%	59	7.7
			% Living in Same County as in 1985	70.8%	57	40.7

Composite: *Rank* 54 / 61 *Score* 48.26   **MOUNT CLEMENS**

CATEGORY	RANK	SCORE	STATISTIC	VALUE	RANK	SCORE
Economics	49	50.80	Median Household Income	$25,716	53	21.3
			% of Families Above Poverty Level	91.9%	44	80.3
Affordable Housing	9	83.45	Median Home Value	$54,200	17	82.0
			Median Rent	$379	5	84.9
Crime	52	57.55	Violent Crimes per 10,000 Population	130	51	74.6
			Property Crimes per 10,000 Population	823	50	40.5
Open Spaces	45	36.90	Population Density (Persons/Sq. Mile)	4370	36	53.8
			Average Rooms per Housing Unit	4.9	54	20.0
Education	60	8.10	% High School Enrollment/Completion	74.0%	61	0.0
			% College Graduates	12.8%	38	16.2
Commute	10	39.75	Average Work Commute in Minutes	20	6	72.7
			% Commuting on Public Transportation	1.6%	14	6.8
Community Stability	38	61.30	% Living in Same House as in 1979	39.0%	40	43.1
			% Living in Same County as in 1985	86.9%	30	79.5

Metropolitan Area Suburb Rankings
DETROIT-ANN ARBOR

Composite: Rank 55 / 61 *Score* 47.56   **HAZEL PARK**

CATEGORY	RANK	SCORE	STATISTIC	VALUE	RANK	SCORE
Economics	53	45.85	Median Household Income	$26,615	51	22.5
			% of Families Above Poverty Level	87.7%	52	69.2
Affordable Housing	12	81.85	Median Home Value	$36,000	6	91.4
			Median Rent	$457	17	72.3
Crime	50	58.90	Violent Crimes per 10,000 Population	129	50	74.8
			Property Crimes per 10,000 Population	797	49	43.0
Open Spaces	57	23.25	Population Density (Persons/Sq. Mile)	7115	59	19.8
			Average Rooms per Housing Unit	5.1	47	26.7
Education	54	19.60	% High School Enrollment/Completion	83.2%	54	36.5
			% College Graduates	4.9%	60	2.7
Commute	15	37.70	Average Work Commute in Minutes	20	6	72.7
			% Commuting on Public Transportation	0.7%	31	2.7
Community Stability	32	65.80	% Living in Same House as in 1979	46.6%	19	61.5
			% Living in Same County as in 1985	83.0%	41	70.1

Composite: Rank 56 / 61 *Score* 47.09   **HARRISON**

CATEGORY	RANK	SCORE	STATISTIC	VALUE	RANK	SCORE
Economics	27	65.35	Median Household Income	$39,210	25	39.4
			% of Families Above Poverty Level	96.1%	31	91.3
Affordable Housing	43	63.90	Median Home Value	$91,600	44	62.7
			Median Rent	$502	33	65.1
Crime	N/A	N/A	Violent Crimes per 10,000 Population	N/A	N/A	N/A
			Property Crimes per 10,000 Population	N/A	N/A	N/A
Open Spaces	19	58.15	Population Density (Persons/Sq. Mile)	1745	8	86.3
			Average Rooms per Housing Unit	5.2	43	30.0
Education	38	40.40	% High School Enrollment/Completion	89.0%	43	59.5
			% College Graduates	15.8%	30	21.3
Commute	58	14.35	Average Work Commute in Minutes	25	57	27.3
			% Commuting on Public Transportation	0.4%	46	1.4
Community Stability	54	40.40	% Living in Same House as in 1979	28.2%	55	16.9
			% Living in Same County as in 1985	80.4%	50	63.9

Composite: Rank 57 / 61 *Score* 46.86   **INKSTER**

CATEGORY	RANK	SCORE	STATISTIC	VALUE	RANK	SCORE
Economics	54	35.30	Median Household Income	$25,198	54	20.6
			% of Families Above Poverty Level	80.4%	55	50.0
Affordable Housing	7	83.60	Median Home Value	$35,800	5	91.5
			Median Rent	$436	14	75.7
Crime	N/A	N/A	Violent Crimes per 10,000 Population	N/A	N/A	N/A
			Property Crimes per 10,000 Population	N/A	N/A	N/A
Open Spaces	53	31.85	Population Density (Persons/Sq. Mile)	4919	42	47.0
			Average Rooms per Housing Unit	4.8	59	16.7
Education	51	26.20	% High School Enrollment/Completion	85.5%	49	45.6
			% College Graduates	7.3%	51	6.8
Commute	45	27.05	Average Work Commute in Minutes	23	43	45.5
			% Commuting on Public Transportation	2.0%	8	8.6
Community Stability	17	77.15	% Living in Same House as in 1979	47.1%	18	62.7
			% Living in Same County as in 1985	91.9%	13	91.6

Composite: *Rank* 58 / 61 *Score* 46.11 — YPSILANTI

CATEGORY	RANK	SCORE	STATISTIC	VALUE	RANK	SCORE
Economics	55	34.50	Median Household Income	$21,219	57	15.3
			% of Families Above Poverty Level	81.8%	54	53.7
Affordable Housing	16	79.30	Median Home Value	$63,000	25	77.4
			Median Rent	$402	8	81.2
Crime	47	60.05	Violent Crimes per 10,000 Population	157	54	69.1
			Property Crimes per 10,000 Population	714	44	51.0
Open Spaces	60	18.65	Population Density (Persons/Sq. Mile)	5701	48	37.3
			Average Rooms per Housing Unit	4.3	61	0.0
Education	13	70.55	% High School Enrollment/Completion	96.3%	8	88.5
			% College Graduates	34.2%	13	52.6
Commute	1	59.75	Average Work Commute in Minutes	17	1	100.0
			% Commuting on Public Transportation	4.4%	3	19.5
Community Stability	61	0.00	% Living in Same House as in 1979	21.2%	61	0.0
			% Living in Same County as in 1985	53.9%	61	0.0

Composite: *Rank* 59 / 61 *Score* 43.27 — PONTIAC

CATEGORY	RANK	SCORE	STATISTIC	VALUE	RANK	SCORE
Economics	57	27.25	Median Household Income	$21,962	55	16.3
			% of Families Above Poverty Level	75.9%	57	38.2
Affordable Housing	8	83.55	Median Home Value	$36,000	6	91.4
			Median Rent	$436	14	75.7
Crime	N/A	N/A	Violent Crimes per 10,000 Population	N/A	N/A	N/A
			Property Crimes per 10,000 Population	N/A	N/A	N/A
Open Spaces	37	41.95	Population Density (Persons/Sq. Mile)	3558	26	63.9
			Average Rooms per Housing Unit	4.9	54	20.0
Education	61	7.45	% High School Enrollment/Completion	75.8%	60	7.1
			% College Graduates	7.9%	49	7.8
Commute	6	42.70	Average Work Commute in Minutes	19	4	81.8
			% Commuting on Public Transportation	0.9%	23	3.6
Community Stability	43	56.75	% Living in Same House as in 1979	35.6%	47	34.9
			% Living in Same County as in 1985	86.5%	33	78.6

Composite: *Rank* 60 / 61 *Score* 41.97 — HIGHLAND PARK

CATEGORY	RANK	SCORE	STATISTIC	VALUE	RANK	SCORE
Economics	61	0.00	Median Household Income	$9,805	61	0.0
			% of Families Above Poverty Level	61.4%	61	0.0
Affordable Housing	1	100.00	Median Home Value	$19,300	1	100.0
			Median Rent	$285	1	100.0
Crime	56	0.00	Violent Crimes per 10,000 Population	497	56	0.0
			Property Crimes per 10,000 Population	1,245	56	0.0
Open Spaces	59	22.10	Population Density (Persons/Sq. Mile)	6759	57	24.2
			Average Rooms per Housing Unit	4.9	54	20.0
Education	34	45.80	% High School Enrollment/Completion	95.5%	12	85.3
			% College Graduates	7.0%	53	6.3
Commute	2	59.10	Average Work Commute in Minutes	26	59	18.2
			% Commuting on Public Transportation	22.2%	1	100.0
Community Stability	31	66.80	% Living in Same House as in 1979	36.2%	46	36.3
			% Living in Same County as in 1985	94.3%	3	97.3

Metropolitan Area Suburb Rankings
DETROIT-ANN ARBOR

Composite: **Rank** 61 / 61 **Score** 41.29 **HAMTRAMCK**

CATEGORY	RANK	SCORE	STATISTIC	VALUE	RANK	SCORE
Economics	59	22.15	Median Household Income	$16,751	60	9.3
			% of Families Above Poverty Level	74.7%	58	35.0
Affordable Housing	2	96.75	Median Home Value	$21,100	2	99.1
			Median Rent	$320	2	94.4
Crime	55	31.80	Violent Crimes per 10,000 Population	271	55	45.9
			Property Crimes per 10,000 Population	1,061	54	17.7
Open Spaces	61	15.00	Population Density (Persons/Sq. Mile)	8717	61	0.0
			Average Rooms per Housing Unit	5.2	43	30.0
Education	59	9.35	% High School Enrollment/Completion	76.4%	59	9.5
			% College Graduates	8.7%	48	9.2
Commute	5	46.30	Average Work Commute in Minutes	20	6	72.7
			% Commuting on Public Transportation	4.5%	2	19.9
Community Stability	29	67.70	% Living in Same House as in 1979	44.8%	25	57.1
			% Living in Same County as in 1985	86.4%	35	78.3

Metropolitan Area Description
GREENSBORO--WINSTON-SALEM--HIGH POINT

STATE: North Carolina
COUNTIES: Davidson, Davie, Forsyth, Guilford, Randolph, Stokes, Yadkin

TOTAL POPULATION:	942,091	
POPULATION IN SUBURBS:	545,589	(57.9%)
POPULATION IN Greensboro:	183,521	(19.5%)
POPULATION IN Winston-Salem:	143,485	(15.2%)
POPULATION IN High Point:	69,496	(7.4%)

The GREENSBORO--WINSTON-SALEM--HIGH POINT metropolitan area is located in the central part of North Carolina. The suburbs range geographically from Kernersville in the west (17 miles from Greensboro), to Asheboro in the south (30 miles from Greensboro), and to Lexington in the southwest (37 miles from Greensboro). The area is growing in population and had an increase of 10.6% between 1980 and 1990. Summer time high temperatures average in the 80's and winter time lows average in the 20's. The suburban area is known for its textile industries. Pharmaceutical companies are also a major presence in the suburbs.

Asheboro is the overall highest rated suburb. **Kernersville** receives the highest scores in economics and education, and is also the safest suburb with the lowest crime rate. **Thomasville** is the suburb with the most affordable housing. The number one scores in open spaces and community stability, as well as the top rated commute belong to **Lexington**.

The highest ranked suburb overall which also has an affordable housing score of at least 50.00 is **Asheboro**.

The highest ranked suburb in the education category which also has an affordable housing score of at least 50.00 is also **Asheboro**.

The county whose suburbs have the highest average overall score is **Randolph County** (66.45).

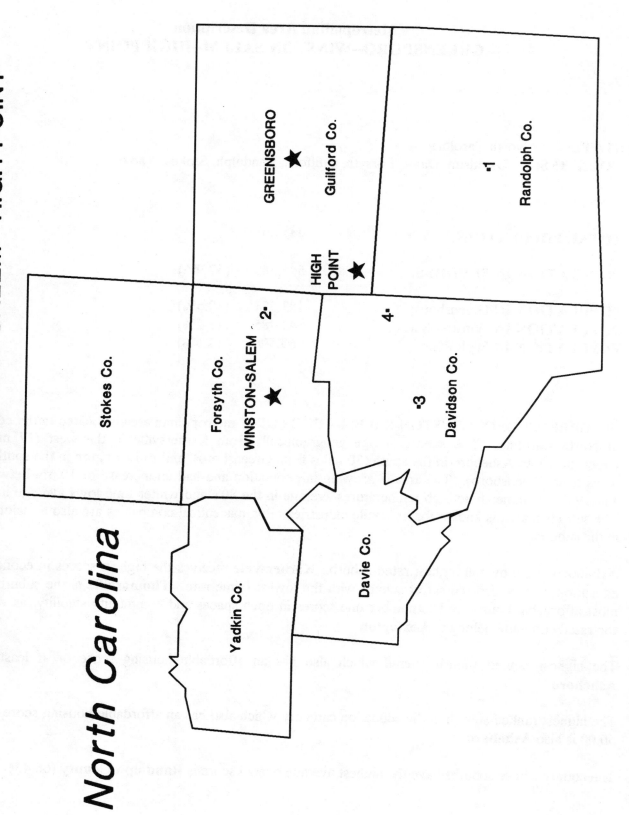

Metropolitan Area Map
GREENSBORO--WINSTON-SALEM--HIGH POINT

North Carolina

Stokes Co.

Yadkin Co.

Forsyth Co.

WINSTON-SALEM

Davie Co.

Davidson Co.

Guilford Co.

GREENSBORO

HIGH POINT

Randolph Co.

Metropolitan Area Suburb Alphabetical Index
GREENSBORO--WINSTON-SALEM--HIGH POINT

SUBURB	PAGE	MAP NO.	STATE	COUNTY	POPU-LATION	RANK
ASHEBORO	254	1	North Carolina	Randolph	16,362	1 / 4
KERNERSVILLE	255	2	North Carolina	Forsyth	10,836	4 / 4
LEXINGTON	254	3	North Carolina	Davidson	16,581	3 / 4
THOMASVILLE	254	4	North Carolina	Davidson	15,915	2 / 4

Metropolitan Area Suburb Rankings
GREENSBORO--WINSTON-SALEM--HIGH POINT

Composite: **Rank** 1 / 4 **Score** 66.45   **ASHEBORO**

CATEGORY	RANK	SCORE	STATISTIC	VALUE	RANK	SCORE
Economics	2	63.85	Median Household Income	$24,294	2	70.8
			% of Families Above Poverty Level	89.9%	3	56.9
Affordable Housing	2	87.20	Median Home Value	$55,600	3	74.4
			Median Rent	$338	1	100.0
Crime	N/A	N/A	Violent Crimes per 10,000 Population	N/A	N/A	N/A
			Property Crimes per 10,000 Population	N/A	N/A	N/A
Open Spaces	2	87.50	Population Density (Persons/Sq. Mile)	1375	1	100.0
			Average Rooms per Housing Unit	5.0	2	75.0
Education	2	38.20	% High School Enrollment/Completion	77.1%	4	0.0
			% College Graduates	15.3%	2	76.4
Commute	3	37.50	Average Work Commute in Minutes	15	2	75.0
			% Commuting on Public Transportation	0.0%	2	0.0
Community Stability	3	84.45	% Living in Same House as in 1979	39.6%	3	82.7
			% Living in Same County as in 1985	81.8%	2	86.2

Composite: **Rank** 2 / 4 **Score** 58.87   **THOMASVILLE**

CATEGORY	RANK	SCORE	STATISTIC	VALUE	RANK	SCORE
Economics	3	40.65	Median Household Income	$21,754	3	16.0
			% of Families Above Poverty Level	90.5%	2	65.3
Affordable Housing	1	98.55	Median Home Value	$46,900	1	100.0
			Median Rent	$339	2	97.1
Crime	2	72.00	Violent Crimes per 10,000 Population	56	2	94.2
			Property Crimes per 10,000 Population	856	2	49.8
Open Spaces	3	37.50	Population Density (Persons/Sq. Mile)	1579	4	0.0
			Average Rooms per Housing Unit	5.0	2	75.0
Education	3	22.00	% High School Enrollment/Completion	80.4%	2	44.0
			% College Graduates	9.8%	4	0.0
Commute	2	50.00	Average Work Commute in Minutes	14	1	100.0
			% Commuting on Public Transportation	0.0%	2	0.0
Community Stability	2	91.40	% Living in Same House as in 1979	43.5%	1	100.0
			% Living in Same County as in 1985	81.1%	3	82.8

Composite: **Rank** 3 / 4 **Score** 54.70   **LEXINGTON**

CATEGORY	RANK	SCORE	STATISTIC	VALUE	RANK	SCORE
Economics	4	0.00	Median Household Income	$21,011	4	0.0
			% of Families Above Poverty Level	85.8%	4	0.0
Affordable Housing	3	77.25	Median Home Value	$47,800	2	97.4
			Median Rent	$353	3	57.1
Crime	3	0.00	Violent Crimes per 10,000 Population	137	3	0.0
			Property Crimes per 10,000 Population	985	3	0.0
Open Spaces	1	98.30	Population Density (Persons/Sq. Mile)	1382	2	96.6
			Average Rooms per Housing Unit	5.1	1	100.0
Education	4	20.05	% High School Enrollment/Completion	77.4%	3	4.0
			% College Graduates	12.4%	3	36.1
Commute	1	87.50	Average Work Commute in Minutes	15	2	75.0
			% Commuting on Public Transportation	0.3%	1	100.0
Community Stability	1	99.80	% Living in Same House as in 1979	43.4%	2	99.6
			% Living in Same County as in 1985	84.6%	1	100.0

Metropolitan Area Suburb Rankings
GREENSBORO--WINSTON-SALEM--HIGH POINT

Composite: Rank 4 / 4 *Score* 45.52   **KERNERSVILLE**

CATEGORY	RANK	SCORE	STATISTIC	VALUE	RANK	SCORE
Economics	1	100.00	Median Household Income	$25,649	1	100.0
			% of Families Above Poverty Level	93.0%	1	100.0
Affordable Housing	4	0.00	Median Home Value	$80,900	4	0.0
			Median Rent	$373	4	0.0
Crime	1	100.00	Violent Crimes per 10,000 Population	51	1	100.0
			Property Crimes per 10,000 Population	726	1	100.0
Open Spaces	4	18.65	Population Density (Persons/Sq. Mile)	1503	3	37.3
			Average Rooms per Housing Unit	4.7	4	0.0
Education	1	100.00	% High School Enrollment/Completion	84.6%	1	100.0
			% College Graduates	17.0%	1	100.0
Commute	4	0.00	Average Work Commute in Minutes	18	4	0.0
			% Commuting on Public Transportation	0.0%	2	0.0
Community Stability	4	0.00	% Living in Same House as in 1979	20.9%	4	0.0
			% Living in Same County as in 1985	64.3%	4	0.0

Metropolitan Area Description
HARTFORD-NEW BRITAIN-MIDDLETOWN-BRISTOL

STATE: Connecticut
COUNTIES: Hartford, Middlesex, Tolland

TOTAL POPULATION: 1,123,678

POPULATION IN SUBURBS: 805,046 (71.6%)

POPULATION IN Hartford: 139,739 (12.4%)
POPULATION IN New Britain: 75,491 (6.7%)
POPULATION IN Middletown: 42,762 (3.8%)
POPULATION IN Bristol: 60,640 (5.4%)

The HARTFORD-NEW BRITAIN-MIDDLETOWN-BRISTOL metropolitan area is located in the central part of Connecticut. The suburbs range geographically from Windsor Locks in the north (14 miles from Hartford), to West Hartford in the west (1 mile from Hartford), to Newington in the south (7 miles from Hartford), and to Storrs in the east (33 miles from Hartford). The area is growing in population and had an increase of 6.9% between 1980 and 1990. Summer time high temperatures average in the 80's and winter time lows average in the teens. The area is known for its insurance companies and some may be found in the suburbs. United Technologies has facilities located in the suburb of Windsor Locks.

Wethersfield is the overall highest rated suburb and also has the highest scores in open spaces and community stability. The number one rating in economics goes to **West Hartford**. The highest score in education belongs to **Storrs**. **East Hartford** is the suburb with the most affordable housing and also has the top rated commute. **Windsor Locks** is rated the safest suburb with the lowest crime rate.

The highest ranked suburb overall which also has an affordable housing score of at least 50.00 is **Wethersfield**.

The highest ranked suburb in the education category which also has an affordable housing score of at least 50.00 is **Storrs**.

The county whose suburbs have the highest average overall score is **Hartford County** (56.00).

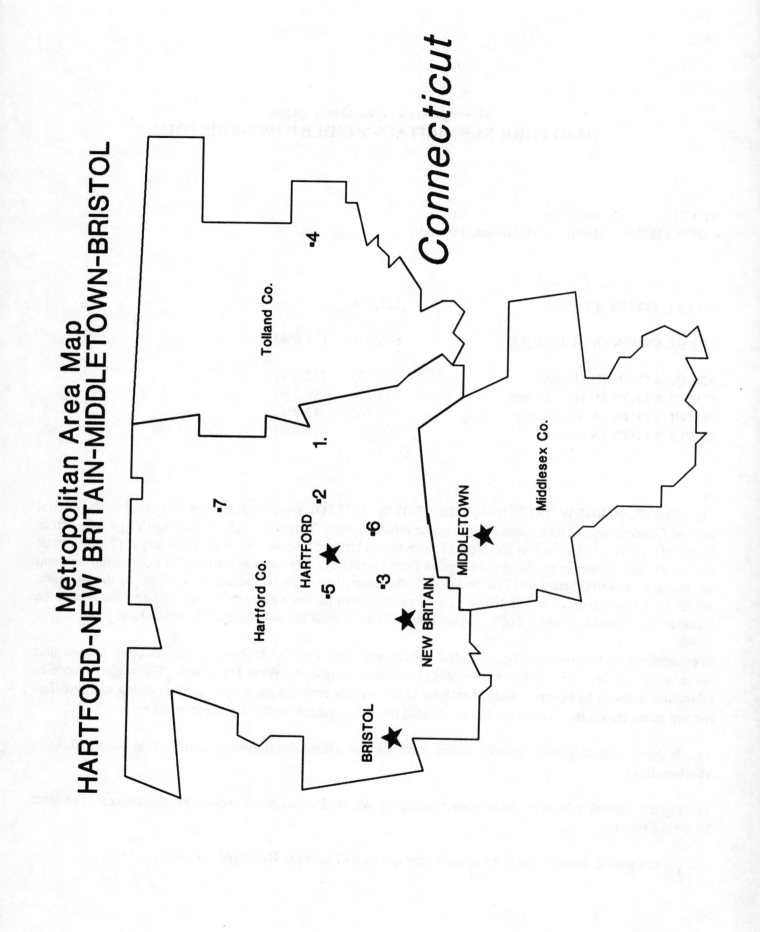

Metropolitan Area Map
HARTFORD–NEW BRITAIN–MIDDLETOWN–BRISTOL

Connecticut

Tolland Co.

Hartford Co.

HARTFORD

NEW BRITAIN

BRISTOL

MIDDLETOWN

Middlesex Co.

.4

1.

.2

.7

.5

.6

.3

Metropolitan Area Suburb Alphabetical Index
HARTFORD-NEW BRITAIN-MIDDLETOWN-BRISTOL

SUBURB	PAGE	MAP NO.	STATE	COUNTY	POPU-LATION	RANK
CENTRAL MANCHESTER	262	1	Connecticut	Hartford	30,934	7 / 7
EAST HARTFORD	261	2	Connecticut	Hartford	50,452	5 / 7
NEWINGTON	261	3	Connecticut	Hartford	29,208	4 / 7
STORRS	261	4	Connecticut	Tolland	12,198	6 / 7
WEST HARTFORD	260	5	Connecticut	Hartford	60,110	3 / 7
WETHERSFIELD	260	6	Connecticut	Hartford	25,651	1 / 7
WINDSOR LOCKS	260	7	Connecticut	Hartford	12,358	2 / 7

Metropolitan Area Suburb Rankings
HARTFORD-NEW BRITAIN-MIDDLETOWN-BRISTOL

Composite: Rank 1 / 7 *Score* 65.68   **WETHERSFIELD**

CATEGORY	RANK	SCORE	STATISTIC	VALUE	RANK	SCORE
Economics	4	80.10	Median Household Income	$43,888	3	76.1
			% of Families Above Poverty Level	97.9%	3	84.1
Affordable Housing	5	54.85	Median Home Value	$180,600	6	34.9
			Median Rent	$606	3	74.8
Crime	3	67.05	Violent Crimes per 10,000 Population	29	4	42.4
			Property Crimes per 10,000 Population	285	2	91.7
Open Spaces	1	80.40	Population Density (Persons/Sq. Mile)	2070	3	79.5
			Average Rooms per Housing Unit	5.9	2	81.3
Education	5	29.30	% High School Enrollment/Completion	90.7%	5	31.6
			% College Graduates	28.3%	3	27.0
Commute	3	48.05	Average Work Commute in Minutes	17	2	42.9
			% Commuting on Public Transportation	3.9%	3	53.2
Community Stability	1	100.00	% Living in Same House as in 1979	57.6%	1	100.0
			% Living in Same County as in 1985	93.9%	1	100.0

Composite: Rank 2 / 7 *Score* 64.29   **WINDSOR LOCKS**

CATEGORY	RANK	SCORE	STATISTIC	VALUE	RANK	SCORE
Economics	3	80.20	Median Household Income	$43,593	4	74.9
			% of Families Above Poverty Level	98.0%	2	85.5
Affordable Housing	4	64.30	Median Home Value	$145,200	2	94.6
			Median Rent	$666	4	34.0
Crime	1	87.90	Violent Crimes per 10,000 Population	18	2	75.8
			Property Crimes per 10,000 Population	268	1	100.0
Open Spaces	3	78.10	Population Density (Persons/Sq. Mile)	1368	1	100.0
			Average Rooms per Housing Unit	5.5	4	56.2
Education	4	30.05	% High School Enrollment/Completion	93.9%	4	55.1
			% College Graduates	16.3%	6	5.0
Commute	5	22.80	Average Work Commute in Minutes	18	3	28.6
			% Commuting on Public Transportation	2.2%	5	17.0
Community Stability	3	86.65	% Living in Same House as in 1979	50.0%	4	78.9
			% Living in Same County as in 1985	89.7%	3	94.4

Composite: Rank 3 / 7 *Score* 59.41   **WEST HARTFORD**

CATEGORY	RANK	SCORE	STATISTIC	VALUE	RANK	SCORE
Economics	1	92.05	Median Household Income	$49,642	1	100.0
			% of Families Above Poverty Level	97.9%	3	84.1
Affordable Housing	7	9.85	Median Home Value	$201,300	7	0.0
			Median Rent	$687	6	19.7
Crime	4	38.30	Violent Crimes per 10,000 Population	23	3	60.6
			Property Crimes per 10,000 Population	441	4	16.0
Open Spaces	2	80.05	Population Density (Persons/Sq. Mile)	2735	5	60.1
			Average Rooms per Housing Unit	6.2	1	100.0
Education	2	64.50	% High School Enrollment/Completion	95.7%	2	68.4
			% College Graduates	46.6%	2	60.6
Commute	4	46.20	Average Work Commute in Minutes	18	3	28.6
			% Commuting on Public Transportation	4.4%	2	63.8
Community Stability	4	84.95	% Living in Same House as in 1979	50.7%	3	80.9
			% Living in Same County as in 1985	85.7%	5	89.0

Metropolitan Area Suburb Rankings
HARTFORD-NEW BRITAIN-MIDDLETOWN-BRISTOL

Composite: **Rank** 4 / 7 *Score* 58.36   **NEWINGTON**

CATEGORY	RANK	SCORE	STATISTIC	VALUE	RANK	SCORE
Economics	2	91.35	Median Household Income	$45,481	2	82.7
			% of Families Above Poverty Level	99.0%	1	100.0
Affordable Housing	6	30.50	Median Home Value	$165,100	4	61.0
			Median Rent	$716	7	0.0
Crime	2	67.25	Violent Crimes per 10,000 Population	10	1	100.0
			Property Crimes per 10,000 Population	403	3	34.5
Open Spaces	4	72.00	Population Density (Persons/Sq. Mile)	2217	4	75.2
			Average Rooms per Housing Unit	5.7	3	68.8
Education	3	41.95	% High School Enrollment/Completion	95.0%	3	63.2
			% College Graduates	24.9%	4	20.7
Commute	7	15.35	Average Work Commute in Minutes	18	3	28.6
			% Commuting on Public Transportation	1.5%	6	2.1
Community Stability	2	90.10	% Living in Same House as in 1979	51.9%	2	84.2
			% Living in Same County as in 1985	90.9%	2	96.0

Composite: **Rank** 5 / 7 *Score* 47.06   **EAST HARTFORD**

CATEGORY	RANK	SCORE	STATISTIC	VALUE	RANK	SCORE
Economics	6	51.15	Median Household Income	$36,584	6	45.8
			% of Families Above Poverty Level	96.0%	6	56.5
Affordable Housing	1	95.45	Median Home Value	$145,400	3	94.3
			Median Rent	$574	2	96.6
Crime	5	0.00	Violent Crimes per 10,000 Population	43	5	0.0
			Property Crimes per 10,000 Population	474	5	0.0
Open Spaces	5	44.70	Population Density (Persons/Sq. Mile)	2800	6	58.2
			Average Rooms per Housing Unit	5.1	6	31.2
Education	7	5.15	% High School Enrollment/Completion	87.8%	6	10.3
			% College Graduates	13.6%	7	0.0
Commute	1	57.15	Average Work Commute in Minutes	19	6	14.3
			% Commuting on Public Transportation	6.1%	1	100.0
Community Stability	5	75.80	% Living in Same House as in 1979	43.2%	5	60.1
			% Living in Same County as in 1985	87.6%	4	91.5

Composite: **Rank** 6 / 7 *Score* 44.45   **STORRS**

CATEGORY	RANK	SCORE	STATISTIC	VALUE	RANK	SCORE
Economics	7	0.00	Median Household Income	$25,554	7	0.0
			% of Families Above Poverty Level	92.1%	7	0.0
Affordable Housing	2	76.40	Median Home Value	$170,000	5	52.8
			Median Rent	$569	1	100.0
Crime	N/A	N/A	Violent Crimes per 10,000 Population	N/A	N/A	N/A
			Property Crimes per 10,000 Population	N/A	N/A	N/A
Open Spaces	6	40.30	Population Density (Persons/Sq. Mile)	2033	2	80.6
			Average Rooms per Housing Unit	4.6	7	0.0
Education	1	100.00	% High School Enrollment/Completion	100.0%	1	100.0
			% College Graduates	68.1%	1	100.0
Commute	2	50.00	Average Work Commute in Minutes	13	1	100.0
			% Commuting on Public Transportation	1.4%	7	0.0
Community Stability	7	0.00	% Living in Same House as in 1979	21.5%	7	0.0
			% Living in Same County as in 1985	19.4%	7	0.0

Metropolitan Area Suburb Rankings
HARTFORD-NEW BRITAIN-MIDDLETOWN-BRISTOL

Composite: **Rank** 7 / 7 **Score** 41.18   **CENTRAL MANCHESTER**

CATEGORY	RANK	SCORE	STATISTIC	VALUE	RANK	SCORE
Economics	5	63.55	Median Household Income	$37,664	5	50.3
			% of Families Above Poverty Level	97.4%	5	76.8
Affordable Housing	3	66.00	Median Home Value	$142,000	1	100.0
			Median Rent	$669	5	32.0
Crime	N/A	N/A	Violent Crimes per 10,000 Population	N/A	N/A	N/A
			Property Crimes per 10,000 Population	N/A	N/A	N/A
Open Spaces	7	18.75	Population Density (Persons/Sq. Mile)	4797	7	0.0
			Average Rooms per Housing Unit	5.2	5	37.5
Education	6	8.35	% High School Enrollment/Completion	86.4%	7	0.0
			% College Graduates	22.7%	5	16.7
Commute	6	20.20	Average Work Commute in Minutes	20	7	0.0
			% Commuting on Public Transportation	3.3%	4	40.4
Community Stability	6	70.25	% Living in Same House as in 1979	40.5%	6	52.6
			% Living in Same County as in 1985	84.9%	6	87.9

Metropolitan Area Description
HOUSTON-GALVESTON-BRAZORIA

STATE: Texas
COUNTIES: Brazoria, Fort Bend, Galveston, Harris, Liberty, Montgomery, Waller

TOTAL POPULATION: 3,711,043

POPULATION IN SUBURBS: 2,018,703   (54.4%)

POPULATION IN Houston: 1,630,553   (43.9%)
POPULATION IN Galveston: 59,070   (1.6%)
POPULATION IN Brazoria: 2,717   (0.1%)

The HOUSTON-GALVESTON-BRAZORIA metropolitan area is located in the southeastern part of Texas near the Gulf of Mexico. The suburbs range geographically from Conroe in the north (41 miles from Houston), to Rosenberg in the west (37 miles from Houston), to Freeport in the south (65 miles from Houston), and to Baytown in the east (24 miles from Houston). The area is growing rapidly in population and had an increase of 19.7% between 1980 and 1990. Summer time high temperatures average in the 90's and winter time lows average in the 40's. The suburban area has many major employers. Dow Chemical has operations in the suburb of Freeport. Amoco and Union Carbide both have facilities in Texas City. Exxon has a major presence in Baytown. In 1992, *Fortune* magazine rated the metropolitan area number two for business. Public transportation in the area is provided on air-conditioned buses by the Metro Transit Authority.

Lake Jackson is the overall highest rated suburb. **West University Place** receives the highest scores in economics and education. **West University Place** is also rated the safest suburb with the lowest crime rate and has the top rated commute. **Freeport** is the suburb with the most affordable housing. The highest score in open spaces belongs to **First Colony**. Finally, the number one rating in community stability goes to **Galena Park**.

The highest ranked suburb overall which also has an affordable housing score of at least 50.00 is **Lake Jackson**.

The highest ranked suburb in the education category which also has an affordable housing score of at least 50.00 is **Mission Bend**.

The county whose suburbs have the highest average overall score is **Galveston County** (60.82).

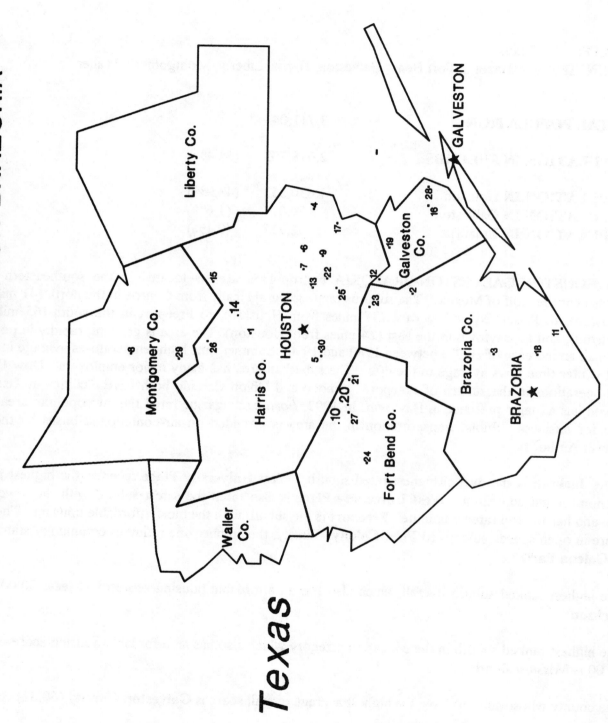

Metropolitan Area Map
HOUSTON-GALVESTON-BRAZORIA

Texas

Liberty Co.

Montgomery Co.

Harris Co.

HOUSTON

Waller Co.

Fort Bend Co.

Galveston Co.

GALVESTON

Brazoria Co.

BRAZORIA

Metropolitan Area Suburb Alphabetical Index
HOUSTON-GALVESTON-BRAZORIA

SUBURB	PAGE	MAP NO.	STATE	COUNTY	POPU-LATION	RANK
ALDINE	273	1	Texas	Harris	11,133	22 / 30
ALVIN	272	2	Texas	Brazoria	19,220	20 / 30
ANGLETON	270	3	Texas	Brazoria	17,140	14 / 30
BAYTOWN	272	4	Texas	Harris	63,850	21 / 30
BELLAIRE	266	5	Texas	Harris	13,842	3 / 30
CHANNELVIEW	271	6	Texas	Harris	25,564	17 / 30
CLOVERLEAF	275	7	Texas	Harris	18,230	30 / 30
CONROE	275	8	Texas	Montgomery	27,610	28 / 30
DEER PARK	268	9	Texas	Harris	27,652	7 / 30
FIRST COLONY	271	10	Texas	Fort Bend	18,327	18 / 30
FREEPORT	273	11	Texas	Brazoria	11,389	23 / 30
FRIENDSWOOD	267	12	Texas	Galveston	22,814	4 / 30
GALENA PARK	270	13	Texas	Harris	10,033	13 / 30
HUMBLE	274	14	Texas	Harris	12,060	25 / 30
KINGWOOD	267	15	Texas	Harris	37,397	5 / 30
LA MARQUE	268	16	Texas	Galveston	14,120	9 / 30
LA PORTE	268	17	Texas	Harris	27,910	8 / 30
LAKE JACKSON	266	18	Texas	Brazoria	22,776	1 / 30
LEAGUE CITY	269	19	Texas	Galveston	30,159	10 / 30
MISSION BEND	273	20	Texas	Fort Bend	24,945	24 / 30
MISSOURI CITY	269	21	Texas	Fort Bend	36,176	11 / 30
PASADENA	274	22	Texas	Harris	119,363	26 / 30
PEARLAND	269	23	Texas	Brazoria	18,697	12 / 30
ROSENBERG	274	24	Texas	Fort Bend	20,183	27 / 30
SOUTH HOUSTON	275	25	Texas	Harris	14,207	29 / 30
SPRING	270	26	Texas	Harris	33,111	15 / 30
SUGAR LAND	267	27	Texas	Fort Bend	24,529	6 / 30
TEXAS CITY	271	28	Texas	Galveston	40,822	16 / 30
THE WOODLANDS	272	29	Texas	Montgomery	29,205	19 / 30
WEST UNIVERSITY PLACE	266	30	Texas	Harris	12,920	2 / 30

Metropolitan Area Suburb Rankings
HOUSTON-GALVESTON-BRAZORIA

Composite: **Rank** 1 / 30 *Score* 68.75   **LAKE JACKSON**

CATEGORY	RANK	SCORE	STATISTIC	VALUE	RANK	SCORE
Economics	10	71.60	Median Household Income	$46,007	10	51.8
			% of Families Above Poverty Level	97.8%	7	91.4
Affordable Housing	17	77.70	Median Home Value	$74,400	22	75.9
			Median Rent	$438	16	79.5
Crime	5	91.90	Violent Crimes per 10,000 Population	24	6	91.6
			Property Crimes per 10,000 Population	343	6	92.2
Open Spaces	10	64.95	Population Density (Persons/Sq. Mile)	1648	15	81.8
			Average Rooms per Housing Unit	5.7	12	48.1
Education	11	66.20	% High School Enrollment/Completion	93.6%	9	86.6
			% College Graduates	33.3%	10	45.8
Commute	5	47.20	Average Work Commute in Minutes	18	3	94.4
			% Commuting on Public Transportation	0.0%	27	0.0
Community Stability	17	61.70	% Living in Same House as in 1979	28.6%	17	51.3
			% Living in Same County as in 1985	77.0%	18	72.1

Composite: **Rank** 2 / 30 *Score* 67.64   **WEST UNIVERSITY PLACE**

CATEGORY	RANK	SCORE	STATISTIC	VALUE	RANK	SCORE
Economics	1	100.00	Median Household Income	$68,783	1	100.0
			% of Families Above Poverty Level	99.5%	1	100.0
Affordable Housing	30	0.00	Median Home Value	$199,200	30	0.0
			Median Rent	$856	30	0.0
Crime	1	100.00	Violent Crimes per 10,000 Population	12	1	100.0
			Property Crimes per 10,000 Population	265	1	100.0
Open Spaces	27	40.75	Population Density (Persons/Sq. Mile)	6427	30	0.0
			Average Rooms per Housing Unit	6.6	3	81.5
Education	1	94.85	% High School Enrollment/Completion	94.3%	7	89.7
			% College Graduates	68.5%	1	100.0
Commute	1	55.20	Average Work Commute in Minutes	17	1	100.0
			% Commuting on Public Transportation	0.8%	15	10.4
Community Stability	7	82.65	% Living in Same House as in 1979	40.7%	6	77.4
			% Living in Same County as in 1985	84.0%	15	87.9

Composite: **Rank** 3 / 30 *Score* 66.79   **BELLAIRE**

CATEGORY	RANK	SCORE	STATISTIC	VALUE	RANK	SCORE
Economics	7	72.75	Median Household Income	$45,892	11	51.6
			% of Families Above Poverty Level	98.3%	2	93.9
Affordable Housing	28	45.50	Median Home Value	$106,200	27	56.6
			Median Rent	$675	25	34.4
Crime	9	81.05	Violent Crimes per 10,000 Population	40	10	80.4
			Property Crimes per 10,000 Population	448	11	81.7
Open Spaces	19	51.90	Population Density (Persons/Sq. Mile)	3830	26	44.5
			Average Rooms per Housing Unit	6.0	9	59.3
Education	5	74.40	% High School Enrollment/Completion	91.9%	12	79.0
			% College Graduates	48.9%	4	69.8
Commute	2	51.60	Average Work Commute in Minutes	19	4	88.9
			% Commuting on Public Transportation	1.1%	10	14.3
Community Stability	3	90.30	% Living in Same House as in 1979	44.7%	3	86.0
			% Living in Same County as in 1985	87.0%	8	94.6

Metropolitan Area Suburb Rankings
HOUSTON-GALVESTON-BRAZORIA

Composite: **Rank** 4 / 30 **Score** 65.76   **FRIENDSWOOD**

CATEGORY	RANK	SCORE	STATISTIC	VALUE	RANK	SCORE
Economics	6	76.10	Median Household Income	$50,492	7	61.3
			% of Families Above Poverty Level	97.7%	8	90.9
Affordable Housing	23	59.20	Median Home Value	$82,300	24	71.1
			Median Rent	$607	22	47.3
Crime	2	98.30	Violent Crimes per 10,000 Population	15	2	97.9
			Property Crimes per 10,000 Population	278	4	98.7
Open Spaces	4	80.80	Population Density (Persons/Sq. Mile)	1102	7	91.2
			Average Rooms per Housing Unit	6.3	6	70.4
Education	8	69.25	% High School Enrollment/Completion	94.4%	6	90.2
			% College Graduates	34.9%	9	48.3
Commute	30	19.75	Average Work Commute in Minutes	30	24	27.8
			% Commuting on Public Transportation	0.9%	13	11.7
Community Stability	22	56.95	% Living in Same House as in 1979	32.4%	12	59.5
			% Living in Same County as in 1985	69.1%	23	54.4

Composite: **Rank** 5 / 30 **Score** 64.27   **KINGWOOD**

CATEGORY	RANK	SCORE	STATISTIC	VALUE	RANK	SCORE
Economics	3	91.10	Median Household Income	$63,976	3	89.8
			% of Families Above Poverty Level	98.0%	5	92.4
Affordable Housing	26	46.50	Median Home Value	$115,300	29	51.0
			Median Rent	$635	24	42.0
Crime	N/A	N/A	Violent Crimes per 10,000 Population	N/A	N/A	N/A
			Property Crimes per 10,000 Population	N/A	N/A	N/A
Open Spaces	2	84.30	Population Density (Persons/Sq. Mile)	2419	23	68.6
			Average Rooms per Housing Unit	7.1	1	100.0
Education	3	86.40	% High School Enrollment/Completion	96.2%	2	98.2
			% College Graduates	52.0%	3	74.6
Commute	4	50.00	Average Work Commute in Minutes	35	30	0.0
			% Commuting on Public Transportation	7.7%	1	100.0
Community Stability	27	27.35	% Living in Same House as in 1979	13.8%	26	19.4
			% Living in Same County as in 1985	60.6%	27	35.3

Composite: **Rank** 6 / 30 **Score** 63.79   **SUGAR LAND**

CATEGORY	RANK	SCORE	STATISTIC	VALUE	RANK	SCORE
Economics	4	84.05	Median Household Income	$56,571	4	74.2
			% of Families Above Poverty Level	98.3%	2	93.9
Affordable Housing	27	45.80	Median Home Value	$90,200	25	66.3
			Median Rent	$723	28	25.3
Crime	6	91.10	Violent Crimes per 10,000 Population	21	5	93.7
			Property Crimes per 10,000 Population	380	7	88.5
Open Spaces	5	76.80	Population Density (Persons/Sq. Mile)	1999	20	75.8
			Average Rooms per Housing Unit	6.5	5	77.8
Education	4	78.65	% High School Enrollment/Completion	95.8%	3	96.4
			% College Graduates	43.1%	6	60.9
Commute	23	28.55	Average Work Commute in Minutes	28	22	38.9
			% Commuting on Public Transportation	1.4%	5	18.2
Community Stability	24	41.55	% Living in Same House as in 1979	25.2%	22	44.0
			% Living in Same County as in 1985	62.3%	25	39.1

Metropolitan Area Suburb Rankings
HOUSTON-GALVESTON-BRAZORIA

Composite: Rank 7 / 30 Score 63.49 **DEER PARK**

CATEGORY	RANK	SCORE	STATISTIC	VALUE	RANK	SCORE
Economics	11	68.30	Median Household Income	$46,199	9	52.3
			% of Families Above Poverty Level	96.4%	11	84.3
Affordable Housing	18	77.40	Median Home Value	$66,300	18	80.8
			Median Rent	$467	18	74.0
Crime	10	79.75	Violent Crimes per 10,000 Population	69	15	60.1
			Property Crimes per 10,000 Population	271	2	99.4
Open Spaces	14	58.15	Population Density (Persons/Sq. Mile)	2667	24	64.4
			Average Rooms per Housing Unit	5.8	11	51.9
Education	16	43.70	% High School Enrollment/Completion	89.7%	16	69.2
			% College Graduates	15.3%	15	18.2
Commute	19	33.35	Average Work Commute in Minutes	23	12	66.7
			% Commuting on Public Transportation	0.0%	27	0.0
Community Stability	6	83.80	% Living in Same House as in 1979	36.6%	7	68.5
			% Living in Same County as in 1985	89.0%	3	99.1

Composite: Rank 8 / 30 Score 61.89 **LA PORTE**

CATEGORY	RANK	SCORE	STATISTIC	VALUE	RANK	SCORE
Economics	15	54.75	Median Household Income	$41,733	14	42.8
			% of Families Above Poverty Level	92.9%	16	66.7
Affordable Housing	16	80.60	Median Home Value	$56,300	14	86.9
			Median Rent	$465	17	74.3
Crime	7	88.55	Violent Crimes per 10,000 Population	38	9	81.8
			Property Crimes per 10,000 Population	312	5	95.3
Open Spaces	13	61.15	Population Density (Persons/Sq. Mile)	1447	12	85.3
			Average Rooms per Housing Unit	5.4	15	37.0
Education	17	41.20	% High School Enrollment/Completion	88.9%	17	65.6
			% College Graduates	14.4%	17	16.8
Commute	14	36.75	Average Work Commute in Minutes	22	8	72.2
			% Commuting on Public Transportation	0.1%	23	1.3
Community Stability	15	70.20	% Living in Same House as in 1979	27.8%	18	49.6
			% Living in Same County as in 1985	85.3%	11	90.8

Composite: Rank 9 / 30 Score 61.71 **LA MARQUE**

CATEGORY	RANK	SCORE	STATISTIC	VALUE	RANK	SCORE
Economics	22	25.25	Median Household Income	$27,914	22	13.6
			% of Families Above Poverty Level	87.0%	21	36.9
Affordable Housing	10	89.30	Median Home Value	$47,200	5	92.5
			Median Rent	$403	11	86.1
Crime	12	71.30	Violent Crimes per 10,000 Population	37	8	82.5
			Property Crimes per 10,000 Population	664	14	60.1
Open Spaces	12	61.35	Population Density (Persons/Sq. Mile)	991	4	93.1
			Average Rooms per Housing Unit	5.2	16	29.6
Education	14	46.90	% High School Enrollment/Completion	92.2%	11	80.4
			% College Graduates	12.2%	21	13.4
Commute	9	41.65	Average Work Commute in Minutes	20	5	83.3
			% Commuting on Public Transportation	0.0%	27	0.0
Community Stability	2	96.25	% Living in Same House as in 1979	47.8%	2	92.7
			% Living in Same County as in 1985	89.3%	2	99.8

Metropolitan Area Suburb Rankings
HOUSTON-GALVESTON-BRAZORIA

Composite: **Rank** 10 / 30 **Score** 61.68   **LEAGUE CITY**

CATEGORY	RANK	SCORE	STATISTIC	VALUE	RANK	SCORE
Economics	12	67.05	Median Household Income	$45,043	12	49.8
			% of Families Above Poverty Level	96.4%	11	84.3
Affordable Housing	20	68.30	Median Home Value	$68,700	20	79.4
			Median Rent	$555	21	57.2
Crime	4	92.90	Violent Crimes per 10,000 Population	15	2	97.9
			Property Crimes per 10,000 Population	386	8	87.9
Open Spaces	7	72.20	Population Density (Persons/Sq. Mile)	586	1	100.0
			Average Rooms per Housing Unit	5.6	14	44.4
Education	10	67.90	% High School Enrollment/Completion	94.7%	5	91.5
			% College Graduates	32.3%	11	44.3
Commute	22	30.00	Average Work Commute in Minutes	27	20	44.4
			% Commuting on Public Transportation	1.2%	7	15.6
Community Stability	26	33.40	% Living in Same House as in 1979	18.6%	25	29.7
			% Living in Same County as in 1985	61.4%	26	37.1

Composite: **Rank** 11 / 30 **Score** 61.65   **MISSOURI CITY**

CATEGORY	RANK	SCORE	STATISTIC	VALUE	RANK	SCORE
Economics	5	78.45	Median Household Income	$51,984	5	64.5
			% of Families Above Poverty Level	98.0%	5	92.4
Affordable Housing	25	51.25	Median Home Value	$77,500	23	74.0
			Median Rent	$706	27	28.5
Crime	8	84.60	Violent Crimes per 10,000 Population	30	7	87.4
			Property Crimes per 10,000 Population	447	10	81.8
Open Spaces	3	82.40	Population Density (Persons/Sq. Mile)	1559	13	83.3
			Average Rooms per Housing Unit	6.6	3	81.5
Education	7	72.55	% High School Enrollment/Completion	94.2%	8	89.3
			% College Graduates	39.8%	7	55.8
Commute	29	21.05	Average Work Commute in Minutes	30	24	27.8
			% Commuting on Public Transportation	1.1%	10	14.3
Community Stability	25	41.25	% Living in Same House as in 1979	24.2%	23	41.8
			% Living in Same County as in 1985	63.0%	24	40.7

Composite: **Rank** 12 / 30 **Score** 58.24   **PEARLAND**

CATEGORY	RANK	SCORE	STATISTIC	VALUE	RANK	SCORE
Economics	13	65.50	Median Household Income	$42,565	13	44.6
			% of Families Above Poverty Level	96.8%	10	86.4
Affordable Housing	19	74.80	Median Home Value	$74,300	21	76.0
			Median Rent	$469	19	73.6
Crime	15	57.95	Violent Crimes per 10,000 Population	91	19	44.8
			Property Crimes per 10,000 Population	554	12	71.1
Open Spaces	8	70.95	Population Density (Persons/Sq. Mile)	950	3	93.8
			Average Rooms per Housing Unit	5.7	12	48.1
Education	12	55.80	% High School Enrollment/Completion	92.8%	10	83.0
			% College Graduates	22.1%	12	28.6
Commute	26	24.00	Average Work Commute in Minutes	28	22	38.9
			% Commuting on Public Transportation	0.7%	16	9.1
Community Stability	18	58.70	% Living in Same House as in 1979	32.8%	10	60.3
			% Living in Same County as in 1985	70.3%	22	57.1

Metropolitan Area Suburb Rankings
HOUSTON-GALVESTON-BRAZORIA

Composite: *Rank* 13 / 30 *Score* 57.82   **GALENA PARK**

CATEGORY	RANK	SCORE	STATISTIC	VALUE	RANK	SCORE
Economics	27	15.10	Median Household Income	$24,103	27	5.5
			% of Families Above Poverty Level	84.6%	27	24.7
Affordable Housing	3	92.60	Median Home Value	$34,800	1	100.0
			Median Rent	$408	13	85.2
Crime	3	97.70	Violent Crimes per 10,000 Population	17	4	96.5
			Property Crimes per 10,000 Population	276	3	98.9
Open Spaces	23	48.90	Population Density (Persons/Sq. Mile)	2011	21	75.6
			Average Rooms per Housing Unit	5.0	21	22.2
Education	28	8.50	% High School Enrollment/Completion	78.0%	27	17.0
			% College Graduates	3.5%	30	0.0
Commute	8	41.95	Average Work Commute in Minutes	22	8	72.2
			% Commuting on Public Transportation	0.9%	13	11.7
Community Stability	1	100.00	% Living in Same House as in 1979	51.2%	1	100.0
			% Living in Same County as in 1985	89.4%	1	100.0

Composite: *Rank* 14 / 30 *Score* 57.81   **ANGLETON**

CATEGORY	RANK	SCORE	STATISTIC	VALUE	RANK	SCORE
Economics	17	42.00	Median Household Income	$32,098	17	22.4
			% of Families Above Poverty Level	91.9%	17	61.6
Affordable Housing	6	90.70	Median Home Value	$52,500	10	89.2
			Median Rent	$371	6	92.2
Crime	11	73.80	Violent Crimes per 10,000 Population	63	14	64.3
			Property Crimes per 10,000 Population	432	9	83.3
Open Spaces	18	52.85	Population Density (Persons/Sq. Mile)	1765	16	79.8
			Average Rooms per Housing Unit	5.1	17	25.9
Education	18	36.50	% High School Enrollment/Completion	86.8%	18	56.2
			% College Graduates	14.4%	17	16.8
Commute	15	36.10	Average Work Commute in Minutes	22	8	72.2
			% Commuting on Public Transportation	0.0%	27	0.0
Community Stability	12	72.75	% Living in Same House as in 1979	30.6%	14	55.6
			% Living in Same County as in 1985	84.9%	12	89.9

Composite: *Rank* 15 / 30 *Score* 55.43   **SPRING**

CATEGORY	RANK	SCORE	STATISTIC	VALUE	RANK	SCORE
Economics	14	60.75	Median Household Income	$40,521	15	40.2
			% of Families Above Poverty Level	95.8%	13	81.3
Affordable Housing	21	66.90	Median Home Value	$54,500	12	88.0
			Median Rent	$615	23	45.8
Crime	N/A	N/A	Violent Crimes per 10,000 Population	N/A	N/A	N/A
			Property Crimes per 10,000 Population	N/A	N/A	N/A
Open Spaces	8	70.95	Population Density (Persons/Sq. Mile)	1387	11	86.3
			Average Rooms per Housing Unit	5.9	10	55.6
Education	13	48.20	% High School Enrollment/Completion	91.0%	14	75.0
			% College Graduates	17.4%	14	21.4
Commute	24	27.35	Average Work Commute in Minutes	31	27	22.2
			% Commuting on Public Transportation	2.5%	3	32.5
Community Stability	19	58.40	% Living in Same House as in 1979	22.6%	24	38.4
			% Living in Same County as in 1985	79.8%	17	78.4

Metropolitan Area Suburb Rankings
HOUSTON-GALVESTON-BRAZORIA

Composite: *Rank* 16 / 30 *Score* 54.13 **TEXAS CITY**

CATEGORY	RANK	SCORE	STATISTIC	VALUE	RANK	SCORE
Economics	25	19.35	Median Household Income	$26,144	24	9.9
			% of Families Above Poverty Level	85.4%	25	28.8
Affordable Housing	4	92.10	Median Home Value	$49,700	9	90.9
			Median Rent	$365	3	93.3
Crime	18	43.65	Violent Crimes per 10,000 Population	72	16	58.0
			Property Crimes per 10,000 Population	971	21	29.3
Open Spaces	11	62.35	Population Density (Persons/Sq. Mile)	657	2	98.8
			Average Rooms per Housing Unit	5.1	17	25.9
Education	22	30.10	% High School Enrollment/Completion	85.5%	20	50.4
			% College Graduates	9.9%	24	9.8
Commute	7	42.30	Average Work Commute in Minutes	20	5	83.3
			% Commuting on Public Transportation	0.1%	23	1.3
Community Stability	4	89.05	% Living in Same House as in 1979	42.4%	4	81.0
			% Living in Same County as in 1985	88.1%	5	97.1

Composite: *Rank* 17 / 30 *Score* 54.05 **CHANNELVIEW**

CATEGORY	RANK	SCORE	STATISTIC	VALUE	RANK	SCORE
Economics	16	43.35	Median Household Income	$33,814	16	26.1
			% of Families Above Poverty Level	91.7%	18	60.6
Affordable Housing	12	88.65	Median Home Value	$47,200	5	92.5
			Median Rent	$410	14	84.8
Crime	N/A	N/A	Violent Crimes per 10,000 Population	N/A	N/A	N/A
			Property Crimes per 10,000 Population	N/A	N/A	N/A
Open Spaces	15	54.60	Population Density (Persons/Sq. Mile)	1562	14	83.3
			Average Rooms per Housing Unit	5.1	17	25.9
Education	23	28.65	% High School Enrollment/Completion	85.2%	21	49.1
			% College Graduates	8.8%	26	8.2
Commute	18	33.80	Average Work Commute in Minutes	24	15	61.1
			% Commuting on Public Transportation	0.5%	19	6.5
Community Stability	10	75.25	% Living in Same House as in 1979	30.1%	15	54.5
			% Living in Same County as in 1985	87.6%	6	96.0

Composite: *Rank* 18 / 30 *Score* 53.76 **FIRST COLONY**

CATEGORY	RANK	SCORE	STATISTIC	VALUE	RANK	SCORE
Economics	2	92.45	Median Household Income	$64,758	2	91.5
			% of Families Above Poverty Level	98.2%	4	93.4
Affordable Housing	29	31.30	Median Home Value	$112,300	28	52.9
			Median Rent	$805	29	9.7
Crime	N/A	N/A	Violent Crimes per 10,000 Population	N/A	N/A	N/A
			Property Crimes per 10,000 Population	N/A	N/A	N/A
Open Spaces	1	84.50	Population Density (Persons/Sq. Mile)	1962	19	76.4
			Average Rooms per Housing Unit	6.9	2	92.6
Education	2	92.60	% High School Enrollment/Completion	96.6%	1	100.0
			% College Graduates	58.9%	2	85.2
Commute	28	21.70	Average Work Commute in Minutes	30	24	27.8
			% Commuting on Public Transportation	1.2%	7	15.6
Community Stability	30	0.00	% Living in Same House as in 1979	4.8%	30	0.0
			% Living in Same County as in 1985	44.9%	30	0.0

Metropolitan Area Suburb Rankings
HOUSTON-GALVESTON-BRAZORIA

Composite: *Rank* 19 / 30 *Score* 53.32   **THE WOODLANDS**

CATEGORY	RANK	SCORE	STATISTIC	VALUE	RANK	SCORE
Economics	9	71.80	Median Household Income	$50,929	6	62.3
			% of Families Above Poverty Level	95.8%	13	81.3
Affordable Housing	22	60.95	Median Home Value	$100,400	26	60.1
			Median Rent	$531	20	61.8
Crime	N/A	N/A	Violent Crimes per 10,000 Population	N/A	N/A	N/A
			Property Crimes per 10,000 Population	N/A	N/A	N/A
Open Spaces	6	73.10	Population Density (Persons/Sq. Mile)	1785	17	79.5
			Average Rooms per Housing Unit	6.2	7	66.7
Education	8	69.25	% High School Enrollment/Completion	90.1%	15	71.0
			% College Graduates	47.4%	5	67.5
Commute	10	41.60	Average Work Commute in Minutes	31	27	22.2
			% Commuting on Public Transportation	4.7%	2	61.0
Community Stability	29	3.25	% Living in Same House as in 1979	6.4%	29	3.4
			% Living in Same County as in 1985	46.3%	29	3.1

Composite: *Rank* 20 / 30 *Score* 51.61   **ALVIN**

CATEGORY	RANK	SCORE	STATISTIC	VALUE	RANK	SCORE
Economics	19	31.55	Median Household Income	$28,860	19	15.6
			% of Families Above Poverty Level	89.1%	19	47.5
Affordable Housing	13	88.15	Median Home Value	$54,700	13	87.9
			Median Rent	$391	10	88.4
Crime	13	66.60	Violent Crimes per 10,000 Population	42	11	79.0
			Property Crimes per 10,000 Population	723	15	54.2
Open Spaces	17	53.45	Population Density (Persons/Sq. Mile)	1050	6	92.1
			Average Rooms per Housing Unit	4.8	24	14.8
Education	21	31.45	% High School Enrollment/Completion	84.9%	22	47.8
			% College Graduates	13.3%	20	15.1
Commute	20	32.50	Average Work Commute in Minutes	24	15	61.1
			% Commuting on Public Transportation	0.3%	21	3.9
Community Stability	21	57.60	% Living in Same House as in 1979	27.4%	19	48.7
			% Living in Same County as in 1985	74.5%	21	66.5

Composite: *Rank* 21 / 30 *Score* 50.79   **BAYTOWN**

CATEGORY	RANK	SCORE	STATISTIC	VALUE	RANK	SCORE
Economics	21	26.55	Median Household Income	$30,151	18	18.3
			% of Families Above Poverty Level	86.6%	23	34.8
Affordable Housing	7	90.35	Median Home Value	$49,300	8	91.2
			Median Rent	$385	9	89.5
Crime	17	47.50	Violent Crimes per 10,000 Population	83	18	50.3
			Property Crimes per 10,000 Population	817	17	44.7
Open Spaces	24	48.65	Population Density (Persons/Sq. Mile)	2040	22	75.1
			Average Rooms per Housing Unit	5.0	21	22.2
Education	20	34.70	% High School Enrollment/Completion	85.9%	19	52.2
			% College Graduates	14.7%	16	17.2
Commute	13	37.40	Average Work Commute in Minutes	22	8	72.2
			% Commuting on Public Transportation	0.2%	22	2.6
Community Stability	14	70.40	% Living in Same House as in 1979	32.7%	11	60.1
			% Living in Same County as in 1985	80.8%	16	80.7

Metropolitan Area Suburb Rankings
HOUSTON-GALVESTON-BRAZORIA

Composite: **Rank** 22 / 30   *Score* 49.75   **ALDINE**

CATEGORY	RANK	SCORE	STATISTIC	VALUE	RANK	SCORE
Economics	24	22.35	Median Household Income	$25,878	25	9.3
			% of Families Above Poverty Level	86.7%	22	35.4
Affordable Housing	8	90.10	Median Home Value	$43,300	4	94.8
			Median Rent	$407	12	85.4
Crime	N/A	N/A	Violent Crimes per 10,000 Population	N/A	N/A	N/A
			Property Crimes per 10,000 Population	N/A	N/A	N/A
Open Spaces	16	54.35	Population Density (Persons/Sq. Mile)	1376	10	86.5
			Average Rooms per Housing Unit	5.0	21	22.2
Education	26	16.40	% High School Enrollment/Completion	81.3%	25	31.7
			% College Graduates	4.2%	28	1.1
Commute	25	26.75	Average Work Commute in Minutes	27	20	44.4
			% Commuting on Public Transportation	0.7%	16	9.1
Community Stability	5	88.55	% Living in Same House as in 1979	41.6%	5	79.3
			% Living in Same County as in 1985	88.4%	4	97.8

Composite: **Rank** 23 / 30   *Score* 49.13   **FREEPORT**

CATEGORY	RANK	SCORE	STATISTIC	VALUE	RANK	SCORE
Economics	30	0.00	Median Household Income	$21,483	30	0.0
			% of Families Above Poverty Level	79.7%	30	0.0
Affordable Housing	1	99.60	Median Home Value	$35,200	2	99.8
			Median Rent	$333	2	99.4
Crime	14	64.10	Violent Crimes per 10,000 Population	58	12	67.8
			Property Crimes per 10,000 Population	661	13	60.4
Open Spaces	21	50.20	Population Density (Persons/Sq. Mile)	992	5	93.0
			Average Rooms per Housing Unit	4.6	29	7.4
Education	30	2.25	% High School Enrollment/Completion	74.2%	30	0.0
			% College Graduates	6.4%	27	4.5
Commute	3	50.65	Average Work Commute in Minutes	17	1	100.0
			% Commuting on Public Transportation	0.1%	23	1.3
Community Stability	9	77.10	% Living in Same House as in 1979	33.6%	8	62.1
			% Living in Same County as in 1985	85.9%	10	92.1

Composite: **Rank** 24 / 30   *Score* 49.03   **MISSION BEND**

CATEGORY	RANK	SCORE	STATISTIC	VALUE	RANK	SCORE
Economics	8	72.70	Median Household Income	$47,515	8	55.0
			% of Families Above Poverty Level	97.6%	9	90.4
Affordable Housing	24	56.35	Median Home Value	$68,600	19	79.4
			Median Rent	$681	26	33.3
Crime	N/A	N/A	Violent Crimes per 10,000 Population	N/A	N/A	N/A
			Property Crimes per 10,000 Population	N/A	N/A	N/A
Open Spaces	25	47.50	Population Density (Persons/Sq. Mile)	4774	28	28.3
			Average Rooms per Housing Unit	6.2	7	66.7
Education	6	73.55	% High School Enrollment/Completion	95.5%	4	95.1
			% College Graduates	37.3%	8	52.0
Commute	27	23.30	Average Work Commute in Minutes	32	29	16.7
			% Commuting on Public Transportation	2.3%	4	29.9
Community Stability	28	20.80	% Living in Same House as in 1979	9.3%	28	9.7
			% Living in Same County as in 1985	59.1%	28	31.9

Metropolitan Area Suburb Rankings
HOUSTON-GALVESTON-BRAZORIA

Composite: **Rank 25 / 30** *Score 47.44* **HUMBLE**

CATEGORY	RANK	SCORE	STATISTIC	VALUE	RANK	SCORE
Economics	18	41.45	Median Household Income	$27,483	23	12.7
			% of Families Above Poverty Level	93.6%	15	70.2
Affordable Housing	15	83.75	Median Home Value	$60,800	16	84.2
			Median Rent	$418	15	83.3
Crime	21	25.85	Violent Crimes per 10,000 Population	81	17	51.7
			Property Crimes per 10,000 Population	1,264	22	0.0
Open Spaces	22	50.10	Population Density (Persons/Sq. Mile)	1223	8	89.1
			Average Rooms per Housing Unit	4.7	27	11.1
Education	15	46.05	% High School Enrollment/Completion	91.2%	13	75.9
			% College Graduates	14.0%	19	16.2
Commute	11	41.15	Average Work Commute in Minutes	23	12	66.7
			% Commuting on Public Transportation	1.2%	7	15.6
Community Stability	23	43.75	% Living in Same House as in 1979	13.8%	26	19.4
			% Living in Same County as in 1985	75.2%	20	68.1

Composite: **Rank 26 / 30** *Score 46.53* **PASADENA**

CATEGORY	RANK	SCORE	STATISTIC	VALUE	RANK	SCORE
Economics	20	30.90	Median Household Income	$28,729	20	15.3
			% of Families Above Poverty Level	88.9%	20	46.5
Affordable Housing	5	90.85	Median Home Value	$48,300	7	91.8
			Median Rent	$383	8	89.9
Crime	19	36.30	Violent Crimes per 10,000 Population	116	21	27.3
			Property Crimes per 10,000 Population	811	16	45.3
Open Spaces	28	39.05	Population Density (Persons/Sq. Mile)	2727	25	63.3
			Average Rooms per Housing Unit	4.8	24	14.8
Education	25	21.55	% High School Enrollment/Completion	81.3%	25	31.7
			% College Graduates	10.9%	23	11.4
Commute	16	35.95	Average Work Commute in Minutes	23	12	66.7
			% Commuting on Public Transportation	0.4%	20	5.2
Community Stability	13	71.10	% Living in Same House as in 1979	29.3%	16	52.8
			% Living in Same County as in 1985	84.7%	13	89.4

Composite: **Rank 27 / 30** *Score 45.02* **ROSENBERG**

CATEGORY	RANK	SCORE	STATISTIC	VALUE	RANK	SCORE
Economics	28	12.65	Median Household Income	$25,773	26	9.1
			% of Families Above Poverty Level	82.9%	28	16.2
Affordable Housing	9	89.85	Median Home Value	$54,100	11	88.3
			Median Rent	$375	7	91.4
Crime	20	35.10	Violent Crimes per 10,000 Population	115	20	28.0
			Property Crimes per 10,000 Population	842	18	42.2
Open Spaces	26	45.25	Population Density (Persons/Sq. Mile)	1788	18	79.4
			Average Rooms per Housing Unit	4.7	27	11.1
Education	24	27.30	% High School Enrollment/Completion	84.4%	24	45.5
			% College Graduates	9.4%	25	9.1
Commute	21	31.20	Average Work Commute in Minutes	24	15	61.1
			% Commuting on Public Transportation	0.1%	23	1.3
Community Stability	11	73.80	% Living in Same House as in 1979	32.1%	13	58.8
			% Living in Same County as in 1985	84.4%	14	88.8

Metropolitan Area Suburb Rankings
HOUSTON-GALVESTON-BRAZORIA

Composite: *Rank* 28 / 30 *Score* 43.81   **CONROE**

CATEGORY	RANK	SCORE	STATISTIC	VALUE	RANK	SCORE
Economics	26	15.40	Median Household Income	$23,634	28	4.5
			% of Families Above Poverty Level	84.9%	26	26.3
Affordable Housing	11	89.25	Median Home Value	$57,900	15	85.9
			Median Rent	$369	5	92.6
Crime	22	15.25	Violent Crimes per 10,000 Population	155	22	0.0
			Property Crimes per 10,000 Population	959	20	30.5
Open Spaces	20	51.15	Population Density (Persons/Sq. Mile)	1318	9	87.5
			Average Rooms per Housing Unit	4.8	24	14.8
Education	19	35.05	% High School Enrollment/Completion	84.8%	23	47.3
			% College Graduates	18.3%	13	22.8
Commute	6	42.80	Average Work Commute in Minutes	21	7	77.8
			% Commuting on Public Transportation	0.6%	18	7.8
Community Stability	20	57.75	% Living in Same House as in 1979	26.3%	21	46.3
			% Living in Same County as in 1985	75.7%	19	69.2

Composite: *Rank* 29 / 30 *Score* 42.29   **SOUTH HOUSTON**

CATEGORY	RANK	SCORE	STATISTIC	VALUE	RANK	SCORE
Economics	29	9.40	Median Household Income	$23,485	29	4.2
			% of Families Above Poverty Level	82.6%	29	14.6
Affordable Housing	2	98.85	Median Home Value	$38,500	3	97.7
			Median Rent	$330	1	100.0
Crime	16	48.20	Violent Crimes per 10,000 Population	61	13	65.7
			Property Crimes per 10,000 Population	957	19	30.7
Open Spaces	30	14.85	Population Density (Persons/Sq. Mile)	4692	27	29.7
			Average Rooms per Housing Unit	4.4	30	0.0
Education	29	7.60	% High School Enrollment/Completion	77.4%	28	14.3
			% College Graduates	4.1%	29	0.9
Commute	12	39.00	Average Work Commute in Minutes	24	15	61.1
			% Commuting on Public Transportation	1.3%	6	16.9
Community Stability	8	78.15	% Living in Same House as in 1979	33.1%	9	61.0
			% Living in Same County as in 1985	87.3%	7	95.3

Composite: *Rank* 30 / 30 *Score* 42.27   **CLOVERLEAF**

CATEGORY	RANK	SCORE	STATISTIC	VALUE	RANK	SCORE
Economics	23	24.05	Median Household Income	$27,989	21	13.8
			% of Families Above Poverty Level	86.5%	24	34.3
Affordable Housing	14	87.30	Median Home Value	$65,000	17	81.6
			Median Rent	$367	4	93.0
Crime	N/A	N/A	Violent Crimes per 10,000 Population	N/A	N/A	N/A
			Property Crimes per 10,000 Population	N/A	N/A	N/A
Open Spaces	29	24.00	Population Density (Persons/Sq. Mile)	5134	29	22.1
			Average Rooms per Housing Unit	5.1	17	25.9
Education	27	13.25	% High School Enrollment/Completion	77.4%	28	14.3
			% College Graduates	11.4%	22	12.2
Commute	17	34.95	Average Work Commute in Minutes	25	19	55.6
			% Commuting on Public Transportation	1.1%	10	14.3
Community Stability	16	70.10	% Living in Same House as in 1979	26.9%	20	47.6
			% Living in Same County as in 1985	86.1%	9	92.6

Metropolitan Area Description
INDIANAPOLIS

STATE: Indiana

COUNTIES: Boone, Hamilton, Hancock, Hendricks, Johnson, Marion, Morgan, Shelby

TOTAL POPULATION: 1,249,822

POPULATION IN SUBURBS: 518,495 (41.5%)

POPULATION IN Indianapolis: 731,327 (58.5%)

The INDIANAPOLIS metropolitan area is located in the central part of Indiana. The suburbs range geographically from Noblesville in the north (27 miles from Indianapolis), to Plainfield in the west (17 miles from Indianapolis), to Franklin in the south (31 miles from Indianapolis), and to Greenfield in the east (24 miles from Indianapolis). The area is growing in population and had an increase of 7.1% between 1980 and 1990. Summer time high temperatures average in the 80's and winter time lows average in the teens. Mayflower Transit has facilities located in the suburb of Carmel. PSI Resources is found in Plainfield. In 1992, *Fortune* magazine rated the metropolitan area number eight for its pro-business attitude, and many new businesses are being attracted to the suburbs. Public transportation in the area is provided on buses by the Indianapolis Metro bus system.

Carmel is the overall highest rated suburb and also has the highest scores in economics, education, and open spaces. **Shelbyville** is the suburb with the most affordable housing. **Greenfield** is rated the safest suburb with the lowest crime rate. The top rated commute belongs to **Speedway**. Finally, the number one rating in community stability goes to **Beech Grove**.

The highest ranked suburb overall which also has an affordable housing score of at least 50.00 is **Greenfield**.

The highest ranked suburb in the education category which also has an affordable housing score of at least 50.00 is **Plainfield**.

The county whose suburbs have the highest average overall score is **Hancock County** (55.00).

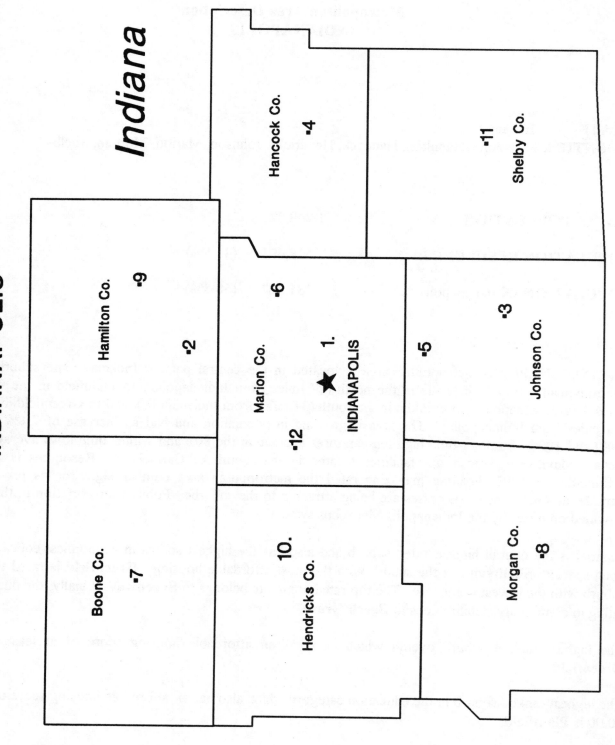

Metropolitan Area Map
INDIANAPOLIS

Indiana

Boone Co.
■7

Hamilton Co.
■9
■2

Hancock Co.
■4

Hendricks Co.
10.

Marion Co.
■12
1.
★
INDIANAPOLIS

Marion Co.
■6

Shelby Co.
■11

Morgan Co.
■8

Johnson Co.
■5
■3

Metropolitan Area Suburb Alphabetical Index
INDIANAPOLIS

SUBURB	PAGE	MAP NO.	STATE	COUNTY	POPU-LATION	RANK
BEECH GROVE	280	1	Indiana	Marion	13,383	3 / 12
CARMEL	280	2	Indiana	Hamilton	25,380	1 / 12
FRANKLIN	282	3	Indiana	Johnson	12,907	9 / 12
GREENFIELD	280	4	Indiana	Hancock	11,657	2 / 12
GREENWOOD	283	5	Indiana	Johnson	26,265	10 / 12
LAWRENCE	282	6	Indiana	Marion	26,763	8 / 12
LEBANON	281	7	Indiana	Boone	12,059	4 / 12
MARTINSVILLE	283	8	Indiana	Morgan	11,677	11 / 12
NOBLESVILLE	283	9	Indiana	Hamilton	17,655	12 / 12
PLAINFIELD	281	10	Indiana	Hendricks	10,433	6 / 12
SHELBYVILLE	282	11	Indiana	Shelby	15,336	7 / 12
SPEEDWAY	281	12	Indiana	Marion	13,092	5 / 12

Metropolitan Area Suburb Rankings
INDIANAPOLIS

Composite: *Rank* 1 / 12 *Score* 56.34 — **CARMEL**

CATEGORY	RANK	SCORE	STATISTIC	VALUE	RANK	SCORE
Economics	1	100.00	Median Household Income	$54,505	1	100.0
			% of Families Above Poverty Level	99.0%	1	100.0
Affordable Housing	12	0.00	Median Home Value	$142,200	12	0.0
			Median Rent	$560	12	0.0
Crime	2	86.30	Violent Crimes per 10,000 Population	10	4	92.1
			Property Crimes per 10,000 Population	279	2	80.5
Open Spaces	1	82.05	Population Density (Persons/Sq. Mile)	2015	5	64.1
			Average Rooms per Housing Unit	6.7	1	100.0
Education	1	100.00	% High School Enrollment/Completion	95.6%	1	100.0
			% College Graduates	51.3%	1	100.0
Commute	8	26.00	Average Work Commute in Minutes	22	8	33.3
			% Commuting on Public Transportation	0.3%	5	18.7
Community Stability	12	0.00	% Living in Same House as in 1979	21.9%	12	0.0
			% Living in Same County as in 1985	56.5%	12	0.0

Composite: *Rank* 2 / 12 *Score* 55.00 — **GREENFIELD**

CATEGORY	RANK	SCORE	STATISTIC	VALUE	RANK	SCORE
Economics	8	22.10	Median Household Income	$29,042	8	14.1
			% of Families Above Poverty Level	93.9%	9	30.1
Affordable Housing	5	80.70	Median Home Value	$57,000	5	84.8
			Median Rent	$403	5	76.6
Crime	1	88.30	Violent Crimes per 10,000 Population	5	1	100.0
			Property Crimes per 10,000 Population	300	3	76.6
Open Spaces	4	54.60	Population Density (Persons/Sq. Mile)	1898	3	70.3
			Average Rooms per Housing Unit	5.6	3	38.9
Education	10	28.15	% High School Enrollment/Completion	83.2%	9	46.8
			% College Graduates	13.0%	9	9.5
Commute	9	22.20	Average Work Commute in Minutes	21	6	44.4
			% Commuting on Public Transportation	0.0%	10	0.0
Community Stability	4	88.95	% Living in Same House as in 1979	39.8%	1	100.0
			% Living in Same County as in 1985	79.8%	6	77.9

Composite: *Rank* 3 / 12 *Score* 54.08 — **BEECH GROVE**

CATEGORY	RANK	SCORE	STATISTIC	VALUE	RANK	SCORE
Economics	3	44.20	Median Household Income	$29,549	6	15.8
			% of Families Above Poverty Level	97.0%	2	72.6
Affordable Housing	6	73.30	Median Home Value	$57,200	6	84.6
			Median Rent	$433	7	62.0
Crime	8	59.05	Violent Crimes per 10,000 Population	19	5	77.8
			Property Crimes per 10,000 Population	496	8	40.3
Open Spaces	12	5.55	Population Density (Persons/Sq. Mile)	3232	12	0.0
			Average Rooms per Housing Unit	5.1	9	11.1
Education	8	35.35	% High School Enrollment/Completion	88.0%	6	67.4
			% College Graduates	10.4%	10	3.3
Commute	2	65.30	Average Work Commute in Minutes	20	3	55.6
			% Commuting on Public Transportation	1.2%	2	75.0
Community Stability	1	95.80	% Living in Same House as in 1979	38.3%	2	91.6
			% Living in Same County as in 1985	86.4%	1	100.0

Metropolitan Area Suburb Rankings
INDIANAPOLIS

Composite: *Rank* 4 / 12 *Score* 52.93   **LEBANON**

CATEGORY	RANK	SCORE	STATISTIC	VALUE	RANK	SCORE
Economics	10	10.75	Median Household Income	$25,537	10	2.3
			% of Families Above Poverty Level	93.1%	10	19.2
Affordable Housing	4	93.75	Median Home Value	$51,300	3	90.4
			Median Rent	$361	2	97.1
Crime	4	69.05	Violent Crimes per 10,000 Population	44	9	38.1
			Property Crimes per 10,000 Population	174	1	100.0
Open Spaces	6	43.40	Population Density (Persons/Sq. Mile)	2006	4	64.6
			Average Rooms per Housing Unit	5.3	5	22.2
Education	7	35.45	% High School Enrollment/Completion	86.4%	8	60.5
			% College Graduates	13.4%	8	10.4
Commute	6	27.80	Average Work Commute in Minutes	20	3	55.6
			% Commuting on Public Transportation	0.0%	10	0.0
Community Stability	3	90.30	% Living in Same House as in 1979	38.3%	2	91.6
			% Living in Same County as in 1985	83.1%	4	89.0

Composite: *Rank* 5 / 12 *Score* 51.84   **SPEEDWAY**

CATEGORY	RANK	SCORE	STATISTIC	VALUE	RANK	SCORE
Economics	5	41.45	Median Household Income	$29,547	7	15.8
			% of Families Above Poverty Level	96.6%	4	67.1
Affordable Housing	8	66.70	Median Home Value	$67,400	8	74.4
			Median Rent	$439	8	59.0
Crime	9	37.30	Violent Crimes per 10,000 Population	21	6	74.6
			Property Crimes per 10,000 Population	713	10	0.0
Open Spaces	11	12.60	Population Density (Persons/Sq. Mile)	2754	9	25.2
			Average Rooms per Housing Unit	4.9	12	0.0
Education	4	51.05	% High School Enrollment/Completion	91.3%	2	81.5
			% College Graduates	17.7%	5	20.6
Commute	1	83.35	Average Work Commute in Minutes	19	2	66.7
			% Commuting on Public Transportation	1.6%	1	100.0
Community Stability	6	70.40	% Living in Same House as in 1979	32.8%	7	60.9
			% Living in Same County as in 1985	80.4%	5	79.9

Composite: *Rank* 6 / 12 *Score* 47.31   **PLAINFIELD**

CATEGORY	RANK	SCORE	STATISTIC	VALUE	RANK	SCORE
Economics	2	51.80	Median Household Income	$34,466	3	32.4
			% of Families Above Poverty Level	96.9%	3	71.2
Affordable Housing	9	62.70	Median Home Value	$68,600	9	73.2
			Median Rent	$453	10	52.2
Crime	7	63.00	Violent Crimes per 10,000 Population	21	6	74.6
			Property Crimes per 10,000 Population	436	6	51.4
Open Spaces	9	25.20	Population Density (Persons/Sq. Mile)	2803	10	22.6
			Average Rooms per Housing Unit	5.4	4	27.8
Education	3	52.15	% High School Enrollment/Completion	91.2%	3	81.1
			% College Graduates	18.8%	3	23.2
Commute	10	19.75	Average Work Commute in Minutes	22	8	33.3
			% Commuting on Public Transportation	0.1%	7	6.2
Community Stability	7	56.55	% Living in Same House as in 1979	33.7%	6	65.9
			% Living in Same County as in 1985	70.6%	9	47.2

Metropolitan Area Suburb Rankings
INDIANAPOLIS

Composite: *Rank* 7 / 12 *Score* 46.68   **SHELBYVILLE**

CATEGORY	RANK	SCORE	STATISTIC	VALUE	RANK	SCORE
Economics	9	17.20	Median Household Income	$24,915	11	0.2
			% of Families Above Poverty Level	94.2%	7	34.2
Affordable Housing	1	96.60	Median Home Value	$41,700	1	100.0
			Median Rent	$369	4	93.2
Crime	N/A	N/A	Violent Crimes per 10,000 Population	N/A	N/A	N/A
			Property Crimes per 10,000 Population	N/A	N/A	N/A
Open Spaces	7	30.25	Population Density (Persons/Sq. Mile)	2400	7	43.8
			Average Rooms per Housing Unit	5.2	7	16.7
Education	12	0.00	% High School Enrollment/Completion	72.3%	12	0.0
			% College Graduates	9.0%	12	0.0
Commute	3	53.10	Average Work Commute in Minutes	16	1	100.0
			% Commuting on Public Transportation	0.1%	7	6.2
Community Stability	5	82.95	% Living in Same House as in 1979	34.9%	5	72.6
			% Living in Same County as in 1985	84.4%	3	93.3

Composite: *Rank* 8 / 12 *Score* 45.81   **LAWRENCE**

CATEGORY	RANK	SCORE	STATISTIC	VALUE	RANK	SCORE
Economics	7	24.50	Median Household Income	$29,652	5	16.1
			% of Families Above Poverty Level	94.1%	8	32.9
Affordable Housing	7	72.25	Median Home Value	$63,600	7	78.2
			Median Rent	$424	6	66.3
Crime	5	65.75	Violent Crimes per 10,000 Population	27	8	65.1
			Property Crimes per 10,000 Population	355	5	66.4
Open Spaces	3	55.55	Population Density (Persons/Sq. Mile)	1334	1	100.0
			Average Rooms per Housing Unit	5.1	9	11.1
Education	9	29.35	% High School Enrollment/Completion	81.4%	11	39.1
			% College Graduates	17.3%	6	19.6
Commute	4	34.70	Average Work Commute in Minutes	21	6	44.4
			% Commuting on Public Transportation	0.4%	4	25.0
Community Stability	9	38.60	% Living in Same House as in 1979	24.4%	10	14.0
			% Living in Same County as in 1985	75.4%	7	63.2

Composite: *Rank* 9 / 12 *Score* 45.07   **FRANKLIN**

CATEGORY	RANK	SCORE	STATISTIC	VALUE	RANK	SCORE
Economics	11	3.35	Median Household Income	$26,040	9	4.0
			% of Families Above Poverty Level	91.9%	11	2.7
Affordable Housing	3	93.85	Median Home Value	$54,100	4	87.7
			Median Rent	$355	1	100.0
Crime	N/A	N/A	Violent Crimes per 10,000 Population	N/A	N/A	N/A
			Property Crimes per 10,000 Population	N/A	N/A	N/A
Open Spaces	5	48.90	Population Density (Persons/Sq. Mile)	1798	2	75.6
			Average Rooms per Housing Unit	5.3	5	22.2
Education	5	47.30	% High School Enrollment/Completion	91.2%	3	81.1
			% College Graduates	14.7%	7	13.5
Commute	6	27.80	Average Work Commute in Minutes	20	3	55.6
			% Commuting on Public Transportation	0.0%	10	0.0
Community Stability	8	49.20	% Living in Same House as in 1979	28.2%	8	35.2
			% Living in Same County as in 1985	75.4%	7	63.2

Metropolitan Area Suburb Rankings
INDIANAPOLIS

Composite: **Rank** 10 / 12 *Score* 42.83   **GREENWOOD**

CATEGORY	RANK	SCORE	STATISTIC	VALUE	RANK	SCORE
Economics	6	40.40	Median Household Income	$32,994	4	27.4
			% of Families Above Poverty Level	95.6%	5	53.4
Affordable Housing	10	62.45	Median Home Value	$73,600	10	68.3
			Median Rent	$444	9	56.6
Crime	3	69.80	Violent Crimes per 10,000 Population	6	2	98.4
			Property Crimes per 10,000 Population	491	7	41.2
Open Spaces	8	29.60	Population Density (Persons/Sq. Mile)	2426	8	42.5
			Average Rooms per Housing Unit	5.2	7	16.7
Education	6	43.65	% High School Enrollment/Completion	87.3%	7	64.4
			% College Graduates	18.7%	4	22.9
Commute	5	32.25	Average Work Commute in Minutes	22	8	33.3
			% Commuting on Public Transportation	0.5%	3	31.2
Community Stability	10	21.65	% Living in Same House as in 1979	25.7%	9	21.2
			% Living in Same County as in 1985	63.1%	11	22.1

Composite: **Rank** 11 / 12 *Score* 42.45   **MARTINSVILLE**

CATEGORY	RANK	SCORE	STATISTIC	VALUE	RANK	SCORE
Economics	12	0.00	Median Household Income	$24,868	12	0.0
			% of Families Above Poverty Level	91.7%	12	0.0
Affordable Housing	2	94.90	Median Home Value	$46,500	2	95.2
			Median Rent	$366	3	94.6
Crime	6	65.60	Violent Crimes per 10,000 Population	9	3	93.7
			Property Crimes per 10,000 Population	511	9	37.5
Open Spaces	10	14.50	Population Density (Persons/Sq. Mile)	2892	11	17.9
			Average Rooms per Housing Unit	5.1	9	11.1
Education	11	20.85	% High School Enrollment/Completion	81.9%	10	41.2
			% College Graduates	9.2%	11	0.5
Commute	12	9.35	Average Work Commute in Minutes	25	12	0.0
			% Commuting on Public Transportation	0.3%	5	18.7
Community Stability	2	91.95	% Living in Same House as in 1979	37.1%	4	84.9
			% Living in Same County as in 1985	86.1%	2	99.0

Composite: **Rank** 12 / 12 *Score* 39.30   **NOBLESVILLE**

CATEGORY	RANK	SCORE	STATISTIC	VALUE	RANK	SCORE
Economics	4	41.80	Median Household Income	$36,652	2	39.8
			% of Families Above Poverty Level	94.9%	6	43.8
Affordable Housing	11	45.20	Median Home Value	$93,600	11	48.4
			Median Rent	$474	11	42.0
Crime	10	36.35	Violent Crimes per 10,000 Population	68	10	0.0
			Property Crimes per 10,000 Population	321	4	72.7
Open Spaces	2	59.10	Population Density (Persons/Sq. Mile)	2043	6	62.6
			Average Rooms per Housing Unit	5.9	2	55.6
Education	2	61.30	% High School Enrollment/Completion	89.8%	5	75.1
			% College Graduates	29.1%	2	47.5
Commute	11	14.20	Average Work Commute in Minutes	23	11	22.2
			% Commuting on Public Transportation	0.1%	7	6.2
Community Stability	11	17.15	% Living in Same House as in 1979	23.5%	11	8.9
			% Living in Same County as in 1985	64.1%	10	25.4

STATE: Florida
COUNTIES: Clay, Duval, Nassau, St. Johns

TOTAL POPULATION: 906,727

POPULATION IN SUBURBS: 271,497   (29.9%)

POPULATION IN Jacksonville: 635,230   (70.1%)

The JACKSONVILLE metropolitan area is located in the northeastern part of Florida near the Atlantic Ocean. The suburbs range geographically from Bellair-Meadowbrook Terrace in the southwest (17 miles from Jacksonville), to St. Augustine in the south (41 miles from Jacksonville), and to Atlantic Beach in the east (16 miles from Jacksonville). The area is growing rapidly in population and had an increase of 25.5% between 1980 and 1990. Summer time high temperatures average in the 90's and winter time lows average in the 40's. Tourism is a major industry in the area. The climate is suited to year-round activities and the metropolitan area includes over 80 miles of white sand beaches. Some of the best known resort towns are the suburbs of Jacksonville Beach and Atlantic Beach.

St. Augustine is the overall highest rated suburb and also has the highest score in community stability. Additionally, **St. Augustine** is the suburb with the most affordable housing. **Lakeside** receives the top scores in economics, education, and open spaces. The top rated commute belongs to **Jacksonville Beach**. Crime rankings were not available for the area.

The highest ranked suburb overall which also has an affordable housing score of at least 50.00 is **St. Augustine**.

The highest ranked suburb in the education category which also has an affordable housing score of at least 50.00 is also **St. Augustine**.

The county whose suburbs have the highest average overall score is **St. Johns County** (59.31).

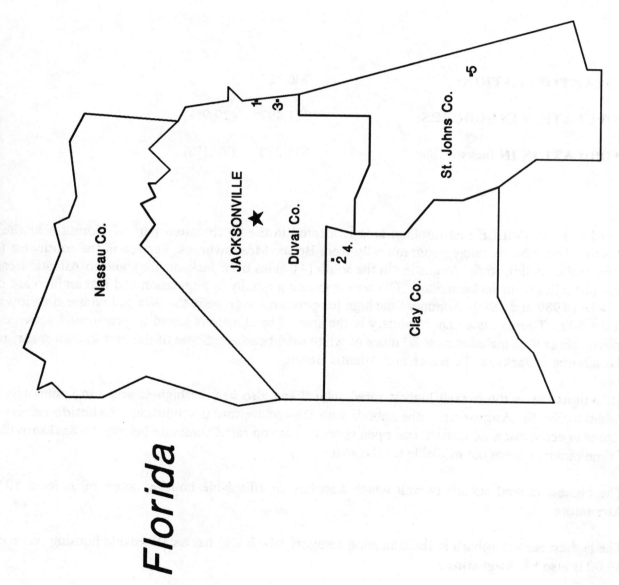

Metropolitan Area Map
JACKSONVILLE

Florida

Nassau Co.

JACKSONVILLE

★

Duval Co.

1
3

St. Johns Co.

5

2
4

Clay Co.

Metropolitan Area Suburb Alphabetical Index
JACKSONVILLE

SUBURB	PAGE	MAP NO.	STATE	COUNTY	POPU-LATION	RANK
ATLANTIC BEACH	289	1	Florida	Duval	11,636	4 / 5
BELLAIR-MEADOWBROOK TERRACE	289	2	Florida	Clay	15,606	5 / 5
JACKSONVILLE BEACH	288	3	Florida	Duval	17,839	2 / 5
LAKESIDE	288	4	Florida	Clay	29,137	3 / 5
ST. AUGUSTINE	288	5	Florida	St. Johns	11,692	1 / 5

Metropolitan Area Suburb Rankings
JACKSONVILLE

Composite: Rank 1 / 5 *Score* 59.31   **ST. AUGUSTINE**

CATEGORY	RANK	SCORE	STATISTIC	VALUE	RANK	SCORE
Economics	5	0.00	Median Household Income	$21,722	5	0.0
			% of Families Above Poverty Level	89.2%	5	0.0
Affordable Housing	1	100.00	Median Home Value	$60,500	1	100.0
			Median Rent	$380	1	100.0
Crime	N/A	N/A	Violent Crimes per 10,000 Population	211	N/A	N/A
			Property Crimes per 10,000 Population	1,294	N/A	N/A
Open Spaces	2	58.35	Population Density (Persons/Sq. Mile)	1666	1	100.0
			Average Rooms per Housing Unit	5.2	4	16.7
Education	2	57.35	% High School Enrollment/Completion	89.2%	2	77.0
			% College Graduates	23.5%	3	37.7
Commute	2	54.00	Average Work Commute in Minutes	15	1	100.0
			% Commuting on Public Transportation	0.3%	4	8.0
Community Stability	1	86.15	% Living in Same House as in 1979	40.4%	1	100.0
			% Living in Same County as in 1985	68.6%	3	72.3

Composite: Rank 2 / 5 *Score* 53.47   **JACKSONVILLE BEACH**

CATEGORY	RANK	SCORE	STATISTIC	VALUE	RANK	SCORE
Economics	3	60.25	Median Household Income	$29,680	4	40.2
			% of Families Above Poverty Level	94.5%	3	80.3
Affordable Housing	2	55.65	Median Home Value	$73,800	3	59.1
			Median Rent	$465	2	52.2
Crime	N/A	N/A	Violent Crimes per 10,000 Population	185	N/A	N/A
			Property Crimes per 10,000 Population	1,051	N/A	N/A
Open Spaces	4	34.65	Population Density (Persons/Sq. Mile)	2324	3	69.3
			Average Rooms per Housing Unit	5.0	5	0.0
Education	4	29.85	% High School Enrollment/Completion	84.6%	4	31.0
			% College Graduates	22.4%	4	28.7
Commute	1	73.10	Average Work Commute in Minutes	22	2	46.2
			% Commuting on Public Transportation	2.6%	1	100.0
Community Stability	2	67.30	% Living in Same House as in 1979	25.5%	3	34.6
			% Living in Same County as in 1985	75.1%	1	100.0

Composite: Rank 3 / 5 *Score* 47.91   **LAKESIDE**

CATEGORY	RANK	SCORE	STATISTIC	VALUE	RANK	SCORE
Economics	1	100.00	Median Household Income	$41,503	1	100.0
			% of Families Above Poverty Level	95.8%	1	100.0
Affordable Housing	5	10.60	Median Home Value	$88,300	4	14.5
			Median Rent	$546	4	6.7
Crime	N/A	N/A	Violent Crimes per 10,000 Population	N/A	N/A	N/A
			Property Crimes per 10,000 Population	N/A	N/A	N/A
Open Spaces	1	94.00	Population Density (Persons/Sq. Mile)	1923	2	88.0
			Average Rooms per Housing Unit	6.2	1	100.0
Education	1	72.15	% High School Enrollment/Completion	91.5%	1	100.0
			% College Graduates	24.3%	2	44.3
Commute	5	6.00	Average Work Commute in Minutes	28	5	0.0
			% Commuting on Public Transportation	0.4%	3	12.0
Community Stability	5	4.70	% Living in Same House as in 1979	17.6%	5	0.0
			% Living in Same County as in 1985	53.8%	4	9.4

Metropolitan Area Suburb Rankings
JACKSONVILLE

Composite: **Rank** 4 / 5 **Score** 40.56   **ATLANTIC BEACH**

CATEGORY	RANK	SCORE	STATISTIC	VALUE	RANK	SCORE
Economics	4	52.20	Median Household Income	$35,486	2	69.6
			% of Families Above Poverty Level	91.5%	4	34.8
Affordable Housing	4	12.35	Median Home Value	$93,000	5	0.0
			Median Rent	$514	3	24.7
Crime	N/A	N/A	Violent Crimes per 10,000 Population	N/A	N/A	N/A
			Property Crimes per 10,000 Population	N/A	N/A	N/A
Open Spaces	5	20.85	Population Density (Persons/Sq. Mile)	3811	5	0.0
			Average Rooms per Housing Unit	5.5	2	41.7
Education	3	50.00	% High School Enrollment/Completion	81.5%	5	0.0
			% College Graduates	31.1%	1	100.0
Commute	3	51.25	Average Work Commute in Minutes	23	3	38.5
			% Commuting on Public Transportation	1.7%	2	64.0
Community Stability	3	56.70	% Living in Same House as in 1979	25.6%	2	35.1
			% Living in Same County as in 1985	70.0%	2	78.3

Composite: **Rank** 5 / 5 **Score** 35.37   **BELLAIR-MEADOWBROOK TERRACE**

CATEGORY	RANK	SCORE	STATISTIC	VALUE	RANK	SCORE
Economics	2	77.45	Median Household Income	$32,590	3	54.9
			% of Families Above Poverty Level	95.8%	1	100.0
Affordable Housing	3	38.75	Median Home Value	$67,800	2	77.5
			Median Rent	$558	5	0.0
Crime	N/A	N/A	Violent Crimes per 10,000 Population	N/A	N/A	N/A
			Property Crimes per 10,000 Population	N/A	N/A	N/A
Open Spaces	3	44.75	Population Density (Persons/Sq. Mile)	2785	4	47.8
			Average Rooms per Housing Unit	5.5	2	41.7
Education	5	25.00	% High School Enrollment/Completion	86.5%	3	50.0
			% College Graduates	18.9%	5	0.0
Commute	4	19.25	Average Work Commute in Minutes	23	3	38.5
			% Commuting on Public Transportation	0.1%	5	0.0
Community Stability	4	7.00	% Living in Same House as in 1979	20.8%	4	14.0
			% Living in Same County as in 1985	51.6%	5	0.0

Metropolitan Area Description
KANSAS CITY

STATE: Kansas
COUNTIES: Johnson, Leavenworth, Miami, Wyandotte

STATE: Missouri
COUNTIES: Cass, Clay, Jackson, Lafayette, Platte, Ray

TOTAL POPULATION:	1,566,280	
POPULATION IN SUBURBS:	981,367	(62.7%)
POPULATION IN Kansas City (MO):	435,146	(27.8%)
POPULATION IN Kansas City (KS):	149,767	(9.6%)

The KANSAS CITY metropolitan area is located in the western part of Missouri and the eastern part of Kansas. The suburbs range geographically from Excelsior Springs (MO) in the north (27 miles from Kansas City), to Leavenworth (KS) in the west (33 miles from Kansas City), to Belton (MO) in the south (24 miles from Kansas City), and to Blue Springs (MO) in the east (18 miles from Kansas City). The area is growing in population and had an increase of 9.3% between 1980 and 1990. Summer time high temperatures average in the 80's and winter time lows average in the teens. Companies located in the suburbs include Peterson Manufacturing located in Grandview (MO) and Ferrell Companies, vendors of liquefied gas, located in Liberty (MO). Clay County (MO) features a concentration of office buildings including the Corporate Woods business park. In 1991, *Fortune* magazine rated the metropolitan area number four for business. Public transportation in the area is provided on buses by the Kansas City Area Transportation Authority.

Prairie Village (KS) is the overall highest rated suburb and also has the highest score in education. **Leawood** (KS) receives the top scores in economics and open spaces, and is also the safest suburb with the lowest crime rate. **Excelsior Springs** (MO) is the suburb with the most affordable housing. The top rated commute belongs to **Gladstone** (MO). Finally, the number one rating in community stability goes to **Raytown** (MO).

The highest ranked suburb overall which also has an affordable housing score of at least 50.00 is **Prairie Village** (KS).

The highest ranked suburb in the education category which also has an affordable housing score of at least 50.00 is also **Prairie Village** (KS).

The county whose suburbs have the highest average overall score is **Johnson County** (KS) (54.42).

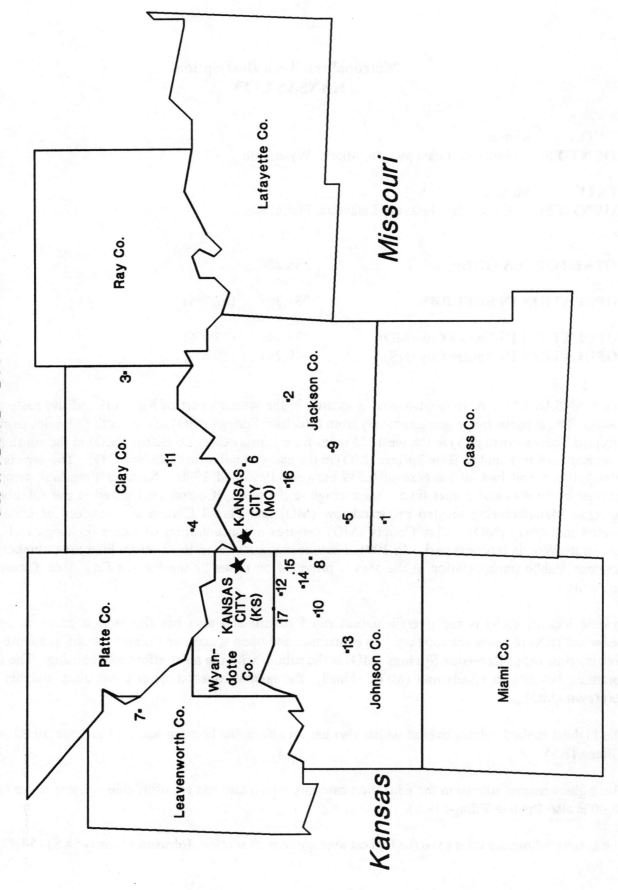

Metropolitan Area Map
KANSAS CITY

Metropolitan Area Suburb Alphabetical Index
KANSAS CITY

SUBURB	PAGE	MAP NO.	STATE	COUNTY	POPU-LATION	RANK
BELTON	299	1	Missouri	Cass	18,150	16 / 17
BLUE SPRINGS	296	2	Missouri	Jackson	40,153	9 / 17
EXCELSIOR SPRINGS	297	3	Missouri	Clay	10,354	11 / 17
GLADSTONE	294	4	Missouri	Clay	26,243	3 / 17
GRANDVIEW	298	5	Missouri	Jackson	24,967	15 / 17
INDEPENDENCE	298	6	Missouri	Jackson	112,301	13 / 17
LEAVENWORTH	298	7	Kansas	Leavenworth	38,495	14 / 17
LEAWOOD	294	8	Kansas	Johnson	19,693	2 / 17
LEE'S SUMMIT	297	9	Missouri	Jackson	46,418	10 / 17
LENEXA	296	10	Kansas	Johnson	34,034	8 / 17
LIBERTY	295	11	Missouri	Clay	20,459	6 / 17
MERRIAM	299	12	Kansas	Johnson	11,821	17 / 17
OLATHE	297	13	Kansas	Johnson	63,352	12 / 17
OVERLAND PARK	295	14	Kansas	Johnson	111,790	5 / 17
PRAIRIE VILLAGE	294	15	Kansas	Johnson	23,186	1 / 17
RAYTOWN	295	16	Missouri	Jackson	30,601	4 / 17
SHAWNEE	296	17	Kansas	Johnson	37,993	7 / 17

Metropolitan Area Suburb Rankings
KANSAS CITY

Composite: **Rank** 1 / 17 *Score* 67.79   **PRAIRIE VILLAGE (KS)**

CATEGORY	RANK	SCORE	STATISTIC	VALUE	RANK	SCORE
Economics	2	67.25	Median Household Income	$43,750	4	38.7
			% of Families Above Poverty Level	98.6%	2	95.8
Affordable Housing	16	58.50	Median Home Value	$85,800	14	67.2
			Median Rent	$623	16	49.8
Crime	2	95.60	Violent Crimes per 10,000 Population	13	1	100.0
			Property Crimes per 10,000 Population	249	2	91.2
Open Spaces	14	25.00	Population Density (Persons/Sq. Mile)	3728	17	0.0
			Average Rooms per Housing Unit	6.4	2	50.0
Education	1	90.70	% High School Enrollment/Completion	97.8%	1	100.0
			% College Graduates	51.1%	2	81.4
Commute	4	58.35	Average Work Commute in Minutes	19	2	66.7
			% Commuting on Public Transportation	0.8%	5	50.0
Community Stability	3	79.10	% Living in Same House as in 1979	43.4%	2	86.8
			% Living in Same County as in 1985	77.8%	4	71.4

Composite: **Rank** 2 / 17 *Score* 67.42   **LEAWOOD (KS)**

CATEGORY	RANK	SCORE	STATISTIC	VALUE	RANK	SCORE
Economics	1	100.00	Median Household Income	$74,980	1	100.0
			% of Families Above Poverty Level	99.0%	1	100.0
Affordable Housing	17	0.00	Median Home Value	$160,700	17	0.0
			Median Rent	$922	17	0.0
Crime	1	100.00	Violent Crimes per 10,000 Population	13	1	100.0
			Property Crimes per 10,000 Population	212	1	100.0
Open Spaces	1	90.60	Population Density (Persons/Sq. Mile)	1315	6	81.2
			Average Rooms per Housing Unit	7.7	1	100.0
Education	2	80.60	% High School Enrollment/Completion	90.9%	11	61.2
			% College Graduates	60.1%	1	100.0
Commute	8	42.70	Average Work Commute in Minutes	19	2	66.7
			% Commuting on Public Transportation	0.3%	9	18.7
Community Stability	7	58.05	% Living in Same House as in 1979	36.0%	4	63.4
			% Living in Same County as in 1985	70.9%	11	52.7

Composite: **Rank** 3 / 17 *Score* 59.49   **GLADSTONE (MO)**

CATEGORY	RANK	SCORE	STATISTIC	VALUE	RANK	SCORE
Economics	5	56.75	Median Household Income	$37,302	9	26.0
			% of Families Above Poverty Level	97.8%	4	87.5
Affordable Housing	7	80.50	Median Home Value	$72,500	7	79.2
			Median Rent	$431	8	81.8
Crime	5	64.50	Violent Crimes per 10,000 Population	34	8	52.3
			Property Crimes per 10,000 Population	310	3	76.7
Open Spaces	16	19.25	Population Density (Persons/Sq. Mile)	3271	16	15.4
			Average Rooms per Housing Unit	5.7	9	23.1
Education	7	53.90	% High School Enrollment/Completion	95.0%	3	84.3
			% College Graduates	23.0%	12	23.5
Commute	1	77.80	Average Work Commute in Minutes	20	7	55.6
			% Commuting on Public Transportation	1.6%	1	100.0
Community Stability	4	63.75	% Living in Same House as in 1979	36.0%	4	63.4
			% Living in Same County as in 1985	75.1%	8	64.1

Composite: **Rank** 4 / 17 *Score* 57.51   **RAYTOWN (MO)**

CATEGORY	RANK	SCORE	STATISTIC	VALUE	RANK	SCORE
Economics	11	45.30	Median Household Income	$32,002	13	15.6
			% of Families Above Poverty Level	96.6%	8	75.0
Affordable Housing	6	84.60	Median Home Value	$64,100	6	86.7
			Median Rent	$427	5	82.5
Crime	6	62.20	Violent Crimes per 10,000 Population	29	7	63.6
			Property Crimes per 10,000 Population	377	6	60.8
Open Spaces	15	24.20	Population Density (Persons/Sq. Mile)	3089	15	21.5
			Average Rooms per Housing Unit	5.8	7	26.9
Education	13	32.80	% High School Enrollment/Completion	89.3%	13	52.2
			% College Graduates	18.1%	13	13.4
Commute	5	53.45	Average Work Commute in Minutes	21	10	44.4
			% Commuting on Public Transportation	1.0%	4	62.5
Community Stability	1	100.00	% Living in Same House as in 1979	47.6%	1	100.0
			% Living in Same County as in 1985	88.4%	1	100.0

Composite: **Rank** 5 / 17 *Score* 54.72   **OVERLAND PARK (KS)**

CATEGORY	RANK	SCORE	STATISTIC	VALUE	RANK	SCORE
Economics	3	65.10	Median Household Income	$44,246	3	39.6
			% of Families Above Poverty Level	98.1%	3	90.6
Affordable Housing	15	60.55	Median Home Value	$95,100	15	58.9
			Median Rent	$549	15	62.2
Crime	8	53.60	Violent Crimes per 10,000 Population	28	6	65.9
			Property Crimes per 10,000 Population	459	9	41.3
Open Spaces	7	46.25	Population Density (Persons/Sq. Mile)	2007	12	57.9
			Average Rooms per Housing Unit	6.0	4	34.6
Education	3	75.55	% High School Enrollment/Completion	94.7%	4	82.6
			% College Graduates	44.8%	4	68.5
Commute	7	45.85	Average Work Commute in Minutes	19	2	66.7
			% Commuting on Public Transportation	0.4%	8	25.0
Community Stability	13	36.15	% Living in Same House as in 1979	25.7%	12	30.9
			% Living in Same County as in 1985	66.7%	13	41.4

Composite: **Rank** 6 / 17 *Score* 53.67   **LIBERTY (MO)**

CATEGORY	RANK	SCORE	STATISTIC	VALUE	RANK	SCORE
Economics	10	49.10	Median Household Income	$36,388	10	24.2
			% of Families Above Poverty Level	96.5%	10	74.0
Affordable Housing	8	79.75	Median Home Value	$76,600	9	75.5
			Median Rent	$418	4	84.0
Crime	N/A	N/A	Violent Crimes per 10,000 Population	N/A	N/A	N/A
			Property Crimes per 10,000 Population	N/A	N/A	N/A
Open Spaces	3	61.55	Population Density (Persons/Sq. Mile)	756	1	100.0
			Average Rooms per Housing Unit	5.7	9	23.1
Education	11	45.80	% High School Enrollment/Completion	91.2%	10	62.9
			% College Graduates	25.5%	10	28.7
Commute	12	34.05	Average Work Commute in Minutes	20	7	55.6
			% Commuting on Public Transportation	0.2%	13	12.5
Community Stability	8	51.75	% Living in Same House as in 1979	30.9%	9	47.3
			% Living in Same County as in 1985	72.2%	9	56.2

Metropolitan Area Suburb Rankings
KANSAS CITY

Composite: Rank 7 / 17 *Score* 52.91 **SHAWNEE (KS)**

CATEGORY	RANK	SCORE	STATISTIC	VALUE	RANK	SCORE
Economics	7	52.85	Median Household Income	$39,206	7	29.7
			% of Families Above Poverty Level	96.7%	6	76.0
Affordable Housing	10	72.60	Median Home Value	$84,400	13	68.5
			Median Rent	$462	9	76.7
Crime	7	55.30	Violent Crimes per 10,000 Population	37	9	45.5
			Property Crimes per 10,000 Population	359	5	65.1
Open Spaces	4	60.90	Population Density (Persons/Sq. Mile)	909	3	94.9
			Average Rooms per Housing Unit	5.8	7	26.9
Education	6	58.60	% High School Enrollment/Completion	94.3%	5	80.3
			% College Graduates	29.5%	7	36.9
Commute	14	22.20	Average Work Commute in Minutes	21	10	44.4
			% Commuting on Public Transportation	0.0%	17	0.0
Community Stability	12	47.90	% Living in Same House as in 1979	28.7%	10	40.4
			% Living in Same County as in 1985	71.9%	10	55.4

Composite: Rank 8 / 17 *Score* 50.68 **LENEXA (KS)**

CATEGORY	RANK	SCORE	STATISTIC	VALUE	RANK	SCORE
Economics	4	62.55	Median Household Income	$46,935	2	44.9
			% of Families Above Poverty Level	97.1%	5	80.2
Affordable Housing	14	60.80	Median Home Value	$103,500	16	51.3
			Median Rent	$500	11	70.3
Crime	N/A	N/A	Violent Crimes per 10,000 Population	N/A	N/A	N/A
			Property Crimes per 10,000 Population	N/A	N/A	N/A
Open Spaces	2	64.15	Population Density (Persons/Sq. Mile)	1173	5	86.0
			Average Rooms per Housing Unit	6.2	3	42.3
Education	4	68.10	% High School Enrollment/Completion	91.8%	8	66.3
			% College Graduates	45.5%	3	69.9
Commute	13	30.90	Average Work Commute in Minutes	20	7	55.6
			% Commuting on Public Transportation	0.1%	15	6.2
Community Stability	17	17.55	% Living in Same House as in 1979	15.9%	17	0.0
			% Living in Same County as in 1985	64.4%	15	35.1

Composite: Rank 9 / 17 *Score* 49.54 **BLUE SPRINGS (MO)**

CATEGORY	RANK	SCORE	STATISTIC	VALUE	RANK	SCORE
Economics	9	50.95	Median Household Income	$39,904	5	31.1
			% of Families Above Poverty Level	96.2%	11	70.8
Affordable Housing	12	72.05	Median Home Value	$77,300	10	74.9
			Median Rent	$507	14	69.2
Crime	4	68.70	Violent Crimes per 10,000 Population	23	4	77.3
			Property Crimes per 10,000 Population	380	7	60.1
Open Spaces	13	38.10	Population Density (Persons/Sq. Mile)	2493	13	41.6
			Average Rooms per Housing Unit	6.0	4	34.6
Education	10	48.85	% High School Enrollment/Completion	92.9%	6	72.5
			% College Graduates	23.8%	11	25.2
Commute	15	18.75	Average Work Commute in Minutes	25	17	0.0
			% Commuting on Public Transportation	0.6%	7	37.5
Community Stability	10	49.35	% Living in Same House as in 1979	23.3%	14	23.3
			% Living in Same County as in 1985	79.3%	3	75.4

Metropolitan Area Suburb Rankings
KANSAS CITY

Composite: *Rank* 10 / 17 *Score* 48.98   **LEE'S SUMMIT (MO)**

CATEGORY	RANK	SCORE	STATISTIC	VALUE	RANK	SCORE
Economics	8	51.95	Median Household Income	$38,800	8	28.9
			% of Families Above Poverty Level	96.6%	8	75.0
Affordable Housing	13	69.05	Median Home Value	$84,100	12	68.8
			Median Rent	$506	12	69.3
Crime	N/A	N/A	Violent Crimes per 10,000 Population	N/A	N/A	N/A
			Property Crimes per 10,000 Population	N/A	N/A	N/A
Open Spaces	5	59.10	Population Density (Persons/Sq. Mile)	785	2	99.0
			Average Rooms per Housing Unit	5.6	11	19.2
Education	9	50.20	% High School Enrollment/Completion	92.1%	7	68.0
			% College Graduates	27.3%	9	32.4
Commute	17	14.20	Average Work Commute in Minutes	23	13	22.2
			% Commuting on Public Transportation	0.1%	15	6.2
Community Stability	9	49.40	% Living in Same House as in 1979	24.6%	13	27.4
			% Living in Same County as in 1985	77.8%	4	71.4

Composite: *Rank* 11 / 17 *Score* 45.97   **EXCELSIOR SPRINGS (MO)**

CATEGORY	RANK	SCORE	STATISTIC	VALUE	RANK	SCORE
Economics	17	0.00	Median Household Income	$24,067	17	0.0
			% of Families Above Poverty Level	89.4%	17	0.0
Affordable Housing	1	100.00	Median Home Value	$49,300	1	100.0
			Median Rent	$322	1	100.0
Crime	9	52.30	Violent Crimes per 10,000 Population	16	3	93.2
			Property Crimes per 10,000 Population	585	12	11.4
Open Spaces	8	44.75	Population Density (Persons/Sq. Mile)	1069	4	89.5
			Average Rooms per Housing Unit	5.1	17	0.0
Education	17	0.20	% High School Enrollment/Completion	80.0%	17	0.0
			% College Graduates	11.8%	16	0.4
Commute	2	61.10	Average Work Commute in Minutes	23	13	22.2
			% Commuting on Public Transportation	1.6%	1	100.0
Community Stability	5	63.45	% Living in Same House as in 1979	35.4%	6	61.5
			% Living in Same County as in 1985	75.6%	7	65.4

Composite: *Rank* 12 / 17 *Score* 45.61   **OLATHE (KS)**

CATEGORY	RANK	SCORE	STATISTIC	VALUE	RANK	SCORE
Economics	6	53.40	Median Household Income	$39,742	6	30.8
			% of Families Above Poverty Level	96.7%	6	76.0
Affordable Housing	11	72.45	Median Home Value	$83,200	11	69.6
			Median Rent	$470	10	75.3
Crime	11	26.00	Violent Crimes per 10,000 Population	50	11	15.9
			Property Crimes per 10,000 Population	481	10	36.1
Open Spaces	6	54.80	Population Density (Persons/Sq. Mile)	1500	9	75.0
			Average Rooms per Housing Unit	6.0	4	34.6
Education	8	53.05	% High School Enrollment/Completion	91.7%	9	65.7
			% College Graduates	31.2%	6	40.4
Commute	11	39.60	Average Work Commute in Minutes	19	2	66.7
			% Commuting on Public Transportation	0.2%	13	12.5
Community Stability	15	20.00	% Living in Same House as in 1979	16.9%	16	3.2
			% Living in Same County as in 1985	65.0%	14	36.8

Metropolitan Area Suburb Rankings
KANSAS CITY

Composite: **Rank** 13 / 17 **Score** 44.99 **INDEPENDENCE (MO)**

CATEGORY	RANK	SCORE	STATISTIC	VALUE	RANK	SCORE
Economics	15	23.35	Median Household Income	$28,242	16	8.2
			% of Families Above Poverty Level	93.1%	15	38.5
Affordable Housing	2	91.75	Median Home Value	$55,700	2	94.3
			Median Rent	$387	2	89.2
Crime	14	3.40	Violent Crimes per 10,000 Population	54	13	6.8
			Property Crimes per 10,000 Population	633	14	0.0
Open Spaces	9	42.40	Population Density (Persons/Sq. Mile)	1436	7	77.1
			Average Rooms per Housing Unit	5.3	14	7.7
Education	16	17.30	% High School Enrollment/Completion	85.4%	15	30.3
			% College Graduates	13.7%	15	4.3
Commute	6	51.70	Average Work Commute in Minutes	23	13	22.2
			% Commuting on Public Transportation	1.3%	3	81.2
Community Stability	2	85.00	% Living in Same House as in 1979	39.7%	3	75.1
			% Living in Same County as in 1985	86.5%	2	94.9

Composite: **Rank** 14 / 17 **Score** 44.07 **LEAVENWORTH (KS)**

CATEGORY	RANK	SCORE	STATISTIC	VALUE	RANK	SCORE
Economics	16	22.65	Median Household Income	$30,156	15	12.0
			% of Families Above Poverty Level	92.6%	16	33.3
Affordable Housing	4	87.90	Median Home Value	$56,800	3	93.3
			Median Rent	$427	5	82.5
Crime	10	32.55	Violent Crimes per 10,000 Population	52	12	11.4
			Property Crimes per 10,000 Population	407	8	53.7
Open Spaces	10	41.90	Population Density (Persons/Sq. Mile)	1695	11	68.4
			Average Rooms per Housing Unit	5.5	12	15.4
Education	12	45.20	% High School Enrollment/Completion	89.6%	12	53.9
			% College Graduates	29.3%	8	36.5
Commute	3	59.35	Average Work Commute in Minutes	16	1	100.0
			% Commuting on Public Transportation	0.3%	9	18.7
Community Stability	16	18.95	% Living in Same House as in 1979	27.9%	11	37.9
			% Living in Same County as in 1985	51.4%	17	0.0

Composite: **Rank** 15 / 17 **Score** 43.54 **GRANDVIEW (MO)**

CATEGORY	RANK	SCORE	STATISTIC	VALUE	RANK	SCORE
Economics	12	39.80	Median Household Income	$32,779	12	17.1
			% of Families Above Poverty Level	95.4%	12	62.5
Affordable Housing	3	88.55	Median Home Value	$62,000	5	88.6
			Median Rent	$391	3	88.5
Crime	12	13.00	Violent Crimes per 10,000 Population	49	10	18.2
			Property Crimes per 10,000 Population	600	13	7.8
Open Spaces	10	41.90	Population Density (Persons/Sq. Mile)	1694	10	68.4
			Average Rooms per Housing Unit	5.5	12	15.4
Education	15	19.10	% High School Enrollment/Completion	84.6%	16	25.8
			% College Graduates	17.6%	14	12.4
Commute	10	41.65	Average Work Commute in Minutes	22	12	33.3
			% Commuting on Public Transportation	0.8%	5	50.0
Community Stability	6	60.80	% Living in Same House as in 1979	32.0%	7	50.8
			% Living in Same County as in 1985	77.6%	6	70.8

Composite: **Rank** 16 / 17 *Score* 42.11   **BELTON (MO)**

CATEGORY	RANK	SCORE	STATISTIC	VALUE	RANK	SCORE
Economics	13	34.80	Median Household Income	$30,896	14	13.4
			% of Families Above Poverty Level	94.8%	13	56.2
Affordable Housing	5	86.20	Median Home Value	$60,500	4	89.9
			Median Rent	$427	5	82.5
Crime	3	71.00	Violent Crimes per 10,000 Population	26	5	70.5
			Property Crimes per 10,000 Population	332	4	71.5
Open Spaces	12	41.35	Population Density (Persons/Sq. Mile)	1498	8	75.0
			Average Rooms per Housing Unit	5.3	14	7.7
Education	14	21.90	% High School Enrollment/Completion	87.8%	14	43.8
			% College Graduates	11.6%	17	0.0
Commute	16	14.90	Average Work Commute in Minutes	24	16	11.1
			% Commuting on Public Transportation	0.3%	9	18.7
Community Stability	14	24.65	% Living in Same House as in 1979	22.7%	15	21.5
			% Living in Same County as in 1985	61.7%	16	27.8

Composite: **Rank** 17 / 17 *Score* 41.83   **MERRIAM (KS)**

CATEGORY	RANK	SCORE	STATISTIC	VALUE	RANK	SCORE
Economics	14	33.20	Median Household Income	$34,013	11	19.5
			% of Families Above Poverty Level	93.9%	14	46.9
Affordable Housing	9	73.50	Median Home Value	$74,100	8	77.7
			Median Rent	$506	12	69.3
Crime	13	10.45	Violent Crimes per 10,000 Population	57	14	0.0
			Property Crimes per 10,000 Population	545	11	20.9
Open Spaces	17	18.20	Population Density (Persons/Sq. Mile)	2759	14	32.6
			Average Rooms per Housing Unit	5.2	16	3.8
Education	5	66.40	% High School Enrollment/Completion	96.3%	2	91.6
			% College Graduates	31.6%	5	41.2
Commute	8	42.70	Average Work Commute in Minutes	19	2	66.7
			% Commuting on Public Transportation	0.3%	9	18.7
Community Stability	11	48.35	% Living in Same House as in 1979	31.3%	8	48.6
			% Living in Same County as in 1985	69.2%	12	48.1

Metropolitan Area Description
LOS ANGELES-ANAHEIM-RIVERSIDE

STATE: California
COUNTIES: Los Angeles, Orange, Riverside, San Bernardino, Ventura

TOTAL POPULATION: 14,531,529

POPULATION IN SUBURBS: 10,553,220 (72.6%)

POPULATION IN Los Angeles: 3,485,398 (24.0%)
POPULATION IN Anaheim: 266,406 (1.8%)
POPULATION IN Riverside: 226,505 (1.6%)

The LOS ANGELES-ANAHEIM-RIVERSIDE metropolitan area is located in the southwestern part of California along the Pacific Ocean. The suburbs range geographically from Ventura in the northwest (78 miles from Los Angeles), to San Clemente in the south (57 miles from Los Angeles), and to Twenty-Nine Palms in the east (159 miles from Los Angeles). The area is growing rapidly in population and had an increase of 26.4% between 1980 and 1990. Summer time high temperatures average in the 80's and winter time lows average in the 40's. The entertainment industry is a big presence in the area. Walt Disney Studios and Warner Brothers are both located in the suburb of Burbank. Aerospace is also a major industry with Rockwell International located in Seal Beach and Aerospace Corporation located in El Segundo. The public transportation system in Los Angeles is not as diversified as in other large cities. Bus service is provided, however, by the Southern California Rapid Transit District.

San Marino is the overall highest rated suburb. **Palos Verdes Estates** receives the highest scores in economics, education, and open spaces. **Coachella** is the suburb with the most affordable housing. **Sierra Madre** is rated the safest suburb with the lowest crime rate. The top rated commute belongs to **East Los Angeles**. Finally, the number one rating in community stability goes to **View Park-Windsor Hills**.

The highest ranked suburb overall which also has an affordable housing score of at least 50.00 is **Claremont**.

The highest ranked suburb in the education category which also has an affordable housing score of at least 50.00 is also **Claremont**.

The county whose suburbs have the highest average overall score is **Orange County** (56.80).

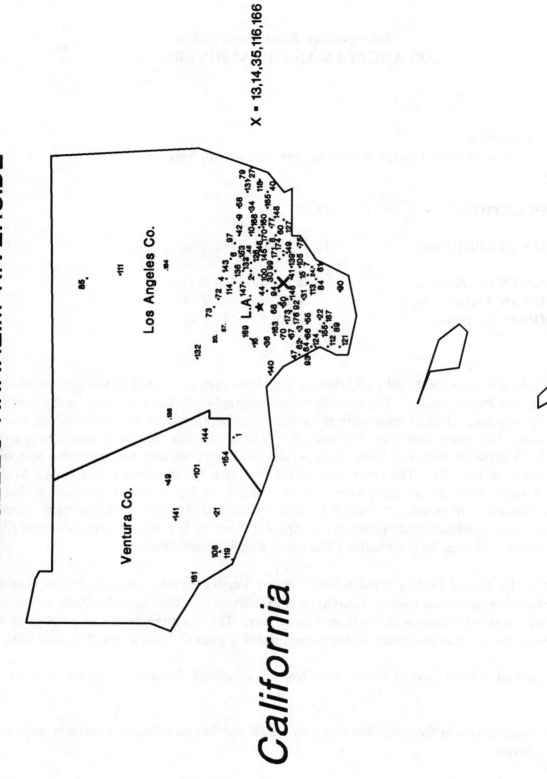

Metropolitan Area Map (Part 1)
LOS ANGELES-ANAHEIM-RIVERSIDE

X = 13,14,35,116,166

Metropolitan Area Map (Part 2)
LOS ANGELES-ANAHEIM-RIVERSIDE

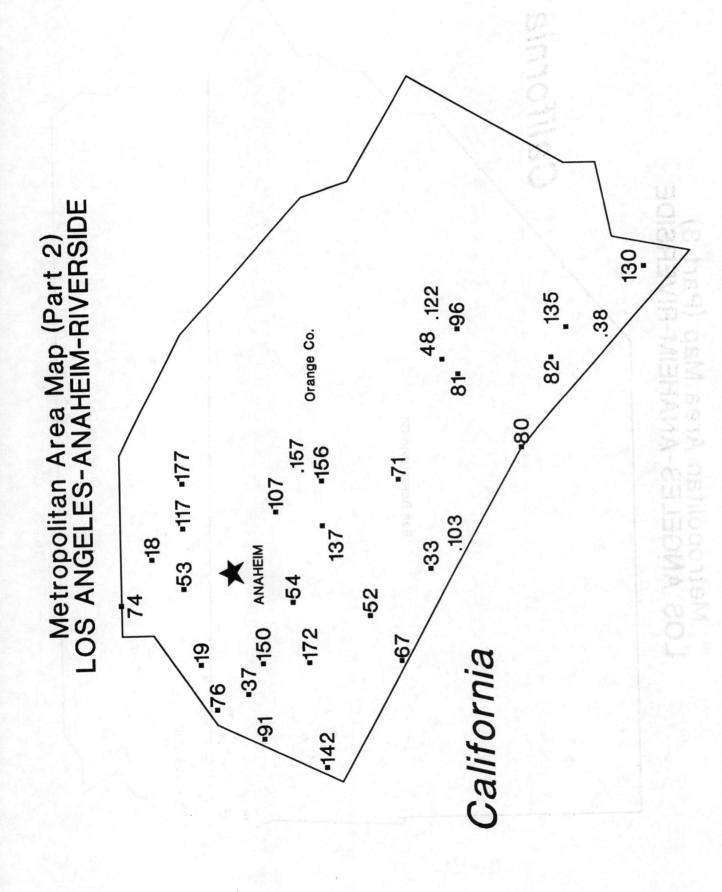

Orange Co.

ANAHEIM

California

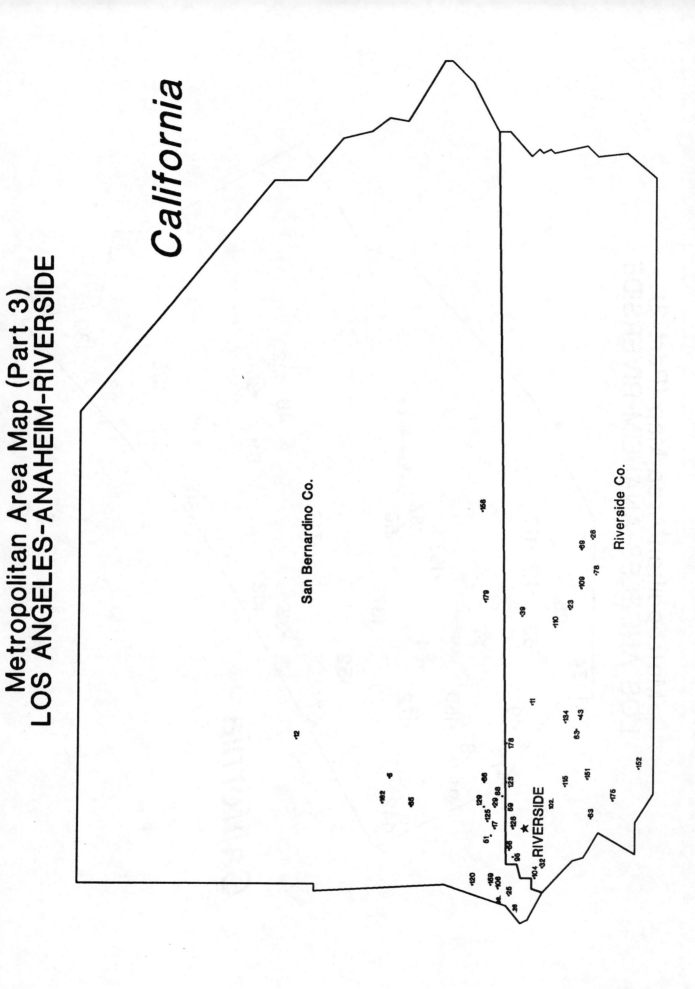

Metropolitan Area Map (Part 3)
LOS ANGELES-ANAHEIM-RIVERSIDE

California

San Bernardino Co.

Riverside Co.

RIVERSIDE

Metropolitan Area Suburb Alphabetical Index
LOS ANGELES-ANAHEIM-RIVERSIDE

SUBURB	PAGE	MAP NO.	STATE	COUNTY	POPU-LATION	RANK
AGOURA HILLS	317	1	California	Los Angeles	20,390	25 / 179
ALHAMBRA	336	2	California	Los Angeles	82,106	83 / 179
ALONDRA PARK	334	3	California	Los Angeles	12,215	77 / 179
ALTADENA	315	4	California	Los Angeles	42,658	19 / 179
APPLE VALLEY	330	5	California	San Bernardino	46,079	65 / 179
ARCADIA	314	6	California	Los Angeles	48,290	17 / 179
ARTESIA	340	7	California	Los Angeles	15,464	94 / 179
AVOCADO HEIGHTS	339	8	California	Los Angeles	14,232	91 / 179
AZUSA	341	9	California	Los Angeles	41,333	97 / 179
BALDWIN PARK	343	10	California	Los Angeles	69,330	105 / 179
BANNING	349	11	California	Riverside	20,570	121 / 179
BARSTOW	335	12	California	San Bernardino	21,472	80 / 179
BELL	363	13	California	Los Angeles	34,365	165 / 179
BELL GARDENS	364	14	California	Los Angeles	42,355	167 / 179
BELLFLOWER	352	15	California	Los Angeles	61,815	132 / 179
BEVERLY HILLS	321	16	California	Los Angeles	31,971	39 / 179
BLOOMINGTON	358	17	California	San Bernardino	15,116	150 / 179
BREA	318	18	California	Orange	32,873	28 / 179
BUENA PARK	337	19	California	Orange	68,784	85 / 179
BURBANK	322	20	California	Los Angeles	93,643	40 / 179
CAMARILLO	314	21	California	Ventura	52,303	16 / 179
CARSON	320	22	California	Los Angeles	83,995	34 / 179
CATHEDRAL CITY	341	23	California	Riverside	30,085	98 / 179
CERRITOS	318	24	California	Los Angeles	53,240	29 / 179
CHINO	343	25	California	San Bernardino	59,682	103 / 179
CHINO HILLS	358	26	California	San Bernardino	27,608	149 / 179
CLAREMONT	310	27	California	Los Angeles	32,503	5 / 179
COACHELLA	338	28	California	Riverside	16,896	89 / 179
COLTON	350	29	California	San Bernardino	40,213	126 / 179
COMMERCE	359	30	California	Los Angeles	12,135	153 / 179
COMPTON	360	31	California	Los Angeles	90,454	155 / 179
CORONA	354	32	California	Riverside	76,095	138 / 179
COSTA MESA	348	33	California	Orange	96,357	120 / 179
COVINA	325	34	California	Los Angeles	43,207	49 / 179
CUDAHY	367	35	California	Los Angeles	22,817	176 / 179
CULVER CITY	323	36	California	Los Angeles	38,793	45 / 179
CYPRESS	321	37	California	Orange	42,655	37 / 179
DANA POINT	330	38	California	Orange	31,896	66 / 179
DESERT HOT SPRINGS	362	39	California	Riverside	11,668	161 / 179
DIAMOND BAR	320	40	California	Los Angeles	53,672	35 / 179
DOWNEY	326	41	California	Los Angeles	91,444	53 / 179
DUARTE	318	42	California	Los Angeles	20,688	30 / 179
EAST HEMET	331	43	California	Riverside	17,611	69 / 179
EAST LOS ANGELES	354	44	California	Los Angeles	126,379	136 / 179
EAST SAN GABRIEL	329	45	California	Los Angeles	12,736	63 / 179
EL MONTE	362	46	California	Los Angeles	106,209	160 / 179
EL SEGUNDO	324	47	California	Los Angeles	15,223	46 / 179
EL TORO	341	48	California	Orange	62,685	99 / 179
FILLMORE	331	49	California	Ventura	11,992	68 / 179
FLORENCE-GRAHAM	366	50	California	Los Angeles	57,147	172 / 179
FONTANA	359	51	California	San Bernardino	87,535	150 / 179

Metropolitan Area Suburb Alphabetical Index
LOS ANGELES-ANAHEIM-RIVERSIDE

SUBURB	PAGE	MAP NO.	STATE	COUNTY	POPU-LATION	RANK
FOUNTAIN VALLEY	312	52	California	Orange	53,691	11 / 179
FULLERTON	329	53	California	Orange	114,144	61 / 179
GARDEN GROVE	342	54	California	Orange	143,050	102 / 179
GARDENA	350	55	California	Los Angeles	49,847	125 / 179
GLEN AVON	360	56	California	Riverside	12,663	154 / 179
GLENDALE	340	57	California	Los Angeles	180,038	95 / 179
GLENDORA	312	58	California	Los Angeles	47,828	10 / 179
GRAND TERRACE	311	59	California	San Bernardino	10,946	9 / 179
HACIENDA HEIGHTS	327	60	California	Los Angeles	52,354	55 / 179
HAWAIIAN GARDENS	367	61	California	Los Angeles	13,639	177 / 179
HAWTHORNE	362	62	California	Los Angeles	71,349	162 / 179
HEMET	356	63	California	Riverside	36,094	144 / 179
HERMOSA BEACH	347	64	California	Los Angeles	18,219	115 / 179
HESPERIA	342	65	California	San Bernardino	50,418	101 / 179
HIGHLAND	337	66	California	San Bernardino	34,439	86 / 179
HUNTINGTON BEACH	327	67	California	Orange	181,519	57 / 179
HUNTINGTON PARK	364	68	California	Los Angeles	56,065	166 / 179
INDIO	352	69	California	Riverside	36,793	131 / 179
INGLEWOOD	359	70	California	Los Angeles	109,602	152 / 179
IRVINE	315	71	California	Orange	110,330	20 / 179
LA CANADA-FLINTRIDGE	309	72	California	Los Angeles	19,378	3 / 179
LA CRESCENTA-MONTROSE	326	73	California	Los Angeles	16,968	52 / 179
LA HABRA	333	74	California	Orange	51,266	75 / 179
LA MIRADA	313	75	California	Los Angeles	40,452	14 / 179
LA PALMA	319	76	California	Orange	15,392	33 / 179
LA PUENTE	348	77	California	Los Angeles	36,955	119 / 179
LA QUINTA	328	78	California	Riverside	11,215	59 / 179
LA VERNE	312	79	California	Los Angeles	30,897	12 / 179
LAGUNA BEACH	323	80	California	Orange	23,170	44 / 179
LAGUNA HILLS	345	81	California	Orange	46,731	110 / 179
LAGUNA NIGUEL	325	82	California	Orange	44,400	50 / 179
LAKE ELSINORE	368	83	California	Riverside	18,285	179 / 179
LAKEWOOD	321	84	California	Los Angeles	73,557	37 / 179
LANCASTER	336	85	California	Los Angeles	97,291	82 / 179
LAWNDALE	361	86	California	Los Angeles	27,331	158 / 179
LENNOX	368	87	California	Los Angeles	22,757	178 / 179
LOMA LINDA	320	88	California	San Bernardino	17,400	36 / 179
LOMITA	349	89	California	Los Angeles	19,382	123 / 179
LONG BEACH	357	90	California	Los Angeles	429,433	145 / 179
LOS ALAMITOS	327	91	California	Orange	11,676	56 / 179
LYNWOOD	364	92	California	Los Angeles	61,945	168 / 179
MANHATTAN BEACH	322	93	California	Los Angeles	32,063	42 / 179
MAYWOOD	365	94	California	Los Angeles	27,850	171 / 179
MIRA LOMA	351	95	California	Riverside	15,786	127 / 179
MISSION VIEJO	316	96	California	Orange	72,820	23 / 179
MONROVIA	338	97	California	Los Angeles	35,761	88 / 179
MONTCLAIR	365	98	California	San Bernardino	28,434	170 / 179
MONTEBELLO	329	99	California	Los Angeles	59,564	62 / 179
MONTEREY PARK	333	100	California	Los Angeles	60,738	74 / 179
MOORPARK	335	101	California	Ventura	25,494	81 / 179
MORENO VALLEY	357	102	California	Riverside	118,779	146 / 179

Metropolitan Area Suburb Alphabetical Index
LOS ANGELES-ANAHEIM-RIVERSIDE

SUBURB	PAGE	MAP. NO.	STATE	COUNTY	POPU-LATION	RANK
NEWPORT BEACH	328	103	California	Orange	66,643	60 / 179
NORCO	331	104	California	Riverside	23,302	66 / 179
NORWALK	344	105	California	Los Angeles	94,279	106 / 179
ONTARIO	361	106	California	San Bernardino	133,179	159 / 179
ORANGE	326	107	California	Orange	110,658	54 / 179
OXNARD	347	108	California	Ventura	142,216	117 / 179
PALM DESERT	338	109	California	Riverside	23,252	90 / 179
PALM SPRINGS	339	110	California	Riverside	40,181	93 / 179
PALMDALE	353	111	California	Los Angeles	68,842	134 / 179
PALOS VERDES ESTATES	309	112	California	Los Angeles	13,512	2 / 179
PARAMOUNT	363	113	California	Los Angeles	47,669	164 / 179
PASADENA	333	114	California	Los Angeles	131,591	73 / 179
PERRIS	367	115	California	Riverside	21,460	175 / 179
PICO RIVERA	335	116	California	Los Angeles	59,177	79 / 179
PLACENTIA	319	117	California	Orange	41,259	31 / 179
POMONA	357	118	California	Los Angeles	131,723	147 / 179
PORT HUENEME	336	119	California	Ventura	20,319	84 / 179
RANCHO CUCAMONGA	332	120	California	San Bernardino	101,409	72 / 179
RANCHO PALOS VERDES	310	121	California	Los Angeles	41,659	6 / 179
RANCHO SANTA MARGARITA	355	122	California	Orange	11,390	139 / 179
REDLANDS	314	123	California	San Bernardino	60,394	18 / 179
REDONDO BEACH	344	124	California	Los Angeles	60,167	107 / 179
RIALTO	348	125	California	San Bernardino	72,388	118 / 179
ROSEMEAD	353	126	California	Los Angeles	51,638	133 / 179
ROWLAND HEIGHTS	342	127	California	Los Angeles	42,647	99 / 179
RUBIDOUX	355	128	California	Riverside	24,367	140 / 179
SAN BERNARDINO	355	129	California	San Bernardino	164,164	141 / 179
SAN CLEMENTE	332	130	California	Orange	41,100	70 / 179
SAN DIMAS	313	131	California	Los Angeles	32,397	15 / 179
SAN FERNANDO	346	132	California	Los Angeles	22,580	114 / 179
SAN GABRIEL	337	133	California	Los Angeles	37,120	87 / 179
SAN JACINTO	349	134	California	Riverside	16,210	122 / 179
SAN JUAN CAPISTRANO	322	135	California	Orange	26,183	41 / 179
SAN MARINO	309	136	California	Los Angeles	12,959	1 / 179
SANTA ANA	360	137	California	Orange	293,742	155 / 179
SANTA CLARITA	324	138	California	Los Angeles	110,642	47 / 179
SANTA FE SPRINGS	351	139	California	Los Angeles	15,520	129 / 179
SANTA MONICA	345	140	California	Los Angeles	86,905	111 / 179
SANTA PAULA	345	141	California	Ventura	25,062	109 / 179
SEAL BEACH	330	142	California	Orange	25,098	64 / 179
SIERRA MADRE	311	143	California	Los Angeles	10,762	7 / 179
SIMI VALLEY	325	144	California	Ventura	100,217	51 / 179
SOUTH EL MONTE	353	145	California	Los Angeles	20,850	134 / 179
SOUTH GATE	352	146	California	Los Angeles	86,284	130 / 179
SOUTH PASADENA	316	147	California	Los Angeles	23,936	24 / 179
SOUTH SAN JOSE HILLS	356	148	California	Los Angeles	17,814	143 / 179
SOUTH WHITTIER	346	149	California	Los Angeles	49,514	113 / 179
STANTON	361	150	California	Orange	30,491	157 / 179
SUN CITY	363	151	California	Riverside	14,930	163 / 179
TEMECULA	354	152	California	Riverside	27,099	137 / 179
TEMPLE CITY	315	153	California	Los Angeles	31,100	21 / 179

Metropolitan Area Suburb Alphabetical Index
LOS ANGELES-ANAHEIM-RIVERSIDE

SUBURB	PAGE	MAP NO.	STATE	COUNTY	POPU-LATION	RANK
THOUSAND OAKS	316	154	California	Ventura	104,352	22 / 179
TORRANCE	324	155	California	Los Angeles	133,107	48 / 179
TUSTIN	334	156	California	Orange	50,689	76 / 179
TUSTIN FOOTHILLS	310	157	California	Orange	24,358	4 / 179
TWENTY-NINE PALMS	344	158	California	San Bernardino	11,821	108 / 179
UPLAND	332	159	California	San Bernardino	63,374	71 / 179
VALINDA	346	160	California	Los Angeles	18,735	112 / 179
VENTURA	323	161	California	Ventura	92,575	43 / 179
VICTORVILLE	358	162	California	San Bernardino	40,674	148 / 179
VIEW PARK-WINDSOR HILLS	311	163	California	Los Angeles	11,769	8 / 179
VINCENT	340	164	California	Los Angeles	13,713	96 / 179
WALNUT	317	165	California	Los Angeles	29,105	27 / 179
WALNUT PARK	356	166	California	Los Angeles	14,722	142 / 179
WEST CARSON	343	167	California	Los Angeles	20,143	104 / 179
WEST COVINA	328	168	California	Los Angeles	96,086	58 / 179
WEST HOLLYWOOD	366	169	California	Los Angeles	36,118	174 / 179
WEST PUENTE VALLEY	347	170	California	Los Angeles	20,254	116 / 179
WEST WHITTIER-LOS NIETOS	334	171	California	Los Angeles	24,164	77 / 179
WESTMINSTER	339	172	California	Orange	78,118	91 / 179
WESTMONT	365	173	California	Los Angeles	31,044	169 / 179
WHITTIER	319	174	California	Los Angeles	77,671	32 / 179
WILDOMAR	366	175	California	Riverside	10,411	173 / 179
WILLOWBROOK	351	176	California	Los Angeles	32,772	128 / 179
YORBA LINDA	313	177	California	Orange	52,422	13 / 179
YUCAIPA	317	178	California	San Bernardino	32,824	26 / 179
YUCCA VALLEY	350	179	California	San Bernardino	13,701	124 / 179

Metropolitan Area Suburb Rankings
LOS ANGELES-ANAHEIM-RIVERSIDE

Composite: *Rank* 1 / 179 *Score* 72.80   **SAN MARINO**

CATEGORY	RANK	SCORE	STATISTIC	VALUE	RANK	SCORE
Economics	2	97.05	Median Household Income	$100,077	2	98.5
			% of Families Above Poverty Level	97.9%	12	95.6
Affordable Housing	176	0.00	Median Home Value	$500,001	172	0.0
			Median Rent	$1,001	175	0.0
Crime	12	91.90	Violent Crimes per 10,000 Population	31	14	92.4
			Property Crimes per 10,000 Population	265	11	91.4
Open Spaces	2	93.20	Population Density (Persons/Sq. Mile)	3441	70	86.4
			Average Rooms per Housing Unit	7.3	1	100.0
Education	2	98.05	% High School Enrollment/Completion	98.4%	3	98.2
			% College Graduates	61.5%	2	97.9
Commute	98	35.90	Average Work Commute in Minutes	24	43	65.4
			% Commuting on Public Transportation	1.0%	112	6.4
Community Stability	3	93.50	% Living in Same House as in 1979	58.1%	1	100.0
			% Living in Same County as in 1985	85.8%	52	87.0

Composite: *Rank* 2 / 179 *Score* 71.82   **PALOS VERDES ESTATES**

CATEGORY	RANK	SCORE	STATISTIC	VALUE	RANK	SCORE
Economics	1	98.75	Median Household Income	$101,320	1	100.0
			% of Families Above Poverty Level	98.5%	4	97.5
Affordable Housing	176	0.00	Median Home Value	$500,001	172	0.0
			Median Rent	$1,001	175	0.0
Crime	2	96.80	Violent Crimes per 10,000 Population	15	3	98.5
			Property Crimes per 10,000 Population	207	4	95.1
Open Spaces	1	93.30	Population Density (Persons/Sq. Mile)	2811	55	89.1
			Average Rooms per Housing Unit	7.2	2	97.5
Education	1	98.95	% High School Enrollment/Completion	98.3%	5	97.9
			% College Graduates	62.8%	1	100.0
Commute	156	22.10	Average Work Commute in Minutes	31	155	38.5
			% Commuting on Public Transportation	0.9%	119	5.7
Community Stability	5	92.85	% Living in Same House as in 1979	54.8%	4	94.3
			% Living in Same County as in 1985	88.7%	20	91.4

Composite: *Rank* 3 / 179 *Score* 70.00   **LA CANADA-FLINTRIDGE**

CATEGORY	RANK	SCORE	STATISTIC	VALUE	RANK	SCORE
Economics	4	84.70	Median Household Income	$78,965	4	72.9
			% of Families Above Poverty Level	98.2%	8	96.5
Affordable Housing	175	0.80	Median Home Value	$500,001	172	0.0
			Median Rent	$991	174	1.6
Crime	7	94.35	Violent Crimes per 10,000 Population	25	9	94.7
			Property Crimes per 10,000 Population	225	7	94.0
Open Spaces	4	88.25	Population Density (Persons/Sq. Mile)	2236	35	91.5
			Average Rooms per Housing Unit	6.7	4	85.0
Education	5	91.20	% High School Enrollment/Completion	97.7%	8	96.1
			% College Graduates	54.4%	5	86.3
Commute	103	35.25	Average Work Commute in Minutes	23	26	69.2
			% Commuting on Public Transportation	0.2%	165	1.3
Community Stability	2	95.45	% Living in Same House as in 1979	56.3%	3	96.9
			% Living in Same County as in 1985	90.4%	13	94.0

Metropolitan Area Suburb Rankings
LOS ANGELES-ANAHEIM-RIVERSIDE

Composite: Rank 4 / 179 *Score* 67.32   **TUSTIN FOOTHILLS**

CATEGORY	RANK	SCORE	STATISTIC	VALUE	RANK	SCORE
Economics	5	81.10	Median Household Income	$74,347	5	67.3
			% of Families Above Poverty Level	97.7%	18	94.9
Affordable Housing	168	22.90	Median Home Value	$369,700	166	30.1
			Median Rent	$900	161	15.7
Crime	N/A	N/A	Violent Crimes per 10,000 Population	N/A	N/A	N/A
			Property Crimes per 10,000 Population	N/A	N/A	N/A
Open Spaces	3	91.60	Population Density (Persons/Sq. Mile)	3615	74	85.7
			Average Rooms per Housing Unit	7.2	2	97.5
Education	14	81.50	% High School Enrollment/Completion	96.0%	18	90.9
			% College Graduates	45.7%	13	72.1
Commute	100	35.85	Average Work Commute in Minutes	23	26	69.2
			% Commuting on Public Transportation	0.4%	155	2.5
Community Stability	6	90.95	% Living in Same House as in 1979	53.5%	5	92.1
			% Living in Same County as in 1985	87.6%	35	89.8

Composite: Rank 5 / 179 *Score* 67.18   **CLAREMONT**

CATEGORY	RANK	SCORE	STATISTIC	VALUE	RANK	SCORE
Economics	23	68.65	Median Household Income	$53,479	26	42.0
			% of Families Above Poverty Level	97.8%	14	95.3
Affordable Housing	116	51.85	Median Home Value	$251,800	127	57.3
			Median Rent	$702	101	46.4
Crime	34	83.45	Violent Crimes per 10,000 Population	41	25	88.6
			Property Crimes per 10,000 Population	467	65	78.3
Open Spaces	20	78.00	Population Density (Persons/Sq. Mile)	2953	60	88.5
			Average Rooms per Housing Unit	6.0	16	67.5
Education	8	87.20	% High School Enrollment/Completion	96.8%	14	93.4
			% College Graduates	51.2%	8	81.0
Commute	112	33.30	Average Work Commute in Minutes	25	62	61.5
			% Commuting on Public Transportation	0.8%	127	5.1
Community Stability	70	67.80	% Living in Same House as in 1979	39.2%	40	67.4
			% Living in Same County as in 1985	73.3%	117	68.2

Composite: Rank 6 / 179 *Score* 66.34   **RANCHO PALOS VERDES**

CATEGORY	RANK	SCORE	STATISTIC	VALUE	RANK	SCORE
Economics	3	84.90	Median Household Income	$79,797	3	73.9
			% of Families Above Poverty Level	98.0%	10	95.9
Affordable Housing	176	0.00	Median Home Value	$500,001	172	0.0
			Median Rent	$1,001	175	0.0
Crime	6	94.50	Violent Crimes per 10,000 Population	31	14	92.4
			Property Crimes per 10,000 Population	185	2	96.6
Open Spaces	9	82.75	Population Density (Persons/Sq. Mile)	3049	65	88.0
			Average Rooms per Housing Unit	6.4	7	77.5
Education	4	91.90	% High School Enrollment/Completion	98.6%	2	98.8
			% College Graduates	53.6%	6	85.0
Commute	151	23.70	Average Work Commute in Minutes	30	148	42.3
			% Commuting on Public Transportation	0.8%	127	5.1
Community Stability	14	86.65	% Living in Same House as in 1979	51.2%	7	88.1
			% Living in Same County as in 1985	84.6%	60	85.2

Metropolitan Area Suburb Rankings
LOS ANGELES-ANAHEIM-RIVERSIDE

SIERRA MADRE

Composite: Rank 7 / 179 Score 66.31

CATEGORY	RANK	SCORE	STATISTIC	VALUE	RANK	SCORE
Economics	41	63.10	Median Household Income	$46,502	45	33.5
			% of Families Above Poverty Level	97.0%	34	92.7
Affordable Housing	139	41.10	Median Home Value	$352,000	164	34.2
			Median Rent	$692	96	48.0
Crime	1	100.00	Violent Crimes per 10,000 Population	11	1	100.0
			Property Crimes per 10,000 Population	132	1	100.0
Open Spaces	48	69.15	Population Density (Persons/Sq. Mile)	3584	73	85.8
			Average Rooms per Housing Unit	5.4	47	52.5
Education	16	78.90	% High School Enrollment/Completion	97.4%	10	95.2
			% College Graduates	39.9%	19	62.6
Commute	107	34.25	Average Work Commute in Minutes	26	82	57.7
			% Commuting on Public Transportation	1.7%	88	10.8
Community Stability	37	77.65	% Living in Same House as in 1979	36.7%	47	63.0
			% Living in Same County as in 1985	89.3%	19	92.3

VIEW PARK-WINDSOR HILLS

Composite: Rank 8 / 179 Score 66.20

CATEGORY	RANK	SCORE	STATISTIC	VALUE	RANK	SCORE
Economics	34	64.90	Median Household Income	$48,419	38	35.8
			% of Families Above Poverty Level	97.4%	26	94.0
Affordable Housing	101	56.30	Median Home Value	$282,100	142	50.3
			Median Rent	$600	48	62.3
Crime	N/A	N/A	Violent Crimes per 10,000 Population	N/A	N/A	N/A
			Property Crimes per 10,000 Population	N/A	N/A	N/A
Open Spaces	38	71.85	Population Density (Persons/Sq. Mile)	6450	115	73.7
			Average Rooms per Housing Unit	6.1	12	70.0
Education	42	62.80	% High School Enrollment/Completion	88.2%	76	67.4
			% College Graduates	37.2%	23	58.2
Commute	59	41.60	Average Work Commute in Minutes	26	82	57.7
			% Commuting on Public Transportation	4.0%	38	25.5
Community Stability	1	99.75	% Living in Same House as in 1979	57.8%	2	99.5
			% Living in Same County as in 1985	94.4%	1	100.0

GRAND TERRACE

Composite: Rank 9 / 179 Score 63.82

CATEGORY	RANK	SCORE	STATISTIC	VALUE	RANK	SCORE
Economics	47	62.10	Median Household Income	$45,127	55	31.8
			% of Families Above Poverty Level	96.9%	36	92.4
Affordable Housing	52	70.15	Median Home Value	$135,700	35	84.1
			Median Rent	$639	69	56.2
Crime	26	85.90	Violent Crimes per 10,000 Population	34	16	91.3
			Property Crimes per 10,000 Population	432	52	80.5
Open Spaces	32	73.80	Population Density (Persons/Sq. Mile)	3156	66	87.6
			Average Rooms per Housing Unit	5.7	29	60.0
Education	60	56.10	% High School Enrollment/Completion	89.4%	67	71.0
			% College Graduates	26.8%	58	41.2
Commute	74	38.80	Average Work Commute in Minutes	22	19	73.1
			% Commuting on Public Transportation	0.7%	136	4.5
Community Stability	104	59.90	% Living in Same House as in 1979	31.8%	75	54.6
			% Living in Same County as in 1985	71.3%	132	65.2

Metropolitan Area Suburb Rankings
LOS ANGELES-ANAHEIM-RIVERSIDE

Composite: *Rank* 10 / 179 *Score* 63.64   **GLENDORA**

CATEGORY	RANK	SCORE	STATISTIC	VALUE	RANK	SCORE
Economics	51	61.75	Median Household Income	$46,116	52	33.0
			% of Families Above Poverty Level	96.3%	49	90.5
Affordable Housing	115	52.15	Median Home Value	$231,000	110	62.1
			Median Rent	$729	118	42.2
Crime	19	88.50	Violent Crimes per 10,000 Population	41	25	88.6
			Property Crimes per 10,000 Population	310	26	88.4
Open Spaces	31	74.00	Population Density (Persons/Sq. Mile)	2457	39	90.5
			Average Rooms per Housing Unit	5.6	37	57.5
Education	54	58.25	% High School Enrollment/Completion	93.3%	37	82.8
			% College Graduates	22.2%	73	33.7
Commute	128	29.45	Average Work Commute in Minutes	28	116	50.0
			% Commuting on Public Transportation	1.4%	94	8.9
Community Stability	23	81.40	% Living in Same House as in 1979	40.4%	30	69.4
			% Living in Same County as in 1985	90.0%	15	93.4

Composite: *Rank* 11 / 179 *Score* 62.69   **FOUNTAIN VALLEY**

CATEGORY	RANK	SCORE	STATISTIC	VALUE	RANK	SCORE
Economics	18	70.30	Median Household Income	$56,255	20	45.3
			% of Families Above Poverty Level	97.8%	14	95.3
Affordable Housing	154	33.10	Median Home Value	$286,300	144	49.4
			Median Rent	$893	157	16.8
Crime	42	82.40	Violent Crimes per 10,000 Population	37	20	90.2
			Property Crimes per 10,000 Population	523	82	74.6
Open Spaces	34	72.75	Population Density (Persons/Sq. Mile)	6023	108	75.5
			Average Rooms per Housing Unit	6.1	12	70.0
Education	26	71.10	% High School Enrollment/Completion	96.9%	12	93.7
			% College Graduates	31.3%	42	48.5
Commute	119	32.05	Average Work Commute in Minutes	26	82	57.7
			% Commuting on Public Transportation	1.0%	112	6.4
Community Stability	40	77.10	% Living in Same House as in 1979	42.6%	23	73.2
			% Living in Same County as in 1985	81.8%	84	81.0

Composite: *Rank* 12 / 179 *Score* 62.64   **LA VERNE**

CATEGORY	RANK	SCORE	STATISTIC	VALUE	RANK	SCORE
Economics	42	63.00	Median Household Income	$46,587	43	33.6
			% of Families Above Poverty Level	96.9%	36	92.4
Affordable Housing	109	53.80	Median Home Value	$253,200	130	57.0
			Median Rent	$675	88	50.6
Crime	23	86.75	Violent Crimes per 10,000 Population	41	25	88.6
			Property Crimes per 10,000 Population	364	34	84.9
Open Spaces	37	72.10	Population Density (Persons/Sq. Mile)	3965	76	84.2
			Average Rooms per Housing Unit	5.7	29	60.0
Education	39	64.20	% High School Enrollment/Completion	94.6%	26	86.7
			% College Graduates	27.1%	57	41.7
Commute	133	28.85	Average Work Commute in Minutes	29	137	46.2
			% Commuting on Public Transportation	1.8%	82	11.5
Community Stability	66	69.80	% Living in Same House as in 1979	29.4%	90	50.4
			% Living in Same County as in 1985	87.2%	44	89.2

Metropolitan Area Suburb Rankings
LOS ANGELES-ANAHEIM-RIVERSIDE

Composite: *Rank* 13 / 179 *Score* 62.49 **YORBA LINDA**

CATEGORY	RANK	SCORE	STATISTIC	VALUE	RANK	SCORE
Economics	7	78.75	Median Household Income	$67,892	7	59.4
			% of Families Above Poverty Level	98.7%	3	98.1
Affordable Housing	166	26.70	Median Home Value	$324,800	156	40.5
			Median Rent	$918	165	12.9
Crime	3	96.05	Violent Crimes per 10,000 Population	17	4	97.7
			Property Crimes per 10,000 Population	218	6	94.4
Open Spaces	6	85.40	Population Density (Persons/Sq. Mile)	2994	62	88.3
			Average Rooms per Housing Unit	6.6	5	82.5
Education	24	71.80	% High School Enrollment/Completion	94.3%	29	85.8
			% College Graduates	37.0%	24	57.8
Commute	154	22.40	Average Work Commute in Minutes	30	148	42.3
			% Commuting on Public Transportation	0.4%	155	2.5
Community Stability	122	56.35	% Living in Same House as in 1979	22.5%	139	38.5
			% Living in Same County as in 1985	77.3%	97	74.2

Composite: *Rank* 14 / 179 *Score* 62.36 **LA MIRADA**

CATEGORY	RANK	SCORE	STATISTIC	VALUE	RANK	SCORE
Economics	36	64.45	Median Household Income	$47,143	42	34.3
			% of Families Above Poverty Level	97.6%	21	94.6
Affordable Housing	122	49.95	Median Home Value	$208,500	97	67.3
			Median Rent	$791	132	32.6
Crime	34	83.45	Violent Crimes per 10,000 Population	70	70	77.7
			Property Crimes per 10,000 Population	298	22	89.2
Open Spaces	58	68.35	Population Density (Persons/Sq. Mile)	5152	94	79.2
			Average Rooms per Housing Unit	5.6	37	57.5
Education	64	55.25	% High School Enrollment/Completion	93.7%	34	84.0
			% College Graduates	17.8%	89	26.5
Commute	122	31.40	Average Work Commute in Minutes	26	82	57.7
			% Commuting on Public Transportation	0.8%	127	5.1
Community Stability	18	83.70	% Living in Same House as in 1979	48.3%	10	83.1
			% Living in Same County as in 1985	84.0%	63	84.3

Composite: *Rank* 15 / 179 *Score* 62.15 **SAN DIMAS**

CATEGORY	RANK	SCORE	STATISTIC	VALUE	RANK	SCORE
Economics	38	64.30	Median Household Income	$50,268	37	38.1
			% of Families Above Poverty Level	96.3%	49	90.5
Affordable Housing	123	49.80	Median Home Value	$241,000	121	59.8
			Median Rent	$745	123	39.8
Crime	40	82.75	Violent Crimes per 10,000 Population	68	67	78.4
			Property Crimes per 10,000 Population	331	28	87.1
Open Spaces	18	78.55	Population Density (Persons/Sq. Mile)	2088	31	92.1
			Average Rooms per Housing Unit	5.9	24	65.0
Education	43	62.05	% High School Enrollment/Completion	93.4%	36	83.1
			% College Graduates	26.7%	59	41.0
Commute	142	27.55	Average Work Commute in Minutes	29	137	46.2
			% Commuting on Public Transportation	1.4%	94	8.9
Community Stability	64	70.05	% Living in Same House as in 1979	30.2%	84	51.8
			% Living in Same County as in 1985	86.6%	48	88.3

Metropolitan Area Suburb Rankings
LOS ANGELES-ANAHEIM-RIVERSIDE

Composite: *Rank* 16 / 179 *Score* 61.70   **CAMARILLO**

CATEGORY	RANK	SCORE	STATISTIC	VALUE	RANK	SCORE
Economics	33	64.95	Median Household Income	$48,219	39	35.6
			% of Families Above Poverty Level	97.5%	23	94.3
Affordable Housing	138	41.15	Median Home Value	$248,500	125	58.1
			Median Rent	$845	147	24.2
Crime	9	92.80	Violent Crimes per 10,000 Population	20	5	96.6
			Property Crimes per 10,000 Population	302	24	89.0
Open Spaces	29	74.45	Population Density (Persons/Sq. Mile)	2836	56	88.9
			Average Rooms per Housing Unit	5.7	29	60.0
Education	51	59.85	% High School Enrollment/Completion	91.7%	45	77.9
			% College Graduates	27.2%	56	41.8
Commute	73	39.10	Average Work Commute in Minutes	21	13	76.9
			% Commuting on Public Transportation	0.2%	165	1.3
Community Stability	107	59.60	% Living in Same House as in 1979	28.2%	100	48.4
			% Living in Same County as in 1985	75.0%	110	70.8

Composite: *Rank* 17 / 179 *Score* 61.62   **ARCADIA**

CATEGORY	RANK	SCORE	STATISTIC	VALUE	RANK	SCORE
Economics	43	62.80	Median Household Income	$47,347	40	34.5
			% of Families Above Poverty Level	96.5%	44	91.1
Affordable Housing	163	29.20	Median Home Value	$438,800	170	14.1
			Median Rent	$716	110	44.3
Crime	31	84.05	Violent Crimes per 10,000 Population	49	41	85.6
			Property Crimes per 10,000 Population	401	42	82.5
Open Spaces	56	68.60	Population Density (Persons/Sq. Mile)	4438	81	82.2
			Average Rooms per Housing Unit	5.5	41	55.0
Education	21	74.05	% High School Enrollment/Completion	96.1%	17	91.2
			% College Graduates	36.4%	27	56.9
Commute	91	36.50	Average Work Commute in Minutes	25	62	61.5
			% Commuting on Public Transportation	1.8%	82	11.5
Community Stability	41	76.15	% Living in Same House as in 1979	40.7%	26	69.9
			% Living in Same County as in 1985	82.7%	76	82.4

Composite: *Rank* 18 / 179 *Score* 61.54   **REDLANDS**

CATEGORY	RANK	SCORE	STATISTIC	VALUE	RANK	SCORE
Economics	92	52.00	Median Household Income	$37,073	96	22.0
			% of Families Above Poverty Level	93.6%	87	82.0
Affordable Housing	41	73.25	Median Home Value	$143,300	43	82.4
			Median Rent	$588	43	64.1
Crime	56	79.30	Violent Crimes per 10,000 Population	64	57	79.9
			Property Crimes per 10,000 Population	460	58	78.7
Open Spaces	39	71.45	Population Density (Persons/Sq. Mile)	2485	41	90.4
			Average Rooms per Housing Unit	5.4	47	52.5
Education	49	59.90	% High School Enrollment/Completion	89.5%	64	71.3
			% College Graduates	31.3%	42	48.5
Commute	71	39.70	Average Work Commute in Minutes	21	13	76.9
			% Commuting on Public Transportation	0.4%	155	2.5
Community Stability	126	55.20	% Living in Same House as in 1979	27.1%	106	46.5
			% Living in Same County as in 1985	70.4%	135	63.9

Metropolitan Area Suburb Rankings
LOS ANGELES-ANAHEIM-RIVERSIDE

Composite: *Rank* 19 / 179 *Score* 61.52   **ALTADENA**

CATEGORY	RANK	SCORE	STATISTIC	VALUE	RANK	SCORE
Economics	77	54.80	Median Household Income	$44,072	59	30.5
			% of Families Above Poverty Level	92.7%	97	79.1
Affordable Housing	104	55.10	Median Home Value	$238,500	118	60.4
			Median Rent	$680	91	49.8
Crime	N/A	N/A	Violent Crimes per 10,000 Population	N/A	N/A	N/A
			Property Crimes per 10,000 Population	N/A	N/A	N/A
Open Spaces	54	68.85	Population Density (Persons/Sq. Mile)	4909	92	80.2
			Average Rooms per Housing Unit	5.6	37	57.5
Education	45	61.55	% High School Enrollment/Completion	89.5%	64	71.3
			% College Graduates	33.3%	35	51.8
Commute	55	42.55	Average Work Commute in Minutes	26	82	57.7
			% Commuting on Public Transportation	4.3%	35	27.4
Community Stability	15	86.25	% Living in Same House as in 1979	46.0%	16	79.1
			% Living in Same County as in 1985	90.0%	15	93.4

Composite: *Rank* 20 / 179 *Score* 61.48   **IRVINE**

CATEGORY	RANK	SCORE	STATISTIC	VALUE	RANK	SCORE
Economics	20	69.70	Median Household Income	$56,307	19	45.4
			% of Families Above Poverty Level	97.4%	26	94.0
Affordable Housing	161	29.85	Median Home Value	$292,600	146	47.9
			Median Rent	$925	167	11.8
Crime	15	90.35	Violent Crimes per 10,000 Population	12	2	99.6
			Property Crimes per 10,000 Population	424	48	81.1
Open Spaces	40	71.20	Population Density (Persons/Sq. Mile)	2607	45	89.9
			Average Rooms per Housing Unit	5.4	47	52.5
Education	6	90.80	% High School Enrollment/Completion	98.3%	5	97.9
			% College Graduates	52.8%	7	83.7
Commute	91	36.50	Average Work Commute in Minutes	23	26	69.2
			% Commuting on Public Transportation	0.6%	141	3.8
Community Stability	161	41.95	% Living in Same House as in 1979	16.2%	164	27.6
			% Living in Same County as in 1985	65.4%	149	56.3

Composite: *Rank* 21 / 179 *Score* 61.25   **TEMPLE CITY**

CATEGORY	RANK	SCORE	STATISTIC	VALUE	RANK	SCORE
Economics	64	57.15	Median Household Income	$38,789	86	24.1
			% of Families Above Poverty Level	96.2%	51	90.2
Affordable Housing	120	50.60	Median Home Value	$253,600	131	56.9
			Median Rent	$716	110	44.3
Crime	21	87.20	Violent Crimes per 10,000 Population	51	44	84.8
			Property Crimes per 10,000 Population	292	20	89.6
Open Spaces	117	55.35	Population Density (Persons/Sq. Mile)	7750	126	68.2
			Average Rooms per Housing Unit	5.0	79	42.5
Education	59	56.35	% High School Enrollment/Completion	92.2%	42	79.5
			% College Graduates	21.9%	74	33.2
Commute	80	38.40	Average Work Commute in Minutes	26	82	57.7
			% Commuting on Public Transportation	3.0%	57	19.1
Community Stability	18	83.70	% Living in Same House as in 1979	45.1%	19	77.5
			% Living in Same County as in 1985	87.7%	34	89.9

Metropolitan Area Suburb Rankings
LOS ANGELES-ANAHEIM-RIVERSIDE

Composite: Rank 22 / 179 *Score* 61.20   **THOUSAND OAKS**

CATEGORY	RANK	SCORE	STATISTIC	VALUE	RANK	SCORE
Economics	19	69.90	Median Household Income	$56,856	17	46.1
			% of Families Above Poverty Level	97.3%	29	93.7
Affordable Housing	157	31.50	Median Home Value	$295,800	148	47.2
			Median Rent	$899	160	15.8
Crime	11	92.00	Violent Crimes per 10,000 Population	27	10	93.9
			Property Crimes per 10,000 Population	285	17	90.1
Open Spaces	12	81.00	Population Density (Persons/Sq. Mile)	2106	32	92.0
			Average Rooms per Housing Unit	6.1	12	70.0
Education	26	71.10	% High School Enrollment/Completion	94.9%	25	87.6
			% College Graduates	35.0%	32	54.6
Commute	141	27.85	Average Work Commute in Minutes	27	104	53.8
			% Commuting on Public Transportation	0.3%	161	1.9
Community Stability	127	55.05	% Living in Same House as in 1979	29.3%	93	50.3
			% Living in Same County as in 1985	67.7%	144	59.8

Composite: Rank 23 / 179 *Score* 61.15   **MISSION VIEJO**

CATEGORY	RANK	SCORE	STATISTIC	VALUE	RANK	SCORE
Economics	9	75.10	Median Household Income	$61,058	11	51.1
			% of Families Above Poverty Level	99.0%	2	99.1
Affordable Housing	159	31.15	Median Home Value	$252,100	128	57.3
			Median Rent	$969	172	5.0
Crime	10	92.15	Violent Crimes per 10,000 Population	24	8	95.1
			Property Crimes per 10,000 Population	299	23	89.2
Open Spaces	22	76.65	Population Density (Persons/Sq. Mile)	4172	77	83.3
			Average Rooms per Housing Unit	6.1	12	70.0
Education	19	74.90	% High School Enrollment/Completion	95.2%	21	88.5
			% College Graduates	39.1%	20	61.3
Commute	149	25.00	Average Work Commute in Minutes	29	137	46.2
			% Commuting on Public Transportation	0.6%	141	3.8
Community Stability	138	53.10	% Living in Same House as in 1979	22.6%	138	38.7
			% Living in Same County as in 1985	72.8%	121	67.5

Composite: Rank 24 / 179 *Score* 61.14   **SOUTH PASADENA**

CATEGORY	RANK	SCORE	STATISTIC	VALUE	RANK	SCORE
Economics	57	60.40	Median Household Income	$43,043	62	29.3
			% of Families Above Poverty Level	96.6%	42	91.5
Affordable Housing	143	38.50	Median Home Value	$371,700	168	29.6
			Median Rent	$696	98	47.4
Crime	49	80.40	Violent Crimes per 10,000 Population	58	53	82.2
			Property Crimes per 10,000 Population	462	61	78.6
Open Spaces	114	55.75	Population Density (Persons/Sq. Mile)	6975	119	71.5
			Average Rooms per Housing Unit	4.9	89	40.0
Education	11	85.10	% High School Enrollment/Completion	96.6%	15	92.7
			% College Graduates	49.0%	10	77.5
Commute	79	38.45	Average Work Commute in Minutes	24	43	65.4
			% Commuting on Public Transportation	1.8%	82	11.5
Community Stability	67	69.35	% Living in Same House as in 1979	32.9%	70	56.5
			% Living in Same County as in 1985	82.6%	79	82.2

Metropolitan Area Suburb Rankings
LOS ANGELES-ANAHEIM-RIVERSIDE

Composite: Rank 25 / 179 Score 61.01 **AGOURA HILLS**

CATEGORY	RANK	SCORE	STATISTIC	VALUE	RANK	SCORE
Economics	6	78.70	Median Household Income	$70,919	6	63.1
			% of Families Above Poverty Level	97.5%	23	94.3
Affordable Housing	170	18.10	Median Home Value	$369,700	166	30.1
			Median Rent	$962	170	6.1
Crime	28	85.35	Violent Crimes per 10,000 Population	62	55	80.7
			Property Crimes per 10,000 Population	286	18	90.0
Open Spaces	5	86.45	Population Density (Persons/Sq. Mile)	2496	43	90.4
			Average Rooms per Housing Unit	6.6	5	82.5
Education	12	83.90	% High School Enrollment/Completion	98.4%	3	98.2
			% College Graduates	44.2%	15	69.6
Commute	158	21.15	Average Work Commute in Minutes	31	155	38.5
			% Commuting on Public Transportation	0.6%	141	3.8
Community Stability	135	53.45	% Living in Same House as in 1979	19.2%	155	32.8
			% Living in Same County as in 1985	77.2%	98	74.1

Composite: Rank 26 / 179 Score 60.32 **YUCAIPA**

CATEGORY	RANK	SCORE	STATISTIC	VALUE	RANK	SCORE
Economics	110	46.95	Median Household Income	$27,182	156	10.0
			% of Families Above Poverty Level	94.2%	79	83.9
Affordable Housing	19	81.10	Median Home Value	$125,000	27	86.6
			Median Rent	$514	19	75.6
Crime	20	87.70	Violent Crimes per 10,000 Population	36	19	90.5
			Property Crimes per 10,000 Population	364	34	84.9
Open Spaces	43	70.35	Population Density (Persons/Sq. Mile)	1238	19	95.7
			Average Rooms per Housing Unit	5.1	72	45.0
Education	91	44.15	% High School Enrollment/Completion	89.3%	68	70.7
			% College Graduates	12.4%	117	17.6
Commute	130	29.15	Average Work Commute in Minutes	26	82	57.7
			% Commuting on Public Transportation	0.1%	172	0.6
Community Stability	89	62.85	% Living in Same House as in 1979	31.6%	77	54.2
			% Living in Same County as in 1985	75.5%	108	71.5

Composite: Rank 27 / 179 Score 60.28 **WALNUT**

CATEGORY	RANK	SCORE	STATISTIC	VALUE	RANK	SCORE
Economics	10	73.60	Median Household Income	$64,333	9	55.1
			% of Families Above Poverty Level	96.8%	38	92.1
Affordable Housing	169	22.45	Median Home Value	$320,100	155	41.5
			Median Rent	$979	173	3.4
Crime	17	88.95	Violent Crimes per 10,000 Population	48	40	86.0
			Property Crimes per 10,000 Population	257	10	91.9
Open Spaces	11	82.30	Population Density (Persons/Sq. Mile)	3284	67	87.1
			Average Rooms per Housing Unit	6.4	7	77.5
Education	17	77.35	% High School Enrollment/Completion	99.0%	1	100.0
			% College Graduates	35.1%	31	54.7
Commute	162	18.85	Average Work Commute in Minutes	34	167	26.9
			% Commuting on Public Transportation	1.7%	88	10.8
Community Stability	116	58.45	% Living in Same House as in 1979	18.1%	160	30.9
			% Living in Same County as in 1985	85.1%	57	86.0

Metropolitan Area Suburb Rankings
LOS ANGELES-ANAHEIM-RIVERSIDE

Composite: *Rank* 28 / 179 *Score* 60.21   **BREA**

CATEGORY	RANK	SCORE	STATISTIC	VALUE	RANK	SCORE
Economics	25	68.05	Median Household Income	$51,253	32	39.3
			% of Families Above Poverty Level	98.3%	7	96.8
Affordable Housing	129	46.80	Median Home Value	$263,900	137	54.5
			Median Rent	$749	126	39.1
Crime	52	79.75	Violent Crimes per 10,000 Population	39	23	89.4
			Property Crimes per 10,000 Population	592	95	70.1
Open Spaces	44	69.75	Population Density (Persons/Sq. Mile)	3292	68	87.0
			Average Rooms per Housing Unit	5.4	47	52.5
Education	41	62.95	% High School Enrollment/Completion	91.7%	45	77.9
			% College Graduates	31.0%	47	48.0
Commute	112	33.30	Average Work Commute in Minutes	25	62	61.5
			% Commuting on Public Transportation	0.8%	127	5.1
Community Stability	101	60.85	% Living in Same House as in 1979	29.0%	96	49.7
			% Living in Same County as in 1985	75.8%	106	72.0

Composite: *Rank* 29 / 179 *Score* 60.11   **CERRITOS**

CATEGORY	RANK	SCORE	STATISTIC	VALUE	RANK	SCORE
Economics	17	70.70	Median Household Income	$59,076	15	48.7
			% of Families Above Poverty Level	97.0%	34	92.7
Affordable Housing	167	23.35	Median Home Value	$297,600	150	46.7
			Median Rent	$1,001	175	0.0
Crime	88	70.45	Violent Crimes per 10,000 Population	80	79	73.9
			Property Crimes per 10,000 Population	640	110	67.0
Open Spaces	41	71.15	Population Density (Persons/Sq. Mile)	6182	109	74.8
			Average Rooms per Housing Unit	6.0	16	67.5
Education	18	74.95	% High School Enrollment/Completion	96.4%	16	92.1
			% College Graduates	37.0%	24	57.8
Commute	138	28.20	Average Work Commute in Minutes	28	116	50.0
			% Commuting on Public Transportation	1.0%	112	6.4
Community Stability	22	81.95	% Living in Same House as in 1979	45.5%	18	78.2
			% Living in Same County as in 1985	84.9%	58	85.7

Composite: *Rank* 30 / 179 *Score* 60.08   **DUARTE**

CATEGORY	RANK	SCORE	STATISTIC	VALUE	RANK	SCORE
Economics	89	52.40	Median Household Income	$37,695	93	22.8
			% of Families Above Poverty Level	93.6%	87	82.0
Affordable Housing	65	64.05	Median Home Value	$171,300	71	75.9
			Median Rent	$665	86	52.2
Crime	54	79.60	Violent Crimes per 10,000 Population	83	83	72.7
			Property Crimes per 10,000 Population	340	31	86.5
Open Spaces	85	63.15	Population Density (Persons/Sq. Mile)	2868	58	88.8
			Average Rooms per Housing Unit	4.8	101	37.5
Education	70	53.30	% High School Enrollment/Completion	90.0%	58	72.8
			% College Graduates	22.3%	72	33.8
Commute	87	37.40	Average Work Commute in Minutes	27	104	53.8
			% Commuting on Public Transportation	3.3%	50	21.0
Community Stability	61	70.65	% Living in Same House as in 1979	29.3%	93	50.3
			% Living in Same County as in 1985	88.4%	26	91.0

Metropolitan Area Suburb Rankings
LOS ANGELES-ANAHEIM-RIVERSIDE

Composite: *Rank* 31 / 179   *Score* 59.99   **PLACENTIA**

CATEGORY	RANK	SCORE	STATISTIC	VALUE	RANK	SCORE
Economics	46	62.35	Median Household Income	$50,945	35	38.9
			% of Families Above Poverty Level	94.8%	68	85.8
Affordable Housing	131	44.25	Median Home Value	$252,800	129	57.1
			Median Rent	$799	134	31.4
Crime	25	86.05	Violent Crimes per 10,000 Population	52	46	84.5
			Property Crimes per 10,000 Population	323	27	87.6
Open Spaces	64	67.25	Population Density (Persons/Sq. Mile)	6259	112	74.5
			Average Rooms per Housing Unit	5.7	29	60.0
Education	58	56.30	% High School Enrollment/Completion	87.7%	78	65.9
			% College Graduates	30.2%	48	46.7
Commute	88	37.15	Average Work Commute in Minutes	24	43	65.4
			% Commuting on Public Transportation	1.4%	94	8.9
Community Stability	72	66.60	% Living in Same House as in 1979	33.8%	63	58.0
			% Living in Same County as in 1985	77.9%	93	75.2

Composite: *Rank* 32 / 179   *Score* 59.93   **WHITTIER**

CATEGORY	RANK	SCORE	STATISTIC	VALUE	RANK	SCORE
Economics	82	54.00	Median Household Income	$38,020	91	23.2
			% of Families Above Poverty Level	94.5%	71	84.8
Affordable Housing	77	61.75	Median Home Value	$209,300	99	67.1
			Median Rent	$638	68	56.4
Crime	47	81.00	Violent Crimes per 10,000 Population	62	55	80.7
			Property Crimes per 10,000 Population	420	46	81.3
Open Spaces	103	58.60	Population Density (Persons/Sq. Mile)	6199	111	74.7
			Average Rooms per Housing Unit	5.0	79	42.5
Education	77	49.25	% High School Enrollment/Completion	88.1%	77	67.1
			% College Graduates	20.8%	81	31.4
Commute	96	36.15	Average Work Commute in Minutes	26	82	57.7
			% Commuting on Public Transportation	2.3%	73	14.6
Community Stability	32	78.75	% Living in Same House as in 1979	39.2%	40	67.4
			% Living in Same County as in 1985	87.8%	32	90.1

Composite: *Rank* 33 / 179   *Score* 59.90   **LA PALMA**

CATEGORY	RANK	SCORE	STATISTIC	VALUE	RANK	SCORE
Economics	35	64.70	Median Household Income	$54,364	23	43.0
			% of Families Above Poverty Level	95.0%	65	86.4
Affordable Housing	145	37.50	Median Home Value	$303,800	151	45.3
			Median Rent	$810	138	29.7
Crime	28	85.35	Violent Crimes per 10,000 Population	38	22	89.8
			Property Crimes per 10,000 Population	426	50	80.9
Open Spaces	70	66.35	Population Density (Persons/Sq. Mile)	8471	134	65.2
			Average Rooms per Housing Unit	6.0	16	67.5
Education	31	67.35	% High School Enrollment/Completion	94.3%	29	85.8
			% College Graduates	31.5%	40	48.9
Commute	130	29.15	Average Work Commute in Minutes	27	104	53.8
			% Commuting on Public Transportation	0.7%	136	4.5
Community Stability	68	68.90	% Living in Same House as in 1979	41.7%	24	71.7
			% Living in Same County as in 1985	71.9%	126	66.1

Metropolitan Area Suburb Rankings
LOS ANGELES-ANAHEIM-RIVERSIDE

Composite: **Rank** 34 / 179 *Score* 59.45   **CARSON**

CATEGORY	RANK	SCORE	STATISTIC	VALUE	RANK	SCORE
Economics	61	58.35	Median Household Income	$43,882	60	30.3
			% of Families Above Poverty Level	95.0%	65	86.4
Affordable Housing	93	57.90	Median Home Value	$186,800	81	72.3
			Median Rent	$721	115	43.5
Crime	105	64.70	Violent Crimes per 10,000 Population	138	117	51.9
			Property Crimes per 10,000 Population	478	69	77.5
Open Spaces	82	63.55	Population Density (Persons/Sq. Mile)	4458	82	82.1
			Average Rooms per Housing Unit	5.1	72	45.0
Education	92	43.60	% High School Enrollment/Completion	86.4%	88	61.9
			% College Graduates	17.1%	91	25.3
Commute	65	40.65	Average Work Commute in Minutes	24	43	65.4
			% Commuting on Public Transportation	2.5%	69	15.9
Community Stability	12	87.40	% Living in Same House as in 1979	46.8%	14	80.5
			% Living in Same County as in 1985	90.6%	12	94.3

Composite: **Rank** 35 / 179 *Score* 59.42   **DIAMOND BAR**

CATEGORY	RANK	SCORE	STATISTIC	VALUE	RANK	SCORE
Economics	12	72.65	Median Household Income	$60,651	12	50.7
			% of Families Above Poverty Level	97.6%	21	94.6
Affordable Housing	159	31.15	Median Home Value	$271,500	139	52.8
			Median Rent	$940	169	9.5
Crime	18	88.80	Violent Crimes per 10,000 Population	46	35	86.7
			Property Crimes per 10,000 Population	273	12	90.9
Open Spaces	15	79.20	Population Density (Persons/Sq. Mile)	3557	72	85.9
			Average Rooms per Housing Unit	6.2	9	72.5
Education	22	73.60	% High School Enrollment/Completion	95.5%	19	89.4
			% College Graduates	37.0%	24	57.8
Commute	167	16.30	Average Work Commute in Minutes	34	167	26.9
			% Commuting on Public Transportation	0.9%	119	5.7
Community Stability	132	54.25	% Living in Same House as in 1979	21.8%	143	37.3
			% Living in Same County as in 1985	75.3%	109	71.2

Composite: **Rank** 36 / 179 *Score* 59.39   **LOMA LINDA**

CATEGORY	RANK	SCORE	STATISTIC	VALUE	RANK	SCORE
Economics	119	44.80	Median Household Income	$33,265	118	17.4
			% of Families Above Poverty Level	90.5%	116	72.2
Affordable Housing	30	76.45	Median Home Value	$151,300	48	80.5
			Median Rent	$535	27	72.4
Crime	36	82.70	Violent Crimes per 10,000 Population	41	25	88.6
			Property Crimes per 10,000 Population	489	74	76.8
Open Spaces	80	63.95	Population Density (Persons/Sq. Mile)	2489	42	90.4
			Average Rooms per Housing Unit	4.8	101	37.5
Education	47	61.05	% High School Enrollment/Completion	84.3%	101	55.6
			% College Graduates	42.3%	17	66.5
Commute	32	48.40	Average Work Commute in Minutes	18	5	88.5
			% Commuting on Public Transportation	1.3%	98	8.3
Community Stability	164	38.40	% Living in Same House as in 1979	16.0%	165	27.3
			% Living in Same County as in 1985	60.9%	163	49.5

Metropolitan Area Suburb Rankings
LOS ANGELES-ANAHEIM-RIVERSIDE

Composite: *Rank* 37 / 179 *Score* 59.23   **CYPRESS**

CATEGORY	RANK	SCORE	STATISTIC	VALUE	RANK	SCORE
Economics	32	65.20	Median Household Income	$50,981	33	38.9
			% of Families Above Poverty Level	96.6%	42	91.5
Affordable Housing	135	43.55	Median Home Value	$250,800	126	57.6
			Median Rent	$811	141	29.5
Crime	41	82.50	Violent Crimes per 10,000 Population	44	29	87.5
			Property Crimes per 10,000 Population	478	69	77.5
Open Spaces	66	66.85	Population Density (Persons/Sq. Mile)	6447	114	73.7
			Average Rooms per Housing Unit	5.7	29	60.0
Education	53	59.20	% High School Enrollment/Completion	91.6%	48	77.6
			% College Graduates	26.6%	60	40.8
Commute	132	28.80	Average Work Commute in Minutes	27	104	53.8
			% Commuting on Public Transportation	0.6%	141	3.8
Community Stability	69	68.50	% Living in Same House as in 1979	40.2%	33	69.1
			% Living in Same County as in 1985	73.1%	119	67.9

Composite: *Rank* 37 / 179 *Score* 59.23   **LAKEWOOD**

CATEGORY	RANK	SCORE	STATISTIC	VALUE	RANK	SCORE
Economics	52	61.70	Median Household Income	$44,700	56	31.3
			% of Families Above Poverty Level	96.8%	38	92.1
Affordable Housing	124	48.55	Median Home Value	$213,500	101	66.2
			Median Rent	$802	136	30.9
Crime	87	70.75	Violent Crimes per 10,000 Population	106	97	64.0
			Property Crimes per 10,000 Population	478	69	77.5
Open Spaces	102	58.95	Population Density (Persons/Sq. Mile)	7830	129	67.9
			Average Rooms per Housing Unit	5.3	57	50.0
Education	68	53.65	% High School Enrollment/Completion	92.7%	38	81.0
			% College Graduates	17.7%	90	26.3
Commute	105	34.90	Average Work Commute in Minutes	25	62	61.5
			% Commuting on Public Transportation	1.3%	98	8.3
Community Stability	16	86.10	% Living in Same House as in 1979	47.7%	11	82.0
			% Living in Same County as in 1985	87.9%	29	90.2

Composite: *Rank* 39 / 179 *Score* 59.22   **BEVERLY HILLS**

CATEGORY	RANK	SCORE	STATISTIC	VALUE	RANK	SCORE
Economics	28	65.95	Median Household Income	$54,348	24	43.0
			% of Families Above Poverty Level	95.8%	56	88.9
Affordable Housing	173	5.90	Median Home Value	$500,001	172	0.0
			Median Rent	$925	167	11.8
Crime	102	65.45	Violent Crimes per 10,000 Population	92	86	69.3
			Property Crimes per 10,000 Population	724	126	61.6
Open Spaces	89	62.30	Population Density (Persons/Sq. Mile)	5632	101	77.1
			Average Rooms per Housing Unit	5.2	62	47.5
Education	10	85.75	% High School Enrollment/Completion	98.1%	7	97.3
			% College Graduates	47.0%	12	74.2
Commute	17	53.10	Average Work Commute in Minutes	21	13	76.9
			% Commuting on Public Transportation	4.6%	32	29.3
Community Stability	42	76.10	% Living in Same House as in 1979	40.6%	27	69.8
			% Living in Same County as in 1985	82.7%	76	82.4

Metropolitan Area Suburb Rankings
LOS ANGELES-ANAHEIM-RIVERSIDE

Composite: *Rank* 40 / 179 *Score* 59.05 **BURBANK**

CATEGORY	RANK	SCORE	STATISTIC	VALUE	RANK	SCORE
Economics	91	52.10	Median Household Income	$35,959	103	20.7
			% of Families Above Poverty Level	94.1%	81	83.5
Affordable Housing	113	52.85	Median Home Value	$260,200	135	55.4
			Median Rent	$677	90	50.3
Crime	44	81.75	Violent Crimes per 10,000 Population	56	50	83.0
			Property Crimes per 10,000 Population	432	52	80.5
Open Spaces	125	52.80	Population Density (Persons/Sq. Mile)	5398	99	78.1
			Average Rooms per Housing Unit	4.4	134	27.5
Education	61	55.60	% High School Enrollment/Completion	91.2%	49	76.4
			% College Graduates	22.9%	69	34.8
Commute	35	47.40	Average Work Commute in Minutes	22	19	73.1
			% Commuting on Public Transportation	3.4%	47	21.7
Community Stability	60	70.85	% Living in Same House as in 1979	33.6%	66	57.7
			% Living in Same County as in 1985	83.8%	65	84.0

Composite: *Rank* 41 / 179 *Score* 58.73 **SAN JUAN CAPISTRANO**

CATEGORY	RANK	SCORE	STATISTIC	VALUE	RANK	SCORE
Economics	44	62.50	Median Household Income	$46,250	50	33.2
			% of Families Above Poverty Level	96.7%	41	91.8
Affordable Housing	153	34.25	Median Home Value	$262,500	136	54.8
			Median Rent	$913	164	13.7
Crime	32	84.00	Violent Crimes per 10,000 Population	46	35	86.7
			Property Crimes per 10,000 Population	420	46	81.3
Open Spaces	23	76.60	Population Density (Persons/Sq. Mile)	1839	26	93.2
			Average Rooms per Housing Unit	5.7	29	60.0
Education	72	52.90	% High School Enrollment/Completion	86.6%	86	62.5
			% College Graduates	28.1%	54	43.3
Commute	59	41.60	Average Work Commute in Minutes	24	43	65.4
			% Commuting on Public Transportation	2.8%	61	17.8
Community Stability	111	59.25	% Living in Same House as in 1979	26.6%	109	45.6
			% Living in Same County as in 1985	76.4%	103	72.9

Composite: *Rank* 42 / 179 *Score* 58.67 **MANHATTAN BEACH**

CATEGORY	RANK	SCORE	STATISTIC	VALUE	RANK	SCORE
Economics	8	78.35	Median Household Income	$67,723	8	59.2
			% of Families Above Poverty Level	98.5%	4	97.5
Affordable Housing	176	0.00	Median Home Value	$500,001	172	0.0
			Median Rent	$1,001	175	0.0
Crime	63	77.85	Violent Crimes per 10,000 Population	49	41	85.6
			Property Crimes per 10,000 Population	593	96	70.1
Open Spaces	108	58.25	Population Density (Persons/Sq. Mile)	8154	132	66.5
			Average Rooms per Housing Unit	5.3	57	50.0
Education	3	92.35	% High School Enrollment/Completion	97.4%	10	95.2
			% College Graduates	56.4%	3	89.5
Commute	120	31.70	Average Work Commute in Minutes	26	82	57.7
			% Commuting on Public Transportation	0.9%	119	5.7
Community Stability	54	72.20	% Living in Same House as in 1979	36.1%	49	62.0
			% Living in Same County as in 1985	82.7%	76	82.4

Metropolitan Area Suburb Rankings
LOS ANGELES-ANAHEIM-RIVERSIDE

Composite: *Rank* 43 / 179   *Score* 58.65   **VENTURA**

CATEGORY	RANK	SCORE	STATISTIC	VALUE	RANK	SCORE
Economics	67	56.85	Median Household Income	$40,307	78	26.0
			% of Families Above Poverty Level	95.4%	61	87.7
Affordable Housing	117	51.60	Median Home Value	$240,300	120	60.0
			Median Rent	$723	116	43.2
Crime	50	79.95	Violent Crimes per 10,000 Population	45	32	87.1
			Property Crimes per 10,000 Population	551	87	72.8
Open Spaces	91	62.15	Population Density (Persons/Sq. Mile)	4517	84	81.8
			Average Rooms per Housing Unit	5.0	79	42.5
Education	66	54.15	% High School Enrollment/Completion	89.3%	68	70.7
			% College Graduates	24.6%	66	37.6
Commute	51	43.25	Average Work Commute in Minutes	20	8	80.8
			% Commuting on Public Transportation	0.9%	119	5.7
Community Stability	90	62.60	% Living in Same House as in 1979	29.4%	90	50.4
			% Living in Same County as in 1985	77.7%	94	74.8

Composite: *Rank* 44 / 179   *Score* 58.60   **LAGUNA BEACH**

CATEGORY	RANK	SCORE	STATISTIC	VALUE	RANK	SCORE
Economics	26	67.45	Median Household Income	$53,419	27	41.9
			% of Families Above Poverty Level	97.1%	33	93.0
Affordable Housing	172	13.70	Median Home Value	$463,200	171	8.5
			Median Rent	$879	155	18.9
Crime	48	80.90	Violent Crimes per 10,000 Population	49	41	85.6
			Property Crimes per 10,000 Population	498	77	76.2
Open Spaces	73	66.10	Population Density (Persons/Sq. Mile)	2668	47	89.7
			Average Rooms per Housing Unit	5.0	79	42.5
Education	9	86.80	% High School Enrollment/Completion	97.7%	8	96.1
			% College Graduates	49.0%	10	77.5
Commute	120	31.70	Average Work Commute in Minutes	28	116	50.0
			% Commuting on Public Transportation	2.1%	76	13.4
Community Stability	87	63.55	% Living in Same House as in 1979	31.6%	77	54.2
			% Living in Same County as in 1985	76.4%	103	72.9

Composite: *Rank* 45 / 179   *Score* 58.44   **CULVER CITY**

CATEGORY	RANK	SCORE	STATISTIC	VALUE	RANK	SCORE
Economics	60	58.45	Median Household Income	$42,971	63	29.2
			% of Families Above Poverty Level	95.4%	61	87.7
Affordable Housing	150	36.25	Median Home Value	$329,400	157	39.4
			Median Rent	$788	131	33.1
Crime	89	69.90	Violent Crimes per 10,000 Population	77	76	75.0
			Property Crimes per 10,000 Population	675	116	64.8
Open Spaces	137	48.15	Population Density (Persons/Sq. Mile)	7600	125	68.8
			Average Rooms per Housing Unit	4.4	134	27.5
Education	25	71.40	% High School Enrollment/Completion	95.1%	23	88.2
			% College Graduates	35.0%	32	54.6
Commute	25	50.90	Average Work Commute in Minutes	22	19	73.1
			% Commuting on Public Transportation	4.5%	33	28.7
Community Stability	50	74.00	% Living in Same House as in 1979	34.1%	61	58.5
			% Living in Same County as in 1985	87.4%	39	89.5

Metropolitan Area Suburb Rankings
LOS ANGELES-ANAHEIM-RIVERSIDE

Composite: *Rank* 46 / 179 *Score* 58.37   **EL SEGUNDO**

CATEGORY	RANK	SCORE	STATISTIC	VALUE	RANK	SCORE
Economics	40	63.50	Median Household Income	$46,352	49	33.3
			% of Families Above Poverty Level	97.3%	29	93.7
Affordable Housing	156	32.55	Median Home Value	$353,000	165	33.9
			Median Rent	$800	135	31.2
Crime	71	75.80	Violent Crimes per 10,000 Population	55	49	83.3
			Property Crimes per 10,000 Population	621	103	68.3
Open Spaces	94	60.90	Population Density (Persons/Sq. Mile)	2744	54	89.3
			Average Rooms per Housing Unit	4.6	118	32.5
Education	29	68.30	% High School Enrollment/Completion	94.4%	28	86.1
			% College Graduates	32.5%	36	50.5
Commute	39	46.80	Average Work Commute in Minutes	18	5	88.5
			% Commuting on Public Transportation	0.8%	127	5.1
Community Stability	103	60.75	% Living in Same House as in 1979	24.7%	121	42.3
			% Living in Same County as in 1985	80.6%	87	79.2

Composite: *Rank* 47 / 179 *Score* 58.30   **SANTA CLARITA**

CATEGORY	RANK	SCORE	STATISTIC	VALUE	RANK	SCORE
Economics	24	68.30	Median Household Income	$52,970	28	41.3
			% of Families Above Poverty Level	97.8%	14	95.3
Affordable Housing	132	44.10	Median Home Value	$231,500	111	62.0
			Median Rent	$832	146	26.2
Crime	33	83.60	Violent Crimes per 10,000 Population	72	72	76.9
			Property Crimes per 10,000 Population	281	15	90.3
Open Spaces	36	72.20	Population Density (Persons/Sq. Mile)	2733	53	89.4
			Average Rooms per Housing Unit	5.5	41	55.0
Education	49	59.90	% High School Enrollment/Completion	92.4%	39	80.1
			% College Graduates	25.9%	62	39.7
Commute	157	21.50	Average Work Commute in Minutes	31	155	38.5
			% Commuting on Public Transportation	0.7%	136	4.5
Community Stability	115	58.50	% Living in Same House as in 1979	20.5%	146	35.1
			% Living in Same County as in 1985	82.4%	83	81.9

Composite: *Rank* 48 / 179 *Score* 57.99   **TORRANCE**

CATEGORY	RANK	SCORE	STATISTIC	VALUE	RANK	SCORE
Economics	45	62.55	Median Household Income	$47,204	41	34.3
			% of Families Above Poverty Level	96.4%	46	90.8
Affordable Housing	152	34.65	Median Home Value	$338,700	159	37.3
			Median Rent	$795	133	32.0
Crime	70	76.30	Violent Crimes per 10,000 Population	70	70	77.7
			Property Crimes per 10,000 Population	519	81	74.9
Open Spaces	116	55.50	Population Density (Persons/Sq. Mile)	6486	117	73.5
			Average Rooms per Housing Unit	4.8	101	37.5
Education	32	66.95	% High School Enrollment/Completion	94.2%	32	85.5
			% College Graduates	31.2%	45	48.4
Commute	83	37.80	Average Work Commute in Minutes	24	43	65.4
			% Commuting on Public Transportation	1.6%	91	10.2
Community Stability	56	72.15	% Living in Same House as in 1979	36.2%	48	62.2
			% Living in Same County as in 1985	82.5%	80	82.1

Metropolitan Area Suburb Rankings
LOS ANGELES-ANAHEIM-RIVERSIDE

Composite: *Rank* 49 / 179 *Score* 57.91 **COVINA**

CATEGORY	RANK	SCORE	STATISTIC	VALUE	RANK	SCORE
Economics	78	54.85	Median Household Income	$38,907	85	24.3
			% of Families Above Poverty Level	94.7%	69	85.4
Affordable Housing	79	61.60	Median Home Value	$201,300	92	69.0
			Median Rent	$652	78	54.2
Crime	66	77.25	Violent Crimes per 10,000 Population	60	54	81.4
			Property Crimes per 10,000 Population	547	85	73.1
Open Spaces	104	58.50	Population Density (Persons/Sq. Mile)	6260	113	74.5
			Average Rooms per Housing Unit	5.0	79	42.5
Education	83	46.25	% High School Enrollment/Completion	88.5%	75	68.3
			% College Graduates	16.4%	93	24.2
Commute	116	32.35	Average Work Commute in Minutes	29	137	46.2
			% Commuting on Public Transportation	2.9%	60	18.5
Community Stability	48	74.60	% Living in Same House as in 1979	33.7%	64	57.9
			% Living in Same County as in 1985	88.6%	22	91.3

Composite: *Rank* 50 / 179 *Score* 57.82 **LAGUNA NIGUEL**

CATEGORY	RANK	SCORE	STATISTIC	VALUE	RANK	SCORE
Economics	11	73.50	Median Household Income	$61,501	10	51.7
			% of Families Above Poverty Level	97.8%	14	95.3
Affordable Housing	162	29.30	Median Home Value	$313,200	153	43.1
			Median Rent	$901	162	15.5
Crime	4	95.35	Violent Crimes per 10,000 Population	21	7	96.2
			Property Crimes per 10,000 Population	217	5	94.5
Open Spaces	25	76.55	Population Density (Persons/Sq. Mile)	3030	63	88.1
			Average Rooms per Housing Unit	5.9	24	65.0
Education	15	79.40	% High School Enrollment/Completion	95.2%	21	88.5
			% College Graduates	44.6%	14	70.3
Commute	165	17.00	Average Work Commute in Minutes	33	161	30.8
			% Commuting on Public Transportation	0.5%	146	3.2
Community Stability	168	33.65	% Living in Same House as in 1979	11.2%	172	19.0
			% Living in Same County as in 1985	60.1%	166	48.3

Composite: *Rank* 51 / 179 *Score* 57.81 **SIMI VALLEY**

CATEGORY	RANK	SCORE	STATISTIC	VALUE	RANK	SCORE
Economics	22	68.70	Median Household Income	$53,967	25	42.5
			% of Families Above Poverty Level	97.7%	18	94.9
Affordable Housing	142	39.05	Median Home Value	$232,200	114	61.8
			Median Rent	$896	158	16.3
Crime	14	91.25	Violent Crimes per 10,000 Population	27	10	93.9
			Property Crimes per 10,000 Population	307	25	88.6
Open Spaces	21	77.80	Population Density (Persons/Sq. Mile)	3034	64	88.1
			Average Rooms per Housing Unit	6.0	16	67.5
Education	67	53.70	% High School Enrollment/Completion	90.9%	53	75.5
			% College Graduates	21.1%	78	31.9
Commute	160	18.90	Average Work Commute in Minutes	32	159	34.6
			% Commuting on Public Transportation	0.5%	146	3.2
Community Stability	125	55.30	% Living in Same House as in 1979	27.2%	105	46.6
			% Living in Same County as in 1985	70.5%	134	64.0

Metropolitan Area Suburb Rankings
LOS ANGELES-ANAHEIM-RIVERSIDE

Composite: **Rank** 52 / 179 *Score* 57.63   **LA CRESCENTA-MONTROSE**

CATEGORY	RANK	SCORE	STATISTIC	VALUE	RANK	SCORE
Economics	55	60.95	Median Household Income	$46,365	48	33.3
			% of Families Above Poverty Level	95.7%	58	88.6
Affordable Housing	134	43.70	Median Home Value	$317,100	154	42.2
			Median Rent	$710	108	45.2
Crime	N/A	N/A	Violent Crimes per 10,000 Population	N/A	N/A	N/A
			Property Crimes per 10,000 Population	N/A	N/A	N/A
Open Spaces	81	63.60	Population Density (Persons/Sq. Mile)	5033	93	79.7
			Average Rooms per Housing Unit	5.2	62	47.5
Education	44	61.70	% High School Enrollment/Completion	90.7%	54	74.9
			% College Graduates	31.3%	42	48.5
Commute	95	36.20	Average Work Commute in Minutes	24	43	65.4
			% Commuting on Public Transportation	1.1%	106	7.0
Community Stability	27	79.65	% Living in Same House as in 1979	39.6%	37	68.0
			% Living in Same County as in 1985	88.6%	22	91.3

Composite: **Rank** 53 / 179 *Score* 57.54   **DOWNEY**

CATEGORY	RANK	SCORE	STATISTIC	VALUE	RANK	SCORE
Economics	85	53.05	Median Household Income	$36,991	97	21.9
			% of Families Above Poverty Level	94.3%	73	84.2
Affordable Housing	90	58.85	Median Home Value	$227,300	108	63.0
			Median Rent	$649	74	54.7
Crime	46	81.45	Violent Crimes per 10,000 Population	57	51	82.6
			Property Crimes per 10,000 Population	436	54	80.3
Open Spaces	129	52.45	Population Density (Persons/Sq. Mile)	7353	123	69.9
			Average Rooms per Housing Unit	4.7	108	35.0
Education	89	44.20	% High School Enrollment/Completion	87.2%	84	64.4
			% College Graduates	16.3%	95	24.0
Commute	89	36.80	Average Work Commute in Minutes	25	62	61.5
			% Commuting on Public Transportation	1.9%	79	12.1
Community Stability	43	76.00	% Living in Same House as in 1979	36.0%	51	61.8
			% Living in Same County as in 1985	87.9%	29	90.2

Composite: **Rank** 54 / 179 *Score* 57.53   **ORANGE**

CATEGORY	RANK	SCORE	STATISTIC	VALUE	RANK	SCORE
Economics	57	60.40	Median Household Income	$46,539	44	33.5
			% of Families Above Poverty Level	95.3%	63	87.3
Affordable Housing	128	47.40	Median Home Value	$247,700	123	58.3
			Median Rent	$766	128	36.5
Crime	68	76.55	Violent Crimes per 10,000 Population	51	44	84.8
			Property Crimes per 10,000 Population	620	102	68.3
Open Spaces	69	66.70	Population Density (Persons/Sq. Mile)	4742	89	80.9
			Average Rooms per Housing Unit	5.4	47	52.5
Education	86	45.00	% High School Enrollment/Completion	82.7%	114	50.8
			% College Graduates	25.6%	63	39.2
Commute	61	41.30	Average Work Commute in Minutes	24	43	65.4
			% Commuting on Public Transportation	2.7%	65	17.2
Community Stability	78	65.35	% Living in Same House as in 1979	30.4%	83	52.2
			% Living in Same County as in 1985	80.1%	88	78.5

Metropolitan Area Suburb Rankings
LOS ANGELES-ANAHEIM-RIVERSIDE

Composite: *Rank* 55 / 179 *Score* 57.43   **HACIENDA HEIGHTS**

CATEGORY	RANK	SCORE	STATISTIC	VALUE	RANK	SCORE
Economics	47	62.10	Median Household Income	$51,837	30	40.0
			% of Families Above Poverty Level	94.3%	73	84.2
Affordable Housing	144	38.05	Median Home Value	$270,400	138	53.0
			Median Rent	$852	148	23.1
Crime	N/A	N/A	Violent Crimes per 10,000 Population	N/A	N/A	N/A
			Property Crimes per 10,000 Population	N/A	N/A	N/A
Open Spaces	30	74.20	Population Density (Persons/Sq. Mile)	4734	88	80.9
			Average Rooms per Housing Unit	6.0	16	67.5
Education	48	60.05	% High School Enrollment/Completion	91.1%	51	76.1
			% College Graduates	28.5%	52	44.0
Commute	143	27.20	Average Work Commute in Minutes	30	148	42.3
			% Commuting on Public Transportation	1.9%	79	12.1
Community Stability	21	83.00	% Living in Same House as in 1979	44.5%	20	76.5
			% Living in Same County as in 1985	87.4%	39	89.5

Composite: *Rank* 56 / 179 *Score* 57.42   **LOS ALAMITOS**

CATEGORY	RANK	SCORE	STATISTIC	VALUE	RANK	SCORE
Economics	39	63.75	Median Household Income	$45,171	54	31.9
			% of Families Above Poverty Level	97.9%	12	95.6
Affordable Housing	147	36.95	Median Home Value	$295,700	147	47.2
			Median Rent	$829	144	26.7
Crime	36	82.70	Violent Crimes per 10,000 Population	46	35	86.7
			Property Crimes per 10,000 Population	461	60	78.7
Open Spaces	59	68.10	Population Density (Persons/Sq. Mile)	2898	59	88.7
			Average Rooms per Housing Unit	5.2	62	47.5
Education	35	65.55	% High School Enrollment/Completion	94.3%	29	85.8
			% College Graduates	29.3%	50	45.3
Commute	122	31.40	Average Work Commute in Minutes	25	62	61.5
			% Commuting on Public Transportation	0.2%	165	1.3
Community Stability	133	53.50	% Living in Same House as in 1979	32.9%	70	56.5
			% Living in Same County as in 1985	61.5%	161	50.5

Composite: *Rank* 57 / 179 *Score* 57.40   **HUNTINGTON BEACH**

CATEGORY	RANK	SCORE	STATISTIC	VALUE	RANK	SCORE
Economics	31	65.30	Median Household Income	$50,633	36	38.5
			% of Families Above Poverty Level	96.8%	38	92.1
Affordable Housing	151	35.75	Median Home Value	$285,300	143	49.6
			Median Rent	$860	151	21.9
Crime	22	86.80	Violent Crimes per 10,000 Population	35	17	90.9
			Property Crimes per 10,000 Population	399	41	82.7
Open Spaces	95	60.95	Population Density (Persons/Sq. Mile)	6871	118	71.9
			Average Rooms per Housing Unit	5.3	57	50.0
Education	46	61.00	% High School Enrollment/Completion	89.8%	60	72.2
			% College Graduates	32.1%	38	49.8
Commute	125	30.70	Average Work Commute in Minutes	27	104	53.8
			% Commuting on Public Transportation	1.2%	102	7.6
Community Stability	98	61.30	% Living in Same House as in 1979	29.5%	88	50.6
			% Living in Same County as in 1985	75.8%	106	72.0

Metropolitan Area Suburb Rankings
LOS ANGELES-ANAHEIM-RIVERSIDE

Composite: **Rank** 58 / 179 *Score* 57.36   **WEST COVINA**

CATEGORY	RANK	SCORE	STATISTIC	VALUE	RANK	SCORE
Economics	68	56.40	Median Household Income	$42,481	65	28.6
			% of Families Above Poverty Level	94.3%	73	84.2
Affordable Housing	103	55.30	Median Home Value	$201,100	91	69.0
			Median Rent	$733	119	41.6
Crime	85	70.90	Violent Crimes per 10,000 Population	80	79	73.9
			Property Crimes per 10,000 Population	626	105	67.9
Open Spaces	92	61.70	Population Density (Persons/Sq. Mile)	5931	107	75.9
			Average Rooms per Housing Unit	5.2	62	47.5
Education	71	53.10	% High School Enrollment/Completion	91.0%	52	75.8
			% College Graduates	20.2%	83	30.4
Commute	128	29.45	Average Work Commute in Minutes	31	155	38.5
			% Commuting on Public Transportation	3.2%	53	20.4
Community Stability	47	74.70	% Living in Same House as in 1979	35.6%	52	61.1
			% Living in Same County as in 1985	86.6%	48	88.3

Composite: **Rank** 59 / 179 *Score* 57.33   **LA QUINTA**

CATEGORY	RANK	SCORE	STATISTIC	VALUE	RANK	SCORE
Economics	76	55.25	Median Household Income	$39,572	82	25.1
			% of Families Above Poverty Level	94.7%	69	85.4
Affordable Housing	76	61.70	Median Home Value	$115,000	23	88.9
			Median Rent	$779	130	34.5
Crime	93	68.55	Violent Crimes per 10,000 Population	79	77	74.2
			Property Crimes per 10,000 Population	703	123	62.9
Open Spaces	19	78.20	Population Density (Persons/Sq. Mile)	467	2	98.9
			Average Rooms per Housing Unit	5.6	37	57.5
Education	56	57.65	% High School Enrollment/Completion	93.5%	35	83.4
			% College Graduates	21.1%	78	31.9
Commute	72	39.40	Average Work Commute in Minutes	22	19	73.1
			% Commuting on Public Transportation	0.9%	119	5.7
Community Stability	162	40.55	% Living in Same House as in 1979	14.6%	168	24.9
			% Living in Same County as in 1985	65.3%	151	56.2

Composite: **Rank** 60 / 179 *Score* 57.28   **NEWPORT BEACH**

CATEGORY	RANK	SCORE	STATISTIC	VALUE	RANK	SCORE
Economics	13	72.60	Median Household Income	$60,374	13	50.3
			% of Families Above Poverty Level	97.7%	18	94.9
Affordable Housing	174	2.65	Median Home Value	$500,001	172	0.0
			Median Rent	$967	171	5.3
Crime	62	78.35	Violent Crimes per 10,000 Population	47	39	86.4
			Property Crimes per 10,000 Population	590	94	70.3
Open Spaces	79	64.15	Population Density (Persons/Sq. Mile)	4755	90	80.8
			Average Rooms per Housing Unit	5.2	62	47.5
Education	13	83.75	% High School Enrollment/Completion	95.0%	24	87.9
			% College Graduates	50.3%	9	79.6
Commute	83	37.80	Average Work Commute in Minutes	23	26	69.2
			% Commuting on Public Transportation	1.0%	112	6.4
Community Stability	95	61.65	% Living in Same House as in 1979	29.4%	90	50.4
			% Living in Same County as in 1985	76.4%	103	72.9

Composite: *Rank* 61 / 179 *Score* 57.24   **FULLERTON**

CATEGORY	RANK	SCORE	STATISTIC	VALUE	RANK	SCORE
Economics	69	56.20	Median Household Income	$41,921	70	27.9
			% of Families Above Poverty Level	94.4%	72	84.5
Affordable Housing	108	53.85	Median Home Value	$231,800	113	61.9
			Median Rent	$706	104	45.8
Crime	74	73.75	Violent Crimes per 10,000 Population	64	57	79.9
			Property Crimes per 10,000 Population	631	109	67.6
Open Spaces	100	59.55	Population Density (Persons/Sq. Mile)	5159	95	79.1
			Average Rooms per Housing Unit	4.9	89	40.0
Education	62	55.55	% High School Enrollment/Completion	87.4%	80	65.0
			% College Graduates	29.8%	49	46.1
Commute	65	40.65	Average Work Commute in Minutes	24	43	65.4
			% Commuting on Public Transportation	2.5%	69	15.9
Community Stability	99	61.15	% Living in Same House as in 1979	31.2%	79	53.5
			% Living in Same County as in 1985	73.7%	115	68.8

Composite: *Rank* 62 / 179 *Score* 57.16   **MONTEBELLO**

CATEGORY	RANK	SCORE	STATISTIC	VALUE	RANK	SCORE
Economics	133	40.35	Median Household Income	$31,441	134	15.2
			% of Families Above Poverty Level	88.4%	135	65.5
Affordable Housing	73	62.70	Median Home Value	$211,200	100	66.7
			Median Rent	$623	60	58.7
Crime	55	79.35	Violent Crimes per 10,000 Population	53	48	84.1
			Property Crimes per 10,000 Population	524	83	74.6
Open Spaces	136	49.00	Population Density (Persons/Sq. Mile)	7215	122	70.5
			Average Rooms per Housing Unit	4.4	134	27.5
Education	96	41.10	% High School Enrollment/Completion	86.1%	92	61.0
			% College Graduates	14.6%	103	21.2
Commute	30	48.60	Average Work Commute in Minutes	26	82	57.7
			% Commuting on Public Transportation	6.2%	21	39.5
Community Stability	30	79.05	% Living in Same House as in 1979	39.4%	39	67.7
			% Living in Same County as in 1985	88.0%	28	90.4

Composite: *Rank* 63 / 179 *Score* 57.15   **EAST SAN GABRIEL**

CATEGORY	RANK	SCORE	STATISTIC	VALUE	RANK	SCORE
Economics	66	56.80	Median Household Income	$41,360	73	27.2
			% of Families Above Poverty Level	95.0%	65	86.4
Affordable Housing	110	53.50	Median Home Value	$286,300	144	49.4
			Median Rent	$630	64	57.6
Crime	N/A	N/A	Violent Crimes per 10,000 Population	N/A	N/A	N/A
			Property Crimes per 10,000 Population	N/A	N/A	N/A
Open Spaces	124	53.05	Population Density (Persons/Sq. Mile)	8244	133	66.1
			Average Rooms per Housing Unit	4.9	89	40.0
Education	40	63.95	% High School Enrollment/Completion	92.1%	43	79.2
			% College Graduates	31.4%	41	48.7
Commute	85	37.75	Average Work Commute in Minutes	26	82	57.7
			% Commuting on Public Transportation	2.8%	61	17.8
Community Stability	36	77.85	% Living in Same House as in 1979	40.4%	30	69.4
			% Living in Same County as in 1985	85.3%	56	86.3

Metropolitan Area Suburb Rankings
LOS ANGELES-ANAHEIM-RIVERSIDE

Composite: Rank 64 / 179 Score 56.91   SEAL BEACH

CATEGORY	RANK	SCORE	STATISTIC	VALUE	RANK	SCORE
Economics	63	57.20	Median Household Income	$32,834	121	16.9
			% of Families Above Poverty Level	98.5%	4	97.5
Affordable Housing	158	31.25	Median Home Value	$350,600	163	34.5
			Median Rent	$821	143	28.0
Crime	8	93.10	Violent Crimes per 10,000 Population	20	5	96.6
			Property Crimes per 10,000 Population	292	20	89.6
Open Spaces	99	59.70	Population Density (Persons/Sq. Mile)	2142	33	91.9
			Average Rooms per Housing Unit	4.4	134	27.5
Education	38	64.40	% High School Enrollment/Completion	92.3%	41	79.8
			% College Graduates	31.6%	39	49.0
Commute	135	28.50	Average Work Commute in Minutes	28	116	50.0
			% Commuting on Public Transportation	1.1%	106	7.0
Community Stability	83	64.25	% Living in Same House as in 1979	37.9%	44	65.1
			% Living in Same County as in 1985	70.1%	136	63.4

Composite: Rank 65 / 179 Score 56.56   APPLE VALLEY

CATEGORY	RANK	SCORE	STATISTIC	VALUE	RANK	SCORE
Economics	115	45.75	Median Household Income	$34,050	112	18.4
			% of Families Above Poverty Level	90.8%	112	73.1
Affordable Housing	23	80.15	Median Home Value	$120,000	24	87.8
			Median Rent	$534	25	72.5
Crime	43	81.80	Violent Crimes per 10,000 Population	45	32	87.1
			Property Crimes per 10,000 Population	494	75	76.5
Open Spaces	16	79.00	Population Density (Persons/Sq. Mile)	686	4	98.0
			Average Rooms per Housing Unit	5.7	29	60.0
Education	85	45.45	% High School Enrollment/Completion	88.8%	73	69.2
			% College Graduates	14.9%	101	21.7
Commute	146	25.95	Average Work Commute in Minutes	28	116	50.0
			% Commuting on Public Transportation	0.3%	161	1.9
Community Stability	165	37.85	% Living in Same House as in 1979	15.8%	166	26.9
			% Living in Same County as in 1985	60.4%	165	48.8

Composite: Rank 66 / 179 Score 56.21   DANA POINT

CATEGORY	RANK	SCORE	STATISTIC	VALUE	RANK	SCORE
Economics	29	65.75	Median Household Income	$54,516	21	43.2
			% of Families Above Poverty Level	95.6%	60	88.3
Affordable Housing	165	26.80	Median Home Value	$337,100	158	37.6
			Median Rent	$898	159	16.0
Crime	27	85.55	Violent Crimes per 10,000 Population	45	32	87.1
			Property Crimes per 10,000 Population	378	36	84.0
Open Spaces	61	67.85	Population Density (Persons/Sq. Mile)	4799	91	80.7
			Average Rooms per Housing Unit	5.5	41	55.0
Education	34	66.15	% High School Enrollment/Completion	91.2%	49	76.4
			% College Graduates	35.8%	29	55.9
Commute	117	32.00	Average Work Commute in Minutes	29	137	46.2
			% Commuting on Public Transportation	2.8%	61	17.8
Community Stability	145	49.40	% Living in Same House as in 1979	19.9%	149	34.0
			% Living in Same County as in 1985	71.0%	133	64.8

Metropolitan Area Suburb Rankings
LOS ANGELES-ANAHEIM-RIVERSIDE

Composite: **Rank** 66 / 179 **Score** 56.21   **NORCO**

CATEGORY	RANK	SCORE	STATISTIC	VALUE	RANK	SCORE
Economics	36	64.45	Median Household Income	$51,594	31	39.7
			% of Families Above Poverty Level	95.9%	53	89.2
Affordable Housing	99	56.70	Median Home Value	$202,000	93	68.8
			Median Rent	$714	109	44.6
Crime	60	78.65	Violent Crimes per 10,000 Population	64	57	79.9
			Property Crimes per 10,000 Population	481	72	77.4
Open Spaces	7	83.10	Population Density (Persons/Sq. Mile)	1701	22	93.7
			Average Rooms per Housing Unit	6.2	9	72.5
Education	90	44.25	% High School Enrollment/Completion	90.5%	56	74.3
			% College Graduates	10.3%	130	14.2
Commute	175	8.65	Average Work Commute in Minutes	37	175	15.4
			% Commuting on Public Transportation	0.3%	161	1.9
Community Stability	118	57.65	% Living in Same House as in 1979	39.5%	38	67.9
			% Living in Same County as in 1985	59.5%	168	47.4

Composite: **Rank** 68 / 179 **Score** 56.11   **FILLMORE**

CATEGORY	RANK	SCORE	STATISTIC	VALUE	RANK	SCORE
Economics	116	45.10	Median Household Income	$33,482	114	17.7
			% of Families Above Poverty Level	90.6%	115	72.5
Affordable Housing	72	62.75	Median Home Value	$193,500	84	70.8
			Median Rent	$649	74	54.7
Crime	16	89.15	Violent Crimes per 10,000 Population	44	29	87.5
			Property Crimes per 10,000 Population	274	13	90.8
Open Spaces	96	60.85	Population Density (Persons/Sq. Mile)	4544	85	81.7
			Average Rooms per Housing Unit	4.9	89	40.0
Education	125	32.00	% High School Enrollment/Completion	83.3%	106	52.6
			% College Graduates	8.6%	144	11.4
Commute	117	32.00	Average Work Commute in Minutes	25	62	61.5
			% Commuting on Public Transportation	0.4%	155	2.5
Community Stability	59	70.90	% Living in Same House as in 1979	33.5%	67	57.5
			% Living in Same County as in 1985	84.0%	63	84.3

Composite: **Rank** 69 / 179 **Score** 56.09   **EAST HEMET**

CATEGORY	RANK	SCORE	STATISTIC	VALUE	RANK	SCORE
Economics	103	48.60	Median Household Income	$32,280	126	16.2
			% of Families Above Poverty Level	93.3%	92	81.0
Affordable Housing	26	79.50	Median Home Value	$110,600	20	89.9
			Median Rent	$556	35	69.1
Crime	N/A	N/A	Violent Crimes per 10,000 Population	N/A	N/A	N/A
			Property Crimes per 10,000 Population	N/A	N/A	N/A
Open Spaces	52	68.90	Population Density (Persons/Sq. Mile)	4291	79	82.8
			Average Rooms per Housing Unit	5.5	41	55.0
Education	101	39.95	% High School Enrollment/Completion	86.3%	90	61.6
			% College Graduates	12.8%	115	18.3
Commute	64	40.70	Average Work Commute in Minutes	20	8	80.8
			% Commuting on Public Transportation	0.1%	172	0.6
Community Stability	112	58.90	% Living in Same House as in 1979	29.3%	93	50.3
			% Living in Same County as in 1985	72.8%	121	67.5

Metropolitan Area Suburb Rankings
LOS ANGELES-ANAHEIM-RIVERSIDE

Composite: *Rank* 70 / 179 *Score* 56.08   **SAN CLEMENTE**

CATEGORY	RANK	SCORE	STATISTIC	VALUE	RANK	SCORE
Economics	59	60.30	Median Household Income	$46,374	47	33.3
			% of Families Above Poverty Level	95.3%	63	87.3
Affordable Housing	140	39.95	Median Home Value	$306,400	152	44.7
			Median Rent	$774	129	35.2
Crime	13	91.70	Violent Crimes per 10,000 Population	28	12	93.6
			Property Crimes per 10,000 Population	289	19	89.8
Open Spaces	60	68.00	Population Density (Persons/Sq. Mile)	2353	36	91.0
			Average Rooms per Housing Unit	5.1	72	45.0
Education	69	53.40	% High School Enrollment/Completion	84.6%	96	56.5
			% College Graduates	32.4%	37	50.3
Commute	134	28.80	Average Work Commute in Minutes	28	116	50.0
			% Commuting on Public Transportation	1.2%	102	7.6
Community Stability	143	50.40	% Living in Same House as in 1979	20.7%	145	35.4
			% Living in Same County as in 1985	71.4%	131	65.4

Composite: *Rank* 71 / 179 *Score* 55.95   **UPLAND**

CATEGORY	RANK	SCORE	STATISTIC	VALUE	RANK	SCORE
Economics	71	55.95	Median Household Income	$41,965	68	28.0
			% of Families Above Poverty Level	94.2%	79	83.9
Affordable Housing	82	61.45	Median Home Value	$227,000	106	63.0
			Median Rent	$615	57	59.9
Crime	83	71.45	Violent Crimes per 10,000 Population	82	81	73.1
			Property Crimes per 10,000 Population	598	99	69.8
Open Spaces	61	67.85	Population Density (Persons/Sq. Mile)	4200	78	83.2
			Average Rooms per Housing Unit	5.4	47	52.5
Education	63	55.40	% High School Enrollment/Completion	89.7%	62	71.9
			% College Graduates	25.4%	65	38.9
Commute	138	28.20	Average Work Commute in Minutes	28	116	50.0
			% Commuting on Public Transportation	1.0%	112	6.4
Community Stability	140	51.35	% Living in Same House as in 1979	25.5%	116	43.7
			% Living in Same County as in 1985	67.2%	145	59.0

Composite: *Rank* 72 / 179 *Score* 55.93   **RANCHO CUCAMONGA**

CATEGORY	RANK	SCORE	STATISTIC	VALUE	RANK	SCORE
Economics	53	61.15	Median Household Income	$46,193	51	33.1
			% of Families Above Poverty Level	95.9%	53	89.2
Affordable Housing	87	59.35	Median Home Value	$183,000	77	73.2
			Median Rent	$708	106	45.5
Crime	36	82.70	Violent Crimes per 10,000 Population	44	29	87.5
			Property Crimes per 10,000 Population	473	68	77.9
Open Spaces	27	74.80	Population Density (Persons/Sq. Mile)	2682	51	89.6
			Average Rooms per Housing Unit	5.7	29	60.0
Education	74	52.35	% High School Enrollment/Completion	90.0%	58	72.8
			% College Graduates	21.1%	78	31.9
Commute	160	18.90	Average Work Commute in Minutes	32	159	34.6
			% Commuting on Public Transportation	0.5%	146	3.2
Community Stability	160	42.25	% Living in Same House as in 1979	18.6%	158	31.8
			% Living in Same County as in 1985	63.0%	157	52.7

Metropolitan Area Suburb Rankings
LOS ANGELES-ANAHEIM-RIVERSIDE

Composite: *Rank* 73 / 179 *Score* 55.89   **PASADENA**

CATEGORY	RANK	SCORE	STATISTIC	VALUE	RANK	SCORE
Economics	123	43.40	Median Household Income	$35,103	108	19.7
			% of Families Above Poverty Level	88.9%	131	67.1
Affordable Housing	107	54.05	Median Home Value	$281,500	141	50.5
			Median Rent	$630	64	57.6
Crime	109	63.60	Violent Crimes per 10,000 Population	126	108	56.4
			Property Crimes per 10,000 Population	582	92	70.8
Open Spaces	120	54.65	Population Density (Persons/Sq. Mile)	5723	103	76.8
			Average Rooms per Housing Unit	4.6	118	32.5
Education	57	56.45	% High School Enrollment/Completion	84.5%	98	56.2
			% College Graduates	36.3%	28	56.7
Commute	14	53.70	Average Work Commute in Minutes	23	26	69.2
			% Commuting on Public Transportation	6.0%	23	38.2
Community Stability	77	65.40	% Living in Same House as in 1979	29.8%	86	51.1
			% Living in Same County as in 1985	80.9%	85	79.7

Composite: *Rank* 74 / 179 *Score* 55.79   **MONTEREY PARK**

CATEGORY	RANK	SCORE	STATISTIC	VALUE	RANK	SCORE
Economics	141	38.20	Median Household Income	$32,605	124	16.6
			% of Families Above Poverty Level	86.6%	148	59.8
Affordable Housing	96	56.95	Median Home Value	$235,400	115	61.1
			Median Rent	$661	85	52.8
Crime	73	75.35	Violent Crimes per 10,000 Population	92	86	69.3
			Property Crimes per 10,000 Population	418	44	81.4
Open Spaces	140	47.40	Population Density (Persons/Sq. Mile)	7954	130	67.3
			Average Rooms per Housing Unit	4.4	134	27.5
Education	73	52.65	% High School Enrollment/Completion	89.5%	64	71.3
			% College Graduates	22.4%	71	34.0
Commute	42	46.65	Average Work Commute in Minutes	25	62	61.5
			% Commuting on Public Transportation	5.0%	31	31.8
Community Stability	52	73.35	% Living in Same House as in 1979	40.0%	36	68.7
			% Living in Same County as in 1985	79.8%	89	78.0

Composite: *Rank* 75 / 179 *Score* 55.74   **LA HABRA**

CATEGORY	RANK	SCORE	STATISTIC	VALUE	RANK	SCORE
Economics	80	54.55	Median Household Income	$39,967	79	25.6
			% of Families Above Poverty Level	94.1%	81	83.5
Affordable Housing	86	59.30	Median Home Value	$199,200	88	69.5
			Median Rent	$685	92	49.1
Crime	36	82.70	Violent Crimes per 10,000 Population	52	46	84.5
			Property Crimes per 10,000 Population	426	50	80.9
Open Spaces	115	55.65	Population Density (Persons/Sq. Mile)	7004	120	71.3
			Average Rooms per Housing Unit	4.9	89	40.0
Education	100	40.35	% High School Enrollment/Completion	83.5%	103	53.2
			% College Graduates	18.4%	86	27.5
Commute	91	36.50	Average Work Commute in Minutes	25	62	61.5
			% Commuting on Public Transportation	1.8%	82	11.5
Community Stability	100	61.10	% Living in Same House as in 1979	32.9%	70	56.5
			% Living in Same County as in 1985	71.6%	129	65.7

Metropolitan Area Suburb Rankings
LOS ANGELES-ANAHEIM-RIVERSIDE

Composite: **Rank** 76 / 179 **Score** 55.72 **TUSTIN**

CATEGORY	RANK	SCORE	STATISTIC	VALUE	RANK	SCORE
Economics	70	56.15	Median Household Income	$38,433	88	23.7
			% of Families Above Poverty Level	95.7%	58	88.6
Affordable Housing	126	48.10	Median Home Value	$255,100	132	56.6
			Median Rent	$746	125	39.6
Crime	52	79.75	Violent Crimes per 10,000 Population	39	23	89.4
			Property Crimes per 10,000 Population	593	96	70.1
Open Spaces	106	58.50	Population Density (Persons/Sq. Mile)	4490	83	82.0
			Average Rooms per Housing Unit	4.7	108	35.0
Education	76	51.90	% High School Enrollment/Completion	87.3%	83	64.7
			% College Graduates	25.5%	64	39.1
Commute	33	48.05	Average Work Commute in Minutes	20	8	80.8
			% Commuting on Public Transportation	2.4%	71	15.3
Community Stability	152	47.60	% Living in Same House as in 1979	19.3%	154	33.0
			% Living in Same County as in 1985	69.3%	137	62.2

Composite: **Rank** 77 / 179 **Score** 55.62 **ALONDRA PARK**

CATEGORY	RANK	SCORE	STATISTIC	VALUE	RANK	SCORE
Economics	108	47.35	Median Household Income	$39,327	83	24.8
			% of Families Above Poverty Level	89.8%	123	69.9
Affordable Housing	65	64.05	Median Home Value	$222,400	103	64.1
			Median Rent	$589	44	64.0
Crime	N/A	N/A	Violent Crimes per 10,000 Population	N/A	N/A	N/A
			Property Crimes per 10,000 Population	N/A	N/A	N/A
Open Spaces	138	47.80	Population Density (Persons/Sq. Mile)	7777	127	68.1
			Average Rooms per Housing Unit	4.4	134	27.5
Education	75	52.15	% High School Enrollment/Completion	92.4%	39	80.1
			% College Graduates	16.4%	93	24.2
Commute	48	44.45	Average Work Commute in Minutes	23	26	69.2
			% Commuting on Public Transportation	3.1%	55	19.7
Community Stability	35	77.90	% Living in Same House as in 1979	37.5%	45	64.4
			% Living in Same County as in 1985	88.7%	20	91.4

Composite: **Rank** 77 / 179 **Score** 55.62 **WEST WHITTIER-LOS NIETOS**

CATEGORY	RANK	SCORE	STATISTIC	VALUE	RANK	SCORE
Economics	87	52.85	Median Household Income	$37,906	92	23.1
			% of Families Above Poverty Level	93.8%	86	82.6
Affordable Housing	68	62.95	Median Home Value	$164,200	64	77.6
			Median Rent	$690	95	48.3
Crime	N/A	N/A	Violent Crimes per 10,000 Population	N/A	N/A	N/A
			Property Crimes per 10,000 Population	N/A	N/A	N/A
Open Spaces	131	52.15	Population Density (Persons/Sq. Mile)	9258	142	61.8
			Average Rooms per Housing Unit	5.0	79	42.5
Education	124	32.35	% High School Enrollment/Completion	84.4%	100	55.9
			% College Graduates	7.0%	153	8.8
Commute	52	43.20	Average Work Commute in Minutes	24	43	65.4
			% Commuting on Public Transportation	3.3%	50	21.0
Community Stability	7	90.25	% Living in Same House as in 1979	48.9%	8	84.1
			% Living in Same County as in 1985	92.0%	4	96.4

Metropolitan Area Suburb Rankings
LOS ANGELES-ANAHEIM-RIVERSIDE

Composite: **Rank** 79 / 179 **Score** 55.48   **PICO RIVERA**

CATEGORY	RANK	SCORE	STATISTIC	VALUE	RANK	SCORE
Economics	114	45.80	Median Household Income	$34,383	110	18.8
			% of Families Above Poverty Level	90.7%	114	72.8
Affordable Housing	56	68.90	Median Home Value	$163,800	62	77.6
			Median Rent	$613	55	60.2
Crime	107	64.15	Violent Crimes per 10,000 Population	165	128	41.7
			Property Crimes per 10,000 Population	339	30	86.6
Open Spaces	134	49.80	Population Density (Persons/Sq. Mile)	7419	124	69.6
			Average Rooms per Housing Unit	4.5	129	30.0
Education	136	29.25	% High School Enrollment/Completion	82.8%	111	51.1
			% College Graduates	6.1%	157	7.4
Commute	65	40.65	Average Work Commute in Minutes	26	82	57.7
			% Commuting on Public Transportation	3.7%	42	23.6
Community Stability	8	89.80	% Living in Same House as in 1979	48.4%	9	83.2
			% Living in Same County as in 1985	92.0%	4	96.4

Composite: **Rank** 80 / 179 **Score** 55.34   **BARSTOW**

CATEGORY	RANK	SCORE	STATISTIC	VALUE	RANK	SCORE
Economics	150	36.55	Median Household Income	$28,289	151	11.4
			% of Families Above Poverty Level	87.2%	144	61.7
Affordable Housing	4	91.15	Median Home Value	$71,800	3	98.9
			Median Rent	$464	7	83.4
Crime	112	62.00	Violent Crimes per 10,000 Population	101	90	65.9
			Property Crimes per 10,000 Population	777	127	58.1
Open Spaces	74	66.00	Population Density (Persons/Sq. Mile)	936	10	97.0
			Average Rooms per Housing Unit	4.7	108	35.0
Education	134	29.55	% High School Enrollment/Completion	80.8%	135	45.0
			% College Graduates	10.2%	132	14.1
Commute	54	42.60	Average Work Commute in Minutes	21	13	76.9
			% Commuting on Public Transportation	1.3%	98	8.3
Community Stability	108	59.55	% Living in Same House as in 1979	30.9%	80	53.0
			% Living in Same County as in 1985	71.9%	126	66.1

Composite: **Rank** 81 / 179 **Score** 55.11   **MOORPARK**

CATEGORY	RANK	SCORE	STATISTIC	VALUE	RANK	SCORE
Economics	14	72.15	Median Household Income	$60,368	14	50.3
			% of Families Above Poverty Level	97.4%	26	94.0
Affordable Housing	155	32.90	Median Home Value	$275,600	140	51.8
			Median Rent	$911	163	14.0
Crime	5	94.65	Violent Crimes per 10,000 Population	29	13	93.2
			Property Crimes per 10,000 Population	192	3	96.1
Open Spaces	13	79.80	Population Density (Persons/Sq. Mile)	2079	30	92.1
			Average Rooms per Housing Unit	6.0	16	67.5
Education	78	47.60	% High School Enrollment/Completion	82.9%	110	51.4
			% College Graduates	28.4%	53	43.8
Commute	148	25.65	Average Work Commute in Minutes	28	116	50.0
			% Commuting on Public Transportation	0.2%	165	1.3
Community Stability	169	33.00	% Living in Same House as in 1979	8.5%	175	14.3
			% Living in Same County as in 1985	62.3%	158	51.7

Metropolitan Area Suburb Rankings
LOS ANGELES-ANAHEIM-RIVERSIDE

Composite: **Rank** 82 / 179 *Score* 54.89   **LANCASTER**

CATEGORY	RANK	SCORE	STATISTIC	VALUE	RANK	SCORE
Economics	98	50.70	Median Household Income	$38,388	89	23.6
			% of Families Above Poverty Level	92.3%	101	77.8
Affordable Housing	45	72.65	Median Home Value	$133,800	30	84.6
			Median Rent	$610	54	60.7
Crime	78	72.80	Violent Crimes per 10,000 Population	108	99	63.3
			Property Crimes per 10,000 Population	404	43	82.3
Open Spaces	33	73.15	Population Density (Persons/Sq. Mile)	1096	15	96.3
			Average Rooms per Housing Unit	5.3	57	50.0
Education	115	34.45	% High School Enrollment/Completion	80.8%	135	45.0
			% College Graduates	16.2%	96	23.9
Commute	135	28.50	Average Work Commute in Minutes	28	116	50.0
			% Commuting on Public Transportation	1.1%	106	7.0
Community Stability	139	51.95	% Living in Same House as in 1979	19.9%	149	34.0
			% Living in Same County as in 1985	74.4%	113	69.9

Composite: **Rank** 83 / 179 *Score* 54.83   **ALHAMBRA**

CATEGORY	RANK	SCORE	STATISTIC	VALUE	RANK	SCORE
Economics	132	40.45	Median Household Income	$31,368	137	15.1
			% of Families Above Poverty Level	88.5%	134	65.8
Affordable Housing	85	59.75	Median Home Value	$227,900	109	62.8
			Median Rent	$636	67	56.7
Crime	58	79.00	Violent Crimes per 10,000 Population	66	61	79.2
			Property Crimes per 10,000 Population	459	57	78.8
Open Spaces	157	38.95	Population Density (Persons/Sq. Mile)	10769	157	55.4
			Average Rooms per Housing Unit	4.2	147	22.5
Education	65	54.85	% High School Enrollment/Completion	90.7%	54	74.9
			% College Graduates	22.9%	69	34.8
Commute	30	48.60	Average Work Commute in Minutes	26	82	57.7
			% Commuting on Public Transportation	6.2%	21	39.5
Community Stability	92	62.20	% Living in Same House as in 1979	27.3%	103	46.8
			% Living in Same County as in 1985	79.5%	90	77.6

Composite: **Rank** 84 / 179 *Score* 54.81   **PORT HUENEME**

CATEGORY	RANK	SCORE	STATISTIC	VALUE	RANK	SCORE
Economics	101	49.70	Median Household Income	$33,554	113	17.8
			% of Families Above Poverty Level	93.5%	89	81.6
Affordable Housing	88	58.95	Median Home Value	$185,600	79	72.6
			Median Rent	$709	107	45.3
Crime	60	78.65	Violent Crimes per 10,000 Population	79	77	74.2
			Property Crimes per 10,000 Population	392	38	83.1
Open Spaces	111	57.00	Population Density (Persons/Sq. Mile)	4589	86	81.5
			Average Rooms per Housing Unit	4.6	118	32.5
Education	84	46.00	% High School Enrollment/Completion	88.6%	74	68.6
			% College Graduates	15.9%	98	23.4
Commute	46	44.85	Average Work Commute in Minutes	20	8	80.8
			% Commuting on Public Transportation	1.4%	94	8.9
Community Stability	150	48.55	% Living in Same House as in 1979	23.8%	129	40.8
			% Living in Same County as in 1985	65.4%	149	56.3

Metropolitan Area Suburb Rankings
LOS ANGELES-ANAHEIM-RIVERSIDE

Composite: Rank 85 / 179 *Score* 54.74   **BUENA PARK**

CATEGORY	RANK	SCORE	STATISTIC	VALUE	RANK	SCORE
Economics	75	55.40	Median Household Income	$41,435	71	27.3
			% of Families Above Poverty Level	94.1%	81	83.5
Affordable Housing	102	55.45	Median Home Value	$204,000	95	68.4
			Median Rent	$727	117	42.5
Crime	75	73.55	Violent Crimes per 10,000 Population	66	61	79.2
			Property Crimes per 10,000 Population	627	106	67.9
Open Spaces	109	58.00	Population Density (Persons/Sq. Mile)	6483	116	73.5
			Average Rooms per Housing Unit	5.0	79	42.5
Education	94	42.35	% High School Enrollment/Completion	86.2%	91	61.3
			% College Graduates	15.9%	98	23.4
Commute	107	34.25	Average Work Commute in Minutes	26	82	57.7
			% Commuting on Public Transportation	1.7%	88	10.8
Community Stability	81	64.20	% Living in Same House as in 1979	35.6%	52	61.1
			% Living in Same County as in 1985	72.7%	123	67.3

Composite: Rank 86 / 179 *Score* 54.66   **HIGHLAND**

CATEGORY	RANK	SCORE	STATISTIC	VALUE	RANK	SCORE
Economics	137	39.50	Median Household Income	$31,561	132	15.4
			% of Families Above Poverty Level	87.8%	138	63.6
Affordable Housing	15	84.20	Median Home Value	$101,500	15	92.0
			Median Rent	$509	18	76.4
Crime	86	70.70	Violent Crimes per 10,000 Population	102	92	65.5
			Property Crimes per 10,000 Population	504	79	75.9
Open Spaces	54	68.85	Population Density (Persons/Sq. Mile)	2539	44	90.2
			Average Rooms per Housing Unit	5.2	62	47.5
Education	131	30.15	% High School Enrollment/Completion	79.3%	144	40.5
			% College Graduates	13.7%	106	19.8
Commute	98	35.90	Average Work Commute in Minutes	24	43	65.4
			% Commuting on Public Transportation	1.0%	112	6.4
Community Stability	137	53.30	% Living in Same House as in 1979	24.0%	126	41.1
			% Living in Same County as in 1985	71.5%	130	65.5

Composite: Rank 87 / 179 *Score* 54.58   **SAN GABRIEL**

CATEGORY	RANK	SCORE	STATISTIC	VALUE	RANK	SCORE
Economics	138	39.45	Median Household Income	$32,559	125	16.6
			% of Families Above Poverty Level	87.4%	143	62.3
Affordable Housing	106	54.65	Median Home Value	$248,000	124	58.2
			Median Rent	$672	87	51.1
Crime	57	79.10	Violent Crimes per 10,000 Population	66	61	79.2
			Property Crimes per 10,000 Population	456	56	79.0
Open Spaces	142	46.50	Population Density (Persons/Sq. Mile)	8977	139	63.0
			Average Rooms per Housing Unit	4.5	129	30.0
Education	87	45.05	% High School Enrollment/Completion	84.8%	94	57.1
			% College Graduates	21.8%	76	33.0
Commute	37	47.00	Average Work Commute in Minutes	25	62	61.5
			% Commuting on Public Transportation	5.1%	30	32.5
Community Stability	62	70.30	% Living in Same House as in 1979	34.1%	61	58.5
			% Living in Same County as in 1985	82.5%	80	82.1

Metropolitan Area Suburb Rankings
LOS ANGELES-ANAHEIM-RIVERSIDE

Composite: *Rank* 88 / 179 *Score* 54.36   **MONROVIA**

CATEGORY	RANK	SCORE	STATISTIC	VALUE	RANK	SCORE
Economics	105	48.35	Median Household Income	$35,684	105	20.4
			% of Families Above Poverty Level	91.8%	104	76.3
Affordable Housing	94	57.95	Median Home Value	$231,500	111	62.0
			Median Rent	$654	79	53.9
Crime	92	68.70	Violent Crimes per 10,000 Population	107	98	63.6
			Property Crimes per 10,000 Population	535	84	73.8
Open Spaces	89	62.30	Population Density (Persons/Sq. Mile)	2675	49	89.6
			Average Rooms per Housing Unit	4.7	108	35.0
Education	114	34.75	% High School Enrollment/Completion	79.1%	146	39.9
			% College Graduates	19.7%	85	29.6
Commute	57	42.20	Average Work Commute in Minutes	25	62	61.5
			% Commuting on Public Transportation	3.6%	45	22.9
Community Stability	74	66.25	% Living in Same House as in 1979	28.3%	99	48.5
			% Living in Same County as in 1985	83.8%	65	84.0

Composite: *Rank* 89 / 179 *Score* 54.26   **COACHELLA**

CATEGORY	RANK	SCORE	STATISTIC	VALUE	RANK	SCORE
Economics	172	18.25	Median Household Income	$23,218	168	5.2
			% of Families Above Poverty Level	77.6%	171	31.3
Affordable Housing	1	99.85	Median Home Value	$68,500	2	99.7
			Median Rent	$357	1	100.0
Crime	115	60.60	Violent Crimes per 10,000 Population	105	95	64.4
			Property Crimes per 10,000 Population	798	128	56.8
Open Spaces	97	59.95	Population Density (Persons/Sq. Mile)	842	7	97.4
			Average Rooms per Housing Unit	4.2	147	22.5
Education	151	22.80	% High School Enrollment/Completion	80.9%	133	45.3
			% College Graduates	1.8%	176	0.3
Commute	50	43.90	Average Work Commute in Minutes	20	8	80.8
			% Commuting on Public Transportation	1.1%	106	7.0
Community Stability	49	74.50	% Living in Same House as in 1979	35.3%	56	60.6
			% Living in Same County as in 1985	86.7%	46	88.4

Composite: *Rank* 90 / 179 *Score* 54.22   **PALM DESERT**

CATEGORY	RANK	SCORE	STATISTIC	VALUE	RANK	SCORE
Economics	72	55.60	Median Household Income	$37,315	94	22.3
			% of Families Above Poverty Level	95.8%	56	88.9
Affordable Housing	81	61.55	Median Home Value	$172,300	73	75.7
			Median Rent	$696	98	47.4
Crime	119	58.70	Violent Crimes per 10,000 Population	72	72	76.9
			Property Crimes per 10,000 Population	1,049	139	40.5
Open Spaces	48	69.15	Population Density (Persons/Sq. Mile)	1220	18	95.8
			Average Rooms per Housing Unit	5.0	79	42.5
Education	95	41.65	% High School Enrollment/Completion	81.6%	129	47.4
			% College Graduates	23.6%	67	35.9
Commute	21	52.55	Average Work Commute in Minutes	15	1	100.0
			% Commuting on Public Transportation	0.8%	127	5.1
Community Stability	163	40.35	% Living in Same House as in 1979	17.5%	162	29.9
			% Living in Same County as in 1985	61.7%	160	50.8

Metropolitan Area Suburb Rankings
LOS ANGELES-ANAHEIM-RIVERSIDE

Composite: *Rank* 91 / 179 *Score* 54.11   **AVOCADO HEIGHTS**

CATEGORY	RANK	SCORE	STATISTIC	VALUE	RANK	SCORE
Economics	94	51.85	Median Household Income	$42,800	64	29.0
			% of Families Above Poverty Level	91.3%	108	74.7
Affordable Housing	96	56.95	Median Home Value	$196,300	86	70.1
			Median Rent	$719	114	43.8
Crime	N/A	N/A	Violent Crimes per 10,000 Population	N/A	N/A	N/A
			Property Crimes per 10,000 Population	N/A	N/A	N/A
Open Spaces	86	62.90	Population Density (Persons/Sq. Mile)	5361	98	78.3
			Average Rooms per Housing Unit	5.2	62	47.5
Education	119	33.80	% High School Enrollment/Completion	82.8%	111	51.1
			% College Graduates	11.7%	121	16.5
Commute	127	30.10	Average Work Commute in Minutes	28	116	50.0
			% Commuting on Public Transportation	1.6%	91	10.2
Community Stability	9	89.05	% Living in Same House as in 1979	47.6%	12	81.9
			% Living in Same County as in 1985	91.9%	6	96.2

Composite: *Rank* 91 / 179 *Score* 54.11   **WESTMINSTER**

CATEGORY	RANK	SCORE	STATISTIC	VALUE	RANK	SCORE
Economics	88	52.75	Median Household Income	$41,364	72	27.3
			% of Families Above Poverty Level	92.4%	100	78.2
Affordable Housing	114	52.25	Median Home Value	$225,500	104	63.4
			Median Rent	$736	120	41.1
Crime	76	73.45	Violent Crimes per 10,000 Population	66	61	79.2
			Property Crimes per 10,000 Population	630	108	67.7
Open Spaces	112	56.55	Population Density (Persons/Sq. Mile)	7780	128	68.1
			Average Rooms per Housing Unit	5.1	72	45.0
Education	99	40.40	% High School Enrollment/Completion	83.7%	102	53.8
			% College Graduates	18.1%	87	27.0
Commute	101	35.55	Average Work Commute in Minutes	26	82	57.7
			% Commuting on Public Transportation	2.1%	76	13.4
Community Stability	71	67.85	% Living in Same House as in 1979	35.5%	55	61.0
			% Living in Same County as in 1985	77.6%	96	74.7

Composite: *Rank* 93 / 179 *Score* 53.80   **PALM SPRINGS**

CATEGORY	RANK	SCORE	STATISTIC	VALUE	RANK	SCORE
Economics	126	42.45	Median Household Income	$27,538	153	10.5
			% of Families Above Poverty Level	91.2%	110	74.4
Affordable Housing	34	75.70	Median Home Value	$138,800	39	83.4
			Median Rent	$563	36	68.0
Crime	128	50.10	Violent Crimes per 10,000 Population	140	119	51.1
			Property Crimes per 10,000 Population	916	132	49.1
Open Spaces	75	65.60	Population Density (Persons/Sq. Mile)	525	3	98.7
			Average Rooms per Housing Unit	4.6	118	32.5
Education	109	35.60	% High School Enrollment/Completion	79.3%	144	40.5
			% College Graduates	20.4%	82	30.7
Commute	12	56.65	Average Work Commute in Minutes	17	2	92.3
			% Commuting on Public Transportation	3.3%	50	21.0
Community Stability	142	50.50	% Living in Same House as in 1979	26.3%	110	45.1
			% Living in Same County as in 1985	65.1%	153	55.9

Metropolitan Area Suburb Rankings
LOS ANGELES-ANAHEIM-RIVERSIDE

Composite: *Rank* 94 / 179 *Score* 53.72 **ARTESIA**

CATEGORY	RANK	SCORE	STATISTIC	VALUE	RANK	SCORE
Economics	97	50.95	Median Household Income	$36,383	98	21.2
			% of Families Above Poverty Level	93.2%	94	80.7
Affordable Housing	95	57.50	Median Home Value	$204,100	96	68.3
			Median Rent	$700	100	46.7
Crime	95	68.05	Violent Crimes per 10,000 Population	144	120	49.6
			Property Crimes per 10,000 Population	340	31	86.5
Open Spaces	139	47.75	Population Density (Persons/Sq. Mile)	9575	146	60.5
			Average Rooms per Housing Unit	4.7	108	35.0
Education	105	37.75	% High School Enrollment/Completion	84.5%	98	56.2
			% College Graduates	13.4%	108	19.3
Commute	76	38.40	Average Work Commute in Minutes	23	26	69.2
			% Commuting on Public Transportation	1.2%	102	7.6
Community Stability	45	75.65	% Living in Same House as in 1979	38.9%	42	66.8
			% Living in Same County as in 1985	84.1%	62	84.5

Composite: *Rank* 95 / 179 *Score* 53.71 **GLENDALE**

CATEGORY	RANK	SCORE	STATISTIC	VALUE	RANK	SCORE
Economics	130	41.05	Median Household Income	$34,372	111	18.8
			% of Families Above Poverty Level	87.7%	140	63.3
Affordable Housing	137	42.60	Median Home Value	$341,700	160	36.6
			Median Rent	$688	94	48.6
Crime	30	84.30	Violent Crimes per 10,000 Population	37	20	90.2
			Property Crimes per 10,000 Population	465	62	78.4
Open Spaces	135	49.30	Population Density (Persons/Sq. Mile)	5882	106	76.1
			Average Rooms per Housing Unit	4.2	147	22.5
Education	55	58.00	% High School Enrollment/Completion	89.7%	62	71.9
			% College Graduates	28.6%	51	44.1
Commute	47	44.75	Average Work Commute in Minutes	25	62	61.5
			% Commuting on Public Transportation	4.4%	34	28.0
Community Stability	123	55.95	% Living in Same House as in 1979	25.5%	116	43.7
			% Living in Same County as in 1985	73.3%	117	68.2

Composite: *Rank* 96 / 179 *Score* 53.69 **VINCENT**

CATEGORY	RANK	SCORE	STATISTIC	VALUE	RANK	SCORE
Economics	83	53.90	Median Household Income	$40,517	75	26.2
			% of Families Above Poverty Level	93.5%	89	81.6
Affordable Housing	121	50.65	Median Home Value	$158,800	55	78.8
			Median Rent	$856	149	22.5
Crime	N/A	N/A	Violent Crimes per 10,000 Population	N/A	N/A	N/A
			Property Crimes per 10,000 Population	N/A	N/A	N/A
Open Spaces	119	54.70	Population Density (Persons/Sq. Mile)	9230	141	61.9
			Average Rooms per Housing Unit	5.2	62	47.5
Education	98	40.90	% High School Enrollment/Completion	89.2%	71	70.4
			% College Graduates	8.6%	144	11.4
Commute	112	33.30	Average Work Commute in Minutes	28	116	50.0
			% Commuting on Public Transportation	2.6%	67	16.6
Community Stability	11	88.70	% Living in Same House as in 1979	46.7%	15	80.3
			% Living in Same County as in 1985	92.5%	2	97.1

Metropolitan Area Suburb Rankings
LOS ANGELES-ANAHEIM-RIVERSIDE

Composite: *Rank* 97 / 179   *Score* 53.61   **AZUSA**

CATEGORY	RANK	SCORE	STATISTIC	VALUE	RANK	SCORE
Economics	127	41.75	Median Household Income	$31,889	130	15.8
			% of Families Above Poverty Level	89.1%	128	67.7
Affordable Housing	60	67.45	Median Home Value	$151,800	49	80.4
			Median Rent	$650	77	54.5
Crime	59	79.05	Violent Crimes per 10,000 Population	57	51	82.6
			Property Crimes per 10,000 Population	509	80	75.5
Open Spaces	122	53.25	Population Density (Persons/Sq. Mile)	4592	87	81.5
			Average Rooms per Housing Unit	4.3	145	25.0
Education	121	33.05	% High School Enrollment/Completion	82.1%	124	48.9
			% College Graduates	12.1%	118	17.2
Commute	86	37.45	Average Work Commute in Minutes	26	82	57.7
			% Commuting on Public Transportation	2.7%	65	17.2
Community Stability	88	63.25	% Living in Same House as in 1979	25.9%	114	44.4
			% Living in Same County as in 1985	82.5%	80	82.1

Composite: *Rank* 98 / 179   *Score* 53.56   **CATHEDRAL CITY**

CATEGORY	RANK	SCORE	STATISTIC	VALUE	RANK	SCORE
Economics	124	43.20	Median Household Income	$30,908	139	14.6
			% of Families Above Poverty Level	90.4%	117	71.8
Affordable Housing	47	71.90	Median Home Value	$114,200	22	89.1
			Median Rent	$649	74	54.7
Crime	102	65.45	Violent Crimes per 10,000 Population	112	102	61.7
			Property Crimes per 10,000 Population	606	101	69.2
Open Spaces	76	64.60	Population Density (Persons/Sq. Mile)	1591	21	94.2
			Average Rooms per Housing Unit	4.7	108	35.0
Education	131	30.15	% High School Enrollment/Completion	79.7%	141	41.7
			% College Graduates	13.0%	113	18.6
Commute	13	55.70	Average Work Commute in Minutes	17	2	92.3
			% Commuting on Public Transportation	3.0%	57	19.1
Community Stability	158	43.95	% Living in Same House as in 1979	18.0%	161	30.7
			% Living in Same County as in 1985	66.0%	148	57.2

Composite: *Rank* 99 / 179   *Score* 53.54   **EL TORO**

CATEGORY	RANK	SCORE	STATISTIC	VALUE	RANK	SCORE
Economics	16	70.95	Median Household Income	$56,324	18	45.4
			% of Families Above Poverty Level	98.2%	8	96.5
Affordable Housing	145	37.50	Median Home Value	$258,900	134	55.7
			Median Rent	$877	154	19.3
Crime	N/A	N/A	Violent Crimes per 10,000 Population	N/A	N/A	N/A
			Property Crimes per 10,000 Population	N/A	N/A	N/A
Open Spaces	42	70.45	Population Density (Persons/Sq. Mile)	5331	97	78.4
			Average Rooms per Housing Unit	5.8	26	62.5
Education	36	64.95	% High School Enrollment/Completion	90.5%	56	74.3
			% College Graduates	35.6%	30	55.6
Commute	145	26.60	Average Work Commute in Minutes	28	116	50.0
			% Commuting on Public Transportation	0.5%	146	3.2
Community Stability	141	50.80	% Living in Same House as in 1979	19.9%	149	34.0
			% Living in Same County as in 1985	72.9%	120	67.6

Metropolitan Area Suburb Rankings
LOS ANGELES-ANAHEIM-RIVERSIDE

Composite: *Rank* 99 / 179 *Score* 53.54   **ROWLAND HEIGHTS**

CATEGORY	RANK	SCORE	STATISTIC	VALUE	RANK	SCORE
Economics	62	57.50	Median Household Income	$46,404	46	33.4
			% of Families Above Poverty Level	93.5%	89	81.6
Affordable Housing	111	53.45	Median Home Value	$236,400	117	60.9
			Median Rent	$705	103	46.0
Crime	N/A	N/A	Violent Crimes per 10,000 Population	N/A	N/A	N/A
			Property Crimes per 10,000 Population	N/A	N/A	N/A
Open Spaces	77	64.40	Population Density (Persons/Sq. Mile)	5231	96	78.8
			Average Rooms per Housing Unit	5.3	57	50.0
Education	52	59.35	% High School Enrollment/Completion	91.9%	44	78.5
			% College Graduates	26.2%	61	40.2
Commute	154	22.40	Average Work Commute in Minutes	33	161	30.8
			% Commuting on Public Transportation	2.2%	75	14.0
Community Stability	84	64.15	% Living in Same House as in 1979	26.7%	108	45.8
			% Living in Same County as in 1985	82.8%	73	82.5

Composite: *Rank* 101 / 179 *Score* 53.31   **HESPERIA**

CATEGORY	RANK	SCORE	STATISTIC	VALUE	RANK	SCORE
Economics	130	41.05	Median Household Income	$30,795	141	14.4
			% of Families Above Poverty Level	89.1%	128	67.7
Affordable Housing	20	80.95	Median Home Value	$105,600	18	91.1
			Median Rent	$545	29	70.8
Crime	24	86.00	Violent Crimes per 10,000 Population	35	17	90.9
			Property Crimes per 10,000 Population	424	48	81.1
Open Spaces	28	74.50	Population Density (Persons/Sq. Mile)	1044	14	96.5
			Average Rooms per Housing Unit	5.4	47	52.5
Education	130	30.60	% High School Enrollment/Completion	83.4%	104	52.9
			% College Graduates	6.7%	155	8.3
Commute	169	15.70	Average Work Commute in Minutes	33	161	30.8
			% Commuting on Public Transportation	0.1%	172	0.6
Community Stability	156	44.35	% Living in Same House as in 1979	19.0%	156	32.5
			% Living in Same County as in 1985	65.3%	151	56.2

Composite: *Rank* 102 / 179 *Score* 53.26   **GARDEN GROVE**

CATEGORY	RANK	SCORE	STATISTIC	VALUE	RANK	SCORE
Economics	95	51.50	Median Household Income	$39,882	80	25.5
			% of Families Above Poverty Level	92.2%	103	77.5
Affordable Housing	105	54.80	Median Home Value	$197,800	87	69.8
			Median Rent	$745	123	39.8
Crime	77	73.15	Violent Crimes per 10,000 Population	69	68	78.0
			Property Crimes per 10,000 Population	621	103	68.3
Open Spaces	130	52.35	Population Density (Persons/Sq. Mile)	7975	131	67.2
			Average Rooms per Housing Unit	4.8	101	37.5
Education	107	36.60	% High School Enrollment/Completion	82.3%	122	49.5
			% College Graduates	16.1%	97	23.7
Commute	75	38.70	Average Work Commute in Minutes	26	82	57.7
			% Commuting on Public Transportation	3.1%	55	19.7
Community Stability	75	65.75	% Living in Same House as in 1979	33.7%	64	57.9
			% Living in Same County as in 1985	76.9%	101	73.6

Metropolitan Area Suburb Rankings
LOS ANGELES-ANAHEIM-RIVERSIDE

Composite: **Rank** 103 / 179 *Score* 53.17   **CHINO**

CATEGORY	RANK	SCORE	STATISTIC	VALUE	RANK	SCORE
Economics	72	55.60	Median Household Income	$41,958	69	28.0
			% of Families Above Poverty Level	94.0%	84	83.2
Affordable Housing	63	64.55	Median Home Value	$173,300	75	75.5
			Median Rent	$656	81	53.6
Crime	63	77.85	Violent Crimes per 10,000 Population	66	61	79.2
			Property Crimes per 10,000 Population	494	75	76.5
Open Spaces	47	69.30	Population Density (Persons/Sq. Mile)	3501	71	86.1
			Average Rooms per Housing Unit	5.4	47	52.5
Education	123	32.95	% High School Enrollment/Completion	82.2%	123	49.2
			% College Graduates	11.8%	120	16.7
Commute	153	22.75	Average Work Commute in Minutes	30	148	42.3
			% Commuting on Public Transportation	0.5%	146	3.2
Community Stability	146	49.20	% Living in Same House as in 1979	28.7%	97	49.2
			% Living in Same County as in 1985	60.7%	164	49.2

Composite: **Rank** 104 / 179 *Score* 53.13   **WEST CARSON**

CATEGORY	RANK	SCORE	STATISTIC	VALUE	RANK	SCORE
Economics	49	62.05	Median Household Income	$44,181	58	30.7
			% of Families Above Poverty Level	97.2%	32	93.4
Affordable Housing	133	43.80	Median Home Value	$236,000	116	61.0
			Median Rent	$830	145	26.6
Crime	N/A	N/A	Violent Crimes per 10,000 Population	N/A	N/A	N/A
			Property Crimes per 10,000 Population	N/A	N/A	N/A
Open Spaces	132	51.70	Population Density (Persons/Sq. Mile)	8892	137	63.4
			Average Rooms per Housing Unit	4.9	89	40.0
Education	79	47.65	% High School Enrollment/Completion	86.6%	86	62.5
			% College Graduates	21.7%	77	32.8
Commute	70	40.00	Average Work Commute in Minutes	24	43	65.4
			% Commuting on Public Transportation	2.3%	73	14.6
Community Stability	51	73.60	% Living in Same House as in 1979	34.6%	60	59.4
			% Living in Same County as in 1985	86.3%	51	87.8

Composite: **Rank** 105 / 179 *Score* 53.08   **BALDWIN PARK**

CATEGORY	RANK	SCORE	STATISTIC	VALUE	RANK	SCORE
Economics	139	39.20	Median Household Income	$32,684	123	16.7
			% of Families Above Poverty Level	87.2%	144	61.7
Affordable Housing	57	67.85	Median Home Value	$149,700	46	80.9
			Median Rent	$648	72	54.8
Crime	50	79.95	Violent Crimes per 10,000 Population	82	81	73.1
			Property Crimes per 10,000 Population	336	29	86.8
Open Spaces	152	42.00	Population Density (Persons/Sq. Mile)	10511	155	56.5
			Average Rooms per Housing Unit	4.4	134	27.5
Education	122	32.90	% High School Enrollment/Completion	83.3%	106	52.6
			% College Graduates	9.7%	139	13.2
Commute	76	38.40	Average Work Commute in Minutes	28	116	50.0
			% Commuting on Public Transportation	4.2%	36	26.8
Community Stability	58	71.25	% Living in Same House as in 1979	30.9%	80	53.0
			% Living in Same County as in 1985	87.4%	39	89.5

Metropolitan Area Suburb Rankings
LOS ANGELES-ANAHEIM-RIVERSIDE

Composite: *Rank* 106 / 179 *Score* 52.95   **NORWALK**

CATEGORY	RANK	SCORE	STATISTIC	VALUE	RANK	SCORE
Economics	96	51.35	Median Household Income	$38,124	90	23.3
			% of Families Above Poverty Level	92.8%	96	79.4
Affordable Housing	79	61.60	Median Home Value	$164,700	65	77.4
			Median Rent	$706	104	45.8
Crime	101	65.55	Violent Crimes per 10,000 Population	148	121	48.1
			Property Crimes per 10,000 Population	394	40	83.0
Open Spaces	144	46.30	Population Density (Persons/Sq. Mile)	9661	148	60.1
-			Average Rooms per Housing Unit	4.6	118	32.5
Education	139	28.40	% High School Enrollment/Completion	80.2%	139	43.2
			% College Graduates	9.9%	136	13.6
Commute	76	38.40	Average Work Commute in Minutes	25	62	61.5
			% Commuting on Public Transportation	2.4%	71	15.3
Community Stability	30	79.05	% Living in Same House as in 1979	40.6%	27	69.8
			% Living in Same County as in 1985	86.6%	48	88.3

Composite: *Rank* 107 / 179 *Score* 52.81   **REDONDO BEACH**

CATEGORY	RANK	SCORE	STATISTIC	VALUE	RANK	SCORE
Economics	30	65.45	Median Household Income	$51,913	29	40.1
			% of Families Above Poverty Level	96.4%	46	90.8
Affordable Housing	164	28.25	Median Home Value	$347,900	162	35.1
			Median Rent	$863	152	21.4
Crime	80	71.85	Violent Crimes per 10,000 Population	69	68	78.0
			Property Crimes per 10,000 Population	660	115	65.7
Open Spaces	143	46.45	Population Density (Persons/Sq. Mile)	9586	147	60.4
			Average Rooms per Housing Unit	4.6	118	32.5
Education	33	66.75	% High School Enrollment/Completion	89.1%	72	70.1
			% College Graduates	40.4%	18	63.4
Commute	111	33.65	Average Work Commute in Minutes	26	82	57.7
			% Commuting on Public Transportation	1.5%	93	9.6
Community Stability	120	57.25	% Living in Same House as in 1979	23.2%	133	39.7
			% Living in Same County as in 1985	77.7%	94	74.8

Composite: *Rank* 108 / 179 *Score* 52.76   **TWENTY-NINE PALMS**

CATEGORY	RANK	SCORE	STATISTIC	VALUE	RANK	SCORE
Economics	149	36.95	Median Household Income	$24,527	164	6.8
			% of Families Above Poverty Level	88.9%	131	67.1
Affordable Housing	2	93.85	Median Home Value	$67,000	1	100.0
			Median Rent	$436	3	87.7
Crime	94	68.40	Violent Crimes per 10,000 Population	102	92	65.5
			Property Crimes per 10,000 Population	575	91	71.3
Open Spaces	72	66.25	Population Density (Persons/Sq. Mile)	218	1	100.0
			Average Rooms per Housing Unit	4.6	118	32.5
Education	112	34.90	% High School Enrollment/Completion	82.5%	116	50.2
			% College Graduates	13.6%	107	19.6
Commute	35	47.40	Average Work Commute in Minutes	17	2	92.3
			% Commuting on Public Transportation	0.4%	155	2.5
Community Stability	176	21.55	% Living in Same House as in 1979	19.6%	152	33.5
			% Living in Same County as in 1985	34.4%	178	9.6

Composite: **Rank** 109 / 179   *Score* 52.60   **SANTA PAULA**

CATEGORY	RANK	SCORE	STATISTIC	VALUE	RANK	SCORE
Economics	125	43.00	Median Household Income	$31,605	131	15.4
			% of Families Above Poverty Level	90.0%	120	70.6
Affordable Housing	64	64.40	Median Home Value	$200,300	89	69.2
			Median Rent	$617	58	59.6
Crime	69	76.45	Violent Crimes per 10,000 Population	64	57	79.9
			Property Crimes per 10,000 Population	548	86	73.0
Open Spaces	118	55.20	Population Density (Persons/Sq. Mile)	5449	100	77.9
			Average Rooms per Housing Unit	4.6	118	32.5
Education	160	20.10	% High School Enrollment/Completion	74.7%	162	26.6
			% College Graduates	9.9%	136	13.6
Commute	90	36.85	Average Work Commute in Minutes	23	26	69.2
			% Commuting on Public Transportation	0.7%	136	4.5
Community Stability	54	72.20	% Living in Same House as in 1979	33.5%	67	57.5
			% Living in Same County as in 1985	85.7%	53	86.9

Composite: **Rank** 110 / 179   *Score* 52.48   **LAGUNA HILLS**

CATEGORY	RANK	SCORE	STATISTIC	VALUE	RANK	SCORE
Economics	54	61.05	Median Household Income	$40,489	76	26.2
			% of Families Above Poverty Level	98.0%	10	95.9
Affordable Housing	148	36.45	Median Home Value	$239,300	119	60.2
			Median Rent	$919	166	12.7
Crime	N/A	N/A	Violent Crimes per 10,000 Population	N/A	N/A	N/A
			Property Crimes per 10,000 Population	N/A	N/A	N/A
Open Spaces	88	62.55	Population Density (Persons/Sq. Mile)	4343	80	82.6
			Average Rooms per Housing Unit	5.0	79	42.5
Education	28	69.00	% High School Enrollment/Completion	94.1%	33	85.2
			% College Graduates	33.9%	34	52.8
Commute	144	27.25	Average Work Commute in Minutes	29	137	46.2
			% Commuting on Public Transportation	1.3%	98	8.3
Community Stability	114	58.55	% Living in Same House as in 1979	29.9%	85	51.3
			% Living in Same County as in 1985	71.7%	128	65.8

Composite: **Rank** 111 / 179   *Score* 52.46   **SANTA MONICA**

CATEGORY	RANK	SCORE	STATISTIC	VALUE	RANK	SCORE
Economics	90	52.45	Median Household Income	$35,997	102	20.7
			% of Families Above Poverty Level	94.3%	73	84.2
Affordable Housing	149	36.40	Median Home Value	$500,001	172	0.0
			Median Rent	$532	24	72.8
Crime	131	45.10	Violent Crimes per 10,000 Population	148	121	48.1
			Property Crimes per 10,000 Population	1,024	138	42.1
Open Spaces	160	37.05	Population Density (Persons/Sq. Mile)	10507	154	56.6
			Average Rooms per Housing Unit	4.0	159	17.5
Education	23	73.10	% High School Enrollment/Completion	91.7%	45	77.9
			% College Graduates	43.4%	16	68.3
Commute	19	53.05	Average Work Commute in Minutes	23	26	69.2
			% Commuting on Public Transportation	5.8%	25	36.9
Community Stability	64	70.05	% Living in Same House as in 1979	31.8%	75	54.6
			% Living in Same County as in 1985	84.8%	59	85.5

Metropolitan Area Suburb Rankings
LOS ANGELES-ANAHEIM-RIVERSIDE

Composite: Rank 112 / 179 *Score* 52.42 VALINDA

CATEGORY	RANK	SCORE	STATISTIC	VALUE	RANK	SCORE
Economics	83	53.90	Median Household Income	$41,028	74	26.8
			% of Families Above Poverty Level	93.3%	92	81.0
Affordable Housing	112	53.25	Median Home Value	$164,100	63	77.6
			Median Rent	$815	142	28.9
Crime	N/A	N/A	Violent Crimes per 10,000 Population	N/A	N/A	N/A
			Property Crimes per 10,000 Population	N/A	N/A	N/A
Open Spaces	123	53.15	Population Density (Persons/Sq. Mile)	9378	143	61.3
			Average Rooms per Housing Unit	5.1	72	45.0
Education	102	39.75	% High School Enrollment/Completion	87.5%	79	65.3
			% College Graduates	10.3%	130	14.2
Commute	125	30.70	Average Work Commute in Minutes	30	148	42.3
			% Commuting on Public Transportation	3.0%	57	19.1
Community Stability	20	83.75	% Living in Same House as in 1979	43.4%	21	74.6
			% Living in Same County as in 1985	89.7%	17	92.9

Composite: Rank 113 / 179 *Score* 52.38 SOUTH WHITTIER

CATEGORY	RANK	SCORE	STATISTIC	VALUE	RANK	SCORE
Economics	93	51.95	Median Household Income	$39,324	84	24.8
			% of Families Above Poverty Level	92.7%	97	79.1
Affordable Housing	77	61.75	Median Home Value	$173,000	74	75.5
			Median Rent	$692	96	48.0
Crime	N/A	N/A	Violent Crimes per 10,000 Population	N/A	N/A	N/A
			Property Crimes per 10,000 Population	N/A	N/A	N/A
Open Spaces	133	51.05	Population Density (Persons/Sq. Mile)	9203	140	62.1
			Average Rooms per Housing Unit	4.9	89	40.0
Education	120	33.65	% High School Enrollment/Completion	83.4%	104	52.9
			% College Graduates	10.4%	129	14.4
Commute	91	36.50	Average Work Commute in Minutes	25	62	61.5
			% Commuting on Public Transportation	1.8%	82	11.5
Community Stability	29	79.35	% Living in Same House as in 1979	40.2%	33	69.1
			% Living in Same County as in 1985	87.5%	36	89.6

Composite: Rank 114 / 179 *Score* 52.31 SAN FERNANDO

CATEGORY	RANK	SCORE	STATISTIC	VALUE	RANK	SCORE
Economics	147	37.25	Median Household Income	$32,128	128	16.0
			% of Families Above Poverty Level	86.2%	154	58.5
Affordable Housing	44	72.75	Median Home Value	$155,900	52	79.5
			Median Rent	$576	39	66.0
Crime	100	65.60	Violent Crimes per 10,000 Population	135	112	53.0
			Property Crimes per 10,000 Population	468	66	78.2
Open Spaces	153	41.75	Population Density (Persons/Sq. Mile)	9454	145	61.0
			Average Rooms per Housing Unit	4.2	147	22.5
Education	162	18.80	% High School Enrollment/Completion	76.3%	154	31.4
			% College Graduates	5.4%	165	6.2
Commute	20	52.75	Average Work Commute in Minutes	23	26	69.2
			% Commuting on Public Transportation	5.7%	26	36.3
Community Stability	39	77.30	% Living in Same House as in 1979	38.0%	43	65.3
			% Living in Same County as in 1985	87.3%	43	89.3

Metropolitan Area Suburb Rankings
LOS ANGELES-ANAHEIM-RIVERSIDE

Composite: **Rank** 115 / 179 **Score** 52.09   **HERMOSA BEACH**

CATEGORY	RANK	SCORE	STATISTIC	VALUE	RANK	SCORE
Economics	27	66.20	Median Household Income	$54,497	22	43.2
			% of Families Above Poverty Level	95.9%	53	89.2
Affordable Housing	171	16.85	Median Home Value	$431,500	169	15.8
			Median Rent	$886	156	17.9
Crime	67	77.20	Violent Crimes per 10,000 Population	46	35	86.7
			Property Crimes per 10,000 Population	629	107	67.7
Open Spaces	161	36.10	Population Density (Persons/Sq. Mile)	12729	165	47.2
			Average Rooms per Housing Unit	4.3	145	25.0
Education	7	90.55	% High School Enrollment/Completion	96.9%	12	93.7
			% College Graduates	55.1%	4	87.4
Commute	135	28.50	Average Work Commute in Minutes	28	116	50.0
			% Commuting on Public Transportation	1.1%	106	7.0
Community Stability	147	49.25	% Living in Same House as in 1979	21.9%	142	37.5
			% Living in Same County as in 1985	68.5%	142	61.0

Composite: **Rank** 116 / 179 **Score** 51.99   **WEST PUENTE VALLEY**

CATEGORY	RANK	SCORE	STATISTIC	VALUE	RANK	SCORE
Economics	102	49.45	Median Household Income	$39,641	81	25.2
			% of Families Above Poverty Level	91.0%	111	73.7
Affordable Housing	119	50.80	Median Home Value	$157,700	53	79.1
			Median Rent	$856	149	22.5
Crime	N/A	N/A	Violent Crimes per 10,000 Population	N/A	N/A	N/A
			Property Crimes per 10,000 Population	N/A	N/A	N/A
Open Spaces	127	52.75	Population Density (Persons/Sq. Mile)	11342	160	53.0
			Average Rooms per Housing Unit	5.4	47	52.5
Education	141	28.00	% High School Enrollment/Completion	82.4%	119	49.8
			% College Graduates	5.4%	165	6.2
Commute	82	38.05	Average Work Commute in Minutes	28	116	50.0
			% Commuting on Public Transportation	4.1%	37	26.1
Community Stability	4	92.90	% Living in Same House as in 1979	52.6%	6	90.5
			% Living in Same County as in 1985	91.3%	9	95.3

Composite: **Rank** 117 / 179 **Score** 51.97   **OXNARD**

CATEGORY	RANK	SCORE	STATISTIC	VALUE	RANK	SCORE
Economics	109	47.00	Median Household Income	$37,174	95	22.2
			% of Families Above Poverty Level	90.4%	117	71.8
Affordable Housing	91	58.80	Median Home Value	$202,600	94	68.7
			Median Rent	$686	93	48.9
Crime	98	66.55	Violent Crimes per 10,000 Population	114	103	61.0
			Property Crimes per 10,000 Population	562	90	72.1
Open Spaces	113	55.70	Population Density (Persons/Sq. Mile)	5818	105	76.4
			Average Rooms per Housing Unit	4.7	108	35.0
Education	137	28.80	% High School Enrollment/Completion	78.8%	148	39.0
			% College Graduates	13.0%	113	18.6
Commute	58	41.95	Average Work Commute in Minutes	21	13	76.9
			% Commuting on Public Transportation	1.1%	106	7.0
Community Stability	79	65.00	% Living in Same House as in 1979	29.5%	88	50.6
			% Living in Same County as in 1985	80.7%	86	79.4

Metropolitan Area Suburb Rankings
LOS ANGELES-ANAHEIM-RIVERSIDE

Composite: **Rank** 118 / 179 *Score* 51.94 **RIALTO**

CATEGORY	RANK	SCORE	STATISTIC	VALUE	RANK	SCORE
Economics	113	46.25	Median Household Income	$36,233	99	21.0
			% of Families Above Poverty Level	90.3%	119	71.5
Affordable Housing	33	75.90	Median Home Value	$123,900	26	86.9
			Median Rent	$583	42	64.9
Crime	91	69.40	Violent Crimes per 10,000 Population	93	88	68.9
			Property Crimes per 10,000 Population	596	98	69.9
Open Spaces	46	69.50	Population Density (Persons/Sq. Mile)	3407	69	86.5
			Average Rooms per Housing Unit	5.4	47	52.5
Education	109	35.60	% High School Enrollment/Completion	84.8%	94	57.1
			% College Graduates	10.2%	132	14.1
Commute	163	17.95	Average Work Commute in Minutes	33	161	30.8
			% Commuting on Public Transportation	0.8%	127	5.1
Community Stability	148	49.00	% Living in Same House as in 1979	24.7%	121	42.3
			% Living in Same County as in 1985	65.0%	154	55.7

Composite: **Rank** 119 / 179 *Score* 51.92 **LA PUENTE**

CATEGORY	RANK	SCORE	STATISTIC	VALUE	RANK	SCORE
Economics	134	40.20	Median Household Income	$33,273	117	17.4
			% of Families Above Poverty Level	87.6%	141	63.0
Affordable Housing	49	70.50	Median Home Value	$154,800	51	79.7
			Median Rent	$606	52	61.3
Crime	121	56.60	Violent Crimes per 10,000 Population	198	132	29.2
			Property Crimes per 10,000 Population	379	37	84.0
Open Spaces	146	44.35	Population Density (Persons/Sq. Mile)	10587	156	56.2
			Average Rooms per Housing Unit	4.6	118	32.5
Education	142	27.90	% High School Enrollment/Completion	81.2%	131	46.2
			% College Graduates	7.5%	149	9.6
Commute	49	44.40	Average Work Commute in Minutes	27	104	53.8
			% Commuting on Public Transportation	5.5%	27	35.0
Community Stability	28	79.50	% Living in Same House as in 1979	40.1%	35	68.9
			% Living in Same County as in 1985	87.8%	32	90.1

Composite: **Rank** 120 / 179 *Score* 51.85 **COSTA MESA**

CATEGORY	RANK	SCORE	STATISTIC	VALUE	RANK	SCORE
Economics	79	54.60	Median Household Income	$40,313	77	26.0
			% of Families Above Poverty Level	94.0%	84	83.2
Affordable Housing	136	43.05	Median Home Value	$255,800	133	56.4
			Median Rent	$810	138	29.7
Crime	104	64.85	Violent Crimes per 10,000 Population	76	75	75.4
			Property Crimes per 10,000 Population	837	131	54.3
Open Spaces	128	52.40	Population Density (Persons/Sq. Mile)	6195	110	74.8
			Average Rooms per Housing Unit	4.5	129	30.0
Education	81	46.85	% High School Enrollment/Completion	83.0%	109	51.7
			% College Graduates	27.3%	55	42.0
Commute	40	46.75	Average Work Commute in Minutes	22	19	73.1
			% Commuting on Public Transportation	3.2%	53	20.4
Community Stability	131	54.45	% Living in Same House as in 1979	23.1%	134	39.6
			% Living in Same County as in 1985	74.0%	114	69.3

Metropolitan Area Suburb Rankings
LOS ANGELES-ANAHEIM-RIVERSIDE

Composite: **Rank** 121 / 179 *Score* 51.82   **BANNING**

CATEGORY	RANK	SCORE	STATISTIC	VALUE	RANK	SCORE
Economics	160	31.80	Median Household Income	$22,514	172	4.4
			% of Families Above Poverty Level	86.4%	153	59.2
Affordable Housing	6	88.55	Median Home Value	$89,300	7	94.8
			Median Rent	$471	8	82.3
Crime	108	63.75	Violent Crimes per 10,000 Population	105	95	64.4
			Property Crimes per 10,000 Population	701	122	63.1
Open Spaces	66	66.85	Population Density (Persons/Sq. Mile)	1116	16	96.2
			Average Rooms per Housing Unit	4.8	101	37.5
Education	147	24.05	% High School Enrollment/Completion	77.4%	152	34.7
			% College Graduates	9.8%	138	13.4
Commute	106	34.30	Average Work Commute in Minutes	24	43	65.4
			% Commuting on Public Transportation	0.5%	146	3.2
Community Stability	135	53.45	% Living in Same House as in 1979	27.1%	106	46.5
			% Living in Same County as in 1985	68.1%	143	60.4

Composite: **Rank** 122 / 179 *Score* 51.63   **SAN JACINTO**

CATEGORY	RANK	SCORE	STATISTIC	VALUE	RANK	SCORE
Economics	154	34.70	Median Household Income	$20,810	175	2.3
			% of Families Above Poverty Level	88.9%	131	67.1
Affordable Housing	5	89.70	Median Home Value	$90,200	8	94.6
			Median Rent	$455	6	84.8
Crime	129	49.65	Violent Crimes per 10,000 Population	160	127	43.6
			Property Crimes per 10,000 Population	815	130	55.7
Open Spaces	83	63.50	Population Density (Persons/Sq. Mile)	1531	20	94.5
			Average Rooms per Housing Unit	4.6	118	32.5
Education	106	37.50	% High School Enrollment/Completion	87.4%	80	65.0
			% College Graduates	7.7%	147	10.0
Commute	81	38.15	Average Work Commute in Minutes	22	19	73.1
			% Commuting on Public Transportation	0.5%	146	3.2
Community Stability	151	48.20	% Living in Same House as in 1979	20.3%	147	34.7
			% Living in Same County as in 1985	69.0%	141	61.7

Composite: **Rank** 123 / 179 *Score* 51.51   **LOMITA**

CATEGORY	RANK	SCORE	STATISTIC	VALUE	RANK	SCORE
Economics	107	47.85	Median Household Income	$36,222	100	21.0
			% of Families Above Poverty Level	91.3%	108	74.7
Affordable Housing	130	46.70	Median Home Value	$296,500	149	47.0
			Median Rent	$702	101	46.4
Crime	72	75.30	Violent Crimes per 10,000 Population	117	105	59.8
			Property Crimes per 10,000 Population	274	13	90.8
Open Spaces	149	43.85	Population Density (Persons/Sq. Mile)	10232	153	57.7
			Average Rooms per Housing Unit	4.5	129	30.0
Education	104	39.05	% High School Enrollment/Completion	81.8%	126	48.0
			% College Graduates	20.0%	84	30.1
Commute	61	41.30	Average Work Commute in Minutes	23	26	69.2
			% Commuting on Public Transportation	2.1%	76	13.4
Community Stability	73	66.55	% Living in Same House as in 1979	25.4%	118	43.5
			% Living in Same County as in 1985	87.5%	36	89.6

Metropolitan Area Suburb Rankings
LOS ANGELES-ANAHEIM-RIVERSIDE

Composite: Rank 124 / 179 Score 51.39 YUCCA VALLEY

CATEGORY	RANK	SCORE	STATISTIC	VALUE	RANK	SCORE
Economics	158	32.10	Median Household Income	$22,563	170	4.4
			% of Families Above Poverty Level	86.6%	148	59.8
Affordable Housing	3	91.85	Median Home Value	$78,200	5	97.4
			Median Rent	$445	5	86.3
Crime	N/A	N/A	Violent Crimes per 10,000 Population	N/A	N/A	N/A
			Property Crimes per 10,000 Population	N/A	N/A	N/A
Open Spaces	65	67.15	Population Density (Persons/Sq. Mile)	984	12	96.8
			Average Rooms per Housing Unit	4.8	101	37.5
Education	129	31.00	% High School Enrollment/Completion	81.4%	130	46.8
			% College Graduates	10.9%	124	15.2
Commute	115	32.70	Average Work Commute in Minutes	24	43	65.4
			% Commuting on Public Transportation	0.0%	175	0.0
Community Stability	134	53.55	% Living in Same House as in 1979	26.2%	112	44.9
			% Living in Same County as in 1985	69.3%	137	62.2

Composite: Rank 125 / 179 Score 51.36 GARDENA

CATEGORY	RANK	SCORE	STATISTIC	VALUE	RANK	SCORE
Economics	111	46.75	Median Household Income	$33,063	120	17.2
			% of Families Above Poverty Level	91.8%	104	76.3
Affordable Housing	75	62.10	Median Home Value	$200,900	90	69.1
			Median Rent	$646	71	55.1
Crime	130	45.20	Violent Crimes per 10,000 Population	212	136	23.9
			Property Crimes per 10,000 Population	649	113	66.5
Open Spaces	155	39.30	Population Density (Persons/Sq. Mile)	9439	144	61.1
			Average Rooms per Housing Unit	4.0	159	17.5
Education	88	44.65	% High School Enrollment/Completion	87.4%	80	65.0
			% College Graduates	16.5%	92	24.3
Commute	41	46.70	Average Work Commute in Minutes	23	26	69.2
			% Commuting on Public Transportation	3.8%	41	24.2
Community Stability	46	74.80	% Living in Same House as in 1979	35.0%	58	60.1
			% Living in Same County as in 1985	87.4%	39	89.5

Composite: Rank 126 / 179 Score 51.13 COLTON

CATEGORY	RANK	SCORE	STATISTIC	VALUE	RANK	SCORE
Economics	152	35.95	Median Household Income	$28,838	148	12.1
			% of Families Above Poverty Level	86.6%	148	59.8
Affordable Housing	17	82.75	Median Home Value	$97,100	11	93.0
			Median Rent	$534	25	72.5
Crime	110	63.20	Violent Crimes per 10,000 Population	90	85	70.1
			Property Crimes per 10,000 Population	806	129	56.3
Open Spaces	107	58.20	Population Density (Persons/Sq. Mile)	2845	57	88.9
			Average Rooms per Housing Unit	4.4	134	27.5
Education	108	35.80	% High School Enrollment/Completion	83.2%	108	52.3
			% College Graduates	13.4%	108	19.3
Commute	104	34.95	Average Work Commute in Minutes	24	43	65.4
			% Commuting on Public Transportation	0.7%	136	4.5
Community Stability	153	47.05	% Living in Same House as in 1979	22.5%	139	38.5
			% Living in Same County as in 1985	64.9%	155	55.6

Metropolitan Area Suburb Rankings
LOS ANGELES-ANAHEIM-RIVERSIDE

Composite: *Rank* 127 / 179 *Score* 51.04   **MIRA LOMA**

CATEGORY	RANK	SCORE	STATISTIC	VALUE	RANK	SCORE
Economics	50	61.95	Median Household Income	$45,913	53	32.8
			% of Families Above Poverty Level	96.5%	44	91.1
Affordable Housing	88	58.95	Median Home Value	$163,300	61	77.8
			Median Rent	$743	122	40.1
Crime	N/A	N/A	Violent Crimes per 10,000 Population	N/A	N/A	N/A
			Property Crimes per 10,000 Population	N/A	N/A	N/A
Open Spaces	17	79.05	Population Density (Persons/Sq. Mile)	2448	38	90.6
			Average Rooms per Housing Unit	6.0	16	67.5
Education	117	34.05	% High School Enrollment/Completion	86.0%	93	60.7
			% College Graduates	6.1%	157	7.4
Commute	174	10.25	Average Work Commute in Minutes	36	172	19.2
			% Commuting on Public Transportation	0.2%	165	1.3
Community Stability	93	62.00	% Living in Same House as in 1979	36.1%	49	62.0
			% Living in Same County as in 1985	69.2%	140	62.0

Composite: *Rank* 128 / 179 *Score* 51.03   **WILLOWBROOK**

CATEGORY	RANK	SCORE	STATISTIC	VALUE	RANK	SCORE
Economics	177	12.05	Median Household Income	$22,323	173	4.2
			% of Families Above Poverty Level	74.0%	177	19.9
Affordable Housing	14	84.95	Median Home Value	$97,600	12	92.9
			Median Rent	$505	16	77.0
Crime	N/A	N/A	Violent Crimes per 10,000 Population	N/A	N/A	N/A
			Property Crimes per 10,000 Population	N/A	N/A	N/A
Open Spaces	141	46.95	Population Density (Persons/Sq. Mile)	8762	136	63.9
			Average Rooms per Housing Unit	4.5	129	30.0
Education	153	22.40	% High School Enrollment/Completion	78.4%	149	37.8
			% College Graduates	5.9%	161	7.0
Commute	26	50.80	Average Work Commute in Minutes	27	104	53.8
			% Commuting on Public Transportation	7.5%	13	47.8
Community Stability	9	89.05	% Living in Same House as in 1979	47.3%	13	81.3
			% Living in Same County as in 1985	92.3%	3	96.8

Composite: *Rank* 129 / 179 *Score* 50.99   **SANTA FE SPRINGS**

CATEGORY	RANK	SCORE	STATISTIC	VALUE	RANK	SCORE
Economics	112	46.40	Median Household Income	$33,313	116	17.5
			% of Families Above Poverty Level	91.5%	107	75.3
Affordable Housing	61	67.20	Median Home Value	$168,200	68	76.6
			Median Rent	$629	61	57.8
Crime	143	21.55	Violent Crimes per 10,000 Population	220	137	20.8
			Property Crimes per 10,000 Population	1,330	143	22.3
Open Spaces	78	64.20	Population Density (Persons/Sq. Mile)	1791	25	93.4
			Average Rooms per Housing Unit	4.7	108	35.0
Education	143	25.20	% High School Enrollment/Completion	79.6%	142	41.4
			% College Graduates	7.1%	152	9.0
Commute	45	45.45	Average Work Commute in Minutes	22	19	73.1
			% Commuting on Public Transportation	2.8%	61	17.8
Community Stability	13	86.90	% Living in Same House as in 1979	46.0%	16	79.1
			% Living in Same County as in 1985	90.9%	11	94.7

Metropolitan Area Suburb Rankings
LOS ANGELES-ANAHEIM-RIVERSIDE

Composite: *Rank* 130 / 179 *Score* 50.90 **SOUTH GATE**

CATEGORY	RANK	SCORE	STATISTIC	VALUE	RANK	SCORE
Economics	157	32.15	Median Household Income	$27,279	155	10.2
			% of Families Above Poverty Level	84.8%	159	54.1
Affordable Housing	38	74.15	Median Home Value	$161,900	60	78.1
			Median Rent	$549	31	70.2
Crime	84	71.00	Violent Crimes per 10,000 Population	108	99	63.3
			Property Crimes per 10,000 Population	460	58	78.7
Open Spaces	164	33.20	Population Density (Persons/Sq. Mile)	11738	161	51.4
			Average Rooms per Housing Unit	3.9	166	15.0
Education	148	24.00	% High School Enrollment/Completion	79.8%	140	42.0
			% College Graduates	5.3%	167	6.0
Commute	24	51.45	Average Work Commute in Minutes	28	116	50.0
			% Commuting on Public Transportation	8.3%	11	52.9
Community Stability	63	70.35	% Living in Same House as in 1979	29.8%	86	51.1
			% Living in Same County as in 1985	87.5%	36	89.6

Composite: *Rank* 131 / 179 *Score* 50.64 **INDIO**

CATEGORY	RANK	SCORE	STATISTIC	VALUE	RANK	SCORE
Economics	163	28.50	Median Household Income	$25,976	158	8.6
			% of Families Above Poverty Level	83.0%	161	48.4
Affordable Housing	9	87.45	Median Home Value	$82,900	6	96.3
			Median Rent	$495	12	78.6
Crime	122	56.50	Violent Crimes per 10,000 Population	100	89	66.3
			Property Crimes per 10,000 Population	954	133	46.7
Open Spaces	110	57.15	Population Density (Persons/Sq. Mile)	2160	34	91.8
			Average Rooms per Housing Unit	4.2	147	22.5
Education	155	21.90	% High School Enrollment/Completion	76.3%	154	31.4
			% College Graduates	9.2%	141	12.4
Commute	33	48.05	Average Work Commute in Minutes	18	5	88.5
			% Commuting on Public Transportation	1.2%	102	7.6
Community Stability	128	54.95	% Living in Same House as in 1979	23.0%	135	39.4
			% Living in Same County as in 1985	74.8%	111	70.5

Composite: *Rank* 132 / 179 *Score* 50.35 **BELLFLOWER**

CATEGORY	RANK	SCORE	STATISTIC	VALUE	RANK	SCORE
Economics	106	47.80	Median Household Income	$32,711	122	16.8
			% of Families Above Poverty Level	92.6%	99	78.8
Affordable Housing	65	64.05	Median Home Value	$194,600	85	70.5
			Median Rent	$630	64	57.6
Crime	113	61.35	Violent Crimes per 10,000 Population	155	124	45.5
			Property Crimes per 10,000 Population	484	73	77.2
Open Spaces	154	40.25	Population Density (Persons/Sq. Mile)	10168	152	58.0
			Average Rooms per Housing Unit	4.2	147	22.5
Education	117	34.05	% High School Enrollment/Completion	82.8%	111	51.1
			% College Graduates	12.0%	119	17.0
Commute	63	41.00	Average Work Commute in Minutes	24	43	65.4
			% Commuting on Public Transportation	2.6%	67	16.6
Community Stability	85	63.95	% Living in Same House as in 1979	26.3%	110	45.1
			% Living in Same County as in 1985	83.0%	72	82.8

Metropolitan Area Suburb Rankings
LOS ANGELES-ANAHEIM-RIVERSIDE

Composite: **Rank** 133 / 179 *Score* 50.17   **ROSEMEAD**

CATEGORY	RANK	SCORE	STATISTIC	VALUE	RANK	SCORE
Economics	159	32.05	Median Household Income	$29,770	144	13.2
			% of Families Above Poverty Level	83.8%	160	50.9
Affordable Housing	71	62.85	Median Home Value	$193,000	83	70.9
			Median Rent	$648	72	54.8
Crime	96	67.90	Violent Crimes per 10,000 Population	136	116	52.7
			Property Crimes per 10,000 Population	393	39	83.1
Open Spaces	156	39.20	Population Density (Persons/Sq. Mile)	10077	150	58.4
			Average Rooms per Housing Unit	4.1	156	20.0
Education	126	31.95	% High School Enrollment/Completion	82.5%	116	50.2
			% College Graduates	10.0%	135	13.7
Commute	43	45.70	Average Work Commute in Minutes	27	104	53.8
			% Commuting on Public Transportation	5.9%	24	37.6
Community Stability	57	71.55	% Living in Same House as in 1979	34.8%	59	59.8
			% Living in Same County as in 1985	83.3%	68	83.3

Composite: **Rank** 134 / 179 *Score* 50.09   **PALMDALE**

CATEGORY	RANK	SCORE	STATISTIC	VALUE	RANK	SCORE
Economics	86	52.90	Median Household Income	$41,974	67	28.0
			% of Families Above Poverty Level	92.3%	101	77.8
Affordable Housing	42	73.15	Median Home Value	$149,500	45	80.9
			Median Rent	$580	41	65.4
Crime	97	67.10	Violent Crimes per 10,000 Population	127	109	56.1
			Property Crimes per 10,000 Population	470	67	78.1
Open Spaces	26	76.10	Population Density (Persons/Sq. Mile)	888	9	97.2
			Average Rooms per Housing Unit	5.5	41	55.0
Education	115	34.45	% High School Enrollment/Completion	82.4%	119	49.8
			% College Graduates	13.3%	110	19.1
Commute	179	2.85	Average Work Commute in Minutes	41	179	0.0
			% Commuting on Public Transportation	0.9%	119	5.7
Community Stability	157	44.05	% Living in Same House as in 1979	8.5%	175	14.3
			% Living in Same County as in 1985	77.0%	100	73.8

Composite: **Rank** 134 / 179 *Score* 50.09   **SOUTH EL MONTE**

CATEGORY	RANK	SCORE	STATISTIC	VALUE	RANK	SCORE
Economics	162	28.85	Median Household Income	$27,074	157	9.9
			% of Families Above Poverty Level	82.8%	162	47.8
Affordable Housing	48	70.85	Median Home Value	$161,600	59	78.2
			Median Rent	$592	45	63.5
Crime	114	61.15	Violent Crimes per 10,000 Population	159	126	43.9
			Property Crimes per 10,000 Population	465	62	78.4
Open Spaces	148	44.00	Population Density (Persons/Sq. Mile)	7206	121	70.5
			Average Rooms per Housing Unit	4.0	159	17.5
Education	169	13.50	% High School Enrollment/Completion	73.8%	166	23.9
			% College Graduates	3.5%	171	3.1
Commute	22	52.10	Average Work Commute in Minutes	23	26	69.2
			% Commuting on Public Transportation	5.5%	27	35.0
Community Stability	26	80.20	% Living in Same House as in 1979	40.3%	32	69.3
			% Living in Same County as in 1985	88.5%	25	91.1

Metropolitan Area Suburb Rankings
LOS ANGELES-ANAHEIM-RIVERSIDE

Composite: **Rank** 136 / 179 *Score* 49.96   **EAST LOS ANGELES**

CATEGORY	RANK	SCORE	STATISTIC	VALUE	RANK	SCORE
Economics	171	19.05	Median Household Income	$22,937	169	4.9
			% of Families Above Poverty Level	78.2%	170	33.2
Affordable Housing	18	81.35	Median Home Value	$141,000	41	82.9
			Median Rent	$487	11	79.8
Crime	N/A	N/A	Violent Crimes per 10,000 Population	N/A	N/A	N/A
			Property Crimes per 10,000 Population	N/A	N/A	N/A
Open Spaces	172	21.20	Population Density (Persons/Sq. Mile)	16818	172	29.9
			Average Rooms per Housing Unit	3.8	169	12.5
Education	165	16.55	% High School Enrollment/Completion	75.9%	158	30.2
			% College Graduates	3.4%	172	2.9
Commute	1	80.75	Average Work Commute in Minutes	25	62	61.5
			% Commuting on Public Transportation	15.7%	1	100.0
Community Stability	24	80.85	% Living in Same House as in 1979	41.6%	25	71.5
			% Living in Same County as in 1985	87.9%	29	90.2

Composite: **Rank** 137 / 179 *Score* 49.87   **TEMECULA**

CATEGORY	RANK	SCORE	STATISTIC	VALUE	RANK	SCORE
Economics	56	60.80	Median Household Income	$44,270	57	30.8
			% of Families Above Poverty Level	96.4%	46	90.8
Affordable Housing	74	62.45	Median Home Value	$190,500	82	71.5
			Median Rent	$657	83	53.4
Crime	90	69.95	Violent Crimes per 10,000 Population	74	74	76.1
			Property Crimes per 10,000 Population	690	120	63.8
Open Spaces	14	79.55	Population Density (Persons/Sq. Mile)	1026	13	96.6
			Average Rooms per Housing Unit	5.8	26	62.5
Education	80	47.55	% High School Enrollment/Completion	86.4%	88	61.9
			% College Graduates	21.9%	74	33.2
Commute	149	25.00	Average Work Commute in Minutes	28	116	50.0
			% Commuting on Public Transportation	0.0%	175	0.0
Community Stability	179	3.80	% Living in Same House as in 1979	4.6%	178	7.6
			% Living in Same County as in 1985	28.0%	179	0.0

Composite: **Rank** 138 / 179 *Score* 49.75   **CORONA**

CATEGORY	RANK	SCORE	STATISTIC	VALUE	RANK	SCORE
Economics	65	57.05	Median Household Income	$43,555	61	29.9
			% of Families Above Poverty Level	94.3%	73	84.2
Affordable Housing	70	62.80	Median Home Value	$186,100	80	72.5
			Median Rent	$659	84	53.1
Crime	81	71.70	Violent Crimes per 10,000 Population	66	61	79.2
			Property Crimes per 10,000 Population	683	117	64.2
Open Spaces	35	72.30	Population Density (Persons/Sq. Mile)	2672	48	89.6
			Average Rooms per Housing Unit	5.5	41	55.0
Education	109	35.60	% High School Enrollment/Completion	80.6%	137	44.4
			% College Graduates	18.0%	88	26.8
Commute	168	16.00	Average Work Commute in Minutes	34	167	26.9
			% Commuting on Public Transportation	0.8%	127	5.1
Community Stability	170	32.80	% Living in Same House as in 1979	18.5%	159	31.6
			% Living in Same County as in 1985	50.6%	173	34.0

Metropolitan Area Suburb Rankings
LOS ANGELES-ANAHEIM-RIVERSIDE

Composite: **Rank** 139 / 179 *Score* 49.56   **RANCHO SANTA MARGARITA**

CATEGORY	RANK	SCORE	STATISTIC	VALUE	RANK	SCORE
Economics	21	69.45	Median Household Income	$50,968	34	38.9
			% of Families Above Poverty Level	99.3%	1	100.0
Affordable Housing	125	48.45	Median Home Value	$209,000	98	67.2
			Median Rent	$810	138	29.7
Crime	N/A	N/A	Violent Crimes per 10,000 Population	N/A	N/A	N/A
			Property Crimes per 10,000 Population	N/A	N/A	N/A
Open Spaces	84	63.45	Population Density (Persons/Sq. Mile)	2731	52	89.4
			Average Rooms per Housing Unit	4.8	101	37.5
Education	20	74.50	% High School Enrollment/Completion	95.5%	19	89.4
			% College Graduates	38.1%	21	59.6
Commute	171	12.80	Average Work Commute in Minutes	35	171	23.1
			% Commuting on Public Transportation	0.4%	155	2.5
Community Stability	173	28.70	% Living in Same House as in 1979	0.2%	179	0.0
			% Living in Same County as in 1985	66.1%	147	57.4

Composite: **Rank** 140 / 179 *Score* 49.43   **RUBIDOUX**

CATEGORY	RANK	SCORE	STATISTIC	VALUE	RANK	SCORE
Economics	145	37.50	Median Household Income	$31,427	135	15.2
			% of Families Above Poverty Level	86.6%	148	59.8
Affordable Housing	21	80.65	Median Home Value	$120,100	25	87.7
			Median Rent	$527	22	73.6
Crime	N/A	N/A	Violent Crimes per 10,000 Population	N/A	N/A	N/A
			Property Crimes per 10,000 Population	N/A	N/A	N/A
Open Spaces	63	67.30	Population Density (Persons/Sq. Mile)	2675	49	89.6
			Average Rooms per Housing Unit	5.1	72	45.0
Education	140	28.20	% High School Enrollment/Completion	79.6%	142	41.4
			% College Graduates	10.8%	125	15.0
Commute	138	28.20	Average Work Commute in Minutes	28	116	50.0
			% Commuting on Public Transportation	1.0%	112	6.4
Community Stability	129	54.75	% Living in Same House as in 1979	27.6%	101	47.3
			% Living in Same County as in 1985	69.3%	137	62.2

Composite: **Rank** 141 / 179 *Score* 49.19   **SAN BERNARDINO**

CATEGORY	RANK	SCORE	STATISTIC	VALUE	RANK	SCORE
Economics	167	24.25	Median Household Income	$25,533	161	8.0
			% of Families Above Poverty Level	80.5%	167	40.5
Affordable Housing	11	86.75	Median Home Value	$95,700	10	93.4
			Median Rent	$485	10	80.1
Crime	N/A	N/A	Violent Crimes per 10,000 Population	N/A	N/A	N/A
			Property Crimes per 10,000 Population	N/A	N/A	N/A
Open Spaces	93	61.65	Population Density (Persons/Sq. Mile)	2980	61	88.3
			Average Rooms per Housing Unit	4.7	108	35.0
Education	145	24.60	% High School Enrollment/Completion	76.2%	156	31.1
			% College Graduates	12.7%	116	18.1
Commute	69	40.35	Average Work Commute in Minutes	23	26	69.2
			% Commuting on Public Transportation	1.8%	82	11.5
Community Stability	119	57.55	% Living in Same House as in 1979	28.4%	98	48.7
			% Living in Same County as in 1985	72.1%	125	66.4

Metropolitan Area Suburb Rankings
LOS ANGELES-ANAHEIM-RIVERSIDE

Composite: **Rank** 142 / 179 *Score* 48.89 **WALNUT PARK**

CATEGORY	RANK	SCORE	STATISTIC	VALUE	RANK	SCORE
Economics	146	37.45	Median Household Income	$30,037	142	13.5
			% of Families Above Poverty Level	87.1%	146	61.4
Affordable Housing	27	77.30	Median Home Value	$165,300	66	77.3
			Median Rent	$503	15	77.3
Crime	N/A	N/A	Violent Crimes per 10,000 Population	N/A	N/A	N/A
			Property Crimes per 10,000 Population	N/A	N/A	N/A
Open Spaces	173	18.20	Population Density (Persons/Sq. Mile)	20026	177	16.4
			Average Rooms per Housing Unit	4.1	156	20.0
Education	149	23.20	% High School Enrollment/Completion	80.3%	138	43.5
			% College Graduates	3.4%	172	2.9
Commute	10	59.05	Average Work Commute in Minutes	27	104	53.8
			% Commuting on Public Transportation	10.1%	7	64.3
Community Stability	34	78.15	% Living in Same House as in 1979	36.9%	46	63.4
			% Living in Same County as in 1985	89.7%	17	92.9

Composite: **Rank** 143 / 179 *Score* 48.72 **SOUTH SAN JOSE HILLS**

CATEGORY	RANK	SCORE	STATISTIC	VALUE	RANK	SCORE
Economics	104	48.40	Median Household Income	$38,467	87	23.7
			% of Families Above Poverty Level	90.8%	112	73.1
Affordable Housing	100	56.65	Median Home Value	$138,400	38	83.5
			Median Rent	$809	137	29.8
Crime	N/A	N/A	Violent Crimes per 10,000 Population	N/A	N/A	N/A
			Property Crimes per 10,000 Population	N/A	N/A	N/A
Open Spaces	147	44.25	Population Density (Persons/Sq. Mile)	12413	164	48.5
			Average Rooms per Housing Unit	4.9	89	40.0
Education	138	28.75	% High School Enrollment/Completion	81.7%	127	47.7
			% College Graduates	7.6%	148	9.8
Commute	109	33.95	Average Work Commute in Minutes	29	137	46.2
			% Commuting on Public Transportation	3.4%	47	21.7
Community Stability	25	80.30	% Living in Same House as in 1979	40.6%	27	69.8
			% Living in Same County as in 1985	88.3%	27	90.8

Composite: **Rank** 144 / 179 *Score* 48.70 **HEMET**

CATEGORY	RANK	SCORE	STATISTIC	VALUE	RANK	SCORE
Economics	151	36.05	Median Household Income	$20,382	178	1.8
			% of Families Above Poverty Level	89.9%	121	70.3
Affordable Housing	13	86.15	Median Home Value	$90,700	9	94.5
			Median Rent	$500	14	77.8
Crime	126	53.00	Violent Crimes per 10,000 Population	116	104	60.2
			Property Crimes per 10,000 Population	967	134	45.8
Open Spaces	98	59.85	Population Density (Persons/Sq. Mile)	2054	29	92.2
			Average Rooms per Housing Unit	4.4	134	27.5
Education	158	21.45	% High School Enrollment/Completion	76.0%	157	30.5
			% College Graduates	9.2%	141	12.4
Commute	101	35.55	Average Work Commute in Minutes	23	26	69.2
			% Commuting on Public Transportation	0.3%	161	1.9
Community Stability	149	48.85	% Living in Same House as in 1979	23.5%	132	40.2
			% Living in Same County as in 1985	66.2%	146	57.5

Metropolitan Area Suburb Rankings
LOS ANGELES-ANAHEIM-RIVERSIDE

Composite: *Rank* 145 / 179 *Score* 48.69   **LONG BEACH**

CATEGORY	RANK	SCORE	STATISTIC	VALUE	RANK	SCORE
Economics	144	37.65	Median Household Income	$31,938	129	15.8
			% of Families Above Poverty Level	86.5%	152	59.5
Affordable Housing	68	62.95	Median Home Value	$221,000	102	64.4
			Median Rent	$605	50	61.5
Crime	133	43.75	Violent Crimes per 10,000 Population	210	135	24.6
			Property Crimes per 10,000 Population	703	123	62.9
Open Spaces	151	42.35	Population Density (Persons/Sq. Mile)	8586	135	64.7
			Average Rooms per Housing Unit	4.1	156	20.0
Education	93	42.90	% High School Enrollment/Completion	82.6%	115	50.5
			% College Graduates	23.2%	68	35.3
Commute	23	51.75	Average Work Commute in Minutes	25	62	61.5
			% Commuting on Public Transportation	6.6%	16	42.0
Community Stability	109	59.50	% Living in Same House as in 1979	26.2%	112	44.9
			% Living in Same County as in 1985	77.2%	98	74.1

Composite: *Rank* 146 / 179 *Score* 48.58   **MORENO VALLEY**

CATEGORY	RANK	SCORE	STATISTIC	VALUE	RANK	SCORE
Economics	81	54.35	Median Household Income	$42,186	66	28.3
			% of Families Above Poverty Level	93.1%	95	80.4
Affordable Housing	62	66.85	Median Home Value	$140,300	40	83.1
			Median Rent	$675	88	50.6
Crime	111	63.05	Violent Crimes per 10,000 Population	119	106	59.1
			Property Crimes per 10,000 Population	640	110	67.0
Open Spaces	23	76.60	Population Density (Persons/Sq. Mile)	2418	37	90.7
			Average Rooms per Housing Unit	5.8	26	62.5
Education	82	46.50	% High School Enrollment/Completion	89.8%	60	72.2
			% College Graduates	14.3%	104	20.8
Commute	172	12.45	Average Work Commute in Minutes	36	172	19.2
			% Commuting on Public Transportation	0.9%	119	5.7
Community Stability	177	20.25	% Living in Same House as in 1979	7.6%	177	12.8
			% Living in Same County as in 1985	46.4%	176	27.7

Composite: *Rank* 147 / 179 *Score* 48.04   **POMONA**

CATEGORY	RANK	SCORE	STATISTIC	VALUE	RANK	SCORE
Economics	148	37.00	Median Household Income	$32,132	127	16.1
			% of Families Above Poverty Level	86.0%	155	57.9
Affordable Housing	39	74.05	Median Home Value	$133,700	29	84.6
			Median Rent	$592	45	63.5
Crime	123	55.05	Violent Crimes per 10,000 Population	171	129	39.4
			Property Crimes per 10,000 Population	583	93	70.7
Open Spaces	121	54.55	Population Density (Persons/Sq. Mile)	5771	104	76.6
			Average Rooms per Housing Unit	4.6	118	32.5
Education	156	21.95	% High School Enrollment/Completion	74.2%	164	25.1
			% College Graduates	13.1%	111	18.8
Commute	109	33.95	Average Work Commute in Minutes	29	137	46.2
			% Commuting on Public Transportation	3.4%	47	21.7
Community Stability	106	59.75	% Living in Same House as in 1979	24.6%	123	42.1
			% Living in Same County as in 1985	79.4%	92	77.4

Metropolitan Area Suburb Rankings
LOS ANGELES-ANAHEIM-RIVERSIDE

Composite: **Rank** 148 / 179 *Score* 47.82   **VICTORVILLE**

CATEGORY	RANK	SCORE	STATISTIC	VALUE	RANK	SCORE
Economics	142	38.25	Median Household Income	$28,698	149	11.9
			% of Families Above Poverty Level	88.1%	137	64.6
Affordable Housing	16	84.25	Median Home Value	$101,900	16	91.9
			Median Rent	$508	17	76.6
Crime	124	54.60	Violent Crimes per 10,000 Population	101	90	65.9
			Property Crimes per 10,000 Population	1,005	136	43.3
Open Spaces	45	69.65	Population Density (Persons/Sq. Mile)	974	11	96.8
			Average Rooms per Housing Unit	5.0	79	42.5
Education	127	31.55	% High School Enrollment/Completion	82.0%	125	48.6
			% College Graduates	10.5%	128	14.5
Commute	152	23.75	Average Work Commute in Minutes	29	137	46.2
			% Commuting on Public Transportation	0.2%	165	1.3
Community Stability	171	32.70	% Living in Same House as in 1979	13.6%	171	23.1
			% Living in Same County as in 1985	56.1%	170	42.3

Composite: **Rank** 149 / 179 *Score* 47.78   **CHINO HILLS**

CATEGORY	RANK	SCORE	STATISTIC	VALUE	RANK	SCORE
Economics	15	70.90	Median Household Income	$58,030	16	47.5
			% of Families Above Poverty Level	97.5%	23	94.3
Affordable Housing	141	39.75	Median Home Value	$244,700	122	59.0
			Median Rent	$869	153	20.5
Crime	N/A	N/A	Violent Crimes per 10,000 Population	N/A	N/A	N/A
			Property Crimes per 10,000 Population	N/A	N/A	N/A
Open Spaces	8	82.95	Population Density (Persons/Sq. Mile)	1777	24	93.4
			Average Rooms per Housing Unit	6.2	9	72.5
Education	30	67.30	% High School Enrollment/Completion	94.5%	27	86.4
			% College Graduates	31.1%	46	48.2
Commute	176	8.30	Average Work Commute in Minutes	38	178	11.5
			% Commuting on Public Transportation	0.8%	127	5.1
Community Stability	178	17.50	% Living in Same House as in 1979	10.7%	174	18.1
			% Living in Same County as in 1985	39.2%	177	16.9

Composite: **Rank** 150 / 179 *Score* 47.65   **BLOOMINGTON**

CATEGORY	RANK	SCORE	STATISTIC	VALUE	RANK	SCORE
Economics	128	41.55	Median Household Income	$31,377	136	15.1
			% of Families Above Poverty Level	89.2%	127	68.0
Affordable Housing	25	79.75	Median Home Value	$97,900	13	92.9
			Median Rent	$572	37	66.6
Crime	N/A	N/A	Violent Crimes per 10,000 Population	N/A	N/A	N/A
			Property Crimes per 10,000 Population	N/A	N/A	N/A
Open Spaces	56	68.60	Population Density (Persons/Sq. Mile)	2665	46	89.7
			Average Rooms per Housing Unit	5.2	62	47.5
Education	171	12.50	% High School Enrollment/Completion	71.8%	171	17.8
			% College Graduates	6.0%	159	7.2
Commute	158	21.15	Average Work Commute in Minutes	30	148	42.3
			% Commuting on Public Transportation	0.0%	175	0.0
Community Stability	91	62.35	% Living in Same House as in 1979	33.5%	67	57.5
			% Living in Same County as in 1985	72.6%	124	67.2

Metropolitan Area Suburb Rankings
LOS ANGELES-ANAHEIM-RIVERSIDE

Composite: Rank 150 / 179 **Score** 47.65 **FONTANA**

CATEGORY	RANK	SCORE	STATISTIC	VALUE	RANK	SCORE
Economics	117	45.05	Median Household Income	$35,558	106	20.2
			% of Families Above Poverty Level	89.8%	123	69.9
Affordable Housing	36	75.15	Median Home Value	$134,300	31	84.5
			Median Rent	$577	40	65.8
Crime	116	60.00	Violent Crimes per 10,000 Population	135	112	53.0
			Property Crimes per 10,000 Population	640	110	67.0
Open Spaces	50	69.00	Population Density (Persons/Sq. Mile)	2457	39	90.5
			Average Rooms per Housing Unit	5.2	62	47.5
Education	135	29.45	% High School Enrollment/Completion	81.2%	131	46.2
			% College Graduates	9.4%	140	12.7
Commute	164	17.30	Average Work Commute in Minutes	33	161	30.8
			% Commuting on Public Transportation	0.6%	141	3.8
Community Stability	166	37.60	% Living in Same House as in 1979	18.8%	157	32.1
			% Living in Same County as in 1985	56.6%	169	43.1

Composite: Rank 152 / 179 **Score** 47.40 **INGLEWOOD**

CATEGORY	RANK	SCORE	STATISTIC	VALUE	RANK	SCORE
Economics	153	35.45	Median Household Income	$29,881	143	13.3
			% of Families Above Poverty Level	85.9%	156	57.6
Affordable Housing	58	67.80	Median Home Value	$170,400	69	76.1
			Median Rent	$618	59	59.5
Crime	136	40.75	Violent Crimes per 10,000 Population	243	140	12.1
			Property Crimes per 10,000 Population	604	100	69.4
Open Spaces	163	33.95	Population Density (Persons/Sq. Mile)	11955	162	50.4
			Average Rooms per Housing Unit	4.0	159	17.5
Education	113	34.70	% High School Enrollment/Completion	81.7%	127	47.7
			% College Graduates	14.9%	101	21.7
Commute	14	53.70	Average Work Commute in Minutes	26	82	57.7
			% Commuting on Public Transportation	7.8%	12	49.7
Community Stability	76	65.45	% Living in Same House as in 1979	25.8%	115	44.2
			% Living in Same County as in 1985	85.6%	54	86.7

Composite: Rank 153 / 179 **Score** 47.32 **COMMERCE**

CATEGORY	RANK	SCORE	STATISTIC	VALUE	RANK	SCORE
Economics	156	33.45	Median Household Income	$27,415	154	10.3
			% of Families Above Poverty Level	85.6%	157	56.6
Affordable Housing	32	76.15	Median Home Value	$150,600	47	80.7
			Median Rent	$540	28	71.6
Crime	144	8.15	Violent Crimes per 10,000 Population	232	139	16.3
			Property Crimes per 10,000 Population	1,673	144	0.0
Open Spaces	125	52.80	Population Density (Persons/Sq. Mile)	1859	28	93.1
			Average Rooms per Housing Unit	3.8	169	12.5
Education	150	23.00	% High School Enrollment/Completion	79.0%	147	39.6
			% College Graduates	5.5%	164	6.4
Commute	8	59.45	Average Work Commute in Minutes	21	13	76.9
			% Commuting on Public Transportation	6.6%	16	42.0
Community Stability	33	78.25	% Living in Same House as in 1979	35.3%	56	60.6
			% Living in Same County as in 1985	91.7%	7	95.9

Metropolitan Area Suburb Rankings
LOS ANGELES-ANAHEIM-RIVERSIDE

Composite: *Rank* 154 / 179 *Score* 47.29 **GLEN AVON**

CATEGORY	RANK	SCORE	STATISTIC	VALUE	RANK	SCORE
Economics	100	49.75	Median Household Income	$31,508	133	15.3
			% of Families Above Poverty Level	94.3%	73	84.2
Affordable Housing	10	86.80	Median Home Value	$136,100	36	84.0
			Median Rent	$424	2	89.6
Crime	N/A	N/A	Violent Crimes per 10,000 Population	N/A	N/A	N/A
			Property Crimes per 10,000 Population	N/A	N/A	N/A
Open Spaces	66	66.85	Population Density (Persons/Sq. Mile)	1714	23	93.7
			Average Rooms per Housing Unit	4.9	89	40.0
Education	166	16.50	% High School Enrollment/Completion	74.5%	163	26.0
			% College Graduates	5.9%	161	7.0
Commute	165	17.00	Average Work Commute in Minutes	33	161	30.8
			% Commuting on Public Transportation	0.5%	146	3.2
Community Stability	155	46.85	% Living in Same House as in 1979	25.2%	119	43.2
			% Living in Same County as in 1985	61.5%	161	50.5

Composite: *Rank* 155 / 179 *Score* 47.09 **COMPTON**

CATEGORY	RANK	SCORE	STATISTIC	VALUE	RANK	SCORE
Economics	174	16.50	Median Household Income	$24,971	163	7.4
			% of Families Above Poverty Level	75.8%	175	25.6
Affordable Housing	22	80.45	Median Home Value	$107,100	19	90.7
			Median Rent	$549	31	70.2
Crime	139	38.00	Violent Crimes per 10,000 Population	275	144	0.0
			Property Crimes per 10,000 Population	502	78	76.0
Open Spaces	145	45.45	Population Density (Persons/Sq. Mile)	8897	138	63.4
			Average Rooms per Housing Unit	4.4	134	27.5
Education	168	14.95	% High School Enrollment/Completion	73.3%	168	22.4
			% College Graduates	6.2%	156	7.5
Commute	29	49.85	Average Work Commute in Minutes	26	82	57.7
			% Commuting on Public Transportation	6.6%	16	42.0
Community Stability	17	84.45	% Living in Same House as in 1979	42.8%	22	73.6
			% Living in Same County as in 1985	91.3%	9	95.3

Composite: *Rank* 155 / 179 *Score* 47.09 **SANTA ANA**

CATEGORY	RANK	SCORE	STATISTIC	VALUE	RANK	SCORE
Economics	129	41.20	Median Household Income	$35,162	107	19.7
			% of Families Above Poverty Level	87.5%	142	62.7
Affordable Housing	96	56.95	Median Home Value	$184,600	78	72.8
			Median Rent	$736	120	41.1
Crime	106	64.30	Violent Crimes per 10,000 Population	110	101	62.5
			Property Crimes per 10,000 Population	655	114	66.1
Open Spaces	158	38.80	Population Density (Persons/Sq. Mile)	10845	158	55.1
			Average Rooms per Housing Unit	4.2	147	22.5
Education	174	8.70	% High School Enrollment/Completion	66.8%	177	2.7
			% College Graduates	10.6%	126	14.7
Commute	5	61.35	Average Work Commute in Minutes	24	43	65.4
			% Commuting on Public Transportation	9.0%	10	57.3
Community Stability	117	58.35	% Living in Same House as in 1979	25.2%	119	43.2
			% Living in Same County as in 1985	76.8%	102	73.5

Metropolitan Area Suburb Rankings
LOS ANGELES-ANAHEIM-RIVERSIDE

Composite: *Rank* 157 / 179 *Score* 47.03 **STANTON**

CATEGORY	RANK	SCORE	STATISTIC	VALUE	RANK	SCORE
Economics	122	43.95	Median Household Income	$33,367	115	17.6
			% of Families Above Poverty Level	89.9%	121	70.3
Affordable Housing	84	60.00	Median Home Value	$170,400	69	76.1
			Median Rent	$718	112	43.9
Crime	117	59.60	Violent Crimes per 10,000 Population	129	111	55.3
			Property Crimes per 10,000 Population	689	119	63.9
Open Spaces	150	43.60	Population Density (Persons/Sq. Mile)	9757	149	59.7
			Average Rooms per Housing Unit	4.4	134	27.5
Education	146	24.20	% High School Enrollment/Completion	75.1%	161	27.8
			% College Graduates	14.2%	105	20.6
Commute	53	43.15	Average Work Commute in Minutes	25	62	61.5
			% Commuting on Public Transportation	3.9%	39	24.8
Community Stability	130	54.70	% Living in Same House as in 1979	23.7%	131	40.6
			% Living in Same County as in 1985	73.7%	115	68.8

Composite: *Rank* 158 / 179 *Score* 47.01 **LAWNDALE**

CATEGORY	RANK	SCORE	STATISTIC	VALUE	RANK	SCORE
Economics	121	44.15	Median Household Income	$34,552	109	19.0
			% of Families Above Poverty Level	89.6%	125	69.3
Affordable Housing	118	51.05	Median Home Value	$227,000	106	63.0
			Median Rent	$749	126	39.1
Crime	125	54.10	Violent Crimes per 10,000 Population	200	134	28.4
			Property Crimes per 10,000 Population	443	55	79.8
Open Spaces	166	30.05	Population Density (Persons/Sq. Mile)	13815	168	42.6
			Average Rooms per Housing Unit	4.0	159	17.5
Education	96	41.10	% High School Enrollment/Completion	86.9%	85	63.4
			% College Graduates	13.1%	111	18.8
Commute	37	47.00	Average Work Commute in Minutes	23	26	69.2
			% Commuting on Public Transportation	3.9%	39	24.8
Community Stability	95	61.65	% Living in Same House as in 1979	23.0%	135	39.4
			% Living in Same County as in 1985	83.7%	67	83.9

Composite: *Rank* 159 / 179 *Score* 46.84 **ONTARIO**

CATEGORY	RANK	SCORE	STATISTIC	VALUE	RANK	SCORE
Economics	120	44.60	Median Household Income	$35,788	104	20.5
			% of Families Above Poverty Level	89.4%	126	68.7
Affordable Housing	51	70.20	Median Home Value	$142,200	42	82.6
			Median Rent	$629	61	57.8
Crime	120	58.60	Violent Crimes per 10,000 Population	135	112	53.0
			Property Crimes per 10,000 Population	683	117	64.2
Open Spaces	87	62.80	Population Density (Persons/Sq. Mile)	3624	75	85.6
			Average Rooms per Housing Unit	4.9	89	40.0
Education	163	18.75	% High School Enrollment/Completion	73.2%	169	22.1
			% College Graduates	11.0%	122	15.4
Commute	146	25.95	Average Work Commute in Minutes	29	137	46.2
			% Commuting on Public Transportation	0.9%	119	5.7
Community Stability	154	47.00	% Living in Same House as in 1979	24.0%	126	41.1
			% Living in Same County as in 1985	63.1%	156	52.9

Metropolitan Area Suburb Rankings
LOS ANGELES-ANAHEIM-RIVERSIDE

Composite: **Rank** 160 / 179 *Score* 46.33 **EL MONTE**

CATEGORY	RANK	SCORE	STATISTIC	VALUE	RANK	SCORE
Economics	164	27.40	Median Household Income	$28,034	152	11.1
			% of Families Above Poverty Level	81.5%	165	43.7
Affordable Housing	55	69.05	Median Home Value	$172,000	72	75.8
			Median Rent	$600	48	62.3
Crime	99	65.70	Violent Crimes per 10,000 Population	135	112	53.0
			Property Crimes per 10,000 Population	465	62	78.4
Open Spaces	162	34.35	Population Density (Persons/Sq. Mile)	11179	159	53.7
			Average Rooms per Housing Unit	3.9	166	15.0
Education	170	12.65	% High School Enrollment/Completion	71.9%	170	18.1
			% College Graduates	6.0%	159	7.2
Commute	27	50.50	Average Work Commute in Minutes	26	82	57.7
			% Commuting on Public Transportation	6.8%	15	43.3
Community Stability	80	64.65	% Living in Same House as in 1979	27.3%	103	46.8
			% Living in Same County as in 1985	82.8%	73	82.5

Composite: **Rank** 161 / 179 *Score* 45.91 **DESERT HOT SPRINGS**

CATEGORY	RANK	SCORE	STATISTIC	VALUE	RANK	SCORE
Economics	166	24.85	Median Household Income	$20,687	177	2.2
			% of Families Above Poverty Level	82.7%	163	47.5
Affordable Housing	8	88.15	Median Home Value	$74,800	4	98.2
			Median Rent	$498	13	78.1
Crime	137	39.75	Violent Crimes per 10,000 Population	181	130	35.6
			Property Crimes per 10,000 Population	996	135	43.9
Open Spaces	101	59.30	Population Density (Persons/Sq. Mile)	1141	17	96.1
			Average Rooms per Housing Unit	4.2	147	22.5
Education	128	31.10	% High School Enrollment/Completion	82.4%	119	49.8
			% College Graduates	9.2%	141	12.4
Commute	65	40.65	Average Work Commute in Minutes	26	82	57.7
			% Commuting on Public Transportation	3.7%	42	23.6
Community Stability	166	37.60	% Living in Same House as in 1979	13.9%	170	23.7
			% Living in Same County as in 1985	62.2%	159	51.5

Composite: **Rank** 162 / 179 *Score* 45.70 **HAWTHORNE**

CATEGORY	RANK	SCORE	STATISTIC	VALUE	RANK	SCORE
Economics	136	39.75	Median Household Income	$30,967	138	14.6
			% of Families Above Poverty Level	88.2%	136	64.9
Affordable Housing	83	60.45	Median Home Value	$226,600	105	63.1
			Median Rent	$629	61	57.8
Crime	135	41.20	Violent Crimes per 10,000 Population	225	138	18.9
			Property Crimes per 10,000 Population	694	121	63.5
Open Spaces	166	30.05	Population Density (Persons/Sq. Mile)	12025	163	50.1
			Average Rooms per Housing Unit	3.7	171	10.0
Education	102	39.75	% High School Enrollment/Completion	84.6%	96	56.5
			% College Graduates	15.7%	100	23.0
Commute	28	49.90	Average Work Commute in Minutes	24	43	65.4
			% Commuting on Public Transportation	5.4%	29	34.4
Community Stability	113	58.80	% Living in Same House as in 1979	20.2%	148	34.5
			% Living in Same County as in 1985	83.2%	69	83.1

Metropolitan Area Suburb Rankings
LOS ANGELES-ANAHEIM-RIVERSIDE

Composite: **Rank** 163 / 179 **Score** 45.49   **SUN CITY**

CATEGORY	RANK	SCORE	STATISTIC	VALUE	RANK	SCORE
Economics	99	50.20	Median Household Income	$24,396	165	6.7
			% of Families Above Poverty Level	97.3%	29	93.7
Affordable Housing	43	72.90	Median Home Value	$100,900	14	92.2
			Median Rent	$656	81	53.6
Crime	N/A	N/A	Violent Crimes per 10,000 Population	N/A	N/A	N/A
			Property Crimes per 10,000 Population	N/A	N/A	N/A
Open Spaces	51	69.05	Population Density (Persons/Sq. Mile)	1852	27	93.1
			Average Rooms per Housing Unit	5.1	72	45.0
Education	133	30.00	% High School Enrollment/Completion	80.9%	133	45.3
			% College Graduates	10.6%	126	14.7
Commute	177	7.70	Average Work Commute in Minutes	37	175	15.4
			% Commuting on Public Transportation	0.0%	175	0.0
Community Stability	159	43.10	% Living in Same House as in 1979	27.4%	102	47.0
			% Living in Same County as in 1985	54.0%	171	39.2

Composite: **Rank** 164 / 179 **Score** 45.44   **PARAMOUNT**

CATEGORY	RANK	SCORE	STATISTIC	VALUE	RANK	SCORE
Economics	155	33.50	Median Household Income	$29,015	147	12.3
			% of Families Above Poverty Level	85.0%	158	54.7
Affordable Housing	59	67.70	Median Home Value	$146,900	44	81.5
			Median Rent	$654	79	53.9
Crime	127	50.65	Violent Crimes per 10,000 Population	199	133	28.8
			Property Crimes per 10,000 Population	556	88	72.5
Open Spaces	159	37.80	Population Density (Persons/Sq. Mile)	10135	151	58.1
			Average Rooms per Housing Unit	4.0	159	17.5
Education	154	22.00	% High School Enrollment/Completion	77.6%	150	35.3
			% College Graduates	6.9%	154	8.7
Commute	55	42.55	Average Work Commute in Minutes	25	62	61.5
			% Commuting on Public Transportation	3.7%	42	23.6
Community Stability	86	63.90	% Living in Same House as in 1979	22.9%	137	39.2
			% Living in Same County as in 1985	86.8%	45	88.6

Composite: **Rank** 165 / 179 **Score** 45.16   **BELL**

CATEGORY	RANK	SCORE	STATISTIC	VALUE	RANK	SCORE
Economics	173	17.05	Median Household Income	$22,515	171	4.4
			% of Families Above Poverty Level	77.1%	173	29.7
Affordable Housing	40	73.50	Median Home Value	$167,800	67	76.7
			Median Rent	$548	30	70.3
Crime	45	81.40	Violent Crimes per 10,000 Population	89	84	70.5
			Property Crimes per 10,000 Population	251	8	92.3
Open Spaces	170	23.35	Population Density (Persons/Sq. Mile)	13433	167	44.2
			Average Rooms per Housing Unit	3.4	174	2.5
Education	179	2.00	% High School Enrollment/Completion	66.1%	178	0.6
			% College Graduates	3.7%	170	3.4
Commute	7	59.40	Average Work Commute in Minutes	27	104	53.8
			% Commuting on Public Transportation	10.2%	6	65.0
Community Stability	110	59.40	% Living in Same House as in 1979	21.2%	144	36.3
			% Living in Same County as in 1985	82.8%	73	82.5

Metropolitan Area Suburb Rankings
LOS ANGELES-ANAHEIM-RIVERSIDE

Composite: *Rank* 166 / 179 *Score* 44.81   **HUNTINGTON PARK**

CATEGORY	RANK	SCORE	STATISTIC	VALUE	RANK	SCORE
Economics	169	19.60	Median Household Income	$23,595	167	5.7
			% of Families Above Poverty Level	78.3%	169	33.5
Affordable Housing	30	76.45	Median Home Value	$160,500	56	78.4
			Median Rent	$521	20	74.5
Crime	118	59.20	Violent Crimes per 10,000 Population	128	110	55.7
			Property Crimes per 10,000 Population	707	125	62.7
Open Spaces	175	11.65	Population Density (Persons/Sq. Mile)	18378	174	23.3
			Average Rooms per Housing Unit	3.3	178	0.0
Education	173	9.20	% High School Enrollment/Completion	70.0%	173	12.4
			% College Graduates	5.3%	167	6.0
Commute	2	75.65	Average Work Commute in Minutes	27	104	53.8
			% Commuting on Public Transportation	15.3%	2	97.5
Community Stability	94	61.95	% Living in Same House as in 1979	23.8%	129	40.8
			% Living in Same County as in 1985	83.2%	69	83.1

Composite: *Rank* 167 / 179 *Score* 44.79   **BELL GARDENS**

CATEGORY	RANK	SCORE	STATISTIC	VALUE	RANK	SCORE
Economics	175	16.45	Median Household Income	$23,819	166	6.0
			% of Families Above Poverty Level	76.2%	174	26.9
Affordable Housing	53	69.95	Median Home Value	$160,500	56	78.4
			Median Rent	$605	50	61.5
Crime	82	71.60	Violent Crimes per 10,000 Population	125	107	56.8
			Property Crimes per 10,000 Population	341	33	86.4
Open Spaces	174	16.10	Population Density (Persons/Sq. Mile)	16856	173	29.7
			Average Rooms per Housing Unit	3.4	174	2.5
Education	143	25.20	% High School Enrollment/Completion	82.5%	116	50.2
			% College Graduates	1.7%	178	0.2
Commute	16	53.35	Average Work Commute in Minutes	25	62	61.5
			% Commuting on Public Transportation	7.1%	14	45.2
Community Stability	101	60.85	% Living in Same House as in 1979	19.5%	153	33.3
			% Living in Same County as in 1985	86.7%	46	88.4

Composite: *Rank* 168 / 179 *Score* 44.47   **LYNWOOD**

CATEGORY	RANK	SCORE	STATISTIC	VALUE	RANK	SCORE
Economics	168	23.60	Median Household Income	$25,961	159	8.6
			% of Families Above Poverty Level	79.9%	168	38.6
Affordable Housing	28	77.00	Median Home Value	$134,700	32	84.4
			Median Rent	$553	34	69.6
Crime	132	43.90	Violent Crimes per 10,000 Population	258	141	6.4
			Property Crimes per 10,000 Population	418	44	81.4
Open Spaces	165	31.05	Population Density (Persons/Sq. Mile)	12757	166	47.1
			Average Rooms per Housing Unit	3.9	166	15.0
Education	164	16.70	% High School Enrollment/Completion	75.7%	159	29.6
			% College Graduates	3.9%	169	3.8
Commute	43	45.70	Average Work Commute in Minutes	28	116	50.0
			% Commuting on Public Transportation	6.5%	19	41.4
Community Stability	52	73.35	% Living in Same House as in 1979	32.3%	74	55.4
			% Living in Same County as in 1985	88.6%	22	91.3

Metropolitan Area Suburb Rankings
LOS ANGELES-ANAHEIM-RIVERSIDE

Composite: *Rank* 169 / 179 *Score* 44.46   **WESTMONT**

CATEGORY	RANK	SCORE	STATISTIC	VALUE	RANK	SCORE
Economics	178	4.45	Median Household Income	$20,785	176	2.3
			% of Families Above Poverty Level	69.8%	178	6.6
Affordable Housing	24	79.90	Median Home Value	$126,600	28	86.2
			Median Rent	$527	22	73.6
Crime	N/A	N/A	Violent Crimes per 10,000 Population	N/A	N/A	N/A
			Property Crimes per 10,000 Population	N/A	N/A	N/A
Open Spaces	169	26.30	Population Density (Persons/Sq. Mile)	16779	171	30.1
			Average Rooms per Housing Unit	4.2	147	22.5
Education	159	20.85	% High School Enrollment/Completion	77.5%	151	35.0
			% College Graduates	5.7%	163	6.7
Commute	9	59.35	Average Work Commute in Minutes	30	148	42.3
			% Commuting on Public Transportation	12.0%	4	76.4
Community Stability	44	75.90	% Living in Same House as in 1979	32.8%	73	56.3
			% Living in Same County as in 1985	91.4%	8	95.5

Composite: *Rank* 170 / 179 *Score* 44.26   **MONTCLAIR**

CATEGORY	RANK	SCORE	STATISTIC	VALUE	RANK	SCORE
Economics	140	39.15	Median Household Income	$33,084	119	17.2
			% of Families Above Poverty Level	87.0%	147	61.1
Affordable Housing	46	72.20	Median Home Value	$135,200	33	84.2
			Median Rent	$613	55	60.2
Crime	138	39.30	Violent Crimes per 10,000 Population	157	125	44.7
			Property Crimes per 10,000 Population	1,151	141	33.9
Open Spaces	105	58.55	Population Density (Persons/Sq. Mile)	5632	101	77.1
			Average Rooms per Housing Unit	4.9	89	40.0
Education	161	19.50	% High School Enrollment/Completion	74.2%	164	25.1
			% College Graduates	10.1%	134	13.9
Commute	124	31.05	Average Work Commute in Minutes	28	116	50.0
			% Commuting on Public Transportation	1.9%	79	12.1
Community Stability	144	50.10	% Living in Same House as in 1979	30.5%	82	52.3
			% Living in Same County as in 1985	59.8%	167	47.9

Composite: *Rank* 171 / 179 *Score* 43.98   **MAYWOOD**

CATEGORY	RANK	SCORE	STATISTIC	VALUE	RANK	SCORE
Economics	165	24.95	Median Household Income	$25,567	160	8.1
			% of Families Above Poverty Level	80.9%	166	41.8
Affordable Housing	29	76.95	Median Home Value	$153,800	50	80.0
			Median Rent	$525	21	73.9
Crime	65	77.75	Violent Crimes per 10,000 Population	103	94	65.2
			Property Crimes per 10,000 Population	281	15	90.3
Open Spaces	179	0.00	Population Density (Persons/Sq. Mile)	23900	179	0.0
			Average Rooms per Housing Unit	3.3	178	0.0
Education	178	3.30	% High School Enrollment/Completion	68.1%	176	6.6
			% College Graduates	1.6%	179	0.0
Commute	6	60.70	Average Work Commute in Minutes	25	62	61.5
			% Commuting on Public Transportation	9.4%	8	59.9
Community Stability	81	64.20	% Living in Same House as in 1979	24.4%	125	41.8
			% Living in Same County as in 1985	85.5%	55	86.6

Metropolitan Area Suburb Rankings
LOS ANGELES-ANAHEIM-RIVERSIDE

Composite: *Rank* 172 / 179   *Score* 43.01   **FLORENCE-GRAHAM**

CATEGORY	RANK	SCORE	STATISTIC	VALUE	RANK	SCORE
Economics	179	0.00	Median Household Income	$18,901	179	0.0
			% of Families Above Poverty Level	67.7%	179	0.0
Affordable Housing	12	86.10	Median Home Value	$103,600	17	91.5
			Median Rent	$481	9	80.7
Crime	N/A	N/A	Violent Crimes per 10,000 Population	N/A	N/A	N/A
			Property Crimes per 10,000 Population	N/A	N/A	N/A
Open Spaces	171	21.50	Population Density (Persons/Sq. Mile)	16092	170	33.0
			Average Rooms per Housing Unit	3.7	171	10.0
Education	177	3.60	% High School Enrollment/Completion	68.2%	175	6.9
			% College Graduates	1.8%	176	0.3
Commute	4	69.30	Average Work Commute in Minutes	29	137	46.2
			% Commuting on Public Transportation	14.5%	3	92.4
Community Stability	38	77.55	% Living in Same House as in 1979	35.6%	52	61.1
			% Living in Same County as in 1985	90.4%	13	94.0

Composite: *Rank* 173 / 179   *Score* 42.94   **WILDOMAR**

CATEGORY	RANK	SCORE	STATISTIC	VALUE	RANK	SCORE
Economics	74	55.50	Median Household Income	$36,049	101	20.8
			% of Families Above Poverty Level	96.2%	51	90.2
Affordable Housing	92	58.60	Median Home Value	$182,800	76	73.3
			Median Rent	$718	112	43.9
Crime	N/A	N/A	Violent Crimes per 10,000 Population	N/A	N/A	N/A
			Property Crimes per 10,000 Population	N/A	N/A	N/A
Open Spaces	10	82.40	Population Density (Persons/Sq. Mile)	857	8	97.3
			Average Rooms per Housing Unit	6.0	16	67.5
Education	152	22.50	% High School Enrollment/Completion	75.7%	159	29.6
			% College Graduates	11.0%	122	15.4
Commute	177	7.70	Average Work Commute in Minutes	37	175	15.4
			% Commuting on Public Transportation	0.0%	175	0.0
Community Stability	172	30.95	% Living in Same House as in 1979	14.0%	169	23.8
			% Living in Same County as in 1985	53.3%	172	38.1

Composite: *Rank* 174 / 179   *Score* 42.41   **WEST HOLLYWOOD**

CATEGORY	RANK	SCORE	STATISTIC	VALUE	RANK	SCORE
Economics	135	40.00	Median Household Income	$29,314	146	12.6
			% of Families Above Poverty Level	89.0%	130	67.4
Affordable Housing	126	48.10	Median Home Value	$347,600	161	35.2
			Median Rent	$608	53	61.0
Crime	142	24.25	Violent Crimes per 10,000 Population	261	142	5.3
			Property Crimes per 10,000 Population	1,008	137	43.2
Open Spaces	176	11.10	Population Density (Persons/Sq. Mile)	19228	175	19.7
			Average Rooms per Housing Unit	3.4	174	2.5
Education	37	64.60	% High School Enrollment/Completion	89.3%	68	70.7
			% College Graduates	37.4%	22	58.5
Commute	17	53.10	Average Work Commute in Minutes	24	43	65.4
			% Commuting on Public Transportation	6.4%	20	40.8
Community Stability	124	55.70	% Living in Same House as in 1979	23.9%	128	40.9
			% Living in Same County as in 1985	74.8%	111	70.5

Metropolitan Area Suburb Rankings
LOS ANGELES-ANAHEIM-RIVERSIDE

Composite: *Rank* 175 / 179 *Score* 41.88   **PERRIS**

CATEGORY	RANK	SCORE	STATISTIC	VALUE	RANK	SCORE
Economics	143	37.70	Median Household Income	$28,611	150	11.8
			% of Families Above Poverty Level	87.8%	138	63.6
Affordable Housing	7	88.30	Median Home Value	$111,300	21	89.8
			Median Rent	$442	4	86.8
Crime	134	42.00	Violent Crimes per 10,000 Population	153	123	46.2
			Property Crimes per 10,000 Population	1,091	140	37.8
Open Spaces	53	68.95	Population Density (Persons/Sq. Mile)	723	5	97.9
			Average Rooms per Housing Unit	4.9	89	40.0
Education	167	16.30	% High School Enrollment/Completion	73.6%	167	23.3
			% College Graduates	7.3%	151	9.3
Commute	173	11.20	Average Work Commute in Minutes	36	172	19.2
			% Commuting on Public Transportation	0.5%	146	3.2
Community Stability	173	28.70	% Living in Same House as in 1979	15.0%	167	25.6
			% Living in Same County as in 1985	49.1%	174	31.8

Composite: *Rank* 176 / 179 *Score* 41.21   **CUDAHY**

CATEGORY	RANK	SCORE	STATISTIC	VALUE	RANK	SCORE
Economics	176	13.90	Median Household Income	$22,279	174	4.1
			% of Families Above Poverty Level	75.2%	176	23.7
Affordable Housing	50	70.35	Median Home Value	$160,800	58	78.3
			Median Rent	$599	47	62.4
Crime	79	71.80	Violent Crimes per 10,000 Population	139	118	51.5
			Property Crimes per 10,000 Population	253	9	92.1
Open Spaces	178	9.20	Population Density (Persons/Sq. Mile)	20728	178	13.4
			Average Rooms per Housing Unit	3.5	173	5.0
Education	172	9.90	% High School Enrollment/Completion	71.8%	171	17.8
			% College Graduates	2.8%	174	2.0
Commute	11	56.85	Average Work Commute in Minutes	27	104	53.8
			% Commuting on Public Transportation	9.4%	8	59.9
Community Stability	121	56.45	% Living in Same House as in 1979	17.5%	162	29.9
			% Living in Same County as in 1985	83.1%	71	83.0

Composite: *Rank* 177 / 179 *Score* 40.37   **HAWAIIAN GARDENS**

CATEGORY	RANK	SCORE	STATISTIC	VALUE	RANK	SCORE
Economics	161	29.70	Median Household Income	$29,510	145	12.9
			% of Families Above Poverty Level	82.4%	164	46.5
Affordable Housing	54	69.80	Median Home Value	$136,100	36	84.0
			Median Rent	$643	70	55.6
Crime	140	36.65	Violent Crimes per 10,000 Population	272	143	1.1
			Property Crimes per 10,000 Population	560	89	72.2
Open Spaces	168	28.85	Population Density (Persons/Sq. Mile)	14377	169	40.2
			Average Rooms per Housing Unit	4.0	159	17.5
Education	157	21.65	% High School Enrollment/Completion	77.1%	153	33.8
			% College Graduates	7.4%	150	9.5
Commute	96	36.15	Average Work Commute in Minutes	28	116	50.0
			% Commuting on Public Transportation	3.5%	46	22.3
Community Stability	105	59.80	% Living in Same House as in 1979	24.5%	124	42.0
			% Living in Same County as in 1985	79.5%	90	77.6

Metropolitan Area Suburb Rankings
LOS ANGELES-ANAHEIM-RIVERSIDE

Composite: **Rank** 178 / 179 **Score** 40.16 **LENNOX**

CATEGORY	RANK	SCORE	STATISTIC	VALUE	RANK	SCORE
Economics	170	19.55	Median Household Income	$25,353	162	7.8
			% of Families Above Poverty Level	77.6%	171	31.3
Affordable Housing	37	74.40	Median Home Value	$158,700	54	78.8
			Median Rent	$550	33	70.0
Crime	N/A	N/A	Violent Crimes per 10,000 Population	N/A	N/A	N/A
			Property Crimes per 10,000 Population	N/A	N/A	N/A
Open Spaces	177	9.95	Population Density (Persons/Sq. Mile)	19785	176	17.4
			Average Rooms per Housing Unit	3.4	174	2.5
Education	175	5.55	% High School Enrollment/Completion	68.9%	174	9.1
			% College Graduates	2.8%	174	2.0
Commute	3	69.95	Average Work Commute in Minutes	23	26	69.2
			% Commuting on Public Transportation	11.1%	5	70.7
Community Stability	97	61.55	% Living in Same House as in 1979	22.3%	141	38.2
			% Living in Same County as in 1985	84.4%	61	84.9

Composite: **Rank** 179 / 179 **Score** 37.47 **LAKE ELSINORE**

CATEGORY	RANK	SCORE	STATISTIC	VALUE	RANK	SCORE
Economics	118	45.00	Median Household Income	$30,801	140	14.4
			% of Families Above Poverty Level	91.6%	106	75.6
Affordable Housing	35	75.40	Median Home Value	$135,400	34	84.2
			Median Rent	$572	37	66.6
Crime	141	32.20	Violent Crimes per 10,000 Population	192	131	31.4
			Property Crimes per 10,000 Population	1,165	142	33.0
Open Spaces	71	66.30	Population Density (Persons/Sq. Mile)	780	6	97.6
			Average Rooms per Housing Unit	4.7	108	35.0
Education	176	5.30	% High School Enrollment/Completion	65.9%	179	0.0
			% College Graduates	8.1%	146	10.6
Commute	170	14.10	Average Work Commute in Minutes	34	167	26.9
			% Commuting on Public Transportation	0.2%	165	1.3
Community Stability	175	24.00	% Living in Same House as in 1979	10.8%	173	18.3
			% Living in Same County as in 1985	47.7%	175	29.7

Metropolitan Area Description
LOUISVILLE

STATE: Kentucky
COUNTIES: Bullitt, Jefferson, Oldham, Shelby

STATE: Indiana
COUNTIES: Clark, Floyd, Harrison

TOTAL POPULATION: 952,662

POPULATION IN SUBURBS: 683,599   (71.8%)

POPULATION IN Louisville (KY):   269,063   (28.2%)

The LOUISVILLE metropolitan area is located in the northern part of Kentucky and the southern part of Indiana. The suburbs range geographically from Clarksville (IN) in the north (3 miles from Louisville), to New Albany (IN) in the west (6 miles from Louisville), to Okolona (KY) in the south (11 miles from Louisville), and to Jeffersontown (KY) in the east (14 miles from Louisville). The area is shrinking in population and had a decrease of 0.4% between 1980 and 1990. Summer time high temperatures average in the 80's and winter time lows average in the 20's. General Electric has facilities in the suburb of Okolona (KY). Professionals have been attracted to Oldham County (KY) for a rural atmosphere which features horse farms famous for Kentucky Derby winners. Public transportation in the area is provided on buses by TARC.

Highview (KY) is the overall highest rated suburb and also has the highest score in open spaces. **Jeffersontown** (KY) receives the top score in economics. **Newburg** (KY) is the suburb with the most affordable housing and also has the top rated commute. The number one score in education belongs to **St. Matthews** (KY). **Valley Station** (KY) has the highest score in community stability. Crime rankings were not available for the area.

The highest ranked suburb overall which also has an affordable housing score of at least 50.00 is **Valley Station** (KY).

The highest ranked suburb in the education category which also has an affordable housing score of at least 50.00 is **Okolona** (KY).

The county whose suburbs have the highest average overall score is **Jefferson County** (KY) (52.56).

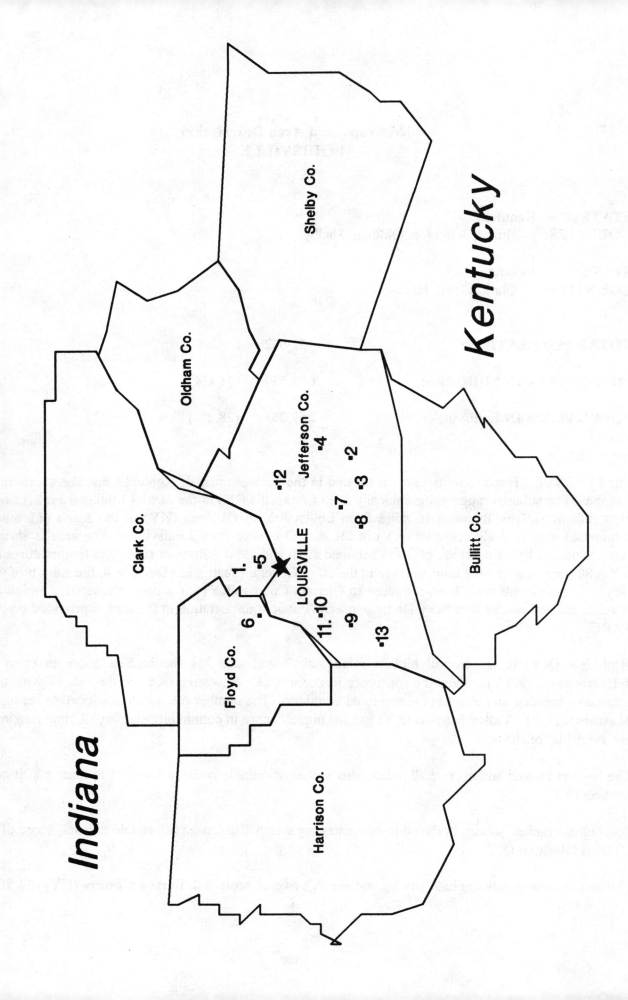

Metropolitan Area Map
LOUISVILLE

Indiana

Kentucky

Clark Co.

Oldham Co.

Shelby Co.

Jefferson Co.

Floyd Co.

Harrison Co.

Bullitt Co.

LOUISVILLE

1.
•5
6.
•12
•7
•4
•3
•2
•8
11. •10
•9
•13

Metropolitan Area Suburb Alphabetical Index
LOUISVILLE

SUBURB	PAGE	MAP NO.	STATE	COUNTY	POPU-LATION	RANK
CLARKSVILLE	376	1	Indiana	Clark	19,833	13 / 13
FERN CREEK	373	2	Kentucky	Jefferson	16,406	5 / 13
HIGHVIEW	372	3	Kentucky	Jefferson	14,814	1 / 13
JEFFERSONTOWN	372	4	Kentucky	Jefferson	23,221	2 / 13
JEFFERSONVILLE	374	5	Indiana	Clark	21,841	9 / 13
NEW ALBANY	375	6	Indiana	Floyd	36,322	12 / 13
NEWBURG	375	7	Kentucky	Jefferson	21,647	11 / 13
OKOLONA	374	8	Kentucky	Jefferson	18,902	7 / 13
PLEASURE RIDGE PARK	373	9	Kentucky	Jefferson	25,131	4 / 13
SHIVELY	373	10	Kentucky	Jefferson	15,535	6 / 13
ST. DENNIS	374	11	Kentucky	Jefferson	10,326	8 / 13
ST. MATTHEWS	375	12	Kentucky	Jefferson	15,800	10 / 13
VALLEY STATION	372	13	Kentucky	Jefferson	22,840	3 / 13

Metropolitan Area Suburb Rankings
LOUISVILLE

Composite: *Rank* 1 / 13 *Score* 67.56   **HIGHVIEW (KY)**

CATEGORY	RANK	SCORE	STATISTIC	VALUE	RANK	SCORE
Economics	2	94.20	Median Household Income	$37,650	2	92.2
			% of Families Above Poverty Level	97.2%	3	96.2
Affordable Housing	10	42.60	Median Home Value	$63,400	10	29.8
			Median Rent	$388	9	55.4
Crime	N/A	N/A	Violent Crimes per 10,000 Population	N/A	N/A	N/A
			Property Crimes per 10,000 Population	N/A	N/A	N/A
Open Spaces	1	91.65	Population Density (Persons/Sq. Mile)	2267	1	100.0
			Average Rooms per Housing Unit	6.0	2	83.3
Education	3	61.15	% High School Enrollment/Completion	95.2%	2	93.9
			% College Graduates	12.8%	5	28.4
Commute	10	40.10	Average Work Commute in Minutes	20	5	66.7
			% Commuting on Public Transportation	1.1%	11	13.5
Community Stability	5	75.65	% Living in Same House as in 1979	50.0%	4	74.0
			% Living in Same County as in 1985	90.3%	6	77.3

Composite: *Rank* 2 / 13 *Score* 56.94   **JEFFERSONTOWN (KY)**

CATEGORY	RANK	SCORE	STATISTIC	VALUE	RANK	SCORE
Economics	1	98.65	Median Household Income	$38,962	1	100.0
			% of Families Above Poverty Level	97.4%	2	97.3
Affordable Housing	12	12.80	Median Home Value	$73,300	13	0.0
			Median Rent	$438	12	25.6
Crime	N/A	N/A	Violent Crimes per 10,000 Population	14	N/A	N/A
			Property Crimes per 10,000 Population	274	N/A	N/A
Open Spaces	3	83.50	Population Density (Persons/Sq. Mile)	2402	4	92.0
			Average Rooms per Housing Unit	5.9	3	75.0
Education	2	81.60	% High School Enrollment/Completion	94.8%	3	90.4
			% College Graduates	27.5%	2	72.8
Commute	7	44.90	Average Work Commute in Minutes	20	5	66.7
			% Commuting on Public Transportation	1.6%	8	23.1
Community Stability	11	20.20	% Living in Same House as in 1979	30.9%	13	0.0
			% Living in Same County as in 1985	83.0%	9	40.4

Composite: *Rank* 3 / 13 *Score* 55.50   **VALLEY STATION (KY)**

CATEGORY	RANK	SCORE	STATISTIC	VALUE	RANK	SCORE
Economics	5	62.90	Median Household Income	$30,236	5	48.0
			% of Families Above Poverty Level	93.8%	5	77.8
Affordable Housing	9	65.20	Median Home Value	$46,800	3	79.8
			Median Rent	$396	10	50.6
Crime	N/A	N/A	Violent Crimes per 10,000 Population	N/A	N/A	N/A
			Property Crimes per 10,000 Population	N/A	N/A	N/A
Open Spaces	4	64.80	Population Density (Persons/Sq. Mile)	2895	8	62.9
			Average Rooms per Housing Unit	5.8	4	66.7
Education	8	24.80	% High School Enrollment/Completion	88.6%	8	36.0
			% College Graduates	7.9%	8	13.6
Commute	12	17.30	Average Work Commute in Minutes	26	13	0.0
			% Commuting on Public Transportation	2.2%	4	34.6
Community Stability	1	98.00	% Living in Same House as in 1979	56.7%	1	100.0
			% Living in Same County as in 1985	94.0%	2	96.0

Metropolitan Area Suburb Rankings
LOUISVILLE

Composite: **Rank** 4 / 13 **Score** 55.41   **PLEASURE RIDGE PARK (KY)**

CATEGORY	RANK	SCORE	STATISTIC	VALUE	RANK	SCORE
Economics	6	56.55	Median Household Income	$28,914	6	40.1
			% of Families Above Poverty Level	92.9%	7	73.0
Affordable Housing	4	84.80	Median Home Value	$49,000	8	73.2
			Median Rent	$319	2	96.4
Crime	N/A	N/A	Violent Crimes per 10,000 Population	N/A	N/A	N/A
			Property Crimes per 10,000 Population	N/A	N/A	N/A
Open Spaces	9	43.85	Population Density (Persons/Sq. Mile)	3182	9	46.0
			Average Rooms per Housing Unit	5.5	5	41.7
Education	6	25.60	% High School Enrollment/Completion	89.4%	7	43.0
			% College Graduates	6.1%	12	8.2
Commute	11	24.55	Average Work Commute in Minutes	24	11	22.2
			% Commuting on Public Transportation	1.8%	6	26.9
Community Stability	2	97.10	% Living in Same House as in 1979	55.2%	2	94.2
			% Living in Same County as in 1985	94.8%	1	100.0

Composite: **Rank** 5 / 13 **Score** 53.41   **FERN CREEK (KY)**

CATEGORY	RANK	SCORE	STATISTIC	VALUE	RANK	SCORE
Economics	3	94.15	Median Household Income	$37,633	3	92.1
			% of Families Above Poverty Level	97.2%	3	96.2
Affordable Housing	11	25.45	Median Home Value	$65,500	11	23.5
			Median Rent	$435	11	27.4
Crime	N/A	N/A	Violent Crimes per 10,000 Population	N/A	N/A	N/A
			Property Crimes per 10,000 Population	N/A	N/A	N/A
Open Spaces	2	83.65	Population Density (Persons/Sq. Mile)	2821	7	67.3
			Average Rooms per Housing Unit	6.2	1	100.0
Education	4	45.40	% High School Enrollment/Completion	90.2%	6	50.0
			% College Graduates	16.9%	3	40.8
Commute	13	15.90	Average Work Commute in Minutes	24	11	22.2
			% Commuting on Public Transportation	0.9%	12	9.6
Community Stability	8	55.90	% Living in Same House as in 1979	44.5%	6	52.7
			% Living in Same County as in 1985	86.7%	8	59.1

Composite: **Rank** 6 / 13 **Score** 51.86   **SHIVELY (KY)**

CATEGORY	RANK	SCORE	STATISTIC	VALUE	RANK	SCORE
Economics	9	38.05	Median Household Income	$24,966	9	16.6
			% of Families Above Poverty Level	90.4%	9	59.5
Affordable Housing	3	85.00	Median Home Value	$47,900	5	76.5
			Median Rent	$324	4	93.5
Crime	N/A	N/A	Violent Crimes per 10,000 Population	56	N/A	N/A
			Property Crimes per 10,000 Population	372	N/A	N/A
Open Spaces	10	30.95	Population Density (Persons/Sq. Mile)	3336	10	36.9
			Average Rooms per Housing Unit	5.3	7	25.0
Education	13	11.45	% High School Enrollment/Completion	85.8%	11	11.4
			% College Graduates	7.2%	9	11.5
Commute	3	59.30	Average Work Commute in Minutes	20	5	66.7
			% Commuting on Public Transportation	3.1%	3	51.9
Community Stability	3	86.40	% Living in Same House as in 1979	51.0%	3	77.9
			% Living in Same County as in 1985	93.8%	3	94.9

Metropolitan Area Suburb Rankings
LOUISVILLE

Composite: *Rank* 7 / 13 *Score* 51.30 — OKOLONA (KY)

CATEGORY	RANK	SCORE	STATISTIC	VALUE	RANK	SCORE
Economics	8	46.70	Median Household Income	$26,704	7	26.9
			% of Families Above Poverty Level	91.7%	8	66.5
Affordable Housing	7	75.45	Median Home Value	$55,000	9	55.1
			Median Rent	$320	3	95.8
Crime	N/A	N/A	Violent Crimes per 10,000 Population	N/A	N/A	N/A
			Property Crimes per 10,000 Population	N/A	N/A	N/A
Open Spaces	6	52.95	Population Density (Persons/Sq. Mile)	2731	6	72.6
			Average Rooms per Housing Unit	5.4	6	33.3
Education	5	31.75	% High School Enrollment/Completion	90.7%	4	54.4
			% College Graduates	6.4%	10	9.1
Commute	9	42.95	Average Work Commute in Minutes	20	5	66.7
			% Commuting on Public Transportation	1.4%	9	19.2
Community Stability	7	58.00	% Living in Same House as in 1979	43.5%	7	48.8
			% Living in Same County as in 1985	88.3%	7	67.2

Composite: *Rank* 8 / 13 *Score* 47.24 — ST. DENNIS (KY)

CATEGORY	RANK	SCORE	STATISTIC	VALUE	RANK	SCORE
Economics	12	16.95	Median Household Income	$23,697	12	9.0
			% of Families Above Poverty Level	84.0%	12	24.9
Affordable Housing	2	89.15	Median Home Value	$47,300	4	78.3
			Median Rent	$313	1	100.0
Crime	N/A	N/A	Violent Crimes per 10,000 Population	N/A	N/A	N/A
			Property Crimes per 10,000 Population	N/A	N/A	N/A
Open Spaces	12	8.35	Population Density (Persons/Sq. Mile)	3962	13	0.0
			Average Rooms per Housing Unit	5.2	8	16.7
Education	7	25.45	% High School Enrollment/Completion	90.3%	5	50.9
			% College Graduates	3.4%	13	0.0
Commute	2	65.30	Average Work Commute in Minutes	21	10	55.6
			% Commuting on Public Transportation	4.3%	2	75.0
Community Stability	4	78.25	% Living in Same House as in 1979	46.8%	5	61.6
			% Living in Same County as in 1985	93.8%	3	94.9

Composite: *Rank* 9 / 13 *Score* 44.22 — JEFFERSONVILLE (IN)

CATEGORY	RANK	SCORE	STATISTIC	VALUE	RANK	SCORE
Economics	10	29.40	Median Household Income	$23,977	10	10.7
			% of Families Above Poverty Level	88.3%	10	48.1
Affordable Housing	5	83.50	Median Home Value	$45,300	2	84.3
			Median Rent	$342	5	82.7
Crime	N/A	N/A	Violent Crimes per 10,000 Population	N/A	N/A	N/A
			Property Crimes per 10,000 Population	N/A	N/A	N/A
Open Spaces	5	53.45	Population Density (Persons/Sq. Mile)	2291	2	98.6
			Average Rooms per Housing Unit	5.1	11	8.3
Education	11	13.45	% High School Enrollment/Completion	84.5%	13	0.0
			% College Graduates	12.3%	6	26.9
Commute	4	57.90	Average Work Commute in Minutes	18	2	88.9
			% Commuting on Public Transportation	1.8%	6	26.9
Community Stability	10	27.65	% Living in Same House as in 1979	38.0%	10	27.5
			% Living in Same County as in 1985	80.5%	10	27.8

Metropolitan Area Suburb Rankings
LOUISVILLE

Composite: Rank 10 / 13 *Score* 43.55   **ST. MATTHEWS (KY)**

CATEGORY	RANK	SCORE	STATISTIC	VALUE	RANK	SCORE
Economics	4	79.60	Median Household Income	$32,108	4	59.2
			% of Families Above Poverty Level	97.9%	1	100.0
Affordable Housing	13	4.05	Median Home Value	$70,600	12	8.1
			Median Rent	$481	13	0.0
Crime	N/A	N/A	Violent Crimes per 10,000 Population	41	N/A	N/A
			Property Crimes per 10,000 Population	495	N/A	N/A
Open Spaces	11	9.10	Population Density (Persons/Sq. Mile)	3937	12	1.5
			Average Rooms per Housing Unit	5.2	8	16.7
Education	1	100.00	% High School Enrollment/Completion	95.9%	1	100.0
			% College Graduates	36.5%	1	100.0
Commute	6	55.25	Average Work Commute in Minutes	19	4	77.8
			% Commuting on Public Transportation	2.1%	5	32.7
Community Stability	12	13.30	% Living in Same House as in 1979	31.9%	12	3.9
			% Living in Same County as in 1985	79.5%	12	22.7

Composite: Rank 11 / 13 *Score* 42.83   **NEWBURG (KY)**

CATEGORY	RANK	SCORE	STATISTIC	VALUE	RANK	SCORE
Economics	13	0.00	Median Household Income	$22,183	13	0.0
			% of Families Above Poverty Level	79.4%	13	0.0
Affordable Housing	1	89.30	Median Home Value	$40,100	1	100.0
			Median Rent	$349	7	78.6
Crime	N/A	N/A	Violent Crimes per 10,000 Population	N/A	N/A	N/A
			Property Crimes per 10,000 Population	N/A	N/A	N/A
Open Spaces	13	5.70	Population Density (Persons/Sq. Mile)	3769	11	11.4
			Average Rooms per Housing Unit	5.0	12	0.0
Education	12	12.75	% High School Enrollment/Completion	86.4%	10	16.7
			% College Graduates	6.3%	11	8.8
Commute	1	83.35	Average Work Commute in Minutes	20	5	66.7
			% Commuting on Public Transportation	5.6%	1	100.0
Community Stability	6	65.90	% Living in Same House as in 1979	41.7%	8	41.9
			% Living in Same County as in 1985	92.8%	5	89.9

Composite: Rank 12 / 13 *Score* 42.20   **NEW ALBANY (IN)**

CATEGORY	RANK	SCORE	STATISTIC	VALUE	RANK	SCORE
Economics	11	25.75	Median Household Income	$23,933	11	10.4
			% of Families Above Poverty Level	87.0%	11	41.1
Affordable Housing	6	77.85	Median Home Value	$47,900	5	76.5
			Median Rent	$348	6	79.2
Crime	N/A	N/A	Violent Crimes per 10,000 Population	101	N/A	N/A
			Property Crimes per 10,000 Population	538	N/A	N/A
Open Spaces	8	45.00	Population Density (Persons/Sq. Mile)	2720	5	73.3
			Average Rooms per Housing Unit	5.2	8	16.7
Education	10	19.15	% High School Enrollment/Completion	85.6%	12	9.6
			% College Graduates	12.9%	4	28.7
Commute	5	57.70	Average Work Commute in Minutes	17	1	100.0
			% Commuting on Public Transportation	1.2%	10	15.4
Community Stability	9	27.75	% Living in Same House as in 1979	38.7%	9	30.2
			% Living in Same County as in 1985	80.0%	11	25.3

Metropolitan Area Suburb Rankings
LOUISVILLE

Composite: *Rank* 13 / 13 *Score* 39.78 **CLARKSVILLE (IN)**

CATEGORY	RANK	SCORE	STATISTIC	VALUE	RANK	SCORE
Economics	7	47.60	Median Household Income	$25,372	8	19.0
			% of Families Above Poverty Level	93.5%	6	76.2
Affordable Housing	8	68.15	Median Home Value	$48,200	7	75.6
			Median Rent	$379	8	60.7
Crime	N/A	N/A	Violent Crimes per 10,000 Population	30	N/A	N/A
			Property Crimes per 10,000 Population	785	N/A	N/A
Open Spaces	7	47.95	Population Density (Persons/Sq. Mile)	2336	3	95.9
			Average Rooms per Housing Unit	5.0	12	0.0
Education	9	21.05	% High School Enrollment/Completion	87.1%	9	22.8
			% College Graduates	9.8%	7	19.3
Commute	8	44.45	Average Work Commute in Minutes	18	2	88.9
			% Commuting on Public Transportation	0.4%	13	0.0
Community Stability	13	9.50	% Living in Same House as in 1979	35.8%	11	19.0
			% Living in Same County as in 1985	75.0%	13	0.0

Metropolitan Area Description
MEMPHIS

STATE: Arkansas
COUNTIES: Crittenden

STATE: Mississippi
COUNTIES: De Soto

STATE: Tennessee
COUNTIES: Shelby, Tipton

TOTAL POPULATION: 981,747

POPULATION IN SUBURBS: 371,410 (37.8%)

POPULATION IN Memphis (TN): 610,337 (62.2%)

The MEMPHIS metropolitan area is located in the southwestern part of Tennessee, the northwestern part of Mississippi, and the northeastern part of Arkansas. The suburbs range geographically from Millington (TN) in the north (17 miles from Memphis), to West Memphis (AR) in the west (9 miles from Memphis), to Southaven (MS) in the south (13 miles from Memphis), and to Collierville (TN) in the east (24 miles from Memphis). The area is growing in population and had an increase of 7.5% between 1980 and 1990. Summer time high temperatures average in the 90's and winter time lows average in the 30's. Suburban Memphis is home to some major area employers. Carrier Air Conditioning Company has facilities located in Collierville (TN). Public transportation in the area is provided on buses by the Memphis Area Transit Authority.

Germantown (TN) is the overall highest rated suburb and also has the highest scores in economics and education. **Germantown** (TN) is also the safest suburb with the lowest crime rate and has the top rated commute. **West Memphis** (AR) is the suburb with the most affordable housing and also has the highest score in community stability. Finally, the number one rating in open spaces goes to **Collierville** (TN).

The highest ranked suburb overall which also has an affordable housing score of at least 50.00 is **Southaven** (MS).

The highest ranked suburb in the education category which also has an affordable housing score of at least 50.00 is **Clarkville** (TN).

The county whose suburbs have the highest average overall score is **Shelby County** (TN) (52.42).

Metropolitan Area Map
MEMPHIS

Tennessee

Mississippi

Arkansas

Tipton Co.

Shelby Co.

•4

•1

3.

•5

De Soto Co.

MEMPHIS

★

•6

•2

Crittenden Co.

Metropolitan Area Suburb Alphabetical Index
MEMPHIS

SUBURB	PAGE	MAP NO.	STATE	COUNTY	POPU-LATION	RANK
BARTLETT	381	1	Tennessee	Shelby	26,989	4 / 6
COLLIERVILLE	380	2	Tennessee	Shelby	14,427	3 / 6
GERMANTOWN	380	3	Tennessee	Shelby	32,893	1 / 6
MILLINGTON	381	4	Tennessee	Shelby	17,866	5 / 6
SOUTHAVEN	380	5	Mississippi	De Soto	17,949	2 / 6
WEST MEMPHIS	381	6	Arkansas	Crittenden	28,259	6 / 6

Metropolitan Area Suburb Rankings
MEMPHIS

Composite: ***Rank*** 1 / 6 ***Score*** 65.68   **GERMANTOWN** (TN)

CATEGORY	RANK	SCORE	STATISTIC	VALUE	RANK	SCORE
Economics	1	100.00	Median Household Income	$69,019	1	100.0
			% of Families Above Poverty Level	99.0%	1	100.0
Affordable Housing	6	0.00	Median Home Value	$145,000	6	0.0
			Median Rent	$631	6	0.0
Crime	1	100.00	Violent Crimes per 10,000 Population	5	1	100.0
			Property Crimes per 10,000 Population	163	1	100.0
Open Spaces	3	50.00	Population Density (Persons/Sq. Mile)	2142	6	0.0
			Average Rooms per Housing Unit	7.7	1	100.0
Education	1	100.00	% High School Enrollment/Completion	97.6%	1	100.0
			% College Graduates	53.5%	1	100.0
Commute	1	55.55	Average Work Commute in Minutes	23	4	11.1
			% Commuting on Public Transportation	0.3%	1	100.0
Community Stability	4	54.20	% Living in Same House as in 1979	22.8%	5	26.6
			% Living in Same County as in 1985	72.9%	3	81.8

Composite: ***Rank*** 2 / 6 ***Score*** 54.04   **SOUTHAVEN** (MS)

CATEGORY	RANK	SCORE	STATISTIC	VALUE	RANK	SCORE
Economics	4	50.10	Median Household Income	$36,469	4	30.7
			% of Families Above Poverty Level	93.7%	4	69.5
Affordable Housing	3	64.20	Median Home Value	$62,600	2	86.4
			Median Rent	$510	4	42.0
Crime	N/A	N/A	Violent Crimes per 10,000 Population	N/A	N/A	N/A
			Property Crimes per 10,000 Population	N/A	N/A	N/A
Open Spaces	2	55.95	Population Density (Persons/Sq. Mile)	1408	2	74.9
			Average Rooms per Housing Unit	6.0	4	37.0
Education	5	34.80	% High School Enrollment/Completion	92.1%	5	65.0
			% College Graduates	12.1%	4	4.6
Commute	4	33.30	Average Work Commute in Minutes	21	3	33.3
			% Commuting on Public Transportation	0.1%	2	33.3
Community Stability	2	85.90	% Living in Same House as in 1979	39.1%	1	100.0
			% Living in Same County as in 1985	67.7%	5	71.8

Composite: ***Rank*** 3 / 6 ***Score*** 53.67   **COLLIERVILLE** (TN)

CATEGORY	RANK	SCORE	STATISTIC	VALUE	RANK	SCORE
Economics	3	64.45	Median Household Income	$47,517	2	54.2
			% of Families Above Poverty Level	94.6%	3	74.7
Affordable Housing	4	52.75	Median Home Value	$104,300	5	42.7
			Median Rent	$450	3	62.8
Crime	2	73.00	Violent Crimes per 10,000 Population	18	2	78.7
			Property Crimes per 10,000 Population	291	2	67.3
Open Spaces	1	77.80	Population Density (Persons/Sq. Mile)	1162	1	100.0
			Average Rooms per Housing Unit	6.5	3	55.6
Education	3	56.40	% High School Enrollment/Completion	94.0%	3	77.1
			% College Graduates	25.6%	2	35.7
Commute	6	0.00	Average Work Commute in Minutes	24	6	0.0
			% Commuting on Public Transportation	0.0%	5	0.0
Community Stability	5	51.30	% Living in Same House as in 1979	23.1%	4	27.9
			% Living in Same County as in 1985	69.2%	4	74.7

Metropolitan Area Suburb Rankings
MEMPHIS

BARTLETT (TN)

Composite: **Rank** 4 / 6 **Score** 53.04

CATEGORY	RANK	SCORE	STATISTIC	VALUE	RANK	SCORE
Economics	2	73.80	Median Household Income	$47,346	3	53.9
			% of Families Above Poverty Level	97.9%	2	93.7
Affordable Housing	5	32.50	Median Home Value	$90,900	4	56.7
			Median Rent	$607	5	8.3
Crime	3	63.75	Violent Crimes per 10,000 Population	28	3	62.3
			Property Crimes per 10,000 Population	299	3	65.2
Open Spaces	4	43.30	Population Density (Persons/Sq. Mile)	1874	4	27.3
			Average Rooms per Housing Unit	6.6	2	59.3
Education	2	56.85	% High School Enrollment/Completion	94.9%	2	82.8
			% College Graduates	23.5%	3	30.9
Commute	5	22.20	Average Work Commute in Minutes	23	4	11.1
			% Commuting on Public Transportation	0.1%	2	33.3
Community Stability	3	78.85	% Living in Same House as in 1979	29.8%	3	58.1
			% Living in Same County as in 1985	82.2%	2	99.6

MILLINGTON (TN)

Composite: **Rank** 5 / 6 **Score** 37.27

CATEGORY	RANK	SCORE	STATISTIC	VALUE	RANK	SCORE
Economics	5	24.60	Median Household Income	$23,815	5	3.8
			% of Families Above Poverty Level	89.5%	5	45.4
Affordable Housing	2	90.60	Median Home Value	$64,200	3	84.7
			Median Rent	$353	2	96.5
Crime	N/A	N/A	Violent Crimes per 10,000 Population	N/A	N/A	N/A
			Property Crimes per 10,000 Population	N/A	N/A	N/A
Open Spaces	5	23.35	Population Density (Persons/Sq. Mile)	1684	3	46.7
			Average Rooms per Housing Unit	5.0	6	0.0
Education	4	35.05	% High School Enrollment/Completion	92.9%	4	70.1
			% College Graduates	10.1%	6	0.0
Commute	2	50.00	Average Work Commute in Minutes	15	1	100.0
			% Commuting on Public Transportation	0.0%	5	0.0
Community Stability	6	0.00	% Living in Same House as in 1979	16.9%	6	0.0
			% Living in Same County as in 1985	30.2%	6	0.0

WEST MEMPHIS (AR)

Composite: **Rank** 6 / 6 **Score** 36.26

CATEGORY	RANK	SCORE	STATISTIC	VALUE	RANK	SCORE
Economics	6	0.00	Median Household Income	$22,052	6	0.0
			% of Families Above Poverty Level	81.6%	6	0.0
Affordable Housing	1	100.00	Median Home Value	$49,600	1	100.0
			Median Rent	$343	1	100.0
Crime	4	0.00	Violent Crimes per 10,000 Population	66	4	0.0
			Property Crimes per 10,000 Population	554	4	0.0
Open Spaces	6	10.70	Population Density (Persons/Sq. Mile)	1969	5	17.7
			Average Rooms per Housing Unit	5.1	5	3.7
Education	6	0.80	% High School Enrollment/Completion	81.9%	6	0.0
			% College Graduates	10.8%	5	1.6
Commute	2	50.00	Average Work Commute in Minutes	18	2	66.7
			% Commuting on Public Transportation	0.1%	2	33.3
Community Stability	1	92.35	% Living in Same House as in 1979	35.7%	2	84.7
			% Living in Same County as in 1985	82.4%	1	100.0

STATE: Florida
COUNTIES: Broward, Dade

TOTAL POPULATION: 3,192,582

POPULATION IN SUBURBS: 2,684,657   (84.1%)

POPULATION IN Miami: 358,548   (11.2%)
POPULATION IN Fort Lauderdale: 149,377   (4.7%)

The MIAMI-FORT LAUDERDALE metropolitan area is located in the southeastern part of Florida along the Atlantic Ocean. The suburbs range geographically from Deerfield Beach in the north (39 miles from Miami), to Westwood Lakes in the west (13 miles from Miami), and to Leisure City in the south (28 miles from Miami). The area is growing rapidly in population and had an increase of 20.8% between 1980 and 1990. Summer time high temperatures average in the 90's and winter time lows average in the 60's. The metropolitan area features many well-known tourist towns. Electronics industries are also located in the area with Racal-Datacom located in Sunrise and Sensormatic Electronics located in Deerfield Beach. In 1992, the area was the site of major damage from Hurricane Andrew. Public transportation in the area is provided by the Metro Transit Authority using buses and a 21-mile elevated railway line.

Cutler is the overall highest rated suburb and also has the highest scores in economics, education, and open spaces. **Gladeview** is the suburb with the most affordable housing and also has the top rated commute. Finally, the number one rating in community stability belongs to **Brownsville**. Crime rankings were not available for the area.

The highest ranked suburb overall which also has an affordable housing score of at least 50.00 is **Miami Shores**.

The highest ranked suburb in the education category which also has an affordable housing score of at least 50.00 is **Hammocks**.

The county whose suburbs have the highest average overall score is **Dade County** (54.14).

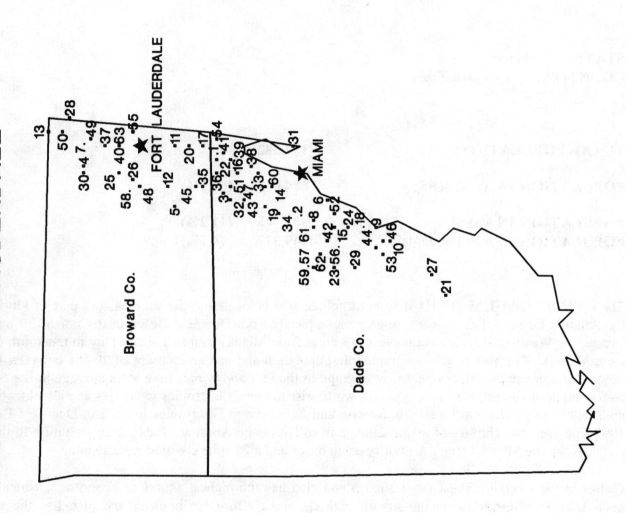

Metropolitan Area Map
MIAMI-FORT LAUDERDALE

Florida

Metropolitan Area Suburb Alphabetical Index
MIAMI-FORT LAUDERDALE

SUBURB	PAGE	MAP NO.	STATE	COUNTY	POPU-LATION	RANK
AVENTURA	406	1	Florida	Dade	14,914	59 / 63
BROWNSVILLE	393	2	Florida	Dade	15,607	19 / 63
CAROL CITY	395	3	Florida	Dade	53,331	25 / 63
COCONUT CREEK	405	4	Florida	Broward	27,485	56 / 63
COOPER CITY	396	5	Florida	Broward	20,791	28 / 63
CORAL GABLES	388	6	Florida	Dade	40,091	4 / 63
CORAL SPRINGS	402	7	Florida	Broward	79,443	47 / 63
CORAL TERRACE	392	8	Florida	Dade	23,255	16 / 63
CUTLER	387	9	Florida	Dade	16,201	1 / 63
CUTLER RIDGE	390	10	Florida	Dade	21,268	10 / 63
DANIA	398	11	Florida	Broward	13,024	35 / 63
DAVIE	401	12	Florida	Broward	47,217	44 / 63
DEERFIELD BEACH	397	13	Florida	Broward	46,325	33 / 63
GLADEVIEW	393	14	Florida	Dade	15,637	20 / 63
GLENVAR HEIGHTS	391	15	Florida	Dade	14,823	14 / 63
GOLDEN GLADES	397	16	Florida	Dade	25,474	31 / 63
HALLANDALE	400	17	Florida	Broward	30,996	41 / 63
HAMMOCKS	406	18	Florida	Dade	10,897	60 / 63
HIALEAH	405	19	Florida	Dade	188,004	57 / 63
HOLLYWOOD	396	20	Florida	Broward	121,697	29 / 63
HOMESTEAD	407	21	Florida	Dade	26,866	61 / 63
IVES ESTATES	394	22	Florida	Dade	13,531	23 / 63
KENDALE LAKES	401	23	Florida	Dade	48,524	45 / 63
KENDALL	388	24	Florida	Dade	87,271	6 / 63
LAUDERDALE LAKES	404	25	Florida	Broward	27,341	52 / 63
LAUDERHILL	405	26	Florida	Broward	49,708	55 / 63
LEISURE CITY	400	27	Florida	Dade	19,379	42 / 63
LIGHTHOUSE POINT	389	28	Florida	Broward	10,378	7 / 63
LINDGREN ACRES	397	29	Florida	Dade	22,290	32 / 63
MARGATE	399	30	Florida	Broward	42,985	37 / 63
MIAMI BEACH	407	31	Florida	Dade	92,639	62 / 63
MIAMI LAKES	392	32	Florida	Dade	12,750	18 / 63
MIAMI SHORES	387	33	Florida	Dade	10,084	2 / 63
MIAMI SPRINGS	391	34	Florida	Dade	13,268	13 / 63
MIRAMAR	398	35	Florida	Broward	40,663	36 / 63
NORLAND	395	36	Florida	Dade	22,109	27 / 63
NORTH LAUDERDALE	404	37	Florida	Broward	26,506	53 / 63
NORTH MIAMI	399	38	Florida	Dade	49,998	39 / 63
NORTH MIAMI BEACH	396	39	Florida	Dade	35,359	30 / 63
OAKLAND PARK	403	40	Florida	Broward	26,326	51 / 63
OJUS	389	41	Florida	Dade	15,519	8 / 63
OLYMPIA HEIGHTS	390	42	Florida	Dade	37,792	11 / 63
OPA-LOCKA	406	43	Florida	Dade	15,283	58 / 63
PALMETTO ESTATES	393	44	Florida	Dade	12,293	21 / 63
PEMBROKE PINES	403	45	Florida	Broward	65,452	49 / 63
PERRINE	392	46	Florida	Dade	15,576	17 / 63
PINEWOOD	402	47	Florida	Dade	15,518	46 / 63
PLANTATION	394	48	Florida	Broward	66,692	22 / 63
POMPANO BEACH	398	49	Florida	Broward	72,411	34 / 63
POMPANO BEACH HIGHLANDS	403	50	Florida	Broward	17,915	50 / 63
SCOTT LAKE	388	51	Florida	Dade	14,588	5 / 63

Metropolitan Area Suburb Alphabetical Index
MIAMI-FORT LAUDERDALE

SUBURB	PAGE	MAP NO.	STATE	COUNTY	POPU-LATION	RANK
SOUTH MIAMI	387	52	Florida	Dade	10,404	3 / 63
SOUTH MIAMI HEIGHTS	402	53	Florida	Dade	30,030	48 / 63
SUNNY ISLES	404	54	Florida	Dade	11,772	54 / 63
SUNRISE	399	55	Florida	Broward	64,407	38 / 63
SUNSET	389	56	Florida	Dade	15,810	9 / 63
SWEETWATER	407	57	Florida	Dade	13,909	63 / 63
TAMARAC	401	58	Florida	Broward	44,822	43 / 63
TAMIAMI	400	59	Florida	Dade	33,845	40 / 63
WEST LITTLE RIVER	394	60	Florida	Dade	33,575	24 / 63
WESTCHESTER	390	61	Florida	Dade	29,883	12 / 63
WESTWOOD LAKES	391	62	Florida	Dade	11,522	15 / 63
WILTON MANORS	395	63	Florida	Broward	11,804	26 / 63

Metropolitan Area Suburb Rankings
MIAMI-FORT LAUDERDALE

Composite: *Rank* 1 / 63 *Score* 71.33 **CUTLER**

CATEGORY	RANK	SCORE	STATISTIC	VALUE	RANK	SCORE
Economics	1	97.90	Median Household Income	$71,898	1	100.0
			% of Families Above Poverty Level	96.0%	9	95.8
Affordable Housing	61	34.50	Median Home Value	$195,300	62	15.2
			Median Rent	$550	29	53.8
Crime	N/A	N/A	Violent Crimes per 10,000 Population	N/A	N/A	N/A
			Property Crimes per 10,000 Population	N/A	N/A	N/A
Open Spaces	1	97.25	Population Density (Persons/Sq. Mile)	2235	4	94.5
			Average Rooms per Housing Unit	6.9	1	100.0
Education	1	97.10	% High School Enrollment/Completion	97.0%	3	94.2
			% College Graduates	52.8%	1	100.0
Commute	50	30.65	Average Work Commute in Minutes	26	42	52.9
			% Commuting on Public Transportation	2.3%	37	8.4
Community Stability	12	70.55	% Living in Same House as in 1979	41.9%	10	75.1
			% Living in Same County as in 1985	83.4%	16	66.0

Composite: *Rank* 2 / 63 *Score* 65.17 **MIAMI SHORES**

CATEGORY	RANK	SCORE	STATISTIC	VALUE	RANK	SCORE
Economics	13	69.25	Median Household Income	$41,670	10	49.8
			% of Families Above Poverty Level	92.8%	29	88.7
Affordable Housing	39	56.55	Median Home Value	$104,500	46	66.9
			Median Rent	$597	38	46.2
Crime	N/A	N/A	Violent Crimes per 10,000 Population	156	N/A	N/A
			Property Crimes per 10,000 Population	867	N/A	N/A
Open Spaces	6	77.75	Population Density (Persons/Sq. Mile)	4038	20	83.0
			Average Rooms per Housing Unit	5.8	3	72.5
Education	8	73.40	% High School Enrollment/Completion	92.4%	18	79.4
			% College Graduates	36.7%	6	67.4
Commute	10	49.75	Average Work Commute in Minutes	20	4	88.2
			% Commuting on Public Transportation	3.0%	28	11.3
Community Stability	18	64.30	% Living in Same House as in 1979	36.0%	19	64.5
			% Living in Same County as in 1985	82.7%	19	64.1

Composite: *Rank* 3 / 63 *Score* 63.81 **SOUTH MIAMI**

CATEGORY	RANK	SCORE	STATISTIC	VALUE	RANK	SCORE
Economics	35	58.05	Median Household Income	$31,741	29	33.2
			% of Families Above Poverty Level	90.2%	42	82.9
Affordable Housing	25	64.90	Median Home Value	$106,800	48	65.5
			Median Rent	$485	12	64.3
Crime	N/A	N/A	Violent Crimes per 10,000 Population	160	N/A	N/A
			Property Crimes per 10,000 Population	881	N/A	N/A
Open Spaces	20	66.15	Population Density (Persons/Sq. Mile)	4528	29	79.8
			Average Rooms per Housing Unit	5.0	19	52.5
Education	9	71.45	% High School Enrollment/Completion	94.7%	8	86.8
			% College Graduates	31.1%	11	56.1
Commute	8	51.40	Average Work Commute in Minutes	23	16	70.6
			% Commuting on Public Transportation	8.0%	8	32.2
Community Stability	11	70.90	% Living in Same House as in 1979	40.3%	13	72.2
			% Living in Same County as in 1985	84.7%	14	69.6

Composite: **Rank** 4 / 63   *Score* 62.65   **CORAL GABLES**

CATEGORY	RANK	SCORE	STATISTIC	VALUE	RANK	SCORE
Economics	3	77.20	Median Household Income	$47,506	3	59.5
			% of Families Above Poverty Level	95.6%	14	94.9
Affordable Housing	62	27.70	Median Home Value	$222,100	63	0.0
			Median Rent	$540	23	55.4
Crime	N/A	N/A	Violent Crimes per 10,000 Population	101	N/A	N/A
			Property Crimes per 10,000 Population	1,244	N/A	N/A
Open Spaces	12	73.55	Population Density (Persons/Sq. Mile)	3390	12	87.1
			Average Rooms per Housing Unit	5.3	12	60.0
Education	2	94.15	% High School Enrollment/Completion	97.5%	2	95.8
			% College Graduates	49.1%	2	92.5
Commute	5	53.55	Average Work Commute in Minutes	19	2	94.1
			% Commuting on Public Transportation	3.4%	24	13.0
Community Stability	37	49.75	% Living in Same House as in 1979	34.9%	27	62.5
			% Living in Same County as in 1985	72.9%	47	37.0

Composite: **Rank** 5 / 63   *Score* 61.31   **SCOTT LAKE**

CATEGORY	RANK	SCORE	STATISTIC	VALUE	RANK	SCORE
Economics	27	63.15	Median Household Income	$38,648	14	44.7
			% of Families Above Poverty Level	89.6%	44	81.6
Affordable Housing	34	60.65	Median Home Value	$72,300	13	85.2
			Median Rent	$659	50	36.1
Crime	N/A	N/A	Violent Crimes per 10,000 Population	N/A	N/A	N/A
			Property Crimes per 10,000 Population	N/A	N/A	N/A
Open Spaces	9	74.00	Population Density (Persons/Sq. Mile)	4430	22	80.5
			Average Rooms per Housing Unit	5.6	6	67.5
Education	29	49.25	% High School Enrollment/Completion	90.0%	27	71.6
			% College Graduates	16.7%	34	26.9
Commute	36	36.70	Average Work Commute in Minutes	26	42	52.9
			% Commuting on Public Transportation	5.2%	14	20.5
Community Stability	3	84.10	% Living in Same House as in 1979	47.6%	4	85.3
			% Living in Same County as in 1985	89.5%	4	82.9

Composite: **Rank** 6 / 63   *Score* 60.32   **KENDALL**

CATEGORY	RANK	SCORE	STATISTIC	VALUE	RANK	SCORE
Economics	6	75.00	Median Household Income	$45,303	6	55.8
			% of Families Above Poverty Level	95.3%	18	94.2
Affordable Housing	52	43.60	Median Home Value	$142,700	55	45.1
			Median Rent	$622	42	42.1
Crime	N/A	N/A	Violent Crimes per 10,000 Population	N/A	N/A	N/A
			Property Crimes per 10,000 Population	N/A	N/A	N/A
Open Spaces	11	73.80	Population Density (Persons/Sq. Mile)	3706	17	85.1
			Average Rooms per Housing Unit	5.4	11	62.5
Education	3	85.40	% High School Enrollment/Completion	95.9%	5	90.6
			% College Graduates	43.0%	3	80.2
Commute	39	35.65	Average Work Commute in Minutes	26	42	52.9
			% Commuting on Public Transportation	4.7%	18	18.4
Community Stability	42	48.50	% Living in Same House as in 1979	25.9%	43	46.4
			% Living in Same County as in 1985	77.8%	33	50.6

Metropolitan Area Suburb Rankings
MIAMI-FORT LAUDERDALE

Composite: **Rank** 7 / 63 **Score** 60.21   **LIGHTHOUSE POINT**

CATEGORY	RANK	SCORE	STATISTIC	VALUE	RANK	SCORE
Economics	9	73.80	Median Household Income	$40,934	12	48.5
			% of Families Above Poverty Level	97.5%	3	99.1
Affordable Housing	59	35.90	Median Home Value	$187,300	60	19.8
			Median Rent	$561	32	52.0
Crime	N/A	N/A	Violent Crimes per 10,000 Population	24	N/A	N/A
			Property Crimes per 10,000 Population	303	N/A	N/A
Open Spaces	15	69.95	Population Density (Persons/Sq. Mile)	4527	28	79.9
			Average Rooms per Housing Unit	5.3	12	60.0
Education	10	71.10	% High School Enrollment/Completion	96.7%	4	93.2
			% College Graduates	27.6%	14	49.0
Commute	26	42.45	Average Work Commute in Minutes	21	8	82.4
			% Commuting on Public Transportation	0.9%	54	2.5
Community Stability	14	68.05	% Living in Same House as in 1979	39.4%	15	70.6
			% Living in Same County as in 1985	83.2%	18	65.5

Composite: **Rank** 8 / 63 **Score** 59.57   **OJUS**

CATEGORY	RANK	SCORE	STATISTIC	VALUE	RANK	SCORE
Economics	30	61.25	Median Household Income	$28,095	39	27.2
			% of Families Above Poverty Level	95.8%	11	95.3
Affordable Housing	51	44.90	Median Home Value	$169,600	59	29.8
			Median Rent	$512	17	60.0
Crime	N/A	N/A	Violent Crimes per 10,000 Population	N/A	N/A	N/A
			Property Crimes per 10,000 Population	N/A	N/A	N/A
Open Spaces	36	58.80	Population Density (Persons/Sq. Mile)	5276	33	75.1
			Average Rooms per Housing Unit	4.6	33	42.5
Education	12	65.55	% High School Enrollment/Completion	93.3%	12	82.3
			% College Graduates	27.5%	16	48.8
Commute	22	44.15	Average Work Commute in Minutes	21	8	82.4
			% Commuting on Public Transportation	1.7%	44	5.9
Community Stability	5	82.80	% Living in Same House as in 1979	50.8%	2	91.0
			% Living in Same County as in 1985	86.5%	9	74.6

Composite: **Rank** 9 / 63 **Score** 59.15   **SUNSET**

CATEGORY	RANK	SCORE	STATISTIC	VALUE	RANK	SCORE
Economics	10	72.80	Median Household Income	$41,984	8	50.3
			% of Families Above Poverty Level	95.8%	11	95.3
Affordable Housing	45	54.25	Median Home Value	$107,400	49	65.2
			Median Rent	$615	41	43.3
Crime	N/A	N/A	Violent Crimes per 10,000 Population	N/A	N/A	N/A
			Property Crimes per 10,000 Population	N/A	N/A	N/A
Open Spaces	13	72.70	Population Density (Persons/Sq. Mile)	4445	24	80.4
			Average Rooms per Housing Unit	5.5	8	65.0
Education	23	53.95	% High School Enrollment/Completion	87.2%	37	62.6
			% College Graduates	25.8%	17	45.3
Commute	44	33.55	Average Work Commute in Minutes	26	42	52.9
			% Commuting on Public Transportation	3.7%	22	14.2
Community Stability	15	67.65	% Living in Same House as in 1979	35.7%	22	64.0
			% Living in Same County as in 1985	85.3%	12	71.3

Metropolitan Area Suburb Rankings
MIAMI-FORT LAUDERDALE

Composite: **Rank** 10 / 63 *Score* 58.38   **CUTLER RIDGE**

CATEGORY	RANK	SCORE	STATISTIC	VALUE	RANK	SCORE
Economics	11	71.25	Median Household Income	$41,019	11	48.7
			% of Families Above Poverty Level	95.1%	22	93.8
Affordable Housing	33	60.75	Median Home Value	$81,800	25	79.8
			Median Rent	$625	43	41.7
Crime	N/A	N/A	Violent Crimes per 10,000 Population	N/A	N/A	N/A
			Property Crimes per 10,000 Population	N/A	N/A	N/A
Open Spaces	10	73.85	Population Density (Persons/Sq. Mile)	4476	26	80.2
			Average Rooms per Housing Unit	5.6	6	67.5
Education	27	50.30	% High School Enrollment/Completion	88.0%	34	65.2
			% College Graduates	20.9%	22	35.4
Commute	50	30.65	Average Work Commute in Minutes	26	42	52.9
			% Commuting on Public Transportation	2.3%	37	8.4
Community Stability	19	63.45	% Living in Same House as in 1979	35.8%	21	64.2
			% Living in Same County as in 1985	82.2%	20	62.7

Composite: **Rank** 11 / 63 *Score* 57.87   **OLYMPIA HEIGHTS**

CATEGORY	RANK	SCORE	STATISTIC	VALUE	RANK	SCORE
Economics	28	63.05	Median Household Income	$35,049	25	38.7
			% of Families Above Poverty Level	92.2%	32	87.4
Affordable Housing	28	62.85	Median Home Value	$95,600	41	71.9
			Median Rent	$550	29	53.8
Crime	N/A	N/A	Violent Crimes per 10,000 Population	N/A	N/A	N/A
			Property Crimes per 10,000 Population	N/A	N/A	N/A
Open Spaces	27	61.50	Population Density (Persons/Sq. Mile)	5606	36	73.0
			Average Rooms per Housing Unit	4.9	21	50.0
Education	17	58.85	% High School Enrollment/Completion	94.0%	9	84.5
			% College Graduates	19.8%	25	33.2
Commute	53	29.80	Average Work Commute in Minutes	26	42	52.9
			% Commuting on Public Transportation	1.9%	43	6.7
Community Stability	10	71.15	% Living in Same House as in 1979	39.5%	14	70.8
			% Living in Same County as in 1985	85.4%	11	71.5

Composite: **Rank** 12 / 63 *Score* 57.59   **WESTCHESTER**

CATEGORY	RANK	SCORE	STATISTIC	VALUE	RANK	SCORE
Economics	29	62.45	Median Household Income	$35,237	24	39.1
			% of Families Above Poverty Level	91.5%	37	85.8
Affordable Housing	29	62.60	Median Home Value	$93,200	36	73.3
			Median Rent	$562	33	51.9
Crime	N/A	N/A	Violent Crimes per 10,000 Population	N/A	N/A	N/A
			Property Crimes per 10,000 Population	N/A	N/A	N/A
Open Spaces	46	55.70	Population Density (Persons/Sq. Mile)	7413	57	61.4
			Average Rooms per Housing Unit	4.9	21	50.0
Education	19	57.50	% High School Enrollment/Completion	93.6%	11	83.2
			% College Graduates	19.1%	28	31.8
Commute	46	33.35	Average Work Commute in Minutes	25	37	58.8
			% Commuting on Public Transportation	2.2%	40	7.9
Community Stability	9	73.95	% Living in Same House as in 1979	43.5%	8	78.0
			% Living in Same County as in 1985	84.8%	13	69.9

Metropolitan Area Suburb Rankings
MIAMI-FORT LAUDERDALE

Composite: Rank 13 / 63 Score 57.25 **MIAMI SPRINGS**

CATEGORY	RANK	SCORE	STATISTIC	VALUE	RANK	SCORE
Economics	33	59.55	Median Household Income	$31,461	31	32.8
			% of Families Above Poverty Level	91.7%	35	86.3
Affordable Housing	23	65.85	Median Home Value	$101,900	45	68.3
			Median Rent	$491	14	63.4
Crime	N/A	N/A	Violent Crimes per 10,000 Population	98	N/A	N/A
			Property Crimes per 10,000 Population	842	N/A	N/A
Open Spaces	24	63.70	Population Density (Persons/Sq. Mile)	4519	27	79.9
			Average Rooms per Housing Unit	4.8	25	47.5
Education	44	40.70	% High School Enrollment/Completion	83.0%	55	49.0
			% College Graduates	19.4%	26	32.4
Commute	7	52.70	Average Work Commute in Minutes	19	2	94.1
			% Commuting on Public Transportation	3.0%	28	11.3
Community Stability	21	61.00	% Living in Same House as in 1979	36.8%	17	65.9
			% Living in Same County as in 1985	79.8%	24	56.1

Composite: Rank 14 / 63 Score 57.20 **GLENVAR HEIGHTS**

CATEGORY	RANK	SCORE	STATISTIC	VALUE	RANK	SCORE
Economics	24	64.45	Median Household Income	$32,182	28	34.0
			% of Families Above Poverty Level	95.6%	14	94.9
Affordable Housing	49	48.75	Median Home Value	$141,200	54	46.0
			Median Rent	$564	34	51.5
Crime	N/A	N/A	Violent Crimes per 10,000 Population	N/A	N/A	N/A
			Property Crimes per 10,000 Population	N/A	N/A	N/A
Open Spaces	30	60.65	Population Density (Persons/Sq. Mile)	3522	13	86.3
			Average Rooms per Housing Unit	4.3	44	35.0
Education	4	82.15	% High School Enrollment/Completion	94.9%	6	87.4
			% College Graduates	41.4%	4	76.9
Commute	23	43.45	Average Work Commute in Minutes	24	25	64.7
			% Commuting on Public Transportation	5.6%	11	22.2
Community Stability	46	43.75	% Living in Same House as in 1979	21.7%	53	38.9
			% Living in Same County as in 1985	77.1%	36	48.6

Composite: Rank 15 / 63 Score 57.14 **WESTWOOD LAKES**

CATEGORY	RANK	SCORE	STATISTIC	VALUE	RANK	SCORE
Economics	25	63.90	Median Household Income	$35,797	22	40.0
			% of Families Above Poverty Level	92.4%	30	87.8
Affordable Housing	43	55.15	Median Home Value	$84,100	27	78.5
			Median Rent	$686	56	31.8
Crime	N/A	N/A	Violent Crimes per 10,000 Population	N/A	N/A	N/A
			Property Crimes per 10,000 Population	N/A	N/A	N/A
Open Spaces	22	65.60	Population Density (Persons/Sq. Mile)	6663	47	66.2
			Average Rooms per Housing Unit	5.5	8	65.0
Education	32	45.60	% High School Enrollment/Completion	90.8%	22	74.2
			% College Graduates	11.8%	49	17.0
Commute	58	23.10	Average Work Commute in Minutes	28	57	41.2
			% Commuting on Public Transportation	1.5%	47	5.0
Community Stability	2	89.50	% Living in Same House as in 1979	55.8%	1	100.0
			% Living in Same County as in 1985	88.1%	6	79.0

Metropolitan Area Suburb Rankings
MIAMI-FORT LAUDERDALE

Composite: **Rank** 16 / 63 *Score* 56.43   **CORAL TERRACE**

CATEGORY	RANK	SCORE	STATISTIC	VALUE	RANK	SCORE
Economics	41	55.20	Median Household Income	$27,300	43	25.9
			% of Families Above Poverty Level	90.9%	40	84.5
Affordable Housing	26	63.90	Median Home Value	$84,100	27	78.5
			Median Rent	$578	36	49.3
Crime	N/A	N/A	Violent Crimes per 10,000 Population	N/A	N/A	N/A
			Property Crimes per 10,000 Population	N/A	N/A	N/A
Open Spaces	42	56.50	Population Density (Persons/Sq. Mile)	6774	49	65.5
			Average Rooms per Housing Unit	4.8	25	47.5
Education	41	42.80	% High School Enrollment/Completion	88.5%	31	66.8
			% College Graduates	12.7%	47	18.8
Commute	29	40.10	Average Work Commute in Minutes	23	16	70.6
			% Commuting on Public Transportation	2.6%	33	9.6
Community Stability	6	80.10	% Living in Same House as in 1979	46.1%	6	82.6
			% Living in Same County as in 1985	87.6%	7	77.6

Composite: **Rank** 17 / 63 *Score* 56.16   **PERRINE**

CATEGORY	RANK	SCORE	STATISTIC	VALUE	RANK	SCORE
Economics	53	46.30	Median Household Income	$30,481	33	31.2
			% of Families Above Poverty Level	80.5%	55	61.4
Affordable Housing	8	75.25	Median Home Value	$89,300	33	75.5
			Median Rent	$419	6	75.0
Crime	N/A	N/A	Violent Crimes per 10,000 Population	N/A	N/A	N/A
			Property Crimes per 10,000 Population	N/A	N/A	N/A
Open Spaces	16	69.55	Population Density (Persons/Sq. Mile)	3862	18	84.1
			Average Rooms per Housing Unit	5.1	17	55.0
Education	39	43.15	% High School Enrollment/Completion	84.5%	49	53.9
			% College Graduates	19.4%	26	32.4
Commute	38	36.05	Average Work Commute in Minutes	26	42	52.9
			% Commuting on Public Transportation	4.9%	17	19.2
Community Stability	16	66.65	% Living in Same House as in 1979	35.7%	22	64.0
			% Living in Same County as in 1985	84.6%	15	69.3

Composite: **Rank** 18 / 63 *Score* 56.15   **MIAMI LAKES**

CATEGORY	RANK	SCORE	STATISTIC	VALUE	RANK	SCORE
Economics	5	75.90	Median Household Income	$45,445	5	56.0
			% of Families Above Poverty Level	96.0%	9	95.8
Affordable Housing	55	41.35	Median Home Value	$137,100	53	48.3
			Median Rent	$670	53	34.4
Crime	N/A	N/A	Violent Crimes per 10,000 Population	N/A	N/A	N/A
			Property Crimes per 10,000 Population	N/A	N/A	N/A
Open Spaces	19	66.55	Population Density (Persons/Sq. Mile)	3231	9	88.1
			Average Rooms per Housing Unit	4.7	31	45.0
Education	7	74.75	% High School Enrollment/Completion	93.3%	12	82.3
			% College Graduates	36.6%	7	67.2
Commute	33	37.20	Average Work Commute in Minutes	23	16	70.6
			% Commuting on Public Transportation	1.2%	50	3.8
Community Stability	48	41.15	% Living in Same House as in 1979	22.3%	50	40.0
			% Living in Same County as in 1985	74.8%	44	42.3

Composite: **Rank** 19 / 63 *Score* 55.90 **BROWNSVILLE**

CATEGORY	RANK	SCORE	STATISTIC	VALUE	RANK	SCORE
Economics	62	8.35	Median Household Income	$12,351	62	1.0
			% of Families Above Poverty Level	59.9%	62	15.7
Affordable Housing	2	96.75	Median Home Value	$46,200	1	100.0
			Median Rent	$305	2	93.5
Crime	N/A	N/A	Violent Crimes per 10,000 Population	N/A	N/A	N/A
			Property Crimes per 10,000 Population	N/A	N/A	N/A
Open Spaces	57	45.15	Population Density (Persons/Sq. Mile)	6812	50	65.3
			Average Rooms per Housing Unit	3.9	55	25.0
Education	59	27.75	% High School Enrollment/Completion	83.3%	54	50.0
			% College Graduates	6.1%	59	5.5
Commute	3	67.70	Average Work Commute in Minutes	24	25	64.7
			% Commuting on Public Transportation	17.2%	2	70.7
Community Stability	1	89.70	% Living in Same House as in 1979	44.3%	7	79.4
			% Living in Same County as in 1985	95.7%	1	100.0

Composite: **Rank** 20 / 63 *Score* 55.83 **GLADEVIEW**

CATEGORY	RANK	SCORE	STATISTIC	VALUE	RANK	SCORE
Economics	63	0.00	Median Household Income	$11,739	63	0.0
			% of Families Above Poverty Level	52.8%	63	0.0
Affordable Housing	1	99.55	Median Home Value	$47,800	2	99.1
			Median Rent	$265	1	100.0
Crime	N/A	N/A	Violent Crimes per 10,000 Population	N/A	N/A	N/A
			Property Crimes per 10,000 Population	N/A	N/A	N/A
Open Spaces	56	45.95	Population Density (Persons/Sq. Mile)	6166	46	69.4
			Average Rooms per Housing Unit	3.8	57	22.5
Education	52	32.75	% High School Enrollment/Completion	88.1%	33	65.5
			% College Graduates	3.4%	63	0.0
Commute	1	73.55	Average Work Commute in Minutes	27	52	47.1
			% Commuting on Public Transportation	24.2%	1	100.0
Community Stability	4	83.15	% Living in Same House as in 1979	41.6%	11	74.6
			% Living in Same County as in 1985	92.7%	2	91.7

Composite: **Rank** 21 / 63 *Score* 55.21 **PALMETTO ESTATES**

CATEGORY	RANK	SCORE	STATISTIC	VALUE	RANK	SCORE
Economics	12	71.20	Median Household Income	$40,427	13	47.7
			% of Families Above Poverty Level	95.5%	16	94.7
Affordable Housing	41	55.75	Median Home Value	$78,700	20	81.5
			Median Rent	$697	58	30.0
Crime	N/A	N/A	Violent Crimes per 10,000 Population	N/A	N/A	N/A
			Property Crimes per 10,000 Population	N/A	N/A	N/A
Open Spaces	14	70.90	Population Density (Persons/Sq. Mile)	5784	38	71.8
			Average Rooms per Housing Unit	5.7	4	70.0
Education	18	58.05	% High School Enrollment/Completion	91.6%	20	76.8
			% College Graduates	22.8%	19	39.3
Commute	56	25.80	Average Work Commute in Minutes	29	59	35.3
			% Commuting on Public Transportation	4.2%	20	16.3
Community Stability	39	49.55	% Living in Same House as in 1979	30.0%	35	53.8
			% Living in Same County as in 1985	75.9%	40	45.3

Metropolitan Area Suburb Rankings
MIAMI-FORT LAUDERDALE

Composite: Rank 22 / 63 *Score* 54.82   **PLANTATION**

CATEGORY	RANK	SCORE	STATISTIC	VALUE	RANK	SCORE
Economics	6	75.00	Median Household Income	$41,832	9	50.0
			% of Families Above Poverty Level	97.9%	1	100.0
Affordable Housing	56	40.35	Median Home Value	$130,600	52	52.0
			Median Rent	$705	59	28.7
Crime	N/A	N/A	Violent Crimes per 10,000 Population	48	N/A	N/A
			Property Crimes per 10,000 Population	826	N/A	N/A
Open Spaces	7	77.10	Population Density (Persons/Sq. Mile)	3066	8	89.2
			Average Rooms per Housing Unit	5.5	8	65.0
Education	14	64.95	% High School Enrollment/Completion	90.3%	24	72.6
			% College Graduates	31.7%	9	57.3
Commute	43	33.60	Average Work Commute in Minutes	24	25	64.7
			% Commuting on Public Transportation	0.9%	54	2.5
Community Stability	50	37.90	% Living in Same House as in 1979	25.8%	44	46.2
			% Living in Same County as in 1985	70.2%	55	29.6

Composite: Rank 23 / 63 *Score* 54.76   **IVES ESTATES**

CATEGORY	RANK	SCORE	STATISTIC	VALUE	RANK	SCORE
Economics	14	69.05	Median Household Income	$38,262	15	44.1
			% of Families Above Poverty Level	95.2%	20	94.0
Affordable Housing	46	53.90	Median Home Value	$91,300	34	74.4
			Median Rent	$676	54	33.4
Crime	N/A	N/A	Violent Crimes per 10,000 Population	N/A	N/A	N/A
			Property Crimes per 10,000 Population	N/A	N/A	N/A
Open Spaces	35	59.20	Population Density (Persons/Sq. Mile)	5154	31	75.9
			Average Rooms per Housing Unit	4.6	33	42.5
Education	13	65.05	% High School Enrollment/Completion	92.2%	19	78.7
			% College Graduates	28.8%	12	51.4
Commute	40	35.30	Average Work Commute in Minutes	24	25	64.7
			% Commuting on Public Transportation	1.7%	44	5.9
Community Stability	44	46.05	% Living in Same House as in 1979	24.7%	45	44.3
			% Living in Same County as in 1985	76.8%	39	47.8

Composite: Rank 24 / 63 *Score* 54.57   **WEST LITTLE RIVER**

CATEGORY	RANK	SCORE	STATISTIC	VALUE	RANK	SCORE
Economics	57	35.85	Median Household Income	$21,779	55	16.7
			% of Families Above Poverty Level	77.6%	59	55.0
Affordable Housing	4	86.40	Median Home Value	$53,300	4	96.0
			Median Rent	$408	4	76.8
Crime	N/A	N/A	Violent Crimes per 10,000 Population	N/A	N/A	N/A
			Property Crimes per 10,000 Population	N/A	N/A	N/A
Open Spaces	52	48.45	Population Density (Persons/Sq. Mile)	7340	55	61.9
			Average Rooms per Housing Unit	4.3	44	35.0
Education	55	30.60	% High School Enrollment/Completion	85.9%	42	58.4
			% College Graduates	4.8%	61	2.8
Commute	14	46.95	Average Work Commute in Minutes	26	42	52.9
			% Commuting on Public Transportation	10.1%	5	41.0
Community Stability	7	79.20	% Living in Same House as in 1979	42.0%	9	75.3
			% Living in Same County as in 1985	89.6%	3	83.1

Metropolitan Area Suburb Rankings
MIAMI-FORT LAUDERDALE

Composite: *Rank* 25 / 63 *Score* 54.55   CAROL CITY

CATEGORY	RANK	SCORE	STATISTIC	VALUE	RANK	SCORE
Economics	46	52.75	Median Household Income	$31,073	32	32.1
			% of Families Above Poverty Level	85.9%	52	73.4
Affordable Housing	13	72.05	Median Home Value	$61,400	7	91.4
			Median Rent	$557	31	52.7
Crime	N/A	N/A	Violent Crimes per 10,000 Population	N/A	N/A	N/A
			Property Crimes per 10,000 Population	N/A	N/A	N/A
Open Spaces	45	55.80	Population Density (Persons/Sq. Mile)	6997	52	64.1
			Average Rooms per Housing Unit	4.8	25	47.5
Education	49	38.50	% High School Enrollment/Completion	88.6%	30	67.1
			% College Graduates	8.3%	57	9.9
Commute	48	32.55	Average Work Commute in Minutes	27	52	47.1
			% Commuting on Public Transportation	4.6%	19	18.0
Community Stability	8	75.65	% Living in Same House as in 1979	41.1%	12	73.7
			% Living in Same County as in 1985	87.6%	7	77.6

Composite: *Rank* 26 / 63 *Score* 54.45   WILTON MANORS

CATEGORY	RANK	SCORE	STATISTIC	VALUE	RANK	SCORE
Economics	42	54.90	Median Household Income	$26,710	46	24.9
			% of Families Above Poverty Level	91.1%	38	84.9
Affordable Housing	22	67.50	Median Home Value	$91,500	35	74.2
			Median Rent	$507	16	60.8
Crime	N/A	N/A	Violent Crimes per 10,000 Population	83	N/A	N/A
			Property Crimes per 10,000 Population	942	N/A	N/A
Open Spaces	44	56.30	Population Density (Persons/Sq. Mile)	6057	43	70.1
			Average Rooms per Housing Unit	4.6	33	42.5
Education	47	39.30	% High School Enrollment/Completion	84.4%	51	53.5
			% College Graduates	15.8%	38	25.1
Commute	4	55.00	Average Work Commute in Minutes	18	1	100.0
			% Commuting on Public Transportation	2.7%	31	10.0
Community Stability	32	53.70	% Living in Same House as in 1979	32.5%	31	58.2
			% Living in Same County as in 1985	77.3%	34	49.2

Composite: *Rank* 27 / 63 *Score* 54.43   NORLAND

CATEGORY	RANK	SCORE	STATISTIC	VALUE	RANK	SCORE
Economics	39	55.60	Median Household Income	$28,233	38	27.4
			% of Families Above Poverty Level	90.6%	41	83.8
Affordable Housing	15	71.55	Median Home Value	$71,300	11	85.7
			Median Rent	$528	21	57.4
Crime	N/A	N/A	Violent Crimes per 10,000 Population	N/A	N/A	N/A
			Property Crimes per 10,000 Population	N/A	N/A	N/A
Open Spaces	47	54.90	Population Density (Persons/Sq. Mile)	6104	45	69.8
			Average Rooms per Housing Unit	4.5	38	40.0
Education	24	53.70	% High School Enrollment/Completion	94.9%	6	87.4
			% College Graduates	13.3%	46	20.0
Commute	28	41.75	Average Work Commute in Minutes	25	37	58.8
			% Commuting on Public Transportation	6.2%	10	24.7
Community Stability	41	49.10	% Living in Same House as in 1979	24.6%	46	44.1
			% Living in Same County as in 1985	79.1%	26	54.1

Metropolitan Area Suburb Rankings
MIAMI-FORT LAUDERDALE

Composite: **Rank** 28 / 63 *Score* 54.42   **COOPER CITY**

CATEGORY	RANK	SCORE	STATISTIC	VALUE	RANK	SCORE
Economics	2	81.15	Median Household Income	$49,750	2	63.2
			% of Families Above Poverty Level	97.5%	3	99.1
Affordable Housing	54	41.30	Median Home Value	$125,400	51	55.0
			Median Rent	$712	60	27.6
Crime	N/A	N/A	Violent Crimes per 10,000 Population	18	N/A	N/A
			Property Crimes per 10,000 Population	281	N/A	N/A
Open Spaces	2	83.85	Population Density (Persons/Sq. Mile)	3290	10	87.7
			Average Rooms per Housing Unit	6.1	2	80.0
Education	11	67.25	% High School Enrollment/Completion	93.8%	10	83.9
			% College Graduates	28.4%	13	50.6
Commute	60	20.60	Average Work Commute in Minutes	28	57	41.2
			% Commuting on Public Transportation	0.3%	63	0.0
Community Stability	58	32.35	% Living in Same House as in 1979	19.9%	55	35.7
			% Living in Same County as in 1985	70.0%	56	29.0

Composite: **Rank** 29 / 63 *Score* 53.73   **HOLLYWOOD**

CATEGORY	RANK	SCORE	STATISTIC	VALUE	RANK	SCORE
Economics	37	56.80	Median Household Income	$27,352	42	26.0
			% of Families Above Poverty Level	92.3%	31	87.6
Affordable Housing	18	69.05	Median Home Value	$81,500	24	79.9
			Median Rent	$523	20	58.2
Crime	N/A	N/A	Violent Crimes per 10,000 Population	80	N/A	N/A
			Property Crimes per 10,000 Population	930	N/A	N/A
Open Spaces	32	60.15	Population Density (Persons/Sq. Mile)	4464	25	80.3
			Average Rooms per Housing Unit	4.5	38	40.0
Education	45	40.35	% High School Enrollment/Completion	85.1%	47	55.8
			% College Graduates	15.7%	40	24.9
Commute	27	42.00	Average Work Commute in Minutes	22	12	76.5
			% Commuting on Public Transportation	2.1%	41	7.5
Community Stability	31	54.05	% Living in Same House as in 1979	36.0%	19	64.5
			% Living in Same County as in 1985	75.3%	41	43.6

Composite: **Rank** 30 / 63 *Score* 53.66   **NORTH MIAMI BEACH**

CATEGORY	RANK	SCORE	STATISTIC	VALUE	RANK	SCORE
Economics	45	53.35	Median Household Income	$24,963	49	22.0
			% of Families Above Poverty Level	91.0%	39	84.7
Affordable Housing	14	71.85	Median Home Value	$74,200	14	84.1
			Median Rent	$514	18	59.6
Crime	N/A	N/A	Violent Crimes per 10,000 Population	121	N/A	N/A
			Property Crimes per 10,000 Population	658	N/A	N/A
Open Spaces	53	48.00	Population Density (Persons/Sq. Mile)	7088	54	63.5
			Average Rooms per Housing Unit	4.2	49	32.5
Education	33	45.35	% High School Enrollment/Completion	88.7%	29	67.4
			% College Graduates	14.9%	41	23.3
Commute	20	45.55	Average Work Commute in Minutes	23	16	70.6
			% Commuting on Public Transportation	5.2%	14	20.5
Community Stability	24	57.85	% Living in Same House as in 1979	35.6%	25	63.8
			% Living in Same County as in 1985	78.3%	31	51.9

Metropolitan Area Suburb Rankings
MIAMI-FORT LAUDERDALE

Composite: *Rank* 31 / 63 *Score* 53.36 **GOLDEN GLADES**

CATEGORY	RANK	SCORE	STATISTIC	VALUE	RANK	SCORE
Economics	44	53.55	Median Household Income	$28,306	37	27.5
			% of Families Above Poverty Level	88.7%	49	79.6
Affordable Housing	19	68.95	Median Home Value	$78,300	18	81.8
			Median Rent	$536	22	56.1
Crime	N/A	N/A	Violent Crimes per 10,000 Population	N/A	N/A	N/A
			Property Crimes per 10,000 Population	N/A	N/A	N/A
Open Spaces	39	57.85	Population Density (Persons/Sq. Mile)	5174	32	75.7
			Average Rooms per Housing Unit	4.5	38	40.0
Education	46	39.50	% High School Enrollment/Completion	84.5%	49	53.9
			% College Graduates	15.8%	38	25.1
Commute	18	45.95	Average Work Commute in Minutes	23	16	70.6
			% Commuting on Public Transportation	5.4%	13	21.3
Community Stability	30	54.35	% Living in Same House as in 1979	31.1%	33	55.7
			% Living in Same County as in 1985	78.7%	29	53.0

Composite: *Rank* 32 / 63 *Score* 53.11 **LINDGREN ACRES**

CATEGORY	RANK	SCORE	STATISTIC	VALUE	RANK	SCORE
Economics	4	77.05	Median Household Income	$46,159	4	57.2
			% of Families Above Poverty Level	96.5%	7	96.9
Affordable Housing	58	39.55	Median Home Value	$101,500	44	68.6
			Median Rent	$817	62	10.5
Crime	N/A	N/A	Violent Crimes per 10,000 Population	N/A	N/A	N/A
			Property Crimes per 10,000 Population	N/A	N/A	N/A
Open Spaces	23	64.20	Population Density (Persons/Sq. Mile)	5935	42	70.9
			Average Rooms per Housing Unit	5.2	15	57.5
Education	6	78.70	% High School Enrollment/Completion	93.2%	14	81.9
			% College Graduates	40.7%	5	75.5
Commute	59	22.90	Average Work Commute in Minutes	29	59	35.3
			% Commuting on Public Transportation	2.8%	30	10.5
Community Stability	54	36.25	% Living in Same House as in 1979	16.4%	59	29.4
			% Living in Same County as in 1985	75.1%	42	43.1

Composite: *Rank* 33 / 63 *Score* 53.04 **DEERFIELD BEACH**

CATEGORY	RANK	SCORE	STATISTIC	VALUE	RANK	SCORE
Economics	34	58.55	Median Household Income	$26,950	44	25.3
			% of Families Above Poverty Level	94.2%	25	91.8
Affordable Housing	37	57.55	Median Home Value	$96,800	42	71.2
			Median Rent	$611	40	43.9
Crime	N/A	N/A	Violent Crimes per 10,000 Population	86	N/A	N/A
			Property Crimes per 10,000 Population	665	N/A	N/A
Open Spaces	40	57.70	Population Density (Persons/Sq. Mile)	4436	23	80.4
			Average Rooms per Housing Unit	4.3	44	35.0
Education	31	46.10	% High School Enrollment/Completion	88.4%	32	66.5
			% College Graduates	16.1%	37	25.7
Commute	15	46.40	Average Work Commute in Minutes	20	4	88.2
			% Commuting on Public Transportation	1.4%	48	4.6
Community Stability	35	51.95	% Living in Same House as in 1979	36.2%	18	64.9
			% Living in Same County as in 1985	73.6%	46	39.0

Metropolitan Area Suburb Rankings
MIAMI-FORT LAUDERDALE

Composite: *Rank* 34 / 63 *Score* 52.89   **POMPANO BEACH**

CATEGORY	RANK	SCORE	STATISTIC	VALUE	RANK	SCORE
Economics	40	55.35	Median Household Income	$29,683	34	29.8
			% of Families Above Poverty Level	89.3%	47	80.9
Affordable Housing	27	63.15	Median Home Value	$96,900	43	71.2
			Median Rent	$542	25	55.1
Crime	N/A	N/A	Violent Crimes per 10,000 Population	230	N/A	N/A
			Property Crimes per 10,000 Population	1,023	N/A	N/A
Open Spaces	31	60.50	Population Density (Persons/Sq. Mile)	3559	16	86.0
			Average Rooms per Housing Unit	4.3	44	35.0
Education	54	32.15	% High School Enrollment/Completion	78.3%	59	33.9
			% College Graduates	18.4%	31	30.4
Commute	12	48.30	Average Work Commute in Minutes	21	8	82.4
			% Commuting on Public Transportation	3.7%	22	14.2
Community Stability	23	57.90	% Living in Same House as in 1979	33.8%	29	60.6
			% Living in Same County as in 1985	79.5%	25	55.2

Composite: *Rank* 35 / 63 *Score* 52.64   **DANIA**

CATEGORY	RANK	SCORE	STATISTIC	VALUE	RANK	SCORE
Economics	55	43.40	Median Household Income	$23,269	52	19.2
			% of Families Above Poverty Level	83.3%	54	67.6
Affordable Housing	16	71.35	Median Home Value	$84,600	29	78.2
			Median Rent	$484	10	64.5
Crime	N/A	N/A	Violent Crimes per 10,000 Population	244	N/A	N/A
			Property Crimes per 10,000 Population	1,490	N/A	N/A
Open Spaces	28	61.30	Population Density (Persons/Sq. Mile)	2531	7	92.6
			Average Rooms per Housing Unit	4.1	51	30.0
Education	50	37.55	% High School Enrollment/Completion	85.8%	44	58.1
			% College Graduates	11.8%	49	17.0
Commute	19	45.60	Average Work Commute in Minutes	21	8	82.4
			% Commuting on Public Transportation	2.4%	36	8.8
Community Stability	26	56.65	% Living in Same House as in 1979	30.7%	34	55.0
			% Living in Same County as in 1985	80.6%	22	58.3

Composite: *Rank* 36 / 63 *Score* 52.48   **MIRAMAR**

CATEGORY	RANK	SCORE	STATISTIC	VALUE	RANK	SCORE
Economics	23	65.10	Median Household Income	$35,794	23	40.0
			% of Families Above Poverty Level	93.5%	27	90.2
Affordable Housing	30	62.35	Median Home Value	$80,300	23	80.6
			Median Rent	$610	39	44.1
Crime	N/A	N/A	Violent Crimes per 10,000 Population	68	N/A	N/A
			Property Crimes per 10,000 Population	541	N/A	N/A
Open Spaces	3	80.00	Population Density (Persons/Sq. Mile)	1370	1	100.0
			Average Rooms per Housing Unit	5.3	12	60.0
Education	42	40.85	% High School Enrollment/Completion	85.9%	42	58.4
			% College Graduates	14.9%	41	23.3
Commute	50	30.65	Average Work Commute in Minutes	25	37	58.8
			% Commuting on Public Transportation	0.9%	54	2.5
Community Stability	55	35.95	% Living in Same House as in 1979	29.8%	36	53.4
			% Living in Same County as in 1985	66.2%	59	18.5

Metropolitan Area Suburb Rankings
MIAMI-FORT LAUDERDALE

Composite: *Rank* 37 / 63 *Score* 52.47 **MARGATE**

CATEGORY	RANK	SCORE	STATISTIC	VALUE	RANK	SCORE
Economics	32	60.35	Median Household Income	$28,465	36	27.8
			% of Families Above Poverty Level	94.7%	23	92.9
Affordable Housing	35	60.15	Median Home Value	$83,100	26	79.0
			Median Rent	$627	44	41.3
Crime	N/A	N/A	Violent Crimes per 10,000 Population	29	N/A	N/A
			Property Crimes per 10,000 Population	390	N/A	N/A
Open Spaces	25	62.60	Population Density (Persons/Sq. Mile)	4861	30	77.7
			Average Rooms per Housing Unit	4.8	25	47.5
Education	48	38.85	% High School Enrollment/Completion	86.3%	40	59.7
			% College Graduates	12.3%	48	18.0
Commute	37	36.55	Average Work Commute in Minutes	23	16	70.6
			% Commuting on Public Transportation	0.9%	54	2.5
Community Stability	27	56.30	% Living in Same House as in 1979	35.7%	22	64.0
			% Living in Same County as in 1985	77.1%	36	48.6

Composite: *Rank* 38 / 63 *Score* 52.43 **SUNRISE**

CATEGORY	RANK	SCORE	STATISTIC	VALUE	RANK	SCORE
Economics	26	63.80	Median Household Income	$31,540	30	32.9
			% of Families Above Poverty Level	95.5%	16	94.7
Affordable Housing	39	56.55	Median Home Value	$89,000	31	75.7
			Median Rent	$651	48	37.4
Crime	N/A	N/A	Violent Crimes per 10,000 Population	46	N/A	N/A
			Property Crimes per 10,000 Population	543	N/A	N/A
Open Spaces	17	68.10	Population Density (Persons/Sq. Mile)	3538	15	86.2
			Average Rooms per Housing Unit	4.9	21	50.0
Education	28	49.40	% High School Enrollment/Completion	90.1%	25	71.9
			% College Graduates	16.7%	34	26.9
Commute	42	34.25	Average Work Commute in Minutes	24	25	64.7
			% Commuting on Public Transportation	1.2%	50	3.8
Community Stability	47	42.50	% Living in Same House as in 1979	27.7%	40	49.6
			% Living in Same County as in 1985	72.3%	49	35.4

Composite: *Rank* 39 / 63 *Score* 52.35 **NORTH MIAMI**

CATEGORY	RANK	SCORE	STATISTIC	VALUE	RANK	SCORE
Economics	50	49.55	Median Household Income	$24,898	50	21.9
			% of Families Above Poverty Level	87.6%	50	77.2
Affordable Housing	10	74.55	Median Home Value	$71,800	12	85.4
			Median Rent	$489	13	63.7
Crime	N/A	N/A	Violent Crimes per 10,000 Population	170	N/A	N/A
			Property Crimes per 10,000 Population	1,097	N/A	N/A
Open Spaces	54	47.95	Population Density (Persons/Sq. Mile)	5934	41	70.9
			Average Rooms per Housing Unit	3.9	55	25.0
Education	37	43.10	% High School Enrollment/Completion	85.4%	45	56.8
			% College Graduates	17.9%	32	29.4
Commute	11	48.65	Average Work Commute in Minutes	24	25	64.7
			% Commuting on Public Transportation	8.1%	7	32.6
Community Stability	36	50.30	% Living in Same House as in 1979	27.6%	41	49.5
			% Living in Same County as in 1985	78.0%	32	51.1

Metropolitan Area Suburb Rankings
MIAMI-FORT LAUDERDALE

Composite: Rank 40 / 63 *Score* 52.22   **TAMIAMI**

CATEGORY	RANK	SCORE	STATISTIC	VALUE	RANK	SCORE
Economics	22	65.55	Median Household Income	$36,584	19	41.3
			% of Families Above Poverty Level	93.3%	28	89.8
Affordable Housing	42	55.25	Median Home Value	$93,800	38	72.9
			Median Rent	$650	47	37.6
Crime	N/A	N/A	Violent Crimes per 10,000 Population	N/A	N/A	N/A
			Property Crimes per 10,000 Population	N/A	N/A	N/A
Open Spaces	28	61.30	Population Density (Persons/Sq. Mile)	5665	37	72.6
			Average Rooms per Housing Unit	4.9	21	50.0
Education	20	56.40	% High School Enrollment/Completion	93.1%	15	81.6
			% College Graduates	18.8%	30	31.2
Commute	61	18.45	Average Work Commute in Minutes	30	61	29.4
			% Commuting on Public Transportation	2.1%	41	7.5
Community Stability	28	56.35	% Living in Same House as in 1979	22.2%	51	39.8
			% Living in Same County as in 1985	85.9%	10	72.9

Composite: Rank 41 / 63 *Score* 52.05   **HALLANDALE**

CATEGORY	RANK	SCORE	STATISTIC	VALUE	RANK	SCORE
Economics	51	48.25	Median Household Income	$20,841	57	15.1
			% of Families Above Poverty Level	89.5%	46	81.4
Affordable Housing	16	71.35	Median Home Value	$75,200	15	83.5
			Median Rent	$517	19	59.2
Crime	N/A	N/A	Violent Crimes per 10,000 Population	124	N/A	N/A
			Property Crimes per 10,000 Population	676	N/A	N/A
Open Spaces	58	40.85	Population Density (Persons/Sq. Mile)	7370	56	61.7
			Average Rooms per Housing Unit	3.7	60	20.0
Education	37	43.10	% High School Enrollment/Completion	87.8%	36	64.5
			% College Graduates	14.1%	45	21.7
Commute	16	46.00	Average Work Commute in Minutes	22	12	76.5
			% Commuting on Public Transportation	4.0%	21	15.5
Community Stability	20	62.75	% Living in Same House as in 1979	46.3%	5	83.0
			% Living in Same County as in 1985	74.9%	43	42.5

Composite: Rank 42 / 63 *Score* 52.02   **LEISURE CITY**

CATEGORY	RANK	SCORE	STATISTIC	VALUE	RANK	SCORE
Economics	47	52.20	Median Household Income	$26,427	48	24.4
			% of Families Above Poverty Level	88.9%	48	80.0
Affordable Housing	7	80.75	Median Home Value	$56,900	5	93.9
			Median Rent	$465	9	67.6
Crime	N/A	N/A	Violent Crimes per 10,000 Population	N/A	N/A	N/A
			Property Crimes per 10,000 Population	N/A	N/A	N/A
Open Spaces	42	56.50	Population Density (Persons/Sq. Mile)	5605	35	73.0
			Average Rooms per Housing Unit	4.5	38	40.0
Education	60	26.45	% High School Enrollment/Completion	82.5%	57	47.4
			% College Graduates	6.1%	59	5.5
Commute	32	38.00	Average Work Commute in Minutes	23	16	70.6
			% Commuting on Public Transportation	1.6%	46	5.4
Community Stability	22	58.25	% Living in Same House as in 1979	33.1%	30	59.3
			% Living in Same County as in 1985	80.2%	23	57.2

Metropolitan Area Suburb Rankings
MIAMI-FORT LAUDERDALE

Composite: *Rank* 43 / 63 *Score* 51.93 **TAMARAC**

CATEGORY	RANK	SCORE	STATISTIC	VALUE	RANK	SCORE
Economics	31	61.00	Median Household Income	$26,703	47	24.9
			% of Families Above Poverty Level	96.6%	6	97.1
Affordable Housing	31	61.40	Median Home Value	$77,100	16	82.4
			Median Rent	$633	45	40.4
Crime	N/A	N/A	Violent Crimes per 10,000 Population	32	N/A	N/A
			Property Crimes per 10,000 Population	394	N/A	N/A
Open Spaces	21	65.65	Population Density (Persons/Sq. Mile)	3901	19	83.8
			Average Rooms per Housing Unit	4.8	25	47.5
Education	43	40.80	% High School Enrollment/Completion	86.3%	40	59.7
			% College Graduates	14.2%	44	21.9
Commute	47	33.20	Average Work Commute in Minutes	24	25	64.7
			% Commuting on Public Transportation	0.7%	61	1.7
Community Stability	40	49.50	% Living in Same House as in 1979	34.6%	28	62.0
			% Living in Same County as in 1985	72.9%	47	37.0

Composite: *Rank* 44 / 63 *Score* 51.27 **DAVIE**

CATEGORY	RANK	SCORE	STATISTIC	VALUE	RANK	SCORE
Economics	16	67.85	Median Household Income	$36,843	18	41.7
			% of Families Above Poverty Level	95.2%	20	94.0
Affordable Housing	38	57.35	Median Home Value	$106,100	47	65.9
			Median Rent	$581	37	48.8
Crime	N/A	N/A	Violent Crimes per 10,000 Population	55	N/A	N/A
			Property Crimes per 10,000 Population	614	N/A	N/A
Open Spaces	5	78.45	Population Density (Persons/Sq. Mile)	1462	2	99.4
			Average Rooms per Housing Unit	5.2	15	57.5
Education	35	43.75	% High School Enrollment/Completion	84.2%	52	52.9
			% College Graduates	20.5%	24	34.6
Commute	55	26.85	Average Work Commute in Minutes	26	42	52.9
			% Commuting on Public Transportation	0.5%	62	0.8
Community Stability	57	33.40	% Living in Same House as in 1979	18.9%	57	33.9
			% Living in Same County as in 1985	71.4%	52	32.9

Composite: *Rank* 45 / 63 *Score* 50.57 **KENDALE LAKES**

CATEGORY	RANK	SCORE	STATISTIC	VALUE	RANK	SCORE
Economics	20	67.05	Median Household Income	$37,412	17	42.7
			% of Families Above Poverty Level	94.0%	26	91.4
Affordable Housing	44	54.80	Median Home Value	$85,200	30	77.8
			Median Rent	$686	56	31.8
Crime	N/A	N/A	Violent Crimes per 10,000 Population	N/A	N/A	N/A
			Property Crimes per 10,000 Population	N/A	N/A	N/A
Open Spaces	34	59.35	Population Density (Persons/Sq. Mile)	5881	39	71.2
			Average Rooms per Housing Unit	4.8	25	47.5
Education	16	61.25	% High School Enrollment/Completion	92.9%	16	81.0
			% College Graduates	23.9%	18	41.5
Commute	62	13.40	Average Work Commute in Minutes	32	62	17.6
			% Commuting on Public Transportation	2.5%	35	9.2
Community Stability	43	47.55	% Living in Same House as in 1979	23.6%	48	42.3
			% Living in Same County as in 1985	78.6%	30	52.8

Metropolitan Area Suburb Rankings
MIAMI-FORT LAUDERDALE

Composite: **Rank** 46 / 63 *Score* 50.47   **PINEWOOD**

CATEGORY	RANK	SCORE	STATISTIC	VALUE	RANK	SCORE
Economics	58	35.70	Median Household Income	$21,503	56	16.2
			% of Families Above Poverty Level	77.7%	58	55.2
Affordable Housing	5	83.10	Median Home Value	$58,900	6	92.8
			Median Rent	$429	8	73.4
Crime	N/A	N/A	Violent Crimes per 10,000 Population	N/A	N/A	N/A
			Property Crimes per 10,000 Population	N/A	N/A	N/A
Open Spaces	59	36.80	Population Density (Persons/Sq. Mile)	9032	59	51.1
			Average Rooms per Housing Unit	3.8	57	22.5
Education	51	33.10	% High School Enrollment/Completion	85.2%	46	56.1
			% College Graduates	8.4%	56	10.1
Commute	13	47.60	Average Work Commute in Minutes	25	37	58.8
			% Commuting on Public Transportation	9.0%	6	36.4
Community Stability	17	66.50	% Living in Same House as in 1979	29.5%	37	52.9
			% Living in Same County as in 1985	88.5%	5	80.1

Composite: **Rank** 47 / 63 *Score* 50.28   **CORAL SPRINGS**

CATEGORY	RANK	SCORE	STATISTIC	VALUE	RANK	SCORE
Economics	8	73.90	Median Household Income	$43,428	7	52.7
			% of Families Above Poverty Level	95.7%	13	95.1
Affordable Housing	60	35.85	Median Home Value	$159,000	58	35.9
			Median Rent	$661	51	35.8
Crime	N/A	N/A	Violent Crimes per 10,000 Population	25	N/A	N/A
			Property Crimes per 10,000 Population	415	N/A	N/A
Open Spaces	4	78.60	Population Density (Persons/Sq. Mile)	3382	11	87.2
			Average Rooms per Housing Unit	5.7	4	70.0
Education	15	64.40	% High School Enrollment/Completion	90.1%	25	71.9
			% College Graduates	31.5%	10	56.9
Commute	45	33.40	Average Work Commute in Minutes	24	25	64.7
			% Commuting on Public Transportation	0.8%	58	2.1
Community Stability	61	15.55	% Living in Same House as in 1979	13.8%	61	24.7
			% Living in Same County as in 1985	61.8%	61	6.4

Composite: **Rank** 48 / 63 *Score* 50.21   **SOUTH MIAMI HEIGHTS**

CATEGORY	RANK	SCORE	STATISTIC	VALUE	RANK	SCORE
Economics	48	52.15	Median Household Income	$28,870	35	28.5
			% of Families Above Poverty Level	87.0%	51	75.8
Affordable Housing	9	74.70	Median Home Value	$66,500	9	88.5
			Median Rent	$506	15	60.9
Crime	N/A	N/A	Violent Crimes per 10,000 Population	N/A	N/A	N/A
			Property Crimes per 10,000 Population	N/A	N/A	N/A
Open Spaces	41	57.45	Population Density (Persons/Sq. Mile)	6082	44	69.9
			Average Rooms per Housing Unit	4.7	31	45.0
Education	52	32.75	% High School Enrollment/Completion	84.8%	48	54.8
			% College Graduates	8.7%	53	10.7
Commute	54	29.60	Average Work Commute in Minutes	27	52	47.1
			% Commuting on Public Transportation	3.2%	26	12.1
Community Stability	29	54.60	% Living in Same House as in 1979	26.2%	42	47.0
			% Living in Same County as in 1985	82.0%	21	62.2

Metropolitan Area Suburb Rankings
MIAMI-FORT LAUDERDALE

Composite: **Rank** 49 / 63 *Score* 50.00   **PEMBROKE PINES**

CATEGORY	RANK	SCORE	STATISTIC	VALUE	RANK	SCORE
Economics	15	68.95	Median Household Income	$36,431	20	41.0
			% of Families Above Poverty Level	96.5%	7	96.9
Affordable Housing	48	52.50	Median Home Value	$93,500	37	73.1
			Median Rent	$685	55	31.9
Crime	N/A	N/A	Violent Crimes per 10,000 Population	32	N/A	N/A
			Property Crimes per 10,000 Population	440	N/A	N/A
Open Spaces	8	74.10	Population Density (Persons/Sq. Mile)	2049	3	95.7
			Average Rooms per Housing Unit	5.0	19	52.5
Education	21	55.95	% High School Enrollment/Completion	91.5%	21	76.5
			% College Graduates	20.9%	22	35.4
Commute	57	24.60	Average Work Commute in Minutes	27	52	47.1
			% Commuting on Public Transportation	0.8%	58	2.1
Community Stability	60	23.90	% Living in Same House as in 1979	22.2%	51	39.8
			% Living in Same County as in 1985	62.4%	60	8.0

Composite: **Rank** 50 / 63 *Score* 49.92   **POMPANO BEACH HIGHLANDS**

CATEGORY	RANK	SCORE	STATISTIC	VALUE	RANK	SCORE
Economics	43	54.45	Median Household Income	$27,500	41	26.2
			% of Families Above Poverty Level	90.1%	43	82.7
Affordable Housing	12	72.60	Median Home Value	$63,600	8	90.1
			Median Rent	$542	25	55.1
Crime	N/A	N/A	Violent Crimes per 10,000 Population	N/A	N/A	N/A
			Property Crimes per 10,000 Population	N/A	N/A	N/A
Open Spaces	38	58.10	Population Density (Persons/Sq. Mile)	5494	34	73.7
			Average Rooms per Housing Unit	4.6	33	42.5
Education	61	15.35	% High School Enrollment/Completion	74.0%	61	20.0
			% College Graduates	8.7%	53	10.7
Commute	16	46.00	Average Work Commute in Minutes	20	4	88.2
			% Commuting on Public Transportation	1.2%	50	3.8
Community Stability	33	53.00	% Living in Same House as in 1979	32.3%	32	57.9
			% Living in Same County as in 1985	76.9%	38	48.1

Composite: **Rank** 51 / 63 *Score* 49.55   **OAKLAND PARK**

CATEGORY	RANK	SCORE	STATISTIC	VALUE	RANK	SCORE
Economics	36	56.95	Median Household Income	$27,708	40	26.5
			% of Families Above Poverty Level	92.2%	32	87.4
Affordable Housing	24	65.50	Median Home Value	$89,000	31	75.7
			Median Rent	$541	24	55.3
Crime	N/A	N/A	Violent Crimes per 10,000 Population	149	N/A	N/A
			Property Crimes per 10,000 Population	1,432	N/A	N/A
Open Spaces	37	58.65	Population Density (Persons/Sq. Mile)	4138	21	82.3
			Average Rooms per Housing Unit	4.3	44	35.0
Education	57	28.60	% High School Enrollment/Completion	76.7%	60	28.7
			% College Graduates	17.5%	33	28.5
Commute	9	49.95	Average Work Commute in Minutes	20	4	88.2
			% Commuting on Public Transportation	3.1%	27	11.7
Community Stability	51	37.65	% Living in Same House as in 1979	23.2%	49	41.6
			% Living in Same County as in 1985	71.7%	50	33.7

Metropolitan Area Suburb Rankings
MIAMI-FORT LAUDERDALE

***Composite: Rank* 52 / 63 *Score* 49.54   LAUDERDALE LAKES**

CATEGORY	RANK	SCORE	STATISTIC	VALUE	RANK	SCORE
Economics	51	48.25	Median Household Income	$20,731	58	14.9
			% of Families Above Poverty Level	89.6%	44	81.6
Affordable Housing	21	67.75	Median Home Value	$80,100	22	80.7
			Median Rent	$544	28	54.8
Crime	N/A	N/A	Violent Crimes per 10,000 Population	134	N/A	N/A
			Property Crimes per 10,000 Population	777	N/A	N/A
Open Spaces	55	46.35	Population Density (Persons/Sq. Mile)	7608	58	60.2
			Average Rooms per Housing Unit	4.2	49	32.5
Education	40	43.00	% High School Enrollment/Completion	90.5%	23	73.2
			% College Graduates	9.7%	52	12.8
Commute	25	42.40	Average Work Commute in Minutes	24	25	64.7
			% Commuting on Public Transportation	5.1%	16	20.1
Community Stability	38	49.50	% Living in Same House as in 1979	37.2%	16	66.7
			% Living in Same County as in 1985	71.2%	54	32.3

***Composite: Rank* 53 / 63 *Score* 49.01   NORTH LAUDERDALE**

CATEGORY	RANK	SCORE	STATISTIC	VALUE	RANK	SCORE
Economics	18	67.50	Median Household Income	$36,297	21	40.8
			% of Families Above Poverty Level	95.3%	18	94.2
Affordable Housing	36	58.95	Median Home Value	$78,600	19	81.6
			Median Rent	$658	49	36.3
Crime	N/A	N/A	Violent Crimes per 10,000 Population	48	N/A	N/A
			Property Crimes per 10,000 Population	517	N/A	N/A
Open Spaces	33	59.95	Population Density (Persons/Sq. Mile)	6873	51	64.9
			Average Rooms per Housing Unit	5.1	17	55.0
Education	34	44.05	% High School Enrollment/Completion	87.9%	35	64.8
			% College Graduates	14.9%	41	23.3
Commute	49	31.70	Average Work Commute in Minutes	25	37	58.8
			% Commuting on Public Transportation	1.4%	48	4.6
Community Stability	59	31.90	% Living in Same House as in 1979	19.6%	56	35.1
			% Living in Same County as in 1985	69.9%	57	28.7

***Composite: Rank* 54 / 63 *Score* 48.48   SUNNY ISLES**

CATEGORY	RANK	SCORE	STATISTIC	VALUE	RANK	SCORE
Economics	49	51.60	Median Household Income	$22,116	54	17.2
			% of Families Above Poverty Level	91.6%	36	86.0
Affordable Housing	57	40.25	Median Home Value	$147,500	56	42.4
			Median Rent	$647	46	38.1
Crime	N/A	N/A	Violent Crimes per 10,000 Population	N/A	N/A	N/A
			Property Crimes per 10,000 Population	N/A	N/A	N/A
Open Spaces	61	31.10	Population Density (Persons/Sq. Mile)	9643	60	47.2
			Average Rooms per Housing Unit	3.5	62	15.0
Education	26	52.95	% High School Enrollment/Completion	92.6%	17	80.0
			% College Graduates	16.2%	36	25.9
Commute	21	45.10	Average Work Commute in Minutes	24	25	64.7
			% Commuting on Public Transportation	6.4%	9	25.5
Community Stability	13	69.90	% Living in Same House as in 1979	48.1%	3	86.2
			% Living in Same County as in 1985	78.9%	27	53.6

Metropolitan Area Suburb Rankings
MIAMI-FORT LAUDERDALE

Composite: *Rank* 55 / 63 *Score* 48.41   **LAUDERHILL**

CATEGORY	RANK	SCORE	STATISTIC	VALUE	RANK	SCORE
Economics	38	56.00	Median Household Income	$26,722	45	24.9
			% of Families Above Poverty Level	92.1%	34	87.1
Affordable Housing	32	61.15	Median Home Value	$94,600	40	72.5
			Median Rent	$575	35	49.8
Crime	N/A	N/A	Violent Crimes per 10,000 Population	103	N/A	N/A
			Property Crimes per 10,000 Population	623	N/A	N/A
Open Spaces	50	51.50	Population Density (Persons/Sq. Mile)	6771	48	65.5
			Average Rooms per Housing Unit	4.4	43	37.5
Education	30	46.75	% High School Enrollment/Completion	87.0%	38	61.9
			% College Graduates	19.0%	29	31.6
Commute	31	38.85	Average Work Commute in Minutes	24	25	64.7
			% Commuting on Public Transportation	3.4%	24	13.0
Community Stability	53	36.20	% Living in Same House as in 1979	21.6%	54	38.7
			% Living in Same County as in 1985	71.7%	50	33.7

Composite: *Rank* 56 / 63 *Score* 47.00   **COCONUT CREEK**

CATEGORY	RANK	SCORE	STATISTIC	VALUE	RANK	SCORE
Economics	18	67.50	Median Household Income	$33,191	26	35.7
			% of Families Above Poverty Level	97.6%	2	99.3
Affordable Housing	52	43.60	Median Home Value	$108,200	50	64.8
			Median Rent	$744	61	22.4
Crime	N/A	N/A	Violent Crimes per 10,000 Population	34	N/A	N/A
			Property Crimes per 10,000 Population	333	N/A	N/A
Open Spaces	18	67.75	Population Density (Persons/Sq. Mile)	2460	6	93.0
			Average Rooms per Housing Unit	4.6	33	42.5
Education	25	53.20	% High School Enrollment/Completion	89.3%	28	69.4
			% College Graduates	21.7%	20	37.0
Commute	30	39.30	Average Work Commute in Minutes	22	12	76.5
			% Commuting on Public Transportation	0.8%	58	2.1
Community Stability	62	10.65	% Living in Same House as in 1979	11.9%	62	21.3
			% Living in Same County as in 1985	59.5%	62	0.0

Composite: *Rank* 57 / 63 *Score* 45.96   **HIALEAH**

CATEGORY	RANK	SCORE	STATISTIC	VALUE	RANK	SCORE
Economics	54	44.90	Median Household Income	$23,443	51	19.5
			% of Families Above Poverty Level	84.5%	53	70.3
Affordable Housing	11	72.70	Median Home Value	$79,800	21	80.9
			Median Rent	$484	10	64.5
Crime	N/A	N/A	Violent Crimes per 10,000 Population	100	N/A	N/A
			Property Crimes per 10,000 Population	717	N/A	N/A
Open Spaces	60	34.45	Population Density (Persons/Sq. Mile)	9770	61	46.4
			Average Rooms per Housing Unit	3.8	57	22.5
Education	58	28.45	% High School Enrollment/Completion	83.0%	55	49.0
			% College Graduates	7.3%	58	7.9
Commute	24	43.25	Average Work Commute in Minutes	22	12	76.5
			% Commuting on Public Transportation	2.7%	31	10.0
Community Stability	34	52.00	% Living in Same House as in 1979	28.3%	38	50.7
			% Living in Same County as in 1985	78.8%	28	53.3

Metropolitan Area Suburb Rankings
MIAMI-FORT LAUDERDALE

Composite: **Rank** 58 / 63 **Score** 45.91   **OPA-LOCKA**

CATEGORY	RANK	SCORE	STATISTIC	VALUE	RANK	SCORE
Economics	61	13.35	Median Household Income	$15,099	61	5.6
			% of Families Above Poverty Level	62.3%	61	21.1
Affordable Housing	3	91.15	Median Home Value	$49,800	3	98.0
			Median Rent	$362	3	84.3
Crime	N/A	N/A	Violent Crimes per 10,000 Population	N/A	N/A	N/A
			Property Crimes per 10,000 Population	N/A	N/A	N/A
Open Spaces	48	51.85	Population Density (Persons/Sq. Mile)	3528	14	86.2
			Average Rooms per Housing Unit	3.6	61	17.5
Education	62	8.00	% High School Enrollment/Completion	72.4%	62	14.8
			% College Graduates	4.0%	62	1.2
Commute	6	53.25	Average Work Commute in Minutes	26	42	52.9
			% Commuting on Public Transportation	13.1%	4	53.6
Community Stability	24	57.85	% Living in Same House as in 1979	27.9%	39	50.0
			% Living in Same County as in 1985	83.3%	17	65.7

Composite: **Rank** 59 / 63 **Score** 45.72   **AVENTURA**

CATEGORY	RANK	SCORE	STATISTIC	VALUE	RANK	SCORE
Economics	21	65.90	Median Household Income	$32,316	27	34.2
			% of Families Above Poverty Level	96.8%	5	97.6
Affordable Housing	63	20.60	Median Home Value	$149,600	57	41.2
			Median Rent	$882	63	0.0
Crime	N/A	N/A	Violent Crimes per 10,000 Population	N/A	N/A	N/A
			Property Crimes per 10,000 Population	N/A	N/A	N/A
Open Spaces	51	50.60	Population Density (Persons/Sq. Mile)	5881	39	71.2
			Average Rooms per Housing Unit	4.1	51	30.0
Education	22	54.80	% High School Enrollment/Completion	86.6%	39	60.6
			% College Graduates	27.6%	14	49.0
Commute	35	36.75	Average Work Commute in Minutes	23	16	70.6
			% Commuting on Public Transportation	1.0%	53	2.9
Community Stability	45	45.65	% Living in Same House as in 1979	35.2%	26	63.1
			% Living in Same County as in 1985	69.7%	58	28.2

Composite: **Rank** 60 / 63 **Score** 43.03   **HAMMOCKS**

CATEGORY	RANK	SCORE	STATISTIC	VALUE	RANK	SCORE
Economics	17	67.75	Median Household Income	$37,936	16	43.5
			% of Families Above Poverty Level	94.3%	24	92.0
Affordable Housing	47	53.80	Median Home Value	$94,100	39	72.8
			Median Rent	$667	52	34.8
Crime	N/A	N/A	Violent Crimes per 10,000 Population	N/A	N/A	N/A
			Property Crimes per 10,000 Population	N/A	N/A	N/A
Open Spaces	48	51.85	Population Density (Persons/Sq. Mile)	7061	53	63.7
			Average Rooms per Housing Unit	4.5	38	40.0
Education	5	80.55	% High School Enrollment/Completion	98.8%	1	100.0
			% College Graduates	33.6%	8	61.1
Commute	63	4.20	Average Work Commute in Minutes	35	63	0.0
			% Commuting on Public Transportation	2.3%	37	8.4
Community Stability	63	0.00	% Living in Same House as in 1979	0.0%	63	0.0
			% Living in Same County as in 1985	59.5%	62	0.0

Metropolitan Area Suburb Rankings
MIAMI-FORT LAUDERDALE

Composite: Rank 61 / 63 *Score* 42.23   **HOMESTEAD**

CATEGORY	RANK	SCORE	STATISTIC	VALUE	RANK	SCORE
Economics	60	32.40	Median Household Income	$20,594	59	14.7
			% of Families Above Poverty Level	75.4%	60	50.1
Affordable Housing	6	82.40	Median Home Value	$66,800	10	88.3
			Median Rent	$410	5	76.5
Crime	N/A	N/A	Violent Crimes per 10,000 Population	288	N/A	N/A
			Property Crimes per 10,000 Population	1,175	N/A	N/A
Open Spaces	26	62.00	Population Density (Persons/Sq. Mile)	2313	5	94.0
			Average Rooms per Housing Unit	4.1	51	30.0
Education	63	5.15	% High School Enrollment/Completion	67.8%	63	0.0
			% College Graduates	8.5%	55	10.3
Commute	34	37.15	Average Work Commute in Minutes	24	25	64.7
			% Commuting on Public Transportation	2.6%	33	9.6
Community Stability	56	34.25	% Living in Same House as in 1979	16.0%	60	28.7
			% Living in Same County as in 1985	73.9%	45	39.8

Composite: Rank 62 / 63 *Score* 40.26   **MIAMI BEACH**

CATEGORY	RANK	SCORE	STATISTIC	VALUE	RANK	SCORE
Economics	59	33.20	Median Household Income	$15,312	60	5.9
			% of Families Above Poverty Level	80.1%	56	60.5
Affordable Housing	50	45.45	Median Home Value	$191,900	61	17.2
			Median Rent	$427	7	73.7
Crime	N/A	N/A	Violent Crimes per 10,000 Population	174	N/A	N/A
			Property Crimes per 10,000 Population	1,307	N/A	N/A
Open Spaces	63	12.35	Population Density (Persons/Sq. Mile)	13172	62	24.7
			Average Rooms per Housing Unit	2.9	63	0.0
Education	36	43.50	% High School Enrollment/Completion	83.6%	53	51.0
			% College Graduates	21.2%	21	36.0
Commute	2	69.40	Average Work Commute in Minutes	23	16	70.6
			% Commuting on Public Transportation	16.6%	3	68.2
Community Stability	51	37.65	% Living in Same House as in 1979	23.8%	47	42.7
			% Living in Same County as in 1985	71.3%	53	32.6

Composite: Rank 63 / 63 *Score* 37.50   **SWEETWATER**

CATEGORY	RANK	SCORE	STATISTIC	VALUE	RANK	SCORE
Economics	56	38.65	Median Household Income	$22,530	53	17.9
			% of Families Above Poverty Level	79.6%	57	59.4
Affordable Housing	20	68.50	Median Home Value	$77,600	17	82.1
			Median Rent	$543	27	54.9
Crime	N/A	N/A	Violent Crimes per 10,000 Population	14	N/A	N/A
			Property Crimes per 10,000 Population	76	N/A	N/A
Open Spaces	62	13.75	Population Density (Persons/Sq. Mile)	17041	63	0.0
			Average Rooms per Housing Unit	4.0	54	27.5
Education	56	28.85	% High School Enrollment/Completion	80.9%	58	42.3
			% College Graduates	11.0%	51	15.4
Commute	41	34.65	Average Work Commute in Minutes	27	52	47.1
			% Commuting on Public Transportation	5.6%	11	22.2
Community Stability	49	40.60	% Living in Same House as in 1979	18.0%	58	32.3
			% Living in Same County as in 1985	77.2%	35	48.9

Metropolitan Area Description
MILWAUKEE-RACINE

STATE: Wisconsin
COUNTIES: Milwaukee, Ozaukee, Racine, Washington, Waukesha

TOTAL POPULATION: 1,607,183

POPULATION IN SUBURBS: 894,797   (55.7%)

POPULATION IN Milwaukee: 628,088   (39.1%)
POPULATION IN Racine: 84,298   (5.2%)

The MILWAUKEE-RACINE metropolitan area is located in the southeastern part of Wisconsin along Lake Michigan. The suburbs range geographically from West Bend in the north (40 miles from Milwaukee), to Oconomowoc in the west (34 miles from Milwaukee), and to Oak Creek in the south (16 miles from Milwaukee). The area is growing in population and had an increase of 2.4% between 1980 and 1990. Summer time high temperatures average in the 80's and winter time lows average in the teens. The electric appliance maker West Bend Company is located in the suburb of West Bend. The engine manufacturing division of Dresser Industries is located in Waukesha. Public transportation in the area is provided on buses by the Milwaukee County Transit System.

Whitefish Bay is the overall highest rated suburb and also has the highest score in education. The top scores in economics and open spaces belong to **Mequon**. **Cudahy** is the suburb with the most affordable housing. **Muskego** is rated the safest suburb with the lowest crime rate. The top rated commute belongs to **Shorewood**. Finally, the number one rating in community stability goes to **Greendale**.

The highest ranked suburb overall which also has an affordable housing score of at least 50.00 is **Greendale**.

The highest ranked suburb in the education category which also has an affordable housing score of at least 50.00 is **Shorewood**.

The county whose suburbs have the highest average overall score is **Ozaukee County** (67.22).

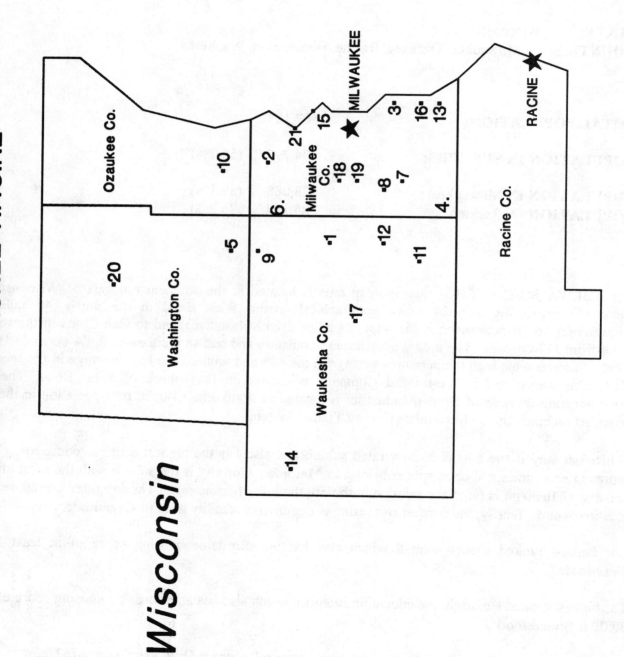

Metropolitan Area Map
MILWAUKEE-RACINE

Wisconsin

Ozaukee Co.

•10

Washington Co.

•20

•5

Waukesha Co.

•17

•14

•9
9•

•1

•12

•11

•6

•2

Milwaukee
Co.

•18
•19

•8
•7

15

21

MILWAUKEE

★

3•

16•
13•

4.

Racine Co.

RACINE

★

Metropolitan Area Suburb Alphabetical Index
MILWAUKEE-RACINE

SUBURB	PAGE	MAP NO.	STATE	COUNTY	POPU-LATION	RANK
BROOKFIELD	413	1	Wisconsin	Waukesha	35,184	6 / 21
BROWN DEER	413	2	Wisconsin	Milwaukee	12,236	4 / 21
CUDAHY	417	3	Wisconsin	Milwaukee	18,659	16 / 21
FRANKLIN	416	4	Wisconsin	Milwaukee	21,855	13 / 21
GERMANTOWN	418	5	Wisconsin	Washington	13,658	19 / 21
GLENDALE	415	6	Wisconsin	Milwaukee	14,088	10 / 21
GREENDALE	412	7	Wisconsin	Milwaukee	15,128	3 / 21
GREENFIELD	416	8	Wisconsin	Milwaukee	33,403	14 / 21
MENOMONEE FALLS	414	9	Wisconsin	Waukesha	26,840	8 / 21
MEQUON	412	10	Wisconsin	Ozaukee	18,885	2 / 21
MUSKEGO	414	11	Wisconsin	Waukesha	16,813	9 / 21
NEW BERLIN	414	12	Wisconsin	Waukesha	33,592	7 / 21
OAK CREEK	415	13	Wisconsin	Milwaukee	19,513	12 / 21
OCONOMOWOC	417	14	Wisconsin	Waukesha	10,993	18 / 21
SHOREWOOD	417	15	Wisconsin	Milwaukee	14,116	17 / 21
SOUTH MILWAUKEE	415	16	Wisconsin	Milwaukee	20,958	11 / 21
WAUKESHA	418	17	Wisconsin	Waukesha	56,958	21 / 21
WAUWATOSA	413	18	Wisconsin	Milwaukee	49,366	5 / 21
WEST ALLIS	418	19	Wisconsin	Milwaukee	63,221	20 / 21
WEST BEND	416	20	Wisconsin	Washington	23,916	15 / 21
WHITEFISH BAY	412	21	Wisconsin	Milwaukee	14,272	1 / 21

Metropolitan Area Suburb Rankings
MILWAUKEE-RACINE

Composite: Rank 1 / 21 *Score* 68.54   **WHITEFISH BAY**

CATEGORY	RANK	SCORE	STATISTIC	VALUE	RANK	SCORE
Economics	3	88.25	Median Household Income	$53,539	3	76.5
			% of Families Above Poverty Level	99.4%	1	100.0
Affordable Housing	19	40.25	Median Home Value	$116,700	19	33.9
			Median Rent	$605	17	46.6
Crime	3	90.45	Violent Crimes per 10,000 Population	6	5	85.7
			Property Crimes per 10,000 Population	173	3	95.2
Open Spaces	14	49.15	Population Density (Persons/Sq. Mile)	6661	20	25.6
			Average Rooms per Housing Unit	6.5	3	72.7
Education	1	95.55	% High School Enrollment/Completion	99.1%	2	91.1
			% College Graduates	61.2%	1	100.0
Commute	7	49.05	Average Work Commute in Minutes	19	5	60.0
			% Commuting on Public Transportation	2.5%	8	38.1
Community Stability	9	67.10	% Living in Same House as in 1979	47.0%	4	81.1
			% Living in Same County as in 1985	80.4%	12	53.1

Composite: Rank 2 / 21 *Score* 67.22   **MEQUON**

CATEGORY	RANK	SCORE	STATISTIC	VALUE	RANK	SCORE
Economics	1	92.20	Median Household Income	$60,900	1	100.0
			% of Families Above Poverty Level	98.7%	4	84.4
Affordable Housing	20	31.60	Median Home Value	$144,400	21	0.0
			Median Rent	$542	13	63.2
Crime	2	98.55	Violent Crimes per 10,000 Population	2	2	97.1
			Property Crimes per 10,000 Population	144	1	100.0
Open Spaces	1	99.95	Population Density (Persons/Sq. Mile)	409	2	99.9
			Average Rooms per Housing Unit	7.1	1	100.0
Education	2	88.10	% High School Enrollment/Completion	100.0%	1	100.0
			% College Graduates	48.8%	3	76.2
Commute	15	27.95	Average Work Commute in Minutes	20	13	40.0
			% Commuting on Public Transportation	1.1%	14	15.9
Community Stability	18	32.20	% Living in Same House as in 1979	42.6%	13	62.2
			% Living in Same County as in 1985	66.3%	20	2.2

Composite: Rank 3 / 21 *Score* 64.68   **GREENDALE**

CATEGORY	RANK	SCORE	STATISTIC	VALUE	RANK	SCORE
Economics	5	66.35	Median Household Income	$44,735	6	48.3
			% of Families Above Poverty Level	98.7%	4	84.4
Affordable Housing	11	66.50	Median Home Value	$93,300	13	62.6
			Median Rent	$515	9	70.4
Crime	8	60.35	Violent Crimes per 10,000 Population	7	6	82.9
			Property Crimes per 10,000 Population	518	20	37.8
Open Spaces	8	61.30	Population Density (Persons/Sq. Mile)	2702	12	72.6
			Average Rooms per Housing Unit	6.0	6	50.0
Education	7	57.70	% High School Enrollment/Completion	97.6%	3	76.2
			% College Graduates	29.5%	8	39.2
Commute	8	43.80	Average Work Commute in Minutes	20	13	40.0
			% Commuting on Public Transportation	3.1%	4	47.6
Community Stability	1	96.75	% Living in Same House as in 1979	51.4%	1	100.0
			% Living in Same County as in 1985	91.6%	2	93.5

Metropolitan Area Suburb Rankings
MILWAUKEE-RACINE

Composite: *Rank* 4 / 21   *Score* 61.54   **BROWN DEER**

CATEGORY	RANK	SCORE	STATISTIC	VALUE	RANK	SCORE
Economics	8	59.35	Median Household Income	$44,495	7	47.6
			% of Families Above Poverty Level	98.1%	9	71.1
Affordable Housing	12	66.25	Median Home Value	$83,100	9	75.1
			Median Rent	$564	15	57.4
Crime	6	73.50	Violent Crimes per 10,000 Population	7	6	82.9
			Property Crimes per 10,000 Population	360	9	64.1
Open Spaces	13	51.75	Population Density (Persons/Sq. Mile)	2779	13	71.7
			Average Rooms per Housing Unit	5.6	12	31.8
Education	6	57.90	% High School Enrollment/Completion	97.4%	4	74.3
			% College Graduates	30.7%	7	41.5
Commute	9	43.50	Average Work Commute in Minutes	19	5	60.0
			% Commuting on Public Transportation	1.8%	10	27.0
Community Stability	4	78.55	% Living in Same House as in 1979	46.2%	5	77.7
			% Living in Same County as in 1985	87.7%	7	79.4

Composite: *Rank* 5 / 21   *Score* 59.54   **WAUWATOSA**

CATEGORY	RANK	SCORE	STATISTIC	VALUE	RANK	SCORE
Economics	11	53.30	Median Household Income	$40,041	12	33.3
			% of Families Above Poverty Level	98.2%	8	73.3
Affordable Housing	10	68.15	Median Home Value	$88,300	11	68.8
			Median Rent	$526	11	67.5
Crime	16	43.00	Violent Crimes per 10,000 Population	23	16	37.1
			Property Crimes per 10,000 Population	451	16	48.9
Open Spaces	15	48.40	Population Density (Persons/Sq. Mile)	3728	16	60.4
			Average Rooms per Housing Unit	5.7	10	36.4
Education	5	61.85	% High School Enrollment/Completion	96.7%	6	67.3
			% College Graduates	38.5%	5	56.4
Commute	3	71.45	Average Work Commute in Minutes	17	1	100.0
			% Commuting on Public Transportation	2.8%	7	42.9
Community Stability	7	70.65	% Living in Same House as in 1979	44.1%	10	68.7
			% Living in Same County as in 1985	85.8%	10	72.6

Composite: *Rank* 6 / 21   *Score* 59.06   **BROOKFIELD**

CATEGORY	RANK	SCORE	STATISTIC	VALUE	RANK	SCORE
Economics	2	91.80	Median Household Income	$57,132	2	88.0
			% of Families Above Poverty Level	99.2%	2	95.6
Affordable Housing	21	14.45	Median Home Value	$120,800	20	28.9
			Median Rent	$781	21	0.0
Crime	15	53.55	Violent Crimes per 10,000 Population	18	13	51.4
			Property Crimes per 10,000 Population	410	14	55.7
Open Spaces	2	92.30	Population Density (Persons/Sq. Mile)	1311	8	89.1
			Average Rooms per Housing Unit	7.0	2	95.5
Education	4	65.45	% High School Enrollment/Completion	96.8%	5	68.3
			% College Graduates	41.7%	4	62.6
Commute	12	38.75	Average Work Commute in Minutes	19	5	60.0
			% Commuting on Public Transportation	1.2%	13	17.5
Community Stability	12	57.10	% Living in Same House as in 1979	49.0%	3	89.7
			% Living in Same County as in 1985	72.5%	18	24.5

Metropolitan Area Suburb Rankings
MILWAUKEE-RACINE

Composite: *Rank* 7 / 21 *Score* 56.44 — NEW BERLIN

CATEGORY	RANK	SCORE	STATISTIC	VALUE	RANK	SCORE
Economics	4	73.80	Median Household Income	$49,394	4	63.2
			% of Families Above Poverty Level	98.7%	4	84.4
Affordable Housing	18	49.25	Median Home Value	$96,400	16	58.8
			Median Rent	$631	20	39.7
Crime	4	83.70	Violent Crimes per 10,000 Population	9	8	77.1
			Property Crimes per 10,000 Population	202	4	90.3
Open Spaces	3	76.50	Population Density (Persons/Sq. Mile)	912	7	93.9
			Average Rooms per Housing Unit	6.2	4	59.1
Education	13	35.65	% High School Enrollment/Completion	93.3%	16	33.7
			% College Graduates	28.7%	9	37.6
Commute	16	25.55	Average Work Commute in Minutes	20	13	40.0
			% Commuting on Public Transportation	0.8%	16	11.1
Community Stability	14	50.65	% Living in Same House as in 1979	45.9%	7	76.4
			% Living in Same County as in 1985	72.6%	17	24.9

Composite: *Rank* 8 / 21 *Score* 53.97 — MENOMONEE FALLS

CATEGORY	RANK	SCORE	STATISTIC	VALUE	RANK	SCORE
Economics	10	54.75	Median Household Income	$42,315	10	40.6
			% of Families Above Poverty Level	98.0%	10	68.9
Affordable Housing	9	71.05	Median Home Value	$87,600	10	69.6
			Median Rent	$507	7	72.5
Crime	10	59.30	Violent Crimes per 10,000 Population	15	11	60.0
			Property Crimes per 10,000 Population	393	12	58.6
Open Spaces	7	68.00	Population Density (Persons/Sq. Mile)	807	6	95.1
			Average Rooms per Housing Unit	5.8	7	40.9
Education	17	21.75	% High School Enrollment/Completion	92.2%	17	22.8
			% College Graduates	19.9%	14	20.7
Commute	13	35.55	Average Work Commute in Minutes	19	5	60.0
			% Commuting on Public Transportation	0.8%	16	11.1
Community Stability	8	67.40	% Living in Same House as in 1979	50.0%	2	94.0
			% Living in Same County as in 1985	77.0%	16	40.8

Composite: *Rank* 9 / 21 *Score* 53.54 — MUSKEGO

CATEGORY	RANK	SCORE	STATISTIC	VALUE	RANK	SCORE
Economics	9	57.45	Median Household Income	$46,119	5	52.7
			% of Families Above Poverty Level	97.7%	11	62.2
Affordable Housing	16	53.65	Median Home Value	$91,600	12	64.7
			Median Rent	$620	19	42.6
Crime	1	99.75	Violent Crimes per 10,000 Population	1	1	100.0
			Property Crimes per 10,000 Population	147	2	99.5
Open Spaces	4	76.40	Population Density (Persons/Sq. Mile)	538	3	98.3
			Average Rooms per Housing Unit	6.1	5	54.5
Education	11	39.05	% High School Enrollment/Completion	96.0%	8	60.4
			% College Graduates	18.3%	16	17.7
Commute	21	3.15	Average Work Commute in Minutes	22	19	0.0
			% Commuting on Public Transportation	0.5%	19	6.3
Community Stability	16	45.30	% Living in Same House as in 1979	43.5%	11	66.1
			% Living in Same County as in 1985	72.5%	18	24.5

Metropolitan Area Suburb Rankings
MILWAUKEE-RACINE

Composite: **Rank** 10 / 21 *Score* 51.51　　**GLENDALE**

CATEGORY	RANK	SCORE	STATISTIC	VALUE	RANK	SCORE
Economics	13	46.45	Median Household Income	$40,602	11	35.1
			% of Families Above Poverty Level	97.5%	13	57.8
Affordable Housing	17	52.50	Median Home Value	$94,800	15	60.8
			Median Rent	$614	18	44.2
Crime	21	12.85	Violent Crimes per 10,000 Population	27	17	25.7
			Property Crimes per 10,000 Population	745	21	0.0
Open Spaces	11	56.10	Population Density (Persons/Sq. Mile)	2432	11	75.8
			Average Rooms per Housing Unit	5.7	10	36.4
Education	8	51.80	% High School Enrollment/Completion	95.3%	12	53.5
			% College Graduates	35.2%	6	50.1
Commute	5	64.30	Average Work Commute in Minutes	17	1	100.0
			% Commuting on Public Transportation	1.9%	9	28.6
Community Stability	5	76.55	% Living in Same House as in 1979	45.6%	8	75.1
			% Living in Same County as in 1985	87.3%	8	78.0

Composite: **Rank** 11 / 21 *Score* 50.51　　**SOUTH MILWAUKEE**

CATEGORY	RANK	SCORE	STATISTIC	VALUE	RANK	SCORE
Economics	18	19.35	Median Household Income	$31,998	19	7.6
			% of Families Above Poverty Level	96.3%	17	31.1
Affordable Housing	3	92.80	Median Home Value	$67,200	3	94.6
			Median Rent	$437	2	91.0
Crime	9	59.90	Violent Crimes per 10,000 Population	16	12	57.1
			Property Crimes per 10,000 Population	368	10	62.7
Open Spaces	18	33.10	Population Density (Persons/Sq. Mile)	4386	18	52.6
			Average Rooms per Housing Unit	5.2	17	13.6
Education	14	33.15	% High School Enrollment/Completion	95.5%	10	55.4
			% College Graduates	14.8%	19	10.9
Commute	14	32.20	Average Work Commute in Minutes	21	16	20.0
			% Commuting on Public Transportation	2.9%	5	44.4
Community Stability	3	83.10	% Living in Same House as in 1979	45.2%	9	73.4
			% Living in Same County as in 1985	91.4%	3	92.8

Composite: **Rank** 12 / 21 *Score* 50.23　　**OAK CREEK**

CATEGORY	RANK	SCORE	STATISTIC	VALUE	RANK	SCORE
Economics	7	63.25	Median Household Income	$39,995	13	33.2
			% of Families Above Poverty Level	99.1%	3	93.3
Affordable Housing	6	74.05	Median Home Value	$81,200	8	77.5
			Median Rent	$514	8	70.6
Crime	14	53.90	Violent Crimes per 10,000 Population	21	14	42.9
			Property Crimes per 10,000 Population	355	8	64.9
Open Spaces	9	59.65	Population Density (Persons/Sq. Mile)	682	5	96.6
			Average Rooms per Housing Unit	5.4	16	22.7
Education	18	16.45	% High School Enrollment/Completion	91.9%	19	19.8
			% College Graduates	15.9%	18	13.1
Commute	17	19.50	Average Work Commute in Minutes	21	16	20.0
			% Commuting on Public Transportation	1.3%	12	19.0
Community Stability	10	64.80	% Living in Same House as in 1979	39.7%	14	49.8
			% Living in Same County as in 1985	87.8%	6	79.8

Metropolitan Area Suburb Rankings
MILWAUKEE-RACINE

Composite: **Rank** 13 / 21 *Score* 50.16   **FRANKLIN**

CATEGORY	RANK	SCORE	STATISTIC	VALUE	RANK	SCORE
Economics	6	64.70	Median Household Income	$43,686	8	45.0
			% of Families Above Poverty Level	98.7%	4	84.4
Affordable Housing	14	59.20	Median Home Value	$94,600	14	61.0
			Median Rent	$564	15	57.4
Crime	5	83.55	Violent Crimes per 10,000 Population	5	3	88.6
			Property Crimes per 10,000 Population	273	5	78.5
Open Spaces	6	69.05	Population Density (Persons/Sq. Mile)	631	4	97.2
			Average Rooms per Housing Unit	5.8	7	40.9
Education	19	14.10	% High School Enrollment/Completion	89.9%	21	0.0
			% College Graduates	23.8%	11	28.2
Commute	19	7.95	Average Work Commute in Minutes	22	19	0.0
			% Commuting on Public Transportation	1.1%	14	15.9
Community Stability	13	52.55	% Living in Same House as in 1979	35.5%	17	31.8
			% Living in Same County as in 1985	86.0%	9	73.3

Composite: **Rank** 14 / 21 *Score* 50.14   **GREENFIELD**

CATEGORY	RANK	SCORE	STATISTIC	VALUE	RANK	SCORE
Economics	14	38.75	Median Household Income	$35,082	15	17.5
			% of Families Above Poverty Level	97.6%	12	60.0
Affordable Housing	8	72.25	Median Home Value	$80,400	5	78.4
			Median Rent	$531	12	66.1
Crime	12	57.35	Violent Crimes per 10,000 Population	12	9	68.6
			Property Crimes per 10,000 Population	468	18	46.1
Open Spaces	17	37.40	Population Density (Persons/Sq. Mile)	2893	14	70.3
			Average Rooms per Housing Unit	5.0	19	4.5
Education	15	30.00	% High School Enrollment/Completion	94.0%	14	40.6
			% College Graduates	19.2%	15	19.4
Commute	6	52.20	Average Work Commute in Minutes	19	5	60.0
			% Commuting on Public Transportation	2.9%	5	44.4
Community Stability	11	63.00	% Living in Same House as in 1979	38.2%	15	43.3
			% Living in Same County as in 1985	88.6%	5	82.7

Composite: **Rank** 15 / 21 *Score* 49.08   **WEST BEND**

CATEGORY	RANK	SCORE	STATISTIC	VALUE	RANK	SCORE
Economics	15	29.75	Median Household Income	$34,337	17	15.1
			% of Families Above Poverty Level	96.9%	15	44.4
Affordable Housing	4	87.15	Median Home Value	$72,500	4	88.1
			Median Rent	$455	4	86.2
Crime	11	58.50	Violent Crimes per 10,000 Population	12	9	68.6
			Property Crimes per 10,000 Population	454	17	48.4
Open Spaces	12	51.85	Population Density (Persons/Sq. Mile)	2385	10	76.4
			Average Rooms per Housing Unit	5.5	14	27.3
Education	16	24.45	% High School Enrollment/Completion	93.4%	15	34.7
			% College Graduates	16.5%	17	14.2
Commute	10	41.60	Average Work Commute in Minutes	18	3	80.0
			% Commuting on Public Transportation	0.3%	20	3.2
Community Stability	15	50.25	% Living in Same House as in 1979	37.4%	16	39.9
			% Living in Same County as in 1985	82.5%	11	60.6

Metropolitan Area Suburb Rankings
MILWAUKEE-RACINE

Composite: Rank 16 / 21 **Score** 48.25   **CUDAHY**

CATEGORY	RANK	SCORE	STATISTIC	VALUE	RANK	SCORE
Economics	21	0.65	Median Household Income	$30,031	20	1.3
			% of Families Above Poverty Level	94.9%	21	0.0
Affordable Housing	1	98.70	Median Home Value	$64,900	2	97.4
			Median Rent	$403	1	100.0
Crime	18	38.95	Violent Crimes per 10,000 Population	29	19	20.0
			Property Crimes per 10,000 Population	397	13	57.9
Open Spaces	19	31.30	Population Density (Persons/Sq. Mile)	3927	17	58.1
			Average Rooms per Housing Unit	5.0	19	4.5
Education	21	11.40	% High School Enrollment/Completion	92.2%	17	22.8
			% College Graduates	9.1%	21	0.0
Commute	4	68.10	Average Work Commute in Minutes	19	5	60.0
			% Commuting on Public Transportation	4.9%	2	76.2
Community Stability	2	88.65	% Living in Same House as in 1979	46.1%	6	77.3
			% Living in Same County as in 1985	93.4%	1	100.0

Composite: Rank 17 / 21 **Score** 44.89   **SHOREWOOD**

CATEGORY	RANK	SCORE	STATISTIC	VALUE	RANK	SCORE
Economics	17	21.00	Median Household Income	$34,417	16	15.3
			% of Families Above Poverty Level	96.1%	18	26.7
Affordable Housing	15	56.90	Median Home Value	$113,300	18	38.1
			Median Rent	$495	6	75.7
Crime	19	38.35	Violent Crimes per 10,000 Population	34	20	5.7
			Property Crimes per 10,000 Population	318	7	71.0
Open Spaces	21	13.65	Population Density (Persons/Sq. Mile)	8812	21	0.0
			Average Rooms per Housing Unit	5.5	14	27.3
Education	3	75.75	% High School Enrollment/Completion	96.5%	7	65.3
			% College Graduates	54.0%	2	86.2
Commute	1	80.00	Average Work Commute in Minutes	19	5	60.0
			% Commuting on Public Transportation	6.4%	1	100.0
Community Stability	19	28.55	% Living in Same House as in 1979	29.8%	20	7.3
			% Living in Same County as in 1985	79.5%	13	49.8

Composite: Rank 18 / 21 **Score** 43.64   **OCONOMOWOC**

CATEGORY	RANK	SCORE	STATISTIC	VALUE	RANK	SCORE
Economics	16	27.10	Median Household Income	$34,061	18	14.2
			% of Families Above Poverty Level	96.7%	16	40.0
Affordable Housing	5	78.00	Median Home Value	$81,000	7	77.7
			Median Rent	$485	5	78.3
Crime	13	56.70	Violent Crimes per 10,000 Population	22	15	40.0
			Property Crimes per 10,000 Population	304	6	73.4
Open Spaces	10	57.00	Population Density (Persons/Sq. Mile)	1898	9	82.2
			Average Rooms per Housing Unit	5.6	12	31.8
Education	10	39.20	% High School Enrollment/Completion	95.5%	10	55.4
			% College Graduates	21.1%	13	23.0
Commute	18	10.00	Average Work Commute in Minutes	21	16	20.0
			% Commuting on Public Transportation	0.1%	21	0.0
Community Stability	17	37.45	% Living in Same House as in 1979	34.1%	18	25.8
			% Living in Same County as in 1985	79.3%	14	49.1

Composite: *Rank* 19 / 21 *Score* 43.56   **GERMANTOWN**

CATEGORY	RANK	SCORE	STATISTIC	VALUE	RANK	SCORE
Economics	12	51.05	Median Household Income	$43,486	9	44.3
			% of Families Above Poverty Level	97.5%	13	57.8
Affordable Housing	13	60.10	Median Home Value	$96,600	17	58.6
			Median Rent	$548	14	61.6
Crime	7	72.10	Violent Crimes per 10,000 Population	5	3	88.6
			Property Crimes per 10,000 Population	411	15	55.6
Open Spaces	5	70.45	Population Density (Persons/Sq. Mile)	397	1	100.0
			Average Rooms per Housing Unit	5.8	7	40.9
Education	9	41.30	% High School Enrollment/Completion	95.8%	9	58.4
			% College Graduates	21.7%	12	24.2
Commute	20	4.75	Average Work Commute in Minutes	22	19	0.0
			% Commuting on Public Transportation	0.7%	18	9.5
Community Stability	21	5.15	% Living in Same House as in 1979	30.5%	19	10.3
			% Living in Same County as in 1985	65.7%	21	0.0

Composite: *Rank* 20 / 21 *Score* 43.07   **WEST ALLIS**

CATEGORY	RANK	SCORE	STATISTIC	VALUE	RANK	SCORE
Economics	20	8.90	Median Household Income	$29,622	21	0.0
			% of Families Above Poverty Level	95.7%	19	17.8
Affordable Housing	2	94.30	Median Home Value	$62,800	1	100.0
			Median Rent	$446	3	88.6
Crime	20	20.30	Violent Crimes per 10,000 Population	36	21	0.0
			Property Crimes per 10,000 Population	501	19	40.6
Open Spaces	20	19.20	Population Density (Persons/Sq. Mile)	5580	19	38.4
			Average Rooms per Housing Unit	4.9	21	0.0
Education	20	11.55	% High School Enrollment/Completion	91.6%	20	16.8
			% College Graduates	12.4%	20	6.3
Commute	2	73.35	Average Work Commute in Minutes	18	3	80.0
			% Commuting on Public Transportation	4.3%	3	66.7
Community Stability	6	73.90	% Living in Same House as in 1979	43.1%	12	64.4
			% Living in Same County as in 1985	88.8%	4	83.4

Composite: *Rank* 21 / 21 *Score* 39.03   **WAUKESHA**

CATEGORY	RANK	SCORE	STATISTIC	VALUE	RANK	SCORE
Economics	19	17.15	Median Household Income	$36,192	14	21.0
			% of Families Above Poverty Level	95.5%	20	13.3
Affordable Housing	7	73.00	Median Home Value	$80,500	6	78.3
			Median Rent	$525	10	67.7
Crime	17	42.05	Violent Crimes per 10,000 Population	28	18	22.9
			Property Crimes per 10,000 Population	377	11	61.2
Open Spaces	16	39.60	Population Density (Persons/Sq. Mile)	3290	15	65.6
			Average Rooms per Housing Unit	5.2	17	13.6
Education	12	38.30	% High School Enrollment/Completion	94.5%	13	45.5
			% College Graduates	25.3%	10	31.1
Commute	11	41.10	Average Work Commute in Minutes	19	5	60.0
			% Commuting on Public Transportation	1.5%	11	22.2
Community Stability	20	22.00	% Living in Same House as in 1979	28.1%	21	0.0
			% Living in Same County as in 1985	77.9%	15	44.0

STATE: Minnesota
COUNTIES: Anoka, Carver, Chisago, Dakota, Hennepin, Isanti, Ramsey, Scott, Washington, Wright

STATE: Wisconsin
COUNTIES: St. Croix

TOTAL POPULATION:	2,464,124	
POPULATION IN SUBURBS:	1,823,506	(74.0%)
POPULATION IN Minneapolis (MN):	368,383	(14.9%)
POPULATION IN St. Paul (MN):	272,235	(11.0%)

The MINNEAPOLIS-ST. PAUL metropolitan area is located in the southeastern part of Minnesota and the northwestern part of Wisconsin. The suburbs range geographically from Andover (MN) in the north (20 miles from Minneapolis), to Chaska (MN) in the west (30 miles from Minneapolis), to Lakeville (MN) in the south (20 miles from Minneapolis), and to Stillwater (MN) in the east (31 miles from Minneapolis). The area is growing in population and had an increase of 15.3% between 1980 and 1990. Summer time high temperatures average in the 80's and winter time lows average between 0 and 10. Many high tech firms are located in the area. Rosemount, a subsidiary of Emerson Electric, is located in the suburb of Eden Prairie. Honeywell has facilities located in Hutchinson. Public transportation in the area is provided on buses by the Metropolitan Transit System.

Golden Valley (MN) is the overall highest rated suburb and also has the highest score in community stability. **Chanhassen** (MN) receives the highest score in economics. **South St. Paul** (MN) is the suburb with the most affordable housing. **Shoreview** (MN) is rated the safest suburb with the lowest crime rate. The number one score in education goes to **Edina** (MN). The top rated commute belongs to **West St. Paul** (MN). Finally, the number one rating in open spaces belongs to **Andover** (MN).

The highest ranked suburb overall which also has an affordable housing score of at least 50.00 is **Golden Valley** (MN).

The highest ranked suburb in the education category which also has an affordable housing score of at least 50.00 is also **Golden Valley** (MN).

The county whose suburbs have the highest average overall score is **Ramsey County** (MN) (60.47).

Metropolitan Area Map
MINNEAPOLIS–ST. PAUL

Minnesota

Wisconsin

Isanti Co.

Chisago Co.

St. Croix Co.

Anoka Co.

Washington Co.

•43

•32

•47

•14

Ramsey
Co.
•40
44
46
•38 31•
•29
•28
•4

ST. PAUL ★

•26

•41

•23

•45

21

Dakota Co.

Hennepin Co.

•13
•19
12
•6
•37
•35
•9
•2
7
•25
•30
•33
15
20
42•

•16

•3

•8

•24

•1

MINNEAPOLIS ★

•18
•36
•5

•22
17
•34

•27
10•
39

11•

Wright Co.

Carver Co.

Scott Co.

Metropolitan Area Suburb Alphabetical Index
MINNEAPOLIS-ST. PAUL

SUBURB	PAGE	MAP NO.	STATE	COUNTY	POPU-LATION	RANK
ANDOVER	429	1	Minnesota	Anoka	15,216	23 / 47
ANOKA	437	2	Minnesota	Anoka	17,192	47 / 47
APPLE VALLEY	427	3	Minnesota	Dakota	34,598	18 / 47
BLAINE	435	4	Minnesota	Anoka	38,975	40 / 47
BLOOMINGTON	424	5	Minnesota	Hennepin	86,335	8 / 47
BROOKLYN CENTER	436	6	Minnesota	Hennepin	28,887	43 / 47
BROOKLYN PARK	436	7	Minnesota	Hennepin	56,381	44 / 47
BURNSVILLE	434	8	Minnesota	Dakota	51,288	39 / 47
CHAMPLIN	428	9	Minnesota	Hennepin	16,849	20 / 47
CHANHASSEN	423	10	Minnesota	Carver	11,732	5 / 47
CHASKA	435	11	Minnesota	Carver	11,339	42 / 47
COLUMBIA HEIGHTS	437	12	Minnesota	Anoka	18,910	46 / 47
COON RAPIDS	433	13	Minnesota	Anoka	52,978	35 / 47
COTTAGE GROVE	426	14	Minnesota	Washington	22,935	13 / 47
CRYSTAL	427	15	Minnesota	Hennepin	23,788	17 / 47
EAGAN	431	16	Minnesota	Dakota	47,409	30 / 47
EDEN PRAIRIE	426	17	Minnesota	Hennepin	39,311	15 / 47
EDINA	422	18	Minnesota	Hennepin	46,070	2 / 47
FRIDLEY	432	19	Minnesota	Anoka	28,335	33 / 47
GOLDEN VALLEY	422	20	Minnesota	Hennepin	20,971	1 / 47
HASTINGS	429	21	Minnesota	Dakota	15,445	22 / 47
HOPKINS	436	22	Minnesota	Hennepin	16,534	45 / 47
INVER GROVE HEIGHTS	433	23	Minnesota	Dakota	22,477	36 / 47
LAKEVILLE	431	24	Minnesota	Dakota	24,854	29 / 47
MAPLE GROVE	424	25	Minnesota	Hennepin	38,736	9 / 47
MAPLEWOOD	432	26	Minnesota	Ramsey	30,954	32 / 47
MINNETONKA	423	27	Minnesota	Hennepin	48,370	4 / 47
MOUNDS VIEW	435	28	Minnesota	Ramsey	12,541	41 / 47
NEW BRIGHTON	425	29	Minnesota	Ramsey	22,207	11 / 47
NEW HOPE	431	30	Minnesota	Hennepin	21,853	28 / 47
NORTH ST. PAUL	430	31	Minnesota	Ramsey	12,376	25 / 47
OAKDALE	433	32	Minnesota	Washington	18,374	34 / 47
PLYMOUTH	425	33	Minnesota	Hennepin	50,889	12 / 47
PRIOR LAKE	430	34	Minnesota	Scott	11,482	26 / 47
RAMSEY	424	35	Minnesota	Anoka	12,408	7 / 47
RICHFIELD	432	36	Minnesota	Hennepin	35,710	31 / 47
ROBBINSDALE	429	37	Minnesota	Hennepin	14,396	24 / 47
ROSEVILLE	425	38	Minnesota	Ramsey	33,485	10 / 47
SHAKOPEE	434	39	Minnesota	Scott	11,739	38 / 47
SHOREVIEW	422	40	Minnesota	Ramsey	24,587	3 / 47
SOUTH ST. PAUL	430	41	Minnesota	Dakota	20,197	27 / 47
ST. LOUIS PARK	428	42	Minnesota	Hennepin	43,787	19 / 47
STILLWATER	428	43	Minnesota	Washington	13,882	21 / 47
VADNAIS HEIGHTS	423	44	Minnesota	Ramsey	11,041	6 / 47
WEST ST. PAUL	434	45	Minnesota	Dakota	19,248	37 / 47
WHITE BEAR LAKE	427	46	Minnesota	Ramsey	24,704	16 / 47
WOODBURY	426	47	Minnesota	Washington	20,075	14 / 47

Metropolitan Area Suburb Rankings
MINNEAPOLIS-ST. PAUL

Composite: *Rank* 1 / 47 *Score* 73.73   GOLDEN VALLEY (MN)

CATEGORY	RANK	SCORE	STATISTIC	VALUE	RANK	SCORE
Economics	16	72.85	Median Household Income	$46,212	12	71.1
			% of Families Above Poverty Level	97.4%	17	74.6
Affordable Housing	31	60.40	Median Home Value	$109,200	40	55.5
			Median Rent	$522	24	65.3
Crime	19	72.85	Violent Crimes per 10,000 Population	13	14	81.7
			Property Crimes per 10,000 Population	384	23	64.0
Open Spaces	14	69.20	Population Density (Persons/Sq. Mile)	2050	22	68.0
			Average Rooms per Housing Unit	6.4	9	70.4
Education	5	78.90	% High School Enrollment/Completion	96.4%	10	83.6
			% College Graduates	42.0%	6	74.2
Commute	12	61.90	Average Work Commute in Minutes	19	7	81.8
			% Commuting on Public Transportation	4.0%	12	42.0
Community Stability	1	100.00	% Living in Same House as in 1979	47.2%	1	100.0
			% Living in Same County as in 1985	86.7%	1	100.0

Composite: *Rank* 2 / 47 *Score* 69.23   EDINA (MN)

CATEGORY	RANK	SCORE	STATISTIC	VALUE	RANK	SCORE
Economics	7	85.45	Median Household Income	$48,936	8	82.8
			% of Families Above Poverty Level	98.2%	4	88.1
Affordable Housing	47	9.70	Median Home Value	$156,400	47	0.0
			Median Rent	$654	43	19.4
Crime	6	80.25	Violent Crimes per 10,000 Population	7	4	91.7
			Property Crimes per 10,000 Population	348	17	68.8
Open Spaces	28	56.80	Population Density (Persons/Sq. Mile)	2927	33	50.6
			Average Rooms per Housing Unit	6.2	15	63.0
Education	1	99.25	% High School Enrollment/Completion	98.4%	2	98.5
			% College Graduates	52.6%	1	100.0
Commute	9	64.35	Average Work Commute in Minutes	19	7	81.8
			% Commuting on Public Transportation	4.4%	9	46.9
Community Stability	8	88.80	% Living in Same House as in 1979	40.7%	12	80.7
			% Living in Same County as in 1985	85.6%	5	96.9

Composite: *Rank* 3 / 47 *Score* 68.62   SHOREVIEW (MN)

CATEGORY	RANK	SCORE	STATISTIC	VALUE	RANK	SCORE
Economics	9	82.70	Median Household Income	$48,828	9	82.3
			% of Families Above Poverty Level	97.9%	10	83.1
Affordable Housing	32	59.30	Median Home Value	$109,900	42	54.7
			Median Rent	$526	26	63.9
Crime	1	100.00	Violent Crimes per 10,000 Population	2	1	100.0
			Property Crimes per 10,000 Population	114	1	100.0
Open Spaces	21	65.90	Population Density (Persons/Sq. Mile)	2197	26	65.1
			Average Rooms per Housing Unit	6.3	13	66.7
Education	7	76.45	% High School Enrollment/Completion	95.7%	19	78.4
			% College Graduates	42.1%	5	74.5
Commute	32	37.35	Average Work Commute in Minutes	21	25	63.6
			% Commuting on Public Transportation	1.5%	37	11.1
Community Stability	29	58.65	% Living in Same House as in 1979	29.2%	30	46.6
			% Living in Same County as in 1985	76.4%	26	70.7

Composite: *Rank* 4 / 47 *Score* 66.85   **MINNETONKA (MN)**

CATEGORY	RANK	SCORE	STATISTIC	VALUE	RANK	SCORE
Economics	2	95.10	Median Household Income	$50,659	5	90.2
			% of Families Above Poverty Level	98.9%	1	100.0
Affordable Housing	45	30.10	Median Home Value	$120,000	43	42.8
			Median Rent	$660	45	17.4
Crime	15	75.25	Violent Crimes per 10,000 Population	13	14	81.7
			Property Crimes per 10,000 Population	348	17	68.8
Open Spaces	18	68.10	Population Density (Persons/Sq. Mile)	1785	18	73.2
			Average Rooms per Housing Unit	6.2	15	63.0
Education	4	82.20	% High School Enrollment/Completion	96.9%	8	87.3
			% College Graduates	43.2%	3	77.1
Commute	21	46.25	Average Work Commute in Minutes	20	15	72.7
			% Commuting on Public Transportation	2.2%	26	19.8
Community Stability	20	70.95	% Living in Same House as in 1979	32.4%	25	56.1
			% Living in Same County as in 1985	81.7%	11	85.8

Composite: *Rank* 5 / 47 *Score* 64.71   **CHANHASSEN (MN)**

CATEGORY	RANK	SCORE	STATISTIC	VALUE	RANK	SCORE
Economics	1	98.00	Median Household Income	$52,011	2	96.0
			% of Families Above Poverty Level	98.9%	1	100.0
Affordable Housing	36	54.45	Median Home Value	$123,400	45	38.8
			Median Rent	$508	19	70.1
Crime	3	90.95	Violent Crimes per 10,000 Population	9	7	88.3
			Property Crimes per 10,000 Population	162	3	93.6
Open Spaces	3	89.45	Population Density (Persons/Sq. Mile)	564	4	97.4
			Average Rooms per Housing Unit	6.7	4	81.5
Education	6	77.20	% High School Enrollment/Completion	96.2%	11	82.1
			% College Graduates	41.2%	8	72.3
Commute	43	23.35	Average Work Commute in Minutes	23	38	45.5
			% Commuting on Public Transportation	0.7%	45	1.2
Community Stability	45	19.60	% Living in Same House as in 1979	24.2%	37	31.8
			% Living in Same County as in 1985	54.2%	46	7.4

Composite: *Rank* 6 / 47 *Score* 64.66   **VADNAIS HEIGHTS (MN)**

CATEGORY	RANK	SCORE	STATISTIC	VALUE	RANK	SCORE
Economics	14	74.75	Median Household Income	$43,929	17	61.4
			% of Families Above Poverty Level	98.2%	4	88.1
Affordable Housing	29	64.80	Median Home Value	$97,000	33	69.9
			Median Rent	$538	27	59.7
Crime	2	96.10	Violent Crimes per 10,000 Population	3	2	98.3
			Property Crimes per 10,000 Population	160	2	93.9
Open Spaces	16	68.95	Population Density (Persons/Sq. Mile)	1515	15	78.6
			Average Rooms per Housing Unit	6.1	18	59.3
Education	12	68.40	% High School Enrollment/Completion	97.6%	5	92.5
			% College Graduates	29.7%	16	44.3
Commute	33	36.75	Average Work Commute in Minutes	21	25	63.6
			% Commuting on Public Transportation	1.4%	38	9.9
Community Stability	38	42.85	% Living in Same House as in 1979	17.7%	45	12.5
			% Living in Same County as in 1985	77.3%	21	73.2

Metropolitan Area Suburb Rankings
MINNEAPOLIS-ST. PAUL

Composite: **Rank** 7 / 47 **Score** 64.12   **RAMSEY** (MN)

CATEGORY	RANK	SCORE	STATISTIC	VALUE	RANK	SCORE
Economics	8	83.65	Median Household Income	$46,101	13	70.7
			% of Families Above Poverty Level	98.7%	3	96.6
Affordable Housing	30	64.15	Median Home Value	$87,200	18	81.4
			Median Rent	$575	35	46.9
Crime	12	77.85	Violent Crimes per 10,000 Population	10	9	86.7
			Property Crimes per 10,000 Population	347	15	69.0
Open Spaces	2	96.30	Population Density (Persons/Sq. Mile)	431	1	100.0
			Average Rooms per Housing Unit	7.0	2	92.6
Education	33	36.75	% High School Enrollment/Completion	94.1%	26	66.4
			% College Graduates	14.4%	43	7.1
Commute	47	6.80	Average Work Commute in Minutes	28	47	0.0
			% Commuting on Public Transportation	1.7%	35	13.6
Community Stability	9	83.35	% Living in Same House as in 1979	43.1%	9	87.8
			% Living in Same County as in 1985	79.3%	17	78.9

Composite: **Rank** 8 / 47 **Score** 63.86   **BLOOMINGTON** (MN)

CATEGORY	RANK	SCORE	STATISTIC	VALUE	RANK	SCORE
Economics	18	65.85	Median Household Income	$41,736	21	52.0
			% of Families Above Poverty Level	97.7%	14	79.7
Affordable Housing	33	58.30	Median Home Value	$97,400	34	69.4
			Median Rent	$574	34	47.2
Crime	24	68.60	Violent Crimes per 10,000 Population	16	23	76.7
			Property Crimes per 10,000 Population	411	27	60.5
Open Spaces	30	54.30	Population Density (Persons/Sq. Mile)	2430	28	60.5
			Average Rooms per Housing Unit	5.8	23	48.1
Education	14	64.85	% High School Enrollment/Completion	96.0%	15	80.6
			% College Graduates	31.7%	15	49.1
Commute	14	56.95	Average Work Commute in Minutes	19	7	81.8
			% Commuting on Public Transportation	3.2%	19	32.1
Community Stability	13	78.15	% Living in Same House as in 1979	36.8%	17	69.1
			% Living in Same County as in 1985	82.2%	9	87.2

Composite: **Rank** 9 / 47 **Score** 63.69   **MAPLE GROVE** (MN)

CATEGORY	RANK	SCORE	STATISTIC	VALUE	RANK	SCORE
Economics	4	89.05	Median Household Income	$50,611	6	90.0
			% of Families Above Poverty Level	98.2%	4	88.1
Affordable Housing	42	35.55	Median Home Value	$96,000	29	71.1
			Median Rent	$710	47	0.0
Crime	4	89.15	Violent Crimes per 10,000 Population	7	4	91.7
			Property Crimes per 10,000 Population	215	4	86.6
Open Spaces	5	87.05	Population Density (Persons/Sq. Mile)	1179	12	85.2
			Average Rooms per Housing Unit	6.9	3	88.9
Education	16	61.75	% High School Enrollment/Completion	96.2%	11	82.1
			% College Graduates	28.5%	18	41.4
Commute	42	26.45	Average Work Commute in Minutes	23	38	45.5
			% Commuting on Public Transportation	1.2%	41	7.4
Community Stability	33	56.85	% Living in Same House as in 1979	23.2%	38	28.8
			% Living in Same County as in 1985	81.4%	13	84.9

Metropolitan Area Suburb Rankings
MINNEAPOLIS-ST. PAUL

Composite: *Rank* 10 / 47 *Score* 63.22   **ROSEVILLE (MN)**

CATEGORY	RANK	SCORE	STATISTIC	VALUE	RANK	SCORE
Economics	21	55.00	Median Household Income	$37,862	29	35.4
			% of Families Above Poverty Level	97.4%	17	74.6
Affordable Housing	23	70.30	Median Home Value	$96,800	32	70.1
			Median Rent	$507	17	70.5
Crime	39	48.80	Violent Crimes per 10,000 Population	17	26	75.0
			Property Crimes per 10,000 Population	695	45	22.6
Open Spaces	32	47.75	Population Density (Persons/Sq. Mile)	2528	29	58.5
			Average Rooms per Housing Unit	5.5	36	37.0
Education	9	74.25	% High School Enrollment/Completion	97.6%	5	92.5
			% College Graduates	34.5%	12	56.0
Commute	10	63.35	Average Work Commute in Minutes	18	2	90.9
			% Commuting on Public Transportation	3.5%	13	35.8
Community Stability	10	83.10	% Living in Same House as in 1979	43.2%	8	88.1
			% Living in Same County as in 1985	79.0%	19	78.1

Composite: *Rank* 11 / 47 *Score* 62.71   **NEW BRIGHTON (MN)**

CATEGORY	RANK	SCORE	STATISTIC	VALUE	RANK	SCORE
Economics	23	53.50	Median Household Income	$40,324	24	46.0
			% of Families Above Poverty Level	96.6%	24	61.0
Affordable Housing	22	70.80	Median Home Value	$101,800	37	64.2
			Median Rent	$487	11	77.4
Crime	7	79.85	Violent Crimes per 10,000 Population	10	9	86.7
			Property Crimes per 10,000 Population	317	9	73.0
Open Spaces	34	43.35	Population Density (Persons/Sq. Mile)	3350	36	42.3
			Average Rooms per Housing Unit	5.7	28	44.4
Education	11	72.05	% High School Enrollment/Completion	97.3%	7	90.3
			% College Graduates	33.6%	14	53.8
Commute	8	64.95	Average Work Commute in Minutes	19	7	81.8
			% Commuting on Public Transportation	4.5%	7	48.1
Community Stability	34	54.50	% Living in Same House as in 1979	36.2%	21	67.4
			% Living in Same County as in 1985	66.2%	39	41.6

Composite: *Rank* 12 / 47 *Score* 62.64   **PLYMOUTH (MN)**

CATEGORY	RANK	SCORE	STATISTIC	VALUE	RANK	SCORE
Economics	6	85.50	Median Household Income	$51,314	3	93.0
			% of Families Above Poverty Level	97.6%	15	78.0
Affordable Housing	44	34.20	Median Home Value	$127,500	46	34.0
			Median Rent	$611	40	34.4
Crime	14	77.15	Violent Crimes per 10,000 Population	13	14	81.7
			Property Crimes per 10,000 Population	320	11	72.6
Open Spaces	13	72.35	Population Density (Persons/Sq. Mile)	1545	16	78.0
			Average Rooms per Housing Unit	6.3	13	66.7
Education	8	75.90	% High School Enrollment/Completion	95.8%	18	79.1
			% College Graduates	41.4%	7	72.7
Commute	23	44.75	Average Work Commute in Minutes	21	25	63.6
			% Commuting on Public Transportation	2.7%	20	25.9
Community Stability	35	48.65	% Living in Same House as in 1979	22.4%	40	26.4
			% Living in Same County as in 1985	76.5%	25	70.9

Metropolitan Area Suburb Rankings
MINNEAPOLIS-ST. PAUL

Composite: Rank 13 / 47 *Score* 62.06　　**COTTAGE GROVE** (MN)

CATEGORY	RANK	SCORE	STATISTIC	VALUE	RANK	SCORE
Economics	11	79.25	Median Household Income	$46,027	14	70.4
			% of Families Above Poverty Level	98.2%	4	88.1
Affordable Housing	35	57.95	Median Home Value	$87,400	19	81.2
			Median Rent	$610	39	34.7
Crime	26	67.05	Violent Crimes per 10,000 Population	24	34	63.3
			Property Crimes per 10,000 Population	333	13	70.8
Open Spaces	4	88.35	Population Density (Persons/Sq. Mile)	675	6	95.2
			Average Rooms per Housing Unit	6.7	4	81.5
Education	34	35.00	% High School Enrollment/Completion	92.1%	33	51.5
			% College Graduates	19.1%	30	18.5
Commute	39	30.75	Average Work Commute in Minutes	23	38	45.5
			% Commuting on Public Transportation	1.9%	33	16.0
Community Stability	15	76.10	% Living in Same House as in 1979	40.6%	13	80.4
			% Living in Same County as in 1985	76.8%	23	71.8

Composite: Rank 14 / 47 *Score* 61.51　　**WOODBURY** (MN)

CATEGORY	RANK	SCORE	STATISTIC	VALUE	RANK	SCORE
Economics	5	88.20	Median Household Income	$51,014	4	91.7
			% of Families Above Poverty Level	98.0%	8	84.7
Affordable Housing	43	35.00	Median Home Value	$109,300	41	55.4
			Median Rent	$668	46	14.6
Crime	5	81.25	Violent Crimes per 10,000 Population	3	2	98.3
			Property Crimes per 10,000 Population	383	22	64.2
Open Spaces	7	83.80	Population Density (Persons/Sq. Mile)	574	5	97.2
			Average Rooms per Housing Unit	6.4	9	70.4
Education	3	85.70	% High School Enrollment/Completion	97.9%	4	94.8
			% College Graduates	43.0%	4	76.6
Commute	27	41.30	Average Work Commute in Minutes	20	15	72.7
			% Commuting on Public Transportation	1.4%	38	9.9
Community Stability	46	15.30	% Living in Same House as in 1979	19.4%	44	17.5
			% Living in Same County as in 1985	56.2%	45	13.1

Composite: Rank 15 / 47 *Score* 61.13　　**EDEN PRAIRIE** (MN)

CATEGORY	RANK	SCORE	STATISTIC	VALUE	RANK	SCORE
Economics	3	89.00	Median Household Income	$52,956	1	100.0
			% of Families Above Poverty Level	97.6%	15	78.0
Affordable Housing	46	29.40	Median Home Value	$122,100	44	40.4
			Median Rent	$657	44	18.4
Crime	17	74.50	Violent Crimes per 10,000 Population	14	19	80.0
			Property Crimes per 10,000 Population	347	15	69.0
Open Spaces	9	77.45	Population Density (Persons/Sq. Mile)	1214	13	84.5
			Average Rooms per Housing Unit	6.4	9	70.4
Education	2	92.95	% High School Enrollment/Completion	98.6%	1	100.0
			% College Graduates	46.8%	2	85.9
Commute	33	36.75	Average Work Commute in Minutes	21	25	63.6
			% Commuting on Public Transportation	1.4%	38	9.9
Community Stability	41	27.85	% Living in Same House as in 1979	15.4%	46	5.6
			% Living in Same County as in 1985	69.2%	38	50.1

Metropolitan Area Suburb Rankings
MINNEAPOLIS-ST. PAUL

Composite: **Rank** 16 / 47 *Score* 61.01 **WHITE BEAR LAKE (MN)**

CATEGORY	RANK	SCORE	STATISTIC	VALUE	RANK	SCORE
Economics	24	53.35	Median Household Income	$39,062	28	40.6
			% of Families Above Poverty Level	96.9%	20	66.1
Affordable Housing	25	70.15	Median Home Value	$87,900	22	80.6
			Median Rent	$538	27	59.7
Crime	25	68.00	Violent Crimes per 10,000 Population	12	12	83.3
			Property Crimes per 10,000 Population	469	33	52.7
Open Spaces	31	48.30	Population Density (Persons/Sq. Mile)	3032	34	48.5
			Average Rooms per Housing Unit	5.8	23	48.1
Education	18	61.10	% High School Enrollment/Completion	96.2%	11	82.1
			% College Graduates	28.0%	19	40.1
Commute	20	46.85	Average Work Commute in Minutes	20	15	72.7
			% Commuting on Public Transportation	2.3%	24	21.0
Community Stability	11	79.30	% Living in Same House as in 1979	39.1%	15	76.0
			% Living in Same County as in 1985	80.6%	15	82.6

Composite: **Rank** 17 / 47 *Score* 60.24 **CRYSTAL (MN)**

CATEGORY	RANK	SCORE	STATISTIC	VALUE	RANK	SCORE
Economics	25	48.25	Median Household Income	$37,093	34	32.1
			% of Families Above Poverty Level	96.8%	22	64.4
Affordable Housing	9	82.30	Median Home Value	$77,300	4	93.1
			Median Rent	$504	16	71.5
Crime	32	62.50	Violent Crimes per 10,000 Population	28	40	56.7
			Property Crimes per 10,000 Population	352	19	68.3
Open Spaces	39	33.70	Population Density (Persons/Sq. Mile)	4137	42	26.7
			Average Rooms per Housing Unit	5.6	31	40.7
Education	26	44.15	% High School Enrollment/Completion	95.1%	20	73.9
			% College Graduates	17.4%	37	14.4
Commute	17	53.65	Average Work Commute in Minutes	20	15	72.7
			% Commuting on Public Transportation	3.4%	16	34.6
Community Stability	2	97.10	% Living in Same House as in 1979	45.6%	3	95.3
			% Living in Same County as in 1985	86.3%	4	98.9

Composite: **Rank** 18 / 47 *Score* 60.23 **APPLE VALLEY (MN)**

CATEGORY	RANK	SCORE	STATISTIC	VALUE	RANK	SCORE
Economics	10	80.95	Median Household Income	$49,981	7	87.3
			% of Families Above Poverty Level	97.4%	17	74.6
Affordable Housing	37	52.90	Median Home Value	$101,300	36	64.8
			Median Rent	$592	37	41.0
Crime	9	79.60	Violent Crimes per 10,000 Population	12	12	83.3
			Property Crimes per 10,000 Population	295	8	75.9
Open Spaces	10	75.30	Population Density (Persons/Sq. Mile)	1995	21	69.1
			Average Rooms per Housing Unit	6.7	4	81.5
Education	15	61.90	% High School Enrollment/Completion	93.6%	29	62.7
			% College Graduates	36.6%	10	61.1
Commute	35	36.50	Average Work Commute in Minutes	22	35	54.5
			% Commuting on Public Transportation	2.1%	27	18.5
Community Stability	39	34.45	% Living in Same House as in 1979	22.8%	39	27.6
			% Living in Same County as in 1985	66.1%	40	41.3

Metropolitan Area Suburb Rankings
MINNEAPOLIS-ST. PAUL

Composite: **Rank** 19 / 47 **Score** 60.16   ST. LOUIS PARK (MN)

CATEGORY	RANK	SCORE	STATISTIC	VALUE	RANK	SCORE
Economics	27	44.15	Median Household Income	$34,778	38	22.2
			% of Families Above Poverty Level	96.9%	20	66.1
Affordable Housing	27	69.80	Median Home Value	$86,700	16	82.0
			Median Rent	$544	30	57.6
Crime	32	62.50	Violent Crimes per 10,000 Population	21	32	68.3
			Property Crimes per 10,000 Population	439	29	56.7
Open Spaces	43	26.80	Population Density (Persons/Sq. Mile)	4087	41	27.7
			Average Rooms per Housing Unit	5.2	44	25.9
Education	17	61.40	% High School Enrollment/Completion	93.9%	27	64.9
			% College Graduates	35.3%	11	57.9
Commute	3	85.55	Average Work Commute in Minutes	18	2	90.9
			% Commuting on Public Transportation	7.1%	2	80.2
Community Stability	20	70.95	% Living in Same House as in 1979	35.4%	22	65.0
			% Living in Same County as in 1985	78.6%	20	76.9

Composite: **Rank** 20 / 47 **Score** 59.36   CHAMPLIN (MN)

CATEGORY	RANK	SCORE	STATISTIC	VALUE	RANK	SCORE
Economics	17	71.50	Median Household Income	$43,218	19	58.3
			% of Families Above Poverty Level	98.0%	8	84.7
Affordable Housing	18	74.80	Median Home Value	$88,200	24	80.2
			Median Rent	$510	21	69.4
Crime	13	77.75	Violent Crimes per 10,000 Population	15	21	78.3
			Property Crimes per 10,000 Population	285	6	77.2
Open Spaces	15	69.10	Population Density (Persons/Sq. Mile)	2061	23	67.8
			Average Rooms per Housing Unit	6.4	9	70.4
Education	28	43.95	% High School Enrollment/Completion	94.5%	24	69.4
			% College Graduates	19.1%	30	18.5
Commute	44	21.45	Average Work Commute in Minutes	26	45	18.2
			% Commuting on Public Transportation	2.6%	22	24.7
Community Stability	32	56.95	% Living in Same House as in 1979	25.2%	35	34.7
			% Living in Same County as in 1985	79.4%	16	79.2

Composite: **Rank** 21 / 47 **Score** 58.84   STILLWATER (MN)

CATEGORY	RANK	SCORE	STATISTIC	VALUE	RANK	SCORE
Economics	33	34.85	Median Household Income	$39,139	27	40.9
			% of Families Above Poverty Level	94.7%	38	28.8
Affordable Housing	8	82.85	Median Home Value	$89,700	26	78.5
			Median Rent	$459	7	87.2
Crime	N/A	N/A	Violent Crimes per 10,000 Population	N/A	N/A	N/A
			Property Crimes per 10,000 Population	N/A	N/A	N/A
Open Spaces	26	58.45	Population Density (Persons/Sq. Mile)	2575	30	57.6
			Average Rooms per Housing Unit	6.1	18	59.3
Education	19	61.00	% High School Enrollment/Completion	95.9%	17	79.9
			% College Graduates	28.8%	17	42.1
Commute	26	42.15	Average Work Commute in Minutes	19	7	81.8
			% Commuting on Public Transportation	0.8%	42	2.5
Community Stability	18	73.75	% Living in Same House as in 1979	39.2%	14	76.3
			% Living in Same County as in 1985	76.6%	24	71.2

Metropolitan Area Suburb Rankings
MINNEAPOLIS-ST. PAUL

Composite: *Rank* 22 / 47 *Score* 58.32   **HASTINGS (MN)**

CATEGORY	RANK	SCORE	STATISTIC	VALUE	RANK	SCORE
Economics	29	39.30	Median Household Income	$36,091	37	27.8
			% of Families Above Poverty Level	96.0%	30	50.8
Affordable Housing	4	89.25	Median Home Value	$83,800	10	85.4
			Median Rent	$442	2	93.1
Crime	16	74.65	Violent Crimes per 10,000 Population	13	14	81.7
			Property Crimes per 10,000 Population	357	20	67.6
Open Spaces	23	61.95	Population Density (Persons/Sq. Mile)	1654	17	75.8
			Average Rooms per Housing Unit	5.8	23	48.1
Education	40	28.35	% High School Enrollment/Completion	91.1%	38	44.0
			% College Graduates	16.7%	39	12.7
Commute	24	43.75	Average Work Commute in Minutes	20	15	72.7
			% Commuting on Public Transportation	1.8%	34	14.8
Community Stability	19	71.00	% Living in Same House as in 1979	33.4%	24	59.1
			% Living in Same County as in 1985	80.7%	14	82.9

Composite: *Rank* 23 / 47 *Score* 58.09   **ANDOVER (MN)**

CATEGORY	RANK	SCORE	STATISTIC	VALUE	RANK	SCORE
Economics	13	76.90	Median Household Income	$46,515	11	72.4
			% of Families Above Poverty Level	97.8%	12	81.4
Affordable Housing	38	52.40	Median Home Value	$96,000	29	71.1
			Median Rent	$613	41	33.7
Crime	18	73.10	Violent Crimes per 10,000 Population	20	30	70.0
			Property Crimes per 10,000 Population	293	7	76.2
Open Spaces	1	99.85	Population Density (Persons/Sq. Mile)	446	3	99.7
			Average Rooms per Housing Unit	7.2	1	100.0
Education	37	29.60	% High School Enrollment/Completion	91.4%	35	46.3
			% College Graduates	16.8%	38	12.9
Commute	46	10.70	Average Work Commute in Minutes	27	46	9.1
			% Commuting on Public Transportation	1.6%	36	12.3
Community Stability	24	64.10	% Living in Same House as in 1979	32.3%	27	55.8
			% Living in Same County as in 1985	77.0%	22	72.4

Composite: *Rank* 24 / 47 *Score* 57.85   **ROBBINSDALE (MN)**

CATEGORY	RANK	SCORE	STATISTIC	VALUE	RANK	SCORE
Economics	30	38.90	Median Household Income	$33,107	41	15.1
			% of Families Above Poverty Level	96.7%	23	62.7
Affordable Housing	10	82.25	Median Home Value	$76,500	3	94.0
			Median Rent	$507	17	70.5
Crime	37	50.75	Violent Crimes per 10,000 Population	26	37	60.0
			Property Crimes per 10,000 Population	553	38	41.5
Open Spaces	44	19.65	Population Density (Persons/Sq. Mile)	5181	45	6.0
			Average Rooms per Housing Unit	5.4	38	33.3
Education	29	43.85	% High School Enrollment/Completion	94.4%	25	68.7
			% College Graduates	19.3%	29	19.0
Commute	5	76.70	Average Work Commute in Minutes	19	7	81.8
			% Commuting on Public Transportation	6.4%	5	71.6
Community Stability	6	92.85	% Living in Same House as in 1979	42.7%	10	86.6
			% Living in Same County as in 1985	86.4%	3	99.1

Metropolitan Area Suburb Rankings
MINNEAPOLIS-ST. PAUL

Composite: *Rank* 25 / 47 *Score* 57.31   **NORTH ST. PAUL (MN)**

CATEGORY	RANK	SCORE	STATISTIC	VALUE	RANK	SCORE
Economics	35	32.45	Median Household Income	$37,617	32	34.4
			% of Families Above Poverty Level	94.8%	37	30.5
Affordable Housing	5	88.45	Median Home Value	$81,000	8	88.7
			Median Rent	$456	5	88.2
Crime	20	72.80	Violent Crimes per 10,000 Population	18	29	73.3
			Property Crimes per 10,000 Population	322	12	72.3
Open Spaces	40	32.20	Population Density (Persons/Sq. Mile)	4287	44	23.7
			Average Rooms per Housing Unit	5.6	31	40.7
Education	42	24.35	% High School Enrollment/Completion	89.7%	44	33.6
			% College Graduates	17.7%	36	15.1
Commute	16	53.85	Average Work Commute in Minutes	19	7	81.8
			% Commuting on Public Transportation	2.7%	20	25.9
Community Stability	3	97.05	% Living in Same House as in 1979	45.4%	5	94.7
			% Living in Same County as in 1985	86.5%	2	99.4

Composite: *Rank* 26 / 47 *Score* 57.09   **PRIOR LAKE (MN)**

CATEGORY	RANK	SCORE	STATISTIC	VALUE	RANK	SCORE
Economics	19	62.00	Median Household Income	$45,489	15	68.1
			% of Families Above Poverty Level	96.3%	26	55.9
Affordable Housing	34	58.25	Median Home Value	$99,900	35	66.5
			Median Rent	$566	33	50.0
Crime	27	66.60	Violent Crimes per 10,000 Population	9	7	88.3
			Property Crimes per 10,000 Population	528	37	44.9
Open Spaces	8	82.65	Population Density (Persons/Sq. Mile)	878	10	91.2
			Average Rooms per Housing Unit	6.5	7	74.1
Education	13	65.75	% High School Enrollment/Completion	98.2%	3	97.0
			% College Graduates	25.7%	21	34.5
Commute	45	18.20	Average Work Commute in Minutes	24	42	36.4
			% Commuting on Public Transportation	0.6%	46	0.0
Community Stability	36	46.20	% Living in Same House as in 1979	26.5%	33	38.6
			% Living in Same County as in 1985	70.5%	37	53.8

Composite: *Rank* 27 / 47 *Score* 56.78   **SOUTH ST. PAUL (MN)**

CATEGORY	RANK	SCORE	STATISTIC	VALUE	RANK	SCORE
Economics	45	14.70	Median Household Income	$30,913	44	5.7
			% of Families Above Poverty Level	94.4%	40	23.7
Affordable Housing	1	100.00	Median Home Value	$71,400	1	100.0
			Median Rent	$422	1	100.0
Crime	29	64.80	Violent Crimes per 10,000 Population	16	23	76.7
			Property Crimes per 10,000 Population	468	31	52.9
Open Spaces	38	34.20	Population Density (Persons/Sq. Mile)	3524	37	38.8
			Average Rooms per Housing Unit	5.3	41	29.6
Education	43	22.00	% High School Enrollment/Completion	91.1%	38	44.0
			% College Graduates	11.5%	47	0.0
Commute	7	67.05	Average Work Commute in Minutes	18	2	90.9
			% Commuting on Public Transportation	4.1%	11	43.2
Community Stability	5	94.70	% Living in Same House as in 1979	46.8%	2	98.8
			% Living in Same County as in 1985	83.4%	8	90.6

Composite: *Rank* 28 / 47 *Score* 56.73   **NEW HOPE** (MN)

CATEGORY	RANK	SCORE	STATISTIC	VALUE	RANK	SCORE
Economics	40	28.35	Median Household Income	$36,096	36	27.9
			% of Families Above Poverty Level	94.7%	38	28.8
Affordable Housing	26	69.90	Median Home Value	$92,700	27	74.9
			Median Rent	$523	25	64.9
Crime	10	77.95	Violent Crimes per 10,000 Population	15	21	78.3
			Property Crimes per 10,000 Population	282	5	77.6
Open Spaces	41	28.65	Population Density (Persons/Sq. Mile)	4273	43	24.0
			Average Rooms per Housing Unit	5.4	38	33.3
Education	22	53.85	% High School Enrollment/Completion	95.1%	20	73.9
			% College Graduates	25.4%	22	33.8
Commute	13	60.40	Average Work Commute in Minutes	20	15	72.7
			% Commuting on Public Transportation	4.5%	7	48.1
Community Stability	14	78.00	% Living in Same House as in 1979	36.7%	18	68.8
			% Living in Same County as in 1985	82.2%	9	87.2

Composite: *Rank* 29 / 47 *Score* 56.41   **LAKEVILLE** (MN)

CATEGORY	RANK	SCORE	STATISTIC	VALUE	RANK	SCORE
Economics	15	74.35	Median Household Income	$44,920	16	65.6
			% of Families Above Poverty Level	97.9%	10	83.1
Affordable Housing	40	50.95	Median Home Value	$96,300	31	70.7
			Median Rent	$620	42	31.2
Crime	10	77.95	Violent Crimes per 10,000 Population	8	6	90.0
			Property Crimes per 10,000 Population	370	21	65.9
Open Spaces	6	84.50	Population Density (Persons/Sq. Mile)	687	7	94.9
			Average Rooms per Housing Unit	6.5	7	74.1
Education	24	47.90	% High School Enrollment/Completion	95.1%	20	73.9
			% College Graduates	20.5%	25	21.9
Commute	40	28.50	Average Work Commute in Minutes	22	35	54.5
			% Commuting on Public Transportation	0.8%	42	2.5
Community Stability	40	30.70	% Living in Same House as in 1979	21.9%	41	24.9
			% Living in Same County as in 1985	64.4%	41	36.5

Composite: *Rank* 30 / 47 *Score* 55.62   **EAGAN** (MN)

CATEGORY	RANK	SCORE	STATISTIC	VALUE	RANK	SCORE
Economics	12	77.15	Median Household Income	$46,612	10	72.9
			% of Families Above Poverty Level	97.8%	12	81.4
Affordable Housing	41	48.70	Median Home Value	$104,900	38	60.6
			Median Rent	$604	38	36.8
Crime	8	79.70	Violent Crimes per 10,000 Population	10	9	86.7
			Property Crimes per 10,000 Population	319	10	72.7
Open Spaces	19	67.50	Population Density (Persons/Sq. Mile)	1470	14	79.4
			Average Rooms per Housing Unit	6.0	21	55.6
Education	10	74.00	% High School Enrollment/Completion	96.0%	15	80.6
			% College Graduates	39.2%	9	67.4
Commute	25	42.30	Average Work Commute in Minutes	21	25	63.6
			% Commuting on Public Transportation	2.3%	24	21.0
Community Stability	47	0.00	% Living in Same House as in 1979	13.5%	47	0.0
			% Living in Same County as in 1985	51.6%	47	0.0

Metropolitan Area Suburb Rankings
MINNEAPOLIS-ST. PAUL

Composite: Rank 31 / 47 ***Score*** 55.54   **RICHFIELD** (MN)

CATEGORY	RANK	SCORE	STATISTIC	VALUE	RANK	SCORE
Economics	36	32.30	Median Household Income	$32,405	42	12.1
			% of Families Above Poverty Level	96.1%	29	52.5
Affordable Housing	7	86.00	Median Home Value	$84,800	12	84.2
			Median Rent	$457	6	87.8
Crime	36	50.85	Violent Crimes per 10,000 Population	33	42	48.3
			Property Crimes per 10,000 Population	464	30	53.4
Open Spaces	45	15.90	Population Density (Persons/Sq. Mile)	5190	46	5.9
			Average Rooms per Housing Unit	5.2	44	25.9
Education	35	31.60	% High School Enrollment/Completion	90.6%	42	40.3
			% College Graduates	20.9%	23	22.9
Commute	4	80.00	Average Work Commute in Minutes	18	2	90.9
			% Commuting on Public Transportation	6.2%	6	69.1
Community Stability	7	92.10	% Living in Same House as in 1979	43.9%	7	90.2
			% Living in Same County as in 1985	84.6%	7	94.0

Composite: Rank 32 / 47 ***Score*** 55.45   **MAPLEWOOD** (MN)

CATEGORY	RANK	SCORE	STATISTIC	VALUE	RANK	SCORE
Economics	37	29.55	Median Household Income	$37,856	30	35.4
			% of Families Above Poverty Level	94.4%	40	23.7
Affordable Housing	19	74.75	Median Home Value	$87,800	21	80.7
			Median Rent	$512	22	68.8
Crime	41	47.65	Violent Crimes per 10,000 Population	21	32	68.3
			Property Crimes per 10,000 Population	662	44	27.0
Open Spaces	27	56.95	Population Density (Persons/Sq. Mile)	1787	19	73.2
			Average Rooms per Housing Unit	5.6	31	40.7
Education	25	46.50	% High School Enrollment/Completion	94.8%	23	71.6
			% College Graduates	20.3%	27	21.4
Commute	17	53.65	Average Work Commute in Minutes	20	15	72.7
			% Commuting on Public Transportation	3.4%	16	34.6
Community Stability	12	79.10	% Living in Same House as in 1979	37.9%	16	72.4
			% Living in Same County as in 1985	81.7%	11	85.8

Composite: Rank 33 / 47 ***Score*** 54.06   **FRIDLEY** (MN)

CATEGORY	RANK	SCORE	STATISTIC	VALUE	RANK	SCORE
Economics	34	33.35	Median Household Income	$36,855	35	31.1
			% of Families Above Poverty Level	95.1%	35	35.6
Affordable Housing	13	80.40	Median Home Value	$86,100	14	82.7
			Median Rent	$485	10	78.1
Crime	40	48.15	Violent Crimes per 10,000 Population	24	34	63.3
			Property Crimes per 10,000 Population	617	42	33.0
Open Spaces	33	46.90	Population Density (Persons/Sq. Mile)	2802	32	53.1
			Average Rooms per Housing Unit	5.6	31	40.7
Education	31	40.45	% High School Enrollment/Completion	93.1%	31	59.0
			% College Graduates	20.5%	25	21.9
Commute	15	54.25	Average Work Commute in Minutes	20	15	72.7
			% Commuting on Public Transportation	3.5%	13	35.8
Community Stability	17	74.95	% Living in Same House as in 1979	42.1%	11	84.9
			% Living in Same County as in 1985	74.4%	32	65.0

Metropolitan Area Suburb Rankings
MINNEAPOLIS-ST. PAUL

Composite: **Rank** 34 / 47 *Score* 53.69   **OAKDALE (MN)**

CATEGORY	RANK	SCORE	STATISTIC	VALUE	RANK	SCORE
Economics	28	43.20	Median Household Income	$41,049	22	49.1
			% of Families Above Poverty Level	95.2%	34	37.3
Affordable Housing	6	86.95	Median Home Value	$87,700	20	80.8
			Median Rent	$442	2	93.1
Crime	34	59.55	Violent Crimes per 10,000 Population	26	37	60.0
			Property Crimes per 10,000 Population	421	28	59.1
Open Spaces	24	59.95	Population Density (Persons/Sq. Mile)	1856	20	71.8
			Average Rooms per Housing Unit	5.8	23	48.1
Education	21	54.00	% High School Enrollment/Completion	96.8%	9	86.6
			% College Graduates	20.3%	27	21.4
Commute	22	45.00	Average Work Commute in Minutes	20	15	72.7
			% Commuting on Public Transportation	2.0%	32	17.3
Community Stability	42	27.20	% Living in Same House as in 1979	25.3%	34	35.0
			% Living in Same County as in 1985	58.4%	44	19.4

Composite: **Rank** 35 / 47 *Score* 53.43   **COON RAPIDS (MN)**

CATEGORY	RANK	SCORE	STATISTIC	VALUE	RANK	SCORE
Economics	22	53.80	Median Household Income	$42,069	20	53.4
			% of Families Above Poverty Level	96.2%	27	54.2
Affordable Housing	24	70.10	Median Home Value	$82,700	9	86.7
			Median Rent	$556	32	53.5
Crime	28	66.45	Violent Crimes per 10,000 Population	14	19	80.0
			Property Crimes per 10,000 Population	468	31	52.9
Open Spaces	22	62.80	Population Density (Persons/Sq. Mile)	2322	27	62.6
			Average Rooms per Housing Unit	6.2	15	63.0
Education	38	28.50	% High School Enrollment/Completion	91.2%	37	44.8
			% College Graduates	16.5%	40	12.2
Commute	36	34.85	Average Work Commute in Minutes	24	42	36.4
			% Commuting on Public Transportation	3.3%	18	33.3
Community Stability	30	57.50	% Living in Same House as in 1979	29.1%	31	46.3
			% Living in Same County as in 1985	75.7%	27	68.7

Composite: **Rank** 36 / 47 *Score* 53.16   **INVER GROVE HEIGHTS (MN)**

CATEGORY	RANK	SCORE	STATISTIC	VALUE	RANK	SCORE
Economics	39	28.60	Median Household Income	$39,378	26	41.9
			% of Families Above Poverty Level	93.9%	43	15.3
Affordable Housing	28	65.65	Median Home Value	$93,500	28	74.0
			Median Rent	$545	31	57.3
Crime	21	70.10	Violent Crimes per 10,000 Population	20	30	70.0
			Property Crimes per 10,000 Population	338	14	70.2
Open Spaces	17	68.70	Population Density (Persons/Sq. Mile)	784	8	93.0
			Average Rooms per Housing Unit	5.7	28	44.4
Education	30	40.75	% High School Enrollment/Completion	93.8%	28	64.2
			% College Graduates	18.6%	32	17.3
Commute	28	41.05	Average Work Commute in Minutes	21	25	63.6
			% Commuting on Public Transportation	2.1%	27	18.5
Community Stability	31	57.30	% Living in Same House as in 1979	30.3%	29	49.9
			% Living in Same County as in 1985	74.3%	33	64.7

Metropolitan Area Suburb Rankings
MINNEAPOLIS-ST. PAUL

Composite: Rank 37 / 47 Score 52.79   WEST ST. PAUL (MN)

CATEGORY	RANK	SCORE	STATISTIC	VALUE	RANK	SCORE
Economics	38	29.45	Median Household Income	$30,683	45	4.7
			% of Families Above Poverty Level	96.2%	27	54.2
Affordable Housing	14	80.20	Median Home Value	$84,700	11	84.4
			Median Rent	$491	13	76.0
Crime	42	47.25	Violent Crimes per 10,000 Population	26	37	60.0
			Property Crimes per 10,000 Population	606	41	34.5
Open Spaces	42	27.35	Population Density (Persons/Sq. Mile)	3845	39	32.5
			Average Rooms per Housing Unit	5.1	46	22.2
Education	36	31.25	% High School Enrollment/Completion	91.3%	36	45.5
			% College Graduates	18.5%	33	17.0
Commute	1	87.05	Average Work Commute in Minutes	17	1	100.0
			% Commuting on Public Transportation	6.6%	3	74.1
Community Stability	23	67.00	% Living in Same House as in 1979	36.7%	18	68.8
			% Living in Same County as in 1985	74.5%	31	65.2

Composite: Rank 38 / 47 Score 51.79   SHAKOPEE (MN)

CATEGORY	RANK	SCORE	STATISTIC	VALUE	RANK	SCORE
Economics	31	38.75	Median Household Income	$37,783	31	35.1
			% of Families Above Poverty Level	95.5%	32	42.4
Affordable Housing	15	80.10	Median Home Value	$86,000	13	82.8
			Median Rent	$487	11	77.4
Crime	38	49.05	Violent Crimes per 10,000 Population	28	40	56.7
			Property Crimes per 10,000 Population	554	39	41.4
Open Spaces	11	73.90	Population Density (Persons/Sq. Mile)	444	2	99.7
			Average Rooms per Housing Unit	5.8	23	48.1
Education	46	11.40	% High School Enrollment/Completion	88.1%	46	21.6
			% College Graduates	12.0%	46	1.2
Commute	31	40.90	Average Work Commute in Minutes	19	7	81.8
			% Commuting on Public Transportation	0.6%	46	0.0
Community Stability	22	68.45	% Living in Same House as in 1979	36.6%	20	68.5
			% Living in Same County as in 1985	75.6%	28	68.4

Composite: Rank 39 / 47 Score 51.12   BURNSVILLE (MN)

CATEGORY	RANK	SCORE	STATISTIC	VALUE	RANK	SCORE
Economics	20	59.70	Median Household Income	$43,620	18	60.1
			% of Families Above Poverty Level	96.5%	25	59.3
Affordable Housing	39	51.85	Median Home Value	$107,800	39	57.2
			Median Rent	$576	36	46.5
Crime	30	63.95	Violent Crimes per 10,000 Population	13	14	81.7
			Property Crimes per 10,000 Population	518	36	46.2
Open Spaces	25	59.80	Population Density (Persons/Sq. Mile)	2062	24	67.7
			Average Rooms per Housing Unit	5.9	22	51.9
Education	20	58.70	% High School Enrollment/Completion	93.5%	30	61.9
			% College Graduates	34.3%	13	55.5
Commute	28	41.05	Average Work Commute in Minutes	21	25	63.6
			% Commuting on Public Transportation	2.1%	27	18.5
Community Stability	44	22.80	% Living in Same House as in 1979	21.5%	42	23.7
			% Living in Same County as in 1985	59.3%	43	21.9

Metropolitan Area Suburb Rankings
MINNEAPOLIS-ST. PAUL

Composite: *Rank* 40 / 47 *Score* 51.02 — BLAINE (MN)

CATEGORY	RANK	SCORE	STATISTIC	VALUE	RANK	SCORE
Economics	26	47.75	Median Household Income	$40,404	23	46.3
			% of Families Above Poverty Level	95.9%	31	49.2
Affordable Housing	20	74.45	Median Home Value	$80,300	7	89.5
			Median Rent	$539	29	59.4
Crime	35	53.80	Violent Crimes per 10,000 Population	16	23	76.7
			Property Crimes per 10,000 Population	633	43	30.9
Open Spaces	12	72.55	Population Density (Persons/Sq. Mile)	1148	11	85.8
			Average Rooms per Housing Unit	6.1	18	59.3
Education	45	19.05	% High School Enrollment/Completion	89.3%	45	30.6
			% College Graduates	14.6%	42	7.5
Commute	41	27.45	Average Work Commute in Minutes	24	42	36.4
			% Commuting on Public Transportation	2.1%	27	18.5
Community Stability	25	62.10	% Living in Same House as in 1979	32.4%	25	56.1
			% Living in Same County as in 1985	75.5%	29	68.1

Composite: *Rank* 41 / 47 *Score* 50.80 — MOUNDS VIEW (MN)

CATEGORY	RANK	SCORE	STATISTIC	VALUE	RANK	SCORE
Economics	32	37.30	Median Household Income	$37,117	33	32.2
			% of Families Above Poverty Level	95.5%	32	42.4
Affordable Housing	16	78.55	Median Home Value	$86,900	17	81.8
			Median Rent	$493	14	75.3
Crime	22	68.90	Violent Crimes per 10,000 Population	17	26	75.0
			Property Crimes per 10,000 Population	393	25	62.8
Open Spaces	36	40.85	Population Density (Persons/Sq. Mile)	3041	35	48.4
			Average Rooms per Housing Unit	5.4	38	33.3
Education	39	28.55	% High School Enrollment/Completion	90.7%	41	41.0
			% College Graduates	18.1%	34	16.1
Commute	28	41.05	Average Work Commute in Minutes	21	25	63.6
			% Commuting on Public Transportation	2.1%	27	18.5
Community Stability	26	60.40	% Living in Same House as in 1979	35.4%	22	65.0
			% Living in Same County as in 1985	71.2%	36	55.8

Composite: *Rank* 42 / 47 *Score* 47.68 — CHASKA (MN)

CATEGORY	RANK	SCORE	STATISTIC	VALUE	RANK	SCORE
Economics	44	15.90	Median Household Income	$34,235	39	19.9
			% of Families Above Poverty Level	93.7%	44	11.9
Affordable Housing	17	76.15	Median Home Value	$88,900	25	79.4
			Median Rent	$500	15	72.9
Crime	23	68.85	Violent Crimes per 10,000 Population	17	26	75.0
			Property Crimes per 10,000 Population	394	26	62.7
Open Spaces	20	66.40	Population Density (Persons/Sq. Mile)	828	9	92.1
			Average Rooms per Housing Unit	5.6	31	40.7
Education	23	48.70	% High School Enrollment/Completion	96.1%	14	81.3
			% College Graduates	18.1%	34	16.1
Commute	38	33.05	Average Work Commute in Minutes	21	25	63.6
			% Commuting on Public Transportation	0.8%	42	2.5
Community Stability	43	24.70	% Living in Same House as in 1979	19.5%	43	17.8
			% Living in Same County as in 1985	62.7%	42	31.6

Metropolitan Area Suburb Rankings
MINNEAPOLIS-ST. PAUL

Composite: **Rank** 43 / 47 **Score** 46.96   **BROOKLYN CENTER** (MN)

CATEGORY	RANK	SCORE	STATISTIC	VALUE	RANK	SCORE
Economics	42	19.95	Median Household Income	$34,168	40	19.6
			% of Families Above Poverty Level	94.2%	42	20.3
Affordable Housing	12	80.60	Median Home Value	$78,700	5	91.4
			Median Rent	$509	20	69.8
Crime	46	6.65	Violent Crimes per 10,000 Population	54	45	13.3
			Property Crimes per 10,000 Population	865	46	0.0
Open Spaces	37	36.80	Population Density (Persons/Sq. Mile)	3636	38	36.6
			Average Rooms per Housing Unit	5.5	36	37.0
Education	44	21.05	% High School Enrollment/Completion	90.0%	43	35.8
			% College Graduates	14.1%	44	6.3
Commute	6	68.85	Average Work Commute in Minutes	21	25	63.6
			% Commuting on Public Transportation	6.6%	3	74.1
Community Stability	4	94.80	% Living in Same House as in 1979	45.6%	3	95.3
			% Living in Same County as in 1985	84.7%	6	94.3

Composite: **Rank** 44 / 47 **Score** 46.75   **BROOKLYN PARK** (MN)

CATEGORY	RANK	SCORE	STATISTIC	VALUE	RANK	SCORE
Economics	41	22.30	Median Household Income	$40,018	25	44.6
			% of Families Above Poverty Level	93.0%	47	0.0
Affordable Housing	11	81.00	Median Home Value	$88,100	23	80.4
			Median Rent	$475	9	81.6
Crime	45	23.30	Violent Crimes per 10,000 Population	62	46	0.0
			Property Crimes per 10,000 Population	515	35	46.6
Open Spaces	29	55.05	Population Density (Persons/Sq. Mile)	2164	25	65.7
			Average Rooms per Housing Unit	5.7	28	44.4
Education	32	36.80	% High School Enrollment/Completion	92.0%	34	50.7
			% College Graduates	20.9%	23	22.9
Commute	19	49.45	Average Work Commute in Minutes	22	35	54.5
			% Commuting on Public Transportation	4.2%	10	44.4
Community Stability	28	59.35	% Living in Same House as in 1979	27.0%	32	40.1
			% Living in Same County as in 1985	79.2%	18	78.6

Composite: **Rank** 45 / 47 **Score** 45.83   **HOPKINS** (MN)

CATEGORY	RANK	SCORE	STATISTIC	VALUE	RANK	SCORE
Economics	43	16.10	Median Household Income	$29,584	47	0.0
			% of Families Above Poverty Level	94.9%	36	32.2
Affordable Housing	21	74.35	Median Home Value	$86,100	14	82.7
			Median Rent	$520	23	66.0
Crime	31	62.80	Violent Crimes per 10,000 Population	25	36	61.7
			Property Crimes per 10,000 Population	385	24	63.9
Open Spaces	47	14.25	Population Density (Persons/Sq. Mile)	4046	40	28.5
			Average Rooms per Housing Unit	4.5	47	0.0
Education	26	44.15	% High School Enrollment/Completion	92.3%	32	53.0
			% College Graduates	26.0%	20	35.3
Commute	10	63.35	Average Work Commute in Minutes	18	2	90.9
			% Commuting on Public Transportation	3.5%	13	35.8
Community Stability	37	45.80	% Living in Same House as in 1979	24.4%	36	32.3
			% Living in Same County as in 1985	72.4%	35	59.3

Metropolitan Area Suburb Rankings
MINNEAPOLIS-ST. PAUL

Composite: **Rank** 46 / 47 **Score** 44.94   COLUMBIA HEIGHTS (MN)

CATEGORY	RANK	SCORE	STATISTIC	VALUE	RANK	SCORE
Economics	47	7.00	Median Household Income	$30,469	46	3.8
			% of Families Above Poverty Level	93.6%	45	10.2
Affordable Housing	2	91.80	Median Home Value	$74,100	2	96.8
			Median Rent	$460	8	86.8
Crime	44	37.40	Violent Crimes per 10,000 Population	41	44	35.0
			Property Crimes per 10,000 Population	566	40	39.8
Open Spaces	46	14.80	Population Density (Persons/Sq. Mile)	5486	47	0.0
			Average Rooms per Housing Unit	5.3	41	29.6
Education	47	1.35	% High School Enrollment/Completion	85.2%	47	0.0
			% College Graduates	12.6%	45	2.7
Commute	2	86.35	Average Work Commute in Minutes	20	15	72.7
			% Commuting on Public Transportation	8.7%	1	100.0
Community Stability	16	75.90	% Living in Same House as in 1979	44.3%	6	91.4
			% Living in Same County as in 1985	72.8%	34	60.4

Composite: **Rank** 47 / 47 **Score** 44.09   ANOKA (MN)

CATEGORY	RANK	SCORE	STATISTIC	VALUE	RANK	SCORE
Economics	46	8.75	Median Household Income	$31,289	43	7.3
			% of Families Above Poverty Level	93.6%	45	10.2
Affordable Housing	3	91.20	Median Home Value	$79,300	6	90.7
			Median Rent	$446	4	91.7
Crime	43	43.85	Violent Crimes per 10,000 Population	39	43	38.3
			Property Crimes per 10,000 Population	494	34	49.4
Open Spaces	34	43.35	Population Density (Persons/Sq. Mile)	2601	31	57.1
			Average Rooms per Housing Unit	5.3	41	29.6
Education	41	27.60	% High School Enrollment/Completion	91.0%	40	43.3
			% College Graduates	16.4%	41	11.9
Commute	37	33.85	Average Work Commute in Minutes	23	38	45.5
			% Commuting on Public Transportation	2.4%	23	22.2
Community Stability	27	60.05	% Living in Same House as in 1979	31.6%	28	53.7
			% Living in Same County as in 1985	74.9%	30	66.4

Metropolitan Area Description
NASHVILLE

STATE: Tennessee

COUNTIES: Cheatham, Davidson, Dickson, Robertson, Rutherford, Sumner, Williamson, Wilson

TOTAL POPULATION: 985,026

POPULATION IN SUBURBS: 496,652 (50.4%)

POPULATION IN Nashville: 488,374 (49.6%)

The NASHVILLE metropolitan area is located in the central part of Tennessee. The suburbs range geographically from Springfield in the north (29 miles from Nashville), to Franklin in the south (20 miles from Nashville), and to Lebanon in the east (31 miles from Nashville). The area is growing in population and had an increase of 15.8% between 1980 and 1990. Summer time high temperatures average in the 80's and winter time lows average in the 20's. Nissan, Tennessee's fifth largest commercial employer, has a automobile manufacturing plant located in the suburb of Smyrna. The high tech firms of AT&T Technologies and Comdata both have facilities located in Brentwood. In 1992, *Fortune* magazine rated the metropolitan area number two for its pro-business attitude. Public transportation in the area is provided on buses by the Metropolitan Transit Authority.

Brentwood is the overall highest rated suburb and also has the highest scores in economics, education, and open spaces. **Brentwood** is also rated the safest suburb with the lowest crime rate. **Springfield** is the suburb with the most affordable housing and also has the highest score in community stability. **Goodlettsville** and **Brentwood** tie for the top rated commute.

The highest ranked suburb overall which also has an affordable housing score of at least 50.00 is **Goodlettsville**.

The highest ranked suburb in the education category which also has an affordable housing score of at least 50.00 is **Franklin**.

The county whose suburbs have the highest average overall score is **Williamson County** (57.73).

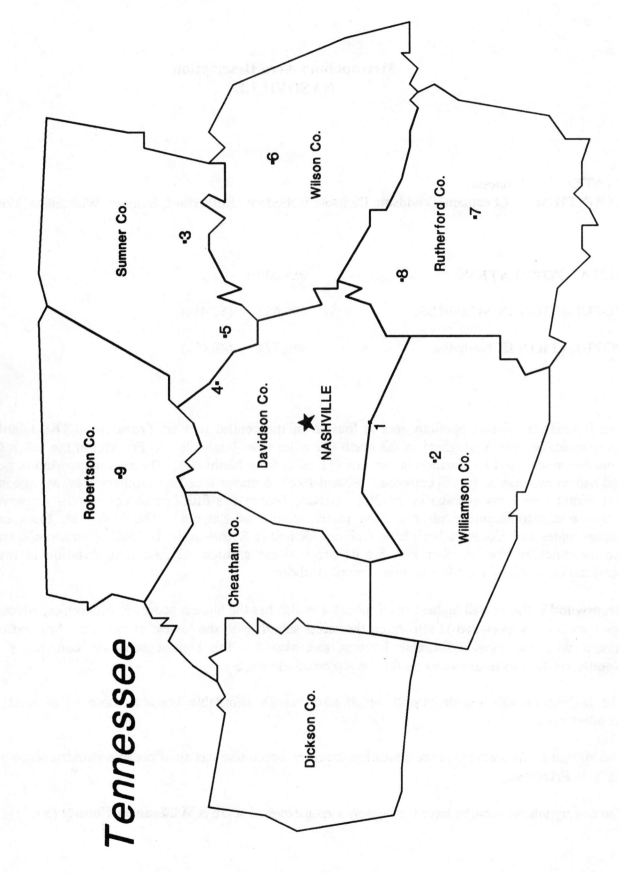

Metropolitan Area Map
NASHVILLE

Tennessee

Robertson Co.

•9

Sumner Co.

•3

Wilson Co.

•6

Cheatham Co.

Davidson Co.

•4

•5

NASHVILLE ★

Dickson Co.

Williamson Co.

•1

•2

Rutherford Co.

•7

•8

Metropolitan Area Suburb Alphabetical Index
NASHVILLE

SUBURB	PAGE	MAP NO.	STATE	COUNTY	POPU-LATION	RANK
BRENTWOOD	442	1	Tennessee	Williamson	16,392	1 / 9
FRANKLIN	443	2	Tennessee	Williamson	20,098	6 / 9
GALLATIN	443	3	Tennessee	Sumner	18,794	5 / 9
GOODLETTSVILLE	442	4	Tennessee	Davidson	11,219	2 / 9
HENDERSONVILLE	442	5	Tennessee	Sumner	32,188	3 / 9
LEBANON	443	6	Tennessee	Wilson	15,208	4 / 9
MURFREESBORO	444	7	Tennessee	Rutherford	44,922	8 / 9
SMYRNA	444	8	Tennessee	Rutherford	13,647	7 / 9
SPRINGFIELD	444	9	Tennessee	Robertson	11,227	9 / 9

Metropolitan Area Suburb Rankings
NASHVILLE

Composite: *Rank* 1 / 9 *Score* 69.01   **BRENTWOOD**

CATEGORY	RANK	SCORE	STATISTIC	VALUE	RANK	SCORE
Economics	1	100.00	Median Household Income	$70,287	1	100.0
			% of Families Above Poverty Level	99.1%	1	100.0
Affordable Housing	9	0.00	Median Home Value	$177,500	9	0.0
			Median Rent	$807	9	0.0
Crime	1	100.00	Violent Crimes per 10,000 Population	14	1	100.0
			Property Crimes per 10,000 Population	259	1	100.0
Open Spaces	1	100.00	Population Density (Persons/Sq. Mile)	564	1	100.0
			Average Rooms per Housing Unit	7.9	1	100.0
Education	1	100.00	% High School Enrollment/Completion	98.8%	1	100.0
			% College Graduates	54.3%	1	100.0
Commute	1	60.00	Average Work Commute in Minutes	20	4	80.0
			% Commuting on Public Transportation	0.5%	3	40.0
Community Stability	7	23.10	% Living in Same House as in 1979	28.0%	6	46.2
			% Living in Same County as in 1985	55.7%	9	0.0

Composite: *Rank* 2 / 9 *Score* 54.55   **GOODLETTSVILLE**

CATEGORY	RANK	SCORE	STATISTIC	VALUE	RANK	SCORE
Economics	3	58.40	Median Household Income	$35,483	3	28.4
			% of Families Above Poverty Level	97.2%	2	88.4
Affordable Housing	6	69.35	Median Home Value	$83,000	6	76.1
			Median Rent	$489	7	62.6
Crime	7	41.30	Violent Crimes per 10,000 Population	57	4	82.6
			Property Crimes per 10,000 Population	1,066	8	0.0
Open Spaces	2	48.60	Population Density (Persons/Sq. Mile)	822	4	75.8
			Average Rooms per Housing Unit	5.7	3	21.4
Education	5	37.40	% High School Enrollment/Completion	90.0%	5	58.1
			% College Graduates	17.8%	5	16.7
Commute	1	60.00	Average Work Commute in Minutes	22	8	60.0
			% Commuting on Public Transportation	0.7%	2	60.0
Community Stability	4	66.80	% Living in Same House as in 1979	33.0%	3	77.5
			% Living in Same County as in 1985	71.7%	4	56.1

Composite: *Rank* 3 / 9 *Score* 54.51   **HENDERSONVILLE**

CATEGORY	RANK	SCORE	STATISTIC	VALUE	RANK	SCORE
Economics	2	60.50	Median Household Income	$38,068	2	33.8
			% of Families Above Poverty Level	97.0%	3	87.2
Affordable Housing	7	67.55	Median Home Value	$85,800	7	73.9
			Median Rent	$496	8	61.2
Crime	2	93.40	Violent Crimes per 10,000 Population	36	2	91.1
			Property Crimes per 10,000 Population	294	2	95.7
Open Spaces	7	24.10	Population Density (Persons/Sq. Mile)	1459	7	16.1
			Average Rooms per Housing Unit	6.0	2	32.1
Education	4	44.50	% High School Enrollment/Completion	91.4%	2	64.8
			% College Graduates	21.1%	4	24.2
Commute	6	50.00	Average Work Commute in Minutes	28	9	0.0
			% Commuting on Public Transportation	1.1%	1	100.0
Community Stability	5	41.50	% Living in Same House as in 1979	28.6%	5	50.0
			% Living in Same County as in 1985	65.1%	6	33.0

Metropolitan Area Suburb Rankings
NASHVILLE

Composite: **Rank** 4 / 9 **Score** 51.57   **LEBANON**

CATEGORY	RANK	SCORE	STATISTIC	VALUE	RANK	SCORE
Economics	7	21.25	Median Household Income	$25,403	8	7.7
			% of Families Above Poverty Level	88.4%	7	34.8
Affordable Housing	3	86.15	Median Home Value	$67,000	3	89.0
			Median Rent	$384	3	83.3
Crime	N/A	N/A	Violent Crimes per 10,000 Population	N/A	N/A	N/A
			Property Crimes per 10,000 Population	N/A	N/A	N/A
Open Spaces	5	40.05	Population Density (Persons/Sq. Mile)	852	5	73.0
			Average Rooms per Housing Unit	5.3	4	7.1
Education	7	15.55	% High School Enrollment/Completion	82.5%	7	22.4
			% College Graduates	14.3%	6	8.7
Commute	4	55.00	Average Work Commute in Minutes	18	1	100.0
			% Commuting on Public Transportation	0.2%	6	10.0
Community Stability	2	91.40	% Living in Same House as in 1979	36.6%	1	100.0
			% Living in Same County as in 1985	79.3%	3	82.8

Composite: **Rank** 5 / 9 **Score** 50.45   **GALLATIN**

CATEGORY	RANK	SCORE	STATISTIC	VALUE	RANK	SCORE
Economics	8	20.25	Median Household Income	$26,498	6	10.0
			% of Families Above Poverty Level	87.7%	8	30.5
Affordable Housing	2	88.50	Median Home Value	$61,700	2	93.3
			Median Rent	$382	2	83.7
Crime	5	67.70	Violent Crimes per 10,000 Population	108	7	61.9
			Property Crimes per 10,000 Population	473	3	73.5
Open Spaces	6	38.25	Population Density (Persons/Sq. Mile)	890	6	69.4
			Average Rooms per Housing Unit	5.3	4	7.1
Education	8	3.75	% High School Enrollment/Completion	78.9%	8	5.2
			% College Graduates	11.5%	7	2.3
Commute	4	55.00	Average Work Commute in Minutes	21	5	70.0
			% Commuting on Public Transportation	0.5%	3	40.0
Community Stability	3	79.70	% Living in Same House as in 1979	32.3%	4	73.1
			% Living in Same County as in 1985	80.3%	2	86.3

Composite: **Rank** 6 / 9 **Score** 46.44   **FRANKLIN**

CATEGORY	RANK	SCORE	STATISTIC	VALUE	RANK	SCORE
Economics	4	47.90	Median Household Income	$32,348	4	22.0
			% of Families Above Poverty Level	94.8%	4	73.8
Affordable Housing	8	65.55	Median Home Value	$95,200	8	66.3
			Median Rent	$478	6	64.8
Crime	4	68.70	Violent Crimes per 10,000 Population	88	6	70.0
			Property Crimes per 10,000 Population	522	4	67.4
Open Spaces	4	43.05	Population Density (Persons/Sq. Mile)	788	3	79.0
			Average Rooms per Housing Unit	5.3	4	7.1
Education	2	52.25	% High School Enrollment/Completion	91.0%	3	62.9
			% College Graduates	28.7%	2	41.6
Commute	8	35.00	Average Work Commute in Minutes	21	5	70.0
			% Commuting on Public Transportation	0.1%	7	0.0
Community Stability	9	12.65	% Living in Same House as in 1979	20.6%	9	0.0
			% Living in Same County as in 1985	62.9%	8	25.3

Metropolitan Area Suburb Rankings
NASHVILLE

Composite: Rank 7 / 9 *Score* 45.09 — SMYRNA

CATEGORY	RANK	SCORE	STATISTIC	VALUE	RANK	SCORE
Economics	5	32.35	Median Household Income	$31,155	5	19.6
			% of Families Above Poverty Level	90.1%	5	45.1
Affordable Housing	5	78.05	Median Home Value	$71,000	4	85.8
			Median Rent	$450	5	70.3
Crime	3	75.70	Violent Crimes per 10,000 Population	36	2	91.1
			Property Crimes per 10,000 Population	579	5	60.3
Open Spaces	3	45.20	Population Density (Persons/Sq. Mile)	742	2	83.3
			Average Rooms per Housing Unit	5.3	4	7.1
Education	6	24.60	% High School Enrollment/Completion	87.8%	6	47.6
			% College Graduates	11.2%	8	1.6
Commute	8	35.00	Average Work Commute in Minutes	21	5	70.0
			% Commuting on Public Transportation	0.1%	7	0.0
Community Stability	6	24.70	% Living in Same House as in 1979	21.7%	8	6.9
			% Living in Same County as in 1985	67.8%	5	42.5

Composite: Rank 8 / 9 *Score* 41.82 — MURFREESBORO

CATEGORY	RANK	SCORE	STATISTIC	VALUE	RANK	SCORE
Economics	6	27.45	Median Household Income	$26,394	7	9.8
			% of Families Above Poverty Level	90.1%	5	45.1
Affordable Housing	4	81.60	Median Home Value	$77,400	5	80.7
			Median Rent	$388	4	82.5
Crime	6	58.20	Violent Crimes per 10,000 Population	78	5	74.1
			Property Crimes per 10,000 Population	725	7	42.3
Open Spaces	8	7.10	Population Density (Persons/Sq. Mile)	1480	8	14.2
			Average Rooms per Housing Unit	5.1	9	0.0
Education	3	50.25	% High School Enrollment/Completion	90.9%	4	62.4
			% College Graduates	27.2%	3	38.1
Commute	7	45.00	Average Work Commute in Minutes	19	3	90.0
			% Commuting on Public Transportation	0.1%	7	0.0
Community Stability	8	23.15	% Living in Same House as in 1979	22.8%	7	13.7
			% Living in Same County as in 1985	65.0%	7	32.6

Composite: Rank 9 / 9 *Score* 39.95 — SPRINGFIELD

CATEGORY	RANK	SCORE	STATISTIC	VALUE	RANK	SCORE
Economics	9	0.00	Median Household Income	$21,645	9	0.0
			% of Families Above Poverty Level	82.7%	9	0.0
Affordable Housing	1	100.00	Median Home Value	$53,400	1	100.0
			Median Rent	$299	1	100.0
Crime	8	26.00	Violent Crimes per 10,000 Population	261	8	0.0
			Property Crimes per 10,000 Population	646	6	52.0
Open Spaces	9	1.80	Population Density (Persons/Sq. Mile)	1631	9	0.0
			Average Rooms per Housing Unit	5.2	8	3.6
Education	9	0.00	% High School Enrollment/Completion	77.8%	9	0.0
			% College Graduates	10.5%	9	0.0
Commute	1	60.00	Average Work Commute in Minutes	18	1	100.0
			% Commuting on Public Transportation	0.3%	5	20.0
Community Stability	1	91.85	% Living in Same House as in 1979	34.0%	2	83.7
			% Living in Same County as in 1985	84.2%	1	100.0

Metropolitan Area Description
NEW ORLEANS

STATE: Louisiana
PARISHES: Jefferson, Orleans, St. Bernard, St. Charles, St. John the Baptist, St. Tammany

TOTAL POPULATION: 1,238,816

POPULATION IN SUBURBS: 741,878   (59.9%)

POPULATION IN New Orleans: 496,938   (40.1%)

The NEW ORLEANS metropolitan area is located in the southeastern part of Louisiana along the Gulf of Mexico. The suburbs range geographically from Slidell in the north (30 miles from New Orleans), to Laplace in the west (28 miles from New Orleans), to Estelle in the south (16 miles from New Orleans), and to Chalmette in the east (9 miles from New Orleans). The area is shrinking in population and had a decrease of 1.4% between 1980 and 1990. The depressed state of the petroleum industry during the 1980's is largely responsible for the decline in population. Summer time high temperatures average in the 90's and winter time lows average in the 40's. Petroleum and port-related industries are the major sources of employment in the area. Avondale Industries, the largest commercial employer in Louisiana, has facilities located in the suburb of Westwego. Public transportation in the area is provided on buses by the Regional Transit Authority.

River Ridge is the overall highest rated suburb and also has the highest scores in economics and education. **Westwego** is the suburb with the most affordable housing. The number one rating in open spaces belongs to **Laplace**. **Chalmette** receives the top score in community stability. **Jefferson** and **Gretna** tie for the top rated commute. Crime rankings were not available for the area.

The highest ranked suburb overall which also has an affordable housing score of at least 50.00 is **Marrero**.

The highest ranked suburb in the education category which also has an affordable housing score of at least 50.00 is **Terrytown**.

The parish whose suburbs have the highest average overall score is **St. Tammany Parish** (59.29).

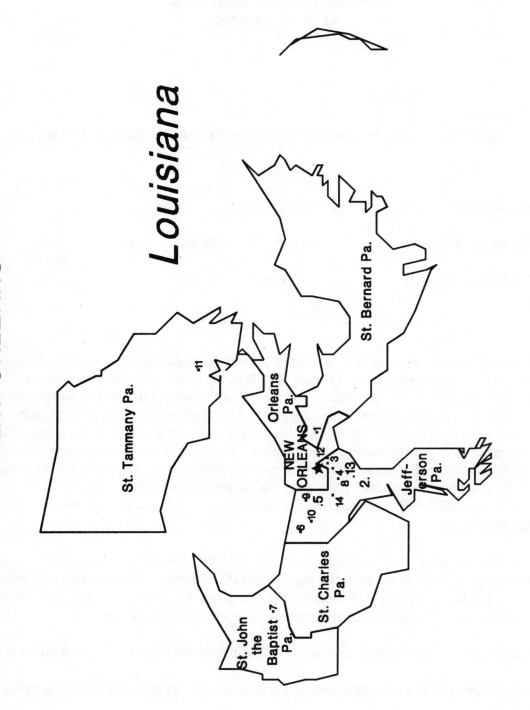

Metropolitan Area Map
NEW ORLEANS

Louisiana

St. Tammany Pa.

St. John
the
Baptist
Pa.

St. Charles
Pa.

Jeff-
erson
Pa.

Orleans
Pa.

NEW
ORLEANS

St. Bernard Pa.

Metropolitan Area Suburb Alphabetical Index
NEW ORLEANS

SUBURB	PAGE	MAP NO.	STATE	COUNTY	POPU-LATION	RANK
CHALMETTE	450	1	Louisiana	St. Bernard	31,860	9 / 14
ESTELLE	450	2	Louisiana	Jefferson	14,091	8 / 14
GRETNA	451	3	Louisiana	Jefferson	17,208	12 / 14
HARVEY	451	4	Louisiana	Jefferson	21,222	11 / 14
JEFFERSON	449	5	Louisiana	Jefferson	14,521	6 / 14
KENNER	452	6	Louisiana	Jefferson	72,033	13 / 14
LAPLACE	451	7	Louisiana	St. John the Baptist	24,194	10 / 14
MARRERO	449	8	Louisiana	Jefferson	36,671	4 / 14
METAIRIE	449	9	Louisiana	Jefferson	149,428	5 / 14
RIVER RIDGE	448	10	Louisiana	Jefferson	14,800	1 / 14
SLIDELL	448	11	Louisiana	St. Tammany	24,124	3 / 14
TERRYTOWN	450	12	Louisiana	Jefferson	23,787	7 / 14
TIMBERLANE	448	13	Louisiana	Jefferson	12,614	2 / 14
WESTWEGO	452	14	Louisiana	Jefferson	11,218	14 / 14

Metropolitan Area Suburb Rankings
NEW ORLEANS

Composite: *Rank* 1 / 14 *Score* 66.08   **RIVER RIDGE**

CATEGORY	RANK	SCORE	STATISTIC	VALUE	RANK	SCORE
Economics	1	96.50	Median Household Income	$33,289	3	93.0
			% of Families Above Poverty Level	94.0%	1	100.0
Affordable Housing	13	32.45	Median Home Value	$91,500	14	0.0
			Median Rent	$389	5	64.9
Crime	N/A	N/A	Violent Crimes per 10,000 Population	N/A	N/A	N/A
			Property Crimes per 10,000 Population	N/A	N/A	N/A
Open Spaces	5	48.50	Population Density (Persons/Sq. Mile)	5261	11	22.0
			Average Rooms per Housing Unit	5.6	4	75.0
Education	1	97.90	% High School Enrollment/Completion	91.3%	3	95.8
			% College Graduates	26.8%	1	100.0
Commute	9	47.80	Average Work Commute in Minutes	23	8	57.1
			% Commuting on Public Transportation	1.7%	8	38.5
Community Stability	4	73.35	% Living in Same House as in 1979	47.9%	2	84.1
			% Living in Same County as in 1985	87.0%	5	62.6

Composite: *Rank* 2 / 14 *Score* 61.87   **TIMBERLANE**

CATEGORY	RANK	SCORE	STATISTIC	VALUE	RANK	SCORE
Economics	2	92.15	Median Household Income	$32,980	4	91.2
			% of Families Above Poverty Level	92.7%	3	93.1
Affordable Housing	12	35.45	Median Home Value	$71,100	11	47.1
			Median Rent	$484	13	23.8
Crime	N/A	N/A	Violent Crimes per 10,000 Population	N/A	N/A	N/A
			Property Crimes per 10,000 Population	N/A	N/A	N/A
Open Spaces	4	51.80	Population Density (Persons/Sq. Mile)	5910	12	9.8
			Average Rooms per Housing Unit	5.9	2	93.8
Education	4	83.80	% High School Enrollment/Completion	88.9%	4	86.5
			% College Graduates	22.5%	4	81.1
Commute	4	79.30	Average Work Commute in Minutes	22	5	71.4
			% Commuting on Public Transportation	3.6%	5	87.2
Community Stability	11	28.70	% Living in Same House as in 1979	38.8%	10	44.8
			% Living in Same County as in 1985	77.9%	11	12.6

Composite: *Rank* 3 / 14 *Score* 59.29   **SLIDELL**

CATEGORY	RANK	SCORE	STATISTIC	VALUE	RANK	SCORE
Economics	3	91.80	Median Household Income	$34,492	1	100.0
			% of Families Above Poverty Level	90.9%	4	83.6
Affordable Housing	9	43.60	Median Home Value	$68,000	9	54.3
			Median Rent	$463	12	32.9
Crime	N/A	N/A	Violent Crimes per 10,000 Population	N/A	N/A	N/A
			Property Crimes per 10,000 Population	N/A	N/A	N/A
Open Spaces	2	86.40	Population Density (Persons/Sq. Mile)	2581	3	72.8
			Average Rooms per Housing Unit	6.0	1	100.0
Education	3	93.20	% High School Enrollment/Completion	92.4%	1	100.0
			% College Graduates	23.7%	3	86.4
Commute	14	6.40	Average Work Commute in Minutes	27	14	0.0
			% Commuting on Public Transportation	0.7%	13	12.8
Community Stability	8	34.35	% Living in Same House as in 1979	42.3%	6	59.9
			% Living in Same County as in 1985	77.2%	12	8.8

Metropolitan Area Suburb Rankings
NEW ORLEANS

Composite: **Rank** 4 / 14 *Score* 58.90 **MARRERO**

CATEGORY	RANK	SCORE	STATISTIC	VALUE	RANK	SCORE
Economics	12	25.20	Median Household Income	$22,074	12	27.6
			% of Families Above Poverty Level	79.4%	13	22.8
Affordable Housing	2	92.85	Median Home Value	$54,400	3	85.7
			Median Rent	$308	1	100.0
Crime	N/A	N/A	Violent Crimes per 10,000 Population	N/A	N/A	N/A
			Property Crimes per 10,000 Population	N/A	N/A	N/A
Open Spaces	11	36.50	Population Density (Persons/Sq. Mile)	4552	7	35.5
			Average Rooms per Housing Unit	5.0	10	37.5
Education	12	41.90	% High School Enrollment/Completion	86.6%	7	77.7
			% College Graduates	5.4%	13	6.1
Commute	5	74.70	Average Work Commute in Minutes	23	8	57.1
			% Commuting on Public Transportation	3.8%	4	92.3
Community Stability	2	82.25	% Living in Same House as in 1979	47.3%	3	81.5
			% Living in Same County as in 1985	90.7%	2	83.0

Composite: **Rank** 5 / 14 *Score* 58.77 **METAIRIE**

CATEGORY	RANK	SCORE	STATISTIC	VALUE	RANK	SCORE
Economics	5	85.10	Median Household Income	$30,024	7	73.9
			% of Families Above Poverty Level	93.3%	2	96.3
Affordable Housing	14	29.05	Median Home Value	$85,500	13	13.9
			Median Rent	$437	10	44.2
Crime	N/A	N/A	Violent Crimes per 10,000 Population	N/A	N/A	N/A
			Property Crimes per 10,000 Population	N/A	N/A	N/A
Open Spaces	12	28.10	Population Density (Persons/Sq. Mile)	6425	13	0.0
			Average Rooms per Housing Unit	5.3	6	56.2
Education	2	95.65	% High School Enrollment/Completion	92.3%	2	99.6
			% College Graduates	24.9%	2	91.7
Commute	7	62.10	Average Work Commute in Minutes	21	3	85.7
			% Commuting on Public Transportation	1.7%	8	38.5
Community Stability	7	52.65	% Living in Same House as in 1979	43.9%	5	66.8
			% Living in Same County as in 1985	82.6%	8	38.5

Composite: **Rank** 6 / 14 *Score* 58.73 **JEFFERSON**

CATEGORY	RANK	SCORE	STATISTIC	VALUE	RANK	SCORE
Economics	10	51.90	Median Household Income	$23,887	10	38.2
			% of Families Above Poverty Level	87.5%	10	65.6
Affordable Housing	5	58.65	Median Home Value	$66,200	6	58.4
			Median Rent	$403	7	58.9
Crime	N/A	N/A	Violent Crimes per 10,000 Population	N/A	N/A	N/A
			Property Crimes per 10,000 Population	N/A	N/A	N/A
Open Spaces	9	39.65	Population Density (Persons/Sq. Mile)	2238	2	79.3
			Average Rooms per Housing Unit	4.4	14	0.0
Education	7	70.70	% High School Enrollment/Completion	86.3%	8	76.5
			% College Graduates	18.8%	6	64.9
Commute	1	100.00	Average Work Commute in Minutes	20	1	100.0
			% Commuting on Public Transportation	4.1%	1	100.0
Community Stability	10	31.45	% Living in Same House as in 1979	39.3%	9	47.0
			% Living in Same County as in 1985	78.5%	10	15.9

Metropolitan Area Suburb Rankings
NEW ORLEANS

Composite: Rank 7 / 14 *Score* 55.08   **TERRYTOWN**

CATEGORY	RANK	SCORE	STATISTIC	VALUE	RANK	SCORE
Economics	7	75.75	Median Household Income	$29,818	8	72.7
			% of Families Above Poverty Level	90.0%	6	78.8
Affordable Housing	8	50.15	Median Home Value	$68,700	10	52.7
			Median Rent	$429	9	47.6
Crime	N/A	N/A	Violent Crimes per 10,000 Population	N/A	N/A	N/A
			Property Crimes per 10,000 Population	N/A	N/A	N/A
Open Spaces	12	28.10	Population Density (Persons/Sq. Mile)	6426	14	0.0
			Average Rooms per Housing Unit	5.3	6	56.2
Education	6	71.30	% High School Enrollment/Completion	88.9%	4	86.5
			% College Graduates	16.8%	7	56.1
Commute	3	92.85	Average Work Commute in Minutes	21	3	85.7
			% Commuting on Public Transportation	4.1%	1	100.0
Community Stability	13	12.35	% Living in Same House as in 1979	32.1%	12	15.9
			% Living in Same County as in 1985	77.2%	12	8.8

Composite: Rank 8 / 14 *Score* 54.85   **ESTELLE**

CATEGORY	RANK	SCORE	STATISTIC	VALUE	RANK	SCORE
Economics	6	77.25	Median Household Income	$30,681	5	77.8
			% of Families Above Poverty Level	89.6%	7	76.7
Affordable Housing	10	42.40	Median Home Value	$54,800	4	84.8
			Median Rent	$539	14	0.0
Crime	N/A	N/A	Violent Crimes per 10,000 Population	N/A	N/A	N/A
			Property Crimes per 10,000 Population	N/A	N/A	N/A
Open Spaces	3	75.10	Population Density (Persons/Sq. Mile)	2783	4	68.9
			Average Rooms per Housing Unit	5.7	3	81.3
Education	10	51.70	% High School Enrollment/Completion	86.9%	6	78.8
			% College Graduates	9.6%	10	24.6
Commute	12	16.10	Average Work Commute in Minutes	26	12	14.3
			% Commuting on Public Transportation	0.9%	11	17.9
Community Stability	5	66.55	% Living in Same House as in 1979	41.3%	8	55.6
			% Living in Same County as in 1985	89.7%	3	77.5

Composite: Rank 9 / 14 *Score* 53.39   **CHALMETTE**

CATEGORY	RANK	SCORE	STATISTIC	VALUE	RANK	SCORE
Economics	9	64.20	Median Household Income	$26,657	9	54.3
			% of Families Above Poverty Level	89.1%	8	74.1
Affordable Housing	7	53.80	Median Home Value	$66,800	7	57.0
			Median Rent	$422	8	50.6
Crime	N/A	N/A	Violent Crimes per 10,000 Population	N/A	N/A	N/A
			Property Crimes per 10,000 Population	N/A	N/A	N/A
Open Spaces	6	45.60	Population Density (Persons/Sq. Mile)	4574	8	35.0
			Average Rooms per Housing Unit	5.3	6	56.2
Education	11	48.20	% High School Enrollment/Completion	86.1%	9	75.8
			% College Graduates	8.7%	11	20.6
Commute	11	22.00	Average Work Commute in Minutes	25	10	28.6
			% Commuting on Public Transportation	0.8%	12	15.4
Community Stability	1	86.55	% Living in Same House as in 1979	51.6%	1	100.0
			% Living in Same County as in 1985	88.9%	4	73.1

Metropolitan Area Suburb Rankings
NEW ORLEANS

Composite: *Rank* 10 / 14 *Score* 50.43 **LAPLACE**

CATEGORY	RANK	SCORE	STATISTIC	VALUE	RANK	SCORE
Economics	4	91.00	Median Household Income	$34,295	2	98.9
			% of Families Above Poverty Level	90.8%	5	83.1
Affordable Housing	6	58.25	Median Home Value	$66,900	8	56.8
			Median Rent	$401	6	59.7
Crime	N/A	N/A	Violent Crimes per 10,000 Population	N/A	N/A	N/A
			Property Crimes per 10,000 Population	N/A	N/A	N/A
Open Spaces	1	87.50	Population Density (Persons/Sq. Mile)	1142	1	100.0
			Average Rooms per Housing Unit	5.6	4	75.0
Education	8	58.70	% High School Enrollment/Completion	85.3%	10	72.7
			% College Graduates	14.2%	8	44.7
Commute	13	7.15	Average Work Commute in Minutes	26	12	14.3
			% Commuting on Public Transportation	0.2%	14	0.0
Community Stability	14	0.00	% Living in Same House as in 1979	28.4%	14	0.0
			% Living in Same County as in 1985	75.6%	14	0.0

Composite: *Rank* 11 / 14 *Score* 50.12 **HARVEY**

CATEGORY	RANK	SCORE	STATISTIC	VALUE	RANK	SCORE
Economics	11	33.25	Median Household Income	$22,490	11	30.0
			% of Families Above Poverty Level	82.0%	11	36.5
Affordable Housing	4	75.55	Median Home Value	$58,700	5	75.8
			Median Rent	$365	4	75.3
Crime	N/A	N/A	Violent Crimes per 10,000 Population	N/A	N/A	N/A
			Property Crimes per 10,000 Population	N/A	N/A	N/A
Open Spaces	8	40.00	Population Density (Persons/Sq. Mile)	3188	5	61.3
			Average Rooms per Housing Unit	4.7	11	18.7
Education	9	53.35	% High School Enrollment/Completion	84.9%	11	71.2
			% College Graduates	12.1%	9	35.5
Commute	6	65.20	Average Work Commute in Minutes	22	5	71.4
			% Commuting on Public Transportation	2.5%	6	59.0
Community Stability	9	33.35	% Living in Same House as in 1979	33.4%	11	21.6
			% Living in Same County as in 1985	83.8%	7	45.1

Composite: *Rank* 12 / 14 *Score* 49.82 **GRETNA**

CATEGORY	RANK	SCORE	STATISTIC	VALUE	RANK	SCORE
Economics	14	0.00	Median Household Income	$17,344	14	0.0
			% of Families Above Poverty Level	75.1%	14	0.0
Affordable Housing	3	89.60	Median Home Value	$51,200	2	93.1
			Median Rent	$340	3	86.1
Crime	N/A	N/A	Violent Crimes per 10,000 Population	166	N/A	N/A
			Property Crimes per 10,000 Population	893	N/A	N/A
Open Spaces	14	20.75	Population Density (Persons/Sq. Mile)	4894	10	29.0
			Average Rooms per Housing Unit	4.6	13	12.5
Education	13	23.15	% High School Enrollment/Completion	73.9%	13	28.8
			% College Graduates	8.0%	12	17.5
Commute	1	100.00	Average Work Commute in Minutes	20	1	100.0
			% Commuting on Public Transportation	4.1%	1	100.0
Community Stability	6	65.45	% Living in Same House as in 1979	46.4%	4	77.6
			% Living in Same County as in 1985	85.3%	6	53.3

Metropolitan Area Suburb Rankings
NEW ORLEANS

Composite: *Rank* 13 / 14 *Score* 48.15   **KENNER**

CATEGORY	RANK	SCORE	STATISTIC	VALUE	RANK	SCORE
Economics	8	71.65	Median Household Income	$30,389	6	76.1
			% of Families Above Poverty Level	87.8%	9	67.2
Affordable Housing	11	40.05	Median Home Value	$73,700	12	41.1
			Median Rent	$449	11	39.0
Crime	N/A	N/A	Violent Crimes per 10,000 Population	134	N/A	N/A
			Property Crimes per 10,000 Population	783	N/A	N/A
Open Spaces	7	40.75	Population Density (Persons/Sq. Mile)	4762	9	31.5
			Average Rooms per Housing Unit	5.2	9	50.0
Education	5	72.95	% High School Enrollment/Completion	84.6%	12	70.0
			% College Graduates	21.3%	5	75.9
Commute	10	39.95	Average Work Commute in Minutes	25	10	28.6
			% Commuting on Public Transportation	2.2%	7	51.3
Community Stability	12	23.55	% Living in Same House as in 1979	31.8%	13	14.7
			% Living in Same County as in 1985	81.5%	9	32.4

Composite: *Rank* 14 / 14 *Score* 47.12   **WESTWEGO**

CATEGORY	RANK	SCORE	STATISTIC	VALUE	RANK	SCORE
Economics	13	19.15	Median Household Income	$18,095	13	4.4
			% of Families Above Poverty Level	81.5%	12	33.9
Affordable Housing	1	98.25	Median Home Value	$48,200	1	100.0
			Median Rent	$316	2	96.5
Crime	N/A	N/A	Violent Crimes per 10,000 Population	84	N/A	N/A
			Property Crimes per 10,000 Population	651	N/A	N/A
Open Spaces	10	36.85	Population Density (Persons/Sq. Mile)	3521	6	55.0
			Average Rooms per Housing Unit	4.7	11	18.7
Education	14	0.00	% High School Enrollment/Completion	66.4%	14	0.0
			% College Graduates	4.0%	14	0.0
Commute	8	48.50	Average Work Commute in Minutes	22	5	71.4
			% Commuting on Public Transportation	1.2%	10	25.6
Community Stability	3	79.95	% Living in Same House as in 1979	42.3%	6	59.9
			% Living in Same County as in 1985	93.8%	1	100.0

NEW YORK-NORTHERN NEW JERSEY-LONG ISLAND

STATE: Connecticut
COUNTIES: Fairfield

STATE: New Jersey
COUNTIES: Bergen, Essex, Hudson, Hunterdon, Middlesex, Monmouth, Morris, Ocean, Passaic, Somerset, Sussex, Union

STATE: New York
COUNTIES: Bronx, Kings, Nassau, New York, Orange, Putnam, Queens, Richmond, Rockland, Suffolk, Westchester

TOTAL POPULATION: 17,953,372

POPULATION IN SUBURBS: 10,630,808 (59.2%)

POPULATION IN New York (NY): 7,322,564 (40.8%)

The NEW YORK-NORTHERN NEW JERSEY-LONG ISLAND metropolitan area is located in the southeastern part of New York, the northeastern part of New Jersey, and the southwestern part of Connecticut along the Atlantic Ocean. The suburbs range geographically from Newburgh (NY) in the north (68 miles from New York), to Hopatcong (NJ) in the west (42 miles from New York), to Point Pleasant (NJ) in the south (67 miles from New York), and to Mastic (NY) in the east (62 miles from New York). The area is growing in population and had an increase of 3.1% between 1980 and 1990. Summer time high temperatures average in the 80's and winter time lows average in the 20's. Some of the leading financial companies in the United States are located in the suburban area. Manufacturing companies are found in many of the New Jersey suburbs. Public transportation in the area is provided by several local transit authorities using buses, trains, and subways.

Livingston (NJ) and **West Caldwell** (NJ) are tied for the overall highest rated suburbs. **Scarsdale** (NY) receives the highest scores in economics and education. **Newark** (NJ) is the community with the most affordable housing. **Berkeley Heights** (NJ) is rated the safest suburb with the lowest crime rate. The top rated commute belongs to **Hoboken** (NJ). The highest score in open spaces goes to **Dix Hills** (NY). Finally, the number one rating in community stability goes to **South Farmingdale** (NY).

The highest ranked suburb overall which also has an affordable housing score of at least 50.00 is **Fair Lawn** (NJ).

The highest ranked suburb in the education category which also has an affordable housing score of at least 50.00 is **South Orange** (NJ).

The county whose suburbs have the highest average overall score is **Union County** (NJ) (62.78).

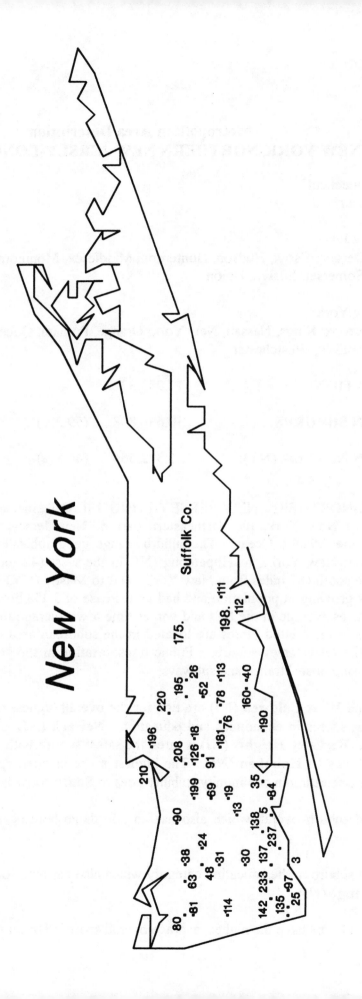

Metropolitan Area Map (Part 1)
NEW YORK-NORTHERN NEW JERSEY-LONG ISLAND

New York

Suffolk Co.

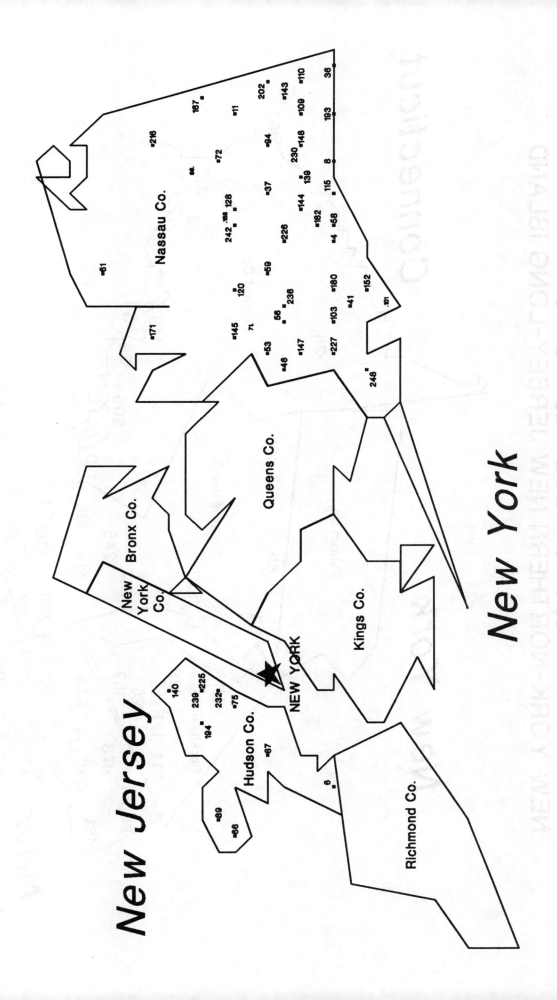

Metropolitan Area Map (Part 2)
NEW YORK-NORTHERN NEW JERSEY-LONG ISLAND

New Jersey

New York

Connecticut

Nassau Co.

Queens Co.

Bronx Co.

New York Co.

Kings Co.

Richmond Co.

Hudson Co.

NEW YORK

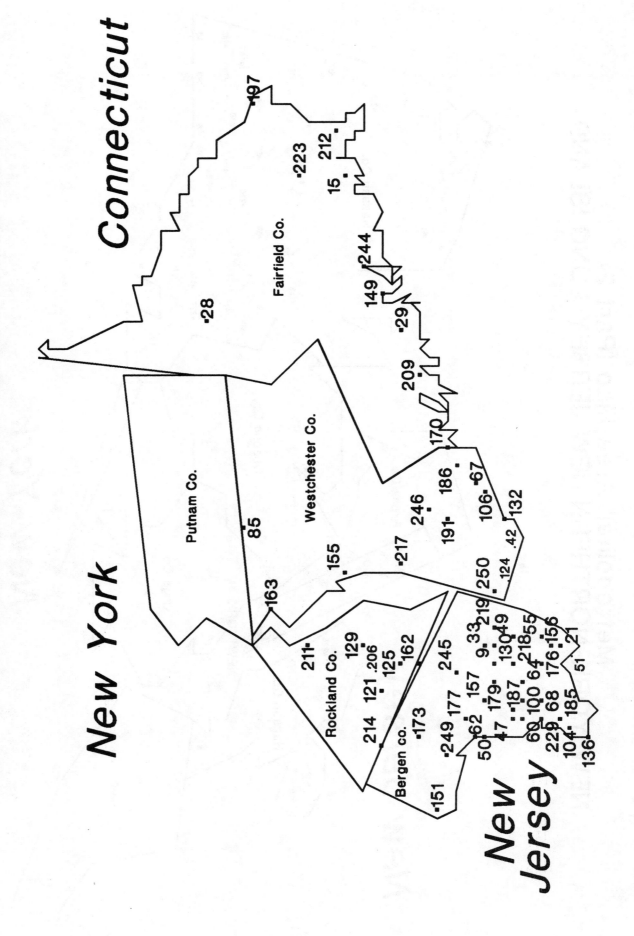

Metropolitan Area Map (Part 3)
NEW YORK–NORTHERN NEW JERSEY–LONG ISLAND

Connecticut

New York

New Jersey

Putnam Co.

Westchester Co.

Fairfield Co.

Rockland Co.

Bergen co.

197

223

212

15

244

149

29

209

170

67

186

191

246

106

42

132

85

155

163

217

250

124

211

219

33

9

49

130

218

55

156

21

129

206

162

245

157

179

187

64

176

51

214

121

125

177

60

100

68

185

173

249

62

47

229

104

136

50

151

28

Metropolitan Area Map (Part 4)
NEW YORK-NORTHERN NEW JERSEY-LONG ISLAND

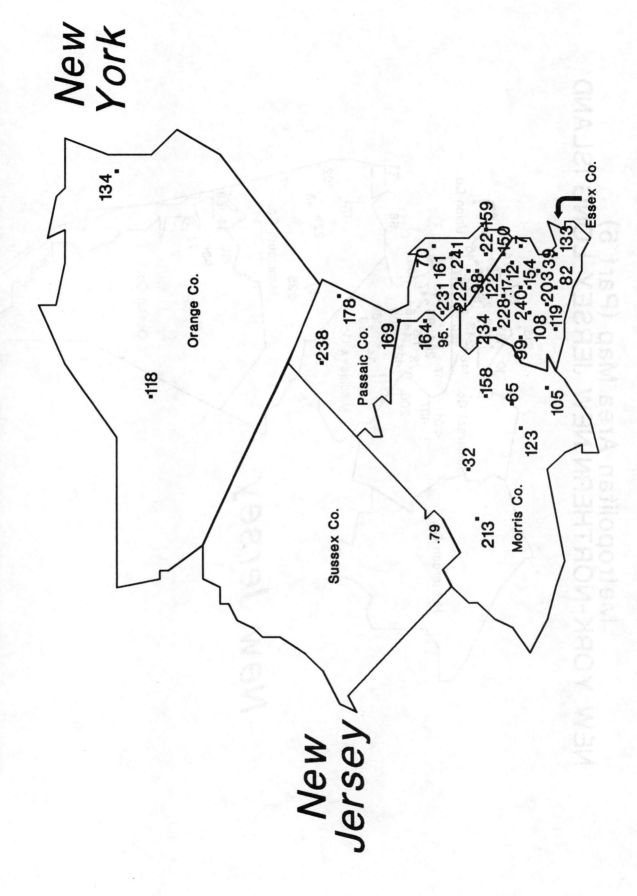

New York

New Jersey

Orange Co.

•134.

•118

•238

•178

Passaic Co.

169

164•

95.

70

•231 161

222• 241

98•

122

•22 •59

150

7

•171 2•

240•

154

108

•119 203 39

82 133

Essex Co.

•158

•65

•99

105•

•32

123•

.79

213•

Morris Co.

Sussex Co.

234•

228•

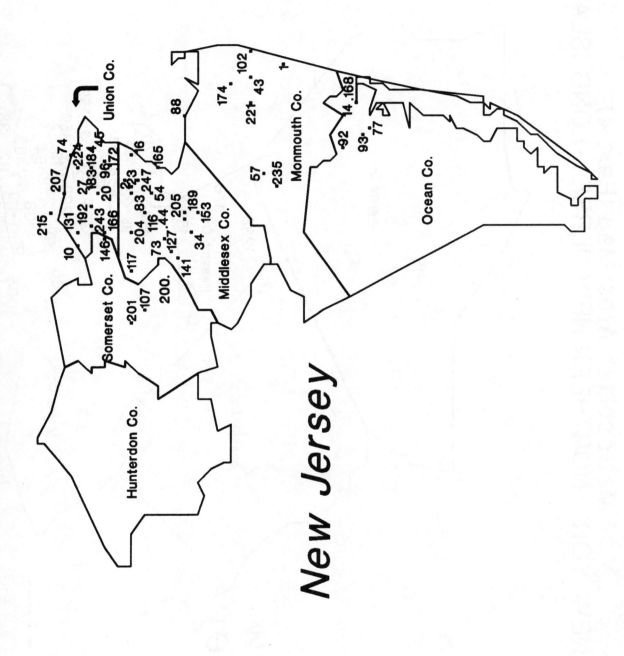

Metropolitan Area Map (Part 5)
NEW YORK–NORTHERN NEW JERSEY–LONG ISLAND

New Jersey

Union Co.

Somerset Co.

Hunterdon Co.

Middlesex Co.

Monmouth Co.

Ocean Co.

Metropolitan Area Suburb Alphabetical Index
NEW YORK-NORTHERN NEW JERSEY-LONG ISLAND

SUBURB	PAGE	MAP NO.	STATE	COUNTY	POPU-LATION	RANK
ASBURY PARK	545	1	New Jersey	Monmouth	16,799	246 / 250
AVENEL	539	2	New Jersey	Middlesex	15,504	227 / 250
BABYLON	511	3	New York	Suffolk	12,249	143 / 250
BALDWIN	507	4	New York	Nassau	22,719	132 / 250
BAY SHORE	534	5	New York	Suffolk	21,279	212 / 250
BAYONNE	488	6	New Jersey	Hudson	61,444	74 / 250
BELLEVILLE	511	7	New Jersey	Essex	34,213	142 / 250
BELLMORE	496	8	New York	Nassau	16,438	97 / 250
BERGENFIELD	480	9	New Jersey	Bergen	24,458	51 / 250
BERKELEY HEIGHTS	470	10	New Jersey	Union	11,980	19 / 250
BETHPAGE	482	11	New York	Nassau	15,761	57 / 250
BLOOMFIELD	498	12	New Jersey	Essex	45,061	104 / 250
BRENTWOOD	526	13	New York	Suffolk	45,218	187 / 250
BRICK TOWNSHIP	518	14	New Jersey	Ocean	66,473	165 / 250
BRIDGEPORT	543	15	Connecticut	Fairfield	141,686	239 / 250
CARTERET	488	16	New Jersey	Middlesex	19,025	75 / 250
CEDAR GROVE	477	17	New Jersey	Essex	12,053	41 / 250
CENTEREACH	518	18	New York	Suffolk	26,720	163 / 250
CENTRAL ISLIP	537	19	New York	Suffolk	26,028	221 / 250
CLARK	465	20	New Jersey	Union	14,629	5 / 250
CLIFFSIDE PARK	528	21	New Jersey	Bergen	20,393	195 / 250
CLIFTON	485	22	New Jersey	Passaic	71,742	64 / 250
COLONIA	478	23	New Jersey	Middlesex	18,238	43 / 250
COMMACK	504	24	New York	Suffolk	36,124	123 / 250
COPIAGUE	535	25	New York	Suffolk	20,769	214 / 250
CORAM	536	26	New York	Suffolk	30,111	217 / 250
CRANFORD	467	27	New Jersey	Union	22,624	11 / 250
DANBURY	519	28	Connecticut	Fairfield	65,585	168 / 250
DARIEN	477	29	Connecticut	Fairfield	18,130	40 / 250
DEER PARK	505	30	New York	Suffolk	28,840	126 / 250
DIX HILLS	487	31	New York	Suffolk	25,849	70 / 250
DOVER	519	32	New Jersey	Morris	15,115	166 / 250
DUMONT	473	33	New Jersey	Bergen	17,187	30 / 250
EAST BRUNSWICK	485	34	New Jersey	Middlesex	43,548	66 / 250
EAST ISLIP	508	35	New York	Suffolk	14,325	135 / 250
EAST MASSAPEQUA	507	36	New York	Nassau	19,550	130 / 250
EAST MEADOW	496	37	New York	Nassau	36,909	98 / 250
EAST NORTHPORT	503	38	New York	Suffolk	20,411	120 / 250
EAST ORANGE	543	39	New Jersey	Essex	73,552	240 / 250
EAST PATCHOGUE	526	40	New York	Suffolk	20,195	188 / 250
EAST ROCKAWAY	515	41	New York	Nassau	10,152	154 / 250
EASTCHESTER	475	42	New York	Westchester	18,537	35 / 250
EATONTOWN	529	43	New Jersey	Monmouth	13,800	197 / 250
EDISON	509	44	New Jersey	Middlesex	88,680	137 / 250
ELIZABETH	541	45	New Jersey	Union	110,002	234 / 250
ELMONT	531	46	New York	Nassau	28,612	203 / 250
ELMWOOD PARK	483	47	New Jersey	Bergen	17,623	58 / 250
ELWOOD	492	48	New York	Suffolk	10,916	86 / 250
ENGLEWOOD	500	49	New Jersey	Bergen	24,850	111 / 250
FAIR LAWN	464	50	New Jersey	Bergen	30,548	3 / 250
FAIRVIEW	530	51	New Jersey	Bergen	10,733	200 / 250

Metropolitan Area Suburb Alphabetical Index
NEW YORK-NORTHERN NEW JERSEY-LONG ISLAND

SUBURB	PAGE	MAP NO.	STATE	COUNTY	POPU-LATION	RANK
FARMINGVILLE	524	52	New York	Suffolk	14,842	182 / 250
FLORAL PARK	479	53	New York	Nassau	15,947	46 / 250
FORDS	505	54	New Jersey	Middlesex	14,392	124 / 250
FORT LEE	537	55	New Jersey	Bergen	31,997	220 / 250
FRANKLIN SQUARE	506	56	New York	Nassau	28,205	127 / 250
FREEHOLD	519	57	New Jersey	Monmouth	10,742	167 / 250
FREEPORT	515	58	New York	Nassau	39,894	155 / 250
GARDEN CITY	472	59	New York	Nassau	21,686	27 / 250
GARFIELD	516	60	New Jersey	Bergen	26,727	157 / 250
GLEN COVE	493	61	New York	Nassau	24,149	88 / 250
GLEN ROCK	469	62	New Jersey	Bergen	10,883	18 / 250
GREENLAWN	482	63	New York	Suffolk	13,208	55 / 250
HACKENSACK	531	64	New Jersey	Bergen	37,049	202 / 250
HANOVER TOWNSHIP	466	65	New Jersey	Morris	11,538	8 / 250
HARRISON	525	66	New Jersey	Hudson	13,425	184 / 250
HARRISON	497	67	New York	Westchester	23,308	100 / 250
HASBROUCK HEIGHTS	473	68	New Jersey	Bergen	11,488	29 / 250
HAUPPAUGE	506	69	New York	Suffolk	19,750	129 / 250
HAWTHORNE	485	70	New Jersey	Passaic	17,084	65 / 250
HEMPSTEAD	537	71	New York	Nassau	49,453	222 / 250
HICKSVILLE	500	72	New York	Nassau	40,174	109 / 250
HIGHLAND PARK	504	73	New Jersey	Middlesex	13,279	121 / 250
HILLSIDE	514	74	New Jersey	Union	21,044	153 / 250
HOBOKEN	543	75	New Jersey	Hudson	33,397	238 / 250
HOLBROOK	520	76	New York	Suffolk	25,273	170 / 250
HOLIDAY CITY-BERKELEY	547	77	New Jersey	Ocean	14,293	250 / 250
HOLTSVILLE	520	78	New York	Suffolk	14,972	171 / 250
HOPATCONG	533	79	New Jersey	Sussex	15,586	209 / 250
HUNTINGTON	507	80	New York	Suffolk	18,243	131 / 250
HUNTINGTON STATION	521	81	New York	Suffolk	28,247	174 / 250
IRVINGTON	546	82	New Jersey	Essex	59,774	247 / 250
ISELIN	528	83	New Jersey	Middlesex	16,141	193 / 250
ISLIP	516	84	New York	Suffolk	18,924	159 / 250
JEFFERSON VALLEY-YORKTOWN	517	85	New York	Westchester	14,118	160 / 250
JERICHO	513	86	New York	Nassau	13,141	149 / 250
JERSEY CITY	540	87	New Jersey	Hudson	228,537	231 / 250
KEANSBURG	535	88	New Jersey	Monmouth	11,069	215 / 250
KEARNY	510	89	New Jersey	Hudson	34,874	139 / 250
KINGS PARK	501	90	New York	Suffolk	17,773	113 / 250
LAKE RONKONKOMA	513	91	New York	Suffolk	18,997	148 / 250
LAKEWOOD	539	92	New Jersey	Ocean	26,095	226 / 250
LEISURE VILLAGE WEST-PINE LAKE PARK	545	93	New Jersey	Ocean	10,139	245 / 250
LEVITTOWN	512	94	New York	Nassau	53,286	146 / 250
LINCOLN PARK	517	95	New Jersey	Morris	10,978	160 / 250
LINDEN	495	96	New Jersey	Union	36,701	94 / 250
LINDENHURST	522	97	New York	Suffolk	26,879	176 / 250
LITTLE FALLS	501	98	New Jersey	Passaic	11,294	114 / 250
LIVINGSTON	464	99	New Jersey	Essex	26,609	1 / 250
LODI	515	100	New Jersey	Bergen	22,355	156 / 250
LONG BEACH	534	101	New York	Nassau	33,510	213 / 250
LONG BRANCH	536	102	New Jersey	Monmouth	28,658	218 / 250

SUBURB	PAGE	MAP NO.	STATE	COUNTY	POPU-LATION	RANK
LYNBROOK	484	103	New York	Nassau	19,208	61 / 250
LYNDHURST	481	104	New Jersey	Bergen	18,262	54 / 250
MADISON	486	105	New Jersey	Morris	15,850	69 / 250
MAMARONECK	491	106	New York	Westchester	17,325	83 / 250
MANVILLE	474	107	New Jersey	Somerset	10,567	32 / 250
MAPLEWOOD	480	108	New Jersey	Essex	21,756	50 / 250
MASSAPEQUA	508	109	New York	Nassau	22,018	134 / 250
MASSAPEQUA PARK	502	110	New York	Nassau	18,044	116 / 250
MASTIC	541	111	New York	Suffolk	13,778	233 / 250
MASTIC BEACH	544	112	New York	Suffolk	10,293	243 / 250
MEDFORD	517	113	New York	Suffolk	21,274	162 / 250
MELVILLE	484	114	New York	Suffolk	12,586	63 / 250
MERRICK	486	115	New York	Nassau	23,042	68 / 250
METUCHEN	466	116	New Jersey	Middlesex	12,804	7 / 250
MIDDLESEX	479	117	New Jersey	Middlesex	13,055	48 / 250
MIDDLETOWN	525	118	New York	Orange	24,160	186 / 250
MILLBURN	469	119	New Jersey	Essex	18,630	17 / 250
MINEOLA	524	120	New York	Nassau	18,994	183 / 250
MONSEY	541	121	New York	Rockland	13,986	232 / 250
MONTCLAIR	506	122	New Jersey	Essex	37,729	127 / 250
MORRISTOWN	533	123	New Jersey	Morris	16,189	210 / 250
MOUNT VERNON	532	124	New York	Westchester	67,153	206 / 250
NANUET	527	125	New York	Rockland	14,065	192 / 250
NESCONSET	502	126	New York	Suffolk	10,712	117 / 250
NEW BRUNSWICK	545	127	New Jersey	Middlesex	41,711	244 / 250
NEW CASSEL	530	128	New York	Nassau	10,257	201 / 250
NEW CITY	489	129	New York	Rockland	33,673	78 / 250
NEW MILFORD	471	130	New Jersey	Bergen	15,990	22 / 250
NEW PROVIDENCE	468	131	New Jersey	Union	11,439	14 / 250
NEW ROCHELLE	495	132	New York	Westchester	67,265	96 / 250
NEWARK	546	133	New Jersey	Essex	275,221	249 / 250
NEWBURGH	544	134	New York	Orange	26,454	242 / 250
NORTH AMITYVILLE	539	135	New York	Suffolk	13,849	228 / 250
NORTH ARLINGTON	476	136	New Jersey	Bergen	13,790	38 / 250
NORTH BABYLON	524	137	New York	Suffolk	18,081	181 / 250
NORTH BAY SHORE	535	138	New York	Suffolk	12,799	216 / 250
NORTH BELLMORE	495	139	New York	Nassau	19,707	95 / 250
NORTH BERGEN	523	140	New Jersey	Hudson	48,414	178 / 250
NORTH BRUNSWICK TOWNSHIP	522	141	New Jersey	Middlesex	31,287	175 / 250
NORTH LINDENHURST	529	142	New York	Suffolk	10,563	196 / 250
NORTH MASSAPEQUA	493	143	New York	Nassau	19,365	89 / 250
NORTH MERRICK	511	144	New York	Nassau	12,113	144 / 250
NORTH NEW HYDE PARK	499	145	New York	Nassau	14,359	106 / 250
NORTH PLAINFIELD	531	146	New Jersey	Somerset	18,820	204 / 250
NORTH VALLEY STREAM	523	147	New York	Nassau	14,574	178 / 250
NORTH WANTAGH	483	148	New York	Nassau	12,276	60 / 250
NORWALK	510	149	Connecticut	Fairfield	78,331	141 / 250
NUTLEY	481	150	New Jersey	Essex	27,099	52 / 250
OAKLAND	476	151	New Jersey	Bergen	11,997	39 / 250
OCEANSIDE	494	152	New York	Nassau	32,423	91 / 250
OLD BRIDGE	475	153	New Jersey	Middlesex	22,151	36 / 250

Metropolitan Area Suburb Alphabetical Index
NEW YORK-NORTHERN NEW JERSEY-LONG ISLAND

SUBURB	PAGE	MAP NO.	STATE	COUNTY	POPU-LATION	RANK
ORANGE	542	154	New Jersey	Essex	29,925	237 / 250
OSSINING	527	155	New York	Westchester	22,582	190 / 250
PALISADES PARK	528	156	New Jersey	Bergen	14,536	194 / 250
PARAMUS	509	157	New Jersey	Bergen	25,067	136 / 250
PARSIPPANY-TROY HILLS TOWNSHIP	498	158	New Jersey	Morris	48,478	103 / 250
PASSAIC	542	159	New Jersey	Passaic	58,041	235 / 250
PATCHOGUE	538	160	New York	Suffolk	11,060	223 / 250
PATERSON	540	161	New Jersey	Passaic	140,891	230 / 250
PEARL RIVER	491	162	New York	Rockland	15,314	84 / 250
PEEKSKILL	532	163	New York	Westchester	19,536	207 / 250
PEQUANNOCK TOWNSHIP	467	164	New Jersey	Morris	12,844	10 / 250
PERTH AMBOY	534	165	New Jersey	Middlesex	41,967	211 / 250
PLAINFIELD	536	166	New Jersey	Union	46,567	219 / 250
PLAINVIEW	469	167	New York	Nassau	26,207	16 / 250
POINT PLEASANT	494	168	New Jersey	Ocean	18,177	92 / 250
POMPTON LAKES	490	169	New Jersey	Passaic	10,539	80 / 250
PORT CHESTER	526	170	New York	Westchester	24,728	189 / 250
PORT WASHINGTON	498	171	New York	Nassau	15,387	104 / 250
RAHWAY	497	172	New Jersey	Union	25,325	102 / 250
RAMSEY	488	173	New Jersey	Bergen	13,228	73 / 250
RED BANK	508	174	New Jersey	Monmouth	10,636	133 / 250
RIDGE	544	175	New York	Suffolk	11,734	241 / 250
RIDGEFIELD PARK	490	176	New Jersey	Bergen	12,454	81 / 250
RIDGEWOOD	470	177	New Jersey	Bergen	24,152	21 / 250
RINGWOOD	494	178	New Jersey	Passaic	12,623	93 / 250
RIVER EDGE	472	179	New Jersey	Bergen	10,603	26 / 250
ROCKVILLE CENTRE	466	180	New York	Nassau	24,727	9 / 250
RONKONKOMA	527	181	New York	Suffolk	20,391	191 / 250
ROOSEVELT	533	182	New York	Nassau	15,030	208 / 250
ROSELLE	499	183	New Jersey	Union	20,314	106 / 250
ROSELLE PARK	499	184	New Jersey	Union	12,805	106 / 250
RUTHERFORD	482	185	New Jersey	Bergen	17,790	56 / 250
RYE	496	186	New York	Westchester	14,936	99 / 250
SADDLE BROOK	478	187	New Jersey	Bergen	13,296	44 / 250
SALISBURY	474	188	New York	Nassau	12,226	32 / 250
SAYREVILLE	500	189	New Jersey	Middlesex	34,986	110 / 250
SAYVILLE	509	190	New York	Suffolk	16,550	138 / 250
SCARSDALE	479	191	New York	Westchester	16,987	46 / 250
SCOTCH PLAINS	470	192	New Jersey	Union	21,160	20 / 250
SEAFORD	503	193	New York	Nassau	15,597	117 / 250
SECAUCUS	512	194	New Jersey	Hudson	14,061	147 / 250
SELDEN	525	195	New York	Suffolk	20,608	185 / 250
SETAUKET-EAST SETAUKET	502	196	New York	Suffolk	13,634	115 / 250
SHELTON	474	197	Connecticut	Fairfield	35,418	30 / 250
SHIRLEY	538	198	New York	Suffolk	22,936	224 / 250
SMITHTOWN	490	199	New York	Suffolk	25,638	79 / 250
SOMERSET	520	200	New Jersey	Somerset	22,070	169 / 250
SOMERVILLE	510	201	New Jersey	Somerset	11,632	139 / 250
SOUTH FARMINGDALE	484	202	New York	Nassau	15,377	62 / 250
SOUTH ORANGE	481	203	New Jersey	Essex	16,390	53 / 250
SOUTH PLAINFIELD	475	204	New Jersey	Middlesex	20,489	34 / 250

Metropolitan Area Suburb Alphabetical Index
NEW YORK-NORTHERN NEW JERSEY-LONG ISLAND

SUBURB	PAGE	MAP NO.	STATE	COUNTY	POPU-LATION	RANK
SOUTH RIVER	487	205	New Jersey	Middlesex	13,692	72 / 250
SPRING VALLEY	540	206	New York	Rockland	21,802	229 / 250
SPRINGFIELD	471	207	New Jersey	Union	13,420	24 / 250
ST. JAMES	514	208	New York	Suffolk	12,703	151 / 250
STAMFORD	518	209	Connecticut	Fairfield	108,056	164 / 250
STONY BROOK	513	210	New York	Suffolk	13,726	150 / 250
STONY POINT	467	211	New York	Rockland	10,587	12 / 250
STRATFORD	468	212	Connecticut	Fairfield	49,389	12 / 250
SUCCASUNNA-KENVIL	486	213	New Jersey	Morris	11,781	67 / 250
SUFFERN	538	214	New York	Rockland	11,055	225 / 250
SUMMIT	489	215	New Jersey	Union	19,757	76 / 250
SYOSSET	503	216	New York	Nassau	18,967	119 / 250
TARRYTOWN	493	217	New York	Westchester	10,739	90 / 250
TEANECK	471	218	New Jersey	Bergen	37,825	23 / 250
TENAFLY	480	219	New Jersey	Bergen	13,326	49 / 250
TERRYVILLE	522	220	New York	Suffolk	10,275	177 / 250
TINTON FALLS	514	221	New Jersey	Monmouth	12,361	152 / 250
TOTOWA	473	222	New Jersey	Passaic	10,177	28 / 250
TRUMBULL	465	223	Connecticut	Fairfield	32,000	6 / 250
UNION	483	224	New Jersey	Union	50,024	59 / 250
UNION CITY	546	225	New Jersey	Hudson	58,012	248 / 250
UNIONDALE	529	226	New York	Nassau	20,328	198 / 250
VALLEY STREAM	512	227	New York	Nassau	33,946	145 / 250
VERONA	465	228	New Jersey	Essex	13,597	4 / 250
WALLINGTON	504	229	New Jersey	Bergen	10,828	122 / 250
WANTAGH	492	230	New York	Nassau	18,567	87 / 250
WAYNE	478	231	New Jersey	Passaic	47,025	45 / 250
WEEHAWKEN	530	232	New Jersey	Hudson	12,385	198 / 250
WEST BABYLON	523	233	New York	Suffolk	42,410	180 / 250
WEST CALDWELL	464	234	New Jersey	Essex	10,422	1 / 250
WEST FREEHOLD	532	235	New Jersey	Monmouth	11,166	205 / 250
WEST HEMPSTEAD	489	236	New York	Nassau	17,689	77 / 250
WEST ISLIP	492	237	New York	Suffolk	28,419	85 / 250
WEST MILFORD	516	238	New Jersey	Passaic	25,430	158 / 250
WEST NEW YORK	542	239	New Jersey	Hudson	38,125	236 / 250
WEST ORANGE	476	240	New Jersey	Essex	39,103	37 / 250
WEST PATERSON	497	241	New Jersey	Passaic	10,982	101 / 250
WESTBURY	501	242	New York	Nassau	13,060	112 / 250
WESTFIELD	468	243	New Jersey	Union	28,870	15 / 250
WESTPORT	487	244	Connecticut	Fairfield	24,407	71 / 250
WESTWOOD	491	245	New Jersey	Bergen	10,446	82 / 250
WHITE PLAINS	505	246	New York	Westchester	48,718	125 / 250
WOODBRIDGE	521	247	New Jersey	Middlesex	17,434	172 / 250
WOODMERE	477	248	New York	Nassau	15,578	42 / 250
WYCKOFF	472	249	New Jersey	Bergen	15,372	25 / 250
YONKERS	521	250	New York	Westchester	188,082	173 / 250

Metropolitan Area Suburb Rankings
NEW YORK-NORTHERN NEW JERSEY-LONG ISLAND

Composite: *Rank* 1 / 250 *Score* 69.61   **LIVINGSTON (NJ)**

CATEGORY	RANK	SCORE	STATISTIC	VALUE	RANK	SCORE
Economics	10	75.10	Median Household Income	$74,401	12	54.0
			% of Families Above Poverty Level	99.0%	16	96.2
Affordable Housing	235	31.30	Median Home Value	$245,200	213	62.6
			Median Rent	$1,001	232	0.0
Crime	77	88.80	Violent Crimes per 10,000 Population	8	22	97.9
			Property Crimes per 10,000 Population	420	89	79.7
Open Spaces	5	92.15	Population Density (Persons/Sq. Mile)	1916	23	96.5
			Average Rooms per Housing Unit	7.4	5	87.8
Education	10	83.00	% High School Enrollment/Completion	97.7%	21	97.7
			% College Graduates	52.5%	12	68.3
Commute	109	36.20	Average Work Commute in Minutes	25	72	61.9
			% Commuting on Public Transportation	6.8%	170	10.5
Community Stability	33	80.75	% Living in Same House as in 1979	62.4%	21	83.1
			% Living in Same County as in 1985	86.2%	87	78.4

Composite: *Rank* 1 / 250 *Score* 69.61   **WEST CALDWELL (NJ)**

CATEGORY	RANK	SCORE	STATISTIC	VALUE	RANK	SCORE
Economics	16	71.75	Median Household Income	$65,920	22	45.6
			% of Families Above Poverty Level	99.4%	4	97.9
Affordable Housing	211	45.50	Median Home Value	$232,900	205	65.6
			Median Rent	$858	202	25.4
Crime	23	94.80	Violent Crimes per 10,000 Population	7	17	98.2
			Property Crimes per 10,000 Population	244	30	91.4
Open Spaces	21	85.90	Population Density (Persons/Sq. Mile)	2064	31	96.2
			Average Rooms per Housing Unit	6.9	26	75.6
Education	35	75.15	% High School Enrollment/Completion	97.6%	24	97.6
			% College Graduates	41.6%	37	52.7
Commute	125	34.65	Average Work Commute in Minutes	25	72	61.9
			% Commuting on Public Transportation	4.9%	201	7.4
Community Stability	38	79.55	% Living in Same House as in 1979	59.4%	36	76.5
			% Living in Same County as in 1985	87.6%	63	82.6

Composite: *Rank* 3 / 250 *Score* 69.30   **FAIR LAWN (NJ)**

CATEGORY	RANK	SCORE	STATISTIC	VALUE	RANK	SCORE
Economics	112	60.05	Median Household Income	$49,658	117	29.5
			% of Families Above Poverty Level	97.7%	116	90.6
Affordable Housing	53	73.30	Median Home Value	$198,000	158	74.2
			Median Rent	$594	33	72.4
Crime	20	95.05	Violent Crimes per 10,000 Population	13	41	96.5
			Property Crimes per 10,000 Population	210	18	93.6
Open Spaces	110	73.15	Population Density (Persons/Sq. Mile)	5908	161	87.8
			Average Rooms per Housing Unit	6.2	91	58.5
Education	88	65.10	% High School Enrollment/Completion	93.6%	124	93.6
			% College Graduates	30.3%	82	36.6
Commute	101	36.80	Average Work Commute in Minutes	26	84	57.1
			% Commuting on Public Transportation	10.6%	109	16.5
Community Stability	26	81.65	% Living in Same House as in 1979	62.8%	18	84.0
			% Living in Same County as in 1985	86.5%	79	79.3

Metropolitan Area Suburb Rankings
NEW YORK-NORTHERN NEW JERSEY-LONG ISLAND

Composite: **Rank** 4 / 250 **Score** 68.87   **VERONA** (NJ)

CATEGORY	RANK	SCORE	STATISTIC	VALUE	RANK	SCORE
Economics	39	67.50	Median Household Income	$55,248	67	35.0
			% of Families Above Poverty Level	99.9%	1	100.0
Affordable Housing	97	65.20	Median Home Value	$213,600	189	70.3
			Median Rent	$663	73	60.1
Crime	43	92.95	Violent Crimes per 10,000 Population	22	74	93.8
			Property Crimes per 10,000 Population	233	27	92.1
Open Spaces	126	70.55	Population Density (Persons/Sq. Mile)	4944	130	89.9
			Average Rooms per Housing Unit	5.9	123	51.2
Education	38	74.40	% High School Enrollment/Completion	95.5%	82	95.5
			% College Graduates	42.0%	36	53.3
Commute	88	38.50	Average Work Commute in Minutes	24	56	66.7
			% Commuting on Public Transportation	6.7%	172	10.3
Community Stability	72	73.00	% Living in Same House as in 1979	53.7%	74	64.0
			% Living in Same County as in 1985	87.4%	67	82.0

Composite: **Rank** 5 / 250 **Score** 68.63   **CLARK** (NJ)

CATEGORY	RANK	SCORE	STATISTIC	VALUE	RANK	SCORE
Economics	85	62.40	Median Household Income	$50,095	110	29.9
			% of Families Above Poverty Level	98.7%	39	94.9
Affordable Housing	125	61.60	Median Home Value	$197,300	156	74.3
			Median Rent	$726	118	48.9
Crime	21	94.95	Violent Crimes per 10,000 Population	5	8	98.8
			Property Crimes per 10,000 Population	248	32	91.1
Open Spaces	103	74.70	Population Density (Persons/Sq. Mile)	3367	80	93.3
			Average Rooms per Housing Unit	6.1	104	56.1
Education	131	60.75	% High School Enrollment/Completion	94.5%	105	94.5
			% College Graduates	23.6%	135	27.0
Commute	82	38.95	Average Work Commute in Minutes	23	40	71.4
			% Commuting on Public Transportation	4.3%	216	6.5
Community Stability	15	87.05	% Living in Same House as in 1979	63.1%	16	84.6
			% Living in Same County as in 1985	89.9%	24	89.5

Composite: **Rank** 6 / 250 **Score** 68.05   **TRUMBULL** (CT)

CATEGORY	RANK	SCORE	STATISTIC	VALUE	RANK	SCORE
Economics	43	67.00	Median Household Income	$60,634	38	40.4
			% of Families Above Poverty Level	98.4%	63	93.6
Affordable Housing	213	44.85	Median Home Value	$241,400	212	63.5
			Median Rent	$854	201	26.2
Crime	60	90.90	Violent Crimes per 10,000 Population	5	8	98.8
			Property Crimes per 10,000 Population	370	81	83.0
Open Spaces	18	86.65	Population Density (Persons/Sq. Mile)	1377	9	97.7
			Average Rooms per Housing Unit	6.9	26	75.6
Education	50	70.60	% High School Enrollment/Completion	96.5%	52	96.5
			% College Graduates	36.0%	52	44.7
Commute	104	36.75	Average Work Commute in Minutes	23	40	71.4
			% Commuting on Public Transportation	1.5%	246	2.1
Community Stability	37	79.60	% Living in Same House as in 1979	57.4%	48	72.1
			% Living in Same County as in 1985	89.1%	39	87.1

Metropolitan Area Suburb Rankings
NEW YORK-NORTHERN NEW JERSEY-LONG ISLAND

Composite: Rank 7 / 250 *Score* 67.96   **METUCHEN (NJ)**

CATEGORY	RANK	SCORE	STATISTIC	VALUE	RANK	SCORE
Economics	66	64.35	Median Household Income	$53,226	80	33.0
			% of Families Above Poverty Level	98.9%	25	95.7
Affordable Housing	72	69.25	Median Home Value	$177,800	105	79.1
			Median Rent	$667	76	59.4
Crime	66	90.25	Violent Crimes per 10,000 Population	13	41	96.5
			Property Crimes per 10,000 Population	355	79	84.0
Open Spaces	109	73.30	Population Density (Persons/Sq. Mile)	4673	121	90.5
			Average Rooms per Housing Unit	6.1	104	56.1
Education	45	71.20	% High School Enrollment/Completion	95.4%	83	95.4
			% College Graduates	37.6%	48	47.0
Commute	90	38.20	Average Work Commute in Minutes	26	84	57.1
			% Commuting on Public Transportation	12.4%	90	19.3
Community Stability	98	69.15	% Living in Same House as in 1979	51.7%	104	59.6
			% Living in Same County as in 1985	86.3%	85	78.7

Composite: Rank 8 / 250 *Score* 67.91   **HANOVER TOWNSHIP (NJ)**

CATEGORY	RANK	SCORE	STATISTIC	VALUE	RANK	SCORE
Economics	28	68.90	Median Household Income	$60,688	37	40.4
			% of Families Above Poverty Level	99.3%	6	97.4
Affordable Housing	231	33.95	Median Home Value	$234,600	207	65.2
			Median Rent	$986	230	2.7
Crime	10	97.50	Violent Crimes per 10,000 Population	5	8	98.8
			Property Crimes per 10,000 Population	171	10	96.2
Open Spaces	15	88.20	Population Density (Persons/Sq. Mile)	1082	5	98.4
			Average Rooms per Housing Unit	7.0	18	78.0
Education	54	69.75	% High School Enrollment/Completion	96.9%	41	96.9
			% College Graduates	34.5%	59	42.6
Commute	49	43.55	Average Work Commute in Minutes	20	5	85.7
			% Commuting on Public Transportation	1.1%	248	1.4
Community Stability	67	73.55	% Living in Same House as in 1979	58.7%	40	75.0
			% Living in Same County as in 1985	84.1%	136	72.1

Composite: Rank 9 / 250 *Score* 67.69   **ROCKVILLE CENTRE (NY)**

CATEGORY	RANK	SCORE	STATISTIC	VALUE	RANK	SCORE
Economics	83	62.95	Median Household Income	$55,476	63	35.3
			% of Families Above Poverty Level	97.7%	116	90.6
Affordable Housing	104	63.80	Median Home Value	$277,500	229	54.6
			Median Rent	$591	31	73.0
Crime	71	89.55	Violent Crimes per 10,000 Population	24	77	93.2
			Property Crimes per 10,000 Population	327	66	85.9
Open Spaces	130	70.15	Population Density (Persons/Sq. Mile)	7538	191	84.2
			Average Rooms per Housing Unit	6.1	104	56.1
Education	27	76.65	% High School Enrollment/Completion	97.3%	32	97.3
			% College Graduates	43.9%	31	56.0
Commute	145	32.45	Average Work Commute in Minutes	32	211	28.6
			% Commuting on Public Transportation	23.1%	19	36.3
Community Stability	43	78.25	% Living in Same House as in 1979	53.0%	89	62.5
			% Living in Same County as in 1985	91.4%	10	94.0

Metropolitan Area Suburb Rankings
NEW YORK-NORTHERN NEW JERSEY-LONG ISLAND

Composite: **Rank** 10 / 250 *Score* 67.54 **PEQUANNOCK TOWNSHIP** (NJ)

CATEGORY	RANK	SCORE	STATISTIC	VALUE	RANK	SCORE
Economics	56	65.20	Median Household Income	$54,935	68	34.7
			% of Families Above Poverty Level	98.9%	25	95.7
Affordable Housing	134	60.30	Median Home Value	$202,300	164	73.1
			Median Rent	$734	123	47.5
Crime	31	94.15	Violent Crimes per 10,000 Population	10	30	97.3
			Property Crimes per 10,000 Population	250	35	91.0
Open Spaces	44	81.30	Population Density (Persons/Sq. Mile)	1824	19	96.7
			Average Rooms per Housing Unit	6.5	62	65.9
Education	102	63.70	% High School Enrollment/Completion	93.0%	141	93.0
			% College Graduates	28.8%	93	34.4
Commute	94	37.85	Average Work Commute in Minutes	23	40	71.4
			% Commuting on Public Transportation	2.9%	231	4.3
Community Stability	86	70.30	% Living in Same House as in 1979	55.2%	63	67.3
			% Living in Same County as in 1985	84.5%	126	73.3

Composite: **Rank** 11 / 250 *Score* 67.51 **CRANFORD** (NJ)

CATEGORY	RANK	SCORE	STATISTIC	VALUE	RANK	SCORE
Economics	63	64.40	Median Household Income	$54,469	71	34.3
			% of Families Above Poverty Level	98.6%	50	94.5
Affordable Housing	158	57.35	Median Home Value	$200,300	161	73.6
			Median Rent	$770	147	41.1
Crime	36	93.70	Violent Crimes per 10,000 Population	7	17	98.2
			Property Crimes per 10,000 Population	277	44	89.2
Open Spaces	74	78.15	Population Density (Persons/Sq. Mile)	4709	123	90.4
			Average Rooms per Housing Unit	6.5	62	65.9
Education	57	69.40	% High School Enrollment/Completion	97.2%	33	97.2
			% College Graduates	33.8%	62	41.6
Commute-	118	35.30	Average Work Commute in Minutes	26	84	57.1
			% Commuting on Public Transportation	8.7%	135	13.5
Community Stability	62	74.30	% Living in Same House as in 1979	56.8%	52	70.8
			% Living in Same County as in 1985	86.0%	98	77.8

Composite: **Rank** 12 / 250 *Score* 67.46 **STONY POINT** (NY)

CATEGORY	RANK	SCORE	STATISTIC	VALUE	RANK	SCORE
Economics	102	60.90	Median Household Income	$50,073	112	29.9
			% of Families Above Poverty Level	98.0%	91	91.9
Affordable Housing	83	67.20	Median Home Value	$194,400	150	75.0
			Median Rent	$667	76	59.4
Crime	3	99.05	Violent Crimes per 10,000 Population	1	1	100.0
			Property Crimes per 10,000 Population	142	5	98.1
Open Spaces	81	77.50	Population Density (Persons/Sq. Mile)	1924	24	96.5
			Average Rooms per Housing Unit	6.2	91	58.5
Education	155	58.40	% High School Enrollment/Completion	94.7%	97	94.7
			% College Graduates	20.2%	163	22.1
Commute	163	30.00	Average Work Commute in Minutes	26	84	57.1
			% Commuting on Public Transportation	2.0%	240	2.9
Community Stability	40	79.15	% Living in Same House as in 1979	51.9%	100	60.1
			% Living in Same County as in 1985	92.8%	3	98.2

Metropolitan Area Suburb Rankings
NEW YORK-NORTHERN NEW JERSEY-LONG ISLAND

Composite: Rank 12 / 250 *Score* 67.46   **STRATFORD (CT)**

CATEGORY	RANK	SCORE	STATISTIC	VALUE	RANK	SCORE
Economics	154	56.40	Median Household Income	$41,745	177	21.7
			% of Families Above Poverty Level	97.8%	111	91.1
Affordable Housing	75	68.55	Median Home Value	$176,900	104	79.3
			Median Rent	$676	82	57.8
Crime	72	89.50	Violent Crimes per 10,000 Population	21	73	94.1
			Property Crimes per 10,000 Population	341	73	84.9
Open Spaces	138	69.25	Population Density (Persons/Sq. Mile)	2809	63	94.6
			Average Rooms per Housing Unit	5.6	154	43.9
Education	132	60.70	% High School Enrollment/Completion	97.8%	19	97.8
			% College Graduates	21.2%	156	23.6
Commute	21	46.70	Average Work Commute in Minutes	19	2	90.5
			% Commuting on Public Transportation	2.0%	240	2.9
Community Stability	32	81.10	% Living in Same House as in 1979	54.8%	64	66.4
			% Living in Same County as in 1985	92.0%	5	95.8

Composite: Rank 14 / 250 *Score* 67.39   **NEW PROVIDENCE (NJ)**

CATEGORY	RANK	SCORE	STATISTIC	VALUE	RANK	SCORE
Economics	32	68.05	Median Household Income	$62,420	31	42.1
			% of Families Above Poverty Level	98.5%	58	94.0
Affordable Housing	185	52.90	Median Home Value	$246,100	215	62.4
			Median Rent	$757	139	43.4
Crime	4	98.90	Violent Crimes per 10,000 Population	4	5	99.1
			Property Crimes per 10,000 Population	133	3	98.7
Open Spaces	49	81.10	Population Density (Persons/Sq. Mile)	3109	73	93.9
			Average Rooms per Housing Unit	6.6	52	68.3
Education	25	77.80	% High School Enrollment/Completion	92.9%	147	92.9
			% College Graduates	48.6%	19	62.7
Commute	99	37.20	Average Work Commute in Minutes	25	72	61.9
			% Commuting on Public Transportation	8.1%	148	12.5
Community Stability	161	55.75	% Living in Same House as in 1979	49.3%	121	54.4
			% Living in Same County as in 1985	79.1%	202	57.1

Composite: Rank 15 / 250 *Score* 67.38   **WESTFIELD (NJ)**

CATEGORY	RANK	SCORE	STATISTIC	VALUE	RANK	SCORE
Economics	20	70.85	Median Household Income	$66,760	17	46.4
			% of Families Above Poverty Level	98.8%	32	95.3
Affordable Housing	208	46.55	Median Home Value	$256,600	219	59.8
			Median Rent	$814	173	33.3
Crime	39	93.60	Violent Crimes per 10,000 Population	6	15	98.5
			Property Crimes per 10,000 Population	285	48	88.7
Open Spaces	34	83.45	Population Density (Persons/Sq. Mile)	4287	107	91.3
			Average Rooms per Housing Unit	6.9	26	75.6
Education	8	84.40	% High School Enrollment/Completion	98.9%	9	98.9
			% College Graduates	53.6%	8	69.9
Commute	138	33.05	Average Work Commute in Minutes	28	127	47.6
			% Commuting on Public Transportation	11.9%	96	18.5
Community Stability	140	59.75	% Living in Same House as in 1979	50.2%	113	56.4
			% Living in Same County as in 1985	81.1%	174	63.1

Metropolitan Area Suburb Rankings
NEW YORK-NORTHERN NEW JERSEY-LONG ISLAND

Composite: **Rank** 16 / 250 **Score** 67.33   **PLAINVIEW (NY)**

CATEGORY	RANK	SCORE	STATISTIC	VALUE	RANK	SCORE
Economics	17	71.60	Median Household Income	$66,095	20	45.8
			% of Families Above Poverty Level	99.3%	6	97.4
Affordable Housing	141	59.75	Median Home Value	$230,900	203	66.1
			Median Rent	$701	104	53.4
Crime	N/A	N/A	Violent Crimes per 10,000 Population	N/A	N/A	N/A
			Property Crimes per 10,000 Population	N/A	N/A	N/A
Open Spaces	31	84.35	Population Density (Persons/Sq. Mile)	4584	118	90.7
			Average Rooms per Housing Unit	7.0	18	78.0
Education	41	74.15	% High School Enrollment/Completion	99.7%	3	99.7
			% College Graduates	38.7%	45	48.6
Commute	206	25.80	Average Work Commute in Minutes	32	211	28.6
			% Commuting on Public Transportation	14.7%	71	23.0
Community Stability	12	88.35	% Living in Same House as in 1979	65.9%	7	90.8
			% Living in Same County as in 1985	88.7%	42	85.9

Composite: **Rank** 17 / 250 **Score** 67.31   **MILLBURN (NJ)**

CATEGORY	RANK	SCORE	STATISTIC	VALUE	RANK	SCORE
Economics	4	78.65	Median Household Income	$83,275	3	62.8
			% of Families Above Poverty Level	98.6%	50	94.5
Affordable Housing	240	28.05	Median Home Value	$381,600	245	29.1
			Median Rent	$849	194	27.0
Crime	74	89.30	Violent Crimes per 10,000 Population	14	48	96.2
			Property Crimes per 10,000 Population	379	83	82.4
Open Spaces	14	88.45	Population Density (Persons/Sq. Mile)	1986	28	96.4
			Average Rooms per Housing Unit	7.1	13	80.5
Education	2	88.95	% High School Enrollment/Completion	97.6%	24	97.6
			% College Graduates	60.9%	2	80.3
Commute	113	35.70	Average Work Commute in Minutes	29	150	42.9
			% Commuting on Public Transportation	18.2%	45	28.5
Community Stability	129	62.05	% Living in Same House as in 1979	53.4%	81	63.4
			% Living in Same County as in 1985	80.3%	188	60.7

Composite: **Rank** 18 / 250 **Score** 67.04   **GLEN ROCK (NJ)**

CATEGORY	RANK	SCORE	STATISTIC	VALUE	RANK	SCORE
Economics	18	70.95	Median Household Income	$65,976	21	45.7
			% of Families Above Poverty Level	99.0%	16	96.2
Affordable Housing	237	30.10	Median Home Value	$254,700	218	60.2
			Median Rent	$1,001	232	0.0
Crime	7	98.20	Violent Crimes per 10,000 Population	5	8	98.8
			Property Crimes per 10,000 Population	150	8	97.6
Open Spaces	28	85.00	Population Density (Persons/Sq. Mile)	3998	99	92.0
			Average Rooms per Housing Unit	7.0	18	78.0
Education	14	80.75	% High School Enrollment/Completion	92.2%	165	92.2
			% College Graduates	53.2%	10	69.3
Commute	147	32.25	Average Work Commute in Minutes	29	150	42.9
			% Commuting on Public Transportation	13.8%	80	21.6
Community Stability	75	72.05	% Living in Same House as in 1979	56.5%	57	70.2
			% Living in Same County as in 1985	84.7%	123	73.9

Metropolitan Area Suburb Rankings
NEW YORK-NORTHERN NEW JERSEY-LONG ISLAND

Composite: **Rank** 19 / 250 *Score* 67.01   **BERKELEY HEIGHTS** (NJ)

CATEGORY	RANK	SCORE	STATISTIC	VALUE	RANK	SCORE
Economics	9	75.45	Median Household Income	$75,122	9	54.7
			% of Families Above Poverty Level	99.0%	16	96.2
Affordable Housing	239	29.15	Median Home Value	$262,800	224	58.3
			Median Rent	$1,001	232	0.0
Crime	1	99.85	Violent Crimes per 10,000 Population	2	2	99.7
			Property Crimes per 10,000 Population	114	1	100.0
Open Spaces	5	92.15	Population Density (Persons/Sq. Mile)	1912	22	96.5
			Average Rooms per Housing Unit	7.4	5	87.8
Education	15	80.55	% High School Enrollment/Completion	99.0%	7	99.0
			% College Graduates	48.2%	22	62.1
Commute	131	33.80	Average Work Commute in Minutes	27	102	52.4
			% Commuting on Public Transportation	9.8%	118	15.2
Community Stability	150	58.10	% Living in Same House as in 1979	52.8%	90	62.1
			% Living in Same County as in 1985	78.1%	213	54.1

Composite: **Rank** 20 / 250 *Score* 66.91   **SCOTCH PLAINS** (NJ)

CATEGORY	RANK	SCORE	STATISTIC	VALUE	RANK	SCORE
Economics	40	67.45	Median Household Income	$58,194	51	37.9
			% of Families Above Poverty Level	99.2%	11	97.0
Affordable Housing	170	55.30	Median Home Value	$208,600	181	71.6
			Median Rent	$782	154	39.0
Crime	40	93.40	Violent Crimes per 10,000 Population	14	48	96.2
			Property Crimes per 10,000 Population	255	39	90.6
Open Spaces	41	81.95	Population Density (Persons/Sq. Mile)	2332	40	95.6
			Average Rooms per Housing Unit	6.6	52	68.3
Education	33	75.55	% High School Enrollment/Completion	98.7%	10	98.7
			% College Graduates	41.4%	38	52.4
Commute	148	32.20	Average Work Commute in Minutes	27	102	52.4
			% Commuting on Public Transportation	7.8%	155	12.0
Community Stability	124	62.50	% Living in Same House as in 1979	51.9%	100	60.1
			% Living in Same County as in 1985	81.7%	166	64.9

Composite: **Rank** 21 / 250 *Score* 66.79   **RIDGEWOOD** (NJ)

CATEGORY	RANK	SCORE	STATISTIC	VALUE	RANK	SCORE
Economics	8	75.50	Median Household Income	$75,221	8	54.8
			% of Families Above Poverty Level	99.0%	16	96.2
Affordable Housing	233	32.90	Median Home Value	$296,400	233	50.0
			Median Rent	$912	218	15.8
Crime	2	99.35	Violent Crimes per 10,000 Population	5	8	98.8
			Property Crimes per 10,000 Population	115	2	99.9
Open Spaces	40	82.40	Population Density (Persons/Sq. Mile)	4179	105	91.6
			Average Rooms per Housing Unit	6.8	36	73.2
Education	5	86.95	% High School Enrollment/Completion	100.0%	1	100.0
			% College Graduates	56.4%	5	73.9
Commute	141	32.85	Average Work Commute in Minutes	29	150	42.9
			% Commuting on Public Transportation	14.6%	73	22.8
Community Stability	152	57.55	% Living in Same House as in 1979	48.2%	138	52.0
			% Living in Same County as in 1985	81.1%	174	63.1

Metropolitan Area Suburb Rankings
NEW YORK-NORTHERN NEW JERSEY-LONG ISLAND

Composite: **Rank** 22 / 250 *Score* 66.76 **NEW MILFORD** (NJ)

CATEGORY	RANK	SCORE	STATISTIC	VALUE	RANK	SCORE
Economics	114	59.70	Median Household Income	$44,600	158	24.5
			% of Families Above Poverty Level	98.7%	39	94.9
Affordable Housing	30	77.50	Median Home Value	$207,900	179	71.7
			Median Rent	$533	13	83.3
Crime	37	93.65	Violent Crimes per 10,000 Population	14	48	96.2
			Property Crimes per 10,000 Population	248	32	91.1
Open Spaces	180	63.50	Population Density (Persons/Sq. Mile)	6914	181	85.5
			Average Rooms per Housing Unit	5.5	162	41.5
Education	108	63.10	% High School Enrollment/Completion	96.5%	52	96.5
			% College Graduates	25.5%	118	29.7
Commute	115	35.60	Average Work Commute in Minutes	26	84	57.1
			% Commuting on Public Transportation	9.1%	127	14.1
Community Stability	62	74.30	% Living in Same House as in 1979	52.7%	92	61.8
			% Living in Same County as in 1985	89.0%	40	86.8

Composite: **Rank** 23 / 250 *Score* 66.71 **TEANECK** (NJ)

CATEGORY	RANK	SCORE	STATISTIC	VALUE	RANK	SCORE
Economics	86	62.45	Median Household Income	$56,598	57	36.4
			% of Families Above Poverty Level	97.2%	145	88.5
Affordable Housing	73	68.85	Median Home Value	$206,900	174	72.0
			Median Rent	$632	53	65.7
Crime	85	86.25	Violent Crimes per 10,000 Population	32	92	90.9
			Property Crimes per 10,000 Population	391	86	81.6
Open Spaces	114	72.75	Population Density (Persons/Sq. Mile)	6249	167	87.0
			Average Rooms per Housing Unit	6.2	91	58.5
Education	43	74.05	% High School Enrollment/Completion	96.4%	59	96.4
			% College Graduates	40.9%	40	51.7
Commute	102	36.85	Average Work Commute in Minutes	28	127	47.6
			% Commuting on Public Transportation	16.7%	50	26.1
Community Stability	113	65.80	% Living in Same House as in 1979	54.8%	64	66.4
			% Living in Same County as in 1985	81.8%	165	65.2

Composite: **Rank** 24 / 250 *Score* 66.65 **SPRINGFIELD** (NJ)

CATEGORY	RANK	SCORE	STATISTIC	VALUE	RANK	SCORE
Economics	96	61.70	Median Household Income	$48,647	123	28.5
			% of Families Above Poverty Level	98.7%	39	94.9
Affordable Housing	165	55.85	Median Home Value	$216,300	191	69.7
			Median Rent	$765	143	42.0
Crime	28	94.30	Violent Crimes per 10,000 Population	7	17	98.2
			Property Crimes per 10,000 Population	258	40	90.4
Open Spaces	105	74.35	Population Density (Persons/Sq. Mile)	2605	59	95.0
			Average Rooms per Housing Unit	6.0	117	53.7
Education	52	70.10	% High School Enrollment/Completion	96.5%	52	96.5
			% College Graduates	35.3%	55	43.7
Commute	71	40.55	Average Work Commute in Minutes	23	40	71.4
			% Commuting on Public Transportation	6.3%	180	9.7
Community Stability	91	69.70	% Living in Same House as in 1979	56.0%	60	69.1
			% Living in Same County as in 1985	83.5%	143	70.3

Metropolitan Area Suburb Rankings
NEW YORK-NORTHERN NEW JERSEY-LONG ISLAND

Composite: **Rank** 25 / 250 **Score** 66.26   **WYCKOFF (NJ)**

CATEGORY	RANK	SCORE	STATISTIC	VALUE	RANK	SCORE
Economics	7	75.85	Median Household Income	$75,905	7	55.5
			% of Families Above Poverty Level	99.0%	16	96.2
Affordable Housing	245	20.65	Median Home Value	$331,800	241	41.3
			Median Rent	$1,001	232	0.0
Crime	5	98.75	Violent Crimes per 10,000 Population	5	8	98.8
			Property Crimes per 10,000 Population	133	3	98.7
Open Spaces	8	90.50	Population Density (Persons/Sq. Mile)	2347	42	95.6
			Average Rooms per Housing Unit	7.3	8	85.4
Education	32	75.65	% High School Enrollment/Completion	93.0%	141	93.0
			% College Graduates	45.5%	28	58.3
Commute	111	36.10	Average Work Commute in Minutes	25	72	61.9
			% Commuting on Public Transportation	6.7%	172	10.3
Community Stability	110	66.35	% Living in Same House as in 1979	53.1%	86	62.7
			% Living in Same County as in 1985	83.4%	144	70.0

Composite: **Rank** 26 / 250 **Score** 66.16   **RIVER EDGE (NJ)**

CATEGORY	RANK	SCORE	STATISTIC	VALUE	RANK	SCORE
Economics	104	60.85	Median Household Income	$52,126	90	31.9
			% of Families Above Poverty Level	97.5%	125	89.8
Affordable Housing	169	55.35	Median Home Value	$220,200	195	68.7
			Median Rent	$765	143	42.0
Crime	35	93.80	Violent Crimes per 10,000 Population	14	48	96.2
			Property Crimes per 10,000 Population	243	29	91.4
Open Spaces	134	69.80	Population Density (Persons/Sq. Mile)	5624	153	88.4
			Average Rooms per Housing Unit	5.9	123	51.2
Education	36	74.55	% High School Enrollment/Completion	100.0%	1	100.0
			% College Graduates	39.1%	44	49.1
Commute	150	31.90	Average Work Commute in Minutes	30	172	38.1
			% Commuting on Public Transportation	16.4%	55	25.7
Community Stability	50	76.85	% Living in Same House as in 1979	59.4%	36	76.5
			% Living in Same County as in 1985	85.8%	106	77.2

Composite: **Rank** 27 / 250 **Score** 66.15   **GARDEN CITY (NY)**

CATEGORY	RANK	SCORE	STATISTIC	VALUE	RANK	SCORE
Economics	11	74.70	Median Household Income	$74,478	11	54.1
			% of Families Above Poverty Level	98.8%	32	95.3
Affordable Housing	247	15.60	Median Home Value	$373,100	244	31.2
			Median Rent	$1,001	232	0.0
Crime	26	94.40	Violent Crimes per 10,000 Population	9	27	97.6
			Property Crimes per 10,000 Population	247	31	91.2
Open Spaces	29	84.90	Population Density (Persons/Sq. Mile)	4057	102	91.8
			Average Rooms per Housing Unit	7.0	18	78.0
Education	6	84.65	% High School Enrollment/Completion	98.2%	15	98.2
			% College Graduates	54.5%	7	71.1
Commute	154	31.55	Average Work Commute in Minutes	33	221	23.8
			% Commuting on Public Transportation	25.0%	14	39.3
Community Stability	47	77.25	% Living in Same House as in 1979	59.9%	33	77.6
			% Living in Same County as in 1985	85.7%	109	76.9

Metropolitan Area Suburb Rankings
NEW YORK-NORTHERN NEW JERSEY-LONG ISLAND

Composite: **Rank** 28 / 250 *Score* 66.11   **TOTOWA** (NJ)

CATEGORY	RANK	SCORE	STATISTIC	VALUE	RANK	SCORE
Economics	123	59.25	Median Household Income	$46,309	143	26.2
			% of Families Above Poverty Level	98.1%	83	92.3
Affordable Housing	105	63.70	Median Home Value	$189,200	133	76.3
			Median Rent	$714	109	51.1
Crime	115	77.35	Violent Crimes per 10,000 Population	23	75	93.5
			Property Crimes per 10,000 Population	699	134	61.2
Open Spaces	97	75.60	Population Density (Persons/Sq. Mile)	2547	54	95.1
			Average Rooms per Housing Unit	6.1	104	56.1
Education	209	51.85	% High School Enrollment/Completion	86.8%	224	86.8
			% College Graduates	16.5%	192	16.9
Commute	40	44.45	Average Work Commute in Minutes	20	5	85.7
			% Commuting on Public Transportation	2.2%	237	3.2
Community Stability	6	90.55	% Living in Same House as in 1979	66.4%	6	91.9
			% Living in Same County as in 1985	89.8%	26	89.2

Composite: **Rank** 29 / 250 *Score* 66.05   **HASBROUCK HEIGHTS** (NJ)

CATEGORY	RANK	SCORE	STATISTIC	VALUE	RANK	SCORE
Economics	132	58.25	Median Household Income	$44,672	156	24.6
			% of Families Above Poverty Level	98.0%	91	91.9
Affordable Housing	94	65.45	Median Home Value	$204,700	171	72.5
			Median Rent	$673	81	58.4
Crime	62	90.70	Violent Crimes per 10,000 Population	4	5	99.1
			Property Crimes per 10,000 Population	381	84	82.3
Open Spaces	171	65.15	Population Density (Persons/Sq. Mile)	7610	193	84.0
			Average Rooms per Housing Unit	5.7	143	46.3
Education	145	59.40	% High School Enrollment/Completion	94.1%	117	94.1
			% College Graduates	22.0%	145	24.7
Commute	26	45.95	Average Work Commute in Minutes	22	27	76.2
			% Commuting on Public Transportation	10.1%	113	15.7
Community Stability	46	77.45	% Living in Same House as in 1979	56.5%	57	70.2
			% Living in Same County as in 1985	88.3%	54	84.7

Composite: **Rank** 30 / 250 *Score* 65.91   **DUMONT** (NJ)

CATEGORY	RANK	SCORE	STATISTIC	VALUE	RANK	SCORE
Economics	122	59.20	Median Household Income	$48,776	121	28.6
			% of Families Above Poverty Level	97.5%	125	89.8
Affordable Housing	80	67.40	Median Home Value	$186,400	123	77.0
			Median Rent	$676	82	57.8
Crime	13	96.45	Violent Crimes per 10,000 Population	8	22	97.9
			Property Crimes per 10,000 Population	190	13	95.0
Open Spaces	169	65.25	Population Density (Persons/Sq. Mile)	8660	208	81.7
			Average Rooms per Housing Unit	5.8	134	48.8
Education	161	57.80	% High School Enrollment/Completion	92.3%	161	92.3
			% College Graduates	21.0%	158	23.3
Commute	123	34.70	Average Work Commute in Minutes	27	102	52.4
			% Commuting on Public Transportation	10.9%	106	17.0
Community Stability	34	80.55	% Living in Same House as in 1979	57.3%	50	71.9
			% Living in Same County as in 1985	89.8%	26	89.2

Metropolitan Area Suburb Rankings
NEW YORK-NORTHERN NEW JERSEY-LONG ISLAND

Composite: *Rank* 30 / 250 *Score* 65.91   **SHELTON (CT)**

CATEGORY	RANK	SCORE	STATISTIC	VALUE	RANK	SCORE
Economics	96	61.70	Median Household Income	$49,965	113	29.8
			% of Families Above Poverty Level	98.4%	63	93.6
Affordable Housing	85	66.75	Median Home Value	$207,800	177	71.8
			Median Rent	$654	65	61.7
Crime	14	96.35	Violent Crimes per 10,000 Population	13	41	96.5
			Property Crimes per 10,000 Population	171	10	96.2
Open Spaces	82	77.15	Population Density (Persons/Sq. Mile)	1159	7	98.2
			Average Rooms per Housing Unit	6.1	104	56.1
Education	128	61.05	% High School Enrollment/Completion	94.7%	97	94.7
			% College Graduates	23.9%	132	27.4
Commute	86	38.75	Average Work Commute in Minutes	22	27	76.2
			% Commuting on Public Transportation	1.0%	249	1.3
Community Stability	141	59.60	% Living in Same House as in 1979	43.1%	176	40.8
			% Living in Same County as in 1985	86.2%	87	78.4

Composite: *Rank* 32 / 250 *Score* 65.88   **MANVILLE (NJ)**

CATEGORY	RANK	SCORE	STATISTIC	VALUE	RANK	SCORE
Economics	172	53.25	Median Household Income	$37,664	206	17.6
			% of Families Above Poverty Level	97.3%	141	88.9
Affordable Housing	43	74.90	Median Home Value	$143,500	37	87.5
			Median Rent	$651	62	62.3
Crime	29	94.20	Violent Crimes per 10,000 Population	14	48	96.2
			Property Crimes per 10,000 Population	232	25	92.2
Open Spaces	177	64.00	Population Density (Persons/Sq. Mile)	4258	106	91.4
			Average Rooms per Housing Unit	5.3	180	36.6
Education	210	51.70	% High School Enrollment/Completion	96.8%	42	96.8
			% College Graduates	9.3%	240	6.6
Commute	48	43.65	Average Work Commute in Minutes	20	5	85.7
			% Commuting on Public Transportation	1.2%	247	1.6
Community Stability	39	79.45	% Living in Same House as in 1979	58.2%	43	73.9
			% Living in Same County as in 1985	88.4%	49	85.0

Composite: *Rank* 32 / 250 *Score* 65.88   **SALISBURY (NY)**

CATEGORY	RANK	SCORE	STATISTIC	VALUE	RANK	SCORE
Economics	36	67.60	Median Household Income	$57,580	54	37.3
			% of Families Above Poverty Level	99.4%	4	97.9
Affordable Housing	88	65.85	Median Home Value	$183,900	118	77.6
			Median Rent	$697	99	54.1
Crime	N/A	N/A	Violent Crimes per 10,000 Population	N/A	N/A	N/A
			Property Crimes per 10,000 Population	N/A	N/A	N/A
Open Spaces	63	79.15	Population Density (Persons/Sq. Mile)	7098	186	85.1
			Average Rooms per Housing Unit	6.8	36	73.2
Education	75	66.55	% High School Enrollment/Completion	96.8%	42	96.8
			% College Graduates	30.1%	85	36.3
Commute	158	30.70	Average Work Commute in Minutes	29	150	42.9
			% Commuting on Public Transportation	11.9%	96	18.5
Community Stability	19	85.40	% Living in Same House as in 1979	63.5%	15	85.5
			% Living in Same County as in 1985	88.5%	46	85.3

Metropolitan Area Suburb Rankings
NEW YORK-NORTHERN NEW JERSEY-LONG ISLAND

Composite: **Rank** 34 / 250 *Score* 65.66   **SOUTH PLAINFIELD** (NJ)

CATEGORY	RANK	SCORE	STATISTIC	VALUE	RANK	SCORE
Economics	93	61.90	Median Household Income	$51,198	103	31.0
			% of Families Above Poverty Level	98.2%	76	92.8
Affordable Housing	96	65.35	Median Home Value	$161,200	75	83.2
			Median Rent	$734	123	47.5
Crime	91	84.75	Violent Crimes per 10,000 Population	20	71	94.4
			Property Crimes per 10,000 Population	489	103	75.1
Open Spaces	56	79.40	Population Density (Persons/Sq. Mile)	2451	50	95.4
			Average Rooms per Housing Unit	6.4	73	63.4
Education	150	59.30	% High School Enrollment/Completion	98.7%	10	98.7
			% College Graduates	18.6%	175	19.9
Commute	116	35.50	Average Work Commute in Minutes	24	56	66.7
			% Commuting on Public Transportation	2.9%	231	4.3
Community Stability	69	73.45	% Living in Same House as in 1979	56.7%	53	70.6
			% Living in Same County as in 1985	85.5%	111	76.3

Composite: **Rank** 35 / 250 *Score* 65.33   **EASTCHESTER** (NY)

CATEGORY	RANK	SCORE	STATISTIC	VALUE	RANK	SCORE
Economics	54	65.45	Median Household Income	$59,274	45	39.0
			% of Families Above Poverty Level	98.0%	91	91.9
Affordable Housing	182	53.25	Median Home Value	$323,500	238	43.3
			Median Rent	$646	60	63.2
Crime	19	95.20	Violent Crimes per 10,000 Population	12	40	96.8
			Property Crimes per 10,000 Population	210	18	93.6
Open Spaces	172	65.05	Population Density (Persons/Sq. Mile)	5543	149	88.6
			Average Rooms per Housing Unit	5.5	162	41.5
Education	30	75.90	% High School Enrollment/Completion	95.8%	76	95.8
			% College Graduates	43.9%	31	56.0
Commute	103	36.70	Average Work Commute in Minutes	31	195	33.3
			% Commuting on Public Transportation	25.5%	11	40.1
Community Stability	114	65.75	% Living in Same House as in 1979	51.3%	107	58.8
			% Living in Same County as in 1985	84.3%	132	72.7

Composite: **Rank** 36 / 250 *Score* 65.31   **OLD BRIDGE** (NJ)

CATEGORY	RANK	SCORE	STATISTIC	VALUE	RANK	SCORE
Economics	50	65.60	Median Household Income	$56,172	60	35.9
			% of Families Above Poverty Level	98.8%	32	95.3
Affordable Housing	20	80.70	Median Home Value	$166,700	86	81.9
			Median Rent	$554	20	79.5
Crime	50	91.90	Violent Crimes per 10,000 Population	19	67	94.7
			Property Crimes per 10,000 Population	278	45	89.1
Open Spaces	46	81.20	Population Density (Persons/Sq. Mile)	3037	71	94.1
			Average Rooms per Housing Unit	6.6	52	68.3
Education	115	62.55	% High School Enrollment/Completion	97.1%	36	97.1
			% College Graduates	24.3%	130	28.0
Commute	229	21.45	Average Work Commute in Minutes	34	234	19.0
			% Commuting on Public Transportation	15.3%	67	23.9
Community Stability	172	53.80	% Living in Same House as in 1979	48.5%	135	52.6
			% Living in Same County as in 1985	78.4%	210	55.0

Metropolitan Area Suburb Rankings
NEW YORK-NORTHERN NEW JERSEY-LONG ISLAND

Composite: Rank 37 / 250 **Score** 65.29 WEST ORANGE (NJ)

CATEGORY	RANK	SCORE	STATISTIC	VALUE	RANK	SCORE
Economics	118	59.50	Median Household Income	$49,777	116	29.6
			% of Families Above Poverty Level	97.4%	132	89.4
Affordable Housing	103	64.05	Median Home Value	$201,700	163	73.3
			Median Rent	$693	92	54.8
Crime	84	86.40	Violent Crimes per 10,000 Population	31	89	91.2
			Property Crimes per 10,000 Population	392	87	81.6
Open Spaces	102	74.85	Population Density (Persons/Sq. Mile)	3228	75	93.6
			Average Rooms per Housing Unit	6.1	104	56.1
Education	51	70.20	% High School Enrollment/Completion	93.3%	133	93.3
			% College Graduates	37.7%	47	47.1
Commute	80	39.45	Average Work Commute in Minutes	24	56	66.7
			% Commuting on Public Transportation	7.9%	153	12.2
Community Stability	123	62.60	% Living in Same House as in 1979	49.8%	115	55.5
			% Living in Same County as in 1985	83.3%	145	69.7

Composite: Rank 38 / 250 **Score** 65.16 NORTH ARLINGTON (NJ)

CATEGORY	RANK	SCORE	STATISTIC	VALUE	RANK	SCORE
Economics	164	54.80	Median Household Income	$39,433	194	19.4
			% of Families Above Poverty Level	97.6%	121	90.2
Affordable Housing	24	79.60	Median Home Value	$179,300	112	78.8
			Median Rent	$549	19	80.4
Crime	50	91.90	Violent Crimes per 10,000 Population	16	56	95.6
			Property Crimes per 10,000 Population	292	55	88.2
Open Spaces	197	60.35	Population Density (Persons/Sq. Mile)	5338	139	89.0
			Average Rooms per Housing Unit	5.1	199	31.7
Education	167	57.10	% High School Enrollment/Completion	97.2%	33	97.2
			% College Graduates	16.6%	190	17.0
Commute	58	42.65	Average Work Commute in Minutes	23	40	71.4
			% Commuting on Public Transportation	9.0%	129	13.9
Community Stability	91	69.70	% Living in Same House as in 1979	57.1%	51	71.5
			% Living in Same County as in 1985	82.7%	153	67.9

Composite: Rank 39 / 250 **Score** 65.06 OAKLAND (NJ)

CATEGORY	RANK	SCORE	STATISTIC	VALUE	RANK	SCORE
Economics	24	69.65	Median Household Income	$63,384	29	43.1
			% of Families Above Poverty Level	99.0%	16	96.2
Affordable Housing	227	35.90	Median Home Value	$215,100	190	70.0
			Median Rent	$991	231	1.8
Crime	8	98.10	Violent Crimes per 10,000 Population	7	17	98.2
			Property Crimes per 10,000 Population	144	7	98.0
Open Spaces	26	85.45	Population Density (Persons/Sq. Mile)	1394	11	97.7
			Average Rooms per Housing Unit	6.8	36	73.2
Education	44	71.40	% High School Enrollment/Completion	97.4%	31	97.4
			% College Graduates	36.5%	51	45.4
Commute	191	27.45	Average Work Commute in Minutes	28	127	47.6
			% Commuting on Public Transportation	4.8%	202	7.3
Community Stability	107	67.50	% Living in Same House as in 1979	53.2%	85	62.9
			% Living in Same County as in 1985	84.1%	136	72.1

Metropolitan Area Suburb Rankings
NEW YORK-NORTHERN NEW JERSEY-LONG ISLAND

Composite: *Rank* 40 / 250   *Score* 65.04   **DARIEN (CT)**

CATEGORY	RANK	SCORE	STATISTIC	VALUE	RANK	SCORE
Economics	2	82.75	Median Household Income	$89,398	2	68.9
			% of Families Above Poverty Level	99.1%	13	96.6
Affordable Housing	249	4.90	Median Home Value	$460,100	248	9.8
			Median Rent	$1,001	232	0.0
Crime	33	93.90	Violent Crimes per 10,000 Population	3	4	99.4
			Property Crimes per 10,000 Population	289	53	88.4
Open Spaces	4	92.70	Population Density (Persons/Sq. Mile)	1412	12	97.6
			Average Rooms per Housing Unit	7.4	5	87.8
Education	4	87.50	% High School Enrollment/Completion	97.0%	39	97.0
			% College Graduates	59.3%	4	78.0
Commute	106	36.55	Average Work Commute in Minutes	31	195	33.3
			% Commuting on Public Transportation	25.3%	12	39.8
Community Stability	158	57.00	% Living in Same House as in 1979	48.4%	137	52.4
			% Living in Same County as in 1985	80.6%	184	61.6

Composite: *Rank* 41 / 250   *Score* 65.00   **CEDAR GROVE (NJ)**

CATEGORY	RANK	SCORE	STATISTIC	VALUE	RANK	SCORE
Economics	77	63.55	Median Household Income	$55,464	64	35.2
			% of Families Above Poverty Level	98.0%	91	91.9
Affordable Housing	156	57.40	Median Home Value	$211,600	186	70.8
			Median Rent	$754	138	44.0
Crime	89	85.00	Violent Crimes per 10,000 Population	55	118	84.1
			Property Crimes per 10,000 Population	326	65	85.9
Open Spaces	79	77.65	Population Density (Persons/Sq. Mile)	2921	66	94.3
			Average Rooms per Housing Unit	6.3	83	61.0
Education	91	64.55	% High School Enrollment/Completion	91.1%	183	91.1
			% College Graduates	31.3%	74	38.0
Commute	89	38.25	Average Work Commute in Minutes	24	56	66.7
			% Commuting on Public Transportation	6.4%	178	9.8
Community Stability	101	68.60	% Living in Same House as in 1979	53.1%	86	62.7
			% Living in Same County as in 1985	84.9%	120	74.5

Composite: *Rank* 42 / 250   *Score* 64.85   **WOODMERE (NY)**

CATEGORY	RANK	SCORE	STATISTIC	VALUE	RANK	SCORE
Economics	3	78.75	Median Household Income	$79,623	5	59.2
			% of Families Above Poverty Level	99.5%	2	98.3
Affordable Housing	229	35.55	Median Home Value	$325,700	239	42.8
			Median Rent	$842	188	28.3
Crime	N/A	N/A	Violent Crimes per 10,000 Population	N/A	N/A	N/A
			Property Crimes per 10,000 Population	N/A	N/A	N/A
Open Spaces	9	90.15	Population Density (Persons/Sq. Mile)	5967	163	87.6
			Average Rooms per Housing Unit	7.6	3	92.7
Education	19	79.55	% High School Enrollment/Completion	94.4%	108	94.4
			% College Graduates	50.0%	15	64.7
Commute	244	16.25	Average Work Commute in Minutes	38	249	0.0
			% Commuting on Public Transportation	20.7%	32	32.5
Community Stability	11	88.85	% Living in Same House as in 1979	66.5%	5	92.1
			% Living in Same County as in 1985	88.6%	44	85.6

Metropolitan Area Suburb Rankings
NEW YORK-NORTHERN NEW JERSEY-LONG ISLAND

Composite: **Rank** 43 / 250 *Score* 64.83   **COLONIA (NJ)**

CATEGORY	RANK	SCORE	STATISTIC	VALUE	RANK	SCORE
Economics	79	63.35	Median Household Income	$53,269	79	33.1
			% of Families Above Poverty Level	98.4%	63	93.6
Affordable Housing	71	69.75	Median Home Value	$174,800	101	79.9
			Median Rent	$666	75	59.6
Crime	N/A	N/A	Violent Crimes per 10,000 Population	N/A	N/A	N/A
			Property Crimes per 10,000 Population	N/A	N/A	N/A
Open Spaces	56	79.40	Population Density (Persons/Sq. Mile)	4674	122	90.5
			Average Rooms per Housing Unit	6.6	52	68.3
Education	133	60.65	% High School Enrollment/Completion	94.4%	108	94.4
			% College Graduates	23.5%	136	26.9
Commute	149	32.05	Average Work Commute in Minutes	26	84	57.1
			% Commuting on Public Transportation	4.6%	206	7.0
Community Stability	23	83.75	% Living in Same House as in 1979	64.3%	12	87.3
			% Living in Same County as in 1985	86.8%	73	80.2

Composite: **Rank** 44 / 250 *Score* 64.78   **SADDLE BROOK (NJ)**

CATEGORY	RANK	SCORE	STATISTIC	VALUE	RANK	SCORE
Economics	141	57.85	Median Household Income	$46,082	146	25.9
			% of Families Above Poverty Level	97.5%	125	89.8
Affordable Housing	132	60.65	Median Home Value	$192,800	145	75.4
			Median Rent	$743	134	45.9
Crime	83	87.65	Violent Crimes per 10,000 Population	13	41	96.5
			Property Crimes per 10,000 Population	433	91	78.8
Open Spaces	147	68.15	Population Density (Persons/Sq. Mile)	4888	127	90.0
			Average Rooms per Housing Unit	5.7	143	46.3
Education	157	58.25	% High School Enrollment/Completion	95.8%	76	95.8
			% College Graduates	19.2%	169	20.7
Commute	45	43.90	Average Work Commute in Minutes	21	14	81.0
			% Commuting on Public Transportation	4.5%	209	6.8
Community Stability	49	77.00	% Living in Same House as in 1979	59.1%	38	75.9
			% Living in Same County as in 1985	86.1%	93	78.1

Composite: **Rank** 45 / 250 *Score* 64.61   **WAYNE (NJ)**

CATEGORY	RANK	SCORE	STATISTIC	VALUE	RANK	SCORE
Economics	44	66.95	Median Household Income	$59,290	44	39.0
			% of Families Above Poverty Level	98.7%	39	94.9
Affordable Housing	172	55.15	Median Home Value	$241,300	211	63.5
			Median Rent	$738	130	46.8
Crime	117	76.95	Violent Crimes per 10,000 Population	29	87	91.7
			Property Crimes per 10,000 Population	684	130	62.2
Open Spaces	33	83.55	Population Density (Persons/Sq. Mile)	1974	26	96.4
			Average Rooms per Housing Unit	6.7	44	70.7
Education	48	70.75	% High School Enrollment/Completion	97.1%	36	97.1
			% College Graduates	35.8%	53	44.4
Commute	107	36.50	Average Work Commute in Minutes	24	56	66.7
			% Commuting on Public Transportation	4.2%	217	6.3
Community Stability	125	62.40	% Living in Same House as in 1979	51.8%	103	59.9
			% Living in Same County as in 1985	81.7%	166	64.9

Metropolitan Area Suburb Rankings
NEW YORK-NORTHERN NEW JERSEY-LONG ISLAND

Composite: **Rank** 46 / 250 **Score** 64.58   **FLORAL PARK** (NY)

CATEGORY	RANK	SCORE	STATISTIC	VALUE	RANK	SCORE
Economics	100	61.55	Median Household Income	$51,344	101	31.2
			% of Families Above Poverty Level	98.0%	91	91.9
Affordable Housing	144	59.55	Median Home Value	$225,200	199	67.5
			Median Rent	$711	107	51.6
Crime	12	96.55	Violent Crimes per 10,000 Population	11	35	97.1
			Property Crimes per 10,000 Population	174	12	96.0
Open Spaces	160	66.15	Population Density (Persons/Sq. Mile)	11184	230	76.2
			Average Rooms per Housing Unit	6.1	104	56.1
Education	104	63.45	% High School Enrollment/Completion	92.6%	155	92.6
			% College Graduates	28.7%	94	34.3
Commute	172	29.50	Average Work Commute in Minutes	33	221	23.8
			% Commuting on Public Transportation	22.4%	23	35.2
Community Stability	54	75.30	% Living in Same House as in 1979	58.5%	41	74.6
			% Living in Same County as in 1985	85.4%	113	76.0

Composite: **Rank** 46 / 250 **Score** 64.58   **SCARSDALE** (NY)

CATEGORY	RANK	SCORE	STATISTIC	VALUE	RANK	SCORE
Economics	1	98.70	Median Household Income	$120,825	1	100.0
			% of Families Above Poverty Level	99.3%	6	97.4
Affordable Housing	250	0.00	Median Home Value	$500,001	250	0.0
			Median Rent	$1,001	232	0.0
Crime	N/A	N/A	Violent Crimes per 10,000 Population	N/A	N/A	N/A
			Property Crimes per 10,000 Population	N/A	N/A	N/A
Open Spaces	2	97.55	Population Density (Persons/Sq. Mile)	2559	55	95.1
			Average Rooms per Housing Unit	7.9	1	100.0
Education	1	98.85	% High School Enrollment/Completion	97.7%	21	97.7
			% College Graduates	74.7%	1	100.0
Commute	189	27.60	Average Work Commute in Minutes	38	249	0.0
			% Commuting on Public Transportation	35.0%	4	55.2
Community Stability	118	64.80	% Living in Same House as in 1979	56.6%	55	70.4
			% Living in Same County as in 1985	79.8%	192	59.2

Composite: **Rank** 48 / 250 **Score** 64.47   **MIDDLESEX** (NJ)

CATEGORY	RANK	SCORE	STATISTIC	VALUE	RANK	SCORE
Economics	109	60.35	Median Household Income	$47,643	130	27.5
			% of Families Above Poverty Level	98.3%	71	93.2
Affordable Housing	52	73.55	Median Home Value	$159,600	70	83.6
			Median Rent	$644	58	63.5
Crime	59	90.95	Violent Crimes per 10,000 Population	17	60	95.3
			Property Crimes per 10,000 Population	316	61	86.6
Open Spaces	120	71.85	Population Density (Persons/Sq. Mile)	3729	93	92.5
			Average Rooms per Housing Unit	5.9	123	51.2
Education	170	56.70	% High School Enrollment/Completion	91.5%	180	91.5
			% College Graduates	20.0%	167	21.9
Commute	78	39.70	Average Work Commute in Minutes	22	27	76.2
			% Commuting on Public Transportation	2.2%	237	3.2
Community Stability	148	58.20	% Living in Same House as in 1979	47.7%	144	50.9
			% Living in Same County as in 1985	81.9%	164	65.5

Metropolitan Area Suburb Rankings
NEW YORK-NORTHERN NEW JERSEY-LONG ISLAND

Composite: *Rank* 49 / 250 *Score* 64.44   **TENAFLY (NJ)**

CATEGORY	RANK	SCORE	STATISTIC	VALUE	RANK	SCORE
Economics	14	72.70	Median Household Income	$68,742	16	48.4
			% of Families Above Poverty Level	99.2%	11	97.0
Affordable Housing	244	21.25	Median Home Value	$355,700	243	35.4
			Median Rent	$961	226	7.1
Crime	6	98.45	Violent Crimes per 10,000 Population	5	8	98.8
			Property Crimes per 10,000 Population	143	6	98.1
Open Spaces	45	81.35	Population Density (Persons/Sq. Mile)	2890	65	94.4
			Average Rooms per Housing Unit	6.6	52	68.3
Education	6	84.65	% High School Enrollment/Completion	96.7%	47	96.7
			% College Graduates	55.5%	6	72.6
Commute	197	26.55	Average Work Commute in Minutes	31	195	33.3
			% Commuting on Public Transportation	12.7%	88	19.8
Community Stability	111	66.15	% Living in Same House as in 1979	54.0%	72	64.7
			% Living in Same County as in 1985	82.6%	154	67.6

Composite: *Rank* 50 / 250 *Score* 64.29   **MAPLEWOOD (NJ)**

CATEGORY	RANK	SCORE	STATISTIC	VALUE	RANK	SCORE
Economics	65	64.30	Median Household Income	$57,361	55	37.1
			% of Families Above Poverty Level	97.9%	102	91.5
Affordable Housing	136	60.00	Median Home Value	$197,600	157	74.3
			Median Rent	$744	135	45.7
Crime	95	83.20	Violent Crimes per 10,000 Population	43	107	87.6
			Property Crimes per 10,000 Population	434	92	78.8
Open Spaces	73	78.30	Population Density (Persons/Sq. Mile)	5638	155	88.3
			Average Rooms per Housing Unit	6.6	52	68.3
Education	22	79.05	% High School Enrollment/Completion	96.7%	47	96.7
			% College Graduates	47.7%	23	61.4
Commute	137	33.25	Average Work Commute in Minutes	30	172	38.1
			% Commuting on Public Transportation	18.1%	46	28.4
Community Stability	180	51.90	% Living in Same House as in 1979	46.6%	151	48.5
			% Living in Same County as in 1985	78.5%	207	55.3

Composite: *Rank* 51 / 250 *Score* 64.26   **BERGENFIELD (NJ)**

CATEGORY	RANK	SCORE	STATISTIC	VALUE	RANK	SCORE
Economics	129	58.55	Median Household Income	$45,713	150	25.6
			% of Families Above Poverty Level	97.9%	102	91.5
Affordable Housing	86	66.30	Median Home Value	$183,100	116	77.8
			Median Rent	$693	92	54.8
Crime	33	93.90	Violent Crimes per 10,000 Population	16	56	95.6
			Property Crimes per 10,000 Population	231	23	92.2
Open Spaces	185	63.05	Population Density (Persons/Sq. Mile)	8454	206	82.2
			Average Rooms per Housing Unit	5.6	154	43.9
Education	126	61.05	% High School Enrollment/Completion	94.8%	95	94.8
			% College Graduates	23.8%	133	27.3
Commute	113	35.70	Average Work Commute in Minutes	27	102	52.4
			% Commuting on Public Transportation	12.2%	93	19.0
Community Stability	81	71.30	% Living in Same House as in 1979	53.5%	78	63.6
			% Living in Same County as in 1985	86.4%	80	79.0

Composite: *Rank* 52 / 250   *Score* 64.21   **NUTLEY (NJ)**

CATEGORY	RANK	SCORE	STATISTIC	VALUE	RANK	SCORE
Economics	169	53.70	Median Household Income	$43,172	168	23.1
			% of Families Above Poverty Level	96.2%	170	84.3
Affordable Housing	70	69.90	Median Home Value	$185,300	122	77.3
			Median Rent	$650	61	62.5
Crime	76	88.95	Violent Crimes per 10,000 Population	31	89	91.2
			Property Crimes per 10,000 Population	315	60	86.7
Open Spaces	190	62.25	Population Density (Persons/Sq. Mile)	8053	202	83.0
			Average Rooms per Housing Unit	5.5	162	41.5
Education	99	64.00	% High School Enrollment/Completion	94.4%	108	94.4
			% College Graduates	28.2%	97	33.6
Commute	73	40.40	Average Work Commute in Minutes	24	56	66.7
			% Commuting on Public Transportation	9.1%	127	14.1
Community Stability	86	70.30	% Living in Same House as in 1979	53.4%	81	63.4
			% Living in Same County as in 1985	85.8%	106	77.2

Composite: *Rank* 53 / 250   *Score* 64.11   **SOUTH ORANGE (NJ)**

CATEGORY	RANK	SCORE	STATISTIC	VALUE	RANK	SCORE
Economics	25	69.45	Median Household Income	$64,338	26	44.0
			% of Families Above Poverty Level	98.7%	39	94.9
Affordable Housing	153	58.10	Median Home Value	$233,400	206	65.5
			Median Rent	$716	112	50.7
Crime	125	72.30	Violent Crimes per 10,000 Population	60	121	82.6
			Property Crimes per 10,000 Population	686	131	62.0
Open Spaces	56	79.40	Population Density (Persons/Sq. Mile)	5729	157	88.1
			Average Rooms per Housing Unit	6.7	44	70.7
Education	11	82.70	% High School Enrollment/Completion	96.3%	62	96.3
			% College Graduates	53.1%	11	69.1
Commute	64	41.45	Average Work Commute in Minutes	26	84	57.1
			% Commuting on Public Transportation	16.5%	53	25.8
Community Stability	202	45.35	% Living in Same House as in 1979	49.3%	121	54.4
			% Living in Same County as in 1985	72.2%	238	36.3

Composite: *Rank* 54 / 250   *Score* 64.06   **LYNDHURST (NJ)**

CATEGORY	RANK	SCORE	STATISTIC	VALUE	RANK	SCORE
Economics	167	54.30	Median Household Income	$41,000	183	20.9
			% of Families Above Poverty Level	97.0%	153	87.7
Affordable Housing	51	73.75	Median Home Value	$174,000	100	80.1
			Median Rent	$622	47	67.4
Crime	87	85.95	Violent Crimes per 10,000 Population	17	60	95.3
			Property Crimes per 10,000 Population	467	96	76.6
Open Spaces	165	65.55	Population Density (Persons/Sq. Mile)	3929	98	92.1
			Average Rooms per Housing Unit	5.4	172	39.0
Education	201	53.25	% High School Enrollment/Completion	91.8%	174	91.8
			% College Graduates	15.0%	208	14.7
Commute	60	42.45	Average Work Commute in Minutes	23	40	71.4
			% Commuting on Public Transportation	8.7%	135	13.5
Community Stability	71	73.15	% Living in Same House as in 1979	55.6%	61	68.2
			% Living in Same County as in 1985	86.1%	93	78.1

Metropolitan Area Suburb Rankings
NEW YORK-NORTHERN NEW JERSEY-LONG ISLAND

Composite: **Rank** 55 / 250 *Score* 63.98   **GREENLAWN (NY)**

CATEGORY	RANK	SCORE	STATISTIC	VALUE	RANK	SCORE
Economics	84	62.80	Median Household Income	$52,601	86	32.4
			% of Families Above Poverty Level	98.3%	71	93.2
Affordable Housing	48	74.15	Median Home Value	$191,600	140	75.7
			Median Rent	$593	32	72.6
Crime	N/A	N/A	Violent Crimes per 10,000 Population	N/A	N/A	N/A
			Property Crimes per 10,000 Population	N/A	N/A	N/A
Open Spaces	59	79.35	Population Density (Persons/Sq. Mile)	3599	86	92.8
			Average Rooms per Housing Unit	6.5	62	65.9
Education	98	64.05	% High School Enrollment/Completion	96.1%	67	96.1
			% College Graduates	27.1%	106	32.0
Commute	177	29.10	Average Work Commute in Minutes	30	172	38.1
			% Commuting on Public Transportation	12.9%	87	20.1
Community Stability	61	74.45	% Living in Same House as in 1979	54.2%	70	65.1
			% Living in Same County as in 1985	88.0%	58	83.8

Composite: **Rank** 56 / 250 *Score* 63.95   **RUTHERFORD (NJ)**

CATEGORY	RANK	SCORE	STATISTIC	VALUE	RANK	SCORE
Economics	146	57.05	Median Household Income	$46,499	141	26.4
			% of Families Above Poverty Level	97.0%	153	87.7
Affordable Housing	102	64.15	Median Home Value	$209,100	182	71.4
			Median Rent	$681	87	56.9
Crime	44	92.80	Violent Crimes per 10,000 Population	10	30	97.3
			Property Crimes per 10,000 Population	290	54	88.3
Open Spaces	168	65.35	Population Density (Persons/Sq. Mile)	6339	168	86.8
			Average Rooms per Housing Unit	5.6	154	43.9
Education	71	67.00	% High School Enrollment/Completion	94.4%	108	94.4
			% College Graduates	32.4%	70	39.6
Commute	44	44.10	Average Work Commute in Minutes	26	84	57.1
			% Commuting on Public Transportation	19.8%	37	31.1
Community Stability	156	57.20	% Living in Same House as in 1979	49.8%	115	55.5
			% Living in Same County as in 1985	79.7%	193	58.9

Composite: **Rank** 57 / 250 *Score* 63.90   **BETHPAGE (NY)**

CATEGORY	RANK	SCORE	STATISTIC	VALUE	RANK	SCORE
Economics	107	60.60	Median Household Income	$52,533	87	32.3
			% of Families Above Poverty Level	97.3%	141	88.9
Affordable Housing	159	56.95	Median Home Value	$193,500	146	75.3
			Median Rent	$784	156	38.6
Crime	N/A	N/A	Violent Crimes per 10,000 Population	N/A	N/A	N/A
			Property Crimes per 10,000 Population	N/A	N/A	N/A
Open Spaces	50	80.95	Population Density (Persons/Sq. Mile)	4330	109	91.2
			Average Rooms per Housing Unit	6.7	44	70.7
Education	143	59.70	% High School Enrollment/Completion	95.4%	83	95.4
			% College Graduates	21.5%	150	24.0
Commute	136	33.30	Average Work Commute in Minutes	28	127	47.6
			% Commuting on Public Transportation	12.2%	93	19.0
Community Stability	5	91.90	% Living in Same House as in 1979	65.7%	8	90.4
			% Living in Same County as in 1985	91.2%	12	93.4

Metropolitan Area Suburb Rankings
NEW YORK-NORTHERN NEW JERSEY-LONG ISLAND

Composite: Rank 58 / 250 *Score* 63.79   **ELMWOOD PARK (NJ)**

CATEGORY	RANK	SCORE	STATISTIC	VALUE	RANK	SCORE
Economics	163	54.85	Median Household Income	$38,248	201	18.2
			% of Families Above Poverty Level	97.9%	102	91.5
Affordable Housing	59	72.45	Median Home Value	$183,900	118	77.6
			Median Rent	$623	49	67.3
Crime	88	85.80	Violent Crimes per 10,000 Population	19	67	94.7
			Property Crimes per 10,000 Population	462	95	76.9
Open Spaces	188	62.55	Population Density (Persons/Sq. Mile)	6639	177	86.1
			Average Rooms per Housing Unit	5.4	172	39.0
Education	214	50.95	% High School Enrollment/Completion	87.2%	221	87.2
			% College Graduates	15.0%	208	14.7
Commute	23	46.50	Average Work Commute in Minutes	20	5	85.7
			% Commuting on Public Transportation	4.8%	202	7.3
Community Stability	69	73.45	% Living in Same House as in 1979	57.8%	44	73.0
			% Living in Same County as in 1985	84.7%	123	73.9

Composite: Rank 59 / 250 *Score* 63.74   **UNION (NJ)**

CATEGORY	RANK	SCORE	STATISTIC	VALUE	RANK	SCORE
Economics	156	56.20	Median Household Income	$42,665	172	22.6
			% of Families Above Poverty Level	97.5%	125	89.8
Affordable Housing	58	72.85	Median Home Value	$175,300	102	79.7
			Median Rent	$630	52	66.0
Crime	112	78.00	Violent Crimes per 10,000 Population	42	104	87.9
			Property Crimes per 10,000 Population	595	123	68.1
Open Spaces	132	69.95	Population Density (Persons/Sq. Mile)	5486	144	88.7
			Average Rooms per Housing Unit	5.9	123	51.2
Education	138	60.20	% High School Enrollment/Completion	96.4%	59	96.4
			% College Graduates	21.5%	150	24.0
Commute	75	40.20	Average Work Commute in Minutes	23	40	71.4
			% Commuting on Public Transportation	5.9%	184	9.0
Community Stability	99	68.80	% Living in Same House as in 1979	56.7%	53	70.6
			% Living in Same County as in 1985	82.4%	156	67.0

Composite: Rank 60 / 250 *Score* 63.68   **NORTH WANTAGH (NY)**

CATEGORY	RANK	SCORE	STATISTIC	VALUE	RANK	SCORE
Economics	46	66.80	Median Household Income	$55,488	62	35.3
			% of Families Above Poverty Level	99.5%	2	98.3
Affordable Housing	79	68.10	Median Home Value	$185,100	121	77.3
			Median Rent	$670	79	58.9
Crime	N/A	N/A	Violent Crimes per 10,000 Population	N/A	N/A	N/A
			Property Crimes per 10,000 Population	N/A	N/A	N/A
Open Spaces	89	76.05	Population Density (Persons/Sq. Mile)	6628	175	86.2
			Average Rooms per Housing Unit	6.5	62	65.9
Education	82	65.50	% High School Enrollment/Completion	96.3%	62	96.3
			% College Graduates	29.0%	91	34.7
Commute	218	22.85	Average Work Commute in Minutes	33	221	23.8
			% Commuting on Public Transportation	14.0%	79	21.9
Community Stability	25	82.80	% Living in Same House as in 1979	58.4%	42	74.3
			% Living in Same County as in 1985	90.5%	16	91.3

Metropolitan Area Suburb Rankings
NEW YORK-NORTHERN NEW JERSEY-LONG ISLAND

Composite: Rank 61 / 250 *Score* 63.58   **LYNBROOK** (NY)

CATEGORY	RANK	SCORE	STATISTIC	VALUE	RANK	SCORE
Economics	130	58.40	Median Household Income	$45,453	152	25.3
			% of Families Above Poverty Level	97.9%	102	91.5
Affordable Housing	123	61.80	Median Home Value	$194,700	151	75.0
			Median Rent	$728	119	48.6
Crime	30	94.10	Violent Crimes per 10,000 Population	16	56	95.6
			Property Crimes per 10,000 Population	225	22	92.6
Open Spaces	186	62.95	Population Density (Persons/Sq. Mile)	9606	215	79.6
			Average Rooms per Housing Unit	5.7	143	46.3
Education	133	60.65	% High School Enrollment/Completion	93.2%	136	93.2
			% College Graduates	24.4%	129	28.1
Commute	142	32.65	Average Work Commute in Minutes	31	195	33.3
			% Commuting on Public Transportation	20.4%	34	32.0
Community Stability	60	74.50	% Living in Same House as in 1979	53.7%	74	64.0
			% Living in Same County as in 1985	88.4%	49	85.0

Composite: Rank 62 / 250 *Score* 63.57   **SOUTH FARMINGDALE** (NY)

CATEGORY	RANK	SCORE	STATISTIC	VALUE	RANK	SCORE
Economics	82	63.05	Median Household Income	$54,437	72	34.2
			% of Families Above Poverty Level	98.0%	91	91.9
Affordable Housing	154	57.95	Median Home Value	$178,800	108	78.9
			Median Rent	$793	160	37.0
Crime	N/A	N/A	Violent Crimes per 10,000 Population	N/A	N/A	N/A
			Property Crimes per 10,000 Population	N/A	N/A	N/A
Open Spaces	61	79.20	Population Density (Persons/Sq. Mile)	7055	185	85.2
			Average Rooms per Housing Unit	6.8	36	73.2
Education	163	57.80	% High School Enrollment/Completion	93.6%	124	93.6
			% College Graduates	20.1%	165	22.0
Commute	181	28.75	Average Work Commute in Minutes	29	150	42.9
			% Commuting on Public Transportation	9.4%	124	14.6
Community Stability	1	94.65	% Living in Same House as in 1979	67.0%	4	93.2
			% Living in Same County as in 1985	92.1%	4	96.1

Composite: Rank 63 / 250 *Score* 63.56   **MELVILLE** (NY)

CATEGORY	RANK	SCORE	STATISTIC	VALUE	RANK	SCORE
Economics	15	72.25	Median Household Income	$72,581	14	52.2
			% of Families Above Poverty Level	98.1%	83	92.3
Affordable Housing	230	35.10	Median Home Value	$269,000	228	56.7
			Median Rent	$925	219	13.5
Crime	N/A	N/A	Violent Crimes per 10,000 Population	N/A	N/A	N/A
			Property Crimes per 10,000 Population	N/A	N/A	N/A
Open Spaces	3	94.25	Population Density (Persons/Sq. Mile)	1112	6	98.3
			Average Rooms per Housing Unit	7.5	4	90.2
Education	29	76.40	% High School Enrollment/Completion	96.5%	52	96.5
			% College Graduates	44.1%	29	56.3
Commute	187	28.05	Average Work Commute in Minutes	29	150	42.9
			% Commuting on Public Transportation	8.5%	140	13.2
Community Stability	54	75.30	% Living in Same House as in 1979	59.9%	33	77.6
			% Living in Same County as in 1985	84.4%	129	73.0

Metropolitan Area Suburb Rankings
NEW YORK-NORTHERN NEW JERSEY-LONG ISLAND

Composite: **Rank** 64 / 250 **Score** 63.54   **CLIFTON** (NJ)

CATEGORY	RANK	SCORE	STATISTIC	VALUE	RANK	SCORE
Economics	170	53.50	Median Household Income	$39,905	190	19.8
			% of Families Above Poverty Level	96.9%	158	87.2
Affordable Housing	54	73.20	Median Home Value	$185,000	120	77.4
			Median Rent	$613	42	69.0
Crime	90	84.80	Violent Crimes per 10,000 Population	28	85	92.0
			Property Crimes per 10,000 Population	452	94	77.6
Open Spaces	191	61.70	Population Density (Persons/Sq. Mile)	6345	169	86.8
			Average Rooms per Housing Unit	5.3	180	36.6
Education	154	58.55	% High School Enrollment/Completion	94.7%	97	94.7
			% College Graduates	20.4%	160	22.4
Commute	35	45.00	Average Work Commute in Minutes	21	14	81.0
			% Commuting on Public Transportation	5.9%	184	9.0
Community Stability	105	68.00	% Living in Same House as in 1979	53.5%	78	63.6
			% Living in Same County as in 1985	84.2%	134	72.4

Composite: **Rank** 65 / 250 **Score** 63.41   **HAWTHORNE** (NJ)

CATEGORY	RANK	SCORE	STATISTIC	VALUE	RANK	SCORE
Economics	146	57.05	Median Household Income	$43,109	169	23.0
			% of Families Above Poverty Level	97.8%	111	91.1
Affordable Housing	122	61.90	Median Home Value	$187,300	126	76.8
			Median Rent	$737	128	47.0
Crime	37	93.65	Violent Crimes per 10,000 Population	13	41	96.5
			Property Crimes per 10,000 Population	252	36	90.8
Open Spaces	164	65.60	Population Density (Persons/Sq. Mile)	5029	132	89.7
			Average Rooms per Housing Unit	5.5	162	41.5
Education	136	60.35	% High School Enrollment/Completion	95.3%	86	95.3
			% College Graduates	22.5%	142	25.4
Commute	52	43.35	Average Work Commute in Minutes	21	14	81.0
			% Commuting on Public Transportation	3.8%	220	5.7
Community Stability	131	61.95	% Living in Same House as in 1979	50.6%	111	57.2
			% Living in Same County as in 1985	82.3%	159	66.7

Composite: **Rank** 66 / 250 **Score** 63.29   **EAST BRUNSWICK** (NJ)

CATEGORY	RANK	SCORE	STATISTIC	VALUE	RANK	SCORE
Economics	47	66.25	Median Household Income	$58,769	48	38.5
			% of Families Above Poverty Level	98.5%	58	94.0
Affordable Housing	120	62.15	Median Home Value	$189,300	134	76.3
			Median Rent	$731	121	48.0
Crime	75	89.15	Violent Crimes per 10,000 Population	16	56	95.6
			Property Crimes per 10,000 Population	375	82	82.7
Open Spaces	53	79.90	Population Density (Persons/Sq. Mile)	1979	27	96.4
			Average Rooms per Housing Unit	6.4	73	63.4
Education	40	74.10	% High School Enrollment/Completion	96.5%	52	96.5
			% College Graduates	40.9%	40	51.7
Commute	225	22.20	Average Work Commute in Minutes	32	211	28.6
			% Commuting on Public Transportation	10.2%	110	15.8
Community Stability	187	49.25	% Living in Same House as in 1979	43.8%	169	42.3
			% Living in Same County as in 1985	78.8%	204	56.2

Metropolitan Area Suburb Rankings
NEW YORK-NORTHERN NEW JERSEY-LONG ISLAND

Composite: *Rank* 67 / 250   *Score* 63.28   **SUCCASUNNA-KENVIL (NJ)**

CATEGORY	RANK	SCORE	STATISTIC	VALUE	RANK	SCORE
Economics	53	65.55	Median Household Income	$61,185	36	40.9
			% of Families Above Poverty Level	97.6%	121	90.2
Affordable Housing	129	61.15	Median Home Value	$203,800	167	72.7
			Median Rent	$722	116	49.6
Crime	N/A	N/A	Violent Crimes per 10,000 Population	N/A	N/A	N/A
			Property Crimes per 10,000 Population	N/A	N/A	N/A
Open Spaces	12	88.65	Population Density (Persons/Sq. Mile)	1793	18	96.8
			Average Rooms per Housing Unit	7.1	13	80.5
Education	61	68.30	% High School Enrollment/Completion	94.7%	97	94.7
			% College Graduates	34.0%	61	41.9
Commute	188	27.70	Average Work Commute in Minutes	27	102	52.4
			% Commuting on Public Transportation	2.1%	239	3.0
Community Stability	104	68.35	% Living in Same House as in 1979	51.1%	108	58.3
			% Living in Same County as in 1985	86.2%	87	78.4

Composite: *Rank* 68 / 250   *Score* 63.21   **MERRICK (NY)**

CATEGORY	RANK	SCORE	STATISTIC	VALUE	RANK	SCORE
Economics	29	68.70	Median Household Income	$65,383	25	45.1
			% of Families Above Poverty Level	98.1%	83	92.3
Affordable Housing	218	40.95	Median Home Value	$236,800	208	64.6
			Median Rent	$904	216	17.3
Crime	N/A	N/A	Violent Crimes per 10,000 Population	N/A	N/A	N/A
			Property Crimes per 10,000 Population	N/A	N/A	N/A
Open Spaces	17	87.05	Population Density (Persons/Sq. Mile)	5488	145	88.7
			Average Rooms per Housing Unit	7.3	8	85.4
Education	47	70.95	% High School Enrollment/Completion	93.6%	124	93.6
			% College Graduates	38.5%	46	48.3
Commute	224	22.30	Average Work Commute in Minutes	35	241	14.3
			% Commuting on Public Transportation	19.3%	38	30.3
Community Stability	9	89.30	% Living in Same House as in 1979	64.6%	10	87.9
			% Living in Same County as in 1985	90.3%	21	90.7

Composite: *Rank* 69 / 250   *Score* 63.18   **MADISON (NJ)**

CATEGORY	RANK	SCORE	STATISTIC	VALUE	RANK	SCORE
Economics	81	63.00	Median Household Income	$56,478	58	36.2
			% of Families Above Poverty Level	97.5%	125	89.8
Affordable Housing	197	49.55	Median Home Value	$247,800	216	61.9
			Median Rent	$792	159	37.2
Crime	11	96.60	Violent Crimes per 10,000 Population	4	5	99.1
			Property Crimes per 10,000 Population	203	16	94.1
Open Spaces	106	74.25	Population Density (Persons/Sq. Mile)	3783	94	92.4
			Average Rooms per Housing Unit	6.1	104	56.1
Education	13	81.10	% High School Enrollment/Completion	98.5%	13	98.5
			% College Graduates	49.3%	17	63.7
Commute	41	44.30	Average Work Commute in Minutes	22	27	76.2
			% Commuting on Public Transportation	8.0%	149	12.4
Community Stability	237	33.45	% Living in Same House as in 1979	44.2%	165	43.2
			% Living in Same County as in 1985	68.0%	246	23.7

Metropolitan Area Suburb Rankings
NEW YORK-NORTHERN NEW JERSEY-LONG ISLAND

Composite: **Rank** 70 / 250   *Score* 63.12   **DIX HILLS (NY)**

CATEGORY	RANK	SCORE	STATISTIC	VALUE	RANK	SCORE
Economics	6	77.20	Median Household Income	$79,154	6	58.7
			% of Families Above Poverty Level	98.9%	25	95.7
Affordable Housing	243	21.20	Median Home Value	$327,200	240	42.4
			Median Rent	$1,001	232	0.0
Crime	N/A	N/A	Violent Crimes per 10,000 Population	N/A	N/A	N/A
			Property Crimes per 10,000 Population	N/A	N/A	N/A
Open Spaces	1	98.60	Population Density (Persons/Sq. Mile)	1621	16	97.2
			Average Rooms per Housing Unit	7.9	1	100.0
Education	18	79.60	% High School Enrollment/Completion	99.3%	4	99.3
			% College Graduates	46.6%	26	59.9
Commute	232	20.80	Average Work Commute in Minutes	32	211	28.6
			% Commuting on Public Transportation	8.4%	142	13.0
Community Stability	30	81.30	% Living in Same House as in 1979	61.0%	27	80.0
			% Living in Same County as in 1985	87.6%	63	82.6

Composite: **Rank** 71 / 250   *Score* 63.09   **WESTPORT (CT)**

CATEGORY	RANK	SCORE	STATISTIC	VALUE	RANK	SCORE
Economics	5	78.20	Median Household Income	$81,998	4	61.5
			% of Families Above Poverty Level	98.7%	39	94.9
Affordable Housing	248	8.55	Median Home Value	$430,200	247	17.1
			Median Rent	$1,001	232	0.0
Crime	58	91.30	Violent Crimes per 10,000 Population	10	30	97.3
			Property Crimes per 10,000 Population	336	71	85.3
Open Spaces	11	89.30	Population Density (Persons/Sq. Mile)	1220	8	98.1
			Average Rooms per Housing Unit	7.1	13	80.5
Education	3	88.65	% High School Enrollment/Completion	97.6%	24	97.6
			% College Graduates	60.5%	3	79.7
Commute	94	37.85	Average Work Commute in Minutes	28	127	47.6
			% Commuting on Public Transportation	17.9%	47	28.1
Community Stability	194	47.80	% Living in Same House as in 1979	45.5%	159	46.1
			% Living in Same County as in 1985	76.6%	220	49.5

Composite: **Rank** 72 / 250   *Score* 63.07   **SOUTH RIVER (NJ)**

CATEGORY	RANK	SCORE	STATISTIC	VALUE	RANK	SCORE
Economics	204	47.25	Median Household Income	$37,998	203	17.9
			% of Families Above Poverty Level	94.4%	206	76.6
Affordable Housing	27	78.75	Median Home Value	$141,400	35	88.1
			Median Rent	$611	40	69.4
Crime	79	88.65	Violent Crimes per 10,000 Population	41	101	88.2
			Property Crimes per 10,000 Population	279	47	89.1
Open Spaces	152	67.00	Population Density (Persons/Sq. Mile)	4856	125	90.1
			Average Rooms per Housing Unit	5.6	154	43.9
Education	221	49.80	% High School Enrollment/Completion	87.6%	219	87.6
			% College Graduates	13.1%	222	12.0
Commute	112	36.05	Average Work Commute in Minutes	24	56	66.7
			% Commuting on Public Transportation	3.6%	222	5.4
Community Stability	64	74.00	% Living in Same House as in 1979	56.1%	59	69.3
			% Living in Same County as in 1985	86.3%	85	78.7

Composite: **Rank** 73 / 250   *Score* 63.03   **RAMSEY (NJ)**

CATEGORY	RANK	SCORE	STATISTIC	VALUE	RANK	SCORE
Economics	22	69.90	Median Household Income	$65,590	24	45.3
			% of Families Above Poverty Level	98.6%	50	94.5
Affordable Housing	234	32.75	Median Home Value	$261,500	222	58.6
			Median Rent	$962	227	6.9
Crime	63	90.75	Violent Crimes per 10,000 Population	14	48	96.2
			Property Crimes per 10,000 Population	335	70	85.3
Open Spaces	36	83.10	Population Density (Persons/Sq. Mile)	2387	43	95.5
			Average Rooms per Housing Unit	6.7	44	70.7
Education	27	76.65	% High School Enrollment/Completion	92.9%	147	92.9
			% College Graduates	47.0%	25	60.4
Commute	140	32.80	Average Work Commute in Minutes	27	102	52.4
			% Commuting on Public Transportation	8.5%	140	13.2
Community Stability	165	55.25	% Living in Same House as in 1979	43.4%	173	41.4
			% Living in Same County as in 1985	83.1%	149	69.1

Composite: **Rank** 74 / 250   *Score* 63.01   **BAYONNE (NJ)**

CATEGORY	RANK	SCORE	STATISTIC	VALUE	RANK	SCORE
Economics	219	42.75	Median Household Income	$31,954	228	11.9
			% of Families Above Poverty Level	93.7%	211	73.6
Affordable Housing	10	87.05	Median Home Value	$169,200	93	81.2
			Median Rent	$479	3	92.9
Crime	86	86.00	Violent Crimes per 10,000 Population	53	116	84.7
			Property Crimes per 10,000 Population	305	57	87.3
Open Spaces	218	53.00	Population Density (Persons/Sq. Mile)	10925	228	76.7
			Average Rooms per Housing Unit	5.0	203	29.3
Education	190	53.95	% High School Enrollment/Completion	90.9%	186	90.9
			% College Graduates	16.6%	190	17.0
Commute	47	43.70	Average Work Commute in Minutes	26	84	57.1
			% Commuting on Public Transportation	19.3%	38	30.3
Community Stability	59	74.60	% Living in Same House as in 1979	49.4%	120	54.6
			% Living in Same County as in 1985	91.6%	8	94.6

Composite: **Rank** 75 / 250   *Score* 62.93   **CARTERET (NJ)**

CATEGORY	RANK	SCORE	STATISTIC	VALUE	RANK	SCORE
Economics	205	47.10	Median Household Income	$40,268	189	20.2
			% of Families Above Poverty Level	93.8%	209	74.0
Affordable Housing	21	80.05	Median Home Value	$148,000	44	86.4
			Median Rent	$587	29	73.7
Crime	61	90.75	Violent Crimes per 10,000 Population	28	85	92.0
			Property Crimes per 10,000 Population	272	42	89.5
Open Spaces	151	67.55	Population Density (Persons/Sq. Mile)	4361	110	91.2
			Average Rooms per Housing Unit	5.6	154	43.9
Education	233	47.80	% High School Enrollment/Completion	89.0%	212	89.0
			% College Graduates	9.3%	240	6.6
Commute	65	41.20	Average Work Commute in Minutes	22	27	76.2
			% Commuting on Public Transportation	4.1%	218	6.2
Community Stability	112	66.05	% Living in Same House as in 1979	54.3%	67	65.4
			% Living in Same County as in 1985	82.3%	159	66.7

Metropolitan Area Suburb Rankings
NEW YORK-NORTHERN NEW JERSEY-LONG ISLAND

Composite: *Rank* 76 / 250 *Score* 62.89   SUMMIT (NJ)

CATEGORY	RANK	SCORE	STATISTIC	VALUE	RANK	SCORE
Economics	19	70.90	Median Household Income	$66,464	19	46.1
			% of Families Above Poverty Level	98.9%	25	95.7
Affordable Housing	223	37.35	Median Home Value	$316,600	235	45.0
			Median Rent	$834	181	29.7
Crime	41	93.30	Violent Crimes per 10,000 Population	8	22	97.9
			Property Crimes per 10,000 Population	285	48	88.7
Open Spaces	55	79.75	Population Density (Persons/Sq. Mile)	3264	76	93.6
			Average Rooms per Housing Unit	6.5	62	65.9
Education	9	83.30	% High School Enrollment/Completion	96.7%	47	96.7
			% College Graduates	53.6%	8	69.9
Commute	127	34.45	Average Work Commute in Minutes	29	150	42.9
			% Commuting on Public Transportation	16.6%	52	26.0
Community Stability	214	41.15	% Living in Same House as in 1979	43.7%	171	42.1
			% Living in Same County as in 1985	73.5%	233	40.2

Composite: *Rank* 77 / 250 *Score* 62.72   WEST HEMPSTEAD (NY)

CATEGORY	RANK	SCORE	STATISTIC	VALUE	RANK	SCORE
Economics	72	63.70	Median Household Income	$52,271	89	32.1
			% of Families Above Poverty Level	98.8%	32	95.3
Affordable Housing	181	53.30	Median Home Value	$200,700	162	73.5
			Median Rent	$815	174	33.1
Crime	N/A	N/A	Violent Crimes per 10,000 Population	N/A	N/A	N/A
			Property Crimes per 10,000 Population	N/A	N/A	N/A
Open Spaces	71	78.40	Population Density (Persons/Sq. Mile)	6660	178	86.1
			Average Rooms per Housing Unit	6.7	44	70.7
Education	76	66.35	% High School Enrollment/Completion	96.0%	68	96.0
			% College Graduates	30.4%	81	36.7
Commute	175	29.40	Average Work Commute in Minutes	31	195	33.3
			% Commuting on Public Transportation	16.3%	57	25.5
Community Stability	22	85.15	% Living in Same House as in 1979	62.3%	22	82.9
			% Living in Same County as in 1985	89.2%	36	87.4

Composite: *Rank* 78 / 250 *Score* 62.62   NEW CITY (NY)

CATEGORY	RANK	SCORE	STATISTIC	VALUE	RANK	SCORE
Economics	13	73.35	Median Household Income	$73,485	13	53.1
			% of Families Above Poverty Level	98.4%	63	93.6
Affordable Housing	209	45.65	Median Home Value	$239,000	209	64.1
			Median Rent	$848	193	27.2
Crime	N/A	N/A	Violent Crimes per 10,000 Population	N/A	N/A	N/A
			Property Crimes per 10,000 Population	N/A	N/A	N/A
Open Spaces	10	89.45	Population Density (Persons/Sq. Mile)	2158	34	96.0
			Average Rooms per Housing Unit	7.2	11	82.9
Education	24	78.80	% High School Enrollment/Completion	98.2%	15	98.2
			% College Graduates	46.3%	27	59.4
Commute	243	16.95	Average Work Commute in Minutes	33	221	23.8
			% Commuting on Public Transportation	6.6%	174	10.1
Community Stability	78	71.50	% Living in Same House as in 1979	54.1%	71	64.9
			% Living in Same County as in 1985	86.1%	93	78.1

Composite: **Rank** 79 / 250 **Score** 62.39   **SMITHTOWN (NY)**

CATEGORY	RANK	SCORE	STATISTIC	VALUE	RANK	SCORE
Economics	36	67.60	Median Household Income	$61,455	34	41.2
			% of Families Above Poverty Level	98.5%	58	94.0
Affordable Housing	188	52.40	Median Home Value	$207,400	176	71.9
			Median Rent	$816	177	32.9
Crime	N/A	N/A	Violent Crimes per 10,000 Population	N/A	N/A	N/A
			Property Crimes per 10,000 Population	N/A	N/A	N/A
Open Spaces	22	85.80	Population Density (Persons/Sq. Mile)	2172	36	96.0
			Average Rooms per Housing Unit	6.9	26	75.6
Education	67	67.50	% High School Enrollment/Completion	95.9%	71	95.9
			% College Graduates	32.1%	72	39.1
Commute	214	24.80	Average Work Commute in Minutes	29	150	42.9
			% Commuting on Public Transportation	4.4%	213	6.7
Community Stability	51	76.25	% Living in Same House as in 1979	55.3%	62	67.5
			% Living in Same County as in 1985	88.4%	49	85.0

Composite: **Rank** 80 / 250 **Score** 62.31   **POMPTON LAKES (NJ)**

CATEGORY	RANK	SCORE	STATISTIC	VALUE	RANK	SCORE
Economics	86	62.45	Median Household Income	$48,864	120	28.7
			% of Families Above Poverty Level	99.0%	16	96.2
Affordable Housing	145	59.30	Median Home Value	$178,100	107	79.1
			Median Rent	$779	152	39.5
Crime	32	94.10	Violent Crimes per 10,000 Population	11	35	97.1
			Property Crimes per 10,000 Population	248	32	91.1
Open Spaces	136	69.60	Population Density (Persons/Sq. Mile)	3551	85	92.9
			Average Rooms per Housing Unit	5.7	143	46.3
Education	152	58.85	% High School Enrollment/Completion	91.0%	185	91.0
			% College Graduates	23.4%	137	26.7
Commute	157	30.95	Average Work Commute in Minutes	26	84	57.1
			% Commuting on Public Transportation	3.2%	227	4.8
Community Stability	135	60.90	% Living in Same House as in 1979	44.7%	162	44.3
			% Living in Same County as in 1985	85.9%	102	77.5

Composite: **Rank** 81 / 250 **Score** 62.22   **RIDGEFIELD PARK (NJ)**

CATEGORY	RANK	SCORE	STATISTIC	VALUE	RANK	SCORE
Economics	177	52.70	Median Household Income	$42,464	173	22.4
			% of Families Above Poverty Level	95.9%	181	83.0
Affordable Housing	82	67.35	Median Home Value	$173,900	99	80.1
			Median Rent	$694	96	54.6
Crime	22	94.85	Violent Crimes per 10,000 Population	17	60	95.3
			Property Crimes per 10,000 Population	198	14	94.4
Open Spaces	210	57.10	Population Density (Persons/Sq. Mile)	7194	188	84.9
			Average Rooms per Housing Unit	5.0	203	29.3
Education	157	58.25	% High School Enrollment/Completion	92.8%	150	92.8
			% College Graduates	21.3%	155	23.7
Commute	25	46.15	Average Work Commute in Minutes	23	40	71.4
			% Commuting on Public Transportation	13.4%	82	20.9
Community Stability	142	59.15	% Living in Same House as in 1979	43.1%	176	40.8
			% Living in Same County as in 1985	85.9%	102	77.5

Metropolitan Area Suburb Rankings
NEW YORK-NORTHERN NEW JERSEY-LONG ISLAND

Composite: *Rank* 82 / 250 *Score* 62.20 WESTWOOD (NJ)

CATEGORY	RANK	SCORE	STATISTIC	VALUE	RANK	SCORE
Economics	105	60.80	Median Household Income	$46,866	138	26.7
			% of Families Above Poverty Level	98.7%	39	94.9
Affordable Housing	185	52.90	Median Home Value	$217,700	193	69.3
			Median Rent	$796	167	36.5
Crime	53	91.85	Violent Crimes per 10,000 Population	20	71	94.4
			Property Crimes per 10,000 Population	276	43	89.3
Open Spaces	144	68.55	Population Density (Persons/Sq. Mile)	4504	114	90.8
			Average Rooms per Housing Unit	5.7	143	46.3
Education	77	66.30	% High School Enrollment/Completion	97.6%	24	97.6
			% College Graduates	29.2%	90	35.0
Commute	123	34.70	Average Work Commute in Minutes	27	102	52.4
			% Commuting on Public Transportation	10.9%	106	17.0
Community Stability	138	60.30	% Living in Same House as in 1979	44.0%	166	42.8
			% Living in Same County as in 1985	86.0%	98	77.8

Composite: *Rank* 83 / 250 *Score* 62.13 MAMARONECK (NY)

CATEGORY	RANK	SCORE	STATISTIC	VALUE	RANK	SCORE
Economics	142	57.65	Median Household Income	$47,321	132	27.2
			% of Families Above Poverty Level	97.1%	150	88.1
Affordable Housing	200	49.30	Median Home Value	$305,000	234	47.9
			Median Rent	$716	112	50.7
Crime	68	89.70	Violent Crimes per 10,000 Population	19	67	94.7
			Property Crimes per 10,000 Population	344	75	84.7
Open Spaces	169	65.25	Population Density (Persons/Sq. Mile)	5356	140	89.0
			Average Rooms per Housing Unit	5.5	162	41.5
Education	85	65.35	% High School Enrollment/Completion	90.8%	189	90.8
			% College Graduates	32.6%	69	39.9
Commute	32	45.45	Average Work Commute in Minutes	25	72	61.9
			% Commuting on Public Transportation	18.5%	43	29.0
Community Stability	128	62.20	% Living in Same House as in 1979	49.6%	117	55.0
			% Living in Same County as in 1985	83.2%	146	69.4

Composite: *Rank* 84 / 250 *Score* 62.02 PEARL RIVER (NY)

CATEGORY	RANK	SCORE	STATISTIC	VALUE	RANK	SCORE
Economics	69	63.90	Median Household Income	$53,095	82	32.9
			% of Families Above Poverty Level	98.7%	39	94.9
Affordable Housing	128	61.45	Median Home Value	$206,900	174	72.0
			Median Rent	$715	111	50.9
Crime	N/A	N/A	Violent Crimes per 10,000 Population	N/A	N/A	N/A
			Property Crimes per 10,000 Population	N/A	N/A	N/A
Open Spaces	90	75.95	Population Density (Persons/Sq. Mile)	2238	38	95.8
			Average Rooms per Housing Unit	6.1	104	56.1
Education	99	64.00	% High School Enrollment/Completion	91.6%	178	91.6
			% College Graduates	30.2%	83	36.4
Commute	139	32.85	Average Work Commute in Minutes	27	102	52.4
			% Commuting on Public Transportation	8.6%	139	13.3
Community Stability	64	74.00	% Living in Same House as in 1979	54.3%	67	65.4
			% Living in Same County as in 1985	87.6%	63	82.6

Metropolitan Area Suburb Rankings
NEW YORK-NORTHERN NEW JERSEY-LONG ISLAND

Composite: **Rank** 85 / 250 *Score* 62.01   WEST ISLIP (NY)

CATEGORY	RANK	SCORE	STATISTIC	VALUE	RANK	SCORE
Economics	62	64.55	Median Household Income	$57,081	56	36.8
			% of Families Above Poverty Level	98.1%	83	92.3
Affordable Housing	212	45.35	Median Home Value	$167,600	89	81.6
			Median Rent	$950	225	9.1
Crime	N/A	N/A	Violent Crimes per 10,000 Population	N/A	N/A	N/A
			Property Crimes per 10,000 Population	N/A	N/A	N/A
Open Spaces	36	83.10	Population Density (Persons/Sq. Mile)	4595	119	90.6
			Average Rooms per Housing Unit	6.9	26	75.6
Education	136	60.35	% High School Enrollment/Completion	96.8%	42	96.8
			% College Graduates	21.4%	152	23.9
Commute	159	30.60	Average Work Commute in Minutes	28	127	47.6
			% Commuting on Public Transportation	8.8%	134	13.6
Community Stability	13	88.10	% Living in Same House as in 1979	61.3%	25	80.7
			% Living in Same County as in 1985	91.9%	6	95.5

Composite: **Rank** 86 / 250 *Score* 61.99   ELWOOD (NY)

CATEGORY	RANK	SCORE	STATISTIC	VALUE	RANK	SCORE
Economics	31	68.30	Median Household Income	$63,700	28	43.4
			% of Families Above Poverty Level	98.3%	71	93.2
Affordable Housing	220	39.70	Median Home Value	$219,300	194	68.9
			Median Rent	$942	224	10.5
Crime	N/A	N/A	Violent Crimes per 10,000 Population	N/A	N/A	N/A
			Property Crimes per 10,000 Population	N/A	N/A	N/A
Open Spaces	7	90.60	Population Density (Persons/Sq. Mile)	2262	39	95.8
			Average Rooms per Housing Unit	7.3	8	85.4
Education	60	68.55	% High School Enrollment/Completion	94.2%	116	94.2
			% College Graduates	34.7%	57	42.9
Commute	200	26.00	Average Work Commute in Minutes	30	172	38.1
			% Commuting on Public Transportation	9.0%	129	13.9
Community Stability	41	78.80	% Living in Same House as in 1979	60.9%	28	79.8
			% Living in Same County as in 1985	86.0%	98	77.8

Composite: **Rank** 87 / 250 *Score* 61.93   WANTAGH (NY)

CATEGORY	RANK	SCORE	STATISTIC	VALUE	RANK	SCORE
Economics	42	67.20	Median Household Income	$60,134	42	39.9
			% of Families Above Poverty Level	98.6%	50	94.5
Affordable Housing	216	43.10	Median Home Value	$199,000	159	73.9
			Median Rent	$932	222	12.3
Crime	N/A	N/A	Violent Crimes per 10,000 Population	N/A	N/A	N/A
			Property Crimes per 10,000 Population	N/A	N/A	N/A
Open Spaces	38	82.85	Population Density (Persons/Sq. Mile)	4836	124	90.1
			Average Rooms per Housing Unit	6.9	26	75.6
Education	85	65.35	% High School Enrollment/Completion	95.1%	88	95.1
			% College Graduates	29.6%	88	35.6
Commute	237	20.00	Average Work Commute in Minutes	35	241	14.3
			% Commuting on Public Transportation	16.4%	55	25.7
Community Stability	3	93.10	% Living in Same House as in 1979	64.5%	11	87.7
			% Living in Same County as in 1985	92.9%	2	98.5

Metropolitan Area Suburb Rankings
NEW YORK-NORTHERN NEW JERSEY-LONG ISLAND

Composite: *Rank* 88 / 250 *Score* 61.91 **GLEN COVE (NY)**

CATEGORY	RANK	SCORE	STATISTIC	VALUE	RANK	SCORE
Economics	176	52.75	Median Household Income	$42,982	170	22.9
			% of Families Above Poverty Level	95.8%	184	82.6
Affordable Housing	196	49.90	Median Home Value	$252,600	217	60.8
			Median Rent	$782	154	39.0
Crime	42	93.25	Violent Crimes per 10,000 Population	23	75	93.5
			Property Crimes per 10,000 Population	219	21	93.0
Open Spaces	124	70.80	Population Density (Persons/Sq. Mile)	3634	88	92.8
			Average Rooms per Housing Unit	5.8	134	48.8
Education	95	64.15	% High School Enrollment/Completion	95.0%	90	95.0
			% College Graduates	28.0%	99	33.3
Commute	118	35.30	Average Work Commute in Minutes	26	84	57.1
			% Commuting on Public Transportation	8.7%	135	13.5
Community Stability	109	67.20	% Living in Same House as in 1979	49.5%	118	54.8
			% Living in Same County as in 1985	86.6%	74	79.6

Composite: *Rank* 89 / 250 *Score* 61.86 **NORTH MASSAPEQUA (NY)**

CATEGORY	RANK	SCORE	STATISTIC	VALUE	RANK	SCORE
Economics	60	64.80	Median Household Income	$55,273	65	35.1
			% of Families Above Poverty Level	98.6%	50	94.5
Affordable Housing	214	44.35	Median Home Value	$189,600	135	76.2
			Median Rent	$931	221	12.5
Crime	N/A	N/A	Violent Crimes per 10,000 Population	N/A	N/A	N/A
			Property Crimes per 10,000 Population	N/A	N/A	N/A
Open Spaces	53	79.90	Population Density (Persons/Sq. Mile)	6430	171	86.6
			Average Rooms per Housing Unit	6.8	36	73.2
Education	149	59.35	% High School Enrollment/Completion	99.0%	7	99.0
			% College Graduates	18.5%	177	19.7
Commute	183	28.40	Average Work Commute in Minutes	31	195	33.3
			% Commuting on Public Transportation	15.0%	68	23.5
Community Stability	2	94.35	% Living in Same House as in 1979	68.1%	2	95.6
			% Living in Same County as in 1985	91.1%	14	93.1

Composite: *Rank* 90 / 250 *Score* 61.79 **TARRYTOWN (NY)**

CATEGORY	RANK	SCORE	STATISTIC	VALUE	RANK	SCORE
Economics	126	58.95	Median Household Income	$48,295	125	28.1
			% of Families Above Poverty Level	97.5%	125	89.8
Affordable Housing	146	59.35	Median Home Value	$268,000	226	57.0
			Median Rent	$654	65	61.7
Crime	56	91.65	Violent Crimes per 10,000 Population	9	27	97.6
			Property Crimes per 10,000 Population	329	68	85.7
Open Spaces	182	63.45	Population Density (Persons/Sq. Mile)	3605	87	92.8
			Average Rooms per Housing Unit	5.2	192	34.1
Education	37	74.45	% High School Enrollment/Completion	94.5%	105	94.5
			% College Graduates	42.8%	34	54.4
Commute	62	42.30	Average Work Commute in Minutes	27	102	52.4
			% Commuting on Public Transportation	20.5%	33	32.2
Community Stability	209	42.35	% Living in Same House as in 1979	41.5%	185	37.3
			% Living in Same County as in 1985	75.9%	225	47.4

Metropolitan Area Suburb Rankings
NEW YORK-NORTHERN NEW JERSEY-LONG ISLAND

Composite: *Rank* 91 / 250 *Score* 61.72   **OCEANSIDE (NY)**

CATEGORY	RANK	SCORE	STATISTIC	VALUE	RANK	SCORE
Economics	78	63.45	Median Household Income	$53,875	75	33.7
			% of Families Above Poverty Level	98.3%	71	93.2
Affordable Housing	189	52.05	Median Home Value	$211,000	185	71.0
			Median Rent	$815	174	33.1
Crime	N/A	N/A	Violent Crimes per 10,000 Population	N/A	N/A	N/A
			Property Crimes per 10,000 Population	N/A	N/A	N/A
Open Spaces	68	78.60	Population Density (Persons/Sq. Mile)	6462	172	86.5
			Average Rooms per Housing Unit	6.7	44	70.7
Education	72	66.90	% High School Enrollment/Completion	95.8%	76	95.8
			% College Graduates	31.3%	74	38.0
Commute	204	25.85	Average Work Commute in Minutes	33	221	23.8
			% Commuting on Public Transportation	17.8%	48	27.9
Community Stability	24	83.45	% Living in Same House as in 1979	60.6%	30	79.2
			% Living in Same County as in 1985	89.3%	33	87.7

Composite: *Rank* 92 / 250 *Score* 61.69   **POINT PLEASANT (NJ)**

CATEGORY	RANK	SCORE	STATISTIC	VALUE	RANK	SCORE
Economics	144	57.15	Median Household Income	$40,798	184	20.7
			% of Families Above Poverty Level	98.4%	63	93.6
Affordable Housing	106	63.55	Median Home Value	$151,400	52	85.6
			Median Rent	$768	146	41.5
Crime	54	91.70	Violent Crimes per 10,000 Population	8	22	97.9
			Property Crimes per 10,000 Population	332	69	85.5
Open Spaces	139	69.10	Population Density (Persons/Sq. Mile)	5142	135	89.4
			Average Rooms per Housing Unit	5.8	134	48.8
Education	159	58.10	% High School Enrollment/Completion	94.1%	117	94.1
			% College Graduates	20.2%	163	22.1
Commute	168	29.80	Average Work Commute in Minutes	26	84	57.1
			% Commuting on Public Transportation	1.8%	243	2.5
Community Stability	125	62.40	% Living in Same House as in 1979	48.0%	141	51.5
			% Living in Same County as in 1985	84.5%	126	73.3

Composite: *Rank* 93 / 250 *Score* 61.68   **RINGWOOD (NJ)**

CATEGORY	RANK	SCORE	STATISTIC	VALUE	RANK	SCORE
Economics	34	67.75	Median Household Income	$60,026	43	39.8
			% of Families Above Poverty Level	98.9%	25	95.7
Affordable Housing	219	40.15	Median Home Value	$188,100	129	76.6
			Median Rent	$980	229	3.7
Crime	9	97.65	Violent Crimes per 10,000 Population	7	17	98.2
			Property Crimes per 10,000 Population	158	9	97.1
Open Spaces	19	86.40	Population Density (Persons/Sq. Mile)	505	2	99.6
			Average Rooms per Housing Unit	6.8	36	73.2
Education	66	67.55	% High School Enrollment/Completion	96.2%	64	96.2
			% College Graduates	31.9%	73	38.9
Commute	247	14.35	Average Work Commute in Minutes	33	221	23.8
			% Commuting on Public Transportation	3.3%	225	4.9
Community Stability	151	57.90	% Living in Same House as in 1979	49.1%	127	53.9
			% Living in Same County as in 1985	80.7%	182	61.9

Metropolitan Area Suburb Rankings
NEW YORK-NORTHERN NEW JERSEY-LONG ISLAND

Composite: *Rank* 94 / 250   *Score* 61.57   **LINDEN (NJ)**

CATEGORY	RANK	SCORE	STATISTIC	VALUE	RANK	SCORE
Economics	195	49.65	Median Household Income	$35,911	212	15.9
			% of Families Above Poverty Level	96.0%	177	83.4
Affordable Housing	26	79.00	Median Home Value	$151,300	51	85.6
			Median Rent	$594	33	72.4
Crime	128	71.70	Violent Crimes per 10,000 Population	70	126	79.6
			Property Crimes per 10,000 Population	660	129	63.8
Open Spaces	174	64.95	Population Density (Persons/Sq. Mile)	3397	82	93.3
			Average Rooms per Housing Unit	5.3	180	36.6
Education	224	49.05	% High School Enrollment/Completion	87.4%	220	87.4
			% College Graduates	12.2%	228	10.7
Commute	56	42.80	Average Work Commute in Minutes	22	27	76.2
			% Commuting on Public Transportation	6.1%	182	9.4
Community Stability	66	73.85	% Living in Same House as in 1979	53.1%	86	62.7
			% Living in Same County as in 1985	88.4%	49	85.0

Composite: *Rank* 95 / 250   *Score* 61.50   **NORTH BELLMORE (NY)**

CATEGORY	RANK	SCORE	STATISTIC	VALUE	RANK	SCORE
Economics	55	65.35	Median Household Income	$56,075	61	35.8
			% of Families Above Poverty Level	98.7%	39	94.9
Affordable Housing	201	48.30	Median Home Value	$197,100	153	74.4
			Median Rent	$876	204	22.2
Crime	N/A	N/A	Violent Crimes per 10,000 Population	N/A	N/A	N/A
			Property Crimes per 10,000 Population	N/A	N/A	N/A
Open Spaces	66	78.65	Population Density (Persons/Sq. Mile)	7562	192	84.1
			Average Rooms per Housing Unit	6.8	36	73.2
Education	113	62.75	% High School Enrollment/Completion	96.4%	59	96.4
			% College Graduates	25.1%	123	29.1
Commute	215	24.50	Average Work Commute in Minutes	33	221	23.8
			% Commuting on Public Transportation	16.1%	59	25.2
Community Stability	8	89.45	% Living in Same House as in 1979	63.9%	13	86.4
			% Living in Same County as in 1985	90.9%	15	92.5

Composite: *Rank* 96 / 250   *Score* 61.44   **NEW ROCHELLE (NY)**

CATEGORY	RANK	SCORE	STATISTIC	VALUE	RANK	SCORE
Economics	182	51.90	Median Household Income	$43,482	165	23.4
			% of Families Above Poverty Level	95.3%	193	80.4
Affordable Housing	137	59.95	Median Home Value	$318,500	236	44.6
			Median Rent	$578	27	75.3
Crime	82	87.75	Violent Crimes per 10,000 Population	45	109	87.0
			Property Crimes per 10,000 Population	287	51	88.5
Open Spaces	193	61.55	Population Density (Persons/Sq. Mile)	6499	173	86.5
			Average Rooms per Housing Unit	5.3	180	36.6
Education	89	65.05	% High School Enrollment/Completion	89.2%	209	89.2
			% College Graduates	33.3%	66	40.9
Commute	72	40.45	Average Work Commute in Minutes	28	127	47.6
			% Commuting on Public Transportation	21.2%	27	33.3
Community Stability	120	63.45	% Living in Same House as in 1979	49.1%	127	53.9
			% Living in Same County as in 1985	84.4%	129	73.0

Metropolitan Area Suburb Rankings
NEW YORK-NORTHERN NEW JERSEY-LONG ISLAND

Composite: *Rank* 97 / 250 *Score* 61.43 **BELLMORE** (NY)

CATEGORY	RANK	SCORE	STATISTIC	VALUE	RANK	SCORE
Economics	49	66.00	Median Household Income	$58,203	50	38.0
			% of Families Above Poverty Level	98.5%	58	94.0
Affordable Housing	195	50.30	Median Home Value	$208,400	180	71.6
			Median Rent	$838	185	29.0
Crime	N/A	N/A	Violent Crimes per 10,000 Population	N/A	N/A	N/A
			Property Crimes per 10,000 Population	N/A	N/A	N/A
Open Spaces	69	78.40	Population Density (Persons/Sq. Mile)	6638	176	86.1
			Average Rooms per Housing Unit	6.7	44	70.7
Education	83	65.40	% High School Enrollment/Completion	96.5%	52	96.5
			% College Graduates	28.7%	94	34.3
Commute	226	22.00	Average Work Commute in Minutes	34	234	19.0
			% Commuting on Public Transportation	16.0%	61	25.0
Community Stability	16	86.45	% Living in Same House as in 1979	61.7%	23	81.6
			% Living in Same County as in 1985	90.5%	16	91.3

Composite: *Rank* 98 / 250 *Score* 61.42 **EAST MEADOW** (NY)

CATEGORY	RANK	SCORE	STATISTIC	VALUE	RANK	SCORE
Economics	80	63.30	Median Household Income	$54,511	70	34.3
			% of Families Above Poverty Level	98.1%	83	92.3
Affordable Housing	87	66.05	Median Home Value	$190,900	138	75.9
			Median Rent	$685	89	56.2
Crime	N/A	N/A	Violent Crimes per 10,000 Population	N/A	N/A	N/A
			Property Crimes per 10,000 Population	N/A	N/A	N/A
Open Spaces	76	78.05	Population Density (Persons/Sq. Mile)	5866	159	87.8
			Average Rooms per Housing Unit	6.6	52	68.3
Education	140	60.10	% High School Enrollment/Completion	90.8%	189	90.8
			% College Graduates	25.3%	121	29.4
Commute	189	27.60	Average Work Commute in Minutes	30	172	38.1
			% Commuting on Public Transportation	11.0%	104	17.1
Community Stability	68	73.40	% Living in Same House as in 1979	57.6%	45	72.6
			% Living in Same County as in 1985	84.8%	121	74.2

Composite: *Rank* 99 / 250 *Score* 61.40 **RYE** (NY)

CATEGORY	RANK	SCORE	STATISTIC	VALUE	RANK	SCORE
Economics	23	69.75	Median Household Income	$69,695	15	49.3
			% of Families Above Poverty Level	97.6%	121	90.2
Affordable Housing	246	17.05	Median Home Value	$428,300	246	17.6
			Median Rent	$908	217	16.5
Crime	15	95.95	Violent Crimes per 10,000 Population	2	2	99.7
			Property Crimes per 10,000 Population	231	23	92.2
Open Spaces	60	79.25	Population Density (Persons/Sq. Mile)	2585	56	95.1
			Average Rooms per Housing Unit	6.4	73	63.4
Education	16	80.45	% High School Enrollment/Completion	94.5%	105	94.5
			% College Graduates	51.2%	14	66.4
Commute	92	38.00	Average Work Commute in Minutes	32	211	28.6
			% Commuting on Public Transportation	30.1%	6	47.4
Community Stability	186	49.35	% Living in Same House as in 1979	46.8%	149	48.9
			% Living in Same County as in 1985	76.7%	219	49.8

Metropolitan Area Suburb Rankings
NEW YORK-NORTHERN NEW JERSEY-LONG ISLAND

Composite: *Rank* 100 / 250 *Score* 61.36 **HARRISON (NY)**

CATEGORY	RANK	SCORE	STATISTIC	VALUE	RANK	SCORE
Economics	89	62.30	Median Household Income	$56,324	59	36.1
			% of Families Above Poverty Level	97.2%	145	88.5
Affordable Housing	241	23.65	Median Home Value	$469,200	249	7.6
			Median Rent	$778	150	39.7
Crime	27	94.35	Violent Crimes per 10,000 Population	8	22	97.9
			Property Crimes per 10,000 Population	252	36	90.8
Open Spaces	75	78.10	Population Density (Persons/Sq. Mile)	1385	10	97.7
			Average Rooms per Housing Unit	6.2	91	58.5
Education	49	70.65	% High School Enrollment/Completion	95.0%	90	95.0
			% College Graduates	37.1%	50	46.3
Commute	24	46.40	Average Work Commute in Minutes	24	56	66.7
			% Commuting on Public Transportation	16.7%	50	26.1
Community Stability	170	54.10	% Living in Same House as in 1979	49.3%	121	54.4
			% Living in Same County as in 1985	78.0%	215	53.8

Composite: *Rank* 101 / 250 *Score* 61.35 **WEST PATERSON (NJ)**

CATEGORY	RANK	SCORE	STATISTIC	VALUE	RANK	SCORE
Economics	145	57.10	Median Household Income	$44,933	155	24.8
			% of Families Above Poverty Level	97.4%	132	89.4
Affordable Housing	100	64.55	Median Home Value	$193,800	147	75.2
			Median Rent	$698	100	53.9
Crime	94	83.55	Violent Crimes per 10,000 Population	24	77	93.2
			Property Crimes per 10,000 Population	508	106	73.9
Open Spaces	153	67.05	Population Density (Persons/Sq. Mile)	3707	92	92.6
			Average Rooms per Housing Unit	5.5	162	41.5
Education	139	60.25	% High School Enrollment/Completion	97.1%	36	97.1
			% College Graduates	21.1%	157	23.4
Commute	54	42.90	Average Work Commute in Minutes	21	14	81.0
			% Commuting on Public Transportation	3.2%	227	4.8
Community Stability	171	54.05	% Living in Same House as in 1979	46.0%	155	47.1
			% Living in Same County as in 1985	80.4%	187	61.0

Composite: *Rank* 102 / 250 *Score* 61.32 **RAHWAY (NJ)**

CATEGORY	RANK	SCORE	STATISTIC	VALUE	RANK	SCORE
Economics	192	50.15	Median Household Income	$40,776	185	20.7
			% of Families Above Poverty Level	95.1%	196	79.6
Affordable Housing	29	77.60	Median Home Value	$150,700	49	85.8
			Median Rent	$611	40	69.4
Crime	96	83.10	Violent Crimes per 10,000 Population	42	104	87.9
			Property Crimes per 10,000 Population	441	93	78.3
Open Spaces	187	62.90	Population Density (Persons/Sq. Mile)	6348	170	86.8
			Average Rooms per Housing Unit	5.4	172	39.0
Education	178	55.75	% High School Enrollment/Completion	92.8%	150	92.8
			% College Graduates	17.8%	181	18.7
Commute	79	39.55	Average Work Commute in Minutes	24	56	66.7
			% Commuting on Public Transportation	8.0%	149	12.4
Community Stability	139	60.20	% Living in Same House as in 1979	47.2%	147	49.8
			% Living in Same County as in 1985	83.6%	140	70.6

Metropolitan Area Suburb Rankings
NEW YORK-NORTHERN NEW JERSEY-LONG ISLAND

Composite: **Rank** 103 / 250 **Score** 61.31   **PARSIPPANY-TROY HILLS TOWNSHIP** (NJ)

CATEGORY	RANK	SCORE	STATISTIC	VALUE	RANK	SCORE
Economics	91	62.15	Median Household Income	$50,475	106	30.3
			% of Families Above Poverty Level	98.5%	58	94.0
Affordable Housing	107	63.45	Median Home Value	$202,700	165	73.0
			Median Rent	$698	100	53.9
Crime	67	89.90	Violent Crimes per 10,000 Population	18	65	95.0
			Property Crimes per 10,000 Population	343	74	84.8
Open Spaces	141	68.90	Population Density (Persons/Sq. Mile)	2029	29	96.3
			Average Rooms per Housing Unit	5.5	162	41.5
Education	62	68.10	% High School Enrollment/Completion	94.8%	95	94.8
			% College Graduates	33.7%	64	41.4
Commute	92	38.00	Average Work Commute in Minutes	23	40	71.4
			% Commuting on Public Transportation	3.1%	229	4.6
Community Stability	223	38.70	% Living in Same House as in 1979	38.2%	201	30.0
			% Living in Same County as in 1985	75.9%	225	47.4

Composite: **Rank** 104 / 250 **Score** 61.26   **BLOOMFIELD** (NJ)

CATEGORY	RANK	SCORE	STATISTIC	VALUE	RANK	SCORE
Economics	186	51.55	Median Household Income	$39,822	191	19.7
			% of Families Above Poverty Level	96.0%	177	83.4
Affordable Housing	35	76.05	Median Home Value	$171,400	96	80.7
			Median Rent	$600	37	71.4
Crime	97	82.85	Violent Crimes per 10,000 Population	34	96	90.3
			Property Crimes per 10,000 Population	484	100	75.4
Open Spaces	211	56.90	Population Density (Persons/Sq. Mile)	8468	207	82.1
			Average Rooms per Housing Unit	5.1	199	31.7
Education	130	60.70	% High School Enrollment/Completion	91.8%	174	91.8
			% College Graduates	25.4%	120	29.6
Commute	85	38.85	Average Work Commute in Minutes	25	72	61.9
			% Commuting on Public Transportation	10.2%	110	15.8
Community Stability	130	61.90	% Living in Same House as in 1979	47.8%	143	51.1
			% Living in Same County as in 1985	84.3%	132	72.7

Composite: **Rank** 104 / 250 **Score** 61.26   **PORT WASHINGTON** (NY)

CATEGORY	RANK	SCORE	STATISTIC	VALUE	RANK	SCORE
Economics	57	65.15	Median Household Income	$64,224	27	43.9
			% of Families Above Poverty Level	96.7%	160	86.4
Affordable Housing	232	33.50	Median Home Value	$337,000	242	40.0
			Median Rent	$849	194	27.0
Crime	64	90.65	Violent Crimes per 10,000 Population	19	67	94.7
			Property Crimes per 10,000 Population	316	61	86.6
Open Spaces	97	75.60	Population Density (Persons/Sq. Mile)	3674	90	92.7
			Average Rooms per Housing Unit	6.2	91	58.5
Education	41	74.15	% High School Enrollment/Completion	92.2%	165	92.2
			% College Graduates	44.0%	30	56.1
Commute	154	31.55	Average Work Commute in Minutes	33	221	23.8
			% Commuting on Public Transportation	25.0%	14	39.3
Community Stability	149	58.25	% Living in Same House as in 1979	49.0%	130	53.7
			% Living in Same County as in 1985	81.0%	177	62.8

Metropolitan Area Suburb Rankings
NEW YORK-NORTHERN NEW JERSEY-LONG ISLAND

Composite: *Rank* 106 / 250 *Score* 61.14   **NORTH NEW HYDE PARK (NY)**

CATEGORY	RANK	SCORE	STATISTIC	VALUE	RANK	SCORE
Economics	92	62.05	Median Household Income	$51,987	95	31.8
			% of Families Above Poverty Level	98.1%	83	92.3
Affordable Housing	204	47.30	Median Home Value	$229,300	202	66.5
			Median Rent	$843	189	28.1
Crime	N/A	N/A	Violent Crimes per 10,000 Population	N/A	N/A	N/A
			Property Crimes per 10,000 Population	N/A	N/A	N/A
Open Spaces	85	76.55	Population Density (Persons/Sq. Mile)	7237	190	84.8
			Average Rooms per Housing Unit	6.6	52	68.3
Education	109	63.00	% High School Enrollment/Completion	96.6%	50	96.6
			% College Graduates	25.3%	121	29.4
Commute	185	28.15	Average Work Commute in Minutes	31	195	33.3
			% Commuting on Public Transportation	14.7%	71	23.0
Community Stability	7	89.80	% Living in Same House as in 1979	70.1%	1	100.0
			% Living in Same County as in 1985	86.6%	74	79.6

Composite: *Rank* 106 / 250 *Score* 61.14   **ROSELLE (NJ)**

CATEGORY	RANK	SCORE	STATISTIC	VALUE	RANK	SCORE
Economics	185	51.65	Median Household Income	$40,431	187	20.3
			% of Families Above Poverty Level	95.9%	181	83.0
Affordable Housing	14	84.75	Median Home Value	$139,500	30	88.5
			Median Rent	$546	18	81.0
Crime	101	81.55	Violent Crimes per 10,000 Population	42	104	87.9
			Property Crimes per 10,000 Population	488	102	75.2
Open Spaces	198	60.20	Population Density (Persons/Sq. Mile)	7690	195	83.8
			Average Rooms per Housing Unit	5.3	180	36.6
Education	175	56.00	% High School Enrollment/Completion	90.6%	193	90.6
			% College Graduates	19.7%	168	21.4
Commute	110	36.25	Average Work Commute in Minutes	26	84	57.1
			% Commuting on Public Transportation	9.9%	116	15.4
Community Stability	152	57.55	% Living in Same House as in 1979	44.8%	161	44.5
			% Living in Same County as in 1985	83.6%	140	70.6

Composite: *Rank* 106 / 250 *Score* 61.14   **ROSELLE PARK (NJ)**

CATEGORY	RANK	SCORE	STATISTIC	VALUE	RANK	SCORE
Economics	149	56.95	Median Household Income	$43,365	167	23.3
			% of Families Above Poverty Level	97.7%	116	90.6
Affordable Housing	56	72.90	Median Home Value	$159,800	71	83.5
			Median Rent	$651	62	62.3
Crime	81	87.90	Violent Crimes per 10,000 Population	29	87	91.7
			Property Crimes per 10,000 Population	354	77	84.1
Open Spaces	214	55.90	Population Density (Persons/Sq. Mile)	10472	225	77.7
			Average Rooms per Housing Unit	5.2	192	34.1
Education	135	60.45	% High School Enrollment/Completion	95.0%	90	95.0
			% College Graduates	22.8%	141	25.9
Commute	66	41.25	Average Work Commute in Minutes	23	40	71.4
			% Commuting on Public Transportation	7.2%	163	11.1
Community Stability	175	52.60	% Living in Same House as in 1979	41.1%	187	36.4
			% Living in Same County as in 1985	83.0%	150	68.8

Metropolitan Area Suburb Rankings
NEW YORK-NORTHERN NEW JERSEY-LONG ISLAND

Composite: **Rank** 109 / 250 *Score* 61.12 **HICKSVILLE** (NY)

CATEGORY	RANK	SCORE	STATISTIC	VALUE	RANK	SCORE
Economics	96	61.70	Median Household Income	$50,794	105	30.6
			% of Families Above Poverty Level	98.2%	76	92.8
Affordable Housing	187	52.65	Median Home Value	$181,300	115	78.3
			Median Rent	$849	194	27.0
Crime	N/A	N/A	Violent Crimes per 10,000 Population	N/A	N/A	N/A
			Property Crimes per 10,000 Population	N/A	N/A	N/A
Open Spaces	95	75.60	Population Density (Persons/Sq. Mile)	5897	160	87.8
			Average Rooms per Housing Unit	6.4	73	63.4
Education	160	57.95	% High School Enrollment/Completion	93.5%	129	93.5
			% College Graduates	20.4%	160	22.4
Commute	134	33.45	Average Work Commute in Minutes	28	127	47.6
			% Commuting on Public Transportation	12.4%	90	19.3
Community Stability	20	85.35	% Living in Same House as in 1979	63.6%	14	85.7
			% Living in Same County as in 1985	88.4%	49	85.0

Composite: **Rank** 110 / 250 *Score* 61.10 **SAYREVILLE** (NJ)

CATEGORY	RANK	SCORE	STATISTIC	VALUE	RANK	SCORE
Economics	136	58.05	Median Household Income	$46,057	147	25.9
			% of Families Above Poverty Level	97.6%	121	90.2
Affordable Housing	57	72.80	Median Home Value	$155,700	62	84.6
			Median Rent	$658	68	61.0
Crime	80	88.50	Violent Crimes per 10,000 Population	26	82	92.6
			Property Crimes per 10,000 Population	349	76	84.4
Open Spaces	117	72.40	Population Density (Persons/Sq. Mile)	2168	35	96.0
			Average Rooms per Housing Unit	5.8	134	48.8
Education	182	55.45	% High School Enrollment/Completion	93.3%	133	93.3
			% College Graduates	17.0%	188	17.6
Commute	200	26.00	Average Work Commute in Minutes	30	172	38.1
			% Commuting on Public Transportation	9.0%	129	13.9
Community Stability	169	54.50	% Living in Same House as in 1979	45.7%	157	46.5
			% Living in Same County as in 1985	80.9%	179	62.5

Composite: **Rank** 111 / 250 *Score* 61.02 **ENGLEWOOD** (NJ)

CATEGORY	RANK	SCORE	STATISTIC	VALUE	RANK	SCORE
Economics	183	51.80	Median Household Income	$46,758	139	26.6
			% of Families Above Poverty Level	94.5%	202	77.0
Affordable Housing	50	73.80	Median Home Value	$207,800	177	71.8
			Median Rent	$575	26	75.8
Crime	116	77.20	Violent Crimes per 10,000 Population	72	128	79.1
			Property Crimes per 10,000 Population	486	101	75.3
Open Spaces	156	66.75	Population Density (Persons/Sq. Mile)	5046	133	89.6
			Average Rooms per Housing Unit	5.6	154	43.9
Education	73	66.80	% High School Enrollment/Completion	90.7%	191	90.7
			% College Graduates	34.7%	57	42.9
Commute	81	39.10	Average Work Commute in Minutes	27	102	52.4
			% Commuting on Public Transportation	16.5%	53	25.8
Community Stability	181	51.70	% Living in Same House as in 1979	46.3%	153	47.8
			% Living in Same County as in 1985	78.6%	205	55.6

Metropolitan Area Suburb Rankings
NEW YORK-NORTHERN NEW JERSEY-LONG ISLAND

Composite: *Rank* 112 / 250 *Score* 60.97 **WESTBURY (NY)**

CATEGORY	RANK	SCORE	STATISTIC	VALUE	RANK	SCORE
Economics	93	61.90	Median Household Income	$52,114	91	31.9
			% of Families Above Poverty Level	98.0%	91	91.9
Affordable Housing	179	53.80	Median Home Value	$206,800	173	72.0
			Median Rent	$801	168	35.6
Crime	N/A	N/A	Violent Crimes per 10,000 Population	N/A	N/A	N/A
			Property Crimes per 10,000 Population	N/A	N/A	N/A
Open Spaces	100	74.90	Population Density (Persons/Sq. Mile)	5436	143	88.8
			Average Rooms per Housing Unit	6.3	83	61.0
Education	78	66.15	% High School Enrollment/Completion	95.9%	71	95.9
			% College Graduates	30.2%	83	36.4
Commute	129	34.25	Average Work Commute in Minutes	28	127	47.6
			% Commuting on Public Transportation	13.4%	82	20.9
Community Stability	58	74.80	% Living in Same House as in 1979	57.4%	48	72.1
			% Living in Same County as in 1985	85.9%	102	77.5

Composite: *Rank* 113 / 250 *Score* 60.92 **KINGS PARK (NY)**

CATEGORY	RANK	SCORE	STATISTIC	VALUE	RANK	SCORE
Economics	67	64.15	Median Household Income	$53,155	81	33.0
			% of Families Above Poverty Level	98.8%	32	95.3
Affordable Housing	118	62.80	Median Home Value	$181,000	114	78.3
			Median Rent	$735	125	47.3
Crime	N/A	N/A	Violent Crimes per 10,000 Population	N/A	N/A	N/A
			Property Crimes per 10,000 Population	N/A	N/A	N/A
Open Spaces	86	76.35	Population Density (Persons/Sq. Mile)	2978	68	94.2
			Average Rooms per Housing Unit	6.2	91	58.5
Education	120	61.95	% High School Enrollment/Completion	95.0%	90	95.0
			% College Graduates	24.9%	125	28.9
Commute	208	25.40	Average Work Commute in Minutes	30	172	38.1
			% Commuting on Public Transportation	8.2%	146	12.7
Community Stability	57	74.90	% Living in Same House as in 1979	53.9%	73	64.5
			% Living in Same County as in 1985	88.5%	46	85.3

Composite: *Rank* 114 / 250 *Score* 60.91 **LITTLE FALLS (NJ)**

CATEGORY	RANK	SCORE	STATISTIC	VALUE	RANK	SCORE
Economics	137	57.95	Median Household Income	$44,970	154	24.8
			% of Families Above Poverty Level	97.8%	111	91.1
Affordable Housing	98	65.00	Median Home Value	$191,600	140	75.7
			Median Rent	$696	98	54.3
Crime	126	72.25	Violent Crimes per 10,000 Population	34	96	90.3
			Property Crimes per 10,000 Population	804	142	54.2
Open Spaces	140	69.00	Population Density (Persons/Sq. Mile)	4105	103	91.7
			Average Rooms per Housing Unit	5.7	143	46.3
Education	95	64.15	% High School Enrollment/Completion	96.0%	68	96.0
			% College Graduates	27.3%	104	32.3
Commute	30	45.50	Average Work Commute in Minutes	21	14	81.0
			% Commuting on Public Transportation	6.5%	175	10.0
Community Stability	177	52.55	% Living in Same House as in 1979	52.2%	99	60.7
			% Living in Same County as in 1985	74.9%	229	44.4

Metropolitan Area Suburb Rankings
NEW YORK-NORTHERN NEW JERSEY-LONG ISLAND

Composite: *Rank* 115 / 250 *Score* 60.83 **SETAUKET-EAST SETAUKET (NY)**

CATEGORY	RANK	SCORE	STATISTIC	VALUE	RANK	SCORE
Economics	21	70.45	Median Household Income	$66,727	18	46.4
			% of Families Above Poverty Level	98.6%	50	94.5
Affordable Housing	226	36.40	Median Home Value	$231,100	204	66.0
			Median Rent	$963	228	6.8
Crime	N/A	N/A	Violent Crimes per 10,000 Population	N/A	N/A	N/A
			Property Crimes per 10,000 Population	N/A	N/A	N/A
Open Spaces	16	87.60	Population Density (Persons/Sq. Mile)	1612	15	97.2
			Average Rooms per Housing Unit	7.0	18	78.0
Education	20	79.35	% High School Enrollment/Completion	94.4%	108	94.4
			% College Graduates	49.7%	16	64.3
Commute	192	27.20	Average Work Commute in Minutes	28	127	47.6
			% Commuting on Public Transportation	4.5%	209	6.8
Community Stability	119	64.00	% Living in Same House as in 1979	47.1%	148	49.6
			% Living in Same County as in 1985	86.2%	87	78.4

Composite: *Rank* 116 / 250 *Score* 60.81 **MASSAPEQUA PARK (NY)**

CATEGORY	RANK	SCORE	STATISTIC	VALUE	RANK	SCORE
Economics	38	67.55	Median Household Income	$58,773	47	38.5
			% of Families Above Poverty Level	99.1%	13	96.6
Affordable Housing	221	38.25	Median Home Value	$188,500	132	76.5
			Median Rent	$1,001	232	0.0
Crime	N/A	N/A	Violent Crimes per 10,000 Population	N/A	N/A	N/A
			Property Crimes per 10,000 Population	N/A	N/A	N/A
Open Spaces	43	81.40	Population Density (Persons/Sq. Mile)	8368	203	82.3
			Average Rooms per Housing Unit	7.1	13	80.5
Education	107	63.15	% High School Enrollment/Completion	99.2%	6	99.2
			% College Graduates	23.7%	134	27.1
Commute	227	21.80	Average Work Commute in Minutes	35	241	14.3
			% Commuting on Public Transportation	18.7%	41	29.3
Community Stability	4	92.70	% Living in Same House as in 1979	67.4%	3	94.1
			% Living in Same County as in 1985	90.5%	16	91.3

Composite: *Rank* 117 / 250 *Score* 60.76 **NESCONSET (NY)**

CATEGORY	RANK	SCORE	STATISTIC	VALUE	RANK	SCORE
Economics	68	64.00	Median Household Income	$60,204	41	39.9
			% of Families Above Poverty Level	97.1%	150	88.1
Affordable Housing	198	49.40	Median Home Value	$192,700	144	75.5
			Median Rent	$870	203	23.3
Crime	N/A	N/A	Violent Crimes per 10,000 Population	N/A	N/A	N/A
			Property Crimes per 10,000 Population	N/A	N/A	N/A
Open Spaces	20	86.30	Population Density (Persons/Sq. Mile)	2799	61	94.6
			Average Rooms per Housing Unit	7.0	18	78.0
Education	78	66.15	% High School Enrollment/Completion	96.2%	64	96.2
			% College Graduates	30.0%	87	36.1
Commute	223	22.45	Average Work Commute in Minutes	30	172	38.1
			% Commuting on Public Transportation	4.5%	209	6.8
Community Stability	51	76.25	% Living in Same House as in 1979	53.5%	78	63.6
			% Living in Same County as in 1985	89.7%	29	88.9

Metropolitan Area Suburb Rankings
NEW YORK-NORTHERN NEW JERSEY-LONG ISLAND

Composite: *Rank* 117 / 250 *Score* 60.76 **SEAFORD** (NY)

CATEGORY	RANK	SCORE	STATISTIC	VALUE	RANK	SCORE
Economics	76	63.65	Median Household Income	$55,259	66	35.0
			% of Families Above Poverty Level	98.1%	83	92.3
Affordable Housing	202	48.10	Median Home Value	$192,000	143	75.6
			Median Rent	$885	209	20.6
Crime	N/A	N/A	Violent Crimes per 10,000 Population	N/A	N/A	N/A
			Property Crimes per 10,000 Population	N/A	N/A	N/A
Open Spaces	63	79.15	Population Density (Persons/Sq. Mile)	5986	165	87.6
			Average Rooms per Housing Unit	6.7	44	70.7
Education	121	61.75	% High School Enrollment/Completion	96.8%	42	96.8
			% College Graduates	23.4%	137	26.7
Commute	216	24.20	Average Work Commute in Minutes	33	221	23.8
			% Commuting on Public Transportation	15.7%	65	24.6
Community Stability	14	87.70	% Living in Same House as in 1979	61.2%	26	80.5
			% Living in Same County as in 1985	91.7%	7	94.9

Composite: *Rank* 119 / 250 *Score* 60.73 **SYOSSET** (NY)

CATEGORY	RANK	SCORE	STATISTIC	VALUE	RANK	SCORE
Economics	29	68.70	Median Household Income	$65,806	23	45.5
			% of Families Above Poverty Level	98.0%	91	91.9
Affordable Housing	238	29.20	Median Home Value	$262,300	223	58.4
			Median Rent	$1,001	232	0.0
Crime	N/A	N/A	Violent Crimes per 10,000 Population	N/A	N/A	N/A
			Property Crimes per 10,000 Population	N/A	N/A	N/A
Open Spaces	27	85.20	Population Density (Persons/Sq. Mile)	3807	95	92.4
			Average Rooms per Housing Unit	7.0	18	78.0
Education	31	75.70	% High School Enrollment/Completion	96.8%	42	96.8
			% College Graduates	42.9%	33	54.6
Commute	194	26.75	Average Work Commute in Minutes	32	211	28.6
			% Commuting on Public Transportation	15.9%	62	24.9
Community Stability	42	78.85	% Living in Same House as in 1979	60.1%	32	78.1
			% Living in Same County as in 1985	86.6%	74	79.6

Composite: *Rank* 120 / 250 *Score* 60.72 **EAST NORTHPORT** (NY)

CATEGORY	RANK	SCORE	STATISTIC	VALUE	RANK	SCORE
Economics	88	62.35	Median Household Income	$52,108	92	31.9
			% of Families Above Poverty Level	98.2%	76	92.8
Affordable Housing	191	51.45	Median Home Value	$190,700	136	76.0
			Median Rent	$850	197	26.9
Crime	N/A	N/A	Violent Crimes per 10,000 Population	N/A	N/A	N/A
			Property Crimes per 10,000 Population	N/A	N/A	N/A
Open Spaces	79	77.65	Population Density (Persons/Sq. Mile)	4002	100	91.9
			Average Rooms per Housing Unit	6.4	73	63.4
Education	83	65.40	% High School Enrollment/Completion	96.2%	64	96.2
			% College Graduates	28.9%	92	34.6
Commute	202	25.95	Average Work Commute in Minutes	30	172	38.1
			% Commuting on Public Transportation	8.9%	133	13.8
Community Stability	29	81.55	% Living in Same House as in 1979	58.9%	39	75.4
			% Living in Same County as in 1985	89.3%	33	87.7

Metropolitan Area Suburb Rankings
NEW YORK-NORTHERN NEW JERSEY-LONG ISLAND

Composite: *Rank* 121 / 250   *Score* 60.59   **HIGHLAND PARK (NJ)**

CATEGORY	RANK	SCORE	STATISTIC	VALUE	RANK	SCORE
Economics	166	54.45	Median Household Income	$39,603	193	19.5
			% of Families Above Poverty Level	97.4%	132	89.4
Affordable Housing	68	70.10	Median Home Value	$170,700	94	80.9
			Median Rent	$668	78	59.3
Crime	46	92.55	Violent Crimes per 10,000 Population	13	41	96.5
			Property Crimes per 10,000 Population	286	50	88.6
Open Spaces	215	55.85	Population Density (Persons/Sq. Mile)	7225	189	84.9
			Average Rooms per Housing Unit	4.9	210	26.8
Education	25	77.80	% High School Enrollment/Completion	93.0%	141	93.0
			% College Graduates	48.5%	20	62.6
Commute	55	42.85	Average Work Commute in Minutes	23	40	71.4
			% Commuting on Public Transportation	9.2%	125	14.3
Community Stability	238	30.55	% Living in Same House as in 1979	35.4%	221	23.9
			% Living in Same County as in 1985	72.5%	237	37.2

Composite: *Rank* 122 / 250   *Score* 60.56   **WALLINGTON (NJ)**

CATEGORY	RANK	SCORE	STATISTIC	VALUE	RANK	SCORE
Economics	203	47.65	Median Household Income	$32,332	227	12.3
			% of Families Above Poverty Level	95.9%	181	83.0
Affordable Housing	37	75.95	Median Home Value	$191,900	142	75.7
			Median Rent	$573	25	76.2
Crime	52	91.95	Violent Crimes per 10,000 Population	9	27	97.6
			Property Crimes per 10,000 Population	320	64	86.3
Open Spaces	227	48.30	Population Density (Persons/Sq. Mile)	10770	227	77.1
			Average Rooms per Housing Unit	4.6	229	19.5
Education	180	55.65	% High School Enrollment/Completion	95.4%	83	95.4
			% College Graduates	15.8%	199	15.9
Commute	28	45.80	Average Work Commute in Minutes	21	14	81.0
			% Commuting on Public Transportation	6.9%	169	10.6
Community Stability	144	58.65	% Living in Same House as in 1979	44.3%	164	43.4
			% Living in Same County as in 1985	84.7%	123	73.9

Composite: *Rank* 123 / 250   *Score* 60.48   **COMMACK (NY)**

CATEGORY	RANK	SCORE	STATISTIC	VALUE	RANK	SCORE
Economics	40	67.45	Median Household Income	$62,014	33	41.7
			% of Families Above Poverty Level	98.3%	71	93.2
Affordable Housing	225	36.90	Median Home Value	$199,400	160	73.8
			Median Rent	$1,001	232	0.0
Crime	N/A	N/A	Violent Crimes per 10,000 Population	N/A	N/A	N/A
			Property Crimes per 10,000 Population	N/A	N/A	N/A
Open Spaces	13	88.55	Population Density (Persons/Sq. Mile)	2995	69	94.2
			Average Rooms per Housing Unit	7.2	11	82.9
Education	80	66.00	% High School Enrollment/Completion	94.7%	97	94.7
			% College Graduates	30.8%	79	37.3
Commute	220	22.45	Average Work Commute in Minutes	31	195	33.3
			% Commuting on Public Transportation	7.5%	158	11.6
Community Stability	28	81.50	% Living in Same House as in 1979	62.8%	18	84.0
			% Living in Same County as in 1985	86.4%	80	79.0

Metropolitan Area Suburb Rankings
NEW YORK-NORTHERN NEW JERSEY-LONG ISLAND

Composite: Rank 124 / 250 **Score** 60.37   **FORDS** (NJ)

CATEGORY	RANK	SCORE	STATISTIC	VALUE	RANK	SCORE
Economics	131	58.30	Median Household Income	$43,913	162	23.8
			% of Families Above Poverty Level	98.2%	76	92.8
Affordable Housing	46	74.30	Median Home Value	$158,800	69	83.8
			Median Rent	$637	55	64.8
Crime	N/A	N/A	Violent Crimes per 10,000 Population	N/A	N/A	N/A
			Property Crimes per 10,000 Population	N/A	N/A	N/A
Open Spaces	159	66.20	Population Density (Persons/Sq. Mile)	5553	150	88.5
			Average Rooms per Housing Unit	5.6	154	43.9
Education	171	56.20	% High School Enrollment/Completion	92.4%	159	92.4
			% College Graduates	18.7%	173	20.0
Commute	83	38.90	Average Work Commute in Minutes	24	56	66.7
			% Commuting on Public Transportation	7.2%	163	11.1
Community Stability	103	68.30	% Living in Same House as in 1979	52.4%	95	61.2
			% Living in Same County as in 1985	85.2%	114	75.4

Composite: Rank 125 / 250 **Score** 60.35   **WHITE PLAINS** (NY)

CATEGORY	RANK	SCORE	STATISTIC	VALUE	RANK	SCORE
Economics	174	53.00	Median Household Income	$44,004	160	23.9
			% of Families Above Poverty Level	95.7%	186	82.1
Affordable Housing	124	61.75	Median Home Value	$295,500	232	50.2
			Median Rent	$589	30	73.3
Crime	119	76.40	Violent Crimes per 10,000 Population	48	111	86.1
			Property Crimes per 10,000 Population	616	126	66.7
Open Spaces	202	58.30	Population Density (Persons/Sq. Mile)	4967	131	89.8
			Average Rooms per Housing Unit	4.9	210	26.8
Education	57	69.40	% High School Enrollment/Completion	91.9%	172	91.9
			% College Graduates	37.5%	49	46.9
Commute	17	47.60	Average Work Commute in Minutes	25	72	61.9
			% Commuting on Public Transportation	21.2%	27	33.3
Community Stability	160	56.00	% Living in Same House as in 1979	44.9%	160	44.7
			% Living in Same County as in 1985	82.5%	155	67.3

Composite: Rank 126 / 250 **Score** 60.31   **DEER PARK** (NY)

CATEGORY	RANK	SCORE	STATISTIC	VALUE	RANK	SCORE
Economics	128	58.70	Median Household Income	$48,117	128	28.0
			% of Families Above Poverty Level	97.4%	132	89.4
Affordable Housing	111	63.25	Median Home Value	$160,900	73	83.3
			Median Rent	$758	140	43.2
Crime	N/A	N/A	Violent Crimes per 10,000 Population	N/A	N/A	N/A
			Property Crimes per 10,000 Population	N/A	N/A	N/A
Open Spaces	92	75.75	Population Density (Persons/Sq. Mile)	4648	120	90.5
			Average Rooms per Housing Unit	6.3	83	61.0
Education	200	53.30	% High School Enrollment/Completion	92.2%	165	92.2
			% College Graduates	14.8%	210	14.4
Commute	176	29.20	Average Work Commute in Minutes	29	150	42.9
			% Commuting on Public Transportation	10.0%	114	15.5
Community Stability	26	81.65	% Living in Same House as in 1979	57.6%	45	72.6
			% Living in Same County as in 1985	90.3%	21	90.7

Metropolitan Area Suburb Rankings
NEW YORK-NORTHERN NEW JERSEY-LONG ISLAND

Composite: *Rank* 127 / 250 *Score* 60.26   **FRANKLIN SQUARE (NY)**

CATEGORY	RANK	SCORE	STATISTIC	VALUE	RANK	SCORE
Economics	119	59.45	Median Household Income	$46,186	145	26.1
			% of Families Above Poverty Level	98.2%	76	92.8
Affordable Housing	101	64.40	Median Home Value	$197,200	154	74.4
			Median Rent	$695	97	54.4
Crime	N/A	N/A	Violent Crimes per 10,000 Population	N/A	N/A	N/A
			Property Crimes per 10,000 Population	N/A	N/A	N/A
Open Spaces	150	67.65	Population Density (Persons/Sq. Mile)	9782	216	79.2
			Average Rooms per Housing Unit	6.1	104	56.1
Education	178	55.75	% High School Enrollment/Completion	95.9%	71	95.9
			% College Graduates	15.6%	200	15.6
Commute	180	28.70	Average Work Commute in Minutes	30	172	38.1
			% Commuting on Public Transportation	12.4%	90	19.3
Community Stability	18	85.60	% Living in Same House as in 1979	62.7%	20	83.8
			% Living in Same County as in 1985	89.2%	36	87.4

Composite: *Rank* 127 / 250 *Score* 60.26   **MONTCLAIR (NJ)**

CATEGORY	RANK	SCORE	STATISTIC	VALUE	RANK	SCORE
Economics	132	58.25	Median Household Income	$52,442	88	32.2
			% of Families Above Poverty Level	96.2%	170	84.3
Affordable Housing	190	51.80	Median Home Value	$266,800	225	57.3
			Median Rent	$741	132	46.3
Crime	109	78.25	Violent Crimes per 10,000 Population	50	114	85.5
			Property Crimes per 10,000 Population	551	115	71.0
Open Spaces	137	69.40	Population Density (Persons/Sq. Mile)	5984	164	87.6
			Average Rooms per Housing Unit	5.9	123	51.2
Education	21	79.20	% High School Enrollment/Completion	94.7%	97	94.7
			% College Graduates	49.3%	17	63.7
Commute	94	37.85	Average Work Commute in Minutes	29	150	42.9
			% Commuting on Public Transportation	20.9%	30	32.8
Community Stability	198	47.10	% Living in Same House as in 1979	40.2%	193	34.4
			% Living in Same County as in 1985	80.0%	190	59.8

Composite: *Rank* 129 / 250 *Score* 60.23   **HAUPPAUGE (NY)**

CATEGORY	RANK	SCORE	STATISTIC	VALUE	RANK	SCORE
Economics	44	66.95	Median Household Income	$57,959	52	37.7
			% of Families Above Poverty Level	99.0%	16	96.2
Affordable Housing	205	47.15	Median Home Value	$195,200	152	74.9
			Median Rent	$892	212	19.4
Crime	N/A	N/A	Violent Crimes per 10,000 Population	N/A	N/A	N/A
			Property Crimes per 10,000 Population	N/A	N/A	N/A
Open Spaces	39	82.50	Population Density (Persons/Sq. Mile)	1825	20	96.7
			Average Rooms per Housing Unit	6.6	52	68.3
Education	70	67.15	% High School Enrollment/Completion	97.2%	33	97.2
			% College Graduates	30.7%	80	37.1
Commute	207	25.75	Average Work Commute in Minutes	29	150	42.9
			% Commuting on Public Transportation	5.6%	188	8.6
Community Stability	76	71.90	% Living in Same House as in 1979	52.4%	95	61.2
			% Living in Same County as in 1985	87.6%	63	82.6

Metropolitan Area Suburb Rankings
NEW YORK-NORTHERN NEW JERSEY-LONG ISLAND

Composite: *Rank* 130 / 250 *Score* 60.19 **EAST MASSAPEQUA (NY)**

CATEGORY	RANK	SCORE	STATISTIC	VALUE	RANK	SCORE
Economics	57	65.15	Median Household Income	$57,717	53	37.5
			% of Families Above Poverty Level	98.2%	76	92.8
Affordable Housing	161	56.70	Median Home Value	$187,600	127	76.7
			Median Rent	$795	165	36.7
Crime	N/A	N/A	Violent Crimes per 10,000 Population	N/A	N/A	N/A
			Property Crimes per 10,000 Population	N/A	N/A	N/A
Open Spaces	82	77.15	Population Density (Persons/Sq. Mile)	5622	152	88.4
			Average Rooms per Housing Unit	6.5	62	65.9
Education	116	62.35	% High School Enrollment/Completion	95.6%	80	95.6
			% College Graduates	25.1%	123	29.1
Commute	239	19.90	Average Work Commute in Minutes	35	241	14.3
			% Commuting on Public Transportation	16.3%	57	25.5
Community Stability	35	79.90	% Living in Same House as in 1979	60.4%	31	78.7
			% Living in Same County as in 1985	87.1%	72	81.1

Composite: *Rank* 131 / 250 *Score* 60.18 **HUNTINGTON (NY)**

CATEGORY	RANK	SCORE	STATISTIC	VALUE	RANK	SCORE
Economics	50	65.60	Median Household Income	$62,121	32	41.8
			% of Families Above Poverty Level	97.4%	132	89.4
Affordable Housing	209	45.65	Median Home Value	$268,900	227	56.8
			Median Rent	$807	169	34.5
Crime	N/A	N/A	Violent Crimes per 10,000 Population	N/A	N/A	N/A
			Property Crimes per 10,000 Population	N/A	N/A	N/A
Open Spaces	42	81.85	Population Density (Persons/Sq. Mile)	2420	47	95.4
			Average Rooms per Housing Unit	6.6	52	68.3
Education	23	78.95	% High School Enrollment/Completion	97.0%	39	97.0
			% College Graduates	47.3%	24	60.9
Commute	204	25.85	Average Work Commute in Minutes	32	211	28.6
			% Commuting on Public Transportation	14.8%	70	23.1
Community Stability	122	63.20	% Living in Same House as in 1979	47.9%	142	51.3
			% Living in Same County as in 1985	85.1%	116	75.1

Composite: *Rank* 132 / 250 *Score* 60.13 **BALDWIN (NY)**

CATEGORY	RANK	SCORE	STATISTIC	VALUE	RANK	SCORE
Economics	90	62.20	Median Household Income	$53,994	74	33.8
			% of Families Above Poverty Level	97.7%	116	90.6
Affordable Housing	119	62.30	Median Home Value	$188,100	129	76.6
			Median Rent	$731	121	48.0
Crime	N/A	N/A	Violent Crimes per 10,000 Population	N/A	N/A	N/A
			Property Crimes per 10,000 Population	N/A	N/A	N/A
Open Spaces	117	72.40	Population Density (Persons/Sq. Mile)	7711	197	83.8
			Average Rooms per Housing Unit	6.3	83	61.0
Education	65	67.60	% High School Enrollment/Completion	97.6%	24	97.6
			% College Graduates	31.0%	78	37.6
Commute	198	26.20	Average Work Commute in Minutes	34	234	19.0
			% Commuting on Public Transportation	21.3%	26	33.4
Community Stability	88	70.10	% Living in Same House as in 1979	54.3%	67	65.4
			% Living in Same County as in 1985	85.0%	119	74.8

Composite: **Rank** 133 / 250 *Score* 60.07   **RED BANK (NJ)**

CATEGORY	RANK	SCORE	STATISTIC	VALUE	RANK	SCORE
Economics	212	45.20	Median Household Income	$36,879	207	16.8
			% of Families Above Poverty Level	93.7%	211	73.6
Affordable Housing	49	74.10	Median Home Value	$154,900	59	84.7
			Median Rent	$644	58	63.5
Crime	102	81.45	Violent Crimes per 10,000 Population	37	98	89.4
			Property Crimes per 10,000 Population	513	108	73.5
Open Spaces	209	57.25	Population Density (Persons/Sq. Mile)	5939	162	87.7
			Average Rooms per Housing Unit	4.9	210	26.8
Education	118	62.10	% High School Enrollment/Completion	90.9%	186	90.9
			% College Graduates	28.0%	99	33.3
Commute	31	45.55	Average Work Commute in Minutes	22	27	76.2
			% Commuting on Public Transportation	9.6%	120	14.9
Community Stability	166	54.85	% Living in Same House as in 1979	38.5%	200	30.7
			% Living in Same County as in 1985	86.4%	80	79.0

Composite: **Rank** 134 / 250 *Score* 60.03   **MASSAPEQUA (NY)**

CATEGORY	RANK	SCORE	STATISTIC	VALUE	RANK	SCORE
Economics	33	67.70	Median Household Income	$60,345	39	40.1
			% of Families Above Poverty Level	98.8%	32	95.3
Affordable Housing	228	35.70	Median Home Value	$209,300	183	71.4
			Median Rent	$1,001	232	0.0
Crime	N/A	N/A	Violent Crimes per 10,000 Population	N/A	N/A	N/A
			Property Crimes per 10,000 Population	N/A	N/A	N/A
Open Spaces	32	83.95	Population Density (Persons/Sq. Mile)	6058	166	87.4
			Average Rooms per Housing Unit	7.1	13	80.5
Education	114	62.60	% High School Enrollment/Completion	94.1%	117	94.1
			% College Graduates	26.5%	110	31.1
Commute	231	21.15	Average Work Commute in Minutes	34	234	19.0
			% Commuting on Public Transportation	14.9%	69	23.3
Community Stability	10	89.05	% Living in Same House as in 1979	63.0%	17	84.4
			% Living in Same County as in 1985	91.3%	11	93.7

Composite: **Rank** 135 / 250 *Score* 60.00   **EAST ISLIP (NY)**

CATEGORY	RANK	SCORE	STATISTIC	VALUE	RANK	SCORE
Economics	109	60.35	Median Household Income	$52,796	84	32.6
			% of Families Above Poverty Level	97.1%	150	88.1
Affordable Housing	166	55.50	Median Home Value	$160,300	72	83.4
			Median Rent	$846	192	27.6
Crime	N/A	N/A	Violent Crimes per 10,000 Population	N/A	N/A	N/A
			Property Crimes per 10,000 Population	N/A	N/A	N/A
Open Spaces	72	78.35	Population Density (Persons/Sq. Mile)	3389	81	93.3
			Average Rooms per Housing Unit	6.4	73	63.4
Education	156	58.20	% High School Enrollment/Completion	92.3%	161	92.3
			% College Graduates	21.6%	149	24.1
Commute	160	30.50	Average Work Commute in Minutes	27	102	52.4
			% Commuting on Public Transportation	5.6%	188	8.6
Community Stability	48	77.10	% Living in Same House as in 1979	49.2%	126	54.2
			% Living in Same County as in 1985	93.4%	1	100.0

Metropolitan Area Suburb Rankings
NEW YORK-NORTHERN NEW JERSEY-LONG ISLAND

Composite: *Rank* 136 / 250 *Score* 59.80   **PARAMUS** (NJ)

CATEGORY	RANK	SCORE	STATISTIC	VALUE	RANK	SCORE
Economics	48	66.15	Median Household Income	$58,995	46	38.7
			% of Families Above Poverty Level	98.4%	63	93.6
Affordable Housing	235	31.30	Median Home Value	$245,200	213	62.6
			Median Rent	$1,001	232	0.0
Crime	148	44.10	Violent Crimes per 10,000 Population	41	101	88.2
			Property Crimes per 10,000 Population	1,621	152	0.0
Open Spaces	24	85.55	Population Density (Persons/Sq. Mile)	2395	46	95.5
			Average Rooms per Housing Unit	6.9	26	75.6
Education	64	67.70	% High School Enrollment/Completion	97.5%	29	97.5
			% College Graduates	31.2%	76	37.9
Commute	94	37.85	Average Work Commute in Minutes	24	56	66.7
			% Commuting on Public Transportation	5.9%	184	9.0
Community Stability	17	85.95	% Living in Same House as in 1979	65.5%	9	89.9
			% Living in Same County as in 1985	87.4%	67	82.0

Composite: *Rank* 137 / 250 *Score* 59.78   **EDISON** (NJ)

CATEGORY	RANK	SCORE	STATISTIC	VALUE	RANK	SCORE
Economics	101	61.10	Median Household Income	$50,075	111	29.9
			% of Families Above Poverty Level	98.1%	83	92.3
Affordable Housing	95	65.30	Median Home Value	$186,500	124	77.0
			Median Rent	$700	103	53.6
Crime	68	89.70	Violent Crimes per 10,000 Population	17	60	95.3
			Property Crimes per 10,000 Population	354	77	84.1
Open Spaces	127	70.30	Population Density (Persons/Sq. Mile)	2938	67	94.3
			Average Rooms per Housing Unit	5.7	143	46.3
Education	74	66.65	% High School Enrollment/Completion	91.7%	177	91.7
			% College Graduates	33.8%	62	41.6
Commute	152	31.70	Average Work Commute in Minutes	28	127	47.6
			% Commuting on Public Transportation	10.2%	110	15.8
Community Stability	236	33.70	% Living in Same House as in 1979	35.8%	219	24.8
			% Living in Same County as in 1985	74.3%	231	42.6

Composite: *Rank* 138 / 250 *Score* 59.73   **SAYVILLE** (NY)

CATEGORY	RANK	SCORE	STATISTIC	VALUE	RANK	SCORE
Economics	73	63.60	Median Household Income	$53,806	76	33.6
			% of Families Above Poverty Level	98.4%	63	93.6
Affordable Housing	170	55.30	Median Home Value	$170,700	94	80.9
			Median Rent	$834	181	29.7
Crime	N/A	N/A	Violent Crimes per 10,000 Population	N/A	N/A	N/A
			Property Crimes per 10,000 Population	N/A	N/A	N/A
Open Spaces	65	78.80	Population Density (Persons/Sq. Mile)	2995	69	94.2
			Average Rooms per Housing Unit	6.4	73	63.4
Education	111	62.85	% High School Enrollment/Completion	94.6%	104	94.6
			% College Graduates	26.5%	110	31.1
Commute	182	28.50	Average Work Commute in Minutes	28	127	47.6
			% Commuting on Public Transportation	6.1%	182	9.4
Community Stability	97	69.30	% Living in Same House as in 1979	49.1%	127	53.9
			% Living in Same County as in 1985	88.3%	54	84.7

Metropolitan Area Suburb Rankings
NEW YORK-NORTHERN NEW JERSEY-LONG ISLAND

Composite: Rank 139 / 250 *Score* 59.63   **KEARNY (NJ)**

CATEGORY	RANK	SCORE	STATISTIC	VALUE	RANK	SCORE
Economics	190	50.60	Median Household Income	$37,840	204	17.8
			% of Families Above Poverty Level	96.0%	177	83.4
Affordable Housing	42	74.95	Median Home Value	$166,500	85	81.9
			Median Rent	$619	46	68.0
Crime	106	79.50	Violent Crimes per 10,000 Population	45	109	87.0
			Property Crimes per 10,000 Population	536	111	72.0
Open Spaces	184	63.25	Population Density (Persons/Sq. Mile)	3814	96	92.4
			Average Rooms per Housing Unit	5.2	192	34.1
Education	205	52.50	% High School Enrollment/Completion	89.9%	202	89.9
			% College Graduates	15.3%	201	15.1
Commute	42	44.20	Average Work Commute in Minutes	23	40	71.4
			% Commuting on Public Transportation	10.9%	106	17.0
Community Stability	178	52.40	% Living in Same House as in 1979	43.8%	169	42.3
			% Living in Same County as in 1985	80.9%	179	62.5

Composite: Rank 139 / 250 *Score* 59.63   **SOMERVILLE (NJ)**

CATEGORY	RANK	SCORE	STATISTIC	VALUE	RANK	SCORE
Economics	179	52.55	Median Household Income	$39,667	192	19.6
			% of Families Above Poverty Level	96.5%	163	85.5
Affordable Housing	65	70.20	Median Home Value	$161,000	74	83.3
			Median Rent	$680	86	57.1
Crime	99	82.80	Violent Crimes per 10,000 Population	25	79	92.9
			Property Crimes per 10,000 Population	525	109	72.7
Open Spaces	196	60.80	Population Density (Persons/Sq. Mile)	4927	129	89.9
			Average Rooms per Housing Unit	5.1	199	31.7
Education	142	59.80	% High School Enrollment/Completion	91.3%	181	91.3
			% College Graduates	24.5%	128	28.3
Commute	14	47.80	Average Work Commute in Minutes	19	2	90.5
			% Commuting on Public Transportation	3.4%	224	5.1
Community Stability	206	43.45	% Living in Same House as in 1979	40.7%	190	35.5
			% Living in Same County as in 1985	77.2%	216	51.4

Composite: Rank 141 / 250 *Score* 59.62   **NORWALK (CT)**

CATEGORY	RANK	SCORE	STATISTIC	VALUE	RANK	SCORE
Economics	157	56.15	Median Household Income	$48,171	127	28.0
			% of Families Above Poverty Level	96.2%	170	84.3
Affordable Housing	168	55.30	Median Home Value	$240,300	210	63.8
			Median Rent	$738	130	46.8
Crime	122	74.10	Violent Crimes per 10,000 Population	58	120	83.2
			Property Crimes per 10,000 Population	642	128	65.0
Open Spaces	161	66.10	Population Density (Persons/Sq. Mile)	3435	83	93.2
			Average Rooms per Housing Unit	5.4	172	39.0
Education	101	63.85	% High School Enrollment/Completion	92.3%	161	92.3
			% College Graduates	29.5%	89	35.4
Commute	19	47.00	Average Work Commute in Minutes	21	14	81.0
			% Commuting on Public Transportation	8.4%	142	13.0
Community Stability	166	54.85	% Living in Same House as in 1979	38.9%	197	31.6
			% Living in Same County as in 1985	86.1%	93	78.1

Metropolitan Area Suburb Rankings
NEW YORK-NORTHERN NEW JERSEY-LONG ISLAND

Composite: **Rank** 142 / 250 *Score* 59.51   **BELLEVILLE** (NJ)

CATEGORY	RANK	SCORE	STATISTIC	VALUE	RANK	SCORE
Economics	181	51.95	Median Household Income	$38,507	199	18.4
			% of Families Above Poverty Level	96.5%	163	85.5
Affordable Housing	36	75.90	Median Home Value	$161,800	77	83.1
			Median Rent	$615	44	68.7
Crime	110	78.15	Violent Crimes per 10,000 Population	62	123	82.0
			Property Crimes per 10,000 Population	501	105	74.3
Open Spaces	216	53.80	Population Density (Persons/Sq. Mile)	10228	220	78.3
			Average Rooms per Housing Unit	5.0	203	29.3
Education	177	55.80	% High School Enrollment/Completion	93.7%	123	93.7
			% College Graduates	17.2%	185	17.9
Commute	70	40.50	Average Work Commute in Minutes	24	56	66.7
			% Commuting on Public Transportation	9.2%	125	14.3
Community Stability	137	60.45	% Living in Same House as in 1979	43.9%	167	42.5
			% Living in Same County as in 1985	86.2%	87	78.4

Composite: **Rank** 143 / 250 *Score* 59.49   **BABYLON** (NY)

CATEGORY	RANK	SCORE	STATISTIC	VALUE	RANK	SCORE
Economics	95	61.85	Median Household Income	$52,023	93	31.8
			% of Families Above Poverty Level	98.0%	91	91.9
Affordable Housing	174	54.95	Median Home Value	$179,900	113	78.6
			Median Rent	$825	180	31.3
Crime	N/A	N/A	Violent Crimes per 10,000 Population	N/A	N/A	N/A
			Property Crimes per 10,000 Population	N/A	N/A	N/A
Open Spaces	107	74.05	Population Density (Persons/Sq. Mile)	5088	134	89.6
			Average Rooms per Housing Unit	6.2	91	58.5
Education	87	65.25	% High School Enrollment/Completion	97.9%	18	97.9
			% College Graduates	27.5%	103	32.6
Commute	172	29.50	Average Work Commute in Minutes	30	172	38.1
			% Commuting on Public Transportation	13.4%	82	20.9
Community Stability	80	71.35	% Living in Same House as in 1979	48.2%	138	52.0
			% Living in Same County as in 1985	90.3%	21	90.7

Composite: **Rank** 144 / 250 *Score* 59.43   **NORTH MERRICK** (NY)

CATEGORY	RANK	SCORE	STATISTIC	VALUE	RANK	SCORE
Economics	35	67.65	Median Household Income	$60,233	40	40.0
			% of Families Above Poverty Level	98.8%	32	95.3
Affordable Housing	222	37.60	Median Home Value	$193,900	149	75.2
			Median Rent	$1,001	232	0.0
Crime	N/A	N/A	Violent Crimes per 10,000 Population	N/A	N/A	N/A
			Property Crimes per 10,000 Population	N/A	N/A	N/A
Open Spaces	52	80.65	Population Density (Persons/Sq. Mile)	6828	180	85.7
			Average Rooms per Housing Unit	6.9	26	75.6
Education	94	64.30	% High School Enrollment/Completion	96.5%	52	96.5
			% College Graduates	27.2%	105	32.1
Commute	211	25.10	Average Work Commute in Minutes	34	234	19.0
			% Commuting on Public Transportation	19.9%	36	31.2
Community Stability	31	81.25	% Living in Same House as in 1979	60.8%	29	79.6
			% Living in Same County as in 1985	87.7%	60	82.9

Metropolitan Area Suburb Rankings
NEW YORK-NORTHERN NEW JERSEY-LONG ISLAND

Composite: *Rank* 145 / 250 *Score* 59.41   **VALLEY STREAM (NY)**

CATEGORY	RANK	SCORE	STATISTIC	VALUE	RANK	SCORE
Economics	124	59.10	Median Household Income	$47,287	133	27.1
			% of Families Above Poverty Level	97.8%	111	91.1
Affordable Housing	133	60.40	Median Home Value	$187,700	128	76.7
			Median Rent	$753	137	44.1
Crime	N/A	N/A	Violent Crimes per 10,000 Population	N/A	N/A	N/A
			Property Crimes per 10,000 Population	N/A	N/A	N/A
Open Spaces	142	68.80	Population Density (Persons/Sq. Mile)	9861	217	79.1
			Average Rooms per Housing Unit	6.2	91	58.5
Education	169	56.90	% High School Enrollment/Completion	93.1%	139	93.1
			% College Graduates	19.2%	169	20.7
Commute	154	31.55	Average Work Commute in Minutes	31	195	33.3
			% Commuting on Public Transportation	19.0%	40	29.8
Community Stability	36	79.70	% Living in Same House as in 1979	59.8%	35	77.4
			% Living in Same County as in 1985	87.4%	67	82.0

Composite: *Rank* 146 / 250 *Score* 59.38   **LEVITTOWN (NY)**

CATEGORY	RANK	SCORE	STATISTIC	VALUE	RANK	SCORE
Economics	73	63.60	Median Household Income	$52,866	83	32.7
			% of Families Above Poverty Level	98.6%	50	94.5
Affordable Housing	206	46.95	Median Home Value	$162,600	78	82.9
			Median Rent	$939	223	11.0
Crime	N/A	N/A	Violent Crimes per 10,000 Population	N/A	N/A	N/A
			Property Crimes per 10,000 Population	N/A	N/A	N/A
Open Spaces	101	74.80	Population Density (Persons/Sq. Mile)	7752	199	83.7
			Average Rooms per Housing Unit	6.5	62	65.9
Education	168	56.95	% High School Enrollment/Completion	95.8%	76	95.8
			% College Graduates	17.4%	183	18.1
Commute	179	28.80	Average Work Commute in Minutes	29	150	42.9
			% Commuting on Public Transportation	9.5%	123	14.7
Community Stability	21	85.20	% Living in Same House as in 1979	61.4%	24	80.9
			% Living in Same County as in 1985	89.9%	24	89.5

Composite: *Rank* 147 / 250 *Score* 59.34   **SECAUCUS (NJ)**

CATEGORY	RANK	SCORE	STATISTIC	VALUE	RANK	SCORE
Economics	137	57.95	Median Household Income	$51,814	98	31.6
			% of Families Above Poverty Level	96.2%	170	84.3
Affordable Housing	127	61.50	Median Home Value	$210,800	184	71.0
			Median Rent	$709	106	52.0
Crime	131	70.80	Violent Crimes per 10,000 Population	31	89	91.2
			Property Crimes per 10,000 Population	862	146	50.4
Open Spaces	176	64.80	Population Density (Persons/Sq. Mile)	2388	44	95.5
			Average Rooms per Housing Unit	5.2	192	34.1
Education	127	61.00	% High School Enrollment/Completion	94.3%	115	94.3
			% College Graduates	24.1%	131	27.7
Commute	37	44.70	Average Work Commute in Minutes	24	56	66.7
			% Commuting on Public Transportation	14.5%	74	22.7
Community Stability	168	54.60	% Living in Same House as in 1979	47.7%	144	50.9
			% Living in Same County as in 1985	79.5%	198	58.3

Metropolitan Area Suburb Rankings
NEW YORK-NORTHERN NEW JERSEY-LONG ISLAND

Composite: *Rank* 148 / 250 *Score* 59.30 **LAKE RONKONKOMA** (NY)

CATEGORY	RANK	SCORE	STATISTIC	VALUE	RANK	SCORE
Economics	171	53.55	Median Household Income	$45,485	151	25.4
			% of Families Above Poverty Level	95.6%	188	81.7
Affordable Housing	64	70.70	Median Home Value	$150,900	50	85.7
			Median Rent	$688	90	55.7
Crime	N/A	N/A	Violent Crimes per 10,000 Population	N/A	N/A	N/A
			Property Crimes per 10,000 Population	N/A	N/A	N/A
Open Spaces	113	72.95	Population Density (Persons/Sq. Mile)	3864	97	92.2
			Average Rooms per Housing Unit	6.0	117	53.7
Education	195	53.75	% High School Enrollment/Completion	92.6%	155	92.6
			% College Graduates	15.1%	207	14.9
Commute	167	29.85	Average Work Commute in Minutes	27	102	52.4
			% Commuting on Public Transportation	4.8%	202	7.3
Community Stability	56	75.00	% Living in Same House as in 1979	52.5%	94	61.4
			% Living in Same County as in 1985	89.6%	30	88.6

Composite: *Rank* 149 / 250 *Score* 59.14 **JERICHO** (NY)

CATEGORY	RANK	SCORE	STATISTIC	VALUE	RANK	SCORE
Economics	12	74.55	Median Household Income	$75,043	10	54.6
			% of Families Above Poverty Level	98.6%	50	94.5
Affordable Housing	242	22.05	Median Home Value	$320,600	237	44.1
			Median Rent	$1,001	232	0.0
Crime	N/A	N/A	Violent Crimes per 10,000 Population	N/A	N/A	N/A
			Property Crimes per 10,000 Population	N/A	N/A	N/A
Open Spaces	23	85.75	Population Density (Persons/Sq. Mile)	3300	78	93.5
			Average Rooms per Housing Unit	7.0	18	78.0
Education	17	80.05	% High School Enrollment/Completion	97.7%	21	97.7
			% College Graduates	48.4%	21	62.4
Commute	217	23.05	Average Work Commute in Minutes	33	221	23.8
			% Commuting on Public Transportation	14.3%	78	22.3
Community Stability	95	69.40	% Living in Same House as in 1979	53.4%	81	63.4
			% Living in Same County as in 1985	85.2%	114	75.4

Composite: *Rank* 150 / 250 *Score* 58.98 **STONY BROOK** (NY)

CATEGORY	RANK	SCORE	STATISTIC	VALUE	RANK	SCORE
Economics	26	69.35	Median Household Income	$63,244	30	43.0
			% of Families Above Poverty Level	98.9%	25	95.7
Affordable Housing	224	37.20	Median Home Value	$197,200	154	74.4
			Median Rent	$1,001	232	0.0
Crime	N/A	N/A	Violent Crimes per 10,000 Population	N/A	N/A	N/A
			Property Crimes per 10,000 Population	N/A	N/A	N/A
Open Spaces	24	85.55	Population Density (Persons/Sq. Mile)	2390	45	95.5
			Average Rooms per Housing Unit	6.9	26	75.6
Education	12	81.30	% High School Enrollment/Completion	95.9%	71	95.9
			% College Graduates	51.4%	13	66.7
Commute	213	24.95	Average Work Commute in Minutes	29	150	42.9
			% Commuting on Public Transportation	4.6%	206	7.0
Community Stability	162	55.50	% Living in Same House as in 1979	46.6%	151	48.5
			% Living in Same County as in 1985	80.9%	179	62.5

Metropolitan Area Suburb Rankings
NEW YORK-NORTHERN NEW JERSEY-LONG ISLAND

Composite: **Rank** 151 / 250 *Score* 58.96   **ST. JAMES (NY)**

CATEGORY	RANK	SCORE	STATISTIC	VALUE	RANK	SCORE
Economics	70	63.80	Median Household Income	$51,571	99	31.4
			% of Families Above Poverty Level	99.0%	16	96.2
Affordable Housing	180	53.40	Median Home Value	$178,900	110	78.9
			Median Rent	$844	191	27.9
Crime	N/A	N/A	Violent Crimes per 10,000 Population	N/A	N/A	N/A
			Property Crimes per 10,000 Population	N/A	N/A	N/A
Open Spaces	78	77.80	Population Density (Persons/Sq. Mile)	2800	62	94.6
			Average Rooms per Housing Unit	6.3	83	61.0
Education	110	62.90	% High School Enrollment/Completion	94.4%	108	94.4
			% College Graduates	26.7%	108	31.4
Commute	209	25.25	Average Work Commute in Minutes	29	150	42.9
			% Commuting on Public Transportation	5.0%	197	7.6
Community Stability	85	70.60	% Living in Same House as in 1979	49.3%	121	54.4
			% Living in Same County as in 1985	89.0%	40	86.8

Composite: **Rank** 152 / 250 *Score* 58.91   **TINTON FALLS (NJ)**

CATEGORY	RANK	SCORE	STATISTIC	VALUE	RANK	SCORE
Economics	71	63.75	Median Household Income	$51,988	94	31.8
			% of Families Above Poverty Level	98.9%	25	95.7
Affordable Housing	167	55.40	Median Home Value	$166,900	87	81.8
			Median Rent	$838	185	29.0
Crime	55	91.75	Violent Crimes per 10,000 Population	14	48	96.2
			Property Crimes per 10,000 Population	305	57	87.3
Open Spaces	86	76.35	Population Density (Persons/Sq. Mile)	792	3	99.0
			Average Rooms per Housing Unit	6.0	117	53.7
Education	34	75.30	% High School Enrollment/Completion	98.3%	14	98.3
			% College Graduates	41.3%	39	52.3
Commute	73	40.40	Average Work Commute in Minutes	22	27	76.2
			% Commuting on Public Transportation	3.1%	229	4.6
Community Stability	249	9.45	% Living in Same House as in 1979	26.3%	248	3.9
			% Living in Same County as in 1985	65.1%	249	15.0

Composite: **Rank** 153 / 250 *Score* 58.90   **HILLSIDE (NJ)**

CATEGORY	RANK	SCORE	STATISTIC	VALUE	RANK	SCORE
Economics	187	51.40	Median Household Income	$41,187	180	21.1
			% of Families Above Poverty Level	95.6%	188	81.7
Affordable Housing	32	77.15	Median Home Value	$138,500	29	88.8
			Median Rent	$633	54	65.5
Crime	135	64.50	Violent Crimes per 10,000 Population	95	134	72.3
			Property Crimes per 10,000 Population	766	139	56.7
Open Spaces	173	64.90	Population Density (Persons/Sq. Mile)	7839	200	83.5
			Average Rooms per Housing Unit	5.7	143	46.3
Education	187	54.45	% High School Enrollment/Completion	91.2%	182	91.2
			% College Graduates	17.1%	187	17.7
Commute	60	42.45	Average Work Commute in Minutes	23	40	71.4
			% Commuting on Public Transportation	8.7%	135	13.5
Community Stability	154	57.45	% Living in Same House as in 1979	48.8%	131	53.3
			% Living in Same County as in 1985	80.6%	184	61.6

Metropolitan Area Suburb Rankings
NEW YORK-NORTHERN NEW JERSEY-LONG ISLAND

Composite: Rank 154 / 250 **Score** 58.76   **EAST ROCKAWAY** (NY)

CATEGORY	RANK	SCORE	STATISTIC	VALUE	RANK	SCORE
Economics	73	63.60	Median Household Income	$50,818	104	30.6
			% of Families Above Poverty Level	99.1%	13	96.6
Affordable Housing	155	57.65	Median Home Value	$222,700	197	68.1
			Median Rent	$736	127	47.2
Crime	N/A	N/A	Violent Crimes per 10,000 Population	N/A	N/A	N/A
			Property Crimes per 10,000 Population	N/A	N/A	N/A
Open Spaces	179	63.85	Population Density (Persons/Sq. Mile)	9941	219	78.9
			Average Rooms per Housing Unit	5.8	134	48.8
Education	90	64.95	% High School Enrollment/Completion	92.2%	165	92.2
			% College Graduates	31.1%	77	37.7
Commute	146	32.35	Average Work Commute in Minutes	32	211	28.6
			% Commuting on Public Transportation	23.0%	20	36.1
Community Stability	89	70.15	% Living in Same House as in 1979	48.6%	134	52.9
			% Living in Same County as in 1985	89.2%	36	87.4

Composite: Rank 155 / 250 **Score** 58.68   **FREEPORT** (NY)

CATEGORY	RANK	SCORE	STATISTIC	VALUE	RANK	SCORE
Economics	190	50.60	Median Household Income	$43,948	161	23.8
			% of Families Above Poverty Level	94.6%	199	77.4
Affordable Housing	47	74.10	Median Home Value	$168,900	92	81.3
			Median Rent	$625	50	66.9
Crime	120	76.25	Violent Crimes per 10,000 Population	93	132	72.9
			Property Crimes per 10,000 Population	422	90	79.6
Open Spaces	192	61.60	Population Density (Persons/Sq. Mile)	8681	209	81.7
			Average Rooms per Housing Unit	5.5	162	41.5
Education	176	55.95	% High School Enrollment/Completion	88.0%	216	88.0
			% College Graduates	21.4%	152	23.9
Commute	133	33.55	Average Work Commute in Minutes	30	172	38.1
			% Commuting on Public Transportation	18.5%	43	29.0
Community Stability	143	58.70	% Living in Same House as in 1979	42.7%	180	39.9
			% Living in Same County as in 1985	85.9%	102	77.5

Composite: Rank 156 / 250 **Score** 58.63   **LODI** (NJ)

CATEGORY	RANK	SCORE	STATISTIC	VALUE	RANK	SCORE
Economics	200	48.80	Median Household Income	$33,311	224	13.3
			% of Families Above Poverty Level	96.2%	170	84.3
Affordable Housing	65	70.20	Median Home Value	$176,500	103	79.4
			Median Rent	$658	68	61.0
Crime	65	90.35	Violent Crimes per 10,000 Population	11	35	97.1
			Property Crimes per 10,000 Population	361	80	83.6
Open Spaces	222	50.50	Population Density (Persons/Sq. Mile)	9877	218	79.0
			Average Rooms per Housing Unit	4.7	219	22.0
Education	235	46.95	% High School Enrollment/Completion	78.8%	246	78.8
			% College Graduates	15.3%	201	15.1
Commute	34	45.35	Average Work Commute in Minutes	21	14	81.0
			% Commuting on Public Transportation	6.3%	180	9.7
Community Stability	147	58.25	% Living in Same House as in 1979	43.4%	173	41.4
			% Living in Same County as in 1985	85.1%	116	75.1

Composite: **Rank** 157 / 250 *Score* 58.49   **GARFIELD (NJ)**

CATEGORY	RANK	SCORE	STATISTIC	VALUE	RANK	SCORE
Economics	213	45.15	Median Household Income	$31,649	230	11.6
			% of Families Above Poverty Level	94.9%	197	78.7
Affordable Housing	40	75.10	Median Home Value	$168,300	91	81.5
			Median Rent	$615	44	68.7
Crime	17	95.35	Violent Crimes per 10,000 Population	10	30	97.3
			Property Crimes per 10,000 Population	214	20	93.4
Open Spaces	229	47.60	Population Density (Persons/Sq. Mile)	12545	234	73.2
			Average Rooms per Housing Unit	4.7	219	22.0
Education	232	47.95	% High School Enrollment/Completion	86.2%	226	86.2
			% College Graduates	11.5%	231	9.7
Commute	22	46.65	Average Work Commute in Minutes	20	5	85.7
			% Commuting on Public Transportation	5.0%	197	7.6
Community Stability	182	51.60	% Living in Same House as in 1979	42.9%	178	40.4
			% Living in Same County as in 1985	81.0%	177	62.8

Composite: **Rank** 158 / 250 *Score* 58.33   **WEST MILFORD (NJ)**

CATEGORY	RANK	SCORE	STATISTIC	VALUE	RANK	SCORE
Economics	125	59.00	Median Household Income	$52,734	85	32.5
			% of Families Above Poverty Level	96.5%	163	85.5
Affordable Housing	159	56.95	Median Home Value	$168,000	90	81.5
			Median Rent	$819	179	32.4
Crime	24	94.65	Violent Crimes per 10,000 Population	11	35	97.1
			Property Crimes per 10,000 Population	232	25	92.2
Open Spaces	62	79.25	Population Density (Persons/Sq. Mile)	337	1	100.0
			Average Rooms per Housing Unit	6.2	91	58.5
Education	129	60.90	% High School Enrollment/Completion	92.9%	147	92.9
			% College Graduates	24.9%	125	28.9
Commute	250	8.95	Average Work Commute in Minutes	35	241	14.3
			% Commuting on Public Transportation	2.5%	235	3.6
Community Stability	189	48.60	% Living in Same House as in 1979	41.7%	184	37.7
			% Living in Same County as in 1985	79.9%	191	59.5

Composite: **Rank** 159 / 250 *Score* 58.32   **ISLIP (NY)**

CATEGORY	RANK	SCORE	STATISTIC	VALUE	RANK	SCORE
Economics	102	60.90	Median Household Income	$50,459	107	30.3
			% of Families Above Poverty Level	97.9%	102	91.5
Affordable Housing	131	60.80	Median Home Value	$154,500	58	84.8
			Median Rent	$794	162	36.8
Crime	N/A	N/A	Violent Crimes per 10,000 Population	N/A	N/A	N/A
			Property Crimes per 10,000 Population	N/A	N/A	N/A
Open Spaces	92	75.75	Population Density (Persons/Sq. Mile)	3506	84	93.0
			Average Rooms per Housing Unit	6.2	91	58.5
Education	172	56.25	% High School Enrollment/Completion	92.1%	170	92.1
			% College Graduates	19.0%	171	20.4
Commute	193	26.85	Average Work Commute in Minutes	29	150	42.9
			% Commuting on Public Transportation	7.0%	168	10.8
Community Stability	96	69.35	% Living in Same House as in 1979	48.7%	132	53.1
			% Living in Same County as in 1985	88.6%	44	85.6

Metropolitan Area Suburb Rankings
NEW YORK-NORTHERN NEW JERSEY-LONG ISLAND

Composite: Rank 160 / 250 *Score* 58.21   **JEFFERSON VALLEY-YORKTOWN (NY)**

CATEGORY	RANK	SCORE	STATISTIC	VALUE	RANK	SCORE
Economics	59	64.85	Median Household Income	$58,403	49	38.2
			% of Families Above Poverty Level	97.9%	102	91.5
Affordable Housing	199	49.35	Median Home Value	$212,700	187	70.6
			Median Rent	$843	189	28.1
Crime	N/A	N/A	Violent Crimes per 10,000 Population	N/A	N/A	N/A
			Property Crimes per 10,000 Population	N/A	N/A	N/A
Open Spaces	66	78.65	Population Density (Persons/Sq. Mile)	2041	30	96.3
			Average Rooms per Housing Unit	6.3	83	61.0
Education	56	69.50	% High School Enrollment/Completion	98.0%	17	98.0
			% College Graduates	33.4%	65	41.0
Commute	245	15.85	Average Work Commute in Minutes	34	234	19.0
			% Commuting on Public Transportation	8.2%	146	12.7
Community Stability	84	71.05	% Living in Same House as in 1979	49.3%	121	54.4
			% Living in Same County as in 1985	89.3%	33	87.7

Composite: Rank 160 / 250 *Score* 58.21   **LINCOLN PARK (NJ)**

CATEGORY	RANK	SCORE	STATISTIC	VALUE	RANK	SCORE
Economics	52	65.50	Median Household Income	$53,781	77	33.6
			% of Families Above Poverty Level	99.3%	6	97.4
Affordable Housing	177	54.30	Median Home Value	$178,800	108	78.9
			Median Rent	$834	181	29.7
Crime	25	94.50	Violent Crimes per 10,000 Population	17	60	95.3
			Property Crimes per 10,000 Population	209	17	93.7
Open Spaces	112	73.00	Population Density (Persons/Sq. Mile)	1632	17	97.2
			Average Rooms per Housing Unit	5.8	134	48.8
Education	91	64.55	% High School Enrollment/Completion	92.8%	150	92.8
			% College Graduates	30.1%	85	36.3
Commute	120	35.05	Average Work Commute in Minutes	25	72	61.9
			% Commuting on Public Transportation	5.4%	191	8.2
Community Stability	246	20.55	% Living in Same House as in 1979	35.7%	220	24.6
			% Living in Same County as in 1985	65.6%	248	16.5

Composite: Rank 162 / 250 *Score* 58.07   **MEDFORD (NY)**

CATEGORY	RANK	SCORE	STATISTIC	VALUE	RANK	SCORE
Economics	106	60.75	Median Household Income	$50,190	109	30.0
			% of Families Above Poverty Level	97.9%	102	91.5
Affordable Housing	194	50.80	Median Home Value	$138,300	28	88.8
			Median Rent	$929	220	12.8
Crime	N/A	N/A	Violent Crimes per 10,000 Population	N/A	N/A	N/A
			Property Crimes per 10,000 Population	N/A	N/A	N/A
Open Spaces	48	81.15	Population Density (Persons/Sq. Mile)	1964	25	96.4
			Average Rooms per Housing Unit	6.5	62	65.9
Education	180	55.65	% High School Enrollment/Completion	94.9%	94	94.9
			% College Graduates	16.2%	194	16.4
Commute	222	22.40	Average Work Commute in Minutes	30	172	38.1
			% Commuting on Public Transportation	4.4%	213	6.7
Community Stability	44	77.65	% Living in Same House as in 1979	52.3%	98	61.0
			% Living in Same County as in 1985	91.5%	9	94.3

Metropolitan Area Suburb Rankings
NEW YORK-NORTHERN NEW JERSEY-LONG ISLAND

Composite: *Rank* 163 / 250   *Score* 58.02   **CENTEREACH** (NY)

CATEGORY	RANK	SCORE	STATISTIC	VALUE	RANK	SCORE
Economics	140	57.80	Median Household Income	$50,224	108	30.1
			% of Families Above Poverty Level	96.5%	163	85.5
Affordable Housing	183	53.05	Median Home Value	$144,300	38	87.4
			Median Rent	$896	213	18.7
Crime	N/A	N/A	Violent Crimes per 10,000 Population	N/A	N/A	N/A
			Property Crimes per 10,000 Population	N/A	N/A	N/A
Open Spaces	35	83.30	Population Density (Persons/Sq. Mile)	3358	79	93.4
			Average Rooms per Housing Unit	6.8	36	73.2
Education	193	53.85	% High School Enrollment/Completion	89.4%	207	89.4
			% College Graduates	17.5%	182	18.3
Commute	219	22.70	Average Work Commute in Minutes	30	172	38.1
			% Commuting on Public Transportation	4.8%	202	7.3
Community Stability	45	77.40	% Living in Same House as in 1979	56.6%	55	70.4
			% Living in Same County as in 1985	88.2%	57	84.4

Composite: *Rank* 164 / 250   *Score* 57.98   **STAMFORD** (CT)

CATEGORY	RANK	SCORE	STATISTIC	VALUE	RANK	SCORE
Economics	150	56.70	Median Household Income	$49,787	115	29.6
			% of Families Above Poverty Level	96.1%	175	83.8
Affordable Housing	215	43.75	Median Home Value	$293,500	231	50.7
			Median Rent	$794	162	36.8
Crime	111	78.05	Violent Crimes per 10,000 Population	52	115	85.0
			Property Crimes per 10,000 Population	549	114	71.1
Open Spaces	157	66.70	Population Density (Persons/Sq. Mile)	2865	64	94.4
			Average Rooms per Housing Unit	5.4	172	39.0
Education	63	67.90	% High School Enrollment/Completion	92.4%	159	92.4
			% College Graduates	35.1%	56	43.4
Commute	18	47.35	Average Work Commute in Minutes	22	27	76.2
			% Commuting on Public Transportation	11.9%	96	18.5
Community Stability	199	45.40	% Living in Same House as in 1979	37.8%	203	29.2
			% Living in Same County as in 1985	80.6%	184	61.6

Composite: *Rank* 165 / 250   *Score* 57.97   **BRICK TOWNSHIP** (NJ)

CATEGORY	RANK	SCORE	STATISTIC	VALUE	RANK	SCORE
Economics	168	53.80	Median Household Income	$38,742	198	18.7
			% of Families Above Poverty Level	97.3%	141	88.9
Affordable Housing	67	70.15	Median Home Value	$131,600	20	90.5
			Median Rent	$721	115	49.8
Crime	47	92.45	Violent Crimes per 10,000 Population	11	35	97.1
			Property Crimes per 10,000 Population	298	56	87.8
Open Spaces	125	70.75	Population Density (Persons/Sq. Mile)	2529	53	95.2
			Average Rooms per Housing Unit	5.7	143	46.3
Education	195	53.75	% High School Enrollment/Completion	90.6%	193	90.6
			% College Graduates	16.5%	192	16.9
Commute	212	25.05	Average Work Commute in Minutes	28	127	47.6
			% Commuting on Public Transportation	1.8%	243	2.5
Community Stability	219	39.85	% Living in Same House as in 1979	37.4%	208	28.3
			% Living in Same County as in 1985	77.2%	216	51.4

Composite: *Rank* 166 / 250 *Score* 57.93 **DOVER (NJ)**

CATEGORY	RANK	SCORE	STATISTIC	VALUE	RANK	SCORE
Economics	202	48.10	Median Household Income	$38,822	197	18.8
			% of Families Above Poverty Level	94.6%	199	77.4
Affordable Housing	62	71.20	Median Home Value	$154,400	57	84.9
			Median Rent	$678	84	57.5
Crime	73	89.35	Violent Crimes per 10,000 Population	25	79	92.9
			Property Crimes per 10,000 Population	328	67	85.8
Open Spaces	200	60.05	Population Density (Persons/Sq. Mile)	5631	154	88.4
			Average Rooms per Housing Unit	5.1	199	31.7
Education	216	50.55	% High School Enrollment/Completion	87.7%	217	87.7
			% College Graduates	14.1%	214	13.4
Commute	29	45.55	Average Work Commute in Minutes	20	5	85.7
			% Commuting on Public Transportation	3.6%	222	5.4
Community Stability	215	40.70	% Living in Same House as in 1979	36.4%	216	26.1
			% Living in Same County as in 1985	78.5%	207	55.3

Composite: *Rank* 167 / 250 *Score* 57.83 **FREEHOLD (NJ)**

CATEGORY	RANK	SCORE	STATISTIC	VALUE	RANK	SCORE
Economics	189	50.75	Median Household Income	$40,327	188	20.2
			% of Families Above Poverty Level	95.5%	190	81.3
Affordable Housing	44	74.60	Median Home Value	$137,000	26	89.1
			Median Rent	$663	73	60.1
Crime	127	72.05	Violent Crimes per 10,000 Population	94	133	72.6
			Property Crimes per 10,000 Population	543	112	71.5
Open Spaces	178	63.95	Population Density (Persons/Sq. Mile)	5378	142	88.9
			Average Rooms per Housing Unit	5.4	172	39.0
Education	190	53.95	% High School Enrollment/Completion	83.6%	234	83.6
			% College Graduates	21.7%	148	24.3
Commute	63	42.20	Average Work Commute in Minutes	22	27	76.2
			% Commuting on Public Transportation	5.4%	191	8.2
Community Stability	196	47.30	% Living in Same House as in 1979	40.8%	189	35.7
			% Living in Same County as in 1985	79.7%	193	58.9

Composite: *Rank* 168 / 250 *Score* 57.81 **DANBURY (CT)**

CATEGORY	RANK	SCORE	STATISTIC	VALUE	RANK	SCORE
Economics	180	52.05	Median Household Income	$43,832	163	23.7
			% of Families Above Poverty Level	95.3%	193	80.4
Affordable Housing	91	65.70	Median Home Value	$188,200	131	76.6
			Median Rent	$693	92	54.8
Crime	100	81.75	Violent Crimes per 10,000 Population	32	92	90.9
			Property Crimes per 10,000 Population	527	110	72.6
Open Spaces	154	66.95	Population Density (Persons/Sq. Mile)	1557	14	97.3
			Average Rooms per Housing Unit	5.3	180	36.6
Education	117	62.15	% High School Enrollment/Completion	92.6%	155	92.6
			% College Graduates	26.9%	107	31.7
Commute	77	39.90	Average Work Commute in Minutes	22	27	76.2
			% Commuting on Public Transportation	2.5%	235	3.6
Community Stability	231	36.20	% Living in Same House as in 1979	34.5%	227	21.9
			% Living in Same County as in 1985	76.9%	218	50.5

Metropolitan Area Suburb Rankings
NEW YORK-NORTHERN NEW JERSEY-LONG ISLAND

Composite: **Rank** 169 / 250 *Score* 57.69   **SOMERSET (NJ)**

CATEGORY	RANK	SCORE	STATISTIC	VALUE	RANK	SCORE
Economics	114	59.70	Median Household Income	$51,896	97	31.7
			% of Families Above Poverty Level	97.0%	153	87.7
Affordable Housing	60	71.85	Median Home Value	$163,300	79	82.7
			Median Rent	$658	68	61.0
Crime	N/A	N/A	Violent Crimes per 10,000 Population	N/A	N/A	N/A
			Property Crimes per 10,000 Population	N/A	N/A	N/A
Open Spaces	115	72.65	Population Density (Persons/Sq. Mile)	4138	104	91.6
			Average Rooms per Housing Unit	6.0	117	53.7
Education	68	67.55	% High School Enrollment/Completion	92.7%	154	92.7
			% College Graduates	34.4%	60	42.4
Commute	128	34.20	Average Work Commute in Minutes	26	84	57.1
			% Commuting on Public Transportation	7.3%	162	11.3
Community Stability	217	40.20	% Living in Same House as in 1979	43.4%	173	41.4
			% Living in Same County as in 1985	73.1%	236	39.0

Composite: **Rank** 170 / 250 *Score* 57.67   **HOLBROOK (NY)**

CATEGORY	RANK	SCORE	STATISTIC	VALUE	RANK	SCORE
Economics	113	59.75	Median Household Income	$51,211	102	31.0
			% of Families Above Poverty Level	97.2%	145	88.5
Affordable Housing	184	53.00	Median Home Value	$156,900	67	84.3
			Median Rent	$879	205	21.7
Crime	N/A	N/A	Violent Crimes per 10,000 Population	N/A	N/A	N/A
			Property Crimes per 10,000 Population	N/A	N/A	N/A
Open Spaces	77	78.00	Population Density (Persons/Sq. Mile)	3705	91	92.6
			Average Rooms per Housing Unit	6.4	73	63.4
Education	166	57.25	% High School Enrollment/Completion	96.6%	50	96.6
			% College Graduates	17.2%	185	17.9
Commute	220	22.45	Average Work Commute in Minutes	31	195	33.3
			% Commuting on Public Transportation	7.5%	158	11.6
Community Stability	53	75.55	% Living in Same House as in 1979	51.9%	100	60.1
			% Living in Same County as in 1985	90.4%	20	91.0

Composite: **Rank** 171 / 250 *Score* 57.49   **HOLTSVILLE (NY)**

CATEGORY	RANK	SCORE	STATISTIC	VALUE	RANK	SCORE
Economics	119	59.45	Median Household Income	$51,400	100	31.2
			% of Families Above Poverty Level	97.0%	153	87.7
Affordable Housing	140	59.70	Median Home Value	$153,600	56	85.1
			Median Rent	$808	171	34.3
Crime	N/A	N/A	Violent Crimes per 10,000 Population	N/A	N/A	N/A
			Property Crimes per 10,000 Population	N/A	N/A	N/A
Open Spaces	50	80.95	Population Density (Persons/Sq. Mile)	2152	33	96.0
			Average Rooms per Housing Unit	6.5	62	65.9
Education	190	53.95	% High School Enrollment/Completion	93.6%	124	93.6
			% College Graduates	14.7%	211	14.3
Commute	240	19.75	Average Work Commute in Minutes	32	211	28.6
			% Commuting on Public Transportation	7.1%	166	10.9
Community Stability	83	71.15	% Living in Same House as in 1979	48.7%	132	53.1
			% Living in Same County as in 1985	89.8%	26	89.2

Metropolitan Area Suburb Rankings
NEW YORK-NORTHERN NEW JERSEY-LONG ISLAND

Composite: **Rank** 172 / 250 *Score* 57.39 **WOODBRIDGE** (NJ)

CATEGORY	RANK	SCORE	STATISTIC	VALUE	RANK	SCORE
Economics	165	54.65	Median Household Income	$43,405	166	23.3
			% of Families Above Poverty Level	96.6%	161	86.0
Affordable Housing	84	67.00	Median Home Value	$155,000	61	84.7
			Median Rent	$724	117	49.3
Crime	105	79.80	Violent Crimes per 10,000 Population	32	92	90.9
			Property Crimes per 10,000 Population	586	120	68.7
Open Spaces	189	62.45	Population Density (Persons/Sq. Mile)	4517	117	90.8
			Average Rooms per Housing Unit	5.2	192	34.1
Education	111	62.85	% High School Enrollment/Completion	96.0%	68	96.0
			% College Graduates	25.5%	118	29.7
Commute	108	36.30	Average Work Commute in Minutes	26	84	57.1
			% Commuting on Public Transportation	10.0%	114	15.5
Community Stability	223	38.70	% Living in Same House as in 1979	37.5%	207	28.5
			% Living in Same County as in 1985	76.4%	224	48.9

Composite: **Rank** 173 / 250 *Score* 57.36 **YONKERS** (NY)

CATEGORY	RANK	SCORE	STATISTIC	VALUE	RANK	SCORE
Economics	224	39.20	Median Household Income	$36,376	210	16.3
			% of Families Above Poverty Level	91.0%	225	62.1
Affordable Housing	34	76.30	Median Home Value	$225,700	200	67.4
			Median Rent	$522	8	85.2
Crime	118	76.70	Violent Crimes per 10,000 Population	70	126	79.6
			Property Crimes per 10,000 Population	509	107	73.8
Open Spaces	223	49.95	Population Density (Persons/Sq. Mile)	10402	224	77.9
			Average Rooms per Housing Unit	4.7	219	22.0
Education	164	57.55	% High School Enrollment/Completion	90.5%	196	90.5
			% College Graduates	21.9%	146	24.6
Commute	68	40.80	Average Work Commute in Minutes	29	150	42.9
			% Commuting on Public Transportation	24.6%	16	38.7
Community Stability	134	61.00	% Living in Same House as in 1979	46.7%	150	48.7
			% Living in Same County as in 1985	84.5%	126	73.3

Composite: **Rank** 174 / 250 *Score* 57.35 **HUNTINGTON STATION** (NY)

CATEGORY	RANK	SCORE	STATISTIC	VALUE	RANK	SCORE
Economics	188	51.30	Median Household Income	$45,775	148	25.6
			% of Families Above Poverty Level	94.5%	202	77.0
Affordable Housing	91	65.70	Median Home Value	$173,000	97	80.3
			Median Rent	$714	109	51.1
Crime	N/A	N/A	Violent Crimes per 10,000 Population	N/A	N/A	N/A
			Property Crimes per 10,000 Population	N/A	N/A	N/A
Open Spaces	129	70.25	Population Density (Persons/Sq. Mile)	5199	136	89.3
			Average Rooms per Housing Unit	5.9	123	51.2
Education	144	59.50	% High School Enrollment/Completion	90.1%	200	90.1
			% College Graduates	24.9%	125	28.9
Commute	130	33.90	Average Work Commute in Minutes	27	102	52.4
			% Commuting on Public Transportation	9.9%	116	15.4
Community Stability	120	63.45	% Living in Same House as in 1979	48.1%	140	51.8
			% Living in Same County as in 1985	85.1%	116	75.1

Metropolitan Area Suburb Rankings
NEW YORK-NORTHERN NEW JERSEY-LONG ISLAND

Composite: Rank 175 / 250 *Score* 57.31   **NORTH BRUNSWICK TOWNSHIP** (NJ)

CATEGORY	RANK	SCORE	STATISTIC	VALUE	RANK	SCORE
Economics	99	61.65	Median Household Income	$49,900	114	29.7
			% of Families Above Poverty Level	98.4%	63	93.6
Affordable Housing	112	63.20	Median Home Value	$177,800	105	79.1
			Median Rent	$735	125	47.3
Crime	92	84.30	Violent Crimes per 10,000 Population	25	79	92.9
			Property Crimes per 10,000 Population	480	98	75.7
Open Spaces	146	68.25	Population Density (Persons/Sq. Mile)	2598	58	95.0
			Average Rooms per Housing Unit	5.5	162	41.5
Education	81	65.55	% High School Enrollment/Completion	91.1%	183	91.1
			% College Graduates	32.7%	67	40.0
Commute	143	32.60	Average Work Commute in Minutes	27	102	52.4
			% Commuting on Public Transportation	8.3%	144	12.8
Community Stability	243	25.60	% Living in Same House as in 1979	29.4%	245	10.7
			% Living in Same County as in 1985	73.6%	232	40.5

Composite: Rank 176 / 250 *Score* 57.28   **LINDENHURST** (NY)

CATEGORY	RANK	SCORE	STATISTIC	VALUE	RANK	SCORE
Economics	137	57.95	Median Household Income	$46,615	140	26.5
			% of Families Above Poverty Level	97.4%	132	89.4
Affordable Housing	93	65.75	Median Home Value	$155,900	65	84.5
			Median Rent	$737	128	47.0
Crime	N/A	N/A	Violent Crimes per 10,000 Population	N/A	N/A	N/A
			Property Crimes per 10,000 Population	N/A	N/A	N/A
Open Spaces	121	71.75	Population Density (Persons/Sq. Mile)	7162	187	85.0
			Average Rooms per Housing Unit	6.2	91	58.5
Education	220	49.85	% High School Enrollment/Completion	89.1%	210	89.1
			% College Graduates	12.1%	229	10.6
Commute	178	28.90	Average Work Commute in Minutes	30	172	38.1
			% Commuting on Public Transportation	12.6%	89	19.7
Community Stability	93	69.50	% Living in Same House as in 1979	52.7%	92	61.8
			% Living in Same County as in 1985	85.8%	106	77.2

Composite: Rank 177 / 250 *Score* 57.20   **TERRYVILLE** (NY)

CATEGORY	RANK	SCORE	STATISTIC	VALUE	RANK	SCORE
Economics	63	64.40	Median Household Income	$54,131	73	33.9
			% of Families Above Poverty Level	98.7%	39	94.9
Affordable Housing	217	42.35	Median Home Value	$154,900	59	84.7
			Median Rent	$1,001	232	0.0
Crime	N/A	N/A	Violent Crimes per 10,000 Population	N/A	N/A	N/A
			Property Crimes per 10,000 Population	N/A	N/A	N/A
Open Spaces	30	84.65	Population Density (Persons/Sq. Mile)	3196	74	93.7
			Average Rooms per Housing Unit	6.9	26	75.6
Education	151	58.90	% High School Enrollment/Completion	93.4%	132	93.4
			% College Graduates	21.8%	147	24.4
Commute	234	20.55	Average Work Commute in Minutes	31	195	33.3
			% Commuting on Public Transportation	5.1%	195	7.8
Community Stability	74	72.35	% Living in Same House as in 1979	51.6%	105	59.4
			% Living in Same County as in 1985	88.5%	46	85.3

Metropolitan Area Suburb Rankings
NEW YORK-NORTHERN NEW JERSEY-LONG ISLAND

Composite: **Rank** 178 / 250 *Score* 57.11 **NORTH BERGEN** (NJ)

CATEGORY	RANK	SCORE	STATISTIC	VALUE	RANK	SCORE
Economics	218	42.90	Median Household Income	$33,488	223	13.5
			% of Families Above Poverty Level	93.4%	213	72.3
Affordable Housing	17	83.50	Median Home Value	$173,200	98	80.3
			Median Rent	$514	5	86.7
Crime	107	79.00	Violent Crimes per 10,000 Population	44	108	87.3
			Property Crimes per 10,000 Population	556	116	70.7
Open Spaces	230	47.40	Population Density (Persons/Sq. Mile)	9324	214	80.2
			Average Rooms per Housing Unit	4.4	237	14.6
Education	184	54.90	% High School Enrollment/Completion	90.5%	196	90.5
			% College Graduates	18.2%	179	19.3
Commute	43	44.25	Average Work Commute in Minutes	27	102	52.4
			% Commuting on Public Transportation	23.0%	20	36.1
Community Stability	193	47.85	% Living in Same House as in 1979	38.7%	199	31.1
			% Living in Same County as in 1985	81.6%	170	64.6

Composite: **Rank** 178 / 250 *Score* 57.11 **NORTH VALLEY STREAM** (NY)

CATEGORY	RANK	SCORE	STATISTIC	VALUE	RANK	SCORE
Economics	111	60.10	Median Household Income	$53,618	78	33.4
			% of Families Above Poverty Level	96.8%	159	86.8
Affordable Housing	152	58.50	Median Home Value	$193,800	147	75.2
			Median Rent	$766	145	41.8
Crime	N/A	N/A	Violent Crimes per 10,000 Population	N/A	N/A	N/A
			Property Crimes per 10,000 Population	N/A	N/A	N/A
Open Spaces	108	73.60	Population Density (Persons/Sq. Mile)	7727	198	83.8
			Average Rooms per Housing Unit	6.4	73	63.4
Education	152	58.85	% High School Enrollment/Completion	92.8%	150	92.8
			% College Graduates	22.1%	144	24.9
Commute	227	21.80	Average Work Commute in Minutes	35	241	14.3
			% Commuting on Public Transportation	18.7%	41	29.3
Community Stability	90	69.80	% Living in Same House as in 1979	57.6%	45	72.6
			% Living in Same County as in 1985	82.4%	156	67.0

Composite: **Rank** 180 / 250 *Score* 57.06 **WEST BABYLON** (NY)

CATEGORY	RANK	SCORE	STATISTIC	VALUE	RANK	SCORE
Economics	135	58.15	Median Household Income	$47,067	136	26.9
			% of Families Above Poverty Level	97.4%	132	89.4
Affordable Housing	139	59.80	Median Home Value	$152,700	55	85.3
			Median Rent	$808	171	34.3
Crime	N/A	N/A	Violent Crimes per 10,000 Population	N/A	N/A	N/A
			Property Crimes per 10,000 Population	N/A	N/A	N/A
Open Spaces	123	71.15	Population Density (Persons/Sq. Mile)	5504	147	88.6
			Average Rooms per Housing Unit	6.0	117	53.7
Education	184	54.90	% High School Enrollment/Completion	97.5%	29	97.5
			% College Graduates	13.3%	219	12.3
Commute	168	29.80	Average Work Commute in Minutes	28	127	47.6
			% Commuting on Public Transportation	7.8%	155	12.0
Community Stability	102	68.55	% Living in Same House as in 1979	51.4%	106	59.0
			% Living in Same County as in 1985	86.1%	93	78.1

Metropolitan Area Suburb Rankings
NEW YORK-NORTHERN NEW JERSEY-LONG ISLAND

Composite: Rank 181 / 250 *Score* 57.02   **NORTH BABYLON** (NY)

CATEGORY	RANK	SCORE	STATISTIC	VALUE	RANK	SCORE
Economics	107	60.60	Median Household Income	$51,976	96	31.8
			% of Families Above Poverty Level	97.4%	132	89.4
Affordable Housing	192	51.10	Median Home Value	$158,400	68	83.9
			Median Rent	$898	215	18.3
Crime	N/A	N/A	Violent Crimes per 10,000 Population	N/A	N/A	N/A
			Property Crimes per 10,000 Population	N/A	N/A	N/A
Open Spaces	99	75.00	Population Density (Persons/Sq. Mile)	5357	141	89.0
			Average Rooms per Housing Unit	6.3	83	61.0
Education	164	57.55	% High School Enrollment/Completion	95.1%	88	95.1
			% College Graduates	18.7%	173	20.0
Commute	196	26.50	Average Work Commute in Minutes	30	172	38.1
			% Commuting on Public Transportation	9.6%	120	14.9
Community Stability	79	71.40	% Living in Same House as in 1979	53.6%	76	63.8
			% Living in Same County as in 1985	86.4%	80	79.0

Composite: Rank 182 / 250 *Score* 56.95   **FARMINGVILLE** (NY)

CATEGORY	RANK	SCORE	STATISTIC	VALUE	RANK	SCORE
Economics	151	56.60	Median Household Income	$47,354	131	27.2
			% of Families Above Poverty Level	96.6%	161	86.0
Affordable Housing	114	63.10	Median Home Value	$147,700	43	86.5
			Median Rent	$778	150	39.7
Crime	N/A	N/A	Violent Crimes per 10,000 Population	N/A	N/A	N/A
			Property Crimes per 10,000 Population	N/A	N/A	N/A
Open Spaces	70	78.45	Population Density (Persons/Sq. Mile)	3286	77	93.5
			Average Rooms per Housing Unit	6.4	73	63.4
Education	199	53.55	% High School Enrollment/Completion	94.0%	121	94.0
			% College Graduates	13.9%	217	13.1
Commute	234	20.55	Average Work Commute in Minutes	31	195	33.3
			% Commuting on Public Transportation	5.1%	195	7.8
Community Stability	94	69.45	% Living in Same House as in 1979	49.9%	114	55.7
			% Living in Same County as in 1985	87.8%	59	83.2

Composite: Rank 183 / 250 *Score* 56.93   **MINEOLA** (NY)

CATEGORY	RANK	SCORE	STATISTIC	VALUE	RANK	SCORE
Economics	153	56.50	Median Household Income	$44,635	157	24.5
			% of Families Above Poverty Level	97.2%	145	88.5
Affordable Housing	115	62.90	Median Home Value	$212,800	188	70.5
			Median Rent	$690	91	55.3
Crime	N/A	N/A	Violent Crimes per 10,000 Population	N/A	N/A	N/A
			Property Crimes per 10,000 Population	N/A	N/A	N/A
Open Spaces	206	57.40	Population Density (Persons/Sq. Mile)	10253	221	78.2
			Average Rooms per Housing Unit	5.3	180	36.6
Education	124	61.10	% High School Enrollment/Completion	91.9%	172	91.9
			% College Graduates	25.9%	115	30.3
Commute	87	38.65	Average Work Commute in Minutes	27	102	52.4
			% Commuting on Public Transportation	15.9%	62	24.9
Community Stability	117	65.00	% Living in Same House as in 1979	50.9%	109	57.9
			% Living in Same County as in 1985	84.1%	136	72.1

Metropolitan Area Suburb Rankings
NEW YORK-NORTHERN NEW JERSEY-LONG ISLAND

Composite: *Rank* 184 / 250 *Score* 56.84 **HARRISON** (NJ)

CATEGORY	RANK	SCORE	STATISTIC	VALUE	RANK	SCORE
Economics	229	37.60	Median Household Income	$33,969	221	13.9
			% of Families Above Poverty Level	90.8%	226	61.3
Affordable Housing	22	80.00	Median Home Value	$140,500	33	88.3
			Median Rent	$598	36	71.7
Crime	45	92.60	Violent Crimes per 10,000 Population	18	65	95.0
			Property Crimes per 10,000 Population	262	41	90.2
Open Spaces	225	49.30	Population Density (Persons/Sq. Mile)	10969	229	76.6
			Average Rooms per Housing Unit	4.7	219	22.0
Education	204	52.65	% High School Enrollment/Completion	90.3%	198	90.3
			% College Graduates	15.2%	205	15.0
Commute	11	49.10	Average Work Commute in Minutes	24	56	66.7
			% Commuting on Public Transportation	20.1%	35	31.5
Community Stability	230	36.60	% Living in Same House as in 1979	36.8%	212	27.0
			% Living in Same County as in 1985	75.5%	227	46.2

Composite: *Rank* 185 / 250 *Score* 56.70 **SELDEN** (NY)

CATEGORY	RANK	SCORE	STATISTIC	VALUE	RANK	SCORE
Economics	143	57.55	Median Household Income	$46,298	144	26.2
			% of Families Above Poverty Level	97.3%	141	88.9
Affordable Housing	110	63.30	Median Home Value	$137,100	27	89.1
			Median Rent	$790	157	37.5
Crime	N/A	N/A	Violent Crimes per 10,000 Population	N/A	N/A	N/A
			Property Crimes per 10,000 Population	N/A	N/A	N/A
Open Spaces	104	74.75	Population Density (Persons/Sq. Mile)	4425	111	91.0
			Average Rooms per Housing Unit	6.2	91	58.5
Education	208	52.20	% High School Enrollment/Completion	93.0%	141	93.0
			% College Graduates	12.7%	225	11.4
Commute	237	20.00	Average Work Commute in Minutes	31	195	33.3
			% Commuting on Public Transportation	4.4%	213	6.7
Community Stability	73	72.40	% Living in Same House as in 1979	50.4%	112	56.8
			% Living in Same County as in 1985	89.4%	32	88.0

Composite: *Rank* 186 / 250 *Score* 56.64 **MIDDLETOWN** (NY)

CATEGORY	RANK	SCORE	STATISTIC	VALUE	RANK	SCORE
Economics	231	33.80	Median Household Income	$30,194	233	10.2
			% of Families Above Poverty Level	89.9%	230	57.4
Affordable Housing	16	84.50	Median Home Value	$118,600	13	93.7
			Median Rent	$578	27	75.3
Crime	103	81.35	Violent Crimes per 10,000 Population	41	101	88.2
			Property Crimes per 10,000 Population	499	104	74.5
Open Spaces	183	63.30	Population Density (Persons/Sq. Mile)	4878	126	90.0
			Average Rooms per Housing Unit	5.3	180	36.6
Education	211	51.75	% High School Enrollment/Completion	87.2%	221	87.2
			% College Graduates	16.1%	196	16.3
Commute	91	38.15	Average Work Commute in Minutes	23	40	71.4
			% Commuting on Public Transportation	3.3%	225	4.9
Community Stability	204	43.65	% Living in Same House as in 1979	36.1%	218	25.4
			% Living in Same County as in 1985	80.7%	182	61.9

Metropolitan Area Suburb Rankings
NEW YORK-NORTHERN NEW JERSEY-LONG ISLAND

Composite: *Rank* 187 / 250 *Score* 56.62   **BRENTWOOD** (NY)

CATEGORY	RANK	SCORE	STATISTIC	VALUE	RANK	SCORE
Economics	162	54.90	Median Household Income	$48,665	122	28.5
			% of Families Above Poverty Level	95.5%	190	81.3
Affordable Housing	149	58.60	Median Home Value	$132,300	21	90.3
			Median Rent	$850	197	26.9
Crime	N/A	N/A	Violent Crimes per 10,000 Population	N/A	N/A	N/A
			Property Crimes per 10,000 Population	N/A	N/A	N/A
Open Spaces	90	75.95	Population Density (Persons/Sq. Mile)	4494	113	90.9
			Average Rooms per Housing Unit	6.3	83	61.0
Education	222	49.25	% High School Enrollment/Completion	90.9%	186	90.9
			% College Graduates	10.0%	238	7.6
Commute	166	29.80	Average Work Commute in Minutes	28	127	47.6
			% Commuting on Public Transportation	7.8%	155	12.0
Community Stability	82	71.25	% Living in Same House as in 1979	54.7%	66	66.2
			% Living in Same County as in 1985	85.5%	111	76.3

Composite: *Rank* 188 / 250 *Score* 56.46   **EAST PATCHOGUE** (NY)

CATEGORY	RANK	SCORE	STATISTIC	VALUE	RANK	SCORE
Economics	172	53.25	Median Household Income	$41,052	181	21.0
			% of Families Above Poverty Level	96.5%	163	85.5
Affordable Housing	108	63.30	Median Home Value	$145,500	40	87.1
			Median Rent	$779	152	39.5
Crime	N/A	N/A	Violent Crimes per 10,000 Population	N/A	N/A	N/A
			Property Crimes per 10,000 Population	N/A	N/A	N/A
Open Spaces	135	69.65	Population Density (Persons/Sq. Mile)	2428	48	95.4
			Average Rooms per Housing Unit	5.6	154	43.9
Education	188	54.10	% High School Enrollment/Completion	91.8%	174	91.8
			% College Graduates	16.2%	194	16.4
Commute	170	29.70	Average Work Commute in Minutes	27	102	52.4
			% Commuting on Public Transportation	4.6%	206	7.0
Community Stability	100	68.75	% Living in Same House as in 1979	44.6%	163	44.1
			% Living in Same County as in 1985	91.2%	12	93.4

Composite: *Rank* 189 / 250 *Score* 56.30   **PORT CHESTER** (NY)

CATEGORY	RANK	SCORE	STATISTIC	VALUE	RANK	SCORE
Economics	207	46.95	Median Household Income	$35,216	216	15.2
			% of Families Above Poverty Level	94.9%	197	78.7
Affordable Housing	148	59.05	Median Home Value	$257,300	220	59.6
			Median Rent	$672	80	58.5
Crime	104	81.15	Violent Crimes per 10,000 Population	49	113	85.8
			Property Crimes per 10,000 Population	468	97	76.5
Open Spaces	224	49.85	Population Density (Persons/Sq. Mile)	10486	226	77.7
			Average Rooms per Housing Unit	4.7	219	22.0
Education	186	54.75	% High School Enrollment/Completion	89.6%	205	89.6
			% College Graduates	18.6%	175	19.9
Commute	5	53.80	Average Work Commute in Minutes	19	2	90.5
			% Commuting on Public Transportation	11.0%	104	17.1
Community Stability	191	48.55	% Living in Same House as in 1979	40.0%	194	34.0
			% Living in Same County as in 1985	81.1%	174	63.1

Metropolitan Area Suburb Rankings
NEW YORK-NORTHERN NEW JERSEY-LONG ISLAND

Composite: *Rank* 190 / 250 *Score* 56.27 **OSSINING** (NY)

CATEGORY	RANK	SCORE	STATISTIC	VALUE	RANK	SCORE
Economics	198	49.20	Median Household Income	$41,901	175	21.8
			% of Families Above Poverty Level	94.4%	206	76.6
Affordable Housing	126	61.55	Median Home Value	$204,000	168	72.7
			Median Rent	$718	114	50.4
Crime	57	91.55	Violent Crimes per 10,000 Population	27	84	92.3
			Property Crimes per 10,000 Population	252	36	90.8
Open Spaces	208	57.30	Population Density (Persons/Sq. Mile)	7015	184	85.3
			Average Rooms per Housing Unit	5.0	203	29.3
Education	124	61.10	% High School Enrollment/Completion	91.6%	178	91.6
			% College Graduates	26.1%	113	30.6
Commute	126	34.50	Average Work Commute in Minutes	28	127	47.6
			% Commuting on Public Transportation	13.7%	81	21.4
Community Stability	223	38.70	% Living in Same House as in 1979	37.2%	209	27.9
			% Living in Same County as in 1985	76.6%	220	49.5

Composite: *Rank* 191 / 250 *Score* 56.22 **RONKONKOMA** (NY)

CATEGORY	RANK	SCORE	STATISTIC	VALUE	RANK	SCORE
Economics	117	59.55	Median Household Income	$47,748	129	27.6
			% of Families Above Poverty Level	97.9%	102	91.5
Affordable Housing	164	55.95	Median Home Value	$152,100	54	85.4
			Median Rent	$852	200	26.5
Crime	N/A	N/A	Violent Crimes per 10,000 Population	N/A	N/A	N/A
			Property Crimes per 10,000 Population	N/A	N/A	N/A
Open Spaces	94	75.70	Population Density (Persons/Sq. Mile)	2494	52	95.3
			Average Rooms per Housing Unit	6.1	104	56.1
Education	207	52.45	% High School Enrollment/Completion	93.2%	136	93.2
			% College Graduates	12.9%	223	11.7
Commute	202	25.95	Average Work Commute in Minutes	29	150	42.9
			% Commuting on Public Transportation	5.9%	184	9.0
Community Stability	106	67.75	% Living in Same House as in 1979	45.9%	156	46.9
			% Living in Same County as in 1985	89.6%	30	88.6

Composite: *Rank* 192 / 250 *Score* 56.15 **NANUET** (NY)

CATEGORY	RANK	SCORE	STATISTIC	VALUE	RANK	SCORE
Economics	61	64.60	Median Household Income	$54,541	69	34.3
			% of Families Above Poverty Level	98.7%	39	94.9
Affordable Housing	206	46.95	Median Home Value	$203,100	166	72.9
			Median Rent	$883	208	21.0
Crime	N/A	N/A	Violent Crimes per 10,000 Population	N/A	N/A	N/A
			Property Crimes per 10,000 Population	N/A	N/A	N/A
Open Spaces	111	73.10	Population Density (Persons/Sq. Mile)	2595	57	95.0
			Average Rooms per Housing Unit	5.9	123	51.2
Education	55	69.65	% High School Enrollment/Completion	99.3%	4	99.3
			% College Graduates	32.7%	67	40.0
Commute	163	30.00	Average Work Commute in Minutes	28	127	47.6
			% Commuting on Public Transportation	8.0%	149	12.4
Community Stability	175	52.60	% Living in Same House as in 1979	45.6%	158	46.3
			% Living in Same County as in 1985	79.7%	193	58.9

Composite: **Rank** 193 / 250 *Score* 56.08   **ISELIN (NJ)**

CATEGORY	RANK	SCORE	STATISTIC	VALUE	RANK	SCORE
Economics	116	59.50	Median Household Income	$47,282	134	27.1
			% of Families Above Poverty Level	98.0%	91	91.9
Affordable Housing	130	60.95	Median Home Value	$156,300	66	84.4
			Median Rent	$790	157	37.5
Crime	N/A	N/A	Violent Crimes per 10,000 Population	N/A	N/A	N/A
			Property Crimes per 10,000 Population	N/A	N/A	N/A
Open Spaces	148	67.80	Population Density (Persons/Sq. Mile)	5200	137	89.3
			Average Rooms per Housing Unit	5.7	143	46.3
Education	148	59.30	% High School Enrollment/Completion	92.3%	161	92.3
			% College Graduates	23.1%	140	26.3
Commute	132	33.75	Average Work Commute in Minutes	27	102	52.4
			% Commuting on Public Transportation	9.7%	119	15.1
Community Stability	164	55.20	% Living in Same House as in 1979	49.5%	118	54.8
			% Living in Same County as in 1985	78.6%	205	55.6

Composite: **Rank** 194 / 250 *Score* 56.07   **PALISADES PARK (NJ)**

CATEGORY	RANK	SCORE	STATISTIC	VALUE	RANK	SCORE
Economics	215	43.95	Median Household Income	$36,019	211	16.0
			% of Families Above Poverty Level	93.3%	214	71.9
Affordable Housing	120	62.15	Median Home Value	$204,100	169	72.7
			Median Rent	$711	107	51.6
Crime	18	95.30	Violent Crimes per 10,000 Population	6	15	98.5
			Property Crimes per 10,000 Population	233	27	92.1
Open Spaces	231	46.90	Population Density (Persons/Sq. Mile)	12032	233	74.3
			Average Rooms per Housing Unit	4.6	229	19.5
Education	91	64.55	% High School Enrollment/Completion	97.8%	19	97.8
			% College Graduates	26.6%	109	31.3
Commute	39	44.50	Average Work Commute in Minutes	25	72	61.9
			% Commuting on Public Transportation	17.3%	49	27.1
Community Stability	234	35.15	% Living in Same House as in 1979	41.5%	185	37.3
			% Living in Same County as in 1985	71.1%	240	33.0

Composite: **Rank** 195 / 250 *Score* 55.87   **CLIFFSIDE PARK (NJ)**

CATEGORY	RANK	SCORE	STATISTIC	VALUE	RANK	SCORE
Economics	178	52.60	Median Household Income	$40,600	186	20.5
			% of Families Above Poverty Level	96.3%	168	84.7
Affordable Housing	113	63.15	Median Home Value	$216,300	191	69.7
			Median Rent	$683	88	56.6
Crime	16	95.45	Violent Crimes per 10,000 Population	13	41	96.5
			Property Crimes per 10,000 Population	198	14	94.4
Open Spaces	246	36.85	Population Density (Persons/Sq. Mile)	21153	247	54.2
			Average Rooms per Housing Unit	4.6	229	19.5
Education	147	59.35	% High School Enrollment/Completion	87.7%	217	87.7
			% College Graduates	26.4%	112	31.0
Commute	69	40.75	Average Work Commute in Minutes	28	127	47.6
			% Commuting on Public Transportation	21.6%	24	33.9
Community Stability	207	42.95	% Living in Same House as in 1979	41.1%	187	36.4
			% Living in Same County as in 1985	76.6%	220	49.5

Metropolitan Area Suburb Rankings
NEW YORK-NORTHERN NEW JERSEY-LONG ISLAND

Composite: **Rank** 196 / 250 *Score* 55.77 **NORTH LINDENHURST (NY)**

CATEGORY	RANK	SCORE	STATISTIC	VALUE	RANK	SCORE
Economics	157	56.15	Median Household Income	$49,025	119	28.9
			% of Families Above Poverty Level	96.0%	177	83.4
Affordable Housing	142	59.60	Median Home Value	$149,200	47	86.1
			Median Rent	$815	174	33.1
Crime	N/A	N/A	Violent Crimes per 10,000 Population	N/A	N/A	N/A
			Property Crimes per 10,000 Population	N/A	N/A	N/A
Open Spaces	133	69.85	Population Density (Persons/Sq. Mile)	5590	151	88.5
			Average Rooms per Housing Unit	5.9	123	51.2
Education	244	44.95	% High School Enrollment/Completion	81.8%	240	81.8
			% College Graduates	10.4%	237	8.1
Commute	144	32.40	Average Work Commute in Minutes	27	102	52.4
			% Commuting on Public Transportation	8.0%	149	12.4
Community Stability	77	71.70	% Living in Same House as in 1979	53.6%	76	63.8
			% Living in Same County as in 1985	86.6%	74	79.6

Composite: **Rank** 197 / 250 *Score* 55.41 **EATONTOWN (NJ)**

CATEGORY	RANK	SCORE	STATISTIC	VALUE	RANK	SCORE
Economics	194	49.70	Median Household Income	$36,864	208	16.8
			% of Families Above Poverty Level	95.8%	184	82.6
Affordable Housing	39	75.35	Median Home Value	$167,200	88	81.7
			Median Rent	$613	42	69.0
Crime	121	75.00	Violent Crimes per 10,000 Population	40	99	88.5
			Property Crimes per 10,000 Population	694	133	61.5
Open Spaces	194	61.20	Population Density (Persons/Sq. Mile)	2333	41	95.6
			Average Rooms per Housing Unit	4.9	210	26.8
Education	118	62.10	% High School Enrollment/Completion	93.6%	124	93.6
			% College Graduates	26.1%	113	30.6
Commute	7	51.90	Average Work Commute in Minutes	17	1	100.0
			% Commuting on Public Transportation	2.6%	234	3.8
Community Stability	248	12.60	% Living in Same House as in 1979	24.5%	250	0.0
			% Living in Same County as in 1985	68.5%	245	25.2

Composite: **Rank** 198 / 250 *Score* 55.22 **UNIONDALE (NY)**

CATEGORY	RANK	SCORE	STATISTIC	VALUE	RANK	SCORE
Economics	134	58.10	Median Household Income	$46,917	137	26.8
			% of Families Above Poverty Level	97.4%	132	89.4
Affordable Housing	150	58.65	Median Home Value	$155,700	62	84.6
			Median Rent	$817	178	32.7
Crime	N/A	N/A	Violent Crimes per 10,000 Population	N/A	N/A	N/A
			Property Crimes per 10,000 Population	N/A	N/A	N/A
Open Spaces	131	70.00	Population Density (Persons/Sq. Mile)	7661	194	83.9
			Average Rooms per Housing Unit	6.1	104	56.1
Education	205	52.50	% High School Enrollment/Completion	89.9%	202	89.9
			% College Graduates	15.3%	201	15.1
Commute	161	30.40	Average Work Commute in Minutes	30	172	38.1
			% Commuting on Public Transportation	14.5%	74	22.7
Community Stability	132	61.65	% Living in Same House as in 1979	50.7%	110	57.5
			% Living in Same County as in 1985	82.0%	163	65.8

Metropolitan Area Suburb Rankings
NEW YORK-NORTHERN NEW JERSEY-LONG ISLAND

Composite: **Rank** 198 / 250 *Score* 55.22   **WEEHAWKEN** (NJ)

CATEGORY	RANK	SCORE	STATISTIC	VALUE	RANK	SCORE
Economics	220	41.80	Median Household Income	$34,716	219	14.7
			% of Families Above Poverty Level	92.6%	219	68.9
Affordable Housing	33	76.60	Median Home Value	$225,900	201	67.3
			Median Rent	$518	6	85.9
Crime	133	67.65	Violent Crimes per 10,000 Population	60	121	82.6
			Property Crimes per 10,000 Population	827	144	52.7
Open Spaces	232	45.40	Population Density (Persons/Sq. Mile)	14534	239	68.8
			Average Rooms per Housing Unit	4.7	219	22.0
Education	105	63.40	% High School Enrollment/Completion	94.1%	117	94.1
			% College Graduates	27.6%	101	32.7
Commute	4	54.25	Average Work Commute in Minutes	29	150	42.9
			% Commuting on Public Transportation	41.6%	2	65.6
Community Stability	229	37.45	% Living in Same House as in 1979	36.2%	217	25.7
			% Living in Same County as in 1985	76.5%	223	49.2

Composite: **Rank** 200 / 250 *Score* 55.16   **FAIRVIEW** (NJ)

CATEGORY	RANK	SCORE	STATISTIC	VALUE	RANK	SCORE
Economics	216	43.85	Median Household Income	$32,846	226	12.8
			% of Families Above Poverty Level	94.0%	208	74.9
Affordable Housing	76	68.35	Median Home Value	$191,300	139	75.8
			Median Rent	$659	71	60.9
Crime	49	92.05	Violent Crimes per 10,000 Population	10	30	97.3
			Property Crimes per 10,000 Population	313	59	86.8
Open Spaces	234	44.95	Population Density (Persons/Sq. Mile)	12717	236	72.8
			Average Rooms per Housing Unit	4.5	235	17.1
Education	218	50.30	% High School Enrollment/Completion	85.5%	227	85.5
			% College Graduates	15.3%	201	15.1
Commute	26	45.95	Average Work Commute in Minutes	27	102	52.4
			% Commuting on Public Transportation	25.1%	13	39.5
Community Stability	216	40.65	% Living in Same House as in 1979	42.0%	183	38.4
			% Living in Same County as in 1985	74.4%	230	42.9

Composite: **Rank** 201 / 250 *Score* 55.12   **NEW CASSEL** (NY)

CATEGORY	RANK	SCORE	STATISTIC	VALUE	RANK	SCORE
Economics	193	50.05	Median Household Income	$48,314	124	28.2
			% of Families Above Poverty Level	93.3%	214	71.9
Affordable Housing	173	55.05	Median Home Value	$161,400	76	83.2
			Median Rent	$850	197	26.9
Crime	N/A	N/A	Violent Crimes per 10,000 Population	N/A	N/A	N/A
			Property Crimes per 10,000 Population	N/A	N/A	N/A
Open Spaces	145	68.30	Population Density (Persons/Sq. Mile)	6995	183	85.4
			Average Rooms per Housing Unit	5.9	123	51.2
Education	229	48.50	% High School Enrollment/Completion	83.7%	233	83.7
			% College Graduates	14.0%	215	13.3
Commute	49	43.55	Average Work Commute in Minutes	25	72	61.9
			% Commuting on Public Transportation	16.1%	59	25.2
Community Stability	115	65.30	% Living in Same House as in 1979	52.4%	95	61.2
			% Living in Same County as in 1985	83.2%	146	69.4

Metropolitan Area Suburb Rankings
NEW YORK-NORTHERN NEW JERSEY-LONG ISLAND

Composite: *Rank* 202 / 250 *Score* 55.10   **HACKENSACK** (NJ)

CATEGORY	RANK	SCORE	STATISTIC	VALUE	RANK	SCORE
Economics	196	49.45	Median Household Income	$38,976	196	18.9
			% of Families Above Poverty Level	95.2%	195	80.0
Affordable Housing	88	65.85	Median Home Value	$186,900	125	76.9
			Median Rent	$693	92	54.8
Crime	108	78.30	Violent Crimes per 10,000 Population	33	95	90.6
			Property Crimes per 10,000 Population	626	127	66.0
Open Spaces	236	44.15	Population Density (Persons/Sq. Mile)	8997	213	81.0
			Average Rooms per Housing Unit	4.1	246	7.3
Education	123	61.25	% High School Enrollment/Completion	92.5%	158	92.5
			% College Graduates	25.7%	117	30.0
Commute	14	47.80	Average Work Commute in Minutes	23	40	71.4
			% Commuting on Public Transportation	15.5%	66	24.2
Community Stability	222	38.90	% Living in Same House as in 1979	33.4%	235	19.5
			% Living in Same County as in 1985	79.5%	198	58.3

Composite: *Rank* 203 / 250 *Score* 54.92   **ELMONT** (NY)

CATEGORY	RANK	SCORE	STATISTIC	VALUE	RANK	SCORE
Economics	146	57.05	Median Household Income	$44,452	159	24.3
			% of Families Above Poverty Level	97.5%	125	89.8
Affordable Housing	88	65.85	Median Home Value	$178,900	110	78.9
			Median Rent	$704	105	52.8
Crime	N/A	N/A	Violent Crimes per 10,000 Population	N/A	N/A	N/A
			Property Crimes per 10,000 Population	N/A	N/A	N/A
Open Spaces	165	65.55	Population Density (Persons/Sq. Mile)	8369	204	82.3
			Average Rooms per Housing Unit	5.8	134	48.8
Education	174	56.05	% High School Enrollment/Completion	94.7%	97	94.7
			% College Graduates	16.9%	189	17.4
Commute	195	26.65	Average Work Commute in Minutes	32	211	28.6
			% Commuting on Public Transportation	15.8%	64	24.7
Community Stability	145	58.40	% Living in Same House as in 1979	52.8%	90	62.1
			% Living in Same County as in 1985	78.3%	212	54.7

Composite: *Rank* 204 / 250 *Score* 54.91   **NORTH PLAINFIELD** (NJ)

CATEGORY	RANK	SCORE	STATISTIC	VALUE	RANK	SCORE
Economics	152	56.65	Median Household Income	$41,875	176	21.8
			% of Families Above Poverty Level	97.9%	102	91.5
Affordable Housing	69	70.05	Median Home Value	$163,700	81	82.6
			Median Rent	$678	84	57.5
Crime	129	71.75	Violent Crimes per 10,000 Population	54	117	84.4
			Property Crimes per 10,000 Population	731	137	59.1
Open Spaces	195	61.25	Population Density (Persons/Sq. Mile)	6747	179	85.9
			Average Rooms per Housing Unit	5.3	180	36.6
Education	106	63.35	% High School Enrollment/Completion	93.3%	133	93.3
			% College Graduates	28.1%	98	33.4
Commute	122	34.90	Average Work Commute in Minutes	25	72	61.9
			% Commuting on Public Transportation	5.2%	193	7.9
Community Stability	242	26.45	% Living in Same House as in 1979	37.8%	203	29.2
			% Living in Same County as in 1985	68.0%	246	23.7

Metropolitan Area Suburb Rankings
NEW YORK-NORTHERN NEW JERSEY-LONG ISLAND

Composite: **Rank** 205 / 250 *Score* 54.80   **WEST FREEHOLD (NJ)**

CATEGORY	RANK	SCORE	STATISTIC	VALUE	RANK	SCORE
Economics	27	69.20	Median Household Income	$61,266	35	41.0
			% of Families Above Poverty Level	99.3%	6	97.4
Affordable Housing	150	58.65	Median Home Value	$204,500	170	72.6
			Median Rent	$750	136	44.7
Crime	N/A	N/A	Violent Crimes per 10,000 Population	N/A	N/A	N/A
			Property Crimes per 10,000 Population	N/A	N/A	N/A
Open Spaces	47	81.25	Population Density (Persons/Sq. Mile)	1887	21	96.6
			Average Rooms per Housing Unit	6.5	62	65.9
Education	39	74.30	% High School Enrollment/Completion	98.6%	12	98.6
			% College Graduates	39.7%	42	50.0
Commute	233	20.85	Average Work Commute in Minutes	33	221	23.8
			% Commuting on Public Transportation	11.5%	99	17.9
Community Stability	245	24.55	% Living in Same House as in 1979	35.0%	224	23.0
			% Living in Same County as in 1985	68.8%	244	26.1

Composite: **Rank** 206 / 250 *Score* 54.53   **MOUNT VERNON (NY)**

CATEGORY	RANK	SCORE	STATISTIC	VALUE	RANK	SCORE
Economics	227	38.70	Median Household Income	$34,850	218	14.8
			% of Families Above Poverty Level	91.1%	224	62.6
Affordable Housing	38	75.80	Median Home Value	$222,800	198	68.1
			Median Rent	$532	11	83.5
Crime	137	63.60	Violent Crimes per 10,000 Population	140	141	59.0
			Property Crimes per 10,000 Population	593	121	68.2
Open Spaces	237	43.30	Population Density (Persons/Sq. Mile)	15319	240	67.1
			Average Rooms per Housing Unit	4.6	229	19.5
Education	173	56.15	% High School Enrollment/Completion	89.9%	202	89.9
			% College Graduates	20.4%	160	22.4
Commute	51	43.40	Average Work Commute in Minutes	29	150	42.9
			% Commuting on Public Transportation	27.9%	8	43.9
Community Stability	136	60.75	% Living in Same House as in 1979	43.9%	167	42.5
			% Living in Same County as in 1985	86.4%	80	79.0

Composite: **Rank** 207 / 250 *Score* 54.51   **PEEKSKILL (NY)**

CATEGORY	RANK	SCORE	STATISTIC	VALUE	RANK	SCORE
Economics	222	40.25	Median Household Income	$35,425	215	15.4
			% of Families Above Poverty Level	91.7%	222	65.1
Affordable Housing	61	71.40	Median Home Value	$164,100	83	82.5
			Median Rent	$662	72	60.3
Crime	93	83.95	Violent Crimes per 10,000 Population	48	111	86.1
			Property Crimes per 10,000 Population	388	85	81.8
Open Spaces	212	56.40	Population Density (Persons/Sq. Mile)	4516	116	90.8
			Average Rooms per Housing Unit	4.7	219	22.0
Education	145	59.40	% High School Enrollment/Completion	93.5%	129	93.5
			% College Graduates	22.4%	143	25.3
Commute	183	28.40	Average Work Commute in Minutes	30	172	38.1
			% Commuting on Public Transportation	12.0%	95	18.7
Community Stability	210	41.75	% Living in Same House as in 1979	33.0%	236	18.6
			% Living in Same County as in 1985	81.7%	166	64.9

Metropolitan Area Suburb Rankings
NEW YORK-NORTHERN NEW JERSEY-LONG ISLAND

Composite: *Rank* 208 / 250 *Score* 54.19 **ROOSEVELT** (NY)

CATEGORY	RANK	SCORE	STATISTIC	VALUE	RANK	SCORE
Economics	214	44.75	Median Household Income	$43,599	164	23.5
			% of Families Above Poverty Level	91.9%	221	66.0
Affordable Housing	175	54.85	Median Home Value	$135,100	23	89.6
			Median Rent	$888	211	20.1
Crime	N/A	N/A	Violent Crimes per 10,000 Population	N/A	N/A	N/A
			Property Crimes per 10,000 Population	N/A	N/A	N/A
Open Spaces	128	70.35	Population Density (Persons/Sq. Mile)	8450	205	82.2
			Average Rooms per Housing Unit	6.2	91	58.5
Education	217	50.40	% High School Enrollment/Completion	89.1%	210	89.1
			% College Graduates	12.9%	223	11.7
Commute	98	37.30	Average Work Commute in Minutes	30	172	38.1
			% Commuting on Public Transportation	23.2%	18	36.5
Community Stability	107	67.50	% Living in Same House as in 1979	53.3%	84	63.2
			% Living in Same County as in 1985	84.0%	139	71.8

Composite: *Rank* 209 / 250 *Score* 54.18 **HOPATCONG** (NJ)

CATEGORY	RANK	SCORE	STATISTIC	VALUE	RANK	SCORE
Economics	121	59.30	Median Household Income	$48,203	126	28.0
			% of Families Above Poverty Level	97.7%	116	90.6
Affordable Housing	176	54.75	Median Home Value	$142,300	36	87.8
			Median Rent	$879	205	21.7
Crime	48	92.20	Violent Crimes per 10,000 Population	15	55	95.9
			Property Crimes per 10,000 Population	287	51	88.5
Open Spaces	96	75.65	Population Density (Persons/Sq. Mile)	1427	13	97.6
			Average Rooms per Housing Unit	6.0	117	53.7
Education	162	57.85	% High School Enrollment/Completion	93.1%	139	93.1
			% College Graduates	20.5%	159	22.6
Commute	249	10.85	Average Work Commute in Minutes	34	234	19.0
			% Commuting on Public Transportation	1.9%	242	2.7
Community Stability	240	28.65	% Living in Same House as in 1979	37.9%	202	29.4
			% Living in Same County as in 1985	69.4%	242	27.9

Composite: *Rank* 210 / 250 *Score* 54.01 **MORRISTOWN** (NJ)

CATEGORY	RANK	SCORE	STATISTIC	VALUE	RANK	SCORE
Economics	184	51.75	Median Household Income	$42,748	171	22.6
			% of Families Above Poverty Level	95.4%	192	80.9
Affordable Housing	78	68.30	Median Home Value	$205,200	172	72.4
			Median Rent	$640	56	64.2
Crime	139	60.10	Violent Crimes per 10,000 Population	124	138	63.7
			Property Crimes per 10,000 Population	769	140	56.5
Open Spaces	204	57.70	Population Density (Persons/Sq. Mile)	5508	148	88.6
			Average Rooms per Housing Unit	4.9	210	26.8
Education	69	67.40	% High School Enrollment/Completion	95.2%	87	95.2
			% College Graduates	32.4%	70	39.6
Commute	33	45.40	Average Work Commute in Minutes	21	14	81.0
			% Commuting on Public Transportation	6.4%	178	9.8
Community Stability	241	27.40	% Living in Same House as in 1979	33.5%	233	19.7
			% Living in Same County as in 1985	71.8%	239	35.1

Metropolitan Area Suburb Rankings
NEW YORK-NORTHERN NEW JERSEY-LONG ISLAND

Composite: **Rank** 211 / 250 *Score* 53.85   **PERTH AMBOY (NJ)**

CATEGORY	RANK	SCORE	STATISTIC	VALUE	RANK	SCORE
Economics	234	27.80	Median Household Income	$28,377	237	8.4
			% of Families Above Poverty Level	87.5%	234	47.2
Affordable Housing	15	84.65	Median Home Value	$124,300	18	92.3
			Median Rent	$568	24	77.0
Crime	130	71.45	Violent Crimes per 10,000 Population	83	131	75.8
			Property Crimes per 10,000 Population	610	125	67.1
Open Spaces	219	52.90	Population Density (Persons/Sq. Mile)	8782	210	81.4
			Average Rooms per Housing Unit	4.8	216	24.4
Education	247	44.20	% High School Enrollment/Completion	83.4%	235	83.4
			% College Graduates	8.2%	246	5.0
Commute	20	47.05	Average Work Commute in Minutes	20	5	85.7
			% Commuting on Public Transportation	5.5%	190	8.4
Community Stability	188	48.90	% Living in Same House as in 1979	36.9%	211	27.2
			% Living in Same County as in 1985	83.6%	140	70.6

Composite: **Rank** 212 / 250 *Score* 53.82   **BAY SHORE (NY)**

CATEGORY	RANK	SCORE	STATISTIC	VALUE	RANK	SCORE
Economics	209	45.80	Median Household Income	$37,702	205	17.6
			% of Families Above Poverty Level	93.8%	209	74.0
Affordable Housing	81	67.30	Median Home Value	$140,500	33	88.3
			Median Rent	$741	132	46.3
Crime	N/A	N/A	Violent Crimes per 10,000 Population	N/A	N/A	N/A
			Property Crimes per 10,000 Population	N/A	N/A	N/A
Open Spaces	167	65.45	Population Density (Persons/Sq. Mile)	4037	101	91.9
			Average Rooms per Housing Unit	5.4	172	39.0
Education	189	54.00	% High School Enrollment/Completion	93.0%	141	93.0
			% College Graduates	15.2%	205	15.0
Commute	121	34.95	Average Work Commute in Minutes	26	84	57.1
			% Commuting on Public Transportation	8.3%	144	12.8
Community Stability	163	55.45	% Living in Same House as in 1979	39.6%	195	33.1
			% Living in Same County as in 1985	86.0%	98	77.8

Composite: **Rank** 213 / 250 *Score* 53.81   **LONG BEACH (NY)**

CATEGORY	RANK	SCORE	STATISTIC	VALUE	RANK	SCORE
Economics	197	49.40	Median Household Income	$41,495	179	21.4
			% of Families Above Poverty Level	94.6%	199	77.4
Affordable Housing	142	59.60	Median Home Value	$190,700	136	76.0
			Median Rent	$758	140	43.2
Crime	77	88.80	Violent Crimes per 10,000 Population	40	99	88.5
			Property Crimes per 10,000 Population	278	45	89.1
Open Spaces	239	42.85	Population Density (Persons/Sq. Mile)	15697	242	66.2
			Average Rooms per Housing Unit	4.6	229	19.5
Education	103	63.65	% High School Enrollment/Completion	93.0%	141	93.0
			% College Graduates	28.7%	94	34.3
Commute	210	25.15	Average Work Commute in Minutes	35	241	14.3
			% Commuting on Public Transportation	22.9%	22	36.0
Community Stability	197	47.20	% Living in Same House as in 1979	37.0%	210	27.4
			% Living in Same County as in 1985	82.4%	156	67.0

Metropolitan Area Suburb Rankings
NEW YORK-NORTHERN NEW JERSEY-LONG ISLAND

Composite: *Rank* 214 / 250 *Score* 53.58   **COPIAGUE** (NY)

CATEGORY	RANK	SCORE	STATISTIC	VALUE	RANK	SCORE
Economics	159	55.15	Median Household Income	$45,738	149	25.6
			% of Families Above Poverty Level	96.3%	168	84.7
Affordable Housing	135	60.05	Median Home Value	$151,500	53	85.6
			Median Rent	$807	169	34.5
Crime	N/A	N/A	Violent Crimes per 10,000 Population	N/A	N/A	N/A
			Property Crimes per 10,000 Population	N/A	N/A	N/A
Open Spaces	149	67.60	Population Density (Persons/Sq. Mile)	6504	174	86.4
			Average Rooms per Housing Unit	5.8	134	48.8
Education	213	51.25	% High School Enrollment/Completion	90.2%	199	90.2
			% College Graduates	13.3%	219	12.3
Commute	161	30.40	Average Work Commute in Minutes	29	150	42.9
			% Commuting on Public Transportation	11.5%	99	17.9
Community Stability	157	57.05	% Living in Same House as in 1979	46.1%	154	47.4
			% Living in Same County as in 1985	82.3%	159	66.7

Composite: *Rank* 215 / 250 *Score* 53.39   **KEANSBURG** (NJ)

CATEGORY	RANK	SCORE	STATISTIC	VALUE	RANK	SCORE
Economics	221	40.35	Median Household Income	$31,769	229	11.8
			% of Families Above Poverty Level	92.6%	219	68.9
Affordable Housing	18	83.00	Median Home Value	$110,400	6	95.7
			Median Rent	$606	39	70.3
Crime	97	82.85	Violent Crimes per 10,000 Population	67	124	80.5
			Property Crimes per 10,000 Population	337	72	85.2
Open Spaces	217	53.70	Population Density (Persons/Sq. Mile)	10305	222	78.1
			Average Rooms per Housing Unit	5.0	203	29.3
Education	238	46.45	% High School Enrollment/Completion	92.0%	171	92.0
			% College Graduates	5.3%	249	0.9
Commute	186	28.00	Average Work Commute in Minutes	30	172	38.1
			% Commuting on Public Transportation	11.5%	99	17.9
Community Stability	221	39.35	% Living in Same House as in 1979	35.3%	222	23.7
			% Living in Same County as in 1985	78.4%	210	55.0

Composite: *Rank* 216 / 250 *Score* 53.32   **NORTH BAY SHORE** (NY)

CATEGORY	RANK	SCORE	STATISTIC	VALUE	RANK	SCORE
Economics	201	48.45	Median Household Income	$47,275	135	27.1
			% of Families Above Poverty Level	92.8%	218	69.8
Affordable Housing	147	59.10	Median Home Value	$135,300	24	89.6
			Median Rent	$840	187	28.6
Crime	N/A	N/A	Violent Crimes per 10,000 Population	N/A	N/A	N/A
			Property Crimes per 10,000 Population	N/A	N/A	N/A
Open Spaces	122	71.25	Population Density (Persons/Sq. Mile)	4298	108	91.3
			Average Rooms per Housing Unit	5.9	123	51.2
Education	230	48.10	% High School Enrollment/Completion	93.8%	122	93.8
			% College Graduates	6.4%	248	2.4
Commute	153	31.65	Average Work Commute in Minutes	27	102	52.4
			% Commuting on Public Transportation	7.1%	166	10.9
Community Stability	133	61.40	% Living in Same House as in 1979	47.5%	146	50.4
			% Living in Same County as in 1985	84.2%	134	72.4

Metropolitan Area Suburb Rankings
NEW YORK-NORTHERN NEW JERSEY-LONG ISLAND

Composite: *Rank* 217 / 250 *Score* 53.15   **CORAM (NY)**

CATEGORY	RANK	SCORE	STATISTIC	VALUE	RANK	SCORE
Economics	127	58.75	Median Household Income	$49,135	118	29.0
			% of Families Above Poverty Level	97.2%	145	88.5
Affordable Housing	115	62.90	Median Home Value	$150,400	48	85.9
			Median Rent	$777	148	39.9
Crime	N/A	N/A	Violent Crimes per 10,000 Population	N/A	N/A	N/A
			Property Crimes per 10,000 Population	N/A	N/A	N/A
Open Spaces	119	72.35	Population Density (Persons/Sq. Mile)	2184	37	95.9
			Average Rooms per Housing Unit	5.8	134	48.8
Education	122	61.65	% High School Enrollment/Completion	93.2%	136	93.2
			% College Graduates	25.8%	116	30.1
Commute	246	14.65	Average Work Commute in Minutes	33	221	23.8
			% Commuting on Public Transportation	3.7%	221	5.5
Community Stability	189	48.60	% Living in Same House as in 1979	33.9%	232	20.6
			% Living in Same County as in 1985	85.6%	110	76.6

Composite: *Rank* 218 / 250 *Score* 53.02   **LONG BRANCH (NJ)**

CATEGORY	RANK	SCORE	STATISTIC	VALUE	RANK	SCORE
Economics	233	32.60	Median Household Income	$30,693	231	10.7
			% of Families Above Poverty Level	89.2%	233	54.5
Affordable Housing	25	79.10	Median Home Value	$145,900	42	87.0
			Median Rent	$601	38	71.2
Crime	141	57.25	Violent Crimes per 10,000 Population	134	139	60.8
			Property Crimes per 10,000 Population	812	143	53.7
Open Spaces	203	57.75	Population Density (Persons/Sq. Mile)	5495	146	88.7
			Average Rooms per Housing Unit	4.9	210	26.8
Education	197	53.70	% High School Enrollment/Completion	85.4%	228	85.4
			% College Graduates	20.1%	165	22.0
Commute	53	43.10	Average Work Commute in Minutes	22	27	76.2
			% Commuting on Public Transportation	6.5%	175	10.0
Community Stability	195	47.65	% Living in Same House as in 1979	34.1%	229	21.1
			% Living in Same County as in 1985	84.8%	121	74.2

Composite: *Rank* 219 / 250 *Score* 52.97   **PLAINFIELD (NJ)**

CATEGORY	RANK	SCORE	STATISTIC	VALUE	RANK	SCORE
Economics	224	39.20	Median Household Income	$38,463	200	18.4
			% of Families Above Poverty Level	90.5%	228	60.0
Affordable Housing	31	77.40	Median Home Value	$140,400	32	88.3
			Median Rent	$627	51	66.5
Crime	138	63.45	Violent Crimes per 10,000 Population	120	137	64.9
			Property Crimes per 10,000 Population	686	131	62.0
Open Spaces	198	60.20	Population Density (Persons/Sq. Mile)	7710	196	83.8
			Average Rooms per Housing Unit	5.3	180	36.6
Education	212	51.30	% High School Enrollment/Completion	82.3%	237	82.3
			% College Graduates	18.9%	172	20.3
Commute	104	36.75	Average Work Commute in Minutes	25	72	61.9
			% Commuting on Public Transportation	7.5%	158	11.6
Community Stability	208	42.50	% Living in Same House as in 1979	36.8%	212	27.0
			% Living in Same County as in 1985	79.4%	200	58.0

Metropolitan Area Suburb Rankings
NEW YORK-NORTHERN NEW JERSEY-LONG ISLAND

Composite: *Rank* 220 / 250 *Score* 52.82 **FORT LEE (NJ)**

CATEGORY	RANK	SCORE	STATISTIC	VALUE	RANK	SCORE
Economics	161	55.05	Median Household Income	$46,395	142	26.3
			% of Families Above Poverty Level	96.1%	175	83.8
Affordable Housing	193	51.05	Median Home Value	$282,300	230	53.5
			Median Rent	$728	119	48.6
Crime	70	89.60	Violent Crimes per 10,000 Population	26	82	92.6
			Property Crimes per 10,000 Population	316	61	86.6
Open Spaces	241	41.35	Population Density (Persons/Sq. Mile)	12652	235	72.9
			Average Rooms per Housing Unit	4.2	245	9.8
Education	59	69.35	% High School Enrollment/Completion	85.1%	231	85.1
			% College Graduates	42.2%	35	53.6
Commute	134	33.45	Average Work Commute in Minutes	31	195	33.3
			% Commuting on Public Transportation	21.4%	25	33.6
Community Stability	239	29.90	% Living in Same House as in 1979	37.7%	205	28.9
			% Living in Same County as in 1985	70.4%	241	30.9

Composite: *Rank* 221 / 250 *Score* 52.48 **CENTRAL ISLIP (NY)**

CATEGORY	RANK	SCORE	STATISTIC	VALUE	RANK	SCORE
Economics	206	46.90	Median Household Income	$42,434	174	22.3
			% of Families Above Poverty Level	93.2%	216	71.5
Affordable Housing	99	64.65	Median Home Value	$123,200	15	92.5
			Median Rent	$794	162	36.8
Crime	N/A	N/A	Violent Crimes per 10,000 Population	N/A	N/A	N/A
			Property Crimes per 10,000 Population	N/A	N/A	N/A
Open Spaces	143	68.65	Population Density (Persons/Sq. Mile)	4444	112	91.0
			Average Rooms per Housing Unit	5.7	143	46.3
Education	228	48.55	% High School Enrollment/Completion	88.1%	215	88.1
			% College Graduates	11.0%	235	9.0
Commute	171	29.60	Average Work Commute in Minutes	28	127	47.6
			% Commuting on Public Transportation	7.5%	158	11.6
Community Stability	159	56.55	% Living in Same House as in 1979	42.8%	179	40.1
			% Living in Same County as in 1985	84.4%	129	73.0

Composite: *Rank* 222 / 250 *Score* 52.39 **HEMPSTEAD (NY)**

CATEGORY	RANK	SCORE	STATISTIC	VALUE	RANK	SCORE
Economics	230	36.45	Median Household Income	$36,715	209	16.7
			% of Families Above Poverty Level	89.6%	231	56.2
Affordable Housing	55	73.10	Median Home Value	$155,700	62	84.6
			Median Rent	$655	67	61.6
Crime	132	68.50	Violent Crimes per 10,000 Population	149	142	56.3
			Property Crimes per 10,000 Population	405	88	80.7
Open Spaces	228	47.80	Population Density (Persons/Sq. Mile)	13425	237	71.2
			Average Rooms per Housing Unit	4.8	216	24.4
Education	202	53.10	% High School Enrollment/Completion	90.1%	200	90.1
			% College Graduates	16.0%	197	16.1
Commute	59	42.50	Average Work Commute in Minutes	28	127	47.6
			% Commuting on Public Transportation	23.8%	17	37.4
Community Stability	201	45.30	% Living in Same House as in 1979	40.6%	191	35.3
			% Living in Same County as in 1985	78.5%	207	55.3

Metropolitan Area Suburb Rankings
NEW YORK-NORTHERN NEW JERSEY-LONG ISLAND

Composite: *Rank* 223 / 250 *Score* 52.23   PATCHOGUE (NY)

CATEGORY	RANK	SCORE	STATISTIC	VALUE	RANK	SCORE
Economics	210	45.55	Median Household Income	$34,173	220	14.1
			% of Families Above Poverty Level	94.5%	202	77.0
Affordable Housing	63	71.15	Median Home Value	$140,000	31	88.4
			Median Rent	$698	100	53.9
Crime	N/A	N/A	Violent Crimes per 10,000 Population	N/A	N/A	N/A
			Property Crimes per 10,000 Population	N/A	N/A	N/A
Open Spaces	213	56.00	Population Density (Persons/Sq. Mile)	4900	128	90.0
			Average Rooms per Housing Unit	4.7	219	22.0
Education	197	53.70	% High School Enrollment/Completion	89.4%	207	89.4
			% College Graduates	17.3%	184	18.0
Commute	83	38.90	Average Work Commute in Minutes	24	56	66.7
			% Commuting on Public Transportation	7.2%	163	11.1
Community Stability	192	48.10	% Living in Same House as in 1979	31.1%	240	14.5
			% Living in Same County as in 1985	87.3%	71	81.7

Composite: *Rank* 224 / 250 *Score* 52.02   SHIRLEY (NY)

CATEGORY	RANK	SCORE	STATISTIC	VALUE	RANK	SCORE
Economics	199	49.25	Median Household Income	$41,602	178	21.5
			% of Families Above Poverty Level	94.5%	202	77.0
Affordable Housing	162	56.50	Median Home Value	$123,500	16	92.5
			Median Rent	$886	210	20.5
Crime	N/A	N/A	Violent Crimes per 10,000 Population	N/A	N/A	N/A
			Property Crimes per 10,000 Population	N/A	N/A	N/A
Open Spaces	88	76.10	Population Density (Persons/Sq. Mile)	2104	32	96.1
			Average Rooms per Housing Unit	6.1	104	56.1
Education	234	47.50	% High School Enrollment/Completion	88.6%	213	88.6
			% College Graduates	9.2%	242	6.4
Commute	236	20.45	Average Work Commute in Minutes	31	195	33.3
			% Commuting on Public Transportation	5.0%	197	7.6
Community Stability	127	62.30	% Living in Same House as in 1979	43.5%	172	41.7
			% Living in Same County as in 1985	87.7%	60	82.9

Composite: *Rank* 225 / 250 *Score* 51.95   SUFFERN (NY)

CATEGORY	RANK	SCORE	STATISTIC	VALUE	RANK	SCORE
Economics	155	56.45	Median Household Income	$45,329	153	25.2
			% of Families Above Poverty Level	97.0%	153	87.7
Affordable Housing	137	59.95	Median Home Value	$183,600	117	77.7
			Median Rent	$764	142	42.2
Crime	N/A	N/A	Violent Crimes per 10,000 Population	N/A	N/A	N/A
			Property Crimes per 10,000 Population	N/A	N/A	N/A
Open Spaces	201	59.20	Population Density (Persons/Sq. Mile)	5292	138	89.1
			Average Rooms per Housing Unit	5.0	203	29.3
Education	53	70.15	% High School Enrollment/Completion	95.9%	71	95.9
			% College Graduates	35.8%	53	44.4
Commute	165	29.90	Average Work Commute in Minutes	28	127	47.6
			% Commuting on Public Transportation	7.9%	153	12.2
Community Stability	232	36.05	% Living in Same House as in 1979	31.6%	239	15.6
			% Living in Same County as in 1985	78.9%	203	56.5

Metropolitan Area Suburb Rankings
NEW YORK-NORTHERN NEW JERSEY-LONG ISLAND

Composite: *Rank* 226 / 250 *Score* 51.86   **LAKEWOOD** (NJ)

CATEGORY	RANK	SCORE	STATISTIC	VALUE	RANK	SCORE
Economics	248	3.35	Median Household Income	$22,306	246	2.4
			% of Families Above Poverty Level	77.4%	248	4.3
Affordable Housing	6	88.15	Median Home Value	$118,300	12	93.7
			Median Rent	$537	16	82.6
Crime	114	77.65	Violent Crimes per 10,000 Population	56	119	83.8
			Property Crimes per 10,000 Population	544	113	71.5
Open Spaces	181	63.40	Population Density (Persons/Sq. Mile)	3655	89	92.7
			Average Rooms per Housing Unit	5.2	192	34.1
Education	223	49.20	% High School Enrollment/Completion	82.3%	237	82.3
			% College Graduates	16.0%	197	16.1
Commute	67	41.05	Average Work Commute in Minutes	22	27	76.2
			% Commuting on Public Transportation	3.9%	219	5.9
Community Stability	217	40.20	% Living in Same House as in 1979	36.5%	215	26.3
			% Living in Same County as in 1985	78.1%	213	54.1

Composite: *Rank* 227 / 250 *Score* 51.16   **AVENEL** (NJ)

CATEGORY	RANK	SCORE	STATISTIC	VALUE	RANK	SCORE
Economics	160	55.00	Median Household Income	$38,112	202	18.1
			% of Families Above Poverty Level	98.0%	91	91.9
Affordable Housing	45	74.35	Median Home Value	$148,200	45	86.4
			Median Rent	$651	62	62.3
Crime	N/A	N/A	Violent Crimes per 10,000 Population	N/A	N/A	N/A
			Property Crimes per 10,000 Population	N/A	N/A	N/A
Open Spaces	205	57.60	Population Density (Persons/Sq. Mile)	4505	115	90.8
			Average Rooms per Housing Unit	4.8	216	24.4
Education	243	45.20	% High School Enrollment/Completion	81.0%	242	81.0
			% College Graduates	11.3%	234	9.4
Commute	100	37.15	Average Work Commute in Minutes	24	56	66.7
			% Commuting on Public Transportation	5.0%	197	7.6
Community Stability	228	37.65	% Living in Same House as in 1979	40.5%	192	35.1
			% Living in Same County as in 1985	73.5%	233	40.2

Composite: *Rank* 228 / 250 *Score* 50.82   **NORTH AMITYVILLE** (NY)

CATEGORY	RANK	SCORE	STATISTIC	VALUE	RANK	SCORE
Economics	217	43.40	Median Household Income	$35,694	214	15.7
			% of Families Above Poverty Level	93.1%	217	71.1
Affordable Housing	156	57.40	Median Home Value	$120,800	14	93.1
			Median Rent	$879	205	21.7
Crime	N/A	N/A	Violent Crimes per 10,000 Population	N/A	N/A	N/A
			Property Crimes per 10,000 Population	N/A	N/A	N/A
Open Spaces	175	64.85	Population Density (Persons/Sq. Mile)	5688	156	88.2
			Average Rooms per Housing Unit	5.5	162	41.5
Education	225	48.95	% High School Enrollment/Completion	90.6%	193	90.6
			% College Graduates	9.8%	239	7.3
Commute	150	31.90	Average Work Commute in Minutes	29	150	42.9
			% Commuting on Public Transportation	13.4%	82	20.9
Community Stability	146	58.45	% Living in Same House as in 1979	48.5%	135	52.6
			% Living in Same County as in 1985	81.5%	171	64.3

Metropolitan Area Suburb Rankings
NEW YORK-NORTHERN NEW JERSEY-LONG ISLAND

Composite: **Rank** 229 / 250 *Score* 50.41 **SPRING VALLEY** (NY)

CATEGORY	RANK	SCORE	STATISTIC	VALUE	RANK	SCORE
Economics	226	39.00	Median Household Income	$33,757	222	13.7
			% of Families Above Poverty Level	91.5%	223	64.3
Affordable Housing	41	75.05	Median Home Value	$163,300	79	82.7
			Median Rent	$622	47	67.4
Crime	113	77.80	Violent Crimes per 10,000 Population	69	125	79.9
			Property Crimes per 10,000 Population	480	98	75.7
Open Spaces	233	45.05	Population Density (Persons/Sq. Mile)	10378	223	77.9
			Average Rooms per Housing Unit	4.3	244	12.2
Education	183	55.20	% High School Enrollment/Completion	90.7%	191	90.7
			% College Graduates	18.5%	177	19.7
Commute	116	35.50	Average Work Commute in Minutes	26	84	57.1
			% Commuting on Public Transportation	9.0%	129	13.9
Community Stability	244	25.25	% Living in Same House as in 1979	27.0%	247	5.5
			% Living in Same County as in 1985	75.1%	228	45.0

Composite: **Rank** 230 / 250 *Score* 50.19 **PATERSON** (NJ)

CATEGORY	RANK	SCORE	STATISTIC	VALUE	RANK	SCORE
Economics	243	20.30	Median Household Income	$26,960	241	7.0
			% of Families Above Poverty Level	84.3%	241	33.6
Affordable Housing	9	87.10	Median Home Value	$136,300	25	89.3
			Median Rent	$524	9	84.9
Crime	140	59.30	Violent Crimes per 10,000 Population	168	145	50.7
			Property Crimes per 10,000 Population	597	124	67.9
Open Spaces	238	43.00	Population Density (Persons/Sq. Mile)	16691	243	64.0
			Average Rooms per Housing Unit	4.7	219	22.0
Education	249	42.55	% High School Enrollment/Completion	79.4%	244	79.4
			% College Graduates	8.7%	244	5.7
Commute	10	49.35	Average Work Commute in Minutes	21	14	81.0
			% Commuting on Public Transportation	11.4%	102	17.7
Community Stability	184	49.75	% Living in Same House as in 1979	34.1%	229	21.1
			% Living in Same County as in 1985	86.2%	87	78.4

Composite: **Rank** 231 / 250 *Score* 49.94 **JERSEY CITY** (NJ)

CATEGORY	RANK	SCORE	STATISTIC	VALUE	RANK	SCORE
Economics	245	19.45	Median Household Income	$29,054	235	9.1
			% of Families Above Poverty Level	83.4%	244	29.8
Affordable Housing	7	87.95	Median Home Value	$126,900	19	91.6
			Median Rent	$527	10	84.3
Crime	146	50.45	Violent Crimes per 10,000 Population	201	147	41.0
			Property Crimes per 10,000 Population	719	136	59.9
Open Spaces	242	40.80	Population Density (Persons/Sq. Mile)	15360	241	67.0
			Average Rooms per Housing Unit	4.4	237	14.6
Education	203	53.05	% High School Enrollment/Completion	82.2%	239	82.2
			% College Graduates	21.4%	152	23.9
Commute	2	54.20	Average Work Commute in Minutes	29	150	42.9
			% Commuting on Public Transportation	41.5%	3	65.5
Community Stability	204	43.65	% Living in Same House as in 1979	34.7%	225	22.4
			% Living in Same County as in 1985	81.7%	166	64.9

Metropolitan Area Suburb Rankings
NEW YORK-NORTHERN NEW JERSEY-LONG ISLAND

Composite: *Rank* 232 / 250 *Score* 49.57   **MONSEY (NY)**

CATEGORY	RANK	SCORE	STATISTIC	VALUE	RANK	SCORE
Economics	244	20.25	Median Household Income	$41,033	182	20.9
			% of Families Above Poverty Level	81.0%	246	19.6
Affordable Housing	178	54.05	Median Home Value	$222,300	196	68.2
			Median Rent	$777	148	39.9
Crime	N/A	N/A	Violent Crimes per 10,000 Population	N/A	N/A	N/A
			Property Crimes per 10,000 Population	N/A	N/A	N/A
Open Spaces	84	76.90	Population Density (Persons/Sq. Mile)	5863	158	87.9
			Average Rooms per Housing Unit	6.5	62	65.9
Education	95	64.15	% High School Enrollment/Completion	95.6%	80	95.6
			% College Graduates	27.6%	101	32.7
Commute	174	29.45	Average Work Commute in Minutes	30	172	38.1
			% Commuting on Public Transportation	13.3%	86	20.8
Community Stability	174	52.65	% Living in Same House as in 1979	42.1%	182	38.6
			% Living in Same County as in 1985	82.3%	159	66.7

Composite: *Rank* 233 / 250 *Score* 49.40   **MASTIC (NY)**

CATEGORY	RANK	SCORE	STATISTIC	VALUE	RANK	SCORE
Economics	223	39.60	Median Household Income	$39,245	195	19.2
			% of Families Above Poverty Level	90.5%	228	60.0
Affordable Housing	163	56.25	Median Home Value	$117,300	10	94.0
			Median Rent	$897	214	18.5
Crime	N/A	N/A	Violent Crimes per 10,000 Population	N/A	N/A	N/A
			Property Crimes per 10,000 Population	N/A	N/A	N/A
Open Spaces	116	72.55	Population Density (Persons/Sq. Mile)	3106	72	93.9
			Average Rooms per Housing Unit	5.9	123	51.2
Education	240	45.95	% High School Enrollment/Completion	88.6%	213	88.6
			% College Graduates	7.0%	247	3.3
Commute	242	16.90	Average Work Commute in Minutes	33	221	23.8
			% Commuting on Public Transportation	6.5%	175	10.0
Community Stability	116	65.15	% Living in Same House as in 1979	42.3%	181	39.0
			% Living in Same County as in 1985	90.5%	16	91.3

Composite: *Rank* 234 / 250 *Score* 49.31   **ELIZABETH (NJ)**

CATEGORY	RANK	SCORE	STATISTIC	VALUE	RANK	SCORE
Economics	236	24.90	Median Household Income	$27,631	239	7.7
			% of Families Above Poverty Level	86.3%	236	42.1
Affordable Housing	11	86.40	Median Home Value	$145,000	39	87.2
			Median Rent	$520	7	85.6
Crime	145	52.20	Violent Crimes per 10,000 Population	150	143	56.0
			Property Crimes per 10,000 Population	891	147	48.4
Open Spaces	226	49.10	Population Density (Persons/Sq. Mile)	8928	212	81.1
			Average Rooms per Housing Unit	4.5	235	17.1
Education	239	46.35	% High School Enrollment/Completion	83.0%	236	83.0
			% College Graduates	11.5%	231	9.7
Commute	38	44.55	Average Work Commute in Minutes	23	40	71.4
			% Commuting on Public Transportation	11.4%	102	17.7
Community Stability	211	41.65	% Living in Same House as in 1979	35.1%	223	23.2
			% Living in Same County as in 1985	80.1%	189	60.1

Metropolitan Area Suburb Rankings
NEW YORK-NORTHERN NEW JERSEY-LONG ISLAND

Composite: **Rank** 235 / 250   *Score* 49.16   **PASSAIC** (NJ)

CATEGORY	RANK	SCORE	STATISTIC	VALUE	RANK	SCORE
Economics	240	22.50	Median Household Income	$26,669	243	6.7
			% of Families Above Poverty Level	85.4%	237	38.3
Affordable Housing	19	83.05	Median Home Value	$163,700	81	82.6
			Median Rent	$532	11	83.5
Crime	134	65.40	Violent Crimes per 10,000 Population	135	140	60.5
			Property Crimes per 10,000 Population	561	117	70.3
Open Spaces	244	37.10	Population Density (Persons/Sq. Mile)	18707	244	59.6
			Average Rooms per Housing Unit	4.4	237	14.6
Education	245	44.85	% High School Enrollment/Completion	76.1%	249	76.1
			% College Graduates	14.2%	213	13.6
Commute	8	51.75	Average Work Commute in Minutes	21	14	81.0
			% Commuting on Public Transportation	14.4%	77	22.5
Community Stability	220	39.50	% Living in Same House as in 1979	34.2%	228	21.3
			% Living in Same County as in 1985	79.3%	201	57.7

Composite: **Rank** 236 / 250   *Score* 49.05   **WEST NEW YORK** (NJ)

CATEGORY	RANK	SCORE	STATISTIC	VALUE	RANK	SCORE
Economics	235	26.20	Median Household Income	$26,361	244	6.4
			% of Families Above Poverty Level	87.2%	235	46.0
Affordable Housing	2	91.10	Median Home Value	$165,400	84	82.2
			Median Rent	$439	1	100.0
Crime	123	73.55	Violent Crimes per 10,000 Population	79	130	77.0
			Property Crimes per 10,000 Population	564	118	70.1
Open Spaces	249	9.15	Population Density (Persons/Sq. Mile)	37502	249	18.3
			Average Rooms per Housing Unit	3.8	250	0.0
Education	231	48.15	% High School Enrollment/Completion	85.3%	229	85.3
			% College Graduates	12.4%	226	11.0
Commute	9	49.80	Average Work Commute in Minutes	27	102	52.4
			% Commuting on Public Transportation	30.0%	7	47.2
Community Stability	199	45.40	% Living in Same House as in 1979	36.6%	214	26.5
			% Living in Same County as in 1985	81.5%	171	64.3

Composite: **Rank** 237 / 250   *Score* 48.74   **ORANGE** (NJ)

CATEGORY	RANK	SCORE	STATISTIC	VALUE	RANK	SCORE
Economics	239	22.60	Median Household Income	$27,301	240	7.3
			% of Families Above Poverty Level	85.3%	238	37.9
Affordable Housing	11	86.40	Median Home Value	$118,200	11	93.8
			Median Rent	$557	21	79.0
Crime	147	46.65	Violent Crimes per 10,000 Population	196	146	42.5
			Property Crimes per 10,000 Population	856	145	50.8
Open Spaces	240	42.75	Population Density (Persons/Sq. Mile)	13555	238	70.9
			Average Rooms per Housing Unit	4.4	237	14.6
Education	226	48.75	% High School Enrollment/Completion	78.4%	247	78.4
			% College Graduates	18.1%	180	19.1
Commute	57	42.75	Average Work Commute in Minutes	27	102	52.4
			% Commuting on Public Transportation	21.1%	29	33.1
Community Stability	183	51.30	% Living in Same House as in 1979	32.1%	238	16.7
			% Living in Same County as in 1985	88.7%	42	85.9

Metropolitan Area Suburb Rankings
NEW YORK-NORTHERN NEW JERSEY-LONG ISLAND

Composite: *Rank* 238 / 250 *Score* 48.46   **HOBOKEN** (NJ)

CATEGORY	RANK	SCORE	STATISTIC	VALUE	RANK	SCORE
Economics	237	23.80	Median Household Income	$34,873	217	14.8
			% of Families Above Poverty Level	84.1%	243	32.8
Affordable Housing	74	68.65	Median Home Value	$260,400	221	58.8
			Median Rent	$560	22	78.5
Crime	136	64.15	Violent Crimes per 10,000 Population	103	135	69.9
			Property Crimes per 10,000 Population	741	138	58.4
Open Spaces	248	23.95	Population Density (Persons/Sq. Mile)	26243	248	43.0
			Average Rooms per Housing Unit	4.0	247	4.9
Education	46	71.10	% High School Enrollment/Completion	92.2%	165	92.2
			% College Graduates	39.7%	42	50.0
Commute	1	69.05	Average Work Commute in Minutes	30	172	38.1
			% Commuting on Public Transportation	63.3%	1	100.0
Community Stability	247	18.55	% Living in Same House as in 1979	29.1%	246	10.1
			% Living in Same County as in 1985	69.1%	243	27.0

Composite: *Rank* 239 / 250 *Score* 48.19   **BRIDGEPORT** (CT)

CATEGORY	RANK	SCORE	STATISTIC	VALUE	RANK	SCORE
Economics	238	22.65	Median Household Income	$28,704	236	8.7
			% of Families Above Poverty Level	85.0%	239	36.6
Affordable Housing	23	79.70	Median Home Value	$145,600	41	87.0
			Median Rent	$594	33	72.4
Crime	149	40.15	Violent Crimes per 10,000 Population	202	148	40.7
			Property Crimes per 10,000 Population	1,024	149	39.6
Open Spaces	220	51.65	Population Density (Persons/Sq. Mile)	8853	211	81.3
			Average Rooms per Housing Unit	4.7	219	22.0
Education	242	45.40	% High School Enrollment/Completion	79.9%	243	79.9
			% College Graduates	12.3%	227	10.9
Commute	12	48.10	Average Work Commute in Minutes	20	5	85.7
			% Commuting on Public Transportation	6.8%	170	10.5
Community Stability	185	49.65	% Living in Same House as in 1979	33.5%	233	19.7
			% Living in Same County as in 1985	86.6%	74	79.6

Composite: *Rank* 240 / 250 *Score* 47.69   **EAST ORANGE** (NJ)

CATEGORY	RANK	SCORE	STATISTIC	VALUE	RANK	SCORE
Economics	242	20.45	Median Household Income	$26,810	242	6.9
			% of Families Above Poverty Level	84.4%	240	34.0
Affordable Housing	5	89.35	Median Home Value	$110,600	7	95.6
			Median Rent	$534	15	83.1
Crime	150	38.90	Violent Crimes per 10,000 Population	267	151	21.5
			Property Crimes per 10,000 Population	772	141	56.3
Open Spaces	245	37.05	Population Density (Persons/Sq. Mile)	18743	245	59.5
			Average Rooms per Housing Unit	4.4	237	14.6
Education	219	49.80	% High School Enrollment/Completion	85.3%	229	85.3
			% College Graduates	14.7%	211	14.3
Commute	36	44.90	Average Work Commute in Minutes	28	127	47.6
			% Commuting on Public Transportation	26.8%	10	42.2
Community Stability	173	53.40	% Living in Same House as in 1979	34.6%	226	22.1
			% Living in Same County as in 1985	88.3%	54	84.7

Composite: *Rank* 241 / 250 *Score* 47.66 **RIDGE** (NY)

CATEGORY	RANK	SCORE	STATISTIC	VALUE	RANK	SCORE
Economics	208	45.90	Median Household Income	$29,634	234	9.7
			% of Families Above Poverty Level	95.7%	186	82.1
Affordable Housing	109	63.35	Median Home Value	$134,800	22	89.7
			Median Rent	$793	160	37.0
Crime	N/A	N/A	Violent Crimes per 10,000 Population	N/A	N/A	N/A
			Property Crimes per 10,000 Population	N/A	N/A	N/A
Open Spaces	158	66.45	Population Density (Persons/Sq. Mile)	889	4	98.8
			Average Rooms per Housing Unit	5.2	192	34.1
Education	193	53.85	% High School Enrollment/Completion	94.4%	108	94.4
			% College Graduates	14.0%	215	13.3
Commute	241	17.90	Average Work Commute in Minutes	31	195	33.3
			% Commuting on Public Transportation	1.8%	243	2.5
Community Stability	226	38.50	% Living in Same House as in 1979	30.3%	243	12.7
			% Living in Same County as in 1985	81.5%	171	64.3

Composite: *Rank* 242 / 250 *Score* 47.48 **NEWBURGH** (NY)

CATEGORY	RANK	SCORE	STATISTIC	VALUE	RANK	SCORE
Economics	250	1.15	Median Household Income	$22,224	247	2.3
			% of Families Above Poverty Level	76.4%	250	0.0
Affordable Housing	4	90.50	Median Home Value	$102,300	3	97.7
			Median Rent	$533	13	83.3
Crime	144	53.40	Violent Crimes per 10,000 Population	209	149	38.6
			Property Crimes per 10,000 Population	593	121	68.2
Open Spaces	206	57.40	Population Density (Persons/Sq. Mile)	6921	182	85.5
			Average Rooms per Housing Unit	5.0	203	29.3
Education	246	44.35	% High School Enrollment/Completion	79.1%	245	79.1
			% College Graduates	11.4%	233	9.6
Commute	45	43.90	Average Work Commute in Minutes	21	14	81.0
			% Commuting on Public Transportation	4.5%	209	6.8
Community Stability	211	41.65	% Living in Same House as in 1979	31.1%	240	14.5
			% Living in Same County as in 1985	83.0%	150	68.8

Composite: *Rank* 243 / 250 *Score* 47.03 **MASTIC BEACH** (NY)

CATEGORY	RANK	SCORE	STATISTIC	VALUE	RANK	SCORE
Economics	228	38.30	Median Household Income	$35,776	213	15.7
			% of Families Above Poverty Level	90.7%	227	60.9
Affordable Housing	115	62.90	Median Home Value	$108,500	5	96.1
			Median Rent	$834	181	29.7
Crime	N/A	N/A	Violent Crimes per 10,000 Population	N/A	N/A	N/A
			Property Crimes per 10,000 Population	N/A	N/A	N/A
Open Spaces	162	66.00	Population Density (Persons/Sq. Mile)	2432	49	95.4
			Average Rooms per Housing Unit	5.3	180	36.6
Education	237	46.50	% High School Enrollment/Completion	87.0%	223	87.0
			% College Graduates	8.9%	243	6.0
Commute	248	11.10	Average Work Commute in Minutes	35	241	14.3
			% Commuting on Public Transportation	5.2%	193	7.9
Community Stability	155	57.35	% Living in Same House as in 1979	39.4%	196	32.7
			% Living in Same County as in 1985	87.4%	67	82.0

Metropolitan Area Suburb Rankings
NEW YORK-NORTHERN NEW JERSEY-LONG ISLAND

Composite: **Rank** 244 / 250 **Score** 46.62 **NEW BRUNSWICK** (NJ)

CATEGORY	RANK	SCORE	STATISTIC	VALUE	RANK	SCORE
Economics	241	20.95	Median Household Income	$28,289	238	8.3
			% of Families Above Poverty Level	84.3%	241	33.6
Affordable Housing	28	78.25	Median Home Value	$124,100	17	92.3
			Median Rent	$640	56	64.2
Crime	143	55.70	Violent Crimes per 10,000 Population	114	136	66.7
			Property Crimes per 10,000 Population	948	148	44.7
Open Spaces	221	51.35	Population Density (Persons/Sq. Mile)	7987	201	83.2
			Average Rooms per Housing Unit	4.6	229	19.5
Education	140	60.10	% High School Enrollment/Completion	93.5%	129	93.5
			% College Graduates	23.4%	137	26.7
Commute	2	54.20	Average Work Commute in Minutes	20	5	85.7
			% Commuting on Public Transportation	14.5%	74	22.7
Community Stability	250	5.80	% Living in Same House as in 1979	29.8%	244	11.6
			% Living in Same County as in 1985	60.1%	250	0.0

Composite: **Rank** 245 / 250 **Score** 46.41 **LEISURE VILLAGE W.-PINE LAKE PARK** (NJ)

CATEGORY	RANK	SCORE	STATISTIC	VALUE	RANK	SCORE
Economics	175	52.85	Median Household Income	$32,963	225	12.9
			% of Families Above Poverty Level	98.2%	76	92.8
Affordable Housing	203	47.45	Median Home Value	$113,600	8	94.9
			Median Rent	$1,001	232	0.0
Crime	N/A	N/A	Violent Crimes per 10,000 Population	N/A	N/A	N/A
			Property Crimes per 10,000 Population	N/A	N/A	N/A
Open Spaces	154	66.95	Population Density (Persons/Sq. Mile)	2663	60	94.9
			Average Rooms per Housing Unit	5.4	172	39.0
Education	215	50.85	% High School Enrollment/Completion	89.6%	205	89.6
			% College Graduates	13.2%	221	12.1
Commute	198	26.20	Average Work Commute in Minutes	27	102	52.4
			% Commuting on Public Transportation	0.2%	250	0.0
Community Stability	235	34.15	% Living in Same House as in 1979	37.6%	206	28.7
			% Living in Same County as in 1985	73.3%	235	39.6

Composite: **Rank** 246 / 250 **Score** 45.88 **ASBURY PARK** (NJ)

CATEGORY	RANK	SCORE	STATISTIC	VALUE	RANK	SCORE
Economics	247	4.50	Median Household Income	$20,754	249	0.9
			% of Families Above Poverty Level	78.3%	247	8.1
Affordable Housing	3	90.70	Median Home Value	$97,500	2	98.8
			Median Rent	$537	16	82.6
Crime	142	56.90	Violent Crimes per 10,000 Population	160	144	53.1
			Property Crimes per 10,000 Population	706	135	60.7
Open Spaces	243	39.90	Population Density (Persons/Sq. Mile)	11731	232	74.9
			Average Rooms per Housing Unit	4.0	247	4.9
Education	241	45.50	% High School Enrollment/Completion	78.4%	247	78.4
			% College Graduates	13.5%	218	12.6
Commute	13	47.95	Average Work Commute in Minutes	21	14	81.0
			% Commuting on Public Transportation	9.6%	120	14.9
Community Stability	233	35.70	% Living in Same House as in 1979	25.8%	249	2.9
			% Living in Same County as in 1985	82.9%	152	68.5

Metropolitan Area Suburb Rankings
NEW YORK-NORTHERN NEW JERSEY-LONG ISLAND

Composite: **Rank** 247 / 250 *Score* 45.73   **IRVINGTON (NJ)**

CATEGORY	RANK	SCORE	STATISTIC	VALUE	RANK	SCORE
Economics	232	33.40	Median Household Income	$30,580	232	10.6
			% of Families Above Poverty Level	89.6%	231	56.2
Affordable Housing	13	86.10	Median Home Value	$115,900	9	94.3
			Median Rent	$563	23	77.9
Crime	151	35.50	Violent Crimes per 10,000 Population	228	150	33.0
			Property Crimes per 10,000 Population	1,049	150	38.0
Open Spaces	247	34.90	Population Density (Persons/Sq. Mile)	20725	246	55.2
			Average Rooms per Housing Unit	4.4	237	14.6
Education	227	48.60	% High School Enrollment/Completion	86.8%	224	86.8
			% College Graduates	12.0%	230	10.4
Commute	76	40.10	Average Work Commute in Minutes	28	127	47.6
			% Commuting on Public Transportation	20.8%	31	32.6
Community Stability	213	41.50	% Living in Same House as in 1979	30.7%	242	13.6
			% Living in Same County as in 1985	83.2%	146	69.4

Composite: **Rank** 248 / 250 *Score* 45.39   **UNION CITY (NJ)**

CATEGORY	RANK	SCORE	STATISTIC	VALUE	RANK	SCORE
Economics	246	17.55	Median Household Income	$25,655	245	5.7
			% of Families Above Poverty Level	83.3%	245	29.4
Affordable Housing	8	87.25	Median Home Value	$149,100	46	86.2
			Median Rent	$505	4	88.3
Crime	124	73.10	Violent Crimes per 10,000 Population	78	129	77.3
			Property Crimes per 10,000 Population	583	119	68.9
Open Spaces	250	1.20	Population Density (Persons/Sq. Mile)	45822	250	0.0
			Average Rooms per Housing Unit	3.9	249	2.4
Education	236	46.75	% High School Enrollment/Completion	84.9%	232	84.9
			% College Graduates	10.7%	236	8.6
Commute	6	53.65	Average Work Commute in Minutes	26	84	57.1
			% Commuting on Public Transportation	31.9%	5	50.2
Community Stability	227	38.20	% Living in Same House as in 1979	32.6%	237	17.8
			% Living in Same County as in 1985	79.6%	196	58.6

Composite: **Rank** 249 / 250 *Score* 43.42   **NEWARK (NJ)**

CATEGORY	RANK	SCORE	STATISTIC	VALUE	RANK	SCORE
Economics	249	2.55	Median Household Income	$21,650	248	1.7
			% of Families Above Poverty Level	77.2%	249	3.4
Affordable Housing	1	97.55	Median Home Value	$108,300	4	96.2
			Median Rent	$445	2	98.9
Crime	152	15.95	Violent Crimes per 10,000 Population	340	152	0.0
			Property Crimes per 10,000 Population	1,141	151	31.9
Open Spaces	234	44.95	Population Density (Persons/Sq. Mile)	11555	231	75.3
			Average Rooms per Housing Unit	4.4	237	14.6
Education	248	43.30	% High School Enrollment/Completion	81.2%	241	81.2
			% College Graduates	8.5%	245	5.4
Commute	16	47.65	Average Work Commute in Minutes	27	102	52.4
			% Commuting on Public Transportation	27.3%	9	42.9
Community Stability	179	52.00	% Living in Same House as in 1979	34.1%	229	21.1
			% Living in Same County as in 1985	87.7%	60	82.9

Metropolitan Area Suburb Rankings
NEW YORK-NORTHERN NEW JERSEY-LONG ISLAND

Composite: *Rank* 250 / 250 *Score* 40.99   HOLIDAY CITY-BERKELEY (NJ)

CATEGORY	RANK	SCORE	STATISTIC	VALUE	RANK	SCORE
Economics	210	45.55	Median Household Income	$19,893	250	0.0
			% of Families Above Poverty Level	97.8%	111	91.1
Affordable Housing	76	68.35	Median Home Value	$92,800	1	100.0
			Median Rent	$795	165	36.7
Crime	N/A	N/A	Violent Crimes per 10,000 Population	N/A	N/A	N/A
			Property Crimes per 10,000 Population	N/A	N/A	N/A
Open Spaces	163	65.95	Population Density (Persons/Sq. Mile)	2483	51	95.3
			Average Rooms per Housing Unit	5.3	180	36.6
Education	250	0.00	% High School Enrollment/Completion	0.0%	250	0.0
			% College Graduates	4.7%	250	0.0
Commute	230	21.10	Average Work Commute in Minutes	30	172	38.1
			% Commuting on Public Transportation	2.8%	233	4.1
Community Stability	203	45.00	% Living in Same House as in 1979	38.8%	198	31.4
			% Living in Same County as in 1985	79.6%	196	58.6

Metropolitan Area Description
NORFOLK-VIRGINIA BEACH-NEWPORT NEWS

STATE: Virginia
COUNTIES: Gloucester, James City, York

INDEPEN-DENT CITIES: Chesapeake, Hampton, Newport News, Norfolk, Poquoson, Portsmouth, Suffolk, Virginia Beach, Williamsburg

TOTAL POPULATION:	1,396,107	
POPULATION IN SUBURBS:	571,764	(41.0%)
POPULATION IN Norfolk:	261,229	(18.7%)
POPULATION IN Newport News:	170,045	(12.2%)
POPULATION IN Virginia Beach:	393,069	(28.2%)

The NORFOLK-VIRGINIA BEACH-NEWPORT NEWS metropolitan area is located in the southeastern part of Virginia along the Atlantic Ocean. The suburbs range geographically from Williamsburg in the northwest (45 miles from Norfolk), to Suffolk in the southwest (19 miles from Norfolk). The area is growing rapidly and had an increase of 20.3% between 1980 and 1990. Summer time high temperatures average in the 80's and winter time lows average in the 20's. The suburb of Williamsburg is the site of the Colonial Williamsburg Foundation, Virginia's seventh largest commercial employer. A research park is located in Hampton, where such firms as Bionetics are located. Public transportation in the area is provided on buses by Tidewater Regional Transit.

Poquoson is the overall highest rated suburb and also has the highest scores in economics and open spaces. **Poquoson** is also rated the safest suburb with the lowest crime rate. **Suffolk** is the suburb with the most affordable housing and also has the top score in community stability. **Williamsburg** receives the highest score in education and also has the number one rated commute.

The highest ranked suburb overall which also has an affordable housing score of at least 50.00 is **Hampton**.

The highest ranked suburb in the education category which also has an affordable housing score of at least 50.00 is also **Hampton**.

All the rated suburbs in this metropolitan area are independent cities and not located in any county.

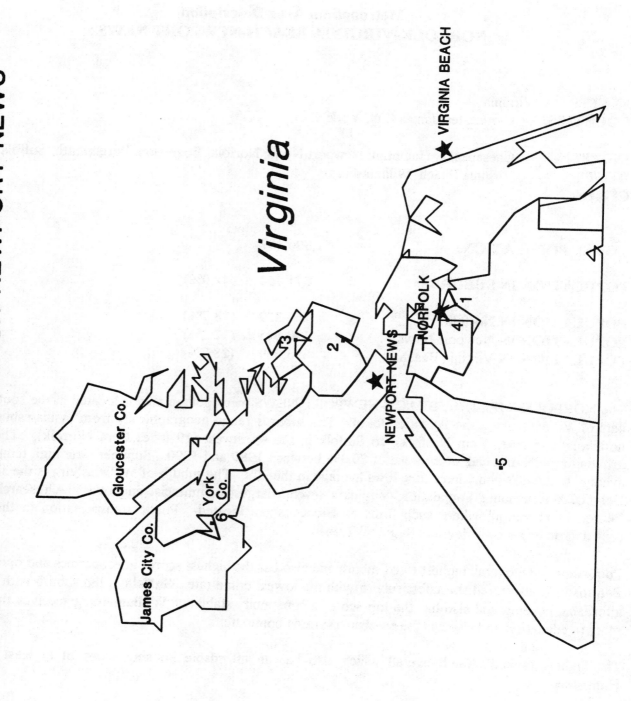

Metropolitan Area Map
NORFOLK-VIRGINIA BEACH-NEWPORT NEWS

Virginia

VIRGINIA BEACH

NORFOLK

NEWPORT NEWS

Gloucester Co.

York Co.

James City Co.

Metropolitan Area Suburb Alphabetical Index
NORFOLK-VIRGINIA BEACH-NEWPORT NEWS

SUBURB	PAGE	MAP NO.	STATE	COUNTY	POPU-LATION	RANK
CHESAPEAKE	553	1	Virginia	Independent City	151,976	4 / 6
HAMPTON	552	2	Virginia	Independent City	133,793	2 / 6
POQUOSON	552	3	Virginia	Independent City	11,005	1 / 6
PORTSMOUTH	553	4	Virginia	Independent City	103,907	6 / 6
SUFFOLK	552	5	Virginia	Independent City	52,141	3 / 6
WILLIAMSBURG	553	6	Virginia	Independent City	11,530	5 / 6

Metropolitan Area Suburb Rankings
NORFOLK-VIRGINIA BEACH-NEWPORT NEWS

Composite: **Rank** 1 / 6 **Score** 65.54 — **POQUOSON**

CATEGORY	RANK	SCORE	STATISTIC	VALUE	RANK	SCORE
Economics	1	100.00	Median Household Income	$43,236	1	100.0
			% of Families Above Poverty Level	97.7%	1	100.0
Affordable Housing	6	4.95	Median Home Value	$113,200	5	9.9
			Median Rent	$574	6	0.0
Crime	1	100.00	Violent Crimes per 10,000 Population	26	1	100.0
			Property Crimes per 10,000 Population	107	1	100.0
Open Spaces	1	90.35	Population Density (Persons/Sq. Mile)	709	3	80.7
			Average Rooms per Housing Unit	6.6	1	100.0
Education	2	76.15	% High School Enrollment/Completion	96.2%	2	95.4
			% College Graduates	29.4%	2	56.9
Commute	6	12.50	Average Work Commute in Minutes	21	3	25.0
			% Commuting on Public Transportation	0.4%	6	0.0
Community Stability	3	74.85	% Living in Same House as in 1979	39.3%	3	81.2
			% Living in Same County as in 1985	65.1%	5	68.5

Composite: **Rank** 2 / 6 **Score** 50.06 — **HAMPTON**

CATEGORY	RANK	SCORE	STATISTIC	VALUE	RANK	SCORE
Economics	3	39.05	Median Household Income	$30,144	3	29.7
			% of Families Above Poverty Level	91.2%	4	48.4
Affordable Housing	3	65.70	Median Home Value	$77,500	3	78.9
			Median Rent	$470	3	52.5
Crime	3	59.45	Violent Crimes per 10,000 Population	46	3	78.5
			Property Crimes per 10,000 Population	562	5	40.4
Open Spaces	5	22.55	Population Density (Persons/Sq. Mile)	2582	5	18.4
			Average Rooms per Housing Unit	5.5	4	26.7
Education	3	47.90	% High School Enrollment/Completion	93.1%	3	71.8
			% College Graduates	19.1%	3	24.0
Commute	3	52.65	Average Work Commute in Minutes	19	2	41.7
			% Commuting on Public Transportation	2.5%	2	63.6
Community Stability	4	63.15	% Living in Same House as in 1979	34.0%	4	55.8
			% Living in Same County as in 1985	66.1%	4	70.5

Composite: **Rank** 3 / 6 **Score** 49.64 — **SUFFOLK**

CATEGORY	RANK	SCORE	STATISTIC	VALUE	RANK	SCORE
Economics	5	8.05	Median Household Income	$26,125	4	8.2
			% of Families Above Poverty Level	86.1%	5	7.9
Affordable Housing	1	96.40	Median Home Value	$70,300	2	92.8
			Median Rent	$376	1	100.0
Crime	5	35.15	Violent Crimes per 10,000 Population	93	5	28.0
			Property Crimes per 10,000 Population	547	4	42.3
Open Spaces	2	73.35	Population Density (Persons/Sq. Mile)	130	1	100.0
			Average Rooms per Housing Unit	5.8	3	46.7
Education	5	14.85	% High School Enrollment/Completion	87.3%	5	27.5
			% College Graduates	12.3%	5	2.2
Commute	4	19.70	Average Work Commute in Minutes	24	6	0.0
			% Commuting on Public Transportation	1.7%	3	39.4
Community Stability	1	100.00	% Living in Same House as in 1979	43.2%	1	100.0
			% Living in Same County as in 1985	80.8%	1	100.0

Metropolitan Area Suburb Rankings
NORFOLK-VIRGINIA BEACH-NEWPORT NEWS

Composite: *Rank* 4 / 6 *Score* 49.23   **CHESAPEAKE**

CATEGORY	RANK	SCORE	STATISTIC	VALUE	RANK	SCORE
Economics	2	61.25	Median Household Income	$35,737	2	59.8
			% of Families Above Poverty Level	93.0%	3	62.7
Affordable Housing	4	49.70	Median Home Value	$87,800	4	59.0
			Median Rent	$494	5	40.4
Crime	4	58.40	Violent Crimes per 10,000 Population	57	4	66.7
			Property Crimes per 10,000 Population	488	2	50.1
Open Spaces	3	71.40	Population Density (Persons/Sq. Mile)	446	2	89.5
			Average Rooms per Housing Unit	5.9	2	53.3
Education	4	29.45	% High School Enrollment/Completion	89.2%	4	42.0
			% College Graduates	16.9%	4	16.9
Commute	5	14.75	Average Work Commute in Minutes	23	5	8.3
			% Commuting on Public Transportation	1.1%	5	21.2
Community Stability	5	59.65	% Living in Same House as in 1979	32.0%	5	46.2
			% Living in Same County as in 1985	67.4%	3	73.1

Composite: *Rank* 5 / 6 *Score* 46.57   **WILLIAMSBURG**

CATEGORY	RANK	SCORE	STATISTIC	VALUE	RANK	SCORE
Economics	4	37.85	Median Household Income	$25,393	5	4.3
			% of Families Above Poverty Level	94.1%	2	71.4
Affordable Housing	5	20.70	Median Home Value	$118,300	6	0.0
			Median Rent	$492	4	41.4
Crime	2	70.90	Violent Crimes per 10,000 Population	28	2	97.8
			Property Crimes per 10,000 Population	534	3	44.0
Open Spaces	4	29.90	Population Density (Persons/Sq. Mile)	1339	4	59.8
			Average Rooms per Housing Unit	5.1	6	0.0
Education	1	100.00	% High School Enrollment/Completion	96.8%	1	100.0
			% College Graduates	42.9%	1	100.0
Commute	1	66.65	Average Work Commute in Minutes	12	1	100.0
			% Commuting on Public Transportation	1.5%	4	33.3
Community Stability	6	0.00	% Living in Same House as in 1979	22.4%	6	0.0
			% Living in Same County as in 1985	30.9%	6	0.0

Composite: *Rank* 6 / 6 *Score* 35.57   **PORTSMOUTH**

CATEGORY	RANK	SCORE	STATISTIC	VALUE	RANK	SCORE
Economics	6	0.00	Median Household Income	$24,601	6	0.0
			% of Families Above Poverty Level	85.1%	6	0.0
Affordable Housing	2	89.90	Median Home Value	$66,600	1	100.0
			Median Rent	$416	2	79.8
Crime	6	0.00	Violent Crimes per 10,000 Population	119	6	0.0
			Property Crimes per 10,000 Population	870	6	0.0
Open Spaces	6	6.65	Population Density (Persons/Sq. Mile)	3135	6	0.0
			Average Rooms per Housing Unit	5.3	5	13.3
Education	6	0.00	% High School Enrollment/Completion	83.7%	6	0.0
			% College Graduates	11.6%	6	0.0
Commute	2	62.50	Average Work Commute in Minutes	21	3	25.0
			% Commuting on Public Transportation	3.7%	1	100.0
Community Stability	2	89.95	% Living in Same House as in 1979	39.9%	2	84.1
			% Living in Same County as in 1985	78.7%	2	95.8

Metropolitan Area Description
OKLAHOMA CITY

STATE: Oklahoma
COUNTIES: Canadian, Cleveland, Logan, McClain, Oklahoma, Pottawatomie

TOTAL POPULATION: 958,839

POPULATION IN SUBURBS: 514,120 (53.6%)

POPULATION IN Oklahoma City: 444,719 (46.4%)

The OKLAHOMA CITY metropolitan area is located in the central part of Oklahoma. The suburbs range geographically from Guthrie in the north (33 miles from Oklahoma City), to El Reno in the west (28 miles from Oklahoma City), to Norman in the south (20 miles from Oklahoma City), and to Shawnee in the east (36 miles from Oklahoma City). The area is growing in population and had an increase of 11.4% between 1980 and 1990. Summer time high temperatures average in the 90's and winter time lows average in the 20's. The suburb of Norman is a college town famous for the nationally-known University of Oklahoma. The Central Environmental Systems division of York International is also located in Norman. Public transportation in the area is provided on buses by the Central Oklahoma Transportation and Parking Authority.

Edmond is the overall highest rated suburb and also has the highest scores in education and open spaces. **Mustang** receives the top score in economics and is also rated the safest suburb with the lowest crime rate. **Guthrie** is the suburb with the most affordable housing. The top rated commute belongs to **Norman**. Finally, the number one rating in community stability goes to **Del City**.

The highest ranked suburb overall which also has an affordable housing score of at least 50.00 is **Bethany**.

The highest ranked suburb in the education category which also has an affordable housing score of at least 50.00 is also **Bethany**.

The county whose suburbs have the highest average overall score is **Canadian County** (55.10).

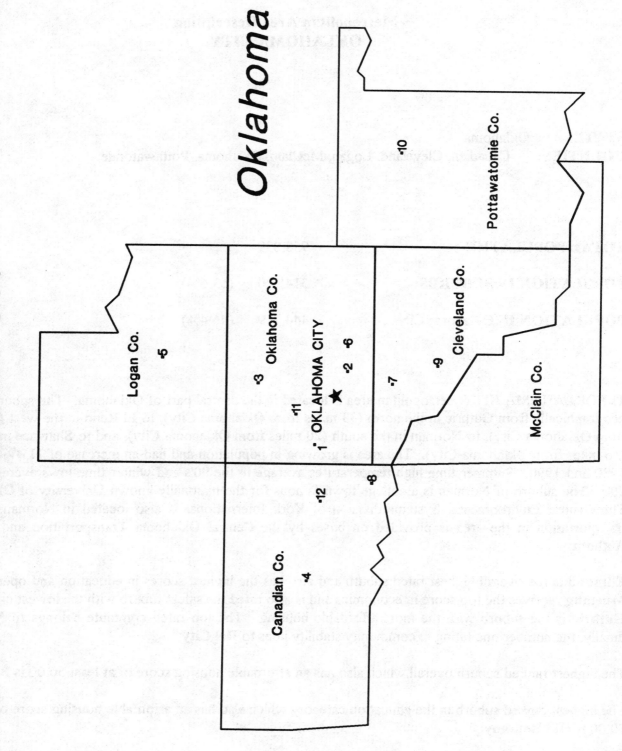

Metropolitan Area Map
OKLAHOMA CITY

Oklahoma

Metropolitan Area Suburb Alphabetical Index
OKLAHOMA CITY

SUBURB	PAGE	MAP NO.	STATE	COUNTY	POPU-LATION	RANK
BETHANY	558	1	Oklahoma	Oklahoma	20,075	3 / 12
DEL CITY	560	2	Oklahoma	Oklahoma	23,928	7 / 12
EDMOND	558	3	Oklahoma	Oklahoma	52,315	1 / 12
EL RENO	559	4	Oklahoma	Canadian	15,414	6 / 12
GUTHRIE	561	5	Oklahoma	Logan	10,518	10 / 12
MIDWEST CITY	560	6	Oklahoma	Oklahoma	52,267	9 / 12
MOORE	561	7	Oklahoma	Cleveland	40,318	12 / 12
MUSTANG	559	8	Oklahoma	Canadian	10,434	5 / 12
NORMAN	559	9	Oklahoma	Cleveland	80,071	4 / 12
SHAWNEE	561	10	Oklahoma	Pottawatomie	26,017	11 / 12
THE VILLAGE	560	11	Oklahoma	Oklahoma	10,353	8 / 12
YUKON	558	12	Oklahoma	Canadian	20,935	2 / 12

Metropolitan Area Suburb Rankings
OKLAHOMA CITY

Composite: *Rank* 1 / 12 *Score* 59.49 — EDMOND

CATEGORY	RANK	SCORE	STATISTIC	VALUE	RANK	SCORE
Economics	2	91.25	Median Household Income	$37,644	1	100.0
			% of Families Above Poverty Level	94.8%	3	82.5
Affordable Housing	12	12.15	Median Home Value	$78,300	12	0.0
			Median Rent	$423	8	24.3
Crime	6	60.75	Violent Crimes per 10,000 Population	41	7	45.9
			Property Crimes per 10,000 Population	458	4	75.6
Open Spaces	1	94.60	Population Density (Persons/Sq. Mile)	613	4	89.2
			Average Rooms per Housing Unit	5.6	1	100.0
Education	1	98.50	% High School Enrollment/Completion	95.0%	2	97.0
			% College Graduates	43.5%	1	100.0
Commute	7	40.10	Average Work Commute in Minutes	20	8	57.1
			% Commuting on Public Transportation	0.3%	2	23.1
Community Stability	11	19.10	% Living in Same House as in 1979	21.8%	12	0.0
			% Living in Same County as in 1985	72.1%	8	38.2

Composite: *Rank* 2 / 12 *Score* 58.21 — YUKON

CATEGORY	RANK	SCORE	STATISTIC	VALUE	RANK	SCORE
Economics	3	85.50	Median Household Income	$35,090	3	86.3
			% of Families Above Poverty Level	95.1%	2	84.7
Affordable Housing	10	31.10	Median Home Value	$56,500	10	54.5
			Median Rent	$453	10	7.7
Crime	2	87.35	Violent Crimes per 10,000 Population	26	4	86.5
			Property Crimes per 10,000 Population	401	2	88.2
Open Spaces	3	77.75	Population Density (Persons/Sq. Mile)	812	6	84.1
			Average Rooms per Housing Unit	5.4	3	71.4
Education	5	53.75	% High School Enrollment/Completion	90.6%	6	78.3
			% College Graduates	19.5%	5	29.2
Commute	4	47.25	Average Work Commute in Minutes	19	5	71.4
			% Commuting on Public Transportation	0.3%	2	23.1
Community Stability	9	24.75	% Living in Same House as in 1979	27.8%	10	22.3
			% Living in Same County as in 1985	69.4%	9	27.2

Composite: *Rank* 3 / 12 *Score* 56.43 — BETHANY

CATEGORY	RANK	SCORE	STATISTIC	VALUE	RANK	SCORE
Economics	6	58.25	Median Household Income	$27,235	6	44.2
			% of Families Above Poverty Level	93.4%	5	72.3
Affordable Housing	6	57.30	Median Home Value	$53,900	8	61.0
			Median Rent	$370	5	53.6
Crime	5	70.75	Violent Crimes per 10,000 Population	23	2	94.6
			Property Crimes per 10,000 Population	587	8	46.9
Open Spaces	12	17.25	Population Density (Persons/Sq. Mile)	3849	11	5.9
			Average Rooms per Housing Unit	5.1	8	28.6
Education	4	62.00	% High School Enrollment/Completion	94.4%	3	94.5
			% College Graduates	19.6%	4	29.5
Commute	3	50.55	Average Work Commute in Minutes	18	2	85.7
			% Commuting on Public Transportation	0.2%	5	15.4
Community Stability	3	78.90	% Living in Same House as in 1979	42.6%	4	77.3
			% Living in Same County as in 1985	82.5%	3	80.5

Metropolitan Area Suburb Rankings
OKLAHOMA CITY

Composite: **Rank** 4 / 12 **Score** 55.72   **NORMAN**

CATEGORY	RANK	SCORE	STATISTIC	VALUE	RANK	SCORE
Economics	8	46.85	Median Household Income	$25,165	9	33.1
			% of Families Above Poverty Level	91.8%	7	60.6
Affordable Housing	7	45.60	Median Home Value	$65,000	11	33.2
			Median Rent	$362	4	58.0
Crime	3	79.35	Violent Crimes per 10,000 Population	21	1	100.0
			Property Crimes per 10,000 Population	534	7	58.7
Open Spaces	8	46.70	Population Density (Persons/Sq. Mile)	452	2	93.4
			Average Rooms per Housing Unit	4.9	12	0.0
Education	2	92.05	% High School Enrollment/Completion	95.7%	1	100.0
			% College Graduates	38.1%	2	84.1
Commute	1	78.55	Average Work Commute in Minutes	20	8	57.1
			% Commuting on Public Transportation	1.3%	1	100.0
Community Stability	12	0.95	% Living in Same House as in 1979	22.3%	11	1.9
			% Living in Same County as in 1985	62.7%	12	0.0

Composite: **Rank** 5 / 12 **Score** 53.88   **MUSTANG**

CATEGORY	RANK	SCORE	STATISTIC	VALUE	RANK	SCORE
Economics	1	96.95	Median Household Income	$36,512	2	93.9
			% of Families Above Poverty Level	97.2%	1	100.0
Affordable Housing	11	29.60	Median Home Value	$54,600	9	59.2
			Median Rent	$467	12	0.0
Crime	1	95.95	Violent Crimes per 10,000 Population	24	3	91.9
			Property Crimes per 10,000 Population	348	1	100.0
Open Spaces	2	91.30	Population Density (Persons/Sq. Mile)	869	7	82.6
			Average Rooms per Housing Unit	5.6	1	100.0
Education	8	41.40	% High School Enrollment/Completion	89.3%	9	72.8
			% College Graduates	13.0%	9	10.0
Commute	12	0.00	Average Work Commute in Minutes	24	12	0.0
			% Commuting on Public Transportation	0.0%	8	0.0
Community Stability	10	21.95	% Living in Same House as in 1979	28.8%	9	26.0
			% Living in Same County as in 1985	67.1%	11	17.9

Composite: **Rank** 6 / 12 **Score** 53.20   **EL RENO**

CATEGORY	RANK	SCORE	STATISTIC	VALUE	RANK	SCORE
Economics	10	9.55	Median Household Income	$22,027	10	16.2
			% of Families Above Poverty Level	83.9%	11	2.9
Affordable Housing	3	85.90	Median Home Value	$38,300	1	100.0
			Median Rent	$337	3	71.8
Crime	4	71.80	Violent Crimes per 10,000 Population	33	5	67.6
			Property Crimes per 10,000 Population	456	3	76.0
Open Spaces	5	71.45	Population Density (Persons/Sq. Mile)	194	1	100.0
			Average Rooms per Housing Unit	5.2	7	42.9
Education	10	37.40	% High School Enrollment/Completion	89.5%	8	73.6
			% College Graduates	10.0%	11	1.2
Commute	6	42.85	Average Work Commute in Minutes	18	2	85.7
			% Commuting on Public Transportation	0.0%	8	0.0
Community Stability	7	53.45	% Living in Same House as in 1979	38.2%	6	61.0
			% Living in Same County as in 1985	74.0%	7	45.9

Metropolitan Area Suburb Rankings
OKLAHOMA CITY

Composite: **Rank** 7 / 12 **Score** 52.44   **DEL CITY**

CATEGORY	RANK	SCORE	STATISTIC	VALUE	RANK	SCORE
Economics	9	32.50	Median Household Income	$25,550	8	35.1
			% of Families Above Poverty Level	87.6%	9	29.9
Affordable Housing	4	69.25	Median Home Value	$42,800	4	88.8
			Median Rent	$377	6	49.7
Crime	7	53.25	Violent Crimes per 10,000 Population	34	6	64.9
			Property Crimes per 10,000 Population	611	9	41.6
Open Spaces	11	18.80	Population Density (Persons/Sq. Mile)	3174	10	23.3
			Average Rooms per Housing Unit	5.0	10	14.3
Education	11	31.70	% High School Enrollment/Completion	87.1%	11	63.4
			% College Graduates	9.6%	12	0.0
Commute	2	61.55	Average Work Commute in Minutes	17	1	100.0
			% Commuting on Public Transportation	0.3%	2	23.1
Community Stability	1	100.00	% Living in Same House as in 1979	48.7%	1	100.0
			% Living in Same County as in 1985	87.3%	1	100.0

Composite: **Rank** 8 / 12 **Score** 51.94   **THE VILLAGE**

CATEGORY	RANK	SCORE	STATISTIC	VALUE	RANK	SCORE
Economics	5	65.65	Median Household Income	$28,097	5	48.8
			% of Families Above Poverty Level	94.8%	3	82.5
Affordable Housing	8	44.35	Median Home Value	$49,900	6	71.0
			Median Rent	$435	9	17.7
Crime	10	24.70	Violent Crimes per 10,000 Population	44	9	37.8
			Property Crimes per 10,000 Population	746	11	11.6
Open Spaces	9	35.70	Population Density (Persons/Sq. Mile)	4079	12	0.0
			Average Rooms per Housing Unit	5.4	3	71.4
Education	3	73.20	% High School Enrollment/Completion	92.1%	4	84.7
			% College Graduates	30.5%	3	61.7
Commute	8	35.70	Average Work Commute in Minutes	19	5	71.4
			% Commuting on Public Transportation	0.0%	8	0.0
Community Stability	2	84.25	% Living in Same House as in 1979	43.3%	3	79.9
			% Living in Same County as in 1985	84.5%	2	88.6

Composite: **Rank** 9 / 12 **Score** 44.77   **MIDWEST CITY**

CATEGORY	RANK	SCORE	STATISTIC	VALUE	RANK	SCORE
Economics	7	49.30	Median Household Income	$27,042	7	43.1
			% of Families Above Poverty Level	91.1%	8	55.5
Affordable Housing	5	59.70	Median Home Value	$48,000	5	75.8
			Median Rent	$388	7	43.6
Crime	11	20.30	Violent Crimes per 10,000 Population	52	10	16.2
			Property Crimes per 10,000 Population	688	10	24.4
Open Spaces	10	32.20	Population Density (Persons/Sq. Mile)	2132	9	50.1
			Average Rooms per Housing Unit	5.0	10	14.3
Education	6	51.25	% High School Enrollment/Completion	91.3%	5	81.3
			% College Graduates	16.8%	6	21.2
Commute	8	35.70	Average Work Commute in Minutes	19	5	71.4
			% Commuting on Public Transportation	0.0%	8	0.0
Community Stability	5	64.95	% Living in Same House as in 1979	35.3%	7	50.2
			% Living in Same County as in 1985	82.3%	4	79.7

Metropolitan Area Suburb Rankings
OKLAHOMA CITY

Composite: *Rank* 10 / 12 *Score* 44.72 **GUTHRIE**

CATEGORY	RANK	SCORE	STATISTIC	VALUE	RANK	SCORE
Economics	11	7.65	Median Household Income	$20,491	11	8.0
			% of Families Above Poverty Level	84.5%	10	7.3
Affordable Housing	1	98.40	Median Home Value	$39,600	2	96.8
			Median Rent	$286	1	100.0
Crime	9	37.00	Violent Crimes per 10,000 Population	58	12	0.0
			Property Crimes per 10,000 Population	465	6	74.0
Open Spaces	4	74.25	Population Density (Persons/Sq. Mile)	529	3	91.4
			Average Rooms per Housing Unit	5.3	6	57.1
Education	12	4.15	% High School Enrollment/Completion	72.2%	12	0.0
			% College Graduates	12.4%	10	8.3
Commute	11	21.45	Average Work Commute in Minutes	21	10	42.9
			% Commuting on Public Transportation	0.0%	8	0.0
Community Stability	4	70.15	% Living in Same House as in 1979	43.6%	2	81.0
			% Living in Same County as in 1985	77.3%	5	59.3

Composite: *Rank* 11 / 12 *Score* 44.62 **SHAWNEE**

CATEGORY	RANK	SCORE	STATISTIC	VALUE	RANK	SCORE
Economics	12	0.00	Median Household Income	$19,002	12	0.0
			% of Families Above Poverty Level	83.5%	12	0.0
Affordable Housing	2	88.45	Median Home Value	$39,600	2	96.8
			Median Rent	$322	2	80.1
Crime	12	20.25	Violent Crimes per 10,000 Population	43	8	40.5
			Property Crimes per 10,000 Population	798	12	0.0
Open Spaces	7	58.80	Population Density (Persons/Sq. Mile)	623	5	89.0
			Average Rooms per Housing Unit	5.1	8	28.6
Education	9	39.25	% High School Enrollment/Completion	87.6%	10	65.5
			% College Graduates	14.0%	7	13.0
Commute	5	46.70	Average Work Commute in Minutes	18	2	85.7
			% Commuting on Public Transportation	0.1%	6	7.7
Community Stability	6	58.90	% Living in Same House as in 1979	38.5%	5	62.1
			% Living in Same County as in 1985	76.4%	6	55.7

Composite: *Rank* 12 / 12 *Score* 43.73 **MOORE**

CATEGORY	RANK	SCORE	STATISTIC	VALUE	RANK	SCORE
Economics	4	73.25	Median Household Income	$32,984	4	75.0
			% of Families Above Poverty Level	93.3%	6	71.5
Affordable Housing	9	35.15	Median Home Value	$50,600	7	69.2
			Median Rent	$465	11	1.1
Crime	8	38.90	Violent Crimes per 10,000 Population	57	11	2.7
			Property Crimes per 10,000 Population	460	5	75.1
Open Spaces	6	64.05	Population Density (Persons/Sq. Mile)	1876	8	56.7
			Average Rooms per Housing Unit	5.4	3	71.4
Education	7	44.45	% High School Enrollment/Completion	90.1%	7	76.2
			% College Graduates	13.9%	8	12.7
Commute	10	25.30	Average Work Commute in Minutes	21	10	42.9
			% Commuting on Public Transportation	0.1%	6	7.7
Community Stability	8	25.00	% Living in Same House as in 1979	29.8%	8	29.7
			% Living in Same County as in 1985	67.7%	10	20.3

Metropolitan Area Description
ORLANDO

STATE: Florida
COUNTIES: Orange, Osceola, Seminole

TOTAL POPULATION: 1,072,748

POPULATION IN SUBURBS: 908,055   (84.6%)

POPULATION IN Orlando: 164,693   (15.4%)

The ORLANDO metropolitan area is located in the central part of Florida.   The suburbs range geographically from Sanford in the north (24 miles from Orlando), to Ocoee in the west (11 miles from Orlando), to St. Cloud in the south (31 miles from Orlando), and to Goldenrod in the east (10 miles from Orlando).   The area is growing rapidly in population and had an increase of 53.3% between 1980 and 1990.   Summer time high temperatures average in the 90's and winter time lows average in the 40's.   Tourism is a major industry in the area.   The Tupperware Company is located in the suburb of Kissimmee.   In 1991, *Fortune* magazine rated the metropolitan area number eight for business.   Public transportation in the area is provided on buses by the Tri-County Transit System.

Conway is the overall highest rated suburb and also has the highest score in community stability.   The top scores in education and economics belong to **Wekiva Springs**.   **Sanford** is the suburb with the most affordable housing.   **Winter Springs** is rated the safest suburb with the lowest crime rate.   The top score in open spaces goes to **Oviedo**.   Finally, the number one rated commute belongs to **Oak Ridge**.

The highest ranked suburb overall which also has an affordable housing score of at least 50.00 is **Conway**.

The highest ranked suburb in the education category which also has an affordable housing score of at least 50.00 is **Oviedo**.

The county whose suburbs have the highest average overall score is **Orange County** (53.68).

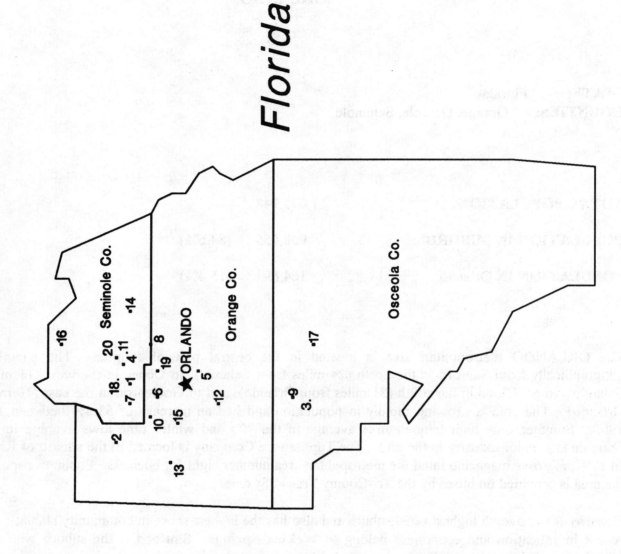

Metropolitan Area Map
ORLANDO

Florida

Metropolitan Area Suburb Alphabetical Index
ORLANDO

SUBURB	PAGE	MAP NO.	STATE	COUNTY	POPU-LATION	RANK
ALTAMONTE SPRINGS	571	1	Florida	Seminole	34,879	17 / 20
APOPKA	571	2	Florida	Orange	13,512	18 / 20
BUENA VENTURA LAKES	572	3	Florida	Osceola	14,148	19 / 20
CASSELBERRY	569	4	Florida	Seminole	18,911	12 / 20
CONWAY	566	5	Florida	Orange	13,159	1 / 20
FAIRVIEW SHORES	567	6	Florida	Orange	13,192	4 / 20
FOREST CITY	570	7	Florida	Seminole	10,638	14 / 20
GOLDENROD	569	8	Florida	Seminole	12,362	11 / 20
KISSIMMEE	572	9	Florida	Osceola	30,050	20 / 20
LOCKHART	570	10	Florida	Orange	11,636	15 / 20
LONGWOOD	567	11	Florida	Seminole	13,316	6 / 20
OAK RIDGE	570	12	Florida	Orange	15,388	13 / 20
OCOEE	568	13	Florida	Orange	12,778	8 / 20
OVIEDO	568	14	Florida	Seminole	11,114	9 / 20
PINE HILLS	569	15	Florida	Orange	35,322	10 / 20
SANFORD	571	16	Florida	Seminole	32,387	16 / 20
ST. CLOUD	568	17	Florida	Osceola	12,453	7 / 20
WEKIVA SPRINGS	567	18	Florida	Seminole	23,026	5 / 20
WINTER PARK	566	19	Florida	Orange	22,242	2 / 20
WINTER SPRINGS	566	20	Florida	Seminole	22,151	3 / 20

Composite: Rank 1 / 20 Score 66.18 — CONWAY

CATEGORY	RANK	SCORE	STATISTIC	VALUE	RANK	SCORE
Economics	5	56.10	Median Household Income	$40,207	4	44.3
			% of Families Above Poverty Level	95.1%	5	67.9
Affordable Housing	16	65.35	Median Home Value	$89,800	16	64.9
			Median Rent	$593	15	65.8
Crime	N/A	N/A	Violent Crimes per 10,000 Population	N/A	N/A	N/A
			Property Crimes per 10,000 Population	N/A	N/A	N/A
Open Spaces	7	55.10	Population Density (Persons/Sq. Mile)	3805	17	24.5
			Average Rooms per Housing Unit	6.3	2	85.7
Education	5	64.95	% High School Enrollment/Completion	93.3%	5	86.0
			% College Graduates	24.3%	7	43.9
Commute	4	58.45	Average Work Commute in Minutes	22	6	75.0
			% Commuting on Public Transportation	1.3%	5	41.9
Community Stability	1	97.15	% Living in Same House as in 1979	41.6%	1	100.0
			% Living in Same County as in 1985	76.6%	3	94.3

Composite: Rank 2 / 20 Score 63.29 — WINTER PARK

CATEGORY	RANK	SCORE	STATISTIC	VALUE	RANK	SCORE
Economics	7	44.85	Median Household Income	$37,080	5	35.9
			% of Families Above Poverty Level	93.6%	11	53.8
Affordable Housing	19	48.75	Median Home Value	$137,100	19	11.2
			Median Rent	$512	6	86.3
Crime	8	44.60	Violent Crimes per 10,000 Population	89	8	49.2
			Property Crimes per 10,000 Population	860	9	40.0
Open Spaces	11	46.15	Population Density (Persons/Sq. Mile)	3199	14	39.9
			Average Rooms per Housing Unit	5.6	7	52.4
Education	2	96.15	% High School Enrollment/Completion	94.7%	3	92.3
			% College Graduates	43.5%	1	100.0
Commute	3	77.40	Average Work Commute in Minutes	20	1	100.0
			% Commuting on Public Transportation	1.7%	4	54.8
Community Stability	3	85.15	% Living in Same House as in 1979	37.4%	2	89.0
			% Living in Same County as in 1985	71.3%	7	81.3

Composite: Rank 3 / 20 Score 61.85 — WINTER SPRINGS

CATEGORY	RANK	SCORE	STATISTIC	VALUE	RANK	SCORE
Economics	2	67.45	Median Household Income	$40,563	2	45.3
			% of Families Above Poverty Level	97.4%	3	89.6
Affordable Housing	17	59.60	Median Home Value	$96,400	18	57.4
			Median Rent	$609	17	61.8
Crime	1	100.00	Violent Crimes per 10,000 Population	24	1	100.0
			Property Crimes per 10,000 Population	348	1	100.0
Open Spaces	3	75.50	Population Density (Persons/Sq. Mile)	1633	4	79.6
			Average Rooms per Housing Unit	6.0	4	71.4
Education	4	72.15	% High School Enrollment/Completion	93.4%	4	86.4
			% College Graduates	29.1%	5	57.9
Commute	18	20.35	Average Work Commute in Minutes	25	15	37.5
			% Commuting on Public Transportation	0.1%	16	3.2
Community Stability	16	37.90	% Living in Same House as in 1979	14.7%	17	29.6
			% Living in Same County as in 1985	57.0%	14	46.2

Composite: *Rank* 4 / 20 *Score* 60.74 **FAIRVIEW SHORES**

CATEGORY	RANK	SCORE	STATISTIC	VALUE	RANK	SCORE
Economics	16	27.35	Median Household Income	$26,198	18	6.6
			% of Families Above Poverty Level	93.0%	14	48.1
Affordable Housing	4	89.40	Median Home Value	$71,100	7	86.1
			Median Rent	$487	4	92.7
Crime	N/A	N/A	Violent Crimes per 10,000 Population	N/A	N/A	N/A
			Property Crimes per 10,000 Population	N/A	N/A	N/A
Open Spaces	15	32.75	Population Density (Persons/Sq. Mile)	3317	15	36.9
			Average Rooms per Housing Unit	5.1	15	28.6
Education	9	43.55	% High School Enrollment/Completion	89.8%	6	70.1
			% College Graduates	15.1%	12	17.0
Commute	2	84.05	Average Work Commute in Minutes	21	2	87.5
			% Commuting on Public Transportation	2.5%	2	80.6
Community Stability	2	87.35	% Living in Same House as in 1979	34.0%	3	80.1
			% Living in Same County as in 1985	76.7%	2	94.6

Composite: *Rank* 5 / 20 *Score* 58.57 **WEKIVA SPRINGS**

CATEGORY	RANK	SCORE	STATISTIC	VALUE	RANK	SCORE
Economics	1	100.00	Median Household Income	$60,850	1	100.0
			% of Families Above Poverty Level	98.5%	1	100.0
Affordable Housing	20	0.00	Median Home Value	$147,000	20	0.0
			Median Rent	$853	20	0.0
Crime	N/A	N/A	Violent Crimes per 10,000 Population	N/A	N/A	N/A
			Property Crimes per 10,000 Population	N/A	N/A	N/A
Open Spaces	2	76.75	Population Density (Persons/Sq. Mile)	2660	11	53.5
			Average Rooms per Housing Unit	6.6	1	100.0
Education	1	99.40	% High School Enrollment/Completion	96.4%	1	100.0
			% College Graduates	43.1%	2	98.8
Commute	16	22.00	Average Work Commute in Minutes	25	15	37.5
			% Commuting on Public Transportation	0.2%	14	6.5
Community Stability	11	53.25	% Living in Same House as in 1979	22.1%	12	49.0
			% Living in Same County as in 1985	61.6%	12	57.5

Composite: *Rank* 6 / 20 *Score* 55.36 **LONGWOOD**

CATEGORY	RANK	SCORE	STATISTIC	VALUE	RANK	SCORE
Economics	3	59.05	Median Household Income	$35,374	6	31.3
			% of Families Above Poverty Level	97.1%	4	86.8
Affordable Housing	18	58.60	Median Home Value	$85,200	14	70.1
			Median Rent	$667	19	47.1
Crime	2	73.50	Violent Crimes per 10,000 Population	48	3	81.2
			Property Crimes per 10,000 Population	640	4	65.8
Open Spaces	5	61.65	Population Density (Persons/Sq. Mile)	2539	9	56.6
			Average Rooms per Housing Unit	5.9	5	66.7
Education	10	42.75	% High School Enrollment/Completion	85.7%	11	51.6
			% College Graduates	20.9%	8	33.9
Commute	14	31.25	Average Work Commute in Minutes	23	8	62.5
			% Commuting on Public Transportation	0.0%	18	0.0
Community Stability	9	60.75	% Living in Same House as in 1979	26.8%	7	61.3
			% Living in Same County as in 1985	62.7%	10	60.2

Composite: *Rank* 7 / 20 *Score* 53.59 — ST. CLOUD

CATEGORY	RANK	SCORE	STATISTIC	VALUE	RANK	SCORE
Economics	13	32.10	Median Household Income	$23,766	20	0.0
			% of Families Above Poverty Level	94.7%	7	64.2
Affordable Housing	2	94.95	Median Home Value	$63,200	2	95.0
			Median Rent	$478	2	94.9
Crime	5	65.25	Violent Crimes per 10,000 Population	46	2	82.8
			Property Crimes per 10,000 Population	795	7	47.7
Open Spaces	9	49.05	Population Density (Persons/Sq. Mile)	1652	5	79.1
			Average Rooms per Housing Unit	4.9	16	19.0
Education	15	22.40	% High School Enrollment/Completion	83.1%	13	39.8
			% College Graduates	11.0%	18	5.0
Commute	10	43.75	Average Work Commute in Minutes	21	2	87.5
			% Commuting on Public Transportation	0.0%	18	0.0
Community Stability	7	67.65	% Living in Same House as in 1979	25.7%	11	58.4
			% Living in Same County as in 1985	69.5%	8	76.9

Composite: *Rank* 8 / 20 *Score* 53.42 — OCOEE

CATEGORY	RANK	SCORE	STATISTIC	VALUE	RANK	SCORE
Economics	8	43.20	Median Household Income	$32,014	9	22.2
			% of Families Above Poverty Level	94.7%	7	64.2
Affordable Housing	8	84.40	Median Home Value	$64,200	3	93.9
			Median Rent	$557	13	74.9
Crime	3	73.35	Violent Crimes per 10,000 Population	66	5	67.2
			Property Crimes per 10,000 Population	523	3	79.5
Open Spaces	4	71.10	Population Density (Persons/Sq. Mile)	1416	2	85.1
			Average Rooms per Housing Unit	5.7	6	57.1
Education	20	0.45	% High School Enrollment/Completion	74.3%	20	0.0
			% College Graduates	9.6%	19	0.9
Commute	16	22.00	Average Work Commute in Minutes	25	15	37.5
			% Commuting on Public Transportation	0.2%	14	6.5
Community Stability	4	79.45	% Living in Same House as in 1979	25.9%	10	58.9
			% Living in Same County as in 1985	78.9%	1	100.0

Composite: *Rank* 9 / 20 *Score* 53.34 — OVIEDO

CATEGORY	RANK	SCORE	STATISTIC	VALUE	RANK	SCORE
Economics	6	49.10	Median Household Income	$40,221	3	44.4
			% of Families Above Poverty Level	93.6%	11	53.8
Affordable Housing	15	67.00	Median Home Value	$92,000	17	62.4
			Median Rent	$570	14	71.6
Crime	4	71.05	Violent Crimes per 10,000 Population	77	7	58.6
			Property Crimes per 10,000 Population	489	2	83.5
Open Spaces	1	88.10	Population Density (Persons/Sq. Mile)	830	1	100.0
			Average Rooms per Housing Unit	6.1	3	76.2
Education	3	84.80	% High School Enrollment/Completion	95.3%	2	95.0
			% College Graduates	34.8%	3	74.6
Commute	20	0.00	Average Work Commute in Minutes	28	20	0.0
			% Commuting on Public Transportation	0.0%	18	0.0
Community Stability	19	13.35	% Living in Same House as in 1979	13.6%	18	26.7
			% Living in Same County as in 1985	38.2%	20	0.0

Metropolitan Area Suburb Rankings
ORLANDO

Composite: **Rank** 10 / 20 **Score** 51.12   **PINE HILLS**

CATEGORY	RANK	SCORE	STATISTIC	VALUE	RANK	SCORE
Economics	12	33.10	Median Household Income	$30,121	13	17.1
			% of Families Above Poverty Level	93.1%	13	49.1
Affordable Housing	5	86.95	Median Home Value	$68,200	6	89.3
			Median Rent	$519	7	84.6
Crime	N/A	N/A	Violent Crimes per 10,000 Population	N/A	N/A	N/A
			Property Crimes per 10,000 Population	N/A	N/A	N/A
Open Spaces	17	24.05	Population Density (Persons/Sq. Mile)	4566	19	5.2
			Average Rooms per Housing Unit	5.4	8	42.9
Education	11	34.20	% High School Enrollment/Completion	87.1%	9	57.9
			% College Graduates	12.9%	14	10.5
Commute	5	51.00	Average Work Commute in Minutes	25	15	37.5
			% Commuting on Public Transportation	2.0%	3	64.5
Community Stability	5	77.45	% Living in Same House as in 1979	30.5%	4	70.9
			% Living in Same County as in 1985	72.4%	5	84.0

Composite: **Rank** 11 / 20 **Score** 50.64   **GOLDENROD**

CATEGORY	RANK	SCORE	STATISTIC	VALUE	RANK	SCORE
Economics	4	58.25	Median Household Income	$33,026	8	25.0
			% of Families Above Poverty Level	97.6%	2	91.5
Affordable Housing	11	77.30	Median Home Value	$84,800	13	70.5
			Median Rent	$521	8	84.1
Crime	N/A	N/A	Violent Crimes per 10,000 Population	N/A	N/A	N/A
			Property Crimes per 10,000 Population	N/A	N/A	N/A
Open Spaces	18	19.05	Population Density (Persons/Sq. Mile)	4769	20	0.0
			Average Rooms per Housing Unit	5.3	10	38.1
Education	6	55.00	% High School Enrollment/Completion	88.0%	7	62.0
			% College Graduates	25.7%	6	48.0
Commute	11	42.55	Average Work Commute in Minutes	23	8	62.5
			% Commuting on Public Transportation	0.7%	8	22.6
Community Stability	13	51.70	% Living in Same House as in 1979	26.0%	9	59.2
			% Living in Same County as in 1985	56.2%	15	44.2

Composite: **Rank** 12 / 20 **Score** 48.66   **CASSELBERRY**

CATEGORY	RANK	SCORE	STATISTIC	VALUE	RANK	SCORE
Economics	9	42.60	Median Household Income	$31,231	11	20.1
			% of Families Above Poverty Level	94.8%	6	65.1
Affordable Housing	10	79.50	Median Home Value	$75,100	10	81.5
			Median Rent	$547	11	77.5
Crime	7	57.20	Violent Crimes per 10,000 Population	75	6	60.2
			Property Crimes per 10,000 Population	739	5	54.2
Open Spaces	14	40.05	Population Density (Persons/Sq. Mile)	3114	13	42.0
			Average Rooms per Housing Unit	5.3	10	38.1
Education	12	31.10	% High School Enrollment/Completion	82.8%	14	38.5
			% College Graduates	17.4%	11	23.7
Commute	13	31.45	Average Work Commute in Minutes	24	13	50.0
			% Commuting on Public Transportation	0.4%	11	12.9
Community Stability	10	58.70	% Living in Same House as in 1979	26.2%	8	59.7
			% Living in Same County as in 1985	61.7%	11	57.7

Metropolitan Area Suburb Rankings
ORLANDO

Composite: Rank 13 / 20 *Score* 48.36   **OAK RIDGE**

CATEGORY	RANK	SCORE	STATISTIC	VALUE	RANK	SCORE
Economics	15	27.85	Median Household Income	$28,672	16	13.2
			% of Families Above Poverty Level	92.4%	15	42.5
Affordable Housing	6	86.40	Median Home Value	$67,200	5	90.5
			Median Rent	$528	9	82.3
Crime	N/A	N/A	Violent Crimes per 10,000 Population	N/A	N/A	N/A
			Property Crimes per 10,000 Population	N/A	N/A	N/A
Open Spaces	19	17.30	Population Density (Persons/Sq. Mile)	3406	16	34.6
			Average Rooms per Housing Unit	4.5	20	0.0
Education	16	20.85	% High School Enrollment/Completion	81.4%	15	32.1
			% College Graduates	12.6%	15	9.6
Commute	1	93.75	Average Work Commute in Minutes	21	2	87.5
			% Commuting on Public Transportation	3.1%	1	100.0
Community Stability	15	44.00	% Living in Same House as in 1979	17.3%	14	36.4
			% Living in Same County as in 1985	59.2%	13	51.6

Composite: Rank 14 / 20 *Score* 47.42   **FOREST CITY**

CATEGORY	RANK	SCORE	STATISTIC	VALUE	RANK	SCORE
Economics	10	42.65	Median Household Income	$35,117	7	30.6
			% of Families Above Poverty Level	93.7%	10	54.7
Affordable Housing	13	69.50	Median Home Value	$82,400	12	73.2
			Median Rent	$593	15	65.8
Crime	N/A	N/A	Violent Crimes per 10,000 Population	N/A	N/A	N/A
			Property Crimes per 10,000 Population	N/A	N/A	N/A
Open Spaces	8	50.55	Population Density (Persons/Sq. Mile)	2476	8	58.2
			Average Rooms per Housing Unit	5.4	8	42.9
Education	8	44.90	% High School Enrollment/Completion	87.3%	8	58.8
			% College Graduates	19.9%	9	31.0
Commute	15	26.60	Average Work Commute in Minutes	24	13	50.0
			% Commuting on Public Transportation	0.1%	16	3.2
Community Stability	14	50.30	% Living in Same House as in 1979	27.2%	6	62.3
			% Living in Same County as in 1985	53.8%	16	38.3

Composite: Rank 15 / 20 *Score* 46.12   **LOCKHART**

CATEGORY	RANK	SCORE	STATISTIC	VALUE	RANK	SCORE
Economics	19	13.45	Median Household Income	$29,559	15	15.6
			% of Families Above Poverty Level	89.1%	19	11.3
Affordable Housing	3	91.10	Median Home Value	$67,100	4	90.6
			Median Rent	$491	5	91.6
Crime	N/A	N/A	Violent Crimes per 10,000 Population	N/A	N/A	N/A
			Property Crimes per 10,000 Population	N/A	N/A	N/A
Open Spaces	13	43.30	Population Density (Persons/Sq. Mile)	2669	12	53.3
			Average Rooms per Housing Unit	5.2	12	33.3
Education	18	18.95	% High School Enrollment/Completion	80.8%	17	29.4
			% College Graduates	12.2%	16	8.5
Commute	8	45.75	Average Work Commute in Minutes	23	8	62.5
			% Commuting on Public Transportation	0.9%	6	29.0
Community Stability	8	64.15	% Living in Same House as in 1979	20.2%	13	44.0
			% Living in Same County as in 1985	72.5%	4	84.3

Metropolitan Area Suburb Rankings
ORLANDO

Composite: *Rank* 16 / 20 *Score* 45.10   **SANFORD**

CATEGORY	RANK	SCORE	STATISTIC	VALUE	RANK	SCORE
Economics	20	1.70	Median Household Income	$25,029	19	3.4
			% of Families Above Poverty Level	87.9%	20	0.0
Affordable Housing	1	100.00	Median Home Value	$58,800	1	100.0
			Median Rent	$458	1	100.0
Crime	9	29.60	Violent Crimes per 10,000 Population	130	9	17.2
			Property Crimes per 10,000 Population	843	8	42.0
Open Spaces	10	46.30	Population Density (Persons/Sq. Mile)	1871	6	73.6
			Average Rooms per Housing Unit	4.9	16	19.0
Education	17	19.65	% High School Enrollment/Completion	81.3%	16	31.7
			% College Graduates	11.9%	17	7.6
Commute	9	44.15	Average Work Commute in Minutes	23	8	62.5
			% Commuting on Public Transportation	0.8%	7	25.8
Community Stability	6	74.30	% Living in Same House as in 1979	28.8%	5	66.5
			% Living in Same County as in 1985	71.6%	6	82.1

Composite: *Rank* 17 / 20 *Score* 43.96   **ALTAMONTE SPRINGS**

CATEGORY	RANK	SCORE	STATISTIC	VALUE	RANK	SCORE
Economics	11	42.10	Median Household Income	$31,538	10	21.0
			% of Families Above Poverty Level	94.6%	9	63.2
Affordable Housing	12	70.55	Median Home Value	$89,500	15	65.2
			Median Rent	$553	12	75.9
Crime	6	60.35	Violent Crimes per 10,000 Population	61	4	71.1
			Property Crimes per 10,000 Population	778	6	49.6
Open Spaces	20	13.35	Population Density (Persons/Sq. Mile)	4093	18	17.2
			Average Rooms per Housing Unit	4.7	18	9.5
Education	7	51.75	% High School Enrollment/Completion	83.8%	12	43.0
			% College Graduates	30.0%	4	60.5
Commute	7	47.20	Average Work Commute in Minutes	22	6	75.0
			% Commuting on Public Transportation	0.6%	9	19.4
Community Stability	18	22.40	% Living in Same House as in 1979	13.0%	19	25.1
			% Living in Same County as in 1985	46.2%	18	19.7

Composite: *Rank* 18 / 20 *Score* 40.24   **APOPKA**

CATEGORY	RANK	SCORE	STATISTIC	VALUE	RANK	SCORE
Economics	17	26.30	Median Household Income	$30,662	12	18.6
			% of Families Above Poverty Level	91.5%	17	34.0
Affordable Housing	7	85.45	Median Home Value	$78,900	11	77.2
			Median Rent	$483	3	93.7
Crime	10	13.10	Violent Crimes per 10,000 Population	152	11	0.0
			Property Crimes per 10,000 Population	978	10	26.2
Open Spaces	6	58.35	Population Density (Persons/Sq. Mile)	1482	3	83.4
			Average Rooms per Housing Unit	5.2	12	33.3
Education	14	26.50	% High School Enrollment/Completion	80.0%	18	25.8
			% College Graduates	18.6%	10	27.2
Commute	19	18.95	Average Work Commute in Minutes	26	19	25.0
			% Commuting on Public Transportation	0.4%	11	12.9
Community Stability	12	53.05	% Living in Same House as in 1979	17.2%	15	36.1
			% Living in Same County as in 1985	66.7%	9	70.0

Metropolitan Area Suburb Rankings
ORLANDO

Composite: **Rank** 19 / 20 **Score** 35.98   **BUENA VENTURA LAKES**

CATEGORY	RANK	SCORE	STATISTIC	VALUE	RANK	SCORE
Economics	14	29.40	Median Household Income	$29,818	14	16.3
			% of Families Above Poverty Level	92.4%	15	42.5
Affordable Housing	14	68.55	Median Home Value	$71,600	8	85.5
			Median Rent	$649	18	51.6
Crime	N/A	N/A	Violent Crimes per 10,000 Population	N/A	N/A	N/A
			Property Crimes per 10,000 Population	N/A	N/A	N/A
Open Spaces	12	44.35	Population Density (Persons/Sq. Mile)	2588	10	55.4
			Average Rooms per Housing Unit	5.2	12	33.3
Education	13	26.90	% High School Enrollment/Completion	86.2%	10	53.8
			% College Graduates	9.3%	20	0.0
Commute	12	40.95	Average Work Commute in Minutes	23	8	62.5
			% Commuting on Public Transportation	0.6%	9	19.4
Community Stability	20	5.75	% Living in Same House as in 1979	3.4%	20	0.0
			% Living in Same County as in 1985	42.9%	19	11.5

Composite: **Rank** 20 / 20 **Score** 33.96   **KISSIMMEE**

CATEGORY	RANK	SCORE	STATISTIC	VALUE	RANK	SCORE
Economics	18	18.85	Median Household Income	$27,591	17	10.3
			% of Families Above Poverty Level	90.8%	18	27.4
Affordable Housing	9	82.30	Median Home Value	$73,700	9	83.1
			Median Rent	$531	10	81.5
Crime	11	8.60	Violent Crimes per 10,000 Population	130	9	17.2
			Property Crimes per 10,000 Population	1,202	11	0.0
Open Spaces	16	32.20	Population Density (Persons/Sq. Mile)	2421	7	59.6
			Average Rooms per Housing Unit	4.6	19	4.8
Education	19	16.65	% High School Enrollment/Completion	79.0%	19	21.3
			% College Graduates	13.4%	13	12.0
Commute	6	50.20	Average Work Commute in Minutes	21	2	87.5
			% Commuting on Public Transportation	0.4%	11	12.9
Community Stability	17	28.90	% Living in Same House as in 1979	15.8%	16	32.5
			% Living in Same County as in 1985	48.5%	17	25.3

Metropolitan Area Description
PHILADELPHIA-WILMINGTON-TRENTON

STATE: Delaware
COUNTIES: New Castle

STATE: Maryland
COUNTIES: Cecil

STATE: New Jersey
COUNTIES: Burlington, Camden, Cumberland, Gloucester, Mercer, Salem

STATE: Pennsylvania
COUNTIES: Bucks, Chester, Delaware, Montgomery, Philadelphia

TOTAL POPULATION: 5,899,345

POPULATION IN SUBURBS: 4,153,564 (70.4%)

POPULATION IN Philadelphia (PA): 1,585,577 (26.9%)
POPULATION IN Wilmington (DE): 71,529 (1.2%)
POPULATION IN Trenton (NJ): 88,675 (1.5%)

The PHILADELPHIA-WILMINGTON-TRENTON metropolitan area is located in the southeastern part of Pennsylvania, the northwestern part of Delaware, the southwestern part of New Jersey, and the northeastern part of Maryland. The suburbs range geographically from Lansdale (PA) in the north (24 miles from Philadelphia), to Coatesville (PA) in the west (36 miles from Philadelphia), to Bridgeton (NJ) in the south (56 miles from Philadelphia), and to Brown Mills (NJ) in the east (41 miles from Philadelphia). The area is growing in population and had an increase of 3.9% between 1980 and 1990. Summer time high temperatures average in the 80's and winter time lows average in the 20's. Many high tech companies are located in the area. Public transportation in the area is provided on buses, trains, trolleys, and subways.

Haddonfield (NJ) is the overall highest rated suburb and also has the highest score in economics. The top score in education belongs to **Princeton** (NJ). **Chester** (PA) is the suburb with the most affordable housing. **Nether Providence Township** (PA) is rated the safest suburb with the lowest crime rate. **Cinnaminson** (NJ) has the number one rating in open spaces. The top rated commute belongs to **Camden** (NJ). Finally, the highest score in community stability goes to **Springfield** (PA).

The highest ranked suburb overall which also has an affordable housing score of at least 50.00 is **Cherry Hill** (NJ).

The highest ranked suburb in the education category which also has an affordable housing score of at least 50.00 is **Newark** (DE).

The county whose suburbs have the highest average overall score is **Mercer County** (NJ) (62.87).

573

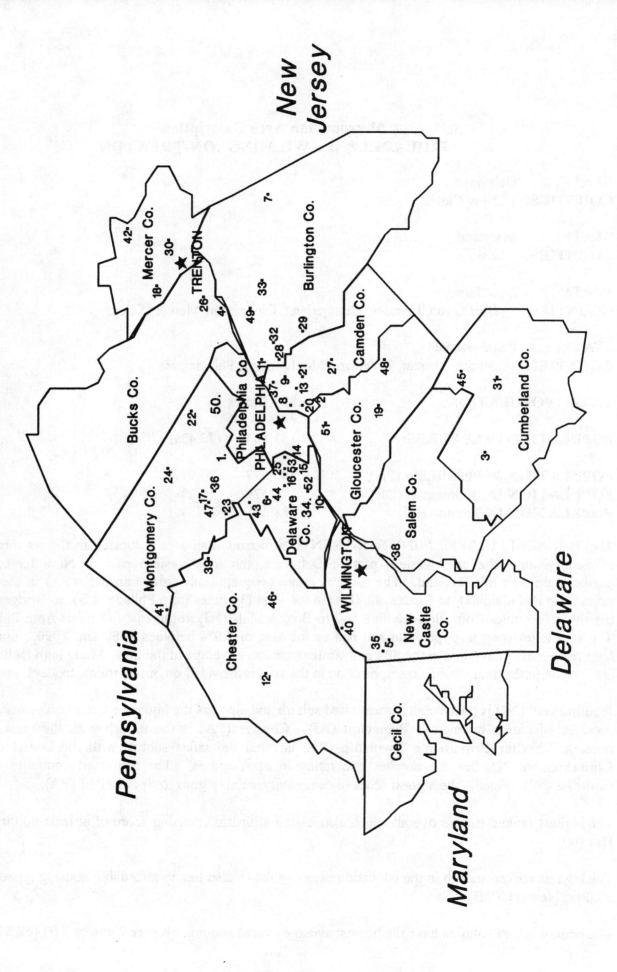

Metropolitan Area Map
PHILADELPHIA–WILMINGTON–TRENTON

Metropolitan Area Suburb Alphabetical Index
PHILADELPHIA-WILMINGTON-TRENTON

SUBURB	PAGE	MAP NO.	STATE	COUNTY	POPU-LATION	RANK
ARDMORE	582	1	Pennsylvania	Montgomery	12,646	18 / 53
BELLMAWR	580	2	New Jersey	Camden	12,603	11 / 53
BRIDGETON	592	3	New Jersey	Cumberland	18,942	48 / 53
BRISTOL	590	4	Pennsylvania	Bucks	10,405	41 / 53
BROOKSIDE	585	5	Delaware	New Castle	15,307	25 / 53
BROOMALL	583	6	Pennsylvania	Delaware	10,930	20 / 53
BROWN MILLS	593	7	New Jersey	Burlington	11,429	51 / 53
CAMDEN	594	8	New Jersey	Camden	87,492	53 / 53
CHERRY HILL	578	9	New Jersey	Camden	69,319	5 / 53
CHESTER	594	10	Pennsylvania	Delaware	41,856	52 / 53
CINNAMINSON	577	11	New Jersey	Burlington	14,583	2 / 53
COATESVILLE	591	12	Pennsylvania	Chester	11,038	45 / 53
COLLINGSWOOD	584	13	New Jersey	Camden	15,289	23 / 53
DARBY	589	14	Pennsylvania	Delaware	11,140	37 / 53
DARBY TOWNSHIP	582	15	Pennsylvania	Delaware	10,955	16 / 53
DREXEL HILL	587	16	Pennsylvania	Delaware	29,744	32 / 53
EAST NORRITON	579	17	Pennsylvania	Montgomery	13,324	7 / 53
EWING	580	18	New Jersey	Mercer	34,185	10 / 53
GLASSBORO	587	19	New Jersey	Gloucester	15,614	33 / 53
GLOUCESTER CITY	586	20	New Jersey	Camden	12,649	29 / 53
HADDONFIELD	577	21	New Jersey	Camden	11,628	1 / 53
HORSHAM	581	22	Pennsylvania	Montgomery	15,051	15 / 53
KING OF PRUSSIA	584	23	Pennsylvania	Montgomery	18,406	24 / 53
LANSDALE	588	24	Pennsylvania	Montgomery	16,362	36 / 53
LANSDOWNE	583	25	Pennsylvania	Delaware	11,712	21 / 53
LEVITTOWN	582	26	Pennsylvania	Bucks	55,362	17 / 53
LINDENWOLD	593	27	New Jersey	Camden	18,734	50 / 53
MAPLE SHADE	589	28	New Jersey	Burlington	19,211	39 / 53
MARLTON	587	29	New Jersey	Burlington	10,228	31 / 53
MERCERVILLE-HAMILTON SQUARE	580	30	New Jersey	Mercer	26,873	12 / 53
MILLVILLE	584	31	New Jersey	Cumberland	25,992	22 / 53
MOORESTOWN-LENOLA	579	32	New Jersey	Burlington	13,242	9 / 53
MOUNT HOLLY	593	33	New Jersey	Burlington	10,639	49 / 53
NETHER PROVIDENCE TOWNSHIP	577	34	Pennsylvania	Delaware	13,229	3 / 53
NEWARK	581	35	Delaware	New Castle	25,098	14 / 53
NORRISTOWN	591	36	Pennsylvania	Montgomery	30,749	43 / 53
PENNSAUKEN	581	37	New Jersey	Camden	34,733	13 / 53
PENNSVILLE	579	38	New Jersey	Salem	12,218	8 / 53
PHOENIXVILLE	590	39	Pennsylvania	Chester	15,066	42 / 53
PIKE CREEK	589	40	Delaware	New Castle	10,163	38 / 53
POTTSTOWN	591	41	Pennsylvania	Montgomery	21,831	44 / 53
PRINCETON	588	42	New Jersey	Mercer	12,016	34 / 53
RADNOR TOWNSHIP	578	43	Pennsylvania	Delaware	28,705	6 / 53
SPRINGFIELD	578	44	Pennsylvania	Delaware	24,160	4 / 53
VINELAND	590	45	New Jersey	Cumberland	54,780	40 / 53
WEST CHESTER	592	46	Pennsylvania	Chester	18,041	47 / 53
WEST NORRITON	588	47	Pennsylvania	Montgomery	15,209	35 / 53
WILLIAMSTOWN	592	48	New Jersey	Gloucester	10,891	46 / 53
WILLINGBORO	586	49	New Jersey	Burlington	36,291	30 / 53
WILLOW GROVE	585	50	Pennsylvania	Montgomery	16,325	26 / 53
WOODBURY	586	51	New Jersey	Gloucester	10,904	28 / 53

SUBURB	PAGE	MAP NO.	STATE	COUNTY	POPU-LATION	RANK
WOODLYN	585	52	Pennsylvania	Delaware	10,151	27 / 53
YEADON	583	53	Pennsylvania	Delaware	11,980	19 / 53

Metropolitan Area Suburb Rankings
PHILADELPHIA-WILMINGTON-TRENTON

Composite: Rank 1 / 53 *Score* 75.36   **HADDONFIELD** (NJ)

CATEGORY	RANK	SCORE	STATISTIC	VALUE	RANK	SCORE
Economics	1	98.50	Median Household Income	$56,585	1	100.0
			% of Families Above Poverty Level	98.3%	12	97.0
Affordable Housing	50	44.15	Median Home Value	$185,600	51	37.4
			Median Rent	$645	41	50.9
Crime	10	91.45	Violent Crimes per 10,000 Population	11	4	98.7
			Property Crimes per 10,000 Population	324	13	84.2
Open Spaces	6	77.35	Population Density (Persons/Sq. Mile)	4112	27	73.2
			Average Rooms per Housing Unit	6.8	3	81.5
Education	5	78.10	% High School Enrollment/Completion	94.2%	24	73.6
			% College Graduates	55.6%	3	82.6
Commute	5	59.15	Average Work Commute in Minutes	22	22	62.5
			% Commuting on Public Transportation	13.9%	9	55.8
Community Stability	13	78.80	% Living in Same House as in 1979	51.6%	9	72.8
			% Living in Same County as in 1985	85.7%	22	84.8

Composite: Rank 2 / 53 *Score* 74.14   **CINNAMINSON** (NJ)

CATEGORY	RANK	SCORE	STATISTIC	VALUE	RANK	SCORE
Economics	6	91.10	Median Household Income	$51,129	5	86.1
			% of Families Above Poverty Level	98.0%	16	96.1
Affordable Housing	46	47.65	Median Home Value	$145,100	44	53.8
			Median Rent	$694	50	41.5
Crime	11	91.35	Violent Crimes per 10,000 Population	20	9	96.8
			Property Crimes per 10,000 Population	305	10	85.9
Open Spaces	1	95.00	Population Density (Persons/Sq. Mile)	1918	7	90.0
			Average Rooms per Housing Unit	7.3	1	100.0
Education	14	60.30	% High School Enrollment/Completion	96.6%	8	84.5
			% College Graduates	27.9%	16	36.1
Commute	33	39.10	Average Work Commute in Minutes	21	17	68.8
			% Commuting on Public Transportation	3.1%	34	9.4
Community Stability	4	94.50	% Living in Same House as in 1979	64.0%	1	100.0
			% Living in Same County as in 1985	87.9%	14	89.0

Composite: Rank 3 / 53 *Score* 73.21   **NETHER PROVIDENCE TOWNSHIP** (PA)

CATEGORY	RANK	SCORE	STATISTIC	VALUE	RANK	SCORE
Economics	3	93.80	Median Household Income	$52,780	3	90.3
			% of Families Above Poverty Level	98.4%	10	97.3
Affordable Housing	48	45.80	Median Home Value	$167,800	49	44.6
			Median Rent	$665	45	47.0
Crime	1	99.45	Violent Crimes per 10,000 Population	10	3	98.9
			Property Crimes per 10,000 Population	149	1	100.0
Open Spaces	4	80.50	Population Density (Persons/Sq. Mile)	2806	15	83.2
			Average Rooms per Housing Unit	6.7	5	77.8
Education	4	80.05	% High School Enrollment/Completion	99.5%	4	97.7
			% College Graduates	43.6%	7	62.4
Commute	38	36.05	Average Work Commute in Minutes	25	42	43.8
			% Commuting on Public Transportation	7.5%	15	28.3
Community Stability	14	76.85	% Living in Same House as in 1979	48.7%	16	66.4
			% Living in Same County as in 1985	87.0%	15	87.3

Metropolitan Area Suburb Rankings
PHILADELPHIA-WILMINGTON-TRENTON

Composite: Rank 4 / 53 *Score* 71.76   **SPRINGFIELD (PA)**

CATEGORY	RANK	SCORE	STATISTIC	VALUE	RANK	SCORE
Economics	8	90.25	Median Household Income	$49,541	8	82.0
			% of Families Above Poverty Level	98.8%	4	98.5
Affordable Housing	47	47.55	Median Home Value	$151,200	47	51.3
			Median Rent	$682	47	43.8
Crime	5	95.40	Violent Crimes per 10,000 Population	13	6	98.3
			Property Crimes per 10,000 Population	232	7	92.5
Open Spaces	5	80.40	Population Density (Persons/Sq. Mile)	3797	25	75.6
			Average Rooms per Housing Unit	6.9	2	85.2
Education	15	56.95	% High School Enrollment/Completion	94.3%	21	74.1
			% College Graduates	30.1%	13	39.8
Commute	43	33.85	Average Work Commute in Minutes	27	47	31.2
			% Commuting on Public Transportation	9.4%	14	36.5
Community Stability	1	97.95	% Living in Same House as in 1979	63.1%	2	98.0
			% Living in Same County as in 1985	92.6%	4	97.9

Composite: Rank 5 / 53 *Score* 69.99   **CHERRY HILL (NJ)**

CATEGORY	RANK	SCORE	STATISTIC	VALUE	RANK	SCORE
Economics	2	96.10	Median Household Income	$54,455	2	94.6
			% of Families Above Poverty Level	98.5%	8	97.6
Affordable Housing	41	53.20	Median Home Value	$149,300	45	52.1
			Median Rent	$627	39	54.3
Crime	19	78.50	Violent Crimes per 10,000 Population	23	11	96.2
			Property Crimes per 10,000 Population	584	24	60.8
Open Spaces	3	82.15	Population Density (Persons/Sq. Mile)	2859	16	82.8
			Average Rooms per Housing Unit	6.8	3	81.5
Education	10	66.45	% High School Enrollment/Completion	94.5%	20	75.0
			% College Graduates	40.9%	9	57.9
Commute	29	41.60	Average Work Commute in Minutes	23	34	56.2
			% Commuting on Public Transportation	7.2%	16	27.0
Community Stability	22	71.95	% Living in Same House as in 1979	49.5%	13	68.2
			% Living in Same County as in 1985	80.9%	36	75.7

Composite: Rank 6 / 53 *Score* 67.82   **RADNOR TOWNSHIP (PA)**

CATEGORY	RANK	SCORE	STATISTIC	VALUE	RANK	SCORE
Economics	5	91.20	Median Household Income	$51,695	4	87.5
			% of Families Above Poverty Level	97.6%	21	94.9
Affordable Housing	52	19.15	Median Home Value	$266,400	52	4.7
			Median Rent	$735	51	33.6
Crime	2	97.55	Violent Crimes per 10,000 Population	12	5	98.5
			Property Crimes per 10,000 Population	187	3	96.6
Open Spaces	7	75.85	Population Density (Persons/Sq. Mile)	2084	8	88.7
			Average Rooms per Housing Unit	6.3	10	63.0
Education	2	93.00	% High School Enrollment/Completion	99.8%	2	99.1
			% College Graduates	58.2%	2	86.9
Commute	7	57.70	Average Work Commute in Minutes	23	34	56.2
			% Commuting on Public Transportation	14.7%	7	59.2
Community Stability	48	40.30	% Living in Same House as in 1979	37.3%	43	41.4
			% Living in Same County as in 1985	61.7%	51	39.2

Metropolitan Area Suburb Rankings
PHILADELPHIA-WILMINGTON-TRENTON

Composite: *Rank* 7 / 53 *Score* 67.59   **EAST NORRITON (PA)**

CATEGORY	RANK	SCORE	STATISTIC	VALUE	RANK	SCORE
Economics	9	87.80	Median Household Income	$47,026	10	75.6
			% of Families Above Poverty Level	99.3%	1	100.0
Affordable Housing	45	48.35	Median Home Value	$144,500	43	54.1
			Median Rent	$688	49	42.6
Crime	9	91.85	Violent Crimes per 10,000 Population	13	6	98.3
			Property Crimes per 10,000 Population	311	12	85.4
Open Spaces	8	75.45	Population Density (Persons/Sq. Mile)	2194	11	87.9
			Average Rooms per Housing Unit	6.3	10	63.0
Education	9	67.45	% High School Enrollment/Completion	100.0%	1	100.0
			% College Graduates	27.2%	18	34.9
Commute	45	32.30	Average Work Commute in Minutes	22	22	62.5
			% Commuting on Public Transportation	1.4%	50	2.1
Community Stability	26	69.90	% Living in Same House as in 1979	44.8%	24	57.9
			% Living in Same County as in 1985	84.2%	25	81.9

Composite: *Rank* 8 / 53 *Score* 67.47   **PENNSVILLE (NJ)**

CATEGORY	RANK	SCORE	STATISTIC	VALUE	RANK	SCORE
Economics	26	70.50	Median Household Income	$37,823	25	52.1
			% of Families Above Poverty Level	95.6%	33	88.9
Affordable Housing	18	77.40	Median Home Value	$87,200	15	77.3
			Median Rent	$506	17	77.5
Crime	8	92.80	Violent Crimes per 10,000 Population	5	1	100.0
			Property Crimes per 10,000 Population	309	11	85.6
Open Spaces	12	68.00	Population Density (Persons/Sq. Mile)	1232	3	95.3
			Average Rooms per Housing Unit	5.7	27	40.7
Education	30	43.00	% High School Enrollment/Completion	95.6%	11	80.0
			% College Graduates	10.0%	42	6.0
Commute	36	38.35	Average Work Commute in Minutes	20	11	75.0
			% Commuting on Public Transportation	1.3%	51	1.7
Community Stability	10	82.25	% Living in Same House as in 1979	49.8%	11	68.9
			% Living in Same County as in 1985	91.4%	6	95.6

Composite: *Rank* 9 / 53 *Score* 67.07   **MOORESTOWN-LENOLA (NJ)**

CATEGORY	RANK	SCORE	STATISTIC	VALUE	RANK	SCORE
Economics	7	90.20	Median Household Income	$50,295	7	84.0
			% of Families Above Poverty Level	98.1%	14	96.4
Affordable Housing	49	45.70	Median Home Value	$174,600	50	41.9
			Median Rent	$652	42	49.5
Crime	N/A	N/A	Violent Crimes per 10,000 Population	N/A	N/A	N/A
			Property Crimes per 10,000 Population	N/A	N/A	N/A
Open Spaces	2	82.20	Population Density (Persons/Sq. Mile)	1880	6	90.3
			Average Rooms per Housing Unit	6.6	7	74.1
Education	7	72.40	% High School Enrollment/Completion	95.9%	10	81.4
			% College Graduates	44.2%	6	63.4
Commute	32	39.55	Average Work Commute in Minutes	21	17	68.8
			% Commuting on Public Transportation	3.3%	33	10.3
Community Stability	20	72.40	% Living in Same House as in 1979	49.3%	14	67.8
			% Living in Same County as in 1985	81.6%	32	77.0

Metropolitan Area Suburb Rankings
PHILADELPHIA-WILMINGTON-TRENTON

Composite: *Rank* 10 / 53 *Score* 66.34   **EWING** (NJ)

CATEGORY	RANK	SCORE	STATISTIC	VALUE	RANK	SCORE
Economics	15	81.55	Median Household Income	$43,191	17	65.8
			% of Families Above Poverty Level	98.4%	10	97.3
Affordable Housing	34	60.80	Median Home Value	$133,500	38	58.5
			Median Rent	$581	32	63.1
Crime	22	76.10	Violent Crimes per 10,000 Population	30	15	94.7
			Property Crimes per 10,000 Population	621	27	57.5
Open Spaces	13	67.85	Population Density (Persons/Sq. Mile)	2229	12	87.6
			Average Rooms per Housing Unit	5.9	18	48.1
Education	19	54.75	% High School Enrollment/Completion	95.0%	15	77.3
			% College Graduates	25.6%	21	32.2
Commute	21	44.05	Average Work Commute in Minutes	19	6	81.2
			% Commuting on Public Transportation	2.5%	42	6.9
Community Stability	12	79.25	% Living in Same House as in 1979	55.3%	7	80.9
			% Living in Same County as in 1985	81.9%	31	77.6

Composite: *Rank* 11 / 53 *Score* 66.32   **BELLMAWR** (NJ)

CATEGORY	RANK	SCORE	STATISTIC	VALUE	RANK	SCORE
Economics	29	69.30	Median Household Income	$34,887	31	44.6
			% of Families Above Poverty Level	97.3%	23	94.0
Affordable Housing	12	82.15	Median Home Value	$88,900	18	76.6
			Median Rent	$453	8	87.7
Crime	7	93.95	Violent Crimes per 10,000 Population	25	13	95.7
			Property Crimes per 10,000 Population	236	8	92.2
Open Spaces	32	53.05	Population Density (Persons/Sq. Mile)	4157	28	72.8
			Average Rooms per Housing Unit	5.5	34	33.3
Education	38	38.65	% High School Enrollment/Completion	94.3%	21	74.1
			% College Graduates	8.3%	47	3.2
Commute	27	41.90	Average Work Commute in Minutes	21	17	68.8
			% Commuting on Public Transportation	4.4%	22	15.0
Community Stability	7	85.25	% Living in Same House as in 1979	54.8%	8	79.8
			% Living in Same County as in 1985	88.8%	13	90.7

Composite: *Rank* 12 / 53 *Score* 64.92   **MERCERVILLE-HAMILTON SQUARE** (NJ)

CATEGORY	RANK	SCORE	STATISTIC	VALUE	RANK	SCORE
Economics	4	92.20	Median Household Income	$51,060	6	85.9
			% of Families Above Poverty Level	98.8%	4	98.5
Affordable Housing	43	50.25	Median Home Value	$149,800	46	51.9
			Median Rent	$657	44	48.6
Crime	N/A	N/A	Violent Crimes per 10,000 Population	N/A	N/A	N/A
			Property Crimes per 10,000 Population	N/A	N/A	N/A
Open Spaces	10	72.30	Population Density (Persons/Sq. Mile)	3496	22	77.9
			Average Rooms per Housing Unit	6.4	8	66.7
Education	24	50.20	% High School Enrollment/Completion	93.5%	27	70.5
			% College Graduates	24.2%	24	29.9
Commute	40	35.55	Average Work Commute in Minutes	22	22	62.5
			% Commuting on Public Transportation	2.9%	37	8.6
Community Stability	6	89.05	% Living in Same House as in 1979	57.4%	6	85.5
			% Living in Same County as in 1985	89.8%	11	92.6

Metropolitan Area Suburb Rankings
PHILADELPHIA-WILMINGTON-TRENTON

Composite: *Rank* 13 / 53 *Score* 64.11   **PENNSAUKEN (NJ)**

CATEGORY	RANK	SCORE	STATISTIC	VALUE	RANK	SCORE
Economics	30	68.75	Median Household Income	$36,097	26	47.7
			% of Families Above Poverty Level	95.9%	32	89.8
Affordable Housing	13	79.60	Median Home Value	$90,600	20	75.9
			Median Rent	$476	13	83.3
Crime	26	72.75	Violent Crimes per 10,000 Population	55	20	89.3
			Property Crimes per 10,000 Population	635	28	56.2
Open Spaces	15	67.50	Population Density (Persons/Sq. Mile)	3297	20	79.4
			Average Rooms per Housing Unit	6.1	13	55.6
Education	36	39.45	% High School Enrollment/Completion	92.8%	31	67.3
			% College Graduates	13.3%	35	11.6
Commute	15	47.15	Average Work Commute in Minutes	20	11	75.0
			% Commuting on Public Transportation	5.4%	19	19.3
Community Stability	16	73.60	% Living in Same House as in 1979	48.5%	17	66.0
			% Living in Same County as in 1985	83.8%	27	81.2

Composite: *Rank* 14 / 53 *Score* 63.18   **NEWARK (DE)**

CATEGORY	RANK	SCORE	STATISTIC	VALUE	RANK	SCORE
Economics	22	75.40	Median Household Income	$38,584	23	54.1
			% of Families Above Poverty Level	98.2%	13	96.7
Affordable Housing	32	65.35	Median Home Value	$133,600	39	58.5
			Median Rent	$534	24	72.2
Crime	25	72.95	Violent Crimes per 10,000 Population	60	23	88.2
			Property Crimes per 10,000 Population	619	26	57.7
Open Spaces	16	67.15	Population Density (Persons/Sq. Mile)	2913	17	82.4
			Average Rooms per Housing Unit	6.0	14	51.9
Education	3	83.65	% High School Enrollment/Completion	99.6%	3	98.2
			% College Graduates	47.6%	5	69.1
Commute	14	48.05	Average Work Commute in Minutes	18	3	87.5
			% Commuting on Public Transportation	2.9%	37	8.6
Community Stability	51	29.70	% Living in Same House as in 1979	30.3%	50	26.1
			% Living in Same County as in 1985	58.6%	52	33.3

Composite: *Rank* 15 / 53 *Score* 62.89   **HORSHAM (PA)**

CATEGORY	RANK	SCORE	STATISTIC	VALUE	RANK	SCORE
Economics	13	82.90	Median Household Income	$43,750	15	67.3
			% of Families Above Poverty Level	98.8%	4	98.5
Affordable Housing	39	53.40	Median Home Value	$135,600	40	57.7
			Median Rent	$654	43	49.1
Crime	3	97.05	Violent Crimes per 10,000 Population	8	2	99.4
			Property Crimes per 10,000 Population	208	5	94.7
Open Spaces	25	62.20	Population Density (Persons/Sq. Mile)	2736	14	83.7
			Average Rooms per Housing Unit	5.7	27	40.7
Education	12	63.70	% High School Enrollment/Completion	98.3%	6	92.3
			% College Graduates	27.3%	17	35.1
Commute	42	34.25	Average Work Commute in Minutes	22	22	62.5
			% Commuting on Public Transportation	2.3%	44	6.0
Community Stability	46	46.70	% Living in Same House as in 1979	30.9%	49	27.4
			% Living in Same County as in 1985	75.8%	43	66.0

Metropolitan Area Suburb Rankings
PHILADELPHIA-WILMINGTON-TRENTON

Composite: *Rank* 16 / 53 *Score* 62.72   **DARBY TOWNSHIP (PA)**

CATEGORY	RANK	SCORE	STATISTIC	VALUE	RANK	SCORE
Economics	48	50.60	Median Household Income	$30,734	42	34.1
			% of Families Above Poverty Level	88.3%	48	67.1
Affordable Housing	21	75.45	Median Home Value	$80,100	10	80.1
			Median Rent	$541	26	70.8
Crime	6	94.25	Violent Crimes per 10,000 Population	46	18	91.2
			Property Crimes per 10,000 Population	179	2	97.3
Open Spaces	40	45.15	Population Density (Persons/Sq. Mile)	7677	45	45.9
			Average Rooms per Housing Unit	5.8	22	44.4
Education	39	33.70	% High School Enrollment/Completion	92.2%	33	64.5
			% College Graduates	8.1%	48	2.9
Commute	19	44.95	Average Work Commute in Minutes	26	44	37.5
			% Commuting on Public Transportation	13.1%	11	52.4
Community Stability	3	94.95	% Living in Same House as in 1979	61.5%	3	94.5
			% Living in Same County as in 1985	91.3%	8	95.4

Composite: *Rank* 17 / 53 *Score* 62.24   **LEVITTOWN (PA)**

CATEGORY	RANK	SCORE	STATISTIC	VALUE	RANK	SCORE
Economics	20	77.40	Median Household Income	$41,458	19	61.4
			% of Families Above Poverty Level	97.1%	25	93.4
Affordable Housing	33	63.60	Median Home Value	$103,100	29	70.8
			Median Rent	$616	36	56.4
Crime	N/A	N/A	Violent Crimes per 10,000 Population	N/A	N/A	N/A
			Property Crimes per 10,000 Population	N/A	N/A	N/A
Open Spaces	26	61.15	Population Density (Persons/Sq. Mile)	5445	37	63.0
			Average Rooms per Housing Unit	6.2	12	59.3
Education	27	44.70	% High School Enrollment/Completion	95.6%	11	80.0
			% College Graduates	12.0%	39	9.4
Commute	48	31.30	Average Work Commute in Minutes	23	34	56.2
			% Commuting on Public Transportation	2.4%	43	6.4
Community Stability	2	95.30	% Living in Same House as in 1979	60.6%	5	92.5
			% Living in Same County as in 1985	92.7%	3	98.1

Composite: *Rank* 18 / 53 *Score* 61.85   **ARDMORE (PA)**

CATEGORY	RANK	SCORE	STATISTIC	VALUE	RANK	SCORE
Economics	21	76.95	Median Household Income	$40,389	20	58.7
			% of Families Above Poverty Level	97.7%	18	95.2
Affordable Housing	37	56.90	Median Home Value	$138,600	41	56.4
			Median Rent	$611	35	57.4
Crime	N/A	N/A	Violent Crimes per 10,000 Population	N/A	N/A	N/A
			Property Crimes per 10,000 Population	N/A	N/A	N/A
Open Spaces	31	53.00	Population Density (Persons/Sq. Mile)	6603	43	54.1
			Average Rooms per Housing Unit	6.0	14	51.9
Education	11	64.55	% High School Enrollment/Completion	94.0%	26	72.7
			% College Graduates	40.0%	10	56.4
Commute	8	55.45	Average Work Commute in Minutes	24	41	50.0
			% Commuting on Public Transportation	15.1%	5	60.9
Community Stability	32	64.25	% Living in Same House as in 1979	46.6%	21	61.8
			% Living in Same County as in 1985	76.2%	40	66.7

Metropolitan Area Suburb Rankings
PHILADELPHIA-WILMINGTON-TRENTON

Composite: **Rank** 19 / 53 **Score** 61.74   **YEADON (PA)**

CATEGORY	RANK	SCORE	STATISTIC	VALUE	RANK	SCORE
Economics	28	69.65	Median Household Income	$35,951	27	47.4
			% of Families Above Poverty Level	96.6%	28	91.9
Affordable Housing	16	77.75	Median Home Value	$77,400	8	81.2
			Median Rent	$523	20	74.3
Crime	16	83.45	Violent Crimes per 10,000 Population	60	23	88.2
			Property Crimes per 10,000 Population	385	15	78.7
Open Spaces	42	42.35	Population Density (Persons/Sq. Mile)	7434	44	47.7
			Average Rooms per Housing Unit	5.6	30	37.0
Education	21	53.45	% High School Enrollment/Completion	94.6%	18	75.5
			% College Graduates	25.1%	23	31.4
Commute	11	50.00	Average Work Commute in Minutes	32	53	0.0
			% Commuting on Public Transportation	24.2%	1	100.0
Community Stability	41	55.50	% Living in Same House as in 1979	39.8%	37	46.9
			% Living in Same County as in 1985	74.8%	44	64.1

Composite: **Rank** 20 / 53 **Score** 61.72   **BROOMALL (PA)**

CATEGORY	RANK	SCORE	STATISTIC	VALUE	RANK	SCORE
Economics	17	80.60	Median Household Income	$43,838	13	67.5
			% of Families Above Poverty Level	97.2%	24	93.7
Affordable Housing	42	52.55	Median Home Value	$155,400	48	49.6
			Median Rent	$621	38	55.5
Crime	N/A	N/A	Violent Crimes per 10,000 Population	N/A	N/A	N/A
			Property Crimes per 10,000 Population	N/A	N/A	N/A
Open Spaces	11	71.30	Population Density (Persons/Sq. Mile)	3763	24	75.9
			Average Rooms per Housing Unit	6.4	8	66.7
Education	28	44.05	% High School Enrollment/Completion	90.9%	37	58.6
			% College Graduates	24.0%	25	29.5
Commute	50	27.70	Average Work Commute in Minutes	25	42	43.8
			% Commuting on Public Transportation	3.6%	29	11.6
Community Stability	5	94.10	% Living in Same House as in 1979	60.7%	4	92.8
			% Living in Same County as in 1985	91.3%	8	95.4

Composite: **Rank** 21 / 53 **Score** 61.69   **LANSDOWNE (PA)**

CATEGORY	RANK	SCORE	STATISTIC	VALUE	RANK	SCORE
Economics	25	71.70	Median Household Income	$35,795	28	47.0
			% of Families Above Poverty Level	98.1%	14	96.4
Affordable Housing	26	71.00	Median Home Value	$105,200	30	70.0
			Median Rent	$535	25	72.0
Crime	4	95.55	Violent Crimes per 10,000 Population	20	9	96.8
			Property Crimes per 10,000 Population	212	6	94.3
Open Spaces	46	36.45	Population Density (Persons/Sq. Mile)	9946	52	28.5
			Average Rooms per Housing Unit	5.8	22	44.4
Education	33	42.40	% High School Enrollment/Completion	87.9%	43	45.0
			% College Graduates	30.1%	13	39.8
Commute	12	49.50	Average Work Commute in Minutes	27	47	31.2
			% Commuting on Public Transportation	16.7%	4	67.8
Community Stability	31	65.25	% Living in Same House as in 1979	40.2%	34	47.8
			% Living in Same County as in 1985	84.6%	24	82.7

Metropolitan Area Suburb Rankings
PHILADELPHIA-WILMINGTON-TRENTON

Composite: **Rank** 22 / 53 **Score** 61.01   **MILLVILLE** (NJ)

CATEGORY	RANK	SCORE	STATISTIC	VALUE	RANK	SCORE
Economics	44	55.00	Median Household Income	$31,266	40	35.4
			% of Families Above Poverty Level	90.8%	44	74.6
Affordable Housing	10	83.55	Median Home Value	$70,000	7	84.2
			Median Rent	$478	14	82.9
Crime	24	74.70	Violent Crimes per 10,000 Population	80	26	84.0
			Property Crimes per 10,000 Population	533	19	65.4
Open Spaces	17	66.65	Population Density (Persons/Sq. Mile)	614	1	100.0
			Average Rooms per Housing Unit	5.5	34	33.3
Education	40	31.15	% High School Enrollment/Completion	89.8%	40	53.6
			% College Graduates	11.6%	41	8.7
Commute	17	45.25	Average Work Commute in Minutes	18	3	87.5
			% Commuting on Public Transportation	1.6%	48	3.0
Community Stability	24	70.75	% Living in Same House as in 1979	43.1%	27	54.2
			% Living in Same County as in 1985	87.0%	15	87.3

Composite: **Rank** 23 / 53 **Score** 60.83   **COLLINGSWOOD** (NJ)

CATEGORY	RANK	SCORE	STATISTIC	VALUE	RANK	SCORE
Economics	33	65.60	Median Household Income	$33,026	35	39.9
			% of Families Above Poverty Level	96.4%	29	91.3
Affordable Housing	23	74.45	Median Home Value	$94,200	23	74.4
			Median Rent	$522	19	74.5
Crime	17	81.20	Violent Crimes per 10,000 Population	23	11	96.2
			Property Crimes per 10,000 Population	524	18	66.2
Open Spaces	47	35.10	Population Density (Persons/Sq. Mile)	8368	46	40.6
			Average Rooms per Housing Unit	5.4	42	29.6
Education	26	45.35	% High School Enrollment/Completion	90.5%	39	56.8
			% College Graduates	26.6%	19	33.9
Commute	3	61.70	Average Work Commute in Minutes	22	22	62.5
			% Commuting on Public Transportation	15.1%	5	60.9
Community Stability	38	62.40	% Living in Same House as in 1979	40.2%	34	47.8
			% Living in Same County as in 1985	81.6%	32	77.0

Composite: **Rank** 24 / 53 **Score** 60.15   **KING OF PRUSSIA** (PA)

CATEGORY	RANK	SCORE	STATISTIC	VALUE	RANK	SCORE
Economics	10	84.50	Median Household Income	$45,157	11	70.8
			% of Families Above Poverty Level	98.7%	7	98.2
Affordable Housing	44	49.25	Median Home Value	$142,500	42	54.9
			Median Rent	$683	48	43.6
Crime	N/A	N/A	Violent Crimes per 10,000 Population	N/A	N/A	N/A
			Property Crimes per 10,000 Population	N/A	N/A	N/A
Open Spaces	24	62.45	Population Density (Persons/Sq. Mile)	2192	10	87.9
			Average Rooms per Housing Unit	5.6	30	37.0
Education	8	67.95	% High School Enrollment/Completion	94.9%	16	76.8
			% College Graduates	41.6%	8	59.1
Commute	30	41.05	Average Work Commute in Minutes	21	17	68.8
			% Commuting on Public Transportation	4.0%	28	13.3
Community Stability	40	55.70	% Living in Same House as in 1979	40.5%	33	48.5
			% Living in Same County as in 1985	74.2%	46	62.9

Metropolitan Area Suburb Rankings
PHILADELPHIA-WILMINGTON-TRENTON

Composite: **Rank** 25 / 53 *Score* 60.08   **BROOKSIDE** (DE)

CATEGORY	RANK	SCORE	STATISTIC	VALUE	RANK	SCORE
Economics	24	73.95	Median Household Income	$39,908	21	57.5
			% of Families Above Poverty Level	96.1%	30	90.4
Affordable Housing	22	74.85	Median Home Value	$88,300	16	76.8
			Median Rent	$530	21	72.9
Crime	N/A	N/A	Violent Crimes per 10,000 Population	N/A	N/A	N/A
			Property Crimes per 10,000 Population	N/A	N/A	N/A
Open Spaces	20	63.30	Population Density (Persons/Sq. Mile)	3918	26	74.7
			Average Rooms per Housing Unit	6.0	14	51.9
Education	32	42.50	% High School Enrollment/Completion	92.4%	32	65.5
			% College Graduates	18.0%	30	19.5
Commute	26	42.10	Average Work Commute in Minutes	19	6	81.2
			% Commuting on Public Transportation	1.6%	48	3.0
Community Stability	33	63.80	% Living in Same House as in 1979	37.4%	42	41.7
			% Living in Same County as in 1985	86.3%	18	85.9

Composite: **Rank** 26 / 53 *Score* 60.07   **WILLOW GROVE** (PA)

CATEGORY	RANK	SCORE	STATISTIC	VALUE	RANK	SCORE
Economics	18	77.90	Median Household Income	$39,604	22	56.7
			% of Families Above Poverty Level	99.0%	2	99.1
Affordable Housing	35	59.45	Median Home Value	$126,500	34	61.3
			Median Rent	$610	34	57.6
Crime	N/A	N/A	Violent Crimes per 10,000 Population	N/A	N/A	N/A
			Property Crimes per 10,000 Population	N/A	N/A	N/A
Open Spaces	28	59.15	Population Density (Persons/Sq. Mile)	4507	30	70.2
			Average Rooms per Housing Unit	5.9	18	48.1
Education	22	52.90	% High School Enrollment/Completion	94.3%	21	74.1
			% College Graduates	25.3%	22	31.7
Commute	35	38.55	Average Work Commute in Minutes	22	22	62.5
			% Commuting on Public Transportation	4.3%	24	14.6
Community Stability	21	72.45	% Living in Same House as in 1979	47.7%	19	64.3
			% Living in Same County as in 1985	83.5%	28	80.6

Composite: **Rank** 27 / 53 *Score* 59.64   **WOODLYN** (PA)

CATEGORY	RANK	SCORE	STATISTIC	VALUE	RANK	SCORE
Economics	36	60.75	Median Household Income	$31,326	39	35.6
			% of Families Above Poverty Level	94.6%	35	85.9
Affordable Housing	7	86.75	Median Home Value	$96,400	27	73.5
			Median Rent	$389	1	100.0
Crime	N/A	N/A	Violent Crimes per 10,000 Population	N/A	N/A	N/A
			Property Crimes per 10,000 Population	N/A	N/A	N/A
Open Spaces	38	47.20	Population Density (Persons/Sq. Mile)	6177	41	57.4
			Average Rooms per Housing Unit	5.6	30	37.0
Education	37	39.05	% High School Enrollment/Completion	94.1%	25	73.2
			% College Graduates	9.3%	44	4.9
Commute	24	42.20	Average Work Commute in Minutes	22	22	62.5
			% Commuting on Public Transportation	6.0%	18	21.9
Community Stability	11	81.90	% Living in Same House as in 1979	48.0%	18	64.9
			% Living in Same County as in 1985	93.1%	2	98.9

Metropolitan Area Suburb Rankings
PHILADELPHIA-WILMINGTON-TRENTON

Composite: *Rank* 28 / 53 *Score* 59.25   **WOODBURY** (NJ)

CATEGORY	RANK	SCORE	STATISTIC	VALUE	RANK	SCORE
Economics	47	51.35	Median Household Income	$28,993	45	29.6
			% of Families Above Poverty Level	90.3%	45	73.1
Affordable Housing	8	85.80	Median Home Value	$90,400	19	76.0
			Median Rent	$412	3	95.6
Crime	20	77.95	Violent Crimes per 10,000 Population	58	22	88.7
			Property Crimes per 10,000 Population	513	17	67.2
Open Spaces	35	48.90	Population Density (Persons/Sq. Mile)	5241	35	64.5
			Average Rooms per Housing Unit	5.5	34	33.3
Education	29	43.10	% High School Enrollment/Completion	91.9%	35	63.2
			% College Graduates	20.1%	27	23.0
Commute	18	45.00	Average Work Commute in Minutes	20	11	75.0
			% Commuting on Public Transportation	4.4%	22	15.0
Community Stability	36	62.65	% Living in Same House as in 1979	40.9%	32	49.3
			% Living in Same County as in 1985	81.1%	35	76.0

Composite: *Rank* 29 / 53 *Score* 59.00   **GLOUCESTER CITY** (NJ)

CATEGORY	RANK	SCORE	STATISTIC	VALUE	RANK	SCORE
Economics	43	55.05	Median Household Income	$28,998	44	29.6
			% of Families Above Poverty Level	92.8%	39	80.5
Affordable Housing	6	87.25	Median Home Value	$62,800	5	87.2
			Median Rent	$455	9	87.3
Crime	12	90.55	Violent Crimes per 10,000 Population	29	14	94.9
			Property Crimes per 10,000 Population	302	9	86.2
Open Spaces	36	48.80	Population Density (Persons/Sq. Mile)	5750	38	60.6
			Average Rooms per Housing Unit	5.6	30	37.0
Education	52	1.35	% High School Enrollment/Completion	78.6%	52	2.7
			% College Graduates	6.4%	52	0.0
Commute	16	46.20	Average Work Commute in Minutes	19	6	81.2
			% Commuting on Public Transportation	3.5%	31	11.2
Community Stability	8	83.80	% Living in Same House as in 1979	50.7%	10	70.8
			% Living in Same County as in 1985	92.0%	5	96.8

Composite: *Rank* 30 / 53 *Score* 58.72   **WILLINGBORO** (NJ)

CATEGORY	RANK	SCORE	STATISTIC	VALUE	RANK	SCORE
Economics	11	84.35	Median Household Income	$47,121	9	75.9
			% of Families Above Poverty Level	96.9%	27	92.8
Affordable Housing	51	37.05	Median Home Value	$95,100	25	74.1
			Median Rent	$910	53	0.0
Crime	15	86.05	Violent Crimes per 10,000 Population	34	17	93.8
			Property Crimes per 10,000 Population	390	16	78.3
Open Spaces	9	73.20	Population Density (Persons/Sq. Mile)	4711	32	68.6
			Average Rooms per Housing Unit	6.7	5	77.8
Education	31	42.85	% High School Enrollment/Completion	91.9%	35	63.2
			% College Graduates	19.8%	28	22.5
Commute	53	18.20	Average Work Commute in Minutes	29	52	18.8
			% Commuting on Public Transportation	5.0%	21	17.6
Community Stability	28	69.35	% Living in Same House as in 1979	49.6%	12	68.4
			% Living in Same County as in 1985	78.1%	39	70.3

Metropolitan Area Suburb Rankings
PHILADELPHIA-WILMINGTON-TRENTON

Composite: ***Rank*** 31 / 53 ***Score*** 58.26   **MARLTON (NJ)**

CATEGORY	RANK	SCORE	STATISTIC	VALUE	RANK	SCORE
Economics	16	81.10	Median Household Income	$43,660	16	67.0
			% of Families Above Poverty Level	97.7%	18	95.2
Affordable Housing	36	57.60	Median Home Value	$131,800	37	59.2
			Median Rent	$618	37	56.0
Crime	N/A	N/A	Violent Crimes per 10,000 Population	N/A	N/A	N/A
			Property Crimes per 10,000 Population	N/A	N/A	N/A
Open Spaces	18	66.20	Population Density (Persons/Sq. Mile)	3163	19	80.5
			Average Rooms per Housing Unit	6.0	14	51.9
Education	16	56.25	% High School Enrollment/Completion	95.4%	13	79.1
			% College Graduates	26.3%	20	33.4
Commute	41	34.95	Average Work Commute in Minutes	23	34	56.2
			% Commuting on Public Transportation	4.1%	26	13.7
Community Stability	44	53.45	% Living in Same House as in 1979	38.2%	41	43.4
			% Living in Same County as in 1985	74.5%	45	63.5

Composite: ***Rank*** 32 / 53 ***Score*** 57.98   **DREXEL HILL (PA)**

CATEGORY	RANK	SCORE	STATISTIC	VALUE	RANK	SCORE
Economics	23	74.25	Median Household Income	$38,294	24	53.3
			% of Families Above Poverty Level	97.7%	18	95.2
Affordable Housing	30	66.85	Median Home Value	$118,400	33	64.6
			Median Rent	$550	30	69.1
Crime	N/A	N/A	Violent Crimes per 10,000 Population	N/A	N/A	N/A
			Property Crimes per 10,000 Population	N/A	N/A	N/A
Open Spaces	43	41.00	Population Density (Persons/Sq. Mile)	9244	49	33.9
			Average Rooms per Housing Unit	5.9	18	48.1
Education	20	53.65	% High School Enrollment/Completion	93.3%	28	69.5
			% College Graduates	28.9%	15	37.8
Commute	34	38.70	Average Work Commute in Minutes	28	51	25.0
			% Commuting on Public Transportation	13.1%	11	52.4
Community Stability	17	73.40	% Living in Same House as in 1979	46.4%	22	61.4
			% Living in Same County as in 1985	86.0%	20	85.4

Composite: ***Rank*** 33 / 53 ***Score*** 57.49   **GLASSBORO (NJ)**

CATEGORY	RANK	SCORE	STATISTIC	VALUE	RANK	SCORE
Economics	39	56.95	Median Household Income	$34,218	32	42.9
			% of Families Above Poverty Level	89.6%	46	71.0
Affordable Housing	15	78.45	Median Home Value	$97,200	28	73.2
			Median Rent	$474	12	83.7
Crime	27	70.45	Violent Crimes per 10,000 Population	68	25	86.5
			Property Crimes per 10,000 Population	655	29	54.4
Open Spaces	23	62.50	Population Density (Persons/Sq. Mile)	1695	4	91.7
			Average Rooms per Housing Unit	5.5	34	33.3
Education	18	55.60	% High School Enrollment/Completion	96.8%	7	85.5
			% College Graduates	21.7%	26	25.7
Commute	47	31.95	Average Work Commute in Minutes	23	34	56.2
			% Commuting on Public Transportation	2.7%	40	7.7
Community Stability	47	46.55	% Living in Same House as in 1979	39.7%	38	46.7
			% Living in Same County as in 1985	65.5%	49	46.4

Metropolitan Area Suburb Rankings
PHILADELPHIA-WILMINGTON-TRENTON

Composite: Rank 34 / 53 *Score* 57.34   **PRINCETON (NJ)**

CATEGORY	RANK	SCORE	STATISTIC	VALUE	RANK	SCORE
Economics	19	77.85	Median Household Income	$43,092	18	65.6
			% of Families Above Poverty Level	96.0%	31	90.1
Affordable Housing	53	16.30	Median Home Value	$277,900	53	0.0
			Median Rent	$740	52	32.6
Crime	18	79.50	Violent Crimes per 10,000 Population	15	8	97.9
			Property Crimes per 10,000 Population	581	23	61.1
Open Spaces	44	40.25	Population Density (Persons/Sq. Mile)	6534	42	54.6
			Average Rooms per Housing Unit	5.3	47	25.9
Education	1	98.85	% High School Enrollment/Completion	99.5%	4	97.7
			% College Graduates	66.0%	1	100.0
Commute	2	72.55	Average Work Commute in Minutes	16	1	100.0
			% Commuting on Public Transportation	11.4%	13	45.1
Community Stability	53	16.10	% Living in Same House as in 1979	33.1%	48	32.2
			% Living in Same County as in 1985	41.1%	53	0.0

Composite: Rank 35 / 53 *Score* 57.33   **WEST NORRITON (PA)**

CATEGORY	RANK	SCORE	STATISTIC	VALUE	RANK	SCORE
Economics	14	82.50	Median Household Income	$43,803	14	67.4
			% of Families Above Poverty Level	98.5%	8	97.6
Affordable Housing	39	53.40	Median Home Value	$128,500	35	60.5
			Median Rent	$669	46	46.3
Crime	N/A	N/A	Violent Crimes per 10,000 Population	N/A	N/A	N/A
			Property Crimes per 10,000 Population	N/A	N/A	N/A
Open Spaces	22	62.75	Population Density (Persons/Sq. Mile)	2596	13	84.8
			Average Rooms per Housing Unit	5.7	27	40.7
Education	17	56.20	% High School Enrollment/Completion	92.1%	34	64.1
			% College Graduates	35.2%	11	48.3
Commute	46	32.20	Average Work Commute in Minutes	23	34	56.2
			% Commuting on Public Transportation	2.8%	39	8.2
Community Stability	39	56.95	% Living in Same House as in 1979	35.5%	46	37.5
			% Living in Same County as in 1985	81.3%	34	76.4

Composite: Rank 36 / 53 *Score* 57.05   **LANSDALE (PA)**

CATEGORY	RANK	SCORE	STATISTIC	VALUE	RANK	SCORE
Economics	27	69.60	Median Household Income	$34,987	30	44.9
			% of Families Above Poverty Level	97.4%	22	94.3
Affordable Housing	28	69.45	Median Home Value	$113,900	31	66.5
			Median Rent	$533	23	72.4
Crime	N/A	N/A	Violent Crimes per 10,000 Population	N/A	N/A	N/A
			Property Crimes per 10,000 Population	N/A	N/A	N/A
Open Spaces	37	48.45	Population Density (Persons/Sq. Mile)	5363	36	63.6
			Average Rooms per Housing Unit	5.5	34	33.3
Education	25	47.50	% High School Enrollment/Completion	94.6%	18	75.5
			% College Graduates	18.0%	30	19.5
Commute	20	44.25	Average Work Commute in Minutes	19	6	81.2
			% Commuting on Public Transportation	2.6%	41	7.3
Community Stability	35	63.05	% Living in Same House as in 1979	38.7%	39	44.5
			% Living in Same County as in 1985	84.0%	26	81.6

Metropolitan Area Suburb Rankings
PHILADELPHIA-WILMINGTON-TRENTON

Composite: *Rank* 37 / 53 *Score* 56.55 **DARBY (PA)**

CATEGORY	RANK	SCORE	STATISTIC	VALUE	RANK	SCORE
Economics	49	39.90	Median Household Income	$26,705	48	23.8
			% of Families Above Poverty Level	84.6%	49	56.0
Affordable Housing	4	89.90	Median Home Value	$46,900	3	93.6
			Median Rent	$461	10	86.2
Crime	13	87.60	Violent Crimes per 10,000 Population	99	27	79.9
			Property Crimes per 10,000 Population	201	4	95.3
Open Spaces	52	22.20	Population Density (Persons/Sq. Mile)	13661	53	0.0
			Average Rooms per Housing Unit	5.8	22	44.4
Education	43	27.80	% High School Enrollment/Completion	89.8%	40	53.6
			% College Graduates	7.6%	50	2.0
Commute	6	58.65	Average Work Commute in Minutes	26	44	37.5
			% Commuting on Public Transportation	19.5%	3	79.8
Community Stability	27	69.80	% Living in Same House as in 1979	45.3%	23	59.0
			% Living in Same County as in 1985	83.5%	28	80.6

Composite: *Rank* 38 / 53 *Score* 56.10 **PIKE CREEK (DE)**

CATEGORY	RANK	SCORE	STATISTIC	VALUE	RANK	SCORE
Economics	12	83.90	Median Household Income	$44,425	12	69.0
			% of Families Above Poverty Level	98.9%	3	98.8
Affordable Housing	38	56.70	Median Home Value	$130,600	36	59.7
			Median Rent	$630	40	53.7
Crime	N/A	N/A	Violent Crimes per 10,000 Population	N/A	N/A	N/A
			Property Crimes per 10,000 Population	N/A	N/A	N/A
Open Spaces	21	63.35	Population Density (Persons/Sq. Mile)	3401	21	78.6
			Average Rooms per Housing Unit	5.9	18	48.1
Education	6	73.95	% High School Enrollment/Completion	94.9%	16	76.8
			% College Graduates	48.8%	4	71.1
Commute	49	30.45	Average Work Commute in Minutes	23	34	56.2
			% Commuting on Public Transportation	2.0%	45	4.7
Community Stability	52	28.25	% Living in Same House as in 1979	18.4%	53	0.0
			% Living in Same County as in 1985	70.8%	48	56.5

Composite: *Rank* 39 / 53 *Score* 56.09 **MAPLE SHADE (NJ)**

CATEGORY	RANK	SCORE	STATISTIC	VALUE	RANK	SCORE
Economics	31	67.90	Median Household Income	$32,955	36	39.7
			% of Families Above Poverty Level	98.0%	16	96.1
Affordable Housing	31	66.70	Median Home Value	$94,900	24	74.1
			Median Rent	$601	33	59.3
Crime	14	86.40	Violent Crimes per 10,000 Population	33	16	94.0
			Property Crimes per 10,000 Population	384	14	78.8
Open Spaces	45	38.75	Population Density (Persons/Sq. Mile)	4992	34	66.4
			Average Rooms per Housing Unit	4.9	51	11.1
Education	34	42.20	% High School Enrollment/Completion	93.1%	30	68.6
			% College Graduates	15.8%	34	15.8
Commute	28	41.70	Average Work Commute in Minutes	21	17	68.8
			% Commuting on Public Transportation	4.3%	24	14.6
Community Stability	45	49.00	% Living in Same House as in 1979	37.0%	44	40.8
			% Living in Same County as in 1985	71.2%	47	57.2

Metropolitan Area Suburb Rankings
PHILADELPHIA-WILMINGTON-TRENTON

Composite: *Rank* 40 / 53 *Score* 55.81 VINELAND (NJ)

CATEGORY	RANK	SCORE	STATISTIC	VALUE	RANK	SCORE
Economics	42	55.15	Median Household Income	$30,733	43	34.0
			% of Families Above Poverty Level	91.4%	43	76.3
Affordable Housing	17	77.60	Median Home Value	$83,900	14	78.6
			Median Rent	$511	18	76.6
Crime	30	62.30	Violent Crimes per 10,000 Population	108	28	78.0
			Property Crimes per 10,000 Population	742	31	46.6
Open Spaces	19	64.10	Population Density (Persons/Sq. Mile)	798	2	98.6
			Average Rooms per Housing Unit	5.4	42	29.6
Education	48	18.60	% High School Enrollment/Completion	83.9%	49	26.8
			% College Graduates	12.6%	38	10.4
Commute	23	42.75	Average Work Commute in Minutes	19	6	81.2
			% Commuting on Public Transportation	1.9%	46	4.3
Community Stability	25	70.15	% Living in Same House as in 1979	44.5%	25	57.2
			% Living in Same County as in 1985	84.8%	23	83.1

Composite: *Rank* 41 / 53 *Score* 55.78 BRISTOL (PA)

CATEGORY	RANK	SCORE	STATISTIC	VALUE	RANK	SCORE
Economics	46	51.60	Median Household Income	$26,265	49	22.7
			% of Families Above Poverty Level	92.8%	39	80.5
Affordable Housing	11	82.35	Median Home Value	$80,700	11	79.9
			Median Rent	$468	11	84.8
Crime	N/A	N/A	Violent Crimes per 10,000 Population	N/A	N/A	N/A
			Property Crimes per 10,000 Population	N/A	N/A	N/A
Open Spaces	41	44.15	Population Density (Persons/Sq. Mile)	6002	40	58.7
			Average Rooms per Housing Unit	5.4	42	29.6
Education	41	30.40	% High School Enrollment/Completion	90.6%	38	57.3
			% College Graduates	8.5%	46	3.5
Commute	22	42.85	Average Work Commute in Minutes	20	11	75.0
			% Commuting on Public Transportation	3.4%	32	10.7
Community Stability	9	83.35	% Living in Same House as in 1979	48.8%	15	66.7
			% Living in Same County as in 1985	93.7%	1	100.0

Composite: *Rank* 42 / 53 *Score* 55.02 PHOENIXVILLE (PA)

CATEGORY	RANK	SCORE	STATISTIC	VALUE	RANK	SCORE
Economics	34	65.00	Median Household Income	$31,848	37	36.9
			% of Families Above Poverty Level	97.0%	26	93.1
Affordable Housing	25	72.30	Median Home Value	$93,500	22	74.7
			Median Rent	$546	28	69.9
Crime	N/A	N/A	Violent Crimes per 10,000 Population	N/A	N/A	N/A
			Property Crimes per 10,000 Population	N/A	N/A	N/A
Open Spaces	33	52.90	Population Density (Persons/Sq. Mile)	4208	29	72.5
			Average Rooms per Housing Unit	5.5	34	33.3
Education	23	51.40	% High School Enrollment/Completion	96.0%	9	81.8
			% College Graduates	18.9%	29	21.0
Commute	44	33.20	Average Work Commute in Minutes	22	22	62.5
			% Commuting on Public Transportation	1.8%	47	3.9
Community Stability	42	55.30	% Living in Same House as in 1979	38.5%	40	44.1
			% Living in Same County as in 1985	76.1%	42	66.5

Metropolitan Area Suburb Rankings
PHILADELPHIA-WILMINGTON-TRENTON

Composite: *Rank* 43 / 53 *Score* 53.62 **NORRISTOWN (PA)**

CATEGORY	RANK	SCORE	STATISTIC	VALUE	RANK	SCORE
Economics	45	54.90	Median Household Income	$28,643	47	28.7
			% of Families Above Poverty Level	93.0%	38	81.1
Affordable Housing	14	79.15	Median Home Value	$79,500	9	80.4
			Median Rent	$504	16	77.9
Crime	N/A	N/A	Violent Crimes per 10,000 Population	N/A	N/A	N/A
			Property Crimes per 10,000 Population	N/A	N/A	N/A
Open Spaces	50	31.85	Population Density (Persons/Sq. Mile)	8723	48	37.8
			Average Rooms per Housing Unit	5.3	47	25.9
Education	35	40.20	% High School Enrollment/Completion	93.3%	28	69.5
			% College Graduates	12.9%	36	10.9
Commute	13	48.85	Average Work Commute in Minutes	20	11	75.0
			% Commuting on Public Transportation	6.2%	17	22.7
Community Stability	29	66.75	% Living in Same House as in 1979	40.1%	36	47.6
			% Living in Same County as in 1985	86.3%	18	85.9

Composite: *Rank* 44 / 53 *Score* 53.51 **POTTSTOWN (PA)**

CATEGORY	RANK	SCORE	STATISTIC	VALUE	RANK	SCORE
Economics	40	56.65	Median Household Income	$28,944	46	29.5
			% of Families Above Poverty Level	93.9%	37	83.8
Affordable Housing	9	84.20	Median Home Value	$80,800	12	79.9
			Median Rent	$449	7	88.5
Crime	N/A	N/A	Violent Crimes per 10,000 Population	N/A	N/A	N/A
			Property Crimes per 10,000 Population	N/A	N/A	N/A
Open Spaces	34	51.65	Population Density (Persons/Sq. Mile)	4524	31	70.0
			Average Rooms per Housing Unit	5.5	34	33.3
Education	46	19.85	% High School Enrollment/Completion	84.4%	48	29.1
			% College Graduates	12.7%	37	10.6
Commute	37	37.50	Average Work Commute in Minutes	20	11	75.0
			% Commuting on Public Transportation	0.9%	53	0.0
Community Stability	23	71.20	% Living in Same House as in 1979	43.8%	26	55.7
			% Living in Same County as in 1985	86.7%	17	86.7

Composite: *Rank* 45 / 53 *Score* 53.24 **COATESVILLE (PA)**

CATEGORY	RANK	SCORE	STATISTIC	VALUE	RANK	SCORE
Economics	50	35.45	Median Household Income	$24,887	50	19.1
			% of Families Above Poverty Level	83.2%	50	51.8
Affordable Housing	5	88.40	Median Home Value	$66,700	6	85.6
			Median Rent	$435	6	91.2
Crime	28	68.50	Violent Crimes per 10,000 Population	121	29	75.2
			Property Crimes per 10,000 Population	573	22	61.8
Open Spaces	39	46.15	Population Density (Persons/Sq. Mile)	5957	39	59.0
			Average Rooms per Housing Unit	5.5	34	33.3
Education	45	20.75	% High School Enrollment/Completion	85.8%	46	35.5
			% College Graduates	10.0%	42	6.0
Commute	31	40.50	Average Work Commute in Minutes	22	22	62.5
			% Commuting on Public Transportation	5.2%	20	18.5
Community Stability	19	72.90	% Living in Same House as in 1979	41.3%	31	50.2
			% Living in Same County as in 1985	91.4%	6	95.6

591

Metropolitan Area Suburb Rankings
PHILADELPHIA-WILMINGTON-TRENTON

Composite: *Rank* 46 / 53 *Score* 53.00   **WILLIAMSTOWN** (NJ)

CATEGORY	RANK	SCORE	STATISTIC	VALUE	RANK	SCORE
Economics	37	59.45	Median Household Income	$33,150	34	40.2
			% of Families Above Poverty Level	92.2%	42	78.7
Affordable Housing	19	76.85	Median Home Value	$95,300	26	74.0
			Median Rent	$495	15	79.7
Crime	N/A	N/A	Violent Crimes per 10,000 Population	N/A	N/A	N/A
			Property Crimes per 10,000 Population	N/A	N/A	N/A
Open Spaces	14	67.80	Population Density (Persons/Sq. Mile)	1767	5	91.2
			Average Rooms per Housing Unit	5.8	22	44.4
Education	42	29.15	% High School Enrollment/Completion	88.8%	42	49.1
			% College Graduates	11.9%	40	9.2
Commute	51	21.40	Average Work Commute in Minutes	27	47	31.2
			% Commuting on Public Transportation	3.6%	29	11.6
Community Stability	34	63.35	% Living in Same House as in 1979	42.1%	30	52.0
			% Living in Same County as in 1985	80.4%	37	74.7

Composite: *Rank* 47 / 53 *Score* 52.96   **WEST CHESTER** (PA)

CATEGORY	RANK	SCORE	STATISTIC	VALUE	RANK	SCORE
Economics	38	57.35	Median Household Income	$31,262	41	35.4
			% of Families Above Poverty Level	92.4%	41	79.3
Affordable Housing	29	67.85	Median Home Value	$116,200	32	65.5
			Median Rent	$544	27	70.2
Crime	23	75.60	Violent Crimes per 10,000 Population	55	20	89.3
			Property Crimes per 10,000 Population	572	21	61.9
Open Spaces	51	25.85	Population Density (Persons/Sq. Mile)	9810	50	29.5
			Average Rooms per Housing Unit	5.2	50	22.2
Education	13	60.50	% High School Enrollment/Completion	95.3%	14	78.6
			% College Graduates	31.7%	12	42.4
Commute	9	51.60	Average Work Commute in Minutes	17	2	93.8
			% Commuting on Public Transportation	3.1%	34	9.4
Community Stability	50	32.00	% Living in Same House as in 1979	29.4%	51	24.1
			% Living in Same County as in 1985	62.1%	50	39.9

Composite: *Rank* 48 / 53 *Score* 52.80   **BRIDGETON** (NJ)

CATEGORY	RANK	SCORE	STATISTIC	VALUE	RANK	SCORE
Economics	51	25.80	Median Household Income	$21,897	51	11.5
			% of Families Above Poverty Level	79.3%	52	40.1
Affordable Housing	3	92.15	Median Home Value	$53,300	4	91.0
			Median Rent	$424	5	93.3
Crime	31	54.35	Violent Crimes per 10,000 Population	208	31	56.6
			Property Crimes per 10,000 Population	681	30	52.1
Open Spaces	30	55.50	Population Density (Persons/Sq. Mile)	3044	18	81.4
			Average Rooms per Housing Unit	5.4	42	29.6
Education	49	17.80	% High School Enrollment/Completion	84.8%	47	30.9
			% College Graduates	9.2%	45	4.7
Commute	10	50.60	Average Work Commute in Minutes	18	3	87.5
			% Commuting on Public Transportation	4.1%	26	13.7
Community Stability	17	73.40	% Living in Same House as in 1979	42.8%	28	53.5
			% Living in Same County as in 1985	90.2%	10	93.3

Composite: **Rank** 49 / 53 **Score** 52.50   **MOUNT HOLLY** (NJ)

CATEGORY	RANK	SCORE	STATISTIC	VALUE	RANK	SCORE
Economics	41	55.95	Median Household Income	$33,527	33	41.2
			% of Families Above Poverty Level	89.5%	47	70.7
Affordable Housing	27	70.40	Median Home Value	$93,400	21	74.8
			Median Rent	$566	31	66.0
Crime	29	63.90	Violent Crimes per 10,000 Population	158	30	67.3
			Property Crimes per 10,000 Population	588	25	60.5
Open Spaces	27	60.40	Population Density (Persons/Sq. Mile)	3694	23	76.4
			Average Rooms per Housing Unit	5.8	22	44.4
Education	50	15.50	% High School Enrollment/Completion	80.8%	50	12.7
			% College Graduates	17.3%	32	18.3
Commute	39	35.75	Average Work Commute in Minutes	22	22	62.5
			% Commuting on Public Transportation	3.0%	36	9.0
Community Stability	30	65.60	% Living in Same House as in 1979	42.6%	29	53.1
			% Living in Same County as in 1985	82.2%	30	78.1

Composite: **Rank** 50 / 53 **Score** 49.34   **LINDENWOLD** (NJ)

CATEGORY	RANK	SCORE	STATISTIC	VALUE	RANK	SCORE
Economics	35	61.20	Median Household Income	$31,793	38	36.8
			% of Families Above Poverty Level	94.5%	36	85.6
Affordable Housing	20	76.25	Median Home Value	$80,900	13	79.8
			Median Rent	$531	22	72.7
Crime	21	77.45	Violent Crimes per 10,000 Population	52	19	90.0
			Property Crimes per 10,000 Population	539	20	64.9
Open Spaces	48	34.15	Population Density (Persons/Sq. Mile)	4748	33	68.3
			Average Rooms per Housing Unit	4.6	53	0.0
Education	51	14.65	% High School Enrollment/Completion	80.8%	50	12.7
			% College Graduates	16.3%	33	16.6
Commute	24	42.20	Average Work Commute in Minutes	27	47	31.2
			% Commuting on Public Transportation	13.3%	10	53.2
Community Stability	49	39.50	% Living in Same House as in 1979	24.0%	52	12.3
			% Living in Same County as in 1985	76.2%	40	66.7

Composite: **Rank** 51 / 53 **Score** 48.32   **BROWN MILLS** (NJ)

CATEGORY	RANK	SCORE	STATISTIC	VALUE	RANK	SCORE
Economics	32	66.80	Median Household Income	$35,483	29	46.2
			% of Families Above Poverty Level	95.1%	34	87.4
Affordable Housing	24	73.05	Median Home Value	$88,400	17	76.8
			Median Rent	$549	29	69.3
Crime	N/A	N/A	Violent Crimes per 10,000 Population	N/A	N/A	N/A
			Property Crimes per 10,000 Population	N/A	N/A	N/A
Open Spaces	29	57.10	Population Density (Persons/Sq. Mile)	2140	9	88.3
			Average Rooms per Housing Unit	5.3	47	25.9
Education	47	19.60	% High School Enrollment/Completion	86.3%	45	37.7
			% College Graduates	7.3%	51	1.5
Commute	52	18.95	Average Work Commute in Minutes	26	44	37.5
			% Commuting on Public Transportation	1.0%	52	0.4
Community Stability	43	54.45	% Living in Same House as in 1979	35.2%	47	36.8
			% Living in Same County as in 1985	79.0%	38	72.1

Metropolitan Area Suburb Rankings
PHILADELPHIA-WILMINGTON-TRENTON

Composite: *Rank* 52 / 53 *Score* 48.09   **CHESTER (PA)**

CATEGORY	RANK	SCORE	STATISTIC	VALUE	RANK	SCORE
Economics	52	24.65	Median Household Income	$20,864	52	8.9
			% of Families Above Poverty Level	79.4%	51	40.4
Affordable Housing	1	98.35	Median Home Value	$37,800	2	97.3
			Median Rent	$392	2	99.4
Crime	32	21.65	Violent Crimes per 10,000 Population	473	33	0.0
			Property Crimes per 10,000 Population	778	32	43.3
Open Spaces	49	34.00	Population Density (Persons/Sq. Mile)	8646	47	38.4
			Average Rooms per Housing Unit	5.4	42	29.6
Education	44	21.80	% High School Enrollment/Completion	87.1%	44	41.4
			% College Graduates	7.7%	49	2.2
Commute	4	59.35	Average Work Commute in Minutes	22	22	62.5
			% Commuting on Public Transportation	14.0%	8	56.2
Community Stability	14	76.85	% Living in Same House as in 1979	46.8%	20	62.3
			% Living in Same County as in 1985	89.2%	12	91.4

Composite: *Rank* 53 / 53 *Score* 37.83   **CAMDEN (NJ)**

CATEGORY	RANK	SCORE	STATISTIC	VALUE	RANK	SCORE
Economics	53	0.00	Median Household Income	$17,386	53	0.0
			% of Families Above Poverty Level	65.9%	53	0.0
Affordable Housing	2	97.60	Median Home Value	$31,100	1	100.0
			Median Rent	$414	4	95.2
Crime	33	11.55	Violent Crimes per 10,000 Population	365	32	23.1
			Property Crimes per 10,000 Population	1,259	33	0.0
Open Spaces	53	19.90	Population Density (Persons/Sq. Mile)	9920	51	28.7
			Average Rooms per Housing Unit	4.9	51	11.1
Education	53	0.00	% High School Enrollment/Completion	78.0%	53	0.0
			% College Graduates	6.4%	52	0.0
Commute	1	73.30	Average Work Commute in Minutes	22	22	62.5
			% Commuting on Public Transportation	20.5%	2	84.1
Community Stability	37	62.45	% Living in Same House as in 1979	36.6%	45	39.9
			% Living in Same County as in 1985	85.8%	21	85.0

Metropolitan Area Description
PHOENIX

STATE: Arizona
COUNTIES: Maricopa

TOTAL POPULATION: 2,122,101

POPULATION IN SUBURBS: 1,138,698 (53.7%)

POPULATION IN Phoenix: 983,403 (46.3%)

The PHOENIX metropolitan area is located in the southcentral part of Arizona. The suburbs range geographically from Sun City in the north (15 miles from Phoenix), to Avondale in the west (8 miles from Phoenix), to Chandler in the south (24 miles from Phoenix), and to Fountain Hills in the east (9 miles from Phoenix). The area is growing rapidly in population and had an increase of 40.6% between 1980 and 1990. Summer time high temperatures average in the 100's and winter time lows average in the 40's. Arizona's largest commercial employer, McDonnell Douglas Helicopter Company, is located in the suburb of Mesa. Sun Health Corporation is located in Sun City. Tempe is the site of Arizona State University. Public transportation is provided using buses by the Phoenix Transit System.

Paradise Valley is the overall highest rated suburb and also has the highest scores in education, economics, and open spaces. **Paradise Valley** is also the safest suburb with the lowest crime rate. **Avondale** is the suburb with the most affordable housing. The top rated commute belongs to **Tempe**. Finally, the number one rating in community stability belongs to **Sun City**.

The highest ranked suburb overall which also has an affordable housing score of at least 50.00 is **Scottsdale**.

The highest ranked suburb in the education category which also has an affordable housing score of at least 50.00 is **Sun City West**.

The metropolitan area contains only one county.

Metropolitan Area Map
PHOENIX

Maricopa Co.

*3

*4

*6

*2

*9

*7

*12

★
PHOENIX

*5

*8

*10

*11

*1

Arizona

Metropolitan Area Suburb Alphabetical Index
PHOENIX

SUBURB	PAGE	MAP NO.	STATE	COUNTY	POPU-LATION	RANK
AVONDALE	601	1	Arizona	Maricopa	16,169	12 / 12
CHANDLER	600	2	Arizona	Maricopa	90,533	7 / 12
FOUNTAIN HILLS	601	3	Arizona	Maricopa	10,030	10 / 12
GILBERT	599	4	Arizona	Maricopa	29,188	5 / 12
GLENDALE	600	5	Arizona	Maricopa	148,134	9 / 12
MESA	601	6	Arizona	Maricopa	288,091	11 / 12
PARADISE VALLEY	598	7	Arizona	Maricopa	11,671	1 / 12
PEORIA	600	8	Arizona	Maricopa	50,618	8 / 12
SCOTTSDALE	598	9	Arizona	Maricopa	130,069	2 / 12
SUN CITY	598	10	Arizona	Maricopa	38,126	3 / 12
SUN CITY WEST	599	11	Arizona	Maricopa	15,997	6 / 12
TEMPE	599	12	Arizona	Maricopa	141,865	4 / 12

Metropolitan Area Suburb Rankings
PHOENIX

Composite: Rank 1 / 12 *Score* 75.25   **PARADISE VALLEY**

CATEGORY	RANK	SCORE	STATISTIC	VALUE	RANK	SCORE
Economics	1	99.30	Median Household Income	$110,550	1	100.0
			% of Families Above Poverty Level	97.7%	2	98.6
Affordable Housing	12	0.00	Median Home Value	$372,500	12	0.0
			Median Rent	$1,001	12	0.0
Crime	1	100.00	Violent Crimes per 10,000 Population	13	1	100.0
			Property Crimes per 10,000 Population	291	1	100.0
Open Spaces	1	97.20	Population Density (Persons/Sq. Mile)	766	4	94.4
			Average Rooms per Housing Unit	7.7	1	100.0
Education	1	98.15	% High School Enrollment/Completion	99.0%	2	96.3
			% College Graduates	58.5%	1	100.0
Commute	8	35.70	Average Work Commute in Minutes	22	4	71.4
			% Commuting on Public Transportation	0.5%	11	0.0
Community Stability	2	96.40	% Living in Same House as in 1979	47.7%	2	92.8
			% Living in Same County as in 1985	83.9%	1	100.0

Composite: Rank 2 / 12 *Score* 61.01   **SCOTTSDALE**

CATEGORY	RANK	SCORE	STATISTIC	VALUE	RANK	SCORE
Economics	4	55.15	Median Household Income	$39,037	4	17.1
			% of Families Above Poverty Level	96.5%	5	93.2
Affordable Housing	9	74.90	Median Home Value	$114,300	10	83.4
			Median Rent	$597	8	66.4
Crime	2	72.50	Violent Crimes per 10,000 Population	25	2	81.8
			Property Crimes per 10,000 Population	528	3	63.2
Open Spaces	4	59.90	Population Density (Persons/Sq. Mile)	705	2	96.5
			Average Rooms per Housing Unit	5.4	4	23.3
Education	4	60.00	% High School Enrollment/Completion	91.5%	5	68.9
			% College Graduates	34.5%	3	51.1
Commute	3	60.70	Average Work Commute in Minutes	22	4	71.4
			% Commuting on Public Transportation	1.1%	3	50.0
Community Stability	5	43.95	% Living in Same House as in 1979	23.1%	4	37.5
			% Living in Same County as in 1985	70.8%	6	50.4

Composite: Rank 3 / 12 *Score* 59.25   **SUN CITY**

CATEGORY	RANK	SCORE	STATISTIC	VALUE	RANK	SCORE
Economics	6	48.30	Median Household Income	$25,714	11	1.6
			% of Families Above Poverty Level	96.9%	4	95.0
Affordable Housing	7	80.35	Median Home Value	$71,700	2	97.2
			Median Rent	$615	9	63.5
Crime	N/A	N/A	Violent Crimes per 10,000 Population	N/A	N/A	N/A
			Property Crimes per 10,000 Population	N/A	N/A	N/A
Open Spaces	9	21.70	Population Density (Persons/Sq. Mile)	2590	9	33.4
			Average Rooms per Housing Unit	5.0	8	10.0
Education	6	50.20	% High School Enrollment/Completion	92.5%	4	72.5
			% College Graduates	23.1%	8	27.9
Commute	4	58.35	Average Work Commute in Minutes	20	1	100.0
			% Commuting on Public Transportation	0.7%	5	16.7
Community Stability	1	96.60	% Living in Same House as in 1979	50.9%	1	100.0
			% Living in Same County as in 1985	82.1%	2	93.2

Metropolitan Area Suburb Rankings
PHOENIX

Composite: Rank 4 / 12 *Score* 51.15 **TEMPE**

CATEGORY	RANK	SCORE	STATISTIC	VALUE	RANK	SCORE
Economics	9	43.00	Median Household Income	$31,885	8	8.8
			% of Families Above Poverty Level	93.0%	9	77.2
Affordable Housing	4	87.00	Median Home Value	$91,300	7	90.9
			Median Rent	$496	5	83.1
Crime	6	28.45	Violent Crimes per 10,000 Population	57	6	33.3
			Property Crimes per 10,000 Population	783	7	23.6
Open Spaces	12	3.35	Population Density (Persons/Sq. Mile)	3590	12	0.0
			Average Rooms per Housing Unit	4.9	10	6.7
Education	3	67.30	% High School Enrollment/Completion	94.2%	3	78.8
			% College Graduates	36.8%	2	55.8
Commute	1	95.85	Average Work Commute in Minutes	20	1	100.0
			% Commuting on Public Transportation	1.6%	2	91.7
Community Stability	8	33.10	% Living in Same House as in 1979	18.5%	6	27.2
			% Living in Same County as in 1985	67.8%	9	39.0

Composite: Rank 5 / 12 *Score* 48.44 **GILBERT**

CATEGORY	RANK	SCORE	STATISTIC	VALUE	RANK	SCORE
Economics	5	52.00	Median Household Income	$41,081	3	19.5
			% of Families Above Poverty Level	94.6%	6	84.5
Affordable Housing	5	85.80	Median Home Value	$107,500	9	85.6
			Median Rent	$478	4	86.0
Crime	4	57.40	Violent Crimes per 10,000 Population	35	4	66.7
			Property Crimes per 10,000 Population	625	4	48.1
Open Spaces	3	60.40	Population Density (Persons/Sq. Mile)	1075	6	84.1
			Average Rooms per Housing Unit	5.8	2	36.7
Education	5	53.85	% High School Enrollment/Completion	91.2%	6	67.8
			% College Graduates	29.0%	4	39.9
Commute	10	21.45	Average Work Commute in Minutes	24	8	42.9
			% Commuting on Public Transportation	0.5%	11	0.0
Community Stability	10	8.15	% Living in Same House as in 1979	6.4%	12	0.0
			% Living in Same County as in 1985	61.8%	10	16.3

Composite: Rank 6 / 12 *Score* 46.84 **SUN CITY WEST**

CATEGORY	RANK	SCORE	STATISTIC	VALUE	RANK	SCORE
Economics	3	56.35	Median Household Income	$35,228	6	12.7
			% of Families Above Poverty Level	98.0%	1	100.0
Affordable Housing	11	60.55	Median Home Value	$106,600	8	85.9
			Median Rent	$787	11	35.2
Crime	N/A	N/A	Violent Crimes per 10,000 Population	N/A	N/A	N/A
			Property Crimes per 10,000 Population	N/A	N/A	N/A
Open Spaces	7	40.95	Population Density (Persons/Sq. Mile)	1740	7	61.9
			Average Rooms per Housing Unit	5.3	5	20.0
Education	2	68.65	% High School Enrollment/Completion	100.0%	1	100.0
			% College Graduates	27.7%	6	37.3
Commute	5	51.20	Average Work Commute in Minutes	21	3	85.7
			% Commuting on Public Transportation	0.7%	5	16.7
Community Stability	12	3.35	% Living in Same House as in 1979	9.4%	9	6.7
			% Living in Same County as in 1985	57.5%	12	0.0

Metropolitan Area Suburb Rankings
PHOENIX

Composite: *Rank* 7 / 12   *Score* 46.41   **CHANDLER**

CATEGORY	RANK	SCORE	STATISTIC	VALUE	RANK	SCORE
Economics	8	46.35	Median Household Income	$38,124	5	16.0
			% of Families Above Poverty Level	92.9%	10	76.7
Affordable Housing	6	85.45	Median Home Value	$89,800	6	91.3
			Median Rent	$517	6	79.6
Crime	5	56.35	Violent Crimes per 10,000 Population	30	3	74.2
			Property Crimes per 10,000 Population	687	5	38.5
Open Spaces	8	36.55	Population Density (Persons/Sq. Mile)	1903	8	56.4
			Average Rooms per Housing Unit	5.2	6	16.7
Education	8	42.55	% High School Enrollment/Completion	86.6%	10	50.9
			% College Graduates	26.2%	7	34.2
Commute	9	29.80	Average Work Commute in Minutes	24	8	42.9
			% Commuting on Public Transportation	0.7%	5	16.7
Community Stability	9	27.80	% Living in Same House as in 1979	9.4%	9	6.7
			% Living in Same County as in 1985	70.4%	7	48.9

Composite: *Rank* 8 / 12   *Score* 45.90   **PEORIA**

CATEGORY	RANK	SCORE	STATISTIC	VALUE	RANK	SCORE
Economics	7	47.30	Median Household Income	$34,205	7	11.5
			% of Families Above Poverty Level	94.3%	7	83.1
Affordable Housing	8	80.15	Median Home Value	$85,500	4	92.7
			Median Rent	$590	7	67.6
Crime	3	57.70	Violent Crimes per 10,000 Population	52	5	40.9
			Property Crimes per 10,000 Population	455	2	74.5
Open Spaces	5	54.60	Population Density (Persons/Sq. Mile)	823	5	92.5
			Average Rooms per Housing Unit	5.2	6	16.7
Education	10	33.85	% High School Enrollment/Completion	87.0%	9	52.4
			% College Graduates	16.9%	11	15.3
Commute	11	11.30	Average Work Commute in Minutes	26	11	14.3
			% Commuting on Public Transportation	0.6%	10	8.3
Community Stability	6	36.40	% Living in Same House as in 1979	10.3%	8	8.8
			% Living in Same County as in 1985	74.4%	5	64.0

Composite: *Rank* 9 / 12   *Score* 44.67   **GLENDALE**

CATEGORY	RANK	SCORE	STATISTIC	VALUE	RANK	SCORE
Economics	11	38.25	Median Household Income	$31,665	9	8.5
			% of Families Above Poverty Level	91.0%	11	68.0
Affordable Housing	2	92.70	Median Home Value	$84,800	3	93.0
			Median Rent	$439	2	92.4
Crime	8	7.30	Violent Crimes per 10,000 Population	79	9	0.0
			Property Crimes per 10,000 Population	841	8	14.6
Open Spaces	10	17.60	Population Density (Persons/Sq. Mile)	2837	11	25.2
			Average Rooms per Housing Unit	5.0	8	10.0
Education	11	33.00	% High School Enrollment/Completion	86.1%	11	49.1
			% College Graduates	17.7%	10	16.9
Commute	2	71.45	Average Work Commute in Minutes	24	8	42.9
			% Commuting on Public Transportation	1.7%	1	100.0
Community Stability	4	52.40	% Living in Same House as in 1979	20.0%	5	30.6
			% Living in Same County as in 1985	77.1%	4	74.2

Metropolitan Area Suburb Rankings
PHOENIX

Composite: *Rank* 10 / 12 *Score* 42.01   **FOUNTAIN HILLS**

CATEGORY	RANK	SCORE	STATISTIC	VALUE	RANK	SCORE
Economics	2	58.35	Median Household Income	$42,231	2	20.8
			% of Families Above Poverty Level	97.1%	3	95.9
Affordable Housing	10	66.45	Median Home Value	$141,000	11	74.8
			Median Rent	$648	10	58.1
Crime	N/A	N/A	Violent Crimes per 10,000 Population	N/A	N/A	N/A
			Property Crimes per 10,000 Population	N/A	N/A	N/A
Open Spaces	2	66.65	Population Density (Persons/Sq. Mile)	600	1	100.0
			Average Rooms per Housing Unit	5.7	3	33.3
Education	7	47.70	% High School Enrollment/Completion	88.3%	8	57.1
			% College Graduates	28.2%	5	38.3
Commute	12	8.35	Average Work Commute in Minutes	27	12	0.0
			% Commuting on Public Transportation	0.7%	5	16.7
Community Stability	11	4.55	% Living in Same House as in 1979	7.9%	11	3.4
			% Living in Same County as in 1985	59.0%	11	5.7

Composite: *Rank* 11 / 12 *Score* 41.91   **MESA**

CATEGORY	RANK	SCORE	STATISTIC	VALUE	RANK	SCORE
Economics	10	42.25	Median Household Income	$30,273	10	6.9
			% of Families Above Poverty Level	93.1%	8	77.6
Affordable Housing	3	89.90	Median Home Value	$86,200	5	92.5
			Median Rent	$470	3	87.3
Crime	7	25.80	Violent Crimes per 10,000 Population	70	7	13.6
			Property Crimes per 10,000 Population	690	6	38.0
Open Spaces	11	15.65	Population Density (Persons/Sq. Mile)	2653	10	31.3
			Average Rooms per Housing Unit	4.7	12	0.0
Education	9	40.90	% High School Enrollment/Completion	88.6%	7	58.2
			% College Graduates	21.0%	9	23.6
Commute	6	45.20	Average Work Commute in Minutes	23	6	57.1
			% Commuting on Public Transportation	0.9%	4	33.3
Community Stability	7	33.65	% Living in Same House as in 1979	17.5%	7	24.9
			% Living in Same County as in 1985	68.7%	8	42.4

Composite: *Rank* 12 / 12 *Score* 35.61   **AVONDALE**

CATEGORY	RANK	SCORE	STATISTIC	VALUE	RANK	SCORE
Economics	12	0.00	Median Household Income	$24,292	12	0.0
			% of Families Above Poverty Level	76.1%	12	0.0
Affordable Housing	1	100.00	Median Home Value	$63,000	1	100.0
			Median Rent	$393	1	100.0
Crime	9	0.75	Violent Crimes per 10,000 Population	78	8	1.5
			Property Crimes per 10,000 Population	935	9	0.0
Open Spaces	6	49.45	Population Density (Persons/Sq. Mile)	731	3	95.6
			Average Rooms per Housing Unit	4.8	11	3.3
Education	12	0.00	% High School Enrollment/Completion	72.7%	12	0.0
			% College Graduates	9.4%	12	0.0
Commute	7	36.90	Average Work Commute in Minutes	23	6	57.1
			% Commuting on Public Transportation	0.7%	5	16.7
Community Stability	3	62.15	% Living in Same House as in 1979	24.8%	3	41.3
			% Living in Same County as in 1985	79.4%	3	83.0

Metropolitan Area Description
PITTSBURGH-BEAVER VALLEY

STATE: Pennsylvania
COUNTIES: Allegheny, Beaver, Fayette, Washington, Westmoreland

TOTAL POPULATION: 2,242,798

POPULATION IN SUBURBS: 1,872,919   (83.5%)

POPULATION IN Pittsburgh: 369,879   (16.5%)

The PITTSBURGH-BEAVER VALLEY metropolitan area is located in the southwestern part of Pennsylvania. The suburbs range geographically from Beaver Falls in the north (34 miles from Pittsburgh), to Carnot-Moon in the west (19 miles from Pittsburgh), to Uniontown in the south (48 miles from Pittsburgh), and to Greensburg in the east (33 miles from Pittsburgh). The area is shrinking in population and had a decrease of 7.4% between 1980 and 1990. Summer time high temperatures average in the 80's and winter time lows average in the teens. The suburban area major employers tend to be industrial. Steel factories are located in the suburbs. Light industries and biotechnology companies have recently moved to the area. Public transportation in the area is provided by Port Authority Transit using buses, trains, and subways.

Shaler Township is the overall highest rated suburb. **Franklin Park** receives the highest scores in economics and open spaces. **McKeesport** is the suburb with the most affordable housing. The top score in education goes to **Mount Lebanon**. The top rated commute belongs to **Wilkinsburg.** Finally, the number one rating in community stability belongs to **West Mifflin**. Crime rankings were not available for the area.

The highest ranked suburb overall which also has an affordable housing score of at least 50.00 is **Shaler Township**.

The highest ranked suburb in the education category which also has an affordable housing score of at least 50.00 is **Mount Lebanon**.

The county whose suburbs have the highest average overall score is **Allegheny County** (54.13).

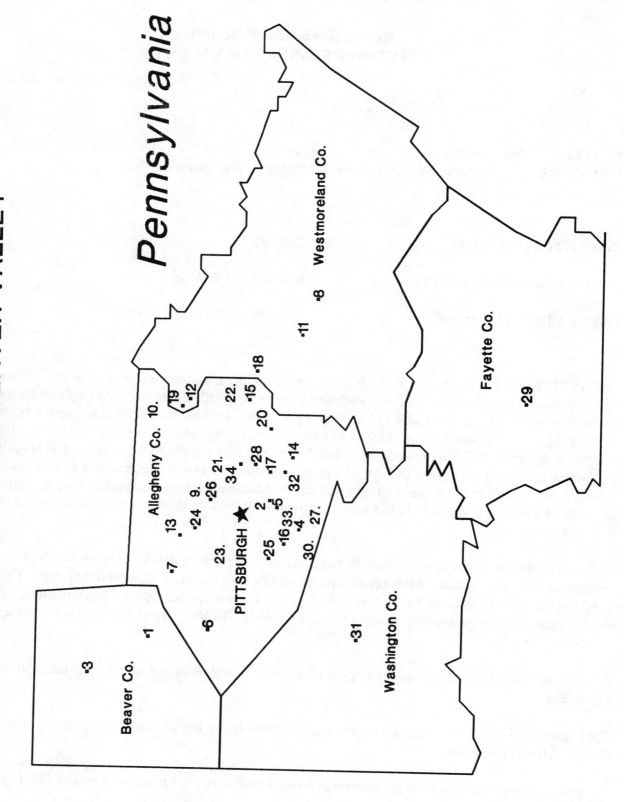

Metropolitan Area Map
PITTSBURGH–BEAVER VALLEY

Pennsylvania

Westmoreland Co.

Fayette Co.

Allegheny Co.

Beaver Co.

Washington Co.

PITTSBURGH

Metropolitan Area Suburb Alphabetical Index
PITTSBURGH-BEAVER VALLEY

SUBURB	PAGE	MAP NO.	STATE	COUNTY	POPU-LATION	RANK
ALIQUIPPA	613	1	Pennsylvania	Beaver	13,374	24 / 34
BALDWIN	608	2	Pennsylvania	Allegheny	21,923	9 / 34
BEAVER FALLS	617	3	Pennsylvania	Beaver	10,687	34 / 34
BETHEL PARK	608	4	Pennsylvania	Allegheny	33,823	7 / 34
BRENTWOOD	614	5	Pennsylvania	Allegheny	10,823	25 / 34
CARNOT-MOON	614	6	Pennsylvania	Allegheny	10,187	26 / 34
FRANKLIN PARK	613	7	Pennsylvania	Allegheny	10,109	22 / 34
GREENSBURG	615	8	Pennsylvania	Westmoreland	16,318	28 / 34
HAMPTON TOWNSHIP	606	9	Pennsylvania	Allegheny	15,568	2 / 34
HARRISON TOWNSHIP	612	10	Pennsylvania	Allegheny	11,763	20 / 34
JEANNETTE	612	11	Pennsylvania	Westmoreland	11,221	19 / 34
LOWER BURRELL	607	12	Pennsylvania	Westmoreland	12,251	5 / 34
MCCANDLESS TOWNSHIP	609	13	Pennsylvania	Allegheny	28,781	11 / 34
MCKEESPORT	615	14	Pennsylvania	Allegheny	26,016	30 / 34
MONROEVILLE	610	15	Pennsylvania	Allegheny	29,169	13 / 34
MOUNT LEBANON	606	16	Pennsylvania	Allegheny	33,362	3 / 34
MUNHALL	611	17	Pennsylvania	Allegheny	13,158	17 / 34
MURRYSVILLE	610	18	Pennsylvania	Westmoreland	17,240	14 / 34
NEW KENSINGTON	614	19	Pennsylvania	Westmoreland	15,894	27 / 34
NORTH VERSAILLES	613	20	Pennsylvania	Allegheny	12,302	23 / 34
PENN HILLS	607	21	Pennsylvania	Allegheny	51,430	4 / 34
PLUM	611	22	Pennsylvania	Allegheny	25,609	16 / 34
ROBINSON TOWNSHIP	610	23	Pennsylvania	Allegheny	10,830	15 / 34
ROSS TOWNSHIP	608	24	Pennsylvania	Allegheny	33,482	8 / 34
SCOTT TOWNSHIP	611	25	Pennsylvania	Allegheny	17,118	18 / 34
SHALER TOWNSHIP	606	26	Pennsylvania	Allegheny	30,533	1 / 34
SOUTH PARK TOWNSHIP	612	27	Pennsylvania	Allegheny	14,292	21 / 34
SWISSVALE	616	28	Pennsylvania	Allegheny	10,637	31 / 34
UNIONTOWN	615	29	Pennsylvania	Fayette	12,034	29 / 34
UPPER ST. CLAIR	609	30	Pennsylvania	Allegheny	19,692	12 / 34
WASHINGTON	616	31	Pennsylvania	Washington	15,864	32 / 34
WEST MIFFLIN	607	32	Pennsylvania	Allegheny	23,644	6 / 34
WHITEHALL	609	33	Pennsylvania	Allegheny	14,451	10 / 34
WILKINSBURG	616	34	Pennsylvania	Allegheny	21,080	33 / 34

Metropolitan Area Suburb Rankings
PITTSBURGH-BEAVER VALLEY

Composite: *Rank* 1 / 34 *Score* 61.40   **SHALER TOWNSHIP**

CATEGORY	RANK	SCORE	STATISTIC	VALUE	RANK	SCORE
Economics	8	68.45	Median Household Income	$36,972	11	42.4
			% of Families Above Poverty Level	97.9%	6	94.5
Affordable Housing	20	67.15	Median Home Value	$70,500	22	67.3
			Median Rent	$460	21	67.0
Crime	N/A	N/A	Violent Crimes per 10,000 Population	N/A	N/A	N/A
			Property Crimes per 10,000 Population	N/A	N/A	N/A
Open Spaces	11	60.90	Population Density (Persons/Sq. Mile)	2749	17	73.7
			Average Rooms per Housing Unit	6.2	8	48.1
Education	16	51.60	% High School Enrollment/Completion	95.4%	14	76.1
			% College Graduates	21.2%	17	27.1
Commute	21	33.60	Average Work Commute in Minutes	23	13	46.7
			% Commuting on Public Transportation	6.2%	15	20.5
Community Stability	5	86.70	% Living in Same House as in 1979	60.5%	5	81.3
			% Living in Same County as in 1985	94.8%	7	92.1

Composite: *Rank* 2 / 34 *Score* 60.56   **HAMPTON TOWNSHIP**

CATEGORY	RANK	SCORE	STATISTIC	VALUE	RANK	SCORE
Economics	5	77.50	Median Household Income	$45,538	6	58.4
			% of Families Above Poverty Level	98.4%	3	96.6
Affordable Housing	31	53.75	Median Home Value	$86,400	29	55.2
			Median Rent	$548	31	52.3
Crime	N/A	N/A	Violent Crimes per 10,000 Population	11	N/A	N/A
			Property Crimes per 10,000 Population	102	N/A	N/A
Open Spaces	4	80.45	Population Density (Persons/Sq. Mile)	971	5	94.2
			Average Rooms per Housing Unit	6.7	4	66.7
Education	3	77.05	% High School Enrollment/Completion	98.2%	1	100.0
			% College Graduates	35.6%	6	54.1
Commute	30	22.20	Average Work Commute in Minutes	25	23	33.3
			% Commuting on Public Transportation	3.4%	22	11.1
Community Stability	21	52.40	% Living in Same House as in 1979	49.2%	19	45.4
			% Living in Same County as in 1985	87.3%	24	59.4

Composite: *Rank* 3 / 34 *Score* 60.02   **MOUNT LEBANON**

CATEGORY	RANK	SCORE	STATISTIC	VALUE	RANK	SCORE
Economics	6	74.20	Median Household Income	$45,801	5	58.9
			% of Families Above Poverty Level	96.7%	12	89.5
Affordable Housing	29	54.55	Median Home Value	$101,300	31	43.8
			Median Rent	$470	23	65.3
Crime	N/A	N/A	Violent Crimes per 10,000 Population	8	N/A	N/A
			Property Crimes per 10,000 Population	112	N/A	N/A
Open Spaces	19	46.85	Population Density (Persons/Sq. Mile)	5521	29	41.8
			Average Rooms per Housing Unit	6.3	7	51.9
Education	1	92.00	% High School Enrollment/Completion	97.8%	5	96.6
			% College Graduates	53.3%	2	87.4
Commute	9	43.15	Average Work Commute in Minutes	25	23	33.3
			% Commuting on Public Transportation	15.9%	4	53.0
Community Stability	23	49.35	% Living in Same House as in 1979	47.0%	23	38.4
			% Living in Same County as in 1985	87.5%	23	60.3

Metropolitan Area Suburb Rankings
PITTSBURGH-BEAVER VALLEY

Composite: *Rank* 4 / 34 *Score* 59.98   **PENN HILLS**

CATEGORY	RANK	SCORE	STATISTIC	VALUE	RANK	SCORE
Economics	17	58.65	Median Household Income	$32,376	17	33.7
			% of Families Above Poverty Level	95.3%	17	83.6
Affordable Housing	18	76.35	Median Home Value	$52,200	15	81.2
			Median Rent	$433	19	71.5
Crime	N/A	N/A	Violent Crimes per 10,000 Population	N/A	N/A	N/A
			Property Crimes per 10,000 Population	N/A	N/A	N/A
Open Spaces	14	57.50	Population Density (Persons/Sq. Mile)	2703	16	74.3
			Average Rooms per Housing Unit	6.0	11	40.7
Education	18	48.20	% High School Enrollment/Completion	94.7%	19	70.1
			% College Graduates	20.8%	20	26.3
Commute	23	31.40	Average Work Commute in Minutes	25	23	33.3
			% Commuting on Public Transportation	8.9%	13	29.5
Community Stability	4	87.75	% Living in Same House as in 1979	61.0%	4	82.9
			% Living in Same County as in 1985	94.9%	6	92.6

Composite: *Rank* 5 / 34 *Score* 59.55   **LOWER BURRELL**

CATEGORY	RANK	SCORE	STATISTIC	VALUE	RANK	SCORE
Economics	20	51.70	Median Household Income	$25,852	21	21.5
			% of Families Above Poverty Level	94.9%	18	81.9
Affordable Housing	16	79.30	Median Home Value	$62,700	18	73.2
			Median Rent	$350	12	85.4
Crime	N/A	N/A	Violent Crimes per 10,000 Population	N/A	N/A	N/A
			Property Crimes per 10,000 Population	N/A	N/A	N/A
Open Spaces	9	63.25	Population Density (Persons/Sq. Mile)	1061	6	93.2
			Average Rooms per Housing Unit	5.8	13	33.3
Education	14	55.10	% High School Enrollment/Completion	97.9%	4	97.4
			% College Graduates	13.6%	23	12.8
Commute	22	32.20	Average Work Commute in Minutes	21	9	60.0
			% Commuting on Public Transportation	1.4%	28	4.4
Community Stability	10	75.75	% Living in Same House as in 1979	61.7%	3	85.1
			% Living in Same County as in 1985	88.9%	20	66.4

Composite: *Rank* 6 / 34 *Score* 59.32   **WEST MIFFLIN**

CATEGORY	RANK	SCORE	STATISTIC	VALUE	RANK	SCORE
Economics	22	45.50	Median Household Income	$26,867	20	23.4
			% of Families Above Poverty Level	91.5%	22	67.6
Affordable Housing	7	90.65	Median Home Value	$49,200	12	83.5
			Median Rent	$276	2	97.8
Crime	N/A	N/A	Violent Crimes per 10,000 Population	N/A	N/A	N/A
			Property Crimes per 10,000 Population	N/A	N/A	N/A
Open Spaces	15	54.20	Population Density (Persons/Sq. Mile)	1670	11	86.2
			Average Rooms per Housing Unit	5.5	19	22.2
Education	26	28.60	% High School Enrollment/Completion	92.2%	26	48.7
			% College Graduates	11.3%	28	8.5
Commute	17	36.95	Average Work Commute in Minutes	23	13	46.7
			% Commuting on Public Transportation	8.2%	14	27.2
Community Stability	1	100.00	% Living in Same House as in 1979	66.4%	1	100.0
			% Living in Same County as in 1985	96.6%	1	100.0

Metropolitan Area Suburb Rankings
PITTSBURGH-BEAVER VALLEY

Composite: **Rank** 7 / 34 *Score* 58.24   **BETHEL PARK**

CATEGORY	RANK	SCORE	STATISTIC	VALUE	RANK	SCORE
Economics	7	70.50	Median Household Income	$41,149	7	50.2
			% of Families Above Poverty Level	97.0%	8	90.8
Affordable Housing	27	58.50	Median Home Value	$82,500	27	58.2
			Median Rent	$509	26	58.8
Crime	N/A	N/A	Violent Crimes per 10,000 Population	N/A	N/A	N/A
			Property Crimes per 10,000 Population	N/A	N/A	N/A
Open Spaces	8	63.85	Population Density (Persons/Sq. Mile)	2894	18	72.1
			Average Rooms per Housing Unit	6.4	6	55.6
Education	10	67.55	% High School Enrollment/Completion	96.5%	9	85.5
			% College Graduates	33.2%	7	49.6
Commute	26	29.95	Average Work Commute in Minutes	27	31	20.0
			% Commuting on Public Transportation	12.0%	7	39.9
Community Stability	15	59.10	% Living in Same House as in 1979	50.8%	14	50.5
			% Living in Same County as in 1985	89.2%	19	67.7

Composite: **Rank** 8 / 34 *Score* 58.19   **ROSS TOWNSHIP**

CATEGORY	RANK	SCORE	STATISTIC	VALUE	RANK	SCORE
Economics	9	67.90	Median Household Income	$36,388	14	41.3
			% of Families Above Poverty Level	97.9%	6	94.5
Affordable Housing	23	65.25	Median Home Value	$73,900	25	64.7
			Median Rent	$467	22	65.8
Crime	N/A	N/A	Violent Crimes per 10,000 Population	N/A	N/A	N/A
			Property Crimes per 10,000 Population	N/A	N/A	N/A
Open Spaces	13	57.75	Population Density (Persons/Sq. Mile)	2332	15	78.5
			Average Rooms per Housing Unit	5.9	12	37.0
Education	12	59.50	% High School Enrollment/Completion	95.6%	13	77.8
			% College Graduates	28.7%	11	41.2
Commute	13	40.05	Average Work Commute in Minutes	21	9	60.0
			% Commuting on Public Transportation	6.1%	16	20.1
Community Stability	17	58.70	% Living in Same House as in 1979	49.6%	18	46.7
			% Living in Same County as in 1985	89.9%	16	70.7

Composite: **Rank** 9 / 34 *Score* 57.83   **BALDWIN**

CATEGORY	RANK	SCORE	STATISTIC	VALUE	RANK	SCORE
Economics	15	61.50	Median Household Income	$31,844	18	32.7
			% of Families Above Poverty Level	96.9%	9	90.3
Affordable Housing	17	77.15	Median Home Value	$60,100	17	75.2
			Median Rent	$388	16	79.1
Crime	N/A	N/A	Violent Crimes per 10,000 Population	N/A	N/A	N/A
			Property Crimes per 10,000 Population	N/A	N/A	N/A
Open Spaces	20	45.65	Population Density (Persons/Sq. Mile)	3794	20	61.7
			Average Rooms per Housing Unit	5.7	15	29.6
Education	22	39.95	% High School Enrollment/Completion	94.8%	18	70.9
			% College Graduates	11.6%	26	9.0
Commute	24	31.30	Average Work Commute in Minutes	27	31	20.0
			% Commuting on Public Transportation	12.8%	6	42.6
Community Stability	2	91.40	% Living in Same House as in 1979	62.1%	2	86.3
			% Living in Same County as in 1985	95.8%	3	96.5

Metropolitan Area Suburb Rankings
PITTSBURGH-BEAVER VALLEY

Composite: *Rank* 10 / 34 *Score* 57.73   **WHITEHALL**

CATEGORY	RANK	SCORE	STATISTIC	VALUE	RANK	SCORE
Economics	14	62.05	Median Household Income	$34,183	16	37.1
			% of Families Above Poverty Level	96.1%	14	87.0
Affordable Housing	19	73.85	Median Home Value	$72,100	24	66.1
			Median Rent	$373	14	81.6
Crime	N/A	N/A	Violent Crimes per 10,000 Population	1	N/A	N/A
			Property Crimes per 10,000 Population	80	N/A	N/A
Open Spaces	21	42.20	Population Density (Persons/Sq. Mile)	4397	24	54.8
			Average Rooms per Housing Unit	5.7	15	29.6
Education	13	57.90	% High School Enrollment/Completion	95.1%	15	73.5
			% College Graduates	29.3%	10	42.3
Commute	19	36.35	Average Work Commute in Minutes	26	27	26.7
			% Commuting on Public Transportation	13.8%	5	46.0
Community Stability	11	74.05	% Living in Same House as in 1979	54.7%	11	62.9
			% Living in Same County as in 1985	93.2%	10	85.2

Composite: *Rank* 11 / 34 *Score* 56.82   **MCCANDLESS TOWNSHIP**

CATEGORY	RANK	SCORE	STATISTIC	VALUE	RANK	SCORE
Economics	4	79.05	Median Household Income	$46,887	4	61.0
			% of Families Above Poverty Level	98.5%	2	97.1
Affordable Housing	32	50.15	Median Home Value	$101,200	30	43.9
			Median Rent	$523	29	56.4
Crime	N/A	N/A	Violent Crimes per 10,000 Population	N/A	N/A	N/A
			Property Crimes per 10,000 Population	N/A	N/A	N/A
Open Spaces	5	72.35	Population Density (Persons/Sq. Mile)	1740	12	85.4
			Average Rooms per Housing Unit	6.5	5	59.3
Education	4	76.20	% High School Enrollment/Completion	96.7%	8	87.2
			% College Graduates	41.5%	4	65.2
Commute	25	30.05	Average Work Commute in Minutes	24	21	40.0
			% Commuting on Public Transportation	6.1%	16	20.1
Community Stability	31	33.15	% Living in Same House as in 1979	40.5%	30	17.8
			% Living in Same County as in 1985	84.8%	28	48.5

Composite: *Rank* 12 / 34 *Score* 55.90   **UPPER ST. CLAIR**

CATEGORY	RANK	SCORE	STATISTIC	VALUE	RANK	SCORE
Economics	2	98.10	Median Household Income	$67,657	1	100.0
			% of Families Above Poverty Level	98.3%	4	96.2
Affordable Housing	34	7.55	Median Home Value	$139,000	33	15.1
			Median Rent	$860	34	0.0
Crime	N/A	N/A	Violent Crimes per 10,000 Population	N/A	N/A	N/A
			Property Crimes per 10,000 Population	N/A	N/A	N/A
Open Spaces	2	91.05	Population Density (Persons/Sq. Mile)	2019	13	82.1
			Average Rooms per Housing Unit	7.6	1	100.0
Education	2	80.35	% High School Enrollment/Completion	93.6%	24	60.7
			% College Graduates	60.0%	1	100.0
Commute	31	20.30	Average Work Commute in Minutes	29	33	6.7
			% Commuting on Public Transportation	10.2%	10	33.9
Community Stability	27	38.05	% Living in Same House as in 1979	47.2%	21	39.0
			% Living in Same County as in 1985	82.2%	31	37.1

Metropolitan Area Suburb Rankings
PITTSBURGH-BEAVER VALLEY

Composite: **Rank** 13 / 34 **Score** 55.43   **MONROEVILLE**

CATEGORY	RANK	SCORE	STATISTIC	VALUE	RANK	SCORE
Economics	10	65.60	Median Household Income	$36,422	13	41.3
			% of Families Above Poverty Level	96.8%	10	89.9
Affordable Housing	25	62.30	Median Home Value	$66,600	20	70.3
			Median Rent	$536	30	54.3
Crime	N/A	N/A	Violent Crimes per 10,000 Population	N/A	N/A	N/A
			Property Crimes per 10,000 Population	N/A	N/A	N/A
Open Spaces	12	60.85	Population Density (Persons/Sq. Mile)	1474	7	88.4
			Average Rooms per Housing Unit	5.8	13	33.3
Education	7	71.25	% High School Enrollment/Completion	97.7%	6	95.7
			% College Graduates	31.7%	8	46.8
Commute	29	24.05	Average Work Commute in Minutes	25	23	33.3
			% Commuting on Public Transportation	4.5%	18	14.8
Community Stability	24	48.55	% Living in Same House as in 1979	47.2%	21	39.0
			% Living in Same County as in 1985	87.0%	26	58.1

Composite: **Rank** 14 / 34 **Score** 55.22   **MURRYSVILLE**

CATEGORY	RANK	SCORE	STATISTIC	VALUE	RANK	SCORE
Economics	3	81.80	Median Household Income	$50,713	3	68.2
			% of Families Above Poverty Level	98.1%	5	95.4
Affordable Housing	28	55.05	Median Home Value	$104,600	32	41.3
			Median Rent	$449	20	68.8
Crime	N/A	N/A	Violent Crimes per 10,000 Population	13	N/A	N/A
			Property Crimes per 10,000 Population	193	N/A	N/A
Open Spaces	3	87.05	Population Density (Persons/Sq. Mile)	468	1	100.0
			Average Rooms per Housing Unit	6.9	3	74.1
Education	6	71.40	% High School Enrollment/Completion	95.8%	12	79.5
			% College Graduates	40.5%	5	63.3
Commute	34	15.20	Average Work Commute in Minutes	26	27	26.7
			% Commuting on Public Transportation	1.2%	29	3.7
Community Stability	32	20.80	% Living in Same House as in 1979	48.0%	20	41.6
			% Living in Same County as in 1985	73.7%	34	0.0

Composite: **Rank** 15 / 34 **Score** 55.19   **ROBINSON TOWNSHIP**

CATEGORY	RANK	SCORE	STATISTIC	VALUE	RANK	SCORE
Economics	12	65.05	Median Household Income	$38,464	8	45.2
			% of Families Above Poverty Level	95.6%	16	84.9
Affordable Housing	30	54.20	Median Home Value	$82,000	26	58.5
			Median Rent	$562	32	49.9
Crime	N/A	N/A	Violent Crimes per 10,000 Population	N/A	N/A	N/A
			Property Crimes per 10,000 Population	N/A	N/A	N/A
Open Spaces	9	63.25	Population Density (Persons/Sq. Mile)	736	2	96.9
			Average Rooms per Housing Unit	5.7	15	29.6
Education	9	68.80	% High School Enrollment/Completion	98.1%	2	99.1
			% College Graduates	27.3%	13	38.5
Commute	20	35.85	Average Work Commute in Minutes	21	9	60.0
			% Commuting on Public Transportation	3.6%	21	11.7
Community Stability	25	44.00	% Living in Same House as in 1979	44.2%	27	29.5
			% Living in Same County as in 1985	87.1%	25	58.5

Metropolitan Area Suburb Rankings
PITTSBURGH-BEAVER VALLEY

Composite: *Rank* 16 / 34 *Score* 55.11   **PLUM**

CATEGORY	RANK	SCORE	STATISTIC	VALUE	RANK	SCORE
Economics	11	65.35	Median Household Income	$36,782	12	42.0
			% of Families Above Poverty Level	96.5%	13	88.7
Affordable Housing	21	65.55	Median Home Value	$63,600	19	72.6
			Median Rent	$511	27	58.5
Crime	N/A	N/A	Violent Crimes per 10,000 Population	N/A	N/A	N/A
			Property Crimes per 10,000 Population	N/A	N/A	N/A
Open Spaces	6	71.60	Population Density (Persons/Sq. Mile)	895	4	95.1
			Average Rooms per Housing Unit	6.2	8	48.1
Education	17	50.95	% High School Enrollment/Completion	94.9%	17	71.8
			% College Graduates	22.8%	16	30.1
Commute	32	18.40	Average Work Commute in Minutes	26	27	26.7
			% Commuting on Public Transportation	3.1%	24	10.1
Community Stability	16	58.80	% Living in Same House as in 1979	50.2%	16	48.6
			% Living in Same County as in 1985	89.5%	18	69.0

Composite: *Rank* 17 / 34 *Score* 53.73   **MUNHALL**

CATEGORY	RANK	SCORE	STATISTIC	VALUE	RANK	SCORE
Economics	21	48.60	Median Household Income	$23,883	24	17.8
			% of Families Above Poverty Level	94.3%	19	79.4
Affordable Housing	5	91.35	Median Home Value	$41,900	9	89.1
			Median Rent	$301	7	93.6
Crime	N/A	N/A	Violent Crimes per 10,000 Population	52	N/A	N/A
			Property Crimes per 10,000 Population	186	N/A	N/A
Open Spaces	27	29.15	Population Density (Persons/Sq. Mile)	5701	30	39.8
			Average Rooms per Housing Unit	5.4	21	18.5
Education	30	21.50	% High School Enrollment/Completion	90.7%	27	35.9
			% College Graduates	10.6%	29	7.1
Commute	11	41.95	Average Work Commute in Minutes	23	13	46.7
			% Commuting on Public Transportation	11.2%	9	37.2
Community Stability	3	89.85	% Living in Same House as in 1979	60.0%	6	79.7
			% Living in Same County as in 1985	96.6%	1	100.0

Composite: *Rank* 18 / 34 *Score* 53.40   **SCOTT TOWNSHIP**

CATEGORY	RANK	SCORE	STATISTIC	VALUE	RANK	SCORE
Economics	13	63.95	Median Household Income	$34,644	15	38.0
			% of Families Above Poverty Level	96.8%	10	89.9
Affordable Housing	24	62.90	Median Home Value	$68,500	21	68.8
			Median Rent	$520	28	57.0
Crime	N/A	N/A	Violent Crimes per 10,000 Population	N/A	N/A	N/A
			Property Crimes per 10,000 Population	N/A	N/A	N/A
Open Spaces	24	37.00	Population Density (Persons/Sq. Mile)	4331	23	55.5
			Average Rooms per Housing Unit	5.4	21	18.5
Education	11	61.65	% High School Enrollment/Completion	95.9%	11	80.3
			% College Graduates	29.7%	9	43.0
Commute	9	43.15	Average Work Commute in Minutes	23	13	46.7
			% Commuting on Public Transportation	11.9%	8	39.6
Community Stability	22	51.75	% Living in Same House as in 1979	46.6%	24	37.1
			% Living in Same County as in 1985	88.9%	20	66.4

Metropolitan Area Suburb Rankings
PITTSBURGH-BEAVER VALLEY

Composite: **Rank** 19 / 34 *Score* 53.04   **JEANNETTE**

CATEGORY	RANK	SCORE	STATISTIC	VALUE	RANK	SCORE
Economics	29	24.60	Median Household Income	$18,482	29	7.6
			% of Families Above Poverty Level	85.3%	29	41.6
Affordable Housing	6	90.85	Median Home Value	$41,800	8	89.2
			Median Rent	$308	9	92.5
Crime	N/A	N/A	Violent Crimes per 10,000 Population	N/A	N/A	N/A
			Property Crimes per 10,000 Population	N/A	N/A	N/A
Open Spaces	26	33.20	Population Density (Persons/Sq. Mile)	4669	25	51.6
			Average Rooms per Housing Unit	5.3	25	14.8
Education	20	45.50	% High School Enrollment/Completion	96.8%	7	88.0
			% College Graduates	8.4%	32	3.0
Commute	6	44.70	Average Work Commute in Minutes	17	2	86.7
			% Commuting on Public Transportation	0.9%	30	2.7
Community Stability	6	79.40	% Living in Same House as in 1979	54.8%	10	63.2
			% Living in Same County as in 1985	95.6%	4	95.6

Composite: **Rank** 20 / 34 *Score* 52.99   **HARRISON TOWNSHIP**

CATEGORY	RANK	SCORE	STATISTIC	VALUE	RANK	SCORE
Economics	23	39.95	Median Household Income	$24,766	23	19.4
			% of Families Above Poverty Level	89.8%	23	60.5
Affordable Housing	10	86.90	Median Home Value	$48,100	11	84.4
			Median Rent	$326	11	89.4
Crime	N/A	N/A	Violent Crimes per 10,000 Population	N/A	N/A	N/A
			Property Crimes per 10,000 Population	N/A	N/A	N/A
Open Spaces	17	52.65	Population Density (Persons/Sq. Mile)	1617	10	86.8
			Average Rooms per Housing Unit	5.4	21	18.5
Education	31	20.20	% High School Enrollment/Completion	90.2%	29	31.6
			% College Graduates	11.5%	27	8.8
Commute	14	39.35	Average Work Commute in Minutes	19	6	73.3
			% Commuting on Public Transportation	1.7%	27	5.4
Community Stability	7	78.90	% Living in Same House as in 1979	59.3%	7	77.5
			% Living in Same County as in 1985	92.1%	14	80.3

Composite: **Rank** 21 / 34 *Score* 52.54   **SOUTH PARK TOWNSHIP**

CATEGORY	RANK	SCORE	STATISTIC	VALUE	RANK	SCORE
Economics	18	58.30	Median Household Income	$37,382	10	43.1
			% of Families Above Poverty Level	92.9%	21	73.5
Affordable Housing	22	65.50	Median Home Value	$71,800	23	66.3
			Median Rent	$474	24	64.7
Crime	N/A	N/A	Violent Crimes per 10,000 Population	N/A	N/A	N/A
			Property Crimes per 10,000 Population	N/A	N/A	N/A
Open Spaces	7	65.95	Population Density (Persons/Sq. Mile)	1558	9	87.5
			Average Rooms per Housing Unit	6.1	10	44.4
Education	15	54.05	% High School Enrollment/Completion	95.1%	15	73.5
			% College Graduates	25.2%	14	34.6
Commute	33	15.60	Average Work Commute in Minutes	30	34	0.0
			% Commuting on Public Transportation	9.4%	12	31.2
Community Stability	19	55.85	% Living in Same House as in 1979	44.5%	26	30.5
			% Living in Same County as in 1985	92.3%	13	81.2

Metropolitan Area Suburb Rankings
PITTSBURGH-BEAVER VALLEY

Composite: *Rank* 22 / 34 *Score* 52.03   **FRANKLIN PARK**

CATEGORY	RANK	SCORE	STATISTIC	VALUE	RANK	SCORE
Economics	1	99.25	Median Household Income	$66,836	2	98.5
			% of Families Above Poverty Level	99.2%	1	100.0
Affordable Housing	33	15.75	Median Home Value	$158,800	34	0.0
			Median Rent	$672	33	31.5
Crime	N/A	N/A	Violent Crimes per 10,000 Population	2	N/A	N/A
			Property Crimes per 10,000 Population	7	N/A	N/A
Open Spaces	1	98.40	Population Density (Persons/Sq. Mile)	745	3	96.8
			Average Rooms per Housing Unit	7.6	1	100.0
Education	5	72.55	% High School Enrollment/Completion	94.4%	22	67.5
			% College Graduates	48.1%	3	77.6
Commute	28	24.70	Average Work Commute in Minutes	23	13	46.7
			% Commuting on Public Transportation	0.9%	30	2.7
Community Stability	34	1.55	% Living in Same House as in 1979	35.6%	33	2.2
			% Living in Same County as in 1985	73.9%	33	0.9

Composite: *Rank* 23 / 34 *Score* 51.69   **NORTH VERSAILLES**

CATEGORY	RANK	SCORE	STATISTIC	VALUE	RANK	SCORE
Economics	24	38.85	Median Household Income	$25,130	22	20.1
			% of Families Above Poverty Level	89.1%	24	57.6
Affordable Housing	12	85.70	Median Home Value	$43,400	10	88.0
			Median Rent	$362	13	83.4
Crime	N/A	N/A	Violent Crimes per 10,000 Population	25	N/A	N/A
			Property Crimes per 10,000 Population	178	N/A	N/A
Open Spaces	18	51.35	Population Density (Persons/Sq. Mile)	1516	8	87.9
			Average Rooms per Housing Unit	5.3	25	14.8
Education	25	30.90	% High School Enrollment/Completion	92.9%	25	54.7
			% College Graduates	10.6%	29	7.1
Commute	27	29.75	Average Work Commute in Minutes	23	13	46.7
			% Commuting on Public Transportation	3.9%	20	12.8
Community Stability	12	73.60	% Living in Same House as in 1979	55.0%	9	63.8
			% Living in Same County as in 1985	92.8%	11	83.4

Composite: *Rank* 24 / 34 *Score* 48.93   **ALIQUIPPA**

CATEGORY	RANK	SCORE	STATISTIC	VALUE	RANK	SCORE
Economics	33	2.25	Median Household Income	$16,804	30	4.5
			% of Families Above Poverty Level	75.4%	34	0.0
Affordable Housing	2	97.30	Median Home Value	$34,700	3	94.6
			Median Rent	$263	1	100.0
Crime	N/A	N/A	Violent Crimes per 10,000 Population	56	N/A	N/A
			Property Crimes per 10,000 Population	429	N/A	N/A
Open Spaces	23	37.60	Population Density (Persons/Sq. Mile)	3269	19	67.8
			Average Rooms per Housing Unit	5.1	30	7.4
Education	21	41.15	% High School Enrollment/Completion	96.0%	10	81.2
			% College Graduates	7.4%	33	1.1
Commute	18	36.55	Average Work Commute in Minutes	21	9	60.0
			% Commuting on Public Transportation	4.0%	19	13.1
Community Stability	8	78.75	% Living in Same House as in 1979	56.6%	8	68.9
			% Living in Same County as in 1985	94.0%	9	88.6

Metropolitan Area Suburb Rankings
PITTSBURGH-BEAVER VALLEY

Composite: **Rank** 25 / 34 **Score** 48.90   **BRENTWOOD**

CATEGORY	RANK	SCORE	STATISTIC	VALUE	RANK	SCORE
Economics	19	55.30	Median Household Income	$27,698	19	24.9
			% of Families Above Poverty Level	95.8%	15	85.7
Affordable Housing	15	80.80	Median Home Value	$51,900	14	81.5
			Median Rent	$382	15	80.1
Crime	N/A	N/A	Violent Crimes per 10,000 Population	N/A	N/A	N/A
			Property Crimes per 10,000 Population	N/A	N/A	N/A
Open Spaces	32	20.75	Population Density (Persons/Sq. Mile)	7481	32	19.3
			Average Rooms per Housing Unit	5.5	19	22.2
Education	29	21.55	% High School Enrollment/Completion	89.5%	31	25.6
			% College Graduates	16.1%	21	17.5
Commute	5	45.55	Average Work Commute in Minutes	26	27	26.7
			% Commuting on Public Transportation	19.3%	2	64.4
Community Stability	13	69.45	% Living in Same House as in 1979	50.6%	15	49.8
			% Living in Same County as in 1985	94.1%	8	89.1

Composite: **Rank** 26 / 34 **Score** 48.71   **CARNOT-MOON**

CATEGORY	RANK	SCORE	STATISTIC	VALUE	RANK	SCORE
Economics	16	61.10	Median Household Income	$37,637	9	43.6
			% of Families Above Poverty Level	94.1%	20	78.6
Affordable Housing	26	58.95	Median Home Value	$82,800	28	57.9
			Median Rent	$502	25	60.0
Crime	N/A	N/A	Violent Crimes per 10,000 Population	N/A	N/A	N/A
			Property Crimes per 10,000 Population	N/A	N/A	N/A
Open Spaces	16	53.65	Population Density (Persons/Sq. Mile)	2086	14	81.4
			Average Rooms per Housing Unit	5.6	18	25.9
Education	8	69.30	% High School Enrollment/Completion	98.1%	2	99.1
			% College Graduates	27.8%	12	39.5
Commute	15	38.90	Average Work Commute in Minutes	20	7	66.7
			% Commuting on Public Transportation	3.4%	22	11.1
Community Stability	33	10.35	% Living in Same House as in 1979	37.0%	32	6.7
			% Living in Same County as in 1985	76.9%	32	14.0

Composite: **Rank** 27 / 34 **Score** 46.78   **NEW KENSINGTON**

CATEGORY	RANK	SCORE	STATISTIC	VALUE	RANK	SCORE
Economics	26	31.45	Median Household Income	$21,525	27	13.3
			% of Families Above Poverty Level	87.2%	26	49.6
Affordable Housing	8	90.25	Median Home Value	$49,300	13	83.5
			Median Rent	$281	4	97.0
Crime	N/A	N/A	Violent Crimes per 10,000 Population	N/A	N/A	N/A
			Property Crimes per 10,000 Population	N/A	N/A	N/A
Open Spaces	22	38.90	Population Density (Persons/Sq. Mile)	4004	22	59.3
			Average Rooms per Housing Unit	5.4	21	18.5
Education	27	25.20	% High School Enrollment/Completion	90.7%	27	35.9
			% College Graduates	14.5%	22	14.5
Commute	16	37.20	Average Work Commute in Minutes	20	7	66.7
			% Commuting on Public Transportation	2.4%	26	7.7
Community Stability	18	57.70	% Living in Same House as in 1979	52.0%	13	54.3
			% Living in Same County as in 1985	87.7%	22	61.1

Metropolitan Area Suburb Rankings
PITTSBURGH-BEAVER VALLEY

Composite: **Rank** 28 / 34 **Score** 45.85   **GREENSBURG**

CATEGORY	RANK	SCORE	STATISTIC	VALUE	RANK	SCORE
Economics	28	26.65	Median Household Income	$20,223	28	10.9
			% of Families Above Poverty Level	85.5%	28	42.4
Affordable Housing	11	85.75	Median Home Value	$55,300	16	78.9
			Median Rent	$307	8	92.6
Crime	N/A	N/A	Violent Crimes per 10,000 Population	46	N/A	N/A
			Property Crimes per 10,000 Population	360	N/A	N/A
Open Spaces	25	36.10	Population Density (Persons/Sq. Mile)	3848	21	61.1
			Average Rooms per Housing Unit	5.2	28	11.1
Education	19	47.95	% High School Enrollment/Completion	94.6%	20	69.2
			% College Graduates	21.0%	18	26.7
Commute	7	44.50	Average Work Commute in Minutes	17	2	86.7
			% Commuting on Public Transportation	0.8%	32	2.3
Community Stability	30	34.15	% Living in Same House as in 1979	39.9%	31	15.9
			% Living in Same County as in 1985	85.7%	27	52.4

Composite: **Rank** 29 / 34 **Score** 45.06   **UNIONTOWN**

CATEGORY	RANK	SCORE	STATISTIC	VALUE	RANK	SCORE
Economics	32	10.35	Median Household Income	$15,383	33	1.8
			% of Families Above Poverty Level	79.9%	30	18.9
Affordable Housing	4	92.80	Median Home Value	$39,700	4	90.8
			Median Rent	$294	6	94.8
Crime	N/A	N/A	Violent Crimes per 10,000 Population	N/A	N/A	N/A
			Property Crimes per 10,000 Population	N/A	N/A	N/A
Open Spaces	30	24.25	Population Density (Persons/Sq. Mile)	5905	31	37.4
			Average Rooms per Housing Unit	5.2	28	11.1
Education	24	35.85	% High School Enrollment/Completion	93.7%	23	61.5
			% College Graduates	12.2%	24	10.2
Commute	8	43.70	Average Work Commute in Minutes	17	2	86.7
			% Commuting on Public Transportation	0.3%	33	0.7
Community Stability	14	63.40	% Living in Same House as in 1979	49.8%	17	47.3
			% Living in Same County as in 1985	91.9%	15	79.5

Composite: **Rank** 30 / 34 **Score** 44.53   **MCKEESPORT**

CATEGORY	RANK	SCORE	STATISTIC	VALUE	RANK	SCORE
Economics	31	10.30	Median Household Income	$16,427	31	3.8
			% of Families Above Poverty Level	79.4%	32	16.8
Affordable Housing	1	98.60	Median Home Value	$27,600	1	100.0
			Median Rent	$280	3	97.2
Crime	N/A	N/A	Violent Crimes per 10,000 Population	N/A	N/A	N/A
			Property Crimes per 10,000 Population	N/A	N/A	N/A
Open Spaces	28	26.50	Population Density (Persons/Sq. Mile)	5195	27	45.6
			Average Rooms per Housing Unit	5.1	30	7.4
Education	33	13.70	% High School Enrollment/Completion	89.7%	30	27.4
			% College Graduates	6.8%	34	0.0
Commute	12	40.30	Average Work Commute in Minutes	23	13	46.7
			% Commuting on Public Transportation	10.2%	10	33.9
Community Stability	9	77.80	% Living in Same House as in 1979	54.2%	12	61.3
			% Living in Same County as in 1985	95.3%	5	94.3

Composite: **Rank** 31 / 34 *Score* 43.05   **SWISSVALE**

CATEGORY	RANK	SCORE	STATISTIC	VALUE	RANK	SCORE
Economics	25	35.70	Median Household Income	$23,773	25	17.6
			% of Families Above Poverty Level	88.2%	25	53.8
Affordable Housing	14	83.35	Median Home Value	$40,700	7	90.0
			Median Rent	$402	18	76.7
Crime	N/A	N/A	Violent Crimes per 10,000 Population	24	N/A	N/A
			Property Crimes per 10,000 Population	325	N/A	N/A
Open Spaces	33	9.00	Population Density (Persons/Sq. Mile)	8873	33	3.2
			Average Rooms per Housing Unit	5.3	25	14.8
Education	28	23.10	% High School Enrollment/Completion	88.8%	32	19.7
			% College Graduates	20.9%	19	26.5
Commute	2	53.05	Average Work Commute in Minutes	23	13	46.7
			% Commuting on Public Transportation	17.8%	3	59.4
Community Stability	20	54.10	% Living in Same House as in 1979	42.7%	28	24.8
			% Living in Same County as in 1985	92.8%	11	83.4

Composite: **Rank** 32 / 34 *Score* 41.06   **WASHINGTON**

CATEGORY	RANK	SCORE	STATISTIC	VALUE	RANK	SCORE
Economics	30	11.05	Median Household Income	$16,365	32	3.6
			% of Families Above Poverty Level	79.8%	31	18.5
Affordable Housing	9	90.20	Median Home Value	$40,600	6	90.1
			Median Rent	$321	10	90.3
Crime	N/A	N/A	Violent Crimes per 10,000 Population	111	N/A	N/A
			Property Crimes per 10,000 Population	608	N/A	N/A
Open Spaces	31	21.65	Population Density (Persons/Sq. Mile)	5389	28	43.3
			Average Rooms per Housing Unit	4.9	34	0.0
Education	23	39.20	% High School Enrollment/Completion	94.5%	21	68.4
			% College Graduates	12.1%	25	10.0
Commute	3	50.00	Average Work Commute in Minutes	15	1	100.0
			% Commuting on Public Transportation	0.1%	34	0.0
Community Stability	29	34.25	% Living in Same House as in 1979	41.2%	29	20.0
			% Living in Same County as in 1985	84.8%	28	48.5

Composite: **Rank** 33 / 34 *Score* 39.97   **WILKINSBURG**

CATEGORY	RANK	SCORE	STATISTIC	VALUE	RANK	SCORE
Economics	27	29.45	Median Household Income	$22,709	26	15.6
			% of Families Above Poverty Level	85.7%	27	43.3
Affordable Housing	13	84.30	Median Home Value	$40,400	5	90.2
			Median Rent	$392	17	78.4
Crime	N/A	N/A	Violent Crimes per 10,000 Population	N/A	N/A	N/A
			Property Crimes per 10,000 Population	N/A	N/A	N/A
Open Spaces	34	3.70	Population Density (Persons/Sq. Mile)	9154	34	0.0
			Average Rooms per Housing Unit	5.1	30	7.4
Education	32	17.45	% High School Enrollment/Completion	87.0%	33	4.3
			% College Graduates	23.1%	15	30.6
Commute	1	70.00	Average Work Commute in Minutes	24	21	40.0
			% Commuting on Public Transportation	29.9%	1	100.0
Community Stability	28	34.95	% Living in Same House as in 1979	34.9%	34	0.0
			% Living in Same County as in 1985	89.7%	17	69.9

Composite: Rank 34 / 34 **Score** 35.55 **BEAVER FALLS**

CATEGORY	RANK	SCORE	STATISTIC	VALUE	RANK	SCORE
Economics	34	0.40	Median Household Income	$14,423	34	0.0
			% of Families Above Poverty Level	75.6%	33	0.8
Affordable Housing	3	97.35	Median Home Value	$29,900	2	98.2
			Median Rent	$284	5	96.5
Crime	N/A	N/A	Violent Crimes per 10,000 Population	112	N/A	N/A
			Property Crimes per 10,000 Population	204	N/A	N/A
Open Spaces	29	25.55	Population Density (Persons/Sq. Mile)	5034	26	47.4
			Average Rooms per Housing Unit	5.0	33	3.7
Education	34	2.05	% High School Enrollment/Completion	86.5%	34	0.0
			% College Graduates	9.0%	31	4.1
Commute	4	47.70	Average Work Commute in Minutes	17	2	86.7
			% Commuting on Public Transportation	2.7%	25	8.7
Community Stability	26	40.25	% Living in Same House as in 1979	46.5%	25	36.8
			% Living in Same County as in 1985	83.7%	30	43.7

Metropolitan Area Description
PORTLAND-VANCOUVER

STATE: Oregon
COUNTIES: Clackamas, Multnomah, Washington, Yamhill

STATE: Washington
COUNTIES: Clark

TOTAL POPULATION: 1,477,895

POPULATION IN SUBURBS: 994,196   (67.3%)

POPULATION IN Portland (OR):   437,319   (29.6%)
POPULATION IN Vancouver (WA): 46,380   (3.1%)

The PORTLAND-VANCOUVER metropolitan area is located in the northwestern part of Oregon and the southwestern part of Washington. The suburbs range geographically from Salmon Creek (WA) in the north (14 miles from Portland), to Forest Grove (OR) in the west (25 miles from Portland), to McMinnville (OR) in the southwest (42 miles from Portland), and to Gresham (OR) in the east (15 miles from Portland). The area is growing in population and had an increase of 13.9% between 1980 and 1990. Summer time high temperatures average in the 70's and winter time lows average in the 30's. High tech companies are located in the suburbs along the Sunset Corridor which extends west of Portland along U.S. Route 26. Tektronix has facilities located in the suburb of Beaverton (OR). Public transportation in the area is provided by Tri-Met and C-TRAN using buses and trains.

Oatfield (OR) is the overall highest rated suburb and also has the highest score in community stability. **Lake Oswego** (OR) receives the top scores in economics and education, and is also rated the safest suburb with the lowest crime rate. **Forest Grove** (OR) is the suburb with the most affordable housing. The top score in open spaces belongs to **West Linn** (OR). Finally, the top rated commute belongs to **Hazelwood** (OR).

The highest ranked suburb overall which also has an affordable housing score of at least 50.00 is **Oatfield** (OR).

The highest ranked suburb in the education category which also has an affordable housing score of at least 50.00 is **Beaverton** (OR).

The county whose suburbs have the highest average overall score is **Clackamas County** (OR) (54.44)

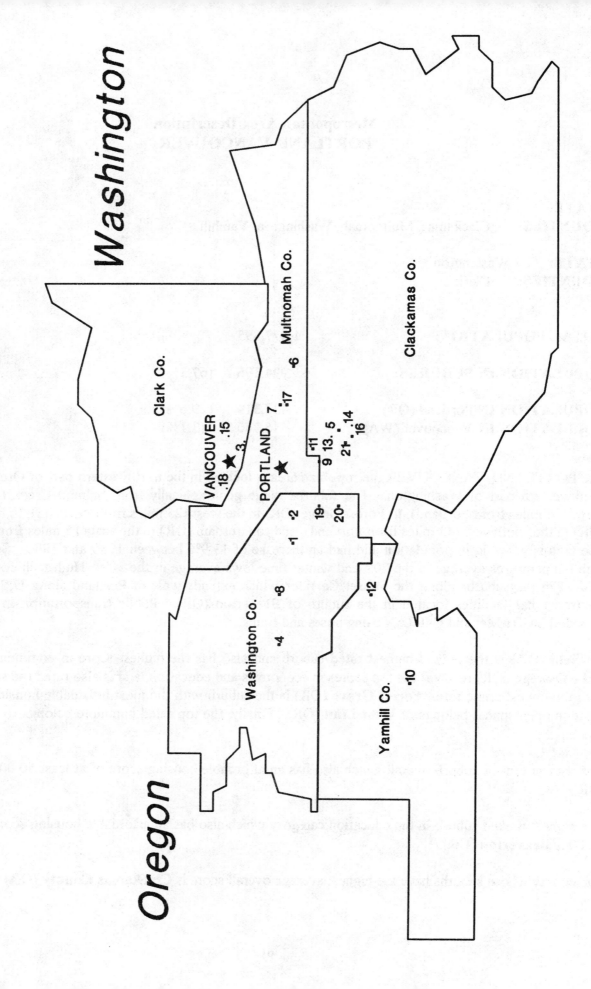

Metropolitan Area Map
PORTLAND–VANCOUVER

Washington

Oregon

Clark Co.

Multnomah Co.

Clackamas Co.

Washington Co.

Yamhill Co.

VANCOUVER
.18 .15
.3

PORTLAND
.7 .17
.6

.11
.9 13. 5
.2 .14
.16

.1
.19
.20

.8

.4

.12

.10

Metropolitan Area Suburb Alphabetical Index
PORTLAND-VANCOUVER

SUBURB	PAGE	MAP NO.	STATE	COUNTY	POPU-LATION	RANK
ALOHA	623	1	Oregon	Washington	34,284	6 / 21
BEAVERTON	625	2	Oregon	Washington	53,310	11 / 21
EVERGREEN	627	3	Washington	Clark	11,249	16 / 21
FOREST GROVE	626	4	Oregon	Washington	13,559	15 / 21
GLADSTONE	623	5	Oregon	Clackamas	10,152	4 / 21
GRESHAM	626	6	Oregon	Multnomah	68,235	13 / 21
HAZELWOOD	624	7	Oregon	Multnomah	11,480	9 / 21
HILLSBORO	624	8	Oregon	Washington	37,520	7 / 21
LAKE OSWEGO	622	9	Oregon	Clackamas	30,576	3 / 21
MCMINNVILLE	625	10	Oregon	Yamhill	17,894	10 / 21
MILWAUKIE	624	11	Oregon	Clackamas	18,692	8 / 21
NEWBERG	627	12	Oregon	Yamhill	13,086	17 / 21
OAK GROVE	628	13	Oregon	Clackamas	12,576	19 / 21
OATFIELD	622	14	Oregon	Clackamas	15,348	1 / 21
ORCHARDS SOUTH	627	15	Washington	Clark	12,956	18 / 21
OREGON CITY	628	16	Oregon	Clackamas	14,698	21 / 21
POWELLHURST-CENTENNIAL	628	17	Oregon	Multnomah	28,756	20 / 21
SALMON CREEK	623	18	Washington	Clark	11,989	5 / 21
TIGARD	625	19	Oregon	Washington	29,344	12 / 21
TUALATIN	626	20	Oregon	Washington	15,013	14 / 21
WEST LINN	622	21	Oregon	Clackamas	16,367	2 / 21

Metropolitan Area Suburb Rankings
PORTLAND-VANCOUVER

Composite: *Rank* 1 / 21 *Score* 68.20   OATFIELD (OR)

CATEGORY	RANK	SCORE	STATISTIC	VALUE	RANK	SCORE
Economics	4	65.85	Median Household Income	$39,451	4	55.9
			% of Families Above Poverty Level	96.6%	5	75.8
Affordable Housing	14	61.70	Median Home Value	$83,000	15	69.2
			Median Rent	$494	14	54.2
Crime	N/A	N/A	Violent Crimes per 10,000 Population	N/A	N/A	N/A
			Property Crimes per 10,000 Population	N/A	N/A	N/A
Open Spaces	2	77.85	Population Density (Persons/Sq. Mile)	3521	14	55.7
			Average Rooms per Housing Unit	6.6	1	100.0
Education	4	62.85	% High School Enrollment/Completion	97.0%	1	100.0
			% College Graduates	20.7%	8	25.7
Commute	9	42.90	Average Work Commute in Minutes	21	5	42.9
			% Commuting on Public Transportation	3.7%	10	42.9
Community Stability	1	98.05	% Living in Same House as in 1979	48.1%	1	100.0
			% Living in Same County as in 1985	79.9%	3	96.1

Composite: *Rank* 2 / 21 *Score* 63.39   WEST LINN (OR)

CATEGORY	RANK	SCORE	STATISTIC	VALUE	RANK	SCORE
Economics	2	78.00	Median Household Income	$45,474	2	78.0
			% of Families Above Poverty Level	96.8%	3	78.0
Affordable Housing	20	47.30	Median Home Value	$102,400	20	46.6
			Median Rent	$511	16	48.0
Crime	2	87.70	Violent Crimes per 10,000 Population	22	4	75.4
			Property Crimes per 10,000 Population	167	1	100.0
Open Spaces	1	92.30	Population Density (Persons/Sq. Mile)	2469	6	84.6
			Average Rooms per Housing Unit	6.6	1	100.0
Education	3	65.80	% High School Enrollment/Completion	93.7%	3	70.5
			% College Graduates	36.5%	3	61.1
Commute	20	26.45	Average Work Commute in Minutes	22	13	28.6
			% Commuting on Public Transportation	2.4%	16	24.3
Community Stability	13	46.20	% Living in Same House as in 1979	27.1%	9	40.8
			% Living in Same County as in 1985	64.9%	17	51.6

Composite: *Rank* 3 / 21 *Score* 59.08   LAKE OSWEGO (OR)

CATEGORY	RANK	SCORE	STATISTIC	VALUE	RANK	SCORE
Economics	1	96.70	Median Household Income	$51,499	1	100.0
			% of Families Above Poverty Level	98.2%	2	93.4
Affordable Housing	21	0.00	Median Home Value	$142,500	21	0.0
			Median Rent	$641	21	0.0
Crime	1	88.05	Violent Crimes per 10,000 Population	7	1	100.0
			Property Crimes per 10,000 Population	288	2	76.1
Open Spaces	3	73.55	Population Density (Persons/Sq. Mile)	3192	12	64.7
			Average Rooms per Housing Unit	6.3	3	82.4
Education	1	84.80	% High School Enrollment/Completion	93.6%	4	69.6
			% College Graduates	53.9%	1	100.0
Commute	11	39.30	Average Work Commute in Minutes	21	5	42.9
			% Commuting on Public Transportation	3.2%	13	35.7
Community Stability	19	31.15	% Living in Same House as in 1979	24.7%	13	34.1
			% Living in Same County as in 1985	57.0%	20	28.2

Metropolitan Area Suburb Rankings
PORTLAND-VANCOUVER

Composite: **Rank** 4 / 21 *Score* 58.60   GLADSTONE (OR)

CATEGORY	RANK	SCORE	STATISTIC	VALUE	RANK	SCORE
Economics	5	64.45	Median Household Income	$32,069	12	28.9
			% of Families Above Poverty Level	98.8%	1	100.0
Affordable Housing	9	77.05	Median Home Value	$72,800	14	81.0
			Median Rent	$443	9	73.1
Crime	N/A	N/A	Violent Crimes per 10,000 Population	N/A	N/A	N/A
			Property Crimes per 10,000 Population	N/A	N/A	N/A
Open Spaces	12	45.65	Population Density (Persons/Sq. Mile)	4147	17	38.4
			Average Rooms per Housing Unit	5.8	5	52.9
Education	12	29.80	% High School Enrollment/Completion	90.0%	10	37.5
			% College Graduates	19.1%	12	22.1
Commute	4	50.00	Average Work Commute in Minutes	20	2	57.1
			% Commuting on Public Transportation	3.7%	10	42.9
Community Stability	3	84.65	% Living in Same House as in 1979	38.6%	3	73.2
			% Living in Same County as in 1985	79.9%	3	96.1

Composite: **Rank** 5 / 21 *Score* 52.50   SALMON CREEK (WA)

CATEGORY	RANK	SCORE	STATISTIC	VALUE	RANK	SCORE
Economics	9	51.80	Median Household Income	$34,170	8	36.6
			% of Families Above Poverty Level	95.8%	7	67.0
Affordable Housing	11	76.60	Median Home Value	$83,800	16	68.3
			Median Rent	$411	3	84.9
Crime	N/A	N/A	Violent Crimes per 10,000 Population	N/A	N/A	N/A
			Property Crimes per 10,000 Population	N/A	N/A	N/A
Open Spaces	3	73.55	Population Density (Persons/Sq. Mile)	1909	1	100.0
			Average Rooms per Housing Unit	5.7	7	47.1
Education	13	27.40	% High School Enrollment/Completion	88.9%	12	27.7
			% College Graduates	21.3%	7	27.1
Commute	13	37.10	Average Work Commute in Minutes	20	2	57.1
			% Commuting on Public Transportation	1.9%	18	17.1
Community Stability	12	48.55	% Living in Same House as in 1979	21.8%	16	25.9
			% Living in Same County as in 1985	71.5%	12	71.2

Composite: **Rank** 6 / 21 *Score* 51.16   ALOHA (OR)

CATEGORY	RANK	SCORE	STATISTIC	VALUE	RANK	SCORE
Economics	6	58.75	Median Household Income	$38,556	5	52.7
			% of Families Above Poverty Level	95.6%	8	64.8
Affordable Housing	15	60.95	Median Home Value	$71,600	12	82.4
			Median Rent	$534	18	39.5
Crime	N/A	N/A	Violent Crimes per 10,000 Population	N/A	N/A	N/A
			Property Crimes per 10,000 Population	N/A	N/A	N/A
Open Spaces	14	44.85	Population Density (Persons/Sq. Mile)	4636	19	25.0
			Average Rooms per Housing Unit	6.0	4	64.7
Education	5	48.05	% High School Enrollment/Completion	93.3%	5	67.0
			% College Graduates	22.2%	6	29.1
Commute	16	30.70	Average Work Commute in Minutes	23	18	14.3
			% Commuting on Public Transportation	4.0%	7	47.1
Community Stability	8	63.65	% Living in Same House as in 1979	30.3%	8	49.9
			% Living in Same County as in 1985	73.6%	9	77.4

Metropolitan Area Suburb Rankings
PORTLAND-VANCOUVER

Composite: Rank 7 / 21 *Score* 51.06   **HILLSBORO** (OR)

CATEGORY	RANK	SCORE	STATISTIC	VALUE	RANK	SCORE
Economics	11	38.95	Median Household Income	$33,125	11	32.8
			% of Families Above Poverty Level	93.8%	13	45.1
Affordable Housing	12	71.15	Median Home Value	$71,200	11	82.9
			Median Rent	$480	12	59.4
Crime	3	71.65	Violent Crimes per 10,000 Population	18	2	82.0
			Property Crimes per 10,000 Population	363	4	61.3
Open Spaces	6	67.10	Population Density (Persons/Sq. Mile)	1948	2	98.9
			Average Rooms per Housing Unit	5.5	8	35.3
Education	19	11.30	% High School Enrollment/Completion	85.8%	20	0.0
			% College Graduates	19.3%	10	22.6
Commute	14	36.45	Average Work Commute in Minutes	22	13	28.6
			% Commuting on Public Transportation	3.8%	9	44.3
Community Stability	10	60.80	% Living in Same House as in 1979	26.7%	12	39.7
			% Living in Same County as in 1985	75.1%	7	81.9

Composite: Rank 8 / 21 *Score* 50.86   **MILWAUKIE** (OR)

CATEGORY	RANK	SCORE	STATISTIC	VALUE	RANK	SCORE
Economics	16	32.65	Median Household Income	$29,693	15	20.2
			% of Families Above Poverty Level	93.8%	13	45.1
Affordable Housing	7	82.20	Median Home Value	$65,500	5	89.5
			Median Rent	$438	7	74.9
Crime	N/A	N/A	Violent Crimes per 10,000 Population	N/A	N/A	N/A
			Property Crimes per 10,000 Population	N/A	N/A	N/A
Open Spaces	16	36.95	Population Density (Persons/Sq. Mile)	3927	16	44.5
			Average Rooms per Housing Unit	5.4	13	29.4
Education	10	31.70	% High School Enrollment/Completion	90.8%	8	44.6
			% College Graduates	17.6%	14	18.8
Commute	3	52.10	Average Work Commute in Minutes	20	2	57.1
			% Commuting on Public Transportation	4.0%	7	47.1
Community Stability	7	69.55	% Living in Same House as in 1979	36.5%	4	67.3
			% Living in Same County as in 1985	71.7%	10	71.8

Composite: Rank 9 / 21 *Score* 49.79   **HAZELWOOD** (OR)

CATEGORY	RANK	SCORE	STATISTIC	VALUE	RANK	SCORE
Economics	15	33.75	Median Household Income	$30,875	14	24.6
			% of Families Above Poverty Level	93.6%	15	42.9
Affordable Housing	3	91.25	Median Home Value	$57,600	2	98.7
			Median Rent	$414	5	83.8
Crime	N/A	N/A	Violent Crimes per 10,000 Population	N/A	N/A	N/A
			Property Crimes per 10,000 Population	N/A	N/A	N/A
Open Spaces	19	17.65	Population Density (Persons/Sq. Mile)	5544	21	0.0
			Average Rooms per Housing Unit	5.5	8	35.3
Education	20	11.05	% High School Enrollment/Completion	87.4%	17	14.3
			% College Graduates	12.7%	19	7.8
Commute	1	57.15	Average Work Commute in Minutes	23	18	14.3
			% Commuting on Public Transportation	7.7%	1	100.0
Community Stability	2	87.90	% Living in Same House as in 1979	39.5%	2	75.8
			% Living in Same County as in 1985	81.2%	1	100.0

Composite: *Rank* 10 / 21 *Score* 49.27 — **MCMINNVILLE (OR)**

CATEGORY	RANK	SCORE	STATISTIC	VALUE	RANK	SCORE
Economics	19	11.95	Median Household Income	$25,878	20	6.3
			% of Families Above Poverty Level	91.3%	19	17.6
Affordable Housing	2	94.00	Median Home Value	$65,900	6	89.1
			Median Rent	$373	2	98.9
Crime	8	44.75	Violent Crimes per 10,000 Population	27	7	67.2
			Property Crimes per 10,000 Population	560	8	22.3
Open Spaces	9	59.15	Population Density (Persons/Sq. Mile)	2098	3	94.8
			Average Rooms per Housing Unit	5.3	15	23.5
Education	8	39.30	% High School Enrollment/Completion	92.1%	6	56.2
			% College Graduates	19.2%	11	22.4
Commute	4	50.00	Average Work Commute in Minutes	17	1	100.0
			% Commuting on Public Transportation	0.7%	21	0.0
Community Stability	14	45.75	% Living in Same House as in 1979	23.5%	14	30.7
			% Living in Same County as in 1985	68.0%	14	60.8

Composite: *Rank* 11 / 21 *Score* 46.61 — **BEAVERTON (OR)**

CATEGORY	RANK	SCORE	STATISTIC	VALUE	RANK	SCORE
Economics	10	45.90	Median Household Income	$33,951	9	35.8
			% of Families Above Poverty Level	94.8%	10	56.0
Affordable Housing	18	55.35	Median Home Value	$89,500	17	61.6
			Median Rent	$508	15	49.1
Crime	7	47.50	Violent Crimes per 10,000 Population	34	8	55.7
			Property Crimes per 10,000 Population	474	6	39.3
Open Spaces	18	32.00	Population Density (Persons/Sq. Mile)	3857	15	46.4
			Average Rooms per Housing Unit	5.2	18	17.6
Education	2	66.60	% High School Enrollment/Completion	94.0%	2	73.2
			% College Graduates	36.0%	4	60.0
Commute	2	54.30	Average Work Commute in Minutes	21	5	42.9
			% Commuting on Public Transportation	5.3%	4	65.7
Community Stability	20	24.60	% Living in Same House as in 1979	16.8%	20	11.8
			% Living in Same County as in 1985	60.1%	19	37.4

Composite: *Rank* 12 / 21 *Score* 46.59 — **TIGARD (OR)**

CATEGORY	RANK	SCORE	STATISTIC	VALUE	RANK	SCORE
Economics	7	57.30	Median Household Income	$35,669	7	42.1
			% of Families Above Poverty Level	96.3%	6	72.5
Affordable Housing	17	59.25	Median Home Value	$90,400	18	60.6
			Median Rent	$484	13	57.9
Crime	10	34.45	Violent Crimes per 10,000 Population	26	5	68.9
			Property Crimes per 10,000 Population	673	11	0.0
Open Spaces	10	54.30	Population Density (Persons/Sq. Mile)	2881	8	73.3
			Average Rooms per Housing Unit	5.5	8	35.3
Education	7	39.90	% High School Enrollment/Completion	89.5%	11	33.0
			% College Graduates	30.1%	5	46.8
Commute	6	48.60	Average Work Commute in Minutes	21	5	42.9
			% Commuting on Public Transportation	4.5%	5	54.3
Community Stability	18	32.30	% Living in Same House as in 1979	21.0%	17	23.7
			% Living in Same County as in 1985	61.3%	18	40.9

Metropolitan Area Suburb Rankings
PORTLAND-VANCOUVER

Composite: *Rank* 13 / 21 *Score* 46.38   **GRESHAM (OR)**

CATEGORY	RANK	SCORE	STATISTIC	VALUE	RANK	SCORE
Economics	12	37.70	Median Household Income	$31,833	13	28.1
			% of Families Above Poverty Level	94.0%	12	47.3
Affordable Housing	8	77.55	Median Home Value	$71,000	10	83.1
			Median Rent	$446	10	72.0
Crime	9	37.55	Violent Crimes per 10,000 Population	37	10	50.8
			Property Crimes per 10,000 Population	550	7	24.3
Open Spaces	11	51.40	Population Density (Persons/Sq. Mile)	3092	9	67.5
			Average Rooms per Housing Unit	5.5	8	35.3
Education	16	13.30	% High School Enrollment/Completion	87.1%	18	11.6
			% College Graduates	15.9%	17	15.0
Commute	8	44.30	Average Work Commute in Minutes	23	18	14.3
			% Commuting on Public Transportation	5.9%	3	74.3
Community Stability	9	62.85	% Living in Same House as in 1979	27.1%	9	40.8
			% Living in Same County as in 1985	76.1%	5	84.9

Composite: *Rank* 14 / 21 *Score* 44.79   **TUALATIN (OR)**

CATEGORY	RANK	SCORE	STATISTIC	VALUE	RANK	SCORE
Economics	3	67.05	Median Household Income	$39,500	3	56.1
			% of Families Above Poverty Level	96.8%	3	78.0
Affordable Housing	19	47.95	Median Home Value	$95,300	19	54.9
			Median Rent	$530	17	41.0
Crime	6	49.70	Violent Crimes per 10,000 Population	18	2	82.0
			Property Crimes per 10,000 Population	585	9	17.4
Open Spaces	8	62.00	Population Density (Persons/Sq. Mile)	2105	4	94.6
			Average Rooms per Housing Unit	5.4	13	29.4
Education	6	45.40	% High School Enrollment/Completion	88.8%	13	26.8
			% College Graduates	37.8%	2	64.0
Commute	10	41.45	Average Work Commute in Minutes	21	5	42.9
			% Commuting on Public Transportation	3.5%	12	40.0
Community Stability	21	0.00	% Living in Same House as in 1979	12.6%	21	0.0
			% Living in Same County as in 1985	47.5%	21	0.0

Composite: *Rank* 15 / 21 *Score* 44.62   **FOREST GROVE (OR)**

CATEGORY	RANK	SCORE	STATISTIC	VALUE	RANK	SCORE
Economics	21	0.00	Median Household Income	$24,162	21	0.0
			% of Families Above Poverty Level	89.7%	21	0.0
Affordable Housing	1	94.35	Median Home Value	$66,200	7	88.7
			Median Rent	$370	1	100.0
Crime	4	70.10	Violent Crimes per 10,000 Population	26	5	68.9
			Property Crimes per 10,000 Population	312	3	71.3
Open Spaces	17	34.00	Population Density (Persons/Sq. Mile)	3287	13	62.1
			Average Rooms per Housing Unit	5.0	20	5.9
Education	14	24.15	% High School Enrollment/Completion	88.4%	14	23.2
			% College Graduates	20.4%	9	25.1
Commute	15	33.60	Average Work Commute in Minutes	21	5	42.9
			% Commuting on Public Transportation	2.4%	16	24.3
Community Stability	11	56.15	% Living in Same House as in 1979	27.1%	9	40.8
			% Living in Same County as in 1985	71.6%	11	71.5

Metropolitan Area Suburb Rankings
PORTLAND-VANCOUVER

Composite: **Rank** 16 / 21 **Score** 43.85   **EVERGREEN (WA)**

CATEGORY	RANK	SCORE	STATISTIC	VALUE	RANK	SCORE
Economics	8	52.10	Median Household Income	$36,145	6	43.8
			% of Families Above Poverty Level	95.2%	9	60.4
Affordable Housing	16	59.55	Median Home Value	$70,500	9	83.7
			Median Rent	$545	20	35.4
Crime	N/A	N/A	Violent Crimes per 10,000 Population	N/A	N/A	N/A
			Property Crimes per 10,000 Population	N/A	N/A	N/A
Open Spaces	5	68.70	Population Density (Persons/Sq. Mile)	2474	7	84.5
			Average Rooms per Housing Unit	5.8	5	52.9
Education	16	13.30	% High School Enrollment/Completion	87.0%	19	10.7
			% College Graduates	16.3%	16	15.9
Commute	17	28.60	Average Work Commute in Minutes	21	5	42.9
			% Commuting on Public Transportation	1.7%	19	14.3
Community Stability	16	40.85	% Living in Same House as in 1979	19.8%	19	20.3
			% Living in Same County as in 1985	68.2%	13	61.4

Composite: **Rank** 17 / 21 **Score** 43.46   **NEWBERG (OR)**

CATEGORY	RANK	SCORE	STATISTIC	VALUE	RANK	SCORE
Economics	18	19.45	Median Household Income	$26,974	18	10.3
			% of Families Above Poverty Level	92.3%	18	28.6
Affordable Housing	4	90.70	Median Home Value	$59,500	3	96.5
			Median Rent	$411	3	84.9
Crime	5	54.60	Violent Crimes per 10,000 Population	35	9	54.1
			Property Crimes per 10,000 Population	394	5	55.1
Open Spaces	15	42.10	Population Density (Persons/Sq. Mile)	3123	10	66.6
			Average Rooms per Housing Unit	5.2	18	17.6
Education	9	33.05	% High School Enrollment/Completion	90.8%	8	44.6
			% College Graduates	18.8%	13	21.5
Commute	21	22.15	Average Work Commute in Minutes	21	5	42.9
			% Commuting on Public Transportation	0.8%	20	1.4
Community Stability	15	42.20	% Living in Same House as in 1979	23.4%	15	30.4
			% Living in Same County as in 1985	65.7%	16	54.0

Composite: **Rank** 18 / 21 **Score** 43.20   **ORCHARDS SOUTH (WA)**

CATEGORY	RANK	SCORE	STATISTIC	VALUE	RANK	SCORE
Economics	13	34.30	Median Household Income	$33,881	10	35.6
			% of Families Above Poverty Level	92.7%	17	33.0
Affordable Housing	13	63.00	Median Home Value	$66,200	7	88.7
			Median Rent	$540	19	37.3
Crime	N/A	N/A	Violent Crimes per 10,000 Population	N/A	N/A	N/A
			Property Crimes per 10,000 Population	N/A	N/A	N/A
Open Spaces	7	63.80	Population Density (Persons/Sq. Mile)	2188	5	92.3
			Average Rooms per Housing Unit	5.5	8	35.3
Education	11	30.60	% High School Enrollment/Completion	91.9%	7	54.5
			% College Graduates	12.2%	20	6.7
Commute	19	27.15	Average Work Commute in Minutes	22	13	28.6
			% Commuting on Public Transportation	2.5%	15	25.7
Community Stability	17	40.35	% Living in Same House as in 1979	20.0%	18	20.8
			% Living in Same County as in 1985	67.7%	15	59.9

Metropolitan Area Suburb Rankings
PORTLAND-VANCOUVER

Composite: Rank 19 / 21 *Score* 42.62   **OAK GROVE (OR)**

CATEGORY	RANK	SCORE	STATISTIC	VALUE	RANK	SCORE
Economics	14	34.10	Median Household Income	$27,510	17	12.2
			% of Families Above Poverty Level	94.8%	10	56.0
Affordable Housing	10	76.75	Median Home Value	$72,100	13	81.9
			Median Rent	$447	11	71.6
Crime	N/A	N/A	Violent Crimes per 10,000 Population	N/A	N/A	N/A
			Property Crimes per 10,000 Population	N/A	N/A	N/A
Open Spaces	20	17.10	Population Density (Persons/Sq. Mile)	4302	18	34.2
			Average Rooms per Housing Unit	4.9	21	0.0
Education	15	17.45	% High School Enrollment/Completion	87.7%	15	17.0
			% College Graduates	17.2%	15	17.9
Commute	12	38.60	Average Work Commute in Minutes	22	13	28.6
			% Commuting on Public Transportation	4.1%	6	48.6
Community Stability	5	71.75	% Living in Same House as in 1979	35.1%	6	63.4
			% Living in Same County as in 1985	74.5%	8	80.1

Composite: Rank 20 / 21 *Score* 40.29   **POWELLHURST-CENTENNIAL (OR)**

CATEGORY	RANK	SCORE	STATISTIC	VALUE	RANK	SCORE
Economics	20	5.65	Median Household Income	$26,638	19	9.1
			% of Families Above Poverty Level	89.9%	20	2.2
Affordable Housing	5	90.60	Median Home Value	$56,500	1	100.0
			Median Rent	$421	6	81.2
Crime	N/A	N/A	Violent Crimes per 10,000 Population	N/A	N/A	N/A
			Property Crimes per 10,000 Population	N/A	N/A	N/A
Open Spaces	21	14.60	Population Density (Persons/Sq. Mile)	5337	20	5.7
			Average Rooms per Housing Unit	5.3	15	23.5
Education	21	0.00	% High School Enrollment/Completion	85.8%	20	0.0
			% College Graduates	9.2%	21	0.0
Commute	7	47.85	Average Work Commute in Minutes	24	21	0.0
			% Commuting on Public Transportation	7.4%	2	95.7
Community Stability	4	83.05	% Living in Same House as in 1979	36.4%	5	67.0
			% Living in Same County as in 1985	80.9%	2	99.1

Composite: Rank 21 / 21 *Score* 38.30   **OREGON CITY (OR)**

CATEGORY	RANK	SCORE	STATISTIC	VALUE	RANK	SCORE
Economics	17	26.45	Median Household Income	$28,687	16	16.6
			% of Families Above Poverty Level	93.0%	16	36.3
Affordable Housing	6	84.90	Median Home Value	$60,900	4	94.9
			Median Rent	$438	7	74.9
Crime	11	1.60	Violent Crimes per 10,000 Population	68	11	0.0
			Property Crimes per 10,000 Population	657	10	3.2
Open Spaces	13	44.95	Population Density (Persons/Sq. Mile)	3132	11	66.4
			Average Rooms per Housing Unit	5.3	15	23.5
Education	18	11.65	% High School Enrollment/Completion	87.5%	16	15.2
			% College Graduates	12.8%	18	8.1
Commute	18	27.85	Average Work Commute in Minutes	22	13	28.6
			% Commuting on Public Transportation	2.6%	14	27.1
Community Stability	6	70.70	% Living in Same House as in 1979	33.3%	7	58.3
			% Living in Same County as in 1985	75.5%	6	83.1

Metropolitan Area Description
PROVIDENCE-PAWTUCKET-WOONSOCKET

STATE: Rhode Island
COUNTIES: Bristol, Kent, Providence, Washington

TOTAL POPULATION: 916,270

POPULATION IN SUBURBS: 639,021 (69.7%)

POPULATION IN Providence: 160,728 (17.5%)
POPULATION IN Pawtucket: 72,644 (7.9%)
POPULATION IN Woonsocket: 43,877 (4.8%)

The PROVIDENCE-PAWTUCKET-WOONSOCKET metropolitan area is located in the northeastern part of Rhode Island. The suburbs range geographically from Valley Falls in the north (8 miles from Providence), to North Providence in the northwest (2 miles from Providence), to Warwick in the south (9 miles from Providence), and to East Providence in the east (3 miles from Providence). The area is growing in population and had an increase of 5.8% between 1980 and 1990. Summer time high temperatures average in the 80's and winter time lows average in the 20's. Metropolitan Property and Liability Insurance Company has major operations in the suburb of Warwick. Industrial companies are also located in the suburban area.

Barrington is the overall highest rated suburb and also has the highest scores in economics, education, and open spaces. **Central Falls** is the suburb with the most affordable housing and also has the top rated commute. **Bristol** is rated the safest suburb with the lowest crime rate. Finally, the number one rating in community stability goes to **Valley Falls**.

The highest ranked suburb overall which also has an affordable housing score of at least 50.00 is **Cranston**.

The highest ranked suburb in the education category which also has an affordable housing score of at least 50.00 is **Warwick**.

The county whose suburbs have the highest average overall score is **Bristol County** (63.36).

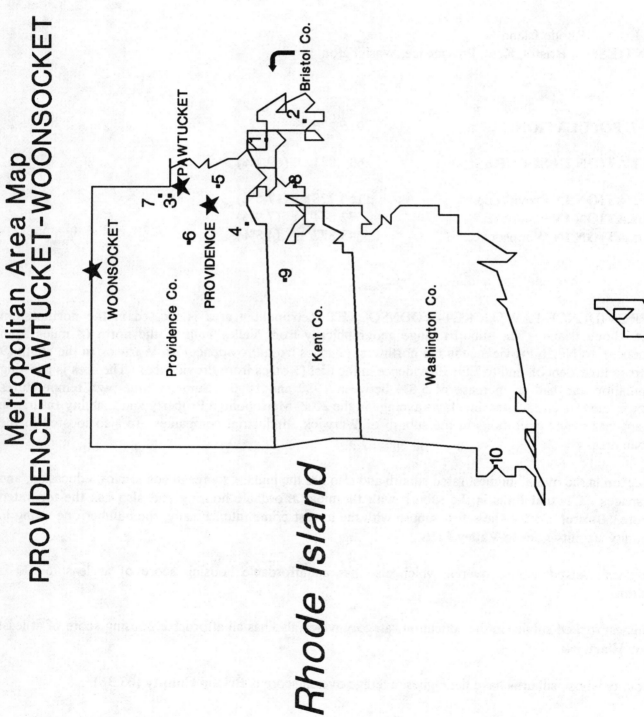

Metropolitan Area Map
PROVIDENCE-PAWTUCKET-WOONSOCKET

WOONSOCKET

Providence Co.

PAWTUCKET

PROVIDENCE

Bristol Co.

Kent Co.

Washington Co.

Rhode Island

Metropolitan Area Suburb Alphabetical Index
PROVIDENCE-PAWTUCKET-WOONSOCKET

SUBURB	PAGE	MAP NO.	STATE	COUNTY	POPU-LATION	RANK
BARRINGTON	632	1	Rhode Island	Bristol	15,849	1 / 10
BRISTOL	633	2	Rhode Island	Bristol	21,625	4 / 10
CENTRAL FALLS	635	3	Rhode Island	Providence	17,637	10 / 10
CRANSTON	632	4	Rhode Island	Providence	76,060	2 / 10
EAST PROVIDENCE	632	5	Rhode Island	Providence	50,380	3 / 10
NORTH PROVIDENCE	633	6	Rhode Island	Providence	32,090	5 / 10
VALLEY FALLS	633	7	Rhode Island	Providence	11,175	6 / 10
WARWICK	634	8	Rhode Island	Kent	85,427	8 / 10
WEST WARWICK	634	9	Rhode Island	Kent	29,268	9 / 10
WESTERLY	634	10	Rhode Island	Washington	16,477	7 / 10

Metropolitan Area Suburb Rankings
PROVIDENCE-PAWTUCKET-WOONSOCKET

Composite: *Rank* 1 / 10 *Score* 65.96 **BARRINGTON**

CATEGORY	RANK	SCORE	STATISTIC	VALUE	RANK	SCORE
Economics	1	100.00	Median Household Income	$53,058	1	100.0
			% of Families Above Poverty Level	99.2%	1	100.0
Affordable Housing	10	0.00	Median Home Value	$190,000	10	0.0
			Median Rent	$674	10	0.0
Crime	3	83.85	Violent Crimes per 10,000 Population	12	3	92.9
			Property Crimes per 10,000 Population	265	3	74.8
Open Spaces	1	97.25	Population Density (Persons/Sq. Mile)	1883	2	94.5
			Average Rooms per Housing Unit	6.7	1	100.0
Education	1	100.00	% High School Enrollment/Completion	95.8%	1	100.0
			% College Graduates	46.4%	1	100.0
Commute	6	30.65	Average Work Commute in Minutes	21	10	0.0
			% Commuting on Public Transportation	2.5%	4	61.3
Community Stability	6	50.00	% Living in Same House as in 1979	54.5%	1	100.0
			% Living in Same County as in 1985	77.5%	10	0.0

Composite: *Rank* 2 / 10 *Score* 65.74 **CRANSTON**

CATEGORY	RANK	SCORE	STATISTIC	VALUE	RANK	SCORE
Economics	5	61.65	Median Household Income	$34,528	4	46.2
			% of Families Above Poverty Level	95.1%	7	77.1
Affordable Housing	6	61.40	Median Home Value	$127,600	7	72.1
			Median Rent	$534	8	50.7
Crime	4	72.35	Violent Crimes per 10,000 Population	14	4	91.1
			Property Crimes per 10,000 Population	332	5	53.6
Open Spaces	5	64.80	Population Density (Persons/Sq. Mile)	2662	5	88.7
			Average Rooms per Housing Unit	5.4	3	40.9
Education	5	49.00	% High School Enrollment/Completion	85.6%	7	60.2
			% College Graduates	21.1%	3	37.8
Commute	3	73.85	Average Work Commute in Minutes	17	2	80.0
			% Commuting on Public Transportation	2.7%	2	67.7
Community Stability	3	77.10	% Living in Same House as in 1979	46.4%	4	66.5
			% Living in Same County as in 1985	88.2%	4	87.7

Composite: *Rank* 3 / 10 *Score* 65.73 **EAST PROVIDENCE**

CATEGORY	RANK	SCORE	STATISTIC	VALUE	RANK	SCORE
Economics	8	56.25	Median Household Income	$31,007	9	36.0
			% of Families Above Poverty Level	95.0%	8	76.5
Affordable Housing	3	76.40	Median Home Value	$121,700	3	78.9
			Median Rent	$470	3	73.9
Crime	5	70.90	Violent Crimes per 10,000 Population	19	5	86.6
			Property Crimes per 10,000 Population	327	4	55.2
Open Spaces	7	53.90	Population Density (Persons/Sq. Mile)	3760	8	80.5
			Average Rooms per Housing Unit	5.1	7	27.3
Education	7	43.70	% High School Enrollment/Completion	86.1%	6	62.1
			% College Graduates	16.0%	7	25.3
Commute	2	80.00	Average Work Commute in Minutes	18	3	60.0
			% Commuting on Public Transportation	3.7%	1	100.0
Community Stability	2	78.95	% Living in Same House as in 1979	45.1%	5	61.2
			% Living in Same County as in 1985	89.3%	2	96.7

Metropolitan Area Suburb Rankings
PROVIDENCE-PAWTUCKET-WOONSOCKET

Composite: *Rank* 4 / 10 *Score* 60.75 **BRISTOL**

CATEGORY	RANK	SCORE	STATISTIC	VALUE	RANK	SCORE
Economics	4	64.75	Median Household Income	$34,165	5	45.1
			% of Families Above Poverty Level	96.4%	4	84.4
Affordable Housing	8	53.40	Median Home Value	$151,800	9	44.1
			Median Rent	$501	5	62.7
Crime	1	97.30	Violent Crimes per 10,000 Population	10	2	94.6
			Property Crimes per 10,000 Population	185	1	100.0
Open Spaces	3	69.05	Population Density (Persons/Sq. Mile)	2140	3	92.6
			Average Rooms per Housing Unit	5.5	2	45.5
Education	3	59.20	% High School Enrollment/Completion	91.7%	2	84.0
			% College Graduates	19.7%	5	34.4
Commute	5	52.25	Average Work Commute in Minutes	19	6	40.0
			% Commuting on Public Transportation	2.6%	3	64.5
Community Stability	9	29.30	% Living in Same House as in 1979	43.3%	6	53.7
			% Living in Same County as in 1985	78.1%	9	4.9

Composite: *Rank* 5 / 10 *Score* 60.13 **NORTH PROVIDENCE**

CATEGORY	RANK	SCORE	STATISTIC	VALUE	RANK	SCORE
Economics	7	60.95	Median Household Income	$32,321	7	39.8
			% of Families Above Poverty Level	96.0%	5	82.1
Affordable Housing	5	63.45	Median Home Value	$126,500	5	73.3
			Median Rent	$526	7	53.6
Crime	7	63.40	Violent Crimes per 10,000 Population	22	6	83.9
			Property Crimes per 10,000 Population	366	7	42.9
Open Spaces	9	44.55	Population Density (Persons/Sq. Mile)	5653	9	66.4
			Average Rooms per Housing Unit	5.0	8	22.7
Education	4	56.35	% High School Enrollment/Completion	89.8%	4	76.6
			% College Graduates	20.4%	4	36.1
Commute	4	59.05	Average Work Commute in Minutes	18	3	60.0
			% Commuting on Public Transportation	2.4%	6	58.1
Community Stability	4	73.15	% Living in Same House as in 1979	41.5%	7	46.3
			% Living in Same County as in 1985	89.7%	1	100.0

Composite: *Rank* 6 / 10 *Score* 59.87 **VALLEY FALLS**

CATEGORY	RANK	SCORE	STATISTIC	VALUE	RANK	SCORE
Economics	2	68.55	Median Household Income	$35,616	3	49.4
			% of Families Above Poverty Level	97.0%	2	87.7
Affordable Housing	2	86.20	Median Home Value	$127,300	6	72.4
			Median Rent	$398	1	100.0
Crime	N/A	N/A	Violent Crimes per 10,000 Population	N/A	N/A	N/A
			Property Crimes per 10,000 Population	N/A	N/A	N/A
Open Spaces	6	63.00	Population Density (Persons/Sq. Mile)	3148	6	85.1
			Average Rooms per Housing Unit	5.4	3	40.9
Education	9	33.65	% High School Enrollment/Completion	82.9%	8	49.6
			% College Graduates	12.9%	9	17.7
Commute	9	28.05	Average Work Commute in Minutes	19	6	40.0
			% Commuting on Public Transportation	1.1%	8	16.1
Community Stability	1	79.75	% Living in Same House as in 1979	47.3%	2	70.2
			% Living in Same County as in 1985	88.4%	3	89.3

Metropolitan Area Suburb Rankings
PROVIDENCE-PAWTUCKET-WOONSOCKET

Composite: **Rank** 7 / 10 *Score* 52.94   **WESTERLY**

CATEGORY	RANK	SCORE	STATISTIC	VALUE	RANK	SCORE
Economics	6	61.20	Median Household Income	$33,469	6	43.1
			% of Families Above Poverty Level	95.5%	6	79.3
Affordable Housing	9	52.10	Median Home Value	$147,100	8	49.5
			Median Rent	$523	6	54.7
Crime	2	87.85	Violent Crimes per 10,000 Population	4	1	100.0
			Property Crimes per 10,000 Population	262	2	75.7
Open Spaces	2	70.45	Population Density (Persons/Sq. Mile)	1144	1	100.0
			Average Rooms per Housing Unit	5.4	3	40.9
Education	8	38.30	% High School Enrollment/Completion	81.3%	9	43.4
			% College Graduates	19.2%	6	33.2
Commute	7	30.00	Average Work Commute in Minutes	18	3	60.0
			% Commuting on Public Transportation	0.6%	10	0.0
Community Stability	8	30.70	% Living in Same House as in 1979	38.4%	8	33.5
			% Living in Same County as in 1985	80.9%	8	27.9

Composite: **Rank** 8 / 10 *Score* 51.61   **WARWICK**

CATEGORY	RANK	SCORE	STATISTIC	VALUE	RANK	SCORE
Economics	3	68.25	Median Household Income	$35,786	2	49.9
			% of Families Above Poverty Level	96.8%	3	86.6
Affordable Housing	6	61.40	Median Home Value	$116,300	2	85.1
			Median Rent	$570	9	37.7
Crime	8	23.95	Violent Crimes per 10,000 Population	63	8	47.3
			Property Crimes per 10,000 Population	500	8	0.6
Open Spaces	4	65.75	Population Density (Persons/Sq. Mile)	2406	4	90.6
			Average Rooms per Housing Unit	5.4	3	40.9
Education	2	59.80	% High School Enrollment/Completion	91.0%	3	81.3
			% College Graduates	21.3%	2	38.3
Commute	8	29.35	Average Work Commute in Minutes	20	9	20.0
			% Commuting on Public Transportation	1.8%	7	38.7
Community Stability	5	52.75	% Living in Same House as in 1979	46.9%	3	68.6
			% Living in Same County as in 1985	82.0%	7	36.9

Composite: **Rank** 9 / 10 *Score* 49.00   **WEST WARWICK**

CATEGORY	RANK	SCORE	STATISTIC	VALUE	RANK	SCORE
Economics	9	52.70	Median Household Income	$31,625	8	37.8
			% of Families Above Poverty Level	93.4%	9	67.6
Affordable Housing	4	72.55	Median Home Value	$123,300	4	77.0
			Median Rent	$486	4	68.1
Crime	6	64.25	Violent Crimes per 10,000 Population	24	7	82.1
			Property Crimes per 10,000 Population	355	6	46.4
Open Spaces	8	51.90	Population Density (Persons/Sq. Mile)	3690	7	81.1
			Average Rooms per Housing Unit	5.0	8	22.7
Education	6	46.05	% High School Enrollment/Completion	88.0%	5	69.5
			% College Graduates	14.9%	8	22.6
Commute	10	21.60	Average Work Commute in Minutes	19	6	40.0
			% Commuting on Public Transportation	0.7%	9	3.2
Community Stability	7	33.95	% Living in Same House as in 1979	36.8%	9	26.9
			% Living in Same County as in 1985	82.5%	6	41.0

Metropolitan Area Suburb Rankings
PROVIDENCE-PAWTUCKET-WOONSOCKET

Composite: *Rank* 10 / 10 *Score* 28.95 **CENTRAL FALLS**

CATEGORY	RANK	SCORE	STATISTIC	VALUE	RANK	SCORE
Economics	10	0.00	Median Household Income	$18,617	10	0.0
			% of Families Above Poverty Level	81.3%	10	0.0
Affordable Housing	1	99.45	Median Home Value	$103,400	1	100.0
			Median Rent	$401	2	98.9
Crime	9	0.00	Violent Crimes per 10,000 Population	116	9	0.0
			Property Crimes per 10,000 Population	502	9	0.0
Open Spaces	10	0.00	Population Density (Persons/Sq. Mile)	14580	10	0.0
			Average Rooms per Housing Unit	4.5	10	0.0
Education	10	0.00	% High School Enrollment/Completion	70.2%	10	0.0
			% College Graduates	5.7%	10	0.0
Commute	1	80.65	Average Work Commute in Minutes	16	1	100.0
			% Commuting on Public Transportation	2.5%	4	61.3
Community Stability	10	22.55	% Living in Same House as in 1979	30.3%	10	0.0
			% Living in Same County as in 1985	83.0%	5	45.1

Metropolitan Area Description
RICHMOND-PETERSBURG

STATE: Virginia

COUNTIES: Charles City, Chesterfield, Dinwiddie, Goochland, Hanover, Henrico, New Kent, Powhatan, Prince George

INDE-PENDENT CITIES: Colonial Heights, Hopewell, Petersburg, Richmond

TOTAL POPULATION: 865,640

POPULATION IN SUBURBS: 624,198   (72.1%)

POPULATION IN Richmond: 203,056   (23.5%)
POPULATION IN Petersburg: 38,386   (4.4%)

The RICHMOND-PETERSBURG metropolitan area is located in the southeastern part of Virginia. The suburbs range geographically from Laurel in the north (10 miles from Richmond), to Tuckahoe in the west (4 miles from Richmond), to Colonial Heights in the south (27 miles from Richmond), and to Highland Springs in the east (12 miles from Richmond). The area is growing in population and had an increase of 13.7% between 1980 and 1990. Summer time high temperatures average in the 80's and winter time lows average in the 20's. Richfood has its headquarters located in the suburb of Mechanicsville. Tobacco companies have facilities in the area. Public transportation in the area is provided by the Greater Richmond Transit Company using buses and trolleys.

Tuckahoe is the overall highest rated suburb and also has the highest score in education. **Bon Air** receives the top score in economics. **Hopewell** is the suburb with the most affordable housing. The number one rating in open spaces belongs to **Mechanicsville**. The top rated commute goes to **Lakeside**. Finally, the number one score in community stability goes to **Colonial Heights**. Crime rankings were not available for the area.

The highest ranked suburb overall which also has an affordable housing score of at least 50.00 is **East Highland Park**.

The highest ranked suburb in the education category which also has an affordable housing score of at least 50.00 is **Highland Springs**.

The county whose suburbs have the highest average overall score is **Hanover County** (52.86).

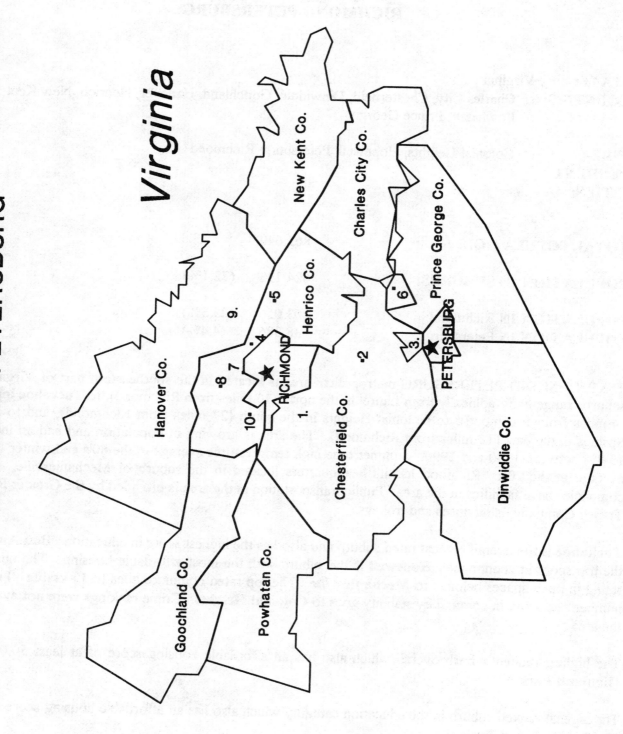

Metropolitan Area Map
RICHMOND–PETERSBURG

Virginia

New Kent Co.

Charles City Co.

Prince George Co.

Henrico Co.

•5

9.

•6

•4

PETERSBURG

Hanover Co.

7

•3

8•

RICHMOND

•2

10•

1.

Chesterfield Co.

Dinwiddie Co.

Goochland Co.

Powhatan Co.

Metropolitan Area Suburb Alphabetical Index
RICHMOND-PETERSBURG

SUBURB	PAGE	MAP NO.	STATE	COUNTY	POPU-LATION	RANK
BON AIR	640	1	Virginia	Chesterfield	16,413	3 / 10
CHESTER	642	2	Virginia	Chesterfield	14,986	9 / 10
COLONIAL HEIGHTS	641	3	Virginia	Independent City	16,064	6 / 10
EAST HIGHLAND PARK	640	4	Virginia	Henrico	11,850	2 / 10
HIGHLAND SPRINGS	642	5	Virginia	Henrico	13,823	7 / 10
HOPEWELL	642	6	Virginia	Independent City	23,101	8 / 10
LAKESIDE	641	7	Virginia	Henrico	12,081	4 / 10
LAUREL	643	8	Virginia	Henrico	13,011	10 / 10
MECHANICSVILLE	641	9	Virginia	Hanover	22,027	5 / 10
TUCKAHOE	640	10	Virginia	Henrico	42,629	1 / 10

Metropolitan Area Suburb Rankings
RICHMOND-PETERSBURG

Composite: *Rank* 1 / 10 *Score* 58.26   **TUCKAHOE**

CATEGORY	RANK	SCORE	STATISTIC	VALUE	RANK	SCORE
Economics	2	87.20	Median Household Income	$42,880	2	76.4
			% of Families Above Poverty Level	98.2%	2	98.0
Affordable Housing	9	22.25	Median Home Value	$108,100	10	0.0
			Median Rent	$525	7	44.5
Crime	N/A	N/A	Violent Crimes per 10,000 Population	N/A	N/A	N/A
			Property Crimes per 10,000 Population	N/A	N/A	N/A
Open Spaces	4	41.95	Population Density (Persons/Sq. Mile)	2071	6	17.2
			Average Rooms per Housing Unit	6.4	2	66.7
Education	1	99.45	% High School Enrollment/Completion	95.2%	1	100.0
			% College Graduates	43.4%	2	98.9
Commute	4	51.15	Average Work Commute in Minutes	20	2	60.0
			% Commuting on Public Transportation	1.3%	4	42.3
Community Stability	6	47.55	% Living in Same House as in 1979	36.1%	7	43.8
			% Living in Same County as in 1985	68.7%	6	51.3

Composite: *Rank* 2 / 10 *Score* 57.80   **EAST HIGHLAND PARK**

CATEGORY	RANK	SCORE	STATISTIC	VALUE	RANK	SCORE
Economics	8	37.75	Median Household Income	$28,918	9	9.5
			% of Families Above Poverty Level	95.0%	7	66.0
Affordable Housing	2	81.60	Median Home Value	$56,500	2	96.3
			Median Rent	$470	4	66.9
Crime	N/A	N/A	Violent Crimes per 10,000 Population	N/A	N/A	N/A
			Property Crimes per 10,000 Population	N/A	N/A	N/A
Open Spaces	6	32.55	Population Density (Persons/Sq. Mile)	1322	3	65.1
			Average Rooms per Housing Unit	5.4	9	0.0
Education	8	31.45	% High School Enrollment/Completion	89.6%	4	62.9
			% College Graduates	8.1%	10	0.0
Commute	2	80.00	Average Work Commute in Minutes	20	2	60.0
			% Commuting on Public Transportation	2.8%	1	100.0
Community Stability	4	83.45	% Living in Same House as in 1979	45.2%	3	95.5
			% Living in Same County as in 1985	71.8%	4	71.4

Composite: *Rank* 3 / 10 *Score* 57.75   **BON AIR**

CATEGORY	RANK	SCORE	STATISTIC	VALUE	RANK	SCORE
Economics	1	96.50	Median Household Income	$47,803	1	100.0
			% of Families Above Poverty Level	97.7%	4	93.0
Affordable Housing	10	14.45	Median Home Value	$92,600	9	28.9
			Median Rent	$634	10	0.0
Crime	N/A	N/A	Violent Crimes per 10,000 Population	N/A	N/A	N/A
			Property Crimes per 10,000 Population	N/A	N/A	N/A
Open Spaces	2	65.40	Population Density (Persons/Sq. Mile)	1858	5	30.8
			Average Rooms per Housing Unit	6.9	1	100.0
Education	2	72.85	% High School Enrollment/Completion	87.0%	5	45.7
			% College Graduates	43.8%	1	100.0
Commute	6	39.60	Average Work Commute in Minutes	20	2	60.0
			% Commuting on Public Transportation	0.7%	6	19.2
Community Stability	5	57.70	% Living in Same House as in 1979	39.8%	5	64.8
			% Living in Same County as in 1985	68.6%	7	50.6

Metropolitan Area Suburb Rankings
RICHMOND-PETERSBURG

Composite: *Rank* 4 / 10 *Score* 54.33   **LAKESIDE**

CATEGORY	RANK	SCORE	STATISTIC	VALUE	RANK	SCORE
Economics	7	50.15	Median Household Income	$30,331	8	16.3
			% of Families Above Poverty Level	96.8%	5	84.0
Affordable Housing	5	64.00	Median Home Value	$66,400	4	77.8
			Median Rent	$511	6	50.2
Crime	N/A	N/A	Violent Crimes per 10,000 Population	N/A	N/A	N/A
			Property Crimes per 10,000 Population	N/A	N/A	N/A
Open Spaces	8	10.00	Population Density (Persons/Sq. Mile)	2340	10	0.0
			Average Rooms per Housing Unit	5.7	6	20.0
Education	7	32.05	% High School Enrollment/Completion	84.4%	9	28.5
			% College Graduates	20.8%	5	35.6
Commute	1	80.75	Average Work Commute in Minutes	18	1	100.0
			% Commuting on Public Transportation	1.8%	3	61.5
Community Stability	2	89.05	% Living in Same House as in 1979	45.8%	2	98.9
			% Living in Same County as in 1985	73.0%	3	79.2

Composite: *Rank* 5 / 10 *Score* 52.86   **MECHANICSVILLE**

CATEGORY	RANK	SCORE	STATISTIC	VALUE	RANK	SCORE
Economics	3	84.20	Median Household Income	$41,203	4	68.4
			% of Families Above Poverty Level	98.4%	1	100.0
Affordable Housing	8	26.20	Median Home Value	$89,200	7	35.3
			Median Rent	$592	9	17.1
Crime	N/A	N/A	Violent Crimes per 10,000 Population	N/A	N/A	N/A
			Property Crimes per 10,000 Population	N/A	N/A	N/A
Open Spaces	1	83.35	Population Density (Persons/Sq. Mile)	776	1	100.0
			Average Rooms per Housing Unit	6.4	2	66.7
Education	3	59.50	% High School Enrollment/Completion	93.5%	2	88.7
			% College Graduates	18.9%	6	30.3
Commute	9	20.00	Average Work Commute in Minutes	21	7	40.0
			% Commuting on Public Transportation	0.2%	9	0.0
Community Stability	7	43.90	% Living in Same House as in 1979	36.3%	6	44.9
			% Living in Same County as in 1985	67.4%	8	42.9

Composite: *Rank* 6 / 10 *Score* 51.12   **COLONIAL HEIGHTS**

CATEGORY	RANK	SCORE	STATISTIC	VALUE	RANK	SCORE
Economics	6	57.05	Median Household Income	$34,472	6	36.1
			% of Families Above Poverty Level	96.2%	6	78.0
Affordable Housing	4	71.70	Median Home Value	$69,700	5	71.6
			Median Rent	$458	3	71.8
Crime	N/A	N/A	Violent Crimes per 10,000 Population	18	N/A	N/A
			Property Crimes per 10,000 Population	492	N/A	N/A
Open Spaces	7	29.35	Population Density (Persons/Sq. Mile)	2153	7	12.0
			Average Rooms per Housing Unit	6.1	4	46.7
Education	6	34.55	% High School Enrollment/Completion	86.9%	7	45.0
			% College Graduates	16.7%	7	24.1
Commute	8	21.90	Average Work Commute in Minutes	21	7	40.0
			% Commuting on Public Transportation	0.3%	8	3.8
Community Stability	1	92.20	% Living in Same House as in 1979	46.0%	1	100.0
			% Living in Same County as in 1985	73.8%	2	84.4

Metropolitan Area Suburb Rankings
RICHMOND-PETERSBURG

Composite: **Rank** 7 / 10 *Score* 48.87   **HIGHLAND SPRINGS**

CATEGORY	RANK	SCORE	STATISTIC	VALUE	RANK	SCORE
Economics	9	36.55	Median Household Income	$30,500	7	17.1
			% of Families Above Poverty Level	94.0%	8	56.0
Affordable Housing	3	74.00	Median Home Value	$62,500	3	85.1
			Median Rent	$480	5	62.9
Crime	N/A	N/A	Violent Crimes per 10,000 Population	N/A	N/A	N/A
			Property Crimes per 10,000 Population	N/A	N/A	N/A
Open Spaces	5	33.55	Population Density (Persons/Sq. Mile)	1603	4	47.1
			Average Rooms per Housing Unit	5.7	6	20.0
Education	4	48.80	% High School Enrollment/Completion	93.4%	3	88.1
			% College Graduates	11.5%	8	9.5
Commute	3	56.55	Average Work Commute in Minutes	21	7	40.0
			% Commuting on Public Transportation	2.1%	2	73.1
Community Stability	8	43.75	% Living in Same House as in 1979	33.4%	8	28.4
			% Living in Same County as in 1985	69.9%	5	59.1

Composite: **Rank** 8 / 10 *Score* 42.16   **HOPEWELL**

CATEGORY	RANK	SCORE	STATISTIC	VALUE	RANK	SCORE
Economics	10	0.00	Median Household Income	$26,934	10	0.0
			% of Families Above Poverty Level	88.4%	10	0.0
Affordable Housing	1	100.00	Median Home Value	$54,500	1	100.0
			Median Rent	$389	1	100.0
Crime	N/A	N/A	Violent Crimes per 10,000 Population	70	N/A	N/A
			Property Crimes per 10,000 Population	535	N/A	N/A
Open Spaces	9	6.10	Population Density (Persons/Sq. Mile)	2254	8	5.5
			Average Rooms per Housing Unit	5.5	8	6.7
Education	9	25.50	% High School Enrollment/Completion	87.0%	5	45.7
			% College Graduates	10.0%	9	5.3
Commute	7	33.85	Average Work Commute in Minutes	20	2	60.0
			% Commuting on Public Transportation	0.4%	7	7.7
Community Stability	3	87.50	% Living in Same House as in 1979	41.6%	4	75.0
			% Living in Same County as in 1985	76.2%	1	100.0

Composite: **Rank** 9 / 10 *Score* 39.70   **CHESTER**

CATEGORY	RANK	SCORE	STATISTIC	VALUE	RANK	SCORE
Economics	5	60.75	Median Household Income	$41,229	3	68.5
			% of Families Above Poverty Level	93.7%	9	53.0
Affordable Housing	6	55.20	Median Home Value	$90,500	8	32.8
			Median Rent	$444	2	77.6
Crime	N/A	N/A	Violent Crimes per 10,000 Population	N/A	N/A	N/A
			Property Crimes per 10,000 Population	N/A	N/A	N/A
Open Spaces	3	57.90	Population Density (Persons/Sq. Mile)	1154	2	75.8
			Average Rooms per Housing Unit	6.0	5	40.0
Education	5	39.45	% High School Enrollment/Completion	84.9%	8	31.8
			% College Graduates	24.9%	3	47.1
Commute	10	0.00	Average Work Commute in Minutes	23	10	0.0
			% Commuting on Public Transportation	0.2%	9	0.0
Community Stability	9	24.90	% Living in Same House as in 1979	31.9%	9	19.9
			% Living in Same County as in 1985	65.4%	9	29.9

Metropolitan Area Suburb Rankings
RICHMOND-PETERSBURG

Composite: **Rank** 10 / 10 *Score* 30.63   **LAUREL**

CATEGORY	RANK	SCORE	STATISTIC	VALUE	RANK	SCORE
Economics	4	67.50	Median Household Income	$35,280	5	40.0
			% of Families Above Poverty Level	97.9%	3	95.0
Affordable Housing	7	50.70	Median Home Value	$75,600	6	60.6
			Median Rent	$534	8	40.8
Crime	N/A	N/A	Violent Crimes per 10,000 Population	N/A	N/A	N/A
			Property Crimes per 10,000 Population	N/A	N/A	N/A
Open Spaces	10	1.50	Population Density (Persons/Sq. Mile)	2293	9	3.0
			Average Rooms per Housing Unit	5.4	9	0.0
Education	10	22.55	% High School Enrollment/Completion	80.1%	10	0.0
			% College Graduates	24.2%	4	45.1
Commute	5	41.55	Average Work Commute in Minutes	20	2	60.0
			% Commuting on Public Transportation	0.8%	5	23.1
Community Stability	10	0.00	% Living in Same House as in 1979	28.4%	10	0.0
			% Living in Same County as in 1985	60.8%	10	0.0

Metropolitan Area Description
ROCHESTER

STATE: New York
COUNTIES: Livingston, Monroe, Ontario, Orleans, Wayne

TOTAL POPULATION: 1,002,410

POPULATION IN SUBURBS: 770,774   (76.9%)

POPULATION IN Rochester: 231,636   (23.1%)

The ROCHESTER metropolitan area is located in the northwestern part of New York along Lake Ontario. The suburbs range geographically from Irondequoit in the north (9 miles from Rochester), to Gates-North Gates in the west (4 miles from Rochester), to Brighton in the south (8 miles from Rochester), and to Geneva in the east (44 miles from Rochester). The area is growing in population and had an increase of 3.2% between 1980 and 1990. Summer time high temperatures average in the 70's and winter time lows average in the teens. Xerox and Mobil Oil both have facilities in the suburbs. Small, high tech companies can also be found in the suburbs. The area produces fruit, with apples, pears, peaches, and cherries as major crops.

Brighton is the overall highest rated suburb and also has the highest scores in economics, education, and open spaces. Additionally, **Brighton** has the top rated commute. **Geneva** is rated the safest suburb with the lowest crime rate, and is also the suburb with the most affordable housing. Finally, the number one rating in community stability goes to **Irondequoit**.

The highest ranked suburb overall which also has an affordable housing score of at least 50.00 is **Gates-North Gates**.

The highest ranked suburb in the education category which also has an affordable housing score of at least 50.00 is **Geneva**.

The county whose suburbs have the highest average overall score is **Monroe County** (57.17)

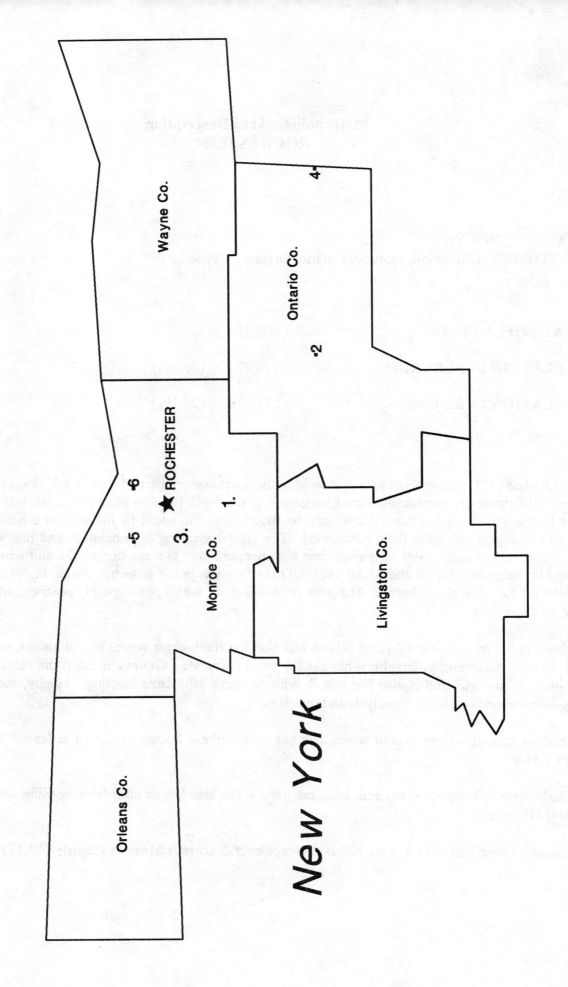

Metropolitan Area Map
ROCHESTER

New York

Orleans Co.

Wayne Co.

Monroe Co.

ROCHESTER

Ontario Co.

Livingston Co.

1.

•2

3.

4•

•5

•6

Metropolitan Area Suburb Alphabetical Index
ROCHESTER

SUBURB	PAGE	MAP NO.	STATE	COUNTY	POPU-LATION	RANK
BRIGHTON	648	1	New York	Monroe	34,455	1 / 6
CANANDAIGUA	649	2	New York	Ontario	10,725	6 / 6
GATES-NORTH GATES	649	3	New York	Monroe	14,995	4 / 6
GENEVA	649	4	New York	Ontario	14,143	5 / 6
GREECE	648	5	New York	Monroe	15,632	2 / 6
IRONDEQUOIT	648	6	New York	Monroe	52,322	3 / 6

Metropolitan Area Suburb Rankings
ROCHESTER

Composite: Rank 1 / 6 *Score* 66.27 — **BRIGHTON**

CATEGORY	RANK	SCORE	STATISTIC	VALUE	RANK	SCORE
Economics	1	100.00	Median Household Income	$41,458	1	100.0
			% of Families Above Poverty Level	97.9%	1	100.0
Affordable Housing	6	0.00	Median Home Value	$115,400	6	0.0
			Median Rent	$538	6	0.0
Crime	3	77.65	Violent Crimes per 10,000 Population	5	1	100.0
			Property Crimes per 10,000 Population	373	3	55.3
Open Spaces	1	71.45	Population Density (Persons/Sq. Mile)	2228	1	100.0
			Average Rooms per Housing Unit	5.6	3	42.9
Education	1	92.25	% High School Enrollment/Completion	96.7%	2	84.5
			% College Graduates	51.6%	1	100.0
Commute	1	87.50	Average Work Commute in Minutes	16	2	75.0
			% Commuting on Public Transportation	3.0%	1	100.0
Community Stability	4	35.05	% Living in Same House as in 1979	38.0%	5	29.6
			% Living in Same County as in 1985	81.2%	4	40.5

Composite: Rank 2 / 6 *Score* 62.17 — **GREECE**

CATEGORY	RANK	SCORE	STATISTIC	VALUE	RANK	SCORE
Economics	2	93.85	Median Household Income	$39,808	2	90.6
			% of Families Above Poverty Level	97.6%	2	97.1
Affordable Housing	4	39.75	Median Home Value	$90,400	5	43.1
			Median Rent	$483	4	36.4
Crime	2	81.50	Violent Crimes per 10,000 Population	8	2	80.0
			Property Crimes per 10,000 Population	264	2	83.0
Open Spaces	2	50.00	Population Density (Persons/Sq. Mile)	3597	6	0.0
			Average Rooms per Housing Unit	6.0	1	100.0
Education	3	47.80	% High School Enrollment/Completion	95.0%	3	69.1
			% College Graduates	20.6%	4	26.5
Commute	5	47.90	Average Work Commute in Minutes	17	4	50.0
			% Commuting on Public Transportation	1.7%	4	45.8
Community Stability	2	74.40	% Living in Same House as in 1979	43.9%	2	51.5
			% Living in Same County as in 1985	93.8%	2	97.3

Composite: Rank 3 / 6 *Score* 50.79 — **IRONDEQUOIT**

CATEGORY	RANK	SCORE	STATISTIC	VALUE	RANK	SCORE
Economics	3	84.90	Median Household Income	$37,006	3	74.7
			% of Families Above Poverty Level	97.4%	3	95.1
Affordable Housing	5	30.05	Median Home Value	$89,000	4	45.5
			Median Rent	$516	5	14.6
Crime	5	6.65	Violent Crimes per 10,000 Population	18	4	13.3
			Property Crimes per 10,000 Population	591	5	0.0
Open Spaces	4	40.90	Population Density (Persons/Sq. Mile)	3454	5	10.4
			Average Rooms per Housing Unit	5.8	2	71.4
Education	4	43.00	% High School Enrollment/Completion	93.4%	4	54.5
			% College Graduates	22.7%	2	31.5
Commute	3	50.00	Average Work Commute in Minutes	18	5	25.0
			% Commuting on Public Transportation	2.4%	2	75.0
Community Stability	1	100.00	% Living in Same House as in 1979	57.0%	1	100.0
			% Living in Same County as in 1985	94.4%	1	100.0

Metropolitan Area Suburb Rankings
ROCHESTER

GATES-NORTH GATES

Composite: Rank 4 / 6 Score 49.44

CATEGORY	RANK	SCORE	STATISTIC	VALUE	RANK	SCORE
Economics	4	79.15	Median Household Income	$35,505	4	66.1
			% of Families Above Poverty Level	97.1%	4	92.2
Affordable Housing	3	50.20	Median Home Value	$82,900	2	56.0
			Median Rent	$471	3	44.4
Crime	N/A	N/A	Violent Crimes per 10,000 Population	N/A	N/A	N/A
			Property Crimes per 10,000 Population	N/A	N/A	N/A
Open Spaces	6	20.85	Population Density (Persons/Sq. Mile)	3222	3	27.4
			Average Rooms per Housing Unit	5.4	5	14.3
Education	6	0.00	% High School Enrollment/Completion	87.4%	6	0.0
			% College Graduates	9.4%	6	0.0
Commute	2	72.90	Average Work Commute in Minutes	16	2	75.0
			% Commuting on Public Transportation	2.3%	3	70.8
Community Stability	3	73.55	% Living in Same House as in 1979	43.7%	3	50.7
			% Living in Same County as in 1985	93.6%	3	96.4

GENEVA

Composite: Rank 5 / 6 Score 48.79

CATEGORY	RANK	SCORE	STATISTIC	VALUE	RANK	SCORE
Economics	6	0.00	Median Household Income	$23,886	6	0.0
			% of Families Above Poverty Level	87.6%	6	0.0
Affordable Housing	1	100.00	Median Home Value	$57,400	1	100.0
			Median Rent	$387	1	100.0
Crime	1	86.65	Violent Crimes per 10,000 Population	9	3	73.3
			Property Crimes per 10,000 Population	197	1	100.0
Open Spaces	5	24.25	Population Density (Persons/Sq. Mile)	3325	4	19.9
			Average Rooms per Housing Unit	5.5	4	28.6
Education	2	59.50	% High School Enrollment/Completion	98.4%	1	100.0
			% College Graduates	17.4%	5	19.0
Commute	3	50.00	Average Work Commute in Minutes	15	1	100.0
			% Commuting on Public Transportation	0.6%	6	0.0
Community Stability	5	21.10	% Living in Same House as in 1979	41.4%	4	42.2
			% Living in Same County as in 1985	72.2%	6	0.0

CANANDAIGUA

Composite: Rank 6 / 6 Score 27.22

CATEGORY	RANK	SCORE	STATISTIC	VALUE	RANK	SCORE
Economics	5	40.55	Median Household Income	$28,428	5	25.8
			% of Families Above Poverty Level	93.3%	5	55.3
Affordable Housing	2	53.35	Median Home Value	$85,000	3	52.4
			Median Rent	$456	2	54.3
Crime	4	17.25	Violent Crimes per 10,000 Population	20	5	0.0
			Property Crimes per 10,000 Population	455	4	34.5
Open Spaces	3	46.20	Population Density (Persons/Sq. Mile)	2332	2	92.4
			Average Rooms per Housing Unit	5.3	6	0.0
Education	5	23.20	% High School Enrollment/Completion	89.3%	5	17.3
			% College Graduates	21.7%	3	29.1
Commute	6	2.10	Average Work Commute in Minutes	19	6	0.0
			% Commuting on Public Transportation	0.7%	5	4.2
Community Stability	6	7.90	% Living in Same House as in 1979	30.0%	6	0.0
			% Living in Same County as in 1985	75.7%	5	15.8

Metropolitan Area Description
SACRAMENTO

STATE: California
COUNTIES: El Dorado, Placer, Sacramento, Yolo

TOTAL POPULATION: 1,481,102

POPULATION IN SUBURBS: 1,111,737   (75.1%)

POPULATION IN Sacramento: 369,365   (24.9%)

The SACRAMENTO metropolitan area is located in the central part of California. The suburbs range geographically from Auburn in the north (35 miles from Sacramento), to Woodland in the west (12 miles from Sacramento), to Elk Grove in the south (15 miles from Sacramento), and to South Lake Tahoe in the east (97 miles from Sacramento). The area is growing rapidly in population and had an increase of 34.7% between 1980 and 1990. Summer time high temperatures average in the 90's and winter time lows average in the 30's. Intel and Avantek have facilities located in the suburb of Folsom. Hewlett-Packard and NEC Electronics have operations in Roseville. A number of food processing and distribution companies are located in West Sacramento. The University of California has a major campus located in Davis.

Fair Oaks is the overall highest rated suburb. **Folsom** receives the top scores in economics and open spaces. **West Sacramento** is the suburb with the most affordable housing. The number one score in education belongs to **Davis**. **South Lake Tahoe** has the top rated commute. Finally, the number one rating in community stability goes to **Parkway-South Sacramento**. Crime rankings were not available for the area.

The highest ranked suburb overall which also has an affordable housing score of at least 50.00 is **Arden-Arcade**.

The highest ranked suburb in the education category which also has an affordable housing score of at least 50.00 is also **Arden-Arcade**.

The county whose suburbs have the highest average overall score is **Sacramento County** (52.79).

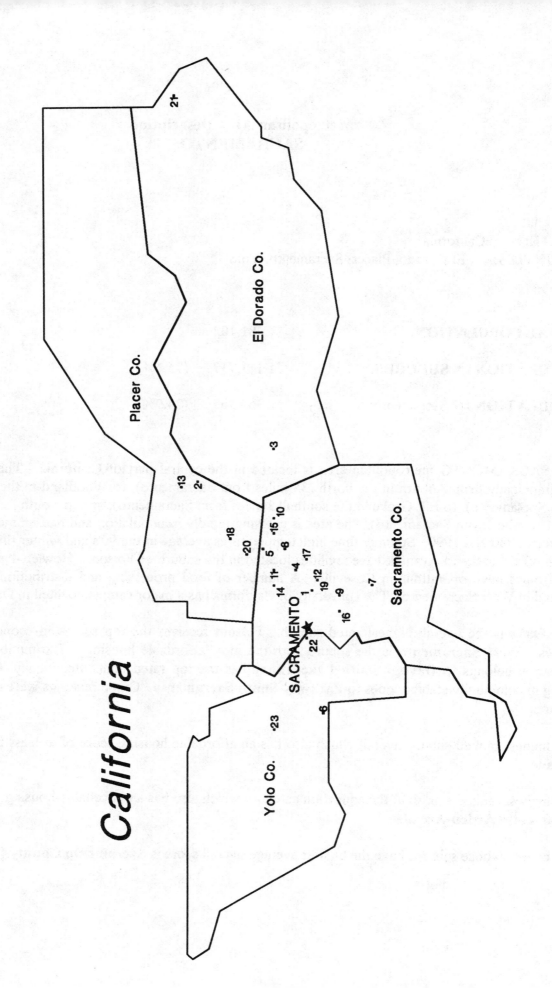

Metropolitan Area Map
SACRAMENTO

California

Yolo Co.

Placer Co.

El Dorado Co.

Sacramento Co.

SACRAMENTO

Metropolitan Area Suburb Alphabetical Index
SACRAMENTO

SUBURB	PAGE	MAP NO.	STATE	COUNTY	POPU-LATION	RANK
ARDEN-ARCADE	655	1	California	Sacramento	92,040	5 / 23
AUBURN	657	2	California	Placer	10,592	12 / 23
CAMERON PARK	661	3	California	El Dorado	11,897	23 / 23
CARMICHAEL	654	4	California	Sacramento	48,702	2 / 23
CITRUS HEIGHTS	659	5	California	Sacramento	107,439	18 / 23
DAVIS	659	6	California	Yolo	46,209	17 / 23
ELK GROVE	655	7	California	Sacramento	17,483	4 / 23
FAIR OAKS	654	8	California	Sacramento	26,867	1 / 23
FLORIN	658	9	California	Sacramento	24,330	14 / 23
FOLSOM	658	10	California	Sacramento	29,802	13 / 23
FOOTHILL FARMS	659	11	California	Sacramento	17,135	16 / 23
LA RIVIERA	654	12	California	Sacramento	10,986	3 / 23
NORTH AUBURN	660	13	California	Placer	10,301	21 / 23
NORTH HIGHLANDS	660	14	California	Sacramento	42,105	20 / 23
ORANGEVALE	656	15	California	Sacramento	26,266	7 / 23
PARKWAY-SOUTH SACRAMENTO	661	16	California	Sacramento	31,903	22 / 23
RANCHO CORDOVA	657	17	California	Sacramento	48,731	10 / 23
ROCKLIN	660	18	California	Placer	19,033	19 / 23
ROSEMONT	655	19	California	Sacramento	22,851	6 / 23
ROSEVILLE	657	20	California	Placer	44,685	11 / 23
SOUTH LAKE TAHOE	656	21	California	El Dorado	21,586	9 / 23
WEST SACRAMENTO	658	22	California	Yolo	28,898	15 / 23
WOODLAND	656	23	California	Yolo	39,802	8 / 23

Metropolitan Area Suburb Rankings
SACRAMENTO

Composite: Rank 1 / 23 *Score* 64.61   **FAIR OAKS**

CATEGORY	RANK	SCORE	STATISTIC	VALUE	RANK	SCORE
Economics	2	97.45	Median Household Income	$47,168	1	100.0
			% of Families Above Poverty Level	95.2%	6	94.9
Affordable Housing	20	20.45	Median Home Value	$206,400	22	1.7
			Median Rent	$564	13	39.2
Crime	N/A	N/A	Violent Crimes per 10,000 Population	N/A	N/A	N/A
			Property Crimes per 10,000 Population	N/A	N/A	N/A
Open Spaces	3	88.80	Population Density (Persons/Sq. Mile)	2717	10	77.6
			Average Rooms per Housing Unit	6.0	1	100.0
Education	2	69.05	% High School Enrollment/Completion	95.4%	2	84.5
			% College Graduates	38.3%	2	53.6
Commute	20	14.95	Average Work Commute in Minutes	25	20	7.7
			% Commuting on Public Transportation	1.7%	13	22.2
Community Stability	3	96.95	% Living in Same House as in 1979	34.4%	2	96.9
			% Living in Same County as in 1985	78.4%	3	97.0

Composite: Rank 2 / 23 *Score* 58.48   **CARMICHAEL**

CATEGORY	RANK	SCORE	STATISTIC	VALUE	RANK	SCORE
Economics	11	69.80	Median Household Income	$34,537	11	49.3
			% of Families Above Poverty Level	94.2%	9	90.3
Affordable Housing	11	45.85	Median Home Value	$160,800	17	38.0
			Median Rent	$531	6	53.7
Crime	N/A	N/A	Violent Crimes per 10,000 Population	N/A	N/A	N/A
			Property Crimes per 10,000 Population	N/A	N/A	N/A
Open Spaces	10	55.40	Population Density (Persons/Sq. Mile)	4524	15	48.3
			Average Rooms per Housing Unit	5.4	8	62.5
Education	3	54.90	% High School Enrollment/Completion	91.7%	8	67.7
			% College Graduates	32.0%	5	42.1
Commute	12	27.90	Average Work Commute in Minutes	22	12	30.8
			% Commuting on Public Transportation	1.9%	10	25.0
Community Stability	2	97.05	% Living in Same House as in 1979	33.7%	4	94.1
			% Living in Same County as in 1985	79.4%	1	100.0

Composite: Rank 3 / 23 *Score* 57.56   **LA RIVIERA**

CATEGORY	RANK	SCORE	STATISTIC	VALUE	RANK	SCORE
Economics	10	71.90	Median Household Income	$37,429	8	60.9
			% of Families Above Poverty Level	92.6%	13	82.9
Affordable Housing	10	46.40	Median Home Value	$127,400	9	64.6
			Median Rent	$589	15	28.2
Crime	N/A	N/A	Violent Crimes per 10,000 Population	N/A	N/A	N/A
			Property Crimes per 10,000 Population	N/A	N/A	N/A
Open Spaces	18	42.25	Population Density (Persons/Sq. Mile)	6147	21	22.0
			Average Rooms per Housing Unit	5.4	8	62.5
Education	7	51.15	% High School Enrollment/Completion	89.9%	15	59.5
			% College Graduates	32.4%	3	42.8
Commute	3	53.95	Average Work Commute in Minutes	21	7	38.5
			% Commuting on Public Transportation	5.1%	2	69.4
Community Stability	9	79.70	% Living in Same House as in 1979	29.8%	7	78.9
			% Living in Same County as in 1985	72.9%	13	80.5

Metropolitan Area Suburb Rankings
SACRAMENTO

Composite: *Rank* 4 / 23 *Score* 57.34   **ELK GROVE**

CATEGORY	RANK	SCORE	STATISTIC	VALUE	RANK	SCORE
Economics	3	92.80	Median Household Income	$44,057	3	87.5
			% of Families Above Poverty Level	95.9%	2	98.1
Affordable Housing	17	28.45	Median Home Value	$138,700	12	55.6
			Median Rent	$650	21	1.3
Crime	N/A	N/A	Violent Crimes per 10,000 Population	N/A	N/A	N/A
			Property Crimes per 10,000 Population	N/A	N/A	N/A
Open Spaces	7	74.75	Population Density (Persons/Sq. Mile)	4451	14	49.5
			Average Rooms per Housing Unit	6.0	1	100.0
Education	8	49.70	% High School Enrollment/Completion	93.5%	4	75.9
			% College Graduates	21.8%	12	23.5
Commute	15	21.95	Average Work Commute in Minutes	23	17	23.1
			% Commuting on Public Transportation	1.6%	14	20.8
Community Stability	12	76.40	% Living in Same House as in 1979	24.2%	15	57.0
			% Living in Same County as in 1985	78.0%	4	95.8

Composite: *Rank* 5 / 23 *Score* 56.70   **ARDEN-ARCADE**

CATEGORY	RANK	SCORE	STATISTIC	VALUE	RANK	SCORE
Economics	15	58.50	Median Household Income	$30,876	16	34.6
			% of Families Above Poverty Level	92.5%	14	82.4
Affordable Housing	9	58.20	Median Home Value	$149,800	14	46.8
			Median Rent	$495	4	69.6
Crime	N/A	N/A	Violent Crimes per 10,000 Population	N/A	N/A	N/A
			Property Crimes per 10,000 Population	N/A	N/A	N/A
Open Spaces	20	33.75	Population Density (Persons/Sq. Mile)	4880	17	42.5
			Average Rooms per Housing Unit	4.8	18	25.0
Education	5	52.65	% High School Enrollment/Completion	90.6%	12	62.7
			% College Graduates	32.3%	4	42.6
Commute	6	48.10	Average Work Commute in Minutes	20	5	46.2
			% Commuting on Public Transportation	3.7%	6	50.0
Community Stability	4	89.00	% Living in Same House as in 1979	33.1%	5	91.8
			% Living in Same County as in 1985	74.8%	8	86.2

Composite: *Rank* 6 / 23 *Score* 54.73   **ROSEMONT**

CATEGORY	RANK	SCORE	STATISTIC	VALUE	RANK	SCORE
Economics	8	77.95	Median Household Income	$36,744	9	58.2
			% of Families Above Poverty Level	95.8%	4	97.7
Affordable Housing	15	36.95	Median Home Value	$124,100	8	67.3
			Median Rent	$638	19	6.6
Crime	N/A	N/A	Violent Crimes per 10,000 Population	N/A	N/A	N/A
			Property Crimes per 10,000 Population	N/A	N/A	N/A
Open Spaces	19	40.80	Population Density (Persons/Sq. Mile)	5934	20	25.4
			Average Rooms per Housing Unit	5.3	10	56.2
Education	4	53.70	% High School Enrollment/Completion	93.5%	4	75.9
			% College Graduates	26.2%	8	31.5
Commute	5	48.40	Average Work Commute in Minutes	21	7	38.5
			% Commuting on Public Transportation	4.3%	5	58.3
Community Stability	14	70.60	% Living in Same House as in 1979	24.0%	16	56.2
			% Living in Same County as in 1985	74.4%	9	85.0

Metropolitan Area Suburb Rankings
SACRAMENTO

Composite: Rank 7 / 23 *Score* 54.55   **ORANGEVALE**

CATEGORY	RANK	SCORE	STATISTIC	VALUE	RANK	SCORE
Economics	7	79.65	Median Household Income	$39,442	7	69.0
			% of Families Above Poverty Level	94.2%	9	90.3
Affordable Housing	18	27.80	Median Home Value	$142,600	13	52.5
			Median Rent	$646	20	3.1
Crime	N/A	N/A	Violent Crimes per 10,000 Population	N/A	N/A	N/A
			Property Crimes per 10,000 Population	N/A	N/A	N/A
Open Spaces	6	80.20	Population Density (Persons/Sq. Mile)	2622	9	79.1
			Average Rooms per Housing Unit	5.7	4	81.3
Education	11	46.55	% High School Enrollment/Completion	92.7%	6	72.3
			% College Graduates	20.3%	13	20.8
Commute	22	8.70	Average Work Commute in Minutes	25	20	7.7
			% Commuting on Public Transportation	0.8%	19	9.7
Community Stability	5	84.40	% Living in Same House as in 1979	30.2%	6	80.5
			% Living in Same County as in 1985	75.5%	7	88.3

Composite: Rank 8 / 23 *Score* 53.54   **WOODLAND**

CATEGORY	RANK	SCORE	STATISTIC	VALUE	RANK	SCORE
Economics	14	58.70	Median Household Income	$31,671	15	37.8
			% of Families Above Poverty Level	91.9%	16	79.6
Affordable Housing	5	68.15	Median Home Value	$130,800	10	61.9
			Median Rent	$484	3	74.4
Crime	N/A	N/A	Violent Crimes per 10,000 Population	48	N/A	N/A
			Property Crimes per 10,000 Population	468	N/A	N/A
Open Spaces	14	44.40	Population Density (Persons/Sq. Mile)	4339	13	51.3
			Average Rooms per Housing Unit	5.0	14	37.5
Education	19	29.45	% High School Enrollment/Completion	86.5%	18	44.1
			% College Graduates	17.0%	16	14.8
Commute	8	38.05	Average Work Commute in Minutes	17	2	69.2
			% Commuting on Public Transportation	0.6%	20	6.9
Community Stability	6	82.50	% Living in Same House as in 1979	28.7%	10	74.6
			% Living in Same County as in 1985	76.2%	6	90.4

Composite: Rank 9 / 23 *Score* 52.23   **SOUTH LAKE TAHOE**

CATEGORY	RANK	SCORE	STATISTIC	VALUE	RANK	SCORE
Economics	19	44.45	Median Household Income	$25,596	21	13.4
			% of Families Above Poverty Level	91.0%	18	75.5
Affordable Housing	4	68.40	Median Home Value	$114,700	7	74.7
			Median Rent	$512	5	62.1
Crime	N/A	N/A	Violent Crimes per 10,000 Population	72	N/A	N/A
			Property Crimes per 10,000 Population	683	N/A	N/A
Open Spaces	13	46.50	Population Density (Persons/Sq. Mile)	2146	8	86.8
			Average Rooms per Housing Unit	4.5	22	6.2
Education	20	27.15	% High School Enrollment/Completion	85.5%	20	39.5
			% College Graduates	17.0%	16	14.8
Commute	1	100.00	Average Work Commute in Minutes	13	1	100.0
			% Commuting on Public Transportation	7.3%	1	100.0
Community Stability	20	26.85	% Living in Same House as in 1979	15.0%	22	21.1
			% Living in Same County as in 1985	56.9%	18	32.6

Metropolitan Area Suburb Rankings
SACRAMENTO

Composite: *Rank* 10 / 23 *Score* 52.08   **RANCHO CORDOVA**

CATEGORY	RANK	SCORE	STATISTIC	VALUE	RANK	SCORE
Economics	16	57.05	Median Household Income	$32,780	12	42.3
			% of Families Above Poverty Level	90.2%	19	71.8
Affordable Housing	8	60.80	Median Home Value	$112,200	5	76.7
			Median Rent	$551	11	44.9
Crime	N/A	N/A	Violent Crimes per 10,000 Population	N/A	N/A	N/A
			Property Crimes per 10,000 Population	N/A	N/A	N/A
Open Spaces	17	43.95	Population Density (Persons/Sq. Mile)	4778	16	44.2
			Average Rooms per Housing Unit	5.1	12	43.7
Education	17	35.75	% High School Enrollment/Completion	89.0%	17	55.5
			% College Graduates	17.7%	15	16.0
Commute	7	42.85	Average Work Commute in Minutes	21	7	38.5
			% Commuting on Public Transportation	3.5%	7	47.2
Community Stability	13	72.05	% Living in Same House as in 1979	25.8%	12	63.3
			% Living in Same County as in 1985	73.0%	12	80.8

Composite: *Rank* 11 / 23 *Score* 50.24   **ROSEVILLE**

CATEGORY	RANK	SCORE	STATISTIC	VALUE	RANK	SCORE
Economics	6	82.10	Median Household Income	$39,975	6	71.1
			% of Families Above Poverty Level	94.8%	7	93.1
Affordable Housing	16	31.75	Median Home Value	$158,000	16	40.2
			Median Rent	$600	17	23.3
Crime	N/A	N/A	Violent Crimes per 10,000 Population	61	N/A	N/A
			Property Crimes per 10,000 Population	622	N/A	N/A
Open Spaces	5	83.00	Population Density (Persons/Sq. Mile)	1496	4	97.3
			Average Rooms per Housing Unit	5.5	7	68.7
Education	12	45.35	% High School Enrollment/Completion	90.7%	11	63.2
			% College Graduates	24.0%	11	27.5
Commute	16	21.65	Average Work Commute in Minutes	22	12	30.8
			% Commuting on Public Transportation	1.0%	18	12.5
Community Stability	18	37.60	% Living in Same House as in 1979	23.4%	17	53.9
			% Living in Same County as in 1985	53.1%	20	21.3

Composite: *Rank* 12 / 23 *Score* 49.62   **AUBURN**

CATEGORY	RANK	SCORE	STATISTIC	VALUE	RANK	SCORE
Economics	12	65.45	Median Household Income	$32,708	13	42.0
			% of Families Above Poverty Level	93.9%	11	88.9
Affordable Housing	12	43.60	Median Home Value	$163,200	18	36.1
			Median Rent	$537	8	51.1
Crime	N/A	N/A	Violent Crimes per 10,000 Population	49	N/A	N/A
			Property Crimes per 10,000 Population	499	N/A	N/A
Open Spaces	8	68.55	Population Density (Persons/Sq. Mile)	1740	6	93.4
			Average Rooms per Housing Unit	5.1	12	43.7
Education	15	37.30	% High School Enrollment/Completion	86.2%	19	42.7
			% College Graduates	26.4%	7	31.9
Commute	17	20.65	Average Work Commute in Minutes	21	7	38.5
			% Commuting on Public Transportation	0.3%	21	2.8
Community Stability	16	62.20	% Living in Same House as in 1979	23.2%	18	53.1
			% Living in Same County as in 1985	69.8%	15	71.3

Metropolitan Area Suburb Rankings
SACRAMENTO

Composite: *Rank* 13 / 23   *Score* 49.48   **FOLSOM**

CATEGORY	RANK	SCORE	STATISTIC	VALUE	RANK	SCORE
Economics	1	97.70	Median Household Income	$46,726	2	98.2
			% of Families Above Poverty Level	95.7%	5	97.2
Affordable Housing	21	13.20	Median Home Value	$208,500	23	0.0
			Median Rent	$593	16	26.4
Crime	N/A	N/A	Violent Crimes per 10,000 Population	18	N/A	N/A
			Property Crimes per 10,000 Population	266	N/A	N/A
Open Spaces	1	96.40	Population Density (Persons/Sq. Mile)	1391	3	99.0
			Average Rooms per Housing Unit	5.9	3	93.8
Education	6	52.35	% High School Enrollment/Completion	93.7%	3	76.8
			% College Graduates	24.2%	10	27.9
Commute	21	14.25	Average Work Commute in Minutes	25	20	7.7
			% Commuting on Public Transportation	1.6%	14	20.8
Community Stability	21	22.95	% Living in Same House as in 1979	15.9%	21	24.6
			% Living in Same County as in 1985	53.1%	20	21.3

Composite: *Rank* 14 / 23   *Score* 49.13   **FLORIN**

CATEGORY	RANK	SCORE	STATISTIC	VALUE	RANK	SCORE
Economics	20	40.05	Median Household Income	$29,406	17	28.7
			% of Families Above Poverty Level	85.8%	21	51.4
Affordable Housing	6	65.50	Median Home Value	$101,100	4	85.6
			Median Rent	$550	10	45.4
Crime	N/A	N/A	Violent Crimes per 10,000 Population	N/A	N/A	N/A
			Property Crimes per 10,000 Population	N/A	N/A	N/A
Open Spaces	14	44.40	Population Density (Persons/Sq. Mile)	4336	12	51.3
			Average Rooms per Housing Unit	5.0	14	37.5
Education	18	35.10	% High School Enrollment/Completion	91.6%	9	67.3
			% College Graduates	10.5%	20	2.9
Commute	11	30.00	Average Work Commute in Minutes	22	12	30.8
			% Commuting on Public Transportation	2.2%	9	29.2
Community Stability	8	79.75	% Living in Same House as in 1979	26.6%	11	66.4
			% Living in Same County as in 1985	77.1%	5	93.1

Composite: *Rank* 15 / 23   *Score* 48.43   **WEST SACRAMENTO**

CATEGORY	RANK	SCORE	STATISTIC	VALUE	RANK	SCORE
Economics	22	24.30	Median Household Income	$23,287	22	4.2
			% of Families Above Poverty Level	84.3%	22	44.4
Affordable Housing	1	97.85	Median Home Value	$88,400	2	95.7
			Median Rent	$426	1	100.0
Crime	N/A	N/A	Violent Crimes per 10,000 Population	124	N/A	N/A
			Property Crimes per 10,000 Population	800	N/A	N/A
Open Spaces	12	49.60	Population Density (Persons/Sq. Mile)	1379	2	99.2
			Average Rooms per Housing Unit	4.4	23	0.0
Education	21	4.55	% High School Enrollment/Completion	78.8%	21	9.1
			% College Graduates	8.9%	22	0.0
Commute	9	36.60	Average Work Commute in Minutes	19	4	53.8
			% Commuting on Public Transportation	1.5%	16	19.4
Community Stability	11	77.70	% Living in Same House as in 1979	33.9%	3	94.9
			% Living in Same County as in 1985	66.2%	16	60.5

Metropolitan Area Suburb Rankings
SACRAMENTO

Composite: **Rank** 16 / 23 **Score** 47.76   **FOOTHILL FARMS**

CATEGORY	RANK	SCORE	STATISTIC	VALUE	RANK	SCORE
Economics	13	59.70	Median Household Income	$32,177	14	39.8
			% of Families Above Poverty Level	91.9%	16	79.6
Affordable Housing	7	64.80	Median Home Value	$112,300	6	76.7
			Median Rent	$533	7	52.9
Crime	N/A	N/A	Violent Crimes per 10,000 Population	N/A	N/A	N/A
			Property Crimes per 10,000 Population	N/A	N/A	N/A
Open Spaces	22	18.75	Population Density (Persons/Sq. Mile)	7503	23	0.0
			Average Rooms per Housing Unit	5.0	14	37.5
Education	16	36.20	% High School Enrollment/Completion	90.0%	14	60.0
			% College Graduates	15.7%	18	12.4
Commute	12	27.90	Average Work Commute in Minutes	22	12	30.8
			% Commuting on Public Transportation	1.9%	10	25.0
Community Stability	10	79.20	% Living in Same House as in 1979	29.4%	8	77.3
			% Living in Same County as in 1985	73.1%	11	81.1

Composite: **Rank** 17 / 23 **Score** 47.65   **DAVIS**

CATEGORY	RANK	SCORE	STATISTIC	VALUE	RANK	SCORE
Economics	17	55.80	Median Household Income	$29,044	18	27.3
			% of Families Above Poverty Level	92.9%	12	84.3
Affordable Housing	19	22.05	Median Home Value	$189,000	21	15.5
			Median Rent	$588	14	28.6
Crime	N/A	N/A	Violent Crimes per 10,000 Population	16	N/A	N/A
			Property Crimes per 10,000 Population	700	N/A	N/A
Open Spaces	21	25.80	Population Density (Persons/Sq. Mile)	5473	18	32.9
			Average Rooms per Housing Unit	4.7	20	18.7
Education	1	100.00	% High School Enrollment/Completion	98.8%	1	100.0
			% College Graduates	63.8%	1	100.0
Commute	2	65.85	Average Work Commute in Minutes	17	2	69.2
			% Commuting on Public Transportation	4.6%	3	62.5
Community Stability	22	16.40	% Living in Same House as in 1979	18.0%	20	32.8
			% Living in Same County as in 1985	46.0%	23	0.0

Composite: **Rank** 18 / 23 **Score** 47.36   **CITRUS HEIGHTS**

CATEGORY	RANK	SCORE	STATISTIC	VALUE	RANK	SCORE
Economics	9	72.45	Median Household Income	$35,748	10	54.2
			% of Families Above Poverty Level	94.3%	8	90.7
Affordable Housing	14	39.55	Median Home Value	$131,900	11	61.0
			Median Rent	$612	18	18.1
Crime	N/A	N/A	Violent Crimes per 10,000 Population	N/A	N/A	N/A
			Property Crimes per 10,000 Population	N/A	N/A	N/A
Open Spaces	16	44.25	Population Density (Persons/Sq. Mile)	5512	19	32.3
			Average Rooms per Housing Unit	5.3	10	56.2
Education	14	40.00	% High School Enrollment/Completion	90.3%	13	61.4
			% College Graduates	19.1%	14	18.6
Commute	18	20.20	Average Work Commute in Minutes	24	19	15.4
			% Commuting on Public Transportation	1.9%	10	25.0
Community Stability	15	67.70	% Living in Same House as in 1979	25.1%	13	60.5
			% Living in Same County as in 1985	71.0%	14	74.9

Metropolitan Area Suburb Rankings
SACRAMENTO

Composite: Rank 19 / 23 *Score* 47.32   **ROCKLIN**

CATEGORY	RANK	SCORE	STATISTIC	VALUE	RANK	SCORE
Economics	5	86.45	Median Household Income	$40,417	5	72.9
			% of Families Above Poverty Level	96.3%	1	100.0
Affordable Housing	22	13.00	Median Home Value	$175,900	19	26.0
			Median Rent	$653	23	0.0
Crime	N/A	N/A	Violent Crimes per 10,000 Population	26	N/A	N/A
			Property Crimes per 10,000 Population	373	N/A	N/A
Open Spaces	2	89.20	Population Density (Persons/Sq. Mile)	1510	5	97.1
			Average Rooms per Housing Unit	5.7	4	81.3
Education	10	47.45	% High School Enrollment/Completion	90.8%	10	63.6
			% College Graduates	26.1%	9	31.3
Commute	19	19.20	Average Work Commute in Minutes	23	17	23.1
			% Commuting on Public Transportation	1.2%	17	15.3
Community Stability	19	28.65	% Living in Same House as in 1979	18.2%	19	33.6
			% Living in Same County as in 1985	53.9%	19	23.7

Composite: Rank 20 / 23 *Score* 46.86   **NORTH HIGHLANDS**

CATEGORY	RANK	SCORE	STATISTIC	VALUE	RANK	SCORE
Economics	21	38.55	Median Household Income	$27,025	19	19.2
			% of Families Above Poverty Level	87.2%	20	57.9
Affordable Housing	3	73.30	Median Home Value	$88,700	3	95.5
			Median Rent	$537	8	51.1
Crime	N/A	N/A	Violent Crimes per 10,000 Population	N/A	N/A	N/A
			Property Crimes per 10,000 Population	N/A	N/A	N/A
Open Spaces	11	49.80	Population Density (Persons/Sq. Mile)	3286	11	68.3
			Average Rooms per Housing Unit	4.9	17	31.3
Education	22	4.40	% High School Enrollment/Completion	78.4%	22	7.3
			% College Graduates	9.7%	21	1.5
Commute	10	34.85	Average Work Commute in Minutes	22	12	30.8
			% Commuting on Public Transportation	2.9%	8	38.9
Community Stability	7	80.25	% Living in Same House as in 1979	29.3%	9	77.0
			% Living in Same County as in 1985	73.9%	10	83.5

Composite: Rank 21 / 23 *Score* 46.37   **NORTH AUBURN**

CATEGORY	RANK	SCORE	STATISTIC	VALUE	RANK	SCORE
Economics	18	49.45	Median Household Income	$26,717	20	17.9
			% of Families Above Poverty Level	92.2%	15	81.0
Affordable Housing	13	41.85	Median Home Value	$153,800	15	43.6
			Median Rent	$562	12	40.1
Crime	N/A	N/A	Violent Crimes per 10,000 Population	N/A	N/A	N/A
			Property Crimes per 10,000 Population	N/A	N/A	N/A
Open Spaces	9	62.50	Population Density (Persons/Sq. Mile)	1332	1	100.0
			Average Rooms per Housing Unit	4.8	18	25.0
Education	13	40.55	% High School Enrollment/Completion	92.2%	7	70.0
			% College Graduates	15.0%	19	11.1
Commute	14	23.80	Average Work Commute in Minutes	20	5	46.2
			% Commuting on Public Transportation	0.2%	22	1.4
Community Stability	17	60.05	% Living in Same House as in 1979	25.0%	14	60.2
			% Living in Same County as in 1985	66.0%	17	59.9

Metropolitan Area Suburb Rankings
SACRAMENTO

PARKWAY-SOUTH SACRAMENTO

Composite: **Rank** 22 / 23 *Score* 42.48

CATEGORY	RANK	SCORE	STATISTIC	VALUE	RANK	SCORE
Economics	23	0.00	Median Household Income	$22,249	23	0.0
			% of Families Above Poverty Level	74.7%	23	0.0
Affordable Housing	2	91.65	Median Home Value	$83,000	1	100.0
			Median Rent	$464	2	83.3
Crime	N/A	N/A	Violent Crimes per 10,000 Population	N/A	N/A	N/A
			Property Crimes per 10,000 Population	N/A	N/A	N/A
Open Spaces	23	12.75	Population Density (Persons/Sq. Mile)	6698	22	13.0
			Average Rooms per Housing Unit	4.6	21	12.5
Education	23	0.00	% High School Enrollment/Completion	76.8%	23	0.0
			% College Graduates	8.9%	22	0.0
Commute	4	50.50	Average Work Commute in Minutes	21	7	38.5
			% Commuting on Public Transportation	4.6%	3	62.5
Community Stability	1	100.00	% Living in Same House as in 1979	35.2%	1	100.0
			% Living in Same County as in 1985	79.4%	1	100.0

CAMERON PARK

Composite: **Rank** 23 / 23 *Score* 39.07

CATEGORY	RANK	SCORE	STATISTIC	VALUE	RANK	SCORE
Economics	4	88.25	Median Household Income	$41,794	4	78.4
			% of Families Above Poverty Level	95.9%	2	98.1
Affordable Housing	23	10.55	Median Home Value	$183,700	20	19.8
			Median Rent	$650	21	1.3
Crime	N/A	N/A	Violent Crimes per 10,000 Population	N/A	N/A	N/A
			Property Crimes per 10,000 Population	N/A	N/A	N/A
Open Spaces	4	86.60	Population Density (Persons/Sq. Mile)	1829	7	91.9
			Average Rooms per Housing Unit	5.7	4	81.3
Education	9	48.30	% High School Enrollment/Completion	89.8%	16	59.1
			% College Graduates	29.5%	6	37.5
Commute	23	0.00	Average Work Commute in Minutes	26	23	0.0
			% Commuting on Public Transportation	0.1%	23	0.0
Community Stability	23	0.75	% Living in Same House as in 1979	9.6%	23	0.0
			% Living in Same County as in 1985	46.5%	22	1.5

Metropolitan Area Description
ST. LOUIS

STATE: Illinois
COUNTIES: Clinton, Jersey, Madison, Monroe, St. Clair

STATE: Missouri
COUNTIES: Franklin, Jefferson, St. Charles, St. Louis

INDE-PENDENT CITIES: St. Louis

TOTAL POPULATION: 2,444,099

POPULATION IN SUBURBS: 2,047,414 (83.8%)

POPULATION IN St. Louis (MO): 396,685 (16.2%)

The ST. LOUIS metropolitan area is located in the eastcentral part of Missouri and the westcentral part of Illinois along the Mississippi River. The suburbs range geographically from Alton (IL) in the north (24 miles from St. Louis), to Washington (MO) in the west (56 miles from St. Louis), to Oakville (MO) in the south (14 miles from St. Louis), and to O'Fallon (IL) in the east (20 miles from St. Louis). The area is growing in population and had an increase of 2.8% between 1980 and 1990. Summer time high temperatures average in the 80's and winter time lows average in the 20's. Since the late 1970's suburban growth has broken past Interstate 270, the ring connecting north and south St. Louis (MO) County, and has reached as far west as Chesterfield (MO). General Motors and Chrysler both have facilities in the suburbs. Public transportation in the area is provided by the Bi-State Transit System using buses and trains.

Webster Groves (MO) is the overall highest rated suburb. **Chesterfield** (MO) receives the highest scores in economics and open spaces. **East St. Louis** (IL) is the suburb with the most affordable housing and also has the top rated commute. **Ballwin** (MO) is rated the safest suburb with the lowest crime rate. The number one score in education belongs to **Clayton** (MO). Finally, the top rating in community stability goes to **Crestwood** (MO).

The highest ranked suburb overall which also has an affordable housing score of at least 50.00 is **Webster Groves** (MO).

The highest ranked suburb in the education category which also has an affordable housing score of at least 50.00 is also **Webster Groves** (MO).

The county whose suburbs have the highest average overall score is **Franklin County** (MO) (56.32).

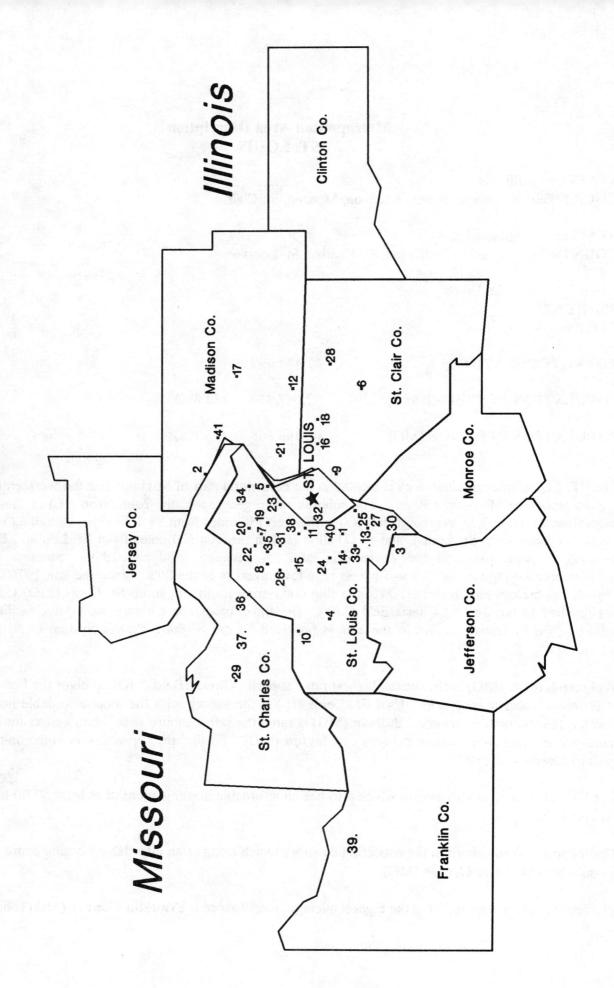

Metropolitan Area Map
ST. LOUIS

Illinois

Missouri

Clinton Co.

Madison Co.

St. Clair Co.

Monroe Co.

Jefferson Co.

Franklin Co.

St. Louis Co.

St. Charles Co.

Jersey Co.

ST. LOUIS

Metropolitan Area Suburb Alphabetical Index
ST. LOUIS

SUBURB	PAGE	MAP NO.	STATE	COUNTY	POPU-LATION	RANK
AFFTON	674	1	Missouri	St. Louis	21,106	26 / 41
ALTON	675	2	Illinois	Madison	32,905	30 / 41
ARNOLD	675	3	Missouri	Jefferson	18,828	28 / 41
BALLWIN	667	4	Missouri	St. Louis	21,816	6 / 41
BELLEFONTAINE NEIGHBORS	668	5	Missouri	St. Louis	10,922	9 / 41
BELLEVILLE	670	6	Illinois	St. Clair	42,785	14 / 41
BERKELEY	673	7	Missouri	St. Louis	12,450	23 / 41
BRIDGETON	668	8	Missouri	St. Louis	17,779	8 / 41
CAHOKIA	676	9	Illinois	St. Clair	17,550	32 / 41
CHESTERFIELD	667	10	Missouri	St. Louis	37,991	5 / 41
CLAYTON	674	11	Missouri	St. Louis	13,874	25 / 41
COLLINSVILLE	673	12	Illinois	Madison	22,446	22 / 41
CONCORD	669	13	Missouri	St. Louis	19,859	11 / 41
CRESTWOOD	666	14	Missouri	St. Louis	11,234	3 / 41
CREVE COEUR	666	15	Missouri	St. Louis	12,304	2 / 41
EAST ST. LOUIS	678	16	Illinois	St. Clair	40,944	38 / 41
EDWARDSVILLE	668	17	Illinois	Madison	14,579	7 / 41
FAIRVIEW HEIGHTS	670	18	Illinois	St. Clair	14,351	13 / 41
FERGUSON	671	19	Missouri	St. Louis	22,286	18 / 41
FLORISSANT	669	20	Missouri	St. Louis	51,206	10 / 41
GRANITE CITY	671	21	Illinois	Madison	32,862	17 / 41
HAZELWOOD	672	22	Missouri	St. Louis	15,324	19 / 41
JENNINGS	678	23	Missouri	St. Louis	15,905	37 / 41
KIRKWOOD	667	24	Missouri	St. Louis	27,291	4 / 41
LEMAY	679	25	Missouri	St. Louis	18,005	40 / 41
MARYLAND HEIGHTS	672	26	Missouri	St. Louis	25,407	20 / 41
MEHLVILLE	678	27	Missouri	St. Louis	27,557	39 / 41
O'FALLON	671	28	Illinois	St. Clair	16,073	16 / 41
O'FALLON	676	29	Missouri	St. Charles	18,698	33 / 41
OAKVILLE	674	30	Missouri	St. Louis	31,750	27 / 41
OVERLAND	676	31	Missouri	St. Louis	17,987	31 / 41
RICHMOND HEIGHTS	673	32	Missouri	St. Louis	10,448	24 / 41
SAPPINGTON	669	33	Missouri	St. Louis	10,917	12 / 41
SPANISH LAKE	677	34	Missouri	St. Louis	20,322	34 / 41
ST. ANN	679	35	Missouri	St. Louis	14,489	41 / 41
ST. CHARLES	677	36	Missouri	St. Charles	54,555	35 / 41
ST. PETERS	677	37	Missouri	St. Charles	45,779	36 / 41
UNIVERSITY CITY	675	38	Missouri	St. Louis	40,087	29 / 41
WASHINGTON	670	39	Missouri	Franklin	10,704	15 / 41
WEBSTER GROVES	666	40	Missouri	St. Louis	22,987	1 / 41
WOOD RIVER	672	41	Illinois	Madison	11,490	21 / 41

Metropolitan Area Suburb Rankings
ST. LOUIS

Composite: Rank 1 / 41 *Score* 66.59   **WEBSTER GROVES (MO)**

CATEGORY	RANK	SCORE	STATISTIC	VALUE	RANK	SCORE
Economics	10	73.70	Median Household Income	$41,489	9	53.1
			% of Families Above Poverty Level	97.1%	16	94.3
Affordable Housing	34	55.50	Median Home Value	$98,100	34	69.0
			Median Rent	$530	36	42.0
Crime	2	99.25	Violent Crimes per 10,000 Population	18	10	98.5
			Property Crimes per 10,000 Population	212	1	100.0
Open Spaces	19	56.30	Population Density (Persons/Sq. Mile)	3897	32	51.7
			Average Rooms per Housing Unit	6.1	5	60.9
Education	4	74.95	% High School Enrollment/Completion	94.8%	9	82.7
			% College Graduates	46.8%	4	67.2
Commute	8	36.20	Average Work Commute in Minutes	20	7	58.3
			% Commuting on Public Transportation	2.1%	12	14.1
Community Stability	11	70.25	% Living in Same House as in 1979	49.7%	10	73.1
			% Living in Same County as in 1985	82.8%	15	67.4

Composite: Rank 2 / 41 *Score* 66.16   **CREVE COEUR (MO)**

CATEGORY	RANK	SCORE	STATISTIC	VALUE	RANK	SCORE
Economics	2	90.70	Median Household Income	$59,913	2	87.1
			% of Families Above Poverty Level	97.1%	16	94.3
Affordable Housing	39	23.20	Median Home Value	$205,500	40	23.2
			Median Rent	$598	40	23.2
Crime	10	86.85	Violent Crimes per 10,000 Population	19	11	98.3
			Property Crimes per 10,000 Population	387	11	75.4
Open Spaces	2	83.00	Population Density (Persons/Sq. Mile)	1621	7	92.1
			Average Rooms per Housing Unit	6.4	2	73.9
Education	2	90.35	% High School Enrollment/Completion	98.4%	2	98.7
			% College Graduates	55.9%	2	82.0
Commute	13	34.35	Average Work Commute in Minutes	19	3	66.7
			% Commuting on Public Transportation	0.3%	36	2.0
Community Stability	24	54.65	% Living in Same House as in 1979	41.5%	23	54.3
			% Living in Same County as in 1985	78.0%	25	55.0

Composite: Rank 3 / 41 *Score* 66.06   **CRESTWOOD (MO)**

CATEGORY	RANK	SCORE	STATISTIC	VALUE	RANK	SCORE
Economics	11	73.35	Median Household Income	$40,926	10	52.1
			% of Families Above Poverty Level	97.2%	14	94.6
Affordable Housing	26	65.40	Median Home Value	$91,200	32	72.0
			Median Rent	$469	20	58.8
Crime	9	87.75	Violent Crimes per 10,000 Population	17	9	98.7
			Property Crimes per 10,000 Population	377	9	76.8
Open Spaces	15	59.65	Population Density (Persons/Sq. Mile)	3524	29	58.4
			Average Rooms per Housing Unit	6.1	5	60.9
Education	13	57.15	% High School Enrollment/Completion	93.2%	15	75.6
			% College Graduates	29.3%	11	38.7
Commute	22	29.05	Average Work Commute in Minutes	21	16	50.0
			% Commuting on Public Transportation	1.2%	20	8.1
Community Stability	1	90.05	% Living in Same House as in 1979	61.5%	1	100.0
			% Living in Same County as in 1985	87.7%	5	80.1

Metropolitan Area Suburb Rankings
ST. LOUIS

Composite: *Rank* 4 / 41 *Score* 65.88   **KIRKWOOD (MO)**

CATEGORY	RANK	SCORE	STATISTIC	VALUE	RANK	SCORE
Economics	8	76.40	Median Household Income	$42,113	8	54.3
			% of Families Above Poverty Level	98.7%	3	98.5
Affordable Housing	37	51.25	Median Home Value	$99,900	35	68.2
			Median Rent	$558	39	34.3
Crime	5	95.00	Violent Crimes per 10,000 Population	12	4	99.6
			Property Crimes per 10,000 Population	280	5	90.4
Open Spaces	12	61.85	Population Density (Persons/Sq. Mile)	3027	24	67.2
			Average Rooms per Housing Unit	6.0	8	56.5
Education	5	73.05	% High School Enrollment/Completion	95.4%	4	85.3
			% College Graduates	42.9%	5	60.8
Commute	12	34.50	Average Work Commute in Minutes	20	7	58.3
			% Commuting on Public Transportation	1.6%	14	10.7
Community Stability	12	69.10	% Living in Same House as in 1979	47.0%	14	66.9
			% Living in Same County as in 1985	84.3%	10	71.3

Composite: *Rank* 5 / 41 *Score* 62.80   **CHESTERFIELD (MO)**

CATEGORY	RANK	SCORE	STATISTIC	VALUE	RANK	SCORE
Economics	1	99.10	Median Household Income	$66,930	1	100.0
			% of Families Above Poverty Level	98.6%	4	98.2
Affordable Housing	41	18.45	Median Home Value	$173,400	39	36.9
			Median Rent	$682	41	0.0
Crime	3	97.85	Violent Crimes per 10,000 Population	16	8	98.9
			Property Crimes per 10,000 Population	235	3	96.8
Open Spaces	1	99.20	Population Density (Persons/Sq. Mile)	1268	4	98.4
			Average Rooms per Housing Unit	7.0	1	100.0
Education	3	80.75	% High School Enrollment/Completion	94.9%	8	83.1
			% College Graduates	53.7%	3	78.4
Commute	36	13.85	Average Work Commute in Minutes	24	34	25.0
			% Commuting on Public Transportation	0.4%	35	2.7
Community Stability	36	30.40	% Living in Same House as in 1979	27.8%	37	23.1
			% Living in Same County as in 1985	71.3%	36	37.7

Composite: *Rank* 6 / 41 *Score* 60.36   **BALLWIN (MO)**

CATEGORY	RANK	SCORE	STATISTIC	VALUE	RANK	SCORE
Economics	4	80.45	Median Household Income	$46,654	4	62.7
			% of Families Above Poverty Level	98.6%	4	98.2
Affordable Housing	35	55.20	Median Home Value	$103,200	36	66.8
			Median Rent	$524	33	43.6
Crime	1	99.30	Violent Crimes per 10,000 Population	10	1	100.0
			Property Crimes per 10,000 Population	222	2	98.6
Open Spaces	7	66.70	Population Density (Persons/Sq. Mile)	3457	28	59.5
			Average Rooms per Housing Unit	6.4	2	73.9
Education	8	62.85	% High School Enrollment/Completion	93.2%	15	75.6
			% College Graduates	36.3%	8	50.1
Commute	40	7.15	Average Work Commute in Minutes	26	39	8.3
			% Commuting on Public Transportation	0.9%	28	6.0
Community Stability	29	50.85	% Living in Same House as in 1979	37.0%	33	44.1
			% Living in Same County as in 1985	79.0%	24	57.6

Metropolitan Area Suburb Rankings
ST. LOUIS

Composite: *Rank* 7 / 41 *Score* 60.24 **EDWARDSVILLE (IL)**

CATEGORY	RANK	SCORE	STATISTIC	VALUE	RANK	SCORE
Economics	27	61.55	Median Household Income	$32,733	24	37.0
			% of Families Above Poverty Level	93.9%	31	86.1
Affordable Housing	14	75.80	Median Home Value	$64,400	16	83.4
			Median Rent	$435	14	68.2
Crime	7	91.30	Violent Crimes per 10,000 Population	13	5	99.4
			Property Crimes per 10,000 Population	331	7	83.2
Open Spaces	9	63.00	Population Density (Persons/Sq. Mile)	1671	8	91.2
			Average Rooms per Housing Unit	5.5	16	34.8
Education	11	57.45	% High School Enrollment/Completion	91.7%	19	68.9
			% College Graduates	33.8%	9	46.0
Commute	33	19.00	Average Work Commute in Minutes	23	27	33.3
			% Commuting on Public Transportation	0.7%	32	4.7
Community Stability	25	53.55	% Living in Same House as in 1979	37.1%	32	44.3
			% Living in Same County as in 1985	81.0%	18	62.8

Composite: *Rank* 8 / 41 *Score* 59.82 **BRIDGETON (MO)**

CATEGORY	RANK	SCORE	STATISTIC	VALUE	RANK	SCORE
Economics	13	72.00	Median Household Income	$38,619	13	47.9
			% of Families Above Poverty Level	97.8%	9	96.1
Affordable Housing	29	61.55	Median Home Value	$90,000	31	72.5
			Median Rent	$499	26	50.6
Crime	27	63.75	Violent Crimes per 10,000 Population	45	26	93.4
			Property Crimes per 10,000 Population	680	27	34.1
Open Spaces	4	73.45	Population Density (Persons/Sq. Mile)	1224	3	99.1
			Average Rooms per Housing Unit	5.8	11	47.8
Education	14	55.80	% High School Enrollment/Completion	94.8%	9	82.7
			% College Graduates	23.3%	17	28.9
Commute	11	35.35	Average Work Commute in Minutes	19	3	66.7
			% Commuting on Public Transportation	0.6%	33	4.0
Community Stability	23	56.85	% Living in Same House as in 1979	38.3%	30	47.0
			% Living in Same County as in 1985	82.5%	16	66.7

Composite: *Rank* 9 / 41 *Score* 59.44 **BELLEFONTAINE NEIGHBORS (MO)**

CATEGORY	RANK	SCORE	STATISTIC	VALUE	RANK	SCORE
Economics	24	64.90	Median Household Income	$31,726	27	35.2
			% of Families Above Poverty Level	97.2%	14	94.6
Affordable Housing	23	66.90	Median Home Value	$57,500	12	86.3
			Median Rent	$510	28	47.5
Crime	12	85.90	Violent Crimes per 10,000 Population	11	2	99.8
			Property Crimes per 10,000 Population	411	14	72.0
Open Spaces	18	57.90	Population Density (Persons/Sq. Mile)	2489	16	76.7
			Average Rooms per Housing Unit	5.6	14	39.1
Education	31	32.50	% High School Enrollment/Completion	88.6%	29	55.1
			% College Graduates	11.6%	30	9.9
Commute	29	21.70	Average Work Commute in Minutes	23	27	33.3
			% Commuting on Public Transportation	1.5%	15	10.1
Community Stability	3	86.30	% Living in Same House as in 1979	61.3%	2	99.5
			% Living in Same County as in 1985	85.0%	9	73.1

Metropolitan Area Suburb Rankings
ST. LOUIS

Composite: *Rank* 10 / 41 *Score* 58.94 **FLORISSANT (MO)**

CATEGORY	RANK	SCORE	STATISTIC	VALUE	RANK	SCORE
Economics	14	70.30	Median Household Income	$36,809	14	44.5
			% of Families Above Poverty Level	97.8%	9	96.1
Affordable Housing	22	67.40	Median Home Value	$66,900	19	82.3
			Median Rent	$492	25	52.5
Crime	4	95.15	Violent Crimes per 10,000 Population	21	12	97.9
			Property Crimes per 10,000 Population	266	4	92.4
Open Spaces	37	33.35	Population Density (Persons/Sq. Mile)	5018	39	31.9
			Average Rooms per Housing Unit	5.5	16	34.8
Education	24	43.25	% High School Enrollment/Completion	91.7%	19	68.9
			% College Graduates	16.3%	25	17.6
Commute	27	24.20	Average Work Commute in Minutes	22	22	41.7
			% Commuting on Public Transportation	1.0%	23	6.7
Community Stability	5	78.95	% Living in Same House as in 1979	52.0%	5	78.3
			% Living in Same County as in 1985	87.5%	6	79.6

Composite: *Rank* 11 / 41 *Score* 58.77 **CONCORD (MO)**

CATEGORY	RANK	SCORE	STATISTIC	VALUE	RANK	SCORE
Economics	7	77.00	Median Household Income	$43,073	7	56.1
			% of Families Above Poverty Level	98.5%	6	97.9
Affordable Housing	33	57.45	Median Home Value	$94,800	33	70.4
			Median Rent	$521	30	44.5
Crime	N/A	N/A	Violent Crimes per 10,000 Population	N/A	N/A	N/A
			Property Crimes per 10,000 Population	N/A	N/A	N/A
Open Spaces	8	65.35	Population Density (Persons/Sq. Mile)	2876	21	69.8
			Average Rooms per Housing Unit	6.1	5	60.9
Education	17	53.95	% High School Enrollment/Completion	93.7%	13	77.8
			% College Graduates	24.0%	16	30.1
Commute	32	20.70	Average Work Commute in Minutes	23	27	33.3
			% Commuting on Public Transportation	1.2%	20	8.1
Community Stability	6	78.20	% Living in Same House as in 1979	56.4%	3	88.4
			% Living in Same County as in 1985	83.0%	11	68.0

Composite: *Rank* 12 / 41 *Score* 56.91 **SAPPINGTON (MO)**

CATEGORY	RANK	SCORE	STATISTIC	VALUE	RANK	SCORE
Economics	9	74.70	Median Household Income	$39,456	11	49.4
			% of Families Above Poverty Level	99.3%	1	100.0
Affordable Housing	38	51.10	Median Home Value	$110,200	37	63.8
			Median Rent	$543	38	38.4
Crime	N/A	N/A	Violent Crimes per 10,000 Population	N/A	N/A	N/A
			Property Crimes per 10,000 Population	N/A	N/A	N/A
Open Spaces	5	68.50	Population Density (Persons/Sq. Mile)	2031	13	84.8
			Average Rooms per Housing Unit	5.9	10	52.2
Education	10	60.70	% High School Enrollment/Completion	95.4%	4	85.3
			% College Graduates	27.7%	13	36.1
Commute	34	18.65	Average Work Commute in Minutes	23	27	33.3
			% Commuting on Public Transportation	0.6%	33	4.0
Community Stability	14	67.80	% Living in Same House as in 1979	50.3%	9	74.4
			% Living in Same County as in 1985	80.4%	19	61.2

Metropolitan Area Suburb Rankings
ST. LOUIS

Composite: **Rank** 13 / 41 *Score* 56.90   **FAIRVIEW HEIGHTS** (IL)

CATEGORY	RANK	SCORE	STATISTIC	VALUE	RANK	SCORE
Economics	20	66.90	Median Household Income	$34,898	19	41.0
			% of Families Above Poverty Level	96.5%	20	92.8
Affordable Housing	28	64.65	Median Home Value	$65,600	18	82.9
			Median Rent	$514	29	46.4
Crime	28	54.05	Violent Crimes per 10,000 Population	32	17	95.8
			Property Crimes per 10,000 Population	835	31	12.3
Open Spaces	6	67.40	Population Density (Persons/Sq. Mile)	1415	5	95.7
			Average Rooms per Housing Unit	5.6	14	39.1
Education	18	52.60	% High School Enrollment/Completion	95.3%	6	84.9
			% College Graduates	18.0%	22	20.3
Commute	18	31.25	Average Work Commute in Minutes	22	22	41.7
			% Commuting on Public Transportation	3.1%	6	20.8
Community Stability	20	61.45	% Living in Same House as in 1979	45.5%	16	63.5
			% Living in Same County as in 1985	79.7%	22	59.4

Composite: **Rank** 14 / 41 *Score* 56.65   **BELLEVILLE** (IL)

CATEGORY	RANK	SCORE	STATISTIC	VALUE	RANK	SCORE
Economics	34	56.25	Median Household Income	$26,668	34	25.9
			% of Families Above Poverty Level	94.1%	30	86.6
Affordable Housing	8	83.00	Median Home Value	$57,900	13	86.2
			Median Rent	$393	7	79.8
Crime	20	76.55	Violent Crimes per 10,000 Population	32	17	95.8
			Property Crimes per 10,000 Population	515	20	57.3
Open Spaces	31	39.85	Population Density (Persons/Sq. Mile)	3055	25	66.7
			Average Rooms per Housing Unit	5.0	34	13.0
Education	26	41.00	% High School Enrollment/Completion	91.1%	23	66.2
			% College Graduates	15.2%	27	15.8
Commute	10	35.40	Average Work Commute in Minutes	21	16	50.0
			% Commuting on Public Transportation	3.1%	6	20.8
Community Stability	17	64.50	% Living in Same House as in 1979	40.7%	26	52.5
			% Living in Same County as in 1985	86.3%	7	76.5

Composite: **Rank** 15 / 41 *Score* 56.32   **WASHINGTON** (MO)

CATEGORY	RANK	SCORE	STATISTIC	VALUE	RANK	SCORE
Economics	25	63.10	Median Household Income	$30,650	29	33.2
			% of Families Above Poverty Level	96.6%	19	93.0
Affordable Housing	6	83.80	Median Home Value	$64,000	15	83.6
			Median Rent	$378	5	84.0
Crime	19	78.35	Violent Crimes per 10,000 Population	71	29	88.5
			Property Crimes per 10,000 Population	438	16	68.2
Open Spaces	13	61.65	Population Density (Persons/Sq. Mile)	1575	6	92.9
			Average Rooms per Housing Unit	5.4	19	30.4
Education	33	27.80	% High School Enrollment/Completion	85.6%	36	41.8
			% College Graduates	14.0%	28	13.8
Commute	25	26.00	Average Work Commute in Minutes	21	16	50.0
			% Commuting on Public Transportation	0.3%	36	2.0
Community Stability	27	53.55	% Living in Same House as in 1979	37.9%	31	46.1
			% Living in Same County as in 1985	80.3%	20	61.0

Metropolitan Area Suburb Rankings
ST. LOUIS

Composite: *Rank* 16 / 41 *Score* 56.28   **O'FALLON (IL)**

CATEGORY	RANK	SCORE	STATISTIC	VALUE	RANK	SCORE
Economics	19	67.05	Median Household Income	$36,041	16	43.1
			% of Families Above Poverty Level	95.8%	24	91.0
Affordable Housing	30	60.95	Median Home Value	$77,800	25	77.7
			Median Rent	$522	32	44.2
Crime	6	94.00	Violent Crimes per 10,000 Population	13	5	99.4
			Property Crimes per 10,000 Population	293	6	88.6
Open Spaces	16	58.95	Population Density (Persons/Sq. Mile)	2620	18	74.4
			Average Rooms per Housing Unit	5.7	13	43.5
Education	7	63.25	% High School Enrollment/Completion	96.0%	3	88.0
			% College Graduates	29.2%	12	38.5
Commute	21	29.35	Average Work Commute in Minutes	21	16	50.0
			% Commuting on Public Transportation	1.3%	18	8.7
Community Stability	39	20.40	% Living in Same House as in 1979	26.2%	38	19.4
			% Living in Same County as in 1985	65.0%	39	21.4

Composite: *Rank* 17 / 41 *Score* 56.27   **GRANITE CITY (IL)**

CATEGORY	RANK	SCORE	STATISTIC	VALUE	RANK	SCORE
Economics	37	49.30	Median Household Income	$25,598	38	23.9
			% of Families Above Poverty Level	89.5%	37	74.7
Affordable Housing	3	92.15	Median Home Value	$42,100	6	92.9
			Median Rent	$351	3	91.4
Crime	21	74.65	Violent Crimes per 10,000 Population	34	20	95.5
			Property Crimes per 10,000 Population	540	21	53.8
Open Spaces	25	43.60	Population Density (Persons/Sq. Mile)	2628	19	74.2
			Average Rooms per Housing Unit	5.0	34	13.0
Education	38	15.15	% High School Enrollment/Completion	81.9%	38	25.3
			% College Graduates	8.6%	35	5.0
Commute	6	39.90	Average Work Commute in Minutes	20	7	58.3
			% Commuting on Public Transportation	3.2%	5	21.5
Community Stability	4	79.15	% Living in Same House as in 1979	48.1%	13	69.4
			% Living in Same County as in 1985	91.1%	2	88.9

Composite: *Rank* 18 / 41 *Score* 56.26   **FERGUSON (MO)**

CATEGORY	RANK	SCORE	STATISTIC	VALUE	RANK	SCORE
Economics	29	60.35	Median Household Income	$29,450	30	31.0
			% of Families Above Poverty Level	95.3%	27	89.7
Affordable Housing	15	74.25	Median Home Value	$56,100	9	86.9
			Median Rent	$459	17	61.6
Crime	17	80.80	Violent Crimes per 10,000 Population	42	25	94.0
			Property Crimes per 10,000 Population	442	17	67.6
Open Spaces	28	41.50	Population Density (Persons/Sq. Mile)	3605	30	56.9
			Average Rooms per Housing Unit	5.3	22	26.1
Education	25	41.10	% High School Enrollment/Completion	90.6%	26	64.0
			% College Graduates	16.7%	24	18.2
Commute	17	31.70	Average Work Commute in Minutes	21	16	50.0
			% Commuting on Public Transportation	2.0%	13	13.4
Community Stability	18	64.10	% Living in Same House as in 1979	44.2%	19	60.5
			% Living in Same County as in 1985	82.9%	13	67.7

Metropolitan Area Suburb Rankings
ST. LOUIS

Composite: Rank 19 / 41 *Score* 55.96   **HAZELWOOD** (MO)

CATEGORY	RANK	SCORE	STATISTIC	VALUE	RANK	SCORE
Economics	15	68.50	Median Household Income	$35,197	17	41.6
			% of Families Above Poverty Level	97.5%	13	95.4
Affordable Housing	27	65.20	Median Home Value	$68,200	20	81.8
			Median Rent	$506	27	48.6
Crime	15	81.80	Violent Crimes per 10,000 Population	15	7	99.1
			Property Crimes per 10,000 Population	464	18	64.5
Open Spaces	29	41.35	Population Density (Persons/Sq. Mile)	3134	26	65.3
			Average Rooms per Housing Unit	5.1	30	17.4
Education	21	45.30	% High School Enrollment/Completion	91.2%	22	66.7
			% College Graduates	20.2%	19	23.9
Commute	9	36.05	Average Work Commute in Minutes	19	3	66.7
			% Commuting on Public Transportation	0.8%	29	5.4
Community Stability	26	53.50	% Living in Same House as in 1979	38.4%	29	47.3
			% Living in Same County as in 1985	79.8%	21	59.7

Composite: Rank 20 / 41 *Score* 55.81   **MARYLAND HEIGHTS** (MO)

CATEGORY	RANK	SCORE	STATISTIC	VALUE	RANK	SCORE
Economics	12	72.30	Median Household Income	$39,211	12	49.0
			% of Families Above Poverty Level	97.6%	12	95.6
Affordable Housing	31	59.95	Median Home Value	$80,500	26	76.5
			Median Rent	$525	34	43.4
Crime	13	84.75	Violent Crimes per 10,000 Population	32	17	95.8
			Property Crimes per 10,000 Population	399	12	73.7
Open Spaces	14	60.50	Population Density (Persons/Sq. Mile)	1212	2	99.3
			Average Rooms per Housing Unit	5.2	25	21.7
Education	20	46.95	% High School Enrollment/Completion	87.1%	32	48.4
			% College Graduates	33.5%	10	45.5
Commute	19	29.80	Average Work Commute in Minutes	20	7	58.3
			% Commuting on Public Transportation	0.2%	38	1.3
Community Stability	35	36.40	% Living in Same House as in 1979	31.8%	35	32.2
			% Living in Same County as in 1985	72.4%	35	40.6

Composite: Rank 21 / 41 *Score* 55.46   **WOOD RIVER** (IL)

CATEGORY	RANK	SCORE	STATISTIC	VALUE	RANK	SCORE
Economics	35	52.55	Median Household Income	$26,317	36	25.2
			% of Families Above Poverty Level	91.5%	34	79.9
Affordable Housing	5	86.85	Median Home Value	$42,000	5	93.0
			Median Rent	$390	6	80.7
Crime	N/A	N/A	Violent Crimes per 10,000 Population	N/A	N/A	N/A
			Property Crimes per 10,000 Population	N/A	N/A	N/A
Open Spaces	26	43.50	Population Density (Persons/Sq. Mile)	2152	14	82.7
			Average Rooms per Housing Unit	4.8	39	4.3
Education	23	43.40	% High School Enrollment/Completion	94.6%	11	81.8
			% College Graduates	8.6%	35	5.0
Commute	15	32.50	Average Work Commute in Minutes	20	7	58.3
			% Commuting on Public Transportation	1.0%	23	6.7
Community Stability	8	73.95	% Living in Same House as in 1979	45.1%	17	62.6
			% Living in Same County as in 1985	89.7%	3	85.3

Composite: *Rank* 22 / 41 *Score* 55.08 **COLLINSVILLE (IL)**

CATEGORY	RANK	SCORE	STATISTIC	VALUE	RANK	SCORE
Economics	28	60.55	Median Household Income	$30,659	28	33.2
			% of Families Above Poverty Level	94.6%	29	87.9
Affordable Housing	11	78.30	Median Home Value	$59,900	14	85.3
			Median Rent	$424	9	71.3
Crime	18	78.30	Violent Crimes per 10,000 Population	31	15	96.0
			Property Crimes per 10,000 Population	492	19	60.6
Open Spaces	21	53.40	Population Density (Persons/Sq. Mile)	2016	12	85.1
			Average Rooms per Housing Unit	5.2	25	21.7
Education	27	40.15	% High School Enrollment/Completion	90.4%	27	63.1
			% College Graduates	16.1%	26	17.2
Commute	28	24.05	Average Work Commute in Minutes	23	27	33.3
			% Commuting on Public Transportation	2.2%	10	14.8
Community Stability	30	50.80	% Living in Same House as in 1979	39.9%	27	50.7
			% Living in Same County as in 1985	76.4%	31	50.9

Composite: *Rank* 23 / 41 *Score* 54.78 **BERKELEY (MO)**

CATEGORY	RANK	SCORE	STATISTIC	VALUE	RANK	SCORE
Economics	39	46.40	Median Household Income	$26,372	35	25.3
			% of Families Above Poverty Level	86.7%	39	67.5
Affordable Housing	13	76.55	Median Home Value	$44,700	7	91.8
			Median Rent	$460	18	61.3
Crime	25	67.70	Violent Crimes per 10,000 Population	102	32	82.6
			Property Crimes per 10,000 Population	547	22	52.8
Open Spaces	23	46.75	Population Density (Persons/Sq. Mile)	2523	17	76.1
			Average Rooms per Housing Unit	5.1	30	17.4
Education	29	36.00	% High School Enrollment/Completion	91.4%	21	67.6
			% College Graduates	8.2%	37	4.4
Commute	5	43.25	Average Work Commute in Minutes	20	7	58.3
			% Commuting on Public Transportation	4.2%	4	28.2
Community Stability	15	66.80	% Living in Same House as in 1979	50.5%	8	74.9
			% Living in Same County as in 1985	79.4%	23	58.7

Composite: *Rank* 24 / 41 *Score* 54.58 **RICHMOND HEIGHTS (MO)**

CATEGORY	RANK	SCORE	STATISTIC	VALUE	RANK	SCORE
Economics	26	63.00	Median Household Income	$32,237	25	36.1
			% of Families Above Poverty Level	95.4%	26	89.9
Affordable Housing	20	69.25	Median Home Value	$82,300	28	75.8
			Median Rent	$455	16	62.7
Crime	32	45.65	Violent Crimes per 10,000 Population	56	27	91.3
			Property Crimes per 10,000 Population	922	33	0.0
Open Spaces	34	34.90	Population Density (Persons/Sq. Mile)	4593	37	39.4
			Average Rooms per Housing Unit	5.4	19	30.4
Education	9	61.80	% High School Enrollment/Completion	91.1%	23	66.2
			% College Graduates	40.8%	7	57.4
Commute	3	50.05	Average Work Commute in Minutes	17	2	83.3
			% Commuting on Public Transportation	2.5%	8	16.8
Community Stability	22	57.40	% Living in Same House as in 1979	44.2%	19	60.5
			% Living in Same County as in 1985	77.7%	26	54.3

Metropolitan Area Suburb Rankings
ST. LOUIS

Composite: *Rank* 25 / 41 *Score* 54.55   **CLAYTON (MO)**

CATEGORY	RANK	SCORE	STATISTIC	VALUE	RANK	SCORE
Economics	6	78.05	Median Household Income	$44,218	6	58.2
			% of Families Above Poverty Level	98.5%	6	97.9
Affordable Housing	40	22.25	Median Home Value	$259,800	41	0.0
			Median Rent	$521	30	44.5
Crime	22	72.85	Violent Crimes per 10,000 Population	35	22	95.3
			Property Crimes per 10,000 Population	564	23	50.4
Open Spaces	36	34.55	Population Density (Persons/Sq. Mile)	5616	40	21.3
			Average Rooms per Housing Unit	5.8	11	47.8
Education	1	100.00	% High School Enrollment/Completion	98.7%	1	100.0
			% College Graduates	67.0%	1	100.0
Commute	2	58.05	Average Work Commute in Minutes	15	1	100.0
			% Commuting on Public Transportation	2.4%	9	16.1
Community Stability	40	16.10	% Living in Same House as in 1979	31.8%	35	32.2
			% Living in Same County as in 1985	56.7%	41	0.0

Composite: *Rank* 26 / 41 *Score* 54.38   **AFFTON (MO)**

CATEGORY	RANK	SCORE	STATISTIC	VALUE	RANK	SCORE
Economics	18	67.10	Median Household Income	$32,860	23	37.3
			% of Families Above Poverty Level	98.1%	8	96.9
Affordable Housing	16	73.95	Median Home Value	$74,400	24	79.1
			Median Rent	$433	13	68.8
Crime	N/A	N/A	Violent Crimes per 10,000 Population	N/A	N/A	N/A
			Property Crimes per 10,000 Population	N/A	N/A	N/A
Open Spaces	32	37.70	Population Density (Persons/Sq. Mile)	4276	35	45.0
			Average Rooms per Housing Unit	5.4	19	30.4
Education	19	47.70	% High School Enrollment/Completion	93.0%	17	74.7
			% College Graduates	18.2%	21	20.7
Commute	26	24.55	Average Work Commute in Minutes	22	22	41.7
			% Commuting on Public Transportation	1.1%	22	7.4
Community Stability	7	75.30	% Living in Same House as in 1979	55.0%	4	85.2
			% Living in Same County as in 1985	82.0%	17	65.4

Composite: *Rank* 27 / 41 *Score* 53.27   **OAKVILLE (MO)**

CATEGORY	RANK	SCORE	STATISTIC	VALUE	RANK	SCORE
Economics	3	82.70	Median Household Income	$48,592	3	66.2
			% of Families Above Poverty Level	99.0%	2	99.2
Affordable Housing	36	52.20	Median Home Value	$112,300	38	63.0
			Median Rent	$532	37	41.4
Crime	N/A	N/A	Violent Crimes per 10,000 Population	N/A	N/A	N/A
			Property Crimes per 10,000 Population	N/A	N/A	N/A
Open Spaces	3	75.50	Population Density (Persons/Sq. Mile)	1978	11	85.8
			Average Rooms per Housing Unit	6.2	4	65.2
Education	12	57.30	% High School Enrollment/Completion	94.4%	12	80.9
			% College Graduates	26.2%	14	33.7
Commute	39	7.50	Average Work Commute in Minutes	26	39	8.3
			% Commuting on Public Transportation	1.0%	23	6.7
Community Stability	34	44.40	% Living in Same House as in 1979	34.1%	34	37.4
			% Living in Same County as in 1985	76.6%	29	51.4

Metropolitan Area Suburb Rankings
ST. LOUIS

Composite: *Rank* 28 / 41 *Score* 52.82 **ARNOLD (MO)**

CATEGORY	RANK	SCORE	STATISTIC	VALUE	RANK	SCORE
Economics	21	65.85	Median Household Income	$34,179	21	39.7
			% of Families Above Poverty Level	96.2%	22	92.0
Affordable Housing	17	71.40	Median Home Value	$65,500	17	82.9
			Median Rent	$465	19	59.9
Crime	13	84.75	Violent Crimes per 10,000 Population	26	13	97.0
			Property Crimes per 10,000 Population	407	13	72.5
Open Spaces	17	58.65	Population Density (Persons/Sq. Mile)	1674	9	91.2
			Average Rooms per Housing Unit	5.3	22	26.1
Education	35	26.35	% High School Enrollment/Completion	86.7%	33	46.7
			% College Graduates	9.2%	33	6.0
Commute	38	11.05	Average Work Commute in Minutes	25	38	16.7
			% Commuting on Public Transportation	0.8%	29	5.4
Community Stability	28	51.70	% Living in Same House as in 1979	41.7%	22	54.8
			% Living in Same County as in 1985	75.5%	32	48.6

Composite: *Rank* 29 / 41 *Score* 52.59 **UNIVERSITY CITY (MO)**

CATEGORY	RANK	SCORE	STATISTIC	VALUE	RANK	SCORE
Economics	31	57.55	Median Household Income	$32,150	26	36.0
			% of Families Above Poverty Level	91.2%	36	79.1
Affordable Housing	24	66.60	Median Home Value	$73,200	23	79.6
			Median Rent	$488	24	53.6
Crime	26	66.90	Violent Crimes per 10,000 Population	59	28	90.7
			Property Crimes per 10,000 Population	616	25	43.1
Open Spaces	41	17.40	Population Density (Persons/Sq. Mile)	6816	41	0.0
			Average Rooms per Housing Unit	5.5	16	34.8
Education	6	65.45	% High School Enrollment/Completion	92.6%	18	72.9
			% College Graduates	41.2%	6	58.0
Commute	4	46.25	Average Work Commute in Minutes	20	7	58.3
			% Commuting on Public Transportation	5.1%	2	34.2
Community Stability	32	48.00	% Living in Same House as in 1979	41.4%	24	54.1
			% Living in Same County as in 1985	72.9%	34	41.9

Composite: *Rank* 30 / 41 *Score* 52.12 **ALTON (IL)**

CATEGORY	RANK	SCORE	STATISTIC	VALUE	RANK	SCORE
Economics	40	39.00	Median Household Income	$22,948	40	19.0
			% of Families Above Poverty Level	83.4%	40	59.0
Affordable Housing	2	96.05	Median Home Value	$37,500	3	94.9
			Median Rent	$330	2	97.2
Crime	29	52.90	Violent Crimes per 10,000 Population	72	30	88.3
			Property Crimes per 10,000 Population	798	28	17.5
Open Spaces	22	47.50	Population Density (Persons/Sq. Mile)	2192	15	82.0
			Average Rooms per Housing Unit	5.0	34	13.0
Education	34	26.75	% High School Enrollment/Completion	86.0%	35	43.6
			% College Graduates	11.6%	30	9.9
Commute	16	31.85	Average Work Commute in Minutes	20	7	58.3
			% Commuting on Public Transportation	0.8%	29	5.4
Community Stability	9	70.80	% Living in Same House as in 1979	44.3%	18	60.7
			% Living in Same County as in 1985	88.0%	4	80.9

Metropolitan Area Suburb Rankings
ST. LOUIS

Composite: *Rank* 31 / 41 *Score* 51.88 — **OVERLAND (MO)**

CATEGORY	RANK	SCORE	STATISTIC	VALUE	RANK	SCORE
Economics	32	57.05	Median Household Income	$28,727	31	29.6
			% of Families Above Poverty Level	93.3%	33	84.5
Affordable Housing	10	78.65	Median Home Value	$53,500	8	88.0
			Median Rent	$431	12	69.3
Crime	23	70.05	Violent Crimes per 10,000 Population	37	23	94.9
			Property Crimes per 10,000 Population	601	24	45.2
Open Spaces	34	34.90	Population Density (Persons/Sq. Mile)	4105	33	48.1
			Average Rooms per Housing Unit	5.2	25	21.7
Education	37	19.85	% High School Enrollment/Completion	83.2%	37	31.1
			% College Graduates	10.8%	32	8.6
Commute	14	33.85	Average Work Commute in Minutes	20	7	58.3
			% Commuting on Public Transportation	1.4%	16	9.4
Community Stability	13	68.80	% Living in Same House as in 1979	48.3%	12	69.9
			% Living in Same County as in 1985	82.9%	13	67.7

Composite: *Rank* 32 / 41 *Score* 51.03 — **CAHOKIA (IL)**

CATEGORY	RANK	SCORE	STATISTIC	VALUE	RANK	SCORE
Economics	38	49.05	Median Household Income	$26,147	37	24.9
			% of Families Above Poverty Level	88.9%	38	73.2
Affordable Housing	7	83.35	Median Home Value	$34,200	2	96.3
			Median Rent	$427	10	70.4
Crime	24	69.30	Violent Crimes per 10,000 Population	34	20	95.5
			Property Crimes per 10,000 Population	616	25	43.1
Open Spaces	20	55.15	Population Density (Persons/Sq. Mile)	1819	10	88.6
			Average Rooms per Housing Unit	5.2	25	21.7
Education	41	0.00	% High School Enrollment/Completion	76.2%	41	0.0
			% College Graduates	5.5%	41	0.0
Commute	20	29.70	Average Work Commute in Minutes	21	16	50.0
			% Commuting on Public Transportation	1.4%	16	9.4
Community Stability	10	70.65	% Living in Same House as in 1979	47.0%	14	66.9
			% Living in Same County as in 1985	85.5%	8	74.4

Composite: *Rank* 33 / 41 *Score* 50.66 — **O'FALLON (MO)**

CATEGORY	RANK	SCORE	STATISTIC	VALUE	RANK	SCORE
Economics	16	68.00	Median Household Income	$36,547	15	44.0
			% of Families Above Poverty Level	96.2%	22	92.0
Affordable Housing	21	69.05	Median Home Value	$70,300	21	80.9
			Median Rent	$475	22	57.2
Crime	8	89.60	Violent Crimes per 10,000 Population	11	2	99.8
			Property Crimes per 10,000 Population	358	8	79.4
Open Spaces	10	63.05	Population Density (Persons/Sq. Mile)	1175	1	100.0
			Average Rooms per Housing Unit	5.3	22	26.1
Education	32	30.25	% High School Enrollment/Completion	87.3%	31	49.3
			% College Graduates	12.4%	29	11.2
Commute	37	12.85	Average Work Commute in Minutes	24	34	25.0
			% Commuting on Public Transportation	0.1%	40	0.7
Community Stability	38	21.85	% Living in Same House as in 1979	23.7%	40	13.7
			% Living in Same County as in 1985	68.3%	38	30.0

Metropolitan Area Suburb Rankings
ST. LOUIS

Composite: **Rank** 34 / 41   *Score* 50.04   **SPANISH LAKE (MO)**

CATEGORY	RANK	SCORE	STATISTIC	VALUE	RANK	SCORE
Economics	22	65.45	Median Household Income	$33,497	22	38.4
			% of Families Above Poverty Level	96.4%	21	92.5
Affordable Housing	18	69.40	Median Home Value	$71,200	22	80.5
			Median Rent	$471	21	58.3
Crime	N/A	N/A	Violent Crimes per 10,000 Population	N/A	N/A	N/A
			Property Crimes per 10,000 Population	N/A	N/A	N/A
Open Spaces	24	44.65	Population Density (Persons/Sq. Mile)	2762	20	71.9
			Average Rooms per Housing Unit	5.1	30	17.4
Education	16	54.30	% High School Enrollment/Completion	95.3%	6	84.9
			% College Graduates	20.1%	20	23.7
Commute	35	15.85	Average Work Commute in Minutes	24	34	25.0
			% Commuting on Public Transportation	1.0%	23	6.7
Community Stability	31	50.60	% Living in Same House as in 1979	39.6%	28	50.0
			% Living in Same County as in 1985	76.5%	30	51.2

Composite: **Rank** 35 / 41   *Score* 49.97   **ST. CHARLES (MO)**

CATEGORY	RANK	SCORE	STATISTIC	VALUE	RANK	SCORE
Economics	23	65.25	Median Household Income	$34,336	20	40.0
			% of Families Above Poverty Level	95.6%	25	90.5
Affordable Housing	25	66.45	Median Home Value	$81,000	27	76.3
			Median Rent	$477	23	56.6
Crime	11	86.15	Violent Crimes per 10,000 Population	31	15	96.0
			Property Crimes per 10,000 Population	380	10	76.3
Open Spaces	27	42.10	Population Density (Persons/Sq. Mile)	3291	27	62.5
			Average Rooms per Housing Unit	5.2	25	21.7
Education	22	43.50	% High School Enrollment/Completion	89.4%	28	58.7
			% College Graduates	22.9%	18	28.3
Commute	30	21.50	Average Work Commute in Minutes	22	22	41.7
			% Commuting on Public Transportation	0.2%	38	1.3
Community Stability	37	24.85	% Living in Same House as in 1979	25.9%	39	18.7
			% Living in Same County as in 1985	68.7%	37	31.0

Composite: **Rank** 36 / 41   *Score* 49.14   **ST. PETERS (MO)**

CATEGORY	RANK	SCORE	STATISTIC	VALUE	RANK	SCORE
Economics	5	78.15	Median Household Income	$45,298	5	60.2
			% of Families Above Poverty Level	97.8%	9	96.1
Affordable Housing	32	58.20	Median Home Value	$86,100	30	74.1
			Median Rent	$529	35	42.3
Crime	15	81.80	Violent Crimes per 10,000 Population	37	23	94.9
			Property Crimes per 10,000 Population	434	15	68.7
Open Spaces	11	63.00	Population Density (Persons/Sq. Mile)	2896	22	69.5
			Average Rooms per Housing Unit	6.0	8	56.5
Education	15	54.70	% High School Enrollment/Completion	93.5%	14	76.9
			% College Graduates	25.5%	15	32.5
Commute	41	0.00	Average Work Commute in Minutes	27	41	0.0
			% Commuting on Public Transportation	0.0%	41	0.0
Community Stability	41	8.15	% Living in Same House as in 1979	17.7%	41	0.0
			% Living in Same County as in 1985	63.0%	40	16.3

Metropolitan Area Suburb Rankings
ST. LOUIS

Composite: **Rank** 37 / 41 *Score* 48.77   **JENNINGS (MO)**

CATEGORY	RANK	SCORE	STATISTIC	VALUE	RANK	SCORE
Economics	36	50.90	Median Household Income	$24,668	39	22.2
			% of Families Above Poverty Level	91.4%	35	79.6
Affordable Housing	4	88.95	Median Home Value	$41,700	4	93.1
			Median Rent	$375	4	84.8
Crime	31	51.45	Violent Crimes per 10,000 Population	72	30	88.3
			Property Crimes per 10,000 Population	818	29	14.6
Open Spaces	38	27.00	Population Density (Persons/Sq. Mile)	4258	34	45.3
			Average Rooms per Housing Unit	4.9	38	8.7
Education	30	34.65	% High School Enrollment/Completion	90.8%	25	64.9
			% College Graduates	8.2%	37	4.4
Commute	24	27.25	Average Work Commute in Minutes	24	34	25.0
			% Commuting on Public Transportation	4.4%	3	29.5
Community Stability	21	61.20	% Living in Same House as in 1979	48.6%	11	70.5
			% Living in Same County as in 1985	76.8%	28	51.9

Composite: **Rank** 38 / 41 *Score* 46.69   **EAST ST. LOUIS (IL)**

CATEGORY	RANK	SCORE	STATISTIC	VALUE	RANK	SCORE
Economics	41	0.00	Median Household Income	$12,627	41	0.0
			% of Families Above Poverty Level	60.5%	41	0.0
Affordable Housing	1	100.00	Median Home Value	$25,500	1	100.0
			Median Rent	$320	1	100.0
Crime	33	6.95	Violent Crimes per 10,000 Population	539	33	0.0
			Property Crimes per 10,000 Population	823	30	13.9
Open Spaces	30	41.10	Population Density (Persons/Sq. Mile)	2913	23	69.2
			Average Rooms per Housing Unit	5.0	34	13.0
Education	36	23.90	% High School Enrollment/Completion	86.3%	34	44.9
			% College Graduates	7.3%	40	2.9
Commute	1	66.65	Average Work Commute in Minutes	23	27	33.3
			% Commuting on Public Transportation	14.9%	1	100.0
Community Stability	2	88.25	% Living in Same House as in 1979	51.2%	6	76.5
			% Living in Same County as in 1985	95.4%	1	100.0

Composite: **Rank** 39 / 41 *Score* 46.40   **MEHLVILLE (MO)**

CATEGORY	RANK	SCORE	STATISTIC	VALUE	RANK	SCORE
Economics	17	67.30	Median Household Income	$35,059	18	41.3
			% of Families Above Poverty Level	96.7%	18	93.3
Affordable Housing	19	69.35	Median Home Value	$83,200	29	75.4
			Median Rent	$453	15	63.3
Crime	N/A	N/A	Violent Crimes per 10,000 Population	N/A	N/A	N/A
			Property Crimes per 10,000 Population	N/A	N/A	N/A
Open Spaces	33	36.05	Population Density (Persons/Sq. Mile)	3731	31	54.7
			Average Rooms per Housing Unit	5.1	30	17.4
Education	28	36.90	% High School Enrollment/Completion	88.3%	30	53.8
			% College Graduates	17.8%	23	20.0
Commute	31	21.00	Average Work Commute in Minutes	23	27	33.3
			% Commuting on Public Transportation	1.3%	18	8.7
Community Stability	33	47.80	% Living in Same House as in 1979	41.0%	25	53.2
			% Living in Same County as in 1985	73.1%	33	42.4

Metropolitan Area Suburb Rankings
ST. LOUIS

Composite: *Rank* 40 / 41 *Score* 44.77   **LEMAY (MO)**

CATEGORY	RANK	SCORE	STATISTIC	VALUE	RANK	SCORE
Economics	33	56.65	Median Household Income	$27,549	32	27.5
			% of Families Above Poverty Level	93.8%	32	85.8
Affordable Housing	9	80.90	Median Home Value	$56,100	9	86.9
			Median Rent	$411	8	74.9
Crime	N/A	N/A	Violent Crimes per 10,000 Population	N/A	N/A	N/A
			Property Crimes per 10,000 Population	N/A	N/A	N/A
Open Spaces	39	23.60	Population Density (Persons/Sq. Mile)	4394	36	42.9
			Average Rooms per Housing Unit	4.8	39	4.3
Education	39	14.20	% High School Enrollment/Completion	81.6%	39	24.0
			% College Graduates	8.2%	37	4.4
Commute	23	28.25	Average Work Commute in Minutes	22	22	41.7
			% Commuting on Public Transportation	2.2%	10	14.8
Community Stability	16	65.00	% Living in Same House as in 1979	51.2%	6	76.5
			% Living in Same County as in 1985	77.4%	27	53.5

Composite: *Rank* 41 / 41 *Score* 44.23   **ST. ANN (MO)**

CATEGORY	RANK	SCORE	STATISTIC	VALUE	RANK	SCORE
Economics	30	58.00	Median Household Income	$27,328	33	27.1
			% of Families Above Poverty Level	95.0%	28	88.9
Affordable Housing	11	78.30	Median Home Value	$56,700	11	86.7
			Median Rent	$429	11	69.9
Crime	30	51.80	Violent Crimes per 10,000 Population	28	14	96.6
			Property Crimes per 10,000 Population	872	32	7.0
Open Spaces	40	19.35	Population Density (Persons/Sq. Mile)	4632	38	38.7
			Average Rooms per Housing Unit	4.7	41	0.0
Education	40	3.50	% High School Enrollment/Completion	76.5%	40	1.3
			% College Graduates	9.0%	34	5.7
Commute	7	36.70	Average Work Commute in Minutes	19	3	66.7
			% Commuting on Public Transportation	1.0%	23	6.7
Community Stability	19	61.95	% Living in Same House as in 1979	42.2%	21	55.9
			% Living in Same County as in 1985	83.0%	11	68.0

Metropolitan Area Description
SALT LAKE CITY-OGDEN

STATE: Utah
COUNTIES: Davis, Salt Lake, Weber

TOTAL POPULATION: 1,072,227

POPULATION IN SUBURBS: 848,382   (79.1%)

POPULATION IN Salt Lake City: 159,936   (14.9%)
POPULATION IN Ogden: 63,909   (6.0%)

The SALT LAKE CITY-OGDEN metropolitan area is located in the northcentral part of Utah along the Great Salt Lake. The suburbs range geographically from North Ogden in the north (42 miles from Salt Lake City), to Magna in the west (17 miles from Salt Lake City), to Riverton in the south (18 miles from Salt Lake City), and to East Millcreek in the east (10 miles from Salt Lake City). The area is growing in population and had an increase of 17.8% between 1980 and 1990. Summer time high temperatures average in the 90's and winter time lows average in the 20's. Many high tech companies are located in the area. Computer device maker Iomega is located in the suburb of Roy. In 1991, *Fortune* magazine rated the metropolitan area number six for business. Public transportation in the area is provided by the Utah Transit Authority using buses.

East Millcreek is the overall highest rated suburb and also has the highest score in community stability. The top scores in economics and open spaces belong to **South Jordan**. **South Salt Lake** is the suburb with the most affordable housing, and also has the top rated commute. Finally, the number one rating in education goes to **Holladay-Cottonwood**. Crime rankings were not available for the area.

The highest ranked suburb overall which also has an affordable housing score of at least 50.00 is **Kaysville**.

The highest ranked suburb in the education category which also has an affordable housing score of at least 50.00 is **North Ogden**.

The county whose suburbs have the highest average overall score is **Weber County** (61.64).

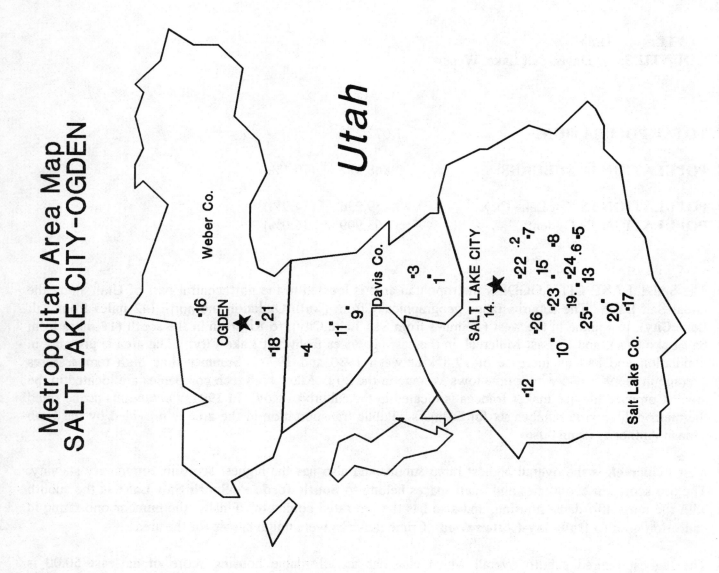

Metropolitan Area Map
SALT LAKE CITY–OGDEN

Utah

Weber Co.

•16

★ OGDEN
•21
•18

•4

Davis Co.

•3
•1

•11
•9

•12

★ SALT LAKE CITY
14.

•22 •2
•7
•15 •8
•23 •24 •6 •5
•26 •19 •13
•10 •25
•20
•17

Salt Lake Co.

Metropolitan Area Suburb Alphabetical Index
SALT LAKE CITY-OGDEN

SUBURB	PAGE	MAP NO.	STATE	COUNTY	POPU-LATION	RANK
BOUNTIFUL	685	1	Utah	Davis	36,659	5 / 26
CANYON RIM	686	2	Utah	Salt Lake	10,527	7 / 26
CENTERVILLE	684	3	Utah	Davis	11,500	3 / 26
CLEARFIELD	691	4	Utah	Davis	21,435	24 / 26
COTTONWOOD HEIGHTS	687	5	Utah	Salt Lake	28,766	11 / 26
COTTONWOOD WEST	688	6	Utah	Salt Lake	17,476	13 / 26
EAST MILLCREEK	684	7	Utah	Salt Lake	21,184	1 / 26
HOLLADAY-COTTONWOOD	685	8	Utah	Salt Lake	14,095	6 / 26
KAYSVILLE	684	9	Utah	Davis	13,961	2 / 26
KEARNS	692	10	Utah	Salt Lake	28,374	26 / 26
LAYTON	690	11	Utah	Davis	41,784	19 / 26
MAGNA	690	12	Utah	Salt Lake	17,829	19 / 26
MIDVALE	692	13	Utah	Salt Lake	11,886	25 / 26
MILLCREEK	691	14	Utah	Salt Lake	32,230	23 / 26
MURRAY	688	15	Utah	Salt Lake	31,282	15 / 26
NORTH OGDEN	685	16	Utah	Weber	11,668	4 / 26
RIVERTON	686	17	Utah	Salt Lake	11,261	9 / 26
ROY	687	18	Utah	Weber	24,603	12 / 26
SANDY	688	19	Utah	Salt Lake	75,058	14 / 26
SOUTH JORDAN	687	20	Utah	Salt Lake	12,220	10 / 26
SOUTH OGDEN	686	21	Utah	Weber	12,105	8 / 26
SOUTH SALT LAKE	691	22	Utah	Salt Lake	10,129	22 / 26
TAYLORSVILLE-BENNION	689	23	Utah	Salt Lake	52,351	17 / 26
UNION	690	24	Utah	Salt Lake	13,684	21 / 26
WEST JORDAN	689	25	Utah	Salt Lake	42,892	16 / 26
WEST VALLEY CITY	689	26	Utah	Salt Lake	86,976	18 / 26

Metropolitan Area Suburb Rankings
SALT LAKE CITY-OGDEN

Composite: Rank 1 / 26 *Score* 71.17   **EAST MILLCREEK**

CATEGORY	RANK	SCORE	STATISTIC	VALUE	RANK	SCORE
Economics	7	85.45	Median Household Income	$37,257	9	73.5
			% of Families Above Poverty Level	97.2%	4	97.4
Affordable Housing	21	42.20	Median Home Value	$96,500	25	31.2
			Median Rent	$413	14	53.2
Crime	N/A	N/A	Violent Crimes per 10,000 Population	N/A	N/A	N/A
			Property Crimes per 10,000 Population	N/A	N/A	N/A
Open Spaces	14	53.50	Population Density (Persons/Sq. Mile)	4757	23	20.8
			Average Rooms per Housing Unit	6.9	5	86.2
Education	2	85.95	% High School Enrollment/Completion	94.3%	8	71.9
			% College Graduates	40.8%	1	100.0
Commute	6	62.30	Average Work Commute in Minutes	18	4	77.8
			% Commuting on Public Transportation	2.9%	13	46.8
Community Stability	1	97.60	% Living in Same House as in 1979	56.0%	1	100.0
			% Living in Same County as in 1985	91.8%	2	95.2

Composite: Rank 2 / 26 *Score* 69.39   **KAYSVILLE**

CATEGORY	RANK	SCORE	STATISTIC	VALUE	RANK	SCORE
Economics	9	81.75	Median Household Income	$39,221	7	81.3
			% of Families Above Poverty Level	94.9%	13	82.2
Affordable Housing	8	67.85	Median Home Value	$80,900	18	52.4
			Median Rent	$357	3	83.3
Crime	N/A	N/A	Violent Crimes per 10,000 Population	16	N/A	N/A
			Property Crimes per 10,000 Population	225	N/A	N/A
Open Spaces	4	81.40	Population Density (Persons/Sq. Mile)	1473	3	83.5
			Average Rooms per Housing Unit	6.7	8	79.3
Education	4	82.40	% High School Enrollment/Completion	97.1%	3	85.7
			% College Graduates	33.9%	4	79.1
Commute	8	58.65	Average Work Commute in Minutes	20	11	55.6
			% Commuting on Public Transportation	3.6%	5	61.7
Community Stability	19	44.30	% Living in Same House as in 1979	36.7%	12	35.9
			% Living in Same County as in 1985	76.8%	24	52.7

Composite: Rank 3 / 26 *Score* 67.48   **CENTERVILLE**

CATEGORY	RANK	SCORE	STATISTIC	VALUE	RANK	SCORE
Economics	3	95.15	Median Household Income	$42,032	4	92.3
			% of Families Above Poverty Level	97.3%	3	98.0
Affordable Housing	22	40.80	Median Home Value	$90,300	21	39.7
			Median Rent	$434	20	41.9
Crime	N/A	N/A	Violent Crimes per 10,000 Population	19	N/A	N/A
			Property Crimes per 10,000 Population	235	N/A	N/A
Open Spaces	3	82.80	Population Density (Persons/Sq. Mile)	1870	5	75.9
			Average Rooms per Housing Unit	7.0	4	89.7
Education	6	76.15	% High School Enrollment/Completion	95.5%	7	77.8
			% College Graduates	32.4%	5	74.5
Commute	4	63.15	Average Work Commute in Minutes	19	6	66.7
			% Commuting on Public Transportation	3.5%	7	59.6
Community Stability	18	46.85	% Living in Same House as in 1979	36.1%	14	33.9
			% Living in Same County as in 1985	79.3%	21	59.8

Metropolitan Area Suburb Rankings
SALT LAKE CITY-OGDEN

Composite: *Rank* 4 / 26 *Score* 67.23   **NORTH OGDEN**

CATEGORY	RANK	SCORE	STATISTIC	VALUE	RANK	SCORE
Economics	5	93.85	Median Household Income	$41,178	5	89.0
			% of Families Above Poverty Level	97.4%	2	98.7
Affordable Housing	17	50.85	Median Home Value	$80,300	17	53.3
			Median Rent	$422	17	48.4
Crime	N/A	N/A	Violent Crimes per 10,000 Population	2	N/A	N/A
			Property Crimes per 10,000 Population	188	N/A	N/A
Open Spaces	2	84.35	Population Density (Persons/Sq. Mile)	1887	6	75.6
			Average Rooms per Housing Unit	7.1	3	93.1
Education	3	85.45	% High School Enrollment/Completion	100.0%	1	100.0
			% College Graduates	31.2%	7	70.9
Commute	24	25.15	Average Work Commute in Minutes	22	19	33.3
			% Commuting on Public Transportation	1.5%	22	17.0
Community Stability	6	63.75	% Living in Same House as in 1979	43.2%	5	57.5
			% Living in Same County as in 1985	82.9%	15	70.0

Composite: *Rank* 5 / 26 *Score* 66.14   **BOUNTIFUL**

CATEGORY	RANK	SCORE	STATISTIC	VALUE	RANK	SCORE
Economics	8	83.00	Median Household Income	$38,346	8	77.8
			% of Families Above Poverty Level	95.8%	10	88.2
Affordable Housing	15	53.20	Median Home Value	$86,700	19	44.6
			Median Rent	$397	11	61.8
Crime	N/A	N/A	Violent Crimes per 10,000 Population	8	N/A	N/A
			Property Crimes per 10,000 Population	322	N/A	N/A
Open Spaces	9	62.65	Population Density (Persons/Sq. Mile)	3440	14	46.0
			Average Rooms per Housing Unit	6.7	8	79.3
Education	7	75.80	% High School Enrollment/Completion	96.5%	5	82.8
			% College Graduates	30.5%	8	68.8
Commute	8	58.65	Average Work Commute in Minutes	20	11	55.6
			% Commuting on Public Transportation	3.6%	5	61.7
Community Stability	7	63.55	% Living in Same House as in 1979	46.0%	3	66.8
			% Living in Same County as in 1985	79.5%	20	60.3

Composite: *Rank* 6 / 26 *Score* 66.00   **HOLLADAY-COTTONWOOD**

CATEGORY	RANK	SCORE	STATISTIC	VALUE	RANK	SCORE
Economics	6	86.55	Median Household Income	$39,667	6	83.0
			% of Families Above Poverty Level	96.1%	9	90.1
Affordable Housing	25	21.25	Median Home Value	$119,500	26	0.0
			Median Rent	$433	19	42.5
Crime	N/A	N/A	Violent Crimes per 10,000 Population	N/A	N/A	N/A
			Property Crimes per 10,000 Population	N/A	N/A	N/A
Open Spaces	6	77.85	Population Density (Persons/Sq. Mile)	2027	7	72.9
			Average Rooms per Housing Unit	6.8	7	82.8
Education	1	95.65	% High School Enrollment/Completion	99.2%	2	96.1
			% College Graduates	39.2%	2	95.2
Commute	18	39.20	Average Work Commute in Minutes	21	16	44.4
			% Commuting on Public Transportation	2.3%	18	34.0
Community Stability	3	75.50	% Living in Same House as in 1979	45.6%	4	65.4
			% Living in Same County as in 1985	88.4%	4	85.6

Metropolitan Area Suburb Rankings
SALT LAKE CITY-OGDEN

Composite: Rank 7 / 26 *Score* 64.01   **CANYON RIM**

CATEGORY	RANK	SCORE	STATISTIC	VALUE	RANK	SCORE
Economics	12	76.25	Median Household Income	$33,284	15	57.8
			% of Families Above Poverty Level	96.8%	5	94.7
Affordable Housing	19	46.90	Median Home Value	$75,000	16	60.5
			Median Rent	$450	21	33.3
Crime	N/A	N/A	Violent Crimes per 10,000 Population	N/A	N/A	N/A
			Property Crimes per 10,000 Population	N/A	N/A	N/A
Open Spaces	20	40.00	Population Density (Persons/Sq. Mile)	5091	25	14.5
			Average Rooms per Housing Unit	6.3	11	65.5
Education	8	70.25	% High School Enrollment/Completion	93.7%	10	69.0
			% College Graduates	31.4%	6	71.5
Commute	3	66.35	Average Work Commute in Minutes	19	6	66.7
			% Commuting on Public Transportation	3.8%	4	66.0
Community Stability	2	84.30	% Living in Same House as in 1979	52.0%	2	86.7
			% Living in Same County as in 1985	87.1%	8	81.9

Composite: Rank 8 / 26 *Score* 61.38   **SOUTH OGDEN**

CATEGORY	RANK	SCORE	STATISTIC	VALUE	RANK	SCORE
Economics	13	71.20	Median Household Income	$33,524	14	58.8
			% of Families Above Poverty Level	95.1%	12	83.6
Affordable Housing	7	69.10	Median Home Value	$71,200	12	65.6
			Median Rent	$377	4	72.6
Crime	N/A	N/A	Violent Crimes per 10,000 Population	14	N/A	N/A
			Property Crimes per 10,000 Population	383	N/A	N/A
Open Spaces	16	49.90	Population Density (Persons/Sq. Mile)	3871	18	37.7
			Average Rooms per Housing Unit	6.2	12	62.1
Education	11	61.35	% High School Enrollment/Completion	93.9%	9	70.0
			% College Graduates	25.2%	11	52.7
Commute	5	62.55	Average Work Commute in Minutes	17	2	88.9
			% Commuting on Public Transportation	2.4%	16	36.2
Community Stability	12	54.15	% Living in Same House as in 1979	40.0%	8	46.8
			% Living in Same County as in 1985	79.9%	18	61.5

Composite: Rank 9 / 26 *Score* 59.09   **RIVERTON**

CATEGORY	RANK	SCORE	STATISTIC	VALUE	RANK	SCORE
Economics	11	78.15	Median Household Income	$36,242	10	69.5
			% of Families Above Poverty Level	95.6%	11	86.8
Affordable Housing	14	58.35	Median Home Value	$72,000	13	64.5
			Median Rent	$415	15	52.2
Crime	N/A	N/A	Violent Crimes per 10,000 Population	N/A	N/A	N/A
			Property Crimes per 10,000 Population	N/A	N/A	N/A
Open Spaces	5	80.55	Population Density (Persons/Sq. Mile)	1385	2	85.2
			Average Rooms per Housing Unit	6.6	10	75.9
Education	14	52.80	% High School Enrollment/Completion	96.9%	4	84.7
			% College Graduates	14.7%	20	20.9
Commute	26	17.25	Average Work Commute in Minutes	24	25	11.1
			% Commuting on Public Transportation	1.8%	21	23.4
Community Stability	4	67.45	% Living in Same House as in 1979	36.4%	13	34.9
			% Living in Same County as in 1985	93.5%	1	100.0

Metropolitan Area Suburb Rankings
SALT LAKE CITY-OGDEN

Composite: *Rank* 10 / 26 *Score* 58.71 — SOUTH JORDAN

CATEGORY	RANK	SCORE	STATISTIC	VALUE	RANK	SCORE
Economics	1	99.65	Median Household Income	$43,804	2	99.3
			% of Families Above Poverty Level	97.6%	1	100.0
Affordable Housing	26	17.60	Median Home Value	$93,600	24	35.2
			Median Rent	$512	26	0.0
Crime	N/A	N/A	Violent Crimes per 10,000 Population	28	N/A	N/A
			Property Crimes per 10,000 Population	318	N/A	N/A
Open Spaces	1	100.00	Population Density (Persons/Sq. Mile)	607	1	100.0
			Average Rooms per Housing Unit	7.3	1	100.0
Education	10	62.55	% High School Enrollment/Completion	95.8%	6	79.3
			% College Graduates	22.9%	13	45.8
Commute	25	17.50	Average Work Commute in Minutes	23	22	22.2
			% Commuting on Public Transportation	1.3%	24	12.8
Community Stability	11	54.95	% Living in Same House as in 1979	33.3%	17	24.6
			% Living in Same County as in 1985	88.3%	5	85.3

Composite: *Rank* 11 / 26 *Score* 57.98 — COTTONWOOD HEIGHTS

CATEGORY	RANK	SCORE	STATISTIC	VALUE	RANK	SCORE
Economics	4	94.35	Median Household Income	$43,429	3	97.9
			% of Families Above Poverty Level	96.2%	8	90.8
Affordable Housing	23	26.50	Median Home Value	$91,600	22	37.9
			Median Rent	$484	23	15.1
Crime	N/A	N/A	Violent Crimes per 10,000 Population	N/A	N/A	N/A
			Property Crimes per 10,000 Population	N/A	N/A	N/A
Open Spaces	11	58.30	Population Density (Persons/Sq. Mile)	4254	19	30.4
			Average Rooms per Housing Unit	6.9	5	86.2
Education	5	76.30	% High School Enrollment/Completion	93.7%	10	69.0
			% College Graduates	35.4%	3	83.6
Commute	20	32.60	Average Work Commute in Minutes	22	19	33.3
			% Commuting on Public Transportation	2.2%	19	31.9
Community Stability	10	59.85	% Living in Same House as in 1979	38.8%	9	42.9
			% Living in Same County as in 1985	85.3%	12	76.8

Composite: *Rank* 12 / 26 *Score* 56.32 — ROY

CATEGORY	RANK	SCORE	STATISTIC	VALUE	RANK	SCORE
Economics	10	79.40	Median Household Income	$35,018	11	64.7
			% of Families Above Poverty Level	96.7%	7	94.1
Affordable Housing	6	71.35	Median Home Value	$65,900	7	72.8
			Median Rent	$382	5	69.9
Crime	N/A	N/A	Violent Crimes per 10,000 Population	36	N/A	N/A
			Property Crimes per 10,000 Population	391	N/A	N/A
Open Spaces	15	52.15	Population Density (Persons/Sq. Mile)	3640	16	42.2
			Average Rooms per Housing Unit	6.2	12	62.1
Education	15	45.30	% High School Enrollment/Completion	93.3%	12	67.0
			% College Graduates	15.6%	18	23.6
Commute	17	39.75	Average Work Commute in Minutes	19	6	66.7
			% Commuting on Public Transportation	1.3%	24	12.8
Community Stability	15	50.00	% Living in Same House as in 1979	37.5%	10	38.5
			% Living in Same County as in 1985	79.9%	18	61.5

Metropolitan Area Suburb Rankings
SALT LAKE CITY-OGDEN

Composite: Rank 13 / 26 Score 54.23   COTTONWOOD WEST

CATEGORY	RANK	SCORE	STATISTIC	VALUE	RANK	SCORE
Economics	14	70.65	Median Household Income	$33,750	13	59.7
			% of Families Above Poverty Level	94.8%	15	81.6
Affordable Housing	20	42.25	Median Home Value	$92,100	23	37.2
			Median Rent	$424	18	47.3
Crime	N/A	N/A	Violent Crimes per 10,000 Population	N/A	N/A	N/A
			Property Crimes per 10,000 Population	N/A	N/A	N/A
Open Spaces	19	41.75	Population Density (Persons/Sq. Mile)	4542	21	24.9
			Average Rooms per Housing Unit	6.1	15	58.6
Education	12	60.95	% High School Enrollment/Completion	91.2%	15	56.7
			% College Graduates	29.3%	10	65.2
Commute	15	46.65	Average Work Commute in Minutes	21	16	44.4
			% Commuting on Public Transportation	3.0%	12	48.9
Community Stability	8	63.15	% Living in Same House as in 1979	41.3%	6	51.2
			% Living in Same County as in 1985	84.7%	13	75.1

Composite: Rank 14 / 26 Score 53.92   SANDY

CATEGORY	RANK	SCORE	STATISTIC	VALUE	RANK	SCORE
Economics	2	97.35	Median Household Income	$43,971	1	100.0
			% of Families Above Poverty Level	96.8%	5	94.7
Affordable Housing	24	24.85	Median Home Value	$87,700	20	43.2
			Median Rent	$500	25	6.5
Crime	N/A	N/A	Violent Crimes per 10,000 Population	13	N/A	N/A
			Property Crimes per 10,000 Population	425	N/A	N/A
Open Spaces	8	68.25	Population Density (Persons/Sq. Mile)	3756	17	39.9
			Average Rooms per Housing Unit	7.2	2	96.6
Education	9	66.25	% High School Enrollment/Completion	93.3%	12	67.0
			% College Graduates	29.4%	9	65.5
Commute	22	29.20	Average Work Commute in Minutes	23	22	22.2
			% Commuting on Public Transportation	2.4%	16	36.2
Community Stability	22	37.65	% Living in Same House as in 1979	29.2%	21	11.0
			% Living in Same County as in 1985	80.9%	17	64.3

Composite: Rank 15 / 26 Score 53.04   MURRAY

CATEGORY	RANK	SCORE	STATISTIC	VALUE	RANK	SCORE
Economics	19	58.85	Median Household Income	$28,950	20	40.7
			% of Families Above Poverty Level	94.1%	16	77.0
Affordable Housing	13	62.95	Median Home Value	$74,300	15	61.4
			Median Rent	$392	8	64.5
Crime	N/A	N/A	Violent Crimes per 10,000 Population	35	N/A	N/A
			Property Crimes per 10,000 Population	1,074	N/A	N/A
Open Spaces	18	43.45	Population Density (Persons/Sq. Mile)	3282	13	49.0
			Average Rooms per Housing Unit	5.5	21	37.9
Education	16	44.45	% High School Enrollment/Completion	90.0%	16	50.7
			% College Graduates	20.4%	15	38.2
Commute	11	54.65	Average Work Commute in Minutes	19	6	66.7
			% Commuting on Public Transportation	2.7%	14	42.6
Community Stability	13	53.90	% Living in Same House as in 1979	34.2%	15	27.6
			% Living in Same County as in 1985	86.5%	10	80.2

Metropolitan Area Suburb Rankings
SALT LAKE CITY-OGDEN

Composite: **Rank** 16 / 26 **Score** 52.85   **WEST JORDAN**

CATEGORY	RANK	SCORE	STATISTIC	VALUE	RANK	SCORE
Economics	17	65.10	Median Household Income	$33,273	16	57.8
			% of Families Above Poverty Level	93.4%	19	72.4
Affordable Housing	11	64.90	Median Home Value	$67,900	9	70.1
			Median Rent	$401	12	59.7
Crime	N/A	N/A	Violent Crimes per 10,000 Population	35	N/A	N/A
			Property Crimes per 10,000 Population	511	N/A	N/A
Open Spaces	7	71.60	Population Density (Persons/Sq. Mile)	1598	4	81.1
			Average Rooms per Housing Unit	6.2	12	62.1
Education	18	34.40	% High School Enrollment/Completion	88.7%	17	44.3
			% College Graduates	15.9%	17	24.5
Commute	20	32.60	Average Work Commute in Minutes	22	19	33.3
			% Commuting on Public Transportation	2.2%	19	31.9
Community Stability	17	48.50	% Living in Same House as in 1979	29.5%	20	12.0
			% Living in Same County as in 1985	88.2%	6	85.0

Composite: **Rank** 17 / 26 **Score** 50.31   **TAYLORSVILLE-BENNION**

CATEGORY	RANK	SCORE	STATISTIC	VALUE	RANK	SCORE
Economics	15	69.20	Median Household Income	$32,866	17	56.2
			% of Families Above Poverty Level	94.9%	13	82.2
Affordable Housing	10	65.65	Median Home Value	$66,800	8	71.6
			Median Rent	$401	12	59.7
Crime	N/A	N/A	Violent Crimes per 10,000 Population	N/A	N/A	N/A
			Property Crimes per 10,000 Population	N/A	N/A	N/A
Open Spaces	21	36.60	Population Density (Persons/Sq. Mile)	4724	22	21.5
			Average Rooms per Housing Unit	5.9	18	51.7
Education	19	33.80	% High School Enrollment/Completion	88.7%	17	44.3
			% College Graduates	15.5%	19	23.3
Commute	14	48.00	Average Work Commute in Minutes	20	11	55.6
			% Commuting on Public Transportation	2.6%	15	40.4
Community Stability	16	48.60	% Living in Same House as in 1979	30.4%	19	15.0
			% Living in Same County as in 1985	87.2%	7	82.2

Composite: **Rank** 18 / 26 **Score** 48.64   **WEST VALLEY CITY**

CATEGORY	RANK	SCORE	STATISTIC	VALUE	RANK	SCORE
Economics	22	46.10	Median Household Income	$29,510	19	42.9
			% of Families Above Poverty Level	89.9%	22	49.3
Affordable Housing	5	74.45	Median Home Value	$58,200	5	83.3
			Median Rent	$390	7	65.6
Crime	N/A	N/A	Violent Crimes per 10,000 Population	N/A	N/A	N/A
			Property Crimes per 10,000 Population	N/A	N/A	N/A
Open Spaces	12	53.80	Population Density (Persons/Sq. Mile)	2556	11	62.8
			Average Rooms per Housing Unit	5.7	19	44.8
Education	22	16.85	% High School Enrollment/Completion	84.2%	21	22.2
			% College Graduates	11.6%	23	11.5
Commute	13	48.80	Average Work Commute in Minutes	21	16	44.4
			% Commuting on Public Transportation	3.2%	11	53.2
Community Stability	14	51.85	% Living in Same House as in 1979	33.5%	16	25.2
			% Living in Same County as in 1985	85.9%	11	78.5

Metropolitan Area Suburb Rankings
SALT LAKE CITY-OGDEN

Composite: *Rank* 19 / 26 *Score* 48.24 **LAYTON**

CATEGORY	RANK	SCORE	STATISTIC	VALUE	RANK	SCORE
Economics	16	69.10	Median Household Income	$34,466	12	62.5
			% of Families Above Poverty Level	93.9%	17	75.7
Affordable Housing	12	63.50	Median Home Value	$72,700	14	63.6
			Median Rent	$394	10	63.4
Crime	N/A	N/A	Violent Crimes per 10,000 Population	N/A	N/A	N/A
			Property Crimes per 10,000 Population	N/A	N/A	N/A
Open Spaces	10	61.55	Population Density (Persons/Sq. Mile)	2289	9	67.9
			Average Rooms per Housing Unit	6.0	17	55.2
Education	17	39.00	% High School Enrollment/Completion	88.2%	19	41.9
			% College Graduates	19.7%	16	36.1
Commute	16	40.80	Average Work Commute in Minutes	19	6	66.7
			% Commuting on Public Transportation	1.4%	23	14.9
Community Stability	25	15.50	% Living in Same House as in 1979	26.7%	23	2.7
			% Living in Same County as in 1985	68.2%	25	28.3

Composite: *Rank* 19 / 26 *Score* 48.24 **MAGNA**

CATEGORY	RANK	SCORE	STATISTIC	VALUE	RANK	SCORE
Economics	20	46.85	Median Household Income	$27,691	22	35.8
			% of Families Above Poverty Level	91.2%	20	57.9
Affordable Housing	4	75.25	Median Home Value	$45,900	1	100.0
			Median Rent	$418	16	50.5
Crime	N/A	N/A	Violent Crimes per 10,000 Population	N/A	N/A	N/A
			Property Crimes per 10,000 Population	N/A	N/A	N/A
Open Spaces	13	53.70	Population Density (Persons/Sq. Mile)	2390	10	66.0
			Average Rooms per Housing Unit	5.6	20	41.4
Education	25	10.15	% High School Enrollment/Completion	83.7%	22	19.7
			% College Graduates	8.0%	25	0.6
Commute	19	38.75	Average Work Commute in Minutes	23	22	22.2
			% Commuting on Public Transportation	3.3%	8	55.3
Community Stability	5	64.75	% Living in Same House as in 1979	40.5%	7	48.5
			% Living in Same County as in 1985	86.8%	9	81.0

Composite: *Rank* 21 / 26 *Score* 48.05 **UNION**

CATEGORY	RANK	SCORE	STATISTIC	VALUE	RANK	SCORE
Economics	18	62.80	Median Household Income	$31,271	18	49.9
			% of Families Above Poverty Level	93.9%	17	75.7
Affordable Housing	18	49.95	Median Home Value	$69,300	10	68.2
			Median Rent	$453	22	31.7
Crime	N/A	N/A	Violent Crimes per 10,000 Population	N/A	N/A	N/A
			Property Crimes per 10,000 Population	N/A	N/A	N/A
Open Spaces	25	25.10	Population Density (Persons/Sq. Mile)	4842	24	19.2
			Average Rooms per Housing Unit	5.3	23	31.0
Education	13	54.45	% High School Enrollment/Completion	91.9%	14	60.1
			% College Graduates	23.9%	12	48.8
Commute	10	55.45	Average Work Commute in Minutes	20	11	55.6
			% Commuting on Public Transportation	3.3%	8	55.3
Community Stability	20	40.55	% Living in Same House as in 1979	27.9%	22	6.6
			% Living in Same County as in 1985	84.5%	14	74.5

Metropolitan Area Suburb Rankings
SALT LAKE CITY-OGDEN

Composite: *Rank* 22 / 26 *Score* 47.14   SOUTH SALT LAKE

CATEGORY	RANK	SCORE	STATISTIC	VALUE	RANK	SCORE
Economics	25	11.50	Median Household Income	$18,627	26	0.0
			% of Families Above Poverty Level	85.9%	25	23.0
Affordable Housing	1	98.50	Median Home Value	$48,100	3	97.0
			Median Rent	$326	1	100.0
Crime	N/A	N/A	Violent Crimes per 10,000 Population	82	N/A	N/A
			Property Crimes per 10,000 Population	1,879	N/A	N/A
Open Spaces	22	34.20	Population Density (Persons/Sq. Mile)	2263	8	68.4
			Average Rooms per Housing Unit	4.4	26	0.0
Education	23	12.10	% High School Enrollment/Completion	83.5%	23	18.7
			% College Graduates	9.6%	24	5.5
Commute	1	93.40	Average Work Commute in Minutes	17	2	88.9
			% Commuting on Public Transportation	5.3%	2	97.9
Community Stability	23	33.15	% Living in Same House as in 1979	25.9%	26	0.0
			% Living in Same County as in 1985	81.6%	16	66.3

Composite: *Rank* 23 / 26 *Score* 42.45   MILLCREEK

CATEGORY	RANK	SCORE	STATISTIC	VALUE	RANK	SCORE
Economics	24	29.15	Median Household Income	$23,709	24	20.1
			% of Families Above Poverty Level	88.2%	24	38.2
Affordable Housing	9	66.10	Median Home Value	$69,300	10	68.2
			Median Rent	$393	9	64.0
Crime	N/A	N/A	Violent Crimes per 10,000 Population	N/A	N/A	N/A
			Property Crimes per 10,000 Population	N/A	N/A	N/A
Open Spaces	26	20.80	Population Density (Persons/Sq. Mile)	4390	20	27.8
			Average Rooms per Housing Unit	4.8	24	13.8
Education	21	19.85	% High School Enrollment/Completion	79.7%	26	0.0
			% College Graduates	20.9%	14	39.7
Commute	2	88.90	Average Work Commute in Minutes	18	4	77.8
			% Commuting on Public Transportation	5.4%	1	100.0
Community Stability	24	29.90	% Living in Same House as in 1979	26.0%	24	0.3
			% Living in Same County as in 1985	79.2%	23	59.5

Composite: *Rank* 24 / 26 *Score* 38.91   CLEARFIELD

CATEGORY	RANK	SCORE	STATISTIC	VALUE	RANK	SCORE
Economics	23	39.30	Median Household Income	$26,875	23	32.5
			% of Families Above Poverty Level	89.4%	23	46.1
Affordable Housing	3	75.50	Median Home Value	$59,800	6	81.1
			Median Rent	$382	5	69.9
Crime	N/A	N/A	Violent Crimes per 10,000 Population	16	N/A	N/A
			Property Crimes per 10,000 Population	338	N/A	N/A
Open Spaces	17	47.30	Population Density (Persons/Sq. Mile)	2875	12	56.7
			Average Rooms per Housing Unit	5.5	21	37.9
Education	20	21.20	% High School Enrollment/Completion	85.6%	20	29.1
			% College Graduates	12.2%	22	13.3
Commute	12	50.00	Average Work Commute in Minutes	16	1	100.0
			% Commuting on Public Transportation	0.7%	26	0.0
Community Stability	26	0.15	% Living in Same House as in 1979	26.0%	24	0.3
			% Living in Same County as in 1985	58.2%	26	0.0

Metropolitan Area Suburb Rankings
SALT LAKE CITY-OGDEN

***Composite: Rank* 25 / 26 *Score* 38.22   MIDVALE**

CATEGORY	RANK	SCORE	STATISTIC	VALUE	RANK	SCORE
Economics	26	5.05	Median Household Income	$21,183	25	10.1
			% of Families Above Poverty Level	82.4%	26	0.0
Affordable Housing	2	86.25	Median Home Value	$57,800	4	83.8
			Median Rent	$347	2	88.7
Crime	N/A	N/A	Violent Crimes per 10,000 Population	33	N/A	N/A
			Property Crimes per 10,000 Population	885	N/A	N/A
Open Spaces	24	26.20	Population Density (Persons/Sq. Mile)	3466	15	45.5
			Average Rooms per Housing Unit	4.6	25	6.9
Education	24	11.40	% High School Enrollment/Completion	81.0%	24	6.4
			% College Graduates	13.2%	21	16.4
Commute	7	61.85	Average Work Commute in Minutes	20	11	55.6
			% Commuting on Public Transportation	3.9%	3	68.1
Community Stability	21	38.55	% Living in Same House as in 1979	31.1%	18	17.3
			% Living in Same County as in 1985	79.3%	21	59.8

***Composite: Rank* 26 / 26 *Score* 36.81   KEARNS**

CATEGORY	RANK	SCORE	STATISTIC	VALUE	RANK	SCORE
Economics	21	46.45	Median Household Income	$28,509	21	39.0
			% of Families Above Poverty Level	90.6%	21	53.9
Affordable Housing	16	52.60	Median Home Value	$48,000	2	97.1
			Median Rent	$497	24	8.1
Crime	N/A	N/A	Violent Crimes per 10,000 Population	N/A	N/A	N/A
			Property Crimes per 10,000 Population	N/A	N/A	N/A
Open Spaces	23	29.30	Population Density (Persons/Sq. Mile)	5850	26	0.0
			Average Rooms per Housing Unit	6.1	15	58.6
Education	26	1.70	% High School Enrollment/Completion	80.4%	25	3.4
			% College Graduates	7.8%	26	0.0
Commute	23	27.65	Average Work Commute in Minutes	25	26	0.0
			% Commuting on Public Transportation	3.3%	8	55.3
Community Stability	8	63.15	% Living in Same House as in 1979	37.5%	10	38.5
			% Living in Same County as in 1985	89.2%	3	87.8

Metropolitan Area Description
SAN ANTONIO

STATE: Texas
COUNTIES: Bexar, Comal, Guadalupe

TOTAL POPULATION: 1,302,099

POPULATION IN SUBURBS: 366,166   (28.1%)

POPULATION IN San Antonio: 935,933   (71.9%)

The SAN ANTONIO metropolitan area is located in the southern part of Texas. The suburbs range geographically from New Braunfels in the north (32 miles from San Antonio), to Seguin in the east (36 miles from San Antonio). The area is growing in population and had an increase of 21.5% between 1980 and 1990. Summer time high temperatures average in the 90's and winter time lows average in the 30's. Motorola has a semiconductor plant in Seguin. Also found in Seguin are poultry processor Tyson Foods, Structural Metals, and farm machinery maker Alamo Group. The San Antonio area has not benefited from the sunbelt business boom of the 1980's to the extent that Houston and Dallas-Fort Worth have. Public transportation in the area is provided by VIA Metropolitan Transit using buses.

Live Oak is the overall highest rated suburb and also has the highest score in economics. Additionally, **Live Oak** has the top rated commute. **Seguin** is the suburb with the most affordable housing, and also has the number one score in community stability. **Schertz** is rated the safest suburb with the lowest crime rate, and also receives the top score in open spaces. Finally, the number one rating in education belongs to **Universal City**.

The highest ranked suburb overall which also has an affordable housing score of at least 50.00 is **Schertz**.

The highest ranked suburb in the education category which also has an affordable housing score of at least 50.00 is also **Schertz**.

The county whose suburbs have the highest average overall score is **Bexar County** (57.38).

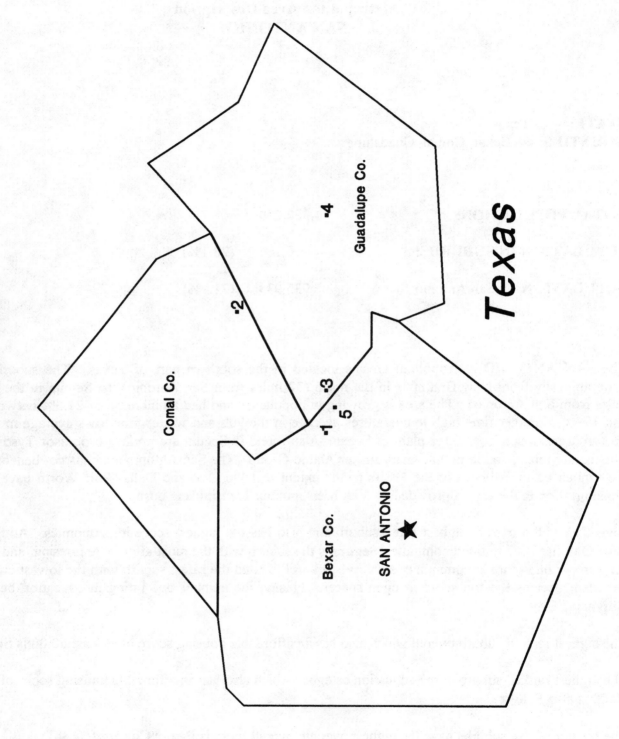

Metropolitan Area Map
SAN ANTONIO

Guadalupe Co.

•4

•2

Comal Co.

•3

•1 •5

Bexar Co.

SAN ANTONIO

★

Texas

Metropolitan Area Suburb Alphabetical Index
SAN ANTONIO

SUBURB	PAGE	MAP NO.	STATE	COUNTY	POPU-LATION	RANK
LIVE OAK	696	1	Texas	Bexar	10,023	1 / 5
NEW BRAUNFELS	697	2	Texas	Comal	27,334	5 / 5
SCHERTZ	696	3	Texas	Guadalupe	10,555	3 / 5
SEGUIN	697	4	Texas	Guadalupe	18,853	4 / 5
UNIVERSAL CITY	696	5	Texas	Bexar	13,057	2 / 5

Metropolitan Area Suburb Rankings
SAN ANTONIO

Composite: **Rank** 1 / 5 **Score** 59.89   **LIVE OAK**

CATEGORY	RANK	SCORE	STATISTIC	VALUE	RANK	SCORE
Economics	1	100.00	Median Household Income	$35,856	1	100.0
			% of Families Above Poverty Level	96.0%	1	100.0
Affordable Housing	4	20.50	Median Home Value	$64,100	2	41.0
			Median Rent	$485	5	0.0
Crime	2	87.55	Violent Crimes per 10,000 Population	42	2	96.0
			Property Crimes per 10,000 Population	475	2	79.1
Open Spaces	2	55.65	Population Density (Persons/Sq. Mile)	2138	4	11.3
			Average Rooms per Housing Unit	5.5	1	100.0
Education	2	61.45	% High School Enrollment/Completion	91.3%	2	69.9
			% College Graduates	21.2%	2	53.0
Commute	1	57.15	Average Work Commute in Minutes	22	4	14.3
			% Commuting on Public Transportation	0.3%	1	100.0
Community Stability	3	36.90	% Living in Same House as in 1979	26.1%	5	0.0
			% Living in Same County as in 1985	75.6%	3	73.8

Composite: **Rank** 2 / 5 **Score** 54.86   **UNIVERSAL CITY**

CATEGORY	RANK	SCORE	STATISTIC	VALUE	RANK	SCORE
Economics	2	92.25	Median Household Income	$35,615	2	98.5
			% of Families Above Poverty Level	93.4%	2	86.0
Affordable Housing	5	15.30	Median Home Value	$77,700	5	0.0
			Median Rent	$444	4	30.6
Crime	3	74.25	Violent Crimes per 10,000 Population	61	3	77.0
			Property Crimes per 10,000 Population	496	3	71.5
Open Spaces	3	42.85	Population Density (Persons/Sq. Mile)	2350	5	0.0
			Average Rooms per Housing Unit	5.4	2	85.7
Education	1	100.00	% High School Enrollment/Completion	94.4%	1	100.0
			% College Graduates	28.9%	1	100.0
Commute	3	38.10	Average Work Commute in Minutes	20	3	42.9
			% Commuting on Public Transportation	0.1%	2	33.3
Community Stability	4	21.30	% Living in Same House as in 1979	27.9%	3	10.7
			% Living in Same County as in 1985	66.0%	4	31.9

Composite: **Rank** 3 / 5 **Score** 52.19   **SCHERTZ**

CATEGORY	RANK	SCORE	STATISTIC	VALUE	RANK	SCORE
Economics	3	76.65	Median Household Income	$31,768	3	74.3
			% of Families Above Poverty Level	92.1%	3	79.0
Affordable Housing	2	50.30	Median Home Value	$66,100	4	34.9
			Median Rent	$397	2	65.7
Crime	1	100.00	Violent Crimes per 10,000 Population	38	1	100.0
			Property Crimes per 10,000 Population	417	1	100.0
Open Spaces	1	85.70	Population Density (Persons/Sq. Mile)	472	1	100.0
			Average Rooms per Housing Unit	5.3	3	71.4
Education	4	31.55	% High School Enrollment/Completion	88.9%	3	46.6
			% College Graduates	15.2%	4	16.5
Commute	5	16.65	Average Work Commute in Minutes	23	5	0.0
			% Commuting on Public Transportation	0.1%	2	33.3
Community Stability	5	4.45	% Living in Same House as in 1979	27.6%	4	8.9
			% Living in Same County as in 1985	58.7%	5	0.0

Metropolitan Area Suburb Rankings
SAN ANTONIO

Composite: *Rank* 4 / 5 *Score* 45.04   **SEGUIN**

CATEGORY	RANK	SCORE	STATISTIC	VALUE	RANK	SCORE
Economics	5	0.00	Median Household Income	$19,970	5	0.0
			% of Families Above Poverty Level	77.4%	5	0.0
Affordable Housing	1	100.00	Median Home Value	$44,500	1	100.0
			Median Rent	$351	1	100.0
Crime	N/A	N/A	Violent Crimes per 10,000 Population	N/A	N/A	N/A
			Property Crimes per 10,000 Population	N/A	N/A	N/A
Open Spaces	5	20.25	Population Density (Persons/Sq. Mile)	1590	3	40.5
			Average Rooms per Housing Unit	4.8	5	0.0
Education	5	0.00	% High School Enrollment/Completion	84.1%	5	0.0
			% College Graduates	12.5%	5	0.0
Commute	2	50.00	Average Work Commute in Minutes	16	1	100.0
			% Commuting on Public Transportation	0.0%	4	0.0
Community Stability	1	100.00	% Living in Same House as in 1979	43.0%	1	100.0
			% Living in Same County as in 1985	81.6%	1	100.0

Composite: *Rank* 5 / 5 *Score* 39.66   **NEW BRAUNFELS**

CATEGORY	RANK	SCORE	STATISTIC	VALUE	RANK	SCORE
Economics	4	49.80	Median Household Income	$26,409	4	40.5
			% of Families Above Poverty Level	88.4%	4	59.1
Affordable Housing	3	44.30	Median Home Value	$64,400	3	40.1
			Median Rent	$420	3	48.5
Crime	4	0.00	Violent Crimes per 10,000 Population	138	4	0.0
			Property Crimes per 10,000 Population	694	4	0.0
Open Spaces	4	41.15	Population Density (Persons/Sq. Mile)	1073	2	68.0
			Average Rooms per Housing Unit	4.9	4	14.3
Education	3	38.70	% High School Enrollment/Completion	88.3%	4	40.8
			% College Graduates	18.5%	3	36.6
Commute	4	35.70	Average Work Commute in Minutes	18	2	71.4
			% Commuting on Public Transportation	0.0%	4	0.0
Community Stability	2	67.95	% Living in Same House as in 1979	36.3%	2	60.4
			% Living in Same County as in 1985	76.0%	2	75.5

Metropolitan Area Description
SAN DIEGO

STATE: California
COUNTIES: San Diego

TOTAL POPULATION: 2,498,016

POPULATION IN SUBURBS: 1,387,467 (55.5%)

POPULATION IN San Diego: 1,110,549 (44.5%)

The SAN DIEGO metropolitan area is located in the southwestern part of California along the Pacific Ocean. The suburbs range geographically from Fallbrook in the north (53 miles from San Diego), to Imperial Beach in the south (11 miles from San Diego), and to Ramona in the east (43 miles from San Diego). The area is growing rapidly in population and had an increase of 34.2% between 1980 and 1990. Summer time high temperatures average in the 70's and winter time lows average in the 40's. Aircraft engine maker Rohr is located in the suburb of Chula Vista. A growth limitation movement, arguing against what is being called the "Los Angelezation of San Diego," is causing a decrease in the issuing of building permits in the area. In 1992, *Fortune* magazine rated the metropolitan area number 57 for its pro-business attitude, nearly at the bottom of its 60-city survey. Public transportation in the area is provided by the San Diego Transit Corporation using buses and trolleys.

Bonita is the overall highest rated suburb and also has the highest scores in economics, education, and community stability. **National City** is the suburb with the most affordable housing. The top rated commute belongs to **Coronado**. Finally, the number one rating in open spaces goes to **Poway**. Crime rankings were not available for the area.

The highest ranked suburb overall which also has an affordable housing score of at least 50.00 is **Casa de Oro-Mount Helix**.

The highest ranked suburb in the education category which also has an affordable housing score of at least 50.00 is **Poway**.

The metropolitan area contains only one county.

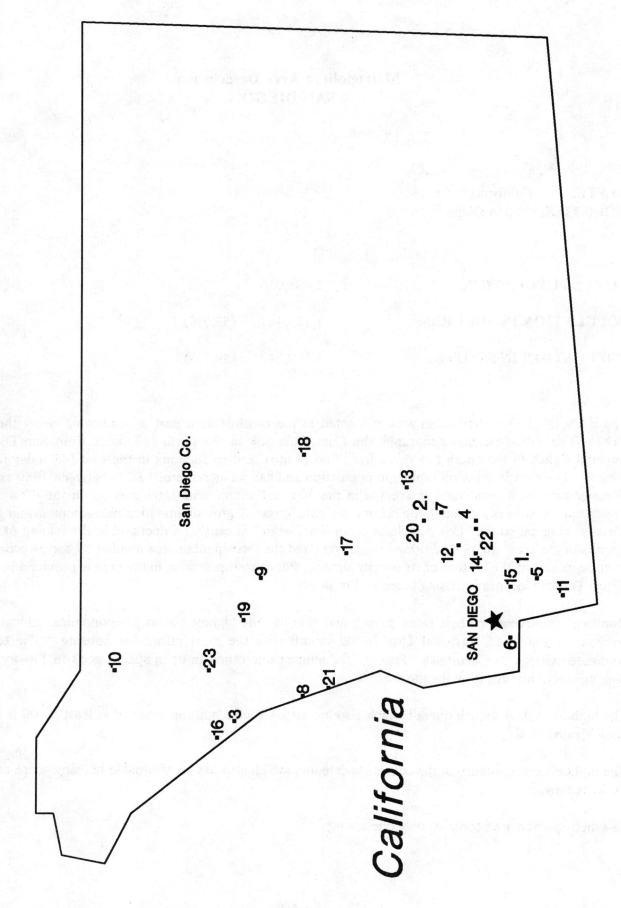

Metropolitan Area Map
SAN DIEGO

San Diego Co.

California

SAN DIEGO

-18

-13

-2.
-7

20. 4

12. 22

14. 1.

-15 -5

-11

-17

-9

-19

-10

-23

-8

-21

-16 -3

-6

Metropolitan Area Suburb Alphabetical Index
SAN DIEGO

SUBURB	PAGE	MAP NO.	STATE	COUNTY	POPU-LATION	RANK
BONITA	702	1	California	San Diego	12,542	1 / 23
BOSTONIA	708	2	California	San Diego	13,670	19 / 23
CARLSBAD	705	3	California	San Diego	63,126	12 / 23
CASA DE ORO-MOUNT HELIX	702	4	California	San Diego	30,727	2 / 23
CHULA VISTA	704	5	California	San Diego	135,163	9 / 23
CORONADO	703	6	California	San Diego	26,540	4 / 23
EL CAJON	708	7	California	San Diego	88,693	20 / 23
ENCINITAS	705	8	California	San Diego	55,386	11 / 23
ESCONDIDO	707	9	California	San Diego	108,635	16 / 23
FALLBROOK	707	10	California	San Diego	22,095	17 / 23
IMPERIAL BEACH	709	11	California	San Diego	26,512	23 / 23
LA MESA	704	12	California	San Diego	52,931	7 / 23
LAKESIDE	705	13	California	San Diego	39,412	10 / 23
LEMON GROVE	703	14	California	San Diego	23,984	6 / 23
NATIONAL CITY	709	15	California	San Diego	54,249	22 / 23
OCEANSIDE	707	16	California	San Diego	128,398	18 / 23
POWAY	702	17	California	San Diego	43,516	3 / 23
RAMONA	706	18	California	San Diego	13,040	14 / 23
SAN MARCOS	706	19	California	San Diego	38,974	15 / 23
SANTEE	704	20	California	San Diego	52,902	8 / 23
SOLANA BEACH	703	21	California	San Diego	12,962	5 / 23
SPRING VALLEY	706	22	California	San Diego	55,331	13 / 23
VISTA	708	23	California	San Diego	71,872	21 / 23

Metropolitan Area Suburb Rankings
SAN DIEGO

Composite: *Rank* 1 / 23 *Score* 73.73   **BONITA**

CATEGORY	RANK	SCORE	STATISTIC	VALUE	RANK	SCORE
Economics	1	96.85	Median Household Income	$56,999	1	100.0
			% of Families Above Poverty Level	96.3%	5	93.7
Affordable Housing	19	40.95	Median Home Value	$265,800	20	55.3
			Median Rent	$757	19	26.6
Crime	N/A	N/A	Violent Crimes per 10,000 Population	N/A	N/A	N/A
			Property Crimes per 10,000 Population	N/A	N/A	N/A
Open Spaces	2	88.20	Population Density (Persons/Sq. Mile)	2541	7	76.4
			Average Rooms per Housing Unit	6.5	1	100.0
Education	1	88.30	% High School Enrollment/Completion	94.8%	1	100.0
			% College Graduates	39.5%	3	76.6
Commute	12	33.70	Average Work Commute in Minutes	21	2	57.1
			% Commuting on Public Transportation	1.1%	21	10.3
Community Stability	1	94.40	% Living in Same House as in 1979	39.3%	1	100.0
			% Living in Same County as in 1985	82.6%	6	88.8

Composite: *Rank* 2 / 23 *Score* 70.12   **CASA DE ORO-MOUNT HELIX**

CATEGORY	RANK	SCORE	STATISTIC	VALUE	RANK	SCORE
Economics	3	89.80	Median Household Income	$52,088	3	85.9
			% of Families Above Poverty Level	96.3%	5	93.7
Affordable Housing	17	55.70	Median Home Value	$258,700	19	57.4
			Median Rent	$652	15	54.0
Crime	N/A	N/A	Violent Crimes per 10,000 Population	N/A	N/A	N/A
			Property Crimes per 10,000 Population	N/A	N/A	N/A
Open Spaces	3	85.55	Population Density (Persons/Sq. Mile)	2391	6	78.8
			Average Rooms per Housing Unit	6.3	2	92.3
Education	5	72.00	% High School Enrollment/Completion	90.2%	7	76.2
			% College Graduates	36.0%	5	67.8
Commute	18	24.90	Average Work Commute in Minutes	24	13	35.7
			% Commuting on Public Transportation	1.4%	19	14.1
Community Stability	3	92.75	% Living in Same House as in 1979	37.2%	2	90.5
			% Living in Same County as in 1985	85.3%	2	95.0

Composite: *Rank* 3 / 23 *Score* 65.53   **POWAY**

CATEGORY	RANK	SCORE	STATISTIC	VALUE	RANK	SCORE
Economics	2	93.80	Median Household Income	$53,252	2	89.3
			% of Families Above Poverty Level	97.1%	2	98.3
Affordable Housing	18	51.40	Median Home Value	$219,400	17	69.1
			Median Rent	$730	18	33.7
Crime	N/A	N/A	Violent Crimes per 10,000 Population	N/A	N/A	N/A
			Property Crimes per 10,000 Population	N/A	N/A	N/A
Open Spaces	1	92.30	Population Density (Persons/Sq. Mile)	1108	1	100.0
			Average Rooms per Housing Unit	6.1	3	84.6
Education	4	76.95	% High School Enrollment/Completion	92.9%	4	90.2
			% College Graduates	34.4%	7	63.7
Commute	20	22.65	Average Work Commute in Minutes	25	16	28.6
			% Commuting on Public Transportation	1.6%	17	16.7
Community Stability	11	56.10	% Living in Same House as in 1979	26.2%	12	40.7
			% Living in Same County as in 1985	75.0%	12	71.5

Metropolitan Area Suburb Rankings
SAN DIEGO

Composite: **Rank** 4 / 23 **Score** 60.58   **CORONADO**

CATEGORY	RANK	SCORE	STATISTIC	VALUE	RANK	SCORE
Economics	5	86.80	Median Household Income	$47,790	5	73.6
			% of Families Above Poverty Level	97.4%	1	100.0
Affordable Housing	23	7.05	Median Home Value	$452,700	23	0.0
			Median Rent	$805	22	14.1
Crime	N/A	N/A	Violent Crimes per 10,000 Population	18	N/A	N/A
			Property Crimes per 10,000 Population	326	N/A	N/A
Open Spaces	11	53.85	Population Density (Persons/Sq. Mile)	3443	13	61.5
			Average Rooms per Housing Unit	5.1	9	46.2
Education	2	85.70	% High School Enrollment/Completion	93.9%	2	95.3
			% College Graduates	39.3%	4	76.1
Commute	1	100.00	Average Work Commute in Minutes	15	1	100.0
			% Commuting on Public Transportation	8.1%	1	100.0
Community Stability	20	30.10	% Living in Same House as in 1979	30.5%	5	60.2
			% Living in Same County as in 1985	43.6%	23	0.0

Composite: **Rank** 5 / 23 **Score** 56.61   **SOLANA BEACH**

CATEGORY	RANK	SCORE	STATISTIC	VALUE	RANK	SCORE
Economics	4	87.15	Median Household Income	$52,000	4	85.7
			% of Families Above Poverty Level	95.4%	8	88.6
Affordable Housing	22	11.00	Median Home Value	$378,400	22	22.0
			Median Rent	$859	23	0.0
Crime	N/A	N/A	Violent Crimes per 10,000 Population	N/A	N/A	N/A
			Property Crimes per 10,000 Population	N/A	N/A	N/A
Open Spaces	12	53.80	Population Density (Persons/Sq. Mile)	3680	14	57.6
			Average Rooms per Housing Unit	5.2	8	50.0
Education	3	81.60	% High School Enrollment/Completion	87.7%	12	63.2
			% College Graduates	48.8%	1	100.0
Commute	6	45.85	Average Work Commute in Minutes	21	2	57.1
			% Commuting on Public Transportation	3.0%	8	34.6
Community Stability	9	60.25	% Living in Same House as in 1979	30.2%	6	58.8
			% Living in Same County as in 1985	70.7%	16	61.7

Composite: **Rank** 6 / 23 **Score** 55.97   **LEMON GROVE**

CATEGORY	RANK	SCORE	STATISTIC	VALUE	RANK	SCORE
Economics	16	49.20	Median Household Income	$31,851	17	27.9
			% of Families Above Poverty Level	92.2%	14	70.5
Affordable Housing	4	80.80	Median Home Value	$135,200	2	94.0
			Median Rent	$600	8	67.6
Crime	N/A	N/A	Violent Crimes per 10,000 Population	N/A	N/A	N/A
			Property Crimes per 10,000 Population	N/A	N/A	N/A
Open Spaces	18	26.20	Population Density (Persons/Sq. Mile)	6323	21	13.9
			Average Rooms per Housing Unit	4.9	13	38.5
Education	13	40.15	% High School Enrollment/Completion	89.4%	9	72.0
			% College Graduates	12.4%	19	8.3
Commute	5	45.80	Average Work Commute in Minutes	23	9	42.9
			% Commuting on Public Transportation	4.1%	6	48.7
Community Stability	2	93.65	% Living in Same House as in 1979	36.5%	3	87.3
			% Living in Same County as in 1985	87.5%	1	100.0

Metropolitan Area Suburb Rankings
SAN DIEGO

Composite: **Rank** 7 / 23 **Score** 55.10   **LA MESA**

CATEGORY	RANK	SCORE	STATISTIC	VALUE	RANK	SCORE
Economics	12	53.30	Median Household Income	$31,171	18	25.9
			% of Families Above Poverty Level	94.0%	10	80.7
Affordable Housing	8	77.35	Median Home Value	$163,800	10	85.5
			Median Rent	$594	7	69.2
Crime	N/A	N/A	Violent Crimes per 10,000 Population	60	N/A	N/A
			Property Crimes per 10,000 Population	606	N/A	N/A
Open Spaces	19	25.20	Population Density (Persons/Sq. Mile)	5742	18	23.5
			Average Rooms per Housing Unit	4.6	19	26.9
Education	8	55.40	% High School Enrollment/Completion	89.5%	8	72.5
			% College Graduates	24.3%	8	38.3
Commute	7	45.20	Average Work Commute in Minutes	21	2	57.1
			% Commuting on Public Transportation	2.9%	9	33.3
Community Stability	4	74.15	% Living in Same House as in 1979	31.3%	4	63.8
			% Living in Same County as in 1985	80.7%	9	84.5

Composite: **Rank** 8 / 23 **Score** 55.06   **SANTEE**

CATEGORY	RANK	SCORE	STATISTIC	VALUE	RANK	SCORE
Economics	8	70.60	Median Household Income	$39,073	8	48.6
			% of Families Above Poverty Level	96.1%	7	92.6
Affordable Housing	13	70.60	Median Home Value	$144,900	5	91.1
			Median Rent	$667	17	50.1
Crime	N/A	N/A	Violent Crimes per 10,000 Population	N/A	N/A	N/A
			Property Crimes per 10,000 Population	N/A	N/A	N/A
Open Spaces	9	58.55	Population Density (Persons/Sq. Mile)	3334	12	63.3
			Average Rooms per Housing Unit	5.3	5	53.8
Education	10	44.95	% High School Enrollment/Completion	90.9%	5	79.8
			% College Graduates	13.1%	18	10.1
Commute	22	18.40	Average Work Commute in Minutes	26	20	21.4
			% Commuting on Public Transportation	1.5%	18	15.4
Community Stability	8	67.25	% Living in Same House as in 1979	26.6%	11	42.5
			% Living in Same County as in 1985	84.0%	3	92.0

Composite: **Rank** 9 / 23 **Score** 54.66   **CHULA VISTA**

CATEGORY	RANK	SCORE	STATISTIC	VALUE	RANK	SCORE
Economics	19	47.10	Median Household Income	$32,012	15	28.3
			% of Families Above Poverty Level	91.4%	18	65.9
Affordable Housing	6	77.75	Median Home Value	$163,000	9	85.8
			Median Rent	$592	6	69.7
Crime	N/A	N/A	Violent Crimes per 10,000 Population	110	N/A	N/A
			Property Crimes per 10,000 Population	672	N/A	N/A
Open Spaces	17	37.95	Population Density (Persons/Sq. Mile)	4663	17	41.3
			Average Rooms per Housing Unit	4.8	16	34.6
Education	11	44.55	% High School Enrollment/Completion	88.5%	11	67.4
			% College Graduates	17.7%	12	21.7
Commute	3	53.20	Average Work Commute in Minutes	22	6	50.0
			% Commuting on Public Transportation	4.7%	4	56.4
Community Stability	7	67.40	% Living in Same House as in 1979	29.3%	7	54.8
			% Living in Same County as in 1985	78.7%	10	80.0

Metropolitan Area Suburb Rankings
SAN DIEGO

Composite: **Rank** 10 / 23 *Score* 54.06   **LAKESIDE**

CATEGORY	RANK	SCORE	STATISTIC	VALUE	RANK	SCORE
Economics	9	59.65	Median Household Income	$36,590	9	41.5
			% of Families Above Poverty Level	93.5%	11	77.8
Affordable Housing	9	76.15	Median Home Value	$160,600	8	86.5
			Median Rent	$607	10	65.8
Crime	N/A	N/A	Violent Crimes per 10,000 Population	N/A	N/A	N/A
			Property Crimes per 10,000 Population	N/A	N/A	N/A
Open Spaces	10	58.10	Population Density (Persons/Sq. Mile)	2929	8	70.0
			Average Rooms per Housing Unit	5.1	9	46.2
Education	12	42.00	% High School Enrollment/Completion	90.6%	6	78.2
			% College Graduates	11.4%	21	5.8
Commute	21	20.05	Average Work Commute in Minutes	25	16	28.6
			% Commuting on Public Transportation	1.2%	20	11.5
Community Stability	6	68.40	% Living in Same House as in 1979	27.1%	10	44.8
			% Living in Same County as in 1985	84.0%	3	92.0

Composite: **Rank** 11 / 23 *Score* 53.61   **ENCINITAS**

CATEGORY	RANK	SCORE	STATISTIC	VALUE	RANK	SCORE
Economics	6	81.80	Median Household Income	$46,069	6	68.7
			% of Families Above Poverty Level	96.5%	3	94.9
Affordable Housing	21	33.15	Median Home Value	$284,200	21	49.9
			Median Rent	$796	21	16.4
Crime	N/A	N/A	Violent Crimes per 10,000 Population	N/A	N/A	N/A
			Property Crimes per 10,000 Population	N/A	N/A	N/A
Open Spaces	8	60.60	Population Density (Persons/Sq. Mile)	3086	10	67.4
			Average Rooms per Housing Unit	5.3	5	53.8
Education	7	67.30	% High School Enrollment/Completion	86.6%	13	57.5
			% College Graduates	39.7%	2	77.1
Commute	9	37.10	Average Work Commute in Minutes	24	13	35.7
			% Commuting on Public Transportation	3.3%	7	38.5
Community Stability	16	41.70	% Living in Same House as in 1979	21.8%	17	20.8
			% Living in Same County as in 1985	71.1%	15	62.6

Composite: **Rank** 12 / 23 *Score* 53.26   **CARLSBAD**

CATEGORY	RANK	SCORE	STATISTIC	VALUE	RANK	SCORE
Economics	7	81.00	Median Household Income	$45,739	7	67.7
			% of Families Above Poverty Level	96.4%	4	94.3
Affordable Housing	20	40.30	Median Home Value	$255,600	18	58.4
			Median Rent	$774	20	22.2
Crime	N/A	N/A	Violent Crimes per 10,000 Population	62	N/A	N/A
			Property Crimes per 10,000 Population	511	N/A	N/A
Open Spaces	4	74.15	Population Density (Persons/Sq. Mile)	1676	3	90.6
			Average Rooms per Housing Unit	5.4	4	57.7
Education	6	69.40	% High School Enrollment/Completion	89.3%	10	71.5
			% College Graduates	35.8%	6	67.3
Commute	16	30.35	Average Work Commute in Minutes	25	16	28.6
			% Commuting on Public Transportation	2.8%	10	32.1
Community Stability	22	24.35	% Living in Same House as in 1979	17.2%	23	0.0
			% Living in Same County as in 1985	65.0%	21	48.7

Metropolitan Area Suburb Rankings
SAN DIEGO

Composite: *Rank* 13 / 23 *Score* 52.11   **SPRING VALLEY**

CATEGORY	RANK	SCORE	STATISTIC	VALUE	RANK	SCORE
Economics	10	57.85	Median Household Income	$36,517	10	41.3
			% of Families Above Poverty Level	92.9%	13	74.4
Affordable Housing	11	74.05	Median Home Value	$144,200	4	91.4
			Median Rent	$642	13	56.7
Crime	N/A	N/A	Violent Crimes per 10,000 Population	N/A	N/A	N/A
			Property Crimes per 10,000 Population	N/A	N/A	N/A
Open Spaces	15	48.50	Population Density (Persons/Sq. Mile)	4548	16	43.2
			Average Rooms per Housing Unit	5.3	5	53.8
Education	14	37.05	% High School Enrollment/Completion	86.4%	14	56.5
			% College Graduates	16.1%	14	17.6
Commute	19	24.80	Average Work Commute in Minutes	26	20	21.4
			% Commuting on Public Transportation	2.5%	11	28.2
Community Stability	5	70.40	% Living in Same House as in 1979	28.7%	8	52.0
			% Living in Same County as in 1985	82.6%	6	88.8

Composite: *Rank* 14 / 23 *Score* 51.00   **RAMONA**

CATEGORY	RANK	SCORE	STATISTIC	VALUE	RANK	SCORE
Economics	18	48.65	Median Household Income	$35,067	11	37.1
			% of Families Above Poverty Level	90.4%	20	60.2
Affordable Housing	3	82.10	Median Home Value	$166,300	11	84.8
			Median Rent	$555	3	79.4
Crime	N/A	N/A	Violent Crimes per 10,000 Population	N/A	N/A	N/A
			Property Crimes per 10,000 Population	N/A	N/A	N/A
Open Spaces	5	70.00	Population Density (Persons/Sq. Mile)	1250	2	97.7
			Average Rooms per Housing Unit	5.0	11	42.3
Education	9	51.65	% High School Enrollment/Completion	93.0%	3	90.7
			% College Graduates	14.1%	17	12.6
Commute	23	0.00	Average Work Commute in Minutes	29	23	0.0
			% Commuting on Public Transportation	0.3%	23	0.0
Community Stability	13	53.60	% Living in Same House as in 1979	21.2%	18	18.1
			% Living in Same County as in 1985	82.7%	5	89.1

Composite: *Rank* 15 / 23 *Score* 47.75   **SAN MARCOS**

CATEGORY	RANK	SCORE	STATISTIC	VALUE	RANK	SCORE
Economics	17	49.05	Median Household Income	$31,961	16	28.2
			% of Families Above Poverty Level	92.1%	16	69.9
Affordable Housing	16	67.85	Median Home Value	$171,900	14	83.2
			Median Rent	$658	16	52.5
Crime	N/A	N/A	Violent Crimes per 10,000 Population	N/A	N/A	N/A
			Property Crimes per 10,000 Population	N/A	N/A	N/A
Open Spaces	6	66.40	Population Density (Persons/Sq. Mile)	1681	4	90.5
			Average Rooms per Housing Unit	5.0	11	42.3
Education	21	17.80	% High School Enrollment/Completion	79.6%	20	21.2
			% College Graduates	14.8%	15	14.4
Commute	8	37.80	Average Work Commute in Minutes	22	6	50.0
			% Commuting on Public Transportation	2.3%	13	25.6
Community Stability	15	47.60	% Living in Same House as in 1979	23.5%	15	28.5
			% Living in Same County as in 1985	72.9%	14	66.7

Metropolitan Area Suburb Rankings
SAN DIEGO

Composite: *Rank* 16 / 23 *Score* 44.76   **ESCONDIDO**

CATEGORY	RANK	SCORE	STATISTIC	VALUE	RANK	SCORE
Economics	14	50.70	Median Household Income	$32,895	13	30.9
			% of Families Above Poverty Level	92.2%	14	70.5
Affordable Housing	12	72.95	Median Home Value	$169,600	12	83.8
			Median Rent	$621	11	62.1
Crime	N/A	N/A	Violent Crimes per 10,000 Population	102	N/A	N/A
			Property Crimes per 10,000 Population	704	N/A	N/A
Open Spaces	14	51.30	Population Density (Persons/Sq. Mile)	3048	9	68.0
			Average Rooms per Housing Unit	4.8	16	34.6
Education	20	21.70	% High School Enrollment/Completion	79.4%	21	20.2
			% College Graduates	18.3%	11	23.2
Commute	13	33.65	Average Work Commute in Minutes	23	9	42.9
			% Commuting on Public Transportation	2.2%	16	24.4
Community Stability	18	38.25	% Living in Same House as in 1979	18.4%	21	5.4
			% Living in Same County as in 1985	74.8%	13	71.1

Composite: *Rank* 17 / 23 *Score* 44.72   **FALLBROOK**

CATEGORY	RANK	SCORE	STATISTIC	VALUE	RANK	SCORE
Economics	20	44.05	Median Household Income	$30,656	19	24.5
			% of Families Above Poverty Level	91.0%	19	63.6
Affordable Housing	10	74.10	Median Home Value	$189,200	16	78.0
			Median Rent	$590	4	70.2
Crime	N/A	N/A	Violent Crimes per 10,000 Population	N/A	N/A	N/A
			Property Crimes per 10,000 Population	N/A	N/A	N/A
Open Spaces	7	61.60	Population Density (Persons/Sq. Mile)	2034	5	84.7
			Average Rooms per Housing Unit	4.9	13	38.5
Education	22	15.90	% High School Enrollment/Completion	77.5%	22	10.4
			% College Graduates	17.6%	13	21.4
Commute	14	32.40	Average Work Commute in Minutes	21	2	57.1
			% Commuting on Public Transportation	0.9%	22	7.7
Community Stability	17	40.25	% Living in Same House as in 1979	22.9%	16	25.8
			% Living in Same County as in 1985	67.6%	18	54.7

Composite: *Rank* 18 / 23 *Score* 43.59   **OCEANSIDE**

CATEGORY	RANK	SCORE	STATISTIC	VALUE	RANK	SCORE
Economics	11	54.60	Median Household Income	$33,453	12	32.5
			% of Families Above Poverty Level	93.3%	12	76.7
Affordable Housing	15	68.90	Median Home Value	$170,600	13	83.5
			Median Rent	$651	14	54.3
Crime	N/A	N/A	Violent Crimes per 10,000 Population	123	N/A	N/A
			Property Crimes per 10,000 Population	515	N/A	N/A
Open Spaces	13	52.35	Population Density (Persons/Sq. Mile)	3157	11	66.2
			Average Rooms per Housing Unit	4.9	13	38.5
Education	17	25.65	% High School Enrollment/Completion	80.7%	19	26.9
			% College Graduates	18.8%	9	24.4
Commute	10	35.70	Average Work Commute in Minutes	26	20	21.4
			% Commuting on Public Transportation	4.2%	5	50.0
Community Stability	22	24.35	% Living in Same House as in 1979	18.8%	20	7.2
			% Living in Same County as in 1985	61.8%	22	41.5

Metropolitan Area Suburb Rankings
SAN DIEGO

Composite: *Rank* 19 / 23 *Score* 43.52   **BOSTONIA**

CATEGORY	RANK	SCORE	STATISTIC	VALUE	RANK	SCORE
Economics	13	53.05	Median Household Income	$29,590	20	21.4
			% of Families Above Poverty Level	94.7%	9	84.7
Affordable Housing	7	77.30	Median Home Value	$157,100	6	87.5
			Median Rent	$602	9	67.1
Crime	N/A	N/A	Violent Crimes per 10,000 Population	N/A	N/A	N/A
			Property Crimes per 10,000 Population	N/A	N/A	N/A
Open Spaces	21	15.30	Population Density (Persons/Sq. Mile)	6946	22	3.7
			Average Rooms per Housing Unit	4.6	19	26.9
Education	19	23.90	% High School Enrollment/Completion	83.9%	17	43.5
			% College Graduates	10.8%	22	4.3
Commute	15	31.95	Average Work Commute in Minutes	24	13	35.7
			% Commuting on Public Transportation	2.5%	11	28.2
Community Stability	10	59.65	% Living in Same House as in 1979	24.7%	13	33.9
			% Living in Same County as in 1985	81.1%	8	85.4

Composite: *Rank* 20 / 23 *Score* 43.45   **EL CAJON**

CATEGORY	RANK	SCORE	STATISTIC	VALUE	RANK	SCORE
Economics	21	35.55	Median Household Income	$28,108	21	17.1
			% of Families Above Poverty Level	89.3%	21	54.0
Affordable Housing	2	84.35	Median Home Value	$157,200	7	87.5
			Median Rent	$548	2	81.2
Crime	N/A	N/A	Violent Crimes per 10,000 Population	89	N/A	N/A
			Property Crimes per 10,000 Population	629	N/A	N/A
Open Spaces	20	21.80	Population Density (Persons/Sq. Mile)	6156	19	16.7
			Average Rooms per Housing Unit	4.6	19	26.9
Education	15	32.10	% High School Enrollment/Completion	85.3%	15	50.8
			% College Graduates	14.4%	16	13.4
Commute	11	34.25	Average Work Commute in Minutes	23	9	42.9
			% Commuting on Public Transportation	2.3%	13	25.6
Community Stability	14	52.65	% Living in Same House as in 1979	23.6%	14	29.0
			% Living in Same County as in 1985	77.1%	11	76.3

Composite: *Rank* 21 / 23 *Score* 41.02   **VISTA**

CATEGORY	RANK	SCORE	STATISTIC	VALUE	RANK	SCORE
Economics	15	49.60	Median Household Income	$32,553	14	29.9
			% of Families Above Poverty Level	92.0%	17	69.3
Affordable Housing	14	69.65	Median Home Value	$183,200	15	79.8
			Median Rent	$631	12	59.5
Crime	N/A	N/A	Violent Crimes per 10,000 Population	N/A	N/A	N/A
			Property Crimes per 10,000 Population	N/A	N/A	N/A
Open Spaces	16	43.40	Population Density (Persons/Sq. Mile)	4006	15	52.2
			Average Rooms per Housing Unit	4.8	16	34.6
Education	16	30.85	% High School Enrollment/Completion	82.9%	18	38.3
			% College Graduates	18.4%	10	23.4
Commute	17	27.10	Average Work Commute in Minutes	25	16	28.6
			% Commuting on Public Transportation	2.3%	13	25.6
Community Stability	21	25.55	% Living in Same House as in 1979	17.5%	22	1.4
			% Living in Same County as in 1985	65.4%	20	49.7

Metropolitan Area Suburb Rankings
SAN DIEGO

Composite: *Rank* 22 / 23 *Score* 40.73 **NATIONAL CITY**

CATEGORY	RANK	SCORE	STATISTIC	VALUE	RANK	SCORE
Economics	23	0.00	Median Household Income	$22,129	23	0.0
			% of Families Above Poverty Level	79.8%	23	0.0
Affordable Housing	1	100.00	Median Home Value	$115,000	1	100.0
			Median Rent	$476	1	100.0
Crime	N/A	N/A	Violent Crimes per 10,000 Population	168	N/A	N/A
			Property Crimes per 10,000 Population	772	N/A	N/A
Open Spaces	23	0.00	Population Density (Persons/Sq. Mile)	7168	23	0.0
			Average Rooms per Housing Unit	3.9	23	0.0
Education	18	25.40	% High School Enrollment/Completion	85.3%	15	50.8
			% College Graduates	9.1%	23	0.0
Commute	2	64.10	Average Work Commute in Minutes	22	6	50.0
			% Commuting on Public Transportation	6.4%	2	78.2
Community Stability	12	54.85	% Living in Same House as in 1979	28.3%	9	50.2
			% Living in Same County as in 1985	69.7%	17	59.5

Composite: *Rank* 23 / 23 *Score* 33.69 **IMPERIAL BEACH**

CATEGORY	RANK	SCORE	STATISTIC	VALUE	RANK	SCORE
Economics	22	21.25	Median Household Income	$26,464	22	12.4
			% of Families Above Poverty Level	85.1%	22	30.1
Affordable Housing	5	80.70	Median Home Value	$144,100	3	91.4
			Median Rent	$591	5	70.0
Crime	N/A	N/A	Violent Crimes per 10,000 Population	N/A	N/A	N/A
			Property Crimes per 10,000 Population	N/A	N/A	N/A
Open Spaces	22	13.45	Population Density (Persons/Sq. Mile)	6237	20	15.4
			Average Rooms per Housing Unit	4.2	22	11.5
Education	23	3.80	% High School Enrollment/Completion	75.5%	23	0.0
			% College Graduates	12.1%	20	7.6
Commute	4	50.95	Average Work Commute in Minutes	23	9	42.9
			% Commuting on Public Transportation	4.9%	3	59.0
Community Stability	19	32.00	% Living in Same House as in 1979	19.6%	19	10.9
			% Living in Same County as in 1985	66.9%	19	53.1

Metropolitan Area Description
SAN FRANCISCO-OAKLAND-SAN JOSE

STATE: California
COUNTIES: Alameda, Contra Costa, Marin, Napa, San Francisco, San Mateo, Santa Clara, Santa Cruz, Solano, Sonoma

TOTAL POPULATION:	6,253,311	
POPULATION IN SUBURBS:	4,374,862	(70.0%)
POPULATION IN San Francisco:	723,959	(11.6%)
POPULATION IN Oakland:	372,242	(6.0%)
POPULATION IN San Jose:	782,248	(12.5%)

The SAN FRANCISCO-OAKLAND-SAN JOSE metropolitan area is located in the westcentral part of California along the Pacific Ocean. The suburbs range geographically from Windsor in the north (68 miles from San Francisco), to Watsonville in the south (93 miles from San Francisco), and to Oakley in the east (53 miles from San Francisco). The area is growing in population and had an increase of 16.5% between 1980 and 1990. Summer time high temperatures average in the 80's and winter time lows average in the 40's. Many major companies are headquartered in the suburbs. Lockheed Missiles and Space Company, Advanced Micro Devices, and Amdahl are all located in the suburb of Sunnyvale. Apple Computer is headquartered in Cupertino. The southern part of the area is known as "Silicon Valley." The University of California's oldest campus is located in Berkeley. Public transportation in the area is provided by many different agencies using buses, trains, subways and ferries.

Hillsborough is the overall highest rated suburb and also has the highest scores in economics and open spaces. **Hillsborough** is also rated the safest suburb with the lowest crime rate. **San Pablo** is the suburb with the most affordable housing. The number one score in education belongs to **Piedmont**. **Berkeley** has the top rated commute. Finally, the number one rating in community stability goes to **San Lorenzo**.

The highest ranked suburb overall which also has an affordable housing score of at least 50.00 is **Walnut Creek**.

The highest ranked suburb in the education category which also has an affordable housing score of at least 50.00 is **Berkeley**.

The county whose suburbs have the highest average overall score is **Marin County** (55.49).

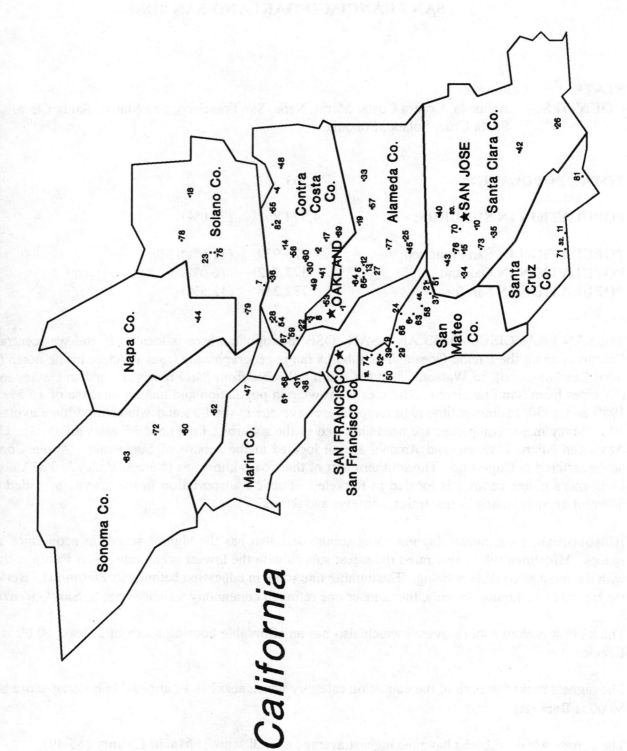

Metropolitan Area Map
SAN FRANCISCO–OAKLAND–SAN JOSE

Sonoma Co.

Napa Co.

Marin Co.

Solano Co.

Contra Costa Co.

Alameda Co.

Santa Clara Co.

San Mateo Co.

Santa Cruz Co.

★ SAN FRANCISCO
San Francisco Co.

★ OAKLAND

★ SAN JOSE

California

Metropolitan Area Suburb Alphabetical Index
SAN FRANCISCO-OAKLAND-SAN JOSE

SUBURB	PAGE	MAP NO.	STATE	COUNTY	POPU-LATION	RANK
ALAMEDA	732	1	California	Alameda	76,459	53 / 83
ALAMO	719	2	California	Contra Costa	12,277	13 / 83
ALBANY	723	3	California	Alameda	16,327	26 / 83
ANTIOCH	735	4	California	Contra Costa	62,195	62 / 83
ASHLAND	738	5	California	Alameda	16,590	72 / 83
BELMONT	721	6	California	San Mateo	24,127	20 / 83
BENICIA	724	7	California	Solano	24,437	30 / 83
BERKELEY	733	8	California	Alameda	102,724	55 / 83
BURLINGAME	730	9	California	San Mateo	26,801	46 / 83
CAMPBELL	734	10	California	Santa Clara	36,048	58 / 83
CAPITOLA	739	11	California	Santa Cruz	10,171	74 / 83
CASTRO VALLEY	720	12	California	Alameda	48,619	17 / 83
CHERRYLAND	741	13	California	Alameda	11,088	81 / 83
CONCORD	727	14	California	Contra Costa	111,348	37 / 83
CUPERTINO	722	15	California	Santa Clara	40,263	23 / 83
DALY CITY	736	16	California	San Mateo	92,311	64 / 83
DANVILLE	717	17	California	Contra Costa	31,306	8 / 83
DIXON	720	18	California	Solano	10,401	18 / 83
DUBLIN	730	19	California	Alameda	23,229	47 / 83
EAST FOOTHILLS	727	20	California	Santa Clara	14,898	38 / 83
EAST PALO ALTO	741	21	California	San Mateo	23,451	79 / 83
EL CERRITO	718	22	California	Contra Costa	22,869	10 / 83
FAIRFIELD	735	23	California	Solano	77,211	63 / 83
FOSTER CITY	733	24	California	San Mateo	28,176	56 / 83
FREMONT	726	25	California	Alameda	173,339	34 / 83
GILROY	736	26	California	Santa Clara	31,487	65 / 83
HAYWARD	734	27	California	Alameda	111,498	59 / 83
HERCULES	735	28	California	Contra Costa	16,829	61 / 83
HILLSBOROUGH	715	29	California	San Mateo	10,667	1 / 83
LAFAYETTE	715	30	California	Contra Costa	23,501	3 / 83
LARKSPUR	732	31	California	Marin	11,070	52 / 83
LIVE OAK	739	32	California	Santa Cruz	15,212	73 / 83
LIVERMORE	723	33	California	Alameda	56,741	25 / 83
LOS ALTOS	716	34	California	Santa Clara	26,303	5 / 83
LOS GATOS	718	35	California	Santa Clara	27,357	12 / 83
MARTINEZ	719	36	California	Contra Costa	31,808	15 / 83
MENLO PARK	730	37	California	San Mateo	28,040	48 / 83
MILL VALLEY	718	38	California	Marin	13,038	11 / 83
MILLBRAE	723	39	California	San Mateo	20,412	27 / 83
MILPITAS	729	40	California	Santa Clara	50,686	43 / 83
MORAGA	717	41	California	Contra Costa	15,852	7 / 83
MORGAN HILL	731	42	California	Santa Clara	23,928	50 / 83
MOUNTAIN VIEW	738	43	California	Santa Clara	67,460	70 / 83
NAPA	725	44	California	Napa	61,842	32 / 83
NEWARK	728	45	California	Alameda	37,861	42 / 83
NORTH FAIR OAKS	742	46	California	San Mateo	13,912	82 / 83
NOVATO	722	47	California	Marin	47,585	24 / 83
OAKLEY	740	48	California	Contra Costa	18,374	76 / 83
ORINDA	716	49	California	Contra Costa	16,642	4 / 83
PACIFICA	722	50	California	San Mateo	37,670	22 / 83
PALO ALTO	721	51	California	Santa Clara	55,900	19 / 83

Metropolitan Area Suburb Alphabetical Index
SAN FRANCISCO-OAKLAND-SAN JOSE

SUBURB	PAGE	MAP NO.	STATE	COUNTY	POPU-LATION	RANK
PETALUMA	726	52	California	Sonoma	43,184	35 / 83
PIEDMONT	715	53	California	Alameda	10,602	2 / 83
PINOLE	725	54	California	Contra Costa	17,460	33 / 83
PITTSBURG	737	55	California	Contra Costa	47,564	69 / 83
PLEASANT HILL	726	56	California	Contra Costa	31,585	35 / 83
PLEASANTON	725	57	California	Alameda	50,553	31 / 83
REDWOOD CITY	736	58	California	San Mateo	66,072	66 / 83
RICHMOND	739	59	California	Contra Costa	87,425	75 / 83
ROHNERT PARK	737	60	California	Sonoma	36,326	67 / 83
SAN ANSELMO	720	61	California	Marin	11,743	16 / 83
SAN BRUNO	731	62	California	San Mateo	38,961	51 / 83
SAN CARLOS	719	63	California	San Mateo	26,167	14 / 83
SAN LEANDRO	721	64	California	Alameda	68,223	21 / 83
SAN LORENZO	724	65	California	Alameda	19,987	28 / 83
SAN MATEO	732	66	California	San Mateo	85,486	54 / 83
SAN PABLO	742	67	California	Contra Costa	25,158	83 / 83
SAN RAFAEL	728	68	California	Marin	48,404	41 / 83
SAN RAMON	729	69	California	Contra Costa	35,303	44 / 83
SANTA CLARA	731	70	California	Santa Clara	93,613	49 / 83
SANTA CRUZ	733	71	California	Santa Cruz	49,040	57 / 83
SANTA ROSA	727	72	California	Sonoma	113,313	39 / 83
SARATOGA	716	73	California	Santa Clara	28,061	6 / 83
SOUTH SAN FRANCISCO	724	74	California	San Mateo	54,312	29 / 83
SUISUN CITY	740	75	California	Solano	22,686	78 / 83
SUNNYVALE	728	76	California	Santa Clara	117,229	40 / 83
UNION CITY	729	77	California	Alameda	53,762	45 / 83
VACAVILLE	734	78	California	Solano	71,479	59 / 83
VALLEJO	738	79	California	Solano	109,199	71 / 83
WALNUT CREEK	717	80	California	Contra Costa	60,569	9 / 83
WATSONVILLE	740	81	California	Santa Cruz	31,099	77 / 83
WEST PITTSBURG	741	82	California	Contra Costa	17,453	80 / 83
WINDSOR	737	83	California	Sonoma	13,371	68 / 83

Metropolitan Area Suburb Rankings
SAN FRANCISCO-OAKLAND-SAN JOSE

Composite: *Rank* 1 / 83 *Score* 71.72   **HILLSBOROUGH**

CATEGORY	RANK	SCORE	STATISTIC	VALUE	RANK	SCORE
Economics	1	95.50	Median Household Income	$123,625	1	100.0
			% of Families Above Poverty Level	98.0%	16	91.0
Affordable Housing	79	0.00	Median Home Value	$500,001	79	0.0
			Median Rent	$1,001	77	0.0
Crime	1	98.90	Violent Crimes per 10,000 Population	12	6	97.8
			Property Crimes per 10,000 Population	93	1	100.0
Open Spaces	1	95.45	Population Density (Persons/Sq. Mile)	1715	7	90.9
			Average Rooms per Housing Unit	8.0	1	100.0
Education	10	82.35	% High School Enrollment/Completion	95.9%	20	88.7
			% College Graduates	56.7%	10	76.0
Commute	52	41.40	Average Work Commute in Minutes	25	36	65.0
			% Commuting on Public Transportation	4.0%	49	17.8
Community Stability	4	88.45	% Living in Same House as in 1979	59.6%	1	100.0
			% Living in Same County as in 1985	81.9%	12	76.9

Composite: *Rank* 2 / 83 *Score* 69.99   **PIEDMONT**

CATEGORY	RANK	SCORE	STATISTIC	VALUE	RANK	SCORE
Economics	4	79.15	Median Household Income	$84,498	4	60.1
			% of Families Above Poverty Level	99.2%	3	98.2
Affordable Housing	79	0.00	Median Home Value	$500,001	79	0.0
			Median Rent	$1,001	77	0.0
Crime	15	86.45	Violent Crimes per 10,000 Population	11	5	98.2
			Property Crimes per 10,000 Population	352	18	74.7
Open Spaces	9	69.80	Population Density (Persons/Sq. Mile)	6294	68	51.5
			Average Rooms per Housing Unit	7.5	2	88.1
Education	1	99.65	% High School Enrollment/Completion	99.1%	3	99.3
			% College Graduates	71.2%	1	100.0
Commute	9	62.05	Average Work Commute in Minutes	22	15	80.0
			% Commuting on Public Transportation	9.6%	20	44.1
Community Stability	2	92.85	% Living in Same House as in 1979	55.7%	4	91.8
			% Living in Same County as in 1985	87.8%	2	93.9

Composite: *Rank* 3 / 83 *Score* 69.20   **LAFAYETTE**

CATEGORY	RANK	SCORE	STATISTIC	VALUE	RANK	SCORE
Economics	11	64.65	Median Household Income	$64,806	9	40.1
			% of Families Above Poverty Level	97.7%	21	89.2
Affordable Housing	63	34.90	Median Home Value	$388,500	65	29.1
			Median Rent	$767	49	40.7
Crime	7	92.25	Violent Crimes per 10,000 Population	9	4	98.9
			Property Crimes per 10,000 Population	240	8	85.6
Open Spaces	7	77.15	Population Density (Persons/Sq. Mile)	1546	5	92.4
			Average Rooms per Housing Unit	6.4	9	61.9
Education	3	89.85	% High School Enrollment/Completion	99.3%	1	100.0
			% College Graduates	58.9%	6	79.7
Commute	20	55.05	Average Work Commute in Minutes	28	55	50.0
			% Commuting on Public Transportation	13.0%	9	60.1
Community Stability	12	70.55	% Living in Same House as in 1979	47.9%	10	75.4
			% Living in Same County as in 1985	78.0%	22	65.7

Metropolitan Area Suburb Rankings
SAN FRANCISCO-OAKLAND-SAN JOSE

Composite: **Rank** 4 / 83 **Score** 68.61   **ORINDA**

CATEGORY	RANK	SCORE	STATISTIC	VALUE	RANK	SCORE
Economics	6	74.95	Median Household Income	$80,968	5	56.5
			% of Families Above Poverty Level	98.4%	10	93.4
Affordable Housing	78	8.65	Median Home Value	$433,600	73	17.3
			Median Rent	$1,001	77	0.0
Crime	3	94.35	Violent Crimes per 10,000 Population	7	2	99.6
			Property Crimes per 10,000 Population	204	5	89.1
Open Spaces	4	84.05	Population Density (Persons/Sq. Mile)	1322	3	94.3
			Average Rooms per Housing Unit	6.9	6	73.8
Education	2	91.85	% High School Enrollment/Completion	97.0%	12	92.3
			% College Graduates	66.0%	2	91.4
Commute	29	52.45	Average Work Commute in Minutes	28	55	50.0
			% Commuting on Public Transportation	11.9%	13	54.9
Community Stability	8	73.95	% Living in Same House as in 1979	52.9%	5	85.9
			% Living in Same County as in 1985	76.7%	31	62.0

Composite: **Rank** 5 / 83 **Score** 66.64   **LOS ALTOS**

CATEGORY	RANK	SCORE	STATISTIC	VALUE	RANK	SCORE
Economics	5	77.55	Median Household Income	$79,579	6	55.1
			% of Families Above Poverty Level	99.5%	1	100.0
Affordable Housing	79	0.00	Median Home Value	$500,001	79	0.0
			Median Rent	$1,001	77	0.0
Crime	6	93.30	Violent Crimes per 10,000 Population	14	8	97.1
			Property Crimes per 10,000 Population	200	4	89.5
Open Spaces	10	68.40	Population Density (Persons/Sq. Mile)	4130	49	70.1
			Average Rooms per Housing Unit	6.6	8	66.7
Education	5	87.05	% High School Enrollment/Completion	97.3%	9	93.3
			% College Graduates	59.6%	4	80.8
Commute	37	48.05	Average Work Commute in Minutes	20	6	90.0
			% Commuting on Public Transportation	1.5%	78	6.1
Community Stability	3	92.10	% Living in Same House as in 1979	59.1%	2	98.9
			% Living in Same County as in 1985	84.8%	6	85.3

Composite: **Rank** 6 / 83 **Score** 66.47   **SARATOGA**

CATEGORY	RANK	SCORE	STATISTIC	VALUE	RANK	SCORE
Economics	3	81.20	Median Household Income	$86,674	3	62.4
			% of Families Above Poverty Level	99.5%	1	100.0
Affordable Housing	79	0.00	Median Home Value	$500,001	79	0.0
			Median Rent	$1,001	77	0.0
Crime	4	93.75	Violent Crimes per 10,000 Population	14	8	97.1
			Property Crimes per 10,000 Population	191	3	90.4
Open Spaces	5	80.85	Population Density (Persons/Sq. Mile)	2344	15	85.5
			Average Rooms per Housing Unit	7.0	5	76.2
Education	7	85.35	% High School Enrollment/Completion	97.1%	10	92.7
			% College Graduates	57.9%	8	78.0
Commute	61	36.65	Average Work Commute in Minutes	24	25	70.0
			% Commuting on Public Transportation	0.9%	82	3.3
Community Stability	5	87.50	% Living in Same House as in 1979	52.1%	6	84.2
			% Living in Same County as in 1985	86.7%	5	90.8

Metropolitan Area Suburb Rankings
SAN FRANCISCO-OAKLAND-SAN JOSE

Composite: **Rank** 7 / 83 **Score** 65.44   **MORAGA**

CATEGORY	RANK	SCORE	STATISTIC	VALUE	RANK	SCORE
Economics	8	69.25	Median Household Income	$69,767	8	45.1
			% of Families Above Poverty Level	98.4%	10	93.4
Affordable Housing	69	23.50	Median Home Value	$406,500	69	24.4
			Median Rent	$871	70	22.6
Crime	2	98.50	Violent Crimes per 10,000 Population	8	3	99.3
			Property Crimes per 10,000 Population	116	2	97.7
Open Spaces	6	80.00	Population Density (Persons/Sq. Mile)	1709	6	91.0
			Average Rooms per Housing Unit	6.7	7	69.0
Education	6	86.80	% High School Enrollment/Completion	98.0%	6	95.7
			% College Graduates	57.8%	9	77.9
Commute	38	47.60	Average Work Commute in Minutes	29	66	45.0
			% Commuting on Public Transportation	10.9%	15	50.2
Community Stability	31	52.40	% Living in Same House as in 1979	42.4%	13	63.9
			% Living in Same County as in 1985	69.4%	64	40.9

Composite: **Rank** 8 / 83 **Score** 61.00   **DANVILLE**

CATEGORY	RANK	SCORE	STATISTIC	VALUE	RANK	SCORE
Economics	7	72.85	Median Household Income	$74,472	7	49.9
			% of Families Above Poverty Level	98.8%	6	95.8
Affordable Housing	74	18.25	Median Home Value	$360,100	64	36.5
			Median Rent	$1,001	77	0.0
Crime	4	93.75	Violent Crimes per 10,000 Population	6	1	100.0
			Property Crimes per 10,000 Population	221	6	87.5
Open Spaces	3	84.50	Population Density (Persons/Sq. Mile)	1770	10	90.4
			Average Rooms per Housing Unit	7.1	4	78.6
Education	14	79.90	% High School Enrollment/Completion	98.6%	5	97.7
			% College Graduates	48.3%	16	62.1
Commute	71	31.65	Average Work Commute in Minutes	29	66	45.0
			% Commuting on Public Transportation	4.1%	45	18.3
Community Stability	49	46.10	% Living in Same House as in 1979	35.2%	28	48.7
			% Living in Same County as in 1985	70.3%	57	43.5

Composite: **Rank** 9 / 83 **Score** 59.47   **WALNUT CREEK**

CATEGORY	RANK	SCORE	STATISTIC	VALUE	RANK	SCORE
Economics	26	55.10	Median Household Income	$45,529	39	20.4
			% of Families Above Poverty Level	97.8%	20	89.8
Affordable Housing	44	51.95	Median Home Value	$289,300	53	55.0
			Median Rent	$720	34	48.9
Crime	30	78.35	Violent Crimes per 10,000 Population	34	28	89.9
			Property Crimes per 10,000 Population	432	33	66.8
Open Spaces	35	57.20	Population Density (Persons/Sq. Mile)	3137	34	78.7
			Average Rooms per Housing Unit	5.3	39	35.7
Education	20	73.90	% High School Enrollment/Completion	95.7%	23	88.0
			% College Graduates	46.9%	19	59.8
Commute	20	55.05	Average Work Commute in Minutes	28	55	50.0
			% Commuting on Public Transportation	13.0%	9	60.1
Community Stability	51	44.75	% Living in Same House as in 1979	33.1%	38	44.3
			% Living in Same County as in 1985	70.9%	55	45.2

Metropolitan Area Suburb Rankings
SAN FRANCISCO-OAKLAND-SAN JOSE

Composite: Rank 10 / 83 *Score* 59.41   **EL CERRITO**

CATEGORY	RANK	SCORE	STATISTIC	VALUE	RANK	SCORE
Economics	37	51.15	Median Household Income	$39,538	59	14.3
			% of Families Above Poverty Level	97.5%	22	88.0
Affordable Housing	30	58.85	Median Home Value	$252,900	39	64.5
			Median Rent	$695	28	53.2
Crime	65	52.55	Violent Crimes per 10,000 Population	82	61	72.6
			Property Crimes per 10,000 Population	783	67	32.5
Open Spaces	60	43.65	Population Density (Persons/Sq. Mile)	6286	67	51.6
			Average Rooms per Housing Unit	5.3	39	35.7
Education	18	75.05	% High School Enrollment/Completion	96.7%	14	91.3
			% College Graduates	46.3%	21	58.8
Commute	3	73.05	Average Work Commute in Minutes	27	47	55.0
			% Commuting on Public Transportation	19.6%	2	91.1
Community Stability	17	61.60	% Living in Same House as in 1979	50.3%	7	80.5
			% Living in Same County as in 1985	70.0%	61	42.7

Composite: Rank 11 / 83 *Score* 59.00   **MILL VALLEY**

CATEGORY	RANK	SCORE	STATISTIC	VALUE	RANK	SCORE
Economics	14	63.30	Median Household Income	$55,748	16	30.8
			% of Families Above Poverty Level	98.8%	6	95.8
Affordable Housing	76	15.95	Median Home Value	$459,000	77	10.7
			Median Rent	$879	71	21.2
Crime	17	84.10	Violent Crimes per 10,000 Population	19	12	95.3
			Property Crimes per 10,000 Population	370	23	72.9
Open Spaces	27	59.90	Population Density (Persons/Sq. Mile)	2791	23	81.7
			Average Rooms per Housing Unit	5.4	32	38.1
Education	11	82.15	% High School Enrollment/Completion	94.5%	34	84.0
			% College Graduates	59.3%	5	80.3
Commute	16	56.90	Average Work Commute in Minutes	28	55	50.0
			% Commuting on Public Transportation	13.8%	7	63.8
Community Stability	36	50.70	% Living in Same House as in 1979	34.6%	31	47.5
			% Living in Same County as in 1985	73.9%	46	53.9

Composite: Rank 12 / 83 *Score* 58.51   **LOS GATOS**

CATEGORY	RANK	SCORE	STATISTIC	VALUE	RANK	SCORE
Economics	16	61.65	Median Household Income	$57,815	14	32.9
			% of Families Above Poverty Level	97.9%	17	90.4
Affordable Housing	70	22.20	Median Home Value	$431,100	72	18.0
			Median Rent	$849	65	26.4
Crime	20	83.65	Violent Crimes per 10,000 Population	20	14	94.9
			Property Crimes per 10,000 Population	375	24	72.4
Open Spaces	19	62.95	Population Density (Persons/Sq. Mile)	2636	18	83.0
			Average Rooms per Housing Unit	5.6	18	42.9
Education	17	78.10	% High School Enrollment/Completion	97.7%	8	94.7
			% College Graduates	47.9%	17	61.5
Commute	59	37.60	Average Work Commute in Minutes	24	25	70.0
			% Commuting on Public Transportation	1.3%	80	5.2
Community Stability	14	63.45	% Living in Same House as in 1979	35.9%	26	50.2
			% Living in Same County as in 1985	81.8%	13	76.7

Metropolitan Area Suburb Rankings
SAN FRANCISCO-OAKLAND-SAN JOSE

Composite: *Rank* 13 / 83 *Score* 58.48   **ALAMO**

CATEGORY	RANK	SCORE	STATISTIC	VALUE	RANK	SCORE
Economics	2	82.35	Median Household Income	$93,089	2	68.9
			% of Families Above Poverty Level	98.8%	6	95.8
Affordable Housing	79	0.00	Median Home Value	$500,001	79	0.0
			Median Rent	$1,001	77	0.0
Crime	N/A	N/A	Violent Crimes per 10,000 Population	N/A	N/A	N/A
			Property Crimes per 10,000 Population	N/A	N/A	N/A
Open Spaces	2	94.05	Population Density (Persons/Sq. Mile)	658	1	100.0
			Average Rooms per Housing Unit	7.5	2	88.1
Education	9	83.70	% High School Enrollment/Completion	97.9%	7	95.3
			% College Graduates	54.3%	13	72.1
Commute	67	34.15	Average Work Commute in Minutes	28	55	50.0
			% Commuting on Public Transportation	4.1%	45	18.3
Community Stability	21	56.65	% Living in Same House as in 1979	38.9%	17	56.5
			% Living in Same County as in 1985	74.9%	40	56.8

Composite: *Rank* 14 / 83 *Score* 58.20   **SAN CARLOS**

CATEGORY	RANK	SCORE	STATISTIC	VALUE	RANK	SCORE
Economics	17	61.25	Median Household Income	$54,658	19	29.7
			% of Families Above Poverty Level	98.3%	13	92.8
Affordable Housing	66	29.40	Median Home Value	$402,000	67	25.6
			Median Rent	$810	59	33.2
Crime	23	82.60	Violent Crimes per 10,000 Population	36	31	89.2
			Property Crimes per 10,000 Population	338	15	76.0
Open Spaces	43	54.30	Population Density (Persons/Sq. Mile)	4648	52	65.7
			Average Rooms per Housing Unit	5.6	18	42.9
Education	25	63.90	% High School Enrollment/Completion	95.2%	24	86.3
			% College Graduates	35.8%	28	41.5
Commute	48	44.15	Average Work Commute in Minutes	24	25	70.0
			% Commuting on Public Transportation	4.1%	45	18.3
Community Stability	11	71.80	% Living in Same House as in 1979	43.3%	11	65.8
			% Living in Same County as in 1985	82.2%	9	77.8

Composite: *Rank* 15 / 83 *Score* 58.07   **MARTINEZ**

CATEGORY	RANK	SCORE	STATISTIC	VALUE	RANK	SCORE
Economics	43	49.30	Median Household Income	$45,964	35	20.9
			% of Families Above Poverty Level	95.8%	47	77.7
Affordable Housing	25	67.10	Median Home Value	$202,200	24	77.7
			Median Rent	$676	23	56.5
Crime	24	82.35	Violent Crimes per 10,000 Population	26	20	92.8
			Property Crimes per 10,000 Population	380	25	71.9
Open Spaces	28	59.60	Population Density (Persons/Sq. Mile)	2860	24	81.1
			Average Rooms per Housing Unit	5.4	32	38.1
Education	35	57.00	% High School Enrollment/Completion	94.3%	36	83.3
			% College Graduates	29.3%	40	30.7
Commute	51	41.80	Average Work Commute in Minutes	27	47	55.0
			% Commuting on Public Transportation	6.3%	35	28.6
Community Stability	40	49.35	% Living in Same House as in 1979	27.7%	53	33.0
			% Living in Same County as in 1985	78.0%	22	65.7

Metropolitan Area Suburb Rankings
SAN FRANCISCO-OAKLAND-SAN JOSE

Composite: Rank 16 / 83   Score 58.06   SAN ANSELMO

CATEGORY	RANK	SCORE	STATISTIC	VALUE	RANK	SCORE
Economics	54	44.50	Median Household Income	$44,770	41	19.7
			% of Families Above Poverty Level	94.4%	59	69.3
Affordable Housing	60	40.00	Median Home Value	$334,000	59	43.3
			Median Rent	$790	55	36.7
Crime	22	82.70	Violent Crimes per 10,000 Population	32	25	90.6
			Property Crimes per 10,000 Population	351	17	74.8
Open Spaces	48	52.50	Population Density (Persons/Sq. Mile)	4224	50	69.3
			Average Rooms per Housing Unit	5.3	39	35.7
Education	19	75.00	% High School Enrollment/Completion	96.3%	19	90.0
			% College Graduates	47.0%	18	60.0
Commute	34	49.35	Average Work Commute in Minutes	30	73	40.0
			% Commuting on Public Transportation	12.7%	11	58.7
Community Stability	16	62.40	% Living in Same House as in 1979	37.8%	21	54.2
			% Living in Same County as in 1985	79.7%	17	70.6

Composite: Rank 17 / 83   Score 57.93   CASTRO VALLEY

CATEGORY	RANK	SCORE	STATISTIC	VALUE	RANK	SCORE
Economics	29	53.60	Median Household Income	$45,636	38	20.5
			% of Families Above Poverty Level	97.3%	25	86.7
Affordable Housing	30	58.85	Median Home Value	$249,300	38	65.4
			Median Rent	$700	29	52.3
Crime	N/A	N/A	Violent Crimes per 10,000 Population	N/A	N/A	N/A
			Property Crimes per 10,000 Population	N/A	N/A	N/A
Open Spaces	30	58.50	Population Density (Persons/Sq. Mile)	3667	44	74.1
			Average Rooms per Housing Unit	5.6	18	42.9
Education	40	54.25	% High School Enrollment/Completion	95.0%	28	85.7
			% College Graduates	24.5%	48	22.8
Commute	47	44.25	Average Work Commute in Minutes	25	36	65.0
			% Commuting on Public Transportation	5.2%	38	23.5
Community Stability	7	78.15	% Living in Same House as in 1979	42.8%	12	64.7
			% Living in Same County as in 1985	87.0%	4	91.6

Composite: Rank 18 / 83   Score 57.36   DIXON

CATEGORY	RANK	SCORE	STATISTIC	VALUE	RANK	SCORE
Economics	59	41.85	Median Household Income	$36,710	63	11.4
			% of Families Above Poverty Level	94.9%	54	72.3
Affordable Housing	2	86.80	Median Home Value	$140,600	6	93.8
			Median Rent	$542	2	79.8
Crime	34	78.00	Violent Crimes per 10,000 Population	29	23	91.7
			Property Crimes per 10,000 Population	458	38	64.3
Open Spaces	23	61.30	Population Density (Persons/Sq. Mile)	2738	21	82.1
			Average Rooms per Housing Unit	5.5	27	40.5
Education	63	41.05	% High School Enrollment/Completion	90.2%	58	69.7
			% College Graduates	18.2%	65	12.4
Commute	60	37.50	Average Work Commute in Minutes	23	21	75.0
			% Commuting on Public Transportation	0.2%	83	0.0
Community Stability	23	55.05	% Living in Same House as in 1979	33.3%	36	44.7
			% Living in Same County as in 1985	77.9%	25	65.4

Metropolitan Area Suburb Rankings
SAN FRANCISCO-OAKLAND-SAN JOSE

Composite: *Rank* 19 / 83 *Score* 57.20   **PALO ALTO**

CATEGORY	RANK	SCORE	STATISTIC	VALUE	RANK	SCORE
Economics	18	61.00	Median Household Income	$55,333	18	30.4
			% of Families Above Poverty Level	98.1%	15	91.6
Affordable Housing	73	18.70	Median Home Value	$456,800	76	11.3
			Median Rent	$851	66	26.1
Crime	42	72.45	Violent Crimes per 10,000 Population	28	22	92.1
			Property Crimes per 10,000 Population	575	53	52.8
Open Spaces	31	58.20	Population Density (Persons/Sq. Mile)	2360	16	85.4
			Average Rooms per Housing Unit	5.1	49	31.0
Education	4	87.70	% High School Enrollment/Completion	94.9%	29	85.3
			% College Graduates	65.2%	3	90.1
Commute	24	54.05	Average Work Commute in Minutes	19	2	95.0
			% Commuting on Public Transportation	3.0%	58	13.1
Community Stability	42	48.30	% Living in Same House as in 1979	38.8%	18	56.3
			% Living in Same County as in 1985	69.2%	65	40.3

Composite: *Rank* 20 / 83 *Score* 56.96   **BELMONT**

CATEGORY	RANK	SCORE	STATISTIC	VALUE	RANK	SCORE
Economics	23	56.00	Median Household Income	$50,859	23	25.9
			% of Families Above Poverty Level	97.2%	27	86.1
Affordable Housing	63	34.90	Median Home Value	$410,500	70	23.4
			Median Rent	$734	39	46.4
Crime	12	87.60	Violent Crimes per 10,000 Population	20	14	94.9
			Property Crimes per 10,000 Population	294	13	80.3
Open Spaces	56	46.55	Population Density (Persons/Sq. Mile)	5327	59	59.8
			Average Rooms per Housing Unit	5.2	45	33.3
Education	22	67.20	% High School Enrollment/Completion	96.7%	14	91.3
			% College Graduates	36.8%	27	43.1
Commute	43	45.80	Average Work Commute in Minutes	24	25	70.0
			% Commuting on Public Transportation	4.8%	40	21.6
Community Stability	18	60.65	% Living in Same House as in 1979	38.3%	20	55.3
			% Living in Same County as in 1985	78.1%	21	66.0

Composite: *Rank* 21 / 83 *Score* 56.56   **SAN LEANDRO**

CATEGORY	RANK	SCORE	STATISTIC	VALUE	RANK	SCORE
Economics	49	46.75	Median Household Income	$35,681	68	10.4
			% of Families Above Poverty Level	96.7%	34	83.1
Affordable Housing	18	70.50	Median Home Value	$193,500	22	80.0
			Median Rent	$650	19	61.0
Crime	56	62.95	Violent Crimes per 10,000 Population	73	56	75.8
			Property Crimes per 10,000 Population	603	57	50.1
Open Spaces	62	42.35	Population Density (Persons/Sq. Mile)	5203	57	60.9
			Average Rooms per Housing Unit	4.8	57	23.8
Education	61	42.25	% High School Enrollment/Completion	91.6%	47	74.3
			% College Graduates	16.9%	68	10.2
Commute	14	57.30	Average Work Commute in Minutes	24	25	70.0
			% Commuting on Public Transportation	9.7%	19	44.6
Community Stability	9	73.85	% Living in Same House as in 1979	42.0%	14	63.0
			% Living in Same County as in 1985	84.6%	7	84.7

Metropolitan Area Suburb Rankings
SAN FRANCISCO-OAKLAND-SAN JOSE

Composite: *Rank* 22 / 83 *Score* 56.32   **PACIFICA**

CATEGORY	RANK	SCORE	STATISTIC	VALUE	RANK	SCORE
Economics	30	53.10	Median Household Income	$47,533	28	22.5
			% of Families Above Poverty Level	96.8%	33	83.7
Affordable Housing	51	44.65	Median Home Value	$266,000	45	61.1
			Median Rent	$839	64	28.2
Crime	13	86.80	Violent Crimes per 10,000 Population	35	30	89.5
			Property Crimes per 10,000 Population	256	10	84.1
Open Spaces	38	56.65	Population Density (Persons/Sq. Mile)	2981	29	80.0
			Average Rooms per Housing Unit	5.2	45	33.3
Education	47	49.85	% High School Enrollment/Completion	93.2%	42	79.7
			% College Graduates	22.8%	54	20.0
Commute	45	45.20	Average Work Commute in Minutes	28	55	50.0
			% Commuting on Public Transportation	8.8%	25	40.4
Community Stability	19	58.00	% Living in Same House as in 1979	38.4%	19	55.5
			% Living in Same County as in 1985	76.2%	37	60.5

Composite: *Rank* 23 / 83 *Score* 56.24   **CUPERTINO**

CATEGORY	RANK	SCORE	STATISTIC	VALUE	RANK	SCORE
Economics	10	65.10	Median Household Income	$64,587	10	39.8
			% of Families Above Poverty Level	97.9%	17	90.4
Affordable Housing	75	16.10	Median Home Value	$406,000	68	24.5
			Median Rent	$957	74	7.7
Crime	26	80.60	Violent Crimes per 10,000 Population	34	28	89.9
			Property Crimes per 10,000 Population	386	27	71.3
Open Spaces	33	57.50	Population Density (Persons/Sq. Mile)	3908	48	72.1
			Average Rooms per Housing Unit	5.6	18	42.9
Education	13	80.05	% High School Enrollment/Completion	96.8%	13	91.7
			% College Graduates	52.1%	14	68.4
Commute	49	43.75	Average Work Commute in Minutes	22	15	80.0
			% Commuting on Public Transportation	1.8%	73	7.5
Community Stability	37	50.60	% Living in Same House as in 1979	34.0%	33	46.2
			% Living in Same County as in 1985	74.3%	45	55.0

Composite: *Rank* 24 / 83 *Score* 55.74   **NOVATO**

CATEGORY	RANK	SCORE	STATISTIC	VALUE	RANK	SCORE
Economics	27	54.40	Median Household Income	$45,890	36	20.8
			% of Families Above Poverty Level	97.5%	22	88.0
Affordable Housing	50	44.75	Median Home Value	$278,800	52	57.7
			Median Rent	$818	61	31.8
Crime	14	86.55	Violent Crimes per 10,000 Population	30	24	91.3
			Property Crimes per 10,000 Population	279	12	81.8
Open Spaces	17	65.65	Population Density (Persons/Sq. Mile)	1726	8	90.8
			Average Rooms per Housing Unit	5.5	27	40.5
Education	33	59.45	% High School Enrollment/Completion	94.5%	34	84.0
			% College Graduates	31.8%	34	34.9
Commute	56	38.55	Average Work Commute in Minutes	30	73	40.0
			% Commuting on Public Transportation	8.1%	28	37.1
Community Stability	59	40.85	% Living in Same House as in 1979	30.2%	45	38.2
			% Living in Same County as in 1985	70.3%	57	43.5

Metropolitan Area Suburb Rankings
SAN FRANCISCO-OAKLAND-SAN JOSE

Composite: Rank 25 / 83 *Score* 55.71   **LIVERMORE**

CATEGORY	RANK	SCORE	STATISTIC	VALUE	RANK	SCORE
Economics	39	50.30	Median Household Income	$49,149	27	24.1
			% of Families Above Poverty Level	95.6%	48	76.5
Affordable Housing	34	57.70	Median Home Value	$217,100	28	73.8
			Median Rent	$762	46	41.6
Crime	38	76.05	Violent Crimes per 10,000 Population	42	40	87.0
			Property Crimes per 10,000 Population	450	35	65.1
Open Spaces	22	61.85	Population Density (Persons/Sq. Mile)	2890	26	80.8
			Average Rooms per Housing Unit	5.6	18	42.9
Education	36	56.85	% High School Enrollment/Completion	95.2%	24	86.3
			% College Graduates	27.3%	43	27.4
Commute	62	35.80	Average Work Commute in Minutes	25	36	65.0
			% Commuting on Public Transportation	1.6%	76	6.6
Community Stability	35	51.40	% Living in Same House as in 1979	31.4%	41	40.8
			% Living in Same County as in 1985	76.7%	31	62.0

Composite: Rank 26 / 83 *Score* 55.65   **ALBANY**

CATEGORY	RANK	SCORE	STATISTIC	VALUE	RANK	SCORE
Economics	64	38.20	Median Household Income	$34,836	72	9.5
			% of Families Above Poverty Level	94.0%	62	66.9
Affordable Housing	28	63.65	Median Home Value	$239,600	35	68.0
			Median Rent	$660	21	59.3
Crime	33	78.20	Violent Crimes per 10,000 Population	40	37	87.7
			Property Crimes per 10,000 Population	413	30	68.7
Open Spaces	77	19.90	Population Density (Persons/Sq. Mile)	9600	79	23.1
			Average Rooms per Housing Unit	4.5	74	16.7
Education	12	80.15	% High School Enrollment/Completion	95.2%	24	86.3
			% College Graduates	55.5%	11	74.0
Commute	2	75.55	Average Work Commute in Minutes	26	42	60.0
			% Commuting on Public Transportation	19.6%	2	91.1
Community Stability	67	33.90	% Living in Same House as in 1979	33.4%	35	45.0
			% Living in Same County as in 1985	63.1%	77	22.8

Composite: Rank 27 / 83 *Score* 55.64   **MILLBRAE**

CATEGORY	RANK	SCORE	STATISTIC	VALUE	RANK	SCORE
Economics	41	49.90	Median Household Income	$45,999	34	20.9
			% of Families Above Poverty Level	96.0%	44	78.9
Affordable Housing	68	27.55	Median Home Value	$397,200	66	26.8
			Median Rent	$838	63	28.3
Crime	18	84.00	Violent Crimes per 10,000 Population	24	18	93.5
			Property Crimes per 10,000 Population	354	19	74.5
Open Spaces	58	44.55	Population Density (Persons/Sq. Mile)	6354	69	51.0
			Average Rooms per Housing Unit	5.4	32	38.1
Education	38	55.60	% High School Enrollment/Completion	95.9%	20	88.7
			% College Graduates	24.3%	50	22.5
Commute	23	54.25	Average Work Commute in Minutes	21	9	85.0
			% Commuting on Public Transportation	5.2%	38	23.5
Community Stability	10	73.65	% Living in Same House as in 1979	48.1%	9	75.8
			% Living in Same County as in 1985	80.0%	16	71.5

Metropolitan Area Suburb Rankings
SAN FRANCISCO-OAKLAND-SAN JOSE

Composite: *Rank* 28 / 83 *Score* 54.88   **SAN LORENZO**

CATEGORY	RANK	SCORE	STATISTIC	VALUE	RANK	SCORE
Economics	38	50.95	Median Household Income	$41,011	53	15.8
			% of Families Above Poverty Level	97.2%	27	86.1
Affordable Housing	32	58.45	Median Home Value	$187,300	19	81.6
			Median Rent	$798	58	35.3
Crime	N/A	N/A	Violent Crimes per 10,000 Population	N/A	N/A	N/A
			Property Crimes per 10,000 Population	N/A	N/A	N/A
Open Spaces	66	39.00	Population Density (Persons/Sq. Mile)	8206	75	35.1
			Average Rooms per Housing Unit	5.6	18	42.9
Education	69	37.85	% High School Enrollment/Completion	90.8%	53	71.7
			% College Graduates	13.1%	77	4.0
Commute	44	45.40	Average Work Commute in Minutes	25	36	65.0
			% Commuting on Public Transportation	5.7%	36	25.8
Community Stability	1	97.60	% Living in Same House as in 1979	57.3%	3	95.2
			% Living in Same County as in 1985	89.9%	1	100.0

Composite: *Rank* 29 / 83 *Score* 54.70   **SOUTH SAN FRANCISCO**

CATEGORY	RANK	SCORE	STATISTIC	VALUE	RANK	SCORE
Economics	52	46.25	Median Household Income	$42,920	44	17.8
			% of Families Above Poverty Level	95.3%	51	74.7
Affordable Housing	40	54.40	Median Home Value	$269,900	48	60.1
			Median Rent	$721	35	48.7
Crime	27	79.35	Violent Crimes per 10,000 Population	33	27	90.3
			Property Crimes per 10,000 Population	416	31	68.4
Open Spaces	67	38.70	Population Density (Persons/Sq. Mile)	6059	64	53.6
			Average Rooms per Housing Unit	4.8	57	23.8
Education	60	42.80	% High School Enrollment/Completion	90.5%	54	70.7
			% College Graduates	19.7%	61	14.9
Commute	15	57.05	Average Work Commute in Minutes	24	25	70.0
			% Commuting on Public Transportation	9.6%	20	44.1
Community Stability	13	64.35	% Living in Same House as in 1979	41.2%	15	61.3
			% Living in Same County as in 1985	78.6%	19	67.4

Composite: *Rank* 30 / 83 *Score* 54.69   **BENICIA**

CATEGORY	RANK	SCORE	STATISTIC	VALUE	RANK	SCORE
Economics	31	52.65	Median Household Income	$49,660	26	24.6
			% of Families Above Poverty Level	96.3%	37	80.7
Affordable Housing	24	67.40	Median Home Value	$202,800	25	77.6
			Median Rent	$672	22	57.2
Crime	18	84.00	Violent Crimes per 10,000 Population	24	18	93.5
			Property Crimes per 10,000 Population	354	19	74.5
Open Spaces	15	66.05	Population Density (Persons/Sq. Mile)	1911	11	89.2
			Average Rooms per Housing Unit	5.6	18	42.9
Education	28	63.45	% High School Enrollment/Completion	96.5%	17	90.7
			% College Graduates	32.6%	33	36.2
Commute	78	27.05	Average Work Commute in Minutes	30	73	40.0
			% Commuting on Public Transportation	3.2%	56	14.1
Community Stability	76	22.25	% Living in Same House as in 1979	21.5%	77	20.0
			% Living in Same County as in 1985	63.7%	75	24.5

Metropolitan Area Suburb Rankings
SAN FRANCISCO-OAKLAND-SAN JOSE

Composite: *Rank* 31 / 83 *Score* 54.54 **PLEASANTON**

CATEGORY	RANK	SCORE	STATISTIC	VALUE	RANK	SCORE
Economics	13	64.30	Median Household Income	$59,458	13	34.6
			% of Families Above Poverty Level	98.5%	9	94.0
Affordable Housing	58	40.95	Median Home Value	$296,100	56	53.2
			Median Rent	$836	62	28.7
Crime	16	85.50	Violent Crimes per 10,000 Population	19	12	95.3
			Property Crimes per 10,000 Population	341	16	75.7
Open Spaces	14	66.80	Population Density (Persons/Sq. Mile)	3118	33	78.8
			Average Rooms per Housing Unit	6.1	10	54.8
Education	24	64.40	% High School Enrollment/Completion	94.8%	31	85.0
			% College Graduates	37.2%	25	43.8
Commute	73	31.00	Average Work Commute in Minutes	27	47	55.0
			% Commuting on Public Transportation	1.7%	74	7.0
Community Stability	73	28.85	% Living in Same House as in 1979	25.2%	65	27.7
			% Living in Same County as in 1985	65.6%	69	30.0

Composite: *Rank* 32 / 83 *Score* 54.44 **NAPA**

CATEGORY	RANK	SCORE	STATISTIC	VALUE	RANK	SCORE
Economics	60	40.95	Median Household Income	$35,479	69	10.2
			% of Families Above Poverty Level	94.8%	56	71.7
Affordable Housing	16	73.85	Median Home Value	$174,100	15	85.1
			Median Rent	$641	17	62.6
Crime	41	72.85	Violent Crimes per 10,000 Population	51	44	83.8
			Property Crimes per 10,000 Population	482	44	61.9
Open Spaces	46	53.05	Population Density (Persons/Sq. Mile)	3549	42	75.1
			Average Rooms per Housing Unit	5.1	49	31.0
Education	62	41.15	% High School Enrollment/Completion	89.8%	61	68.3
			% College Graduates	19.2%	62	14.0
Commute	42	46.00	Average Work Commute in Minutes	21	9	85.0
			% Commuting on Public Transportation	1.7%	74	7.0
Community Stability	29	53.20	% Living in Same House as in 1979	33.3%	36	44.7
			% Living in Same County as in 1985	76.6%	34	61.7

Composite: *Rank* 33 / 83 *Score* 54.36 **PINOLE**

CATEGORY	RANK	SCORE	STATISTIC	VALUE	RANK	SCORE
Economics	28	54.35	Median Household Income	$45,820	37	20.7
			% of Families Above Poverty Level	97.5%	22	88.0
Affordable Housing	29	62.50	Median Home Value	$192,400	20	80.3
			Median Rent	$744	42	44.7
Crime	60	59.20	Violent Crimes per 10,000 Population	90	64	69.7
			Property Crimes per 10,000 Population	617	59	48.7
Open Spaces	24	60.85	Population Density (Persons/Sq. Mile)	3393	38	76.5
			Average Rooms per Housing Unit	5.7	16	45.2
Education	45	50.50	% High School Enrollment/Completion	94.8%	31	85.0
			% College Graduates	20.4%	60	16.0
Commute	74	30.20	Average Work Commute in Minutes	31	78	35.0
			% Commuting on Public Transportation	5.6%	37	25.4
Community Stability	15	62.90	% Living in Same House as in 1979	40.3%	16	59.5
			% Living in Same County as in 1985	78.2%	20	66.3

Metropolitan Area Suburb Rankings
SAN FRANCISCO-OAKLAND-SAN JOSE

Composite: **Rank** 34 / 83 *Score* 53.97   **FREMONT**

CATEGORY	RANK	SCORE	STATISTIC	VALUE	RANK	SCORE
Economics	24	55.55	Median Household Income	$51,231	22	26.2
			% of Families Above Poverty Level	97.0%	30	84.9
Affordable Housing	48	48.80	Median Home Value	$263,400	44	61.8
			Median Rent	$795	57	35.8
Crime	25	81.35	Violent Crimes per 10,000 Population	36	31	89.2
			Property Crimes per 10,000 Population	364	21	73.5
Open Spaces	21	62.20	Population Density (Persons/Sq. Mile)	2250	13	86.3
			Average Rooms per Housing Unit	5.4	32	38.1
Education	39	54.70	% High School Enrollment/Completion	92.6%	44	77.7
			% College Graduates	29.9%	39	31.7
Commute	57	38.30	Average Work Commute in Minutes	27	47	55.0
			% Commuting on Public Transportation	4.8%	40	21.6
Community Stability	64	36.90	% Living in Same House as in 1979	26.4%	60	30.3
			% Living in Same County as in 1985	70.3%	57	43.5

Composite: **Rank** 35 / 83 *Score* 53.84   **PETALUMA**

CATEGORY	RANK	SCORE	STATISTIC	VALUE	RANK	SCORE
Economics	36	51.20	Median Household Income	$40,926	56	15.7
			% of Families Above Poverty Level	97.3%	25	86.7
Affordable Housing	26	64.00	Median Home Value	$204,300	26	77.2
			Median Rent	$709	31	50.8
Crime	28	79.00	Violent Crimes per 10,000 Population	41	38	87.4
			Property Crimes per 10,000 Population	393	28	70.6
Open Spaces	32	58.00	Population Density (Persons/Sq. Mile)	3508	40	75.5
			Average Rooms per Housing Unit	5.5	27	40.5
Education	52	47.95	% High School Enrollment/Completion	91.3%	48	73.3
			% College Graduates	24.4%	49	22.6
Commute	70	32.35	Average Work Commute in Minutes	29	66	45.0
			% Commuting on Public Transportation	4.4%	43	19.7
Community Stability	53	44.35	% Living in Same House as in 1979	31.2%	42	40.3
			% Living in Same County as in 1985	72.0%	52	48.4

Composite: **Rank** 35 / 83 *Score* 53.84   **PLEASANT HILL**

CATEGORY	RANK	SCORE	STATISTIC	VALUE	RANK	SCORE
Economics	22	56.10	Median Household Income	$46,885	30	21.8
			% of Families Above Poverty Level	97.9%	17	90.4
Affordable Housing	37	56.50	Median Home Value	$228,500	32	70.9
			Median Rent	$759	43	42.1
Crime	57	62.35	Violent Crimes per 10,000 Population	54	46	82.7
			Property Crimes per 10,000 Population	686	64	42.0
Open Spaces	51	50.70	Population Density (Persons/Sq. Mile)	4651	53	65.7
			Average Rooms per Housing Unit	5.3	39	35.7
Education	30	61.75	% High School Enrollment/Completion	94.1%	39	82.7
			% College Graduates	35.4%	29	40.8
Commute	33	49.90	Average Work Commute in Minutes	28	55	50.0
			% Commuting on Public Transportation	10.8%	16	49.8
Community Stability	61	39.55	% Living in Same House as in 1979	28.5%	52	34.7
			% Living in Same County as in 1985	70.6%	56	44.4

Metropolitan Area Suburb Rankings
SAN FRANCISCO-OAKLAND-SAN JOSE

Composite: *Rank* 37 / 83 *Score* 53.79   **CONCORD**

CATEGORY	RANK	SCORE	STATISTIC	VALUE	RANK	SCORE
Economics	53	45.00	Median Household Income	$41,675	51	16.5
			% of Families Above Poverty Level	95.1%	52	73.5
Affordable Housing	22	68.10	Median Home Value	$193,900	23	79.9
			Median Rent	$677	25	56.3
Crime	52	66.45	Violent Crimes per 10,000 Population	54	46	82.7
			Property Crimes per 10,000 Population	602	56	50.2
Open Spaces	42	54.45	Population Density (Persons/Sq. Mile)	3778	47	73.2
			Average Rooms per Housing Unit	5.3	39	35.7
Education	41	51.60	% High School Enrollment/Completion	92.6%	44	77.7
			% College Graduates	26.1%	46	25.5
Commute	41	46.45	Average Work Commute in Minutes	29	66	45.0
			% Commuting on Public Transportation	10.4%	18	47.9
Community Stability	52	44.45	% Living in Same House as in 1979	30.2%	45	38.2
			% Living in Same County as in 1985	72.8%	48	50.7

Composite: *Rank* 38 / 83 *Score* 53.32   **EAST FOOTHILLS**

CATEGORY	RANK	SCORE	STATISTIC	VALUE	RANK	SCORE
Economics	51	46.50	Median Household Income	$46,339	32	21.3
			% of Families Above Poverty Level	94.8%	56	71.7
Affordable Housing	36	56.70	Median Home Value	$227,000	31	71.3
			Median Rent	$759	43	42.1
Crime	N/A	N/A	Violent Crimes per 10,000 Population	N/A	N/A	N/A
			Property Crimes per 10,000 Population	N/A	N/A	N/A
Open Spaces	40	54.85	Population Density (Persons/Sq. Mile)	4791	55	64.5
			Average Rooms per Housing Unit	5.7	16	45.2
Education	64	41.00	% High School Enrollment/Completion	90.4%	55	70.3
			% College Graduates	17.8%	66	11.7
Commute	66	34.45	Average Work Commute in Minutes	26	42	60.0
			% Commuting on Public Transportation	2.1%	68	8.9
Community Stability	6	86.45	% Living in Same House as in 1979	49.7%	8	79.2
			% Living in Same County as in 1985	87.7%	3	93.7

Composite: *Rank* 39 / 83 *Score* 53.01   **SANTA ROSA**

CATEGORY	RANK	SCORE	STATISTIC	VALUE	RANK	SCORE
Economics	62	39.90	Median Household Income	$35,237	70	9.9
			% of Families Above Poverty Level	94.5%	58	69.9
Affordable Housing	17	71.65	Median Home Value	$192,800	21	80.2
			Median Rent	$638	16	63.1
Crime	51	68.45	Violent Crimes per 10,000 Population	58	49	81.2
			Property Crimes per 10,000 Population	546	51	55.7
Open Spaces	44	53.85	Population Density (Persons/Sq. Mile)	3362	37	76.7
			Average Rooms per Housing Unit	5.1	49	31.0
Education	56	44.40	% High School Enrollment/Completion	87.9%	68	62.0
			% College Graduates	26.9%	45	26.8
Commute	32	50.40	Average Work Commute in Minutes	20	6	90.0
			% Commuting on Public Transportation	2.5%	62	10.8
Community Stability	57	42.45	% Living in Same House as in 1979	26.1%	63	29.6
			% Living in Same County as in 1985	74.4%	41	55.3

Metropolitan Area Suburb Rankings
SAN FRANCISCO-OAKLAND-SAN JOSE

Composite: *Rank* 40 / 83 *Score* 52.98   SUNNYVALE

CATEGORY	RANK	SCORE	STATISTIC	VALUE	RANK	SCORE
Economics	33	52.20	Median Household Income	$46,403	31	21.3
			% of Families Above Poverty Level	96.7%	34	83.1
Affordable Housing	59	40.80	Median Home Value	$332,000	58	43.9
			Median Rent	$784	53	37.7
Crime	21	83.50	Violent Crimes per 10,000 Population	23	16	93.9
			Property Crimes per 10,000 Population	368	22	73.1
Open Spaces	64	39.30	Population Density (Persons/Sq. Mile)	5354	60	59.6
			Average Rooms per Housing Unit	4.6	66	19.0
Education	34	58.45	% High School Enrollment/Completion	91.3%	48	73.3
			% College Graduates	37.1%	26	43.6
Commute	27	53.35	Average Work Commute in Minutes	19	2	95.0
			% Commuting on Public Transportation	2.7%	60	11.7
Community Stability	55	43.25	% Living in Same House as in 1979	29.4%	50	36.6
			% Living in Same County as in 1985	72.5%	51	49.9

Composite: *Rank* 41 / 83 *Score* 52.96   SAN RAFAEL

CATEGORY	RANK	SCORE	STATISTIC	VALUE	RANK	SCORE
Economics	50	46.65	Median Household Income	$41,922	50	16.8
			% of Families Above Poverty Level	95.6%	48	76.5
Affordable Housing	53	44.10	Median Home Value	$342,700	60	41.1
			Median Rent	$730	38	47.1
Crime	50	68.60	Violent Crimes per 10,000 Population	50	43	84.1
			Property Crimes per 10,000 Population	572	52	53.1
Open Spaces	41	54.60	Population Density (Persons/Sq. Mile)	2918	27	80.6
			Average Rooms per Housing Unit	5.0	56	28.6
Education	43	51.25	% High School Enrollment/Completion	86.3%	71	56.7
			% College Graduates	38.4%	24	45.8
Commute	11	59.35	Average Work Commute in Minutes	26	42	60.0
			% Commuting on Public Transportation	12.7%	11	58.7
Community Stability	48	46.20	% Living in Same House as in 1979	33.1%	38	44.3
			% Living in Same County as in 1985	71.9%	54	48.1

Composite: *Rank* 42 / 83 *Score* 52.81   NEWARK

CATEGORY	RANK	SCORE	STATISTIC	VALUE	RANK	SCORE
Economics	34	51.90	Median Household Income	$50,471	24	25.5
			% of Families Above Poverty Level	95.9%	45	78.3
Affordable Housing	41	54.00	Median Home Value	$224,900	30	71.8
			Median Rent	$793	56	36.2
Crime	55	64.30	Violent Crimes per 10,000 Population	56	48	81.9
			Property Crimes per 10,000 Population	638	60	46.7
Open Spaces	26	60.20	Population Density (Persons/Sq. Mile)	2712	19	82.3
			Average Rooms per Housing Unit	5.4	32	38.1
Education	49	48.75	% High School Enrollment/Completion	93.4%	41	80.3
			% College Graduates	21.1%	58	17.2
Commute	64	35.50	Average Work Commute in Minutes	27	47	55.0
			% Commuting on Public Transportation	3.6%	54	16.0
Community Stability	24	55.00	% Living in Same House as in 1979	36.1%	25	50.6
			% Living in Same County as in 1985	75.8%	38	59.4

Metropolitan Area Suburb Rankings
SAN FRANCISCO-OAKLAND-SAN JOSE

Composite: **Rank** 43 / 83 *Score* 52.78   **MILPITAS**

CATEGORY	RANK	SCORE	STATISTIC	VALUE	RANK	SCORE
Economics	20	57.55	Median Household Income	$55,730	17	30.8
			% of Families Above Poverty Level	96.9%	32	84.3
Affordable Housing	54	43.45	Median Home Value	$255,100	40	63.9
			Median Rent	$869	68	23.0
Crime	36	76.65	Violent Crimes per 10,000 Population	38	34	88.4
			Property Crimes per 10,000 Population	452	36	64.9
Open Spaces	45	53.65	Population Density (Persons/Sq. Mile)	3685	46	74.0
			Average Rooms per Housing Unit	5.2	45	33.3
Education	53	46.75	% High School Enrollment/Completion	90.3%	57	70.0
			% College Graduates	24.9%	47	23.5
Commute	46	44.30	Average Work Commute in Minutes	23	21	75.0
			% Commuting on Public Transportation	3.1%	57	13.6
Community Stability	46	47.10	% Living in Same House as in 1979	26.5%	58	30.5
			% Living in Same County as in 1985	77.3%	28	63.7

Composite: **Rank** 44 / 83 *Score* 52.74   **SAN RAMON**

CATEGORY	RANK	SCORE	STATISTIC	VALUE	RANK	SCORE
Economics	9	67.60	Median Household Income	$63,607	11	38.8
			% of Families Above Poverty Level	98.9%	5	96.4
Affordable Housing	65	32.60	Median Home Value	$315,400	57	48.2
			Median Rent	$903	73	17.0
Crime	10	88.60	Violent Crimes per 10,000 Population	12	6	97.8
			Property Crimes per 10,000 Population	304	14	79.4
Open Spaces	13	66.90	Population Density (Persons/Sq. Mile)	3101	32	79.0
			Average Rooms per Housing Unit	6.1	10	54.8
Education	21	71.95	% High School Enrollment/Completion	96.5%	17	90.7
			% College Graduates	42.9%	22	53.2
Commute	72	31.50	Average Work Commute in Minutes	27	47	55.0
			% Commuting on Public Transportation	1.9%	72	8.0
Community Stability	82	10.00	% Living in Same House as in 1979	18.5%	79	13.7
			% Living in Same County as in 1985	57.4%	82	6.3

Composite: **Rank** 45 / 83 *Score* 52.48   **UNION CITY**

CATEGORY	RANK	SCORE	STATISTIC	VALUE	RANK	SCORE
Economics	48	47.10	Median Household Income	$46,988	29	21.9
			% of Families Above Poverty Level	94.9%	54	72.3
Affordable Housing	38	55.65	Median Home Value	$228,900	33	70.8
			Median Rent	$768	50	40.5
Crime	44	72.35	Violent Crimes per 10,000 Population	52	45	83.4
			Property Crimes per 10,000 Population	489	47	61.3
Open Spaces	37	57.15	Population Density (Persons/Sq. Mile)	2867	25	81.0
			Average Rooms per Housing Unit	5.2	45	33.3
Education	55	44.70	% High School Enrollment/Completion	91.2%	50	73.0
			% College Graduates	20.6%	59	16.4
Commute	53	40.95	Average Work Commute in Minutes	28	55	50.0
			% Commuting on Public Transportation	7.0%	31	31.9
Community Stability	39	49.45	% Living in Same House as in 1979	29.7%	48	37.2
			% Living in Same County as in 1985	76.6%	34	61.7

Metropolitan Area Suburb Rankings
SAN FRANCISCO-OAKLAND-SAN JOSE

Composite: *Rank* 46 / 83 *Score* 52.38 BURLINGAME

CATEGORY	RANK	SCORE	STATISTIC	VALUE	RANK	SCORE
Economics	35	51.40	Median Household Income	$42,487	47	17.3
			% of Families Above Poverty Level	97.1%	29	85.5
Affordable Housing	67	28.90	Median Home Value	$461,800	78	10.0
			Median Rent	$726	36	47.8
Crime	35	76.75	Violent Crimes per 10,000 Population	32	25	90.6
			Property Crimes per 10,000 Population	472	41	62.9
Open Spaces	68	37.00	Population Density (Persons/Sq. Mile)	6168	65	52.6
			Average Rooms per Housing Unit	4.7	61	21.4
Education	31	60.35	% High School Enrollment/Completion	94.2%	37	83.0
			% College Graduates	33.5%	32	37.7
Commute	18	55.80	Average Work Commute in Minutes	23	21	75.0
			% Commuting on Public Transportation	8.0%	29	36.6
Community Stability	22	56.45	% Living in Same House as in 1979	35.4%	27	49.2
			% Living in Same County as in 1985	77.3%	28	63.7

Composite: *Rank* 47 / 83 *Score* 52.11 DUBLIN

CATEGORY	RANK	SCORE	STATISTIC	VALUE	RANK	SCORE
Economics	21	56.85	Median Household Income	$53,710	20	28.8
			% of Families Above Poverty Level	97.0%	30	84.9
Affordable Housing	52	44.30	Median Home Value	$238,300	34	68.3
			Median Rent	$884	72	20.3
Crime	9	90.60	Violent Crimes per 10,000 Population	18	11	95.7
			Property Crimes per 10,000 Population	241	9	85.5
Open Spaces	12	67.35	Population Density (Persons/Sq. Mile)	2712	19	82.3
			Average Rooms per Housing Unit	6.0	12	52.4
Education	42	51.55	% High School Enrollment/Completion	93.6%	40	81.0
			% College Graduates	24.1%	52	22.1
Commute	65	34.70	Average Work Commute in Minutes	26	42	60.0
			% Commuting on Public Transportation	2.2%	66	9.4
Community Stability	78	19.40	% Living in Same House as in 1979	24.7%	67	26.7
			% Living in Same County as in 1985	59.4%	81	12.1

Composite: *Rank* 48 / 83 *Score* 52.06 MENLO PARK

CATEGORY	RANK	SCORE	STATISTIC	VALUE	RANK	SCORE
Economics	32	52.50	Median Household Income	$50,468	25	25.5
			% of Families Above Poverty Level	96.1%	42	79.5
Affordable Housing	72	19.20	Median Home Value	$451,500	75	12.7
			Median Rent	$853	67	25.7
Crime	45	72.10	Violent Crimes per 10,000 Population	61	52	80.1
			Property Crimes per 10,000 Population	460	39	64.1
Open Spaces	39	56.35	Population Density (Persons/Sq. Mile)	2783	22	81.7
			Average Rooms per Housing Unit	5.1	49	31.0
Education	27	63.80	% High School Enrollment/Completion	85.7%	72	54.7
			% College Graduates	54.8%	12	72.9
Commute	25	53.90	Average Work Commute in Minutes	20	6	90.0
			% Commuting on Public Transportation	4.0%	49	17.8
Community Stability	47	46.60	% Living in Same House as in 1979	36.6%	23	51.7
			% Living in Same County as in 1985	69.6%	62	41.5

Metropolitan Area Suburb Rankings
SAN FRANCISCO-OAKLAND-SAN JOSE

Composite: Rank 49 / 83 *Score* 52.05 **SANTA CLARA**

CATEGORY	RANK	SCORE	STATISTIC	VALUE	RANK	SCORE
Economics	40	50.15	Median Household Income	$44,707	42	19.6
			% of Families Above Poverty Level	96.3%	37	80.7
Affordable Housing	47	49.40	Median Home Value	$269,400	47	60.2
			Median Rent	$779	52	38.6
Crime	49	68.95	Violent Crimes per 10,000 Population	46	41	85.6
			Property Crimes per 10,000 Population	581	54	52.3
Open Spaces	65	39.20	Population Density (Persons/Sq. Mile)	5115	56	61.7
			Average Rooms per Housing Unit	4.5	74	16.7
Education	37	56.10	% High School Enrollment/Completion	93.0%	43	79.0
			% College Graduates	30.8%	37	33.2
Commute	28	53.15	Average Work Commute in Minutes	19	2	95.0
			% Commuting on Public Transportation	2.6%	61	11.3
Community Stability	45	47.40	% Living in Same House as in 1979	30.8%	44	39.5
			% Living in Same County as in 1985	74.4%	41	55.3

Composite: Rank 50 / 83 *Score* 51.99 **MORGAN HILL**

CATEGORY	RANK	SCORE	STATISTIC	VALUE	RANK	SCORE
Economics	25	55.20	Median Household Income	$53,480	21	28.5
			% of Families Above Poverty Level	96.5%	36	81.9
Affordable Housing	55	43.30	Median Home Value	$294,700	55	53.6
			Median Rent	$811	60	33.0
Crime	48	71.40	Violent Crimes per 10,000 Population	58	49	81.2
			Property Crimes per 10,000 Population	485	45	61.6
Open Spaces	11	68.00	Population Density (Persons/Sq. Mile)	2287	14	86.0
			Average Rooms per Housing Unit	5.9	13	50.0
Education	49	48.75	% High School Enrollment/Completion	89.9%	60	68.7
			% College Graduates	28.1%	41	28.8
Commute	79	25.40	Average Work Commute in Minutes	30	73	40.0
			% Commuting on Public Transportation	2.5%	62	10.8
Community Stability	33	51.85	% Living in Same House as in 1979	25.3%	64	27.9
			% Living in Same County as in 1985	81.5%	14	75.8

Composite: Rank 51 / 83 *Score* 51.76 **SAN BRUNO**

CATEGORY	RANK	SCORE	STATISTIC	VALUE	RANK	SCORE
Economics	47	48.50	Median Household Income	$42,019	49	16.9
			% of Families Above Poverty Level	96.2%	39	80.1
Affordable Housing	49	47.85	Median Home Value	$291,800	54	54.3
			Median Rent	$763	47	41.4
Crime	38	76.05	Violent Crimes per 10,000 Population	23	16	93.9
			Property Crimes per 10,000 Population	520	48	58.2
Open Spaces	69	36.30	Population Density (Persons/Sq. Mile)	6056	63	53.6
			Average Rooms per Housing Unit	4.6	66	19.0
Education	57	43.90	% High School Enrollment/Completion	90.4%	55	70.3
			% College Graduates	21.3%	57	17.5
Commute	22	54.80	Average Work Commute in Minutes	22	15	80.0
			% Commuting on Public Transportation	6.5%	33	29.6
Community Stability	25	54.95	% Living in Same House as in 1979	34.8%	30	47.9
			% Living in Same County as in 1985	76.7%	31	62.0

Metropolitan Area Suburb Rankings
SAN FRANCISCO-OAKLAND-SAN JOSE

Composite: *Rank* 52 / 83 *Score* 51.71 **LARKSPUR**

CATEGORY	RANK	SCORE	STATISTIC	VALUE	RANK	SCORE
Economics	19	58.90	Median Household Income	$45,304	40	20.2
			% of Families Above Poverty Level	99.1%	4	97.6
Affordable Housing	71	19.40	Median Home Value	$438,600	74	16.0
			Median Rent	$870	69	22.8
Crime	N/A	N/A	Violent Crimes per 10,000 Population	N/A	N/A	N/A
			Property Crimes per 10,000 Population	N/A	N/A	N/A
Open Spaces	53	48.35	Population Density (Persons/Sq. Mile)	3531	41	75.3
			Average Rooms per Housing Unit	4.7	61	21.4
Education	16	78.25	% High School Enrollment/Completion	97.1%	10	92.7
			% College Graduates	49.3%	15	63.8
Commute	12	57.40	Average Work Commute in Minutes	28	55	50.0
			% Commuting on Public Transportation	14.0%	6	64.8
Community Stability	43	47.95	% Living in Same House as in 1979	33.8%	34	45.8
			% Living in Same County as in 1985	72.6%	50	50.1

Composite: *Rank* 53 / 83 *Score* 51.43 **ALAMEDA**

CATEGORY	RANK	SCORE	STATISTIC	VALUE	RANK	SCORE
Economics	61	40.80	Median Household Income	$38,122	61	12.9
			% of Families Above Poverty Level	94.3%	60	68.7
Affordable Housing	33	58.35	Median Home Value	$269,300	46	60.2
			Median Rent	$676	23	56.5
Crime	54	64.85	Violent Crimes per 10,000 Population	64	54	79.1
			Property Crimes per 10,000 Population	598	55	50.6
Open Spaces	72	34.15	Population Density (Persons/Sq. Mile)	7114	73	44.5
			Average Rooms per Housing Unit	4.8	57	23.8
Education	32	60.15	% High School Enrollment/Completion	95.2%	24	86.3
			% College Graduates	31.3%	35	34.0
Commute	4	71.15	Average Work Commute in Minutes	24	25	70.0
			% Commuting on Public Transportation	15.6%	5	72.3
Community Stability	72	30.55	% Living in Same House as in 1979	28.6%	51	34.9
			% Living in Same County as in 1985	64.3%	73	26.2

Composite: *Rank* 54 / 83 *Score* 51.42 **SAN MATEO**

CATEGORY	RANK	SCORE	STATISTIC	VALUE	RANK	SCORE
Economics	46	48.60	Median Household Income	$42,894	45	17.7
			% of Families Above Poverty Level	96.1%	42	79.5
Affordable Housing	61	38.25	Median Home Value	$348,800	62	39.5
			Median Rent	$788	54	37.0
Crime	30	78.35	Violent Crimes per 10,000 Population	38	34	88.4
			Property Crimes per 10,000 Population	417	32	68.3
Open Spaces	74	33.40	Population Density (Persons/Sq. Mile)	7002	72	45.4
			Average Rooms per Housing Unit	4.7	61	21.4
Education	51	48.25	% High School Enrollment/Completion	88.6%	66	64.3
			% College Graduates	30.2%	38	32.2
Commute	17	56.20	Average Work Commute in Minutes	22	15	80.0
			% Commuting on Public Transportation	7.1%	30	32.4
Community Stability	20	56.90	% Living in Same House as in 1979	35.2%	28	48.7
			% Living in Same County as in 1985	77.8%	26	65.1

Metropolitan Area Suburb Rankings
SAN FRANCISCO-OAKLAND-SAN JOSE

Composite: *Rank* 55 / 83   *Score* 51.23   **BERKELEY**

CATEGORY	RANK	SCORE	STATISTIC	VALUE	RANK	SCORE
Economics	75	25.35	Median Household Income	$29,737	78	4.3
			% of Families Above Poverty Level	90.6%	73	46.4
Affordable Housing	7	81.80	Median Home Value	$256,500	41	63.6
			Median Rent	$426	1	100.0
Crime	69	24.60	Violent Crimes per 10,000 Population	148	68	48.7
			Property Crimes per 10,000 Population	1,110	70	0.5
Open Spaces	76	20.10	Population Density (Persons/Sq. Mile)	9824	81	21.2
			Average Rooms per Housing Unit	4.6	66	19.0
Education	8	83.80	% High School Enrollment/Completion	95.8%	22	88.3
			% College Graduates	58.7%	7	79.3
Commute	1	85.00	Average Work Commute in Minutes	24	25	70.0
			% Commuting on Public Transportation	21.5%	1	100.0
Community Stability	63	37.95	% Living in Same House as in 1979	34.4%	32	47.1
			% Living in Same County as in 1985	65.2%	70	28.8

Composite: *Rank* 56 / 83   *Score* 51.07   **FOSTER CITY**

CATEGORY	RANK	SCORE	STATISTIC	VALUE	RANK	SCORE
Economics	12	64.50	Median Household Income	$60,462	12	35.6
			% of Families Above Poverty Level	98.4%	10	93.4
Affordable Housing	77	14.35	Median Home Value	$411,500	71	23.1
			Median Rent	$969	75	5.6
Crime	11	88.20	Violent Crimes per 10,000 Population	26	20	92.8
			Property Crimes per 10,000 Population	261	11	83.6
Open Spaces	63	40.85	Population Density (Persons/Sq. Mile)	7492	74	41.2
			Average Rooms per Housing Unit	5.5	27	40.5
Education	15	79.25	% High School Enrollment/Completion	99.0%	4	99.0
			% College Graduates	46.7%	20	59.5
Commute	55	38.90	Average Work Commute in Minutes	26	42	60.0
			% Commuting on Public Transportation	4.0%	49	17.8
Community Stability	70	31.45	% Living in Same House as in 1979	24.5%	68	26.3
			% Living in Same County as in 1985	67.9%	67	36.6

Composite: *Rank* 57 / 83   *Score* 50.68   **SANTA CRUZ**

CATEGORY	RANK	SCORE	STATISTIC	VALUE	RANK	SCORE
Economics	71	33.05	Median Household Income	$31,857	76	6.5
			% of Families Above Poverty Level	92.8%	67	59.6
Affordable Housing	35	56.90	Median Home Value	$259,800	42	62.7
			Median Rent	$707	30	51.1
Crime	63	56.50	Violent Crimes per 10,000 Population	77	57	74.4
			Property Crimes per 10,000 Population	721	65	38.6
Open Spaces	57	46.50	Population Density (Persons/Sq. Mile)	3679	45	74.0
			Average Rooms per Housing Unit	4.6	66	19.0
Education	29	62.90	% High School Enrollment/Completion	94.9%	29	85.3
			% College Graduates	35.2%	30	40.5
Commute	6	64.55	Average Work Commute in Minutes	21	9	85.0
			% Commuting on Public Transportation	9.6%	20	44.1
Community Stability	66	34.35	% Living in Same House as in 1979	27.3%	54	32.1
			% Living in Same County as in 1985	67.9%	67	36.6

Metropolitan Area Suburb Rankings
SAN FRANCISCO-OAKLAND-SAN JOSE

Composite: **Rank** 58 / 83 **Score** 50.44   **CAMPBELL**

CATEGORY	RANK	SCORE	STATISTIC	VALUE	RANK	SCORE
Economics	44	48.70	Median Household Income	$42,489	46	17.3
			% of Families Above Poverty Level	96.2%	39	80.1
Affordable Housing	45	51.80	Median Home Value	$275,200	51	58.7
			Median Rent	$743	41	44.9
Crime	37	76.25	Violent Crimes per 10,000 Population	38	34	88.4
			Property Crimes per 10,000 Population	460	39	64.1
Open Spaces	71	34.70	Population Density (Persons/Sq. Mile)	6427	71	50.4
			Average Rooms per Housing Unit	4.6	66	19.0
Education	46	50.15	% High School Enrollment/Completion	89.3%	62	66.7
			% College Graduates	31.0%	36	33.6
Commute	50	42.90	Average Work Commute in Minutes	23	21	75.0
			% Commuting on Public Transportation	2.5%	62	10.8
Community Stability	41	48.60	% Living in Same House as in 1979	24.8%	66	26.9
			% Living in Same County as in 1985	79.6%	18	70.3

Composite: **Rank** 59 / 83 **Score** 49.70   **HAYWARD**

CATEGORY	RANK	SCORE	STATISTIC	VALUE	RANK	SCORE
Economics	70	34.00	Median Household Income	$36,058	67	10.8
			% of Families Above Poverty Level	92.4%	69	57.2
Affordable Housing	21	68.40	Median Home Value	$184,500	17	82.4
			Median Rent	$688	26	54.4
Crime	61	58.30	Violent Crimes per 10,000 Population	84	62	71.8
			Property Crimes per 10,000 Population	657	61	44.8
Open Spaces	48	52.50	Population Density (Persons/Sq. Mile)	2566	17	83.6
			Average Rooms per Housing Unit	4.7	61	21.4
Education	73	35.05	% High School Enrollment/Completion	87.2%	69	59.7
			% College Graduates	17.0%	67	10.4
Commute	40	46.50	Average Work Commute in Minutes	27	47	55.0
			% Commuting on Public Transportation	8.3%	27	38.0
Community Stability	30	53.15	% Living in Same House as in 1979	32.0%	40	42.0
			% Living in Same County as in 1985	77.5%	27	64.3

Composite: **Rank** 59 / 83 **Score** 49.70   **VACAVILLE**

CATEGORY	RANK	SCORE	STATISTIC	VALUE	RANK	SCORE
Economics	54	44.50	Median Household Income	$40,679	58	15.5
			% of Families Above Poverty Level	95.1%	52	73.5
Affordable Housing	11	78.30	Median Home Value	$147,900	9	91.9
			Median Rent	$629	14	64.7
Crime	28	79.00	Violent Crimes per 10,000 Population	41	38	87.4
			Property Crimes per 10,000 Population	393	28	70.6
Open Spaces	29	59.50	Population Density (Persons/Sq. Mile)	3157	35	78.5
			Average Rooms per Housing Unit	5.5	27	40.5
Education	67	39.75	% High School Enrollment/Completion	90.1%	59	69.3
			% College Graduates	16.9%	68	10.2
Commute	76	27.35	Average Work Commute in Minutes	28	55	50.0
			% Commuting on Public Transportation	1.2%	81	4.7
Community Stability	77	19.50	% Living in Same House as in 1979	22.9%	73	22.9
			% Living in Same County as in 1985	60.8%	79	16.1

Metropolitan Area Suburb Rankings
SAN FRANCISCO-OAKLAND-SAN JOSE

Composite: *Rank* 61 / 83 *Score* 49.52 **HERCULES**

CATEGORY	RANK	SCORE	STATISTIC	VALUE	RANK	SCORE
Economics	15	61.70	Median Household Income	$56,098	15	31.2
			% of Families Above Poverty Level	98.2%	14	92.2
Affordable Housing	62	37.50	Median Home Value	$224,700	29	71.9
			Median Rent	$983	76	3.1
Crime	8	91.35	Violent Crimes per 10,000 Population	17	10	96.0
			Property Crimes per 10,000 Population	229	7	86.7
Open Spaces	18	64.75	Population Density (Persons/Sq. Mile)	3040	30	79.5
			Average Rooms per Housing Unit	5.9	13	50.0
Education	23	65.50	% High School Enrollment/Completion	96.7%	14	91.3
			% College Graduates	34.7%	31	39.7
Commute	82	14.55	Average Work Commute in Minutes	38	83	0.0
			% Commuting on Public Transportation	6.4%	34	29.1
Community Stability	81	11.30	% Living in Same House as in 1979	13.7%	82	3.6
			% Living in Same County as in 1985	61.8%	78	19.0

Composite: *Rank* 62 / 83 *Score* 49.20 **ANTIOCH**

CATEGORY	RANK	SCORE	STATISTIC	VALUE	RANK	SCORE
Economics	67	34.95	Median Household Income	$40,936	55	15.7
			% of Families Above Poverty Level	91.9%	71	54.2
Affordable Housing	12	76.80	Median Home Value	$155,600	10	89.9
			Median Rent	$635	15	63.7
Crime	59	59.85	Violent Crimes per 10,000 Population	90	64	69.7
			Property Crimes per 10,000 Population	604	58	50.0
Open Spaces	25	60.60	Population Density (Persons/Sq. Mile)	3176	36	78.3
			Average Rooms per Housing Unit	5.6	18	42.9
Education	68	39.45	% High School Enrollment/Completion	90.9%	51	72.0
			% College Graduates	14.9%	74	6.9
Commute	77	27.20	Average Work Commute in Minutes	29	66	45.0
			% Commuting on Public Transportation	2.2%	66	9.4
Community Stability	50	45.55	% Living in Same House as in 1979	26.4%	60	30.3
			% Living in Same County as in 1985	76.3%	36	60.8

Composite: *Rank* 63 / 83 *Score* 49.11 **FAIRFIELD**

CATEGORY	RANK	SCORE	STATISTIC	VALUE	RANK	SCORE
Economics	63	38.35	Median Household Income	$36,886	62	11.6
			% of Families Above Poverty Level	93.7%	64	65.1
Affordable Housing	3	85.20	Median Home Value	$139,300	4	94.2
			Median Rent	$563	3	76.2
Crime	61	58.30	Violent Crimes per 10,000 Population	80	59	73.3
			Property Crimes per 10,000 Population	672	63	43.3
Open Spaces	20	62.60	Population Density (Persons/Sq. Mile)	2154	12	87.1
			Average Rooms per Housing Unit	5.4	32	38.1
Education	66	39.90	% High School Enrollment/Completion	90.9%	51	72.0
			% College Graduates	15.4%	72	7.8
Commute	62	35.80	Average Work Commute in Minutes	25	36	65.0
			% Commuting on Public Transportation	1.6%	76	6.6
Community Stability	75	23.60	% Living in Same House as in 1979	23.4%	71	23.9
			% Living in Same County as in 1985	63.3%	76	23.3

Metropolitan Area Suburb Rankings
SAN FRANCISCO-OAKLAND-SAN JOSE

Composite: *Rank* 64 / 83 *Score* 49.09   **DALY CITY**

CATEGORY	RANK	SCORE	STATISTIC	VALUE	RANK	SCORE
Economics	58	41.95	Median Household Income	$41,533	52	16.4
			% of Families Above Poverty Level	94.1%	61	67.5
Affordable Housing	43	53.20	Median Home Value	$270,000	49	60.0
			Median Rent	$734	39	46.4
Crime	30	78.35	Violent Crimes per 10,000 Population	47	42	85.2
			Property Crimes per 10,000 Population	384	26	71.5
Open Spaces	82	9.50	Population Density (Persons/Sq. Mile)	12286	83	0.0
			Average Rooms per Housing Unit	4.6	66	19.0
Education	48	49.00	% High School Enrollment/Completion	92.0%	46	75.7
			% College Graduates	24.2%	51	22.3
Commute	5	70.55	Average Work Commute in Minutes	28	55	50.0
			% Commuting on Public Transportation	19.6%	2	91.1
Community Stability	58	41.10	% Living in Same House as in 1979	37.7%	22	54.0
			% Living in Same County as in 1985	65.0%	71	28.2

Composite: *Rank* 65 / 83 *Score* 48.91   **GILROY**

CATEGORY	RANK	SCORE	STATISTIC	VALUE	RANK	SCORE
Economics	74	27.20	Median Household Income	$40,955	54	15.8
			% of Families Above Poverty Level	89.3%	75	38.6
Affordable Housing	27	63.70	Median Home Value	$239,800	36	67.9
			Median Rent	$659	20	59.5
Crime	53	65.25	Violent Crimes per 10,000 Population	80	59	73.3
			Property Crimes per 10,000 Population	530	49	57.2
Open Spaces	33	57.50	Population Density (Persons/Sq. Mile)	3069	31	79.3
			Average Rooms per Housing Unit	5.3	39	35.7
Education	71	36.40	% High School Enrollment/Completion	88.4%	67	63.7
			% College Graduates	16.2%	70	9.1
Commute	58	37.80	Average Work Commute in Minutes	24	25	70.0
			% Commuting on Public Transportation	1.4%	79	5.6
Community Stability	26	54.50	% Living in Same House as in 1979	27.0%	56	31.5
			% Living in Same County as in 1985	82.1%	10	77.5

Composite: *Rank* 66 / 83 *Score* 48.42   **REDWOOD CITY**

CATEGORY	RANK	SCORE	STATISTIC	VALUE	RANK	SCORE
Economics	57	42.05	Median Household Income	$42,962	43	17.8
			% of Families Above Poverty Level	93.9%	63	66.3
Affordable Housing	56	43.20	Median Home Value	$351,100	63	38.9
			Median Rent	$728	37	47.5
Crime	46	71.85	Violent Crimes per 10,000 Population	69	55	77.3
			Property Crimes per 10,000 Population	436	34	66.4
Open Spaces	54	47.40	Population Density (Persons/Sq. Mile)	3469	39	75.8
			Average Rooms per Housing Unit	4.6	66	19.0
Education	72	35.20	% High School Enrollment/Completion	82.3%	77	43.3
			% College Graduates	27.1%	44	27.1
Commute	36	49.15	Average Work Commute in Minutes	22	15	80.0
			% Commuting on Public Transportation	4.1%	45	18.3
Community Stability	38	50.10	% Living in Same House as in 1979	29.5%	49	36.8
			% Living in Same County as in 1985	77.2%	30	63.4

Metropolitan Area Suburb Rankings
SAN FRANCISCO-OAKLAND-SAN JOSE

Composite: *Rank* 67 / 83 *Score* 46.80 **ROHNERT PARK**

CATEGORY	RANK	SCORE	STATISTIC	VALUE	RANK	SCORE
Economics	56	43.35	Median Household Income	$36,097	66	10.8
			% of Families Above Poverty Level	95.5%	50	75.9
Affordable Housing	23	67.80	Median Home Value	$185,000	18	82.2
			Median Rent	$694	27	53.4
Crime	47	71.60	Violent Crimes per 10,000 Population	60	51	80.5
			Property Crimes per 10,000 Population	474	42	62.7
Open Spaces	59	43.95	Population Density (Persons/Sq. Mile)	5669	62	56.9
			Average Rooms per Housing Unit	5.1	49	31.0
Education	44	50.65	% High School Enrollment/Completion	94.2%	37	83.0
			% College Graduates	21.8%	56	18.3
Commute	68	34.05	Average Work Commute in Minutes	27	47	55.0
			% Commuting on Public Transportation	3.0%	58	13.1
Community Stability	80	16.20	% Living in Same House as in 1979	15.6%	81	7.6
			% Living in Same County as in 1985	63.8%	74	24.8

Composite: *Rank* 68 / 83 *Score* 46.32 **WINDSOR**

CATEGORY	RANK	SCORE	STATISTIC	VALUE	RANK	SCORE
Economics	69	34.60	Median Household Income	$36,702	64	11.4
			% of Families Above Poverty Level	92.5%	68	57.8
Affordable Housing	19	70.25	Median Home Value	$210,200	27	75.6
			Median Rent	$628	12	64.9
Crime	N/A	N/A	Violent Crimes per 10,000 Population	N/A	N/A	N/A
			Property Crimes per 10,000 Population	N/A	N/A	N/A
Open Spaces	16	66.00	Population Density (Persons/Sq. Mile)	1366	4	93.9
			Average Rooms per Housing Unit	5.4	32	38.1
Education	75	32.45	% High School Enrollment/Completion	85.0%	75	52.3
			% College Graduates	18.3%	64	12.6
Commute	54	39.95	Average Work Commute in Minutes	24	25	70.0
			% Commuting on Public Transportation	2.3%	65	9.9
Community Stability	65	34.65	% Living in Same House as in 1979	20.7%	78	18.3
			% Living in Same County as in 1985	72.9%	47	51.0

Composite: *Rank* 69 / 83 *Score* 46.23 **PITTSBURG**

CATEGORY	RANK	SCORE	STATISTIC	VALUE	RANK	SCORE
Economics	72	32.55	Median Household Income	$38,532	60	13.3
			% of Families Above Poverty Level	91.5%	72	51.8
Affordable Housing	10	80.15	Median Home Value	$138,300	3	94.4
			Median Rent	$622	10	65.9
Crime	58	62.00	Violent Crimes per 10,000 Population	95	66	67.9
			Property Crimes per 10,000 Population	542	50	56.1
Open Spaces	52	49.50	Population Density (Persons/Sq. Mile)	4375	51	68.0
			Average Rooms per Housing Unit	5.1	49	31.0
Education	77	30.05	% High School Enrollment/Completion	85.5%	74	54.0
			% College Graduates	14.4%	75	6.1
Commute	80	25.35	Average Work Commute in Minutes	32	80	30.0
			% Commuting on Public Transportation	4.6%	42	20.7
Community Stability	54	44.00	% Living in Same House as in 1979	26.6%	57	30.7
			% Living in Same County as in 1985	75.1%	39	57.3

Metropolitan Area Suburb Rankings
SAN FRANCISCO-OAKLAND-SAN JOSE

Composite: **Rank** 70 / 83 **Score** 46.19   **MOUNTAIN VIEW**

CATEGORY	RANK	SCORE	STATISTIC	VALUE	RANK	SCORE
Economics	44	48.70	Median Household Income	$42,431	48	17.3
			% of Families Above Poverty Level	96.2%	39	80.1
Affordable Housing	57	41.50	Median Home Value	$342,700	60	41.1
			Median Rent	$760	45	41.9
Crime	40	75.45	Violent Crimes per 10,000 Population	37	33	88.8
			Property Crimes per 10,000 Population	480	43	62.1
Open Spaces	73	33.45	Population Density (Persons/Sq. Mile)	5606	61	57.4
			Average Rooms per Housing Unit	4.2	77	9.5
Education	54	46.15	% High School Enrollment/Completion	82.1%	78	42.7
			% College Graduates	40.7%	23	49.6
Commute	10	59.85	Average Work Commute in Minutes	18	1	100.0
			% Commuting on Public Transportation	4.4%	43	19.7
Community Stability	79	18.20	% Living in Same House as in 1979	21.9%	75	20.8
			% Living in Same County as in 1985	60.6%	80	15.6

Composite: **Rank** 71 / 83 *Score* 45.96   **VALLEJO**

CATEGORY	RANK	SCORE	STATISTIC	VALUE	RANK	SCORE
Economics	65	36.35	Median Household Income	$36,605	65	11.3
			% of Families Above Poverty Level	93.1%	66	61.4
Affordable Housing	6	83.70	Median Home Value	$140,600	6	93.8
			Median Rent	$578	6	73.6
Crime	66	47.25	Violent Crimes per 10,000 Population	144	67	50.2
			Property Crimes per 10,000 Population	662	62	44.3
Open Spaces	47	52.80	Population Density (Persons/Sq. Mile)	3614	43	74.6
			Average Rooms per Housing Unit	5.1	49	31.0
Education	65	40.00	% High School Enrollment/Completion	89.1%	64	66.0
			% College Graduates	19.2%	62	14.0
Commute	75	28.70	Average Work Commute in Minutes	30	73	40.0
			% Commuting on Public Transportation	3.9%	52	17.4
Community Stability	68	32.90	% Living in Same House as in 1979	29.9%	47	37.6
			% Living in Same County as in 1985	65.0%	71	28.2

Composite: **Rank** 72 / 83 *Score* 44.26   **ASHLAND**

CATEGORY	RANK	SCORE	STATISTIC	VALUE	RANK	SCORE
Economics	79	18.25	Median Household Income	$27,626	82	2.2
			% of Families Above Poverty Level	88.6%	77	34.3
Affordable Housing	13	76.35	Median Home Value	$163,800	12	87.8
			Median Rent	$628	12	64.9
Crime	N/A	N/A	Violent Crimes per 10,000 Population	N/A	N/A	N/A
			Property Crimes per 10,000 Population	N/A	N/A	N/A
Open Spaces	78	19.10	Population Density (Persons/Sq. Mile)	8952	76	28.7
			Average Rooms per Housing Unit	4.2	77	9.5
Education	59	42.85	% High School Enrollment/Completion	94.8%	31	85.0
			% College Graduates	11.1%	81	0.7
Commute	12	57.40	Average Work Commute in Minutes	25	36	65.0
			% Commuting on Public Transportation	10.8%	16	49.8
Community Stability	34	51.60	% Living in Same House as in 1979	26.3%	62	30.0
			% Living in Same County as in 1985	80.6%	15	73.2

Composite: **Rank** 73 / 83 *Score* 43.57   **LIVE OAK**

CATEGORY	RANK	SCORE	STATISTIC	VALUE	RANK	SCORE
Economics	73	27.75	Median Household Income	$35,031	71	9.7
			% of Families Above Poverty Level	90.5%	74	45.8
Affordable Housing	42	53.65	Median Home Value	$240,900	37	67.6
			Median Rent	$773	51	39.7
Crime	N/A	N/A	Violent Crimes per 10,000 Population	N/A	N/A	N/A
			Property Crimes per 10,000 Population	N/A	N/A	N/A
Open Spaces	61	42.30	Population Density (Persons/Sq. Mile)	4659	54	65.6
			Average Rooms per Housing Unit	4.6	66	19.0
Education	58	43.25	% High School Enrollment/Completion	89.2%	63	66.3
			% College Graduates	22.9%	53	20.2
Commute	31	51.20	Average Work Commute in Minutes	21	9	85.0
			% Commuting on Public Transportation	3.9%	52	17.4
Community Stability	55	43.25	% Living in Same House as in 1979	21.9%	75	20.8
			% Living in Same County as in 1985	78.0%	22	65.7

Composite: **Rank** 74 / 83 *Score* 43.36   **CAPITOLA**

CATEGORY	RANK	SCORE	STATISTIC	VALUE	RANK	SCORE
Economics	68	34.90	Median Household Income	$30,138	77	4.7
			% of Families Above Poverty Level	93.7%	64	65.1
Affordable Housing	46	50.45	Median Home Value	$270,300	50	60.0
			Median Rent	$766	48	40.9
Crime	68	37.00	Violent Crimes per 10,000 Population	78	58	74.0
			Property Crimes per 10,000 Population	1,115	71	0.0
Open Spaces	75	31.75	Population Density (Persons/Sq. Mile)	6281	66	51.6
			Average Rooms per Housing Unit	4.3	76	11.9
Education	25	63.90	% High School Enrollment/Completion	99.3%	1	100.0
			% College Graduates	27.5%	42	27.8
Commute	39	47.30	Average Work Commute in Minutes	22	15	80.0
			% Commuting on Public Transportation	3.3%	55	14.6
Community Stability	62	38.25	% Living in Same House as in 1979	24.3%	69	25.8
			% Living in Same County as in 1985	72.8%	48	50.7

Composite: **Rank** 75 / 83 *Score* 43.14   **RICHMOND**

CATEGORY	RANK	SCORE	STATISTIC	VALUE	RANK	SCORE
Economics	81	14.25	Median Household Income	$32,165	74	6.8
			% of Families Above Poverty Level	86.5%	81	21.7
Affordable Housing	5	84.50	Median Home Value	$142,600	8	93.3
			Median Rent	$566	5	75.7
Crime	71	8.25	Violent Crimes per 10,000 Population	283	71	0.0
			Property Crimes per 10,000 Population	946	69	16.5
Open Spaces	50	50.90	Population Density (Persons/Sq. Mile)	2941	28	80.4
			Average Rooms per Housing Unit	4.7	61	21.4
Education	70	36.85	% High School Enrollment/Completion	85.7%	72	54.7
			% College Graduates	22.2%	55	19.0
Commute	26	53.95	Average Work Commute in Minutes	29	66	45.0
			% Commuting on Public Transportation	13.6%	8	62.9
Community Stability	28	53.30	% Living in Same House as in 1979	36.4%	24	51.3
			% Living in Same County as in 1985	74.4%	41	55.3

Metropolitan Area Suburb Rankings
SAN FRANCISCO-OAKLAND-SAN JOSE

Composite: **Rank** 76 / 83 **Score** 42.98   **OAKLEY**

CATEGORY	RANK	SCORE	STATISTIC	VALUE	RANK	SCORE
Economics	42	49.65	Median Household Income	$46,091	33	21.0
			% of Families Above Poverty Level	95.9%	45	78.3
Affordable Housing	20	68.60	Median Home Value	$164,800	14	87.5
			Median Rent	$715	32	49.7
Crime	N/A	N/A	Violent Crimes per 10,000 Population	N/A	N/A	N/A
			Property Crimes per 10,000 Population	N/A	N/A	N/A
Open Spaces	8	70.95	Population Density (Persons/Sq. Mile)	1320	2	94.3
			Average Rooms per Housing Unit	5.8	15	47.6
Education	76	31.65	% High School Enrollment/Completion	87.0%	70	59.0
			% College Graduates	13.3%	76	4.3
Commute	83	9.25	Average Work Commute in Minutes	36	82	10.0
			% Commuting on Public Transportation	2.0%	70	8.5
Community Stability	74	27.75	% Living in Same House as in 1979	17.7%	80	12.0
			% Living in Same County as in 1985	70.3%	57	43.5

Composite: **Rank** 77 / 83 **Score** 41.19   **WATSONVILLE**

CATEGORY	RANK	SCORE	STATISTIC	VALUE	RANK	SCORE
Economics	76	19.60	Median Household Income	$27,980	81	2.5
			% of Families Above Poverty Level	89.0%	76	36.7
Affordable Housing	15	74.15	Median Home Value	$182,500	16	82.9
			Median Rent	$625	11	65.4
Crime	64	53.75	Violent Crimes per 10,000 Population	84	62	71.8
			Property Crimes per 10,000 Population	750	66	35.7
Open Spaces	70	35.00	Population Density (Persons/Sq. Mile)	5253	58	60.5
			Average Rooms per Housing Unit	4.2	77	9.5
Education	83	0.00	% High School Enrollment/Completion	69.3%	83	0.0
			% College Graduates	10.7%	83	0.0
Commute	30	51.95	Average Work Commute in Minutes	19	2	95.0
			% Commuting on Public Transportation	2.1%	68	8.9
Community Stability	27	53.85	% Living in Same House as in 1979	26.5%	58	30.5
			% Living in Same County as in 1985	82.0%	11	77.2

Composite: **Rank** 78 / 83 **Score** 41.07   **SUISUN CITY**

CATEGORY	RANK	SCORE	STATISTIC	VALUE	RANK	SCORE
Economics	66	35.85	Median Household Income	$40,865	57	15.7
			% of Families Above Poverty Level	92.2%	70	56.0
Affordable Housing	8	81.00	Median Home Value	$139,800	5	94.0
			Median Rent	$610	9	68.0
Crime	43	72.40	Violent Crimes per 10,000 Population	61	52	80.1
			Property Crimes per 10,000 Population	454	37	64.7
Open Spaces	55	46.90	Population Density (Persons/Sq. Mile)	6370	70	50.9
			Average Rooms per Housing Unit	5.6	18	42.9
Education	74	34.60	% High School Enrollment/Completion	89.0%	65	65.7
			% College Graduates	12.8%	78	3.5
Commute	81	16.75	Average Work Commute in Minutes	33	81	25.0
			% Commuting on Public Transportation	2.0%	70	8.5
Community Stability	83	0.00	% Living in Same House as in 1979	12.0%	83	0.0
			% Living in Same County as in 1985	55.2%	83	0.0

Metropolitan Area Suburb Rankings
SAN FRANCISCO-OAKLAND-SAN JOSE

Composite: **Rank** 79 / 83   *Score* 40.41   **EAST PALO ALTO**

CATEGORY	RANK	SCORE	STATISTIC	VALUE	RANK	SCORE
Economics	82	9.15	Median Household Income	$29,206	79	3.8
			% of Families Above Poverty Level	85.3%	82	14.5
Affordable Housing	9	80.75	Median Home Value	$157,900	11	89.3
			Median Rent	$586	7	72.2
Crime	67	43.35	Violent Crimes per 10,000 Population	213	70	25.3
			Property Crimes per 10,000 Population	487	46	61.4
Open Spaces	81	13.25	Population Density (Persons/Sq. Mile)	9206	77	26.5
			Average Rooms per Housing Unit	3.8	83	0.0
Education	78	26.40	% High School Enrollment/Completion	82.7%	76	44.7
			% College Graduates	15.6%	71	8.1
Commute	8	62.45	Average Work Commute in Minutes	21	9	85.0
			% Commuting on Public Transportation	8.7%	26	39.9
Community Stability	44	47.50	% Living in Same House as in 1979	30.9%	43	39.7
			% Living in Same County as in 1985	74.4%	41	55.3

Composite: **Rank** 80 / 83   *Score* 39.59   **WEST PITTSBURG**

CATEGORY	RANK	SCORE	STATISTIC	VALUE	RANK	SCORE
Economics	78	18.55	Median Household Income	$32,322	73	7.0
			% of Families Above Poverty Level	87.9%	79	30.1
Affordable Housing	4	84.65	Median Home Value	$118,200	2	99.7
			Median Rent	$601	8	69.6
Crime	N/A	N/A	Violent Crimes per 10,000 Population	N/A	N/A	N/A
			Property Crimes per 10,000 Population	N/A	N/A	N/A
Open Spaces	36	57.25	Population Density (Persons/Sq. Mile)	1739	9	90.7
			Average Rooms per Housing Unit	4.8	57	23.8
Education	81	12.30	% High School Enrollment/Completion	76.0%	81	22.3
			% College Graduates	12.1%	79	2.3
Commute	69	32.50	Average Work Commute in Minutes	31	78	35.0
			% Commuting on Public Transportation	6.6%	32	30.0
Community Stability	69	32.30	% Living in Same House as in 1979	23.0%	72	23.1
			% Living in Same County as in 1985	69.6%	62	41.5

Composite: **Rank** 81 / 83   *Score* 38.07   **CHERRYLAND**

CATEGORY	RANK	SCORE	STATISTIC	VALUE	RANK	SCORE
Economics	80	14.60	Median Household Income	$28,763	80	3.3
			% of Families Above Poverty Level	87.2%	80	25.9
Affordable Housing	14	75.05	Median Home Value	$164,600	13	87.5
			Median Rent	$641	17	62.6
Crime	N/A	N/A	Violent Crimes per 10,000 Population	N/A	N/A	N/A
			Property Crimes per 10,000 Population	N/A	N/A	N/A
Open Spaces	79	15.55	Population Density (Persons/Sq. Mile)	9500	78	24.0
			Average Rooms per Housing Unit	4.1	80	7.1
Education	79	15.15	% High School Enrollment/Completion	78.3%	79	30.0
			% College Graduates	10.9%	82	0.3
Commute	19	55.65	Average Work Commute in Minutes	24	25	70.0
			% Commuting on Public Transportation	9.0%	23	41.3
Community Stability	31	52.40	% Living in Same House as in 1979	24.3%	69	25.8
			% Living in Same County as in 1985	82.6%	8	79.0

Metropolitan Area Suburb Rankings
SAN FRANCISCO-OAKLAND-SAN JOSE

Composite: Rank 82 / 83 *Score* 32.40   **NORTH FAIR OAKS**

CATEGORY	RANK	SCORE	STATISTIC	VALUE	RANK	SCORE
Economics	77	18.95	Median Household Income	$31,961	75	6.6
			% of Families Above Poverty Level	88.1%	78	31.3
Affordable Housing	39	55.45	Median Home Value	$262,800	43	61.9
			Median Rent	$719	33	49.0
Crime	N/A	N/A	Violent Crimes per 10,000 Population	N/A	N/A	N/A
			Property Crimes per 10,000 Population	N/A	N/A	N/A
Open Spaces	83	5.30	Population Density (Persons/Sq. Mile)	11884	82	3.5
			Average Rooms per Housing Unit	4.1	80	7.1
Education	82	11.65	% High School Enrollment/Completion	74.0%	82	15.7
			% College Graduates	15.3%	73	7.6
Commute	7	62.90	Average Work Commute in Minutes	21	9	85.0
			% Commuting on Public Transportation	8.9%	24	40.8
Community Stability	60	40.15	% Living in Same House as in 1979	27.2%	55	31.9
			% Living in Same County as in 1985	72.0%	52	48.4

Composite: Rank 83 / 83 *Score* 31.57   **SAN PABLO**

CATEGORY	RANK	SCORE	STATISTIC	VALUE	RANK	SCORE
Economics	83	0.00	Median Household Income	$25,479	83	0.0
			% of Families Above Poverty Level	82.9%	83	0.0
Affordable Housing	1	88.00	Median Home Value	$116,900	1	100.0
			Median Rent	$564	4	76.0
Crime	70	23.35	Violent Crimes per 10,000 Population	211	69	26.0
			Property Crimes per 10,000 Population	903	68	20.7
Open Spaces	80	14.55	Population Density (Persons/Sq. Mile)	9733	80	22.0
			Average Rooms per Housing Unit	4.1	80	7.1
Education	80	15.10	% High School Enrollment/Completion	77.9%	80	28.7
			% College Graduates	11.6%	80	1.5
Commute	35	49.25	Average Work Commute in Minutes	29	66	45.0
			% Commuting on Public Transportation	11.6%	14	53.5
Community Stability	71	30.75	% Living in Same House as in 1979	22.1%	74	21.2
			% Living in Same County as in 1985	69.2%	65	40.3

Metropolitan Area Description
SEATTLE-TACOMA

STATE: Washington
COUNTIES: King, Pierce, Snohomish

TOTAL POPULATION: 2,559,164

POPULATION IN SUBURBS: 1,866,241 (72.9%)

POPULATION IN Seattle: 516,259 (20.2%)
POPULATION IN Tacoma: 176,664 (6.9%)

The SEATTLE-TACOMA metropolitan area is located in the westcentral part of Washington along Puget Sound. The suburbs range geographically from North Marysville in the north (40 miles from Seattle), to Elk Plain in the south (44 miles from Seattle), and to Redmond in the east (14 miles from Seattle). The area is growing in population and had an increase of 22.3% between 1980 and 1990. Summer time high temperatures average in the 70's and winter time lows average in the 30's. Computer software maker Microsoft is located in the suburb of Redmond. Aircraft maker Boeing, the area's largest employer, has divisions in Renton and Everett. In 1992, *Fortune* magazine rated the metropolitan area number one for business. Public transportation in the area is provided on buses by METRO Transit.

Mercer Island is the overall highest rated suburb and also has the highest score in education. The top scores in economics and open spaces belong to **Sahalee**. **Parkland** is the suburb with the most affordable housing. The top rated commute belongs to **Tukwila**. Finally, the number one rating in community stability goes to **East Renton Highlands**. Crime rankings were not available for the area.

The highest ranked suburb overall which also has an affordable housing score of at least 50.00 is **Newport Hills**.

The highest ranked suburb in the education category which also has an affordable housing score of at least 50.00 is **Bellevue**.

The county whose suburbs have the highest average overall score is **King County** (56.12).

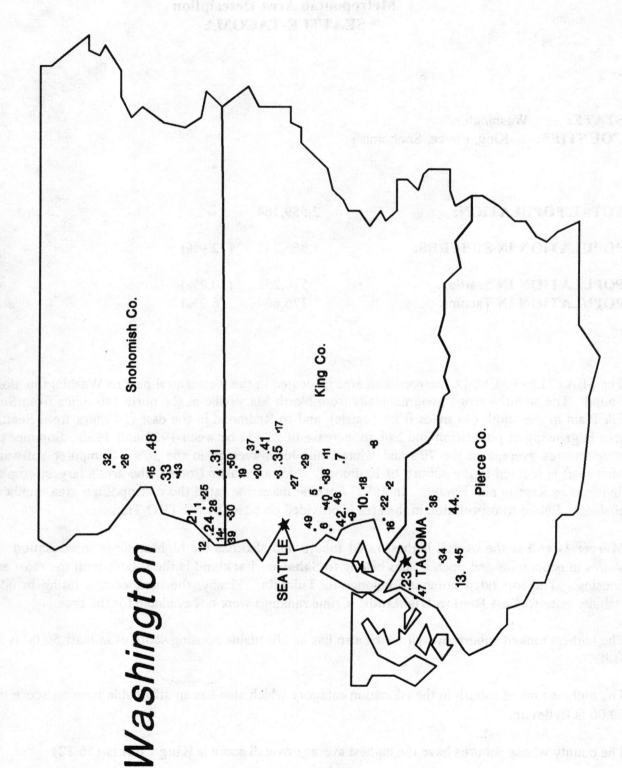

Metropolitan Area Map
SEATTLE-TACOMA

Washington

Metropolitan Area Suburb Alphabetical Index
SEATTLE-TACOMA

SUBURB	PAGE	MAP NO.	STATE	COUNTY	POPU-LATION	RANK
ALDERWOOD MANOR-BOTHELL NORTH	757	1	Washington	Snohomish	22,945	36 / 50
AUBURN	759	2	Washington	King	33,102	40 / 50
BELLEVUE	747	3	Washington	King	86,874	4 / 50
BOTHELL	752	4	Washington	King	12,345	19 / 50
BRYN MAWR-SKYWAY	747	5	Washington	King	12,514	6 / 50
BURIEN	752	6	Washington	King	25,089	20 / 50
CASCADE-FAIRWOOD	749	7	Washington	King	30,107	10 / 50
COVINGTON-SAWYER-WILDERNESS	752	8	Washington	King	24,321	21 / 50
DES MOINES	762	9	Washington	King	17,283	49 / 50
EAST HILL-MERIDIAN	753	10	Washington	King	42,696	23 / 50
EAST RENTON HIGHLANDS	746	11	Washington	King	13,218	3 / 50
EDMONDS	750	12	Washington	Snohomish	30,744	14 / 50
ELK PLAIN	759	13	Washington	Pierce	12,197	41 / 50
ESPERANCE	754	14	Washington	Snohomish	11,236	25 / 50
EVERETT	758	15	Washington	Snohomish	69,961	38 / 50
FEDERAL WAY	758	16	Washington	King	67,554	37 / 50
INGLEWOOD-FINN HILL	749	17	Washington	King	29,132	11 / 50
KENT	761	18	Washington	King	37,960	46 / 50
KINGSGATE	749	19	Washington	King	14,259	12 / 50
KIRKLAND	755	20	Washington	King	40,052	29 / 50
LAKE SERENE-NORTH LYNNWOOD	760	21	Washington	Snohomish	14,290	44 / 50
LAKELAND NORTH	748	22	Washington	King	14,402	7 / 50
LAKEWOOD	761	23	Washington	Pierce	58,412	48 / 50
LYNNWOOD	761	24	Washington	Snohomish	28,695	47 / 50
MARTHA LAKE	751	25	Washington	Snohomish	10,155	17 / 50
MARYSVILLE	760	26	Washington	Snohomish	10,328	43 / 50
MERCER ISLAND	746	27	Washington	King	20,816	1 / 50
MOUNTLAKE TERRACE	758	28	Washington	Snohomish	19,320	39 / 50
NEWPORT HILLS	746	29	Washington	King	14,736	2 / 50
NORTH CITY-RIDGECREST	751	30	Washington	King	13,832	16 / 50
NORTH CREEK-CANYON PARK	756	31	Washington	Snohomish	23,236	33 / 50
NORTH MARYSVILLE	748	32	Washington	Snohomish	18,711	9 / 50
PAINE FIELD-LAKE STICKNEY	762	33	Washington	Snohomish	18,670	50 / 50
PARKLAND	757	34	Washington	Pierce	20,882	35 / 50
PINE LAKE	748	35	Washington	King	13,940	8 / 50
PUYALLUP	756	36	Washington	Pierce	23,875	32 / 50
REDMOND	751	37	Washington	King	35,800	18 / 50
RENTON	754	38	Washington	King	41,688	26 / 50
RICHMOND HIGHLANDS	750	39	Washington	King	26,037	13 / 50
RIVERTON-BOULEVARD PARK	753	40	Washington	King	15,337	24 / 50
SAHALEE	753	41	Washington	King	13,951	22 / 50
SEA-TAC	754	42	Washington	King	22,694	27 / 50
SILVER LAKE-FIRCREST	750	43	Washington	Snohomish	24,474	15 / 50
SOUTH HILL	757	44	Washington	Pierce	12,963	34 / 50
SPANAWAY	760	45	Washington	Pierce	15,001	45 / 50
TUKWILA	755	46	Washington	King	11,874	30 / 50
UNIVERSITY PLACE	755	47	Washington	Pierce	27,701	28 / 50
WEST LAKE STEVENS	756	48	Washington	Snohomish	12,453	31 / 50
WHITE CENTER-SHOREWOOD	759	49	Washington	King	20,531	42 / 50
WOODINVILLE	747	50	Washington	King	23,654	5 / 50

Metropolitan Area Suburb Rankings
SEATTLE-TACOMA

Composite: *Rank* 1 / 50 *Score* 74.10 — MERCER ISLAND

CATEGORY	RANK	SCORE	STATISTIC	VALUE	RANK	SCORE
Economics	2	96.95	Median Household Income	$61,572	1	100.0
			% of Families Above Poverty Level	98.4%	5	93.9
Affordable Housing	48	32.60	Median Home Value	$332,500	50	0.0
			Median Rent	$607	31	65.2
Crime	N/A	N/A	Violent Crimes per 10,000 Population	5	N/A	N/A
			Property Crimes per 10,000 Population	192	N/A	N/A
Open Spaces	13	65.10	Population Density (Persons/Sq. Mile)	3261	32	47.4
			Average Rooms per Housing Unit	7.0	3	82.8
Education	1	95.65	% High School Enrollment/Completion	96.8%	2	91.3
			% College Graduates	60.3%	1	100.0
Commute	9	74.35	Average Work Commute in Minutes	22	5	85.7
			% Commuting on Public Transportation	6.6%	13	63.0
Community Stability	3	79.95	% Living in Same House as in 1979	45.6%	2	98.6
			% Living in Same County as in 1985	79.0%	9	61.3

Composite: *Rank* 2 / 50 *Score* 68.42 — NEWPORT HILLS

CATEGORY	RANK	SCORE	STATISTIC	VALUE	RANK	SCORE
Economics	5	81.95	Median Household Income	$50,632	5	69.2
			% of Families Above Poverty Level	98.5%	3	94.7
Affordable Housing	45	57.85	Median Home Value	$167,200	44	63.4
			Median Rent	$685	46	52.3
Crime	N/A	N/A	Violent Crimes per 10,000 Population	N/A	N/A	N/A
			Property Crimes per 10,000 Population	N/A	N/A	N/A
Open Spaces	12	65.35	Population Density (Persons/Sq. Mile)	2518	26	65.2
			Average Rooms per Housing Unit	6.5	8	65.5
Education	5	72.00	% High School Enrollment/Completion	94.0%	10	76.0
			% College Graduates	43.8%	5	68.0
Commute	12	68.80	Average Work Commute in Minutes	23	12	78.6
			% Commuting on Public Transportation	6.2%	15	59.0
Community Stability	11	64.55	% Living in Same House as in 1979	35.1%	10	68.8
			% Living in Same County as in 1985	78.7%	11	60.3

Composite: *Rank* 3 / 50 *Score* 67.66 — EAST RENTON HIGHLANDS

CATEGORY	RANK	SCORE	STATISTIC	VALUE	RANK	SCORE
Economics	7	77.00	Median Household Income	$47,135	8	59.3
			% of Families Above Poverty Level	98.5%	3	94.7
Affordable Housing	38	65.10	Median Home Value	$120,000	28	81.5
			Median Rent	$707	47	48.7
Crime	N/A	N/A	Violent Crimes per 10,000 Population	N/A	N/A	N/A
			Property Crimes per 10,000 Population	N/A	N/A	N/A
Open Spaces	4	83.55	Population Density (Persons/Sq. Mile)	1288	5	94.7
			Average Rooms per Housing Unit	6.7	6	72.4
Education	29	42.75	% High School Enrollment/Completion	92.2%	24	66.1
			% College Graduates	18.8%	36	19.4
Commute	39	37.55	Average Work Commute in Minutes	26	32	57.1
			% Commuting on Public Transportation	2.1%	40	18.0
Community Stability	1	100.00	% Living in Same House as in 1979	46.1%	1	100.0
			% Living in Same County as in 1985	90.5%	1	100.0

Metropolitan Area Suburb Rankings
SEATTLE-TACOMA

Composite: **Rank** 4 / 50 **Score** 62.48   **BELLEVUE**

CATEGORY	RANK	SCORE	STATISTIC	VALUE	RANK	SCORE
Economics	16	65.10	Median Household Income	$43,800	15	49.9
			% of Families Above Poverty Level	96.6%	20	80.3
Affordable Housing	44	58.95	Median Home Value	$193,800	46	53.2
			Median Rent	$610	32	64.7
Crime	N/A	N/A	Violent Crimes per 10,000 Population	22	N/A	N/A
			Property Crimes per 10,000 Population	536	N/A	N/A
Open Spaces	24	45.75	Population Density (Persons/Sq. Mile)	3290	34	46.7
			Average Rooms per Housing Unit	5.9	19	44.8
Education	3	77.40	% High School Enrollment/Completion	95.3%	7	83.1
			% College Graduates	45.7%	4	71.7
Commute	4	79.95	Average Work Commute in Minutes	21	2	92.9
			% Commuting on Public Transportation	7.0%	8	67.0
Community Stability	23	47.75	% Living in Same House as in 1979	29.1%	21	51.7
			% Living in Same County as in 1985	73.8%	26	43.8

Composite: **Rank** 5 / 50 **Score** 61.53   **WOODINVILLE**

CATEGORY	RANK	SCORE	STATISTIC	VALUE	RANK	SCORE
Economics	4	88.80	Median Household Income	$57,403	4	88.2
			% of Families Above Poverty Level	97.8%	12	89.4
Affordable Housing	47	50.15	Median Home Value	$223,300	47	41.9
			Median Rent	$648	40	58.4
Crime	N/A	N/A	Violent Crimes per 10,000 Population	N/A	N/A	N/A
			Property Crimes per 10,000 Population	N/A	N/A	N/A
Open Spaces	2	90.15	Population Density (Persons/Sq. Mile)	1314	7	94.1
			Average Rooms per Housing Unit	7.1	2	86.2
Education	4	74.95	% High School Enrollment/Completion	95.8%	5	85.8
			% College Graduates	41.8%	6	64.1
Commute	43	35.00	Average Work Commute in Minutes	27	38	50.0
			% Commuting on Public Transportation	2.3%	36	20.0
Community Stability	40	30.15	% Living in Same House as in 1979	19.9%	45	25.6
			% Living in Same County as in 1985	71.1%	36	34.7

Composite: **Rank** 6 / 50 **Score** 61.51   **BRYN MAWR-SKYWAY**

CATEGORY	RANK	SCORE	STATISTIC	VALUE	RANK	SCORE
Economics	31	47.90	Median Household Income	$34,535	31	23.8
			% of Families Above Poverty Level	95.5%	26	72.0
Affordable Housing	18	83.65	Median Home Value	$98,600	13	89.8
			Median Rent	$533	21	77.5
Crime	N/A	N/A	Violent Crimes per 10,000 Population	N/A	N/A	N/A
			Property Crimes per 10,000 Population	N/A	N/A	N/A
Open Spaces	41	29.40	Population Density (Persons/Sq. Mile)	3936	41	31.2
			Average Rooms per Housing Unit	5.4	31	27.6
Education	21	46.95	% High School Enrollment/Completion	93.1%	17	71.0
			% College Graduates	20.6%	29	22.9
Commute	5	77.35	Average Work Commute in Minutes	22	5	85.7
			% Commuting on Public Transportation	7.2%	7	69.0
Community Stability	2	83.80	% Living in Same House as in 1979	40.6%	3	84.4
			% Living in Same County as in 1985	85.5%	2	83.2

Metropolitan Area Suburb Rankings
SEATTLE-TACOMA

Composite: Rank 7 / 50 *Score* 59.95   **LAKELAND NORTH**

CATEGORY	RANK	SCORE	STATISTIC	VALUE	RANK	SCORE
Economics	15	67.25	Median Household Income	$46,410	10	57.2
			% of Families Above Poverty Level	96.2%	23	77.3
Affordable Housing	30	73.05	Median Home Value	$110,100	23	85.3
			Median Rent	$634	38	60.8
Crime	N/A	N/A	Violent Crimes per 10,000 Population	N/A	N/A	N/A
			Property Crimes per 10,000 Population	N/A	N/A	N/A
Open Spaces	9	71.40	Population Density (Persons/Sq. Mile)	2161	16	73.8
			Average Rooms per Housing Unit	6.6	7	69.0
Education	26	44.30	% High School Enrollment/Completion	92.3%	22	66.7
			% College Graduates	20.1%	30	21.9
Commute	44	34.50	Average Work Commute in Minutes	27	38	50.0
			% Commuting on Public Transportation	2.2%	38	19.0
Community Stability	7	69.20	% Living in Same House as in 1979	35.8%	7	70.7
			% Living in Same County as in 1985	80.9%	8	67.7

Composite: Rank 8 / 50 *Score* 58.52   **PINE LAKE**

CATEGORY	RANK	SCORE	STATISTIC	VALUE	RANK	SCORE
Economics	3	96.50	Median Household Income	$59,077	3	93.0
			% of Families Above Poverty Level	99.2%	1	100.0
Affordable Housing	49	31.85	Median Home Value	$234,900	49	37.5
			Median Rent	$843	49	26.2
Crime	N/A	N/A	Violent Crimes per 10,000 Population	N/A	N/A	N/A
			Property Crimes per 10,000 Population	N/A	N/A	N/A
Open Spaces	3	86.70	Population Density (Persons/Sq. Mile)	1313	6	94.1
			Average Rooms per Housing Unit	6.9	4	79.3
Education	7	67.15	% High School Enrollment/Completion	90.0%	31	54.1
			% College Graduates	50.1%	3	80.2
Commute	41	36.45	Average Work Commute in Minutes	28	41	42.9
			% Commuting on Public Transportation	3.3%	30	30.0
Community Stability	37	32.50	% Living in Same House as in 1979	21.2%	43	29.3
			% Living in Same County as in 1985	71.4%	35	35.7

Composite: Rank 9 / 50 *Score* 58.51   **NORTH MARYSVILLE**

CATEGORY	RANK	SCORE	STATISTIC	VALUE	RANK	SCORE
Economics	17	63.10	Median Household Income	$39,984	20	39.1
			% of Families Above Poverty Level	97.5%	14	87.1
Affordable Housing	26	74.70	Median Home Value	$106,600	19	86.7
			Median Rent	$622	35	62.7
Crime	N/A	N/A	Violent Crimes per 10,000 Population	N/A	N/A	N/A
			Property Crimes per 10,000 Population	N/A	N/A	N/A
Open Spaces	8	73.25	Population Density (Persons/Sq. Mile)	1284	4	94.8
			Average Rooms per Housing Unit	6.1	16	51.7
Education	32	35.10	% High School Enrollment/Completion	92.0%	26	65.0
			% College Graduates	11.5%	48	5.2
Commute	42	36.15	Average Work Commute in Minutes	25	22	64.3
			% Commuting on Public Transportation	1.1%	48	8.0
Community Stability	9	68.75	% Living in Same House as in 1979	32.5%	13	61.4
			% Living in Same County as in 1985	83.4%	4	76.1

Metropolitan Area Suburb Rankings
SEATTLE-TACOMA

Composite: *Rank* 10 / 50 *Score* 58.40 — CASCADE-FAIRWOOD

CATEGORY	RANK	SCORE	STATISTIC	VALUE	RANK	SCORE
Economics	12	69.60	Median Household Income	$44,826	12	52.8
			% of Families Above Poverty Level	97.4%	16	86.4
Affordable Housing	27	74.35	Median Home Value	$124,900	30	79.7
			Median Rent	$584	28	69.0
Crime	N/A	N/A	Violent Crimes per 10,000 Population	N/A	N/A	N/A
			Property Crimes per 10,000 Population	N/A	N/A	N/A
Open Spaces	20	51.00	Population Density (Persons/Sq. Mile)	3285	33	46.8
			Average Rooms per Housing Unit	6.2	14	55.2
Education	12	59.40	% High School Enrollment/Completion	95.3%	7	83.1
			% College Graduates	27.2%	14	35.7
Commute	34	40.55	Average Work Commute in Minutes	26	32	57.1
			% Commuting on Public Transportation	2.7%	33	24.0
Community Stability	13	55.50	% Living in Same House as in 1979	29.7%	18	53.4
			% Living in Same County as in 1985	77.9%	15	57.6

Composite: *Rank* 11 / 50 *Score* 58.24 — INGLEWOOD-FINN HILL

CATEGORY	RANK	SCORE	STATISTIC	VALUE	RANK	SCORE
Economics	8	76.35	Median Household Income	$47,731	7	61.0
			% of Families Above Poverty Level	98.1%	8	91.7
Affordable Housing	41	62.45	Median Home Value	$153,300	40	68.8
			Median Rent	$662	42	56.1
Crime	N/A	N/A	Violent Crimes per 10,000 Population	N/A	N/A	N/A
			Property Crimes per 10,000 Population	N/A	N/A	N/A
Open Spaces	17	56.95	Population Density (Persons/Sq. Mile)	3220	31	48.4
			Average Rooms per Housing Unit	6.5	8	65.5
Education	9	61.85	% High School Enrollment/Completion	93.9%	12	75.4
			% College Graduates	33.7%	10	48.3
Commute	37	37.95	Average Work Commute in Minutes	28	41	42.9
			% Commuting on Public Transportation	3.6%	26	33.0
Community Stability	15	53.90	% Living in Same House as in 1979	30.0%	16	54.3
			% Living in Same County as in 1985	76.7%	17	53.5

Composite: *Rank* 12 / 50 *Score* 57.97 — KINGSGATE

CATEGORY	RANK	SCORE	STATISTIC	VALUE	RANK	SCORE
Economics	21	59.25	Median Household Income	$42,865	16	47.3
			% of Families Above Poverty Level	95.4%	28	71.2
Affordable Housing	42	62.30	Median Home Value	$152,500	39	69.1
			Median Rent	$666	43	55.5
Crime	N/A	N/A	Violent Crimes per 10,000 Population	N/A	N/A	N/A
			Property Crimes per 10,000 Population	N/A	N/A	N/A
Open Spaces	27	45.10	Population Density (Persons/Sq. Mile)	4209	43	24.7
			Average Rooms per Housing Unit	6.5	8	65.5
Education	13	58.90	% High School Enrollment/Completion	92.3%	22	66.7
			% College Graduates	35.1%	9	51.1
Commute	10	73.15	Average Work Commute in Minutes	25	22	64.3
			% Commuting on Public Transportation	8.5%	3	82.0
Community Stability	21	49.10	% Living in Same House as in 1979	29.7%	18	53.4
			% Living in Same County as in 1985	74.1%	24	44.8

Metropolitan Area Suburb Rankings
SEATTLE-TACOMA

Composite: Rank 13 / 50 *Score* 57.77   **RICHMOND HIGHLANDS**

CATEGORY	RANK	SCORE	STATISTIC	VALUE	RANK	SCORE
Economics	24	55.55	Median Household Income	$37,300	27	31.6
			% of Families Above Poverty Level	96.5%	21	79.5
Affordable Housing	29	73.40	Median Home Value	$136,000	35	75.4
			Median Rent	$570	26	71.4
Crime	N/A	N/A	Violent Crimes per 10,000 Population	N/A	N/A	N/A
			Property Crimes per 10,000 Population	N/A	N/A	N/A
Open Spaces	46	20.50	Population Density (Persons/Sq. Mile)	5110	48	3.1
			Average Rooms per Housing Unit	5.7	23	37.9
Education	23	46.10	% High School Enrollment/Completion	89.9%	32	53.6
			% College Graduates	28.7%	13	38.6
Commute	2	82.15	Average Work Commute in Minutes	25	22	64.3
			% Commuting on Public Transportation	10.3%	1	100.0
Community Stability	8	68.95	% Living in Same House as in 1979	38.2%	4	77.6
			% Living in Same County as in 1985	78.7%	11	60.3

Composite: Rank 14 / 50 *Score* 57.10   **EDMONDS**

CATEGORY	RANK	SCORE	STATISTIC	VALUE	RANK	SCORE
Economics	18	62.35	Median Household Income	$40,515	19	40.6
			% of Families Above Poverty Level	97.1%	17	84.1
Affordable Housing	31	71.80	Median Home Value	$159,600	43	66.3
			Median Rent	$534	22	77.3
Crime	N/A	N/A	Violent Crimes per 10,000 Population	11	N/A	N/A
			Property Crimes per 10,000 Population	340	N/A	N/A
Open Spaces	38	36.50	Population Density (Persons/Sq. Mile)	4210	44	24.7
			Average Rooms per Housing Unit	6.0	18	48.3
Education	14	57.35	% High School Enrollment/Completion	93.2%	16	71.6
			% College Graduates	31.0%	11	43.1
Commute	20	60.65	Average Work Commute in Minutes	25	22	64.3
			% Commuting on Public Transportation	6.0%	17	57.0
Community Stability	14	53.95	% Living in Same House as in 1979	35.7%	9	70.5
			% Living in Same County as in 1985	71.9%	31	37.4

Composite: Rank 15 / 50 *Score* 56.99   **SILVER LAKE-FIRCREST**

CATEGORY	RANK	SCORE	STATISTIC	VALUE	RANK	SCORE
Economics	6	80.15	Median Household Income	$49,891	6	67.1
			% of Families Above Poverty Level	98.3%	6	93.2
Affordable Housing	46	55.40	Median Home Value	$140,400	37	73.7
			Median Rent	$777	48	37.1
Crime	N/A	N/A	Violent Crimes per 10,000 Population	N/A	N/A	N/A
			Property Crimes per 10,000 Population	N/A	N/A	N/A
Open Spaces	6	80.30	Population Density (Persons/Sq. Mile)	1705	11	84.7
			Average Rooms per Housing Unit	6.8	5	75.9
Education	28	43.40	% High School Enrollment/Completion	90.7%	28	57.9
			% College Graduates	23.7%	22	28.9
Commute	35	40.05	Average Work Commute in Minutes	26	32	57.1
			% Commuting on Public Transportation	2.6%	34	23.0
Community Stability	30	42.65	% Living in Same House as in 1979	26.1%	30	43.2
			% Living in Same County as in 1985	73.3%	28	42.1

Metropolitan Area Suburb Rankings
SEATTLE-TACOMA

Composite: *Rank* 16 / 50 *Score* 56.67   **NORTH CITY-RIDGECREST**

CATEGORY	RANK	SCORE	STATISTIC	VALUE	RANK	SCORE
Economics	28	51.75	Median Household Income	$34,051	32	22.4
			% of Families Above Poverty Level	96.7%	19	81.1
Affordable Housing	20	81.30	Median Home Value	$113,600	25	84.0
			Median Rent	$526	19	78.6
Crime	N/A	N/A	Violent Crimes per 10,000 Population	N/A	N/A	N/A
			Property Crimes per 10,000 Population	N/A	N/A	N/A
Open Spaces	47	18.10	Population Density (Persons/Sq. Mile)	5023	46	5.2
			Average Rooms per Housing Unit	5.5	29	31.0
Education	30	38.55	% High School Enrollment/Completion	89.9%	32	53.6
			% College Graduates	20.9%	26	23.5
Commute	3	80.20	Average Work Commute in Minutes	24	19	71.4
			% Commuting on Public Transportation	9.2%	2	89.0
Community Stability	6	70.15	% Living in Same House as in 1979	36.0%	6	71.3
			% Living in Same County as in 1985	81.3%	7	69.0

Composite: *Rank* 17 / 50 *Score* 56.28   **MARTHA LAKE**

CATEGORY	RANK	SCORE	STATISTIC	VALUE	RANK	SCORE
Economics	11	70.20	Median Household Income	$44,200	14	51.0
			% of Families Above Poverty Level	97.8%	12	89.4
Affordable Housing	37	66.30	Median Home Value	$139,600	36	74.0
			Median Rent	$647	39	58.6
Crime	N/A	N/A	Violent Crimes per 10,000 Population	N/A	N/A	N/A
			Property Crimes per 10,000 Population	N/A	N/A	N/A
Open Spaces	14	63.80	Population Density (Persons/Sq. Mile)	2070	15	75.9
			Average Rooms per Housing Unit	6.1	16	51.7
Education	10	60.60	% High School Enrollment/Completion	96.1%	4	87.4
			% College Graduates	26.2%	18	33.8
Commute	32	44.05	Average Work Commute in Minutes	26	32	57.1
			% Commuting on Public Transportation	3.4%	28	31.0
Community Stability	36	32.75	% Living in Same House as in 1979	27.2%	26	46.3
			% Living in Same County as in 1985	66.5%	42	19.2

Composite: *Rank* 18 / 50 *Score* 55.83   **REDMOND**

CATEGORY	RANK	SCORE	STATISTIC	VALUE	RANK	SCORE
Economics	13	68.70	Median Household Income	$42,299	17	45.7
			% of Families Above Poverty Level	98.1%	8	91.7
Affordable Housing	43	59.40	Median Home Value	$169,500	45	62.5
			Median Rent	$661	41	56.3
Crime	N/A	N/A	Violent Crimes per 10,000 Population	21	N/A	N/A
			Property Crimes per 10,000 Population	428	N/A	N/A
Open Spaces	21	50.30	Population Density (Persons/Sq. Mile)	2480	25	66.1
			Average Rooms per Housing Unit	5.6	24	34.5
Education	6	69.15	% High School Enrollment/Completion	94.0%	10	76.0
			% College Graduates	40.9%	7	62.3
Commute	18	62.80	Average Work Commute in Minutes	23	12	78.6
			% Commuting on Public Transportation	5.0%	22	47.0
Community Stability	43	24.60	% Living in Same House as in 1979	19.3%	47	23.9
			% Living in Same County as in 1985	68.3%	39	25.3

751

Metropolitan Area Suburb Rankings
SEATTLE-TACOMA

Composite: **Rank** 19 / 50 **Score** 55.73   **BOTHELL**

CATEGORY	RANK	SCORE	STATISTIC	VALUE	RANK	SCORE
Economics	19	61.80	Median Household Income	$37,159	28	31.2
			% of Families Above Poverty Level	98.2%	7	92.4
Affordable Housing	34	68.95	Median Home Value	$157,800	41	67.0
			Median Rent	$573	27	70.9
Crime	N/A	N/A	Violent Crimes per 10,000 Population	13	N/A	N/A
			Property Crimes per 10,000 Population	442	N/A	N/A
Open Spaces	19	52.15	Population Density (Persons/Sq. Mile)	2325	20	69.8
			Average Rooms per Housing Unit	5.6	24	34.5
Education	17	55.30	% High School Enrollment/Completion	93.8%	13	74.9
			% College Graduates	27.2%	14	35.7
Commute	19	62.05	Average Work Commute in Minutes	26	32	57.1
			% Commuting on Public Transportation	7.0%	8	67.0
Community Stability	35	34.10	% Living in Same House as in 1979	22.0%	42	31.5
			% Living in Same County as in 1985	71.7%	34	36.7

Composite: **Rank** 20 / 50 **Score** 55.66   **BURIEN**

CATEGORY	RANK	SCORE	STATISTIC	VALUE	RANK	SCORE
Economics	36	37.85	Median Household Income	$32,261	38	17.4
			% of Families Above Poverty Level	93.7%	37	58.3
Affordable Housing	15	86.70	Median Home Value	$106,700	20	86.6
			Median Rent	$477	10	86.8
Crime	N/A	N/A	Violent Crimes per 10,000 Population	N/A	N/A	N/A
			Property Crimes per 10,000 Population	N/A	N/A	N/A
Open Spaces	42	26.10	Population Density (Persons/Sq. Mile)	3924	40	31.5
			Average Rooms per Housing Unit	5.2	35	20.7
Education	35	33.60	% High School Enrollment/Completion	88.1%	38	43.7
			% College Graduates	20.9%	26	23.5
Commute	8	75.85	Average Work Commute in Minutes	22	5	85.7
			% Commuting on Public Transportation	6.9%	10	66.0
Community Stability	5	73.85	% Living in Same House as in 1979	34.9%	11	68.2
			% Living in Same County as in 1985	84.4%	3	79.5

Composite: **Rank** 21 / 50 **Score** 55.61   **COVINGTON-SAWYER-WILDERNESS**

CATEGORY	RANK	SCORE	STATISTIC	VALUE	RANK	SCORE
Economics	10	71.05	Median Household Income	$46,660	9	58.0
			% of Families Above Poverty Level	97.1%	17	84.1
Affordable Housing	36	68.25	Median Home Value	$115,200	26	83.4
			Median Rent	$680	45	53.1
Crime	N/A	N/A	Violent Crimes per 10,000 Population	N/A	N/A	N/A
			Property Crimes per 10,000 Population	N/A	N/A	N/A
Open Spaces	5	81.20	Population Density (Persons/Sq. Mile)	1197	3	96.9
			Average Rooms per Housing Unit	6.5	8	65.5
Education	16	55.40	% High School Enrollment/Completion	95.7%	6	85.2
			% College Graduates	22.0%	23	25.6
Commute	49	7.50	Average Work Commute in Minutes	34	50	0.0
			% Commuting on Public Transportation	1.8%	42	15.0
Community Stability	19	50.25	% Living in Same House as in 1979	25.3%	32	40.9
			% Living in Same County as in 1985	78.5%	14	59.6

Metropolitan Area Suburb Rankings
SEATTLE-TACOMA

Composite: *Rank* 22 / 50 *Score* 55.45   **SAHALEE**

CATEGORY	RANK	SCORE	STATISTIC	VALUE	RANK	SCORE
Economics	1	99.95	Median Household Income	$61,524	2	99.9
			% of Families Above Poverty Level	99.2%	1	100.0
Affordable Housing	50	20.65	Median Home Value	$224,800	48	41.3
			Median Rent	$1,001	50	0.0
Crime	N/A	N/A	Violent Crimes per 10,000 Population	N/A	N/A	N/A
			Property Crimes per 10,000 Population	N/A	N/A	N/A
Open Spaces	1	91.90	Population Density (Persons/Sq. Mile)	1741	12	83.8
			Average Rooms per Housing Unit	7.5	1	100.0
Education	2	90.30	% High School Enrollment/Completion	98.4%	1	100.0
			% College Graduates	50.3%	2	80.6
Commute	47	23.85	Average Work Commute in Minutes	29	46	35.7
			% Commuting on Public Transportation	1.5%	44	12.0
Community Stability	50	6.05	% Living in Same House as in 1979	10.9%	50	0.0
			% Living in Same County as in 1985	64.4%	43	12.1

Composite: *Rank* 23 / 50 *Score* 55.17   **EAST HILL-MERIDIAN**

CATEGORY	RANK	SCORE	STATISTIC	VALUE	RANK	SCORE
Economics	22	57.15	Median Household Income	$44,623	13	52.2
			% of Families Above Poverty Level	94.2%	35	62.1
Affordable Housing	28	73.85	Median Home Value	$126,700	31	79.0
			Median Rent	$586	29	68.7
Crime	N/A	N/A	Violent Crimes per 10,000 Population	N/A	N/A	N/A
			Property Crimes per 10,000 Population	N/A	N/A	N/A
Open Spaces	15	62.90	Population Density (Persons/Sq. Mile)	2434	23	67.2
			Average Rooms per Housing Unit	6.3	12	58.6
Education	19	50.20	% High School Enrollment/Completion	92.9%	19	69.9
			% College Graduates	24.5%	20	30.5
Commute	36	38.55	Average Work Commute in Minutes	26	32	57.1
			% Commuting on Public Transportation	2.3%	36	20.0
Community Stability	22	48.35	% Living in Same House as in 1979	26.9%	27	45.5
			% Living in Same County as in 1985	76.0%	20	51.2

Composite: *Rank* 24 / 50 *Score* 54.78   **RIVERTON-BOULEVARD PARK**

CATEGORY	RANK	SCORE	STATISTIC	VALUE	RANK	SCORE
Economics	43	31.40	Median Household Income	$30,353	43	12.0
			% of Families Above Poverty Level	92.7%	40	50.8
Affordable Housing	4	92.35	Median Home Value	$89,400	6	93.3
			Median Rent	$449	4	91.4
Crime	N/A	N/A	Violent Crimes per 10,000 Population	N/A	N/A	N/A
			Property Crimes per 10,000 Population	N/A	N/A	N/A
Open Spaces	43	26.15	Population Density (Persons/Sq. Mile)	3633	38	38.5
			Average Rooms per Housing Unit	5.0	40	13.8
Education	33	34.35	% High School Enrollment/Completion	90.3%	30	55.7
			% College Graduates	15.5%	39	13.0
Commute	7	75.95	Average Work Commute in Minutes	21	2	92.9
			% Commuting on Public Transportation	6.2%	15	59.0
Community Stability	10	68.50	% Living in Same House as in 1979	33.9%	12	65.3
			% Living in Same County as in 1985	82.1%	6	71.7

Metropolitan Area Suburb Rankings
SEATTLE-TACOMA

Composite: **Rank** 25 / 50   *Score* 54.20   **ESPERANCE**

CATEGORY	RANK	SCORE	STATISTIC	VALUE	RANK	SCORE
Economics	20	61.65	Median Household Income	$38,935	21	36.2
			% of Families Above Poverty Level	97.5%	14	87.1
Affordable Housing	33	69.75	Median Home Value	$135,400	34	75.6
			Median Rent	$615	34	63.9
Crime	N/A	N/A	Violent Crimes per 10,000 Population	N/A	N/A	N/A
			Property Crimes per 10,000 Population	N/A	N/A	N/A
Open Spaces	45	21.00	Population Density (Persons/Sq. Mile)	5213	49	0.6
			Average Rooms per Housing Unit	5.8	20	41.4
Education	8	61.95	% High School Enrollment/Completion	96.4%	3	89.1
			% College Graduates	26.7%	16	34.8
Commute	22	60.00	Average Work Commute in Minutes	27	38	50.0
			% Commuting on Public Transportation	7.3%	6	70.0
Community Stability	18	50.85	% Living in Same House as in 1979	35.8%	7	70.7
			% Living in Same County as in 1985	70.0%	38	31.0

Composite: **Rank** 26 / 50   *Score* 53.97   **RENTON**

CATEGORY	RANK	SCORE	STATISTIC	VALUE	RANK	SCORE
Economics	34	40.65	Median Household Income	$32,393	35	17.7
			% of Families Above Poverty Level	94.4%	33	63.6
Affordable Housing	16	85.90	Median Home Value	$105,800	17	87.0
			Median Rent	$489	14	84.8
Crime	N/A	N/A	Violent Crimes per 10,000 Population	52	N/A	N/A
			Property Crimes per 10,000 Population	943	N/A	N/A
Open Spaces	36	37.20	Population Density (Persons/Sq. Mile)	2566	27	64.1
			Average Rooms per Housing Unit	4.9	43	10.3
Education	20	48.65	% High School Enrollment/Completion	93.3%	15	72.1
			% College Graduates	21.8%	24	25.2
Commute	17	63.80	Average Work Commute in Minutes	23	12	78.6
			% Commuting on Public Transportation	5.2%	20	49.0
Community Stability	24	47.60	% Living in Same House as in 1979	23.2%	36	34.9
			% Living in Same County as in 1985	78.7%	11	60.3

Composite: **Rank** 27 / 50   *Score* 53.90   **SEA-TAC**

CATEGORY	RANK	SCORE	STATISTIC	VALUE	RANK	SCORE
Economics	35	39.20	Median Household Income	$32,437	34	17.8
			% of Families Above Poverty Level	94.0%	36	60.6
Affordable Housing	10	88.35	Median Home Value	$93,700	9	91.6
			Median Rent	$487	12	85.1
Crime	N/A	N/A	Violent Crimes per 10,000 Population	N/A	N/A	N/A
			Property Crimes per 10,000 Population	N/A	N/A	N/A
Open Spaces	29	41.95	Population Density (Persons/Sq. Mile)	2314	18	70.1
			Average Rooms per Housing Unit	5.0	40	13.8
Education	40	26.20	% High School Enrollment/Completion	87.8%	39	42.1
			% College Graduates	14.1%	43	10.3
Commute	14	66.85	Average Work Commute in Minutes	22	5	85.7
			% Commuting on Public Transportation	5.1%	21	48.0
Community Stability	12	60.85	% Living in Same House as in 1979	32.3%	15	60.8
			% Living in Same County as in 1985	78.9%	10	60.9

Metropolitan Area Suburb Rankings
SEATTLE-TACOMA

Composite: *Rank* 28 / 50 *Score* 53.78   UNIVERSITY PLACE

CATEGORY	RANK	SCORE	STATISTIC	VALUE	RANK	SCORE
Economics	33	43.75	Median Household Income	$34,576	30	23.9
			% of Families Above Poverty Level	94.4%	33	63.6
Affordable Housing	9	88.50	Median Home Value	$100,300	14	89.1
			Median Rent	$470	7	87.9
Crime	N/A	N/A	Violent Crimes per 10,000 Population	N/A	N/A	N/A
			Property Crimes per 10,000 Population	N/A	N/A	N/A
Open Spaces	34	37.80	Population Density (Persons/Sq. Mile)	3523	37	41.1
			Average Rooms per Housing Unit	5.6	24	34.5
Education	15	55.60	% High School Enrollment/Completion	92.6%	20	68.3
			% College Graduates	30.9%	12	42.9
Commute	31	44.80	Average Work Commute in Minutes	23	12	78.6
			% Commuting on Public Transportation	1.4%	45	11.0
Community Stability	17	52.25	% Living in Same House as in 1979	28.7%	22	50.6
			% Living in Same County as in 1985	76.8%	16	53.9

Composite: *Rank* 29 / 50 *Score* 53.25   KIRKLAND

CATEGORY	RANK	SCORE	STATISTIC	VALUE	RANK	SCORE
Economics	23	56.80	Median Household Income	$38,437	23	34.8
			% of Families Above Poverty Level	96.4%	22	78.8
Affordable Housing	39	63.90	Median Home Value	$159,400	42	66.4
			Median Rent	$630	36	61.4
Crime	N/A	N/A	Violent Crimes per 10,000 Population	24	N/A	N/A
			Property Crimes per 10,000 Population	544	N/A	N/A
Open Spaces	40	30.00	Population Density (Persons/Sq. Mile)	3742	39	35.9
			Average Rooms per Housing Unit	5.3	33	24.1
Education	11	60.05	% High School Enrollment/Completion	92.2%	24	66.1
			% College Graduates	36.6%	8	54.0
Commute	11	69.80	Average Work Commute in Minutes	23	12	78.6
			% Commuting on Public Transportation	6.4%	14	61.0
Community Stability	33	38.95	% Living in Same House as in 1979	23.6%	35	36.1
			% Living in Same County as in 1985	73.2%	29	41.8

Composite: *Rank* 30 / 50 *Score* 53.17   TUKWILA

CATEGORY	RANK	SCORE	STATISTIC	VALUE	RANK	SCORE
Economics	45	30.70	Median Household Income	$30,141	44	11.4
			% of Families Above Poverty Level	92.6%	41	50.0
Affordable Housing	11	88.05	Median Home Value	$94,900	10	91.2
			Median Rent	$488	13	84.9
Crime	N/A	N/A	Violent Crimes per 10,000 Population	201	N/A	N/A
			Property Crimes per 10,000 Population	2,538	N/A	N/A
Open Spaces	26	45.35	Population Density (Persons/Sq. Mile)	1455	9	90.7
			Average Rooms per Housing Unit	4.6	49	0.0
Education	38	28.25	% High School Enrollment/Completion	86.7%	41	36.1
			% College Graduates	19.3%	33	20.4
Commute	1	82.85	Average Work Commute in Minutes	22	5	85.7
			% Commuting on Public Transportation	8.3%	4	80.0
Community Stability	28	43.80	% Living in Same House as in 1979	24.2%	34	37.8
			% Living in Same County as in 1985	75.6%	21	49.8

Metropolitan Area Suburb Rankings
SEATTLE-TACOMA

Composite: **Rank** 31 / 50 **Score** 52.97   **WEST LAKE STEVENS**

CATEGORY	RANK	SCORE	STATISTIC	VALUE	RANK	SCORE
Economics	26	52.60	Median Household Income	$37,641	25	32.5
			% of Families Above Poverty Level	95.6%	25	72.7
Affordable Housing	24	79.05	Median Home Value	$111,600	24	84.8
			Median Rent	$558	24	73.3
Crime	N/A	N/A	Violent Crimes per 10,000 Population	N/A	N/A	N/A
			Property Crimes per 10,000 Population	N/A	N/A	N/A
Open Spaces	10	70.55	Population Density (Persons/Sq. Mile)	1077	2	99.7
			Average Rooms per Housing Unit	5.8	20	41.4
Education	37	28.50	% High School Enrollment/Completion	88.8%	36	47.5
			% College Graduates	13.7%	44	9.5
Commute	40	37.15	Average Work Commute in Minutes	25	22	64.3
			% Commuting on Public Transportation	1.3%	46	10.0
Community Stability	20	49.95	% Living in Same House as in 1979	27.6%	25	47.4
			% Living in Same County as in 1985	76.4%	18	52.5

Composite: **Rank** 32 / 50 **Score** 52.73   **PUYALLUP**

CATEGORY	RANK	SCORE	STATISTIC	VALUE	RANK	SCORE
Economics	32	44.75	Median Household Income	$32,849	33	19.0
			% of Families Above Poverty Level	95.3%	29	70.5
Affordable Housing	6	91.95	Median Home Value	$84,200	4	95.3
			Median Rent	$466	5	88.6
Crime	N/A	N/A	Violent Crimes per 10,000 Population	25	N/A	N/A
			Property Crimes per 10,000 Population	771	N/A	N/A
Open Spaces	22	48.75	Population Density (Persons/Sq. Mile)	2321	19	69.9
			Average Rooms per Housing Unit	5.4	31	27.6
Education	33	34.35	% High School Enrollment/Completion	89.5%	35	51.4
			% College Graduates	17.7%	38	17.3
Commute	33	43.20	Average Work Commute in Minutes	24	19	71.4
			% Commuting on Public Transportation	1.8%	42	15.0
Community Stability	16	53.40	% Living in Same House as in 1979	30.0%	16	54.3
			% Living in Same County as in 1985	76.4%	18	52.5

Composite: **Rank** 33 / 50 **Score** 51.97   **NORTH CREEK-CANYON PARK**

CATEGORY	RANK	SCORE	STATISTIC	VALUE	RANK	SCORE
Economics	9	72.55	Median Household Income	$45,341	11	54.2
			% of Families Above Poverty Level	98.0%	11	90.9
Affordable Housing	40	62.80	Median Home Value	$145,800	38	71.6
			Median Rent	$675	44	54.0
Crime	N/A	N/A	Violent Crimes per 10,000 Population	N/A	N/A	N/A
			Property Crimes per 10,000 Population	N/A	N/A	N/A
Open Spaces	7	75.25	Population Density (Persons/Sq. Mile)	1405	8	91.9
			Average Rooms per Housing Unit	6.3	12	58.6
Education	18	52.90	% High School Enrollment/Completion	93.6%	14	73.8
			% College Graduates	25.3%	19	32.0
Commute	45	31.35	Average Work Commute in Minutes	29	46	35.7
			% Commuting on Public Transportation	3.0%	31	27.0
Community Stability	48	17.00	% Living in Same House as in 1979	22.4%	40	32.7
			% Living in Same County as in 1985	61.2%	49	1.3

Metropolitan Area Suburb Rankings
SEATTLE-TACOMA

Composite: *Rank* 34 / 50 *Score* 51.42   **SOUTH HILL**

CATEGORY	RANK	SCORE	STATISTIC	VALUE	RANK	SCORE
Economics	25	54.85	Median Household Income	$38,704	22	35.5
			% of Families Above Poverty Level	95.8%	24	74.2
Affordable Housing	14	87.05	Median Home Value	$95,300	11	91.0
			Median Rent	$499	16	83.1
Crime	N/A	N/A	Violent Crimes per 10,000 Population	N/A	N/A	N/A
			Property Crimes per 10,000 Population	N/A	N/A	N/A
Open Spaces	16	61.40	Population Density (Persons/Sq. Mile)	1843	13	81.4
			Average Rooms per Housing Unit	5.8	20	41.4
Education	27	43.90	% High School Enrollment/Completion	92.5%	21	67.8
			% College Graduates	19.1%	35	20.0
Commute	48	17.85	Average Work Commute in Minutes	29	46	35.7
			% Commuting on Public Transportation	0.3%	49	0.0
Community Stability	29	43.45	% Living in Same House as in 1979	25.0%	33	40.1
			% Living in Same County as in 1985	74.7%	23	46.8

Composite: *Rank* 35 / 50 *Score* 49.29   **PARKLAND**

CATEGORY	RANK	SCORE	STATISTIC	VALUE	RANK	SCORE
Economics	48	15.15	Median Household Income	$27,704	48	4.5
			% of Families Above Poverty Level	89.4%	48	25.8
Affordable Housing	1	98.70	Median Home Value	$71,900	1	100.0
			Median Rent	$413	2	97.4
Crime	N/A	N/A	Violent Crimes per 10,000 Population	N/A	N/A	N/A
			Property Crimes per 10,000 Population	N/A	N/A	N/A
Open Spaces	37	36.75	Population Density (Persons/Sq. Mile)	3036	30	52.8
			Average Rooms per Housing Unit	5.2	35	20.7
Education	24	45.75	% High School Enrollment/Completion	94.7%	9	79.8
			% College Graduates	14.8%	40	11.7
Commute	27	52.35	Average Work Commute in Minutes	22	5	85.7
			% Commuting on Public Transportation	2.2%	38	19.0
Community Stability	25	47.05	% Living in Same House as in 1979	32.4%	14	61.1
			% Living in Same County as in 1985	70.6%	37	33.0

Composite: *Rank* 36 / 50 *Score* 49.14   **ALDERWOOD MANOR-BOTHELL NORTH**

CATEGORY	RANK	SCORE	STATISTIC	VALUE	RANK	SCORE
Economics	14	67.45	Median Household Income	$41,445	18	43.2
			% of Families Above Poverty Level	98.1%	8	91.7
Affordable Housing	35	68.55	Median Home Value	$135,100	32	75.7
			Median Rent	$630	36	61.4
Crime	N/A	N/A	Violent Crimes per 10,000 Population	N/A	N/A	N/A
			Property Crimes per 10,000 Population	N/A	N/A	N/A
Open Spaces	18	56.05	Population Density (Persons/Sq. Mile)	2866	28	56.9
			Average Rooms per Housing Unit	6.2	14	55.2
Education	31	37.15	% High School Enrollment/Completion	88.3%	37	44.8
			% College Graduates	24.0%	21	29.5
Commute	37	37.95	Average Work Commute in Minutes	28	41	42.9
			% Commuting on Public Transportation	3.6%	26	33.0
Community Stability	41	27.70	% Living in Same House as in 1979	29.2%	20	52.0
			% Living in Same County as in 1985	61.8%	47	3.4

Metropolitan Area Suburb Rankings
SEATTLE-TACOMA

Composite: Rank 37 / 50 *Score* 48.23 **FEDERAL WAY**

CATEGORY	RANK	SCORE	STATISTIC	VALUE	RANK	SCORE
Economics	27	52.05	Median Household Income	$38,311	24	34.4
			% of Families Above Poverty Level	95.2%	31	69.7
Affordable Housing	23	79.20	Median Home Value	$119,000	27	81.9
			Median Rent	$539	23	76.5
Crime	N/A	N/A	Violent Crimes per 10,000 Population	N/A	N/A	N/A
			Property Crimes per 10,000 Population	N/A	N/A	N/A
Open Spaces	32	38.85	Population Density (Persons/Sq. Mile)	3435	36	43.2
			Average Rooms per Housing Unit	5.6	24	34.5
Education	22	46.80	% High School Enrollment/Completion	90.9%	27	59.0
			% College Graduates	26.6%	17	34.6
Commute	28	47.95	Average Work Commute in Minutes	28	41	42.9
			% Commuting on Public Transportation	5.6%	19	53.0
Community Stability	44	24.50	% Living in Same House as in 1979	20.1%	44	26.1
			% Living in Same County as in 1985	67.6%	40	22.9

Composite: Rank 38 / 50 *Score* 46.09 **EVERETT**

CATEGORY	RANK	SCORE	STATISTIC	VALUE	RANK	SCORE
Economics	47	18.80	Median Household Income	$28,415	47	6.5
			% of Families Above Poverty Level	90.1%	47	31.1
Affordable Housing	12	87.85	Median Home Value	$97,700	12	90.1
			Median Rent	$484	11	85.6
Crime	N/A	N/A	Violent Crimes per 10,000 Population	51	N/A	N/A
			Property Crimes per 10,000 Population	698	N/A	N/A
Open Spaces	30	39.90	Population Density (Persons/Sq. Mile)	2341	21	69.5
			Average Rooms per Housing Unit	4.9	43	10.3
Education	48	18.35	% High School Enrollment/Completion	84.9%	45	26.2
			% College Graduates	14.2%	42	10.5
Commute	13	67.50	Average Work Commute in Minutes	20	1	100.0
			% Commuting on Public Transportation	3.8%	25	35.0
Community Stability	27	44.15	% Living in Same House as in 1979	26.7%	29	44.9
			% Living in Same County as in 1985	73.7%	27	43.4

Composite: Rank 39 / 50 *Score* 45.93 **MOUNTLAKE TERRACE**

CATEGORY	RANK	SCORE	STATISTIC	VALUE	RANK	SCORE
Economics	30	48.35	Median Household Income	$35,391	29	26.2
			% of Families Above Poverty Level	95.3%	29	70.5
Affordable Housing	25	77.00	Median Home Value	$106,100	18	86.9
			Median Rent	$596	30	67.1
Crime	N/A	N/A	Violent Crimes per 10,000 Population	25	N/A	N/A
			Property Crimes per 10,000 Population	480	N/A	N/A
Open Spaces	48	14.50	Population Density (Persons/Sq. Mile)	4894	45	8.3
			Average Rooms per Housing Unit	5.2	35	20.7
Education	25	45.45	% High School Enrollment/Completion	93.0%	18	70.5
			% College Graduates	19.3%	33	20.4
Commute	15	64.15	Average Work Commute in Minutes	25	22	64.3
			% Commuting on Public Transportation	6.7%	11	64.0
Community Stability	42	26.15	% Living in Same House as in 1979	27.9%	24	48.3
			% Living in Same County as in 1985	62.0%	46	4.0

Metropolitan Area Suburb Rankings
SEATTLE-TACOMA

Composite: *Rank* 40 / 50 *Score* 45.82   **AUBURN**

CATEGORY	RANK	SCORE	STATISTIC	VALUE	RANK	SCORE
Economics	46	27.85	Median Household Income	$30,007	45	11.0
			% of Families Above Poverty Level	91.9%	46	44.7
Affordable Housing	7	90.60	Median Home Value	$90,600	7	92.8
			Median Rent	$467	6	88.4
Crime	N/A	N/A	Violent Crimes per 10,000 Population	57	N/A	N/A
			Property Crimes per 10,000 Population	698	N/A	N/A
Open Spaces	23	47.80	Population Density (Persons/Sq. Mile)	1680	10	85.3
			Average Rooms per Housing Unit	4.9	43	10.3
Education	42	25.05	% High School Enrollment/Completion	87.8%	39	42.1
			% College Graduates	12.9%	47	8.0
Commute	29	47.65	Average Work Commute in Minutes	25	22	64.3
			% Commuting on Public Transportation	3.4%	28	31.0
Community Stability	34	35.95	% Living in Same House as in 1979	22.1%	41	31.8
			% Living in Same County as in 1985	72.7%	30	40.1

Composite: *Rank* 41 / 50 *Score* 45.33   **ELK PLAIN**

CATEGORY	RANK	SCORE	STATISTIC	VALUE	RANK	SCORE
Economics	40	33.75	Median Household Income	$32,319	37	17.5
			% of Families Above Poverty Level	92.6%	41	50.0
Affordable Housing	8	90.65	Median Home Value	$78,300	3	97.5
			Median Rent	$495	15	83.8
Crime	N/A	N/A	Violent Crimes per 10,000 Population	N/A	N/A	N/A
			Property Crimes per 10,000 Population	N/A	N/A	N/A
Open Spaces	11	67.25	Population Density (Persons/Sq. Mile)	1066	1	100.0
			Average Rooms per Housing Unit	5.6	24	34.5
Education	39	28.15	% High School Enrollment/Completion	90.4%	29	56.3
			% College Graduates	8.8%	50	0.0
Commute	50	7.15	Average Work Commute in Minutes	32	49	14.3
			% Commuting on Public Transportation	0.3%	49	0.0
Community Stability	26	45.00	% Living in Same House as in 1979	26.8%	28	45.2
			% Living in Same County as in 1985	74.1%	24	44.8

Composite: *Rank* 42 / 50 *Score* 45.16   **WHITE CENTER-SHOREWOOD**

CATEGORY	RANK	SCORE	STATISTIC	VALUE	RANK	SCORE
Economics	49	4.80	Median Household Income	$29,497	46	9.6
			% of Families Above Poverty Level	86.0%	50	0.0
Affordable Housing	5	92.10	Median Home Value	$92,500	8	92.1
			Median Rent	$445	3	92.1
Crime	N/A	N/A	Violent Crimes per 10,000 Population	N/A	N/A	N/A
			Property Crimes per 10,000 Population	N/A	N/A	N/A
Open Spaces	49	8.60	Population Density (Persons/Sq. Mile)	5240	50	0.0
			Average Rooms per Housing Unit	5.1	38	17.2
Education	49	15.00	% High School Enrollment/Completion	83.6%	49	19.1
			% College Graduates	14.4%	41	10.9
Commute	6	76.30	Average Work Commute in Minutes	23	12	78.6
			% Commuting on Public Transportation	7.7%	5	74.0
Community Stability	4	74.15	% Living in Same House as in 1979	37.6%	5	75.9
			% Living in Same County as in 1985	82.3%	5	72.4

Metropolitan Area Suburb Rankings
SEATTLE-TACOMA

Composite: *Rank* 43 / 50   *Score* 44.97   **MARYSVILLE**

CATEGORY	RANK	SCORE	STATISTIC	VALUE	RANK	SCORE
Economics	39	36.00	Median Household Income	$26,107	50	0.0
			% of Families Above Poverty Level	95.5%	26	72.0
Affordable Housing	13	87.20	Median Home Value	$105,100	16	87.3
			Median Rent	$475	8	87.1
Crime	N/A	N/A	Violent Crimes per 10,000 Population	25	N/A	N/A
			Property Crimes per 10,000 Population	579	N/A	N/A
Open Spaces	31	39.60	Population Density (Persons/Sq. Mile)	2221	17	72.3
			Average Rooms per Housing Unit	4.8	47	6.9
Education	36	28.65	% High School Enrollment/Completion	89.8%	34	53.0
			% College Graduates	11.0%	49	4.3
Commute	30	47.35	Average Work Commute in Minutes	22	5	85.7
			% Commuting on Public Transportation	1.2%	47	9.0
Community Stability	38	31.05	% Living in Same House as in 1979	19.6%	46	24.7
			% Living in Same County as in 1985	71.9%	31	37.4

Composite: *Rank* 44 / 50   *Score* 44.95   **LAKE SERENE-NORTH LYNNWOOD**

CATEGORY	RANK	SCORE	STATISTIC	VALUE	RANK	SCORE
Economics	29	49.95	Median Household Income	$37,360	26	31.7
			% of Families Above Poverty Level	95.0%	32	68.2
Affordable Housing	32	69.90	Median Home Value	$135,300	33	75.7
			Median Rent	$614	33	64.1
Crime	N/A	N/A	Violent Crimes per 10,000 Population	N/A	N/A	N/A
			Property Crimes per 10,000 Population	N/A	N/A	N/A
Open Spaces	25	45.40	Population Density (Persons/Sq. Mile)	2456	24	66.7
			Average Rooms per Housing Unit	5.3	33	24.1
Education	46	21.35	% High School Enrollment/Completion	83.9%	48	20.8
			% College Graduates	20.1%	30	21.9
Commute	21	60.15	Average Work Commute in Minutes	25	22	64.3
			% Commuting on Public Transportation	5.9%	18	56.0
Community Stability	45	22.95	% Living in Same House as in 1979	22.8%	38	33.8
			% Living in Same County as in 1985	64.4%	43	12.1

Composite: *Rank* 45 / 50   *Score* 43.10   **SPANAWAY**

CATEGORY	RANK	SCORE	STATISTIC	VALUE	RANK	SCORE
Economics	41	32.65	Median Household Income	$32,082	41	16.8
			% of Families Above Poverty Level	92.4%	44	48.5
Affordable Housing	3	92.95	Median Home Value	$74,600	2	99.0
			Median Rent	$476	9	86.9
Crime	N/A	N/A	Violent Crimes per 10,000 Population	N/A	N/A	N/A
			Property Crimes per 10,000 Population	N/A	N/A	N/A
Open Spaces	28	43.35	Population Density (Persons/Sq. Mile)	2915	29	55.7
			Average Rooms per Housing Unit	5.5	29	31.0
Education	47	20.00	% High School Enrollment/Completion	85.9%	44	31.7
			% College Graduates	13.1%	46	8.3
Commute	46	29.95	Average Work Commute in Minutes	28	41	42.9
			% Commuting on Public Transportation	2.0%	41	17.0
Community Stability	32	39.70	% Living in Same House as in 1979	25.7%	31	42.0
			% Living in Same County as in 1985	71.9%	31	37.4

Metropolitan Area Suburb Rankings
SEATTLE-TACOMA

Composite: **Rank** 46 / 50 **Score** 42.80   **KENT**

CATEGORY	RANK	SCORE	STATISTIC	VALUE	RANK	SCORE
Economics	38	36.85	Median Household Income	$32,341	36	17.6
			% of Families Above Poverty Level	93.4%	39	56.1
Affordable Housing	19	83.20	Median Home Value	$106,800	21	86.6
			Median Rent	$519	18	79.8
Crime	N/A	N/A	Violent Crimes per 10,000 Population	50	N/A	N/A
			Property Crimes per 10,000 Population	1,042	N/A	N/A
Open Spaces	33	38.75	Population Density (Persons/Sq. Mile)	2006	14	77.5
			Average Rooms per Housing Unit	4.6	49	0.0
Education	44	23.60	% High School Enrollment/Completion	84.4%	47	23.5
			% College Graduates	21.0%	25	23.7
Commute	25	54.65	Average Work Commute in Minutes	25	22	64.3
			% Commuting on Public Transportation	4.8%	23	45.0
Community Stability	46	19.75	% Living in Same House as in 1979	17.0%	48	17.3
			% Living in Same County as in 1985	67.4%	41	22.2

Composite: **Rank** 47 / 50 *Score* 40.08   **LYNNWOOD**

CATEGORY	RANK	SCORE	STATISTIC	VALUE	RANK	SCORE
Economics	44	30.80	Median Household Income	$30,512	42	12.4
			% of Families Above Poverty Level	92.5%	43	49.2
Affordable Housing	22	79.70	Median Home Value	$120,600	29	81.3
			Median Rent	$529	20	78.1
Crime	N/A	N/A	Violent Crimes per 10,000 Population	41	N/A	N/A
			Property Crimes per 10,000 Population	956	N/A	N/A
Open Spaces	44	22.05	Population Density (Persons/Sq. Mile)	4119	42	26.9
			Average Rooms per Housing Unit	5.1	38	17.2
Education	41	25.50	% High School Enrollment/Completion	86.0%	43	32.2
			% College Graduates	18.5%	37	18.8
Commute	15	64.15	Average Work Commute in Minutes	25	22	64.3
			% Commuting on Public Transportation	6.7%	11	64.0
Community Stability	47	18.30	% Living in Same House as in 1979	23.2%	36	34.9
			% Living in Same County as in 1985	61.3%	48	1.7

Composite: **Rank** 48 / 50 *Score* 39.98   **LAKEWOOD**

CATEGORY	RANK	SCORE	STATISTIC	VALUE	RANK	SCORE
Economics	50	0.55	Median Household Income	$26,228	49	0.3
			% of Families Above Poverty Level	86.1%	49	0.8
Affordable Housing	2	97.15	Median Home Value	$86,800	5	94.3
			Median Rent	$397	1	100.0
Crime	N/A	N/A	Violent Crimes per 10,000 Population	N/A	N/A	N/A
			Property Crimes per 10,000 Population	N/A	N/A	N/A
Open Spaces	39	30.10	Population Density (Persons/Sq. Mile)	3304	35	46.4
			Average Rooms per Housing Unit	5.0	40	13.8
Education	43	24.40	% High School Enrollment/Completion	84.8%	46	25.7
			% College Graduates	20.7%	28	23.1
Commute	24	56.95	Average Work Commute in Minutes	21	2	92.9
			% Commuting on Public Transportation	2.4%	35	21.0
Community Stability	39	30.75	% Living in Same House as in 1979	28.4%	23	49.7
			% Living in Same County as in 1985	64.3%	45	11.8

Metropolitan Area Suburb Rankings
SEATTLE-TACOMA

Composite: **Rank** 49 / 50 *Score* 39.80   **DES MOINES**

CATEGORY	RANK	SCORE	STATISTIC	VALUE	RANK	SCORE
Economics	37	37.30	Median Household Income	$32,145	39	17.0
			% of Families Above Poverty Level	93.6%	38	57.6
Affordable Housing	17	83.80	Median Home Value	$107,600	22	86.3
			Median Rent	$510	17	81.3
Crime	N/A	N/A	Violent Crimes per 10,000 Population	30	N/A	N/A
			Property Crimes per 10,000 Population	627	N/A	N/A
Open Spaces	50	7.05	Population Density (Persons/Sq. Mile)	5083	47	3.8
			Average Rooms per Housing Unit	4.9	43	10.3
Education	50	10.80	% High School Enrollment/Completion	80.1%	50	0.0
			% College Graduates	19.9%	32	21.6
Commute	23	58.20	Average Work Commute in Minutes	24	19	71.4
			% Commuting on Public Transportation	4.8%	23	45.0
Community Stability	31	41.65	% Living in Same House as in 1979	22.8%	38	33.8
			% Living in Same County as in 1985	75.5%	22	49.5

Composite: **Rank** 50 / 50 *Score* 38.33   **PAINE FIELD-LAKE STICKNEY**

CATEGORY	RANK	SCORE	STATISTIC	VALUE	RANK	SCORE
Economics	42	32.00	Median Household Income	$32,134	40	17.0
			% of Families Above Poverty Level	92.2%	45	47.0
Affordable Housing	21	79.95	Median Home Value	$104,600	15	87.5
			Median Rent	$564	25	72.4
Crime	N/A	N/A	Violent Crimes per 10,000 Population	N/A	N/A	N/A
			Property Crimes per 10,000 Population	N/A	N/A	N/A
Open Spaces	35	37.30	Population Density (Persons/Sq. Mile)	2414	22	67.7
			Average Rooms per Housing Unit	4.8	47	6.9
Education	45	22.30	% High School Enrollment/Completion	86.6%	42	35.5
			% College Graduates	13.5%	45	9.1
Commute	26	52.30	Average Work Commute in Minutes	23	12	78.6
			% Commuting on Public Transportation	2.9%	32	26.0
Community Stability	49	6.10	% Living in Same House as in 1979	15.2%	49	12.2
			% Living in Same County as in 1985	60.8%	50	0.0

Metropolitan Area Description
TAMPA-ST. PETERSBURG-CLEARWATER

STATE: Florida
COUNTIES: Hernando, Hillsborough, Pasco, Pinellas

TOTAL POPULATION: 2,067,959

POPULATION IN SUBURBS: 1,450,531   (70.1%)

POPULATION IN Tampa: 280,015   (13.5%)
POPULATION IN St. Petersburg: 238,629   (11.5%)
POPULATION IN Clearwater: 98,784   (4.8%)

The TAMPA-ST. PETERSBURG-CLEARWATER metropolitan area is located in the westcentral part of Florida along Tampa Bay. The suburbs range geographically from Spring Hill in the north (49 miles from Tampa), to Largo in the west (22 miles from Tampa), to Gulfport in the southwest (26 miles from Tampa), and to Plant City in the east (23 miles from Tampa). The area is growing rapidly in population and had an increase of 28.2% between 1980 and 1990. Summer time high temperatures average in the 90's and winter time lows average in the 50's. Many electronics and computer-related businesses are located in Pinellas County. General Electric and Paradyne have facilities in the suburb of Largo. The West Shore area, close to the airport, is one of the state's largest business districts. Public transportation in the area is provided on buses by PSTA.

Lutz is the overall highest rated suburb and also has the highest score in open spaces. **Bloomingdale** receives the highest score in economics. **New Port Richey** is the suburb with the most affordable housing. The number one score in education belongs to **Carrollwood Village**. **University West** has the top rated commute. Finally, the number one rating in community stability goes to **Palm River-Clair Mel**. Crime rankings were not available for the area.

The highest ranked suburb overall which also has an affordable housing score of at least 50.00 is **Lake Magdalene**.

The highest ranked suburb in the education category which also has an affordable housing score of at least 50.00 is also **Lake Magdalene**.

The county whose suburbs have the highest average overall score is **Hillsborough County** (55.88).

763

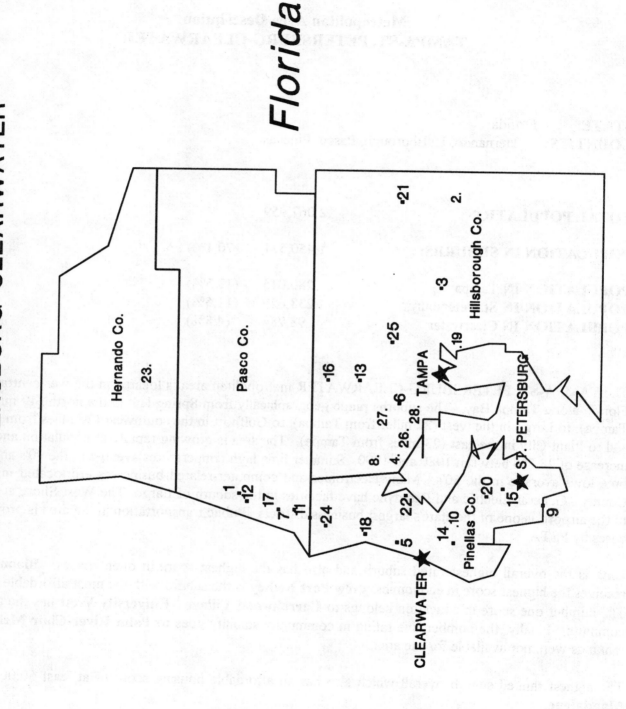

Metropolitan Area Map
TAMPA-ST. PETERSBURG-CLEARWATER

Florida

Hernando Co.

23.

Pasco Co.

•21

2.

Hillsborough Co.

•3

•25

•16

•13

•19

TAMPA

ST. PETERSBURG

•6

27.

26. 28.

1

•12

•24

22•

•20

15

9

7• f1

17

•18

•10

14

•5

Pinellas Co.

CLEARWATER

8.

4.

SUBURB	PAGE	MAP NO.	STATE	COUNTY	POPULATION	RANK
BAYONET POINT	772	1	Florida	Pasco	21,860	21 / 28
BLOOMINGDALE	770	2	Florida	Hillsborough	13,912	15 / 28
BRANDON	767	3	Florida	Hillsborough	57,985	5 / 28
CARROLLWOOD VILLAGE	768	4	Florida	Hillsborough	15,051	8 / 28
DUNEDIN	768	5	Florida	Pinellas	34,012	9 / 28
EGYPT LAKE	769	6	Florida	Hillsborough	14,580	10 / 28
ELFERS	769	7	Florida	Pasco	12,356	11 / 28
GREATER NORTHDALE	769	8	Florida	Hillsborough	16,318	12 / 28
GULFPORT	768	9	Florida	Pinellas	11,727	7 / 28
HIGHPOINT	774	10	Florida	Pinellas	13,818	25 / 28
HOLIDAY	772	11	Florida	Pasco	19,360	20 / 28
JASMINE ESTATES	773	12	Florida	Pasco	17,136	23 / 28
LAKE MAGDALENE	766	13	Florida	Hillsborough	15,973	2 / 28
LARGO	772	14	Florida	Pinellas	65,674	19 / 28
LEALMAN	773	15	Florida	Pinellas	21,748	22 / 28
LUTZ	766	16	Florida	Hillsborough	10,552	1 / 28
NEW PORT RICHEY	774	17	Florida	Pasco	14,044	27 / 28
PALM HARBOR	773	18	Florida	Pinellas	50,256	24 / 28
PALM RIVER-CLAIR MEL	767	19	Florida	Hillsborough	13,691	4 / 28
PINELLAS PARK	770	20	Florida	Pinellas	43,426	13 / 28
PLANT CITY	771	21	Florida	Hillsborough	22,754	18 / 28
SAFETY HARBOR	771	22	Florida	Pinellas	15,124	16 / 28
SPRING HILL	774	23	Florida	Hernando	31,117	26 / 28
TARPON SPRINGS	771	24	Florida	Pinellas	17,906	17 / 28
TEMPLE TERRACE	766	25	Florida	Hillsborough	16,444	3 / 28
TOWN 'N' COUNTRY	770	26	Florida	Hillsborough	60,946	14 / 28
UNIVERSITY WEST	775	27	Florida	Hillsborough	23,760	28 / 28
WEST PARK	767	28	Florida	Hillsborough	10,347	6 / 28

Metropolitan Area Suburb Rankings
TAMPA-ST. PETERSBURG-CLEARWATER

Composite: Rank 1 / 28 Score 63.85 — LUTZ

CATEGORY	RANK	SCORE	STATISTIC	VALUE	RANK	SCORE
Economics	4	86.50	Median Household Income	$43,988	4	80.0
			% of Families Above Poverty Level	96.4%	7	93.0
Affordable Housing	24	41.55	Median Home Value	$96,700	23	37.8
			Median Rent	$565	25	45.3
Crime	N/A	N/A	Violent Crimes per 10,000 Population	N/A	N/A	N/A
			Property Crimes per 10,000 Population	N/A	N/A	N/A
Open Spaces	1	93.75	Population Density (Persons/Sq. Mile)	796	1	100.0
			Average Rooms per Housing Unit	6.4	2	87.5
Education	5	69.85	% High School Enrollment/Completion	90.4%	7	77.9
			% College Graduates	28.4%	5	61.8
Commute	25	18.35	Average Work Commute in Minutes	27	26	11.1
			% Commuting on Public Transportation	1.1%	6	25.6
Community Stability	6	73.10	% Living in Same House as in 1979	28.0%	16	56.5
			% Living in Same County as in 1985	81.8%	3	89.7

Composite: Rank 2 / 28 Score 61.94 — LAKE MAGDALENE

CATEGORY	RANK	SCORE	STATISTIC	VALUE	RANK	SCORE
Economics	9	68.75	Median Household Income	$31,429	10	42.9
			% of Families Above Poverty Level	96.7%	6	94.6
Affordable Housing	19	65.15	Median Home Value	$82,700	20	54.7
			Median Rent	$458	10	75.6
Crime	N/A	N/A	Violent Crimes per 10,000 Population	N/A	N/A	N/A
			Property Crimes per 10,000 Population	N/A	N/A	N/A
Open Spaces	14	51.15	Population Density (Persons/Sq. Mile)	3342	18	52.3
			Average Rooms per Housing Unit	5.2	11	50.0
Education	6	69.60	% High School Enrollment/Completion	91.4%	6	81.2
			% College Graduates	26.9%	7	58.0
Commute	12	45.25	Average Work Commute in Minutes	23	17	55.6
			% Commuting on Public Transportation	1.5%	3	34.9
Community Stability	7	71.75	% Living in Same House as in 1979	32.0%	9	65.9
			% Living in Same County as in 1985	77.2%	6	77.6

Composite: Rank 3 / 28 Score 61.31 — TEMPLE TERRACE

CATEGORY	RANK	SCORE	STATISTIC	VALUE	RANK	SCORE
Economics	8	71.25	Median Household Income	$37,156	6	59.8
			% of Families Above Poverty Level	94.5%	15	82.7
Affordable Housing	23	45.95	Median Home Value	$99,200	25	34.7
			Median Rent	$523	21	57.2
Crime	N/A	N/A	Violent Crimes per 10,000 Population	47	N/A	N/A
			Property Crimes per 10,000 Population	492	N/A	N/A
Open Spaces	13	57.55	Population Density (Persons/Sq. Mile)	3326	15	52.6
			Average Rooms per Housing Unit	5.6	7	62.5
Education	4	86.80	% High School Enrollment/Completion	92.0%	4	83.2
			% College Graduates	39.7%	2	90.4
Commute	9	54.90	Average Work Commute in Minutes	20	4	88.9
			% Commuting on Public Transportation	0.9%	12	20.9
Community Stability	19	51.40	% Living in Same House as in 1979	23.2%	19	45.3
			% Living in Same County as in 1985	69.6%	17	57.5

Metropolitan Area Suburb Rankings
TAMPA-ST. PETERSBURG-CLEARWATER

Composite: *Rank* 4 / 28 *Score* 59.68   **PALM RIVER-CLAIR MEL**

CATEGORY	RANK	SCORE	STATISTIC	VALUE	RANK	SCORE
Economics	26	30.10	Median Household Income	$25,723	16	26.1
			% of Families Above Poverty Level	85.5%	27	34.1
Affordable Housing	7	87.00	Median Home Value	$48,000	3	96.7
			Median Rent	$452	9	77.3
Crime	N/A	N/A	Violent Crimes per 10,000 Population	N/A	N/A	N/A
			Property Crimes per 10,000 Population	N/A	N/A	N/A
Open Spaces	7	68.15	Population Density (Persons/Sq. Mile)	1691	4	83.2
			Average Rooms per Housing Unit	5.3	8	53.1
Education	25	21.10	% High School Enrollment/Completion	79.6%	21	42.2
			% College Graduates	4.0%	28	0.0
Commute	7	56.35	Average Work Commute in Minutes	21	10	77.8
			% Commuting on Public Transportation	1.5%	3	34.9
Community Stability	1	95.35	% Living in Same House as in 1979	42.6%	3	90.7
			% Living in Same County as in 1985	85.7%	1	100.0

Composite: *Rank* 5 / 28 *Score* 58.85   **BRANDON**

CATEGORY	RANK	SCORE	STATISTIC	VALUE	RANK	SCORE
Economics	5	81.65	Median Household Income	$39,798	5	67.6
			% of Families Above Poverty Level	96.9%	4	95.7
Affordable Housing	21	51.60	Median Home Value	$84,500	21	52.5
			Median Rent	$546	23	50.7
Crime	N/A	N/A	Violent Crimes per 10,000 Population	N/A	N/A	N/A
			Property Crimes per 10,000 Population	N/A	N/A	N/A
Open Spaces	3	74.75	Population Density (Persons/Sq. Mile)	1994	6	77.6
			Average Rooms per Housing Unit	5.9	4	71.9
Education	9	63.25	% High School Enrollment/Completion	89.8%	9	75.9
			% College Graduates	24.0%	8	50.6
Commute	22	27.10	Average Work Commute in Minutes	25	23	33.3
			% Commuting on Public Transportation	0.9%	12	20.9
Community Stability	18	54.75	% Living in Same House as in 1979	25.7%	17	51.2
			% Living in Same County as in 1985	69.9%	14	58.3

Composite: *Rank* 6 / 28 *Score* 57.49   **WEST PARK**

CATEGORY	RANK	SCORE	STATISTIC	VALUE	RANK	SCORE
Economics	20	46.20	Median Household Income	$26,781	11	29.2
			% of Families Above Poverty Level	90.9%	23	63.2
Affordable Housing	11	80.35	Median Home Value	$54,400	7	89.0
			Median Rent	$472	16	71.7
Crime	N/A	N/A	Violent Crimes per 10,000 Population	N/A	N/A	N/A
			Property Crimes per 10,000 Population	N/A	N/A	N/A
Open Spaces	22	37.20	Population Density (Persons/Sq. Mile)	4502	24	30.6
			Average Rooms per Housing Unit	5.0	17	43.8
Education	16	37.55	% High School Enrollment/Completion	86.1%	13	63.7
			% College Graduates	8.5%	22	11.4
Commute	8	55.20	Average Work Commute in Minutes	21	10	77.8
			% Commuting on Public Transportation	1.4%	5	32.6
Community Stability	2	88.45	% Living in Same House as in 1979	39.9%	4	84.3
			% Living in Same County as in 1985	82.9%	2	92.6

Metropolitan Area Suburb Rankings
TAMPA-ST. PETERSBURG-CLEARWATER

Composite: Rank 7 / 28 *Score* 56.48   **GULFPORT**

CATEGORY	RANK	SCORE	STATISTIC	VALUE	RANK	SCORE
Economics	19	46.45	Median Household Income	$21,397	22	13.4
			% of Families Above Poverty Level	93.9%	18	79.5
Affordable Housing	4	89.50	Median Home Value	$49,800	4	94.6
			Median Rent	$427	7	84.4
Crime	N/A	N/A	Violent Crimes per 10,000 Population	73	N/A	N/A
			Property Crimes per 10,000 Population	684	N/A	N/A
Open Spaces	24	35.95	Population Density (Persons/Sq. Mile)	4132	23	37.5
			Average Rooms per Housing Unit	4.7	21	34.4
Education	20	27.80	% High School Enrollment/Completion	74.9%	25	26.7
			% College Graduates	15.4%	14	28.9
Commute	2	63.05	Average Work Commute in Minutes	20	4	88.9
			% Commuting on Public Transportation	1.6%	2	37.2
Community Stability	5	76.10	% Living in Same House as in 1979	36.9%	5	77.3
			% Living in Same County as in 1985	76.2%	7	74.9

Composite: Rank 8 / 28 *Score* 56.42   **CARROLLWOOD VILLAGE**

CATEGORY	RANK	SCORE	STATISTIC	VALUE	RANK	SCORE
Economics	3	93.15	Median Household Income	$47,600	2	90.6
			% of Families Above Poverty Level	96.9%	4	95.7
Affordable Housing	27	22.95	Median Home Value	$127,900	28	0.0
			Median Rent	$563	24	45.9
Crime	N/A	N/A	Violent Crimes per 10,000 Population	N/A	N/A	N/A
			Property Crimes per 10,000 Population	N/A	N/A	N/A
Open Spaces	8	62.90	Population Density (Persons/Sq. Mile)	2920	11	60.2
			Average Rooms per Housing Unit	5.7	5	65.6
Education	1	98.50	% High School Enrollment/Completion	96.2%	2	97.0
			% College Graduates	43.5%	1	100.0
Commute	23	24.80	Average Work Commute in Minutes	25	23	33.3
			% Commuting on Public Transportation	0.7%	14	16.3
Community Stability	24	36.20	% Living in Same House as in 1979	10.4%	25	15.4
			% Living in Same County as in 1985	69.4%	18	57.0

Composite: Rank 9 / 28 *Score* 56.41   **DUNEDIN**

CATEGORY	RANK	SCORE	STATISTIC	VALUE	RANK	SCORE
Economics	11	57.15	Median Household Income	$25,906	15	26.7
			% of Families Above Poverty Level	95.4%	9	87.6
Affordable Housing	18	67.35	Median Home Value	$77,300	18	61.3
			Median Rent	$466	13	73.4
Crime	N/A	N/A	Violent Crimes per 10,000 Population	50	N/A	N/A
			Property Crimes per 10,000 Population	370	N/A	N/A
Open Spaces	17	45.40	Population Density (Persons/Sq. Mile)	3289	14	53.3
			Average Rooms per Housing Unit	4.8	20	37.5
Education	11	54.35	% High School Enrollment/Completion	88.3%	11	71.0
			% College Graduates	18.9%	13	37.7
Commute	11	47.05	Average Work Commute in Minutes	21	10	77.8
			% Commuting on Public Transportation	0.7%	14	16.3
Community Stability	12	67.15	% Living in Same House as in 1979	31.9%	10	65.7
			% Living in Same County as in 1985	73.8%	11	68.6

Metropolitan Area Suburb Rankings
TAMPA-ST. PETERSBURG-CLEARWATER

Composite: *Rank* 10 / 28 *Score* 54.73 **EGYPT LAKE**

CATEGORY	RANK	SCORE	STATISTIC	VALUE	RANK	SCORE
Economics	13	52.05	Median Household Income	$26,685	12	29.0
			% of Families Above Poverty Level	93.1%	19	75.1
Affordable Housing	14	71.05	Median Home Value	$70,900	14	69.0
			Median Rent	$467	14	73.1
Crime	N/A	N/A	Violent Crimes per 10,000 Population	N/A	N/A	N/A
			Property Crimes per 10,000 Population	N/A	N/A	N/A
Open Spaces	27	21.10	Population Density (Persons/Sq. Mile)	5381	27	14.1
			Average Rooms per Housing Unit	4.5	24	28.1
Education	7	66.65	% High School Enrollment/Completion	92.0%	4	83.2
			% College Graduates	23.8%	9	50.1
Commute	5	57.25	Average Work Commute in Minutes	20	4	88.9
			% Commuting on Public Transportation	1.1%	6	25.6
Community Stability	15	60.25	% Living in Same House as in 1979	24.1%	18	47.4
			% Living in Same County as in 1985	75.5%	9	73.1

Composite: *Rank* 11 / 28 *Score* 54.65 **ELFERS**

CATEGORY	RANK	SCORE	STATISTIC	VALUE	RANK	SCORE
Economics	23	42.35	Median Household Income	$18,461	27	4.7
			% of Families Above Poverty Level	94.0%	17	80.0
Affordable Housing	5	88.95	Median Home Value	$45,300	1	100.0
			Median Rent	$450	8	77.9
Crime	N/A	N/A	Violent Crimes per 10,000 Population	N/A	N/A	N/A
			Property Crimes per 10,000 Population	N/A	N/A	N/A
Open Spaces	16	48.30	Population Density (Persons/Sq. Mile)	3483	19	49.7
			Average Rooms per Housing Unit	5.1	13	46.9
Education	24	23.10	% High School Enrollment/Completion	79.8%	20	42.9
			% College Graduates	5.3%	26	3.3
Commute	13	44.45	Average Work Commute in Minutes	20	4	88.9
			% Commuting on Public Transportation	0.0%	25	0.0
Community Stability	3	80.75	% Living in Same House as in 1979	46.6%	1	100.0
			% Living in Same County as in 1985	71.1%	12	61.5

Composite: *Rank* 12 / 28 *Score* 54.58 **GREATER NORTHDALE**

CATEGORY	RANK	SCORE	STATISTIC	VALUE	RANK	SCORE
Economics	2	94.20	Median Household Income	$46,841	3	88.4
			% of Families Above Poverty Level	97.7%	1	100.0
Affordable Housing	26	28.45	Median Home Value	$93,500	22	41.6
			Median Rent	$671	27	15.3
Crime	N/A	N/A	Violent Crimes per 10,000 Population	N/A	N/A	N/A
			Property Crimes per 10,000 Population	N/A	N/A	N/A
Open Spaces	4	72.80	Population Density (Persons/Sq. Mile)	2700	9	64.3
			Average Rooms per Housing Unit	6.2	3	81.3
Education	3	89.10	% High School Enrollment/Completion	95.8%	3	95.7
			% College Graduates	36.6%	4	82.5
Commute	26	17.20	Average Work Commute in Minutes	27	26	11.1
			% Commuting on Public Transportation	1.0%	10	23.3
Community Stability	25	25.75	% Living in Same House as in 1979	9.1%	26	12.4
			% Living in Same County as in 1985	62.6%	25	39.1

Metropolitan Area Suburb Rankings
TAMPA-ST. PETERSBURG-CLEARWATER

Composite: Rank 13 / 28 *Score* 54.49   **PINELLAS PARK**

CATEGORY	RANK	SCORE	STATISTIC	VALUE	RANK	SCORE
Economics	14	51.20	Median Household Income	$26,109	13	27.3
			% of Families Above Poverty Level	93.1%	19	75.1
Affordable Housing	12	72.05	Median Home Value	$62,000	12	79.8
			Median Rent	$498	19	64.3
Crime	N/A	N/A	Violent Crimes per 10,000 Population	48	N/A	N/A
			Property Crimes per 10,000 Population	700	N/A	N/A
Open Spaces	15	48.45	Population Density (Persons/Sq. Mile)	3131	13	56.3
			Average Rooms per Housing Unit	4.9	19	40.6
Education	22	26.60	% High School Enrollment/Completion	77.7%	23	36.0
			% College Graduates	10.8%	19	17.2
Commute	4	58.15	Average Work Commute in Minutes	19	1	100.0
			% Commuting on Public Transportation	0.7%	14	16.3
Community Stability	9	70.50	% Living in Same House as in 1979	29.6%	13	60.3
			% Living in Same County as in 1985	78.4%	5	80.7

Composite: Rank 14 / 28 *Score* 54.48   **TOWN 'N' COUNTRY**

CATEGORY	RANK	SCORE	STATISTIC	VALUE	RANK	SCORE
Economics	10	68.50	Median Household Income	$33,820	9	50.0
			% of Families Above Poverty Level	95.3%	11	87.0
Affordable Housing	20	60.00	Median Home Value	$73,700	16	65.6
			Median Rent	$533	22	54.4
Crime	N/A	N/A	Violent Crimes per 10,000 Population	N/A	N/A	N/A
			Property Crimes per 10,000 Population	N/A	N/A	N/A
Open Spaces	11	58.30	Population Density (Persons/Sq. Mile)	2578	8	66.6
			Average Rooms per Housing Unit	5.2	11	50.0
Education	12	48.50	% High School Enrollment/Completion	84.3%	15	57.8
			% College Graduates	19.5%	12	39.2
Commute	16	40.60	Average Work Commute in Minutes	23	17	55.6
			% Commuting on Public Transportation	1.1%	6	25.6
Community Stability	20	51.00	% Living in Same House as in 1979	22.7%	20	44.2
			% Living in Same County as in 1985	69.7%	16	57.8

Composite: Rank 15 / 28 *Score* 53.07   **BLOOMINGDALE**

CATEGORY	RANK	SCORE	STATISTIC	VALUE	RANK	SCORE
Economics	1	98.90	Median Household Income	$50,790	1	100.0
			% of Families Above Poverty Level	97.3%	2	97.8
Affordable Housing	28	13.10	Median Home Value	$106,300	27	26.2
			Median Rent	$725	28	0.0
Crime	N/A	N/A	Violent Crimes per 10,000 Population	N/A	N/A	N/A
			Property Crimes per 10,000 Population	N/A	N/A	N/A
Open Spaces	2	90.80	Population Density (Persons/Sq. Mile)	1781	5	81.6
			Average Rooms per Housing Unit	6.8	1	100.0
Education	2	92.30	% High School Enrollment/Completion	97.1%	1	100.0
			% College Graduates	37.4%	3	84.6
Commute	28	11.65	Average Work Commute in Minutes	28	28	0.0
			% Commuting on Public Transportation	1.0%	10	23.3
Community Stability	27	11.70	% Living in Same House as in 1979	7.6%	27	8.9
			% Living in Same County as in 1985	53.3%	26	14.5

Metropolitan Area Suburb Rankings
TAMPA-ST. PETERSBURG-CLEARWATER

Composite: *Rank* 16 / 28 *Score* 52.80 — **SAFETY HARBOR**

CATEGORY	RANK	SCORE	STATISTIC	VALUE	RANK	SCORE
Economics	7	73.10	Median Household Income	$36,935	7	59.2
			% of Families Above Poverty Level	95.3%	11	87.0
Affordable Housing	22	46.20	Median Home Value	$99,600	26	34.3
			Median Rent	$520	20	58.1
Crime	N/A	N/A	Violent Crimes per 10,000 Population	35	N/A	N/A
			Property Crimes per 10,000 Population	380	N/A	N/A
Open Spaces	10	59.00	Population Density (Persons/Sq. Mile)	3338	16	52.4
			Average Rooms per Housing Unit	5.7	5	65.6
Education	8	66.05	% High School Enrollment/Completion	88.2%	12	70.6
			% College Graduates	28.3%	6	61.5
Commute	21	29.20	Average Work Commute in Minutes	24	21	44.4
			% Commuting on Public Transportation	0.6%	18	14.0
Community Stability	21	43.25	% Living in Same House as in 1979	18.0%	21	33.2
			% Living in Same County as in 1985	68.0%	21	53.3

Composite: *Rank* 17 / 28 *Score* 52.69 — **TARPON SPRINGS**

CATEGORY	RANK	SCORE	STATISTIC	VALUE	RANK	SCORE
Economics	18	49.30	Median Household Income	$25,380	17	25.1
			% of Families Above Poverty Level	92.8%	21	73.5
Affordable Housing	13	71.60	Median Home Value	$80,100	19	57.9
			Median Rent	$424	6	85.3
Crime	N/A	N/A	Violent Crimes per 10,000 Population	108	N/A	N/A
			Property Crimes per 10,000 Population	642	N/A	N/A
Open Spaces	9	60.05	Population Density (Persons/Sq. Mile)	2062	7	76.3
			Average Rooms per Housing Unit	5.0	17	43.8
Education	15	39.15	% High School Enrollment/Completion	82.0%	17	50.2
			% College Graduates	15.1%	15	28.1
Commute	19	35.95	Average Work Commute in Minutes	23	17	55.6
			% Commuting on Public Transportation	0.7%	14	16.3
Community Stability	16	60.10	% Living in Same House as in 1979	29.4%	14	59.8
			% Living in Same County as in 1985	70.7%	13	60.4

Composite: *Rank* 18 / 28 *Score* 52.23 — **PLANT CITY**

CATEGORY	RANK	SCORE	STATISTIC	VALUE	RANK	SCORE
Economics	25	30.50	Median Household Income	$25,268	18	24.8
			% of Families Above Poverty Level	85.9%	26	36.2
Affordable Housing	6	87.50	Median Home Value	$59,400	10	82.9
			Median Rent	$400	2	92.1
Crime	N/A	N/A	Violent Crimes per 10,000 Population	242	N/A	N/A
			Property Crimes per 10,000 Population	1,299	N/A	N/A
Open Spaces	6	70.85	Population Density (Persons/Sq. Mile)	1075	2	94.8
			Average Rooms per Housing Unit	5.1	13	46.9
Education	26	17.70	% High School Enrollment/Completion	70.3%	26	11.6
			% College Graduates	13.4%	18	23.8
Commute	17	38.90	Average Work Commute in Minutes	21	10	77.8
			% Commuting on Public Transportation	0.0%	25	0.0
Community Stability	10	67.95	% Living in Same House as in 1979	29.9%	12	61.0
			% Living in Same County as in 1985	76.2%	7	74.9

Metropolitan Area Suburb Rankings
TAMPA-ST. PETERSBURG-CLEARWATER

Composite: *Rank* 19 / 28 *Score* 51.65   **LARGO**

CATEGORY	RANK	SCORE	STATISTIC	VALUE	RANK	SCORE
Economics	12	55.25	Median Household Income	$24,296	19	21.9
			% of Families Above Poverty Level	95.6%	8	88.6
Affordable Housing	15	69.65	Median Home Value	$71,800	15	67.9
			Median Rent	$473	17	71.4
Crime	N/A	N/A	Violent Crimes per 10,000 Population	58	N/A	N/A
			Property Crimes per 10,000 Population	453	N/A	N/A
Open Spaces	26	29.55	Population Density (Persons/Sq. Mile)	4647	25	27.9
			Average Rooms per Housing Unit	4.6	23	31.2
Education	17	36.50	% High School Enrollment/Completion	81.4%	18	48.2
			% College Graduates	13.8%	17	24.8
Commute	10	51.45	Average Work Commute in Minutes	20	4	88.9
			% Commuting on Public Transportation	0.6%	18	14.0
Community Stability	11	67.50	% Living in Same House as in 1979	30.3%	11	61.9
			% Living in Same County as in 1985	75.5%	9	73.1

Composite: *Rank* 20 / 28 *Score* 51.32   **HOLIDAY**

CATEGORY	RANK	SCORE	STATISTIC	VALUE	RANK	SCORE
Economics	21	45.85	Median Household Income	$18,623	25	5.2
			% of Families Above Poverty Level	95.2%	13	86.5
Affordable Housing	3	92.25	Median Home Value	$46,400	2	98.7
			Median Rent	$422	5	85.8
Crime	N/A	N/A	Violent Crimes per 10,000 Population	N/A	N/A	N/A
			Property Crimes per 10,000 Population	N/A	N/A	N/A
Open Spaces	21	39.70	Population Density (Persons/Sq. Mile)	3733	20	45.0
			Average Rooms per Housing Unit	4.7	21	34.4
Education	18	33.80	% High School Enrollment/Completion	85.9%	14	63.0
			% College Graduates	5.8%	25	4.6
Commute	24	24.55	Average Work Commute in Minutes	24	21	44.4
			% Commuting on Public Transportation	0.2%	22	4.7
Community Stability	7	71.75	% Living in Same House as in 1979	43.3%	2	92.3
			% Living in Same County as in 1985	67.2%	22	51.2

Composite: *Rank* 21 / 28 *Score* 51.04   **BAYONET POINT**

CATEGORY	RANK	SCORE	STATISTIC	VALUE	RANK	SCORE
Economics	16	49.95	Median Household Income	$21,408	21	13.4
			% of Families Above Poverty Level	95.2%	13	86.5
Affordable Housing	10	80.70	Median Home Value	$55,900	9	87.2
			Median Rent	$463	11	74.2
Crime	N/A	N/A	Violent Crimes per 10,000 Population	N/A	N/A	N/A
			Property Crimes per 10,000 Population	N/A	N/A	N/A
Open Spaces	18	44.40	Population Density (Persons/Sq. Mile)	3897	21	41.9
			Average Rooms per Housing Unit	5.1	13	46.9
Education	23	26.10	% High School Enrollment/Completion	79.1%	22	40.6
			% College Graduates	8.6%	21	11.6
Commute	15	41.25	Average Work Commute in Minutes	21	10	77.8
			% Commuting on Public Transportation	0.2%	22	4.7
Community Stability	13	63.85	% Living in Same House as in 1979	35.1%	6	73.1
			% Living in Same County as in 1985	68.5%	20	54.6

Metropolitan Area Suburb Rankings
TAMPA-ST. PETERSBURG-CLEARWATER

Composite: Rank 22 / 28 **Score** 50.60   **LEALMAN**

CATEGORY	RANK	SCORE	STATISTIC	VALUE	RANK	SCORE
Economics	24	37.30	Median Household Income	$19,080	24	6.5
			% of Families Above Poverty Level	91.8%	22	68.1
Affordable Housing	2	92.55	Median Home Value	$50,100	5	94.2
			Median Rent	$404	3	90.9
Crime	N/A	N/A	Violent Crimes per 10,000 Population	N/A	N/A	N/A
			Property Crimes per 10,000 Population	N/A	N/A	N/A
Open Spaces	25	29.75	Population Density (Persons/Sq. Mile)	4126	22	37.6
			Average Rooms per Housing Unit	4.3	27	21.9
Education	28	4.70	% High School Enrollment/Completion	67.5%	27	2.3
			% College Graduates	6.8%	24	7.1
Commute	3	62.80	Average Work Commute in Minutes	19	1	100.0
			% Commuting on Public Transportation	1.1%	6	25.6
Community Stability	4	76.50	% Living in Same House as in 1979	32.7%	8	67.5
			% Living in Same County as in 1985	80.2%	4	85.5

Composite: Rank 23 / 28 **Score** 49.74   **JASMINE ESTATES**

CATEGORY	RANK	SCORE	STATISTIC	VALUE	RANK	SCORE
Economics	15	50.25	Median Household Income	$21,220	23	12.9
			% of Families Above Poverty Level	95.4%	9	87.6
Affordable Housing	9	81.60	Median Home Value	$54,400	7	89.0
			Median Rent	$463	11	74.2
Crime	N/A	N/A	Violent Crimes per 10,000 Population	N/A	N/A	N/A
			Property Crimes per 10,000 Population	N/A	N/A	N/A
Open Spaces	23	36.20	Population Density (Persons/Sq. Mile)	4776	26	25.5
			Average Rooms per Housing Unit	5.1	13	46.9
Education	19	29.55	% High School Enrollment/Completion	83.8%	16	56.1
			% College Graduates	5.2%	27	3.0
Commute	17	38.90	Average Work Commute in Minutes	21	10	77.8
			% Commuting on Public Transportation	0.0%	25	0.0
Community Stability	14	61.95	% Living in Same House as in 1979	32.9%	7	68.0
			% Living in Same County as in 1985	69.0%	19	55.9

Composite: Rank 24 / 28 **Score** 47.95   **PALM HARBOR**

CATEGORY	RANK	SCORE	STATISTIC	VALUE	RANK	SCORE
Economics	6	74.55	Median Household Income	$34,281	8	51.3
			% of Families Above Poverty Level	97.3%	2	97.8
Affordable Housing	25	41.25	Median Home Value	$97,200	24	37.2
			Median Rent	$565	25	45.3
Crime	N/A	N/A	Violent Crimes per 10,000 Population	N/A	N/A	N/A
			Property Crimes per 10,000 Population	N/A	N/A	N/A
Open Spaces	12	57.75	Population Density (Persons/Sq. Mile)	2803	10	62.4
			Average Rooms per Housing Unit	5.3	8	53.1
Education	10	62.50	% High School Enrollment/Completion	90.0%	8	76.6
			% College Graduates	23.1%	10	48.4
Commute	27	14.60	Average Work Commute in Minutes	26	25	22.2
			% Commuting on Public Transportation	0.3%	21	7.0
Community Stability	23	37.05	% Living in Same House as in 1979	15.2%	24	26.6
			% Living in Same County as in 1985	65.8%	24	47.5

Composite: *Rank* 25 / 28 *Score* 46.38   **HIGHPOINT**

CATEGORY	RANK	SCORE	STATISTIC	VALUE	RANK	SCORE
Economics	22	44.80	Median Household Income	$25,988	14	26.9
			% of Families Above Poverty Level	90.8%	24	62.7
Affordable Housing	17	68.95	Median Home Value	$73,900	17	65.4
			Median Rent	$469	15	72.5
Crime	N/A	N/A	Violent Crimes per 10,000 Population	N/A	N/A	N/A
			Property Crimes per 10,000 Population	N/A	N/A	N/A
Open Spaces	19	40.65	Population Density (Persons/Sq. Mile)	3127	12	56.3
			Average Rooms per Housing Unit	4.4	26	25.0
Education	21	27.50	% High School Enrollment/Completion	75.4%	24	28.4
			% College Graduates	14.5%	16	26.6
Commute	6	57.00	Average Work Commute in Minutes	19	1	100.0
			% Commuting on Public Transportation	0.6%	18	14.0
Community Stability	22	39.40	% Living in Same House as in 1979	16.5%	22	29.7
			% Living in Same County as in 1985	66.4%	23	49.1

Composite: *Rank* 26 / 28 *Score* 46.27   **SPRING HILL**

CATEGORY	RANK	SCORE	STATISTIC	VALUE	RANK	SCORE
Economics	17	49.80	Median Household Income	$23,349	20	19.1
			% of Families Above Poverty Level	94.1%	16	80.5
Affordable Housing	16	69.60	Median Home Value	$66,900	13	73.8
			Median Rent	$494	18	65.4
Crime	N/A	N/A	Violent Crimes per 10,000 Population	N/A	N/A	N/A
			Property Crimes per 10,000 Population	N/A	N/A	N/A
Open Spaces	5	71.15	Population Density (Persons/Sq. Mile)	1372	3	89.2
			Average Rooms per Housing Unit	5.3	8	53.1
Education	14	43.50	% High School Enrollment/Completion	89.4%	10	74.6
			% College Graduates	8.9%	20	12.4
Commute	20	30.15	Average Work Commute in Minutes	23	17	55.6
			% Commuting on Public Transportation	0.2%	22	4.7
Community Stability	26	13.45	% Living in Same House as in 1979	15.3%	23	26.9
			% Living in Same County as in 1985	47.8%	28	0.0

Composite: *Rank* 27 / 28 *Score* 45.66   **NEW PORT RICHEY**

CATEGORY	RANK	SCORE	STATISTIC	VALUE	RANK	SCORE
Economics	27	29.50	Median Household Income	$18,514	26	4.9
			% of Families Above Poverty Level	89.2%	25	54.1
Affordable Housing	1	96.05	Median Home Value	$51,800	6	92.1
			Median Rent	$372	1	100.0
Crime	N/A	N/A	Violent Crimes per 10,000 Population	40	N/A	N/A
			Property Crimes per 10,000 Population	860	N/A	N/A
Open Spaces	20	40.20	Population Density (Persons/Sq. Mile)	3341	17	52.3
			Average Rooms per Housing Unit	4.5	24	28.1
Education	27	5.30	% High School Enrollment/Completion	66.8%	28	0.0
			% College Graduates	8.2%	23	10.6
Commute	13	44.45	Average Work Commute in Minutes	20	4	88.9
			% Commuting on Public Transportation	0.0%	25	0.0
Community Stability	17	58.45	% Living in Same House as in 1979	28.9%	15	58.6
			% Living in Same County as in 1985	69.9%	14	58.3

Metropolitan Area Suburb Rankings
TAMPA-ST. PETERSBURG-CLEARWATER

Composite: **Rank** 28 / 28 **Score** 37.85   **UNIVERSITY WEST**

CATEGORY	RANK	SCORE	STATISTIC	VALUE	RANK	SCORE
Economics	28	0.00	Median Household Income	$16,859	28	0.0
			% of Families Above Poverty Level	79.2%	28	0.0
Affordable Housing	8	84.45	Median Home Value	$61,400	11	80.5
			Median Rent	$413	4	88.4
Crime	N/A	N/A	Violent Crimes per 10,000 Population	N/A	N/A	N/A
			Property Crimes per 10,000 Population	N/A	N/A	N/A
Open Spaces	28	0.00	Population Density (Persons/Sq. Mile)	6135	28	0.0
			Average Rooms per Housing Unit	3.6	28	0.0
Education	13	47.30	% High School Enrollment/Completion	80.8%	19	46.2
			% College Graduates	23.1%	10	48.4
Commute	1	88.90	Average Work Commute in Minutes	21	10	77.8
			% Commuting on Public Transportation	4.3%	1	100.0
Community Stability	28	6.45	% Living in Same House as in 1979	3.8%	28	0.0
			% Living in Same County as in 1985	52.7%	27	12.9

Metropolitan Area Description
WASHINGTON

DISTRICT: District of Columbia

STATE: Maryland
COUNTIES: Calvert, Charles, Frederick, Montgomery, Prince George's

STATE: Virginia
COUNTIES: Arlington, Fairfax, Loudoun, Prince William, Stafford

INDE-PENDENT CITIES: Alexandria, Fairfax, Falls Church, Manassas, Manassas Park

TOTAL POPULATION: 3,923,574

POPULATION IN SUBURBS: 3,316,674 (84.5%)

POPULATION IN Washington (DC): 606,900 (15.5%)

The WASHINGTON metropolitan area is located in the District of Columbia, the northeastern part of Virginia, and the southwestern part of Maryland. The suburbs range geographically from Frederick (MD) in the north (45 miles from Washington), to Leesburg (VA) in the west (38 miles from Washington), to St. Charles (MD) in the south (29 miles from Washington), and to Bowie (MD) in the east (20 miles from Washington). The area is growing in population and had an increase of 20.7% between 1980 and 1990. Summer time high temperatures average in the 80's and winter time lows average in the 20's. The suburban area contains many government offices and commercial companies. The Pentagon is located in Arlington (VA). Mobil Oil has its headquarters in the suburb of Fairfax (VA). Public transportation in the area is provided by the Washington Metropolitan Area Transit Authority using buses and trains.

Fort Hunt (VA) is the overall highest rated suburb and also has the highest score in community stability. **Wolf Trap** (VA) receives the top scores in economics and open spaces. **Hyattsville** (MD) is the suburb with the most affordable housing. **Potomac** (MD) has the number one score in education. Finally, the top rated commute belongs to **Arlington** (VA). Crime rankings were not available for the area.

The highest ranked suburb overall which also has an affordable housing score of at least 50.00 is **Fort Washington** (MD).

The highest ranked suburb in the education category which also has an affordable housing score of at least 50.00 is **Annandale** (VA).

The county whose suburbs have the highest average overall score is **Montgomery County** (MD) (57.93).

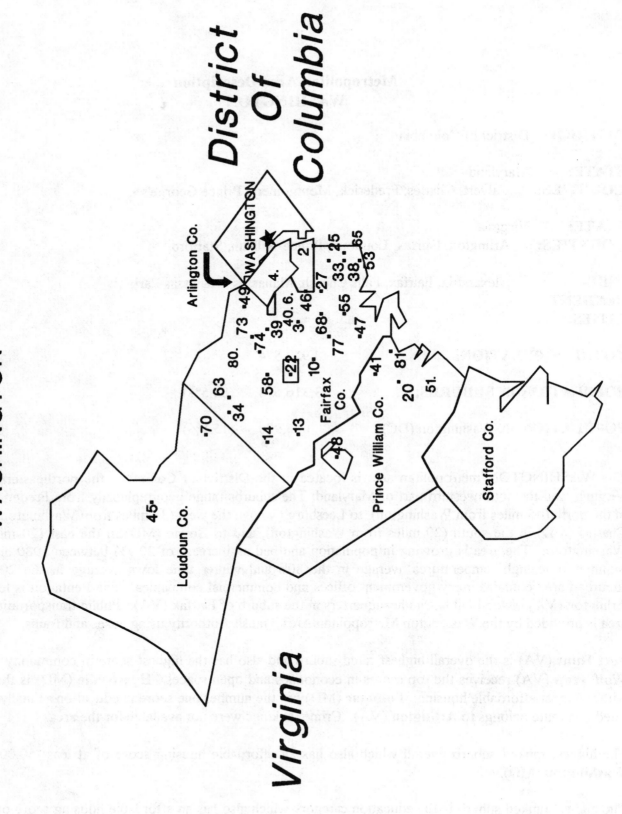

Metropolitan Area Map (Part 1)
WASHINGTON

District
Of
Columbia

WASHINGTON

Arlington Co.

Virginia

Loudoun Co.

Fairfax
Co.

Prince William Co.

Stafford Co.

Metropolitan Area Map (Part 2)
WASHINGTON

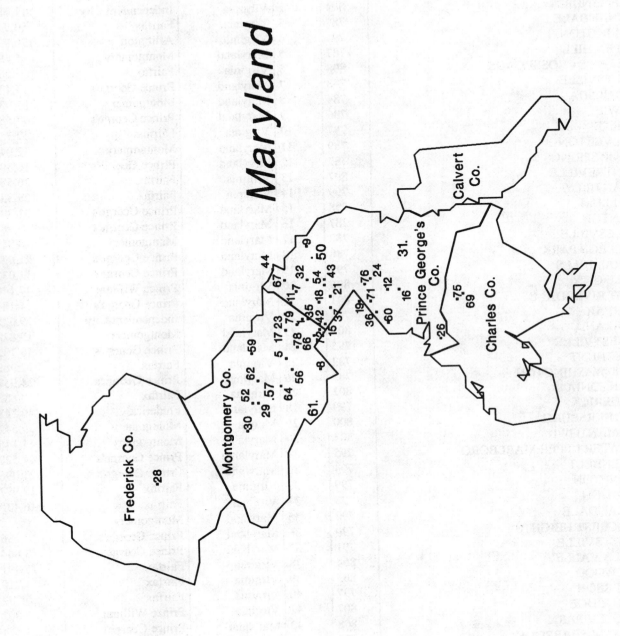

Maryland

Frederick Co.

•28

Montgomery Co.

•30 52 62
    29 57
      64
        56
      66
    •78
  5 17 23
    •79
  •59
      44
      67
    11 7 32
      35
      42 •18 54 •9
        12 15 37 21 43 50
        •8
    61.

19 •76
36 •71 24
    •60 •12
      16 • 31.

Prince George's
Co.

•26

Charles Co.

•75
69

Calvert
Co.

Metropolitan Area Suburb Alphabetical Index
WASHINGTON

SUBURB	PAGE	MAP NO.	STATE	COUNTY	POPU-LATION	RANK
ADELPHI	800	1	Maryland	Prince George's	13,524	57 / 81
ALEXANDRIA	804	2	Virginia	Independent City	111,183	69 / 81
ANNANDALE	787	3	Virginia	Fairfax	50,975	16 / 81
ARLINGTON	794	4	Virginia	Arlington	170,936	38 / 81
ASPEN HILL	787	5	Maryland	Montgomery	45,494	17 / 81
BAILEY'S CROSSROADS	808	6	Virginia	Fairfax	19,507	80 / 81
BELTSVILLE	788	7	Maryland	Prince George's	14,476	21 / 81
BETHESDA	784	8	Maryland	Montgomery	62,936	8 / 81
BOWIE	786	9	Maryland	Prince George's	37,589	15 / 81
BURKE	797	10	Virginia	Fairfax	57,734	47 / 81
CALVERTON	789	11	Maryland	Montgomery	12,046	22 / 81
CAMP SPRINGS	783	12	Maryland	Prince George's	16,392	6 / 81
CENTREVILLE	807	13	Virginia	Fairfax	26,585	76 / 81
CHANTILLY	799	14	Virginia	Fairfax	29,337	52 / 81
CHILLUM	798	15	Maryland	Prince George's	31,309	51 / 81
CLINTON	787	16	Maryland	Prince George's	19,987	18 / 81
COLESVILLE	782	17	Maryland	Montgomery	18,819	2 / 81
COLLEGE PARK	788	18	Maryland	Prince George's	21,927	18 / 81
CORAL HILLS	793	19	Maryland	Prince George's	11,032	36 / 81
DALE CITY	806	20	Virginia	Prince William	47,170	73 / 81
EAST RIVERDALE	801	21	Maryland	Prince George's	14,187	60 / 81
FAIRFAX	793	22	Virginia	Independent City	19,622	35 / 81
FAIRLAND	805	23	Maryland	Montgomery	19,828	69 / 81
FORESTVILLE	795	24	Maryland	Prince George's	16,731	42 / 81
FORT HUNT	782	25	Virginia	Fairfax	12,989	1 / 81
FORT WASHINGTON	783	26	Maryland	Prince George's	24,032	5 / 81
FRANCONIA	802	27	Virginia	Fairfax	19,882	63 / 81
FREDERICK	799	28	Maryland	Frederick	40,148	53 / 81
GAITHERSBURG	800	29	Maryland	Montgomery	39,542	56 / 81
GERMANTOWN	803	30	Maryland	Montgomery	41,145	66 / 81
GREATER UPPER MARLBORO	795	31	Maryland	Prince George's	11,528	40 / 81
GREENBELT	794	32	Maryland	Prince George's	21,096	37 / 81
GROVETON	799	33	Virginia	Fairfax	19,997	54 / 81
HERNDON	796	34	Virginia	Fairfax	16,139	45 / 81
HILLANDALE	790	35	Maryland	Montgomery	10,318	27 / 81
HILLCREST HEIGHTS	790	36	Maryland	Prince George's	17,136	25 / 81
HYATTSVILLE	791	37	Maryland	Prince George's	13,864	29 / 81
HYBLA VALLEY	804	38	Virginia	Fairfax	15,491	68 / 81
IDYLWOOD	805	39	Virginia	Fairfax	14,710	71 / 81
JEFFERSON	797	40	Virginia	Fairfax	25,782	48 / 81
LAKE RIDGE	807	41	Virginia	Prince William	23,862	77 / 81
LANGLEY PARK	808	42	Maryland	Prince George's	17,474	81 / 81
LANHAM-SEABROOK	784	43	Maryland	Prince George's	16,792	9 / 81
LAUREL	801	44	Maryland	Prince George's	19,438	59 / 81
LEESBURG	804	45	Virginia	Loudoun	16,202	67 / 81
LINCOLNIA	801	46	Virginia	Fairfax	13,041	58 / 81
LORTON	808	47	Virginia	Fairfax	15,385	79 / 81
MANASSAS	807	48	Virginia	Independent City	27,957	78 / 81
MCLEAN	784	49	Virginia	Fairfax	38,168	7 / 81
MITCHELLVILLE	789	50	Maryland	Prince George's	12,593	24 / 81
MONTCLAIR	805	51	Virginia	Prince William	11,399	72 / 81

Metropolitan Area Suburb Alphabetical Index
WASHINGTON

SUBURB	PAGE	MAP NO.	STATE	COUNTY	POPU-LATION	RANK
MONTGOMERY VILLAGE	795	52	Maryland	Montgomery	32,315	41 / 81
MOUNT VERNON	797	53	Virginia	Fairfax	27,485	46 / 81
NEW CARROLLTON	792	54	Maryland	Prince George's	12,002	33 / 81
NEWINGTON	803	55	Virginia	Fairfax	17,965	65 / 81
NORTH BETHESDA	792	56	Maryland	Montgomery	29,656	31 / 81
NORTH POTOMAC	794	57	Maryland	Montgomery	18,456	39 / 81
OAKTON	791	58	Virginia	Fairfax	24,610	28 / 81
OLNEY	786	59	Maryland	Montgomery	23,019	13 / 81
OXON HILL-GLASSMANOR	798	60	Maryland	Prince George's	35,794	49 / 81
POTOMAC	783	61	Maryland	Montgomery	45,634	4 / 81
REDLAND	785	62	Maryland	Montgomery	16,145	10 / 81
RESTON	796	63	Virginia	Fairfax	48,556	43 / 81
ROCKVILLE	786	64	Maryland	Montgomery	44,835	14 / 81
ROSE HILL	785	65	Virginia	Fairfax	12,675	11 / 81
SILVER SPRING	788	66	Maryland	Montgomery	76,046	20 / 81
SOUTH LAUREL	803	67	Maryland	Prince George's	18,591	64 / 81
SPRINGFIELD	792	68	Virginia	Fairfax	23,706	32 / 81
ST. CHARLES	806	69	Maryland	Charles	28,717	75 / 81
STERLING	800	70	Virginia	Loudoun	20,512	55 / 81
SUITLAND-SILVER HILL	802	71	Maryland	Prince George's	35,111	60 / 81
TAKOMA PARK	789	72	Maryland	Montgomery	16,700	23 / 81
TYSONS CORNER	802	73	Virginia	Fairfax	13,124	62 / 81
VIENNA	785	74	Virginia	Fairfax	14,852	12 / 81
WALDORF	798	75	Maryland	Charles	15,058	49 / 81
WALKER MILL	793	76	Maryland	Prince George's	10,920	34 / 81
WEST SPRINGFIELD	791	77	Virginia	Fairfax	28,126	30 / 81
WHEATON-GLENMONT	790	78	Maryland	Montgomery	53,720	26 / 81
WHITE OAK	796	79	Maryland	Montgomery	18,671	44 / 81
WOLF TRAP	782	80	Virginia	Fairfax	13,133	3 / 81
WOODBRIDGE	806	81	Virginia	Prince William	26,401	74 / 81

Metropolitan Area Suburb Rankings
WASHINGTON

Composite: *Rank* 1 / 81 *Score* 68.22 — FORT HUNT (VA)

CATEGORY	RANK	SCORE	STATISTIC	VALUE	RANK	SCORE
Economics	5	75.05	Median Household Income	$71,274	6	59.7
			% of Families Above Poverty Level	98.7%	18	90.4
Affordable Housing	77	25.10	Median Home Value	$250,400	74	50.2
			Median Rent	$1,001	72	0.0
Crime	N/A	N/A	Violent Crimes per 10,000 Population	N/A	N/A	N/A
			Property Crimes per 10,000 Population	N/A	N/A	N/A
Open Spaces	4	87.90	Population Density (Persons/Sq. Mile)	2620	24	86.9
			Average Rooms per Housing Unit	8.0	2	88.9
Education	5	90.65	% High School Enrollment/Completion	100.0%	1	100.0
			% College Graduates	58.5%	7	81.3
Commute	53	38.05	Average Work Commute in Minutes	29	31	60.0
			% Commuting on Public Transportation	6.0%	53	16.1
Community Stability	1	92.55	% Living in Same House as in 1979	59.7%	1	100.0
			% Living in Same County as in 1985	78.1%	11	85.1

Composite: *Rank* 2 / 81 *Score* 67.83 — COLESVILLE (MD)

CATEGORY	RANK	SCORE	STATISTIC	VALUE	RANK	SCORE
Economics	4	80.00	Median Household Income	$76,122	4	66.7
			% of Families Above Poverty Level	99.0%	12	93.3
Affordable Housing	64	42.20	Median Home Value	$233,000	72	55.3
			Median Rent	$867	62	29.1
Crime	N/A	N/A	Violent Crimes per 10,000 Population	N/A	N/A	N/A
			Property Crimes per 10,000 Population	N/A	N/A	N/A
Open Spaces	3	89.55	Population Density (Persons/Sq. Mile)	2038	11	90.2
			Average Rooms per Housing Unit	8.0	2	88.9
Education	6	84.35	% High School Enrollment/Completion	97.9%	8	92.8
			% College Graduates	55.1%	12	75.9
Commute	67	27.35	Average Work Commute in Minutes	32	51	45.0
			% Commuting on Public Transportation	3.9%	67	9.7
Community Stability	3	83.55	% Living in Same House as in 1979	44.8%	5	72.5
			% Living in Same County as in 1985	82.2%	3	94.6

Composite: *Rank* 3 / 81 *Score* 67.59 — WOLF TRAP (VA)

CATEGORY	RANK	SCORE	STATISTIC	VALUE	RANK	SCORE
Economics	1	97.00	Median Household Income	$97,846	2	97.8
			% of Families Above Poverty Level	99.3%	6	96.2
Affordable Housing	80	9.55	Median Home Value	$356,700	80	19.1
			Median Rent	$1,001	72	0.0
Crime	N/A	N/A	Violent Crimes per 10,000 Population	N/A	N/A	N/A
			Property Crimes per 10,000 Population	N/A	N/A	N/A
Open Spaces	1	96.90	Population Density (Persons/Sq. Mile)	1409	6	93.8
			Average Rooms per Housing Unit	8.5	1	100.0
Education	3	94.70	% High School Enrollment/Completion	98.1%	6	93.5
			% College Graduates	67.6%	3	95.9
Commute	54	37.75	Average Work Commute in Minutes	29	31	60.0
			% Commuting on Public Transportation	5.8%	55	15.5
Community Stability	14	69.65	% Living in Same House as in 1979	35.1%	21	54.5
			% Living in Same County as in 1985	78.0%	12	84.8

Metropolitan Area Suburb Rankings
WASHINGTON

Composite: *Rank* 4 / 81 *Score* 67.56   **POTOMAC** (MD)

CATEGORY	RANK	SCORE	STATISTIC	VALUE	RANK	SCORE
Economics	2	93.75	Median Household Income	$99,371	1	100.0
			% of Families Above Poverty Level	98.4%	21	87.5
Affordable Housing	81	0.00	Median Home Value	$421,800	81	0.0
			Median Rent	$1,001	72	0.0
Crime	N/A	N/A	Violent Crimes per 10,000 Population	N/A	N/A	N/A
			Property Crimes per 10,000 Population	N/A	N/A	N/A
Open Spaces	2	91.25	Population Density (Persons/Sq. Mile)	1436	7	93.6
			Average Rooms per Housing Unit	8.0	2	88.9
Education	1	97.75	% High School Enrollment/Completion	98.7%	2	95.5
			% College Graduates	70.2%	1	100.0
Commute	45	41.45	Average Work Commute in Minutes	28	26	65.0
			% Commuting on Public Transportation	6.6%	49	17.9
Community Stability	6	81.15	% Living in Same House as in 1979	43.0%	7	69.1
			% Living in Same County as in 1985	81.6%	5	93.2

Composite: *Rank* 5 / 81 *Score* 66.67   **FORT WASHINGTON** (MD)

CATEGORY	RANK	SCORE	STATISTIC	VALUE	RANK	SCORE
Economics	10	72.05	Median Household Income	$62,378	15	47.0
			% of Families Above Poverty Level	99.4%	4	97.1
Affordable Housing	25	74.30	Median Home Value	$151,500	34	79.2
			Median Rent	$681	23	69.4
Crime	N/A	N/A	Violent Crimes per 10,000 Population	N/A	N/A	N/A
			Property Crimes per 10,000 Population	N/A	N/A	N/A
Open Spaces	10	82.50	Population Density (Persons/Sq. Mile)	1775	8	91.7
			Average Rooms per Housing Unit	7.3	10	73.3
Education	37	64.65	% High School Enrollment/Completion	95.8%	17	85.6
			% College Graduates	34.9%	49	43.7
Commute	69	25.25	Average Work Commute in Minutes	34	69	35.0
			% Commuting on Public Transportation	5.8%	55	15.5
Community Stability	5	81.25	% Living in Same House as in 1979	43.7%	6	70.4
			% Living in Same County as in 1985	81.1%	6	92.1

Composite: *Rank* 6 / 81 *Score* 65.61   **CAMP SPRINGS** (MD)

CATEGORY	RANK	SCORE	STATISTIC	VALUE	RANK	SCORE
Economics	21	64.45	Median Household Income	$53,775	30	34.7
			% of Families Above Poverty Level	99.1%	11	94.2
Affordable Housing	18	76.50	Median Home Value	$131,600	24	85.1
			Median Rent	$688	25	67.9
Crime	N/A	N/A	Violent Crimes per 10,000 Population	N/A	N/A	N/A
			Property Crimes per 10,000 Population	N/A	N/A	N/A
Open Spaces	15	78.85	Population Density (Persons/Sq. Mile)	2286	15	88.8
			Average Rooms per Housing Unit	7.1	16	68.9
Education	59	50.25	% High School Enrollment/Completion	92.6%	39	74.7
			% College Graduates	23.7%	66	25.8
Commute	56	36.55	Average Work Commute in Minutes	29	31	60.0
			% Commuting on Public Transportation	5.0%	61	13.1
Community Stability	2	87.05	% Living in Same House as in 1979	45.7%	2	74.1
			% Living in Same County as in 1985	84.5%	1	100.0

Metropolitan Area Suburb Rankings
WASHINGTON

Composite: Rank 7 / 81 *Score* 65.33   **MCLEAN (VA)**

CATEGORY	RANK	SCORE	STATISTIC	VALUE	RANK	SCORE
Economics	3	83.60	Median Household Income	$79,832	3	72.0
			% of Families Above Poverty Level	99.2%	8	95.2
Affordable Housing	79	9.65	Median Home Value	$355,900	79	19.3
			Median Rent	$1,001	72	0.0
Crime	N/A	N/A	Violent Crimes per 10,000 Population	N/A	N/A	N/A
			Property Crimes per 10,000 Population	N/A	N/A	N/A
Open Spaces	5	86.15	Population Density (Persons/Sq. Mile)	2060	12	90.1
			Average Rooms per Housing Unit	7.7	6	82.2
Education	4	92.40	% High School Enrollment/Completion	97.7%	9	92.1
			% College Graduates	65.6%	4	92.7
Commute	27	50.85	Average Work Commute in Minutes	24	2	85.0
			% Commuting on Public Transportation	6.2%	51	16.7
Community Stability	15	69.35	% Living in Same House as in 1979	45.2%	3	73.2
			% Living in Same County as in 1985	69.7%	28	65.5

Composite: Rank 8 / 81 *Score* 65.23   **BETHESDA (MD)**

CATEGORY	RANK	SCORE	STATISTIC	VALUE	RANK	SCORE
Economics	12	71.65	Median Household Income	$65,889	8	52.0
			% of Families Above Poverty Level	98.8%	13	91.3
Affordable Housing	76	30.20	Median Home Value	$325,900	78	28.1
			Median Rent	$852	60	32.3
Crime	N/A	N/A	Violent Crimes per 10,000 Population	N/A	N/A	N/A
			Property Crimes per 10,000 Population	N/A	N/A	N/A
Open Spaces	45	62.20	Population Density (Persons/Sq. Mile)	4245	54	77.7
			Average Rooms per Housing Unit	6.1	38	46.7
Education	2	95.25	% High School Enrollment/Completion	98.3%	4	94.2
			% College Graduates	67.9%	2	96.3
Commute	5	67.05	Average Work Commute in Minutes	25	5	80.0
			% Commuting on Public Transportation	18.5%	15	54.1
Community Stability	18	65.05	% Living in Same House as in 1979	40.8%	9	65.1
			% Living in Same County as in 1985	69.5%	29	65.0

Composite: Rank 9 / 81 *Score* 64.77   **LANHAM-SEABROOK (MD)**

CATEGORY	RANK	SCORE	STATISTIC	VALUE	RANK	SCORE
Economics	29	60.45	Median Household Income	$52,201	34	32.4
			% of Families Above Poverty Level	98.5%	20	88.5
Affordable Housing	19	76.55	Median Home Value	$127,400	18	86.3
			Median Rent	$693	26	66.8
Crime	N/A	N/A	Violent Crimes per 10,000 Population	N/A	N/A	N/A
			Property Crimes per 10,000 Population	N/A	N/A	N/A
Open Spaces	28	69.60	Population Density (Persons/Sq. Mile)	3209	37	83.6
			Average Rooms per Housing Unit	6.5	26	55.6
Education	54	52.50	% High School Enrollment/Completion	92.0%	46	72.6
			% College Graduates	27.8%	60	32.4
Commute	29	50.35	Average Work Commute in Minutes	27	16	70.0
			% Commuting on Public Transportation	10.8%	35	30.7
Community Stability	7	79.20	% Living in Same House as in 1979	40.1%	12	63.8
			% Living in Same County as in 1985	82.2%	3	94.6

Metropolitan Area Suburb Rankings
WASHINGTON

Composite: *Rank* 10 / 81 *Score* 61.85   **REDLAND (MD)**

CATEGORY	RANK	SCORE	STATISTIC	VALUE	RANK	SCORE
Economics	39	53.80	Median Household Income	$59,700	18	43.2
			% of Families Above Poverty Level	96.0%	57	64.4
Affordable Housing	50	57.15	Median Home Value	$193,900	58	66.8
			Median Rent	$782	45	47.5
Crime	N/A	N/A	Violent Crimes per 10,000 Population	N/A	N/A	N/A
			Property Crimes per 10,000 Population	N/A	N/A	N/A
Open Spaces	14	79.80	Population Density (Persons/Sq. Mile)	2332	16	88.5
			Average Rooms per Housing Unit	7.2	13	71.1
Education	18	73.80	% High School Enrollment/Completion	95.5%	19	84.6
			% College Graduates	47.0%	26	63.0
Commute	26	50.90	Average Work Commute in Minutes	30	38	55.0
			% Commuting on Public Transportation	16.1%	18	46.8
Community Stability	29	55.65	% Living in Same House as in 1979	25.7%	46	37.2
			% Living in Same County as in 1985	73.4%	20	74.1

Composite: *Rank* 11 / 81 *Score* 61.77   **ROSE HILL (VA)**

CATEGORY	RANK	SCORE	STATISTIC	VALUE	RANK	SCORE
Economics	25	62.70	Median Household Income	$56,731	22	38.9
			% of Families Above Poverty Level	98.3%	24	86.5
Affordable Housing	56	53.50	Median Home Value	$185,200	54	69.3
			Median Rent	$827	56	37.7
Crime	N/A	N/A	Violent Crimes per 10,000 Population	N/A	N/A	N/A
			Property Crimes per 10,000 Population	N/A	N/A	N/A
Open Spaces	20	75.30	Population Density (Persons/Sq. Mile)	2740	29	86.2
			Average Rooms per Housing Unit	6.9	18	64.4
Education	28	70.60	% High School Enrollment/Completion	98.3%	4	94.2
			% College Graduates	37.0%	45	47.0
Commute	37	45.20	Average Work Commute in Minutes	29	31	60.0
			% Commuting on Public Transportation	10.7%	36	30.4
Community Stability	20	63.30	% Living in Same House as in 1979	40.8%	9	65.1
			% Living in Same County as in 1985	68.0%	30	61.5

Composite: *Rank* 12 / 81 *Score* 61.65   **VIENNA (VA)**

CATEGORY	RANK	SCORE	STATISTIC	VALUE	RANK	SCORE
Economics	19	65.00	Median Household Income	$61,271	16	45.4
			% of Families Above Poverty Level	98.1%	29	84.6
Affordable Housing	68	38.45	Median Home Value	$212,000	64	61.5
			Median Rent	$930	69	15.4
Crime	N/A	N/A	Violent Crimes per 10,000 Population	14	N/A	N/A
			Property Crimes per 10,000 Population	374	N/A	N/A
Open Spaces	18	75.65	Population Density (Persons/Sq. Mile)	3405	39	82.4
			Average Rooms per Housing Unit	7.1	16	68.9
Education	30	70.30	% High School Enrollment/Completion	94.3%	29	80.5
			% College Graduates	45.2%	30	60.1
Commute	28	50.55	Average Work Commute in Minutes	26	9	75.0
			% Commuting on Public Transportation	9.3%	41	26.1
Community Stability	13	69.95	% Living in Same House as in 1979	45.1%	4	73.0
			% Living in Same County as in 1985	70.3%	27	66.9

Metropolitan Area Suburb Rankings
WASHINGTON

Composite: Rank 13 / 81 *Score* 61.29   **OLNEY** (MD)

CATEGORY	RANK	SCORE	STATISTIC	VALUE	RANK	SCORE
Economics	8	74.55	Median Household Income	$67,218	7	53.9
			% of Families Above Poverty Level	99.2%	8	95.2
Affordable Housing	69	37.55	Median Home Value	$225,000	68	57.7
			Median Rent	$921	67	17.4
Crime	N/A	N/A	Violent Crimes per 10,000 Population	N/A	N/A	N/A
			Property Crimes per 10,000 Population	N/A	N/A	N/A
Open Spaces	7	84.80	Population Density (Persons/Sq. Mile)	2533	22	87.4
			Average Rooms per Housing Unit	7.7	6	82.2
Education	12	79.15	% High School Enrollment/Completion	97.6%	11	91.8
			% College Graduates	49.2%	22	66.5
Commute	66	28.60	Average Work Commute in Minutes	32	51	45.0
			% Commuting on Public Transportation	4.7%	62	12.2
Community Stability	21	63.10	% Living in Same House as in 1979	28.5%	36	42.3
			% Living in Same County as in 1985	77.6%	13	83.9

Composite: Rank 14 / 81 *Score* 60.70   **ROCKVILLE** (MD)

CATEGORY	RANK	SCORE	STATISTIC	VALUE	RANK	SCORE
Economics	47	49.75	Median Household Income	$52,073	35	32.2
			% of Families Above Poverty Level	96.3%	52	67.3
Affordable Housing	51	57.10	Median Home Value	$182,400	52	70.2
			Median Rent	$798	48	44.0
Crime	N/A	N/A	Violent Crimes per 10,000 Population	N/A	N/A	N/A
			Property Crimes per 10,000 Population	N/A	N/A	N/A
Open Spaces	40	65.95	Population Density (Persons/Sq. Mile)	3696	45	80.8
			Average Rooms per Housing Unit	6.3	32	51.1
Education	38	64.45	% High School Enrollment/Completion	90.8%	50	68.5
			% College Graduates	45.4%	29	60.4
Commute	17	56.30	Average Work Commute in Minutes	27	16	70.0
			% Commuting on Public Transportation	14.7%	21	42.6
Community Stability	12	70.65	% Living in Same House as in 1979	39.4%	14	62.5
			% Living in Same County as in 1985	75.4%	16	78.8

Composite: Rank 15 / 81 *Score* 60.14   **BOWIE** (MD)

CATEGORY	RANK	SCORE	STATISTIC	VALUE	RANK	SCORE
Economics	13	70.60	Median Household Income	$59,622	19	43.1
			% of Families Above Poverty Level	99.5%	2	98.1
Affordable Housing	62	45.30	Median Home Value	$142,900	29	81.7
			Median Rent	$960	70	8.9
Crime	N/A	N/A	Violent Crimes per 10,000 Population	N/A	N/A	N/A
			Property Crimes per 10,000 Population	N/A	N/A	N/A
Open Spaces	23	73.70	Population Density (Persons/Sq. Mile)	2923	32	85.2
			Average Rooms per Housing Unit	6.8	21	62.2
Education	33	68.35	% High School Enrollment/Completion	96.7%	13	88.7
			% College Graduates	37.6%	44	48.0
Commute	65	29.65	Average Work Commute in Minutes	32	51	45.0
			% Commuting on Public Transportation	5.4%	58	14.3
Community Stability	10	73.25	% Living in Same House as in 1979	38.7%	15	61.2
			% Living in Same County as in 1985	78.2%	10	85.3

Metropolitan Area Suburb Rankings
WASHINGTON

Composite: *Rank* 16 / 81   *Score* 59.84   **ANNANDALE (VA)**

CATEGORY	RANK	SCORE	STATISTIC	VALUE	RANK	SCORE
Economics	28	60.40	Median Household Income	$56,167	24	38.1
			% of Families Above Poverty Level	97.9%	32	82.7
Affordable Housing	54	55.25	Median Home Value	$221,400	67	58.7
			Median Rent	$762	43	51.8
Crime	N/A	N/A	Violent Crimes per 10,000 Population	N/A	N/A	N/A
			Property Crimes per 10,000 Population	N/A	N/A	N/A
Open Spaces	35	67.05	Population Density (Persons/Sq. Mile)	3691	44	80.8
			Average Rooms per Housing Unit	6.4	29	53.3
Education	13	78.75	% High School Enrollment/Completion	97.7%	9	92.1
			% College Graduates	48.5%	23	65.4
Commute	41	44.40	Average Work Commute in Minutes	27	16	70.0
			% Commuting on Public Transportation	6.9%	47	18.8
Community Stability	31	53.20	% Living in Same House as in 1979	33.8%	26	52.1
			% Living in Same County as in 1985	64.9%	35	54.3

Composite: *Rank* 17 / 81   *Score* 59.82   **ASPEN HILL (MD)**

CATEGORY	RANK	SCORE	STATISTIC	VALUE	RANK	SCORE
Economics	32	58.40	Median Household Income	$52,645	32	33.1
			% of Families Above Poverty Level	98.0%	31	83.7
Affordable Housing	53	56.40	Median Home Value	$187,200	56	68.8
			Median Rent	$798	48	44.0
Crime	N/A	N/A	Violent Crimes per 10,000 Population	N/A	N/A	N/A
			Property Crimes per 10,000 Population	N/A	N/A	N/A
Open Spaces	38	66.35	Population Density (Persons/Sq. Mile)	4347	56	77.1
			Average Rooms per Housing Unit	6.5	26	55.6
Education	35	67.55	% High School Enrollment/Completion	93.1%	37	76.4
			% College Graduates	44.3%	34	58.7
Commute	42	43.60	Average Work Commute in Minutes	30	38	55.0
			% Commuting on Public Transportation	11.3%	33	32.2
Community Stability	16	66.60	% Living in Same House as in 1979	36.9%	19	57.9
			% Living in Same County as in 1985	73.9%	19	75.3

Composite: *Rank* 18 / 81   *Score* 59.34   **CLINTON (MD)**

CATEGORY	RANK	SCORE	STATISTIC	VALUE	RANK	SCORE
Economics	20	64.75	Median Household Income	$56,266	23	38.2
			% of Families Above Poverty Level	98.8%	13	91.3
Affordable Housing	47	60.45	Median Home Value	$129,100	21	85.8
			Median Rent	$839	58	35.1
Crime	N/A	N/A	Violent Crimes per 10,000 Population	N/A	N/A	N/A
			Property Crimes per 10,000 Population	N/A	N/A	N/A
Open Spaces	11	81.15	Population Density (Persons/Sq. Mile)	1860	9	91.2
			Average Rooms per Housing Unit	7.2	13	71.1
Education	60	49.15	% High School Enrollment/Completion	93.8%	33	78.8
			% College Graduates	19.7%	69	19.5
Commute	71	23.95	Average Work Commute in Minutes	33	66	40.0
			% Commuting on Public Transportation	3.3%	69	7.9
Community Stability	8	76.60	% Living in Same House as in 1979	40.7%	11	64.9
			% Living in Same County as in 1985	79.5%	7	88.3

Metropolitan Area Suburb Rankings
WASHINGTON

Composite: Rank 18 / 81 **Score** 59.34   **COLLEGE PARK (MD)**

CATEGORY	RANK	SCORE	STATISTIC	VALUE	RANK	SCORE
Economics	60	40.10	Median Household Income	$39,250	66	13.9
			% of Families Above Poverty Level	96.2%	53	66.3
Affordable Housing	14	82.05	Median Home Value	$124,700	17	87.1
			Median Rent	$646	13	77.0
Crime	N/A	N/A	Violent Crimes per 10,000 Population	N/A	N/A	N/A
			Property Crimes per 10,000 Population	N/A	N/A	N/A
Open Spaces	48	60.45	Population Density (Persons/Sq. Mile)	4067	51	78.7
			Average Rooms per Housing Unit	5.9	45	42.2
Education	23	71.80	% High School Enrollment/Completion	98.4%	3	94.5
			% College Graduates	38.3%	41	49.1
Commute	11	59.40	Average Work Commute in Minutes	21	1	100.0
			% Commuting on Public Transportation	6.9%	47	18.8
Community Stability	45	42.25	% Living in Same House as in 1979	40.1%	12	63.8
			% Living in Same County as in 1985	50.5%	71	20.7

Composite: Rank 20 / 81 **Score** 59.29   **SILVER SPRING (MD)**

CATEGORY	RANK	SCORE	STATISTIC	VALUE	RANK	SCORE
Economics	56	41.85	Median Household Income	$42,357	60	18.3
			% of Families Above Poverty Level	96.1%	55	65.4
Affordable Housing	28	71.95	Median Home Value	$178,700	50	71.2
			Median Rent	$666	15	72.7
Crime	N/A	N/A	Violent Crimes per 10,000 Population	N/A	N/A	N/A
			Property Crimes per 10,000 Population	N/A	N/A	N/A
Open Spaces	68	48.75	Population Density (Persons/Sq. Mile)	6238	70	66.4
			Average Rooms per Housing Unit	5.4	60	31.1
Education	25	71.25	% High School Enrollment/Completion	94.0%	31	79.5
			% College Graduates	47.0%	26	63.0
Commute	6	66.10	Average Work Commute in Minutes	30	38	55.0
			% Commuting on Public Transportation	26.1%	5	77.2
Community Stability	28	55.85	% Living in Same House as in 1979	34.1%	24	52.7
			% Living in Same County as in 1985	66.9%	33	59.0

Composite: Rank 21 / 81 **Score** 59.06   **BELTSVILLE (MD)**

CATEGORY	RANK	SCORE	STATISTIC	VALUE	RANK	SCORE
Economics	42	52.30	Median Household Income	$45,545	52	22.9
			% of Families Above Poverty Level	97.8%	35	81.7
Affordable Housing	23	75.15	Median Home Value	$142,700	28	81.8
			Median Rent	$685	24	68.5
Crime	N/A	N/A	Violent Crimes per 10,000 Population	N/A	N/A	N/A
			Property Crimes per 10,000 Population	N/A	N/A	N/A
Open Spaces	43	64.60	Population Density (Persons/Sq. Mile)	2207	13	89.2
			Average Rooms per Housing Unit	5.8	46	40.0
Education	43	61.45	% High School Enrollment/Completion	94.9%	24	82.5
			% College Graduates	32.8%	56	40.4
Commute	44	42.30	Average Work Commute in Minutes	27	16	70.0
			% Commuting on Public Transportation	5.5%	57	14.6
Community Stability	27	58.55	% Living in Same House as in 1979	31.5%	30	47.9
			% Living in Same County as in 1985	71.3%	25	69.2

Composite: *Rank* 22 / 81 *Score* 58.59   **CALVERTON (MD)**

CATEGORY	RANK	SCORE	STATISTIC	VALUE	RANK	SCORE
Economics	26	62.00	Median Household Income	$55,023	26	36.5
			% of Families Above Poverty Level	98.4%	21	87.5
Affordable Housing	34	68.80	Median Home Value	$163,300	42	75.8
			Median Rent	$716	33	61.8
Crime	N/A	N/A	Violent Crimes per 10,000 Population	N/A	N/A	N/A
			Property Crimes per 10,000 Population	N/A	N/A	N/A
Open Spaces	30	69.30	Population Density (Persons/Sq. Mile)	2517	20	87.5
			Average Rooms per Housing Unit	6.3	32	51.1
Education	39	63.25	% High School Enrollment/Completion	90.5%	56	67.5
			% College Graduates	44.5%	33	59.0
Commute	51	38.90	Average Work Commute in Minutes	30	38	55.0
			% Commuting on Public Transportation	8.2%	42	22.8
Community Stability	34	49.30	% Living in Same House as in 1979	25.8%	45	37.3
			% Living in Same County as in 1985	67.9%	31	61.3

Composite: *Rank* 23 / 81 *Score* 58.10   **TAKOMA PARK (MD)**

CATEGORY	RANK	SCORE	STATISTIC	VALUE	RANK	SCORE
Economics	75	31.40	Median Household Income	$37,144	72	10.9
			% of Families Above Poverty Level	94.7%	76	51.9
Affordable Housing	10	85.85	Median Home Value	$160,800	38	76.5
			Median Rent	$562	2	95.2
Crime	N/A	N/A	Violent Crimes per 10,000 Population	N/A	N/A	N/A
			Property Crimes per 10,000 Population	N/A	N/A	N/A
Open Spaces	77	39.55	Population Density (Persons/Sq. Mile)	8299	78	54.7
			Average Rooms per Housing Unit	5.1	70	24.4
Education	29	70.50	% High School Enrollment/Completion	94.5%	28	81.2
			% College Graduates	45.0%	31	59.8
Commute	2	75.45	Average Work Commute in Minutes	29	31	60.0
			% Commuting on Public Transportation	30.6%	2	90.9
Community Stability	40	45.85	% Living in Same House as in 1979	29.6%	33	44.4
			% Living in Same County as in 1985	61.9%	43	47.3

Composite: *Rank* 24 / 81 *Score* 58.03   **MITCHELLVILLE (MD)**

CATEGORY	RANK	SCORE	STATISTIC	VALUE	RANK	SCORE
Economics	7	74.50	Median Household Income	$65,809	9	51.9
			% of Families Above Poverty Level	99.4%	4	97.1
Affordable Housing	70	36.55	Median Home Value	$172,400	46	73.1
			Median Rent	$1,001	72	0.0
Crime	N/A	N/A	Violent Crimes per 10,000 Population	N/A	N/A	N/A
			Property Crimes per 10,000 Population	N/A	N/A	N/A
Open Spaces	9	83.10	Population Density (Persons/Sq. Mile)	1170	3	95.1
			Average Rooms per Housing Unit	7.2	13	71.1
Education	24	71.60	% High School Enrollment/Completion	96.7%	13	88.7
			% College Graduates	41.7%	37	54.5
Commute	57	36.20	Average Work Commute in Minutes	32	51	45.0
			% Commuting on Public Transportation	9.7%	39	27.4
Community Stability	39	46.25	% Living in Same House as in 1979	17.2%	62	21.4
			% Living in Same County as in 1985	72.1%	23	71.1

Metropolitan Area Suburb Rankings
WASHINGTON

Composite: *Rank* 25 / 81 *Score* 57.84   **HILLCREST HEIGHTS** (MD)

CATEGORY	RANK	SCORE	STATISTIC	VALUE	RANK	SCORE
Economics	65	37.40	Median Household Income	$36,122	74	9.4
			% of Families Above Poverty Level	96.1%	55	65.4
Affordable Housing	2	93.35	Median Home Value	$94,800	2	95.8
			Median Rent	$582	3	90.9
Crime	N/A	N/A	Violent Crimes per 10,000 Population	N/A	N/A	N/A
			Property Crimes per 10,000 Population	N/A	N/A	N/A
Open Spaces	71	45.35	Population Density (Persons/Sq. Mile)	7044	73	61.8
			Average Rooms per Housing Unit	5.3	63	28.9
Education	64	46.45	% High School Enrollment/Completion	94.0%	31	79.5
			% College Graduates	15.9%	75	13.4
Commute	22	52.50	Average Work Commute in Minutes	33	66	40.0
			% Commuting on Public Transportation	22.1%	9	65.0
Community Stability	11	72.00	% Living in Same House as in 1979	37.0%	18	58.0
			% Living in Same County as in 1985	78.5%	9	86.0

Composite: *Rank* 26 / 81 *Score* 57.23   **WHEATON-GLENMONT** (MD)

CATEGORY	RANK	SCORE	STATISTIC	VALUE	RANK	SCORE
Economics	48	49.50	Median Household Income	$47,622	47	25.9
			% of Families Above Poverty Level	96.9%	49	73.1
Affordable Housing	41	62.25	Median Home Value	$154,500	35	78.3
			Median Rent	$788	46	46.2
Crime	N/A	N/A	Violent Crimes per 10,000 Population	N/A	N/A	N/A
			Property Crimes per 10,000 Population	N/A	N/A	N/A
Open Spaces	52	59.35	Population Density (Persons/Sq. Mile)	5250	67	72.0
			Average Rooms per Housing Unit	6.1	38	46.7
Education	45	59.05	% High School Enrollment/Completion	92.6%	39	74.7
			% College Graduates	34.7%	51	43.4
Commute	34	47.70	Average Work Commute in Minutes	30	38	55.0
			% Commuting on Public Transportation	14.0%	23	40.4
Community Stability	17	65.55	% Living in Same House as in 1979	37.8%	17	59.5
			% Living in Same County as in 1985	72.3%	22	71.6

Composite: *Rank* 27 / 81 *Score* 57.19   **HILLANDALE** (MD)

CATEGORY	RANK	SCORE	STATISTIC	VALUE	RANK	SCORE
Economics	58	41.05	Median Household Income	$45,876	50	23.4
			% of Families Above Poverty Level	95.4%	65	58.7
Affordable Housing	24	74.75	Median Home Value	$160,400	37	76.6
			Median Rent	$665	14	72.9
Crime	N/A	N/A	Violent Crimes per 10,000 Population	N/A	N/A	N/A
			Property Crimes per 10,000 Population	N/A	N/A	N/A
Open Spaces	59	55.60	Population Density (Persons/Sq. Mile)	5007	62	73.4
			Average Rooms per Housing Unit	5.7	51	37.8
Education	40	62.95	% High School Enrollment/Completion	94.9%	24	82.5
			% College Graduates	34.7%	51	43.4
Commute	18	54.95	Average Work Commute in Minutes	31	46	50.0
			% Commuting on Public Transportation	20.4%	11	59.9
Community Stability	30	53.85	% Living in Same House as in 1979	34.5%	23	53.4
			% Living in Same County as in 1985	64.9%	35	54.3

Metropolitan Area Suburb Rankings
WASHINGTON

Composite: Rank 28 / 81 *Score* 57.09   **OAKTON** (VA)

CATEGORY	RANK	SCORE	STATISTIC	VALUE	RANK	SCORE
Economics	18	65.35	Median Household Income	$59,715	17	43.2
			% of Families Above Poverty Level	98.4%	21	87.5
Affordable Housing	66	39.65	Median Home Value	$247,400	73	51.1
			Median Rent	$871	63	28.2
Crime	N/A	N/A	Violent Crimes per 10,000 Population	N/A	N/A	N/A
			Property Crimes per 10,000 Population	N/A	N/A	N/A
Open Spaces	24	71.60	Population Density (Persons/Sq. Mile)	2499	18	87.6
			Average Rooms per Housing Unit	6.5	26	55.6
Education	9	81.65	% High School Enrollment/Completion	95.8%	17	85.6
			% College Graduates	56.2%	11	77.7
Commute	30	50.05	Average Work Commute in Minutes	29	31	60.0
			% Commuting on Public Transportation	13.9%	24	40.1
Community Stability	54	34.25	% Living in Same House as in 1979	22.1%	52	30.5
			% Living in Same County as in 1985	57.9%	57	38.0

Composite: Rank 29 / 81 *Score* 56.92   **HYATTSVILLE** (MD)

CATEGORY	RANK	SCORE	STATISTIC	VALUE	RANK	SCORE
Economics	73	33.55	Median Household Income	$32,793	80	4.6
			% of Families Above Poverty Level	95.8%	58	62.5
Affordable Housing	1	95.85	Median Home Value	$108,800	10	91.7
			Median Rent	$540	1	100.0
Crime	N/A	N/A	Violent Crimes per 10,000 Population	67	N/A	N/A
			Property Crimes per 10,000 Population	543	N/A	N/A
Open Spaces	69	45.85	Population Density (Persons/Sq. Mile)	6475	71	65.0
			Average Rooms per Housing Unit	5.2	68	26.7
Education	73	39.00	% High School Enrollment/Completion	85.7%	72	51.0
			% College Graduates	24.4%	63	27.0
Commute	8	63.25	Average Work Commute in Minutes	27	16	70.0
			% Commuting on Public Transportation	19.3%	13	56.5
Community Stability	19	64.00	% Living in Same House as in 1979	35.9%	20	56.0
			% Living in Same County as in 1985	72.5%	21	72.0

Composite: Rank 30 / 81 *Score* 56.67   **WEST SPRINGFIELD** (VA)

CATEGORY	RANK	SCORE	STATISTIC	VALUE	RANK	SCORE
Economics	15	70.00	Median Household Income	$63,559	12	48.7
			% of Families Above Poverty Level	98.8%	13	91.3
Affordable Housing	74	32.95	Median Home Value	$197,000	60	65.9
			Median Rent	$1,001	72	0.0
Crime	N/A	N/A	Violent Crimes per 10,000 Population	N/A	N/A	N/A
			Property Crimes per 10,000 Population	N/A	N/A	N/A
Open Spaces	17	75.85	Population Density (Persons/Sq. Mile)	4124	53	78.4
			Average Rooms per Housing Unit	7.3	10	73.3
Education	8	81.95	% High School Enrollment/Completion	97.0%	12	89.7
			% College Graduates	54.0%	13	74.2
Commute	62	32.40	Average Work Commute in Minutes	32	51	45.0
			% Commuting on Public Transportation	7.2%	46	19.8
Community Stability	36	46.85	% Living in Same House as in 1979	30.7%	32	46.4
			% Living in Same County as in 1985	61.9%	43	47.3

Metropolitan Area Suburb Rankings
WASHINGTON

Composite: Rank 31 / 81 *Score* 56.43 **NORTH BETHESDA (MD)**

CATEGORY	RANK	SCORE	STATISTIC	VALUE	RANK	SCORE
Economics	36	56.15	Median Household Income	$52,948	31	33.5
			% of Families Above Poverty Level	97.5%	38	78.8
Affordable Housing	65	40.10	Median Home Value	$277,900	76	42.2
			Median Rent	$826	55	38.0
Crime	N/A	N/A	Violent Crimes per 10,000 Population	N/A	N/A	N/A
			Property Crimes per 10,000 Population	N/A	N/A	N/A
Open Spaces	61	55.10	Population Density (Persons/Sq. Mile)	3986	50	79.1
			Average Rooms per Housing Unit	5.4	60	31.1
Education	11	80.85	% High School Enrollment/Completion	93.6%	35	78.1
			% College Graduates	59.9%	6	83.6
Commute	7	64.05	Average Work Commute in Minutes	27	16	70.0
			% Commuting on Public Transportation	19.8%	12	58.1
Community Stability	44	42.35	% Living in Same House as in 1979	23.3%	50	32.7
			% Living in Same County as in 1985	63.9%	38	52.0

Composite: Rank 32 / 81 *Score* 56.30 **SPRINGFIELD (VA)**

CATEGORY	RANK	SCORE	STATISTIC	VALUE	RANK	SCORE
Economics	38	53.95	Median Household Income	$51,178	37	31.0
			% of Families Above Poverty Level	97.3%	40	76.9
Affordable Housing	38	64.20	Median Home Value	$171,600	45	73.3
			Median Rent	$747	40	55.1
Crime	N/A	N/A	Violent Crimes per 10,000 Population	N/A	N/A	N/A
			Property Crimes per 10,000 Population	N/A	N/A	N/A
Open Spaces	29	69.55	Population Density (Persons/Sq. Mile)	2419	17	88.0
			Average Rooms per Housing Unit	6.3	32	51.1
Education	49	55.75	% High School Enrollment/Completion	90.6%	54	67.8
			% College Graduates	34.9%	49	43.7
Commute	40	44.50	Average Work Commute in Minutes	26	9	75.0
			% Commuting on Public Transportation	5.3%	59	14.0
Community Stability	33	49.85	% Living in Same House as in 1979	34.7%	22	53.8
			% Living in Same County as in 1985	61.3%	45	45.9

Composite: Rank 33 / 81 *Score* 56.13 **NEW CARROLLTON (MD)**

CATEGORY	RANK	SCORE	STATISTIC	VALUE	RANK	SCORE
Economics	52	47.40	Median Household Income	$42,071	61	17.9
			% of Families Above Poverty Level	97.3%	40	76.9
Affordable Housing	17	77.35	Median Home Value	$131,600	24	85.1
			Median Rent	$680	22	69.6
Crime	N/A	N/A	Violent Crimes per 10,000 Population	N/A	N/A	N/A
			Property Crimes per 10,000 Population	N/A	N/A	N/A
Open Spaces	73	44.00	Population Density (Persons/Sq. Mile)	7904	77	56.9
			Average Rooms per Housing Unit	5.4	60	31.1
Education	61	49.00	% High School Enrollment/Completion	90.5%	56	67.5
			% College Graduates	26.6%	61	30.5
Commute	16	56.60	Average Work Commute in Minutes	31	46	50.0
			% Commuting on Public Transportation	21.5%	10	63.2
Community Stability	22	62.45	% Living in Same House as in 1979	31.0%	31	47.0
			% Living in Same County as in 1985	75.0%	17	77.9

Metropolitan Area Suburb Rankings
WASHINGTON

Composite: **Rank** 34 / 81 *Score* 56.09   **WALKER MILL** (MD)

CATEGORY	RANK	SCORE	STATISTIC	VALUE	RANK	SCORE
Economics	80	5.70	Median Household Income	$37,560	70	11.4
			% of Families Above Poverty Level	89.3%	80	0.0
Affordable Housing	6	87.95	Median Home Value	$104,600	7	93.0
			Median Rent	$619	7	82.9
Crime	N/A	N/A	Violent Crimes per 10,000 Population	N/A	N/A	N/A
			Property Crimes per 10,000 Population	N/A	N/A	N/A
Open Spaces	47	61.05	Population Density (Persons/Sq. Mile)	3459	40	82.1
			Average Rooms per Housing Unit	5.8	46	40.0
Education	72	40.05	% High School Enrollment/Completion	90.8%	50	68.5
			% College Graduates	14.8%	78	11.6
Commute	12	58.80	Average Work Commute in Minutes	32	51	45.0
			% Commuting on Public Transportation	24.6%	6	72.6
Community Stability	4	83.00	% Living in Same House as in 1979	41.7%	8	66.7
			% Living in Same County as in 1985	84.2%	2	99.3

Composite: **Rank** 35 / 81 *Score* 56.05   **FAIRFAX** (VA)

CATEGORY	RANK	SCORE	STATISTIC	VALUE	RANK	SCORE
Economics	40	53.30	Median Household Income	$50,913	41	30.6
			% of Families Above Poverty Level	97.2%	43	76.0
Affordable Housing	55	54.30	Median Home Value	$182,900	53	70.0
			Median Rent	$823	54	38.6
Crime	N/A	N/A	Violent Crimes per 10,000 Population	N/A	N/A	N/A
			Property Crimes per 10,000 Population	N/A	N/A	N/A
Open Spaces	32	67.40	Population Density (Persons/Sq. Mile)	3183	36	83.7
			Average Rooms per Housing Unit	6.3	32	51.1
Education	34	68.05	% High School Enrollment/Completion	94.8%	27	82.2
			% College Graduates	41.3%	38	53.9
Commute	33	48.00	Average Work Commute in Minutes	26	9	75.0
			% Commuting on Public Transportation	7.6%	44	21.0
Community Stability	42	45.25	% Living in Same House as in 1979	34.1%	24	52.7
			% Living in Same County as in 1985	57.8%	58	37.8

Composite: **Rank** 36 / 81 *Score* 56.03   **CORAL HILLS** (MD)

CATEGORY	RANK	SCORE	STATISTIC	VALUE	RANK	SCORE
Economics	78	25.65	Median Household Income	$35,140	77	8.0
			% of Families Above Poverty Level	93.8%	78	43.3
Affordable Housing	3	91.95	Median Home Value	$80,600	1	100.0
			Median Rent	$614	6	83.9
Crime	N/A	N/A	Violent Crimes per 10,000 Population	N/A	N/A	N/A
			Property Crimes per 10,000 Population	N/A	N/A	N/A
Open Spaces	72	44.75	Population Density (Persons/Sq. Mile)	7252	74	60.6
			Average Rooms per Housing Unit	5.3	63	28.9
Education	75	38.35	% High School Enrollment/Completion	93.2%	36	76.7
			% College Graduates	7.5%	81	0.0
Commute	10	61.70	Average Work Commute in Minutes	32	51	45.0
			% Commuting on Public Transportation	26.5%	4	78.4
Community Stability	9	73.75	% Living in Same House as in 1979	38.5%	16	60.8
			% Living in Same County as in 1985	78.8%	8	86.7

Metropolitan Area Suburb Rankings
WASHINGTON

Composite: Rank 37 / 81 *Score* 55.68   **GREENBELT** (MD)

CATEGORY	RANK	SCORE	STATISTIC	VALUE	RANK	SCORE
Economics	55	43.25	Median Household Income	$38,956	68	13.4
			% of Families Above Poverty Level	96.9%	49	73.1
Affordable Housing	15	80.00	Median Home Value	$95,100	3	95.8
			Median Rent	$705	31	64.2
Crime	N/A	N/A	Violent Crimes per 10,000 Population	66	N/A	N/A
			Property Crimes per 10,000 Population	468	N/A	N/A
Open Spaces	66	49.70	Population Density (Persons/Sq. Mile)	3550	41	81.6
			Average Rooms per Housing Unit	4.8	75	17.8
Education	15	76.25	% High School Enrollment/Completion	98.0%	7	93.2
			% College Graduates	44.7%	32	59.3
Commute	32	48.85	Average Work Commute in Minutes	27	16	70.0
			% Commuting on Public Transportation	9.8%	38	27.7
Community Stability	50	36.00	% Living in Same House as in 1979	18.8%	58	24.4
			% Living in Same County as in 1985	62.0%	42	47.6

Composite: Rank 38 / 81 *Score* 55.29   **ARLINGTON** (VA)

CATEGORY	RANK	SCORE	STATISTIC	VALUE	RANK	SCORE
Economics	57	41.50	Median Household Income	$44,600	55	21.5
			% of Families Above Poverty Level	95.7%	61	61.5
Affordable Housing	48	60.25	Median Home Value	$231,000	70	55.9
			Median Rent	$703	30	64.6
Crime	N/A	N/A	Violent Crimes per 10,000 Population	44	N/A	N/A
			Property Crimes per 10,000 Population	639	N/A	N/A
Open Spaces	75	41.05	Population Density (Persons/Sq. Mile)	6605	72	64.3
			Average Rooms per Housing Unit	4.8	75	17.8
Education	26	71.00	% High School Enrollment/Completion	91.4%	49	70.5
			% College Graduates	52.3%	14	71.5
Commute	1	84.00	Average Work Commute in Minutes	24	2	85.0
			% Commuting on Public Transportation	28.0%	3	83.0
Community Stability	55	33.95	% Living in Same House as in 1979	26.2%	40	38.1
			% Living in Same County as in 1985	54.4%	67	29.8

Composite: Rank 39 / 81 *Score* 54.99   **NORTH POTOMAC** (MD)

CATEGORY	RANK	SCORE	STATISTIC	VALUE	RANK	SCORE
Economics	6	74.60	Median Household Income	$73,367	5	62.7
			% of Families Above Poverty Level	98.3%	24	86.5
Affordable Housing	78	23.75	Median Home Value	$259,700	75	47.5
			Median Rent	$1,001	72	0.0
Crime	N/A	N/A	Violent Crimes per 10,000 Population	N/A	N/A	N/A
			Property Crimes per 10,000 Population	N/A	N/A	N/A
Open Spaces	8	84.40	Population Density (Persons/Sq. Mile)	3060	33	84.4
			Average Rooms per Housing Unit	7.8	5	84.4
Education	10	81.20	% High School Enrollment/Completion	92.3%	43	73.6
			% College Graduates	63.2%	5	88.8
Commute	59	33.50	Average Work Commute in Minutes	31	46	50.0
			% Commuting on Public Transportation	6.3%	50	17.0
Community Stability	57	32.50	% Living in Same House as in 1979	9.5%	77	7.2
			% Living in Same County as in 1985	66.4%	34	57.8

Metropolitan Area Suburb Rankings
WASHINGTON

Composite: Rank 40 / 81 *Score* 54.71   **GREATER UPPER MARLBORO (MD)**

CATEGORY	RANK	SCORE	STATISTIC	VALUE	RANK	SCORE
Economics	27	61.10	Median Household Income	$54,515	28	35.7
			% of Families Above Poverty Level	98.3%	24	86.5
Affordable Housing	16	77.95	Median Home Value	$129,000	20	85.8
			Median Rent	$678	19	70.1
Crime	N/A	N/A	Violent Crimes per 10,000 Population	N/A	N/A	N/A
			Property Crimes per 10,000 Population	N/A	N/A	N/A
Open Spaces	12	81.10	Population Density (Persons/Sq. Mile)	307	1	100.0
			Average Rooms per Housing Unit	6.8	21	62.2
Education	77	27.00	% High School Enrollment/Completion	78.9%	78	27.7
			% College Graduates	24.0%	64	26.3
Commute	72	21.15	Average Work Commute in Minutes	34	69	35.0
			% Commuting on Public Transportation	3.1%	71	7.3
Community Stability	24	59.95	% Living in Same House as in 1979	26.2%	40	38.1
			% Living in Same County as in 1985	76.7%	15	81.8

Composite: Rank 41 / 81 *Score* 54.67   **MONTGOMERY VILLAGE (MD)**

CATEGORY	RANK	SCORE	STATISTIC	VALUE	RANK	SCORE
Economics	37	55.95	Median Household Income	$50,647	42	30.2
			% of Families Above Poverty Level	97.8%	35	81.7
Affordable Housing	36	64.50	Median Home Value	$134,200	26	84.3
			Median Rent	$795	47	44.7
Crime	N/A	N/A	Violent Crimes per 10,000 Population	N/A	N/A	N/A
			Property Crimes per 10,000 Population	N/A	N/A	N/A
Open Spaces	50	60.10	Population Density (Persons/Sq. Mile)	4991	61	73.5
			Average Rooms per Housing Unit	6.1	38	46.7
Education	17	75.60	% High School Enrollment/Completion	95.2%	21	83.6
			% College Graduates	49.9%	19	67.6
Commute	48	40.90	Average Work Commute in Minutes	32	51	45.0
			% Commuting on Public Transportation	12.8%	27	36.8
Community Stability	59	31.00	% Living in Same House as in 1979	14.3%	68	16.1
			% Living in Same County as in 1985	61.3%	45	45.9

Composite: Rank 42 / 81 *Score* 54.28   **FORESTVILLE (MD)**

CATEGORY	RANK	SCORE	STATISTIC	VALUE	RANK	SCORE
Economics	67	37.30	Median Household Income	$41,350	63	16.9
			% of Families Above Poverty Level	95.3%	66	57.7
Affordable Housing	13	82.55	Median Home Value	$99,800	5	94.4
			Median Rent	$675	18	70.7
Crime	N/A	N/A	Violent Crimes per 10,000 Population	N/A	N/A	N/A
			Property Crimes per 10,000 Population	N/A	N/A	N/A
Open Spaces	56	57.05	Population Density (Persons/Sq. Mile)	3689	43	80.8
			Average Rooms per Housing Unit	5.5	58	33.3
Education	63	47.15	% High School Enrollment/Completion	94.1%	30	79.8
			% College Graduates	16.6%	74	14.5
Commute	49	40.75	Average Work Commute in Minutes	32	51	45.0
			% Commuting on Public Transportation	12.7%	28	36.5
Community Stability	23	60.90	% Living in Same House as in 1979	26.5%	39	38.6
			% Living in Same County as in 1985	77.3%	14	83.2

Metropolitan Area Suburb Rankings
WASHINGTON

Composite: Rank 43 / 81 *Score* 54.18   **RESTON (VA)**

CATEGORY	RANK	SCORE	STATISTIC	VALUE	RANK	SCORE
Economics	35	57.55	Median Household Income	$56,884	21	39.1
			% of Families Above Poverty Level	97.2%	43	76.0
Affordable Housing	57	52.65	Median Home Value	$198,100	61	65.6
			Median Rent	$818	53	39.7
Crime	N/A	N/A	Violent Crimes per 10,000 Population	N/A	N/A	N/A
			Property Crimes per 10,000 Population	N/A	N/A	N/A
Open Spaces	33	67.35	Population Density (Persons/Sq. Mile)	2817	31	85.8
			Average Rooms per Housing Unit	6.2	36	48.9
Education	16	76.10	% High School Enrollment/Completion	92.3%	43	73.6
			% College Graduates	56.8%	9	78.6
Commute	43	43.05	Average Work Commute in Minutes	27	16	70.0
			% Commuting on Public Transportation	6.0%	53	16.1
Community Stability	64	28.40	% Living in Same House as in 1979	15.9%	64	19.0
			% Living in Same County as in 1985	57.8%	58	37.8

Composite: Rank 44 / 81 *Score* 54.04   **WHITE OAK (MD)**

CATEGORY	RANK	SCORE	STATISTIC	VALUE	RANK	SCORE
Economics	63	38.35	Median Household Income	$44,144	56	20.9
			% of Families Above Poverty Level	95.1%	69	55.8
Affordable Housing	37	64.35	Median Home Value	$190,800	57	67.7
			Median Rent	$720	35	61.0
Crime	N/A	N/A	Violent Crimes per 10,000 Population	N/A	N/A	N/A
			Property Crimes per 10,000 Population	N/A	N/A	N/A
Open Spaces	53	59.15	Population Density (Persons/Sq. Mile)	3749	46	80.5
			Average Rooms per Housing Unit	5.7	51	37.8
Education	31	70.10	% High School Enrollment/Completion	94.9%	24	82.5
			% College Graduates	43.7%	35	57.7
Commute	39	45.05	Average Work Commute in Minutes	31	46	50.0
			% Commuting on Public Transportation	13.9%	24	40.1
Community Stability	35	47.25	% Living in Same House as in 1979	29.5%	34	44.2
			% Living in Same County as in 1985	63.2%	40	50.3

Composite: Rank 45 / 81 *Score* 53.93   **HERNDON (VA)**

CATEGORY	RANK	SCORE	STATISTIC	VALUE	RANK	SCORE
Economics	24	63.05	Median Household Income	$53,840	29	34.8
			% of Families Above Poverty Level	98.8%	13	91.3
Affordable Housing	35	66.75	Median Home Value	$166,100	44	74.9
			Median Rent	$731	37	58.6
Crime	N/A	N/A	Violent Crimes per 10,000 Population	20	N/A	N/A
			Property Crimes per 10,000 Population	415	N/A	N/A
Open Spaces	37	66.70	Population Density (Persons/Sq. Mile)	3817	47	80.1
			Average Rooms per Housing Unit	6.4	29	53.3
Education	46	56.80	% High School Enrollment/Completion	89.8%	60	65.1
			% College Graduates	37.9%	43	48.5
Commute	45	41.45	Average Work Commute in Minutes	26	9	75.0
			% Commuting on Public Transportation	3.3%	69	7.9
Community Stability	62	28.80	% Living in Same House as in 1979	14.2%	69	15.9
			% Living in Same County as in 1985	59.5%	50	41.7

Metropolitan Area Suburb Rankings
WASHINGTON

Composite: *Rank* 46 / 81 *Score* 53.64   **MOUNT VERNON** (VA)

CATEGORY	RANK	SCORE	STATISTIC	VALUE	RANK	SCORE
Economics	41	52.70	Median Household Income	$50,079	43	29.4
			% of Families Above Poverty Level	97.2%	43	76.0
Affordable Housing	42	61.90	Median Home Value	$175,500	47	72.2
			Median Rent	$763	44	51.6
Crime	N/A	N/A	Violent Crimes per 10,000 Population	N/A	N/A	N/A
			Property Crimes per 10,000 Population	N/A	N/A	N/A
Open Spaces	44	64.00	Population Density (Persons/Sq. Mile)	3610	42	81.3
			Average Rooms per Housing Unit	6.1	38	46.7
Education	41	62.85	% High School Enrollment/Completion	95.2%	21	83.6
			% College Graduates	33.9%	53	42.1
Commute	50	39.50	Average Work Commute in Minutes	32	51	45.0
			% Commuting on Public Transportation	11.9%	30	34.0
Community Stability	46	40.90	% Living in Same House as in 1979	27.8%	38	41.0
			% Living in Same County as in 1985	59.1%	51	40.8

Composite: *Rank* 47 / 81 *Score* 53.12   **BURKE** (VA)

CATEGORY	RANK	SCORE	STATISTIC	VALUE	RANK	SCORE
Economics	14	70.50	Median Household Income	$64,878	10	50.6
			% of Families Above Poverty Level	98.7%	18	90.4
Affordable Housing	75	32.15	Median Home Value	$202,400	62	64.3
			Median Rent	$1,001	72	0.0
Crime	N/A	N/A	Violent Crimes per 10,000 Population	N/A	N/A	N/A
			Property Crimes per 10,000 Population	N/A	N/A	N/A
Open Spaces	19	75.50	Population Density (Persons/Sq. Mile)	5031	63	73.2
			Average Rooms per Housing Unit	7.5	9	77.8
Education	7	81.90	% High School Enrollment/Completion	95.9%	16	86.0
			% College Graduates	56.3%	10	77.8
Commute	70	24.50	Average Work Commute in Minutes	34	69	35.0
			% Commuting on Public Transportation	5.3%	59	14.0
Community Stability	53	34.20	% Living in Same House as in 1979	19.5%	56	25.7
			% Living in Same County as in 1985	59.9%	49	42.7

Composite: *Rank* 48 / 81 *Score* 53.03   **JEFFERSON** (VA)

CATEGORY	RANK	SCORE	STATISTIC	VALUE	RANK	SCORE
Economics	44	51.35	Median Household Income	$49,611	44	28.7
			% of Families Above Poverty Level	97.0%	46	74.0
Affordable Housing	52	56.80	Median Home Value	$179,200	51	71.1
			Median Rent	$805	51	42.5
Crime	N/A	N/A	Violent Crimes per 10,000 Population	N/A	N/A	N/A
			Property Crimes per 10,000 Population	N/A	N/A	N/A
Open Spaces	57	56.50	Population Density (Persons/Sq. Mile)	5067	64	73.0
			Average Rooms per Housing Unit	5.8	46	40.0
Education	50	55.50	% High School Enrollment/Completion	89.5%	62	64.0
			% College Graduates	37.0%	45	47.0
Commute	23	52.40	Average Work Commute in Minutes	26	9	75.0
			% Commuting on Public Transportation	10.5%	37	29.8
Community Stability	41	45.60	% Living in Same House as in 1979	33.6%	27	51.8
			% Living in Same County as in 1985	58.5%	53	39.4

Metropolitan Area Suburb Rankings
WASHINGTON

Composite: **Rank** 49 / 81 **Score** 52.71   **OXON HILL-GLASSMANOR** (MD)

CATEGORY	RANK	SCORE	STATISTIC	VALUE	RANK	SCORE
Economics	71	34.70	Median Household Income	$39,041	67	13.6
			% of Families Above Poverty Level	95.1%	69	55.8
Affordable Housing	9	85.90	Median Home Value	$105,800	8	92.6
			Median Rent	$636	12	79.2
Crime	N/A	N/A	Violent Crimes per 10,000 Population	N/A	N/A	N/A
			Property Crimes per 10,000 Population	N/A	N/A	N/A
Open Spaces	63	51.55	Population Density (Persons/Sq. Mile)	4067	51	78.7
			Average Rooms per Housing Unit	5.1	70	24.4
Education	71	40.40	% High School Enrollment/Completion	90.0%	59	65.8
			% College Graduates	16.9%	73	15.0
Commute	38	45.00	Average Work Commute in Minutes	32	51	45.0
			% Commuting on Public Transportation	15.5%	20	45.0
Community Stability	26	58.70	% Living in Same House as in 1979	28.0%	37	41.4
			% Living in Same County as in 1985	74.2%	18	76.0

Composite: **Rank** 49 / 81 **Score** 52.71   **WALDORF** (MD)

CATEGORY	RANK	SCORE	STATISTIC	VALUE	RANK	SCORE
Economics	31	58.65	Median Household Income	$51,082	39	30.8
			% of Families Above Poverty Level	98.3%	24	86.5
Affordable Housing	32	70.80	Median Home Value	$128,700	19	85.9
			Median Rent	$744	39	55.7
Crime	N/A	N/A	Violent Crimes per 10,000 Population	N/A	N/A	N/A
			Property Crimes per 10,000 Population	N/A	N/A	N/A
Open Spaces	16	76.85	Population Density (Persons/Sq. Mile)	1027	2	95.9
			Average Rooms per Housing Unit	6.6	24	57.8
Education	57	51.20	% High School Enrollment/Completion	95.3%	20	83.9
			% College Graduates	19.1%	70	18.5
Commute	77	13.55	Average Work Commute in Minutes	36	75	25.0
			% Commuting on Public Transportation	1.4%	75	2.1
Community Stability	43	45.20	% Living in Same House as in 1979	25.9%	44	37.5
			% Living in Same County as in 1985	64.3%	37	52.9

Composite: **Rank** 51 / 81 **Score** 52.47   **CHILLUM** (MD)

CATEGORY	RANK	SCORE	STATISTIC	VALUE	RANK	SCORE
Economics	72	34.40	Median Household Income	$35,993	75	9.2
			% of Families Above Poverty Level	95.5%	63	59.6
Affordable Housing	11	85.70	Median Home Value	$114,500	13	90.1
			Median Rent	$626	8	81.3
Crime	N/A	N/A	Violent Crimes per 10,000 Population	N/A	N/A	N/A
			Property Crimes per 10,000 Population	N/A	N/A	N/A
Open Spaces	78	38.15	Population Density (Persons/Sq. Mile)	7629	76	58.5
			Average Rooms per Housing Unit	4.8	75	17.8
Education	67	43.00	% High School Enrollment/Completion	88.7%	65	61.3
			% College Graduates	23.0%	67	24.7
Commute	9	62.90	Average Work Commute in Minutes	30	38	55.0
			% Commuting on Public Transportation	24.0%	7	70.8
Community Stability	32	50.65	% Living in Same House as in 1979	32.8%	28	50.3
			% Living in Same County as in 1985	63.5%	39	51.0

Metropolitan Area Suburb Rankings
WASHINGTON

Composite: **Rank** 52 / 81 **Score** 52.44   **CHANTILLY** (VA)

CATEGORY	RANK	SCORE	STATISTIC	VALUE	RANK	SCORE
Economics	11	71.70	Median Household Income	$62,495	13	47.2
			% of Families Above Poverty Level	99.3%	6	96.2
Affordable Housing	63	42.40	Median Home Value	$195,200	59	66.4
			Median Rent	$916	66	18.4
Crime	N/A	N/A	Violent Crimes per 10,000 Population	N/A	N/A	N/A
			Property Crimes per 10,000 Population	N/A	N/A	N/A
Open Spaces	21	74.85	Population Density (Persons/Sq. Mile)	2511	19	87.5
			Average Rooms per Housing Unit	6.8	21	62.2
Education	14	77.30	% High School Enrollment/Completion	96.3%	15	87.3
			% College Graduates	49.7%	21	67.3
Commute	64	30.85	Average Work Commute in Minutes	32	51	45.0
			% Commuting on Public Transportation	6.2%	51	16.7
Community Stability	73	17.55	% Living in Same House as in 1979	12.1%	74	12.0
			% Living in Same County as in 1985	51.5%	70	23.1

Composite: **Rank** 53 / 81 **Score** 52.12   **FREDERICK** (MD)

CATEGORY	RANK	SCORE	STATISTIC	VALUE	RANK	SCORE
Economics	77	25.90	Median Household Income	$34,891	78	7.6
			% of Families Above Poverty Level	93.9%	77	44.2
Affordable Housing	4	90.85	Median Home Value	$112,000	11	90.8
			Median Rent	$582	3	90.9
Crime	N/A	N/A	Violent Crimes per 10,000 Population	108	N/A	N/A
			Property Crimes per 10,000 Population	517	N/A	N/A
Open Spaces	46	61.25	Population Density (Persons/Sq. Mile)	2207	13	89.2
			Average Rooms per Housing Unit	5.5	58	33.3
Education	69	42.95	% High School Enrollment/Completion	88.2%	67	59.6
			% College Graduates	24.0%	64	26.3
Commute	36	45.25	Average Work Commute in Minutes	24	2	85.0
			% Commuting on Public Transportation	2.5%	73	5.5
Community Stability	38	46.50	% Living in Same House as in 1979	23.4%	49	32.9
			% Living in Same County as in 1985	67.4%	32	60.1

Composite: **Rank** 54 / 81 **Score** 51.43   **GROVETON** (VA)

CATEGORY	RANK	SCORE	STATISTIC	VALUE	RANK	SCORE
Economics	64	37.55	Median Household Income	$45,051	53	22.2
			% of Families Above Poverty Level	94.8%	74	52.9
Affordable Housing	33	69.00	Median Home Value	$161,200	39	76.4
			Median Rent	$717	34	61.6
Crime	N/A	N/A	Violent Crimes per 10,000 Population	N/A	N/A	N/A
			Property Crimes per 10,000 Population	N/A	N/A	N/A
Open Spaces	49	60.15	Population Density (Persons/Sq. Mile)	3401	38	82.5
			Average Rooms per Housing Unit	5.7	51	37.8
Education	55	51.55	% High School Enrollment/Completion	88.9%	64	62.0
			% College Graduates	33.3%	54	41.1
Commute	24	51.80	Average Work Commute in Minutes	30	38	55.0
			% Commuting on Public Transportation	16.7%	16	48.6
Community Stability	47	38.55	% Living in Same House as in 1979	29.4%	35	44.0
			% Living in Same County as in 1985	55.8%	63	33.1

Metropolitan Area Suburb Rankings
WASHINGTON

Composite: *Rank* 55 / 81 *Score* 50.99   **STERLING (VA)**

CATEGORY	RANK	SCORE	STATISTIC	VALUE	RANK	SCORE
Economics	16	67.70	Median Household Income	$55,593	25	37.3
			% of Families Above Poverty Level	99.5%	2	98.1
Affordable Housing	61	47.45	Median Home Value	$156,300	36	77.8
			Median Rent	$922	68	17.1
Crime	N/A	N/A	Violent Crimes per 10,000 Population	N/A	N/A	N/A
			Property Crimes per 10,000 Population	N/A	N/A	N/A
Open Spaces	25	71.05	Population Density (Persons/Sq. Mile)	3085	34	84.3
			Average Rooms per Housing Unit	6.6	24	57.8
Education	53	52.75	% High School Enrollment/Completion	90.8%	50	68.5
			% College Graduates	30.7%	58	37.0
Commute	63	30.90	Average Work Commute in Minutes	29	31	60.0
			% Commuting on Public Transportation	1.3%	76	1.8
Community Stability	49	36.10	% Living in Same House as in 1979	24.0%	47	34.0
			% Living in Same County as in 1985	58.0%	55	38.2

Composite: *Rank* 56 / 81 *Score* 50.20   **GAITHERSBURG (MD)**

CATEGORY	RANK	SCORE	STATISTIC	VALUE	RANK	SCORE
Economics	68	37.00	Median Household Income	$43,644	58	20.2
			% of Families Above Poverty Level	94.9%	71	53.8
Affordable Housing	22	75.30	Median Home Value	$147,100	30	80.5
			Median Rent	$678	19	70.1
Crime	N/A	N/A	Violent Crimes per 10,000 Population	N/A	N/A	N/A
			Property Crimes per 10,000 Population	N/A	N/A	N/A
Open Spaces	58	56.40	Population Density (Persons/Sq. Mile)	4333	55	77.2
			Average Rooms per Housing Unit	5.6	55	35.6
Education	56	51.30	% High School Enrollment/Completion	85.8%	70	51.4
			% College Graduates	39.6%	39	51.2
Commute	31	49.20	Average Work Commute in Minutes	28	26	65.0
			% Commuting on Public Transportation	11.7%	31	33.4
Community Stability	58	32.00	% Living in Same House as in 1979	13.5%	72	14.6
			% Living in Same County as in 1985	62.8%	41	49.4

Composite: *Rank* 57 / 81 *Score* 50.18   **ADELPHI (MD)**

CATEGORY	RANK	SCORE	STATISTIC	VALUE	RANK	SCORE
Economics	70	35.15	Median Household Income	$37,051	73	10.7
			% of Families Above Poverty Level	95.5%	63	59.6
Affordable Housing	20	76.05	Median Home Value	$141,100	27	82.3
			Median Rent	$679	21	69.8
Crime	N/A	N/A	Violent Crimes per 10,000 Population	N/A	N/A	N/A
			Property Crimes per 10,000 Population	N/A	N/A	N/A
Open Spaces	67	49.20	Population Density (Persons/Sq. Mile)	4514	58	76.2
			Average Rooms per Housing Unit	5.0	74	22.2
Education	52	53.20	% High School Enrollment/Completion	85.8%	70	51.4
			% College Graduates	42.0%	36	55.0
Commute	20	53.15	Average Work Commute in Minutes	28	26	65.0
			% Commuting on Public Transportation	14.3%	22	41.3
Community Stability	52	34.30	% Living in Same House as in 1979	26.2%	40	38.1
			% Living in Same County as in 1985	54.7%	65	30.5

Metropolitan Area Suburb Rankings
WASHINGTON

Composite: **Rank** 58 / 81 *Score* 49.88 **LINCOLNIA (VA)**

CATEGORY	RANK	SCORE	STATISTIC	VALUE	RANK	SCORE
Economics	53	43.75	Median Household Income	$51,090	38	30.8
			% of Families Above Poverty Level	95.2%	68	56.7
Affordable Housing	49	58.90	Median Home Value	$204,700	63	63.6
			Median Rent	$751	41	54.2
Crime	N/A	N/A	Violent Crimes per 10,000 Population	N/A	N/A	N/A
			Property Crimes per 10,000 Population	N/A	N/A	N/A
Open Spaces	54	58.25	Population Density (Persons/Sq. Mile)	4448	57	76.5
			Average Rooms per Housing Unit	5.8	46	40.0
Education	44	59.10	% High School Enrollment/Completion	90.6%	54	67.8
			% College Graduates	39.1%	40	50.4
Commute	19	53.90	Average Work Commute in Minutes	26	9	75.0
			% Commuting on Public Transportation	11.5%	32	32.8
Community Stability	67	25.40	% Living in Same House as in 1979	23.0%	51	32.2
			% Living in Same County as in 1985	49.6%	74	18.6

Composite: **Rank** 59 / 81 *Score* 49.51 **LAUREL (MD)**

CATEGORY	RANK	SCORE	STATISTIC	VALUE	RANK	SCORE
Economics	43	51.70	Median Household Income	$44,002	57	20.7
			% of Families Above Poverty Level	97.9%	32	82.7
Affordable Housing	12	84.85	Median Home Value	$119,400	15	88.6
			Median Rent	$627	9	81.1
Crime	N/A	N/A	Violent Crimes per 10,000 Population	54	N/A	N/A
			Property Crimes per 10,000 Population	587	N/A	N/A
Open Spaces	70	45.70	Population Density (Persons/Sq. Mile)	6137	69	67.0
			Average Rooms per Housing Unit	5.1	70	24.4
Education	65	46.10	% High School Enrollment/Completion	84.4%	73	46.6
			% College Graduates	36.1%	47	45.6
Commute	47	40.95	Average Work Commute in Minutes	27	16	70.0
			% Commuting on Public Transportation	4.6%	64	11.9
Community Stability	65	27.75	% Living in Same House as in 1979	14.6%	66	16.6
			% Living in Same County as in 1985	58.3%	54	38.9

Composite: **Rank** 60 / 81 *Score* 49.50 **EAST RIVERDALE (MD)**

CATEGORY	RANK	SCORE	STATISTIC	VALUE	RANK	SCORE
Economics	69	35.40	Median Household Income	$35,394	76	8.3
			% of Families Above Poverty Level	95.8%	58	62.5
Affordable Housing	7	87.75	Median Home Value	$95,800	4	95.5
			Median Rent	$632	10	80.0
Crime	N/A	N/A	Violent Crimes per 10,000 Population	N/A	N/A	N/A
			Property Crimes per 10,000 Population	N/A	N/A	N/A
Open Spaces	76	40.40	Population Density (Persons/Sq. Mile)	8406	79	54.1
			Average Rooms per Housing Unit	5.2	68	26.7
Education	79	18.05	% High School Enrollment/Completion	77.6%	79	23.3
			% College Graduates	15.5%	76	12.8
Commute	15	56.65	Average Work Commute in Minutes	28	26	65.0
			% Commuting on Public Transportation	16.6%	17	48.3
Community Stability	25	58.75	% Living in Same House as in 1979	32.5%	29	49.7
			% Living in Same County as in 1985	70.7%	26	67.8

Metropolitan Area Suburb Rankings
WASHINGTON

Composite: *Rank* 60 / 81 *Score* 49.50 **SUITLAND-SILVER HILL (MD)**

CATEGORY	RANK	SCORE	STATISTIC	VALUE	RANK	SCORE
Economics	76	29.80	Median Household Income	$34,264	79	6.7
			% of Families Above Poverty Level	94.8%	74	52.9
Affordable Housing	8	86.55	Median Home Value	$103,300	6	93.3
			Median Rent	$633	11	79.8
Crime	N/A	N/A	Violent Crimes per 10,000 Population	N/A	N/A	N/A
			Property Crimes per 10,000 Population	N/A	N/A	N/A
Open Spaces	74	42.55	Population Density (Persons/Sq. Mile)	5289	68	71.8
			Average Rooms per Housing Unit	4.6	78	13.3
Education	74	38.70	% High School Enrollment/Completion	90.1%	58	66.1
			% College Graduates	14.6%	79	11.3
Commute	21	52.65	Average Work Commute in Minutes	33	66	40.0
			% Commuting on Public Transportation	22.2%	8	65.3
Community Stability	37	46.75	% Living in Same House as in 1979	18.1%	60	23.1
			% Living in Same County as in 1985	71.8%	24	70.4

Composite: *Rank* 62 / 81 *Score* 49.19 **TYSONS CORNER (VA)**

CATEGORY	RANK	SCORE	STATISTIC	VALUE	RANK	SCORE
Economics	33	58.35	Median Household Income	$51,299	36	31.1
			% of Families Above Poverty Level	98.2%	28	85.6
Affordable Housing	73	33.95	Median Home Value	$290,700	77	38.4
			Median Rent	$865	61	29.5
Crime	N/A	N/A	Violent Crimes per 10,000 Population	N/A	N/A	N/A
			Property Crimes per 10,000 Population	N/A	N/A	N/A
Open Spaces	60	55.50	Population Density (Persons/Sq. Mile)	2679	26	86.6
			Average Rooms per Housing Unit	5.1	70	24.4
Education	20	72.80	% High School Enrollment/Completion	89.8%	60	65.1
			% College Graduates	58.0%	8	80.5
Commute	25	51.25	Average Work Commute in Minutes	25	5	80.0
			% Commuting on Public Transportation	8.1%	43	22.5
Community Stability	69	23.30	% Living in Same House as in 1979	14.4%	67	16.3
			% Living in Same County as in 1985	54.6%	66	30.3

Composite: *Rank* 63 / 81 *Score* 48.87 **FRANCONIA (VA)**

CATEGORY	RANK	SCORE	STATISTIC	VALUE	RANK	SCORE
Economics	17	66.45	Median Household Income	$58,607	20	41.6
			% of Families Above Poverty Level	98.8%	13	91.3
Affordable Housing	67	39.10	Median Home Value	$177,800	49	71.5
			Median Rent	$970	71	6.7
Crime	N/A	N/A	Violent Crimes per 10,000 Population	N/A	N/A	N/A
			Property Crimes per 10,000 Population	N/A	N/A	N/A
Open Spaces	27	69.80	Population Density (Persons/Sq. Mile)	2728	27	86.3
			Average Rooms per Housing Unit	6.4	29	53.3
Education	27	70.80	% High School Enrollment/Completion	91.7%	47	71.6
			% College Graduates	51.4%	15	70.0
Commute	58	35.70	Average Work Commute in Minutes	32	51	45.0
			% Commuting on Public Transportation	9.4%	40	26.4
Community Stability	77	11.35	% Living in Same House as in 1979	13.7%	71	15.0
			% Living in Same County as in 1985	44.9%	79	7.7

Metropolitan Area Suburb Rankings
WASHINGTON

Composite: **Rank** 64 / 81 **Score** 48.65   **SOUTH LAUREL (MD)**

CATEGORY	RANK	SCORE	STATISTIC	VALUE	RANK	SCORE
Economics	62	39.00	Median Household Income	$40,398	64	15.5
			% of Families Above Poverty Level	95.8%	58	62.5
Affordable Housing	26	73.70	Median Home Value	$163,100	41	75.8
			Median Rent	$671	17	71.6
Crime	N/A	N/A	Violent Crimes per 10,000 Population	N/A	N/A	N/A
			Property Crimes per 10,000 Population	N/A	N/A	N/A
Open Spaces	62	52.50	Population Density (Persons/Sq. Mile)	4531	59	76.1
			Average Rooms per Housing Unit	5.3	63	28.9
Education	51	54.35	% High School Enrollment/Completion	90.8%	50	68.5
			% College Graduates	32.7%	57	40.2
Commute	52	38.45	Average Work Commute in Minutes	28	26	65.0
			% Commuting on Public Transportation	4.6%	64	11.9
Community Stability	56	33.90	% Living in Same House as in 1979	18.4%	59	23.7
			% Living in Same County as in 1985	60.5%	47	44.1

Composite: **Rank** 65 / 81 **Score** 48.62   **NEWINGTON (VA)**

CATEGORY	RANK	SCORE	STATISTIC	VALUE	RANK	SCORE
Economics	23	63.35	Median Household Income	$63,660	11	48.8
			% of Families Above Poverty Level	97.4%	39	77.9
Affordable Housing	72	34.55	Median Home Value	$186,000	55	69.1
			Median Rent	$1,001	72	0.0
Crime	N/A	N/A	Violent Crimes per 10,000 Population	N/A	N/A	N/A
			Property Crimes per 10,000 Population	N/A	N/A	N/A
Open Spaces	13	80.00	Population Density (Persons/Sq. Mile)	2662	25	86.7
			Average Rooms per Housing Unit	7.3	10	73.3
Education	22	71.90	% High School Enrollment/Completion	92.6%	39	74.7
			% College Graduates	50.8%	18	69.1
Commute	74	18.60	Average Work Commute in Minutes	36	75	25.0
			% Commuting on Public Transportation	4.7%	62	12.2
Community Stability	69	23.30	% Living in Same House as in 1979	12.9%	73	13.5
			% Living in Same County as in 1985	55.8%	63	33.1

Composite: **Rank** 66 / 81 **Score** 48.35   **GERMANTOWN (MD)**

CATEGORY	RANK	SCORE	STATISTIC	VALUE	RANK	SCORE
Economics	51	47.85	Median Household Income	$46,037	49	23.6
			% of Families Above Poverty Level	96.8%	51	72.1
Affordable Housing	29	71.30	Median Home Value	$129,600	22	85.6
			Median Rent	$738	38	57.0
Crime	N/A	N/A	Violent Crimes per 10,000 Population	N/A	N/A	N/A
			Property Crimes per 10,000 Population	N/A	N/A	N/A
Open Spaces	51	60.00	Population Density (Persons/Sq. Mile)	3838	48	80.0
			Average Rooms per Housing Unit	5.8	46	40.0
Education	47	56.00	% High School Enrollment/Completion	89.2%	63	63.0
			% College Graduates	38.2%	42	49.0
Commute	61	32.85	Average Work Commute in Minutes	32	51	45.0
			% Commuting on Public Transportation	7.5%	45	20.7
Community Stability	71	22.10	% Living in Same House as in 1979	6.3%	80	1.3
			% Living in Same County as in 1985	60.0%	48	42.9

Metropolitan Area Suburb Rankings
WASHINGTON

Composite: **Rank** 67 / 81 **Score** 47.77 **LEESBURG (VA)**

CATEGORY	RANK	SCORE	STATISTIC	VALUE	RANK	SCORE
Economics	59	40.55	Median Household Income	$39,887	65	14.8
			% of Families Above Poverty Level	96.2%	53	66.3
Affordable Housing	30	71.00	Median Home Value	$163,300	42	75.8
			Median Rent	$696	28	66.2
Crime	N/A	N/A	Violent Crimes per 10,000 Population	19	N/A	N/A
			Property Crimes per 10,000 Population	392	N/A	N/A
Open Spaces	41	65.80	Population Density (Persons/Sq. Mile)	1404	5	93.8
			Average Rooms per Housing Unit	5.7	51	37.8
Education	68	43.05	% High School Enrollment/Completion	86.1%	69	52.4
			% College Graduates	28.6%	59	33.7
Commute	55	37.50	Average Work Commute in Minutes	26	9	75.0
			% Commuting on Public Transportation	0.7%	81	0.0
Community Stability	63	28.75	% Living in Same House as in 1979	15.0%	65	17.4
			% Living in Same County as in 1985	58.8%	52	40.1

Composite: **Rank** 68 / 81 **Score** 47.69 **HYBLA VALLEY (VA)**

CATEGORY	RANK	SCORE	STATISTIC	VALUE	RANK	SCORE
Economics	74	32.40	Median Household Income	$37,272	71	11.0
			% of Families Above Poverty Level	94.9%	71	53.8
Affordable Housing	40	63.70	Median Home Value	$232,800	71	55.4
			Median Rent	$669	16	72.0
Crime	N/A	N/A	Violent Crimes per 10,000 Population	N/A	N/A	N/A
			Property Crimes per 10,000 Population	N/A	N/A	N/A
Open Spaces	64	50.90	Population Density (Persons/Sq. Mile)	5082	65	72.9
			Average Rooms per Housing Unit	5.3	63	28.9
Education	48	56.05	% High School Enrollment/Completion	91.7%	47	71.6
			% College Graduates	32.9%	55	40.5
Commute	35	47.55	Average Work Commute in Minutes	30	38	55.0
			% Commuting on Public Transportation	13.9%	24	40.1
Community Stability	51	35.55	% Living in Same House as in 1979	24.0%	47	34.0
			% Living in Same County as in 1985	57.5%	60	37.1

Composite: **Rank** 69 / 81 **Score** 47.23 **ALEXANDRIA (VA)**

CATEGORY	RANK	SCORE	STATISTIC	VALUE	RANK	SCORE
Economics	65	37.40	Median Household Income	$41,472	62	17.1
			% of Families Above Poverty Level	95.3%	66	57.7
Affordable Housing	44	60.95	Median Home Value	$228,000	69	56.8
			Median Rent	$701	29	65.1
Crime	N/A	N/A	Violent Crimes per 10,000 Population	65	N/A	N/A
			Property Crimes per 10,000 Population	688	N/A	N/A
Open Spaces	79	36.90	Population Density (Persons/Sq. Mile)	7281	75	60.5
			Average Rooms per Housing Unit	4.6	78	13.3
Education	58	50.85	% High School Enrollment/Completion	81.4%	75	36.3
			% College Graduates	48.5%	23	65.4
Commute	4	67.80	Average Work Commute in Minutes	25	5	80.0
			% Commuting on Public Transportation	19.0%	14	55.6
Community Stability	61	29.50	% Living in Same House as in 1979	21.4%	53	29.2
			% Living in Same County as in 1985	54.4%	67	29.8

Metropolitan Area Suburb Rankings
WASHINGTON

Composite: **Rank** 69 / 81 *Score* 47.23 **FAIRLAND (MD)**

CATEGORY	RANK	SCORE	STATISTIC	VALUE	RANK	SCORE
Economics	54	43.50	Median Household Income	$47,970	45	26.4
			% of Families Above Poverty Level	95.6%	62	60.6
Affordable Housing	46	60.80	Median Home Value	$150,000	32	79.7
			Median Rent	$808	52	41.9
Crime	N/A	N/A	Violent Crimes per 10,000 Population	N/A	N/A	N/A
			Property Crimes per 10,000 Population	N/A	N/A	N/A
Open Spaces	55	57.40	Population Density (Persons/Sq. Mile)	3973	49	79.2
			Average Rooms per Housing Unit	5.6	55	35.6
Education	19	73.00	% High School Enrollment/Completion	93.7%	34	78.4
			% College Graduates	49.9%	19	67.6
Commute	60	33.30	Average Work Commute in Minutes	34	69	35.0
			% Commuting on Public Transportation	11.1%	34	31.6
Community Stability	74	15.40	% Living in Same House as in 1979	7.0%	78	2.6
			% Living in Same County as in 1985	53.7%	69	28.2

Composite: **Rank** 71 / 81 *Score* 46.52 **IDYLWOOD (VA)**

CATEGORY	RANK	SCORE	STATISTIC	VALUE	RANK	SCORE
Economics	61	39.90	Median Household Income	$47,687	46	26.0
			% of Families Above Poverty Level	94.9%	71	53.8
Affordable Housing	60	48.25	Median Home Value	$221,100	65	58.8
			Median Rent	$827	56	37.7
Crime	N/A	N/A	Violent Crimes per 10,000 Population	N/A	N/A	N/A
			Property Crimes per 10,000 Population	N/A	N/A	N/A
Open Spaces	65	50.65	Population Density (Persons/Sq. Mile)	5174	66	72.4
			Average Rooms per Housing Unit	5.3	63	28.9
Education	41	62.85	% High School Enrollment/Completion	87.3%	68	56.5
			% College Graduates	50.9%	17	69.2
Commute	14	58.10	Average Work Commute in Minutes	25	5	80.0
			% Commuting on Public Transportation	12.6%	29	36.2
Community Stability	72	19.40	% Living in Same House as in 1979	19.1%	57	25.0
			% Living in Same County as in 1985	47.5%	76	13.8

Composite: **Rank** 72 / 81 *Score* 46.05 **MONTCLAIR (VA)**

CATEGORY	RANK	SCORE	STATISTIC	VALUE	RANK	SCORE
Economics	9	73.50	Median Household Income	$62,390	14	47.0
			% of Families Above Poverty Level	99.7%	1	100.0
Affordable Housing	71	35.95	Median Home Value	$176,600	48	71.9
			Median Rent	$1,001	72	0.0
Crime	N/A	N/A	Violent Crimes per 10,000 Population	N/A	N/A	N/A
			Property Crimes per 10,000 Population	N/A	N/A	N/A
Open Spaces	6	85.50	Population Density (Persons/Sq. Mile)	1887	10	91.0
			Average Rooms per Housing Unit	7.6	8	80.0
Education	36	65.20	% High School Enrollment/Completion	88.6%	66	61.0
			% College Graduates	51.0%	16	69.4
Commute	81	0.75	Average Work Commute in Minutes	41	80	0.0
			% Commuting on Public Transportation	1.2%	78	1.5
Community Stability	74	15.40	% Living in Same House as in 1979	11.8%	75	11.5
			% Living in Same County as in 1985	49.9%	73	19.3

Metropolitan Area Suburb Rankings
WASHINGTON

Composite: **Rank** 73 / 81 **Score** 45.83   **DALE CITY (VA)**

CATEGORY	RANK	SCORE	STATISTIC	VALUE	RANK	SCORE
Economics	34	57.60	Median Household Income	$50,940	40	30.6
			% of Families Above Poverty Level	98.1%	29	84.6
Affordable Housing	45	60.90	Median Home Value	$121,600	16	88.0
			Median Rent	$845	59	33.8
Crime	N/A	N/A	Violent Crimes per 10,000 Population	N/A	N/A	N/A
			Property Crimes per 10,000 Population	N/A	N/A	N/A
Open Spaces	22	74.25	Population Density (Persons/Sq. Mile)	3109	35	84.1
			Average Rooms per Housing Unit	6.9	18	64.4
Education	62	48.50	% High School Enrollment/Completion	92.1%	45	72.9
			% College Graduates	22.6%	68	24.1
Commute	80	3.05	Average Work Commute in Minutes	41	80	0.0
			% Commuting on Public Transportation	2.7%	72	6.1
Community Stability	60	30.70	% Living in Same House as in 1979	20.4%	54	27.4
			% Living in Same County as in 1985	56.2%	62	34.0

Composite: **Rank** 74 / 81 **Score** 45.49   **WOODBRIDGE (VA)**

CATEGORY	RANK	SCORE	STATISTIC	VALUE	RANK	SCORE
Economics	45	50.90	Median Household Income	$42,900	59	19.1
			% of Families Above Poverty Level	97.9%	32	82.7
Affordable Housing	21	75.40	Median Home Value	$112,900	12	90.5
			Median Rent	$723	36	60.3
Crime	N/A	N/A	Violent Crimes per 10,000 Population	N/A	N/A	N/A
			Property Crimes per 10,000 Population	N/A	N/A	N/A
Open Spaces	34	67.10	Population Density (Persons/Sq. Mile)	2519	21	87.5
			Average Rooms per Housing Unit	6.1	38	46.7
Education	78	23.10	% High School Enrollment/Completion	81.3%	76	36.0
			% College Graduates	13.9%	80	10.2
Commute	75	18.40	Average Work Commute in Minutes	34	69	35.0
			% Commuting on Public Transportation	1.3%	76	1.8
Community Stability	48	38.05	% Living in Same House as in 1979	26.1%	43	37.9
			% Living in Same County as in 1985	58.0%	55	38.2

Composite: **Rank** 75 / 81 **Score** 44.98   **ST. CHARLES (MD)**

CATEGORY	RANK	SCORE	STATISTIC	VALUE	RANK	SCORE
Economics	49	48.60	Median Household Income	$45,767	51	23.2
			% of Families Above Poverty Level	97.0%	46	74.0
Affordable Housing	31	70.90	Median Home Value	$115,700	14	89.7
			Median Rent	$761	42	52.1
Crime	N/A	N/A	Violent Crimes per 10,000 Population	N/A	N/A	N/A
			Property Crimes per 10,000 Population	N/A	N/A	N/A
Open Spaces	36	66.80	Population Density (Persons/Sq. Mile)	2617	23	86.9
			Average Rooms per Housing Unit	6.1	38	46.7
Education	66	46.05	% High School Enrollment/Completion	92.7%	38	75.0
			% College Graduates	18.2%	72	17.1
Commute	78	10.30	Average Work Commute in Minutes	37	78	20.0
			% Commuting on Public Transportation	0.9%	80	0.6
Community Stability	66	27.25	% Living in Same House as in 1979	16.4%	63	20.0
			% Living in Same County as in 1985	56.4%	61	34.5

Metropolitan Area Suburb Rankings
WASHINGTON

Composite: **Rank** 76 / 81 *Score* 44.63 CENTREVILLE (VA)

CATEGORY	RANK	SCORE	STATISTIC	VALUE	RANK	SCORE
Economics	30	58.95	Median Household Income	$54,848	27	36.2
			% of Families Above Poverty Level	97.8%	35	81.7
Affordable Housing	59	48.80	Median Home Value	$161,400	40	76.3
			Median Rent	$903	64	21.3
Crime	N/A	N/A	Violent Crimes per 10,000 Population	N/A	N/A	N/A
			Property Crimes per 10,000 Population	N/A	N/A	N/A
Open Spaces	31	67.55	Population Density (Persons/Sq. Mile)	2735	28	86.2
			Average Rooms per Housing Unit	6.2	36	48.9
Education	32	68.80	% High School Enrollment/Completion	92.4%	42	74.0
			% College Graduates	47.4%	25	63.6
Commute	76	18.10	Average Work Commute in Minutes	36	75	25.0
			% Commuting on Public Transportation	4.4%	66	11.2
Community Stability	79	5.55	% Living in Same House as in 1979	6.7%	79	2.0
			% Living in Same County as in 1985	45.5%	78	9.1

Composite: **Rank** 77 / 81 *Score* 44.27 LAKE RIDGE (VA)

CATEGORY	RANK	SCORE	STATISTIC	VALUE	RANK	SCORE
Economics	22	63.95	Median Household Income	$52,410	33	32.7
			% of Families Above Poverty Level	99.2%	8	95.2
Affordable Housing	58	49.70	Median Home Value	$148,500	31	80.1
			Median Rent	$912	65	19.3
Crime	N/A	N/A	Violent Crimes per 10,000 Population	N/A	N/A	N/A
			Property Crimes per 10,000 Population	N/A	N/A	N/A
Open Spaces	26	69.90	Population Density (Persons/Sq. Mile)	4646	60	75.4
			Average Rooms per Housing Unit	6.9	18	64.4
Education	21	72.05	% High School Enrollment/Completion	95.0%	23	82.9
			% College Graduates	45.9%	28	61.2
Commute	79	4.80	Average Work Commute in Minutes	40	79	5.0
			% Commuting on Public Transportation	2.2%	74	4.6
Community Stability	80	5.20	% Living in Same House as in 1979	10.2%	76	8.5
			% Living in Same County as in 1985	42.4%	80	1.9

Composite: **Rank** 78 / 81 *Score* 43.21 MANASSAS (VA)

CATEGORY	RANK	SCORE	STATISTIC	VALUE	RANK	SCORE
Economics	46	50.70	Median Household Income	$46,674	48	24.5
			% of Families Above Poverty Level	97.3%	40	76.9
Affordable Housing	27	72.95	Median Home Value	$150,600	33	79.5
			Median Rent	$695	27	66.4
Crime	N/A	N/A	Violent Crimes per 10,000 Population	20	N/A	N/A
			Property Crimes per 10,000 Population	445	N/A	N/A
Open Spaces	39	66.30	Population Density (Persons/Sq. Mile)	2793	30	85.9
			Average Rooms per Housing Unit	6.1	38	46.7
Education	76	28.80	% High School Enrollment/Completion	79.1%	77	28.4
			% College Graduates	25.8%	62	29.2
Commute	68	25.45	Average Work Commute in Minutes	31	46	50.0
			% Commuting on Public Transportation	1.0%	79	0.9
Community Stability	76	15.05	% Living in Same House as in 1979	14.2%	69	15.9
			% Living in Same County as in 1985	47.7%	75	14.2

Metropolitan Area Suburb Rankings
WASHINGTON

Composite: **Rank** 79 / 81 *Score* 35.22   **LORTON (VA)**

CATEGORY	RANK	SCORE	STATISTIC	VALUE	RANK	SCORE
Economics	50	47.90	Median Household Income	$44,769	54	21.8
			% of Families Above Poverty Level	97.0%	46	74.0
Affordable Housing	39	64.15	Median Home Value	$131,300	23	85.1
			Median Rent	$802	50	43.2
Crime	N/A	N/A	Violent Crimes per 10,000 Population	N/A	N/A	N/A
			Property Crimes per 10,000 Population	N/A	N/A	N/A
Open Spaces	42	65.15	Population Density (Persons/Sq. Mile)	1238	4	94.7
			Average Rooms per Housing Unit	5.6	55	35.6
Education	81	9.10	% High School Enrollment/Completion	70.8%	81	0.0
			% College Graduates	18.9%	71	18.2
Commute	73	19.85	Average Work Commute in Minutes	35	74	30.0
			% Commuting on Public Transportation	3.9%	67	9.7
Community Stability	81	5.15	% Living in Same House as in 1979	5.6%	81	0.0
			% Living in Same County as in 1985	46.0%	77	10.3

Composite: **Rank** 80 / 81 *Score* 35.06   **BAILEY'S CROSSROADS (VA)**

CATEGORY	RANK	SCORE	STATISTIC	VALUE	RANK	SCORE
Economics	79	10.10	Median Household Income	$38,291	69	12.5
			% of Families Above Poverty Level	90.1%	79	7.7
Affordable Housing	43	61.40	Median Home Value	$221,200	66	58.8
			Median Rent	$706	32	64.0
Crime	N/A	N/A	Violent Crimes per 10,000 Population	N/A	N/A	N/A
			Property Crimes per 10,000 Population	N/A	N/A	N/A
Open Spaces	80	28.50	Population Density (Persons/Sq. Mile)	9463	80	48.1
			Average Rooms per Housing Unit	4.4	80	8.9
Education	70	41.30	% High School Enrollment/Completion	81.6%	74	37.0
			% College Graduates	36.1%	47	45.6
Commute	13	58.25	Average Work Commute in Minutes	27	16	70.0
			% Commuting on Public Transportation	16.0%	19	46.5
Community Stability	78	10.80	% Living in Same House as in 1979	17.3%	61	21.6
			% Living in Same County as in 1985	41.6%	81	0.0

Composite: **Rank** 81 / 81 *Score* 32.72   **LANGLEY PARK (MD)**

CATEGORY	RANK	SCORE	STATISTIC	VALUE	RANK	SCORE
Economics	81	0.00	Median Household Income	$29,570	81	0.0
			% of Families Above Poverty Level	89.3%	80	0.0
Affordable Housing	5	88.30	Median Home Value	$108,700	9	91.8
			Median Rent	$610	5	84.8
Crime	N/A	N/A	Violent Crimes per 10,000 Population	N/A	N/A	N/A
			Property Crimes per 10,000 Population	N/A	N/A	N/A
Open Spaces	81	0.00	Population Density (Persons/Sq. Mile)	17952	81	0.0
			Average Rooms per Housing Unit	4.0	81	0.0
Education	80	12.05	% High School Enrollment/Completion	74.3%	80	12.0
			% College Graduates	15.1%	77	12.1
Commute	3	72.50	Average Work Commute in Minutes	32	51	45.0
			% Commuting on Public Transportation	33.6%	1	100.0
Community Stability	68	23.45	% Living in Same House as in 1979	19.9%	55	26.4
			% Living in Same County as in 1985	50.4%	72	20.5

Metropolitan Area Description
WEST PALM BEACH-BOCA RATON-DELRAY BEACH

STATE: Florida
COUNTIES: Palm Beach

TOTAL POPULATION: 863,518

POPULATION IN SUBURBS: 687,202   (79.6%)

POPULATION IN West Palm Beach: 67,643   (7.8%)
POPULATION IN Boca Raton: 61,492   (7.1%)
POPULATION IN Delray Beach: 47,181   (5.5%)

The WEST PALM BEACH-BOCA RATON-DELRAY BEACH metropolitan area is located in the southeastern part of Florida along the Atlantic Ocean. The suburbs range geographically from Jupiter in the north (20 miles from West Palm Beach), to Belle Glade in the west (43 miles from West Palm Beach), and to Boca Del Mar in the south (45 miles from West Palm Beach). The area is growing rapidly in population and had an increase of 49.7% between 1980 and 1990. Summer time high temperatures average in the 90's and winter time lows average in the 50's. Tourism is a major industry in the area. High tech companies also have a major presence. Both IBM and Pratt & Whitney have large facilities in the area, which has been nicknamed "Silicon Beach." Public transportation in the area is provided by Cotran using buses.

North Palm Beach is the overall highest rated suburb. **Wellington** receives the highest scores in economics and open spaces. **Belle Glade** is the suburb with the most affordable housing, and also has the top rated commute. **Royal Palm Beach** is rated the safest suburb with the lowest crime rate. The top score in education belongs to **Palm Beach Gardens**. Finally, the number one rating in community stability goes to **Riviera Beach**.

The highest ranked suburb overall which also has an affordable housing score of at least 50.00 is **Riviera Beach**.

The highest ranked suburb in the education category which also has an affordable housing score of at least 50.00 is **Kings Point**.

The metropolitan area contains only one county.

Metropolitan Area Map
WEST PALM BEACH–BOCA RATON–DELRAY BEACH

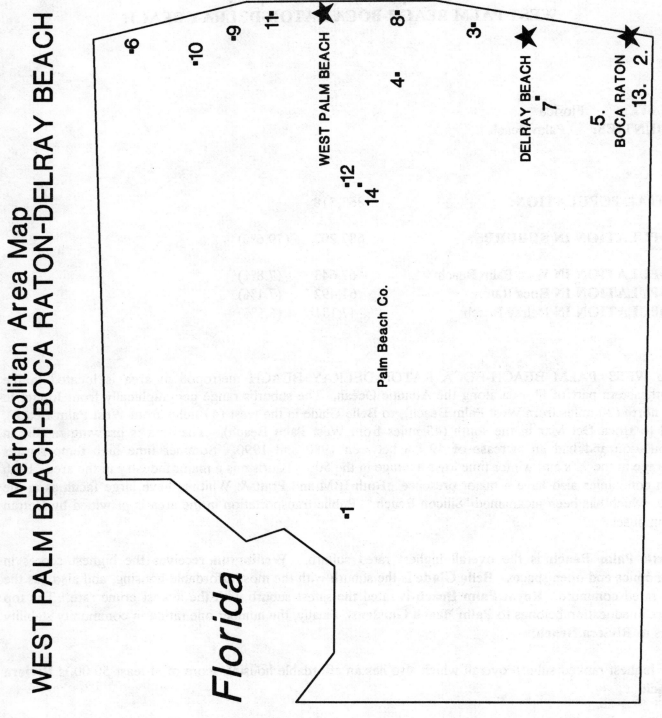

Florida

Palm Beach Co.

WEST PALM BEACH

DELRAY BEACH

BOCA RATON

Metropolitan Area Suburb Alphabetical Index
WEST PALM BEACH-BOCA RATON-DELRAY BEACH

SUBURB	PAGE	MAP NO.	STATE	COUNTY	POPU-LATION	RANK
BELLE GLADE	815	1	Florida	Palm Beach	16,177	11 / 14
BOCA DEL MAR	815	2	Florida	Palm Beach	17,754	10 / 14
BOYNTON BEACH	814	3	Florida	Palm Beach	46,194	7 / 14
GREENACRES CITY	814	4	Florida	Palm Beach	18,683	9 / 14
HAMPTONS AT BOCA RATON	815	5	Florida	Palm Beach	11,686	12 / 14
JUPITER	813	6	Florida	Palm Beach	24,986	4 / 14
KINGS POINT	813	7	Florida	Palm Beach	12,422	6 / 14
LAKE WORTH	816	8	Florida	Palm Beach	28,564	13 / 14
NORTH PALM BEACH	812	9	Florida	Palm Beach	11,343	1 / 14
PALM BEACH GARDENS	812	10	Florida	Palm Beach	22,965	2 / 14
RIVIERA BEACH	813	11	Florida	Palm Beach	27,639	5 / 14
ROYAL PALM BEACH	812	12	Florida	Palm Beach	14,589	3 / 14
SANDALFOOT COVE	816	13	Florida	Palm Beach	14,214	14 / 14
WELLINGTON	814	14	Florida	Palm Beach	20,670	8 / 14

Metropolitan Area Suburb Rankings
WEST PALM BEACH-BOCA RATON-DELRAY BEACH

Composite: *Rank* 1 / 14 *Score* 68.23   **NORTH PALM BEACH**

CATEGORY	RANK	SCORE	STATISTIC	VALUE	RANK	SCORE
Economics	5	75.55	Median Household Income	$38,464	5	57.0
			% of Families Above Poverty Level	96.9%	4	94.1
Affordable Housing	9	34.00	Median Home Value	$125,700	11	29.9
			Median Rent	$648	8	38.1
Crime	2	97.25	Violent Crimes per 10,000 Population	22	2	97.2
			Property Crimes per 10,000 Population	467	2	97.3
Open Spaces	5	54.05	Population Density (Persons/Sq. Mile)	3430	6	58.1
			Average Rooms per Housing Unit	5.0	6	50.0
Education	4	78.10	% High School Enrollment/Completion	97.2%	2	88.5
			% College Graduates	31.1%	4	67.7
Commute	6	50.00	Average Work Commute in Minutes	19	1	100.0
			% Commuting on Public Transportation	0.0%	14	0.0
Community Stability	2	88.65	% Living in Same House as in 1979	42.7%	2	98.9
			% Living in Same County as in 1985	79.2%	3	78.4

Composite: *Rank* 2 / 14 *Score* 63.61   **PALM BEACH GARDENS**

CATEGORY	RANK	SCORE	STATISTIC	VALUE	RANK	SCORE
Economics	3	84.00	Median Household Income	$44,688	3	75.6
			% of Families Above Poverty Level	96.5%	6	92.4
Affordable Housing	12	21.35	Median Home Value	$136,200	12	20.8
			Median Rent	$724	10	21.9
Crime	5	68.45	Violent Crimes per 10,000 Population	37	4	91.1
			Property Crimes per 10,000 Population	832	6	45.8
Open Spaces	2	84.60	Population Density (Persons/Sq. Mile)	874	1	100.0
			Average Rooms per Housing Unit	5.5	2	69.2
Education	1	88.45	% High School Enrollment/Completion	96.7%	3	86.5
			% College Graduates	38.2%	2	90.4
Commute	5	51.45	Average Work Commute in Minutes	19	1	100.0
			% Commuting on Public Transportation	0.4%	9	2.9
Community Stability	7	46.95	% Living in Same House as in 1979	21.0%	7	41.7
			% Living in Same County as in 1985	69.1%	7	52.2

Composite: *Rank* 3 / 14 *Score* 55.72   **ROYAL PALM BEACH**

CATEGORY	RANK	SCORE	STATISTIC	VALUE	RANK	SCORE
Economics	4	82.10	Median Household Income	$40,885	4	64.2
			% of Families Above Poverty Level	98.3%	1	100.0
Affordable Housing	8	42.00	Median Home Value	$90,100	7	61.0
			Median Rent	$719	9	23.0
Crime	1	100.00	Violent Crimes per 10,000 Population	15	1	100.0
			Property Crimes per 10,000 Population	448	1	100.0
Open Spaces	3	76.30	Population Density (Persons/Sq. Mile)	1657	2	87.2
			Average Rooms per Housing Unit	5.4	3	65.4
Education	6	58.25	% High School Enrollment/Completion	95.3%	4	80.7
			% College Graduates	21.1%	6	35.8
Commute	14	0.35	Average Work Commute in Minutes	29	14	0.0
			% Commuting on Public Transportation	0.1%	13	0.7
Community Stability	9	31.05	% Living in Same House as in 1979	11.6%	11	16.9
			% Living in Same County as in 1985	66.4%	10	45.2

Metropolitan Area Suburb Rankings
WEST PALM BEACH-BOCA RATON-DELRAY BEACH

Composite: Rank 4 / 14 *Score* 55.64   **JUPITER**

CATEGORY	RANK	SCORE	STATISTIC	VALUE	RANK	SCORE
Economics	6	73.50	Median Household Income	$38,211	6	56.2
			% of Families Above Poverty Level	96.1%	7	90.8
Affordable Housing	10	30.80	Median Home Value	$108,400	9	45.0
			Median Rent	$749	11	16.6
Crime	3	87.80	Violent Crimes per 10,000 Population	33	3	92.7
			Property Crimes per 10,000 Population	569	3	82.9
Open Spaces	4	68.45	Population Density (Persons/Sq. Mile)	1905	4	83.1
			Average Rooms per Housing Unit	5.1	4	53.8
Education	5	61.20	% High School Enrollment/Completion	91.9%	8	66.8
			% College Graduates	27.3%	5	55.6
Commute	10	40.70	Average Work Commute in Minutes	21	8	80.0
			% Commuting on Public Transportation	0.2%	11	1.4
Community Stability	11	27.05	% Living in Same House as in 1979	13.3%	9	21.4
			% Living in Same County as in 1985	61.6%	11	32.7

Composite: Rank 5 / 14 *Score* 53.04   **RIVIERA BEACH**

CATEGORY	RANK	SCORE	STATISTIC	VALUE	RANK	SCORE
Economics	13	24.10	Median Household Income	$24,847	11	16.3
			% of Families Above Poverty Level	82.1%	13	31.9
Affordable Housing	4	78.40	Median Home Value	$61,200	3	86.2
			Median Rent	$495	3	70.6
Crime	N/A	N/A	Violent Crimes per 10,000 Population	N/A	N/A	N/A
			Property Crimes per 10,000 Population	N/A	N/A	N/A
Open Spaces	9	40.35	Population Density (Persons/Sq. Mile)	3690	8	53.8
			Average Rooms per Housing Unit	4.4	10	26.9
Education	10	31.60	% High School Enrollment/Completion	86.5%	9	44.7
			% College Graduates	15.7%	9	18.5
Commute	3	52.85	Average Work Commute in Minutes	20	4	90.0
			% Commuting on Public Transportation	2.2%	2	15.7
Community Stability	1	90.95	% Living in Same House as in 1979	38.7%	3	88.4
			% Living in Same County as in 1985	85.0%	2	93.5

Composite: Rank 6 / 14 *Score* 52.07   **KINGS POINT**

CATEGORY	RANK	SCORE	STATISTIC	VALUE	RANK	SCORE
Economics	11	47.05	Median Household Income	$19,373	14	0.0
			% of Families Above Poverty Level	96.9%	4	94.1
Affordable Housing	2	82.45	Median Home Value	$45,400	1	100.0
			Median Rent	$522	4	64.9
Crime	N/A	N/A	Violent Crimes per 10,000 Population	N/A	N/A	N/A
			Property Crimes per 10,000 Population	N/A	N/A	N/A
Open Spaces	14	5.75	Population Density (Persons/Sq. Mile)	6970	14	0.0
			Average Rooms per Housing Unit	4.0	13	11.5
Education	7	50.00	% High School Enrollment/Completion	100.0%	1	100.0
			% College Graduates	9.9%	14	0.0
Commute	7	47.15	Average Work Commute in Minutes	20	4	90.0
			% Commuting on Public Transportation	0.6%	6	4.3
Community Stability	3	80.00	% Living in Same House as in 1979	43.1%	1	100.0
			% Living in Same County as in 1985	72.1%	6	60.0

Metropolitan Area Suburb Rankings
WEST PALM BEACH-BOCA RATON-DELRAY BEACH

Composite: *Rank* 7 / 14 *Score* 51.12   **BOYNTON BEACH**

CATEGORY	RANK	SCORE	STATISTIC	VALUE	RANK	SCORE
Economics	10	54.65	Median Household Income	$28,824	9	28.2
			% of Families Above Poverty Level	93.8%	11	81.1
Affordable Housing	6	55.90	Median Home Value	$79,400	6	70.3
			Median Rent	$632	7	41.5
Crime	6	51.40	Violent Crimes per 10,000 Population	148	7	45.9
			Property Crimes per 10,000 Population	753	5	56.9
Open Spaces	6	51.35	Population Density (Persons/Sq. Mile)	3054	5	64.2
			Average Rooms per Housing Unit	4.7	8	38.5
Education	11	22.10	% High School Enrollment/Completion	81.3%	13	23.4
			% College Graduates	16.4%	8	20.8
Commute	2	53.95	Average Work Commute in Minutes	19	1	100.0
			% Commuting on Public Transportation	1.1%	5	7.9
Community Stability	5	68.50	% Living in Same House as in 1979	33.7%	4	75.2
			% Living in Same County as in 1985	72.8%	5	61.8

Composite: *Rank* 8 / 14 *Score* 50.21   **WELLINGTON**

CATEGORY	RANK	SCORE	STATISTIC	VALUE	RANK	SCORE
Economics	1	95.15	Median Household Income	$52,863	1	100.0
			% of Families Above Poverty Level	96.0%	9	90.3
Affordable Housing	13	9.30	Median Home Value	$145,600	13	12.6
			Median Rent	$799	12	6.0
Crime	N/A	N/A	Violent Crimes per 10,000 Population	N/A	N/A	N/A
			Property Crimes per 10,000 Population	N/A	N/A	N/A
Open Spaces	1	92.15	Population Density (Persons/Sq. Mile)	1833	3	84.3
			Average Rooms per Housing Unit	6.3	1	100.0
Education	3	81.60	% High School Enrollment/Completion	95.0%	5	79.5
			% College Graduates	36.1%	3	83.7
Commute	13	10.70	Average Work Commute in Minutes	27	13	20.0
			% Commuting on Public Transportation	0.2%	11	1.4
Community Stability	13	12.35	% Living in Same House as in 1979	7.1%	13	5.0
			% Living in Same County as in 1985	56.6%	12	19.7

Composite: *Rank* 9 / 14 *Score* 46.24   **GREENACRES CITY**

CATEGORY	RANK	SCORE	STATISTIC	VALUE	RANK	SCORE
Economics	9	58.65	Median Household Income	$29,241	8	29.5
			% of Families Above Poverty Level	95.4%	10	87.8
Affordable Housing	5	62.45	Median Home Value	$68,100	5	80.2
			Median Rent	$617	6	44.7
Crime	4	77.15	Violent Crimes per 10,000 Population	40	5	89.8
			Property Crimes per 10,000 Population	699	4	64.5
Open Spaces	10	36.65	Population Density (Persons/Sq. Mile)	4610	10	38.7
			Average Rooms per Housing Unit	4.6	9	34.6
Education	12	22.15	% High School Enrollment/Completion	84.0%	10	34.4
			% College Graduates	13.0%	11	9.9
Commute	12	31.05	Average Work Commute in Minutes	23	11	60.0
			% Commuting on Public Transportation	0.3%	10	2.1
Community Stability	8	35.60	% Living in Same House as in 1979	12.4%	10	19.0
			% Living in Same County as in 1985	69.1%	7	52.2

Metropolitan Area Suburb Rankings
WEST PALM BEACH-BOCA RATON-DELRAY BEACH

Composite: Rank 10 / 14 Score 44.48 **BOCA DEL MAR**

CATEGORY	RANK	SCORE	STATISTIC	VALUE	RANK	SCORE
Economics	2	86.75	Median Household Income	$45,264	2	77.3
			% of Families Above Poverty Level	97.4%	3	96.2
Affordable Housing	14	1.30	Median Home Value	$160,000	14	0.0
			Median Rent	$815	13	2.6
Crime	N/A	N/A	Violent Crimes per 10,000 Population	N/A	N/A	N/A
			Property Crimes per 10,000 Population	N/A	N/A	N/A
Open Spaces	7	45.80	Population Density (Persons/Sq. Mile)	4436	9	41.6
			Average Rooms per Housing Unit	5.0	6	50.0
Education	2	86.25	% High School Enrollment/Completion	93.3%	7	72.5
			% College Graduates	41.2%	1	100.0
Commute	8	46.80	Average Work Commute in Minutes	20	4	90.0
			% Commuting on Public Transportation	0.5%	8	3.6
Community Stability	14	0.00	% Living in Same House as in 1979	5.2%	14	0.0
			% Living in Same County as in 1985	49.0%	14	0.0

Composite: Rank 11 / 14 Score 44.06 **BELLE GLADE**

CATEGORY	RANK	SCORE	STATISTIC	VALUE	RANK	SCORE
Economics	14	0.40	Median Household Income	$19,629	13	0.8
			% of Families Above Poverty Level	74.5%	14	0.0
Affordable Housing	1	94.70	Median Home Value	$57,500	2	89.4
			Median Rent	$357	1	100.0
Crime	8	0.35	Violent Crimes per 10,000 Population	261	8	0.0
			Property Crimes per 10,000 Population	1,151	7	0.7
Open Spaces	12	27.65	Population Density (Persons/Sq. Mile)	3599	7	55.3
			Average Rooms per Housing Unit	3.7	14	0.0
Education	13	15.65	% High School Enrollment/Completion	83.0%	11	30.3
			% College Graduates	10.2%	13	1.0
Commute	1	90.00	Average Work Commute in Minutes	21	8	80.0
			% Commuting on Public Transportation	14.0%	1	100.0
Community Stability	4	79.70	% Living in Same House as in 1979	27.7%	6	59.4
			% Living in Same County as in 1985	87.5%	1	100.0

Composite: Rank 12 / 14 Score 40.86 **HAMPTONS AT BOCA RATON**

CATEGORY	RANK	SCORE	STATISTIC	VALUE	RANK	SCORE
Economics	8	60.05	Median Household Income	$26,370	10	20.9
			% of Families Above Poverty Level	98.1%	2	99.2
Affordable Housing	7	45.70	Median Home Value	$119,900	10	35.0
			Median Rent	$562	5	56.4
Crime	N/A	N/A	Violent Crimes per 10,000 Population	N/A	N/A	N/A
			Property Crimes per 10,000 Population	N/A	N/A	N/A
Open Spaces	11	32.10	Population Density (Persons/Sq. Mile)	4698	11	37.3
			Average Rooms per Housing Unit	4.4	10	26.9
Education	8	43.15	% High School Enrollment/Completion	93.6%	6	73.8
			% College Graduates	13.8%	10	12.5
Commute	11	35.35	Average Work Commute in Minutes	23	11	60.0
			% Commuting on Public Transportation	1.5%	4	10.7
Community Stability	10	28.80	% Living in Same House as in 1979	9.6%	12	11.6
			% Living in Same County as in 1985	66.7%	9	46.0

Metropolitan Area Suburb Rankings
WEST PALM BEACH-BOCA RATON-DELRAY BEACH

Composite: **Rank** 13 / 14 *Score* 40.64   **LAKE WORTH**

CATEGORY	RANK	SCORE	STATISTIC	VALUE	RANK	SCORE
Economics	12	28.40	Median Household Income	$21,665	12	6.8
			% of Families Above Poverty Level	86.4%	12	50.0
Affordable Housing	3	80.70	Median Home Value	$66,300	4	81.8
			Median Rent	$453	2	79.6
Crime	7	25.00	Violent Crimes per 10,000 Population	138	6	50.0
			Property Crimes per 10,000 Population	1,156	8	0.0
Open Spaces	13	27.00	Population Density (Persons/Sq. Mile)	5087	13	30.9
			Average Rooms per Housing Unit	4.3	12	23.1
Education	14	4.15	% High School Enrollment/Completion	75.6%	14	0.0
			% College Graduates	12.5%	12	8.3
Commute	3	52.85	Average Work Commute in Minutes	20	4	90.0
			% Commuting on Public Transportation	2.2%	2	15.7
Community Stability	6	66.40	% Living in Same House as in 1979	30.5%	5	66.8
			% Living in Same County as in 1985	74.4%	4	66.0

Composite: **Rank** 14 / 14 *Score* 39.20   **SANDALFOOT COVE**

CATEGORY	RANK	SCORE	STATISTIC	VALUE	RANK	SCORE
Economics	7	68.10	Median Household Income	$34,585	7	45.4
			% of Families Above Poverty Level	96.1%	7	90.8
Affordable Housing	11	27.95	Median Home Value	$95,900	8	55.9
			Median Rent	$827	14	0.0
Crime	N/A	N/A	Violent Crimes per 10,000 Population	N/A	N/A	N/A
			Property Crimes per 10,000 Population	N/A	N/A	N/A
Open Spaces	8	44.50	Population Density (Persons/Sq. Mile)	4822	12	35.2
			Average Rooms per Housing Unit	5.1	4	53.8
Education	9	32.25	% High School Enrollment/Completion	83.0%	11	30.3
			% College Graduates	20.6%	7	34.2
Commute	9	42.15	Average Work Commute in Minutes	21	8	80.0
			% Commuting on Public Transportation	0.6%	6	4.3
Community Stability	12	20.25	% Living in Same House as in 1979	17.8%	8	33.2
			% Living in Same County as in 1985	51.8%	13	7.3

Index

SUBURB	STATE	METROPOLITAN AREA	PAGE
			42
ABERDEEN	Maryland	BALTIMORE	69
ABINGTON	Massachusetts	BOSTON-LAWRENCE-SALEM-LOWELL-BROCKTON	131
ADDISON	Illinois	CHICAGO-GARY-LAKE COUNTY	800
ADELPHI	Maryland	WASHINGTON	674
AFFTON	Missouri	ST. LOUIS	317
AGOURA HILLS	California	LOS ANGELES-ANAHEIM-RIVERSIDE	54
ALABASTER	Alabama	BIRMINGHAM	732
ALAMEDA	California	SAN FRANCISCO-OAKLAND-SAN JOSE	719
ALAMO	California	SAN FRANCISCO-OAKLAND-SAN JOSE	723
ALBANY	California	SAN FRANCISCO-OAKLAND-SAN JOSE	757
ALDERWOOD MANOR-BOTHELL NORTH	Washington	SEATTLE-TACOMA	273
ALDINE	Texas	HOUSTON-GALVESTON-BRAZORIA	804
ALEXANDRIA	Virginia	WASHINGTON	124
ALGONQUIN	Illinois	CHICAGO-GARY-LAKE COUNTY	336
ALHAMBRA	California	LOS ANGELES-ANAHEIM-RIVERSIDE	613
ALIQUIPPA	Pennsylvania	PITTSBURGH-BEAVER VALLEY	194
ALLEN	Texas	DALLAS-FORT WORTH	230
ALLEN PARK	Michigan	DETROIT-ANN ARBOR	623
ALOHA	Oregon	PORTLAND-VANCOUVER	334
ALONDRA PARK	California	LOS ANGELES-ANAHEIM-RIVERSIDE	24
ALPHARETTA	Georgia	ATLANTA	132
ALSIP	Illinois	CHICAGO-GARY-LAKE COUNTY	315
ALTADENA	California	LOS ANGELES-ANAHEIM-RIVERSIDE	571
ALTAMONTE SPRINGS	Florida	ORLANDO	675
ALTON	Illinois	ST. LOUIS	272
ALVIN	Texas	HOUSTON-GALVESTON-BRAZORIA	73
AMESBURY	Massachusetts	BOSTON-LAWRENCE-SALEM-LOWELL-BROCKTON	163
AMHERST	Ohio	CLEVELAND-AKRON-LORAIN	13
AMSTERDAM	New York	ALBANY-SCHENECTADY-TROY	429
ANDOVER	Minnesota	MINNEAPOLIS-ST. PAUL	270
ANGLETON	Texas	HOUSTON-GALVESTON-BRAZORIA	787
ANNANDALE	Virginia	WASHINGTON	45
ANNAPOLIS	Maryland	BALTIMORE	437
ANOKA	Minnesota	MINNEAPOLIS-ST. PAUL	735
ANTIOCH	California	SAN FRANCISCO-OAKLAND-SAN JOSE	571
APOPKA	Florida	ORLANDO	330
APPLE VALLEY	California	LOS ANGELES-ANAHEIM-RIVERSIDE	427
APPLE VALLEY	Minnesota	MINNEAPOLIS-ST. PAUL	216
APPLEWOOD	Colorado	DENVER-BOULDER	36
ARBUTUS	Maryland	BALTIMORE	314
ARCADIA	California	LOS ANGELES-ANAHEIM-RIVERSIDE	655
ARDEN-ARCADE	California	SACRAMENTO	582
ARDMORE	Pennsylvania	PHILADELPHIA-WILMINGTON-TRENTON	67
ARLINGTON	Massachusetts	BOSTON-LAWRENCE-SALEM-LOWELL-BROCKTON	203
ARLINGTON	Texas	DALLAS-FORT WORTH	794
ARLINGTON	Virginia	WASHINGTON	111
ARLINGTON HEIGHTS	Illinois	CHICAGO-GARY-LAKE COUNTY	38
ARNOLD	Maryland	BALTIMORE	675
ARNOLD	Missouri	ST. LOUIS	340
ARTESIA	California	LOS ANGELES-ANAHEIM-RIVERSIDE	218
ARVADA	Colorado	DENVER-BOULDER	545
ASBURY PARK	New Jersey	NEW YORK-NORTHERN NEW JERSEY-LONG ISLAND	254
ASHEBORO	North Carolina	GREENSBORO--WINSTON-SALEM--HIGH POINT	738
ASHLAND	California	SAN FRANCISCO-OAKLAND-SAN JOSE	787
ASPEN HILL	Maryland	WASHINGTON	289
ATLANTIC BEACH	Florida	JACKSONVILLE	657
AUBURN	California	SACRAMENTO	759
AUBURN	Washington	SEATTLE-TACOMA	242
AUBURN HILLS	Michigan	DETROIT-ANN ARBOR	222
AURORA	Colorado	DENVER-BOULDER	

817

Index

SUBURB	STATE	METROPOLITAN AREA	PAGE
AURORA	Illinois	CHICAGO-GARY-LAKE COUNTY	141
AVENEL	New Jersey	NEW YORK-NORTHERN NEW JERSEY-LONG ISLAND	539
AVENTURA	Florida	MIAMI-FORT LAUDERDALE	406
AVOCADO HEIGHTS	California	LOS ANGELES-ANAHEIM-RIVERSIDE	339
AVON LAKE	Ohio	CLEVELAND-AKRON-LORAIN	172
AVONDALE	Arizona	PHOENIX	601
AZUSA	California	LOS ANGELES-ANAHEIM-RIVERSIDE	341
BABYLON	New York	NEW YORK-NORTHERN NEW JERSEY-LONG ISLAND	511
BAILEY'S CROSSROADS	Virginia	WASHINGTON	808
BALCH SPRINGS	Texas	DALLAS-FORT WORTH	203
BALDWIN	New York	NEW YORK-NORTHERN NEW JERSEY-LONG ISLAND	507
BALDWIN	Pennsylvania	PITTSBURGH-BEAVER VALLEY	608
BALDWIN PARK	California	LOS ANGELES-ANAHEIM-RIVERSIDE	343
BALLWIN	Missouri	ST. LOUIS	667
BANNING	California	LOS ANGELES-ANAHEIM-RIVERSIDE	349
BARBERTON	Ohio	CLEVELAND-AKRON-LORAIN	176
BARRINGTON	Rhode Island	PROVIDENCE-PAWTUCKET-WOONSOCKET	632
BARSTOW	California	LOS ANGELES-ANAHEIM-RIVERSIDE	335
BARTLETT	Illinois	CHICAGO-GARY-LAKE COUNTY	123
BARTLETT	Tennessee	MEMPHIS	381
BATAVIA	Illinois	CHICAGO-GARY-LAKE COUNTY	122
BAY SHORE	New York	NEW YORK-NORTHERN NEW JERSEY-LONG ISLAND	534
BAY VILLAGE	Ohio	CLEVELAND-AKRON-LORAIN	161
BAYONET POINT	Florida	TAMPA-ST. PETERSBURG-CLEARWATER	772
BAYONNE	New Jersey	NEW YORK-NORTHERN NEW JERSEY-LONG ISLAND	488
BAYTOWN	Texas	HOUSTON-GALVESTON-BRAZORIA	272
BEACHWOOD	Ohio	CLEVELAND-AKRON-LORAIN	171
BEAVER FALLS	Pennsylvania	PITTSBURGH-BEAVER VALLEY	617
BEAVERCREEK	Ohio	DAYTON-SPRINGFIELD	208
BEAVERTON	Oregon	PORTLAND-VANCOUVER	625
BEDFORD	Ohio	CLEVELAND-AKRON-LORAIN	172
BEDFORD	Texas	DALLAS-FORT WORTH	197
BEDFORD HEIGHTS	Ohio	CLEVELAND-AKRON-LORAIN	177
BEECH GROVE	Indiana	INDIANAPOLIS	280
BEL AIR NORTH	Maryland	BALTIMORE	37
BEL AIR SOUTH	Maryland	BALTIMORE	40
BELL	California	LOS ANGELES-ANAHEIM-RIVERSIDE	363
BELL GARDENS	California	LOS ANGELES-ANAHEIM-RIVERSIDE	364
BELLAIR-MEADOWBROOK TERRACE	Florida	JACKSONVILLE	289
BELLAIRE	Texas	HOUSTON-GALVESTON-BRAZORIA	266
BELLE GLADE	Florida	WEST PALM BEACH-BOCA RATON-DELRAY BEACH	815
BELLEFONTAINE NEIGHBORS	Missouri	ST. LOUIS	668
BELLEVILLE	Illinois	ST. LOUIS	670
BELLEVILLE	New Jersey	NEW YORK-NORTHERN NEW JERSEY-LONG ISLAND	511
BELLEVUE	Washington	SEATTLE-TACOMA	747
BELLFLOWER	California	LOS ANGELES-ANAHEIM-RIVERSIDE	352
BELLMAWR	New Jersey	PHILADELPHIA-WILMINGTON-TRENTON	580
BELLMORE	New York	NEW YORK-NORTHERN NEW JERSEY-LONG ISLAND	496
BELLWOOD	Illinois	CHICAGO-GARY-LAKE COUNTY	139
BELMONT	California	SAN FRANCISCO-OAKLAND-SAN JOSE	721
BELMONT	Massachusetts	BOSTON-LAWRENCE-SALEM-LOWELL-BROCKTON	65
BELTON	Missouri	KANSAS CITY	299
BELTSVILLE	Maryland	WASHINGTON	788
BELVEDERE PARK	Georgia	ATLANTA	25
BENBROOK	Texas	DALLAS-FORT WORTH	191
BENICIA	California	SAN FRANCISCO-OAKLAND-SAN JOSE	724
BENSENVILLE	Illinois	CHICAGO-GARY-LAKE COUNTY	141
BEREA	Ohio	CLEVELAND-AKRON-LORAIN	165
BERGENFIELD	New Jersey	NEW YORK-NORTHERN NEW JERSEY-LONG ISLAND	480
BERKELEY	California	SAN FRANCISCO-OAKLAND-SAN JOSE	733

Index

Index

SUBURB	STATE	METROPOLITAN AREA	PAGE
BROOKSIDE	Delaware	PHILADELPHIA-WILMINGTON-TRENTON	585
BROOMALL	Pennsylvania	PHILADELPHIA-WILMINGTON-TRENTON	583
BROOMFIELD	Colorado	DENVER-BOULDER	216
BROWN DEER	Wisconsin	MILWAUKEE-RACINE	413
BROWN MILLS	New Jersey	PHILADELPHIA-WILMINGTON-TRENTON	593
BROWNSVILLE	Florida	MIAMI-FORT LAUDERDALE	393
BRUNSWICK	Ohio	CLEVELAND-AKRON-LORAIN	175
BRYN MAWR-SKYWAY	Washington	SEATTLE-TACOMA	747
BUENA PARK	California	LOS ANGELES-ANAHEIM-RIVERSIDE	337
BUENA VENTURA LAKES	Florida	ORLANDO	572
BUFFALO GROVE	Illinois	CHICAGO-GARY-LAKE COUNTY	125
BURBANK	California	LOS ANGELES-ANAHEIM-RIVERSIDE	322
BURBANK	Illinois	CHICAGO-GARY-LAKE COUNTY	123
BURIEN	Washington	SEATTLE-TACOMA	752
BURKE	Virginia	WASHINGTON	797
BURLESON	Texas	DALLAS-FORT WORTH	196
BURLINGAME	California	SAN FRANCISCO-OAKLAND-SAN JOSE	730
BURLINGTON	Massachusetts	BOSTON-LAWRENCE-SALEM-LOWELL-BROCKTON	64
BURNSVILLE	Minnesota	MINNEAPOLIS-ST. PAUL	434
CAHOKIA	Illinois	ST. LOUIS	676
CALUMET CITY	Illinois	CHICAGO-GARY-LAKE COUNTY	135
CALVERTON	Maryland	WASHINGTON	789
CAMARILLO	California	LOS ANGELES-ANAHEIM-RIVERSIDE	314
CAMBRIDGE	Massachusetts	BOSTON-LAWRENCE-SALEM-LOWELL-BROCKTON	77
CAMDEN	New Jersey	PHILADELPHIA-WILMINGTON-TRENTON	594
CAMERON PARK	California	SACRAMENTO	661
CAMP SPRINGS	Maryland	WASHINGTON	783
CAMPBELL	California	SAN FRANCISCO-OAKLAND-SAN JOSE	734
CANANDAIGUA	New York	ROCHESTER	649
CANDLER-MCAFEE	Georgia	ATLANTA	21
CANTON	Michigan	DETROIT-ANN ARBOR	236
CANYON RIM	Utah	SALT LAKE CITY-OGDEN	686
CAPITOLA	California	SAN FRANCISCO-OAKLAND-SAN JOSE	739
CARLSBAD	California	SAN DIEGO	705
CARMEL	Indiana	INDIANAPOLIS	280
CARMICHAEL	California	SACRAMENTO	654
CARNEY	Maryland	BALTIMORE	44
CARNOT-MOON	Pennsylvania	PITTSBURGH-BEAVER VALLEY	614
CAROL CITY	Florida	MIAMI-FORT LAUDERDALE	395
CAROL STREAM	Illinois	CHICAGO-GARY-LAKE COUNTY	138
CARPENTERSVILLE	Illinois	CHICAGO-GARY-LAKE COUNTY	140
CARROLLTON	Texas	DALLAS-FORT WORTH	195
CARROLLWOOD VILLAGE	Florida	TAMPA-ST. PETERSBURG-CLEARWATER	768
CARSON	California	LOS ANGELES-ANAHEIM-RIVERSIDE	320
CARTERET	New Jersey	NEW YORK-NORTHERN NEW JERSEY-LONG ISLAND	488
CARY	Illinois	CHICAGO-GARY-LAKE COUNTY	108
CASA DE ORO-MOUNT HELIX	California	SAN DIEGO	702
CASCADE-FAIRWOOD	Washington	SEATTLE-TACOMA	749
CASSELBERRY	Florida	ORLANDO	569
CASTLEWOOD	Colorado	DENVER-BOULDER	217
CASTRO VALLEY	California	SAN FRANCISCO-OAKLAND-SAN JOSE	720
CATHEDRAL CITY	California	LOS ANGELES-ANAHEIM-RIVERSIDE	341
CATONSVILLE	Maryland	BALTIMORE	33
CEDAR GROVE	New Jersey	NEW YORK-NORTHERN NEW JERSEY-LONG ISLAND	477
CEDAR HILL	Texas	DALLAS-FORT WORTH	193
CENTER POINT	Alabama	BIRMINGHAM	55
CENTEREACH	New York	NEW YORK-NORTHERN NEW JERSEY-LONG ISLAND	518
CENTERVILLE	Ohio	DAYTON-SPRINGFIELD	208
CENTERVILLE	Utah	SALT LAKE CITY-OGDEN	684
CENTRAL FALLS	Rhode Island	PROVIDENCE-PAWTUCKET-WOONSOCKET	635

Index

Index

SUBURB	STATE	METROPOLITAN AREA	PAGE
COLUMBINE	Colorado	DENVER-BOULDER	218
COMMACK	New York	NEW YORK-NORTHERN NEW JERSEY-LONG ISLAND	504
COMMERCE	California	LOS ANGELES-ANAHEIM-RIVERSIDE	359
COMMERCE CITY	Colorado	DENVER-BOULDER	223
COMPTON	California	LOS ANGELES-ANAHEIM-RIVERSIDE	360
CONCORD	California	SAN FRANCISCO-OAKLAND-SAN JOSE	727
CONCORD	Missouri	ST. LOUIS	669
CONCORD	North Carolina	CHARLOTTE-GASTONIA-ROCK HILL	91
CONROE	Texas	HOUSTON-GALVESTON-BRAZORIA	275
CONWAY	Florida	ORLANDO	566
COON RAPIDS	Minnesota	MINNEAPOLIS-ST. PAUL	433
COOPER CITY	Florida	MIAMI-FORT LAUDERDALE	396
COPIAGUE	New York	NEW YORK-NORTHERN NEW JERSEY-LONG ISLAND	535
COPPELL	Texas	DALLAS-FORT WORTH	192
CORAL GABLES	Florida	MIAMI-FORT LAUDERDALE	388
CORAL HILLS	Maryland	WASHINGTON	793
CORAL SPRINGS	Florida	MIAMI-FORT LAUDERDALE	402
CORAL TERRACE	Florida	MIAMI-FORT LAUDERDALE	392
CORAM	New York	NEW YORK-NORTHERN NEW JERSEY-LONG ISLAND	536
CORONA	California	LOS ANGELES-ANAHEIM-RIVERSIDE	354
CORONADO	California	SAN DIEGO	703
COSTA MESA	California	LOS ANGELES-ANAHEIM-RIVERSIDE	348
COTTAGE GROVE	Minnesota	MINNEAPOLIS-ST. PAUL	426
COTTONWOOD HEIGHTS	Utah	SALT LAKE CITY-OGDEN	687
COTTONWOOD WEST	Utah	SALT LAKE CITY-OGDEN	688
COUNTRY CLUB HILLS	Illinois	CHICAGO-GARY-LAKE COUNTY	120
COVINA	California	LOS ANGELES-ANAHEIM-RIVERSIDE	325
COVINGTON	Georgia	ATLANTA	20
COVINGTON	Kentucky	CINCINNATI-HAMILTON	155
COVINGTON-SAWYER-WILDERNESS	Washington	SEATTLE-TACOMA	752
CRANFORD	New Jersey	NEW YORK-NORTHERN NEW JERSEY-LONG ISLAND	467
CRANSTON	Rhode Island	PROVIDENCE-PAWTUCKET-WOONSOCKET	632
CREST HILL	Illinois	CHICAGO-GARY-LAKE COUNTY	128
CRESTWOOD	Illinois	CHICAGO-GARY-LAKE COUNTY	128
CRESTWOOD	Missouri	ST. LOUIS	666
CREVE COEUR	Missouri	ST. LOUIS	666
CROFTON	Maryland	BALTIMORE	42
CROWN POINT	Indiana	CHICAGO-GARY-LAKE COUNTY	107
CRYSTAL	Minnesota	MINNEAPOLIS-ST. PAUL	427
CRYSTAL LAKE	Illinois	CHICAGO-GARY-LAKE COUNTY	119
CUDAHY	California	LOS ANGELES-ANAHEIM-RIVERSIDE	367
CUDAHY	Wisconsin	MILWAUKEE-RACINE	417
CULVER CITY	California	LOS ANGELES-ANAHEIM-RIVERSIDE	323
CUPERTINO	California	SAN FRANCISCO-OAKLAND-SAN JOSE	722
CUTLER	Florida	MIAMI-FORT LAUDERDALE	387
CUTLER RIDGE	Florida	MIAMI-FORT LAUDERDALE	390
CUYAHOGA FALLS	Ohio	CLEVELAND-AKRON-LORAIN	171
CYPRESS	California	LOS ANGELES-ANAHEIM-RIVERSIDE	321
DALE CITY	Virginia	WASHINGTON	806
DALY CITY	California	SAN FRANCISCO-OAKLAND-SAN JOSE	736
DANA POINT	California	LOS ANGELES-ANAHEIM-RIVERSIDE	330
DANBURY	Connecticut	NEW YORK-NORTHERN NEW JERSEY-LONG ISLAND	519
DANIA	Florida	MIAMI-FORT LAUDERDALE	398
DANVERS	Massachusetts	BOSTON-LAWRENCE-SALEM-LOWELL-BROCKTON	67
DANVILLE	California	SAN FRANCISCO-OAKLAND-SAN JOSE	717
DARBY	Pennsylvania	PHILADELPHIA-WILMINGTON-TRENTON	589
DARBY TOWNSHIP	Pennsylvania	PHILADELPHIA-WILMINGTON-TRENTON	582
DARIEN	Connecticut	NEW YORK-NORTHERN NEW JERSEY-LONG ISLAND	477
DARIEN	Illinois	CHICAGO-GARY-LAKE COUNTY	109
DAVIE	Florida	MIAMI-FORT LAUDERDALE	401

Index

Index

Index

SUBURB	STATE	METROPOLITAN AREA	PAGE
FAIRFIELD	Ohio	CINCINNATI-HAMILTON	153
FAIRLAND	Maryland	WASHINGTON	805
FAIRVIEW	New Jersey	NEW YORK-NORTHERN NEW JERSEY-LONG ISLAND	530
FAIRVIEW HEIGHTS	Illinois	ST. LOUIS	670
FAIRVIEW PARK	Ohio	CLEVELAND-AKRON-LORAIN	164
FAIRVIEW SHORES	Florida	ORLANDO	567
FALLBROOK	California	SAN DIEGO	707
FARMERS BRANCH	Texas	DALLAS-FORT WORTH	190
FARMINGTON	Michigan	DETROIT-ANN ARBOR	235
FARMINGTON HILLS	Michigan	DETROIT-ANN ARBOR	239
FARMINGVILLE	New York	NEW YORK-NORTHERN NEW JERSEY-LONG ISLAND	524
FEDERAL WAY	Washington	SEATTLE-TACOMA	758
FERGUSON	Missouri	ST. LOUIS	671
FERN CREEK	Kentucky	LOUISVILLE	373
FERNDALE	Maryland	BALTIMORE	41
FERNDALE	Michigan	DETROIT-ANN ARBOR	244
FILLMORE	California	LOS ANGELES-ANAHEIM-RIVERSIDE	331
FINNEYTOWN	Ohio	CINCINNATI-HAMILTON	148
FIRST COLONY	Texas	HOUSTON-GALVESTON-BRAZORIA	271
FLORAL PARK	New York	NEW YORK-NORTHERN NEW JERSEY-LONG ISLAND	479
FLORENCE	Kentucky	CINCINNATI-HAMILTON	153
FLORENCE-GRAHAM	California	LOS ANGELES-ANAHEIM-RIVERSIDE	366
FLORIN	California	SACRAMENTO	658
FLORISSANT	Missouri	ST. LOUIS	669
FLOWER MOUND	Texas	DALLAS-FORT WORTH	199
FOLSOM	California	SACRAMENTO	658
FONTANA	California	LOS ANGELES-ANAHEIM-RIVERSIDE	359
FOOTHILL FARMS	California	SACRAMENTO	659
FORDS	New Jersey	NEW YORK-NORTHERN NEW JERSEY-LONG ISLAND	505
FOREST CITY	Florida	ORLANDO	570
FOREST GROVE	Oregon	PORTLAND-VANCOUVER	626
FOREST HILL	Texas	DALLAS-FORT WORTH	200
FOREST PARK	Georgia	ATLANTA	23
FOREST PARK	Illinois	CHICAGO-GARY-LAKE COUNTY	137
FOREST PARK	Ohio	CINCINNATI-HAMILTON	151
FORESTDALE	Alabama	BIRMINGHAM	52
FORESTVILLE	Maryland	WASHINGTON	795
FORT HUNT	Virginia	WASHINGTON	782
FORT LEE	New Jersey	NEW YORK-NORTHERN NEW JERSEY-LONG ISLAND	537
FORT THOMAS	Kentucky	CINCINNATI-HAMILTON	148
FORT WASHINGTON	Maryland	WASHINGTON	783
FOSTER CITY	California	SAN FRANCISCO-OAKLAND-SAN JOSE	733
FOUNTAIN HILLS	Arizona	PHOENIX	601
FOUNTAIN VALLEY	California	LOS ANGELES-ANAHEIM-RIVERSIDE	312
FRAMINGHAM	Massachusetts	BOSTON-LAWRENCE-SALEM-LOWELL-BROCKTON	74
FRANCONIA	Virginia	WASHINGTON	802
FRANKLIN	Indiana	INDIANAPOLIS	282
FRANKLIN	Ohio	CINCINNATI-HAMILTON	152
FRANKLIN	Tennessee	NASHVILLE	443
FRANKLIN	Wisconsin	MILWAUKEE-RACINE	416
FRANKLIN PARK	Illinois	CHICAGO-GARY-LAKE COUNTY	127
FRANKLIN PARK	Pennsylvania	PITTSBURGH-BEAVER VALLEY	613
FRANKLIN SQUARE	New York	NEW YORK-NORTHERN NEW JERSEY-LONG ISLAND	506
FRASER	Michigan	DETROIT-ANN ARBOR	238
FREDERICK	Maryland	WASHINGTON	799
FREEHOLD	New Jersey	NEW YORK-NORTHERN NEW JERSEY-LONG ISLAND	519
FREEPORT	New York	NEW YORK-NORTHERN NEW JERSEY-LONG ISLAND	515
FREEPORT	Texas	HOUSTON-GALVESTON-BRAZORIA	273
FREMONT	California	SAN FRANCISCO-OAKLAND-SAN JOSE	726
FRIDLEY	Minnesota	MINNEAPOLIS-ST. PAUL	432

Index

SUBURB	STATE	METROPOLITAN AREA	PAGE
FRIENDSWOOD	Texas	HOUSTON-GALVESTON-BRAZORIA	267
FULLERTON	California	LOS ANGELES-ANAHEIM-RIVERSIDE	329
GAHANNA	Ohio	COLUMBUS	183
GAITHERSBURG	Maryland	WASHINGTON	800
GALENA PARK	Texas	HOUSTON-GALVESTON-BRAZORIA	270
GALLATIN	Tennessee	NASHVILLE	443
GARDEN CITY	Michigan	DETROIT-ANN ARBOR	233
GARDEN CITY	New York	NEW YORK-NORTHERN NEW JERSEY-LONG ISLAND	472
GARDEN GROVE	California	LOS ANGELES-ANAHEIM-RIVERSIDE	342
GARDENA	California	LOS ANGELES-ANAHEIM-RIVERSIDE	350
GARFIELD	New Jersey	NEW YORK-NORTHERN NEW JERSEY-LONG ISLAND	516
GARFIELD HEIGHTS	Ohio	CLEVELAND-AKRON-LORAIN	168
GARLAND	Texas	DALLAS-FORT WORTH	193
GATES-NORTH GATES	New York	ROCHESTER	649
GENEVA	Illinois	CHICAGO-GARY-LAKE COUNTY	106
GENEVA	New York	ROCHESTER	649
GERMANTOWN	Maryland	WASHINGTON	803
GERMANTOWN	Tennessee	MEMPHIS	380
GERMANTOWN	Wisconsin	MILWAUKEE-RACINE	418
GILBERT	Arizona	PHOENIX	599
GILROY	California	SAN FRANCISCO-OAKLAND-SAN JOSE	736
GLADEVIEW	Florida	MIAMI-FORT LAUDERDALE	393
GLADSTONE	Missouri	KANSAS CITY	294
GLADSTONE	Oregon	PORTLAND-VANCOUVER	623
GLASSBORO	New Jersey	PHILADELPHIA-WILMINGTON-TRENTON	587
GLEN AVON	California	LOS ANGELES-ANAHEIM-RIVERSIDE	360
GLEN BURNIE	Maryland	BALTIMORE	43
GLEN COVE	New York	NEW YORK-NORTHERN NEW JERSEY-LONG ISLAND	493
GLEN ELLYN	Illinois	CHICAGO-GARY-LAKE COUNTY	105
GLEN ROCK	New Jersey	NEW YORK-NORTHERN NEW JERSEY-LONG ISLAND	469
GLENDALE	Arizona	PHOENIX	600
GLENDALE	California	LOS ANGELES-ANAHEIM-RIVERSIDE	340
GLENDALE	Wisconsin	MILWAUKEE-RACINE	415
GLENDALE HEIGHTS	Illinois	CHICAGO-GARY-LAKE COUNTY	131
GLENDORA	California	LOS ANGELES-ANAHEIM-RIVERSIDE	312
GLENVAR HEIGHTS	Florida	MIAMI-FORT LAUDERDALE	391
GLENVIEW	Illinois	CHICAGO-GARY-LAKE COUNTY	104
GLOUCESTER	Massachusetts	BOSTON-LAWRENCE-SALEM-LOWELL-BROCKTON	71
GLOUCESTER CITY	New Jersey	PHILADELPHIA-WILMINGTON-TRENTON	586
GOLDEN	Colorado	DENVER-BOULDER	219
GOLDEN GLADES	Florida	MIAMI-FORT LAUDERDALE	397
GOLDEN VALLEY	Minnesota	MINNEAPOLIS-ST. PAUL	422
GOLDENROD	Florida	ORLANDO	569
GOODINGS GROVE	Illinois	CHICAGO-GARY-LAKE COUNTY	135
GOODLETTSVILLE	Tennessee	NASHVILLE	442
GRAND PRAIRIE	Texas	DALLAS-FORT WORTH	202
GRAND TERRACE	California	LOS ANGELES-ANAHEIM-RIVERSIDE	311
GRANDVIEW	Missouri	KANSAS CITY	298
GRANITE CITY	Illinois	ST. LOUIS	671
GRAPEVINE	Texas	DALLAS-FORT WORTH	196
GREATER NORTHDALE	Florida	TAMPA-ST. PETERSBURG-CLEARWATER	769
GREATER UPPER MARLBORO	Maryland	WASHINGTON	795
GREECE	New York	ROCHESTER	648
GREEN HAVEN	Maryland	BALTIMORE	46
GREENACRES CITY	Florida	WEST PALM BEACH-BOCA RATON-DELRAY BEACH	814
GREENBELT	Maryland	WASHINGTON	794
GREENDALE	Wisconsin	MILWAUKEE-RACINE	412
GREENFIELD	Indiana	INDIANAPOLIS	280
GREENFIELD	Wisconsin	MILWAUKEE-RACINE	416
GREENLAWN	New York	NEW YORK-NORTHERN NEW JERSEY-LONG ISLAND	482

Index

Index

SUBURB	STATE	METROPOLITAN AREA	PAGE
HIGHLAND PARK	Michigan	DETROIT-ANN ARBOR	248
HIGHLAND PARK	New Jersey	NEW YORK-NORTHERN NEW JERSEY-LONG ISLAND	504
HIGHLAND SPRINGS	Virginia	RICHMOND-PETERSBURG	642
HIGHLANDS RANCH	Colorado	DENVER-BOULDER	223
HIGHPOINT	Florida	TAMPA-ST. PETERSBURG-CLEARWATER	774
HIGHVIEW	Kentucky	LOUISVILLE	372
HILLANDALE	Maryland	WASHINGTON	790
HILLCREST HEIGHTS	Maryland	WASHINGTON	790
HILLIARD	Ohio	COLUMBUS	184
HILLSBORO	Oregon	PORTLAND-VANCOUVER	624
HILLSBOROUGH	California	SAN FRANCISCO-OAKLAND-SAN JOSE	715
HILLSIDE	New Jersey	NEW YORK-NORTHERN NEW JERSEY-LONG ISLAND	514
HINSDALE	Illinois	CHICAGO-GARY-LAKE COUNTY	100
HOBART	Indiana	CHICAGO-GARY-LAKE COUNTY	108
HOBOKEN	New Jersey	NEW YORK-NORTHERN NEW JERSEY-LONG ISLAND	543
HOFFMAN ESTATES	Illinois	CHICAGO-GARY-LAKE COUNTY	125
HOLBROOK	Massachusetts	BOSTON-LAWRENCE-SALEM-LOWELL-BROCKTON	68
HOLBROOK	New York	NEW YORK-NORTHERN NEW JERSEY-LONG ISLAND	520
HOLIDAY	Florida	TAMPA-ST. PETERSBURG-CLEARWATER	772
HOLIDAY CITY-BERKELEY	New Jersey	NEW YORK-NORTHERN NEW JERSEY-LONG ISLAND	547
HOLLADAY-COTTONWOOD	Utah	SALT LAKE CITY-OGDEN	685
HOLLYWOOD	Florida	MIAMI-FORT LAUDERDALE	396
HOLTSVILLE	New York	NEW YORK-NORTHERN NEW JERSEY-LONG ISLAND	520
HOMESTEAD	Florida	MIAMI-FORT LAUDERDALE	407
HOMEWOOD	Alabama	BIRMINGHAM	54
HOMEWOOD	Illinois	CHICAGO-GARY-LAKE COUNTY	101
HOOVER	Alabama	BIRMINGHAM	53
HOPATCONG	New Jersey	NEW YORK-NORTHERN NEW JERSEY-LONG ISLAND	533
HOPEWELL	Virginia	RICHMOND-PETERSBURG	642
HOPKINS	Minnesota	MINNEAPOLIS-ST. PAUL	436
HORSHAM	Pennsylvania	PHILADELPHIA-WILMINGTON-TRENTON	581
HUBER HEIGHTS	Ohio	DAYTON-SPRINGFIELD	211
HUDSON	Massachusetts	BOSTON-LAWRENCE-SALEM-LOWELL-BROCKTON	66
HUEYTOWN	Alabama	BIRMINGHAM	53
HULL	Massachusetts	BOSTON-LAWRENCE-SALEM-LOWELL-BROCKTON	77
HUMBLE	Texas	HOUSTON-GALVESTON-BRAZORIA	274
HUNTINGTON	New York	NEW YORK-NORTHERN NEW JERSEY-LONG ISLAND	507
HUNTINGTON BEACH	California	LOS ANGELES-ANAHEIM-RIVERSIDE	327
HUNTINGTON PARK	California	LOS ANGELES-ANAHEIM-RIVERSIDE	364
HUNTINGTON STATION	New York	NEW YORK-NORTHERN NEW JERSEY-LONG ISLAND	521
HURST	Texas	DALLAS-FORT WORTH	198
HYATTSVILLE	Maryland	WASHINGTON	791
HYBLA VALLEY	Virginia	WASHINGTON	804
IDYLWOOD	Virginia	WASHINGTON	805
IMPERIAL BEACH	California	SAN DIEGO	709
INDEPENDENCE	Kentucky	CINCINNATI-HAMILTON	149
INDEPENDENCE	Missouri	KANSAS CITY	298
INDIO	California	LOS ANGELES-ANAHEIM-RIVERSIDE	352
INGLEWOOD	California	LOS ANGELES-ANAHEIM-RIVERSIDE	359
INGLEWOOD-FINN HILL	Washington	SEATTLE-TACOMA	749
INKSTER	Michigan	DETROIT-ANN ARBOR	247
INVER GROVE HEIGHTS	Minnesota	MINNEAPOLIS-ST. PAUL	433
IRONDEQUOIT	New York	ROCHESTER	648
IRVINE	California	LOS ANGELES-ANAHEIM-RIVERSIDE	315
IRVING	Texas	DALLAS-FORT WORTH	200
IRVINGTON	New Jersey	NEW YORK-NORTHERN NEW JERSEY-LONG ISLAND	546
ISELIN	New Jersey	NEW YORK-NORTHERN NEW JERSEY-LONG ISLAND	528
ISLIP	New York	NEW YORK-NORTHERN NEW JERSEY-LONG ISLAND	516
IVES ESTATES	Florida	MIAMI-FORT LAUDERDALE	394
JACKSONVILLE BEACH	Florida	JACKSONVILLE	288

Index

SUBURB	STATE	METROPOLITAN AREA	PAGE
JASMINE ESTATES	Florida	TAMPA-ST. PETERSBURG-CLEARWATER	773
JASPER	Alabama	BIRMINGHAM	53
JEANNETTE	Pennsylvania	PITTSBURGH-BEAVER VALLEY	612
JEFFERSON	Louisiana	NEW ORLEANS	449
JEFFERSON	Virginia	WASHINGTON	797
JEFFERSON VALLEY-YORKTOWN	New York	NEW YORK-NORTHERN NEW JERSEY-LONG ISLAND	517
JEFFERSONTOWN	Kentucky	LOUISVILLE	372
JEFFERSONVILLE	Indiana	LOUISVILLE	374
JENNINGS	Missouri	ST. LOUIS	678
JERICHO	New York	NEW YORK-NORTHERN NEW JERSEY-LONG ISLAND	513
JERSEY CITY	New Jersey	NEW YORK-NORTHERN NEW JERSEY-LONG ISLAND	540
JOLIET	Illinois	CHICAGO-GARY-LAKE COUNTY	137
JOPPATOWNE	Maryland	BALTIMORE	36
JUPITER	Florida	WEST PALM BEACH-BOCA RATON-DELRAY BEACH	813
JUSTICE	Illinois	CHICAGO-GARY-LAKE COUNTY	141
KANNAPOLIS	North Carolina	CHARLOTTE-GASTONIA-ROCK HILL	91
KAYSVILLE	Utah	SALT LAKE CITY-OGDEN	684
KEANSBURG	New Jersey	NEW YORK-NORTHERN NEW JERSEY-LONG ISLAND	535
KEARNS	Utah	SALT LAKE CITY-OGDEN	692
KEARNY	New Jersey	NEW YORK-NORTHERN NEW JERSEY-LONG ISLAND	510
KELLER	Texas	DALLAS-FORT WORTH	193
KEN CARYL	Colorado	DENVER-BOULDER	223
KENDALE LAKES	Florida	MIAMI-FORT LAUDERDALE	401
KENDALL	Florida	MIAMI-FORT LAUDERDALE	388
KENMORE	New York	BUFFALO-NIAGARA FALLS	82
KENNER	Louisiana	NEW ORLEANS	452
KENOSHA	Wisconsin	CHICAGO-GARY-LAKE COUNTY	131
KENT	Ohio	CLEVELAND-AKRON-LORAIN	177
KENT	Washington	SEATTLE-TACOMA	761
KERNERSVILLE	North Carolina	GREENSBORO--WINSTON-SALEM--HIGH POINT	255
KETTERING	Ohio	DAYTON-SPRINGFIELD	209
KING OF PRUSSIA	Pennsylvania	PHILADELPHIA-WILMINGTON-TRENTON	584
KINGS PARK	New York	NEW YORK-NORTHERN NEW JERSEY-LONG ISLAND	501
KINGS POINT	Florida	WEST PALM BEACH-BOCA RATON-DELRAY BEACH	813
KINGSGATE	Washington	SEATTLE-TACOMA	749
KINGWOOD	Texas	HOUSTON-GALVESTON-BRAZORIA	267
KIRKLAND	Washington	SEATTLE-TACOMA	755
KIRKWOOD	Missouri	ST. LOUIS	667
KISSIMMEE	Florida	ORLANDO	572
LA CANADA-FLINTRIDGE	California	LOS ANGELES-ANAHEIM-RIVERSIDE	309
LA CRESCENTA-MONTROSE	California	LOS ANGELES-ANAHEIM-RIVERSIDE	326
LA GRANGE	Illinois	CHICAGO-GARY-LAKE COUNTY	105
LA GRANGE PARK	Illinois	CHICAGO-GARY-LAKE COUNTY	104
LA HABRA	California	LOS ANGELES-ANAHEIM-RIVERSIDE	333
LA MARQUE	Texas	HOUSTON-GALVESTON-BRAZORIA	268
LA MESA	California	SAN DIEGO	704
LA MIRADA	California	LOS ANGELES-ANAHEIM-RIVERSIDE	313
LA PALMA	California	LOS ANGELES-ANAHEIM-RIVERSIDE	319
LA PORTE	Texas	HOUSTON-GALVESTON-BRAZORIA	268
LA PUENTE	California	LOS ANGELES-ANAHEIM-RIVERSIDE	348
LA QUINTA	California	LOS ANGELES-ANAHEIM-RIVERSIDE	328
LA RIVIERA	California	SACRAMENTO	654
LA VERNE	California	LOS ANGELES-ANAHEIM-RIVERSIDE	312
LACKAWANNA	New York	BUFFALO-NIAGARA FALLS	84
LAFAYETTE	California	SAN FRANCISCO-OAKLAND-SAN JOSE	715
LAFAYETTE	Colorado	DENVER-BOULDER	221
LAGUNA BEACH	California	LOS ANGELES-ANAHEIM-RIVERSIDE	323
LAGUNA HILLS	California	LOS ANGELES-ANAHEIM-RIVERSIDE	345
LAGUNA NIGUEL	California	LOS ANGELES-ANAHEIM-RIVERSIDE	325
LAKE ELSINORE	California	LOS ANGELES-ANAHEIM-RIVERSIDE	368

Index

SUBURB	STATE	METROPOLITAN AREA	PAGE
LAKE FOREST	Illinois	CHICAGO-GARY-LAKE COUNTY	101
LAKE JACKSON	Texas	HOUSTON-GALVESTON-BRAZORIA	266
LAKE MAGDALENE	Florida	TAMPA-ST. PETERSBURG-CLEARWATER	766
LAKE OSWEGO	Oregon	PORTLAND-VANCOUVER	622
LAKE RIDGE	Virginia	WASHINGTON	807
LAKE RONKONKOMA	New York	NEW YORK-NORTHERN NEW JERSEY-LONG ISLAND	513
LAKE SERENE-NORTH LYNNWOOD	Washington	SEATTLE-TACOMA	760
LAKE SHORE	Maryland	BALTIMORE	35
LAKE STATION	Indiana	CHICAGO-GARY-LAKE COUNTY	138
LAKE WORTH	Florida	WEST PALM BEACH-BOCA RATON-DELRAY BEACH	816
LAKE ZURICH	Illinois	CHICAGO-GARY-LAKE COUNTY	119
LAKELAND NORTH	Washington	SEATTLE-TACOMA	748
LAKESIDE	California	SAN DIEGO	705
LAKESIDE	Florida	JACKSONVILLE	288
LAKESIDE	Virginia	RICHMOND-PETERSBURG	641
LAKEVILLE	Minnesota	MINNEAPOLIS-ST. PAUL	431
LAKEWOOD	California	LOS ANGELES-ANAHEIM-RIVERSIDE	321
LAKEWOOD	Colorado	DENVER-BOULDER	218
LAKEWOOD	New Jersey	NEW YORK-NORTHERN NEW JERSEY-LONG ISLAND	539
LAKEWOOD	Ohio	CLEVELAND-AKRON-LORAIN	174
LAKEWOOD	Washington	SEATTLE-TACOMA	761
LANCASTER	California	LOS ANGELES-ANAHEIM-RIVERSIDE	336
LANCASTER	New York	BUFFALO-NIAGARA FALLS	83
LANCASTER	Ohio	COLUMBUS	186
LANCASTER	Texas	DALLAS-FORT WORTH	195
LANGLEY PARK	Maryland	WASHINGTON	808
LANHAM-SEABROOK	Maryland	WASHINGTON	784
LANSDALE	Pennsylvania	PHILADELPHIA-WILMINGTON-TRENTON	588
LANSDOWNE	Pennsylvania	PHILADELPHIA-WILMINGTON-TRENTON	583
LANSDOWNE-BALTIMORE HIGHLANDS	Maryland	BALTIMORE	42
LANSING	Illinois	CHICAGO-GARY-LAKE COUNTY	113
LAPLACE	Louisiana	NEW ORLEANS	451
LARGO	Florida	TAMPA-ST. PETERSBURG-CLEARWATER	772
LARKSPUR	California	SAN FRANCISCO-OAKLAND-SAN JOSE	732
LATHAM	New York	ALBANY-SCHENECTADY-TROY	12
LAUDERDALE LAKES	Florida	MIAMI-FORT LAUDERDALE	404
LAUDERHILL	Florida	MIAMI-FORT LAUDERDALE	405
LAUREL	Maryland	WASHINGTON	801
LAUREL	Virginia	RICHMOND-PETERSBURG	643
LAWNDALE	California	LOS ANGELES-ANAHEIM-RIVERSIDE	361
LAWRENCE	Indiana	INDIANAPOLIS	282
LAWRENCEVILLE	Georgia	ATLANTA	25
LAYTON	Utah	SALT LAKE CITY-OGDEN	690
LEAGUE CITY	Texas	HOUSTON-GALVESTON-BRAZORIA	269
LEALMAN	Florida	TAMPA-ST. PETERSBURG-CLEARWATER	773
LEAVENWORTH	Kansas	KANSAS CITY	298
LEAWOOD	Kansas	KANSAS CITY	294
LEBANON	Indiana	INDIANAPOLIS	281
LEBANON	Ohio	CINCINNATI-HAMILTON	152
LEBANON	Tennessee	NASHVILLE	443
LEE'S SUMMIT	Missouri	KANSAS CITY	297
LEESBURG	Virginia	WASHINGTON	804
LEISURE CITY	Florida	MIAMI-FORT LAUDERDALE	400
LEISURE VILLAGE WEST-PINE LAKE PARK	New Jersey	NEW YORK-NORTHERN NEW JERSEY-LONG ISLAND	545
LEMAY	Missouri	ST. LOUIS	679
LEMON GROVE	California	SAN DIEGO	703
LENEXA	Kansas	KANSAS CITY	296
LENNOX	California	LOS ANGELES-ANAHEIM-RIVERSIDE	368
LEVITTOWN	New York	NEW YORK-NORTHERN NEW JERSEY-LONG ISLAND	512
LEVITTOWN	Pennsylvania	PHILADELPHIA-WILMINGTON-TRENTON	582

Index

SUBURB	STATE	METROPOLITAN AREA	PAGE
LEWISVILLE	Texas	DALLAS-FORT WORTH	203
LEXINGTON	Massachusetts	BOSTON-LAWRENCE-SALEM-LOWELL-BROCKTON	62
LEXINGTON	North Carolina	GREENSBORO--WINSTON-SALEM--HIGH POINT	254
LIBERTY	Missouri	KANSAS CITY	295
LIBERTYVILLE	Illinois	CHICAGO-GARY-LAKE COUNTY	116
LIGHTHOUSE POINT	Florida	MIAMI-FORT LAUDERDALE	389
LINCOLN PARK	Michigan	DETROIT-ANN ARBOR	240
LINCOLN PARK	New Jersey	NEW YORK-NORTHERN NEW JERSEY-LONG ISLAND	517
LINCOLNIA	Virginia	WASHINGTON	801
LINCOLNWOOD	Illinois	CHICAGO-GARY-LAKE COUNTY	107
LINDEN	New Jersey	NEW YORK-NORTHERN NEW JERSEY-LONG ISLAND	495
LINDENHURST	New York	NEW YORK-NORTHERN NEW JERSEY-LONG ISLAND	522
LINDENWOLD	New Jersey	PHILADELPHIA-WILMINGTON-TRENTON	593
LINDGREN ACRES	Florida	MIAMI-FORT LAUDERDALE	397
LISLE	Illinois	CHICAGO-GARY-LAKE COUNTY	121
LITHIA SPRINGS	Georgia	ATLANTA	24
LITTLE FALLS	New Jersey	NEW YORK-NORTHERN NEW JERSEY-LONG ISLAND	501
LITTLETON	Colorado	DENVER-BOULDER	217
LIVE OAK	California	SAN FRANCISCO-OAKLAND-SAN JOSE	739
LIVE OAK	Texas	SAN ANTONIO	696
LIVERMORE	California	SAN FRANCISCO-OAKLAND-SAN JOSE	723
LIVINGSTON	New Jersey	NEW YORK-NORTHERN NEW JERSEY-LONG ISLAND	464
LIVONIA	Michigan	DETROIT-ANN ARBOR	231
LOCHEARN	Maryland	BALTIMORE	34
LOCKHART	Florida	ORLANDO	570
LOCKPORT	New York	BUFFALO-NIAGARA FALLS	85
LODI	New Jersey	NEW YORK-NORTHERN NEW JERSEY-LONG ISLAND	515
LOMA LINDA	California	LOS ANGELES-ANAHEIM-RIVERSIDE	320
LOMBARD	Illinois	CHICAGO-GARY-LAKE COUNTY	128
LOMITA	California	LOS ANGELES-ANAHEIM-RIVERSIDE	349
LONG BEACH	California	LOS ANGELES-ANAHEIM-RIVERSIDE	357
LONG BEACH	New York	NEW YORK-NORTHERN NEW JERSEY-LONG ISLAND	534
LONG BRANCH	New Jersey	NEW YORK-NORTHERN NEW JERSEY-LONG ISLAND	536
LONGMONT	Colorado	DENVER-BOULDER	220
LONGWOOD	Florida	ORLANDO	567
LORTON	Virginia	WASHINGTON	808
LOS ALAMITOS	California	LOS ANGELES-ANAHEIM-RIVERSIDE	327
LOS ALTOS	California	SAN FRANCISCO-OAKLAND-SAN JOSE	716
LOS GATOS	California	SAN FRANCISCO-OAKLAND-SAN JOSE	718
LOUDONVILLE	New York	ALBANY-SCHENECTADY-TROY	12
LOUISVILLE	Colorado	DENVER-BOULDER	216
LOWER BURRELL	Pennsylvania	PITTSBURGH-BEAVER VALLEY	607
LUTHERVILLE-TIMONIUM	Maryland	BALTIMORE	32
LUTZ	Florida	TAMPA-ST. PETERSBURG-CLEARWATER	766
LYNBROOK	New York	NEW YORK-NORTHERN NEW JERSEY-LONG ISLAND	484
LYNDHURST	New Jersey	NEW YORK-NORTHERN NEW JERSEY-LONG ISLAND	481
LYNDHURST	Ohio	CLEVELAND-AKRON-LORAIN	161
LYNN	Massachusetts	BOSTON-LAWRENCE-SALEM-LOWELL-BROCKTON	77
LYNNFIELD	Massachusetts	BOSTON-LAWRENCE-SALEM-LOWELL-BROCKTON	61
LYNNWOOD	Washington	SEATTLE-TACOMA	761
LYNWOOD	California	LOS ANGELES-ANAHEIM-RIVERSIDE	364
MABLETON	Georgia	ATLANTA	19
MADISON	New Jersey	NEW YORK-NORTHERN NEW JERSEY-LONG ISLAND	486
MADISON HEIGHTS	Michigan	DETROIT-ANN ARBOR	240
MAGNA	Utah	SALT LAKE CITY-OGDEN	690
MALDEN	Massachusetts	BOSTON-LAWRENCE-SALEM-LOWELL-BROCKTON	76
MAMARONECK	New York	NEW YORK-NORTHERN NEW JERSEY-LONG ISLAND	491
MANASSAS	Virginia	WASHINGTON	807
MANHATTAN BEACH	California	LOS ANGELES-ANAHEIM-RIVERSIDE	322
MANSFIELD	Texas	DALLAS-FORT WORTH	199

Index

Index

Index

SUBURB	STATE	METROPOLITAN AREA	PAGE
MOUNTLAKE TERRACE	Washington	SEATTLE-TACOMA	758
MUNDELEIN	Illinois	CHICAGO-GARY-LAKE COUNTY	134
MUNHALL	Pennsylvania	PITTSBURGH-BEAVER VALLEY	611
MUNSTER	Indiana	CHICAGO-GARY-LAKE COUNTY	102
MURFREESBORO	Tennessee	NASHVILLE	444
MURRAY	Utah	SALT LAKE CITY-OGDEN	688
MURRYSVILLE	Pennsylvania	PITTSBURGH-BEAVER VALLEY	610
MUSKEGO	Wisconsin	MILWAUKEE-RACINE	414
MUSTANG	Oklahoma	OKLAHOMA CITY	559
NANUET	New York	NEW YORK-NORTHERN NEW JERSEY-LONG ISLAND	527
NAPA	California	SAN FRANCISCO-OAKLAND-SAN JOSE	725
NAPERVILLE	Illinois	CHICAGO-GARY-LAKE COUNTY	112
NATIONAL CITY	California	SAN DIEGO	709
NEEDHAM	Massachusetts	BOSTON-LAWRENCE-SALEM-LOWELL-BROCKTON	62
NESCONSET	New York	NEW YORK-NORTHERN NEW JERSEY-LONG ISLAND	502
NETHER PROVIDENCE TOWNSHIP	Pennsylvania	PHILADELPHIA-WILMINGTON-TRENTON	577
NEW ALBANY	Indiana	LOUISVILLE	375
NEW BERLIN	Wisconsin	MILWAUKEE-RACINE	414
NEW BRAUNFELS	Texas	SAN ANTONIO	697
NEW BRIGHTON	Minnesota	MINNEAPOLIS-ST. PAUL	425
NEW BRUNSWICK	New Jersey	NEW YORK-NORTHERN NEW JERSEY-LONG ISLAND	545
NEW CARROLLTON	Maryland	WASHINGTON	792
NEW CASSEL	New York	NEW YORK-NORTHERN NEW JERSEY-LONG ISLAND	530
NEW CITY	New York	NEW YORK-NORTHERN NEW JERSEY-LONG ISLAND	489
NEW HOPE	Minnesota	MINNEAPOLIS-ST. PAUL	431
NEW KENSINGTON	Pennsylvania	PITTSBURGH-BEAVER VALLEY	614
NEW MILFORD	New Jersey	NEW YORK-NORTHERN NEW JERSEY-LONG ISLAND	471
NEW PORT RICHEY	Florida	TAMPA-ST. PETERSBURG-CLEARWATER	774
NEW PROVIDENCE	New Jersey	NEW YORK-NORTHERN NEW JERSEY-LONG ISLAND	468
NEW ROCHELLE	New York	NEW YORK-NORTHERN NEW JERSEY-LONG ISLAND	495
NEWARK	California	SAN FRANCISCO-OAKLAND-SAN JOSE	728
NEWARK	Delaware	PHILADELPHIA-WILMINGTON-TRENTON	581
NEWARK	New Jersey	NEW YORK-NORTHERN NEW JERSEY-LONG ISLAND	546
NEWARK	Ohio	COLUMBUS	186
NEWBERG	Oregon	PORTLAND-VANCOUVER	627
NEWBURG	Kentucky	LOUISVILLE	375
NEWBURGH	New York	NEW YORK-NORTHERN NEW JERSEY-LONG ISLAND	544
NEWBURYPORT	Massachusetts	BOSTON-LAWRENCE-SALEM-LOWELL-BROCKTON	74
NEWINGTON	Connecticut	HARTFORD-NEW BRITAIN-MIDDLETOWN-BRISTOL	261
NEWINGTON	Virginia	WASHINGTON	803
NEWNAN	Georgia	ATLANTA	22
NEWPORT	Kentucky	CINCINNATI-HAMILTON	155
NEWPORT BEACH	California	LOS ANGELES-ANAHEIM-RIVERSIDE	328
NEWPORT HILLS	Washington	SEATTLE-TACOMA	746
NEWTON	Massachusetts	BOSTON-LAWRENCE-SALEM-LOWELL-BROCKTON	66
NILES	Illinois	CHICAGO-GARY-LAKE COUNTY	114
NOBLESVILLE	Indiana	INDIANAPOLIS	283
NORCO	California	LOS ANGELES-ANAHEIM-RIVERSIDE	331
NORLAND	Florida	MIAMI-FORT LAUDERDALE	395
NORMAN	Oklahoma	OKLAHOMA CITY	559
NORRIDGE	Illinois	CHICAGO-GARY-LAKE COUNTY	124
NORRISTOWN	Pennsylvania	PHILADELPHIA-WILMINGTON-TRENTON	591
NORTH AMITYVILLE	New York	NEW YORK-NORTHERN NEW JERSEY-LONG ISLAND	539
NORTH ARLINGTON	New Jersey	NEW YORK-NORTHERN NEW JERSEY-LONG ISLAND	476
NORTH ATLANTA	Georgia	ATLANTA	26
NORTH AUBURN	California	SACRAMENTO	660
NORTH BABYLON	New York	NEW YORK-NORTHERN NEW JERSEY-LONG ISLAND	524
NORTH BAY SHORE	New York	NEW YORK-NORTHERN NEW JERSEY-LONG ISLAND	535
NORTH BELLMORE	New York	NEW YORK-NORTHERN NEW JERSEY-LONG ISLAND	495
NORTH BERGEN	New Jersey	NEW YORK-NORTHERN NEW JERSEY-LONG ISLAND	523

Index

Index

SUBURB	STATE	METROPOLITAN AREA	PAGE
OAKVILLE	Missouri	ST. LOUIS	674
OATFIELD	Oregon	PORTLAND-VANCOUVER	622
OCEANSIDE	California	SAN DIEGO	707
OCEANSIDE	New York	NEW YORK-NORTHERN NEW JERSEY-LONG ISLAND	494
OCOEE	Florida	ORLANDO	568
OCONOMOWOC	Wisconsin	MILWAUKEE-RACINE	417
ODENTON	Maryland	BALTIMORE	36
OJUS	Florida	MIAMI-FORT LAUDERDALE	389
OKOLONA	Kentucky	LOUISVILLE	374
OLATHE	Kansas	KANSAS CITY	297
OLD BRIDGE	New Jersey	NEW YORK-NORTHERN NEW JERSEY-LONG ISLAND	475
OLNEY	Maryland	WASHINGTON	786
OLYMPIA HEIGHTS	Florida	MIAMI-FORT LAUDERDALE	390
ONTARIO	California	LOS ANGELES-ANAHEIM-RIVERSIDE	361
OPA-LOCKA	Florida	MIAMI-FORT LAUDERDALE	406
ORANGE	California	LOS ANGELES-ANAHEIM-RIVERSIDE	326
ORANGE	New Jersey	NEW YORK-NORTHERN NEW JERSEY-LONG ISLAND	542
ORANGEVALE	California	SACRAMENTO	656
ORCHARDS SOUTH	Washington	PORTLAND-VANCOUVER	627
OREGON CITY	Oregon	PORTLAND-VANCOUVER	628
ORINDA	California	SAN FRANCISCO-OAKLAND-SAN JOSE	716
ORLAND PARK	Illinois	CHICAGO-GARY-LAKE COUNTY	111
OSSINING	New York	NEW YORK-NORTHERN NEW JERSEY-LONG ISLAND	527
OVERLAND	Missouri	ST. LOUIS	676
OVERLAND PARK	Kansas	KANSAS CITY	295
OVERLEA	Maryland	BALTIMORE	35
OVERLOOK-PAGE MANOR	Ohio	DAYTON-SPRINGFIELD	209
OVIEDO	Florida	ORLANDO	568
OXFORD	Ohio	CINCINNATI-HAMILTON	154
OXNARD	California	LOS ANGELES-ANAHEIM-RIVERSIDE	347
OXON HILL-GLASSMANOR	Maryland	WASHINGTON	798
PACIFICA	California	SAN FRANCISCO-OAKLAND-SAN JOSE	722
PAINE FIELD-LAKE STICKNEY	Washington	SEATTLE-TACOMA	762
PAINESVILLE	Ohio	CLEVELAND-AKRON-LORAIN	178
PALATINE	Illinois	CHICAGO-GARY-LAKE COUNTY	121
PALISADES PARK	New Jersey	NEW YORK-NORTHERN NEW JERSEY-LONG ISLAND	528
PALM BEACH GARDENS	Florida	WEST PALM BEACH-BOCA RATON-DELRAY BEACH	812
PALM DESERT	California	LOS ANGELES-ANAHEIM-RIVERSIDE	338
PALM HARBOR	Florida	TAMPA-ST. PETERSBURG-CLEARWATER	773
PALM RIVER-CLAIR MEL	Florida	TAMPA-ST. PETERSBURG-CLEARWATER	767
PALM SPRINGS	California	LOS ANGELES-ANAHEIM-RIVERSIDE	339
PALMDALE	California	LOS ANGELES-ANAHEIM-RIVERSIDE	353
PALMETTO ESTATES	Florida	MIAMI-FORT LAUDERDALE	393
PALO ALTO	California	SAN FRANCISCO-OAKLAND-SAN JOSE	721
PALOS HEIGHTS	Illinois	CHICAGO-GARY-LAKE COUNTY	103
PALOS HILLS	Illinois	CHICAGO-GARY-LAKE COUNTY	113
PALOS VERDES ESTATES	California	LOS ANGELES-ANAHEIM-RIVERSIDE	309
PARADISE VALLEY	Arizona	PHOENIX	598
PARAMOUNT	California	LOS ANGELES-ANAHEIM-RIVERSIDE	363
PARAMUS	New Jersey	NEW YORK-NORTHERN NEW JERSEY-LONG ISLAND	509
PARK FOREST	Illinois	CHICAGO-GARY-LAKE COUNTY	117
PARK RIDGE	Illinois	CHICAGO-GARY-LAKE COUNTY	103
PARKLAND	Washington	SEATTLE-TACOMA	757
PARKVILLE	Maryland	BALTIMORE	39
PARKWAY-SOUTH SACRAMENTO	California	SACRAMENTO	661
PARMA	Ohio	CLEVELAND-AKRON-LORAIN	168
PARMA HEIGHTS	Ohio	CLEVELAND-AKRON-LORAIN	176
PAROLE	Maryland	BALTIMORE	40
PARSIPPANY-TROY HILLS TOWNSHIP	New Jersey	NEW YORK-NORTHERN NEW JERSEY-LONG ISLAND	498
PASADENA	California	LOS ANGELES-ANAHEIM-RIVERSIDE	333

Index

SUBURB	STATE	METROPOLITAN AREA	PAGE
PASADENA	Maryland	BALTIMORE	34
PASADENA	Texas	HOUSTON-GALVESTON-BRAZORIA	274
PASSAIC	New Jersey	NEW YORK-NORTHERN NEW JERSEY-LONG ISLAND	542
PATCHOGUE	New York	NEW YORK-NORTHERN NEW JERSEY-LONG ISLAND	538
PATERSON	New Jersey	NEW YORK-NORTHERN NEW JERSEY-LONG ISLAND	540
PEABODY	Massachusetts	BOSTON-LAWRENCE-SALEM-LOWELL-BROCKTON	69
PEACHTREE CITY	Georgia	ATLANTA	21
PEARL RIVER	New York	NEW YORK-NORTHERN NEW JERSEY-LONG ISLAND	491
PEARLAND	Texas	HOUSTON-GALVESTON-BRAZORIA	269
PEEKSKILL	New York	NEW YORK-NORTHERN NEW JERSEY-LONG ISLAND	532
PEMBROKE PINES	Florida	MIAMI-FORT LAUDERDALE	403
PENN HILLS	Pennsylvania	PITTSBURGH-BEAVER VALLEY	607
PENNSAUKEN	New Jersey	PHILADELPHIA-WILMINGTON-TRENTON	581
PENNSVILLE	New Jersey	PHILADELPHIA-WILMINGTON-TRENTON	579
PEORIA	Arizona	PHOENIX	600
PEQUANNOCK TOWNSHIP	New Jersey	NEW YORK-NORTHERN NEW JERSEY-LONG ISLAND	467
PERRINE	Florida	MIAMI-FORT LAUDERDALE	392
PERRIS	California	LOS ANGELES-ANAHEIM-RIVERSIDE	367
PERRY HALL	Maryland	BALTIMORE	39
PERTH AMBOY	New Jersey	NEW YORK-NORTHERN NEW JERSEY-LONG ISLAND	534
PETALUMA	California	SAN FRANCISCO-OAKLAND-SAN JOSE	726
PHOENIXVILLE	Pennsylvania	PHILADELPHIA-WILMINGTON-TRENTON	590
PICO RIVERA	California	LOS ANGELES-ANAHEIM-RIVERSIDE	335
PIEDMONT	California	SAN FRANCISCO-OAKLAND-SAN JOSE	715
PIKE CREEK	Delaware	PHILADELPHIA-WILMINGTON-TRENTON	589
PIKESVILLE	Maryland	BALTIMORE	33
PINE HILLS	Florida	ORLANDO	569
PINE LAKE	Washington	SEATTLE-TACOMA	748
PINELLAS PARK	Florida	TAMPA-ST. PETERSBURG-CLEARWATER	770
PINEWOOD	Florida	MIAMI-FORT LAUDERDALE	402
PINOLE	California	SAN FRANCISCO-OAKLAND-SAN JOSE	725
PINSON-CLAY-CHALKVILLE	Alabama	BIRMINGHAM	54
PIQUA	Ohio	DAYTON-SPRINGFIELD	212
PITTSBURG	California	SAN FRANCISCO-OAKLAND-SAN JOSE	737
PLACENTIA	California	LOS ANGELES-ANAHEIM-RIVERSIDE	319
PLAINFIELD	Indiana	INDIANAPOLIS	281
PLAINFIELD	New Jersey	NEW YORK-NORTHERN NEW JERSEY-LONG ISLAND	536
PLAINVIEW	New York	NEW YORK-NORTHERN NEW JERSEY-LONG ISLAND	469
PLANO	Texas	DALLAS-FORT WORTH	192
PLANT CITY	Florida	TAMPA-ST. PETERSBURG-CLEARWATER	771
PLANTATION	Florida	MIAMI-FORT LAUDERDALE	394
PLEASANT HILL	California	SAN FRANCISCO-OAKLAND-SAN JOSE	726
PLEASANT PRAIRIE	Wisconsin	CHICAGO-GARY-LAKE COUNTY	106
PLEASANTON	California	SAN FRANCISCO-OAKLAND-SAN JOSE	725
PLEASURE RIDGE PARK	Kentucky	LOUISVILLE	373
PLUM	Pennsylvania	PITTSBURGH-BEAVER VALLEY	611
PLYMOUTH	Minnesota	MINNEAPOLIS-ST. PAUL	425
PLYMOUTH TOWNSHIP	Michigan	DETROIT-ANN ARBOR	230
POINT PLEASANT	New Jersey	NEW YORK-NORTHERN NEW JERSEY-LONG ISLAND	494
POMONA	California	LOS ANGELES-ANAHEIM-RIVERSIDE	357
POMPANO BEACH	Florida	MIAMI-FORT LAUDERDALE	398
POMPANO BEACH HIGHLANDS	Florida	MIAMI-FORT LAUDERDALE	403
POMPTON LAKES	New Jersey	NEW YORK-NORTHERN NEW JERSEY-LONG ISLAND	490
PONTIAC	Michigan	DETROIT-ANN ARBOR	248
POQUOSON	Virginia	NORFOLK-VIRGINIA BEACH-NEWPORT NEWS	552
PORT CHESTER	New York	NEW YORK-NORTHERN NEW JERSEY-LONG ISLAND	526
PORT HUENEME	California	LOS ANGELES-ANAHEIM-RIVERSIDE	336
PORT HURON	Michigan	DETROIT-ANN ARBOR	242
PORT WASHINGTON	New York	NEW YORK-NORTHERN NEW JERSEY-LONG ISLAND	498
PORTAGE	Indiana	CHICAGO-GARY-LAKE COUNTY	124

Index

SUBURB	STATE	METROPOLITAN AREA	PAGE
PORTAGE LAKES	Ohio	CLEVELAND-AKRON-LORAIN	171
PORTSMOUTH	Virginia	NORFOLK-VIRGINIA BEACH-NEWPORT NEWS	553
POTOMAC	Maryland	WASHINGTON	783
POTTSTOWN	Pennsylvania	PHILADELPHIA-WILMINGTON-TRENTON	591
POWAY	California	SAN DIEGO	702
POWELLHURST-CENTENNIAL	Oregon	PORTLAND-VANCOUVER	628
PRAIRIE VILLAGE	Kansas	KANSAS CITY	294
PRINCETON	New Jersey	PHILADELPHIA-WILMINGTON-TRENTON	588
PRIOR LAKE	Minnesota	MINNEAPOLIS-ST. PAUL	430
PROSPECT HEIGHTS	Illinois	CHICAGO-GARY-LAKE COUNTY	138
PUYALLUP	Washington	SEATTLE-TACOMA	756
QUINCY	Massachusetts	BOSTON-LAWRENCE-SALEM-LOWELL-BROCKTON	73
RADNOR TOWNSHIP	Pennsylvania	PHILADELPHIA-WILMINGTON-TRENTON	578
RAHWAY	New Jersey	NEW YORK-NORTHERN NEW JERSEY-LONG ISLAND	497
RAMONA	California	SAN DIEGO	706
RAMSEY	Minnesota	MINNEAPOLIS-ST. PAUL	424
RAMSEY	New Jersey	NEW YORK-NORTHERN NEW JERSEY-LONG ISLAND	488
RANCHO CORDOVA	California	SACRAMENTO	657
RANCHO CUCAMONGA	California	LOS ANGELES-ANAHEIM-RIVERSIDE	332
RANCHO PALOS VERDES	California	LOS ANGELES-ANAHEIM-RIVERSIDE	310
RANCHO SANTA MARGARITA	California	LOS ANGELES-ANAHEIM-RIVERSIDE	355
RANDALLSTOWN	Maryland	BALTIMORE	34
RANDOLPH	Massachusetts	BOSTON-LAWRENCE-SALEM-LOWELL-BROCKTON	72
RAVENNA	Ohio	CLEVELAND-AKRON-LORAIN	175
RAYTOWN	Missouri	KANSAS CITY	295
READING	Massachusetts	BOSTON-LAWRENCE-SALEM-LOWELL-BROCKTON	61
READING	Ohio	CINCINNATI-HAMILTON	149
RED BANK	New Jersey	NEW YORK-NORTHERN NEW JERSEY-LONG ISLAND	508
REDAN	Georgia	ATLANTA	26
REDFORD	Michigan	DETROIT-ANN ARBOR	234
REDLAND	Maryland	WASHINGTON	785
REDLANDS	California	LOS ANGELES-ANAHEIM-RIVERSIDE	314
REDMOND	Washington	SEATTLE-TACOMA	751
REDONDO BEACH	California	LOS ANGELES-ANAHEIM-RIVERSIDE	344
REDWOOD CITY	California	SAN FRANCISCO-OAKLAND-SAN JOSE	736
REISTERSTOWN	Maryland	BALTIMORE	39
RENTON	Washington	SEATTLE-TACOMA	754
RESTON	Virginia	WASHINGTON	796
REVERE	Massachusetts	BOSTON-LAWRENCE-SALEM-LOWELL-BROCKTON	76
REYNOLDSBURG	Ohio	COLUMBUS	185
RIALTO	California	LOS ANGELES-ANAHEIM-RIVERSIDE	348
RICHARDSON	Texas	DALLAS-FORT WORTH	190
RICHFIELD	Minnesota	MINNEAPOLIS-ST. PAUL	432
RICHMOND	California	SAN FRANCISCO-OAKLAND-SAN JOSE	739
RICHMOND HEIGHTS	Missouri	ST. LOUIS	673
RICHMOND HIGHLANDS	Washington	SEATTLE-TACOMA	750
RICHTON PARK	Illinois	CHICAGO-GARY-LAKE COUNTY	119
RIDGE	New York	NEW YORK-NORTHERN NEW JERSEY-LONG ISLAND	544
RIDGEFIELD PARK	New Jersey	NEW YORK-NORTHERN NEW JERSEY-LONG ISLAND	490
RIDGEWOOD	New Jersey	NEW YORK-NORTHERN NEW JERSEY-LONG ISLAND	470
RINGWOOD	New Jersey	NEW YORK-NORTHERN NEW JERSEY-LONG ISLAND	494
RIVER EDGE	New Jersey	NEW YORK-NORTHERN NEW JERSEY-LONG ISLAND	472
RIVER FOREST	Illinois	CHICAGO-GARY-LAKE COUNTY	101
RIVER RIDGE	Louisiana	NEW ORLEANS	448
RIVER ROUGE	Michigan	DETROIT-ANN ARBOR	245
RIVERDALE	Illinois	CHICAGO-GARY-LAKE COUNTY	140
RIVERTON	Utah	SALT LAKE CITY-OGDEN	686
RIVERTON-BOULEVARD PARK	Washington	SEATTLE-TACOMA	753
RIVERVIEW	Michigan	DETROIT-ANN ARBOR	231
RIVIERA BEACH	Florida	WEST PALM BEACH-BOCA RATON-DELRAY BEACH	813

Index

SUBURB	STATE	METROPOLITAN AREA	PAGE
RIVIERA BEACH	Maryland	BALTIMORE	41
ROBBINSDALE	Minnesota	MINNEAPOLIS-ST. PAUL	429
ROBINSON TOWNSHIP	Pennsylvania	PITTSBURGH-BEAVER VALLEY	610
ROCHESTER HILLS	Michigan	DETROIT-ANN ARBOR	246
ROCKLIN	California	SACRAMENTO	660
ROCKVILLE	Maryland	WASHINGTON	786
ROCKVILLE CENTRE	New York	NEW YORK-NORTHERN NEW JERSEY-LONG ISLAND	466
ROCKWALL	Texas	DALLAS-FORT WORTH	198
ROCKY RIVER	Ohio	CLEVELAND-AKRON-LORAIN	167
ROESSLEVILLE	New York	ALBANY-SCHENECTADY-TROY	13
ROHNERT PARK	California	SAN FRANCISCO-OAKLAND-SAN JOSE	737
ROLLING MEADOWS	Illinois	CHICAGO-GARY-LAKE COUNTY	130
ROMEOVILLE	Illinois	CHICAGO-GARY-LAKE COUNTY	133
ROMULUS	Michigan	DETROIT-ANN ARBOR	241
RONKONKOMA	New York	NEW YORK-NORTHERN NEW JERSEY-LONG ISLAND	527
ROOSEVELT	New York	NEW YORK-NORTHERN NEW JERSEY-LONG ISLAND	533
ROSE HILL	Virginia	WASHINGTON	785
ROSEDALE	Maryland	BALTIMORE	35
ROSELLE	Illinois	CHICAGO-GARY-LAKE COUNTY	120
ROSELLE	New Jersey	NEW YORK-NORTHERN NEW JERSEY-LONG ISLAND	499
ROSELLE PARK	New Jersey	NEW YORK-NORTHERN NEW JERSEY-LONG ISLAND	499
ROSEMEAD	California	LOS ANGELES-ANAHEIM-RIVERSIDE	353
ROSEMONT	California	SACRAMENTO	655
ROSENBERG	Texas	HOUSTON-GALVESTON-BRAZORIA	274
ROSEVILLE	California	SACRAMENTO	657
ROSEVILLE	Michigan	DETROIT-ANN ARBOR	244
ROSEVILLE	Minnesota	MINNEAPOLIS-ST. PAUL	425
ROSS TOWNSHIP	Pennsylvania	PITTSBURGH-BEAVER VALLEY	608
ROSWELL	Georgia	ATLANTA	20
ROTTERDAM	New York	ALBANY-SCHENECTADY-TROY	12
ROUND LAKE BEACH	Illinois	CHICAGO-GARY-LAKE COUNTY	142
ROWLAND HEIGHTS	California	LOS ANGELES-ANAHEIM-RIVERSIDE	342
ROWLETT	Texas	DALLAS-FORT WORTH	195
ROY	Utah	SALT LAKE CITY-OGDEN	687
ROYAL OAK	Michigan	DETROIT-ANN ARBOR	238
ROYAL PALM BEACH	Florida	WEST PALM BEACH-BOCA RATON-DELRAY BEACH	812
RUBIDOUX	California	LOS ANGELES-ANAHEIM-RIVERSIDE	355
RUTHERFORD	New Jersey	NEW YORK-NORTHERN NEW JERSEY-LONG ISLAND	482
RYE	New York	NEW YORK-NORTHERN NEW JERSEY-LONG ISLAND	496
SADDLE BROOK	New Jersey	NEW YORK-NORTHERN NEW JERSEY-LONG ISLAND	478
SAFETY HARBOR	Florida	TAMPA-ST. PETERSBURG-CLEARWATER	771
SAHALEE	Washington	SEATTLE-TACOMA	753
SALISBURY	New York	NEW YORK-NORTHERN NEW JERSEY-LONG ISLAND	474
SALISBURY	North Carolina	CHARLOTTE-GASTONIA-ROCK HILL	90
SALMON CREEK	Washington	PORTLAND-VANCOUVER	623
SAN ANSELMO	California	SAN FRANCISCO-OAKLAND-SAN JOSE	720
SAN BERNARDINO	California	LOS ANGELES-ANAHEIM-RIVERSIDE	355
SAN BRUNO	California	SAN FRANCISCO-OAKLAND-SAN JOSE	731
SAN CARLOS	California	SAN FRANCISCO-OAKLAND-SAN JOSE	719
SAN CLEMENTE	California	LOS ANGELES-ANAHEIM-RIVERSIDE	332
SAN DIMAS	California	LOS ANGELES-ANAHEIM-RIVERSIDE	313
SAN FERNANDO	California	LOS ANGELES-ANAHEIM-RIVERSIDE	346
SAN GABRIEL	California	LOS ANGELES-ANAHEIM-RIVERSIDE	337
SAN JACINTO	California	LOS ANGELES-ANAHEIM-RIVERSIDE	349
SAN JUAN CAPISTRANO	California	LOS ANGELES-ANAHEIM-RIVERSIDE	322
SAN LEANDRO	California	SAN FRANCISCO-OAKLAND-SAN JOSE	721
SAN LORENZO	California	SAN FRANCISCO-OAKLAND-SAN JOSE	724
SAN MARCOS	California	SAN DIEGO	706
SAN MARINO	California	LOS ANGELES-ANAHEIM-RIVERSIDE	309
SAN MATEO	California	SAN FRANCISCO-OAKLAND-SAN JOSE	732

Index

SUBURB	STATE	METROPOLITAN AREA	PAGE
SAN PABLO	California	SAN FRANCISCO-OAKLAND-SAN JOSE	742
SAN RAFAEL	California	SAN FRANCISCO-OAKLAND-SAN JOSE	728
SAN RAMON	California	SAN FRANCISCO-OAKLAND-SAN JOSE	729
SANDALFOOT COVE	Florida	WEST PALM BEACH-BOCA RATON-DELRAY BEACH	816
SANDY	Utah	SALT LAKE CITY-OGDEN	688
SANDY SPRINGS	Georgia	ATLANTA	22
SANFORD	Florida	ORLANDO	571
SANTA ANA	California	LOS ANGELES-ANAHEIM-RIVERSIDE	360
SANTA CLARA	California	SAN FRANCISCO-OAKLAND-SAN JOSE	731
SANTA CLARITA	California	LOS ANGELES-ANAHEIM-RIVERSIDE	324
SANTA CRUZ	California	SAN FRANCISCO-OAKLAND-SAN JOSE	733
SANTA FE SPRINGS	California	LOS ANGELES-ANAHEIM-RIVERSIDE	351
SANTA MONICA	California	LOS ANGELES-ANAHEIM-RIVERSIDE	345
SANTA PAULA	California	LOS ANGELES-ANAHEIM-RIVERSIDE	345
SANTA ROSA	California	SAN FRANCISCO-OAKLAND-SAN JOSE	727
SANTEE	California	SAN DIEGO	704
SAPPINGTON	Missouri	ST. LOUIS	669
SARATOGA	California	SAN FRANCISCO-OAKLAND-SAN JOSE	716
SARATOGA SPRINGS	New York	ALBANY-SCHENECTADY-TROY	14
SAUGUS	Massachusetts	BOSTON-LAWRENCE-SALEM-LOWELL-BROCKTON	70
SAYREVILLE	New Jersey	NEW YORK-NORTHERN NEW JERSEY-LONG ISLAND	500
SAYVILLE	New York	NEW YORK-NORTHERN NEW JERSEY-LONG ISLAND	509
SCARSDALE	New York	NEW YORK-NORTHERN NEW JERSEY-LONG ISLAND	479
SCHAUMBURG	Illinois	CHICAGO-GARY-LAKE COUNTY	133
SCHERERVILLE	Indiana	CHICAGO-GARY-LAKE COUNTY	133
SCHERTZ	Texas	SAN ANTONIO	696
SCHILLER PARK	Illinois	CHICAGO-GARY-LAKE COUNTY	134
SCOTCH PLAINS	New Jersey	NEW YORK-NORTHERN NEW JERSEY-LONG ISLAND	470
SCOTT LAKE	Florida	MIAMI-FORT LAUDERDALE	388
SCOTT TOWNSHIP	Pennsylvania	PITTSBURGH-BEAVER VALLEY	611
SCOTTSDALE	Arizona	PHOENIX	598
SEA-TAC	Washington	SEATTLE-TACOMA	754
SEAFORD	New York	NEW YORK-NORTHERN NEW JERSEY-LONG ISLAND	503
SEAL BEACH	California	LOS ANGELES-ANAHEIM-RIVERSIDE	330
SECAUCUS	New Jersey	NEW YORK-NORTHERN NEW JERSEY-LONG ISLAND	512
SEGUIN	Texas	SAN ANTONIO	697
SELDEN	New York	NEW YORK-NORTHERN NEW JERSEY-LONG ISLAND	525
SETAUKET-EAST SETAUKET	New York	NEW YORK-NORTHERN NEW JERSEY-LONG ISLAND	502
SEVEN HILLS	Ohio	CLEVELAND-AKRON-LORAIN	161
SEVERN	Maryland	BALTIMORE	43
SEVERNA PARK	Maryland	BALTIMORE	33
SHAKER HEIGHTS	Ohio	CLEVELAND-AKRON-LORAIN	166
SHAKOPEE	Minnesota	MINNEAPOLIS-ST. PAUL	434
SHALER TOWNSHIP	Pennsylvania	PITTSBURGH-BEAVER VALLEY	606
SHARONVILLE	Ohio	CINCINNATI-HAMILTON	151
SHAWNEE	Kansas	KANSAS CITY	296
SHAWNEE	Oklahoma	OKLAHOMA CITY	561
SHELBY	Michigan	DETROIT-ANN ARBOR	235
SHELBYVILLE	Indiana	INDIANAPOLIS	282
SHELTON	Connecticut	NEW YORK-NORTHERN NEW JERSEY-LONG ISLAND	474
SHERRELWOOD	Colorado	DENVER-BOULDER	222
SHILOH	Ohio	DAYTON-SPRINGFIELD	210
SHIRLEY	New York	NEW YORK-NORTHERN NEW JERSEY-LONG ISLAND	538
SHIVELY	Kentucky	LOUISVILLE	373
SHOREVIEW	Minnesota	MINNEAPOLIS-ST. PAUL	422
SHOREWOOD	Wisconsin	MILWAUKEE-RACINE	417
SIERRA MADRE	California	LOS ANGELES-ANAHEIM-RIVERSIDE	311
SILVER LAKE-FIRCREST	Washington	SEATTLE-TACOMA	750
SILVER SPRING	Maryland	WASHINGTON	788
SIMI VALLEY	California	LOS ANGELES-ANAHEIM-RIVERSIDE	325

Index

SUBURB	STATE	METROPOLITAN AREA	PAGE
SKOKIE	Illinois	CHICAGO-GARY-LAKE COUNTY	109
SLIDELL	Louisiana	NEW ORLEANS	448
SMITHTOWN	New York	NEW YORK-NORTHERN NEW JERSEY-LONG ISLAND	490
SMYRNA	Georgia	ATLANTA	25
SMYRNA	Tennessee	NASHVILLE	444
SNELLVILLE	Georgia	ATLANTA	20
SOLANA BEACH	California	SAN DIEGO	703
SOLON	Ohio	CLEVELAND-AKRON-LORAIN	164
SOMERSET	New Jersey	NEW YORK-NORTHERN NEW JERSEY-LONG ISLAND	520
SOMERVILLE	Massachusetts	BOSTON-LAWRENCE-SALEM-LOWELL-BROCKTON	76
SOMERVILLE	New Jersey	NEW YORK-NORTHERN NEW JERSEY-LONG ISLAND	510
SOUTH EL MONTE	California	LOS ANGELES-ANAHEIM-RIVERSIDE	353
SOUTH EUCLID	Ohio	CLEVELAND-AKRON-LORAIN	163
SOUTH FARMINGDALE	New York	NEW YORK-NORTHERN NEW JERSEY-LONG ISLAND	484
SOUTH GATE	California	LOS ANGELES-ANAHEIM-RIVERSIDE	352
SOUTH GATE	Maryland	BALTIMORE	47
SOUTH HILL	Washington	SEATTLE-TACOMA	757
SOUTH HOLLAND	Illinois	CHICAGO-GARY-LAKE COUNTY	100
SOUTH HOUSTON	Texas	HOUSTON-GALVESTON-BRAZORIA	275
SOUTH JORDAN	Utah	SALT LAKE CITY-OGDEN	687
SOUTH LAKE TAHOE	California	SACRAMENTO	656
SOUTH LAUREL	Maryland	WASHINGTON	803
SOUTH MIAMI	Florida	MIAMI-FORT LAUDERDALE	387
SOUTH MIAMI HEIGHTS	Florida	MIAMI-FORT LAUDERDALE	402
SOUTH MILWAUKEE	Wisconsin	MILWAUKEE-RACINE	415
SOUTH OGDEN	Utah	SALT LAKE CITY-OGDEN	686
SOUTH ORANGE	New Jersey	NEW YORK-NORTHERN NEW JERSEY-LONG ISLAND	481
SOUTH PARK TOWNSHIP	Pennsylvania	PITTSBURGH-BEAVER VALLEY	612
SOUTH PASADENA	California	LOS ANGELES-ANAHEIM-RIVERSIDE	316
SOUTH PLAINFIELD	New Jersey	NEW YORK-NORTHERN NEW JERSEY-LONG ISLAND	475
SOUTH RIVER	New Jersey	NEW YORK-NORTHERN NEW JERSEY-LONG ISLAND	487
SOUTH SALT LAKE	Utah	SALT LAKE CITY-OGDEN	691
SOUTH SAN FRANCISCO	California	SAN FRANCISCO-OAKLAND-SAN JOSE	724
SOUTH SAN JOSE HILLS	California	LOS ANGELES-ANAHEIM-RIVERSIDE	356
SOUTH ST. PAUL	Minnesota	MINNEAPOLIS-ST. PAUL	430
SOUTH WHITTIER	California	LOS ANGELES-ANAHEIM-RIVERSIDE	346
SOUTHAVEN	Mississippi	MEMPHIS	380
SOUTHFIELD	Michigan	DETROIT-ANN ARBOR	242
SOUTHGATE	Michigan	DETROIT-ANN ARBOR	238
SOUTHGLENN	Colorado	DENVER-BOULDER	217
SPANAWAY	Washington	SEATTLE-TACOMA	760
SPANISH LAKE	Missouri	ST. LOUIS	677
SPEEDWAY	Indiana	INDIANAPOLIS	281
SPRING	Texas	HOUSTON-GALVESTON-BRAZORIA	270
SPRING HILL	Florida	TAMPA-ST. PETERSBURG-CLEARWATER	774
SPRING VALLEY	California	SAN DIEGO	706
SPRING VALLEY	New York	NEW YORK-NORTHERN NEW JERSEY-LONG ISLAND	540
SPRINGDALE	Ohio	CINCINNATI-HAMILTON	151
SPRINGFIELD	New Jersey	NEW YORK-NORTHERN NEW JERSEY-LONG ISLAND	471
SPRINGFIELD	Pennsylvania	PHILADELPHIA-WILMINGTON-TRENTON	578
SPRINGFIELD	Tennessee	NASHVILLE	444
SPRINGFIELD	Virginia	WASHINGTON	792
ST. ANN	Missouri	ST. LOUIS	679
ST. AUGUSTINE	Florida	JACKSONVILLE	288
ST. CHARLES	Illinois	CHICAGO-GARY-LAKE COUNTY	115
ST. CHARLES	Maryland	WASHINGTON	806
ST. CHARLES	Missouri	ST. LOUIS	677
ST. CLAIR SHORES	Michigan	DETROIT-ANN ARBOR	236
ST. CLOUD	Florida	ORLANDO	568
ST. DENNIS	Kentucky	LOUISVILLE	374

Index

Index

SUBURB	STATE	METROPOLITAN AREA	PAGE
TIMBERLANE	Louisiana	NEW ORLEANS	448
TINLEY PARK	Illinois	CHICAGO-GARY-LAKE COUNTY	114
TINTON FALLS	New Jersey	NEW YORK-NORTHERN NEW JERSEY-LONG ISLAND	514
TONAWANDA	New York	BUFFALO-NIAGARA FALLS	82
TORRANCE	California	LOS ANGELES-ANAHEIM-RIVERSIDE	324
TOTOWA	New Jersey	NEW YORK-NORTHERN NEW JERSEY-LONG ISLAND	473
TOWN 'N' COUNTRY	Florida	TAMPA-ST. PETERSBURG-CLEARWATER	770
TOWSON	Maryland	BALTIMORE	32
TRENTON	Michigan	DETROIT-ANN ARBOR	231
TROY	Michigan	DETROIT-ANN ARBOR	233
TROY	Ohio	DAYTON-SPRINGFIELD	210
TRUMBULL	Connecticut	NEW YORK-NORTHERN NEW JERSEY-LONG ISLAND	465
TUALATIN	Oregon	PORTLAND-VANCOUVER	626
TUCKAHOE	Virginia	RICHMOND-PETERSBURG	640
TUCKER	Georgia	ATLANTA	18
TUKWILA	Washington	SEATTLE-TACOMA	755
TUSTIN	California	LOS ANGELES-ANAHEIM-RIVERSIDE	334
TUSTIN FOOTHILLS	California	LOS ANGELES-ANAHEIM-RIVERSIDE	310
TWENTY-NINE PALMS	California	LOS ANGELES-ANAHEIM-RIVERSIDE	344
TYSONS CORNER	Virginia	WASHINGTON	802
UNION	New Jersey	NEW YORK-NORTHERN NEW JERSEY-LONG ISLAND	483
UNION	Utah	SALT LAKE CITY-OGDEN	690
UNION CITY	California	SAN FRANCISCO-OAKLAND-SAN JOSE	729
UNION CITY	New Jersey	NEW YORK-NORTHERN NEW JERSEY-LONG ISLAND	546
UNIONDALE	New York	NEW YORK-NORTHERN NEW JERSEY-LONG ISLAND	529
UNIONTOWN	Pennsylvania	PITTSBURGH-BEAVER VALLEY	615
UNIVERSAL CITY	Texas	SAN ANTONIO	696
UNIVERSITY CITY	Missouri	ST. LOUIS	675
UNIVERSITY HEIGHTS	Ohio	CLEVELAND-AKRON-LORAIN	162
UNIVERSITY PARK	Texas	DALLAS-FORT WORTH	191
UNIVERSITY PLACE	Washington	SEATTLE-TACOMA	755
UNIVERSITY WEST	Florida	TAMPA-ST. PETERSBURG-CLEARWATER	775
UPLAND	California	LOS ANGELES-ANAHEIM-RIVERSIDE	332
UPPER ARLINGTON	Ohio	COLUMBUS	182
UPPER ST. CLAIR	Pennsylvania	PITTSBURGH-BEAVER VALLEY	609
VACAVILLE	California	SAN FRANCISCO-OAKLAND-SAN JOSE	734
VADNAIS HEIGHTS	Minnesota	MINNEAPOLIS-ST. PAUL	423
VALINDA	California	LOS ANGELES-ANAHEIM-RIVERSIDE	346
VALLEJO	California	SAN FRANCISCO-OAKLAND-SAN JOSE	738
VALLEY FALLS	Rhode Island	PROVIDENCE-PAWTUCKET-WOONSOCKET	633
VALLEY STATION	Kentucky	LOUISVILLE	372
VALLEY STREAM	New York	NEW YORK-NORTHERN NEW JERSEY-LONG ISLAND	512
VALPARAISO	Indiana	CHICAGO-GARY-LAKE COUNTY	115
VANDALIA	Ohio	DAYTON-SPRINGFIELD	210
VENTURA	California	LOS ANGELES-ANAHEIM-RIVERSIDE	323
VERMILION	Ohio	CLEVELAND-AKRON-LORAIN	172
VERNON HILLS	Illinois	CHICAGO-GARY-LAKE COUNTY	136
VERONA	New Jersey	NEW YORK-NORTHERN NEW JERSEY-LONG ISLAND	465
VESTAVIA HILLS	Alabama	BIRMINGHAM	52
VICTORVILLE	California	LOS ANGELES-ANAHEIM-RIVERSIDE	358
VIENNA	Virginia	WASHINGTON	785
VIEW PARK-WINDSOR HILLS	California	LOS ANGELES-ANAHEIM-RIVERSIDE	311
VILLA PARK	Illinois	CHICAGO-GARY-LAKE COUNTY	121
VINCENT	California	LOS ANGELES-ANAHEIM-RIVERSIDE	340
VINELAND	New Jersey	PHILADELPHIA-WILMINGTON-TRENTON	590
VISTA	California	SAN DIEGO	708
WADSWORTH	Ohio	CLEVELAND-AKRON-LORAIN	167
WAKEFIELD	Massachusetts	BOSTON-LAWRENCE-SALEM-LOWELL-BROCKTON	65
WALDORF	Maryland	WASHINGTON	798
WALKER MILL	Maryland	WASHINGTON	793

Index

SUBURB	STATE	METROPOLITAN AREA	PAGE
WALLINGTON	New Jersey	NEW YORK-NORTHERN NEW JERSEY-LONG ISLAND	504
WALNUT	California	LOS ANGELES-ANAHEIM-RIVERSIDE	317
WALNUT CREEK	California	SAN FRANCISCO-OAKLAND-SAN JOSE	717
WALNUT PARK	California	LOS ANGELES-ANAHEIM-RIVERSIDE	356
WALTHAM	Massachusetts	BOSTON-LAWRENCE-SALEM-LOWELL-BROCKTON	72
WANTAGH	New York	NEW YORK-NORTHERN NEW JERSEY-LONG ISLAND	492
WARREN	Michigan	DETROIT-ANN ARBOR	239
WARRENSVILLE HEIGHTS	Ohio	CLEVELAND-AKRON-LORAIN	177
WARRENVILLE	Illinois	CHICAGO-GARY-LAKE COUNTY	116
WARWICK	Rhode Island	PROVIDENCE-PAWTUCKET-WOONSOCKET	634
WASHINGTON	Missouri	ST. LOUIS	670
WASHINGTON	Pennsylvania	PITTSBURGH-BEAVER VALLEY	616
WATAUGA	Texas	DALLAS-FORT WORTH	202
WATERFORD	Michigan	DETROIT-ANN ARBOR	240
WATERTOWN	Massachusetts	BOSTON-LAWRENCE-SALEM-LOWELL-BROCKTON	73
WATERVLIET	New York	ALBANY-SCHENECTADY-TROY	13
WATSONVILLE	California	SAN FRANCISCO-OAKLAND-SAN JOSE	740
WAUKEGAN	Illinois	CHICAGO-GARY-LAKE COUNTY	139
WAUKESHA	Wisconsin	MILWAUKEE-RACINE	418
WAUWATOSA	Wisconsin	MILWAUKEE-RACINE	413
WAXAHACHIE	Texas	DALLAS-FORT WORTH	201
WAYNE	Michigan	DETROIT-ANN ARBOR	239
WAYNE	New Jersey	NEW YORK-NORTHERN NEW JERSEY-LONG ISLAND	478
WEATHERFORD	Texas	DALLAS-FORT WORTH	194
WEBSTER GROVES	Missouri	ST. LOUIS	666
WEEHAWKEN	New Jersey	NEW YORK-NORTHERN NEW JERSEY-LONG ISLAND	530
WEKIVA SPRINGS	Florida	ORLANDO	567
WELBY	Colorado	DENVER-BOULDER	221
WELLESLEY	Massachusetts	BOSTON-LAWRENCE-SALEM-LOWELL-BROCKTON	63
WELLINGTON	Florida	WEST PALM BEACH-BOCA RATON-DELRAY BEACH	814
WEST ALLIS	Wisconsin	MILWAUKEE-RACINE	418
WEST BABYLON	New York	NEW YORK-NORTHERN NEW JERSEY-LONG ISLAND	523
WEST BEND	Wisconsin	MILWAUKEE-RACINE	416
WEST BLOOMFIELD TOWNSHIP	Michigan	DETROIT-ANN ARBOR	237
WEST CALDWELL	New Jersey	NEW YORK-NORTHERN NEW JERSEY-LONG ISLAND	464
WEST CARROLLTON CITY	Ohio	DAYTON-SPRINGFIELD	211
WEST CARSON	California	LOS ANGELES-ANAHEIM-RIVERSIDE	343
WEST CHESTER	Pennsylvania	PHILADELPHIA-WILMINGTON-TRENTON	592
WEST CHICAGO	Illinois	CHICAGO-GARY-LAKE COUNTY	132
WEST COVINA	California	LOS ANGELES-ANAHEIM-RIVERSIDE	328
WEST FREEHOLD	New Jersey	NEW YORK-NORTHERN NEW JERSEY-LONG ISLAND	532
WEST HARTFORD	Connecticut	HARTFORD-NEW BRITAIN-MIDDLETOWN-BRISTOL	260
WEST HEMPSTEAD	New York	NEW YORK-NORTHERN NEW JERSEY-LONG ISLAND	489
WEST HOLLYWOOD	California	LOS ANGELES-ANAHEIM-RIVERSIDE	366
WEST ISLIP	New York	NEW YORK-NORTHERN NEW JERSEY-LONG ISLAND	492
WEST JORDAN	Utah	SALT LAKE CITY-OGDEN	689
WEST LAKE STEVENS	Washington	SEATTLE-TACOMA	756
WEST LINN	Oregon	PORTLAND-VANCOUVER	622
WEST LITTLE RIVER	Florida	MIAMI-FORT LAUDERDALE	394
WEST MEMPHIS	Arkansas	MEMPHIS	381
WEST MIFFLIN	Pennsylvania	PITTSBURGH-BEAVER VALLEY	607
WEST MILFORD	New Jersey	NEW YORK-NORTHERN NEW JERSEY-LONG ISLAND	516
WEST NEW YORK	New Jersey	NEW YORK-NORTHERN NEW JERSEY-LONG ISLAND	542
WEST NORRITON	Pennsylvania	PHILADELPHIA-WILMINGTON-TRENTON	588
WEST ORANGE	New Jersey	NEW YORK-NORTHERN NEW JERSEY-LONG ISLAND	476
WEST PARK	Florida	TAMPA-ST. PETERSBURG-CLEARWATER	767
WEST PATERSON	New Jersey	NEW YORK-NORTHERN NEW JERSEY-LONG ISLAND	497
WEST PITTSBURG	California	SAN FRANCISCO-OAKLAND-SAN JOSE	741
WEST PUENTE VALLEY	California	LOS ANGELES-ANAHEIM-RIVERSIDE	347
WEST SACRAMENTO	California	SACRAMENTO	658

Index

SUBURB	STATE	METROPOLITAN AREA	PAGE
WEST SENECA	New York	BUFFALO-NIAGARA FALLS	82
WEST SPRINGFIELD	Virginia	WASHINGTON	791
WEST ST. PAUL	Minnesota	MINNEAPOLIS-ST. PAUL	434
WEST UNIVERSITY PLACE	Texas	HOUSTON-GALVESTON-BRAZORIA	266
WEST VALLEY CITY	Utah	SALT LAKE CITY-OGDEN	689
WEST WARWICK	Rhode Island	PROVIDENCE-PAWTUCKET-WOONSOCKET	634
WEST WHITTIER-LOS NIETOS	California	LOS ANGELES-ANAHEIM-RIVERSIDE	334
WESTBURY	New York	NEW YORK-NORTHERN NEW JERSEY-LONG ISLAND	501
WESTCHESTER	Florida	MIAMI-FORT LAUDERDALE	390
WESTCHESTER	Illinois	CHICAGO-GARY-LAKE COUNTY	105
WESTERLY	Rhode Island	PROVIDENCE-PAWTUCKET-WOONSOCKET	634
WESTERN SPRINGS	Illinois	CHICAGO-GARY-LAKE COUNTY	99
WESTERVILLE	Ohio	COLUMBUS	183
WESTFIELD	New Jersey	NEW YORK-NORTHERN NEW JERSEY-LONG ISLAND	468
WESTLAKE	Ohio	CLEVELAND-AKRON-LORAIN	164
WESTLAND	Michigan	DETROIT-ANN ARBOR	243
WESTMINSTER	California	LOS ANGELES-ANAHEIM-RIVERSIDE	339
WESTMINSTER	Colorado	DENVER-BOULDER	220
WESTMINSTER	Maryland	BALTIMORE	46
WESTMONT	California	LOS ANGELES-ANAHEIM-RIVERSIDE	365
WESTMONT	Illinois	CHICAGO-GARY-LAKE COUNTY	132
WESTPORT	Connecticut	NEW YORK-NORTHERN NEW JERSEY-LONG ISLAND	487
WESTWEGO	Louisiana	NEW ORLEANS	452
WESTWOOD	New Jersey	NEW YORK-NORTHERN NEW JERSEY-LONG ISLAND	491
WESTWOOD LAKES	Florida	MIAMI-FORT LAUDERDALE	391
WETHERSFIELD	Connecticut	HARTFORD-NEW BRITAIN-MIDDLETOWN-BRISTOL	260
WEYMOUTH	Massachusetts	BOSTON-LAWRENCE-SALEM-LOWELL-BROCKTON	71
WHEAT RIDGE	Colorado	DENVER-BOULDER	219
WHEATON	Illinois	CHICAGO-GARY-LAKE COUNTY	110
WHEATON-GLENMONT	Maryland	WASHINGTON	790
WHEELING	Illinois	CHICAGO-GARY-LAKE COUNTY	129
WHITE BEAR LAKE	Minnesota	MINNEAPOLIS-ST. PAUL	427
WHITE CENTER-SHOREWOOD	Washington	SEATTLE-TACOMA	759
WHITE OAK	Maryland	WASHINGTON	796
WHITE OAK	Ohio	CINCINNATI-HAMILTON	150
WHITE PLAINS	New York	NEW YORK-NORTHERN NEW JERSEY-LONG ISLAND	505
WHITE SETTLEMENT	Texas	DALLAS-FORT WORTH	199
WHITEFISH BAY	Wisconsin	MILWAUKEE-RACINE	412
WHITEHALL	Ohio	COLUMBUS	186
WHITEHALL	Pennsylvania	PITTSBURGH-BEAVER VALLEY	609
WHITTIER	California	LOS ANGELES-ANAHEIM-RIVERSIDE	319
WICKLIFFE	Ohio	CLEVELAND-AKRON-LORAIN	162
WILDOMAR	California	LOS ANGELES-ANAHEIM-RIVERSIDE	366
WILKINSBURG	Pennsylvania	PITTSBURGH-BEAVER VALLEY	616
WILLIAMSBURG	Virginia	NORFOLK-VIRGINIA BEACH-NEWPORT NEWS	553
WILLIAMSTOWN	New Jersey	PHILADELPHIA-WILMINGTON-TRENTON	592
WILLINGBORO	New Jersey	PHILADELPHIA-WILMINGTON-TRENTON	586
WILLOUGHBY	Ohio	CLEVELAND-AKRON-LORAIN	174
WILLOW GROVE	Pennsylvania	PHILADELPHIA-WILMINGTON-TRENTON	585
WILLOWBROOK	California	LOS ANGELES-ANAHEIM-RIVERSIDE	351
WILLOWICK	Ohio	CLEVELAND-AKRON-LORAIN	173
WILMETTE	Illinois	CHICAGO-GARY-LAKE COUNTY	99
WILMINGTON	Massachusetts	BOSTON-LAWRENCE-SALEM-LOWELL-BROCKTON	63
WILTON MANORS	Florida	MIAMI-FORT LAUDERDALE	395
WINCHESTER	Massachusetts	BOSTON-LAWRENCE-SALEM-LOWELL-BROCKTON	62
WINDSOR	California	SAN FRANCISCO-OAKLAND-SAN JOSE	737
WINDSOR LOCKS	Connecticut	HARTFORD-NEW BRITAIN-MIDDLETOWN-BRISTOL	260
WINNETKA	Illinois	CHICAGO-GARY-LAKE COUNTY	99
WINTER PARK	Florida	ORLANDO	566
WINTER SPRINGS	Florida	ORLANDO	566

Index